wake up and smell the savings.

Nothing gets me started like a free hot breakfast. And when I show my AAA/CAA card, I get AAA/CAA rates.* Throw in all the other extras I appreciate, and my stay's even more tantalizing. Real value from my friends at Hampton. For reservations, call your AAA/CAA agent, visit **hampton.com** or call 1-800-hampton.

we love having you here.™

free high-speed internet

free hot breakfast

preferred hotels

Western Canada & Alaska

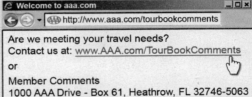

Published by AAA Publishing
1000 AAA Drive, Heathrow, FL 32746-5063
Copyright AAA 2010, All rights reserved

Advertising Rate and Circulation Information: (407) 444-8280

Printed in the USA by Worldcolor, Buffalo, NY

Photo Credit: (Cover & Title Page)
Lake Clark National Park and Preserve, AK
© 2009 Michael DeYoung / AlaskaStock

Printed on recyclable paper.
Please recycle whenever possible.

Stock #4601

Mixed Sources
Product group from well-managed forests and other controlled sources
www.fsc.org Cert no. SW - COC - 002550
© 1996 Forest Stewardship Council

Western Canada & Alaska

What do these items have in common?
AAA/CAA members spend less.

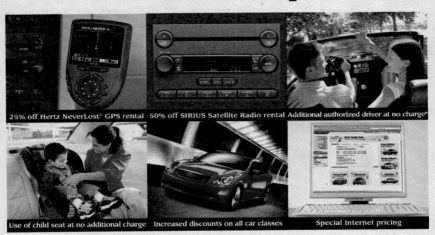

25% off Hertz NeverLost® GPS rental   50% off SIRIUS Satellite Radio rental   Additional authorized driver at no charge*

Use of child seat at no additional charge   Increased discounts on all car classes   Special Internet pricing

Hertz offers AAA/CAA members exclusive discounts on a variety of products and services. Benefits include:

- 25% off Hertz NeverLost® GPS rental
- 50% off SIRIUS Satellite Radio rental
- Additional authorized driver at no charge*
- Free use of child seat
- Discounts on all car classes
- Special Internet pricing
- Member Satisfaction Guarantee

Show Your Card & Save

SHOW YOUR AAA/CAA CARD AND SAVE

THE ONLY CAR RENTAL COMPANY ENDORSED BY AAA/CAA

AAA.com/Hertz or CAA.ca/Hertz

FOR YOUR INFORMATION: Advance reservations are required. Discounts and benefits are valid at participating locations in the U.S., Canada and Puerto Rico. One child seat at no additional charge. Hertz NeverLost and SIRIUS Satellite Radio subject to availability. SIRIUS not available in Alaska, Hawaii or Puerto Rico. Discounts valued in local currency upon redemption and exclude applicable taxes and surcharges. Your valid AAA/CAA membership card or Hertz/AAA/CAA discount card must be presented at time of pickup. SIRIUS is a registered trademark of SIRIUS Satellite Radio, Inc.

*No charge for an additional authorized driver who is a AAA/CAA member, holds a major credit card in their name and meets standard rental qualifications.   ® Reg. U.S. Pat. Off. © 2009 Hertz System, Inc.

Visit	Over 1,100 AAA/CAA Offices		
Click	AAA.com/Hertz or CAA.ca/Hertz	Call	800-654-3080 or 888-333-3120

Attractions, lodgings and restaurants are listed on the basis of merit alone after careful evaluation and approval by one of AAA/CAA's full-time, professionally trained inspectors. Evaluations are unannounced to ensure that we see an establishment just as you would see it.

An establishment's decision to advertise in the TourBook guide has no bearing on its evaluation or rating. Advertising for services or products does not imply AAA endorsement.

Information in this guide was believed accurate at the time of publication. However, since changes inevitably occur between annual editions, we suggest you work with your AAA travel professional or check on AAA.com to confirm prices and schedules.

How the TourBook Guide is Organized

The TourBook guide is organized into three distinct sections.

The **Points of Interest** section helps you plan daily activities and sightseeing excursions and provides details about the city or attraction you are visiting.

The **Lodgings and Restaurants** section helps you select AAA Approved accommodations and dining facilities meeting your specific needs and expectations.

The **Reference** section provides indexes for locating information within this guide and items to aid the trip planning process.

Locating the Attractions, Lodgings and Restaurants

Attractions, lodgings and restaurants are listed under the city in which they physically are located - or in some cases under the nearest recognized city. Most listings are alphabetically organized by state, province, region or island, then by city and establishment name.

A color is assigned to each state or province so that you can match the color bars at the top of the page to switch from the **Points of Interest** section to the **Lodgings and Restaurants** section.

Spotting maps help you physically locate points of interest, lodgings and restaurants in the major destinations.

The Comprehensive City Index located in the **Reference** section contains an A-to-Z list of cities.

Destination Cities and Destination Areas

Destination cities, established based on government models and local expertise, include metropolitan areas plus nearby vicinity cities. **Destination areas** are regions with broad tourist appeal; several cities will comprise the area.

If a city falls within a destination's vicinity, the city name will appear at its alphabetical location in the book, and a cross reference will give you the exact page on which listings for that city begin.

An Orientation map appears at the beginning of each destination section to familiarize you with that destination.

Understanding the Points of Interest Listing

GEM Designation

A ☆ indicates the attraction has been rated a AAA GEM, a "must see" point of interest that offers a *Great Experience for Members®*. These attractions have been judged to be of exceptional interest and quality by AAA inspectors.

Discount Savings

The SAVE icon denotes those attractions offering AAA/CAA, AAA MasterCard, AAA VISA or international Show Your Card & Save discount cardholders a discount off the attraction's standard admission. Present your card at the attraction's admission desk.

A list of participating points of interest appears in the Reference section of this guide.

Shopping establishments preceded by a SAVE icon also provide to AAA/CAA members a discount and/or gift with purchase; present your card at the mall's customer service center to receive your benefit.

Exceptions

- Members should inquire in advance concerning the validity of the discount for special rates.
- The SAVE discount may not be used in conjunction with other discounts.
- Attractions that already provide a reduced senior or child rate may not honor the SAVE discount for those age groups.
- All offers are subject to change and may not apply during special events, particular days or seasons or for the entire validity period of the TourBook guide.

Adventure Travel

There are inherent risks with adventure travel activities like air tours, hiking, skiing and white-water rafting. For your own safety, please read and adhere to all safety instructions. Mentions of these activities are for information only and do **not** imply endorsement by AAA.

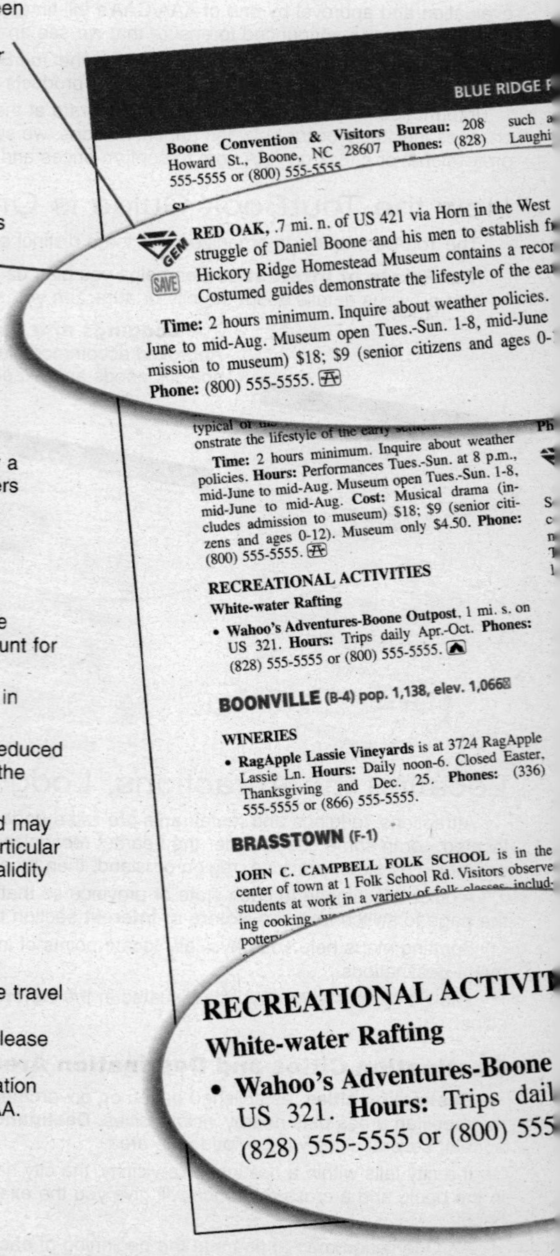

BLUE RIDGE P

Boone Convention & Visitors Bureau: 208 such a
Howard St., Boone, NC 28607 **Phones:** (828) Laughi
555-5555 or (800) 555-5555

☆ SAVE **RED OAK,** .7 mi. n. of US 421 via Horn in the West
struggle of Daniel Boone and his men to establish fi
Hickory Ridge Homestead Museum contains a recor
Costumed guides demonstrate the lifestyle of the ear

Time: 2 hours minimum. Inquire about weather policies.
June to mid-Aug. Museum open Tues.-Sun. 1-8, mid-June
mission to museum) $18; $9 (senior citizens and ages 0-
Phone: (800) 555-5555. 🆓

typical or the
onstrate the lifestyle of the early sch...

Time: 2 hours minimum. Inquire about weather
policies. **Hours:** Performances Tues.-Sun. at 8 p.m.,
mid-June to mid-Aug. Museum open Tues.-Sun. 1-8,
mid-June to mid-Aug. **Cost:** Musical drama (includes admission to museum) $18; $9 (senior citizens and ages 0-12). Museum only $4.50. **Phone:**
(800) 555-5555. 🆓

RECREATIONAL ACTIVITIES

White-water Rafting

- **Wahoo's Adventures-Boone Outpost**, 1 mi. s. on
US 321. **Hours:** Trips daily Apr.-Oct. **Phones:**
(828) 555-5555 or (800) 555-5555. 🅰

BOONVILLE (B-4) pop. 1,138, elev. 1,066☒

WINERIES

- **RagApple Lassie Vineyards** is at 3724 RagApple
Lassie Ln. **Hours:** Daily noon-6. Closed Easter,
Thanksgiving and Dec. 25. **Phones:** (336)
555-5555 or (866) 555-5555.

BRASSTOWN (F-1)

JOHN C. CAMPBELL FOLK SCHOOL is in the
center of town at 1 Folk School Rd. Visitors observe
students at work in a variety of folk classes, including cooking, w...
potter...

RECREATIONAL ACTIVIT

White-water Rafting

- **Wahoo's Adventures-Boone**
US 321. **Hours:** Trips dail
(828) 555-5555 or (800) 555

— BRYSON CITY, NC   129

Falls, Courthouse Falls and

...f Commerce

...tdoor musical drama portraying the
...e Southern Appalachian Highlands.
...g village typical of the 18th century.

...formances Tues.-Sun. at 8 p.m. mid-
... **Cost:** Musical drama (includes ad-
...m only $4.50. **Cards:** AX, MC, VI.

...210
...ryson City, NC 28713
555-5555 or (800) 555-5555.

Smoky Mountains Railroad, departing
...ryson City depot, operates various
...ay and full-day round-trip excursions.
...fered in open cars, coaches, crown
...lub cars. On weekends there are Gour-
... Trains and Mystery Theatre Dinner
...Polar Express runs early Nov. through

...–The Easter Beagle Express" and
... Tank," rides with kid-oriented themes,
... in the spring and summer with limited
...nuts— The Great Pumpkin Patch Ex-
... weekends in October. An animal petting
...usical entertainment also are offered.

... hours, 30 minutes minimum. **Hours:**
... year-round. Phone ahead to confirm
...**Cost:** Sightseeing fares begin at $34; $19
...2). **Reservations:** recommended. **Phone:**
...-5555, or (800) 555-5555 for reservations.

...er Ltd. **Raft & Rail Excursion,** departing
...ad depot in Bryson City, combines rail and
...ater excursions in one outing. The adventure
...with a scenic 2-hour train trip across Fontana
... the top of Nantahala Gorge. Rafts are then
... for a guided 3-hour trip down the Nan-
...Lunch is included.

...minimum. Children under 60
...d. **Hours:** Trips daily mid-
...times vary. **Cost:** Fares
...3–12). **Phone:** (828)

...ES

...ost, 1 mi. s. on   3 mi. s.w. on US
...-Oct. **Phones:**   daily 8-8, Apr.-Oct.
...   ...ec. 25. **Phones:** (828)
...   ...55.

Directions

Unless otherwise specified, directions are given from the center of town, using the following highway designations:

I=interstate highway	**US**=federal highway
SR=state route	**CR**=county road
FM=farm to market	**FR**=forest road
Mex.=Mexican highway	**Hwy.**=Canadian or Caribbean highway

Prices and Dates of Operation

Admission prices are quoted without sales tax. Children under the lowest age specified are admitted free when accompanied by an adult. Days, months and age groups written with a hyphen are inclusive.

Prices pertaining to points of interest in the United States are quoted in U.S. dollars; points of interest in Canada are quoted in Canadian dollars; prices for points of interest in Mexico and the Caribbean are quoted as an approximate U.S. dollar equivalent.

Schedules and admission rates may change throughout the validity period of this guide. Check AAA.com for the most current information.

Credit Card Information

Most establishments accept credit cards, but a small number require cash. If you want to use a specific credit card, call ahead to ensure it's accepted.

Icons

Attraction icons represent some of the services and facilities offered:

⛰ Camping facilities available

🍴 Food available on premises

🎿 Recreational activities available

🐕 Pets on leash allowed

🏕 Picnicking permitted

Bulleted Listings

Gambling establishments within hotels are presented for member information regardless of whether the lodging is AAA Approved.

Recreational activities of a participatory nature (requiring physical exertion or special skills) are not inspected.

Wineries are evaluated by AAA inspectors to ensure they meet listing requirements and offer tours.

All are presented in an abbreviated bulleted format for informational purposes.

Local Member Value

AAA or CAA and SAVE identify hotels that offer members a rate guarantee and up to two free special amenities as part of their Official Appointment partnership with AAA. Rate guarantee: Discounted standard room rate (usually based on last standard room availability) or the lowest public rate available at time of booking for dates of stay. Free special amenity options such as breakfast, local telephone calls, newspaper, room upgrade, preferred room or high-speed Internet are included in the listing.

Diamond Rating

The number of Diamonds informs you of the overall complexity of a lodging's amenities and service. Red indicates an Official Appointment lodging. An fyi in place of Diamonds indicates the property has not been rated but is included as an "information only" service. A detailed description of each rating level appears on page 18.

Classification

All Diamond Rated lodgings are classified using three key elements: style of operation, overall concept and service level. See pages 20-21 for details on our classifications.

Rates

The property's standard 2-person rates and effective dates are shown.

Rates provided to AAA for each lodging represent the publicly available rate or ranges for a standard room. Rates are rounded to the nearest dollar and do not include taxes. U.S., Mexican and Caribbean rates are in U.S. dollars; rates for Canadian lodgings are in Canadian dollars.

Information about cancellation and minimum stay policies is provided in the **Terms** section of the property's listing.

Online Reservations

This notation indicates AAA/CAA members can conveniently check room availability, validate room rates and make reservations for this property in a secure online environment at AAA.com.

Service Availability

Unit types, amenities and room features preceded by the word "Some" indicate the item is available in **some units**, potentially within only one unit. The term "fee" appearing beside an amenity indicates an extra charge applies.

Phone: (555)555-5555 **75**

I-4, exit 72, just e
Facility: Spacious

Phone: 555/555-5555 **11**

Hilton

AAA Benefit:
mbers save 5%
more everyday!

aundry, airport transportation, beach shuttle,
, business center. **Free Special Amenities:**
76)

aundry, airport transportation, beach shuttle,
, business center. **Free Special Amenities:**
76)

Phone: (555)555-5555 **9**

-275, exit 16,
recreational
one-bedroom
2 stories,
ding: on-site
nternet, dual
ideo games
oor. **Leisure**
nnis courts,
ch cruisers,
oin laundry,
PC, fax.

Phone: 555/555-5555

n Palace; downtown; in historic district.
d with antiques and family heirlooms; a
. Smoke free premises. 6 one-bedroom
. **Bath:** combo or shower only. **Parking:**
brary, hair dryers. *Some:* DVD players.
t. **Business Services:** meeting rooms,

Phone: 555/555-5555 **18**

w. **Facility:** The large facility boasts
nd a 90,000-square-foot casino with a
d units, some with whirlpools. 2 one-
: combo or shower only. **Parking:** on-
ames (fee), high-speed Internet, dual
rs. *Some:* DVD players. **Dining:** 4
e separate listing, entertainment.
nrooms, exercise room, spa. **Guest**
conference facilities, business center.
t Internet.

Nationwide Member Value
The blue box in the listing identifies hotel brands that offer an everyday member benefit at all AAA Approved locations. (See page 17 for additional program benefits.)

Spotting Symbol
Black ovals with white numbers are used to locate, or "spot," lodgings on maps we provide for larger cities.

Credit Card Information
Most establishments accept credit cards, but a small number require cash. If you want to use a specific credit card, call ahead to ensure it's accepted.

Icons
Lodging icons represent some of the member values, services and facilities offered. The term "FEE" appearing to the left of an amenity icon indicates an extra charge applies.

The **ECO** icon indicates lodgings that have been certified by well-established government and/or private eco-certification organizations. For more information about these organizations and their programs, visit AAA.com/eco.

Discounts
ASK May offer discount

Member Services
✦ Airport transportation
☞ Pets allowed (call property for restrictions and fees)
🍴 Restaurant on premises
🍴▶ Restaurant off premises (walking distance)
24🍴 24-hour room service
🍸 Full bar
👶 Child care
&M Accessible features (call property for available services and amenities)

Leisure Activities
🎰 Full-service casino
🏊 Pool
🏋 Health club on premises

🏋↪ Health club off premises
🎿 Recreational activities

In-Room Amenities
☒ Designated non-smoking rooms
🎬 Movies
🍴 Refrigerator
📡 Microwave
☕ Coffee maker
🅐🅒 No air conditioning
📺 No TV
📺 No cable TV
☎ No telephones

Safety Features
(see page 22)
(Mexico and Caribbean only)

S Sprinklers
D Smoke detectors

Understanding the Restaurant Listing

Official Appointment

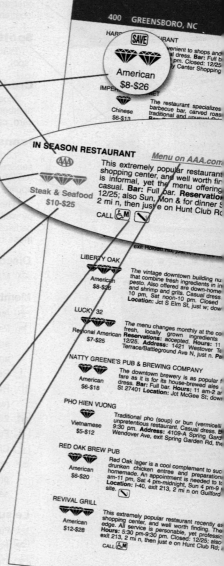

AAA or CAA indicates Official Appointment (OA) restaurants. The OA program permits restaurants to display and advertise the AAA or CAA emblem. These establishments are highlighted in red to help you quickly identify them. The AAA or CAA Approved sign helps traveling members find restaurants that want member business.

Local Member Value

SAVE identifies restaurants that offer a Show Your Card & Save® discount to AAA/CAA members.

Diamond Rating

The number of Diamonds informs you of the overall complexity of food, presentation, service and ambience. Red indicates an Official Appointment restaurant. A detailed description of each Diamond level appears on page 19.

Cuisine Type

The cuisine type helps you select a dining facility that caters to your individual taste. AAA currently recognizes more than 120 different cuisine types.

Prices

Prices shown represent the minimum and maximum entree cost per person. Exceptions may include one-of-a-kind or special market priced items. Prices are rounded to the nearest dollar and do not include taxes. U.S., Mexican and Caribbean prices are in U.S. dollars; prices for Canadian restaurants are in Canadian dollars.

Icons

Icons provide additional information about services and facilities.

- No air-conditioning
- Accessible features offered
  (call property for available services and amenities)
- Designated smoking section available

Menus

This notation indicates AAA/CAA members can conveniently view the restaurant's menu in a secure online environment at AAA.com.

The left side shows sample restaurant listings (partially cut off):

asual eatery prepares tasty steak, seafood, chicken and salads.
accepted. **Hours:** 11:15 am-10 pm, Fri & Sat-11 pm, Sun 10:30
ndly Center Rd 27408 **Location:** Jct Wendover Ave, just w; in
n-site. **Phone:** 555/555-5555

buffets for lunch and dinner. Included in the buffet are a
l and dim sum selection. Buffet items include a variety of
also available. Casual dress.
r Rd 27407 **Phone:** 555/555-5555

Phone: 555/555-5555 43
anded to this newly constructed building, located behind a
ecialize in all-you-can-eat buffets for lunch. The atmosphere
edge. All service is personable, yet professional. Dressy
Hours: 11 am-8:30 pm, Thurs & Fri 5 pm-9 pm. Closed
un. **Address:** 604 Milner Dr 27410 **Location:** I-40, exit 213,
ker Village Shopping Center. **Parking:** on-site. **Classic**

1.8 mi e on Wendover Ave, Closed: 12/25;

Phone: 555/555-5555
pscale dining atmosphere. The menu features dishes
n as in stuffed rainbow trout and lamb with honey-mint
with flair, including roasted pulled pork, fried chicken
servations: accepted. **Hours:** 11:30 am-9:30 pm, Fri-
so Sun. **Address:** 100-D W Washington St 27401
treet.

Phone: 555/555-5555
eatery, with the focus of the cuisine on incorporating
American fare. Casual dress. **Bar:** Full bar.
& Sat-11 pm, Sun 10 am-10 pm. Closed: 11/26,
cation: Wendover Ave, exit US 220 N/Westover

Phone: 555/555-5555
nu of burgers, wraps, sandwiches and hearty pub
r seating is offered during warm weather. Casual
Closed: 11/26, 12/24, 12/25. **Address:** 345 S Elm
treet.

Phone: 555/555-5555
and is served with a smile in the comfortable.
Hours: 11 am-3:30 & 5-9:30 pm, Fri-Sun 11 am-
cation: I-40, exit 214 or 214 B, 1.8 mi ne on
ng: on-site.

Phone: 555/555-5555
urmet sandwiches, fish and chips, the signature
us beef. Sauces, dressings and soups are
ewery. Casual dress. **Bar:** Full bar. **Hours:** 11
6, 12/25. **Address:** 714 Francis King St 27410
w on Hunt Club Rd, then just n. **Parking:** on-

Phone: 555/555-5555
newly constructed building, located behind a
informal, yet the menu offerings are cutting
ual. **Bar:** Full bar. **Reservations:** accepted.
dress: 604 Milner Dr 27410 **Location:** I-40,
illage Shopping Center. **Parking:** on-site.

Spotting Symbol

White ovals with black numbers serve as restaurant locators and are used to locate, or "spot," restaurants on maps for larger cities.

Classifications

If applicable, a restaurant may be defined as:

Classic - renowned and/or landmark restaurant in business longer than 25 years, known for unique style and ambience.

Historic - establishments must meet one of the following criteria:
- Listed on the National Register of Historic Places
- Designated a National Historic Landmark
- Located in a National Register Historic District

Separate criteria designate historic properties in Canada, Mexico and the Caribbean.

Credit Card Information

Most establishments accept credit cards, but a small number require cash. If you want to use a specific credit card, call ahead to ensure it's accepted.

AAA/CAA members can generally expect to pay no more than the maximum regular rate printed in the TourBook guide in each rate range for a standard room. On rare occasions AAA receives or inadvertently publishes incorrect rates.

Obtain current AAA/CAA member rates and make reservations at AAA.com. Rates may vary within the range, depending on season and room type. Listed rates are usually based on last standard room availability.

Discounts

Member discounts, when offered, will apply to rates quoted within the rate range and are applicable at the time of booking. Special rates used in advertising, as well as special short-term promotional rates lower than the lowest listed rate in the range, are not subject to additional member discounts.

Exceptions

Rates for properties operating as concessionaires for the U.S. National Park Service are not guaranteed due to governing regulations. Rates in the Mexico TourBook are not guaranteed and may fluctuate based on the exchange rate of the peso.

Lodgings may temporarily increase room rates, not recognize discounts or modify pricing policies during special events. Examples of special events range from Mardi Gras and the Kentucky Derby (including pre-Derby events) to college football games, holidays, holiday periods and state fairs. Although some special events are listed in AAA/CAA TourBook guides and on AAA.com, it is always wise to check in advance with AAA travel professionals for specific dates.

Meeting Your Travel Needs

AAA is proud to stand behind the Approved hotels, restaurants, attractions and campgrounds listed in the TourBook and CampBook guides. If, however, your visit doesn't meet your expectations, now you can tell us about it immediately. Visit AAA.com/TourBookComments to complete an easy online form, or send written comments to: AAA Member Comments, 1000 AAA Dr., Heathrow, FL 32746.

Get the Room You Reserved

When making your reservation, identify yourself as a AAA or CAA member and request written confirmation to guarantee: type of room, rate, dates of stay, and cancellation and refund policies. At registration, show your membership card.

When you find your room is not as specified, and you have written confirmation of reservations for a certain type of accommodation, you should be given the option of choosing a different room or finding one elsewhere. Should you choose to go elsewhere and a refund is refused or resisted, submit the matter to AAA/CAA within 30 days, along with complete documentation, including your

reasons for refusing the room and copies of your written confirmation and any receipts or canceled checks associated with this problem.

If you are charged more than the maximum rate listed in the TourBook guide for a standard room, question the additional charge. If management refuses to adhere to the published rate, pay for the room and submit your receipt and membership number to AAA/CAA within 30 days. Include all pertinent information: dates of stay, rate paid, itemized paid receipts, number of persons in your party and the room number you occupied, and list any extra room equipment used. A refund of the amount paid in excess of the stated maximum will be made if our investigation indicates that unjustified charging occurred.

Deposit, Refund and Cancellation Policies

Most establishments give full deposit refunds if they have been notified at least 48 hours before the normal check-in time. Listing prose will note if more than 48 hours' notice is required for cancellation. Some properties may charge a cancellation or handling fee. When this applies, "cancellation fee imposed" will appear in the **Terms** section of the listing. If you cancel too late, you have little recourse if a refund is denied.

When an establishment requires full or partial payment in advance and your trip is cut short, a refund may not be given.

When canceling a reservation, phone the lodging immediately. Make a note of the date and time you called, the cancellation number if there is one, and the name of the person who handled the cancellation. If your AAA/CAA club made your reservation, allow them to make the cancellation for you as well, so you will have proof of cancellation.

Check-in and Check-out Times

Check-in and check-out times are shown in the lodging listings, under **Terms**, only if they are before 3 p.m. or after 10 a.m. respectively.

Members Save With Our Partners

These Show Your Card & Save® partners provide the listed member benefits. Visit AAA.com/Discounts to discover all the great Show Your Card & Save® discounts in your area. Even greater discounts on theme park tickets may be available at your local AAA/CAA club. Discounts apply to a maximum of six tickets for Amtrak, Gray Line and the theme parks. Restaurant savings apply to AAA/CAA members and up to five guests.

SeaWorld, Busch Gardens, Sesame Place

- Save on admission at the gate, at participating offices or online AAA.com/SeaWorld
- Save 10% on up-close dining; visit Guest Relations for details

Six Flags

- Save on admission at the gate, at participating offices or online AAA.com/SixFlags
- Save 10% on merchandise purchases of $15 or more at in-park stores

Universal Orlando Resort and Universal Studios Hollywood

- Save on admission at the gate, at participating offices or online AAA.com/Universal

- Save 10% at select food and merchandise venues in-park and at Universal CityWalk®

The Entertainment Capital of L.A.™

Hard Rock Cafe

- Save 10% on food, non-alcoholic beverages and merchandise at all U.S., Canadian and select international locations

Landry's Seafood House, The Crab House, Chart House, Saltgrass Steak House, Muer Seafood Restaurants and Aquarium Restaurants

- Save 10% on food and non-alcoholic beverages at all of the above restaurants
- Save 10% on merchandise at Aquarium and Downtown Aquarium restaurants

Amtrak

- 10% discount on rail fare when booked at least 3 days in advance of travel date

EagleRider

- We Rent Dreams® 12% off motorcycle rentals 1-877-869-5023

Fetch! Pet Care

- Save 10% off pet-sitting and dog-walking services AAA.com/Fetchpetcare 1-877-533-8242 code AAAPETS

We've got your tail covered.™

Grand Canyon Railway

- Save up to 20% on rail fare, hotel accommodations, restaurant and gift shop purchases sold outside of Grand Canyon National Park

GRAND CANYON Railway

Gray Line

AAA.com/GrayLine

- Save 10% on sightseeing tours of 1 day or less worldwide

Hertz

- Exclusive AAA member savings on daily, weekend, weekly and monthly rentals AAA.com/hertz or 1-800-654-3080

Tanger Outlet Centers www.tangeroutlet.com

- Save up to 20% on total purchase at select merchants with FREE coupon booklet
- Member BONUS: FREE $5 gift card for each additional Tanger Outlet Center visited after first within same calendar year

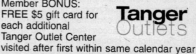

- Show membership card and register at the AAA customer service desk when you visit

AAA Preferred Lodging Partners

EXPECT SAVINGS, SELECTION, AND SATISFACTION

- **Best AAA/CAA member rates for your dates of stay.** Provide a valid membership number when placing your reservation and show your card at hotel check-in.

- **Satisfaction guarantee.** Notify the property if you are dissatisfied with any part of your stay. If the matter cannot be resolved, you may be entitled to compensation (see page 15).

- **Seasonal promotions and special member offers.** Visit AAA.com to view current offers.

- **Everyday member benefit.** Look for the blue boxes in the TourBook listings for everyday values offered at all AAA Approved locations. *Offer good at time of publication: Chains and offers may change without notice. Preferred Hotel Partner discounts may vary in Mexico and the Caribbean.*

10% Off Best Available Rates
Best Western International

5% or More Off Best Available Rates
Conrad, DoubleTree, Embassy Suites, Hampton, Hilton, Hilton Garden Inn, Hilton Grand Vacations, Home2 Suites, Homewood Suites, and Waldorf=Astoria Collection

10% Off Best Available Rates
ANdAZ, Grand Hyatt, Hyatt Place, Hyatt Regency, Hyatt Summerfield Suites, and Park Hyatt

5% or More Off Best Available Rates
Courtyard, Fairfield Inn, JW Marriott, Marriott, Renaissance Hotels & Resorts, Residence Inn, SpringHill Suites, and TownePlace Suites

5-15% Off Best Available Rates
aloft, element, Four Points, Le Meridien, Sheraton, St. Regis, The Luxury Collection, Westin, and W Hotels

Understanding the Diamond Ratings

AAA/CAA inspectors have evaluated and rated each of the 58,000 lodging and restaurant establishments in the TourBook series to ensure quality travel information for our members. All properties must meet AAA's minimum requirements (for lodgings) concerning cleanliness, comfort and security - or - AAA's minimum requirements (for restaurants) pertaining to cleanliness, food preparation and service.

Eligible applicants receive an unannounced evaluation by a AAA/CAA inspector that includes two distinct components:

- **AAA Approval:** The inspector first must determine whether the property meets the criteria required to be AAA Approved. Every establishment that meets these strict guidelines offers AAA members the assurance that, regardless of the Diamond Rating, it provides acceptable quality, cleanliness, service and value.
- **AAA Diamond Rating:** Once an establishment becomes AAA Approved, it is then assigned a rating of one to five Diamonds, indicating the extensiveness of its facilities, amenities and services, from basic to moderate to luxury. These Diamond Ratings guide members in selecting establishments appropriately matched to their needs and expectations.

LODGINGS

1 Diamond

One Diamond lodgings typically appeal to the budget-minded traveler. They provide essential, no-frills accommodations and basic comfort and hospitality.

2 Diamond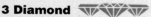

Two Diamond lodgings appeal to travelers seeking affordable yet more than the basic accommodations. Facilities, decor and amenities are modestly enhanced.

3 Diamond

Three Diamond lodgings offer a distinguished style. Properties are multi-faceted, with marked upgrades in physical attributes, amenities and guest comforts.

4 Diamond

Four Diamond lodgings are refined and stylish. Physical attributes are upscale. The fundamental hallmarks at this level include an extensive array of amenities combined with a high degree of hospitality, service and attention to detail.

5 Diamond

Five Diamond lodgings provide the ultimate in luxury and sophistication. Physical attributes are extraordinary in every manner. Service is meticulous, exceeding guest expectations and maintaining impeccable standards of excellence. Extensive personalized services and amenities provide first-class comfort.

The lodging listings with **fyi** in place of Diamonds are included as an *information only* service for members. The icon indicates that a property has not been rated for one or more of the following reasons: too new to rate, under construction, under major renovation, not evaluated, may not meet all AAA requirements.

A property not meeting all AAA requirements is included for either its member value or because it may be the only accommodation available in the area. Listing prose will give insight as to why the **fyi** designation was assigned.

4 Diamond

Four Diamond restaurants provide a distinctive fine-dining experience that is typically expensive. Surroundings are highly refined with upscale enhancements throughout. Highly creative chefs use imaginative presentations to augment fresh, top-quality ingredients. A proficient service staff meets or exceeds guest expectations. A wine steward may offer menu-specific knowledge to guide selection.

5 Diamond

Five Diamond restaurants are luxurious and renowned for consistently providing a world-class experience. Highly acclaimed chefs offer artistic menu selections that are imaginative and unique, using only the finest ingredients available. A maitre d' leads an expert service staff in exceeding guest expectations, attending to every detail in an effortless and unobtrusive manner.

RESTAURANTS

1 Diamond

One Diamond restaurants provide simple, familiar specialty food (such as burgers, chicken, pizza or tacos) at an economical price. Often self-service, basic surroundings complement a no-nonsense approach.

The restaurants with 【fyi】 in place of Diamonds are included as an *information only* service for members. These listings provide additional dining choices but have not yet been evaluated.

2 Diamond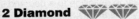

Two Diamond restaurants offer a familiar, family-oriented experience. Menu selection includes home-style foods and family favorites, often cooked to order, modestly enhanced and reasonably priced. Service is accommodating yet relaxed, a perfect complement to casual surroundings.

3 Diamond

Three Diamond restaurants convey an entry into fine dining and are often positioned as adult-oriented experiences. The atypical menu may feature the latest cooking trends and/or traditional cuisine. Expanded beverage offerings complement the menu. The ambience is well coordinated, comfortable and enhanced by a professional service staff.

Understanding the Lodging Classifications

To ensure that your lodging needs and preferences are met, we recommend that you consider an establishment's classification when making your travel choices. While the quality and comfort at properties with the same Diamond Rating should be consistent (regardless of the classification), there are differences in typical decor/theme elements, range of facilities and service levels.

Lodging Classifications

Bed & Breakfast

Typically smaller scale properties emphasizing a high degree of personal touches that provide guests an "at home" feeling. Guest units tend to be individually decorated. Rooms may not include some modern amenities such as televisions and telephones, and may have a shared bathroom. Usually owner-operated with a common room or parlor separate from the innkeeper's living quarters, where guests and operators can interact during evening and breakfast hours. Evening office closures are normal. A continental or full, hot breakfast is served and is included in the room rate.

1884 Paxton House Inn
Thomasville, GA

Cabin

Vacation-oriented, typically smaller scale, freestanding units of simple construction—roughly finished logs or stone—and basic design or décor. Often located in wooded, rural, or waterfront locations. As a rule, basic cleaning supplies, kitchen utensils, and complete bed and bath linens are supplied. The guest registration area may be located off site.

Greenbrier Valley Resorts
Gatlinburg, TN

Condominium

Vacation-oriented—commonly for extended-stay purposes—apartment-style accommodations of varying design or décor. Routinely available for rent through a management company, units often contain one or more bedrooms, a living room, full kitchen, and an eating area. Studio-type models combine the

Sands of Kahana
Kahana, Maui, HI

sleeping and living areas into one room. As a rule, basic cleaning supplies, kitchen utensils, and complete bed and bath linens are supplied. The guest registration area may be located off site.

Cottage

Vacation-oriented, typically smaller scale, freestanding units with home style enhancements in architectural design and interior décor. Often located in wooded, rural, or waterfront locations. Units may vary in design and décor. As a rule, basic cleaning supplies, kitchen utensils, and complete bed and bath linens are supplied. The guest registration area may be located off site.

Paradise Villas, Little Cayman Island

Country Inn

Although similar in definition to a bed and breakfast, country inns are usually larger in scale with spacious public areas and offer a dining facility that serves—at a minimum—breakfast and dinner.

Greenville Inn, Greenville, ME

Hotel

Commonly, a multistory establishment with interior room entrances offering a variety of guest unit styles. The magnitude of the public areas is determined by the overall theme, location and service level, but may include a variety of facilities such as a restaurant, shops, fitness center, spa, business center, and/or meeting rooms.

The Grand America Hotel
Salt Lake City, UT

Motel

Commonly, a one- or two-story establishment with exterior room entrances and drive up parking. Typically, guest units have one bedroom with a bathroom of similar décor and design. Public areas and facilities are often limited in size and/or availability.

Best Western Deltona Inn, Deltona, FL

Ranch

Typically a working ranch with an obvious rustic, Western theme featuring equestrian-related activities and a variety of guest unit styles.

Lost Valley Ranch, Deckers, CO

Vacation Rental House

Vacation-oriented—commonly for extended-stay purposes—typically larger scale, freestanding, and of varying design or décor. Routinely available for rent through a management company, houses often contain two or more bedrooms, a living room, full kitchen, dining room, and multiple bathrooms. As a rule, basic cleaning supplies, kitchen utensils, and complete bed and bath linens are supplied. The guest registration area may be located off site.

ResortQuest, Hilton Head Island, SC

Lodging Sub-classifications

The following are sub-classifications that may appear along with the classifications listed previously to provide a more specific description of the lodging.

Boutique

Often thematic and typically an informal, yet highly personalized experience; may have a luxurious or quirky style which is fashionable or unique.

Casino

Extensive gambling facilities are available, such as: blackjack, craps, keno, and slot machines. **Note:** This sub-classification will not appear beneath its Diamond Rating in the listing. It will be indicated by a 🎲 icon and will be included in the row of icons following the lodging listing.

Classic

Renowned and landmark properties, older than 50 years, well-known for their unique style and ambience.

Contemporary

Overall design and theme reflects characteristics of the present era's mainstream tastes and style.

Extended Stay

Offers a predominance of long-term accommodations with a designated full-service kitchen area within each unit.

Historic

These properties are typically over 75 years of age and exhibit many features of a historic nature with respect to architecture, design, furnishings, public record, or acclaim. Properties must meet one of the following criteria:

- Maintain the integrity of the historical nature
- Be listed on the National Register of Historic Places
- Have a National Historic Landmark designation or be located in a National Register Historic District

Separate criteria designate historic properties in Canada, Mexico and the Caribbean.

Resort

Recreation-oriented, geared to vacation travelers seeking a specific destination experience. Travel packages, meal plans, themed entertainment, and social and recreational programs are typically available. Recreational facilities are extensive and may include spa treatments, golf, tennis, skiing, fishing, or water sports. Larger resorts may offer a variety of guest accommodations.

Retro

Overall design and theme reflect a contemporary design reinterpreting styles from a bygone era.

Vacation Rental

Typically houses, condos, cottages or cabins; these properties are a "home away from home" offering more room and greater value for the money. In general, they provide the conveniences of home, such as full kitchens and washers/dryers. Located in resort or popular destination areas within close proximity to major points of interest, attractions, or recreation areas, these properties may require a pre-arranged reservation and check-in at an off-site location. Housekeeping services may be limited or not included.

Vintage

Offers a window to the past and provides an experience reflecting a predominance of traits associated with the era of their origin.

Guest Safety

Room Security

In order to be approved for listing in AAA/CAA TourBook guides for the United States and Canada, accommodations must have deadbolt locks on all guest room entry doors and connecting room doors.

If the area outside the guest room door is not visible from inside the room through a window or door panel, viewports must be installed on all guest room entry doors. Bed and breakfast properties and country inns are not required to have viewports. Ground floor and easily accessible sliding doors must be equipped with some type of secondary security locks.

Even with those approval requirements, AAA cannot guarantee guest safety. AAA inspectors view a percentage of rooms at each property since it is not feasible to evaluate every room in every lodging establishment. Therefore, AAA cannot guarantee that there are working locks on all doors and windows in all guest rooms.

Fire Safety

Because of the highly specialized skills needed to conduct professional fire safety inspections, AAA/CAA inspectors cannot assess fire safety.

Properties must meet all federal, state/province and local fire codes. Each guest unit in all U.S. and Canadian lodging properties must be equipped with an operational, single-station smoke detector. A AAA/CAA inspector has evaluated a sampling of the rooms to verify this equipment is in place.

Mexico and the Caribbean

Requirements for some features, such as door locks and smoke detectors/sprinkler systems, differ in Mexico and the Caribbean. If a property met AAA's security requirements at the time of the evaluation, the phrase "Meets AAA guest room security requirements" appears in the listing.

Service Animals

The Americans with Disabilities Act (ADA) prohibits U.S. businesses that serve the public from discriminating against persons with disabilities. Some businesses have mistakenly denied access to persons who use service animals. Businesses must permit entry to guests and their service animals, as well as allow service animals to accompany guests to all public areas of a property.

A property is permitted to ask whether the animal is a service animal or a pet, and whether the guest has a disability. The property may not, however, ask questions about the nature of the disability, the service provided by the animal, or require proof of a disability or certification that the animal is a service animal. These regulations may not apply in Canada, Mexico or the Caribbean.

No fees or deposits, even those normally charged for pets, may be charged for service animals. Service animals fulfill a critical need for their owners—they are not pets.

Frank Frand with his seeing eye dog, Cardinal.

*A*lberta

Camping
Doesn't get better than in Alberta

Shop 'til You Drop
In a mall so large it has a hotel and a water park

The Old West is Alive and Well
For 10 days in the Canadian Rockies during The Calgary Stampede

Variety Unsurpassed
Placid lakes, prairies, red rock canyons, lush forests, and soaring mountains

Lake Louise
Ski it in winter, hike it in summer, admire it all year

Athabasca River, Jasper National Park of Canada
© Daryl Benson
Masterfile

Lake Louise, Banff National Park of Canada / © Brad Wrobleski / Masterfile

Alberta is a *happening* place.
In any season you're bound to
find Albertans commemorating
some aspect of their multifaceted province.
And with the Canadian Rockies blocking
eastbound Pacific moisture, odds are
great that whatever the event, it will
take place in sunshine.

Winter festivals in Jasper and Banff
showcase such snowy weather sports as
skiing, sledding and ice-skating against
a backdrop of postcard-beautiful
alpine scenery.

As spring and summer heat things
up, Edmonton earns its reputation as
"Canada's Festival City," with events
celebrating local culture. Laughter and
applause punctuate the Edmonton
International Street Performers Festival,
while food lovers can take a gastronomic

trip around the world as they sample from a spectrum of cuisines during the Edmonton Heritage Festival.

The bronc-buckin' Calgary Stampede all but steals the spotlight. Much more than a big-time rodeo, this Wild West exhibition turns into a huge outdoor party with parades and a carnival midway.

In autumn Calgary's Spruce Meadows hosts another exciting equestrian event—the Masters Tournament, one of the world's most distinguished show jumping competitions.

Of course, you don't have to rope a steer if you travel to Alberta. Just visiting Canada's sunniest province is a special event.

Mirror images of mountain peaks reflected in calm, clear lakes. The twinkling, shimmering dance of lights known as aurora borealis. Blankets of golden wheat and vivid canola pulled up snugly over the rolling countryside.

Typical visions of the Wild West? Hardly.

But Alberta urges you to stretch the definition of what the Canadian West is all about.

Plenty in the province fits neatly into the Western mold. Take Calgary, for instance. The former cow town's very roots are in ranching and meatpacking. Thousands of folks in denim and 10-gallon hats gather to watch the rough-and-tumble rodeo and chuck wagon races of the 10-day Calgary Stampede. Even the roof of the Pengrowth Saddledome, home of the National Hockey League's Calgary Flames, is in the shape of—you guessed it—a saddle.

But although Calgary is decidedly Western in many ways, it prides itself on having cultivated a personality that's much more well-rounded.

A Multifaceted Identity

In 1988 the world's best athletes united in the city for the Olympic Winter Games. From grizzly bears to wood bison, the renowned Calgary Zoo, Botanical Garden & Prehistoric Park offers the best chance to see native wildlife. It also is home to more than 4,000 plants and a collection of life-size replicas of dinosaurs in a simulated Mesozoic landscape. Futuristic elevated "pedways" link nearly half of the buildings downtown.

And so it goes with the rest of the province, where such dichotomies are commonplace.

The faintly sweet aroma of 18 varieties of orchids in Cypress Hills Interprovincial Park lends to an air of tranquility and peace. But just a scant hop and skip to the northwest, volatile Medicine Hat harnesses an extensive reserve of natural gas that prompted Rudyard Kipling to describe the city as having "all hell for a basement."

Rafters steel themselves against the raging rapids of the Elbow, Highwood and Kananaskis rivers in Kananaskis Country. Turbulent rushes of water sweeping over rock at Athabasca and Sunwapta falls become imposing towers of irresistible ice to climbers who chink away at them in winter. Amid the chaos, however, canoeists ply the placid, emerald waters of Banff National Park of Canada's

The Hudson's Bay Co. gets fur-trading rights in a portion of what is now Alberta.
1670

Anthony Henday is the first European to visit the area.
1754

Calgary is established as a North West Mounted Police fort.
1875

Library of Congress

1795
Edmonton is founded as a Hudson's Bay trading fort.

Library of Congress

1883
The Canadian Pacific Railway reaches Calgary.

Alberta Historical Timeline

Moraine Lake and gaze upon the 10 glaciated summits that rise around it to provide a serene habitat for elk, deer and bighorn sheep.

The ground in Fort McMurray holds a significant reserve of lucrative oil sands deposits, but most people visit the town for its treasure in the sky: a spectacular view of the northern lights.

A Canadian Melting Pot

Alberta's diversity also stems from the many ethnic currents that run through it.

A strong Ukrainian heritage marks the area east of Edmonton. At the Ukrainian Cultural Heritage Village costumed interpreters demonstrate what life was like for settlers from the 1890s to 1930. The design of Vegreville's famed bronze, gold and silver pysanka, or Ukrainian Easter egg, depicts the people's faith and commemorates the protection provided to them by the Royal Canadian Mounted Police. Museums in Edmonton and Mundare hold collections of cultural items.

West of Edmonton, English-, French- and German-speaking emigrants from central Europe established villages. Murals and a living-history museum in Stony Plain tell their stories.

The history of native cultures is evident at the Head-Smashed-In Buffalo Jump Interpretive Centre near Fort Macleod and in the petroglyphs and pictographs at Writing-on-Stone Provincial Park, near Milk River. Indian Battle Park in Lethbridge details a significant battle between the Cree and Blackfoot Indians.

Traditions of the aboriginal people are remembered in Edmonton's Royal Alberta Museum. The territory around Cypress Hills Interprovincial Park—now home to ruminants, beavers and coyotes—nurtured a community of aborigines more than 7,000 years ago.

Prehistoric denizens of the Red Deer Valley, the dinosaurs, left their mark on the region by way of the fossils left behind in walls of sediment. Drumheller best captures the age along the Dinosaur Trail (hwys. 838 and 837) and through displays in its museums. To the southeast, a fertile fossil bed at Dinosaur Provincial Park near Patricia contains the remains of 39 species of dinosaurs.

Alberta weaves a rich, vibrant tapestry of cultures, geography and a wealth of experiences. Westward ho.

The province of Alberta is formed.
1905

Great Canadian Oil Sands, the first commercial plant to successfully mine oil sands and extract bitumen, starts production in Fort McMurray.
1967

Construction of West Edmonton Mall, one of the world's largest malls, is completed.
1998

Travel Alberta

1988
Calgary hosts the Winter Olympic Games.

2005
Alberta celebrates its 100th year as a Canadian province.

1914
Oil is discovered in the Turner Valley.

Recreation

Alberta is a nature lover's paradise. A place where unspoiled landscapes lend themselves to exploration in any season. A place where midnight summer sunsets in the north cap off long days of rest and relaxation. A place where towering mountains in the west beckon to all who appreciate unrestrained beauty.

Outdoor enthusiasts often look to Alberta's five national parks. Hikers, golfers, boaters, bicyclists, horseback riders, anglers and skiers are among the people who trek to them: Banff, Canada's first national park; Elk Island, an oasis for rare and endangered species; Jasper, a land of glaciers; Waterton Lakes, where the Rockies and prairie meet; and Wood Buffalo, which reaches north into Northwest Territories.

And although the national parks are arguably the most popular spots for recreational escape, sites throughout the grand expanse of untamed Alberta are equally as irresistible.

Experienced guides lead half-day to multi-week **trail riding** expeditions through the Elbow and Sheep valleys in the Kananaskis high country, west of Calgary; Ram Falls, southwest of Rocky Mountain House National Historic Site of Canada; and Cooking Lake-Blackfoot Provincial Recreational Area, east of Edmonton.

Only your imagination limits what you can do in the challenging Rockies. **Hiking, mountain climbing** and **mountain biking** are among the ways to get to know the peaks.

High-Octane Excitement

Pulse-pounding thrills await the adventurous who take on raging rivers for a **whitewater rafting** diversion. Beginners and veterans alike appreciate the draw of the Athabasca, Elbow, Highwood, Kananaskis, Kicking Horse, Red Deer and Sunwapta rivers.

The Blackstone River, a hot spot for **kayaking** in inflatable boats, cuts through the foothills of the Rockies. Slip into the North Saskatchewan River for a memorable **canoeing** experience.

When a blanket of snow covers the majestic Rockies, bundle up and head for the mountains. **Snowshoeing, tobogganing, crosscountry skiing** and **sledding,** which can be done nearly anywhere there's snow, are mainstays of Canadian family fun.

To up the exhilaration factor, take advantage of one of North America's longest ski seasons, which can range from early November to late May in places. Some of the best **downhill skiing** and **snowboarding** the province has to offer is at Marmot Basin, 19 kilometres (12 mi.) south of Jasper; Lake Louise, 57 kilometres (35 mi.) northwest of Banff; Sunshine Village and Banff Mount Norquay, both within 15 minutes of Banff; Fortress Mountain, in Kananaskis Country; and Nakiska, at 90 kilometres (55 mi.) west the closest mountain ski area to Calgary. The boldest of the bold tackle waterfall **ice climbing** or **heli-skiing,** in which a helicopter takes skiers to untouched powder.

Leaving a Wake of Powder

Wide, open expanses of windswept grasslands, rolling hills and heavily dusted valleys make for lots of good **snowmobiling,** too. For cheek-reddening mirth, zip through the region around Grande Prairie.

One of Alberta's more popular winter adventures is a trip to Fort McMurray to catch the best view of the awe-inspiring aurora borealis, or "northern lights."

Nearly anywhere you go in the province, you'll find opportunities galore for **fishing.** Alberta's numerous trophy lakes, so designated because of the huge fish that inhabit them, brim with pike, whitefish, perch and walleye. Some notable fly-in trophy lakes are Gardiner and Namur, northwest of Fort McMurray, and Winefred, northeast of Lac La Biche. Head to the Bow River for exceptional trout fly-fishing. Phone (888) 944-5494 for information about regulations and licensing.

For an unforgettable **camping** experience, charter a plane out of Cold Lake, Fort McMurray, Fort Smith, Fort Vermilion, High Level or Lac La Biche and fly to a lodge or camp in the northern lakes.

Recreational Activities

Throughout the TourBook, you may notice a Recreational Activities heading with bulleted listings of recreation-oriented establishments listed underneath. Similar operations also may be mentioned in Destination City recreation sections. Since normal AAA inspection criteria cannot be applied, these establishments are presented only for information. Age, height and weight restrictions may apply. Reservations often are recommended and sometimes are required. Addresses and/or phone numbers are provided so visitors can contact the attraction for additional information.

Fast Facts

POPULATION: 3,290,350.

AREA: 640,045 sq km (247,123 sq mi); ranks 6th.

CAPITAL: Edmonton.

HIGHEST POINT: 3,747 m/12,293 ft., Mount Columbia.

LOWEST POINT: 152 m/499 ft., Salt River at border with the Northwest Territories.

TIME ZONE(S): Mountain. DST.

TEEN DRIVING LAWS: For probationary licensees, driving is not permitted daily midnight-5 a.m. The minimum age for an unrestricted driver's license is 18. Phone (780) 422-8839 for more information about Alberta driver's license regulations.

MINIMUM AGE FOR GAMBLING: 18.

SEAT BELT/CHILD RESTRAINT LAWS: Seat belts are required for driver and all passengers ages 16 and older. Children ages 6 until 16 and over 17 kilograms (38 lbs.) are required to be in a child restraint or seat belt. Child restraints are required for those under age 6 and under 18 kilograms (40 lbs.).

HELMETS FOR MOTORCYCLISTS: Required for all riders.

RADAR DETECTORS: Permitted.

FIREARMS LAWS: By federal law, all nonresidents entering Canada with a firearm must declare their weapon in writing and pay a fee of $25 (Canadian). Contact the Canadian Firearms Centre at (800) 731-4000 to receive a declaration form or for additional information.

HOLIDAYS: Jan. 1; Family Day, Feb. (3rd Mon.); Good Friday; Easter Monday; Victoria Day, May 24 (if a Mon.) or the closest prior Mon.; Canada Day, July 1; Heritage Day, Aug. (1st Mon.); Labour Day, Sept. (1st Mon.); Thanksgiving, Oct. (2nd Mon.); Remembrance Day, Nov. 11; Christmas, Dec. 25; Boxing Day, Dec. 26.

TAXES: Alberta has no provincial sales tax. However, there is a 4 percent hotel tax, plus a 1-2 percent tourism levy in some areas. In addition there is a 5 percent national Goods and Service Tax (GST).

INFORMATION CENTERS: Travel Alberta Visitor Centres provide information about accommodations and campgrounds as well as maps. They are located at Canmore on Hwy. 1; Crowsnest Pass on Hwy. 3; Field, British Columbia, on Hwy. 1; Grande Prairie on 106th St.; Hinton on Hwy. 16; Lloydminster on Hwy. 16; Milk River on Hwy. 4; Oyen at the junction of hwys. 9 and 41; Walsh on Hwy. 1; and West Glacier, Mont., at the junction of Hwy. 2 and Going-to-the-Sun Road. Most centers are open daily 9-6, mid-May through Labour Day. A tourism office is open year-round in Canmore.

FURTHER INFORMATION FOR VISITORS:

Travel Alberta
P.O. Box 2500
Edmonton, AB, Canada T5J 2Z4
(780) 427-4321
(800) 252-3782
See color ad page 41 and on insert

RECREATION INFORMATION:

Alberta Tourism, Parks and Recreation
Parks & Protected Areas
9820 106th St., 2nd Floor
Edmonton, AB, Canada T5K 2J6
(780) 427-9470
(866) 427-3582

FISHING AND HUNTING REGULATIONS:

Sustainable Resource Development
   Information Centre
9920 108th St., Main Floor
Edmonton, AB, Canada T5K 2M4
(780) 944-0313
(877) 944-0313 (in Alberta)

ALCOHOL CONSUMPTION: Legal age 18.

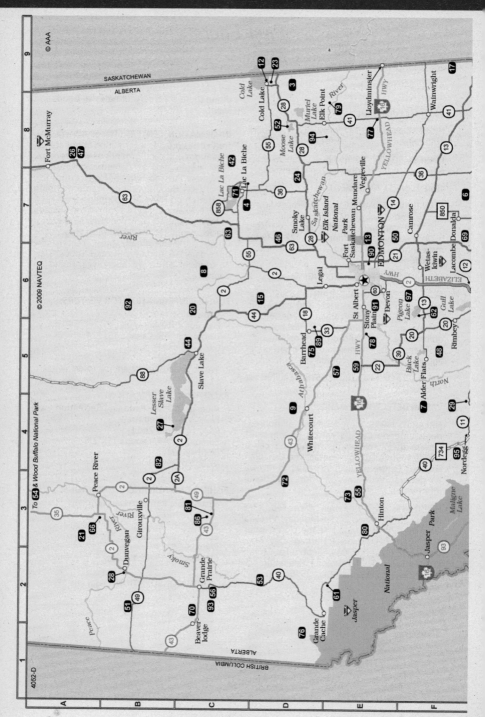

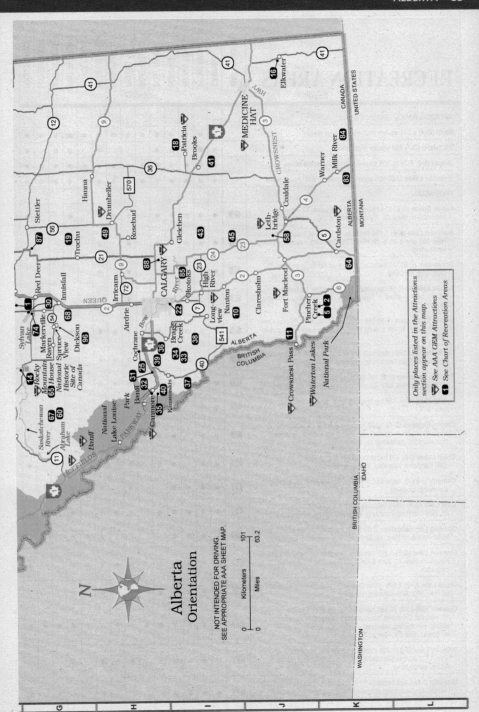

Alberta Orientation

NOT INTENDED FOR DRIVING. SEE APPROPRIATE AAA SHEET MAP.

Kilometers 101
Miles 63.2

Only places listed in the Attractions section appear on this map.

See AAA GEM Attractions
See Chart of Recreation Areas

RECREATION AREAS

	MAP LOCATION	CAMPING	PICNICKING	HIKING TRAILS	BOATING	BOAT RAMP	BOAT RENTAL	FISHING	SWIMMING	PETS ON LEASH	BICYCLE TRAILS	WINTER SPORTS	VISITOR CENTER	LODGE/CABINS	FOOD SERVICE
NATIONAL PARKS *(See place listings)*															
Banff (G-4) 6,641 square kilometres. Horse rental.		•	•	•	•	•	•	•	•	•	•	•	•	•	•
Elk Island (D-7) 194 square kilometres.		•	•	•	•	•				•		•	•		•
Jasper (E-2, F-2) 11,228 square kilometres. Horse rental.		•	•	•	•	•	•	•	•	•	•	•	•	•	•
Waterton Lakes (J-5) 505 square kilometres. Golf; horse rental.		•	•	•	•	•	•	•	•	•	•	•	•	•	•
PROVINCIAL															
Aspen Beach (G-6) 214 hectares on Gull Lake, 17 km w. of Lacombe on Hwy. 12. *(See Lacombe p. 84)*	1	•	•					•	•	•		•			•
Beauvais Lake (K-6) 1,160 hectares 11 km w. of Pincher Creek on Hwy. 507 and 8 km s. on Hwy. 775. Canoeing, kayaking, sailing, windsurfing.	2	•	•	•	•	•		•		•		•			
Beaverdam (D-9) 110 hectares 5 km e. of Nordegg on Hwy. 11. Canoeing, kayaking.	3	•	•					•	•						
Beaver Lake (C-7) 96 hectares 6 km s.e. of Lac La Biche off Hwy. 36, on the n.e. shore of Beaver Lake. Bird-watching, canoeing, kayaking.	4	•			•	•	•	•							•
Beaver Mines Lake (K-6) 118 hectares 20 km w. of Pincher Creek on Hwy. 507, 10 km s.w. on Hwy. 774, then 5 km s. on access road.	5	•	•	•	•			•		•		•			
Big Knife (F-7) 295 hectares 8 km w. and 13 km s. of Forestburg on Hwy. 855. Bird-watching, canoeing, kayaking.	6	•	•	•				•	•						
Brazeau Reservoir (F-4) 130 hectares 60 km s.w. of Drayton Valley along Hwy. 620. Canoeing, kayaking, sailing, windsurfing.	7	•			•	•		•							
Calling Lake (C-6) 738 hectares 55 km n. of Athabasca on Hwy. 813.	8	•	•			•		•	•						
Carson-Pegasus (D-4) 1,209 hectares 6 km w. of Whitecourt on Hwy. 43, 11 km n. on Hwy. 32, then 5 km e. on access road. Bird-watching, canoeing, kayaking, wildlife observation.	9	•	•	•	•	•	•	•		•					•
Chain Lakes (I-6) 409 hectares 38 km s.w. of Nanton on Hwy. 533. Canoeing, kayaking, sailing, windsurfing.	10	•	•	•	•	•		•		•		•			•
Chinook (J-5) 48 hectares 8 km w. of Crowsnest Pass off Hwy. 3. Canoeing, kayaking.	11	•	•	•				•				•			
Cold Lake (D-9) 5,849 hectares 3 km n.e. of Cold Lake off Hwy. 28. Bird-watching, canoeing, kayaking, sailing, windsurfing.	12	•	•	•	•	•		•	•	•		•			
Cooking Lake-Blackfoot (E-7) 9,700 hectares 24 km e. of Sherwood Park s. of Hwy. 16. Bird-watching, canoeing, kayaking.	13		•	•	•					•	•	•			
Crimson Lake (G-5) 3,209 hectares 14 km w. of Rocky Mountain House on Hwy. 11, then 6 km n. on Hwy. 756. Interpretive programs.	14	•	•	•	•	•		•	•	•		•			•
Cross Lake (D-6) 2,076 hectares 8 km n. and 19 km n.e. of Jarvie off Hwy. 663. Bird-watching, canoeing, kayaking.	15	•	•	•	•	•		•	•	•		•			
Cypress Hills (J-9) 20,451 hectares 1.5 km s. of Elkwater on Hwy. 41. Historic. Canoeing, cross-country skiing, golf, kayaking, sailing, windsurfing; interpretive programs. Five horsepower limit for boats. *(See Elkwater p. 76)*	16	•	•	•	•	•		•	•	•		•	•	•	•
Dillberry Lake (F-9) 1,205 hectares 15 km s.e. of Chauvin on Hwy. 17 at Alberta/Saskatchewan border. Canoeing, kayaking, sailing, windsurfing.	17	•	•	•	•			•	•	•		•			
Dinosaur (I-8) 8,085 hectares 13 km n.e. of Patricia via Hwy. 210. Historic. Bird-watching, canoeing, kayaking; interpretive programs. *(See Patricia p. 88)*	18	•	•							•			•		•

RECREATION AREAS

	MAP LOCATION	CAMPING	PICNICKING	HIKING TRAILS	BOATING	BOAT RAMP	BOAT RENTAL	FISHING	SWIMMING	PETS ON LEASH	BICYCLE TRAILS	WINTER SPORTS	VISITOR CENTER	LODGE/CABINS	FOOD SERVICE
Dry Island Buffalo Jump (G-7) 1,598 hectares 15 km n.e. of Huxley off Hwy. 21 on an access road. Bird-watching, canoeing, kayaking.	19	•	•	•				•		•					
Fawcett Lake (West) (C-6) 48 hectares 55 km s.e. of Slave Lake on Hwy. 2, 20 km n. on Hwy. 2A, then 18 km n. on access road.	20	•	•		•	•		•	•	•					•
Figure Eight Lake (A-3) 90 hectares 25 km w. of Peace River off Hwy. 35.	21	•	•	•	•	•		•	•	•			•		
Fish Creek (I-6) 1,355 hectares in Calgary between 37th St. S.W. and the Bow River. Golf; interpretive programs.	22		•					•	•	•	•		•		•
French Bay (D-9) 449 hectares 11 km e. and 3 km n. of Cold Lake off Hwy. 55. Canoeing, kayaking, sailing, windsurfing.	23	•	•		•	•		•	•	•					
Garner Lake (D-7) 74 hectares 5 km n. of Spedden off Hwy. 28.	24	•	•	•	•	•		•	•	•					
Ghost Reservoir (H-5) 24 hectares 18 km w. of Cochrane on Hwy. 1A. Sailing, windsurfing.	25	•	•		•	•	•	•	•	•					
Gregoire Lake (A-8) 696 hectares 19 km s. of Fort McMurray on Hwy. 63, then 10 km e. on Hwy. 881. Bird-watching.	26	•	•	•	•	•		•	•	•			•		
Hilliard's Bay (B-4) 2,323 hectares 10 km e. of Grouard off Hwy. 750. Canoeing, kayaking, sailing, windsurfing.	27	•	•	•	•	•		•	•	•					
Historic Dunvegan (B-2) 9 hectares off Queen Elizabeth II Hwy. on the n. side of the Peace River beside Dunvegan Suspension Bridge. Historic. *(See Dunvegan p. 63)*	28	•	•		•			•		•			•		
Jackfish Lake (F-4) 203 hectares 50 km w. of Rocky Mountain House on Hwy. 11, then 2 km n. on access road. Pier.	29	•	•		•	•		•		•					
Jarvis Bay (G-6) 86 hectares 4 km n. of Sylvan Lake townsite on Hwy. 20.	30	•		•						•			•	•	
Kananaskis Country (I-4) *(See place listing p. 83)*															
Bow Valley (H-5) 3,129 hectares 25 km e. of Canmore on Hwy. 1 and :5 km n. on Hwy. 1X. Canoeing, kayaking; bicycle rental, interpretive programs.	31	•	•	•	•	•	•	•		•	•	•	•		•
Canmore Nordic Centre (H-5) 804 hectares 3 km s. of Canmore on Spray Lakes Rd.	32		•	•						•	•	•	•		•
Elbow Falls (I-5) 106 hectares 30 km w. of Bragg Creek on Hwy. 66. Bird-watching, canoeing, kayaking.	33	•	•	•				•		•					
Elbow River (I-5) 245 hectares 20 km w. of Bragg Creek on Hwy. 66. Interpretive programs.	34	•	•	•				•		•	•				
Evan-Thomas (H-4) 2,571 hectares 30 km e. of Canmore on Spray Lakes Rd.	35		•	•				•		•			•	•	
McLean Creek (H-5) 238 hectares 12 km w. of Bragg Creek on Hwy. 66, then 1.3 km s. on McLean Creek Trail. Bird-watching.	36	•	•					•		•					•
Peter Lougheed (I-5) 50,142 hectares 43 km s.e. of Canmore on Hwy. 40. Canoeing, kayaking; interpretive programs.	37	•	•	•	•	•		•		•	•	•	•		•
Sheep River (I-5) 6,191 hectares 25 km w. of Turner Valley on Hwy. 546. Horseback riding.	38		•	•				•		•		•			
Sibbald Lake (H-5) 79 hectares 30 km e. of Canmore on Hwy. 1, 6 km s. on Hwy. 40, then 12 km e. on Hwy. 68. Canoeing, kayaking; amphitheater, interpretive programs.	39	•	•	•	•			•		•		•			
Spray Valley (H-5) 27,471 hectares s.w. of Canmore, surrounding the Spray Lakes Reservoir. Golf; interpretive programs.	40	•	•	•				•		•			•		
Kinbrook Island (I-8) 540 hectares 13 km s. of Brooks off Hwy. 873. Bird-watching, canoeing, kayaking, sailing, windsurfing.	41	•	•		•	•		•	•	•		•			•

RECREATION AREAS

	MAP LOCATION	CAMPING	PICNICKING	HIKING TRAILS	BOATING	BOAT RAMP	BOAT RENTAL	FISHING	SWIMMING	PETS ON LEASH	BICYCLE TRAILS	WINTER SPORTS	VISITOR CENTER	LODGE/CABINS	FOOD SERVICE
Lakeland (C-8) 59,030 hectares 13 km e. of Lac La Biche off Hwy. 663. Bird-watching, canoeing, kayaking. *(See Lac La Biche p. 84)*	42	•	•	•	•	•	•		•	•	•	•	•		
Lake McGregor (I-7) 140 hectares 20 km n. of Vulcan on Hwy. 23, then 25 km e. on Hwy. 542. Canoeing, kayaking, sailing, windsurfing.	43	•	•		•	•		•		•	•	•			
Lesser Slave Lake (C-5) 7,566 hectares 6 km n. of Slave Lake on Hwy. 88. Bird-watching; interpretive programs. *(See Slave Lake p. 90)*	44	•	•	•	•			•	•	•	•	•	•		
Little Bow (I-7) 110 hectares 20 km s. of Vulcan on Hwy. 23, 16 km e. on Hwy. 529, then 1 km s. on access road. Bird-watching, canoeing, kayaking.	45	•	•		•	•	•	•	•	•		•			•
Long Lake (D-7) 769 hectares 20 km s. of Boyle on Hwy. 831, then 2 km n.e. on access road.	46	•	•		•	•	•	•	•	•		•			•
Maqua Lake (A-8) 191 hectares 27 km s. of Fort McMurray on Hwy. 63, 15 km s. on Hwy. 881, then 10 km s.w. on access road. Canoeing, kayaking.	47		•	•	•					•		•			
Medicine Lake (F-5) 24 hectares 47 km n. of Rocky Mountain House on Hwy. 22, then 8 km s.e. on access road. Canoeing, kayaking.	48	•	•		•	•		•	•	•		•			•
Midland (H-7) 599 hectares 6 km w. of Drumheller on Hwy. 838. Historic. Canoeing, golf, kayaking; interpretive programs, outdoor exhibits. *(See Drumheller p. 62)*	49			•	•			•							•
Miquelon Lake (E-7) 1,299 hectares 3 km s. of New Sarepta on Hwy. 21, then 20 km e. on Hwy. 623. Bird-watching, canoeing, kayaking, sailing, windsurfing; interpretive programs.	50	•	•	•	•			•	•	•		•	•	•	•
Moonshine Lake (B-2) 1,103 hectares 27 km w. of Spirit River on Hwy. 49, then 7 km n. on Hwy. 725.	51	•	•	•	•			•	•	•		•			
Moose Lake (D-8) 736 hectares 5 km n. of Bonnyville on Hwy. 41, 10 km w. on Hwy. 660, then 2 km s. on access road. Canoeing, kayaking, sailing, windsurfing.	52	•	•		•	•		•	•	•					
Musreau Lake (D-2) 1,803 hectares 80 km s. of Grande Prairie on Hwy. 40, then 2 km e. on access road. Canoeing, kayaking.	53	•	•		•	•		•		•					
Notikewin (A-3) 9,697 hectares 37 km n. of Manning via Hwy. 35, then 30 km e. on Hwy. 692. Historic. Bird-watching, canoeing, golf, kayaking.	54	•	•		•			•		•		•		•	
Obed Lake (E-3) 3,402 hectares 55 km w. of Edson off Hwy. 16. Canoeing, kayaking.	55	•	•		•	•		•		•					
O'Brien (C-2) 65 hectares 10 km s. of Grande Prairie on Hwy. 40. Canoeing, kayaking.	56		•		•			•	•	•					
Paddle River Dam (E-5) 70 hectares 10 km n.w. of Sangudo on Hwy. 43. Canoeing, kayaking.	57		•		•	•		•	•	•		•			
Park Lake (J-7) 224 hectares 17 km n.w. of Lethbridge on Hwy. 25, then 5 km n.w. on Hwy. 101. Canoeing, kayaking, sailing.	58	•	•		•	•		•	•	•		•			•
Pembina River (E-5) 167 hectares 2 km n.e. of Entwistle on Hwy. 16A. Canoeing, kayaking; interpretive programs.	59	•	•		•			•	•	•					
Peppers Lake (G-4) 18 hectares 84 km s.e. of Nordegg on Forestry Trunk Rd. (Hwy. 734). Canoeing, horseback riding, kayaking.	60	•			•	•		•		•					
Pierre Grey's Lakes (E-2) 633 hectares 37 km s. of Grande Cache off Hwy. 40 on access road. Historic. Scenic.	61	•	•	•	•	•	•	•	•			•			
Pigeon Lake (F-6) 443 hectares 5 km w. and 10 km n. of Westerose off Hwy. 771.	62	•	•		•	•		•	•	•	•	•	•		•

RECREATION AREAS

	MAP LOCATION	CAMPING	PICNICKING	HIKING TRAILS	BOATING	BOAT RAMP	BOAT RENTAL	FISHING	SWIMMING	PETS ON LEASH	BICYCLE TRAILS	WINTER SPORTS	VISITOR CENTER	LODGE/CABINS	FOOD SERVICE
Poachers' Landing (C-7) 1,518 hectares 35 km n.e. of Athabasca on Hwy. 55, then 25 km n. on access road. Horseback riding.	63	•	•					•		•					
Police Outpost (K-6) 223 hectares 10 km s. and 23 km w. of Cardston on Queen Elizabeth II Hwy. Historic. Canoeing, kayaking.	64	•	•	•	•	•		•		•			•		
Prairie Creek (G-5) 38 hectares 41 km s.w. of Rocky Mountain House on Hwy. 752. Horseback riding.	65	•						•							
Queen Elizabeth (A-3) 86 hectares 3 km n. and 5 km w. of Grimshaw off Hwy. 35. Historic. Bird-watching, canoeing, kayaking, sailing.	66	•	•					•	•				•	•	
Ram Falls (G-4) 409 hectares 64 km s. of Nordegg on Forestry Trunk Rd. (Hwy. 734).	67	•	•	•				•		•					•
Red Lodge (G-6) 129 hectares 15 km w. of Bowden on Hwy. 587. Canoeing, kayaking.	68	•	•	•				•	•	•			•		
Rochon Sands (F-7) 119 hectares 12 km w. of Stettler on Hwy. 12, then 16 km n. on Hwy. 835. Canoeing, kayaking, sailing, windsurfing.	69	•	•	•	•	•		•	•	•					
Saskatoon Island (C-2) 101 hectares 21 km w. of Grande Prairie on Hwy. 43, then 4 km n. on an access road. Water sports; interpretive programs.	70	•	•	•	•			•	•	•	•		•		
Sir Winston Churchill (C-7) 239 hectares 13 km n.e. of Lac La Biche off Hwy. 881. Bird-watching, canoeing, kayaking. *(See Lac La Biche p. 84)*	71	•	•	•	•	•		•	•	•			•		•
Smoke Lake (D-3) 102 hectares 9 km s.w. of Fox Creek off Hwy. 43. Canoeing, kayaking.	72	•	•		•	•		•	•	•					
Sundance (E-3) 151 hectares 56 km n.e. of Hinton on Emerson Creek Rd. Canoeing, kayaking.	73	•	•	•				•		•					
Sylvan Lake (G-5) 85 hectares 18 km n.w. of Red Deer on Hwy. 11 in town of Sylvan Lake. Canoeing, golf, kayaking, sailing, windsurfing. *(See Red Deer p. 89)*	74	•	•		•			•	•				•		•
Thunder Lake (D-5) 208 hectares 21 km w. of Barrhead on Hwy. 18.	75	•	•		•	•		•	•	•					•
Two Lakes (D-1) 1,566 hectares 130 km s.w. of Grande Prairie on Two Lakes Rd. Canoeing, kayaking.	76	•		•	•	•		•		•			•		
Vermilion (E-8) 759 hectares 1.5 km n. of Vermilion on Hwy. 41 from jct. Hwy. 16, then w. on 50th Ave. following signs. Historic. Canoeing, golf, kayaking.	77	•	•	•	•			•	•	•			•		•
Wabamun Lake (E-5) 231 hectares 3 km e. and 1 km s. of Wabamun off Hwy. 16A. Historic. Bird-watching, kayaking, sailing, windsurfing.	78	•	•	•	•	•		•	•	•					
Whitney Lakes (E-8) 1,489 hectares 24 km e. of Elk Point off Hwy. 646. Historic. Bird-watching, canoeing, kayaking, sailing, windsurfing.	79	•	•	•	•	•		•	•	•					
William A. Switzer (E-3) 6,268 hectares 3 km w. of Hinton on Hwy. 16, then 19 km n. on Hwy. 40. Historic. Bird-watching, canoeing, kayaking; interpretive programs.	80	•	•	•	•	•	•	•	•	•	•	•	•	•	
Williamson (C-3) 17 hectares 17 km w. of Valleyview on Hwy. 43, then 2 km n. on an access road. Canoeing, kayaking, sailing, windsurfing.	81	•	•		•	•		•	•	•			•		
Winagami Lake (B-4) 6,542 hectares 20 km n. of High Prairie on Hwy. 749, 10 km w. on Hwy. 679, then 7 km n. on access road. Bird-watching, canoeing, kayaking.	82	•	•	•	•	•		•		•					
Woolford (K-7) 35 hectares 50 km s.w. of Lethbridge on Hwy. 5, then 17 km e. on Hwy. 503. Historic. Canoeing, kayaking.	83	•	•	•	•			•		•					

RECREATION AREAS

	MAP LOCATION	CAMPING	PICNICKING	HIKING TRAILS	BOATING	BOAT RAMP	BOAT RENTAL	FISHING	SWIMMING	PETS ON LEASH	BICYCLE TRAILS	WINTER SPORTS	VISITOR CENTER	LODGE/CABINS	FOOD SERVICE
Writing-on-Stone (K-8) 1,718 hectares 35 km e. of Milk River off Hwy. 501. Historic. Bird-watching, canoeing, kayaking; interpretive programs. *(See Milk River p. 87)*	84	•	•	•	•			•	•	•			•		•
Wyndham-Carseland (I-6) 178 hectares 2 km e. and 2 km s. of Carseland on Hwy. 24. Canoeing, kayaking.	85	•	•	•	•	•			•		•		•		
Young's Point (C-3) 3,072 hectares 26 km w. of Valleyview on Hwy. 43, then 10 km n.e. on an access road. Water sports.	86	•	•	•	•	•	•		•	•	•		•		
OTHER															
Content Bridge (G-7) 12 hectares 6 km s. of Nevis on Hwy. 21. Canoeing, kayaking.	87	•	•	•		•			•		•				•
Eagle Lake Park (H-6) 7 km e. and 6 km s. of Strathmore via Hwy. 1.	88	•	•		•	•	•	•	•	•	•				•
Elks Beach (D-5) 14 km s. of Barrhead on Hwy. 33, then e. on Hwy. 651.	89	•	•		•	•		•	•	•	•				•
Half Moon Lake (E-6) 4 hectares 3 km e. of Sherwood Park on Hwy. 630. Canoeing, kayaking; horse rental.	90	•	•	•	•		•	•	•	•	•				•
Hasse Lake (E-6) 81 hectares 5 km w. and 10 km s. of Stony Plain on Hwy. 16.	91		•	•	•			•	•	•	•		•		
North Wabasca (B-6) 77 hectares 38 km n. of Slave Lake on Hwy. 88, 100 km n.e. on Hwy. 754, then 7 km. n. on access road.	92	•	•		•	•		•	•	•	•				
Pipestone Creek (C-2) 15 km s. of Wembley. Interpretive trails.	93	•	•	•		•			•		•				
Stony Lake (D-8) 158 hectares on Stony Lake, 16 km s.w. of Elk Point off Hwy. 646.	94	•	•		•	•		•	•	•	•				
Upper Shunda Creek (F-4) 47 hectares 3 km w. of Nordegg off Hwy. 11.	95	•		•				•		•	•	•			
Westward Ho (G-5) 8 km e. of Sundre on Hwy. 27. Canoeing, kayaking.	96	•	•		•			•							•
Wizard Lake (F-6) 33 hectares 19 km s. of Calmar on Hwy. 795.	97	•	•		•	•		•	•	•	•				

Alberta Temperature Averages
Maximum/Minimum (Celsius)
From the records of The Weather Channel Interactive, Inc.

	JAN	FEB	MAR	APR	MAY	JUNE	JULY	AUG	SEPT	OCT	NOV	DEC
Banff	-5 / -15	0 / -11	4 / -8	9 / -3	14 / 2	19 / 6	22 / 7	22 / 7	16 / 3	10 / -1	1 / -8	-5 / -14
Calgary	-3 / -16	-1 / -12	3 / -8	11 / -2	17 / 3	21 / 7	23 / 9	23 / 9	17 / 4	13 / -1	3 / -9	-2 / -14
Edmonton	-8 / -17	-4 / -14	1 / -9	10 / -1	17 / 6	21 / 9	23 / 12	22 / 11	16 / 6	11 / -1	-1 / -9	-7 / -15
Jasper	-6 / -16	-1 / -12	4 / -8	10 / -3	15 / 2	19 / 6	22 / 8	22 / 7	16 / 3	10 / -1	0 / -9	-6 / -14

Points of Interest

AIRDRIE—*see Calgary p. 57.*

ALDER FLATS (F-5)
pop. 148, elev. 953 m/3,125'

EM-TE TOWN is 3 km (1.9 mi.) s. of jct. hwys. 13 and 22, then 10 km (6.2 mi.) w. on a gravel road following signs. This replica of an 1880s Western ghost town has 27 buildings including a saloon, gazebo, church, blacksmith shop, school, emporium, jail and restaurant. **Time:** Allow 1 hour minimum. **Hours:** Town open Sun.- Thurs. 9-7, Fri.-Sat. 9 a.m.-11 p.m. **Cost:** $7; $5 (ages 13-17 and 65+); $4 (ages 8-12). Prices may vary; phone ahead. **Phone:** (780) 388-2166. 🍴 🏕

BANFF NATIONAL PARK OF CANADA (G-4)

Elevations in the park range from 1,326 metres (4,350 ft.) around the Bow River to 3,612 metres (11,851 ft.) at Mount Forbes. Refer to CAA/AAA maps for additional elevation information.

Banff National Park of Canada is approached from the southeast via the Trans-Canada Hwy. west of Canmore, from the northeast via Hwy. 11 southwest of Abraham Lake, or from the north via Hwy. 93 from Jasper. The park's majestic beauty is inescapable. These routes lead to a region where mountains and the forces of nature inspire awe and command respect.

This is Canada's oldest national park: Evidence suggests that prehistoric habitation dates back 11,000 years. Remnants of the more recent Assiniboine, Blackfoot, Cree, Kootenai and Stoney settlements also have been found in the park. European explorers did not arrive until the early 1800s, and when they did, they argued over the land's resources, prompting the government to establish the park in 1885.

In this 6,641-square-kilometre (2,564-sq.-mi.) section of the Canadian Rockies there are only two main centers of activity: Banff and Lake Louise. The glacial-green Bow River flows through the mountain-ringed valley that is the setting for Banff. The dry, bracing climate, alpine grandeur and mineral hot spring pools enhance Banff's attractiveness.

The town of Banff, granted autonomy from federal jurisdiction Jan. 1, 1990, is within the park. Development within the town is strictly controlled; residents do not own their land but lease it from the park.

Situated 58 kilometres (36 mi.) west of Banff at an elevation of 1,731 metres (5,679 ft.) is icy, blue-green Lake Louise. About 2.4 kilometres (1.5 mi.) long, .6 kilometres (.4 mi.) wide and 90 metres (295 ft.) deep, Lake Louise springs from Victoria Glacier, whose meltwater carries the silt and rock flour that give the lake the opaque turquoise color common to most of the area's waters. The upper portion of the glacier is 60 to 90 metres (197 to 295 ft.) thick; the lower part is 90 metres (295 ft.) at its deepest.

The park's well-known peaks include Rundle, Cascade, Victoria, Lefroy, Temple, Castle, Forbes, Chephren, Hector and the Ten Peaks, all ranging from 2,752 to 3,618 metres (9,030 to 11,870 ft.) above sea level. The upper slopes of the ranges are either bare and rugged or glacier crowned, while the lower slopes are forested. Many mountains are mirrored in Moraine, Peyto and other lakes.

Banff National Park of Canada is a wildlife refuge. Animals are especially visible in the fall; elk, deer and bighorn sheep are most common, while sightings of mountain goats and moose often require binoculars. Bears, wolves, coyotes, lynx and other predators are seen occasionally. Black magpies and other members of the crow family, including the gray jay, Clark's nutcracker and raven, dart through the trees.

Although most of the park's lakes and rivers—particularly the Bow River—sustain healthy fish populations, some lakes cannot due to the "winter kill." This phenomenon occurs when a lake freezes to such a great depth that oxygen is depleted at the bottom of the lake, thereby killing all fish.

Note: Night travelers should be alert for animals on the highways. It is not only dangerous but also against park regulations to feed, molest, touch or tease the animals.

General Information and Activities

The park, which is open all year, has about 354 kilometres (219 mi.) of scenic roads. Hwy. 1 to Vancouver and Hwy. 93S (Banff-Windermere Hwy.) are open year-round, as is the northern end of Hwy.

93N (Icefields Parkway) from Lake Louise to Jasper; check locally for road conditions. One- or multiple-day bus tours of the park's major points of interest also are available.

More than 1,300 kilometres (800 mi.) of trails traverse the park. All activities involving an overnight stay in the back country require a wilderness permit offered at information centers and park warden offices in the Banff and Lake Louise townsites. Public campgrounds in the park are available by reservation, with some sites set aside on a first-come, first-served basis; phone (877) 737-3783, or TTY (866) 787-6221 in Canada.

If such potentially risky activities as mountain climbing or hiking away from designated trails are planned, visitors should register their trips in person at a park warden office or information center. Upon return, notify the warden office or information center in person or by phone. Phone (403) 762-1550 for back-country travel information, including weather and avalanche bulletins.

Lake Louise's waters, about 4 C (39 F), are too cold for swimming but are ideal for boating. Motors are not permitted; motorboats may be used only on Lake Minnewanka. Cruises on Lake Minnewanka are offered during the summer. Skating, skiing, curling and hockey are available in the park in winter.

Park naturalists conduct interpretive programs at major campgrounds most evenings and at key attractions daily throughout the summer. Bankhead, a once-booming mining town 4.8 kilometres (3 mi.) northeast of Banff, has a self-guiding trail with explanatory signs and a mining exhibit. The trail is open daily 24 hours.

Special events include the Banff Mountain Film Festival and the Banff Mountain Book Festival. Both are held late October through early November. From May through August, The Banff Centre, a performing arts venue off Tunnel Mountain Drive in the town of Banff, hosts the ☞Banff Summer Arts Festival.

Throughout the summer guides and outfitters offer fishing, hiking and float trips. Saddle horses are available for treks through the mountains to glacier-fed lakes. White-water rafting trips and helicopter tours can be arranged outside the park boundaries in Canmore and in Golden, British Columbia *(see place listings p. 59 and p. 122, respectively).*

Information, interpretive program schedules and back-country trail tips are available at Banff Information Centre, (403) 762-1550, 224 Banff Ave., and Lake Louise Information Centre, (403) 522-3833, on Village Road; topographical maps and trail guides are sold at both locations. The Banff center is open daily 8-8, late June to mid-Sept.; hours vary rest of year. The Lake Louise center is open daily 9-8, late June to mid-Sept.; hours vary rest of year. GPS Audio Tours are available at The Bear & The Butterfly, a retail outlet at 214 Banff Ave.; phone (403) 762-8911.

Fishing is permitted; national park fishing permits are sold at park information, administration and warden offices as well as at some boat concessionaires and tackle shops. Check at the information centers

With all the amazing things Alberta has to offer we took our vacation to new and unexpected heights.

Plan your dream vacation today
TravelAlberta.com

in Banff or Lake Louise for a summary of park fishing regulations.

Hunting is strictly prohibited; visitors entering the area must have firearms dismantled. *See Recreation Chart and the AAA/CAA Western Canada & Alaska CampBook.*

ADMISSION to the park is $19.60 per private vehicle (two to seven persons). Otherwise admission per person is $9.80; $8.30 (ages 65+); $4.90 (ages 6-16). An annual pass, valid at all Canadian national parks, is available.

PETS are allowed in the park but must be leashed, crated or physically restrained.

ADDRESS inquiries to the Superintendent, Banff National Park of Canada, P.O. Box 900, Banff, AB, Canada T1L 1K2; phone (403) 762-1550.

Points of Interest

Natural points of interest within the park include hoodoos—mushroom-shaped pillars of glacial silt and clay—east of Banff; Vermilion Lakes and Johnston Canyon to the west; Bow Falls to the south; Mount Norquay, Lake Louise, Moraine Lake and Valley of the Ten Peaks to the northwest via the Trans-Canada Hwy.; and Hector, Bow and Peyto lakes and Bow Summit to the northwest on the Icefields Parkway.

BANFF GONDOLA is 3.2 km (2 mi.) s. of Banff on Mountain Ave. (lower terminal next to the Upper Hot Springs). An enclosed gondola journeys along the eastern slope of Sulphur Mountain. The lift rises 698 metres (2,290 ft.) from the 1,583-metre (5,194-ft.) level to the 2,281-metre (7,484-ft.) summit ridge in 8 minutes. An open-air observation deck affords spectacular views of Banff and the surrounding mountains. A self-guiding nature walk affords other panoramic views and leads to a historic cosmic ray station and an old weather observatory.

Hours: Daily 8:30 a.m.-9 p.m., early June-day before Labour Day; otherwise varies. Closed 12 days in January for maintenance and Dec. 25. **Cost:** Round-trip fare $27.62; $13.33 (ages 6-15). **Phone:** (403) 762-2523. [T]

BANFF PARK MUSEUM NATIONAL HISTORIC SITE OF CANADA is at 91 Banff Ave. Established in 1895, the collection moved to its present building in 1903. The museum depicts the way natural history exhibits were presented and interpreted at the beginning of the 20th century. Exhibits include mounted animals and mineral specimens.

Time: Allow 30 minutes minimum. **Hours:** Daily 10-6, mid-May to mid-Sept.; 1-5, rest of year. Guided tours are given daily at 3, mid-May to mid-Sept. Closed Jan. 1 and Dec. 25-26. **Cost:** $3.90; $3.40 (ages 65+); $1.90 (ages 6-18); $9.80 (family). **Phone:** (403) 762-1558.

BANFF UPPER HOT SPRINGS is 4 km (2.5 mi.) s. of Banff via Mountain Ave. Natural hot springs feed this bathing pool with temperatures ranging between 34 C (93 F) and 42 C (108 F). A day spa is on the

premises. Swimsuit, towel and locker rentals are available. **Time:** Allow 1 hour minimum. **Hours:** Daily 9 a.m.-11 p.m., mid-May to early Sept.; 10-10 (also Fri.-Sat. 10-11 p.m.), rest of year. **Cost:** $7.30; $6.30 (ages 3-17 and 65+); $22.50 (family, two adults and two children, $3.40 for each additional child). Prices may vary; phone ahead. **Phone:** (403) 762-1515 or (800) 767-1611. [T]

BOW VALLEY PARKWAY (HWY. 1A) is 5 km (3 mi.) w. of Banff off Hwy. 1. The parkway, the original road between the villages of Banff and Lake Louise, runs along the Bow River parallel to the Trans-Canada Hwy. The parkway's speed limit of 60 kph (37 mph) provides a slower, more scenic alternative to Hwy. 1. Each curve in the road brings postcard-like images of snow-capped mountains, glaciers and ice fields.

There are frequent pull-offs with viewpoints, interpretive panels, picnic sites and trailheads. Wildlife such as bears, bighorn sheep, elks and deer can frequently be spotted. **Note:** In order to help protect wildlife, there is a voluntary restriction on driving the section of the parkway between Banff and Johnston Canyon daily 6-9 p.m., Mar. 1-June 25. Use Hwy. 1 instead.

[SAVE] **BREWSTER SIGHTSEEING EXCURSIONS** departs from several area hotels. Guides discuss local history during the 3-hour Discover Banff tour, which offers views of wildlife and such points of interest as the Banff Gondola and Lake Minnewanka. A variety of full- and half-day narrated excursions of and from Banff to Lake Louise, the Columbia Icefield and Jasper also are offered. **Time:** Allow 3 hours, 30 minutes minimum. **Hours:** Tours are offered daily, May 1 to mid-Oct. Departure times vary; phone ahead. **Cost:** Discover Banff tour $49; $24.50 (children). **Phone:** (403) 762-6700 or (866) 606-6700.

BUFFALO NATIONS LUXTON MUSEUM is just w. of Banff Ave. at 1 Birch Ave. This log-fort museum re-creates the era when Europeans first arrived on the Plains to find a culture rich in ceremonies, songs and legends. Arts, crafts, dioramas and displays showcase the historical journey of the Northern Plains people, their culture and the flora and fauna of the surrounding area.

Tours: Guided tours are available. **Time:** Allow 30 minutes minimum. **Hours:** Daily 10-6, May 1 to mid-Oct.; 1-5, rest of year. Closed Dec. 25. **Cost:** $8; $6 (ages 65+ and students with ID); $2.50 (ages 6-12); $16.50 (family). **Phone:** (403) 762-2388.

CASCADE GARDENS encircle the Banff National Park of Canada administration building at 101 Mountain Ave. These gardens are built in a series of rock terraces connected by small cascades that highlight flowers, plants and shrubs, rustic bridges, pavilions and flagged walks. Traditional dancing and drumming performances are held on the grounds at the Siksika Nation Interpretive Centre.

Time: Allow 30 minutes minimum. **Hours:** Gardens daily dawn-dusk, June-Sept. Dancing and drumming performances take place Tues. at 2, July-Aug. **Cost:** Free. **Phone:** (403) 760-1338. 🅿️

CAVE AND BASIN NATIONAL HISTORIC SITE OF CANADA is at 311 Cave Ave. The beginnings of Canada's national park system are founded on a cave and hot springs discovered in 1883 by three Canadian Pacific Railway workers. Disputes over the ownership of the area prompted the Canadian government to declare the area a national reserve 2 years later. The site consists of naturally occurring warm mineral springs inside the cave and an emerald-colored basin outside. Exhibits, interpretive trails and a 30-minute videotape presentation explain the history of the springs and the development of the national park.

Time: Allow 1 hour minimum. **Hours:** Daily 9-6, mid-May through Sept. 30; Mon.-Fri. 11-4, Sat.-Sun. 9:30-5, rest of year. Guided tours are given daily at 11, 2 and 4, mid-May through Sept. 30; Sat.-Sun. at 11, rest of year. Closed Jan. 1 and Dec. 25-26. **Cost:** $3.90; $3.40 (ages 65+); $1.90 (ages 6-18); $9.80 (family). **Phone:** (403) 762-1566.

DISCOVER BANFF TOURS is at 215 Banff Ave. in the Sundance Mall. Passengers also are picked up at area hotels. Various year-round guided tours are offered, including ice walks, snowshoe treks, dog sled trips, sleigh rides, mountain hikes, wildlife safaris, horseback riding, white-water rafting and nature walks. Some tours include lunch. Canoe rentals and self-guiding tours also are available.

Inquire about cancellation policies. Allow 3-9 hours minimum, depending on tour. **Hours:** Tours depart daily (weather permitting) 7:30 a.m.-10 p.m. Tour times vary; phone ahead. **Cost:** Fees vary, depending on activity. **Phone:** (403) 760-5007 or (877) 565-9372. *See color ad on insert.*

▼ᴳᴱᴹ **ICEFIELDS PARKWAY (HWY. 93)** crosses Banff and Jasper national parks. The 230-kilometre (143-mi.) route, which connects the towns of Lake Louise and Jasper, offers spectacular vistas of snowcapped mountains, waterfalls, lakes and rivers that drain the Columbia Icefields' glacial meltwater to the oceans. While the terrain is rugged, the road is well-engineered to provide a relatively easy drive.

Those who wish to pause and experience the area more intimately will not be disappointed—in addition to several campgrounds along the route, numerous turnouts at viewpoints provide opportunities to relax and enjoy more of the scenery. Roadside signs explain the terrain. Long hikes through the wilderness are available, as are shorter trails leading to scenic Sunwapta Falls and Athabasca Falls.

About 76 kilometres (47 mi.) north of Lake Louise at the Saskatchewan River crossing, David Thompson Hwy. (Hwy. 11) meets the Icefields Parkway. Just inside Jasper National Park of Canada is the Athabasca Glacier, a tongue of the Columbia Icefield (*see Jasper National Park of Canada p. 81*); it comes to within 1.5 kilometres (.9 mi.) of the parkway. Across the road, ice explorer trips onto the

Athabasca Glacier are available April 15 to mid-October (weather permitting). Columbia Icefield Centre offers information and interpretive displays.

Note: Drivers should be alert for slow or stopped vehicles and animals. Snow tires and/or chains are recommended in winter; check for weather and road conditions. **Cost:** Parkway free; drivers must pay the national park entrance fee regardless of whether they stop inside the park. **Phone:** (403) 762-2088 for weather information, or (403) 762-1450 for road condition information.

JOHNSTON CANYON is 18 km (11 mi.) w. of the town of Banff on the Bow Valley Pkwy. (Hwy. 1A). An uphill hike to one or both of the two waterfalls at this canyon follows a paved pathway through a wooded area along Johnston Creek. Observation points along the way allow for scenic views of the rushing water. The pathway soon becomes more of a catwalk that is literally attached to the canyon wall.

The Lower Falls are reached after a hike of about 1.1 kilometres (.7 mi.); the trail continues another 1.7 kilometres (1 mi.) to the Upper Falls. **Note:** This is a popular day-use area, and the parking lot can become crowded.

▼ᴳᴱᴹ **LAKE LOUISE** is 4 km (2.4 mi.) w. of Hwy. 1/93 in the village of Lake Louise behind The Fairmont Chateau Lake Louise hotel. Incredibly aqua in summer and glistening with snow and ice in winter, the lake has been the subject of countless photographs. Perfectly framed behind The Fairmont Chateau Lake Louise hotel with snow-capped mountains and Victoria Glacier as backdrops, the lake is 2.4 kilometres (1.5 mi.) long, .6 kilometres (.4 mi.) wide and 90 metres (295 ft.) deep. It is named for Queen Victoria's daughter Princess Louise Caroline Alberta.

The water, at its warmest, is never more than 4 C (39 F). Trails rim the lake providing scenic views, and canoes can be rented at the boathouse on the lake's west shore. The Lake Louise Visitor Centre in nearby Samson Mall has maps and information. **Note:** Due to the popularity of the lake, the parking lot tends to be crowded in summer. **Phone:** (403) 522-3833 for the visitor center.

LAKE LOUISE SIGHTSEEING GONDOLA AND INTERPRETIVE CENTRE is just n. of Hwy. 1 interchange. A lift offers an impressive aerial view of Lake Louise and the mountains of the Continental Divide. At the interpretive center staff members present a brief visitor orientation session; interpretive programs, including guided walks, are offered daily for an additional fee. Ride and dine packages also are offered. **Hours:** Daily 9-4:30, May 15-Sept. 30. **Cost:** Gondola $25; $12.50 (ages 6-15). Interpretive center free. **Phone:** (403) 522-3555. ⓣ

LAKE MINNEWANKA BOAT TOURS is on Lake Minnewanka, 8 km (5 mi.) n.e. of Banff on Hwy. 1, then n. 7 km (4 mi.) from the beginning of Lake Minnewanka Loop. The interpretive sightseeing cruises, in glass-enclosed, heated boats, last 1 hour, 30 minutes. Motorboats also can be rented. Charter fishing is available as well. **Hours:** Cruises depart daily at 10, noon, 2, 4 and 6, mid-May to early Oct. **Cost:** Fare $41.91; $18.10 (ages 6-15). **Phone:** (403) 762-3473.

MORAINE LAKE is 13 km (8 mi.) s. of Lake Louise. Though roughly half the size of better-known nearby Lake Louise, many believe blue-green Moraine Lake is equally beautiful. Known as "the jewel of the Rockies," the lake is in the Valley of the Ten Peaks, which provides the ten saw-toothed ridges that rise dramatically from the lakeshore. A short hike to the top of a rockslide leads to panoramic views of the lake and valley. A number of hikes begin at the lake, and canoe rentals are available. **Phone:** (403) 522-3833 for the Lake Louise Visitor Centre.

ROCKY MOUNTAIN RAFT TOURS launch area is reached by buses departing the Banff Park Lodge and the Banff Springs Hotel. Tickets are available at the Banff Springs Hotel concierge desk and at the launch point meeting area below Bow Falls. Scenic 1-hour guided raft tours travel the river in the section of the Bow Valley below Tunnel and Rundle mountains. **Hours:** Raft trips depart daily at 9:20, 11:20, 1:20, 3:20 and 5:20, mid-May through Labour Day. **Cost:** Fare $42; $21 (ages 0-15). **Phone:** (403) 762-3632.

WALTER PHILLIPS GALLERY is in Glyde Hall at The Banff Centre, 107 Tunnel Mountain Dr. Exhibits contain international and Canadian contemporary art. Media include painting, sculpture, printmaking, textiles, ceramics, photography, video and performance art. Works by established and emerging artists are featured. **Hours:** Wed.-Sun. 12:30-5 (also Thurs. 5-9). Closed holidays and between exhibitions. **Cost:** Donations. **Phone:** (403) 762-6281.

[SAVE] **WHYTE MUSEUM OF THE CANADIAN ROCKIES,** 111 Bear St., presents the heritage of the region through four galleries exhibiting cultural and natural history displays and artwork. Docents also lead visitors through several historic houses on-site, including the former residence of the museum's founders, Peter and Catharine Whyte.

Guided tours include the Luxton Home & Garden Tour; the Heritage Gallery Tour; and the Art Gallery Tour, which focuses on creative works that illustrate the beauty of the Canadian Rockies landscape. **Time:** Allow 30 minutes minimum. **Hours:** Museum daily 10-5. Heritage Homes Tour is given daily at 11 and 2:30, June 1-Labour Day; Sun. at 2:30, rest of year. Luxton Home & Garden Tour is given daily at 1, June 1-Labour Day. Heritage Gallery Tour is given daily at 11, June 1-Labour Day; Sun. at 1:30, rest of year. Art Gallery Tour is given daily at 1:30, June 1-Labour Day. Closed Jan. 1 and Dec. 25.

Cost: $7; $4 (ages 65+ and students with ID); free (ages 0-6); $16 (family, two adults and two children). Guided house tours $8-$13. Gallery tours free. **Phone:** (403) 762-2291.

RECREATIONAL ACTIVITIES
Skiing
- **Lake Louise Ski Area** is 60 km (36 mi.) w. of the town of Banff. Other activities are offered.

Hours: Daily, early Nov.-May 31. Hours vary; phone ahead. **Phone:** (403) 522-3555 or (877) 956-8473.

- **Ski Norquay** is 6 km (4 mi.) n. of the town of Banff on the Mount Norquay access road. **Hours:** Daily 9-4, early Dec. to mid-Apr. (also Fri. 4-9, Jan.-Mar.). **Phone:** (403) 762-4421.

- **Sunshine Village Ski Resort** is 8 km (5 mi.) w. of the town of Banff on Hwy. 1. **Hours:** Daily 9-4, mid-Nov. to late May. **Phone:** (403) 762-6500 or (877) 542-2633.

BARRHEAD (D-5)
pop. 4,209, elev. 648 m/2,125′

BARRHEAD CENTENNIAL MUSEUM is at 5629 49th St. Displays depict early area history. Exhibits include farm equipment, pioneer furniture, tools, woodcrafts, a wildlife display, Native artifacts and a collection of African trophies. The museum also serves as a visitor information center. **Time:** Allow 1 hour minimum. **Hours:** Tues.-Sat. 10-5, May-Sept.; by appointment rest of year. **Cost:** Donations. **Phone:** (780) 674-5203.

BEAVERLODGE (C-1) pop. 2,264

First settled in 1908, Beaverlodge derives its name from the Beaver Indians who made their temporary home, or lodge, in the area. With the arrival of the railway in 1928, a new townsite was created about 1.6 kilometres (1 mi.) northwest of the original hamlet; many original buildings were moved. In the Beaverlodge Valley, the town serves as a gateway to Monkman Pass and is a large agricultural center.

Beaverlodge & District Chamber of Commerce: P.O. Box 303, Beaverlodge, AB, Canada T0H 0C0. **Phone:** (780) 354-8785.

SOUTH PEACE CENTENNIAL MUSEUM is 3 km (1.9 mi.) n.w. on Hwy. 43. Pioneer items, equipment and furnishings used in the early 1900s are displayed. A 1928 pioneer house is furnished in period. Other exhibits include a trading post, a general store, a flour mill, a schoolhouse, an Anglican church, a railway caboose, antique steam engines, and vintage cars and trucks. **Hours:** Daily 10-6, mid-May to early Sept. **Cost:** $5; free (ages 0-10). **Phone:** (780) 354-8869.

BRAGG CREEK—see Calgary p. 57.

BROOKS (I-8) pop. 12,498

Brooks is surrounded by 105,222 hectares (260,000 acres) of irrigated farmland and more than 404,700 hectares (1 million acres) of rangeland used for cattle grazing. This semiarid shortgrass section of the province is the setting for wildlife and horticultural research centers.

Newell Regional Tourism Association Office and Tourism Information Centre: 208 2nd Ave. W., P.O. Box 1597, Brooks, AB, Canada T1R 1C4. **Phone:** (403) 793-8064.

BROOKS AQUEDUCT is 2 km (1 mi.) s.e. of Hwy. 1 exit Cassils Rd. (Hwy. 542), then 3 km (2 mi.) s. on a gravel road, following signs. Hailed as an engineering marvel when it was built in the early 1900s, the concrete aqueduct carried water to farmers and ranchers who settled in the region following the arrival of the Canadian Pacific Railway.

Operational until 1979, it has been preserved as a monument to the engineers and agriculturalists who developed the region. Signage and brochures offer information for self-guiding tours. **Tours:** Guided tours are available. **Time:** Allow 30 minutes minimum. **Hours:** Daily 10-5, May 15-Labour Day. **Cost:** Donations. **Phone:** (403) 362-4451. 🎫

BROOKS AND DISTRICT MUSEUM is .4 km (.2 mi.) w. of Trans-Canada Hwy. Exhibits about early ranchers, homesteaders, the Royal Canadian Mounted Police, railroading and irrigation trace local history from the late 19th and early 20th centuries. Seventeen buildings, including a log cabin, a schoolhouse and a church, are on the grounds. **Time:** Allow 1 hour, 30 minutes minimum. **Hours:** Daily 9-5, Victoria Day weekend-Labour Day; by appointment rest of year. **Cost:** Donations. **Phone:** (403) 362-5073.

DINOSAUR PROVINCIAL PARK—
see Patricia p. 88.

©Disney/Pixar

Calgary

City Population: 988,193
Elevation: 1,048 m/3,440 ft.

Editor's Picks:

© Robin Smith / age fotostock

Calgary, once considered a cow town, now is a city of skyscrapers, light-rail transit, shopping complexes and contemporary houses. The city's economy began with—and still includes—ranching and the subsequent meatpacking industry, but the discovery of oil just south of the city in 1914 and just north in 1947 fueled a spurt of growth that turned an agricultural community into a metropolis.

Calgary today boasts a high concentration of head offices, the second largest in Canada. Energy, agriculture, tourism, manufacturing, research and development, and advanced technology comprise Calgary's industrial base.

The region's history of human habitation began almost 10,000 years before the first 19th-century fur and whiskey traders arrived. Indian tribes chose the confluence of the Bow and Elbow rivers as a campsite; emerging as the dominant tribe was the Blackfoot. Their acquisition of horses allowed them to hunt buffalo and fight almost every other prairie tribe with great success. As European settlement increased, so did the friction between the natives and the newcomers.

An 1877 treaty calmed the rough waters, and relative peace among all factions has existed since. Several reservations, including the Tsuu T'ina Reserve south of the city, are near Calgary. Native North Americans have sought to assimilate themselves into Canadian culture while retaining their native heritage.

Chinese were recruited abroad in the early 1900s to build the railroads; once the trains were running, however, Chinese immigration was restricted severely. Oil and money lured many American entrepreneurs who brought the technology and investment funds needed to get Calgary's petroleum industry started. But many of those who came for the money enjoyed the area and stayed, becoming Canadian citizens.

Calgary's modern sophistication is offset by a romantic perception of the past—a past in which the city was established as a North West Mounted Police fort in 1875. The Calgary Stampede, a 10-day Western wingding, is attended by more than a million residents and visitors who relive the days of chuck wagons and lassos. Those days existed more than a century ago, after the North West Mounted Police—the forerunner of today's Royal Canadian Mounted Police—and the railroad brought law, order and homesteaders to a region previously settled by trappers, buffalo hunters and whiskey traders.

Although Calgary's growth has been rapid, it has been practical. The bustling downtown district was designed to accommodate a large amount of activity, even during winter when below-freezing temperatures normally would inhibit commerce. Enclosed walkways called "plus-15s" (they are 15 feet above street level) connect almost half the downtown buildings, making it possible to eat, work, shop or visit neighbors without donning so much as a mitten.

The Stephen Avenue Walk, a pedestrian mall in the city center lined with trees, benches and fountains, is an urban refuge from traffic as well as a nice place to enjoy lunch or a stroll in warm weather.

Getting There — *starting on p. 47*

Getting Around — *starting on p. 47*

What To See — *starting on p. 47*

What To Do — *starting on p. 55*

Where To Stay — *starting on p. 397*

Where To Dine — *starting on p. 401*

Bowness Park / Travel Alberta

All is not business in Calgary. Music, ballet, theater and plenty of outdoor recreation are readily available. In addition Calgary distinguished itself as host city of the 1988 Winter Olympic Games. Such educational institutions as Mount Royal College, Southern Alberta Institute of Technology and the University of Calgary prepare Canadians for the future. The city also is home to the Rothney Astrophysical Observatory, where one of Canada's largest telescopes resides. Natural resources and man-made technology continue to drive Calgary in the 21st century.

Getting There

By Car

Two major highways pass through Calgary. Queen Elizabeth II Hwy. runs north and south through the city; Trans-Canada Hwy. provides access from the east and west. Hwy. 1A, which connects Calgary and Cochrane, also serves as an alternate route between Calgary and the towns of Canmore and Banff. Hwy. 8 connects Calgary with Bragg Creek.

Getting Around

Street System

Calgary is divided into quadrants, with Centre Street separating the east and west sectors and the Bow River and Memorial Drive delineating north and south. Streets run north and south, avenues east and west. All are numbered from the intersection of Centre Street and Centre Avenue, just north of downtown. Roads in suburban areas are numbered where they form grids and named where they do not.

The speed limit is 50 kilometres per hour (30 mph) or as posted. A right turn on red after stopping is permitted unless otherwise posted; U-turns are not. Other restrictions apply during rush hours in certain areas; be aware of signs, especially in school and playground zones. Pedestrian crosswalks are designated by "X" signs, and motorists must yield to pedestrians.

Parking

Parking is not permitted on major roads in the downtown core during rush hours, between 6:30 and 9 a.m. and 3:30 and 6 p.m. Downtown metered street parking usually is limited to 2 hours at a maximum cost of $5 per hour. Pay parking for extended periods is available at numerous locations. Rates for downtown parking lots range from $1.75-$2.75 per half-hour during the day.

What To See

SAVE **AERO SPACE MUSEUM OF CALGARY** is at 4629 McCall Way N.E. In a former Royal Air Force drill hall, the museum contains exhibits about western Canada's aviation history. Aircraft displayed

Destination Calgary

*A*lthough a thriving ranching industry and the discovery of oil helped put Calgary on the map, it was the 1988 Olympic Games that turned all eyes on the former cow town.

*T*oday visitors can travel to an observation terrace in the sky, peruse museums and historic sites and ski in the same park where the games were held.

© Darby Sawchuk / Alamy

Calgary Zoo, Botanical Garden & Prehistoric Park.
(See listing page 52)

Travel Alberta

Canada Olympic Park, Calgary.
(See listing page 52)

Travel Alberta

Calgary Tower.
(See listing page 51)

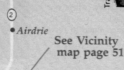

See Vicinity map page 51

② Airdrie

•Cochrane

22

①

22

•Bragg Creek

①A

①

Calgary

②A

Okotoks•

②

Travel Alberta

Heritage Park Historical Village, Calgary.
(See listing page 53)

*P*laces included in this AAA Destination City:

The Informed Traveler

Sales Tax: The federal Goods and Service Tax is 5 percent and applies to most goods, food/beverages and services, including lodgings. Alberta does not have a provincial sales tax but does impose a 4 percent hotel tax. A 1-2 percent tourism levy also is charged in some areas.

WHOM TO CALL

Emergency: 911

Police (non-emergency): (403) 266-1234

Fire: (403) 287-4299

Weather: (403) 299-7878

Road Conditions: (877) 262-4997

Hospitals: Foothills Medical Centre, (403) 670-1110, and Rockyview General Hospital, (403) 541-3000.

WHERE TO LOOK

Newspapers

Calgary's daily newspapers are the *Calgary Herald* and the *Calgary Sun,* both morning papers. The national newspapers are *The Globe and Mail* and the *National Post.*

Radio

Calgary radio station CBC (1010 AM) is a member of the Canadian Broadcasting Corp.

Visitor Information

Tourism Calgary: 238 11th Ave. S.E., Room 200, Calgary, AB, Canada T2G 0X8. **Phone:** (403) 263-8510 or (800) 661-1678.

Visitor information also is available at the Calgary International Airport on the arrivals level and at the Riley & McCormick Western Store at 220 Stephen Ave. in the Eau Claire Market.

TRANSPORTATION

Air Travel

Calgary International Airport is northeast of downtown off Hwy. 2 exit 266. Public bus transportation to and from the airport is offered by Calgary Transit via Route 57, with service to and from the Whitehorn light-rail rapid transit station. Taxi service between the airport and downtown typically costs $27-$30. Many hotels also offer free shuttle service for their guests.

Rental Cars

Hertz, downtown or at the airport, offers discounts to CAA and AAA members; phone (403) 221-1676, (800) 263-0600 in Canada, or (800) 654-3080 out of Canada.

Rail Service

The nearest VIA Rail stations are in Jasper and Edmonton; phone (506) 857-9830 or (888) 842-7245.

Buses

Greyhound Lines Inc. operates from the depot at 850 16th St. S.W.; phone (800) 661-8747. Red Arrow Express operates luxury motor coaches between Calgary, Red Deer, Edmonton and Fort McMurray; phone (403) 531-0350 or (403) 571-2578.

Taxis

Taxi companies include Checker Yellow Cab, (403) 299-9999; Mayfair Taxi, (403) 255-6555; Prestige Limousine, (403) 730-6666; and Yellow Cab, (403) 974-1111. Rates begin at $3.40 for the first 150 metres (about $1/10$ mi.) or portion thereof, plus 20c for each additional 150 metres (about $1/10$ mi.) or portion thereof. Cabs can be hailed on the street, but phoning ahead is recommended.

Public Transport

Calgary has both bus and light-rail rapid transit (LRT) service; the latter is free in the downtown core. Calgary Transit's office, 240 7th Ave. S.W., has schedules and maps and sells transit passes. Fare is $2.50; $1.75 (ages 6-14). A 1-day pass is $7.50; $5.25 (ages 6-14). Phone (403) 262-1000.

include an F86 Sabre jet, a Bell 47G helicopter and one of the few remaining World War I Sopwith Triplanes. Also featured are piston and jet aircraft engines, aviation artwork and a Martin Baker ejection seat.

Time: Allow 30 minutes minimum. **Hours:** Daily 10-5. Closed Jan. 1, Good Friday, Easter and Dec. 24-26. **Cost:** $7; $4.50 (ages 60+ and students with ID); $3.50 (ages 6-11); $18 (family). **Phone:** (403) 250-3752.

ART GALLERY OF CALGARY is at 117 8th Ave. S.W. Housed in two joined, historic buildings, the art gallery presents four to five exhibitions of contemporary work each year. Such mediums as painting, photography and sculpture are represented, with pieces from both emerging and established artists displayed.

Time: Allow 30 minutes minimum. **Hours:** Tues.-Sat. 10-5 (also Thurs. 5-9), July-Aug.; Tues.-Sat. 10-5 (also first Thurs. of the month 5-9), rest of year. Closed major holidays. **Cost:** $5; $2.50 (ages 6-11, ages 65+ and students with ID); free (first Thurs. of the month 4-9 p.m.). **Phone:** (403) 770-1350.

BOW HABITAT STATION is at 1440 17A St. S.E. in Pearce Estate City Park. This eco-park is located along the Bow River and features the Sam Livingston Fish Hatchery, the Pearce Estate Park Interpretive Wetland and a visitor center. The hatchery is one of the largest of its kind, producing 2 to 3 million trout a year, while the wetland showcases Albertan aquatic habitats. In the visitor center interactive exhibits tell about fisheries management and fish culture programs in Alberta.

Note: At press time, the site was closed for renovations and reopening was scheduled for late 2009. Phone ahead for more information. **Cost:** Donations. **Phone:** (403) 297-6561.

BUTTERFIELD ACRES CHILDREN'S FARM is 3 km (1.9 mi.) n. of Crowchild Tr. at 254077 Rocky Ridge Rd. Visitors can meet and play with animals such as baby goats, rabbits, chicks, calves, sheep, llamas and a 450-pound pig named Scarlet at this whimsical, educational farm. In addition to interactive displays and pony and wagon rides, children also will enjoy trying to milk a goat and playing on a tractor.

Time: Allow 2 hours minimum. **Hours:** Daily 10-4, July-Aug.; Mon.-Fri. 10-2, Sat.-Sun. 10-4, Apr.-June and in Sept. **Cost:** $12.99; $10.99 (ages 65+); $9.99 (ages 1-17). Pony ride $1. **Phone:** (403) 547-3595 or (403) 239-0638. 🍴 🍽

CALAWAY PARK is 10 km (6 mi.) w. off Trans-Canada Hwy. Springbank Rd. exit. Said to be western Canada's largest outdoor amusement park, it features 32 rides, including a roller coaster, a log ride, bumper boats and skill games. Live stage shows are presented daily. The landscaped grounds include an interactive maze, a miniature golf course and a fishing hole.

Calgary Zoo, Botanical Garden & Prehistoric Park / Travel Alberta

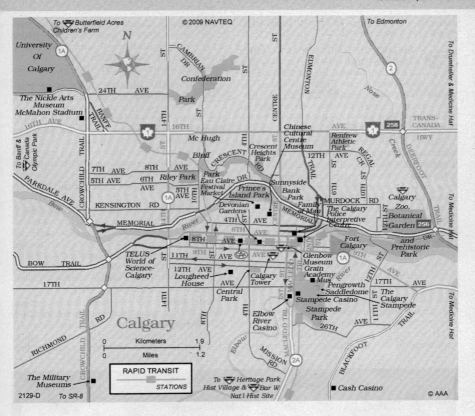

© 2009 NAVTEQ

To Butterfield Acres Children's Farm

To Edmonton

University Of Calgary

The Nickle Arts Museum
McMahon Stadium

Confederation Park

Mc Hugh

Crescent Heights Park

Chinese Cultural Centre Museum

Renfrew Athletic Park

TRANS-CANADA HWY

7TH AVE
5TH AVE
8TH AVE
6TH AVE
Riley Park

Park Eau Claire
Festival Market

Prince's Island Park

Sunnyside Bank Park

Family of Man

Calgary Zoo, Botanical Garden and Prehistoric Park

KENSINGTON RD

Devonian Gardens

The Calgary Police Interpretive Centre

MEMORIAL

Fort Calgary

BOW TRAIL

TELUS World of Science-Calgary

Glenbow Museum
Grain Academy Mus.

17TH

Calgary Tower

Pengrowth Saddledome

The Calgary Stampede

Central Park

Stampede Casino

Calgary

Elbow River Casino

Stampede Park

The Military Museums

RAPID TRANSIT
STATIONS

To Heritage Park Hist Village & Bar W Nat'l Hist Site

Cash Casino

2129-D   To SR-8

© AAA

Kilometers   0 — 1.9
Miles   0 — 1.2

Kennel, stroller and wheelchair rentals are available. **Time:** Allow 4 hours minimum. **Hours:** Daily 10-7, July 1-Labour Day; Fri. 5-9, Sat.-Sun. and Mon. holidays 10-7, Victoria Day weekend-June 30; Sat.-Sun. and Mon. holidays 11-6, day after Labour Day-late Nov. Phone ahead to confirm schedule. **Cost:** $31.95; $25 (ages 3-6); $23 (ages 50+); $75 (family). After 2 p.m. $16.95; free (ages 0-2). After 4 p.m. $14.95; free (ages 0-2). Admission includes unlimited rides; prices for individual games, the maze, fishing and miniature golf vary. **Phone:** (403) 240-3822. *See color ad on insert.*

THE CALGARY POLICE INTERPRETIVE CENTRE is on the second floor of the Police Administration Building at 316 7th Ave. S.E. Interactive displays help children to understand the role of police officers in society. Exhibit galleries detail the early days of police work through artifacts and photos. Visitors also learn how to deal with serious issues facing society today, including substance abuse and domestic violence.

Time: Allow 45 minutes minimum. **Hours:** Mon.-Fri. 10-4, Sat. noon-4, July-Aug.; Mon. 9:30-4, Fri.-Sat. noon-4, rest of year. Closed major holidays. Phone ahead to confirm schedule. **Cost:**

$5; free (ages 0-17). Under 13 must be with an adult. **Phone:** (403) 206-4566.

THE CALGARY SPACEPORT is on the third floor of the Calgary International Airport off Hwy. 2 (Deerfoot Tr. N.E.). The entertaining educational facility offers exhibits focusing on space and aeronautics.

Hands-on displays, NASA and Canadian Space Agency items and simulator rides are featured. Visitors can view a moon rock, learn about flight tracking systems and control a live camera used on the airport's runways. **Time:** Allow 30 minutes minimum. **Hours:** Mon.-Fri. 9-9, Sat.-Sun. 9-5. **Cost:** Free. Simulator rides $3-$14. **Phone:** (403) 717-7678.

CALGARY TOWER is in Tower Centre at 101 9th Ave. S.W. at Centre St. S. The tower rises 191 metres (626 ft.) above the city. An observation deck and revolving restaurant provide a panorama of the city and the nearby Rocky Mountains. The observation deck features a glass floor and glass walls, which create in visitors the sensation of floating high above the city.

A torch atop the tower burned nonstop during the 1988 Olympic Games; it is illuminated on special occasions. **Hours:** Daily 9 a.m.-10:30 p.m., June-Sept.; 9 a.m.-9:30 p.m., rest of year. Hours may vary Oct.-May; phone ahead. **Cost:** $12.95; $10.95

(ages 65+); $9.95 (ages 13-17); $5 (ages 4-12). **Phone:** (403) 266-7171.

CALGARY ZOO, BOTANICAL GARDEN & PREHISTORIC PARK is at 1300 Zoo Rd. N.E. at Memorial Dr. and 12th St. E. In five themed areas—Destination Africa, Canadian Wilds, South America, Australia and Eurasia—visitors observe more than 900 animals, including such rare and endangered species as the Siberian tiger and the whooping crane.

Nestled in the tree canopy, sharp-eyed lemurs watch inquisitively as bold guests thump their chests along with the resident gorillas of Destination Africa's rainforest. Nearby, apprehensive visitors shiver over too-close-for-comfort encounters with boas, crocodiles and giant snails. Black bears, cougars and bison are among the creatures you'll learn about in the Canadian Wilds, and at the South America habitat, fruit-loving squirrel monkeys and preening flamingos frequently draw crowds. Bouncing children *and* parents emulate Australia's most famous furry inhabitants at the ZooVenture Playground, while family members of a larger variety frolic in Eurasia's Elephant Crossing pavilion.

In addition to purring big cats and yawning hippos, the site features a tropical aviary and conservatory containing a butterfly garden and more than 4,000 plants. A 2.6-hectare (6.5-acre) prehistoric park dotted by life-size dinosaur replicas transports you to western Canada's bygone Mesozoic landscape. **Time:** Allow 3 hours minimum. **Hours:** Daily 9-6. Last admission 1 hour before closing. Closed Dec. 25. **Cost:** $18; $16 (ages 60+); $10 (ages 3-12). **Phone:** (403) 232-9300. *See color ad.*

CANADA OLYMPIC PARK is off Trans-Canada Hwy. Bowfort Rd. exit. The park, the host area for ski jumping, freestyle skiing, bobsled and luge events at the 1988 Winter Olympic Games, remains a site for year-round sports activities. In winter visitors can learn to ski and snowboard. During summer guests can try the bobsled/luge track, at speeds up to 95 kilometres per hour (59 mph). Also on the premises is a mountain bike park with more than 25 kilometres (15 mi.) of trails.

A 2-hour self-guiding audio tour is available in several different languages and includes visitor access to the Olympic Hall of Fame and Museum; the Ice House, a training facility where bobsled, skeleton-sled and luge athletes practice; the Olympic bobsled track; the observation level of the 90-metre (295-ft.) ski-jump tower; and, in summer, a chairlift offering breathtaking scenic views.

Note: Public luge rides have been discontinued due to athletic training leading up to the Vancouver 2010 Winter Olympics. In addition, immediately following the Olympic games, the Ice House will be closed for renovations; no reopening date has been

set. **Time:** Allow 2 hours minimum. **Hours:** Self-guiding audio tours are available daily 9-5, July-Aug.; 10-4, rest of year. **Cost:** Self-guiding tour $16; $49 (family). Prices for activities and rides vary. **Phone:** (403) 247-5452. ⓘ

(SAVE) **Olympic Hall of Fame and Museum** is at Canada Olympic Park, off Trans-Canada Hwy. Bowfort Rd. exit. Exhibits focus on Canada's participation in the Winter Olympic Games from 1924 to the present. A large collection of Olympic torches is on display.

The facility also offers such hands-on displays as the Virtual Reality Hockey Shootout, which lets visitors experience firsthand what it's like to be a member of a Canadian Olympic hockey team. **Hours:** Daily 10-5. **Cost:** $6. Combination ticket with Canada Olympic Park self-guiding tour $16; $49 (family). **Phone:** (403) 247-5452.

CHINESE CULTURAL CENTRE MUSEUM is at 197 1st St. S.W. Exhibits represent Chinese culture and history and include sculptures, ceramics and other artifacts dating back thousands of years. Permanently displayed is a replica of the army of terracotta soldiers found during a 1974 excavation at Mount Li in China. The clay archers, bowmen, cavalry, chariots and saddled cavalry horses were found in battle-ready formation guarding the Tomb of Qin Shihuang; each figure is unique. **Hours:** Daily 9-5. Closed major holidays. **Cost:** $4; $2 (ages 6-12 and 65+); free (students with ID). **Phone:** (403) 262-5071.

DEVONIAN GARDENS is on the fourth level of Toronto Dominion Square, 317 7th Ave. S.W. These 1-hectare (2.5-acre) glassed-in, indoor gardens contain 15,700 subtropical trees, plants, fish and turtles as well as waterfalls, fountains and a reflecting pool. Monthly exhibits display works by local artists. A 100-seat amphitheater occasionally hosts shows at noon. **Note:** The gardens are closed for renovations; reopening is scheduled for summer 2010. **Hours:** Daily 9:30-6 (also Thurs.-Fri. 6-8 p.m.). **Cost:** Free. **Phone:** (403) 221-4681.

FAMILY OF MAN is outside the Calgary Board of Education Building at 515 Macleod Tr. S.E. This grouping of sculpted metal figures stands 6.5 metres (21 ft.) tall. Originally commissioned as part of Great Britain's exhibit for Expo 67, the statues were created by Mario Armengol. Nude and lacking a discernible race, the figures extend their arms and hands in gestures of goodwill and friendship. **Hours:** Daily 24 hours. **Cost:** Free. **Phone:** (403) 268-2489.

(SAVE) **FORT CALGARY** is at 806 9th Ave. S.E. The 16-hectare (40-acre) riverside park contains a reconstruction of an 1875 North West Mounted Police fort and its 1888 barracks and the Deane House Historic Site, the last remaining building from the site's days as a garrison. Interactive exhibits, costumed interpreters, hands-on activities and audio-visual presentations tell the story of the site, the settlement and the people of Calgary.

Hours: Daily 9-5. Closed Jan. 1, Good Friday and Dec. 24-26. **Cost:** $11; $10 (ages 65+ and college students with ID); $7 (ages 7-17); $5 (ages 3-6). Prices may vary; phone ahead. **Phone:** (403) 290-1875. ⓘ

GLENBOW MUSEUM is at 130 9th Ave. S.E., across from the Calgary Tower. The complex includes a museum, an art gallery, a library and archives. Fascinating men and women who contributed to the development of the province are highlighted in Mavericks: An Incorrigible History of Alberta. Niitsitapiisinni: Our Way of Life features artifacts and interactive displays illustrating Blackfoot traditions and values.

Other galleries feature exhibits about warriors, gemstones and West Africa. An Asian sculpture gallery and a hands-on art studio also are on-site. **Time:** Allow 2 hours minimum. **Hours:** Mon.-Sat. 9-5, Sun. noon-5. Closed Dec. 25. **Cost:** $14; $10 (ages 65+); $9 (ages 7-17 and college students with ID); $28 (family, two adults and four children). **Phone:** (403) 268-4100. ⓘ

GRAIN ACADEMY MUSEUM is at Stampede Park off 4th St. S.E. on the second level of Round Up Centre. Visitors can learn about the processes of bringing grain from the field to the table. Highlights include a miniature grain elevator and a working model train that depicts the transportation of grain from the prairie to the Pacific coast. A movie theater and displays describing the history of grain also are featured. **Time:** Allow 1 hour minimum. **Hours:** Mon.-Fri. 10-4. Closed major holidays. **Cost:** Donations. **Parking:** $12. **Phone:** (403) 263-4594.

HERITAGE PARK HISTORICAL VILLAGE is 2.5 km (1.5 mi.) w. off Queen Elizabeth II Hwy. to 1900 Heritage Dr. S.W. The re-created pre-1914 village is on 27 hectares (66 acres). The village reflects the fur trade of

DID YOU KNOW

There are more than 400 campgrounds in Alberta.

the 1860s, the pre-railway settlements of the 1880s and businesses and residences 1900-14.

Among the park's more than 150 exhibits are a general store, an antique midway, pioneer farm machinery and a Hudson's Bay Co. trading post. Most of the buildings are originals that have been moved to the park. An antique steam train circles the park, and a 200-passenger stern-wheeler cruises Glenmore Reservoir.

Hours: Historical village daily 9:30-5, late May-Labour Day; Sat.-Sun. 9:30-5, day after Labour Day to mid-Oct. Heritage Town Square and Gasoline Alley Museum daily 9:30-5, year-round. **Cost:** May-Sept. $20; $16 (senior citizens); $15 (ages 3-17);

$70 (family, two adults and two children). Rest of year $13.95; $11.95 (senior citizens); $8.95 (ages 3-17); $45.85 (family, two adults and children). Unlimited rides pass $12. Individual ride $4. Prices may vary; phone ahead. **Phone:** (403) 268-8500. *See color ad.*

INGLEWOOD BIRD SANCTUARY is at 2425 9th Ave. S.E. on the Bow River. Self-guiding trails wind throughout the forest, where some 280 species of birds and various mammals have been sighted. Natural history programs and guided nature walks also are offered. **Time:** Allow 1 hour minimum. **Hours:** Trails daily dawn-dusk. Visitor center daily 10-5, May-Sept.; Tues.-Sun. 10-4, rest of year.

Closed Jan. 1, Easter, Nov. 11 and Dec. 24-26. **Cost:** Donations. **Phone:** (403) 268-2489.

SAVE **LOUGHEED HOUSE** is at 707 13th Ave. S.W. Built in 1891 and enlarged in 1907, the sandstone mansion was the residence of Sir James Alexander Lougheed, a cabinet minister and party leader in the Senate, and his family. It later served as a barracks for the Canadian Women's Army Corps and as a blood donor clinic and dormitory for the Canadian Red Cross Society; today it houses interpretive exhibits detailing the structure's history and architecture.

The lovely 1.1-hectare (2.8-acre) estate includes the formal Beaulieu Gardens. Redesigned every year, the green space dazzles onlookers with such flora as yellow cannas and marigolds, red dahlias, and white and pink peonies. **Tours:** Guided tours are available. **Time:** Allow 30 minutes minimum. **Hours:** House Wed.-Fri. 11-4, Sat.-Sun. 10-4. Gardens daily 7 a.m.-dusk. Closed major holidays. **Cost:** House $8.50; $6.50 (students with ID and senior citizens); $5 (ages 6-12); $25 (family). Gardens free. **Phone:** (403) 244-6333. ⊤⊥

THE MILITARY MUSEUMS is at 4520 Crowchild Tr. S.W., off Flanders Ave. exit. This 5.3-hectare (13-acre) site is home to several museums detailing the history of the Canadian Forces. Exhibits highlight Lord Strathcona's Horse Regiment—the Royal Canadians; Princess Patricia's Canadian Light Infantry; The King's Own Calgary Regiment; and The Calgary Highlanders. Vintage tanks and carriers are outside. Visitors also can view a mural in the Queen Elizabeth II Atrium while watching videos that explain how the mosaic piece was created.

Time: Allow 1 hour, 30 minutes minimum. **Hours:** Mon.-Fri. 9-5, Sat.-Sun. 9:30-4. Closed Jan. 1 and Dec. 24-25. **Cost:** $6; $4 (senior citizens); $3 (ages 7-17); free (ages 0-6 and veterans and active military with ID and their families); $15 (family). **Phone:** (403) 974-2850. ⊤⊥

THE NICKLE ARTS MUSEUM is on the University of Calgary campus at 2500 University Dr. N.W. Four galleries present changing exhibits of contemporary art textile and numismatic collections. Lectures, gallery talks and other events are offered throughout the year. **Time:** Allow 1 hour minimum. **Hours:** Mon.-Fri. 10-5 (also Thurs. 5-9), Sept.-May; Mon.-Fri. 10-5, rest of year. Closed major holidays. **Cost:** $5; $2 (ages 66+); free (ages 0-6, students ages 7-17 with ID and to all Tues.). **Phone:** (403) 220-7234.

TELUS WORLD OF SCIENCE—CALGARY is at 11th St. and 7th Ave. S.W. Science is at the core of hands-on exhibits, demonstrations and live theater. The center presents multimedia productions and large-format films in the Discovery Dome. The Creative Kids Museum's five exhibit areas focus on the literary, performing and visual arts.

Hours: Daily 9-5:30, late June-Aug. 31; Mon.-Thurs. 9:45-4, Fri. 9:45-5; Sat.-Sun. 10-5, rest of

year. Closed Dec. 25. **Cost:** $14.25; $10 (ages 3-17 and 65+). Under 12 must be with an adult. **Parking:** $1.25 per hour, up to $5 for 6 hours. **Phone:** (403) 268-8300.

GAMBLING ESTABLISHMENTS

- **Cash Casino** is at 4040 Blackfoot Tr. S.E. **Hours:** Daily 9:30 a.m.-2 a.m. Closed Dec. 25. **Phone:** (403) 287-1635.

- **Casino Calgary** is at 1420 Meridian Rd. N.E. **Hours:** Daily 10 a.m.-3 a.m. Closed Dec. 25. **Phone:** (403) 248-9467.

- **Elbow River Casino** is at 218 18th Ave. S.E. **Hours:** Table games daily noon-3 a.m. Poker daily 24 hours. Closed Dec. 25. **Phone:** (403) 289-8880.

- SAVE **Frank Sisson's Silver Dollar Casino** is at 1010 42nd Ave. S.E. **Hours:** Casino daily 9:30 a.m.-3 a.m. Table games daily noon-2 a.m. Slots daily 10 a.m.-3 a.m. Closed Dec. 25. **Phone:** (403) 287-1183.

- **Stampede Casino** is at 421 12th Ave. S.E. in the Big Four Building in Stampede Park. **Hours:** Daily 9:30 a.m.-3 a.m. A 24-hour poker room is available. Closed Dec. 25. **Phone:** (403) 261-0422.

What To Do

Sightseeing

Bus, Train and Van Tours

Brewster Transportation and Tours offers a 4-hour bus tour of Calgary's attractions as well as trips to Banff, Lake Louise, Jasper and the Columbia Icefield; phone (403) 221-8242 for schedules and fares.

Rocky Mountaineer Vacations offers scenic vacation packages, including the Rocky Mountaineer, a 2-day, all-daylight, narrated rail tour between Canada's west and the Canadian Rockies. The Rocky Mountaineer tour departs mid-April to mid-October, with winter rail trips available in December; phone (604) 606-7245 or (877) 460-3200.

Walking Tours

Free pamphlets detailing a self-guiding tour of the Stephen Avenue Walk are available at the City of Calgary Municipal Building, 800 Macleod Tr. S.E. This pedestrian mall, which extends from Macleod Trail west along 8th Avenue to 3rd Street S.W., is a showcase for historic buildings, many of which are restored. Other pamphlets describing self-guiding walking tours and historic sites also are available.

Sports and Recreation

Calgary was an appropriate choice as host of the 1988 Winter Olympic Games—opportunities for indoor and outdoor recreation abound. For information about recreational activities, programs and facilities visitors can phone the city's recreation department by dialing 311 in Calgary or (403) 268-2489.

In winter public **skiing** facilities at Canada Olympic Park and in numerous areas nearby are available. Canada Olympic Park *(see attraction listing p. 52)* also is where to go for other **winter sports,** such as bobsledding, ski jumping and snowboarding.

At Talisman Centre, 2225 Macleod Tr. S., **swimming, track events** and **weight lifting** are among the popular activities; phone (403) 233-8393. Similar facilities are offered at the following leisure centers: Eau Claire YMCA, 101 3rd St. S.W.; YWCA, 320 5th Ave. S.E.; Southland Leisure Center, 2000 Southland Dr. S.W.; and Village Square Leisure Center, 2623 56th St. N.E. The latter two offer wave pools.

Ice-skating is featured during the winter at Olympic Plaza as well as year-round at more than two dozen other locations. The Olympic Oval, at 2500 University Dr. N.W., is the site of the 1988 Olympic speedskating events; skate rentals are available.

Several parks are in the city, particularly along the Bow River. Fish Creek Provincial Park *(see Recreation Chart)* has a visitor center and a small lake providing swimming in summer and ice-skating in winter. Joggers and bicyclists use the park's extensive trail system. Other recreation sites include Bowness, Edworthy and Riley parks in northwest Calgary and Prince's Island Park in the city center. The 145-hectare (360-acre) Glenmore Reservoir provides ample space for **sailing** and **canoeing;** the Dragon Boat races are held in late July.

With spectacular natural areas nearby, many visitors to Calgary will be lured to the wilds to enjoy canoeing, **camping, rafting, hiking** and other outdoor pursuits. **Walking** and **bicycling** trails meander through these regions, as do **cross-country skiing** routes. **Tennis** and swimming enthusiasts will find courts and pools throughout Calgary.

Golf lovers can play at more than 40 local courses, including 18 holes at Maple Ridge, 1240 Mapleglade Dr. S.E.; McCall Lake, 1600 32nd Ave. N.E.; McKenzie Meadows, 17215 McKenzie Meadows Dr. S.E.; and Shaganappi Point, 1200 26th St. S.W. Nine-hole courses are at Confederation, 3204 Collingwood Dr. N.W.; Lakeview, 5840 19th St. S.W.; and Richmond Green, 2539 33rd Ave. S.W. Some private courses accept visiting golfers; check locally for greens fees and restrictions.

With names like Flames, Stampeders Roughnecks and Hitmen, Calgary's major sports teams cannot help but be exciting. The Flames play **ice hockey** at Pengrowth Saddledome, 555 Saddledome Rise S.E. in Stampede Park; phone (403) 777-2177.

The local Canadian **Football** League team, the Calgary Stampeders, pounds the turf at McMahon Stadium, off 16th Avenue at 1817 Crowchild Tr. N.W. Tickets can be obtained by phoning the box office at (403) 289-0258. Ticket prices are $27-$80; $23-$80 (ages 0-18 and 61+).

Race City Speedway, 11550 68th St. S.E., features professional and amateur **auto racing** on a

drag strip, a high-banked oval and a 3-kilometre (2-mi.) road course; phone (403) 272-7223. For those wishing to get behind the wheel, Kart World Family Fun Center, 5202 1st St. S.W., offers **go-carts,** which can be rented. Helmets, clothing and instructions are provided. Tamer tracks for children also are available; phone (403) 253-8301.

Spruce Meadows, an outdoor equestrian center and show jumping venue 3 kilometres (2 mi.) west on Hwy. 22X (Spruce Meadows Trail) from Macleod Trail at 18011 Spruce Meadows Way S.W., has world-class programs, including international show jumping events. On days when no shows are scheduled the grounds are open free to the public, daily 9-6. Visitors are invited to wander the grounds, picnic and view horses in the stables; phone (403) 974-4200 for a schedule of Spruce Meadows events.

Shopping

Stephen Avenue Walk, a downtown pedestrian mall, extends from Bankers Hall to the city municipal buildings. This popular spot for people-watching features shops, galleries and restaurants housed within historic buildings. Also downtown, a five-block shopping complex linked by an indoor walkway includes the more than 200 boutiques, department stores and retail chains of Calgary Eaton Centre/TD Square, Bankers Hall and Scotia Centre.

Unique specialty shops, kiosks and restaurants are the draw at Eau Claire Market, adjacent to the Bow River and Prince's Island Park at 2nd Avenue and 2nd Street S.W.

The trendy Uptown 17th Avenue, a scenic neighborhood and upscale shopping district, features stylish fashion shops, antiques stores and eclectic craft boutiques. The avenue also is home to the exclusive shops at Mount Royal Village. The Kensington district features smaller stores in new and old buildings. Originally Atlantic Avenue, Ninth Avenue S.E. now is lined with antiques and home-furnishings stores, bookstores and cappuccino bars.

Major department stores and a wide variety of chain and specialty stores occupy the city's shopping centers: Chinook Centre at 6455 Macleod Tr. S.W., Deerfoot Outlet Mall at 901 64th Ave. N.E., Market Mall at 3625 Shaganappi Tr. N.W., North Hill Mall at 1632 14th Ave. N.W., Northland Village Shoppes at 5111 Northland Dr. N.W., Shawnessy Centre at 162nd Avenue and Macleod Trail, Southcentre Mall at Macleod Trail and Anderson Road S.E., Sunridge Mall at 2525 36th St. N.E., Westhills Towne Centre at Stewart Green S.W. off Richmond Road and Sarcee Trail S.W. and Willow Park Village on Macleod Trail S.

Performing Arts

Four of Calgary's most illustrious theater and music companies perform in the Epcor Centre for the Performing Arts at 205 8th Ave. S.E. The center is shared by Alberta Theatre Projects, Theatre Calgary, One Yellow Rabbit Theatre Company and Calgary Philharmonic Orchestra. In addition to four theaters and a concert hall, it contains shops, a restaurant and a coffee bar. For information about performance schedules and ticket sales phone Ticketmaster at (403) 777-0000 or (403) 299-8888.

Southern Alberta Jubilee Auditorium, 1415 14th Ave. N.W., stages a variety of performing arts, including touring companies of Broadway musicals and presentations by Calgary Opera; for details phone the opera company at (403) 262-7286 or the auditorium at (403) 297-8000.

Loose Moose Theatre Company, 1235 26th Ave. S.E., performs adult comedy and drama as well as children's theater; phone (403) 265-5682. Pumphouse Theatre, 2140 Pumphouse Ave. S.W., gets its name from the 1913 former pumphouse that the city converted into two theaters; phone (403) 263-0079 for schedule and ticket information. Midday performances take place in the aptly named Lunchbox Theatre on the second level in Bow Valley Square, 205 Fifth Ave. S.W.; phone (403) 265-4292.

A popular dinner theater that often showcases well-known performers in its productions is Stage West, 727 42nd Ave. S.E.; phone (403) 243-6642. Other theater, dance and music companies operate locally; check newspapers for performance schedules.

Special Events

To celebrate the season and showcase local arts, culture and sports, Calgary Winter Festival takes place for 11 days in February. The festival, which takes advantage of the venues from the 1988 Winter Olympics, features dog sledding, snowboarding and the Winter Village.

Calgary International Children's Festival, which begins the third Wednesday in May and continues

for 5 days, draws performers from such locales as Peru, Germany, Russia and Zimbabwe. The festival's many offerings include music, puppetry, dance and storytelling. Jazz musicians and jazz enthusiasts gather in June at the C-Jazz Festival.

Despite a focus on the modern oil and gas industry, Calgary citizens recall their past with The Calgary Stampede (officially known as The Calgary Exhibition & Stampede). This 10-day Wild West exhibition in July features a rodeo, chuck wagon races, livestock shows, a re-creation of a Plains Indian village, beach-themed attractions, educational displays, shopping, extreme sports events and a midway. Parades, fireworks, street dancing, pancake breakfasts and other activities create a carnival-like atmosphere. Families enjoy the cultural and musical events that take place during the Calgary Folk Music Festival, held over 4 days in late July.

GlobalFest takes place in August and features such events as an international fireworks competition and a multicultural celebration. Afrikadey! celebrates African culture through traditional and contemporary music, crafts, food and special scheduled events. Venues for the popular mid-August event are found throughout the area, with festivities concluding at Prince's Island Park. Visitors can sample fine foods and beverages at the Eau Claire Market during Taste of Calgary, which also occurs in mid-August.

During Labour Day weekend BBQ on the Bow offers a barbecue competition, live performances by local bands, a children's craft tent, and vendors selling food samples and take-home goods. The Masters Tournament takes place in September at the Spruce Meadows outdoor equestrian center, off Hwy. 22X (Spruce Meadows Trail) and Macleod Trail. Other racing and dressage events are held at the center throughout the year.

The Calgary Vicinity

AIRDRIE (H-5)
pop. 28,927, elev. 1,077 m/3,533′

NOSE CREEK VALLEY MUSEUM is just w. off Hwy. 2 Big Hill Springs Rd. exit, then 1 km (.6 mi.) n. to 1701 Main St. S. Located in Nose Creek Park's visitor center, this museum contains exhibits about early farming and ranching, wildlife, military history and native peoples. A topographical map, replicas of a pioneer house and a blacksmith shop, and antique vehicles are on display. Also included is an extensive collection of Indian artifacts and crafts.

Time: Allow 30 minutes minimum. **Hours:** Mon.-Fri. 10-5, Sat.-Sun. 1-5, June-Aug.; daily 1-5, rest of year. Closed Easter, Canadian Thanksgiving and Dec. 25. **Cost:** $2; free (ages 0-11). **Phone:** (403) 948-6685. 🎫

BRAGG CREEK (I-5) pop. 550

Bragg Creek, 40 kilometres (25 mi.) southwest of Calgary on Hwy. 22, was named after Albert Bragg,

a rancher who settled in the area in 1894. Known as the "Gateway to the Kananaskis" for its proximity to the Northern Rockies, the town has been a popular weekend getaway and year-round recreation area since the 1920s. Bragg Creek offers picnic areas, hiking trails, cross-country skiing, campgrounds and scenic Elbow Falls. The area has evolved as an artist's community with sculptors, potters, weavers, painters and other artisans practicing their crafts.

Bragg Creek Chamber of Commerce: P.O. Box 216, Bragg Creek, AB, Canada T0L 0K0. **Phone:** (403) 949-0004.

COCHRANE (H-5) pop. 13,760

Cochrane—named for Sen. Matthew Henry Cochrane, who began the first large-scale cattle ranch in the area in the 1880s—is known locally for its homemade ice cream, made by the same family since 1948; hang gliding; horseback riding; and canoe trips down the Bow River. Stoney Indian Reserve, 16 kilometres (10 mi.) west on Hwy. 1A, was the filming site of several movies, including Arthur Penn's "Legends of the Fall" and "Little Big Man," and of the television series "Lonesome Dove."

The downtown's Western-style architecture provides a backdrop for local arts and crafts and specialty shops. Of particular interest is Studio West, a foundry and art gallery where visitors can view the 3,000-year-old sculpting technique known as the "lost wax" process.

Also noteworthy is the town's "Trust" mural, on display at The Cochrane RancheHouse at 101 Ranchehouse Rd. A montage of small paintings, the collective work of nearly 200 artists, forms a large Western image of a cowboy and his horse. The mural is accessible Mon.-Fri. 8:30-4:30. Closed holidays.

Cochrane & District Chamber of Commerce: Unit 5 205 First St. E., Cochrane, AB, Canada T4C 1X6. **Phone:** (403) 932-0320.

COCHRANE RANCHE HISTORIC SITE is near jct. hwys. 1A and 22. This 60-hectare (150-acre) site is where Sen. Matthew Cochrane began his large-scale cattle operation in 1881. A visitor center, interpretive programs and walking trails are available. The "Men of Vision" bronze statue overlooks the grounds. **Time:** Allow 30 minutes minimum. **Hours:** Daily 9-5, mid-May through Labour Day. **Cost:** Free. **Phone:** (403) 932-4705. 🆓

OKOTOKS (I-6)
pop. 17,145, elev. 1,036 m/3,400'

Incorporated in 1904, Okotoks thrived on brick making, lumber and oil distribution in its early days. Today Okotoks is a commuter community of Calgary. The town gets its name from the Blackfoot name *okatoks*, meaning "rocks." Big Rock, 7 kilometres (4 mi.) west, is the continent's largest known glacial boulder, having been carried here during an ice age.

A popular recreational retreat, Okotoks offers such leisure pursuits as fishing and hiking. Events include a parade and Youth Festival in mid-June and the Coors Pro Rodeo and Western Art Show on Labour Day.

Okotoks & District Chamber of Commerce: 14 McRae St., P.O. Box 1053, Okotoks, AB, Canada T1S 1B1. **Phone:** (403) 938-2848.

Self-guiding tours: Heritage Walking Tour brochures are available from the information desk at The Station Cultural Centre, 53 N. Railway St.

Stampede Park / © Hans-Peter Merten / age fotostock

This ends listings for the Calgary Vicinity.
The following page resumes the alphabetical listings of cities in Alberta.

CAMROSE (F-7) pop. 15,620

Camrose, first settled around 1900 as a trading post, has a strong sense of its Scandinavian heritage. Known originally as the Hamlet of Sparling, its name was changed to Camrose in 1906. Camrose salutes country music during ☞ Big Valley Jamboree the first week in August.

Camrose Chamber of Commerce and Tourist Information Centre: 5402 48th Ave., Camrose, AB, Canada T4V 0J7. **Phone:** (780) 672-4217.

CAMROSE AND DISTRICT CENTENNIAL MUSEUM is 2 blks. s. of Hwy. 13 at 4522 53rd St. at jct. 46th Ave. The museum houses items from Camrose's pioneer days. Buildings include a country school; a fire hall; and a restored log pioneer house and church, both furnished in period. A steam engine, a replica of the first newspaper building and a working model of an early threshing machine are displayed.

Hours: Tues.-Sun. 10-5, Victoria Day-Labour Day; by appointment rest of year. **Cost:** Donations. **Phone:** (780) 672-3298 Victoria Day-Labour Day, or (780) 672-5377 for appointments rest of year.

CANMORE (H-4)
pop. 12,039, elev. 1,341 m/4,400′

Established in 1883 as a coal-mining center, Canmore was the first Canadian Pacific Railroad divisional point west of Calgary. The town also was the site of the biathlon and cross-country ski events of the 1988 Winter Olympics. Year-round recreational activities are abundant; fly fishing, rock climbing, snowshoeing and dog sledding are just a few activities visitors can enjoy. Hiking, mountain biking and cross-country skiing are popular along the area's numerous trails. The Canmore Highland Games in September also keeps sports enthusiasts entertained with a variety of athletic competitions. Scottish and Celtic dance and musical performances take place during the daylong festival as well.

Tourism Canmore: 907 7th Ave., P.O. Box 8608, Canmore, AB, Canada T1W 3K1. **Phone:** (403) 678-1295 or (866) 226-6673.

ALPINE HELICOPTERS LTD. is off Hwy. 1 Canmore exit, following signs to Canmore Municipal Heliport at 91 Bow Valley Tr. Scenic flights over the Canadian Rockies are offered. Passengers can view alpine valleys, glaciers, the Continental Divide, Banff National Park of Canada and towering Mount Assiniboine—"the Matterhorn of the Canadian Rockies." Helicopters carry four to six passengers.

Hours: Sightseeing flights are offered daily (weather permitting). Closed Jan. 1 and Dec. 25-26. Phone ahead to confirm schedule. **Cost:** Sightseeing flight $249 per passenger (30-minute tour); $219 per passenger (25-minute tour); $109 per passenger (12-minute tour). Reservations are required. **Phone:** (403) 678-4802.

CANMORE MUSEUM AND GEOSCIENCE CENTRE is at 902B 7th Ave. Displays detail Canmore's past through photographs and coal-mining artifacts. The museum also presents a geology exhibit with fossils, rocks, photographs and videos.

Time: Allow 30 minutes minimum. **Hours:** Mon.-Tues. noon-5, Wed.-Sun. 10-6, Victoria Day weekend-Labour Day; Mon.-Fri. noon-5, Sat.-Sun. 11-5, rest of year. Closed Jan. 1 and Dec. 25. **Cost:** $5; $3 (ages 65+ and students with ID); free (ages 0-7); $10 (family, two adults and two children). **Phone:** (403) 678-2462.

☞ **OH CANADA EH?! DINNER SHOW** is at 125 Kananaskis Way. The interactive show provides guests with a humorous take on Canadian culture and tradition. Singing Mounties, lumberjacks, a hockey player and other characters serve guests a family-style, traditional Canadian meal during the boisterous musical performance. Other shows are featured in the off-season.

Time: Allow 3 hours minimum. **Hours:** Shows are presented Fri.-Wed. at 6:15 p.m., Apr.-Oct.; otherwise varies. Phone ahead to confirm schedule. **Cost:** $65; $59 (senior citizens); $32.50 (ages 0-16). Ticket prices vary. Reservations are required. **Phone:** (403) 609-0004 or (800) 773-0004. 🍴

RECREATIONAL ACTIVITIES
Dog Sledding

- **Snowy Owl Sled Dog Tours** is at #104 602 Bow Valley Tr. **Hours:** Trips are offered daily, Nov.-Apr. (weather permitting). Departure times vary. **Phone:** (403) 678-4369 or (888) 311-6874.

White-water Rafting

- **Blast Adventures Inc.** is at 120 B Rundle Dr. **Hours:** Trips are offered daily, June 1 to mid-Sept. Departure times vary. **Phone:** (403) 609-2009, or (888) 802-5278 in Alberta and British Columbia.

- **Inside Out Experience** departs Fort Chiniki, just s. of Hwy. 1. Other activities are offered. **Hours:** Trips are offered daily, May 1-early Oct. Departure times vary. **Phone:** (403) 949-3305 or (877) 999-7238.

CARDSTON (K-6)
pop. 3,452, elev. 1,185 m/3,888′

A son-in-law of Brigham Young, Charles Ora Card, led 10 Mormon families from Utah into Canada in 1887, hoping to find freedom from American anti-polygamy laws. Settling in Cardston, the immigrants founded the country's first Mormon settlement and named the town after their leader, who became its first mayor.

Cardston Alberta Temple of the Church of Jesus Christ of Latter-day Saints, 348 3rd St. W., was completed and dedicated in 1923. The temple serves a large area of western Canada and Montana; a large percentage of Cardston residents are Mormon. Non-Mormons are not permitted to enter the structure but can tour the grounds, where a visitor center offers information; phone (403) 653-1696.

Cardston & District Chamber of Commerce: P.O. Box 1212, Cardston, AB, Canada T0K 0K0. **Phone:** (403) 653-2798.

CHARLES ORA CARD HOME is at 337 Main St. The log cabin of this Mormon leader has been restored and refurnished with hand-carved furniture. **Time:** Allow 30 minutes minimum. **Hours:** Mon.-Sat. 9-5, July-Aug. **Cost:** Donations. **Phone:** (403) 653-3366.

COURTHOUSE MUSEUM is at 89 3rd Ave. W. Displays include local pioneer memorabilia in a stone courthouse dating from 1907. **Time:** Allow 1 hour minimum. **Hours:** Mon.-Sat. 9-12:30, July-Aug. **Cost:** Donations. **Phone:** (403) 653-3366.

REMINGTON CARRIAGE MUSEUM is at 623 Main St. More than 250 19th- and early 20th-century horse-drawn vehicles are showcased. Interactive displays and exhibit galleries provide the feeling of riding in the horse-drawn transportation of that era, and an introductory multimedia presentation provides an overview of that time.

The exhibit galleries, which include a blacksmith shop and livery stable, carriage factory, carriage dealership, working restoration shop, frontier settlement and racetrack, depict 19th-century society and its dependence on this mode of transportation. Sound effects, lighting and audiovisual presentations enhance many of the presentations. Horses may be seen being groomed and harnessed in a working stable. In summer visitors may schedule 15-minute rides on vintage and reproduction carriages.

Tours: Guided tours are available. **Time:** Allow 1 hour, 30 minutes minimum. **Hours:** Daily 9-6, July 1-Labour Day; 10-5, rest of year. Carriage rides are offered daily 11-noon and 1-5, May 15-Labour Day. Closed Jan. 1, Easter and Dec. 24-25. **Cost:** $9; $8 (ages 65+); $5 (ages 7-17); $22 (family, two adults and two children). Carriage ride $4; $2.50 (ages 4-17); $12 (family, two adults and two children). **Phone:** (403) 653-5139.

RECREATIONAL ACTIVITIES
White-water Rafting
• **Kimball River Sports** is 9 km (5.5 mi.) s.e. on Hwy. 501. **Hours:** Trips are offered June-Aug. Schedule varies; phone ahead. **Phone:** (403) 653-1099.

CLARESHOLM (J-6) pop. 3,700

CLARESHOLM MUSEUM is on Hwy. 2 at 5126 1st St. W. Displays are housed in a former Canadian Pacific Railway station. The sandstone building features early 20th-century items that represent pioneer life. Town history is highlighted in railway, medical and educational displays. On the grounds are a visitor center, a one-room schoolhouse, a historic log cabin, a caboose, a playground and the Louise McKinney Memorial Gardens. **Hours:** Daily 9:30-5:30, mid-May through the second Mon. in Oct.; by appointment rest of year. **Cost:** Donations. **Phone:** (403) 625-3131.

COALDALE (J-7) pop. 6,177

THE ALBERTA BIRDS OF PREY CENTRE is 3 blks. n. of jct. hwys. 3 and 845, then w. on 16th Ave. The facility, a working conservation center, rehabilitates injured and orphaned birds of prey and prepares them for release back into the wild. A captive breeding program returns threatened and endangered species to their native habitats. A self-guiding nature walk provides a close-up view of captive hawks, falcons, owls, eagles and vultures. Birds fly freely during daily demonstrations at this 28-hectare (70-acre) prairie wetland site.

Tours: Guided tours are available. **Time:** Allow 1 hour, 30 minutes minimum. **Hours:** Daily 9:30-5, early May-early Sept. **Cost:** $9; $8 (ages 60+); $6 (ages 6-17); $5 (ages 3-5). **Phone:** (403) 345-4262.

COCHRANE—see Calgary p. 57.

COLD LAKE (D-8)
pop. 11,991, elev. 555 m/1,820′

COLD LAKE MUSEUMS is 5.1 km (3.12 mi.) s.w. on Hwy. 28 (8th Ave.)/Hwy. 55 (51st St.) at 6503 51st St. Four separate buildings connected by an enclosed passageway are situated on the site of a former radar facility. Showcased is the original 42-foot radar height finder antenna, part of the Distant Early Warning Line during the Cold War.

The Aboriginal Museum displays Dene Suline and Cree artifacts and crafts. Interactive exhibits focusing on the area's oil sands industry are featured in The Oil & Gas Gallery, while the Heritage Museum highlights some of Cold Lake's other industries in addition to local history. Several aircraft and military vehicles are parked just outside the Cold Lake Air Force Museum, which relates the story of the Canadian Forces in the region.

Tours: Guided tours are available. **Time:** Allow 1 hour minimum. **Hours:** Daily 10-4, Victoria Day weekend-Labour Day. **Cost:** Donations. **Phone:** (780) 594-3546, or (800) 840-6140, off-season.

COLUMBIA ICEFIELD—
see Jasper National Park of Canada p. 81.

CROWSNEST PASS (J-5) pop. 5,749

An area of wild beauty and haunting legends, the municipality of Crowsnest Pass is an amalgamation of the former coal-mining towns of Bellevue, Blairmore, Coleman, Frank and Hillcrest. Scenic Hwy. 3 through Crowsnest Pass connects Burmis to Fernie, British Columbia, via the Rocky Mountain Range and the Continental Divide.

The area provides visitors with recreational opportunities and stimulates the imagination with such stories as the curse of the Lost Lemon Gold Mine, rum-running and the shoot-out at Bellevue Cafe.

The town of Frank made national headlines April 29, 1903, when close to 70 residents were killed in the dramatic slide of Turtle Mountain on the east side of the pass. Ninety million tons of limestone swept over 1.5 kilometres (.9 mi.) of the valley before dawn, destroying part of the town and burying a mine plant and railway. The old town was at the western edge of the slide; many cellars still are visible.

BELLEVUE UNDERGROUND MINE TOUR is n. off Hwy. 3 Bellevue exit, following signs to the Bellevue Underground Mine access road at 21814 28th Ave. Participants don a miner's helmet and lamp, strap on a battery pack and follow guides along the same path taken by coal miners 1903-61, when this was an active coal mine. The 1-hour tour provides insights into the process of coal mining and the events that led to the mine's closing.

Note: The temperature in the mine can reach 7 C (45 F); dress in warm clothing and wear sturdy footwear. **Time:** Allow 1 hour minimum. **Hours:** Tours depart daily every 30 minutes 10-5:30, May 15-Labour Day. **Cost:** Fee $10; $9 (ages 65+); $8 (ages 6-17); $25 (family). **Phone:** (403) 564-4700.

FRANK SLIDE INTERPRETIVE CENTRE is 1.5 km (.9 mi.) n. off Hwy. 3 at w. edge of Frank Slide. The center overlooks the site of the 1903 rockslide. Visitors experience the impact of Canada's deadliest rockslide through interactive exhibits and multimedia presentations. Walkways outside the center provide spectacular views of the surrounding Canadian Rockies. A 1.5-kilometre (.9-mi.) self-guiding trail over the slide allows visitors to view the debris. Interpretive programs are offered in summer.

Time: Allow 1 hour, 30 minutes minimum. **Hours:** Daily 9-6, July 1-Labour Day; 10-5, rest of year. Closed Jan. 1, Easter and Dec. 24-25. **Cost:** $9; $8 (ages 65+); $5 (ages 7-17); $22 (family, two adults and children). **Phone:** (403) 562-7388.

LEITCH COLLIERIES PROVINCIAL HISTORIC SITE is 3 km (1.9 mi.) e. of Bellevue on Hwy. 3. Founded in 1907, this was the first wholly Canadian-owned mine. The area was the site of a sophisticated early colliery—a coal mine and the buildings and equipment connected with it. The remains of the power house, washery, mine manager's residence and coke ovens still stand.

Interpretive signs explain the mining and processing methods. **Hours:** Self-guiding tours are available year-round. Interpreters are on-site daily 10-5 and offer guided tours at 11 and 2, mid-May through Labour Day. **Cost:** Donations. **Phone:** (403) 562-7388.

DEVON—*see Edmonton p. 74.*

DICKSON (G-5) pop. 77

DICKSON STORE MUSEUM is at 1928 2nd Ave. Renovated to a style typical of the 1930s, this general store once served as the town post office and a local gathering place. Now operating as a museum, it features exhibits of dry goods, hardware and groceries common to that time. Costumed interpreters also lead visitors through the restored second-floor living quarters.

Time: Allow 30 minutes minimum. **Hours:** Mon.-Sat. 10-5:30, Sun. 12:30-5:30, mid-May through Labour Day; Sat. 10-5:30, Sun. 12:30-5:30, day after Labour Day-last Sun. in Sept. **Cost:** Donations. **Phone:** (403) 728-3355.

DONALDA (F-7) pop. 224

Situated in the heart of Alberta, Donalda was established in 1911 and named after the niece of Donald A. Mann, an official with the Canadian National Railway. It overlooks the scenic Meeting Creek Coulee. The region's unusual Paskapoo sandstone rock formations attract sportsman, hikers, artists and photographers. Donalda also claims an unusual man-made distinction. A 12.8-metre (42-ft.) lamp, said to be the world's largest, was built in the town center by local residents. It glows at the east end of Main Street each evening.

DONALDA & DISTRICT MUSEUM is at Main St. and Railway Ave. More than 900 lamps ranging from the antique bicycle variety to colorful living room types are displayed. Some 40 tiny courting lamps, which hold only an hour's worth of fuel and were used in the 1800s to signal the end of a suitor's visit, also can be seen. In addition more than 4,000 artifacts depicting the area's history are exhibited. An art gallery, a 1909 railway station and a creamery are on-site.

Time: Allow 30 minutes minimum. **Hours:** Mon.-Fri. 9-5, Sat.-Sun. 11-5, early May-second

DID YOU KNOW

Alberta is Canada's sunniest province.

Mon. in Oct.; Mon.-Fri. 9-5, rest of year. **Cost:** $3; free (ages 0-14). **Phone:** (403) 883-2100.

DRUMHELLER (H-7) pop. 7,932

About 65 million years before Sam Drumheller began promoting the 1910 townsite later named for him, the surrounding Red Deer Valley was the home of immense dinosaurs. Plant-eating hadrosaurs, flesh-eating tyrannosaurs and their formidable cousins stomped through the swampy lowlands and forests bordering the Mowry Sea, which once covered the North American plains. Fossils of prehistoric creatures often are discovered in the multi-layered sedimentary walls of the valley; several life-size dinosaur replicas can be seen in town.

A larger-than-life version of one of these prehistoric beings, a 25-metre-tall (84-ft.) facsimile of a tyrannosaurus rex, has been built over the top of the Drumheller & District Chamber of Commerce at 60 First Ave. W. Visitors can climb up to a viewing platform in the dinosaur's mouth.

Although the local coal industry founded in 1911 by American Jesse Gouge has declined, remnants of old mines still exist. Six kilometres (3.7 mi.) w. on N. Dinosaur Trail (Hwy. 838), Midland Provincial Park *(see Recreation Chart)* features a self-guiding walking trail that leads to the former site of Midland Mine. Gas and oil wells sporadically dot the nearby rolling prairies, but the shortgrass country is occupied mostly by geese and antelope.

Hoodoos—mushroom-shaped pillars of rock that have been carved into unusual formations by centuries of wind and rain—can be seen 18 kilometres (11 mi.) southeast on Hwy. 10. Because of their fragile nature, climbing these formations is not permitted.

Another nearby remarkable natural site is Horseshoe Canyon, 17 kilometres (11 mi.) southwest on Hwy. 9. Deriving its name from its horseshoe shape, the canyon is in an area of badlands amidst the Alberta prairies. Viewpoints provide opportunities to survey multicolored canyon walls and unusual rock formations.

A natural amphitheater is the site in early July for six performances of The Canadian Badlands Passion Play. In a setting closely resembling the Holy Land, a cast of 150 and a 100-voice choir relate the life of Christ; phone (403) 823-2001 or (888) 823-2001.

Stretching over the Red Deer River, the Rosedale Suspension Bridge on Hwy. 10 originally was used to carry miners across the river to the now-abandoned Star Mine. In 1931 the swinging bridge replaced the original cable car system and was used until the mine closed in 1957. A park with picnic facilities is available.

Drumheller & District Chamber of Commerce: 60 First Ave. W., P.O. Box 999, Drumheller, AB, Canada T0J 0Y0. **Phone:** (866) 823-8100.

ATLAS COAL MINE NATIONAL HISTORIC SITE is 18 km (11 mi.) s.e. on Hwy. 10. This site explores the coal mining history of the Drumheller Valley.

Visitors can take a guided tour of what is said to be the last remaining wooden tipple (coal screening plant) in Canada; take a ride on a 1936 Mancha locomotive; see restored mine offices, a lamp house and a miner's shack; hike on interpretive trails; and climb on antique mining machines. An underground tunnel tour also is offered.

Time: Allow 1 hour, 30 minutes minimum. **Hours:** Daily 9:30-8:30, July-Aug.; 9:30-5:30, May-June; 10-4, Sept. 1-second Mon. in Oct. (weather permitting). Tour times vary; phone ahead. **Cost:** $7; free (ages 0-6); $21 (family, two adults and two children). Tunnel tour additional $5; free (ages 0-6); $15 (family, two adults and two children). Tipple tour (includes mine train) additional $2; free (ages 0-6); $6 (family, two adults and two children). Combination ticket (includes historic site, tunnel tour, tipple tour and mine train) $14; free (ages 0-6); $42 (family, two adults and two children). **Phone:** (403) 822-2220.

DINOSAUR TRAIL (HWYS. 838 AND 837) is a 48-km (30-mi.) looping drive trip that connects Drumheller with the Red Deer River Valley, part of Alberta's Canadian Badlands. The trail is marked, and several museums, parks and observation points are along the route. The arid terrain is distinguished by hoodoos—mushroom-shaped rock pillars carved by thousands of years of wind and rain.

On the north side of the trail is The Little Church, a meditation chapel that holds six visitors. The cable-run Bleriot Ferry crosses the Red Deer River. **Hours:** Highway open daily. The ferry departs daily as needed dawn-dusk, early May to mid-Oct. **Cost:** Highway and ferry free. **Phone:** (866) 823-8100.

Badlands Historical Centre is at 335 1st St. E. Displays focus on pioneer history, the coal-mining boom and the region's ecology. A lapidary collection includes fossils, gems and minerals. Interactive exhibits also are featured. **Hours:** Daily 10-6, May-Oct. **Cost:** $4; $3 (ages 8-18 and 65+); $10 (family). **Phone:** (403) 823-2593.

HOMESTEAD MUSEUM is .7 km (.5 mi.) n.w. via Hwy. 9 to 901 N. Dinosaur Tr. Pioneer and First Nations items as well as clocks, gramophones, radios, early cars, fine china, jewelry, tractors and farm implements are displayed. There also are collections of military badges, medals and early 20th-century clothing. **Time:** Allow 1 hour, 30 minutes minimum. **Hours:** Daily 10-5, May 1 to mid-Oct. (also Fri.-Sun. 5-8, Victoria Day weekend-Labour Day). **Cost:** $5; $3 (ages 6-17 and 65+); $12 (family). **Phone:** (403) 823-2600.

REPTILE WORLD is at 95 3rd Ave. E. Home to more than 150 species of reptiles and amphibians—including snakes, frogs and turtles—the facility features Fred, a 318-kilogram (700-lb.) alligator. **Time:** Allow 30 minutes minimum. **Hours:** Daily 9 a.m.-10 p.m., July-Aug.; Thurs.-Mon. 10-5, Sun. noon-5, Apr.; Thurs.-Mon. 10-6, May-June; Thurs.-Mon. 10-5, rest of year. Closed major holidays. Phone ahead to confirm schedule. **Cost:** $7;

$5 (ages 5-17 and 65+); $20 (family, two adults and children). **Phone:** (403) 823-8623.

ROYAL TYRRELL MUSEUM is 6 km (4 mi.) n.w. on N. Dinosaur Tr. (Hwy. 838) in Midland Provincial Park. The museum is in the badlands of the Red Deer River Valley, surrounded by one of the richest fossil deposits in the world. Dinosaurs that once roamed Alberta are now showcased in the museum's Dinosaur Hall, where more than 35 skeletons and lifelike models are displayed.

Fossils, models, computers, DVD centers, a preparation laboratory, hands-on exhibits and an indoor garden illustrate millions of years of geological and biological development. Educational programs are offered Victoria Day weekend through Labour Day. The Cretaceous Garden contains plants that are virtually the same today as they were more than 65 million years ago. The museum also houses a research center and operates a field station near Patricia *(see attraction listing p. 88)*.

Time: Allow 3 hours minimum. **Hours:** Daily 9-9, Victoria Day weekend-Labour Day; daily 10-5, day after Labour Day-second Mon. in Oct.; Tues.-Sun. 10-5, rest of year. Closed Jan. 1 and Dec. 25. **Cost:** $10; $8 (ages 65+); $6 (ages 7-17); $30 (family, two adults and children). **Phone:** (403) 823-7707, or (888) 440-4240 out of Alberta. *See color ad on insert.*

VALLEY DOLL MUSEUM is at 60-249 3rd Ave. W. More than 700 dolls are displayed in themed settings. Celebrity dolls include Marilyn Monroe, Elvis Presley and John Wayne. Unusual figures fashioned from such materials as coal, wax and felt also are exhibited. **Time:** Allow 30 minutes minimum. **Hours:** Mon.-Sat. 10-7, Sun. noon-5, in summer; Tues.-Sat. 10-5, rest of year. Closed Jan. 1, third Mon. in Feb., Thanksgiving and Dec. 25-26. **Cost:** $5.50; $4.50 (ages 12-17); $3.50 (ages 5-11). **Phone:** (403) 823-3655.

DUNVEGAN (B-2)

HISTORIC DUNVEGAN PROVINCIAL PARK is off Queen Elizabeth II Hwy. on the n. side of the Peace River beside Dunvegan Suspension Bridge. The park was a fur-trading post and the site of one of the first Roman Catholic missions in Alberta. Three original buildings remain: the 1877-78 Factor's House, part of the Hudson's Bay Co.'s fort; the 1885 church of St. Charles Mission; and its 1889 rectory.

Guided walks and educational programs explain the site's history. A visitor center offers a video about the history of Dunvegan. *See Recreation Chart.* **Time:** Allow 1 hour minimum. **Hours:** Daily 10-6, May 15-Labour Day. **Cost:** $3; $2 (ages 65+); $1.50 (ages 7-17); $8 (family). **Phone:** (780) 835-7150.

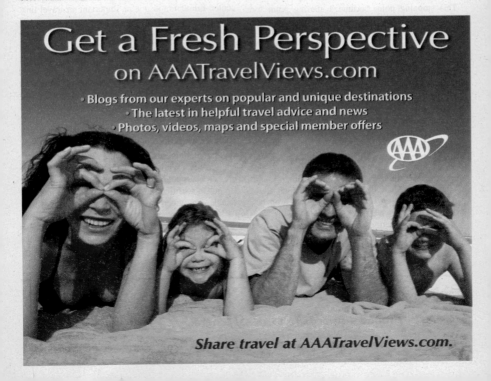

Edmonton

City Population: 730,372
Elevation: 670 m/2,198 ft.

Editor's Picks:

Fort Edmonton Park.................*(see p. 69)*
Royal Alberta Museum ....*(see p. 70)*
West Edmonton Mall ....*(see p. 71)*

© George Hunter / SuperStock

Few first-time visitors to Edmonton are prepared for what they discover when they arrive. From trading post to metropolis within some 200 years, this capital city continues to surprise visitors by its size, quality of life, sophistication and its beautiful river valley location.

Edmonton owes its existence to an abundant and varied supply of natural resources, which prompted each of its three major booms. In 1795 the Hudson's Bay Co. founded Fort Edmonton on the banks of the North Saskatchewan River. Traders bartered with Cree and Blackfoot Indians for luxuriant and sought-after pelts of otters, beavers, muskrats, minks and foxes. A trading settlement developed and became the main stopping point on routes to the north and to the Pacific.

This stopping point became a starting point for prospectors rushing to the Klondike for gold; they stocked up on supplies in Edmonton for the harsh trip northward. When gold failed to materialize and many prospectors realized they were not going to get rich, let alone get rich quick, they headed back to Edmonton to settle for a slower but surer way of life.

A bust for prospectors was a boom for Edmonton. The city grew to six times its previous size, making it a prime choice for the provincial capital when Alberta was formed in 1905.

In the years that followed, the capital city earned its nickname, "Gateway to the North," because of its status as a transportation hub and gateway to the regions beyond. In 1915 Edmonton became a major link in the Canadian Pacific Transcontinental Railroad, emerging as an important crossroads stop between east and west as well as north and south.

The city's reputation as a transportation center was reinforced during the 1930s as bush pilots transported vital medical supplies, food and mail to northern communities. And when construction began on the Alaska Hwy. in 1942, Edmonton found itself again in the role of a major distribution and supply center. Edmonton also is an important air travel link.

When the last big boom was fading from memory, the Leduc No. 1 Well gushed forth black crude oil only 40 kilometres (25 mi.) southwest of Edmonton. This discovery in February 1947 was just the beginning. Since then more than 2,250 wells within a 40-kilometre (25-mi.) radius of Edmonton have coaxed the precious natural resource to the surface. Enormous industrial growth resulted; the city's population quadrupled in the 25 years following the Leduc gusher. Today more than 450,000 barrels of crude oil are refined daily in Greater Edmonton.

Edmonton is a city growing in both prosperity and beauty. With about 938,000 residents in the greater metropolitan area, Edmonton has been careful not to sacrifice the natural resource that makes it livable—its green space. Edmonton's river valley parkland is reputed to be the largest stretch of urban parkland in North America, encompassing 7,340 hectares (18,348 acres). The city contains more than 11,000 hectares (27,181 acres) of parkland, playgrounds and open areas.

Stretches of parks along the North Saskatchewan River Valley let residents spend long summer days enjoying the outdoors. The city park system provides a winter playground for such activities as cross-country skiing, ice-skating, dog sledding and snowshoeing. For visitors who prefer the indoors, an extensive system of underground and overhead "pedways" in the downtown area makes it possible to travel in climate-controlled comfort regardless of the weather; Edmonton Tourism provides pedway maps.

William Hawrelak Park / Travel Alberta

Getting There

By Car

Two major highways run through Edmonton. The Trans-Canada Yellowhead Hwy. (Hwy. 16) provides access from the east and west; Queen Elizabeth II Hwy. runs north and south between Edmonton and Calgary.

Getting Around

Street System

Edmonton's street system is a grid with streets running north and south and avenues running east and west. Most streets and avenues are numbered starting from the southeast corner of the city; a few are named.

Edmonton's street plan includes several traffic circles. When approaching a traffic circle, make sure you are in the correct lane. Use the right lane if you plan to exit, the left lane if you are traveling around the circle. When in the circle, the vehicle on the outside must yield to the vehicle on the inside.

The city speed limit is 50 kilometres per hour (30 mph) or as posted. A right turn on red after stopping is permitted; U-turns are not. A sign that reads "Bus and Taxi Lane Only" means it is illegal to drive, park or stop any vehicle other than the above in that lane.

Parking

Street parking restrictions vary throughout the city; watch for and heed the signs. Parking is not permitted in the residential areas surrounding Northlands Park, TELUS Field and Commonwealth Stadium during major events; cars parked there will be towed.

Rates for city-operated parking meters are $1-$2 per hour. Most meters are free after 6 p.m. and on Sundays and holidays; however, there are some 24-hour meters.

Rates for downtown parking lots range $2-$4 per half-hour during the day. At lots participating in the city's Park in the Heart program, parking costs $2 from 6 p.m. to midnight Monday through Friday and for the first 3 hours on Saturdays and Sundays.

Destination Edmonton

*O*nce a tiny settlement where traders sought to swap for furs with Cree and Blackfoot Indians, today's bustling Edmonton holds its heritage in high regard.

*R*eminders of the city's past can be found at museums, living-history demonstrations, historic sites and archives. But don't forget to step into the present for a visit to one of the world's largest malls.

Travel Alberta

Sea Life Caverns at West Edmonton Mall.
(See listing page 71)

Valley Zoo, Edmonton.
(See listing page 71)

Travel Alberta

Francis Winspear Centre, Edmonton.
(See mention page 73)

Edmonton

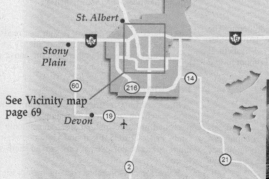

St. Albert

Stony Plain

See Vicinity map page 69

Devon

Travel Alberta

Edmonton Heritage Festival.
(See mention page 73)

*P*laces included in this AAA Destination City:

The Informed Traveler

Sales Tax: The federal Goods and Service Tax is 5 percent and applies to most goods, food/beverages and services, including lodgings. Alberta does not have a provincial sales tax but does impose a 4 percent hotel tax. A 1-2 percent tourism levy also is charged in some areas.

WHOM TO CALL

Emergency: 911 or (780) 426-3232
Police (non-emergency): (780) 423-4567
Fire: (780) 496-3900
Ambulance: 911 or (780) 426-3232
Distress Line: (780) 482-4357
Weather: (780) 468-4940
Road Reports: (780) 471-6056
Hospitals: Grey Nuns Community Hospital, (780) 735-7000; Misericordia, (780) 735-2000; Royal Alexandra Hospital, (780) 735-4111; University of Alberta Hospital, (780) 407-8822.

WHERE TO LOOK

Newspapers

Edmonton has two daily newspapers, the *Edmonton Journal* and the *Edmonton Sun,* both distributed in the morning. Canada's national newspapers, *The Globe and Mail* and the *National Post,* also are available at newsstands.

Radio

Radio station CBC (740 AM) is a member of Canadian Broadcasting Corp.

Visitor Information

Edmonton Tourism: 9990 Jasper Ave. N.W., Edmonton, AB, Canada T5J 1P7. **Phone:** (780) 496-8400 or (800) 463-4667. *See color ad on insert.*

Gateway Park Information Center: 2404 Gateway Blvd. S.W./Queen Elizabeth II Hwy., Edmonton, AB, Canada T6W 1A1. **Phone:** (780) 496-8400 or (800) 463-4667.

Visitor information also is available at the Edmonton International Airport.

TRANSPORTATION

Air Travel

Edmonton International Airport is 29 kilometres (18 mi.) south of the city center; for information phone (780) 890-8382 or (800) 268-7134. Sky Shuttle service to downtown costs $15 one way and $30 round-trip (phone to confirm fares); phone (780) 465-8515 or (888) 438-2342. Taxi service between the airport and downtown typically costs $49; a limousine costs $60. In addition many hotels offer free shuttle service for their guests.

Rental Cars

Hertz, downtown or at the airport, offers discounts to CAA and AAA members; phone (780) 423-3431 downtown, (780) 890-4435 at the airport, (800) 263-0600 in Canada or (800) 654-3080 out of Canada.

Rail Service

The VIA Rail station is at 12360 121st St.; phone (780) 448-2575 for baggage information, (888) 842-7245 for arrival and departure information.

Buses

The downtown depot for Greyhound Lines Inc. is at 10324 103rd St.; phone (780) 413-8747 or (800) 661-8747. The south side depot is at 5723 104th St. Red Arrow Express offers luxury motor coach service between Edmonton, Calgary, Fort McMurray and Red Deer; phone (780) 424-3339 or (800) 232-1958.

Taxis

Taxi companies include Alberta Co-Op Taxi, (780) 425-2525; Barrel Taxi (780) 489-7777; and Yellow Cab, (780) 462-3456. Taxi rates start at $2.50, plus 20c is charged for each additional 210 metres (about ⅛ mile) or a portion thereof. Taxis can be hailed, but phoning is recommended.

Public Transport

Edmonton Transit System's Churchill Station Information Centre, 99th Street and 102A Avenue, is open Mon.-Fri. 8:30-5:30; phone (780) 496-1611. Buses operate 6 a.m.-1 a.m., Mon.-Sat., 6:30 a.m.-12:30 a.m., Sun. and holidays; hours may be extended for special events. The Light-Rail Transit (LRT) operates 5:30 a.m. to 1 a.m. Fare is $2.50. A 1-day pass is $7.50. Disabled Adult Transit System (DATS) serves those who can't use other transit facilities. Visitors may request a temporary registration number by phoning (780) 496-4570. DATS reservations are accepted up to 3 days in advance.

What To See

ALBERTA AVIATION MUSEUM is at 11410 Kingsway Ave. This hangar was part of a training facility for air crews during World War II. The museum displays more than 30 historic aircraft including a carefully restored Fairchild 71, a fighter-bomber version of the De Havilland Mosquito, a fully operational Boeing 737 airliner, as well as 1920s biplanes and jet fighters from the Cold War era. Other displays detail the history of aviation in Edmonton and Alberta.

Guided tours are available by appointment. **Time:** Allow 1 hour minimum. **Hours:** Mon.-Fri. 10-6, Sat.-Sun. and holidays 10-4. Closed Jan. 1 and Dec. 25-26 and 31. **Cost:** $9; $7 (ages 60+); $6 (ages 13-17); $5 (ages 6-12); $24 (family, two adults and four children). **Phone:** (780) 451-1175.

ALBERTA LEGISLATURE BUILDING is at 10800 97th Ave. Public-use parkland, monuments, reflecting pools and fountains surround the building, which was built with sandstone and marble and completed in 1912. Displays outline Alberta's history and parliamentary traditions. Guided 45-minute tours begin in the Legislature Interpretive Centre.

Time: Allow 1 hour minimum. **Hours:** Guided tours are offered daily on the hour 9-noon and every 30 minutes 12:30-4, May 1-Oct. 15; on the hour Mon.-Fri. 9-3, Sat.-Sun. and holidays noon-4, rest of year. Closed Jan. 1, Good Friday and Dec. 25. **Cost:** Free. **Phone:** (780) 427-7362.

ALBERTA RAILWAY MUSEUM is 2 km (1.2 mi.) s. of Hwy. 37 at 24215 34th St. The museum resembles a railway terminal, with a train yard, locomotive and car shops, a water tank and a station. More than 60 pieces of rolling stock are displayed. There are many exhibits about railway history, including telegraph systems and railway technology. Some weekends in July and August a 20-minute ride aboard a steam or diesel-powered train is offered (weather permitting).

Tours: Guided tours are available. **Time:** Allow 1 hour, 30 minutes minimum. **Hours:** Sat.-Sun. 10-5, Victoria Day weekend-Labour Day. **Cost:** $5; $3.50 (students with ID and senior citizens); $2 (ages 3-12). Train ride $4. **Phone:** (780) 472-6229.

ART GALLERY OF ALBERTA is at 100-10230 Jasper Ave. at Enterprise Square. The gallery exhibits fine and applied arts and is dedicated to the exhibition and preservation of Canadian art and visual culture.

Note: At press time, the museum's collections were being displayed in an interim gallery; a new permanent facility was being constructed on Sir Winston Churchill Square and was set to open in early 2010. Phone ahead for updates and to confirm schedule and location. **Time:** Allow 1 hour minimum. **Hours:** Mon.-Fri. 10:30-5 (also Thurs. 5-8), Sat.-Sun. 11-5. Closed major holidays. **Cost:** $10; $7 (ages 65+ and students with ID); $5 (ages 6-12); free (ages 0-5 and to all Thurs. 4-8 p.m.); $20 (family, two adults and four children). **Phone:** (780) 422-6223.

Fort Edmonton Park / Travel Alberta

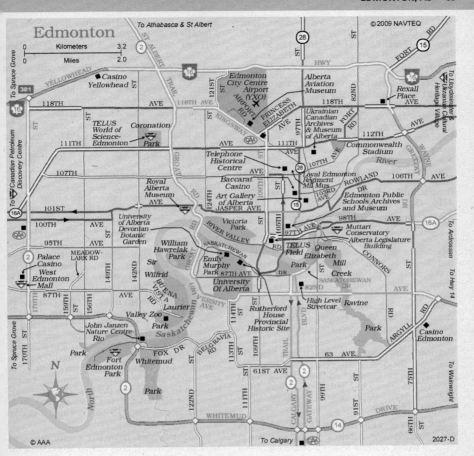

Edmonton

© 2009 NAVTEQ

© AAA

2027-D

EDMONTON PUBLIC SCHOOLS ARCHIVES AND MUSEUM is at 10425 99th Ave. The archives and museum is in historic 1905 McKay Avenue School, site of the first two sessions of the Alberta Legislature. The building has been carefully restored and features the 1906 legislative chamber, period classrooms and displays tracing the history of Edmonton public schools.

Also on the grounds is the restored Edmonton 1881 Schoolhouse, the first free public school in Alberta. **Time:** Allow 1 hour minimum. **Hours:** Tues.-Fri. 12:30-4 (also Wed. 4-9), Sun. 1-4, May-Sept.; Tues.-Fri. 12:30-4, rest of year. Closed major holidays. **Cost:** Free. **Phone:** (780) 422-1970.

FORT EDMONTON PARK is at jct. Fox and Whitemud drs. at 7000 143rd. St. Reputed to be Canada's largest living-history park, it depicts Edmonton in four eras: as an 1846 Hudson's Bay Co. fur-trading fort and Cree encampment, as an 1885 settlement, as a developing capital in 1905 and as a 1920 business community.

Costumed interpreters give demonstrations. Visitors may play horseshoes and old-time children's games, ride in antique cars, fire a round in the shooting gallery, learn to bead and sample pioneer foods such as bannock. Steam train and streetcar rides as well as a 1920s-style midway are included.

Pets are not permitted. **Time:** Allow 3 hours minimum. **Hours:** Daily 10-6, late June-Labour Day; Mon.-Fri. 10-4, Sat.-Sun. 10-6, late May-late June; Sun. 10-6, day after Labour Day-Sept. 30. Guided tours are available at 11, noon, 1, 2 and 3. **Cost:** $13.50; $10.25 (ages 13-17 and 65+); $6.75 (ages 2-12); $40.50 (family, two adults and children). Prices may vary; phone ahead. **Phone:** (780) 496-8787. [TI]

JOHN JANZEN NATURE CENTRE is at jct. Fox and Whitemud drs., adjacent to Fort Edmonton Park. The center has exhibits, self-guiding nature trails through the river valley, small animals, hands-on exhibits for children, and interpretive programs and events designed to promote awareness and appreciation of wildlife and the environment.

Time: Allow 1 hour minimum. **Hours:** Mon.-Fri. 9-6, Sat.-Sun. and holidays 11-6, July 1-Labour

Day; Mon.-Fri. 9-4, Sat.-Sun. and holidays 1-4, rest of year. Closed Jan. 1 and Dec. 25. **Cost:** $2; $1.65 (ages 13-17 and 65+); $1.35 (ages 2-12); $6 (family). Prices may vary; phone ahead. **Phone:** (780) 496-8787.

THE LOYAL EDMONTON REGIMENT MILITARY MUSEUM is 2 km (1.2 mi.) n. on 105th St., then just w. to 10440 108th Ave. in the Prince of Wales Armouries Heritage Centre. The museum's two galleries examine the history of The Loyal Edmonton Regiment, Alberta's oldest infantry unit, and explore military life. Displays include weapons, military equipment, uniforms, medals and badges, photographs and documents. **Time:** Allow 1 hour minimum. **Hours:** Mon.-Fri. 10-4. Phone ahead to confirm schedule. **Cost:** Donations. **Phone:** (780) 421-9943.

MUTTART CONSERVATORY is at 9626 96A St., at the e. end of the James MacDonald Bridge. Four pyramid-shaped glass greenhouses showcase a variety of flora. Palm trees, orchids and hibiscus, typical of warm, moist climates, thrive in the rain forest atmosphere of the Tropical Pyramid, while the Arid Pyramid displays vegetation indigenous to parts of North America and Africa. The Temperate Pyramid shows seasonal changes, and the Show Pyramid features changing floral displays. The conservatory's outdoor grounds can be enjoyed on a stroll.

Time: Allow 1 hour minimum. **Hours:** Mon.-Fri. 9:30-5:30, Sat.-Sun. and holidays 11-5:30. Closed Dec. 25. Phone ahead to confirm schedule. **Cost:** $9.75; $7.25 (ages 13-17 and 65+); $5 (ages 2-12); $29.25 (family). Prices may vary. **Phone:** (780) 496-8787.

ROYAL ALBERTA MUSEUM is at 12845 102nd Ave. Alberta's natural and human history museum houses a permanent collection in three main galleries, with changing displays and events scheduled throughout the year.

The Natural History Gallery offers specimens of plants, animals, birds, live insects, fossils and minerals depicting the 1 billion-year odyssey from dinosaurs to rare minerals and gems. A fossil gallery displays extinct beasts from ancient Alberta, while The Bug Room contains live specimens from around the world.

The Syncrude Gallery of Aboriginal Culture tells the story of 11,000 years of aboriginal history. The Wild Alberta gallery encourages visitors to look at Alberta's environment from a different perspective. **Time:** Allow 2 hours minimum. **Hours:** Daily 9-5. Hours may vary during special exhibits. Closed Dec. 24-25. **Cost:** $10; $8 (ages 65+); $7 (students with ID); $5 (ages 7-17); $28 (family, two adults and children); half-price (Sat.-Sun. 9-11 a.m.). An additional fee may be charged during special exhibitions. **Phone:** (780) 453-9100.

RUTHERFORD HOUSE PROVINCIAL HISTORIC SITE is at 11153 Saskatchewan Dr. on the University of Alberta campus. The structure was home to A.C. Rutherford, Alberta's first premier and a founder of the University of Alberta. Completed in 1911, the elegant Jacobethan (a blend of Jacobean and Elizabethan styles) Revival house established a new standard in domestic architecture and marked the end of the pioneer style in Alberta. Historical interpreters in period dress conduct house tours upon request. Events are scheduled throughout the year.

Time: Allow 1 hour minimum. **Hours:** Daily 9-5, May 15-Labour Day; Tues.-Sun. noon-5, rest of year. Closed Jan. 1, Good Friday and Dec. 25. **Cost:** $4; $3 (ages 7-17 and 65+); $12 (family, two adults and two children). **Phone:** (780) 427-3995.

TELEPHONE HISTORICAL CENTRE is in the Prince of Wales Armouries Heritage Centre at 10440 108th Ave. The center presents the history of telecommunications in Edmonton dating from the introduction of telephone service in 1885. The facility features numerous interactive exhibits and a 30-minute theater presentation with Xeldon the Robot.

Time: Allow 1 hour minimum. **Hours:** Tues.-Thurs. 10-3 (also Fri. 10-3, Victoria Day-Labour Day). Phone ahead to confirm schedule. **Cost:** Donations. **Phone:** (780) 433-1010.

TELUS WORLD OF SCIENCE—EDMONTON is at 142nd St. and 111th Ave. Five galleries house exhibits that explain and explore unusual phenomena: Space Place, which focuses on space exploration; The Body Fantastic, which includes large-scale models of body parts; Mystery Avenue, where visitors must collect and analyze clues to solve a crime; The Greens' House, a living backyard that teaches visitors about nature and conservation; and Discoveryland, an interactive area designed for children ages 2 through 8.

In addition visitors enjoy live science demonstrations, an observatory, films offered in an IMAX theater, and digital shows presented in the Margaret Zeidler Star Theatre.

Hours: Center daily 10-7, Victoria Day weekend-Labour Day; 10-5, rest of year. Observatory daily 1-5 and 6:30-10, Victoria Day weekend-Labour Day; Fri. 7-10, Sat. 1-4 and 7-10, Sun. and holidays 1-4, rest of year (weather permitting). Science demonstrations are given daily on the hour noon-4, July 1-Labour Day; Sat.-Sun. and holidays on the hour noon-4, rest of year. IMAX shows are offered daily on the hour beginning at 11. Closed Dec. 25.

Cost: Exhibit galleries (includes Margaret Zeidler Star Theatre) or one IMAX film $13.95; $11.95 (ages 13-17 and 65+); $9.50 (ages 4-12); $54.95 (family, two adults and four children). Combination ticket (includes exhibit galleries, Margaret Zeidler Star Theatre and one IMAX film) $22.50; $19 (ages 13-17 and 65+); $15.25 (ages 4-12); $84.95 (family, two adults and four children). Prices may vary; phone ahead. **Phone:** (780) 451-3344.

UKRAINIAN CANADIAN ARCHIVES & MUSEUM OF ALBERTA is at 9543 110th Ave. Exhibits trace the history of Alberta's Ukrainian pioneers. Displays include traditional apparel and musical instruments, costumes, Ukrainian currency, photographs, church artifacts and folk art. **Time:** Allow 1 hour minimum. **Hours:** Tues.-Fri. 10-5, Sat. noon-5. Closed major holidays. Phone ahead to confirm schedule. **Cost:** $5. **Phone:** (780) 424-7580.

UKRAINIAN CULTURAL HERITAGE VILLAGE is 50 km (31 mi.) e. on Hwy. 16, 3 km e. of the entrance to Elk Island National Park of Canada. The lifestyle of the region's Ukrainian immigrant population is portrayed in a village re-created to resemble a typical east central Alberta settlement 1892-1930.

Living-history demonstrations center around more than 30 restored historic buildings, including houses, farm buildings, churches and stores. Costumed interpreters depicting a wide variety of characters from the turn of the 20th century re-create the lives of those who lived in each of the buildings, demonstrating the settlers' daily routines. Special events are held throughout the summer.

Time: Allow 2 hours minimum. **Hours:** Daily 10-6, Victoria Day weekend-Labour Day; Sat.-Sun. 10-6, day after Labour Day-second Mon. in Oct. **Cost:** $8; $7 (ages 65+); $4 (ages 7-17); $20 (family, two adults and children). Rates may be increased during special events. **Phone:** (780) 662-3640. 🅿️

UNIVERSITY OF ALBERTA DEVONIAN BOTANIC GARDEN is 14 km (9 mi.) s. on Hwy. 60 from jct. Hwy. 16W and the Devon Hwy. overpass. Comprising 32 hectares (80 acres) of cultivated gardens and 44.5 hectares (110 acres) of natural area, the garden includes a Japanese garden, a butterfly house, ecological reserves and collections of native and alpine plants. Nature trails and guided tram tours also are offered.

Time: Allow 2 hours minimum. **Hours:** Mon.-Wed. 10-6, Thurs.-Sun. 10-8, June 1-early Sept.; Mon.-Wed. 10-5, Thurs.-Sun. 10-6 in May and early Sept. to mid-Oct. Tram tours are given daily on the hour 11-3, July 1-Labour Day (also daily at 4, July-Aug.); Thurs.-Sun. on the hour 11-3, in June; Sat.-Sun. on the hour 11-3, in May. Tram tour schedule may vary; phone ahead. **Cost:** $13; $8.50 (ages 65+); $5 (ages 13-17); $3 (ages 7-12); $26 (family, two adults and four children). Tram tour $5; $2 (ages 0-17). Prices may vary. **Phone:** (780) 987-3054 or (780) 987-3055. 🍴 🅿️

VALLEY ZOO is at Buena Vista Rd. (87th Ave.) and 134th St. More than 300 domestic, endangered and exotic animals from around the world call the zoo home. Animal interpretive programs are featured year-round. A merry-go-round, paddle boats, a miniature train and a children's discovery zoo are available in summer.

Time: Allow 1 hour, 30 minutes minimum. **Hours:** Daily 9:30-6, early May-late Aug.; Mon.-Fri. 9:30-4, Sat.-Sun. and holidays 9:30-6, late Aug. to mid-Oct.; daily 9:30-4, rest of year. Closed Dec. 25. Phone ahead to confirm schedule. **Cost:** early May to mid-Oct. $9.75; $7.25 (ages 13-17 and 65+);

$5 (ages 2-12); $29.25 (family). Rest of year $7.25; $5.50 (ages 13-17 and 65+); $3.75 (ages 2-12); $21.25 (family). Prices may vary. **Phone:** (780) 496-8787, ext. 2. 🍴

WEST EDMONTON MALL is at jct. 87th Ave. and 170th St. The huge, two-level complex is one of the world's largest shopping and entertainment centers. It contains more than 800 stores and services, 19 movie theaters, more than 100 eateries and nine major theme attractions.

Galaxyland features 25 rides and attractions. Sea Life Caverns contains approximately 200 species of marine life. World Waterpark offers more than 2 hectares (5 acres) of indoor fun, including a giant wave pool. The mall also is home to three sea lions (a program allowing patrons to swim with the creatures is offered); the Ice Palace, an NHL-size ice rink; two miniature golf courses; and a recreation center offering bowling, billiards and arcade games.

Allow a full day. **Hours:** Shops open Mon.-Sat. 10-9, Sun. 11-5, most holidays 10-6. Hours for attractions, theaters and restaurants vary; phone ahead. **Cost:** Prices for individual attractions vary. **Phone:** (780) 444-5200 for general mall information, (780) 444-5300, or (800) 661-8890 for more information about attractions, including hours of operation and prices. *See color ad on insert.*

GAMBLING ESTABLISHMENTS

- **Baccarat Casino** is at 10128 104th Ave. N.W. **Hours:** Slot machines daily 10 a.m.-3 a.m. Table games daily noon-2 a.m. Poker daily 24 hours. Closed Dec. 25. **Phone:** (780) 413-3178 or (877) 616-5695.

- **Casino Edmonton** is at 7055 Argyll Rd. **Hours:** Slot machines daily 10 a.m.-3 a.m. Table games daily noon-2 a.m. Poker daily 24 hours. Closed Dec. 25. **Phone:** (780) 463-9467.

- **Casino Yellowhead** is at 12464 153rd St. N.W. **Hours:** Slot machines daily 10 a.m.-3 a.m. Table games daily noon-2 a.m. Poker daily 24 hours. Closed Dec. 25. **Phone:** (780) 424-9467.

- **Palace Casino** is at 2710 West Edmonton Mall, 8882 170th St. N.W., Upper Level Entrance #9. **Hours:** Slot machines daily 10 a.m.-3 a.m. Table games daily noon-2 a.m. Poker daily 24 hours. **Phone:** (780) 444-2112.

What To Do

Sightseeing

Bus, Streetcar and Van Tours

Nite Tours offers pub crawls and ghost and graveyard tours; phone (780) 454-0303 or (877) 600-6483.

HIGH LEVEL STREETCAR departs from the Old Strathcona stop at 103rd St. and 84th Ave. and from downtown s. of Jasper Ave. and w. of 109th St. A vintage streetcar takes passengers along the old CPR rail line across the High Level Bridge built 1911-13 to link Old Strathcona and Edmonton. The narrated, 6-kilometre (3.7-mi.) trip offers excellent views of the city and the river valley.

Time: Allow 45 minutes minimum. **Hours:** Sun.-Fri. 11-4, Sat. 9-4, late May-Labour Day; Fri.-Sun. 11-4, day after Labour Day-early Oct. Hours extended to 10 p.m. during the Fringe Festival in Aug. Phone ahead to confirm schedule. **Cost:** Fare $4; free (ages 0-5); $12 (family, two adults and children). **Phone:** (780) 442-5311.

Driving Tours

The most scenic areas in Edmonton are along the North Saskatchewan River Valley. On the south side, the drive north along Saskatchewan Drive from 76th Avenue and 120th Street to 99th Street offers a picturesque trip around the University of Alberta campus. The views from the Royal Alberta Museum, 102nd Avenue and 128th Street, and the residential district of Glenora are impressive.

Walking Tours

Heritage Trail leads from the Shaw Conference Centre to the Alberta Legislature Building, a route that links government and industry by way of Edmonton's past. Old Strathcona, south of the North Saskatchewan River, offers a view of many original buildings and street scenes characteristic of an early 20th-century prairie town. Edmonton Gallery Walk joins nine private art galleries around Jasper Avenue and 124th Street.

Guided walking tours of the 30,000-student University of Alberta are available year-round; phone (780) 492-4086.

Sports and Recreation

Whatever the season, there are opportunities for both indoor and outdoor recreation. The North Saskatchewan River Valley is an oasis of parkland, with 122 kilometres (76 mi.) of trails, four lake systems and 22 parks. Depending on the time of year, you can **golf, hike, jog, cycle, ride horseback, fish, ski (cross-country** and **downhill), skate** or even pan for gold in a park.

The largest park is Capital City Recreation Park, composed of many smaller areas in the center and on the east side of the city. Within the park are 30 kilometres (19 mi.) of paths for **bicycling** and **jogging.** For information about activities and facilities phone Community Services at (780) 496-7275 Monday through Friday.

Playing host to three major sporting events—the Commonwealth Games in 1978, the World University Games in 1983 and the World Championships in Athletics in 2001—has provided Edmonton with a legacy of world-class sporting facilities. Several multiple-purpose centers—including Commonwealth Stadium Sport & Fitness Centre, 11000 Stadium Rd. at 91st Street, (780) 944-7400; Kinsmen Sports Centre, 9100 Walterdale Hill, (780) 944-7400; and Mill Woods Recreation Centre, 7207 28th Ave., (780)

496-2900—offer such activities as **swimming, diving, racquetball, squash** and **track** events.

Bring your set of clubs and try out one of more than 70 **golf** courses scattered about the Edmonton area. Three courses in the city's river valley are Riverside, on Rowland Road (106th Avenue) on the south side of the Dawson Bridge; Rundle Park, in the east end of Edmonton off 118th Avenue and Victoria Trail; and Victoria, said to be the oldest municipal golf course in Canada, on River Valley Road, accessible from Groat Road or from either 109th Street via the Walterdale Bridge from the south, or from 101st Street from the north.

Spectator sports can be enjoyed throughout the year. Castrol Motorsports Park, 2 kilometres (1.2 mi.) west of Queen Elizabeth II Hwy. on Hwy. 19, offers motorsport racing May through September; phone (780) 461-5801 or (780) 955-5540. Northlands Park, 7300 116th Ave., offers a chance to watch **harness racing** from early March to mid-June and from October to mid-December; phone (780) 471-7379 to confirm the dates for the racing schedule. **Thoroughbred racing** takes place from June to October; phone (780) 471-7379.

Note: Policies concerning admittance of children to pari-mutuel betting facilities vary. Phone for information.

Home to four professional sports teams, Edmonton is referred to fondly as the City of Champions. The Edmonton Oilers, several-time Stanley Cup champions of the National **Hockey** League, play from September to April in Rexall Place at 118th Avenue and 74th Street; phone (780) 414-4625. The Edmonton Eskimos **football** team, many times the Grey Cup champions of the Canadian Football League, play at Commonwealth Stadium, 111th Avenue and Stadium Road, from June to November; phone (780) 448-3757.

Golden League **Baseball** is played by the Edmonton Capitals from April to September at TELUS Field, south of downtown at 96th Avenue and 102nd Street; phone (780) 414-4625. National League **Lacrosse** is played by the Edmonton Rush from January through April in Rexall Place at 118th Avenue and 74th Street; phone (780) 732-7874.

Shopping

For the intrepid shopper, there is nothing like **West Edmonton Mall** *(see attraction listing p. 71),* which occupies a 44-hectare (110-acre) site at 87th Avenue and 170th Street. Inside are more than 800 stores and services.

Once complete, South Edmonton Common will offer about 130 hectares (320 acres) of retail space. Construction of the massive outdoor shopping complex at 23rd Avenue and Calgary Trail is ongoing; currently there are more than 100 stores available to shoppers, including IKEA, Liz Claiborne, Nike and Sears Home.

For those who want shopping on a less imposing scale, other popular malls include Kingsway Garden Mall, 109th Street and Princess Elizabeth Avenue;

Londonderry Mall, 137th Avenue and 66th Street; and Southgate Centre, 111th Street and 51st Avenue.

Downtown offers boutiques and restaurants as well as covered shopping areas joined by enclosed walkways or pedways. The Edmonton City Centre complex between 100th and 103rd streets on 102nd Avenue contains Hudson's Bay Co., 140 other shops and a nine-screen theater among its four glittering floors.

ManuLife Place, 102nd Avenue and 101st Street, contains designer boutiques and Holt Renfrew, an elegant retail store with a quaint in-store cafe. Connected to ManuLife Place is Commerce Place, which features several shops with signature fashions.

Rice Howard Way, an attractive outdoor pedestrian area lined with sidewalk seating and eateries, is downtown at 100th Street and 101A Avenue. It is particularly popular in summer.

At 102nd Avenue and 97th Street, the Chinatown Gate symbolizes friendship and welcomes visitors to Chinatown, which features several ethnic restaurants, shops and outdoor vendors selling fresh produce.

Old Strathcona at Whyte Avenue (82nd Avenue from 99th to 109th streets), the main outdoor shopping street on the south side of the city, has the look of historic Edmonton and offers boutiques, specialty shops, restaurants, bistros and coffee bars.

Don't forget that the major museums have interesting shops with items sometimes impossible to find elsewhere. Of particular interest are the six period shops in Fort Edmonton Park and the shop in the interpretive center at the Alberta Legislature Building.

Performing Arts

Theater season runs from September through May. For live theater visit the Citadel Theatre complex, 99th Street and 101A Avenue, which consists of four theaters, an amphitheater and a beautiful atrium; phone (780) 425-1820. Family-themed theater, produced by Fringe Theatre Adventures, can be enjoyed by all ages in October, December and February at the Arts Barns in Old Strathcona at 103rd Street and 84th Avenue; phone (780) 448-9000.

Prominent Canadian and American performers take to the stage at Mayfield Dinner Theatre at Mayfield Inn & Suites, 166th Street and 109th Avenue; phone (780) 483-4051 or (877) 529-7829. Jubilations Dinner Theatre, in the West Edmonton Mall at the intersection of 87th Avenue and 170th Street, features musical comedy; phone (780) 484-2424.

The Alberta Ballet, (780) 428-6839, and the Edmonton Opera, (780) 429-1000, perform in Northern Alberta Jubilee Auditorium on the University of Alberta campus at 87th Avenue and 114th Street; phone (780) 427-2760 for auditorium information. Phone ahead for updates. The Edmonton Symphony Orchestra, (780)

428-1414, performs at Francis Winspear Centre, 4 Sir Winston Churchill Sq.; phone (780) 428-1414 for concert information. Shaw Conference Centre, Francis Winspear Centre, Northern Alberta Jubilee Auditorium and Rexall Place play host to a variety of concerts ranging from classical music to rock.

The free publications *See Magazine, Vue Magazine* and *Where Edmonton* give detailed, up-to-date information about arts and entertainment in Edmonton, and local newspapers provide current performance information. Ticketmaster outlets handle ticket sales for most sports, recreation, theater and concert events; phone (780) 451-8000.

Special Events

Edmonton offers a smorgasbord of events. Concerts, workshops, club dates and outdoor events characterize the Yardbird Jazz-Festival, held mid- to late June. Also in June The Works Art and Design Festival brings together artists and artisans.

Edmonton Celebrate Canada is a 12-day celebration, beginning late June with National Aboriginal Day. On June 24 are Francophone festivities honoring St. Jean Baptiste. The celebration concludes on Canada Day (July 1), with a full day of events and the Fireworks Finale.

During late June to mid-July the River City Shakespeare Festival presents two shows on alternating nights in William Hawrelak Park. Edmonton International Street Performers Festival in early July offers 10 days of free performances by street acts including magicians, clowns, jugglers, mime artists, musicians and comics.

The city's biggest event is ⬥ Edmonton's Capital EX, a 10-day celebration held in July. Parades, casinos, gold panning, a chuck wagon derby and various other forms of entertainment keep the city alive with activities such as Sunday in the City and A Taste of Edmonton. Another major draw in July is the Rexall Edmonton Indy, offering racing excitement, concerts, exhibits and live demonstrations.

Colored lights illuminate Great Divide Waterfall on Sunday evenings of summer holiday weekends; the best view is northeast of the High Level Bridge at 109th Street and 97th Avenue.

August brings the world to Canada during the 3-day ⬥ Edmonton Heritage Festival, which offers more than 60 outdoor ethnic pavilions showcasing international music, dance, art and cuisine. Also in August are the ⬥ Edmonton Folk Music Festival; the Cariwest Caribbean Arts Festival; the Labatt Blues Festival; the Dragon Boat Festival; and the ⬥ Edmonton International Fringe Theatre Festival, an 11-day extravaganza of plays, dance, music, mime and street performances.

In September is the Edmonton Symphony Orchestra's 5-day Symphony Under the Sky Festival at Hawrelak Park. Post-summer events include the Edmonton International Film Festival, featuring independent short and feature-length movies in October, the ⬥ Canadian Finals Rodeo in early November, and New Year's Eve special events.

The Edmonton Vicinity

DEVON (E-6) pop. 6,256, elev. 680 m/2,230′

Canada's first planned community, Devon was created by Imperial Oil Resources Ltd. in 1948 to provide accommodations for the workers employed in the company's oilfields. Imperial Leduc No. 1, the area's first well, had just put the town of Devon on the map. The town's name was derived from the Devonian formation, the oil's source, a stratum 1,524 metres (5,000 ft.) underground.

Devon is on the banks of the North Saskatchewan River, where fishing often yields northern pike, walleye and goldeye. Year-round recreational activities include canoeing, cross-country skiing, golf, hiking, ice-skating and swimming.

Town of Devon: 1 Columbia Ave. W., Devon, AB, Canada T9G 1A1. **Phone:** (780) 987-8300.

CANADIAN PETROLEUM DISCOVERY CENTRE is 2 km (1.2 mi.) s. on Hwy. 60. The center not only provides insight into the workings of the oil industry but also looks at area history, the story behind Leduc No. 1 and how Canada became self-sufficient in oil production. A 15-minute video presentation, interactive energy displays, geological exhibits, equipment, artifacts, photographs, scale models, murals and an outdoor interpretive trail help explain how oil is produced and refined.

A 53-metre (174-ft.) replica of the original derrick has been erected on the discovery site. **Time:** Allow 1 hour minimum. **Hours:** Mon.-Sat. 9-5. **Cost:** $8; $7 (ages 65+); $5 (ages 6-18); $20 (family). **Phone:** (780) 987-4323 or (866) 987-4323.

ST. ALBERT (E-6) pop. 57,719

Alberta's oldest non-fortified community, St. Albert was established in 1861. The city is the site of the first cathedral west of Winnipeg. Its founder—Father Albert Lacombe—devoted 62 years to acting as a peacemaker between the Cree and the Blackfoot and as a negotiator between the Blood Indians and the Canadian Pacific Railway.

St. Albert lays claim to western Canada's largest outdoor farmers' market, which operates every Saturday July through September, as well as an interactive water play park and a vibrant arts community. Grain Elevator Park, 4 Meadowview Dr., features two grain elevators from the early 20th century and a replica of a 1920s-era train station. The site is open Wed.-Sun. 10-5, late May-Labour Day; phone (780) 419-7354 for more information.

The Rainmaker Rodeo & Exhibition takes place the fourth weekend in May. The Northern Alberta International Children's Festival—a showcase for performers in theater, music, dance, storytelling and puppetry—is traditionally held the weekend after the rodeo.

St. Albert Business and Tourism Development: 71 St. Albert Rd., St. Albert, AB, Canada T8N 6L5. **Phone:** (780) 459-1724.

[SAVE] **FATHER LACOMBE CHAPEL** is just w. of Queen Elizabeth II Hwy. on St. Vital Ave. The log chapel, built by Father Albert Lacombe and his Métis helpers in 1861, is said to be Alberta's oldest building. Guided tours explain the importance of Lacombe and the St. Albert Roman Catholic Mission to the French/Métis community as well as the priest's role as spiritual leader, peacemaker and negotiator in the 1860s. Conducted in English and French, tours include the chapel, crypt, cemetery and grotto.

Time: Allow 30 minutes minimum. **Hours:** Tours are given daily by request 10-6, May 15-Labour Day. **Cost:** Fee $2; $1.50 (ages 7-17 and senior citizens); $5 (family). **Phone:** (780) 459-7663, or (780) 431-2300 off-season.

MUSÉE HERITAGE MUSEUM is w. of Queen Elizabeth II Hwy. at 5 St. Anne St. in St. Albert Place. Exhibits are dedicated to the heritage of St. Albert. Changing displays are featured. **Time:** Allow 1 hour minimum. **Hours:** Tues.-Sat. 10-5 (also Sun. 1-5, Sept.-June). Closed major holidays. **Cost:** Donations. **Phone:** (780) 459-1528.

STONY PLAIN (E-6) pop. 12,363

Plentiful water and abundant fish and game attracted the first settlers to the region in 1881. By 1892 the name of the community itself was changed from Dog Creek to Stony Plain. The Stony Plain of today is an agricultural community.

Murals depicting historical remembrances, events and pioneers prominent in the early settlement of Stony Plain have been painted by local artists on 26 buildings in town. Memories of an early 1900s Christmas from a child's point of view are the basis for one mural, while another shows the multiculturalism of the area's early residents. The Heritage Walk Murals can be seen on a walking tour.

Town of Stony Plain: 4905 51st Ave., Stony Plain, AB, Canada T7Z 1Y1. **Phone:** (780) 963-2151.

MULTICULTURAL HERITAGE CENTRE AND OPPERTSHAUSER HOUSE is at 5411 51st St. Restored buildings feature local history and art exhibits, programs and events. The center, built as the area's first high school in 1925, offers regional archives as well as a living-history museum, a demonstration farm, an art gallery and the 1910 Oppertshauser House. **Time:** Allow 30 minutes minimum. **Hours:** Daily 10-4 (also Sun. 4-6). Closed Dec. 24-Jan. 2. A country market takes place Sat. 9-1, May-Oct. **Cost:** Donations. **Phone:** (780) 963-2777. [H]

The previous listings were for the Edmonton Vicinity.
This page resumes the alphabetical listings of cities in Alberta.

ELK ISLAND NATIONAL PARK OF CANADA (D-7)

Elevations in the park range from 709 metres (2,326 ft.) at Goose Lake to 754 metres (2,475 ft.) at Tawayik Lake. Refer to CAA/AAA maps for additional elevation information.

About 35 kilometres (22 mi.) east of Edmonton, Elk Island National Park of Canada is reached by Hwy. 15 from the north and Hwy. 16 from the south. The lakes, ponds, forests and meadows of this 194-square-kilometre (75-sq.-mi.) park provide a haven for many species of animals and plants.

The park occupies the Beaver Hills region, which first was settled by Sarcee and Plains Cree Indians. They trapped beavers and hunted bison and elk, as did the European fur traders who arrived between the late 18th and the mid-19th centuries. Soon the animals became nearly extinct, and the natives were forced to seek sustenance elsewhere.

In 1906 five local men asked that the government establish a wildlife refuge to preserve the remaining elk. A year later 400 plains bison were added, while another preserve near Wainwright was being established. Most of these animals later were transferred, but about 50 stayed and produced the plains bison herd of more than 300 that remains today north of Hwy. 16. A herd of several hundred wood bison, a threatened subspecies, is kept separate from this herd south of Hwy. 16.

As the wildlife populations grew, so did the park's area; more land was added to the refuge in 1922, 1947, 1956 and 1978. Many small lakes dot the landscape, but the major bodies are Tawayik and Astotin, the latter being the larger. The lakes and marshes support the more than 250 bird species, including ducks, grebes, gulls, loons, pelicans, rare trumpeter swans and terns.

Marsh marigolds and several types of lilies are among several plants rarely seen outside the park. Song birds occupy the many aspen, spruce and birch forests, but few fish inhabit the waters due to low oxygen levels. The herd of elk for which the park was established flourish among the meadows and forests, as do reintroduced colonies of beavers. Deer, moose and coyotes also roam the park.

General Information and Activities

The park is open daily all year. Most recreation facilities center on Astotin Lake, which offers non-motorized boating, wildlife observations, picnic facilities, a nine-hole golf course, camping, hiking and walking trails. A campground is on the east side of the lake. Interpretive talks, events and displays explain the park's history and features.

A visitor information center is .8 kilometres (.5 mi.) north of Hwy. 16 before the park's south gate entrance. Staff members and displays describe Elk Island and other national parks. The center is open Thursday through Monday, mid-May through Labour Day; phone (780) 922-5790 to confirm schedule.

Camping and picnicking are popular in summer. The park's approximately 100 kilometres (60 mi.) of trails are popular with hikers and cross-country skiers. Hunting and fishing are prohibited. *See Recreation Chart and the AAA/CAA Western Canada & Alaska CampBook.*

ADMISSION to the park is $19.60 per private vehicle (three to seven persons). Otherwise admission per person is $7.80; $6.80 (ages 65+); $3.90 (ages 6-16). An annual pass, valid at all Canadian national parks, is available.

PETS must be kept on a leash at all times.

ADDRESS inquiries for additional information to Elk Island National Park of Canada, Site 4, R.R. 1, Fort Saskatchewan, AB, Canada T8L 2N7; phone (780) 992-2950.

UKRAINIAN CULTURAL HERITAGE VILLAGE— *see Edmonton p. 71.*

ELK POINT (D-8)
pop. 1,487, elev. 594 m/1,948'

SAVE **FORT GEORGE AND BUCKINGHAM HOUSE PROVINCIAL HISTORIC SITE,** 13 km (8 mi.) s.e. on Hwy. 646, encompasses the archeological remains of two fur trade forts. A scenic interpretive trail complemented by wild flowers—including the rare yellow lady's slipper orchid—allows for closer inspection of the site and its various structural remains. Staff members are available at the visitor center, which offers displays about the area's heritage and fur trading industry.

Educational programs are offered. **Tours:** Guided tours are available. **Time:** Allow 2 hours minimum. **Hours:** Daily 10-6, May 15-Labour Day. **Cost:** $3; $2 (senior citizens); $1.50 (ages 7-17); $8 (family, two adults and two children). **Phone:** (780) 724-2611, or (780) 645-6256 off-season.

ELKWATER (J-9) pop. 107

Before Europeans came to the Elkwater region, Assiniboine, Blackfoot, Cree and Sioux shared the land with grizzly bears, wolves, bison and a large number of elk. After settlers and trappers arrived, the wolves and elk were hunted to extinction; the elk population since has been reintroduced. An 1873 massacre of Assiniboine Indians by wolf hunters and whiskey traders prompted the formation of the North West Mounted Police and the establishment of Fort Walsh.

The Cypress Hills area, shared by Alberta and Saskatchewan, is noted for its lodgepole pine forests, water resources and wildlife. The hills, which rise to more than 1,466 metres (4,810 ft.), offer visitors a cool climate, scenic views and diverse flora and fauna. Elkwater serves as the area's hub.

CYPRESS HILLS INTERPROVINCIAL PARK is 1.5 km (.9 mi.) s. on Hwy. 41. Fossils of early mammals dating back 40 million years have been found in the hills. An aboriginal culture flourished in the area for more than 7,000 years. Ruminants, beavers, coyotes and varied birds and plants now live in the park. Park interpreters schedule programs May through September. The visitor center offers information, displays and audiovisual presentations. *See Recreation Chart and Medicine Hat in the AAA/ CAA Western Canada & Alaska CampBook.*

Hours: Grounds daily 24 hours. Visitor center daily 10-5, mid-May through Labour Day. Special events are offered year-round. **Cost:** Free. **Phone:** (403) 893-3833, (403) 893-3777 for the visitor center, or (403) 893-3782 for camping reservations.

FORT MACLEOD (J-6)
pop. 3,072, elev. 955 m/3,133'

In 1874 at the end of their 1,126-kilometre (700-mi.) march through the prairie wilderness to rid western Canada of whiskey traders, the North West Mounted Police, now the Royal Canadian Mounted Police, chose the site of what is now Fort Macleod as their first headquarters.

A commanding view of the countryside and the natural protection afforded by the Oldman River made Fort Macleod an important outpost; a cairn at 2nd Avenue and 25th Street commemorates the fort's founding. Guided walking tours of the historic district, ranging from 30 minutes to 1 hour, can be arranged in advance during the summer by contacting the Main Street Office; phone (403) 553-2500, or The Fort Museum of the North West Mounted Police *(see attraction listing).*

The highland physical geography that made the Fort Macleod outpost successful also helped the Plains Indians survive long before the first traders appeared in the area. In order to kill the buffalo for food, the Plains hunters stampeded them over the high cliffs.

SAVE **THE FORT MUSEUM OF THE NORTH WEST MOUNTED POLICE,** 219 25th St., creates the atmosphere of the original Fort Macleod. Exhibits set among historic structures focus on the history of the North West Mounted Police, southern Alberta natives and pioneer settlers. Of particular interest are the summer Mounted Patrol Musical Rides in which horseback riders in replicas of 1878 RCMP uniforms perform precision movements to music.

Time: Allow 1 hour minimum. **Hours:** Daily 9-6, July 1-Labour Day; daily 9-5, early June-June 30; Tues.-Fri. 9-5, early May-early June; Wed.-Sun. 10-4, day after Labour Day to mid-Oct. Musical rides are presented Wed.-Mon. (weather permitting) at 10, 11:30, 2 and 3:30, July 1-Labour Day.

Cost: July 1-Labour Day $8; $7.50 (ages 65+); $6 (ages 12-17); $5 (ages 6-11); $25 (family, two

adults and four children). Early May-June 30 and day after Labour Day to mid-Oct. $7.50; $6.50 (ages 65+); $5 (ages 12-17); $4 (ages 6-11); $20 (family, two adults and four children). **Phone:** (403) 553-4703 or (866) 273-6841.

GEM **HEAD-SMASHED-IN BUFFALO JUMP IN-TERPRETIVE CENTRE** is 3 km (1.9 mi.) SAVE n. on Queen Elizabeth II Hwy., then 16 km (10 mi.) w. on Hwy. 785. For at least 6,000 years the Plains Indians stampeded herds of buffalo over sandstone cliffs to their deaths. The hunters then butchered the kill at their campsite below the cliffs. This is one of the oldest, best-preserved buffalo jump sites. A 12-minute film re-creates the hunts.

The site's name is derived from a young brave who stood under a ledge of the cliff to watch the buffalo as they fell past him. As the number of carcasses multiplied, his skull was crushed as he became trapped between the animals and the cliff.

Built into that cliff today is a seven-story interpretive center with displays. Exhibits focus on the geographical and climatic factors affecting these tribes as well as their lifestyle and history. The hunting site is preserved; short trails lead to the main areas. A re-created archeological dig provides additional insights into this way of life.

Time: Allow 2 hours minimum. **Hours:** Daily 9-6, July 1-Labour Day; 10-5, rest of year. Closed Jan. 1, Easter and Dec. 24-25. **Cost:** $9; $8 (ages 66+); $5 (ages 7-17); $22 (family). **Phone:** (403) 553-2731.

FORT McMURRAY (A-8) pop. 47,705

At the confluence of the Clearwater and Athabasca rivers in the fur country of northern Alberta, Fort McMurray began as the home of the Woodland Cree and Chipewyan Indians. In 1778 explorers and fur traders led by Peter Pond opened the vast fur trade region of the Mackenzie River basin. In 1870 Henry John Moberly built a post and named it Fort McMurray after his chief factor, William McMurray of Hudson's Bay Co.

Soon after a steamboat terminus was established near Fort McMurray in 1884, the region's vast resources began to attract attention. Oil sands containing some 1.7 trillion barrels of oil were found around Lake Athabasca. The first commercially successful extractions, however, did not take place until the late 1960s. Since then Fort McMurray has boomed, serving oil recovery plants that now extract from the sands more than 600,000 barrels of synthetic crude oil per day.

The city is the southern terminus of the vast water transportation system that navigates Great Slave Lake and the Mackenzie River en route to the Arctic. Logging and tourism further bolster the economy. Fort McMurray is a service center for surrounding areas and the oil sands plants.

Re-creating the city's past is Heritage Park, on the banks of the Hangingstone River just off King Street on Tolen Drive. A museum highlights the history of boat building, aviation, river travel, lumbering, fishing, salt production and fur trading; phone (780) 791-7575.

Fort McMurray Tourism: 400 Sakitawaw Tr., Fort McMurray, AB, Canada T9H 4Z3. **Phone:** (780) 791-4336 or (800) 565-3947.

OIL SANDS DISCOVERY CENTRE is at jct. Hwy. 63 and MacKenzie Blvd. Exhibits relate the geology, history and technology of the Athabasca Oil Sands, said to be the world's single largest oil deposit. Oil sands mining, technology and new methods of exploration are explained through interpretive displays, demonstrations and the video presentation "Quest for Energy." Outside in the Industrial Garden are a seven-story bucket-wheel excavator and other pieces of massive mining equipment.

Seasonal bus tours to view the production facilities of Suncor Energy depart from the discovery center; reservations for the 3.5-hour tours can be arranged through Fort McMurray Tourism.

Note: Photo ID is required for the bus tour. **Time:** Allow 1 hour, 30 minutes minimum. **Hours:** Daily 9-5, mid-May through Labour Day; Tues.-Sun. 10-4, rest of year. Closed Jan. 1, Good Friday and Dec. 24-26. Bus tours to Suncor, generally one per day, are given Fri.-Sat., Victoria Day weekend-Labour Day. Phone ahead to confirm schedule.

Cost: Discovery center $6; $5 (ages 65+); $4 (ages 7-17); $20 (family, two adults and children). Bus tour (includes admission to Heritage Park and Oil Sands Discovery Centre) $35. Tour prices may vary. Under 12 are not permitted on the bus tour. Because tours are generally given only once a day and are in high demand, make reservations well in advance of your visit. In any event, reservations for the bus tour are required and must be made at least 24 hours in advance. **Phone:** (780) 743-7167 for the Oil Sands Discovery Centre, (780) 791-4336 for Fort McMurray Tourism, or (800) 565-3947 for tour reservations.

GIROUXVILLE (B-3) pop. 282

GIROUXVILLE MUSEUM is on Main St. (Hwy. 49). More than 6,000 artifacts tell the story of the indigenous people, devout missionaries and rugged pioneers who lived here. The museum also displays mounted birds and fur-bearing animals and the works of local artists Leon Tremblay and Alfred Gaboury.

Transportation Means of Yesterday includes sleighs, an antique snowmobile, a birch bark canoe and a 1927 Chevrolet truck. **Time:** Allow 1 hour minimum. **Hours:** Mon.-Fri. 10-5, May-Sept.; by appointment rest of year. **Cost:** $3; $1.50 (ages 6-17). **Phone:** (780) 323-4252.

GLEICHEN (I-6) pop. 348, elev. 899 m/2,952'

BLACKFOOT CROSSING HISTORICAL PARK is 11 km (7 mi.) e. on Hwy. 1, then 9.7 km (6 mi.) s. on Hwy. 842. Used by the Siksika (Blackfoot) Indians as a wintering grounds, Blackfoot Crossing was the site of the signing of Treaty No. 7 by representatives of the Blackfoot Confederacy and the Canadian and British governments in 1877. An on-site cultural center offers several galleries that describe the culture and history of the Siksika people.

Housed in a striking, eco-friendly edifice are exhibits about hunting, early life, societies, storytelling and warriors. The collection features such artifacts as tools, weapons, clothing and utensils as well as multimedia displays. The building's architectural features also document First Nations heritage, with tepee-shaped skylights and stained-glass eagle feather fans incorporated into the structure's design.

Self-guiding tours of the Blackfoot Crossing area are offered; guided tours of the cultural center and of the surroundings also are available by appointment. **Time:** Allow 1 hour, 30 minutes minimum. **Hours:** Daily 9-6, mid-May through Sept. 30; Mon.-Fri. 9-5, rest of year. **Cost:** $10.50; $8 (ages 8-17 and 65+). **Phone:** (780) 734-5171 or (888) 654-6274.

GRANDE CACHE (D-1) pop. 3,783

Grande Cache was named after a large shipment of furs cached nearby in 1821 by Ignace Giasson, an Iroquois working for Hudson Bay Co. The Grande Cache area historically served as a major trading area for marten, lynx and beaver pelts.

Grande Cache is known for the many recreational activities available nearby. The town is surrounded on three sides by Willmore Wilderness Park, which has the Continental Divide and Jasper National Park of Canada as its western and southern borders, respectively; the park can be accessed only by horseback, mountain bike or by hiking.

Lakes, rivers and mountains are favorites with outdoor enthusiasts, who come for white-water rafting, horseback riding, hiking, kayaking, fishing, canoeing and mountain biking. Pacific Western Helicopter Tours offers various sightseeing trips; phone (780) 827-3911.

Local events accommodate those with an adventurous streak. During the Canadian Death Race, held the first weekend in August, runners must travel 125 kilometres (78 mi.) over rough mountain trails—with part of the race occurring after dusk—and then cross a major river by raft. An accompanying festival offers food, concerts and carnival rides and games.

Interpretive displays in the tourism center, on the south side of Grande Cache, feature dinosaur tracks, artifacts from the ice age and memorabilia from the fur trade era.

Grande Cache Tourism and Interpretive Centre: 9701 100th St., P.O. Box 300, Grande Cache, AB, Canada T0E 0Y0. **Phone:** (780) 827-3300 or (888) 827-3790.

RECREATIONAL ACTIVITIES
White-water Rafting

- **Wild Blue Yonder White Water Rafting** is w. off Hwy. 40. **Hours:** Trips are offered daily, May-Sept. Departure times vary. **Phone:** (780) 827-5450 or (877) 945-3786.

GRANDE PRAIRIE (C-2) pop. 47,076

Surrounded by a colorful checkerboard of rich farmland along the gateway to the Alaska Hwy., Grande Prairie serves as the business and transportation center of Alberta's Peace River country.

Glimpses into the Peace River region's past are evident in the Kleskun Hills, just east via Hwy. 43. Erosion of the glacial drift of clay, sand, gravel and boulders has uncovered dinosaur tracks and aquatic fossils embedded in a prehistoric river delta formed more than 70 million years ago.

Local culture and artistry are displayed at The Prairie Art Gallery, 9856 97th Ave., Suite 103; phone (780) 532-8111. Muskoseepi Park has hiking and bicycling trails, picnicking areas and recreation facilities. Other area recreational pursuits include swimming, boating, bird-watching and fishing. A pioneer-oriented event is the Grande Prairie Stompede the first weekend in June. Other festivals celebrated throughout the summer highlight the region's diversity.

Grande Prairie Regional Tourism Association: 11330 106th St., Suite 217, Grande Prairie, AB, Canada T8V 7X9. **Phone:** (780) 539-7688 or (866) 202-2202.

Shopping areas: Prairie Mall, 11801 100th St., features Shopper's and Zellers.

GRANDE PRAIRIE MUSEUM is at 102nd St. and 102nd Ave. in Muskoseepi Park. The 10-building village features a one-room schoolhouse, a country store, a church and a log homesteader's cabin. The main exhibit building houses artifacts depicting the life of Peace River area pioneers 1908-16. The gallery also features natural history items and aboriginal artifacts. **Hours:** Mon.-Fri. 8:30-4:30, Sat. 10-4:30, Sun. noon-4:30. **Cost:** $5; $4 (ages 66+); $3 (ages 6-17); $12 (family, two adults and children); $10 (family, one adult and children). **Phone:** (780) 532-5482.

HERITAGE DISCOVERY CENTRE is at 11330 106th St. on the lower level of Centre 2000, Grand Prairie's visitor information center. Operated by the Grand Prairie Museum *(see attraction listing)*, the hands-on interpretive center depicts regional history through pioneer artifacts, a geology timeline, an animatronic dinosaur named Piper, a tepee, photographs, films, a caboose and computer games. Changing exhibits also are featured. **Tours:** Guided tours are available. **Hours:** Mon.-Fri. 8:30-4:30 (also Wed. 4:30-6:30), Sat.-Sun. 10-4:30. Closed Jan. 1, third Mon. in Feb., Good Friday and Dec. 25-26. **Cost:** $5; $4 (senior citizens); $3 (students with ID); free (ages 0-6). **Phone:** (780) 532-5790.

GAMBLING ESTABLISHMENTS

- **Great Northern Casino** is at 10910-107 A Ave. **Hours:** Mon.-Sat. 10 a.m.-2 a.m., Sun. 10 a.m.-1 a.m. **Phone:** (780) 539-4454.

HANNA (G-7) pop. 2,847

HANNA PIONEER VILLAGE & MUSEUM is at Pioneer Tr. and 4th Ave. E. Restored and partially furnished 19th-century buildings, arranged in a pioneer village setting, include a general store, a school, a four-room hospital, a church, a power windmill, a Canadian National Railway station, a telephone office, a ranch house and smithy, and the Hanna archives. Among the displays are antique automobiles and farm machinery.

Tours: Guided tours are available. **Time:** Allow 1 hour, 30 minutes minimum. **Hours:** Daily 10-6, June-Aug.; by appointment in May and Sept. Last tour begins 1 hour, 30 minutes before closing. **Cost:** $4; $1 (ages 0-11). **Phone:** (403) 854-4244.

HIGH RIVER (I-6) pop. 10,716

A ranching and farming town, High River counts among its events Little Britches Rodeo and Parade, held Victoria Day weekend in late May, as well as the North American Chuckwagon Championship and the Guy Weadick Memorial Rodeo, both held in June. The winter holiday season is ushered in the first weekend in December with the evening Santa Claus Parade.

High River Tourism and Economic Development: 309B Macleod Tr. S.W., High River, AB, Canada T1V 1Z5. **Phone:** (403) 652-8622.

HIGH RIVER HISTORICAL MURALS are at various locations throughout town. Many colorful paintings illustrate area history. The murals present a variety of subjects, ranging from cattle ranching and

DID YOU KNOW

Alberta was named for Louise Caroline Alberta, daughter of Queen Victoria and Prince Albert.

polo to well-known residents, including author W.O. Mitchell and former Prime Minister Joe Clark.

Hours: Murals visible daily 24 hours. Brochures are available at the High River Tourism and Economic Development office and from the Museum of the Highwood Mon.-Fri. 10-6, Sat.-Sun. 12:30-5, May-Oct.; otherwise varies. Closed Jan. 1 and Dec. 25. **Cost:** Free. **Phone:** (403) 603-3101.

MUSEUM OF THE HIGHWOOD is at 406 1st St. S.W. The museum takes its name from the nearby Highwood River. Changing exhibits are housed in a 1911 sandstone building once used as a Canadian Pacific Railway station. Displays detail local history, primarily from the mid-19th century to the present. A family discovery room has interactive exhibits.

Time: Allow 30 minutes minimum. **Hours:** Mon.-Sat. 10-4, Sun. noon-4, Victoria Day-Labour Day; Wed.-Sat. 11-3, Sun. noon-3, rest of year. Closed statutory holidays in the off-season. **Cost:** $3; $2.50 (senior citizens); free (ages 0-16). **Phone:** (403) 652-7156.

HINTON (E-3) pop. 9,738, elev. 1,049 m/3,444'

RECREATIONAL ACTIVITIES

Horseback Riding

- **Larry's Riding Stables** is 8 km (5 mi.) w. off Hwy. 16. Other activities are offered. **Hours:** Daily 10-6. **Phone:** (780) 865-9223.

INNISFAIL (G-6)
pop. 7,316, elev. 945 m/3,100'

DISCOVERY WILDLIFE PARK is off Queen Elizabeth II Hwy. N. Innisfail exit; take Hwy. 2A 2 blks. n.e., then just n.w. on 42nd Ave., following signs. The 36-hectare (90-acre) park is home to a variety of rescued exotic and native animals, including jaguars, lions, bears, monkeys, tigers and wolves. Some of the creatures are trained to work in show business and have been featured in major film and television productions. Educational shows and interactive programs are offered daily. A children's train also is on-site.

Time: Allow 1 hour, 30 minutes minimum. **Hours:** Daily 10-7, May 1 to mid-Oct. **Cost:** $13; $11 (ages 13-17 and senior citizens); $7 (ages 3-12). **Phone:** (403) 227-3211. 🍽 🎁

INNISFAIL & DISTRICT HISTORICAL VILLAGE, at 52nd Ave. and 42nd St., is home to 17 buildings, including a blacksmith shop, barn and pioneer church. The 2-acre site features several furnished structures as well as The Bowden Train Station, which displays various relics. Originally located about 6 kilometres (4 mi.) north of Innisfail, the 19th-century "Spruces" building once served as a depot on the stagecoach trail between Calgary and Edmonton and is purportedly the last surviving stopping house from the route. Historical gardens also grace the village grounds.

Time: Allow 30 minutes minimum. **Hours:** Mon.-Sat. 10-6, Sun. and holidays noon-5, Victoria Day weekend-Labour Day. **Cost:** Donations. **Phone:** (403) 227-2906. 🍽 🎁

IRRICANA (H-6) pop. 1,243

PIONEER ACRES OF ALBERTA MUSEUM is off Hwy. 9, 1 km n., then 1 km w. The museum features one of the largest collections of antique farm equipment in western Canada. It also displays furniture, tools, memorabilia, clothing and vehicles. A collection of early buildings includes a school, a steam-engine shop and a blacksmith shop. **Tours:** Guided tours are available. **Time:** Allow 1 hour, 30 minutes minimum. **Hours:** Daily 9-5, May 15-Sept. 30. **Cost:** $7; free (ages 0-11). **Phone:** (403) 935-4357.

⬗ GEM JASPER NATIONAL PARK OF CANADA (E-2, F-2)

See map page 80.

Elevations in the park range from 1,067 metres (3,500 ft.) in the town of Jasper to 3,747 metres (12,293 ft.) at Mount Columbia. Refer to CAA/AAA maps for additional elevation information.

Reached from the east and west via the Yellowhead Hwy. (Hwy. 16) and from the south by the Icefields Parkway (Hwy. 93), Jasper National Park of Canada, Banff National Park of Canada's northern neighbor, was established in 1907. The park was named after Jasper Haws, who was in charge of a Hudson's Bay Co. trading post in 1817.

Less developed and less crowded than Banff National Park of Canada, its 11,228 square kilometres (4,335 sq. mi.) of majestic mountains, valleys and lakes offer equally spectacular views of the Rocky Mountain wilderness. The variety and beauty of its numerous lakes, of which Maligne Lake is the largest, are perhaps the area's chief attractions.

Nature's scenic sculpting process at work can be seen at Athabasca Falls and Sunwapta Falls, both just west of Icefields Parkway south of Jasper. To the east off Hwy. 16 is Miette Hot Springs, where mineral pools are open for bathing Victoria Day weekend through the second Monday in October. Northeast of Jasper 51-metre-deep (170-ft.) Maligne Canyon surrounds the river that carved it over the years.

Park wildlife is as diverse as its peaks and valleys. Mountain goats and bighorn sheep inhabit the crags and highlands, although the sheep frequently wander down within good viewing distance.

The lower slopes and meadows are home to deer, elk, moose and bears, which never should be fed or approached. More elusive are coyotes, wolves, lynx and other predators that usually avoid humans. Lodgepole pines, spruces, poplars and firs forest the area, and eagles, jays, magpies and other birds dot the skies.

Note: Since hunting is illegal, some animals may have lost their fear of human activity; be alert for animals on the highways both day and night, and never feed them.

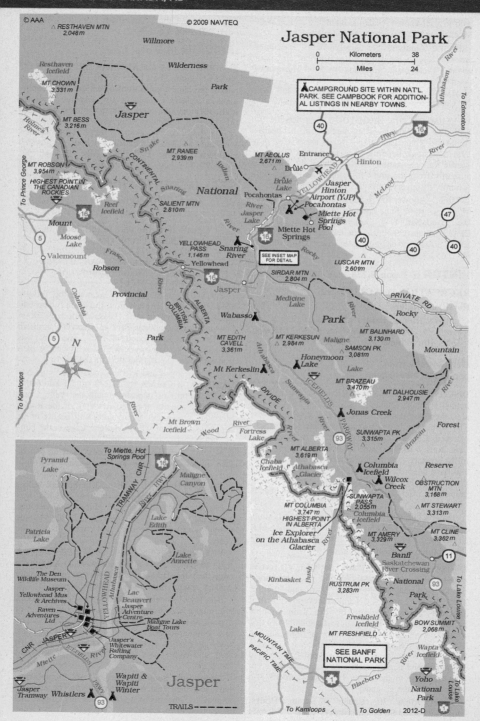

Jasper National Park

General Information and Activities

The park is open all year, though weather conditions in winter make some portions inaccessible except to cross-country skiers and those on snowshoes. Some facilities are open only from May to September or October. A Parks Canada information center is in the townsite of Jasper.

Many hiking trails, including the 11.2-kilometre (7-mi.) trip to Valley of Five Lakes and the loop to Lac Beauvert, depart from Old Fort Point, 1.6 kilometres (1 mi.) east of Jasper on Hwy. 93. The Valley of Five Lakes also can be accessed from the trailhead on the Icefields Parkway, 9 km (6 mi.) south of the townsite.

Hikers and skiers staying overnight in the back country must have a valid back-country use permit. These permits are available at the Parks Canada information center in Jasper and at the Columbia Icefield Centre from early June to mid-October.

Campgrounds are open varying durations: Whistler early May through the second Monday in October; Snaring River mid-May to late September; Wapiti mid-June to mid-September; and Wabasso late June through Labour Day. Limited camping facilities are available in winter at the Wapiti campgrounds. For campground information phone (780) 852-6176.

There are many ways to explore the park's features, either alone or with a guide. One- or multiple-day bus tours to attractions within the park depart from Jasper. Several stables in the Jasper area offer 1-hour and half- and full-day trail rides from mid-May to mid-September and sleigh rides in winter.

Winter sports include curling, skating, tobogganing, ice climbing, snowshoeing and hockey. Cross-country skiing tours operate out of Jasper. Downhill skiing is available at Marmot Basin; cross-country trails also traverse the Maligne and Pyramid lake areas. Interpretive guides share their insights in theatrical productions. Wildlife tours also are available. Audiotape tours by CCInc. Auto Tape Tours are available at the Friends of Jasper store in the Parks Canada information center, 415 Connaught Dr.; phone (780) 852-4767.

Fishing permits can be obtained at information centers, campgrounds and local sport fishing shops. Boats with electric motors are allowed on lakes unless signs indicate otherwise. *See Recreation Chart and the AAA/CAA Western Canada & Alaska Camp-Book.*

ADMISSION to the park is $19.60 per private vehicle (two to seven persons). Otherwise admission per person is $9.80; $8.30 (ages 65+); $4.90 (ages 6-16). An annual pass, valid at Jasper and 10 other western Canada national parks, is available.

PETS are allowed in some areas of the park but must be leashed, crated or physically restrained at all times.

ADDRESS inquiries to the Jasper National Park Information Centre, Jasper National Park of Canada,

P.O. Box 10, Jasper, AB, Canada T0E 1E0; phone (780) 852-6176. For other area information contact Jasper Park Chamber of Commerce, P.O. Box 98, Jasper, AB, Canada T0E 1E0; phone (780) 852-3858.

Points of Interest

Natural points of interest include Edith and Annette lakes to the east of Jasper; Maligne Canyon, Maligne Lake and Medicine Lake to the northeast; Pyramid and Patricia lakes to the north; and Mount Edith Cavell, with its Angel Glacier, and Athabasca and Sunwapta falls to the south.

COLUMBIA ICEFIELD, just inside the Jasper National Park of Canada boundary next to Banff National Park of Canada, is the largest ice mass in the Rocky Mountains. Its main bulk, about 16 by 24 kilometres (10 by 15 mi.), straddles the Great Divide, part of the British Columbia border and portions of Banff and Jasper national parks. The ice covers about 325 square kilometres (130 sq. mi.) to an estimated depth of 300 metres (984 ft.). Three glaciers—Stutfield, Athabasca and Dome—can be seen from Icefields Parkway.

Columbia Icefield Centre is 105 km (64 mi.) s. of Jasper on Hwy. 93. The center overlooks Athabasca and Dome glaciers and offers views of major mountain peaks surrounding the Columbia Icefield. An interpretive center contains models of the ice field and an ice cave. The center offers maps, information and details about interpretive programs. **Time:** Allow 30 minutes minimum. **Hours:** Daily 9-6, May-Sept.; 10-4 in Apr. and Oct. **Cost:** Free. **Phone:** (780) 852-5288 or (877) 423-7433. 🏛

COLUMBIA ICEFIELD GLACIER EXPERIENCE departs from Columbia Icefield Centre, 105 km (64 mi.) s. of Jasper on Hwy. 93N. Tours provide an opportunity to see and walk on a field of moving glacier ice formed by snow falling as long ago as 400 years. The bus driver provides anecdotes and information during this 80-minute excursion. **Time:** Allow 1 hour, 30 minutes minimum. **Hours:** Tours depart daily every 15-30 minutes (weather permitting) 9-6, June-Aug.; 10-5 in May and Sept.; 10-4, mid-Apr. through Apr. 30 and Oct. 1 to mid-Oct. **Cost:** Fare $46.67; $22.86 (ages 6-15); free (ages 0-5 in lap). **Phone:** (403) 762-6700 or (877) 423-7433.

THE DEN WILDLIFE MUSEUM is in the lower level of Whistler's Inn at 105 Miette Ave. in Jasper. Displayed are more than 150 mounted animals in simulated habitats. Nearly all of the animals shown were native to the area. **Time:** Allow 30 minutes minimum. **Hours:** Daily 8 a.m.-10 p.m. **Cost:** $3; free (ages 0-6); $6 (family). **Phone:** (780) 852-3361.

 ICEFIELDS PARKWAY— *see Banff National Park of Canada p. 43.*

JASPER ADVENTURE CENTRE is on Connaught Dr. in Jasper National Park of Canada. The company offers guided interpretive van tours, wildlife tours

and walking tours. Summer adventures include exploration of the Columbia Icefield, Maligne Valley and Morro Peak. Some winter treks encompass such activities as snowshoeing, dog sledding and cross-country skiing. Horseback riding trips, rafting tours and icewalks also are offered seasonally. **Hours:** Daily 8-6. Closed Dec. 25. **Cost:** Fare \$55-\$130. **Phone:** (780) 852-5595 or (800) 565-7547.

JASPER TRAMWAY is 3 km (1.8 mi.) s. on Hwy. 93, then 4 km (2.5 mi.) w. at Whistlers Mountain Rd. Passengers take a short, narrated tram ride 973 m (3,243 ft.) up into the alpine zone on Whistlers Mountain, where scenic views await. Six surrounding mountain ranges, glacial-fed lakes and the Jasper townsite are visible. Once at the top, visitors may hike to the summit. Interpretive panels describe natural features.

Time: Allow 1 hour minimum. **Hours:** Daily 9-8, late June-late Aug.; 9:30-6:30, late May-late June; 10-5, mid-Apr. to late May and late Aug.-second Mon. in Oct. **Cost:** Fare \$28; \$14 (ages 5-14). **Phone:** (780) 852-3093. *See color ad.*

JASPER-YELLOWHEAD MUSEUM AND ARCHIVES is at 400 Pyramid Lake Rd. Exhibits depict Jasper history, highlighting the area's fur trade, pioneers and railways. Early tourism within Jasper National Park of Canada also is documented. An art gallery features the works of local artists, while the archives contain photographs, maps and documents.

Time: Allow 30 minutes minimum. **Hours:** Daily 10-5, Victoria Day-second Mon. in Oct.; Thurs.-Sun. 10-5, rest of year. Closed Jan. 1 and Dec. 25-26. **Cost:** \$5; \$4 (ages 65+ and students with ID); free (ages 0-5); \$12 (family). **Phone:** (780) 852-3013.

MALIGNE LAKE BOAT TOURS is 48 km (30 mi.) s.e. via Maligne Lake Rd.; tickets can be purchased from the office at 616 Patricia St. in the town of Jasper. The 90-minute tours, which offer a brief stop at Spirit Island, provide exceptional views of Maligne Narrows and insight into area geology and wildlife. Hiking and trout-fishing trips as well as boat, canoe and sea kayak rentals are available June to September. Shuttles are available from the town of Jasper.

Time: Allow 1 hour, 30 minutes minimum. **Hours:** Boat tours depart daily on the hour (weather permitting) 10-5, July-Aug.; 10-4 in June and Sept. **Cost:** Boat fare \$55; \$27.50 (ages 6-12). Round-trip shuttle fare \$40. One-way shuttle fare \$20. **Phone:** (780) 852-3370 for information and shuttle schedule. *See color ad.*

MIETTE HOT SPRINGS POOL is e. on Hwy. 16 from Jasper for 44 km (27.3 mi.) to the Pocahontas Bungalows and jct. Miette Rd., then s. 17 km (11 mi.) on Miette Rd. Man-made pools are fed by sulfur hot springs, with the water temperature ranging between 38 C (100 F) and 42 C (108 F). One pool is about 1.5 metres (5 ft.) deep; another pool averages one-half metre (18 in.) deep. Visitors also can cool off in two swimming pools.

Wildlife viewing opportunities often are available in the area, and hiking trails are nearby. Changing rooms and bathing suit and towel rentals are available. **Time:** Allow 30 minutes minimum. **Hours:** Daily 8:30 a.m.-10:30 p.m., mid-June through Labour Day; 10:30-9, early May to mid-June and day after Labour Day to mid-Oct. **Cost:** \$6.05; \$5.15 (ages 3-17 and 65+); \$18.35 (family, two adults and two children). Prices may vary; phone ahead. **Phone:** (780) 866-3939 or (800) 767-1611.

RECREATIONAL ACTIVITIES

Horseback Riding

- **Pyramid Stables** is 4 km (2.5 mi.) n. on Pyramid Lake Rd. **Hours:** Daily 8:30-4:30, mid-May to mid-Oct. **Phone:** (780) 852-7433.

- **Skyline Trail Rides Ltd.** departs The Fairmont Jasper Park Lodge on Old Lodge Rd. **Hours:** Daily 9:30-6:30, late Apr.-late Oct. **Phone:** (780) 852-4215 or (888) 852-7787.

White-water Rafting

- **SAVE** **Jasper Raft Tours** is at 604 Connaught Dr. **Hours:** Trips are offered daily, May 15-Sept. 30. Departure times vary. **Phone:** (780) 852-2665 or (888) 553-5628.

- **Jasper's Whitewater Rafting Co.** departs from the parking lot .3 km (.19 mi.) s. of Sunwapta Falls Resort off Hwy. 93. **Hours:** Trips are offered May 1-early Oct. Schedule varies; phone ahead. **Phone:** (780) 852-7238.

- **Raven Adventures Ltd.** is at 610 Patricia St. Other activities are offered. **Hours:** Trips are offered daily, May-Sept. Departure times vary. **Phone:** (780) 852-4292 or (866) 496-7238.

- **Rocky Mountain River Guides** is at 626 Connaught Dr. **Hours:** Trips are offered daily, mid-May through Sept. 30. Departure times vary. **Phone:** (780) 852-3777 or (866) 952-3777.

KANANASKIS COUNTRY (I-4) pop. 429

Kananaskis Country is a four-season, multiuse recreation area encompassing more than 4,200 square kilometres (1,622 sq. mi.) of mountains and foothills. West of Calgary, the area contains Bow Valley, Bragg Creek, Canmore Nordic Centre, Peter Lougheed, Sheep River and Spray Valley provincial parks. In addition there are Blue Rock, Bow Valley, Don Getty and Elbow-Sheep wildland parks. There are also numerous provincial recreation areas with campgrounds, day use areas and trails *(see Recreation Chart)*.

Year-round recreational activities are offered, including hiking, horseback riding, snowmobiling, kayaking, mountain biking, fishing, snowshoeing and downhill and cross-country skiing. The area begins just south of Hwy. 1 and extends south to the intersection of hwys. 940 and 532. Animals, including elk, deer, bighorn sheep, lynx, moose, mountain goats, bears and porcupines, can be observed in the area.

Three major visitor information centers within Kananaskis Country provide brochures, maps, displays and other travel information. The Barrier Lake Visitor Information Centre is 6.5 kilometres (4 mi.) south of Hwy. 1 on Hwy. 40, and Peter Lougheed Provincial Park Visitor Information Centre is 50 kilometres (31 mi.) south off Hwy. 40 on Kananaskis Lakes Trail. Elbow Valley Visitor Information Centre is 5 kilometres (3 mi.) west of Hwy. 22 on Hwy. 66. Campground amphitheaters offer interpretive programs Wednesday through Sunday evenings in July and August. The area is open daily; however, Hwy. 40 is closed December 1 to June 15 between the Kananaskis Lakes Trail and the junction of hwys. 541 and 940.

Kananaskis Country General Inquiries: Provincial Building, 800 Railway Ave., Suite 201, Canmore, AB, Canada T1W 1P1. **Phone:** (403) 678-5508 or (403) 673-3985.

PASSING OF THE LEGENDS MUSEUM is at Rafter Six Ranch Resort, 2 km (1.2 mi.) s. of Hwy. 1 overpass after the Seebe exit. Exhibits include

First Nations, North West Mounted Police and pioneer memorabilia; antique carriages; and artwork. Movies and television commercials have been filmed on the property. Adventure programs, including trail riding, white-water rafting and hiking tours, can be organized at the ranch.

Tours require a minimum of five people. **Hours:** Museum daily 9-5, May-Sept. **Cost:** $5; $3 (ages 5-12 and senior citizens). **Phone:** (403) 673-3622, (403) 264-1251, or (888) 267-2624 (Rafter Six Ranch Resort).

RECREATIONAL ACTIVITIES

Skiing

- **Nakiska Ski Resort** is just n. of Kananaskis Village on Hwy. 40. **Hours:** Daily 9-4, early Dec. to mid-Apr. **Phone:** (403) 591-7777, (403) 256-8473 or (800) 258-7669.

LAC LA BICHE (C-7) pop. 2,758

South of town, Portage La Biche was discovered in 1798 by renowned geographer and explorer David Thompson of the North West Co. This area encompasses the land between the Churchill and Athabasca-Mackenzie basins. Soon after its discovery the portage became a key link in Canada's main fur trade routes and a passageway to the Pacific Ocean.

The 1853 founding of Lac La Biche Mission played a vital role in the settlement of the area, which quickly developed into a major transportation center of the north.

Lakeland Provincial Park (see Recreation Chart), 13 kilometres (8 mi.) east off Hwy. 663, provides such recreational opportunities as bicycling, birdwatching, camping, cross-country skiing, fishing, hiking and swimming. The park also offers Alberta's only back-country canoe circuit. Sir Winston Churchill Provincial Park (see Recreation Chart and the AAA/CAA Western Canada & Alaska CampBook), 13 kilometres (8 mi.) northeast off Hwy. 881, is the largest of the 12 islands on Lac La Biche and offers opportunities for camping, hiking and bird-watching.

Lac La Biche Regional Community Development Corp.: 10106 102nd Ave., P.O. Box 2188, Lac La Biche, AB, Canada T0A 2C0. **Phone:** (780) 623-2662 or (877) 623-9696.

LACOMBE (F-6)

pop. 10,742, elev. 846 m/2,775'

Lacombe is the site of the Canadian Agriculture Department's experimental farm; visitors can tour the facility. At Gull Lake is Aspen Beach Provincial Park, a noteworthy area resort affording such recreational activities as cross-country skiing, ice fishing and water skiing (see Recreation Chart and the AAA/CAA Western Canada & Alaska CampBook).

ELLIS BIRD FARM, 8 km (5 mi.) e. on Hwy. 12, then 8 km (5 mi.) s. on Prentiss Rd., is a working bird-conservation facility encouraging the propagation of mountain bluebirds and tree swallows. Such species as house wrens, owls and warblers also are attracted to the vibrant grounds. A network of trails afford access to butterfly, native wildflower, hummingbird and water gardens. A visitor center displaying mounted bird specimens is on-site as is a pond where children can try to net beetles and damselflies.

Time: Allow 1 hour minimum. **Hours:** Tues.-Sun. and Mon. holidays 11-5, Victoria Day weekend-Labour Day. Guided tours are offered Sun. at 2, June-July. **Cost:** Admission by donation. Guided tour $2. **Phone:** (403) 885-4477, or (403) 346-2211 off-season. ⟨†⟩ ⟨⼼⟩

LAKE LOUISE—

see Banff National Park of Canada p. 43.

LEGAL (D-6) pop. 1,192

Best known for its collection of building-sized historical murals, the small town of Legal is 50 kilometres (31 mi.) north of Edmonton. The Francophone community is named after Father Emile Legal, a French bishop, missionary and architect.

The town takes pride in its Francophone pioneer history, as is depicted by its huge outdoor murals. Subject matter ranges from the Grey Nuns—who built the first educational center for rural children—to Alexandre Lavoie, whose court battle helped French-Canadians throughout the country obtain federal services in French.

ACFA and Centralta Community Centre: 5109-46 St., P.O. Box 328, Legal, AB, Canada T0G 1L0. **Phone:** (780) 961-3665.

LETHBRIDGE (J-7)

pop. 74,637, elev. 930 m/3,051'

Founded in the 1870s, abundant agricultural resources helped Lethbridge to become one of Alberta's major feedlot and grain distribution centers. The region reportedly receives more hours of sunshine annually than any other spot in Canada and therefore requires irrigation to counterbalance the semiarid climate; more than 400,000 hectares (988,000 acres) produce crops of grain and sugar beets. Livestock, oil and gas also support the economic base.

Numerous parks and green spaces complement the city's commercial enterprises. Two popular areas are Lethbridge Nature Preserve in Indian Battle Park at 3rd Avenue S. and Scenic Drive, and Henderson Park at S. Parkside Drive and Mayor Magrath. The park has a golf course, a 60-acre lake with tennis courts, a picnic area and a campground. Rose and Japanese gardens, a stadium and an ice-skating center are included. Lethbridge holds Whoop-Up Days in summer.

Chinook Country Tourist Association: 2805 Scenic Dr. S., Lethbridge, AB, Canada T1K 5B7. **Phone:** (403) 320-1222 or (800) 661-1222.

Shopping areas: Hudson's Bay Co. anchors Lethbridge Centre, off Hwy. 3 at 200 4th Ave. S. Park

Place Mall, 1st Avenue S. on Scenic Drive, has more than 100 stores and features Sears.

BREWERY GARDENS is just w. off 1st Ave. S. at Brewery Hill on Scenic Dr. Developed by a former brewery, the gardens present eight floral displays May through the first frost, as well as displays for Easter, Halloween, Remembrance Day and Christmas. The gardens are not walk-through gardens, but are a 1 hectare (2.5 acre) plot on the side of a coulee. Visitors view them across the coulee. **Hours:** Daily dawn-dusk. **Cost:** Free. **Phone:** (403) 320-1223.

GALT MUSEUM & ARCHIVES is at the w. end of 5th Ave. S. Housed in a 1910 building that once served as a hospital, the museum is named for the founder of North Western Coal and Navigation Co. The Discovery Hall exhibit gallery highlights the history of the Kainai people and southern Alberta. The High Level Bridge can be seen from the Viewing Gallery, which overlooks the Oldman River Valley.

Time: Allow 30 minutes minimum. **Hours:** Museum Mon.-Sat. 10-5, Sun. and holidays 1-5, May 15-Aug. 31; Mon.-Sat. 10-4:30, Sun. and holidays 1-4:30, rest of year. Closed Jan. 1, Easter, Aug. 31 and Dec. 25-26. Archives Mon.-Fri. 10-4:30; closed statutory holidays. **Cost:** $5; $4 (students with ID and senior citizens); $3 (ages 7-17); $12 (family, two adults and two children). **Phone:** (403) 320-3898, (403) 320-4258 for recorded information, or (866) 320-3898 in Canada.

INDIAN BATTLE PARK is 1 km (.6 mi.) w. of jct. Scenic Dr. and 3rd Ave. S. under the High Level Bridge. This was the 1870 site of the last intertribal battle in North America, between the Cree and Blackfoot Indians. Within the park are attractions, self-guiding trails and playground facilities. **Hours:** Daily 7 a.m.-10:30 p.m., May-Sept.; 7 a.m.-8:30 p.m., rest of year. **Cost:** Free. 🏕

Coal Banks Interpretive Sites are scattered throughout the city. Five informational signs explain the origin of coal mining in the area. Three of the signs are in or near the park at Helen Schuler Coulee Centre *(see attraction listing)*, by the Elks Recreation Centre, and between the Lodge and the Galt Museum & Archives *(see attraction listing)*. The others are at Brewery Gardens *(see attraction listing)* and on Queen Elizabeth II Hwy. near Kipp. **Hours:** Daily 24 hours. **Phone:** (403) 320-3898 (Galt Museum & Archives).

Fort Whoop-Up is on the river in Indian Battle Park, 1 km (.6 mi.) w. of jct. Scenic Dr. and 3rd Ave. S. This is a replica of a fort built in 1869 by American traders in Canadian territory. Trade in guns and illegal alcohol, in addition to reports of an American flag flying in Canada, led to the formation of the North West Mounted Police and to their march west in 1874. Wagon rides through the park are available in summer; they must be booked in advance during winter months.

Time: Allow 30 minutes minimum. **Hours:** Daily 10-5, June-Sept.; Wed.-Sun. 1-4, Apr.-May and in Oct.; Sat.-Sun. 1-4, rest of year. Guided tours are available Tues.-Sun. at 10:30, 1:30 and 2:30, July-Aug. **Cost:** June-Sept. $7; $6 (ages 65+); $5 (ages 13-18); $3 (ages 5-12); $18.69 (family). Rest of year $5; $4 (ages 65+); $3 (ages 13-18); $2 (ages 5-12); $14 (family). **Phone:** (403) 329-0444.

Helen Schuler Coulee Centre is at the n. of Indian Battle Park, 1 km (.6 mi.) w. of jct. Scenic Dr. and 3rd Ave. S. Desertlike flora and fauna are found on the coulee slopes and in cottonwood forests along the Oldman River. The center is surrounded by the 79-hectare (196-acre) Lethbridge Nature Reserve, home to the great horned owl, porcupines and white-tailed deer. Most of the park is accessible via three self-guiding trails. The center offers seasonal exhibits.

Pets, bicycles, inline skates and skateboards are not permitted. **Time:** Allow 30 minutes minimum. **Hours:** Daily 10-6, June-Aug.; Tues.-Sun. 1-4, rest of year. Closed Jan. 1 and Dec. 25. Phone ahead to confirm schedule. **Cost:** Free. **Phone:** (403) 320-3064.

The High Level Bridge spans the Oldman River in Indian Battle Park, 1 km (.6 mi.) w. of jct. Scenic Dr. and 3rd Ave. S. Reputedly this is the longest and highest bridge of its type and construction in North America. The 1909 trestle bridge extends 1.6 kilometres (1 mi.) across the coulees and is 97 metres high (300 ft.). The best place to view the bridge is from the information center/rest area on the west end of 1st Avenue, south of Hwy. 3 on Brewery Hill. **Hours:** Daily 24 hours. **Cost:** Free.

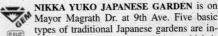 **NIKKA YUKO JAPANESE GARDEN** is on Mayor Magrath Dr. at 9th Ave. Five basic types of traditional Japanese gardens are incorporated into the overall design, which is one of the most authentic of its kind in North America. A pavilion, bridges, a bell tower imported from Japan and cypress wood from Taiwan are featured; paths punctuated by footbridges over ponds and streams weave through the gardens.

A variety of ongoing activities are offered. Visitors can take in art exhibitions or learn pruning and gardening techniques. Guides in traditional kimonos also conduct half-hour tours as needed. Special events, which take place on select Saturdays at 2, include traditional Japanese art demonstrations of bonsai, flower arranging, origami, sand art and calligraphy. A tea ceremony is offered Sundays at 2.

Time: Allow 1 hour minimum. **Hours:** Daily 9-8, July-Aug.; 9-5, early May-June 30 and Sept.-Oct. Phone ahead to confirm schedule. **Cost:** $7; $5 (ages 65+); $4 (ages 6-17). **Phone:** (403) 328-3511.

ST. MARY'S RIVER DAM is 78 km (47 mi.) s. off Hwy. 5. This earth-filled dam is one of the largest in Canada. Water sports and a campground are available. **Phone:** (403) 382-4097 (Park Lake Provincial Park).

SOUTHERN ALBERTA ART GALLERY is at 601 3rd Ave. S. Exhibits showcase works of Canadian and international artists with an emphasis on contemporary art. **Time:** Allow 30 minutes minimum. **Hours:** Tues.-Sat. 10-5, Sun. 1-5. **Cost:** $5; $4 (students with ID and senior citizens); free (ages 0-11 and to all Sun.). **Phone:** (403) 327-8770.

GAMBLING ESTABLISHMENTS

• **Casino Lethbridge** is at 3756 2nd Ave. S. **Hours:** Daily 9:30 a.m.-3 a.m. Closed Dec. 25. **Phone:** (403) 381-9467.

LLOYDMINSTER—*see Saskatchewan p. 276.*

LONGVIEW (I-6) pop. 300

BAR U RANCH NATIONAL HISTORIC SITE OF CANADA is 15 km (9 mi.) s. on Hwy. 22. The site focuses on the history of ranching in Canada and the role that occupation played in the country's development. Visitors learn the history of the Bar U Ranch, from the days of open range ranching through its prominence as a breeding center for cattle and Percheron horses to its position as part of a multiple-ranch cattle operation.

The visitor center has exhibits and a presentation about the site, one of Canada's largest ranching operations 1882-1950. Guests can tour the 158-hectare (390-acre) site on foot or via a hay wagon. Historic structures include the 1882-83 saddle horse barn, blacksmith shop, stud horse barn, wintering pens, 1910 cook house, storage sheds and ranch office/post office. Ranch chores also are demonstrated.

Hours: Daily 9-5, Victoria Day-Sept. 30. **Cost:** $7.80; $6.55 (ages 65+); $3.90 (ages 6-16); $19.60 (family). **Phone:** (403) 395-2212, (403) 395-3044 or (888) 773-8888. ⒯

MARKERVILLE (G-5) pop. 50

On June 27, 1888, 50 Icelanders from the drought-plagued Dakota Territory crossed the Red Deer River to settle in Markerville, where they hoped to maintain their language and customs. For a time they produced woolen outerwear, pastries, sweets and smoked mutton in the traditional Icelandic manner.

During the 1920s, however, an increase in intermarriage with other ethnic groups and improved transportation diluted their cultural isolation. Less than 10 percent of the population is now of purely Icelandic descent, but many traditional customs are celebrated during heritage days.

HISTORIC MARKERVILLE CREAMERY MUSEUM is off hwys. 781 and 592 on Creamery Way. Begun by 34 Icelandic farmers as a cooperative in 1899 and in operation until 1972, the creamery has been restored to depict the operation as it was in the 1930s. Costumed guides offer tours. **Time:** Allow 30 minutes minimum. **Hours:** Mon.-Sat. 10-5:30, Sun. noon-5:30, May 15-Labour Day; by appointment rest of year. **Cost:** $3; $2 (ages 7-17 and 65+); $10 (family, two adults and two children). **Phone:** (403) 728-3006. ⒯ Ⓐ

STEPHANSSON HOUSE PROVINCIAL HISTORIC SITE is 7 km (4 mi.) n., following signs. Historical displays highlight the Icelanders who founded Markerville, including Stephan G. Stephansson, a prominent poet and farmer. His home, restored to its 1927 appearance, contains original furnishings. Costumed guides give 15- to 30-minute tours and demonstrations of 1920s homemaking chores such as spinning.

Self-guiding tours are available. **Time:** Allow 30 minutes minimum. **Hours:** Daily 10-6, May 15-Labour Day. **Cost:** $3; $2 (ages 7-17 and 65+); $8 (family, two adults and children). **Phone:** (403) 728-3929 May 15-Labour Day, or (780) 427-1787 rest of year. Ⓐ

MEDICINE HAT (J-8)
pop. 56,997, elev. 715 m/2,346′

According to popular legend the name Medicine Hat originated because of a battle between Cree and Blackfoot Indians on the banks of a southern Alberta river. The Cree fought bravely until their medicine man deserted them, losing his headdress in midstream. Believing this to be a bad omen, the Cree put down their weapons and were killed by the Blackfoot. This site became known as "Saamis," which translates as "medicine man's hat."

A buried prehistoric river, or aquifer, serves as a source of unlimited cool water. More than 20 billion cubic metres (26 billion cu. yd.) of natural gas reserves inspired Rudyard Kipling in 1907 to describe Medicine Hat as possessing "all hell for a basement."

Guided tours of Medicine Hat are available through Tourism Medicine Hat. Outdoor opportunities include swimming, boating and fishing at Echo Dale Regional Park. Circuit cowboys and spectators gather for 4 days in late July for the Medicine Hat Exhibition & Stampede.

Tourism Medicine Hat: 8 Gehring Rd. S.W., Medicine Hat, AB, Canada T1B 4W1. **Phone:** (403) 527-6422 or (800) 481-2822.

Shopping areas: Medicine Hat Mall, 3292 Dunmore Rd. S.E., features The Bay, Sears and Zellers among its more than 100 stores.

ESPLANADE ARTS & HERITAGE CENTRE, 401 First St. S.E., houses a state-of-the-art theater, art galleries featuring works by both local and national artists, a museum and archives. The museum presents audiovisual displays detailing the region's cultural heritage as well as a collection encompassing more than 25,000 artifacts. Included are pioneer items and pieces related to the area's petroleum industry.

Time: Allow 1 hour minimum. **Hours:** Exhibit galleries and box office Mon.-Fri. 10-5, Sat.-Sun. and holidays noon-5. Closed Jan. 1, Good Friday and Dec. 25-26. **Cost:** Exhibit galleries $4; $3 (ages 7-17 and students with ID); free (ages 0-6 and to all

Thurs.); $12 (family). Prices for shows vary; phone ahead. **Phone:** (403) 502-8580. 🍴

▲ **MEDICINE HAT CLAY INDUSTRIES NATIONAL HISTORIC DISTRICT** is at 713 Medalta Ave. S.E. Brick, tile and pottery manufacturing were prominent industries in Medicine Hat starting in the late 19th century due to a supply of clay deposits, natural gas and the availability of railroad transportation. The city once boasted several potteries, such as Medalta Potteries and Medicine Hat Potteries (later Hycroft China Ltd.). Today only the brick industry remains.

At the Medalta Potteries site, visitors can see beehive kilns constructed in the early 1920s. Artifacts and production machines also are displayed. Self-guiding tours are available. Semiguided tours are offered in summer. **Time:** Allow 1 hour minimum. **Hours:** Daily 9:30-5, mid-May through Labour Day; Tues.-Sat. 10-4, rest of year. **Cost:** $10; $8 (ages 7-16, ages 65+ and students with ID); $25 (family, two adults and two children). **Phone:** (403) 529-1070.

SAAMIS TEEPEE is at jct. Hwy. 1 and South Ridge Dr. Made of steel, the tepee stands approximately 20 stories high. Storyboards incorporated in the tepee stand 3.6 metres (12 ft.) high and depict Indian history. Used during the 1988 Olympics in Calgary, the tepee was moved to Medicine Hat where it now stands on Saamis Archaeological Site—the location of a 16th-century buffalo camp. **Time:** Allow 1 hour minimum. **Hours:** Daily 24 hours. **Cost:** Free. **Phone:** (403) 527-6422.

GAMBLING ESTABLISHMENTS

- **Casino by Van Shaw** is at 1051 Ross Glen Dr. S.E. **Hours:** Daily 10 a.m.-3 a.m. Closed Dec. 25. **Phone:** (403) 504-4584.

MILK RIVER (K-8) pop. 816

Milk River is on the east side of Milk River Ridge, an area more than 1,200 metres (3,900 ft.) high, 39 kilometres (24 mi.) long and 29 kilometres (18 mi.) wide. Quartzite, granite and gneiss rock formations indicate prehistoric glacial action; meltwater carved the Milk River Valley 10,000 years ago. The river, formed from small streams and springs in southwest Alberta and northern Montana, joins the Missouri and Mississippi rivers to flow to the Gulf of Mexico.

Throughout the area and predominantly in Writing-on-Stone Provincial Park (see attraction listing) are mushroom-shaped sandstone hoodoos, odd rock formations that once led Indians to believe spirits inhabited the valley.

The Alberta Tourism Information and Interpretive Centre: General Delivery, Milk River, AB, Canada T0K 1M0. **Phone:** (800) 252-3782.

WRITING-ON-STONE PROVINCIAL PARK is 35 km (21.9 mi.) e. on Hwy. 501, 7 km (4.5 mi.) s. on Hwy. 130, then 6 km (3.9 mi.) e. on Hwy. 500, following signs. The archeological preserve overlooks the Milk River. Massive sandstone outcrops display pictographs and petroglyphs created by nomadic Shoshone and Blackfoot Indians. Fire-burned stones, broken bones, horn tools and other implements have been found at former campsites. Interpretive programs are presented mid-May to early September. *See Recreation Chart and the AAA/CAA Western Canada & Alaska CampBook.*

Note: Temperatures in excess of 40 C (104 F) are often recorded along the trail. **Hours:** Grounds daily 24 hours. Guided 90-minute tours depart Sat.-Sun. at 2, mid-May to early Sept. Tour departure times vary; phone ahead. **Cost:** Grounds free. Guided tour $8; $6 (ages 7-17); $25 (family). **Phone:** (403) 647-2364. 🍴 🎪 ⛺

MUNDARE (E-7) pop. 712

BASILIAN FATHERS MUSEUM is 2 km (1.2 mi.) n. of Hwy. 16 on Hwy. 855. Operated by the Basilian Fathers, the museum houses exhibits about Ukrainian immigration and the religious order's work in east central Alberta and throughout Canada. **Tours:** Guided tours are available. **Hours:** Mon.-Fri. 10-4 (also Sat.-Sun. 1-5, July-Aug.). Closed holidays Sept.-June. **Cost:** Donations. **Phone:** (780) 764-3887.

NANTON (I-6) pop. 2,055

NANTON LANCASTER SOCIETY AIR MUSEUM is s. on Queen Elizabeth II Hwy. following signs. Exhibits honor Royal Canadian Air Force and Royal Air Force members who waged bombing operations during World War II. The highlight of the museum's collection is a Canadian-built Lancaster bomber.

Other bombers also are displayed, along with training planes, simulators, gun turrets and instrumentation and photographs of training aircraft in action. **Time:** Allow 1 hour minimum. **Hours:** Daily 9-5, mid-Apr. to mid-Oct.; Sat.-Sun. 10-4, rest of year. Closed Jan. 1 and Dec. 25-26. **Cost:** Donations. **Phone:** (403) 646-2270.

NORDEGG (F-4) elev. 1,453 m/4,470′

NORDEGG HERITAGE CENTRE AND THE BRAZEAU COLLIERIES is .5 km s. of Hwy. 11. The center offers a small museum that documents Nordegg's heritage and coal mining industry history through a collection of photos and artifacts. In addition guided tours of the Brazeau Collieries, once Canada's largest producer of coal briquettes, depart from the museum.

The mine site and processing plant operated until 1955. Brazeau's technical aspects are explored during the 2.5-hour Technical Tour, which takes visitors to the mine portals (but not underground) and through the briquette processing plant buildings; a 1-hour overview tour also is offered some months.

Note: Guided tours of the Brazeau Collieries involve a lot of walking and climbing; in addition it is necessary to maneuver through remnants of the eration and ascend steep ladders in tight spaces

tours are organized at the museum, but visitors must drive their own private vehicles to the mine site.

Hours: Museum daily 9-5, Victoria Day weekend to mid-Sept. Technical tours are given daily at 1, Victoria Day weekend-Aug. 31; Sat.-Sun. at 1, Sept. 1 to mid-Sept. Overview tours are given daily at 10, July-Aug. **Cost:** Museum admission by donation. Technical tour $8; $2 (ages 7-12). Overview tour $5. **Phone:** (403) 845-4444. 🎫 🎫

OKOTOKS—*see Calgary p. 58.*

PATRICIA (I-8) pop. 114

DINOSAUR PROVINCIAL PARK is 13 km (8 mi.) n.e. via Hwy. 210, following signs. The park, declared a UNESCO World Heritage Site in 1979, covers 81 square kilometres (31 sq. mi.) of badlands and prairie along the Red Deer River. One of the richest fossil beds in the world, it contains the remains of 39 species of dinosaurs from 75 million years ago as well as crocodile, fish, flying reptile, small mammal and turtle fossils.

Five self-guiding trails explore three habitats: prairie grassland, badlands and riverside. Each offers opportunities for bird-watching. The visitor center contains exhibits, a theater and a preparation lab. Interpretive programs are offered seasonally. *See Recreation Chart and Brooks in the AAA/CAA Western Canada & Alaska CampBook.*

Allow a full day. **Hours:** Grounds daily 24 hours. Visitor center daily 8:30-7, Victoria Day weekend-day before Labour Day; daily 9-4, Labour Day-second Mon. in Oct.; Mon.-Fri. 9-4, rest of year. **Cost:** Grounds free. Visitor center (includes Royal Tyrrell Museum Field Station) $4; $2 (ages 7-17); $8 (family). Interpretive programs $8; $6 (ages 7-17); $25 (family). Reservations are recommended for interpretive programs. **Phone:** (403) 378-4344, or (403) 378-3700 for camping reservations. 🎫 🎫 🏕

Royal Tyrrell Museum Field Station is at the back of the visitor center building at Dinosaur Provincial Park, 13 km (8 mi.) n.e. via Hwy. 210. The interpretive center and research facility contains dinosaur skeletons, interpretive displays depicting the park's geological and paleontological resources, a preparation lab and the park administration office.

Hours: Daily 8:30-7, Victoria Day weekend-day before Labour Day; daily 9-4, Labour Day-second Mon. in Oct.; Mon.-Fri. 9-4, rest of year. **Cost:** (includes Dinosaur Provincial Park visitor center) $4; $2 (ages 7-17); $8 (family). **Phone:** (403) 378-4342.

PEACE RIVER (A-3) pop. 6,315

Formed by the confluence of the Smoky and Heart rivers, the Peace River flows north and east of the town of the same name to Lake Athabasca and to the west into British Columbia. The area was known as "The Forks" by trappers and traders in the 1700s and "Sagitawa" (meeting of the waters) by the Cree Indians. On his historic trek across the northern continent, Alexander Mackenzie explored

the region and built a fort and wintered here 1792-93.

A wooden statue honors prospector and local legend Henry Fuller "Twelve-Foot" Davis. The Vermont native, known for his generosity and hospitality, achieved great social stature when he mined $15,000 worth of gold from a 3.5-metre (12-ft.) plot between two gold claims. Davis said on his deathbed that he was not afraid to die because "I never kilt nobody, I never stole from nobody and I kept open house for travelers all my life." His grave overlooks the confluence of the Peace, Heart and Smoky rivers.

Nearby forests, rivers and streams make Peace River a popular center for year-round recreation in northern Alberta. Golfing, swimming, canoeing, downhill skiing and dog sledding are all options.

Peace River and District Chamber of Commerce: 9309 100th St., P.O. Box 6599, Peace River, AB, Canada T8S 1S4. **Phone:** (780) 624-4166.

PINCHER CREEK (J-6) pop. 3,625

Pincher Creek was established in 1878 by the North West Mounted Police as a horse farm to provide remounts for Fort Macleod *(see place listing p. 76)*. The town was named for a pair of pincers that presumably were left behind by prospectors. After hearing that the area had ample grassland, other settlers soon arrived.

Pincher Creek & District Chamber of Economic Development and Information Centre: 1037 Beverly McLachlin Dr., P.O. Box 2287, Pincher Creek, AB, Canada T0K 1W0. **Phone:** (403) 627-5855.

KOOTENAI BROWN PIONEER VILLAGE is at 1037 Bev McLachlin Dr. Displays include more than 16,000 local relics—including military uniforms, agricultural equipment, jewelry, clothing and books about local history—in 12 historical buildings. On the grounds is the restored log cabin of George "Kootenai" Brown, an Irish adventurer and one of the region's first settlers who helped establish Waterton Lakes National Park of Canada. Other period buildings are on the grounds.

Time: Allow 2 hours minimum. **Hours:** Daily 10-6, Victoria Day weekend-Labour Day; Mon.-Fri. 10-4:30, rest of year. Closed Dec. 24-Jan. 2. **Cost:** $6; $5 (ages 65+); $4 (ages 7-17); free (ages 0-6 with adult); $18 (family). **Phone:** (403) 627-3684.

RECREATIONAL ACTIVITIES
Skiing

• **Castle Mountain Resort** is off CR 507, just w. on CR 774. **Hours:** Daily 9-4, mid-Dec. to early Apr. **Phone:** (403) 627-5101.

RAVEN (G-5)

MEDICINE RIVER WILDLIFE CENTRE is 4 km (2.5 mi.) s. of Hwy. 54, then 2 km (1.2 mi.) e. The organization provides rehabilitation for injured and orphaned wildlife. It also serves as an environmental education center, offering a videotape presentation and displays about wildlife. A trail leads to an observation tower that affords excellent bird-watching around a 30-hectare (75-acre) marsh. **Time:** Allow 1 hour minimum. **Hours:** Daily 10-5, May 1-Labour Day; by appointment rest of year. **Cost:** Donations. **Phone:** (403) 728-3467.

RED DEER (G-6)
pop. 82,772, elev. 905 m/2,969'

Red Deer's name comes from the Cree Indian word *waskasoo,* meaning "elk." Early Scottish settlers mistook the native elk for the red deer of their homeland and the name stuck. A creek and park running through Red Deer still bear the name Waskasoo.

The original settlement was several kilometres upstream on the Red Deer River where the water was shallow and easy to cross. Dr. Leonard Gaetz, a Methodist minister who arrived in 1884, persuaded the Calgary and Edmonton Railway to cross the river on his property by donating half of his land for use as a townsite. The trains came through, and the town took root at its current site. Agriculture and petroleum products are the major local industries.

City Hall Park, 48th Avenue and Ross Street, is a landscaped oasis known for its Christmas light and flower displays. West of town is Sylvan Lake, which accommodates Jarvis Bay and Sylvan Lake provincial parks *(see Recreation Chart).*

Tourism Red Deer: 30A Riverview Park, Red Deer, AB, Canada T4N 1E3. **Phone:** (403) 346-0180 or (800) 215-8946.

Self-guiding tours: A brochure outlining a walking tour of historic downtown is available from the visitor information center west of Heritage Ranch in Waskasoo Park *(see attraction listing).*

Shopping areas: Bower Place, Gaetz Avenue and 28th Street, is anchored by The Bay and Zellers. Parkland Mall, 67th Street and Gaetz Avenue, has Sears and 120 smaller shops.

ALBERTA SPORTS HALL OF FAME & MUSEUM is on Queen Elizabeth II Hwy., n. of 32nd St. by Heritage Ranch. Alberta's sports history and heroes are celebrated through the display of 7,000 artifacts, archival material and interactive exhibits, including an Alpine ski racer game and a 200-metre (656-ft.) wheelchair race.

Time: Allow 1 hour, 30 minutes minimum. **Hours:** Daily 9-6, Victoria Day weekend-second Mon. in Oct.; 10-5, rest of year. Closed Jan. 1, Good Friday, Easter and Dec. 25-26. **Cost:** $3; $2 (ages 6-17 and 56+); $9 (family, two adults and children). **Phone:** (403) 341-8614. 🅃 🄐

RED DEER MUSEUM + ART GALLERY is in the Parkland Mall at 4747 67th St. Its collections tell the story of diverse cultures who lived in the Red Deer River Valley from the days of the First Nations

to the start of modern civilization. Changing art exhibits are featured. **Note:** The museum's collections currently are displayed in an interim gallery while renovations to its permanent exhibit space at 4525 47A Ave. take place. The renovations are expected to be completed sometime in 2010; phone ahead to confirm schedule and location. **Hours:** Mon.-Fri. noon-8, Sat.-Sun. noon-5. Closed major holidays. **Cost:** Donations. **Phone:** (403) 309-8405.

ST. MARY'S CHURCH is at 6 McMillan Ave. This ultramodern 1968 structure of unusual design is the work of architect Douglas Cardinal. Local architect Graham Leadbeater designed the parish center addition. Alois Peter Marx of Germany created the sculpture displays. **Hours:** Mon.-Fri. 8:30-4. Closed major holidays. **Cost:** Free. **Phone:** (403) 347-3114.

SUNNYBROOK FARM MUSEUM AND INTERPRETIVE CENTRE, 4701 30th St., features several structures, including a windmill, a sawmill and a replica log house. Various types of farm equipment and tools are on display throughout the 10-acre site. The highlight of the museum and interpretive center's exhibits is its large collection of vintage tractors. Chickens, goats, pigs, sheep and other barnyard animals can be seen.

Tours: Guided tours are available. **Time:** Allow 30 minutes minimum. **Hours:** Daily 10-4, June-Aug.; Mon.-Fri. 10-4, rest of year. Closed Jan. 1 and Dec. 25. **Cost:** Donations. **Phone:** (403) 340-3511. 🄐

WASKASOO PARK borders the Red Deer River and runs throughout the city. The park has about 100 kilometres (62 mi.) of both paved and unpaved walking trails. Also within the park are Bower Ponds; the 1911 Victorian Cronquist House Multicultural Centre; Fort Normandeau, with an interpretive center; Heritage Ranch; Kerry Wood Nature Centre, which houses nature displays; and Gaetz Lake Sanctuary, a wildlife preserve. **Hours:** Grounds daily dawn-11 p.m. **Cost:** Grounds free. **Phone:** (403) 342-8159. 🄐 🄧

GAMBLING ESTABLISHMENTS
- **Cash Casino** is at 6350 67th St. **Hours:** Daily 10 a.m.-2 a.m. (also Fri.-Sat. 2-3 a.m.). Closed Dec. 25. **Phone:** (403) 346-3339.
- **Jackpot Casino Ltd.** is at 4950 47th Ave. **Hours:** Daily 10 a.m.-3 a.m. **Phone:** (403) 342-5825.

RECREATIONAL ACTIVITIES
Recreational Complex
- **Collicutt Centre** is at 3031 30th Ave. **Hours:** Mon.-Fri. 5:30 a.m.-10:30 p.m., Sat.-Sun. 6:30 a.m.-10:30 p.m., holidays 10-8. Closed Dec. 25. **Phone:** (403) 358-7529.

RIMBEY (F-5) pop. 2,252

PAS-KA-POO HISTORICAL PARK is at 5620 51st St. The park's Smithson International Truck Museum features 19 half-ton trucks, a collection of license plates, farm machinery and photographs. A restored village features 10 historic structures and two museums. A 1902 schoolhouse, a 1915 town office, a train station, a replica trapper's cabin, a 1932 homesteader's cottage, a 1908 church, a barbershop and a blacksmith shop are on-site. Each building contains artifacts and memorabilia.

Tours: Guided tours are available. **Hours:** Truck museum daily 10-5. Village daily 10-5, mid-May to early Sept. Closed Jan. 1 and Dec. 25. **Cost:** $5; free (ages 0-11 with adult). **Phone:** (403) 843-2004.

◥GEM ROCKY MOUNTAIN HOUSE NATIONAL HISTORIC SITE OF CANADA (G-5)

In west central Alberta about 80 kilometres (50 mi.) west of Red Deer on Hwy. 11 and 6 kilometres (4 mi.) west from the town of Rocky Mountain House via Hwy. 11A, following signs, Rocky Mountain House National Historic Site of Canada tells the story of the fur trade era that existed 1799-1875. The site, on the banks of the North Saskatchewan River, protects the remains of four fur-trading posts.

Both the North West Co. and Hudson's Bay Co. were expanding in an attempt to reach the area's native peoples. The two rivals arrived here within a week of each other in 1799, their goal being to stimulate trade with the Kootenai, who were on the western side of the Rocky Mountains. The Blackfoot people blocked the planned trade. Rocky Mountain House traded with eight different aboriginal groups in its 76 years of operation.

Well-known cartographer and fur trader David Thompson used Rocky Mountain House for a time as a base for exploring routes over the mountains. Thompson was the first person of European descent to cross Howse Pass, accomplishing this feat in 1807.

Trade competition remained intense between the two companies until their merger in 1821. The influx of illegal whiskey traders into southern Alberta in 1869 disrupted trade with the aboriginal people, and in 1875 the last of the four posts was abandoned.

Two walking trails along the North Saskatchewan River and through a scenic wooded area connect the remains of the four forts. Eight listening stations and illustrated interpretive panels are spaced along the trail system. A 30-minute walk leads past the two later forts, the reconstructed chimneys at the last fort site, a replica flat-bottom York boat, a Red River cart and a fur press. A longer 90-minute walk travels to the first two forts built at Rocky Mountain House, passing tepees, the 1967 Centennial Canoe Race exhibit and a buffalo viewing area. Visitors often can see deer, coyotes, bluebirds and hawks along the trails.

The visitor center contains exhibits of trade items and aboriginal objects and a theater presenting films. Interpretive programs and special events are offered daily during July and August. Bicycle rentals are available.

The visitor center is open daily 10-5, Victoria Day weekend-Labour Day; hours vary, day after Labour Day-Sept. 30. Admission is $3.90; $3.40 (ages 65+); $1.90 (ages 6-16); $9.80 (family, two adults and four children). Phone (403) 845-2412.

ROSEBUD (H-7) pop. 109

A pioneer ranching settlement founded in the 1880s, Rosebud has become a thriving cultural center. The community participates in the activities of Rosebud School of the Arts. Rosebud Theatre offers dinner and theater entertainment at matinees and evening performances Wednesday through Saturday from March through December. Matinees also are offered on Sundays from July through August; phone (403) 677-2350 or (800) 267-7553.

Among Rosebud's historic buildings is an early 20th-century Chinese laundry, which now is home to Centennial Museum. The museum displays local memorabilia and an array of western Canadiana. Works by Alberta artists are exhibited in Akokiniskway Art Gallery and other shops along the town's self-guiding historic walking tour.

ST. ALBERT—*see Edmonton p. 74.*

SLAVE LAKE (C-5) pop. 6,703

Slave Lake is on the southeast shore of Lesser Slave Lake, Alberta's largest auto-accessible lake. Lesser Slave Lake Provincial Park *(see Recreation Chart)*, which hugs the lake's east shore, provides snowshoeing and cross-country skiing opportunities in winter and camping, hiking and bird-watching during the summer. The park is home to the Lesser Slave Lake Bird Observatory and the Boreal Centre for Bird Conservation. Riverboat Daze takes place the second week in July, and the Alberta Open Sand Sculpture Championship is held the third weekend in July.

SMOKY LAKE (D-7) pop. 1,010

SAVE VICTORIA SETTLEMENT PROVINCIAL HISTORIC SITE is 10 km (6 mi.) s. on Hwy. 855 and 6 km (3.6 mi.) e. on Victoria Tr. Settlement began in 1862 as a Methodist mission. A Hudson's Bay Co. fur-trading post soon followed, and by the beginning of the 20th century the village was known as Pakan. Guided tours are offered of the 1906 Methodist Church and the 1864 Clerk's Quarters, which is furnished with pioneer articles. A videotape presentation describes local history.

Time: Allow 1 hour minimum. **Hours:** Daily 10-6, May 15-Labour Day. **Cost:** $3; $2 (ages 65+); $1.50 (ages 7-17); $8 (family, two adults and children). **Phone:** (780) 656-2333.

SPRUCE VIEW (G-5)

Founded at the turn of the 20th century, Spruce View was named for its omnipresent spruce trees. Such recreational opportunities as boating, camping, fishing and picnicking are available at Dickson Dam-North Valley Provincial Recreation Area *(see Innisfail in the AAA/CAA Western Canada & Alaska CampBook).*

DICKSON DAM VISITOR CENTRE is 6 km (4 mi.) e. on Hwy. 54, following signs. Perched on a hillside, the center offers a bird's-eye view of Dickson

Dam. Exhibits and a short video focus on the dam's history and topography. **Hours:** Tues. and Fri. 8:15-3:30; June-Oct. **Cost:** Free. **Phone:** (403) 227-1106.

STETTLER (G-7) pop. 5,418

Stettler is named after Carl Stettler, a Swiss immigrant who arrived in Alberta in 1903. He helped establish a Swiss community known as Blumenau not far from present-day Stettler. With the arrival of the railroad, the Stettler settlement was established and the residents of Blumenau relocated there.

ALBERTA PRAIRIE RAILWAY EXCURSIONS depart the train station at 47th Ave. and 46th St. Steam- and diesel-powered rail excursions are offered through the Alberta countryside in vintage passenger coaches. Trips last 5 to 6 hours; all include a buffet-style meal at the destination in the summer or on-board dining during the winter. Theme trips also are scheduled.

Hours: Trains operate Sat.-Sun. and selected weekdays, May-Oct. Departure times vary. **Cost:** Fare $85-$135; $65-$120 (ages 11-17); $35-$120 (ages 4-10). Prices may vary. Reservations are required. **Phone:** (403) 742-2811.

STONY PLAIN—*see Edmonton p. 74.*

TROCHU (G-6) pop. 1,005

ST. ANN RANCH TRADING CO. PROVINCIAL HISTORIC SITE is .5 km (.3 mi.) s. on King George Ave. This reconstructed 1905 French settlement contains restored historic houses and reproductions of period buildings. The site includes a small school, post office, hospital and chapel.

An interpretive center contains displays recounting the history of the settlement, which was founded by aristocratic officers from the French cavalry. **Time:** Allow 30 minutes minimum. **Hours:** Museum and interpretive center open daily 9-9. **Cost:** $2. **Phone:** (888) 442-3924 in Canada.

VEGREVILLE (E-7) pop. 5,519

The center of eastern Alberta's Ukrainian culture, Vegreville has the distinction of possessing the largest known *pysanka*, or Easter egg, in the world. The 9.4-metre-high (31-ft.) egg, decorated to reflect Ukrainian folk art, was erected in 1975 for the centennial of the formation of the Royal Canadian Mounted Police in Alberta.

The egg's bronze, gold and silver design, made from more than 3,500 pieces of aluminum, illustrates the local settlers' struggles and the protection the mounted police provided them. Queen Elizabeth and Prince Phillip unveiled the plaque next to the giant egg in Elks/Kinsmen Park during their visit in 1978. The Ukrainian Pysanka Festival is held in early July.

Town of Vegreville Parks, Recreation & Tourism: 4509 48th St., P.O. Box 640, Vegreville, AB, Canada T9C 1K8. **Phone:** (780) 632-3100.

WAINWRIGHT (F-8) pop. 5,426

WAINWRIGHT & DISTRICT MUSEUM is at 1001 1st Ave. Displays include items and memorabilia relating to family life in the town since its founding in 1908. The histories of a local prisoner of war camp and the now defunct Buffalo National Park also are presented. The museum is housed in an original Canadian National Railway station built in 1929. **Time:** Allow 30 minutes minimum. **Hours:** Daily 9-5, May-Aug.; 1-5, rest of year. Closed Jan. 1, Good Friday and Dec. 25. **Cost:** $5; $3 (ages 6-17). **Phone:** (780) 842-3115.

WARNER (K-7) pop. 307, elev. 1,017 m/3,336′

DEVIL'S COULEE DINOSAUR HERITAGE MUSEUM is in the County of Warner Administration Building w. off Hwy. 4, following signs. Embryonic fossils in their nests were found on the Milk River Ridge in 1987. The specimens were from a hadrosaur (a duck-billed dinosaur); the location was the first nesting site found in Canada. A 2-hour walking tour allows for first-hand inspection of the dinosaur egg site, where ongoing excavations often yield new scientific discoveries. Museum displays feature a hadrosaur nest, embryo, fossils and models of dinosaurs. Also included is an exhibit about early area settlement.

Note: The guided hikes are organized at the museum, but visitors must drive their own private vehicles to the dig site. The nesting site is in a primitive area not suitable for small children or those with mobility or medical problems. Allow 30 minutes minimum for the museum, 3 hours minimum for tour and museum. **Hours:** Museum daily 9-5, July 1-Labour Day; Wed.-Mon. 9-5, Victoria Day-June 30; by appointment rest of year. Tours of the nesting site are given daily at 10 and 1, July 1-Labour Day; Sat.-Sun. at 10 and 1, Victoria Day-June 30 (weather permitting). Phone ahead to confirm schedule.

Cost: Museum $4; free (ages 0-5); $12 (family). Tour of dig site $12; $30 (family). Reservations are recommended for the tour. **Phone:** (403) 642-2118.

▼ WATERTON LAKES NATIONAL PARK OF CANADA (J-5)

Elevations in the park range from 1,279 metres (4,200 ft.) in the town of Waterton Park to 2,920 metres (9,580 ft.) at Mount Blakiston. Refer to CAA/AAA maps for additional elevation information.

The most direct approach into the national park from the south is over Chief Mountain International Hwy. (SR 17/Hwy. 6) from Glacier National Park in Montana; the park also is accessible via Hwy. 5 from Cardston or Hwy. 6 from Pincher Creek. Covering 505 square kilometres (195 sq. mi.), Waterton Lakes National Park of Canada adjoins Glacier National Park. Together the two parks form Waterton-Glacier International Peace Park. The customs office is open daily 7 a.m.-10 p.m., June 1-Sept. 1; 9-6, Victoria Day weekend-May 31 and Sept. 2-30.

For thousands of years this was aboriginal territory, where the Kootenai and Blackfoot were the primary aboriginal tribes. In 1858 Lt. Thomas Blakiston became the first European on record to explore the area; he named the lakes for Charles Waterton, an 18th-century English naturalist.

Local rancher Fred Godsal, American journalist and naturalist George Bird Grinnell and others lobbied their respective governments in the late 19th century to set aside parts of this wilderness area for future generations. They succeeded, and Waterton Lakes and Glacier national parks were established in 1895 and 1910, respectively.

Waterton Lake is divided into three parts: Upper, Middle and Lower Waterton lakes. The townsite, the location of park headquarters, is on the north shore of Upper Waterton Lake, which juts 4.7 kilometres (3 mi.) into Glacier National Park. The mountains on either side tower 900 to 1,200 metres (3,000 to 4,000 ft.) above the lake. Mount Crandell rises to the north; Sofa Mountain and Vimy Peak are east across the lake.

Wildlife ranging from squirrels and marmots to deer and bears inhabits the park. A small herd of plains bison is in the buffalo paddocks on the northern boundary, 1.6 kilometres (1 mi.) north of the Waterton River Bridge on Hwy. 6. Thousands of waterfowl visit the lakes during spring and fall migrations. Hunting is prohibited.

Among the many rare wildflowers that grace prairie and mountain landscapes are bear grass, pygmy poppy and mountain lady-slipper. Evergreens blanket the slopes and peaks below mountain goat country at an altitude of about 2,286 metres (7,500 ft.).

General Information and Activities

The park is open all year, though most concessions operate only from Victoria Day weekend through the second Monday in October. Red Rock Canyon, 15 kilometres (11 mi.) northwest of Waterton, offers a .7-kilometre (.4-mi.) loop trail along the canyon and a 1-kilometre (.6-mi.) trail to Blakiston Falls. Riding stables are 2.5 kilometres (1.5 mi.) north of town near the main entrance road; horses can be rented.

Just north of the townsite is an 18-hole public golf course that is open daily, Victoria Day weekend through the second Monday in October. A free four-court tennis facility is on Cameron Falls Drive.

The park visitor center, at the junction of the entrance road and Prince of Wales Road, is open daily 8-7, mid-June through Labour Day; 9-5, mid-May to mid-June; 9-4:30, day after Labour Day-second Mon. in Oct. Interpretive display centers at Cameron Lake and the Waterton townsite describe the park's subalpine forest and the history of the International Peace Park. All are open daily 24 hours.

Illustrated talks are given every evening at 8 at the park's indoor theaters. There also are guided walks and other interpretive programs; phone (403) 859-5133.

Those wishing to camp in Waterton's backcountry campsites must obtain a park use permit ($9.80) at the visitor center. You also can register your outing with the Park Warden Service.

Hunting is prohibited. Anglers need a fishing license, which can be obtained along with fishing regulations at the park offices, information center, campgrounds, from park wardens and at service stations in the townsite. Motorboats are permitted on both Upper and Middle Waterton lakes; water skiing, however, is permitted only on Middle Waterton Lake. *See Recreation Chart and the AAA/CAA Western Canada & Alaska CampBook.*

ADMISSION to the park is $19.60 per private vehicle (up to seven persons). Otherwise admission per person is $7.80; $6.80 (ages 65+); $3.90 (ages 6-16). An annual pass, valid at all Canadian national parks, is available.

PETS must be leashed at all times while in the park.

ADDRESS inquiries to the Superintendent, Waterton Lakes National Park of Canada, P.O. Box 200, Waterton Park, AB, Canada T0K 2M0; phone (403) 859-2224.

WATERTON INTER-NATION SHORELINE CRUISE CO. departs from the Waterton Marina. Narrated sightseeing trips lasting 2.25 hours cross Waterton Lake, which is surrounded by the majestic scenery of the Rocky Mountains. From early June through late September the cruise includes a 30-minute stop at Goat Haunt in Montana; passengers also may stay at Goat Haunt for day-long hiking trips and return on a later boat. Hikes to Crypt Lake also may be enjoyed, with a shuttle picking up and dropping off patrons at Crypt Landing mid-May to early October.

Note: A valid Canadian or U.S. photo ID must be presented by any passenger choosing to disembark at Goat Haunt for the day-long hiking trips. **Hours:** Sightseeing trips landing at Goat Haunt depart daily at 10, 1 and 4, early June-late Sept. (also at 7 p.m., July-Aug.). Non-landing sightseeing trips depart daily at 10 and 2:30, early May-early June and late Sept.-second Mon. in Oct. Crypt Landing shuttle trips depart daily at 9 and 10, mid-May to early Oct. **Cost:** Sightseeing trip $34; $17 (ages 13-17); $11 (ages 4-12). Crypt Landing shuttle $17; $8.50 (ages 4-12). **Phone:** (403) 859-2362.

RECREATIONAL ACTIVITIES
Horseback Riding

- **Alpine Stables** is in Waterton Lakes National Park of Canada, following signs. **Hours:** Daily 9-5, July-Aug.; 10-5, May-Sept. Phone ahead to confirm schedule. **Phone:** (403) 859-2462, or (403) 653-2449 off-season.

WETASKIWIN (F-6) pop. 11,673

Wetaskiwin got its name from a Cree phrase meaning "the hills where peace was made." It is believed that a peace agreement between the warring

Cree and Blackfoot tribes was made in the area. A stop between the growing outposts of Calgary and Edmonton, Wetaskiwin flourished due to its proximity to the Canadian Pacific Railway; the city was incorporated in 1906. Today Wetaskiwin boasts progressive commercial, agricultural and industrial ties, while a restored downtown area highlights the community's historic roots.

Wetaskiwin City Hall: 4705 50th Ave., P.O. Box 6210, Wetaskiwin, AB, Canada T9A 2E9. **Phone:** (780) 361-4417.

REYNOLDS-ALBERTA MUSEUM is 2 km (1.2 mi.) w. on Hwy. 13. Displays interpret the history of ground and air transportation, agriculture and industry in Alberta. Audiovisual presentations, displays and demonstrations supplement the actual operation of vintage automobiles, bicycles, and farm and industrial machinery. One area features a reproduction of a small drive-in theater, complete with old films, metal speakers and seats shaped like the back end of 1950-era automobiles.

The museum also is home to Canada's Aviation Hall of Fame, situated in a separate exhibit building. Vintage aircraft are displayed. Canadians who have contributed significantly to aviation history are recognized. **Time:** Allow 2 hours minimum. **Hours:** Daily 10-6, July 1-Labour Day; Tues.-Sun. 10-5, rest of year. Closed Jan. 1 and Dec. 24-25. **Cost:** $9; $7 (ages 65+); $5 (ages 7-17); $25 (family, two adults and children). **Phone:** (780) 361-1351 or (800) 661-4726.

WETASKIWIN & DISTRICT HERITAGE MUSEUM is at 5007 50th Ave. Housed in a historic building, the museum depicts local history and includes displays about the military, hospitals, early businesses, and Swedish and Chinese immigrants. The Origins Exhibit offers interactive games as well as such archeological finds as dinosaur fossils and Cree Indian artifacts. Women of Aspenland profiles notable women from the community.

A hands-on gallery for children features a blacksmith's shop, a one-room schoolhouse and a pioneer kitchen. **Time:** Allow 30 minutes minimum. **Hours:** Tues.-Sat. 10-5, Victoria Day weekend-Labour Day; Tues.-Fri. 10-5, rest of year. Closed Jan. 1, Good Friday and Dec. 25. **Cost:** Donations. **Phone:** (780) 352-0227.

WHITECOURT (D-4)
pop. 8,971, elev. 732 m/2,404'

THE WHITECOURT AND DISTRICT FOREST INTERPRETIVE CENTRE is 1 km (.6 mi.) e. on Hwy. 43. The center includes multimedia exhibits detailing the role of the forest in the evolution of Whitecourt. Visitors can view a storyboard describing the manufacturing process of wood products, a tepee, and a variety of wood artifacts and tools.

Next to the building, Heritage Park re-creates an early 20th-century logging town through a collection of restored buildings and vehicles. Tools and other artifacts from this period also are on display. Guided tours are available by appointment. **Time:** Allow 30 minutes minimum. **Hours:** Daily 9-6, June 1-early Sept.; Mon.-Fri. 8:30-4:30, rest of year. Closed statutory holidays in winter. **Cost:** $1.50; 50c (ages 6-10). **Phone:** (780) 778-5363.

WOOD BUFFALO NATIONAL PARK OF CANADA—
see Northwest Territories and Nunavut p. 258.

See how we got here.

Immerse yourself in the newly renovated museum and explore how transportation has changed America. National Museum of American History, Washington, D.C.

http://americanhistory.si.edu/onthemove

AMERICA
ON THE MOVE

America on the Move is made possible by generous support from General Motors Corporation, AAA, State Farm Companies Foundation, The History Channel, United States Congress, U.S. Department of Transportation, ExxonMobil, American Public Transportation Association, American Road & Transportation Builders Association, Association of American Railroads, National Asphalt Pavement Association, The UPS Foundation.

British Columbia

Tearooms & Totem Poles
British and Indian influences profile a cultural potpourri

Beautiful Victoria
English gardens and turreted buildings reflect a distinctive British essence

Splendid by Nature
The Canadian Rockies create a mountain playground amid glacial lakes and parks

Relaxing Hot Springs
Soak your stresses away and get an invigorating rush in warm mineral baths

A Land of Plenty
Orchards, vineyards and farms produce bountiful harvests

Gulf Islands National Park
Reserve of Canada
© Chris Cheadle
age fotostock

Elk River, near Fernie / © Henry Georgi / age fotostock

S ailing along Vancouver Island's untamed coast in 1842, James Douglas visited the site of present-day Victoria and reported: "The place itself appears a perfect Eden... one might be pardoned for supposing it had been dropped from the clouds..."

Prophetic words considering that Douglas, who later became colonial governor of British Columbia, was describing the "Garden City" many years before its first flower beds were planted.

Today, Edenic gardens are the province's forte: From Victoria's renowned, blossom-loaded Butchart Gardens to lush Queen Elizabeth Park atop the city of Vancouver's tallest hill, horticultural delights are everywhere.

And if a single apple was enough to tempt Adam and Eve, then they would no doubt have found BC's fertile Okanagan Valley irresistible. Not only do orchards here produce more than a third of Canada's apples, the valley also lures vacationers with sunny weather, sandy lakefront beaches and picturesque rolling hills striped by orderly rows of grapevines. According to legend, Okanagan Lake even harbors a serpentlike monster called Ogopogo, although unlike the biblical serpent, this elusive beast seems quite shy.

If you were searching for the Garden of Eden on Earth, British Columbia wouldn't be a bad place to start.

"Once upon a time. . ."

For generations, parents have used these four words to introduce children to the fantastic, magic-filled realms of fairy tales. Say them, and a spell is cast, transforming restless young ones into an attentive audience eagerly awaiting a story. Maybe you remember feeling such anticipation yourself.

If not, then a trip to British Columbia might just help recapture that youthful expectation of adventure. Though far removed from the Old World settings popularized in the works of Hans Christian Andersen and the Brothers Grimm, this far western province—with its daunting, snowcapped mountains and mist-filled rain forests—seems to have sprung from the pages of a storybook.

Into the Woods

Walk among centuries-old Douglas firs in MacMillan Provincial Park's Cathedral Grove and it's easy to imagine bumping into Little Red Riding Hood on her way to grandmother's house. Not only will these giants make you feel child-size by comparison; the perpetual twilight created by their lofty, intertwining branches can play tricks on your eyes, too. Look up at the high, dim ceiling of needle-heavy boughs arching overhead, and you'll understand how this grove got its name. Logging may have taken its toll on British Columbia's old-growth forests, but many stands continue to thrive in such havens as Pacific Rim National Park Reserve of Canada and Strathcona Provincial Park, both on Vancouver Island.

Another of these sylvan sanctuaries is in the city of Vancouver's Stanley Park. This urban wilderness embraces an evergreen woodland so extensive that while wandering its paths you might forget you're in the heart of Canada's third largest city. A miniature railway, children's petting zoo and the Vancouver Aquarium make this park a great Sunday getaway for families—and a perfect backdrop for storytelling.

Some of the most interesting tales told in Stanley Park are silently portrayed by stylized figures carved into totem poles. A thicket of these cedar columns loom at the park's eastern edge, and each one communicates its own story, whether it be a family history, a notable event or an age-old myth. Travel along the mainland coast or among British Columbia's offshore islands and you'll find more outstanding examples carved by the Bella Coola,

---

British Columbia Historical Timeline

The Queen Charlotte Islands are occupied by Haida Indians.
1750

Spanish explorers first sight the coast of Vancouver Island.
1774

George Vancouver, an English explorer, surveys the British Columbian coast.
1792

Vancouver Island becomes a crown colony.
1849

1820
The powerful Hudson's Bay Co. controls fur trading in the Pacific Northwest.

Haida, Kwakwaka'wakw, Nootka, Salish, Tlingit and Tsimshian peoples.

Symbolizing strength and authority, the bears glaring down from totem poles may not be the only ones you see in British Columbia: Grizzlies are common within Mount Revelstoke and Glacier national parks. Part of the Columbia Mountains, the terrain here consists of narrow, steep-walled valleys that fill with snow in winter to create icebound Shangri-Las.

Not far away, in the Canadian Rockies, Kootenay National Park of Canada preserves land that seems equally imbued with magic. At the park's southern end are the Radium Hot Springs, which bubble forth hot, mineral-tinged water no matter what time of year it is.

Enchanted Gardens

On the other hand, changing seasons mean a world of difference at Victoria's flower-crowded Butchart Gardens. As some plants bloom, others fade, producing a dramatic shift in hues seemingly conjured by a wizard's wand. Meandering paths thread among blossoming trees and shrubs, past softly splashing fountains and around countless flower beds in this rainbow-saturated wonderland. Rhododendrons and azaleas enjoy the limelight in spring and early summer; roses steal the show in late June.

Across the Straits of Georgia, Vancouver's VanDusen Botanical Garden is similarly endowed with floral color. Careful tending has transfigured this former golf course into a city showplace of lakes, streams, hedge mazes and whimsical topiary figures.

And what childhood fantasy would be complete without a castle? Victoria boasts two. Turrets, columns and rough sandstone walls lend 19th-century Craigdarroch Castle a medieval air that greatly pleased its builder, Robert Dunsmuir, a wealthy Scottish immigrant and industrialist. Hatley Castle, on the Royal Roads University campus, looks even more like a genuine fortress from the Middle Ages. Topped by battlements, this imposing mansion would be at home in a European fable.

To anyone who has ever been mesmerized by fanciful storybook illustrations, British Columbia should seem delightfully familiar.

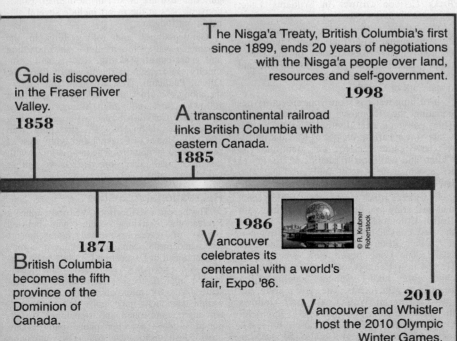

The Nisga'a Treaty, British Columbia's first since 1899, ends 20 years of negotiations with the Nisga'a people over land, resources and self-government.
1998

Gold is discovered in the Fraser River Valley.
1858

A transcontinental railroad links British Columbia with eastern Canada.
1885

1871
British Columbia becomes the fifth province of the Dominion of Canada.

1986
Vancouver celebrates its centennial with a world's fair, Expo '86.

© R. Krubner Robertstock

2010
Vancouver and Whistler host the 2010 Olympic Winter Games.

Recreation

The Rocky Mountain and Cascade ranges, a lush valley, and a system of rivers, lakes and protected ocean waterways are the hallmarks of British Columbia's natural beauty and the sources of unlimited recreational possibilities.

Summer Sojourns

Extended **canoeing** trips await you on the Outside Trail, a chain of lakes in the Kootenay region's Champion Lakes Provincial Park. The coastal area's 57-kilometre (35-mi.) Powell Forest Canoe Route, eight lakes connected by portage routes, begins on Lois Lake and ends at the marina on Powell Lake.

The 116-kilometre (72-mi.) canoeing and **kayaking** circuit (plus portage routes) in Bowron Lake Provincial Park is so popular that reservations are required and daily access is limited to 25 boats. Paddling through this unspoiled wildlife sanctuary could take up to 7 days, depending on the weather or how much time you spend gawking at bears, deer, moose, mountain goats or the beautiful Cariboo Mountains. Approach the park from Wells, which is just north of Barkerville Historic Town. For more information contact BC Parks Cariboo District in Williams Lake; phone (250) 398-4530.

In addition to spectacular mountain scenery, canoeists will find calm, turquoise-colored glacial lakes nestled in the snow-capped Rockies; two of these—O'Hara and the aptly named Emerald—are in Yoho National Park of Canada.

If rushing water is more your speed, try negotiating the Thompson and Fraser rivers. They converge near Lytton, said to be the **white-water rafting** capital of Canada; outfitters and guide services are plentiful. The Chilko and Chilcotin tributaries of the Fraser River, which lie west of Williams Lake, also have a reputation for adventure.

Every region has a network of **hiking** trails that will bring you up close and personal with British Columbia's natural wonders. One of the best coastal hikes is in Pacific Rim National Park Reserve of Canada, on Vancouver Island. The Long Beach Unit, accessed off Hwy. 4 near Ucluelet, offers eight moderately challenging hiking venues ranging from beaches to rain forests. The park's pride and joy—the rugged West Coast Trail—follows the shoreline from Port Renfrew to Bamfield. Only experienced hikers need apply for reservations, which are restricted to 50 per day during the season, May through September.

But that's just the tip of the iceberg when it comes to trekking around the province. Five national and nearly 650 provincial parks and recreation areas are your gateways to discovery.

Take the family **swimming, water skiing** or **windsurfing** inland at one of seven provincial beach parks on Okanagan Lake, or to Osoyoos Lake, the warmest in the province; both are in the desertlike Okanagan Valley.

The valley's climate and terrain invite other types of activities. The Kettle Valley Railway bed, west of Penticton, provides easy **mountain biking,** while tougher trails cross nearby Campbell Mountain and Ellis Ridge.

World-class Wintering

The **skiing** amenities at Whistler and Blackcomb mountains, north of Vancouver, are world renowned. Some 32 high-speed lifts, 200 trails and 12 alpine bowls—all on more than 2,800 hectares (7,000 acres)—make up one of the largest ski resorts in North America. **Snowboarding** and skiing lessons keep the children happy. Off the slopes, adults have unlimited après ski options in Whistler Village's eclectic mix of pubs, dance clubs and culinary nightspots; shops, spas and art galleries also are tucked in the hamlet. Bonus conveniences at the resort include several ski-in/ski-out lodgings.

Gentle slopes and rolling hills in the Okanagan Valley are ideal for snowboarding and **cross-country skiing.** Resorts and community ski areas near the towns of Osoyoos, Oliver, Penticton, West Kelowna and Kelowna, along the Hwy. 97 corridor, have quite a following; most offer night skiing, too. Some of western Canada's best cross-country skiing is farther north on Hwy. 97, stretching from 100 Mile House to Quesnel and lying west of the Cariboo Mountains. The area is laced with dozens of marked, groomed trails as well as wilderness paths.

Recreational Activities

Throughout the TourBook, you may notice a Recreational Activities heading with bulleted listings of recreation-oriented establishments listed underneath. Similar operations also may be mentioned in Destination City recreation sections. Since normal AAA inspection criteria cannot be applied, these establishments are presented only for information. Age, height and weight restrictions may apply. Reservations often are recommended and sometimes are required. Addresses and/or phone numbers are provided so visitors can contact the attraction for additional information.

Fast Facts

POPULATION: 3,907,738.

AREA: 944,735 sq km (364,762 sq mi); ranks 5th.

CAPITAL: Victoria.

HIGHEST POINT: 4,663 m/15,295 ft., Mount Fairweather.

LOWEST POINT: Sea level, Pacific Ocean.

TIME ZONE(S): Mountain/Pacific. DST in portions of the province.

TEEN DRIVING LAWS: The minimum age for an unrestricted driver's license is 19. No more than one unrelated passenger is permitted unless accompanied by a driver age 25 or older. For more information about British Columbia driver's license regulations phone (800) 663-3051.

MINIMUM AGE FOR GAMBLING: 19.

SEAT BELT/CHILD RESTRAINT LAWS: Seat belts required for driver and all passengers age 16 and older. Children ages 9-15 or 145 cm (57 inches) and over are required to be in a child restraint or seat belt; child restraints are required for under 145 cm (57 inches).

HELMETS FOR MOTORCYCLISTS: Required for all riders.

RADAR DETECTORS: Permitted.

FIREARMS LAWS: By federal law, all nonresidents entering Canada with a firearm must declare their weapon in writing and pay a fee of $25 (Canadian). Contact the Canadian Firearms Centre at (800) 731-4000 to receive a declaration form or for additional information.

HOLIDAYS: Jan. 1; Good Friday; Easter Monday; Victoria Day, May 24 (if a Mon.) or closest prior Mon.; Canada Day, July 1; British Columbia Day, Aug. (1st Mon.); Labour Day, Sept. (1st Mon.); Thanksgiving, Oct. (2nd Mon.); Remembrance Day, Nov. 11; Christmas, Dec. 25; Boxing Day, Dec. 26.

TAXES: British Columbia's provincial sales tax is 7 percent. A 5 percent Goods and Services Tax (GST) also is levied, and there is a provincial room tax of 8 percent to 10 percent on lodgings. This tax structure will be in effect until July 1, 2010, when the province will change to a harmonized sales tax, creating a single tax of 12 per cent. The separate lodgings tax will be discontinued, and hotel accommodations will be subject to the harmonized tax.

ROAD CONDITIONS: DriveBC provides current information about road conditions; phone (800) 550-4997 in British Columbia or anywhere in North America.

INFORMATION CENTERS: British Columbia has more than 125 visitor information centers throughout the province. Of these more than 80 are open all year and can be found in all major cities including Victoria and Vancouver. The smaller community travel information centers are open June through August. For further information phone Hello BC at (800) 435-5622.

FURTHER INFORMATION FOR VISITORS:
1-800-HELLO BC
1166 Alberni St., Unit 600
Vancouver, BC, Canada V6C 3L6
(604) 435-5622 (in Greater Vancouver)
(800) 435-5622

RECREATION INFORMATION:
BC Parks
P.O. Box 9398, Stn. Prov. Gov't.
Victoria, BC, Canada V8W 9M9
(604) 689-9025 (camping reservations in Greater Vancouver)
(800) 689-9025 (camping reservations)

FISHING AND HUNTING REGULATIONS:
Ministry of Environment
Fish and Wildlife Branch
P.O. Box 9391, Stn. Prov. Gov't.
Victoria, BC, Canada V8W 9M8
(250) 387-9771

ALCOHOL CONSUMPTION: Legal age 19.

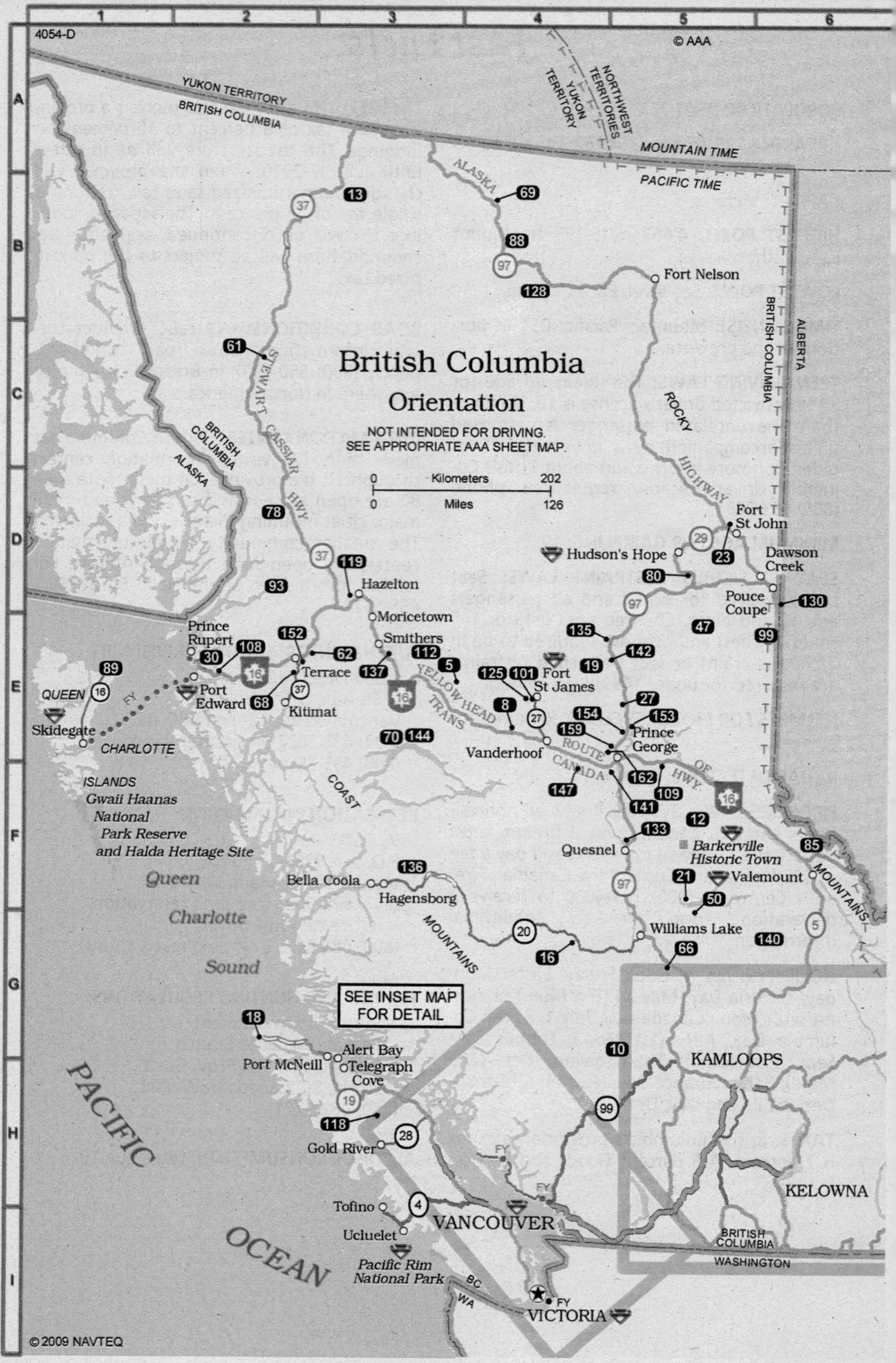

4054-D

© AAA

British Columbia

Orientation

NOT INTENDED FOR DRIVING.
SEE APPROPRIATE AAA SHEET MAP.

Kilometers 0 — 202
Miles 0 — 126

YUKON TERRITORY
BRITISH COLUMBIA

NORTHWEST TERRITORIES
UKON TERRITORY

MOUNTAIN TIME
PACIFIC TIME

Fort Nelson

BRITISH COLUMBIA
ALBERTA

ALASKA
BRITISH COLUMBIA

STEWART CASSIAR HWY.

ROCKY MOUNTAIN HIGHWAY

37   13
69
88
97
128
61
78
37   119   Hazelton
93   Moricetown
Prince Rupert   152   Smithers
30   108   62   112   5
Terrace   137   16   125   101   Fort St James   19   142
Port Edward   68   37   Kitimat   8   27
70   144   27   154   153   Prince George
Vanderhoof   159   Prince George
Skidegate   89   18   16   147   162   109
QUEEN   FY   141   12
CHARLOTTE   133   Barkerville Historic Town
ISLANDS   Quesnel   21   Valemount
Gwaii Haanas   National   136   97   50   140
Park Reserve   Bella Coola   Hagensborg   Williams Lake
and Halda Heritage Site   20   66
Queen   16
Charlotte
Sound   SEE INSET MAP
FOR DETAIL
18   10   KAMLOOPS
Port McNeill   Alert Bay
Telegraph Cove   99
19   KELOWNA
118   28
Gold River
4
Tofino   VANCOUVER
Ucluelet
Pacific Rim   BRITISH COLUMBIA
National Park   WASHINGTON
VICTORIA

Hudson's Hope
Fort St John
29   23   Dawson Creek
80   Pouce Coupe
97   47   99   130
135
85

PACIFIC

OCEAN

COAST MOUNTAINS

YELLOWHEAD TRANS CANADA ROUTE OF HWY.

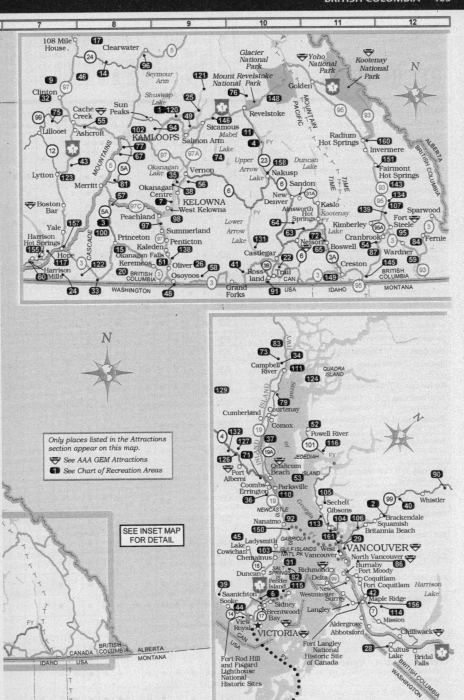

Only places listed in the Attractions section appear on this map.

See AAA GEM Attractions

See Chart of Recreation Areas

SEE INSET MAP FOR DETAIL

RECREATION AREAS

	MAP LOCATION	CAMPING	PICNICKING	HIKING TRAILS	BOATING	BOAT RAMP	BOAT RENTAL	FISHING	SWIMMING	PETS ON LEASH	BICYCLE TRAILS	WINTER SPORTS	VISITOR CENTER	LODGE/CABINS	FOOD SERVICE
NATIONAL PARKS (See place listings)															
Glacier (A-10) 1,350 square kilometres. Camping, wildlife viewing.		•	•	•				•		•		•	•	•	•
Gulf Islands (G-10) 33 square kilometres. Golf, kayaking, scuba diving. Recreational activities vary on each island.		•	•	•	•		•		•	•					
Gwaii Haanas (F-1) 1,495 square kilometres. Kayaking.		•		•			•						•		
Kootenay (A-11) 1,406 square kilometres. Horseback riding, mountain biking, wildlife viewing.		•	•	•				•	•	•	•	•	•	•	•
Mount Revelstoke (A-9) 260 square kilometres.		•	•	•				•		•		•	•	•	
Pacific Rim (I-3) 510 square kilometres.		•	•	•	•	•		•	•	•			•		
Yoho (A-11) 1,313 square kilometres. Cross-country skiing; horse rental. Power boats prohibited.		•	•	•		•	•	•	•	•					•
PROVINCIAL															
Adams Lake (B-9) 56 hectares 30 km n. of Chase off Hwy. 1. Archeological sites. Canoeing, scuba diving, water skiing, windsurfing.	❶	•				•		•	•	•					
Alice Lake (G-11) 396 hectares 13 km n. of Squamish on Hwy. 99. Canoeing.	❷	•	•	•				•	•	•					
Allison Lake (C-8) 23 hectares 28 km n. of Princeton on Hwy. 5A.	❸	•	•					•	•	•					
Arrow Lakes (Shelter Bay) (B-10) 93 hectares on Hwy. 23.	❹	•	•		•	•		•	•						
Babine Lake-Pendleton Bay Marine (E-3) 37 hectares 45 km n. of Burns Lake off Hwy. 16.	❺	•			•	•		•							
Bamberton (H-10) 28 hectares 45 km n. of Victoria off Hwy. 1.	❻	•	•	•				•	•	•					
Bear Creek (C-9) 178 hectares 9 km n. off Hwy. 97 w. of Kelowna.	❼	•	•	•				•	•	•					
Beaumont (E-4) 192 hectares 134 km w. of Prince George on Hwy. 16.	❽	•	•	•	•	•		•	•	•					
Big Bar Lake (A-7) 332 hectares 42 km n.w. of Clinton off Hwy. 97.	❾	•	•	•	•	•		•	•						
Birkenhead Lake (G-5) 10,439 hectares 54 km n.e. of Pemberton. Cross-country skiing, windsurfing.	❿	•	•	•	•			•	•	•		•			
Blanket Creek (B-10) 318 hectares 25 km s. of Revelstoke on Hwy. 23.	⓫	•	•					•	•	•					
Bowron Lake (F-5) 149,207 hectares 120 km e. of Quesnel via a gravel access road off Hwy. 26. Water circuit of connecting lakes.	⓬	•		•	•	•		•	•	•		•		•	
Boya Lake (B-3) 4,597 hectares 150 km n. of Dease Lake. Canoeing, kayaking.	⓭	•			•			•	•	•					
Bridge Lake (A-8) 11 hectares 51 km e. of 100 Mile House off Hwy. 24.	⓮	•	•		•	•		•	•						
Bromley Rock (C-8) 149 hectares 21 km e. of Princeton on Hwy. 3.	⓯	•	•					•	•	•					
Bull Canyon (G-4) 369 hectares 6 km w. of Alexis Creek off Hwy. 20.	⓰	•	•	•				•		•					
Canim Beach (A-8) 6 hectares on Canim Lake, 43 km n.e. of 100 Mile House off Hwy. 97. Canoeing, kayaking.	⓱		•		•	•		•	•						
Cape Scott (G-2) 22,294 hectares 64 km w. of Port Hardy. Canoeing, hunting, kayaking.	⓲	•		•				•	•	•					
Carp Lake (E-4) 38,149 hectares 32 km s.w. of McLeod Lake off Hwy. 97. Canoeing, hunting, ice fishing, kayaking.	⓳	•	•	•	•	•		•	•	•			•		
Cathedral (D-8) 33,272 hectares 24 km w. of Keremeos off Hwy. 3. Horseback riding, hunting, mountaineering.	⓴	•	•	•				•	•	•					
Cedar Point (F-5) 8 hectares 118 km n.e. of Williams Lake off Hwy. 97 on Quesnel Lake. Water skiing; mining displays.	㉑	•	•		•	•		•	•						
Champion Lakes (D-10) 1,426 hectares 10 km s. of Castlegar off Hwy. 3B. Cross-country skiing, ice fishing. Power boats prohibited.	㉒	•	•	•	•			•	•	•	•	•			
Charlie Lake (D-5) 85 hectares 11 km n. of Fort St. John off Hwy. 97.	㉓	•	•	•	•	•		•	•	•		•			

RECREATION AREAS

	MAP LOCATION	CAMPING	PICNICKING	HIKING TRAILS	BOATING	BOAT RAMP	BOAT RENTAL	FISHING	SWIMMING	PETS ON LEASH	BICYCLE TRAILS	WINTER SPORTS	VISITOR CENTER	LODGE/CABINS	FOOD SERVICE
Chilliwack Lake (D-7) 9,528 hectares 64 km s.e. of Chilliwack via an access road off Hwy. 1. Hunting, water skiing. ATVs or unlicensed motorbikes prohibited.	24	•	•	•	•	•		•	•	•					
Cinnemousun Narrows (A-9) 176 hectares 22.5 km n. of Sicamous via boat. Houseboating, scuba diving, water skiing, windsurfing.	25	•	•	•	•	•		•	•	•				•	
Conkle Lake (D-9) 587 hectares 28 km n.e. of Osoyoos via Hwy. 3, then 26 km to entrance. Windsurfing.	26	•	•	•	•	•	•	•	•	•			•		
Crooked River (E-5) 970 hectares 70 km n. of Prince George on Hwy. 97. Cross-country skiing, ice fishing, windsurfing. Power boats prohibited.	27	•	•	•				•	•	•		•			
Cultus Lake (I-11) 2,561 hectares 11 km s.w. of Chilliwack off Hwy. 1. Water skiing, windsurfing. *(See Cultus Lake p. 117)*	28	•	•	•	•	•	•	•	•	•					
Cypress (G-11) 3,012 hectares off Hwy. 1 exit 8 in West Vancouver, then w. following signs. Cross-country and downhill skiing, snowmobiling, wilderness camping. *(See West Vancouver p. 188)*	29	•	•	•						•		•	•		
Diana Lake (E-2) 233 hectares 16 km e. of Prince Rupert on Hwy. 16. Canoeing, kayaking and paddling.	30		•	•				•	•	•					
Dionisio Point (H-10) 142 hectares on Galiano Island via car ferry. Scuba diving, winter camping.	31	•	•					•	•	•		•			
Downing (A-7) 100 hectares 18 km s.w. of Clinton off Hwy. 97.	32	•	•		•	•		•	•						
E.C. Manning (D-8) 70,844 hectares on Hwy. 3 between Hope and Princeton. Scenic. Cross-country and downhill skiing, mountain biking, snowshoeing; canoe, horse and kayak rentals. *(See Hope p. 125)*	33	•	•	•	•	•	•	•	•	•	•	•	•	•	•
Elk Falls (E-10) 1,087 hectares 3 km n.w. of Campbell River off Hwy. 28. Mountain biking (on designated trails), winter camping; waterfall.	34	•	•	•				•	•	•		•			
Ellison (B-9) 200 hectares on Okanagan Lake, 16 km s.w. of Vernon off Hwy. 97. Rock climbing.	35	•	•	•	•	•		•	•	•				•	
Englishman River Falls (G-10) 97 hectares 13 km s.w. of Parksville off Hwy. 4.	36	•	•	•				•	•	•					
Filongley (F-10) 23 hectares on Denman Island via ferry from Buckley Bay. Canoeing, kayaking, winter camping.	37	•	•					•	•	•					
Fintry (C-9) 361 hectares 34 km n. of Kelowna off Hwy. 97. Hunting, scuba diving, water skiing.	38	•	•	•	•	•		•	•	•				•	
French Beach (H-9) 59 hectares 20 km w. of Sooke off Hwy. 14. Windsurfing.	39	•	•	•				•	•	•					
Garibaldi (G-12) 194,650 hectares accessible by five trails from Hwy. 99 in Squamish. Cross-country skiing, winter camping. Snowmobiling prohibited. *(See Squamish p. 154)*	40	•	•	•				•	•	•		•	•	•	
Gladstone (D-10) 39,387 hectares 5 km e. of Christina Lake on Hwy. 3. Cross-country skiing, hunting, scuba diving, snowshoeing, water skiing.	41	•	•	•	•	•		•	•	•		•			
Golden Ears (H-11) 62,540 hectares 11 km n. of Maple Ridge off Hwy. 7. Water skiing, windsurfing. Horse rental.	42	•	•	•	•	•	•	•	•	•					
Goldpan (B-8) 5 hectares 10 km s. of Spences Bridge adjacent to Hwy. 1 on the e. bank of the Thompson River. Canoeing, kayaking.	43	•	•					•	•	•					
Goldstream (H-10) 477 hectares 16 km n.w. of Victoria via Hwy. 1. Wildlife viewing, winter camping. Salmon spawning in fall.	44	•	•						•	•					
Gordon Bay (G-10) 51 hectares 14 km w. of Lake Cowichan off Hwy. 18. Freshwater diving, water skiing, windsurfing, winter camping.	45	•	•	•	•	•		•	•	•					
Green Lake (A-8) 347 hectares 16 km n.e. of Hwy. 97 at 70 Mile House. Horseback riding, water skiing.	46	•	•	•	•	•		•	•	•		•			
Gwillim Lake (E-5) 32,458 hectares 56 km. s.e. of Chetwynd on Hwy. 29. Canoeing, kayaking, rock climbing, scuba diving, water skiing, windsurfing.	47	•	•	•	•	•		•	•	•			•		

RECREATION AREAS

	MAP LOCATION	CAMPING	PICNICKING	HIKING TRAILS	BOATING	BOAT RAMP	BOAT RENTAL	FISHING	SWIMMING	PETS ON LEASH	BICYCLE TRAILS	WINTER SPORTS	VISITOR CENTER	LODGE/CABINS	FOOD SERVICE
Haynes Point (D-9) 38 hectares 2 km s. of Osoyoos on Hwy. 97. Water skiing, wildlife viewing.	48	•	•	•	•	•		•	•	•					
Herald (B-9) 79 hectares 14 km e. of Tappen off Hwy. 1. Scuba diving, water skiing, windsurfing.	49	•	•	•	•	•		•	•	•					
Horsefly Lake (F-5) 148 hectares 65 km e. of 150 Mile House off Hwy. 97. Scuba diving, water skiing, windsurfing.	50	•	•	•	•	•	•	•	•	•					
Inkaneep (D-9) 21 hectares 6 km n. of Oliver on Hwy. 97. Canoeing, kayaking.	51	•	•	•				•	•						
Inland Lake (F-11) 2,763 hectares 12 km n. of Powell River on Inland Lake Rd. Canoeing, kayaking; wheelchair accessible trail. *(See Powell River p. 148)*	52	•	•	•	•	•		•	•	•	•				
Jedediah Island Marine (F-10) 243 hectares between Lasqueti and Texada islands in the Sabine Channel of the Strait of Georgia. Accessible only via boat from Lasqueti Island. Kayaking, wilderness camping, winter camping; sandy bays.	53	•						•	•						
Jimsmith Lake (C-11) 14 hectares 5 km e. of Cranbrook off Hwy. 3. Power boats prohibited.	54	•	•	•	•	•		•	•	•					
Juniper Beach (B-8) 260 hectares 19 km e. of Cache Creek on Hwy. 1.	55	•	•	•				•	•	•					
Kalamalka Lake (C-9) 4,209 hectares 8 km s. of Vernon off Hwy. 6. Canoeing, cross-country skiing, horseback riding, kayaking, snowshoeing, water skiing, wildlife viewing. *(See Vernon p. 144)*	56		•	•				•	•	•	•	•	•		
Kentucky Alleyne (C-8) 144 hectares 38 km s. of Merritt on Hwy. 5A.	57	•		•	•	•		•	•	•					
Kettle River (D-9) 179 hectares 5 km n. of Rock Creek on Hwy. 33. Cross-country skiing, snowshoeing.	58	•	•	•				•	•	•					
Kikomun Creek (D-12) 682 hectares 64 km s.e. of Cranbrook via Hwy. 3, then 11 km s. to entrance. Canoeing; playground.	59	•	•	•	•	•		•	•	•					•
Kilby (D-7) 3 hectares 2 km e. of Harrison Mills on Hwy. 7. Historic. Water skiing, wildlife viewing.	60	•	•		•	•		•	•	•					
Kinaskan Lake (C-2) 1,800 hectares on Hwy. 37 100 km s. of Dease Lake.	61	•	•	•	•	•		•							
Kleanza Creek (E-3) 269 hectares 15 km e. of Terrace on Hwy. 16. Snowshoeing.	62	•	•	•						•		•			
Kokanee Creek (C-10) 260 hectares 19 km e. of Nelson on Hwy. 3A. Cross-country skiing, snowshoeing, water skiing, windsurfing; adventure playground.	63	•	•	•	•	•		•	•	•			•	•	
Kokanee Glacier (C-10) 32,035 hectares 19 km n.e. of Nelson on Hwy. 3A. Back- and cross-country skiing, snowshoeing. No pets allowed.	64	•	•	•				•				•		•	
Kootenay Lake (Davis Creek/Lost Ledge) (C-11) 343 hectares n. of Kaslo on Hwy. 31. Water skiing, windsurfing.	65	•	•		•	•		•	•	•					
Lac La Hache (G-5) 24 hectares 13 km n. of Lac la Hache on Hwy. 97. Water skiing; adventure playground	66	•	•	•				•	•	•					
Lac Le Jeune (B-8) 213 hectares 37 km s. of Kamloops off Hwy. 5. Nature programs. Cross-country skiing, ice skating, snowshoeing; canoe and paddleboat rental, playground.	67	•	•	•	•	•	•	•	•	•		•	•		
Lakelse Lake (E-2) 354 hectares 20 km s. of Terrace on Hwy. 37. Canoeing, water skiing, windsurfing.	68	•	•	•				•	•	•			•		
Liard River Hot Springs (B-4) 1,082 hectares at Liard River at Km-post 765 on Hwy. 97 (Alaska Hwy.). Winter camping; playground.	69	•	•	•					•	•			•		
Little Andrews Bay (E-3) 45 hectares 95 km s. of Houston on Oosta Lake.	70	•			•	•									
Little Qualicum Falls (F-10) 440 hectares 19 km w. of Parksville off Hwy. 4. Canoeing, kayaking, scuba diving, water skiing, windsurfing; adventure playground.	71	•	•	•				•	•	•					
Lockhart Beach (C-11) 3 hectares 40 km n. of Creston on Hwy. 3A.	72	•	•	•	•			•	•	•					

RECREATION AREAS

	MAP LOCATION	CAMPING	PICNICKING	HIKING TRAILS	BOATING	BOAT RAMP	BOAT RENTAL	FISHING	SWIMMING	PETS ON LEASH	BICYCLE TRAILS	WINTER SPORTS	VISITOR CENTER	LODGE/CABINS	FOOD SERVICE
Loveland Bay (E-10) 30 hectares 16 km w. of Campbell River off Hwy. 28. Water skiing, windsurfing.	73	•		•		•		•	•	•					
Mabel Lake (B-9) 187 hectares 60 km n.e. of Vernon via an access road off Hwy. 6.	74	•	•	•	•	•		•	•	•					
Marble Canyon (B-7) 355 hectares 40 km n.w. of Cache Creek off Hwy. 99. Rock climbing, scuba diving.	75	•	•	•				•	•	•					
Martha Creek (A-10) 71 hectares 20 km n. of Revelstoke on Hwy. 23. Canoeing, kayaking.	76	•	•		•	•		•	•	•					
McConnell Lake (B-8) 102 hectares 35 km s. of Kamloops off Hwy. 5. Canoeing, cross-country skiing, ice fishing, kayaking, snowshoeing.	77		•	•	•			•	•	•			•		
Meziadin Lake (D-2) 335 hectares 50 km e. of Stewart off Hwy. 37.	78	•	•		•	•		•	•	•					
Miracle Beach (E-10) 137 hectares 22 km n. of Courtenay off Hwy. 19. Winter camping.	79	•	•	•				•	•	•					•
Moberly Lake (D-5) 104 hectares 25 km n.w. of Chetwynd on Hwy. 29. Water skiing, windsurfing; playground.	80	•	•		•	•		•	•	•					
Monck (C-8) 92 hectares 22 km n. of Merritt off Hwy. 5A. Water skiing, windsurfing; playground.	81	•	•	•	•	•		•	•	•			•		
Montague Harbour Marine (H-10) 97 hectares on Galiano Island via car ferry. Indian middens.	82	•	•	•	•	•		•	•						
Morton Lake (E-10) 74 hectares 27 km n.w. of Campbell River on Hwy. 19. Winter camping.	83	•	•	•	•	•		•	•	•					
Mount Fernie (C-12) 259 hectares 3 km s. of Fernie on Hwy. 3.	84	•	•	•				•		•					
Mount Robson (F-6) 224,866 hectares bordering Jasper National Park of Canada on Hwy. 16. Rock climbing, spelunking, winter camping; horse rental, playground. (See Valemount p. 157)	85	•	•	•	•			•	•	•		•	•	•	
Mount Seymour (H-12) 3,508 hectares 24 km n.e. of North Vancouver off Hwy. 1. Cross-country skiing, horseback riding, winter camping. (See North Vancouver p. 183)	86	•	•	•				•	•	•		•		•	•
Moyie Lake (C-11) 91 hectares 20 km s. of Cranbrook on Hwy. 3. Canoeing, ice fishing, kayaking, windsurfing; playground.	87	•	•	•	•	•		•	•	•					
Muncho Lake (B-4) 86,079 hectares on Hwy. 97 at Muncho Lake at Km-post 681 of the Alaska Hwy. Canoeing, kayaking, scuba diving, water skiing.	88	•	•	•	•	•		•	•	•				•	
Naikoon (E-1) 69,166 hectares on n. tip of Graham Island in the Queen Charlotte Islands.	89	•	•	•	•	•		•	•	•					
Nairn Falls (F-12) 170 hectares 32 km n. of Whistler on Hwy. 99. Wildlife viewing.	90	•	•	•				•		•					
Nancy Greene (D-10) 203 hectares 29 km n.w. of Rossland via Hwy. 3B. Cross-country skiing.	91	•	•	•				•	•	•		•			
Newcastle Island Marine (G-10) 336 hectares e. of Nanaimo via foot passenger ferry. (See Nanaimo p. 131)	92	•	•	•				•	•	•					•
Nisga'a Memorial Lava Bed (D-2) 17,683 hectares 100 km n. of Terrace on Nisga'a Hwy. (first 70 km is paved). (See Terrace p. 156)	93	•	•	•	•	•		•	•	•			•		
Niskonlith Lake (B-9) 238 hectares 8 km n.w. of Chase off Hwy. 1. Cross-country skiing, ice fishing, scuba diving, snowshoeing, windsurfing.	94	•			•	•		•	•	•		•			
Norbury Lake (C-12) 97 hectares 16 km s. of jct. hwys. 93 and 95 at Fort Steele.	95	•	•	•	•			•	•	•					
North Thompson River (A-8) 126 hectares 5 km s. of Clearwater off Hwy. 5. Playground.	96	•	•	•				•	•	•					
Okanagan Lake (C-8) 98 hectares 11 km n. of Summerland off Hwy. 97. Water skiing, windsurfing; playground.	97	•	•	•	•	•		•	•	•					•
Okanagan Mountain (C-9) 11,038 hectares 25 km n. of Penticton off Hwy. 97. Canoeing, horseback riding, hunting, kayaking, water skiing.	98	•	•	•				•	•	•				•	

RECREATION AREAS

	MAP LOCATION	CAMPING	PICNICKING	HIKING TRAILS	BOATING	BOAT RAMP	BOAT RENTAL	FISHING	SWIMMING	PETS ON LEASH	BICYCLE TRAILS	WINTER SPORTS	VISITOR CENTER	LODGE/CABINS	FOOD SERVICE
One Island Lake (E-6) 59 hectares 30 km s. of Tupper off Hwy. 2. Canoeing, kayaking, scuba diving, water skiing, windsurfing; playground.	99	•	•		•	•		•	•	•					
Otter Lake (C-8) 51 hectares on Otter Lake, 33 km w. of Princeton off Hwy. 5A. Ice fishing, water skiing.	100	•	•	•	•	•		•	•	•			•		
Paarens Beach (E-4) 43 hectares 11 km s.w. of Fort St. James off Hwy. 27. Water skiing, windsurfing; playground.	101	•	•		•	•		•	•	•					
Paul Lake (B-8) 670 hectares 5 km n. of Kamloops off Hwy. 5. Cross-country skiing, snowshoeing; paddleboat rentals.	102	•	•	•	•	•	•	•	•	•		•			
Pirates Cove Marine (G-10) 31 hectares 16 km s.e. of Nanaimo on DeCourcy Island via boat.	103	•	•	•	•			•	•	•					
Plumper Cove Marine (G-11) 66 hectares on Keats Island. Boat and ferry access only. Winter camping.	104	•	•	•	•			•	•	•	•	•			
Porpoise Bay (G-11) 61 hectares 4 km n. of Sechelt on East Porpoise Bay Rd. Playground.	105	•	•	•	•			•	•	•					
Porteau Cove (G-11) 50 hectares 38 km n. of Vancouver on Hwy. 99. Scuba diving, windsurfing, winter camping.	106	•	•		•	•		•	•	•					
Premier Lake (C-12) 662 hectares 12 km s. of Skookumchuck via Hwy. 95. Hunting, winter camping; playground.	107	•	•	•	•	•		•	•	•					
Prudhomme Lake (E-2) 7 hectares 16 km e. of Prince Rupert on Hwy. 16.	108	•			•			•	•	•					
Purden Lake (F-5) 2,521 hectares 64 km e. of Prince George off Hwy. 16. Hunting, water skiing, windsurfing; playground.	109	•	•	•	•	•		•	•	•					
Rathtrevor Beach (G-10) 347 hectares 3 km s. of Parksville on Hwy. 19. Nature programs. Windsurfing, winter camping; playground.	110	•	•	•				•	•	•					
Rebecca Spit Marine (E-10) 177 hectares on Quadra Island via ferry from Campbell River, then 5 km e. on Heriot Bay Rd. Scuba diving, windsurfing.	111		•	•	•	•		•	•	•					
Red Bluff (E-3) 148 hectares 45 km n. of Topley via Hwy. 118.	112	•	•	•	•	•		•	•	•					
Roberts Creek (G-11) 40 hectares 9 km s. of Sechelt on Hwy. 101.	113	•	•					•	•	•					
Rolley Lake (H-12) 115 hectares 23 km n.w. of Mission off Hwy. 7.	114	•	•	•				•	•	•					
Ruckle (H-10) 486 hectares at Beaver Point on Salt Spring Island via ferry from Swartz Bay. Scuba diving, wildlife viewing, windsurfing, winter camping. (See Salt Spring Island p. 123)	115	•	•	•	•			•		•					
Saltery Bay (F-11) 69 hectares 1 km n. of Saltery Bay ferry landing on Hwy. 101. Scuba diving.	116	•	•	•	•			•	•	•					
Sasquatch (D-7) 1,217 hectares 6.4 km n. of Harrison Hot Springs via an access road off Hwy. 7. Canoeing, water skiing, windsurfing; playground.	117	•	•	•	•	•		•	•	•					
Schoen Lake (H-3) 8,430 hectares 45 km s. of Sayward, 38 km s. of Hwy. 19. Back-country skiing, snowshoeing.	118	•	•	•	•			•	•	•			•		
Seeley Lake (D-3) 24 hectares 10 km w. of Hazelton on Hwy. 16.	119	•	•	•	•			•	•	•					
Shuswap Lake (B-9) 149 hectares 19 km n. of Squilax. Nature programs. Canoeing, cross-country skiing, kayaking, snorkeling, snowshoeing, water skiing, windsurfing; playground.	120	•	•	•	•	•	•	•	•	•	•	•	•		
Silver Beach (A-9) 130 hectares at n. end of Shuswap Lake at Seymour Arm.	121	•		•	•	•		•	•	•					
Skagit Valley (D-8) 27,948 hectares 3 km w. of Hope via Hwy. 1, then 37 km s. on entrance portal via Silver Skagit Rd. Interpretive programs. Hunting; horse trails, playground.	122	•	•	•				•	•	•					
Skihist (B-7) 33 hectares 6 km e. of Lytton on Hwy. 1.	123	•	•	•				•		•	•				
Smelt Bay (E-11) 16 hectares on s.w. side of Cortes Island via ferry from Campbell River. Canoeing, kayaking.	124	•	•		•	•		•	•	•					
Sowchea Bay (E-4) 13 hectares on Stuart Lake, 20 km w. of Fort St. James off Hwy. 27.	125	•			•	•		•	•	•					

RECREATION AREAS

	MAP LOCATION	CAMPING	PICNICKING	HIKING TRAILS	BOATING	BOAT RAMP	BOAT RENTAL	FISHING	SWIMMING	PETS ON LEASH	BICYCLE TRAILS	WINTER SPORTS	VISITOR CENTER	LODGE/CABINS	FOOD SERVICE
Sproat Lake (F-9) 43 hectares 13 km n.w. of Port Alberni on Sproat Lake Rd. Water skiing. Indian carvings.	126	•	•	•	•	•		•	•	•					
Stamp River (F-10) 327 hectares 14 km w. of Port Alberni on Stamp River Rd. Winter camping.	127	•		•				•		•					
Stone Mountain (B-4) 25,690 hectares 140 km w. of Fort Nelson on Hwy. 97. Canoeing, horseback riding, kayaking.	128	•	•	•	•	•		•		•			•		
Strathcona (E-9) 245,807 hectares 48 km w. of Campbell River via Hwy. 28. Cross-country skiing, mountain biking, rock climbing, snowshoeing, water skiing, windsurfing. Snowmobiles prohibited.	129	•	•	•	•	•		•	•	•		•		•	
Swan Lake (D-6) 65 hectares at Tupper, 35 km s.e. of Dawson Creek via Hwy. 2. Canoeing, kayaking, scuba diving, water skiing, windsurfing; playground.	130	•	•	•	•	•		•	•	•					
Syringa (C-10) 4,417 hectares 19 km n.w. of Castlegar off Hwy. 3. Canoeing, kayaking, water skiing, windsurfing; playground.	131	•	•	•	•	•		•	•	•					
Taylor Arm (F-10) 71 hectares 23 km n.w. of Port Alberni on Hwy. 4. Winter camping.	132	•	•	•	•	•		•	•	•					
Ten Mile Lake (F-5) 260 hectares 12 km n. of Quesnel on Hwy. 97. Cross-country and water skiing.	133	•	•	•	•	•		•	•	•					
Top of the World (C-12) 8,790 hectares 48 km n.e. of Kimberley off Hwy. 93. Cross-country skiing, mountain biking, snowshoeing, winter camping; horse trails.	134	•		•				•		•	•	•	•		•
Tudyah Lake (E-4) 56 hectares 9 km n. of McLeod Lake on Hwy. 97. Ice fishing.	135	•	•	•				•	•	•					
Tweedsmuir South (F-3) 506,000 hectares 365 km n.w. of Williams Lake on Hwy. 20. Canoeing circuit, cross-country and downhill skiing.	136	•		•	•	•		•	•	•		•	•		
Tyhee Lake (E-3) 33 hectares 10 km e. of Smithers off Hwy. 16. Canoeing, cross-country skiing, ice skating, kayaking.	137	•	•	•				•	•	•		•			
Vaseux Lake (C-9) 12 hectares 25 km s. of Penticton on Hwy. 97. Canoeing, ice skating, kayaking.	138	•	•	•	•			•		•			•		
Wasa Lake (C-11) 144 hectares 21 km n. of Fort Steele off Hwy. 93/95. Canoeing, water skiing, windsurfing; playground.	139	•	•	•	•	•		•	•	•	•				
Wells Gray (G-6) 540,000 hectares 67 km n. of Clearwater via an access road off Hwy. 5. Interpretive programs. Canoeing, cross-country skiing, horseback riding, kayaking, snowshoeing; horse rental. *(See Clearwater p. 115)*	140	•	•	•	•	•	•	•	•	•		•	•	•	•
West Lake (F-5) 256 hectares 22 km s.w. of Prince George off Hwy. 16. Cross-country skiing, water skiing, windsurfing.	141		•	•	•	•		•	•	•					
Whiskers Point (E-5) 116 hectares 130 km n. of Prince George off Hwy. 97. Canoeing, kayaking, water skiing, windsurfing; nature trail, playground.	142	•	•	•	•	•		•	•	•					
Whiteswan Lake (C-12) 1,994 hectares 22 km e. of Canal Flats off Hwy. 93/95. Canoeing, kayaking.	143	•	•	•	•	•		•	•	•					
Wistaria (E-3) 40 hectares 60 km w. of Hwy. 35, s.w. of Burns Lake on Ootsa Lake.	144		•		•	•		•		•					
Yahk (D-12) 9 hectares on Hwy. 3/93 at Yahk.	145	•	•					•		•					
Yard Creek (B-9) 175 hectares 15 km e. of Sicamous on Hwy. 1.	146	•	•	•				•	•	•					
OTHER															
Berman Lake (F-4) 38 hectares 45 km w. of Prince George. Canoeing.	147		•	•					•	•					
Canyon Hot Springs (A-10) Hot mineral springs 35 km e. of Revelstoke on Hwy. 1. *(See Revelstoke p. 152)*	148	•	•	•					•	•				•	•
Creston Valley Wildlife Management Area (D-11) 7,000 hectares 13 km w. of Creston on Hwy. 3. Bird-watching, hunting. *(See Creston p. 117)*	149		•	•				•				•	•	•	
Descanso Bay Regional Park (G-10) 16 hectares 1 km e. of Nanaimo on Gabriola Island via ferry. Kayaking.	150	•	•	•	•			•	•	•					

RECREATION AREAS

	MAP LOCATION	CAMPING	PICNICKING	HIKING TRAILS	BOATING	BOAT RAMP	BOAT RENTAL	FISHING	SWIMMING	PETS ON LEASH	BICYCLE TRAILS	WINTER SPORTS	VISITOR CENTER	LODGE/CABINS	FOOD SERVICE
Fairmont Hot Springs (B-12) Hot mineral springs on Hwy. 95 in Fairmont Hot Springs. Downhill skiing, fly fishing, ice fishing, rock climbing, snowshoeing, wildlife viewing, winter camping; horse rental. *(See place listing p. 118)*	151	•	•	•				•	•	•		•		•	•
Ferry Island (E-2) 61 hectares 1 km e. of Terrace off Hwy. 16. Cross-country skiing.	152	•	•	•	•	•	•	•	•	•			•	•	
Giscome Portage (E-5) 160 hectares 40 km n. of Prince George. Historic. Cross-country skiing, snowshoeing.	153			•					•	•		•			
Harold Mann (E-4) 13 hectares 50 km n.e. of Prince George. Canoeing; nature trail.	154			•				•	•	•					
Harrison Hot Springs (C-7) Hot mineral springs on Harrison Lake, 5 km n. of Hwy. 7 on Hwy. 9. Canoeing, golf, hunting, rock hunting; horse rental. *(See place listing p. 124)*	155	•	•	•	•	•	•	•	•	•	•	•	•	•	•
Kanaka Creek (H-12) 400 hectares 2 km e. of Haney. Canoeing; fish hatchery, horse trails. *(See Maple Ridge p. 180)*	156		•	•				•		•					
Kawkawa Lake (C-7) 7 hectares 5 km e. of Hope off Hwy. 5. Jet skiing, tubing.	157	•	•		•	•	•	•	•	•					
Nakusp Hot Springs (B-10) Hot mineral springs 12 km n. of Nakusp on Nakusp Hot Springs Rd. Cross-country skiing, kayaking, mountain biking, snowmobiling. *(See Nakusp p. 131)*	158	•	•	•				•	•	•		•	•	•	•
Ness Lake (E-4) 14 hectares 35 km n.w. of Prince George. Canoeing, cross-country skiing, ice fishing.	159	•	•	•	•			•	•	•					
Radium Hot Springs (B-12) Hot mineral springs near the w. entrance of Kootenay National Park of Canada. Hunting, skiing; horse rental. *(See place listing p. 152 and Kootenay National Park of Canada p. 129)*	160	•	•	•				•	•	•		•	•	•	•
Whytecliff Park (G-11) 16 hectares near Horseshoe Bay in West Vancouver. Scuba diving; playground.	161		•	•				•	•	•					•
Wilkins Park (F-5) 57 hectares 15 km w. of Prince George. Cross-country skiing; nature trail.	162	•	•	•	•					•		•		•	

British Columbia Temperature Averages Maximum/Minimum (Celsius)

From the records of The Weather Channel Interactive, Inc.

	JAN	FEB	MAR	APR	MAY	JUNE	JULY	AUG	SEPT	OCT	NOV	DEC
Fort St. John	-11/-19	-7/-16	-1/-11	8/-2	15/3	19/8	21/10	20/9	14/4	8/-1	-3/-11	-9/-18
Kamloops	-2/-9	3/-5	10/-2	16/2	21/7	25/11	28/13	28/13	22/8	14/3	5/-2	0/-7
Prince George	-6/-14	-1/-11	4/-6	11/-2	16/3	19/6	22/8	21/7	16/3	9/-1	1/-7	-5/-13
Prince Rupert	4/-3	6/-1	7/0	9/1	12/4	14/7	16/9	16/10	15/7	11/4	7/1	4/-2
Vancouver	6/0	8/1	9/2	12/4	16/8	19/11	22/12	22/13	18/10	13/6	9/3	6/1
Victoria	6/0	8/1	10/2	13/3	16/6	19/9	22/11	22/11	19/8	14/5	9/2	7/1

Points of Interest

108 MILE HOUSE (A-7)

South Cariboo Visitor Info Centre: 422 Hwy. 97, Box 340, 100 Mile House, BC, Canada V0K 2E0. **Phone:** (250) 395-5353 or (877) 511-5353.

108 MILE HOUSE HERITAGE SITE is at 4690 Cariboo Tr. The site comprises 8 historical buildings depicting the famous mile houses, which were established as a stopover for weary travelers. With the discovery of gold in 1858 and the influx of miners increasing, the houses served a need by providing meals or a place to sleep. A 1908 log barn and 1890 church also are on-site. **Time:** Allow 30 minutes minimum. **Hours:** Daily 10-5, Victoria Day-Labour Day weekend. **Cost:** Donations. **Phone:** (250) 791-5288 or (250) 791-1971.

ABBOTSFORD (H-11)
pop. 115,463, elev. 58 m/190′

Abbotsford is the regional shopping center as well as the center of trade and industry for the fruit, livestock, poultry and dairy farms of the surrounding Fraser Valley. Several area industries and farms offer tours, including Clayburn Industries Ltd., at Railway and Pine streets, which produces refractory products. Castle Park Golf and Games Amusement Park, 36165 N. Parallel Rd., provides a range of family entertainment.

The city is also the site of the ✈ Abbotsford International Air Show, held in early August. In addition to more than 2 dozen planes on display, more than 30 planes, both military and civilian, take to the air.

Tourism Abbotsford Visitor Centre: 34561 Delair Rd., Abbotsford, BC, Canada V2S 2E1. **Phone:** (604) 859-1721 or (888) 332-2229.

TRETHEWEY HOUSE HERITAGE SITE ON MILL LAKE is at 2313 Ware St., next to John Mahoney Park. Restored and furnished to its 1925 appearance, this Arts and Crafts-style house features reconstructions of a playhouse and a carriage house as well as period gardens.

Tours: Guided tours are available. **Time:** Allow 30 minutes minimum. **Hours:** House open daily 9-5, Victoria Day-Labour Day; by appointment rest of year. Closed statutory holidays. **Cost:** Donations. **Phone:** (604) 853-0313.

AINSWORTH HOT SPRINGS (C-10)
elev. 538 m/1766′

AINSWORTH HOT SPRINGS RESORT is on Hwy. 31. Overlooking Kootenay Lake, the springs feature a natural, odorless mineral cave pool with an average temperature of 40-44 C (104-111 F), and a main pool averaging 35 C (97 F). The cold plunge pool, fed by a natural spring, has an average temperature of 4 C (40 F). Towels can be rented. **Hours:** Daily 10-9. Last admission 30 minutes before closing. **Cost:** $9; $8 (ages 13-17 and 65+); $7 (ages 3-12). **Phone:** (250) 229-4212 or (800) 668-1171. ⓣ

ALDERGROVE—see Vancouver p. 178.

ALERT BAY (G-3) pop. 556, elev. 15 m/49′

On crescent-shaped Cormorant Island off Vancouver Island's northeast coast, Alert Bay is a fishing village reached by ferry from Port McNeill (see place listing p. 148). The influence of native cultures is evident in the many totem poles, including a memorial pole for totem carver Chief Mungo Martin.

Christ Church on Front Street is an 1881 cedar church with stained-glass windows that reflect the blending of Indian and European cultures; phone the Travel InfoCentre for information.

Alert Bay Travel InfoCentre: 116 Fir St., Bag Service 2800, Alert Bay, BC, Canada V0N 1A0. **Phone:** (250) 974-5024.

ALERT BAY PUBLIC LIBRARY AND MUSEUM is at 118 Fir St. This small museum houses Kwakwaka'wakw artifacts and items depicting local history. Its archives include Alert Bay newspapers and more than 6,000 photographs. **Time:** Allow 30 minutes minimum. **Hours:** Mon.-Sat. 1-4, July-Aug.; Mon., Wed. and Fri.-Sat. 1-4, rest of year. Closed major holidays. **Cost:** Donations. **Phone:** (250) 974-5721.

TOTEM POLE is near the corner of Park and Wood sts. Erected in 1973, the 53-metre (173-ft.) pole is considered to be the world's tallest. It features 22 figures, including a sun at the top. Binoculars are recommended for viewing. The totem pole stands near the 'Namgis Big House, a Kwakwaka'wakw ceremonial center not open to the public. **Time:** Allow 30 minutes minimum. **Hours:** Daily dawn-dusk. **Cost:** Free.

U'MISTA CULTURAL CENTRE & MUSEUM is 2 km (1.2 mi.) w. of the ferry on Front St. The collection includes elaborately carved masks, traditional and historical carvings, woven cedar pieces, ceremonial regalia, paintings and other artifacts from Indian potlatches—the gift-giving ceremonies that mark such important occasions as birth, marriage and death. There also are films and small galleries with short-term exhibits. Traditional dancing may be seen July through August.

Hours: Daily 9-5, Victoria Day-Sept. 30; Tues.-Sat. 9-5, rest of year. Traditional dancing Thurs.-Sat. at 1:15, July-Aug. **Cost:** $8; $7 (ages 65+ and students with ID); $1 (ages 0-11). Admission to dances in ceremonial house $15. **Phone:** (250) 974-5403 or (800) 690-8222.

ASHCROFT (B-7)
pop. 1,664, elev. 305 m/1,000'

Ashcroft Manor, a roadside house on Cariboo Waggon Road, was named for the English home of its settlers, Clement and Henry Cornwall. The Cornwalls established themselves as cattlemen in 1862 and lived the pioneer life in the style of gentlemen, practicing such rituals as afternoon tea and riding to hounds through sagebrush and scrub in pursuit of coyotes. The manor is south of town on Hwy. 1.

ASHCROFT MUSEUM is at 404 Brink St. Exhibits recount the history of the southern Cariboo, the Indian tribes that first settled Ashcroft. Artifacts and photographs are displayed in the windows of old shops, churches and houses along a board sidewalk, depicting life as it was in Ashcroft's glory days between the first settlement in 1884 and the great fire in 1916. A re-creation of the Hat Creek Mine also is displayed. **Hours:** Daily 9-5, June 15-Aug. 31; Thurs.-Mon. 9-5, Apr. 15-June 14 and Sept.-Oct. Closed major holidays. **Cost:** Donations. **Phone:** (250) 453-9232.

▼ BARKERVILLE HISTORIC TOWN (F-5)

Barkerville is approximately 80 kilometres (50 mi.) east of Quesnel via Hwy. 26. The restored 1870s gold rush town once had the largest population north of San Francisco and west of Chicago. In those days when more than $50 million of gold—at $16 per ounce—had been mined from the area, soap cost $1 a bar and a dance with a hurdy-gurdy girl cost $1 a whirl.

The town was named for Billy Barker, a Cornish miner who first found gold in large quantities in the early 1860s. Barkerville became a virtual ghost town a few years later when the gold ran out.

The Barkerville Hotel, St. Saviours Church, the Mason and Daly General Store and the Wake Up Jake Cafe are just a few of the 125 original or reconstructed buildings in the town; many are manned by attendants in period dress. Board sidewalks and dirt streets help preserve the essence of the original site.

Theatre Royale presents period melodrama, dance and music Victoria Day through September 30. Treasure seekers can pan for gold at Eldorado Mine. A visitor center presents videos and exhibits about the history of Barkerville. Guided town, Chinatown and cemetery tours as well as living-history programs are offered.

The townsite is open daily 8-8. Full visitor services operate daily, mid-May through Sept. 27. Pets are not permitted. Admission mid-May through Sept. 27, $13.33; $12.14 (ages 65+); $8.10 (ages 13-18); $4.05 (ages 6-12); $32.25 (family). Free rest of year. Phone (250) 994-3332 or (888) 994-3332.

BELLA COOLA (F-2) pop. 135, elev. 590'

BELLA COOLA VALLEY MUSEUM is just e. of jct. MacKenzie Hwy. and Bentinck Ave. at 269 Hwy. 20. The museum, in an 1892 heritage building, contains artifacts and interpretive exhibits about the Bella Coola Valley from the late 18th century, when Europeans first discovered the area's aboriginal people, to the mid-20th century. **Tours:** Guided tours are available. **Time:** Allow 30 minutes minimum. **Hours:** Daily 9-noon and 1-5, early June-early Sept. **Cost:** $2.50; $2 (students with ID). **Phone:** (250) 799-5767.

BOSTON BAR (C-7)
pop. 188, elev. 309 m/1,013'

Boston Bar, which began as a gold mining town, was named for a Dutchman who came from Boston to prospect in the 1860s. Because Boston was the home port to many of the ships bringing prospectors, local Indians called the newcomers Boston men. Boston Bar is a logging and trade center, with the Canadian National Railway passing through town. The Canadian Pacific Railway parallels the National on the other side of Fraser River Canyon and passes through the village of North Bend.

Boston Bar is the access point for the Nahatlach Valley, which features the Nahatlach River and a chain of lakes. Recreation includes camping, fishing and white-water rafting.

▼ HELL'S GATE AIRTRAM is 11 km (7 mi.) s. on Hwy. 1 to 43111 Trans-Canada Hwy. in Fraser River Canyon. The 25-passenger gondola descends 153 metres (502 ft.) across the river to the narrowest part of Fraser Canyon and across Hell's Gate Fishways, where millions of salmon annually swim upstream to their spawning grounds.

Visitors can see eight fishways from observation decks or a suspension bridge. A film about the life cycle of the salmon is shown at the education center. Simon's Wall is an interactive photo exhibit that pays tribute to the 200th anniversary of explorer Simon Fraser's journey. Panning for gold is available. **Time:** Allow 1 hour minimum. **Hours:** Daily 10-5, June-Aug.; 10-4, mid-Apr. through May 31 and Sept. 1 to mid-Oct. **Cost:** $17.14; $15.24 (ages 65+ and students with ID); $11.43 (ages 6-18). **Phone:** (604) 867-9277.

RECREATIONAL ACTIVITIES
White-water Rafting

• REO Rafting Adventure Resort is 18 km (11 mi.) n.w. on Hwy. 1 in Fraser Canyon. **Hours:** Nahatlatch River trips operate May-Sept. **Phone:** (604) 461-7238 or (800) 736-7238.

BOSWELL (C-11) elev. 533 m/1,748'

THE GLASS HOUSE is on Hwy. 3A (Southern Trans-Canada Hwy.). This six-room, castlelike house is made of empty 16-ounce embalming fluid bottles.

A funeral director built the house, archway and several terraces on the landscaped lakefront grounds. **Time:** Allow 30 minutes minimum. **Hours:** Daily 8-8, July-Aug.; 9-5, May-June and Sept. 1 to mid-Oct. **Cost:** $8; $6 (ages 13-19); $5 (ages 5-12). **Phone:** (250) 223-8372.

BRACKENDALE (G-12)

GLACIER AIR TOURS is at 46001 Government Rd. at Squamish Municipal Airport. Helicopter and airplane sightseeing flights and glacier-landing flights are offered. The latter may include dining on a glacier. **Hours:** Daily dawn-dusk (departure times vary). Closed Jan. 1 and Dec. 25-26. **Cost:** Sightseeing flights start at $79. Reservations are recommended. **Phone:** (604) 898-9016, or (800) 265-0088 within Canada.

RECREATIONAL ACTIVITIES
White-water Rafting

• **Sunwolf Outdoor Centre** is at 70002 Squamish Valley Rd. Other activities are available. **Hours:** Daily 8-8, May-Sept. (weather permitting). **Phone:** (604) 898-1537 or (877) 806-8046.

BRENTWOOD BAY —see Victoria p. 200.

BRIDAL FALLS (I-12) elev. 61 m/200'

BRIDAL FALLS WATER PARK is at jct. hwys. 1 and 9 on Bridal Falls Rd. The park features 10 waterslides, a giant hot pool, miniature golf course, river ride, and picnic and barbecue facilities. **Time:** Allow 2 hours minimum. **Hours:** Daily 10-7, mid-June through Labour Day; Sat.-Sun. 10-6, Victoria Day to mid-June. Phone ahead to confirm schedule. **Cost:** $17; free (ages 0-3). Admission may vary; phone ahead. **Phone:** (604) 794-7455, or (888) 883-8852 to verify schedule or rates. ⑪

DINOTOWN is off Hwy. 1 exit 135, following signs. Geared for ages 2-12, this 5-hectare (12-acre) amusement park features live shows, a train, paddleboats, bumper cars, miniature golf, a parade and a water park.

Time: Allow 3 hours minimum. **Hours:** Mon.-Fri. 10-5, Sat.-Sun. 10-7, July-Aug.; Mon.-Fri. 10-5, day after Father's Day-Labour Day; Sat.-Sun. 10-5, Mother's Day weekend-Father's Day. **Cost:** $16; free (ages 0-2). **Phone:** (604) 794-7410 or (604) 794-3733. ⑪ 🏞

BRITANNIA BEACH (G-11) elev. 6 m/20'

From 1930 to 1935 the Britannia Mine at Britannia Beach was the largest producer of copper in the British Empire. No longer in operation, the mine is now part of the British Columbia Museum of Mining.

BRITISH COLUMBIA MUSEUM OF MINING is on Hwy. 99. An underground mine tunnel ride is a highlight of the museum, which chronicles mining history through hands-on demonstrations and exhibits. On site is a 1921 concentrator mill and a 235-ton super mine truck. Gold panning is included with admission.

Note: The tunnel temperature is a constant 12 C (54 F); warm clothing and comfortable walking shoes are recommended. Hard hats are provided. **Time:** Allow 1 hour, 30 minutes minimum. **Hours:** Daily 9-4:30, Feb. 12-Oct. 14; Mon.-Fri. 9-4:30, rest of year. **Cost:** $18.50; $13.95 (ages 13-18 and 65+); $11.95 (ages 6-12); $55 (family, two adults and three children). **Phone:** (604) 896-2233 or (800) 896-4044.

BURNABY —see Vancouver p. 178.

CACHE CREEK (B-7)
pop. 1,037, elev. 450 m/1,500'

◆ GEM **HISTORIC HAT CREEK RANCH** is 11 km (7 mi.) n. on Hwy. 97 at jct. hwys. 97 and 99. The 130-hectare (320-acre) ranch, on one of the few sections of the Cariboo Waggon Road still accessible to the public, consists of more than 20 historic buildings constructed 1863-1915 when the ranch served as a roadhouse for the horse-drawn stagecoaches and freight wagons of the B.C. Express line (known as the B.X.).

Docents in period costumes conduct guided tours of the 1860s roadhouse, and visitors can explore a heritage apple orchard, a Shuswap village, a blacksmith shop and a collection of pioneer agricultural machinery. Visitors also can enjoy stagecoach rides and try their hand at gold panning.

Hours: Daily 9-6, July-Aug.; 9-5, May-June and in Sept. **Cost:** $9; $8 (ages 55+); $6 (ages 6-11); $20 (family, two adults and three children). Camping $10-$15 per night. **Phone:** (250) 457-9722 or (800) 782-0922. ⑪ 🏞

CAMPBELL RIVER (E-10)
pop. 28,456, elev. 18 m/59'

An important lumber, mining and commercial fishing center, Campbell River is near a noted Vancouver Island timber stand. The Elk Falls Pulp and Paper Mill offers tours in the summer. Campbell River is headquarters of the Tyee Club, whose members must catch a salmon of 14 kilograms (30 lbs.) or more while fishing from a rowboat in the raging waters of Discovery Passage.

Provincial parks preserve the area's natural beauty, typified by waterfalls and mountainous wilderness. At Elk Falls Provincial Park the Campbell River drops 27 metres (90 ft.) into a deep canyon. Strathcona Provincial Park contains Mount Golden Hinde, at 2,200 metres (7,218 ft.) the highest mountain on Vancouver Island, and 440-metre (1,445-ft.) Della Falls, the highest waterfall in Canada. Scuba diving is popular during the winter when the waters are particularly clear. *See Recreation Chart and the AAA/CAA Western Canada & Alaska CampBook.*

The 183-metre-long (600-ft.) Campbell River Fishing Pier, 655 Island Hwy., is available for fishing, strolling or watching the cruise ships pass through the Strait of Georgia.

Campbell River Visitor Centre: 1235 Shoppers Row, Campbell River, BC, Canada V9W 2C7. **Phone:** (250) 830-0411 or (877) 286-5705.

MUSEUM AT CAMPBELL RIVER is at 470 Island Hwy. with an entrance off 5th Ave. The museum displays artifacts crafted by First Nations peoples of northern Vancouver Island. Exhibits also follow the island's pioneer and industrial history, including vintage logging and fishing equipment and replicas of a pioneer cabin and a float house. The outdoor historical interpretation park includes indigenous plant gardens, a cod fishing boat and a logging steam donkey.

Time: Allow 1 hour minimum. **Hours:** Daily 10-5, mid-May through Sept. 30; Tues.-Sun. noon-5, rest of year. Closed Jan 1, Good Friday and Dec. 25. **Cost:** $6; $4 (students with ID); free (ages 0-5); $15 (family). **Phone:** (250) 287-3103.

QUINSAM RIVER SALMON HATCHERY is .5 km (.3 mi.) w. on Hwy. 28, then 2.4 km (1.5 mi.) s. on Quinsam Rd. to 4217 Argonaut Rd. The salmon enhancement project produces pink, coho and chinook salmon and steelhead trout. A display room chronicles the life cycle of a salmon. Facilities include various hatchery sensing containers. Adult salmon viewing is best from mid-September to mid-November. Also available are picnic sites and a network of hiking trails along the river. **Hours:** Daily 8-4; closed Jan. 1 and Dec. 25-26. **Cost:** Free. **Phone:** (250) 287-9564.

CASTLEGAR (D-10)
pop. 7,002, elev. 494 m/1,620′

At the junction of hwys. 3 and 3A, Castlegar is considered the crossroads of the Kootenays. Just north is the 51-metre-high (167-ft.) Hugh Keenleyside Dam. The upper and lower Arrow Lakes, created by the dam, offer popular summer recreation areas including Arrow Lakes Provincial Park (Shelter Bay) and Syringa Provincial Park *(see Recreation Chart and the AAA/CAA Western Canada & Alaska CampBook).*

Castlegar Chamber of Commerce: 1995 Sixth Ave., Castlegar, BC, Canada V1N 4B7. **Phone:** (250) 365-6313.

DOUKHOBOR DISCOVERY CENTRE is opposite the airport just off Hwy. 3A to 112 Heritage Way. The site is a ten-building replica of the communal settlement of the Doukhobors, a pacifist group of Russian immigrants who settled in the area 1908-13. There were about 90 such villages. Highlights include thousands of artifacts reflecting the settlement and an art gallery depicting Doukhobor life.

Spinning and weaving demonstrations occur July through September. **Time:** Allow 30 minutes minimum. **Hours:** Daily 10-5, May-Sept. **Cost:** $8; $5 (students with ID); free (ages 0-5). Cash only. **Phone:** (250) 365-5327.

KOOTENAY GALLERY OF ART is opposite the airport just off Hwy. 3A at 120 Heritage Way, next to Doukhobor Discovery Centre. Two galleries feature rotating exhibitions of local, national and international origin. Workshops and musical events are held throughout the year.

Time: Allow 30 minutes minimum. **Hours:** Daily 10-5, June-Aug. and in Dec.; Wed.-Sat. 10-5, Sun. noon-4, Mar.-May and Sept.-Nov. Closed Easter and Dec. 25-31. Phone ahead to confirm schedule. **Cost:** $2; $1 (ages 60+ and students with ID); free (ages 0-11). **Phone:** (250) 365-3337.

ZUCKERBERG ISLAND HERITAGE PARK is at 7th Ave. and 9th St. A suspension bridge leads to the island at the confluence of the Columbia and Kootenay rivers. Walking tours offers such sights as an Indian Kekuli or pit house, a cemetery, a log house, a sculpture of a seated woman carved from a tree stump and the Chapel House with its Russian Orthodox onion dome. The Castlegar Station Museum is in a restored 19th-century Canadian Pacific Railway (CPR) station.

Time: Allow 30 minutes minimum. **Hours:** Zuckerberg Island Wed.-Sun. 10-5, May-Sept. Station museum Mon.-Sat. 10-5. Island tours are available year-round. Phone ahead to confirm schedule. **Cost:** $2. **Phone:** (250) 365-6440. 🏮

CHEMAINUS (G-10) pop. 2,937, elev. 6 m/20′

A lumber and manufacturing town, Chemainus added tourism to its economy with the creation of murals. More than 30 professional paintings on the walls of buildings portray the history of the Chemainus Valley. Subjects range from North American Indians to dramatic depictions of the logging industry.

Begun by local artists, the series of murals has attracted artists from around the world. Walking tour maps can be bought at the kiosk in the central parking area. Prearranged guided tours and horse-drawn carriage tours also are available for a fee; phone (250) 246-5055 or (250) 246-0063.

Chemainus Theatre offers dramas, comedies and musical productions; phone (250) 246-9820 or (800) 565-7738.

Chemainus Chamber of Commerce: 9796 Willow St., P.O. Box 575, Chemainus, BC, Canada V0R 1K0. **Phone:** (250) 246-3944.

CHILLIWACK (H-12)
pop. 62,927, elev. 10 m/33′

In the heart of the upper Fraser River Valley, Chilliwack is the center of a prosperous farming and dairy region. The surrounding lakes, rivers, mountains and nearby provincial parks offer such varied recreation as skiing, hiking, fishing, rock hunting and white-water rafting. Scenic views and picnic facilities are available at Chilliwack Lake Provincial Park, 84 kilometres (54 mi.) southeast off Hwy. 1 *(see Recreation Chart),* and Cultus Lake Provincial Park, 11 kilometres (7 mi.) southwest off Hwy. 1 *(see Recreation Chart).*

Tourism Chilliwack Visitor Information Centre: 44150 Luckakuck Way, Chilliwack, BC, Canada V2R 4A7. **Phone:** (604) 858-8121 or (800) 567-9535.

BRIDAL VEIL FALLS PROVINCIAL PARK is 16 km (10 mi.) e. off Hwy. 1 exit 135, following signs. An easy 15-minute hike leads visitors to a lovely view of the area, characterized by valleys and emerald-colored rounded mountains. The main attraction is the falls, Canada's sixth-highest, which cascade 60 metres (197 ft.) over slick rock and create the appearance of a glassy bridal veil. The park is the former site of Popkum, a 1700s village.

Note: In winter, the falls may freeze and cause the base to be slippery as well as allow rock and ice to fall. **Time:** Allow 30 minutes minimum. **Hours:** Daily dawn-dusk. **Cost:** Free. 🅰️

CHILLIWACK MUSEUM is at 45820 Spadina Ave. between Main St. and Yale Rd. Books, pictures, clothing and farming supplies are among the approximately 7,500 objects that tell the story of Chilliwack's history. Housed in the old city hall building, the exhibits focus on life in the area from the late 1800s, when it was settled, to World War II. **Time:** Allow 30 minutes minimum. **Hours:** Mon.-Fri. 9-4:30, Sat. 11-3:30. Closed Jan. 1 and Dec. 25. **Cost:** Donations. **Phone:** (604) 795-5210.

GREAT BLUE HERON NATURE RESERVE is at 5200 Sumas Prairie Rd. This 130-hectare (321-acre) site includes an interpretive center, an observation tower, fish-spawning channels and a self-guiding interpretive walking trail. More than 90 herons build nests here; painted turtles, tailed frogs, beavers, bald eagles and a variety of other birds also dwell at the reserve.

Time: Allow 1 hour minimum. **Hours:** Nature reserve open daily 8-8. Interpretive center open daily 10-4; phone ahead in winter. **Cost:** Donations. **Phone:** (604) 823-6603.

◤GEM◢ **MINTER GARDENS** is 19 km (12 mi.) e. on Hwy. 1 to exit 135 (Hwy. 9) at 52892 Bunker Rd. Covering nearly 11 hectares (27 acres), 11 thematic gardens display seasonal colors and plants from around the world. Highlights include an evergreen living maze, topiary sculptures, a Penjing rock collection and two Victorian-style conservatories.

Time: Allow 1 hour minimum. **Hours:** Daily 9-7, July-Aug.; 9-6, in June; 9-5:30 in May and Sept.; 10-5 in Apr. and Oct. (weather permitting). Phone ahead to confirm schedule. **Cost:** $16; $14 (ages 65+); $9 (ages 13-18); $6 (ages 6-12); $35 (family). **Phone:** (604) 794-7191 or (888) 646-8377. 🆃

CLEARWATER (A-8)

Clearwater gets its name from the clear waters of the nearby Clearwater River. Opportunities for riding, hiking, canoeing, skiing and fishing abound in the surrounding North Thompson Valley.

Wells Gray Provincial Park, north off Hwy. 5, offers a variety of scenery, particularly with regard to water. Scattered throughout its boundaries are five large lakes, two river systems, many streams and waterways and a multitude of waterfalls. Helmcken Falls, which drops 141 metres (465 ft.), is said to be the fourth highest in Canada. At Bailey's Chute Loop in late summer, visitors can view salmon jumping upstream to spawn. Extinct volcanoes and lava beds recall the region's fiery past. *See Recreation Chart and the AAA/CAA Western Canada & Alaska CampBook.*

Clearwater Chamber of Commerce: 425 E. Yellowhead Hwy., P.O. Box 1988, Clearwater, BC, Canada V0E 1N0. **Phone:** (250) 674-2646.

RECREATIONAL ACTIVITIES
White-water Rafting

- **Interior Whitewater Expeditions** is w. of Hwy. 5 at Old N. Thompson Hwy. **Hours:** Daily 8-8, May-Sept. (depending on water level). **Phone:** (250) 674-3727.

CLINTON (A-7) pop. 621, elev. 274 m/898'

During the gold rush of the late 1850s and early 1860s Clinton was the junction of several wagon roads leading to northern goldfields. In 1863 Queen Victoria changed the town's name from Junction to Clinton. Retaining much of its frontier look, Clinton is a supply center for surrounding resorts, fishing camps and ranches. Summer activities include boating, fishing and camping at area lakes, which also attract various wildlife.

The Village of Clinton: 1423 Cariboo Hwy., P.O. Box 309, Clinton, BC, Canada V0K 1K0. **Phone:** (250) 459-2261.

CLINTON MUSEUM is at 1419 Cariboo Hwy. Built in 1892, this building has served as the town's schoolhouse and courthouse. Displays include photographs and pioneer artifacts. **Time:** Allow 30 minutes minimum. **Hours:** Wed.-Sun. 9-7, May-Sept. Phone ahead to confirm schedule. **Cost:** Donations. **Phone:** (250) 459-2442.

COMOX (F-10) pop. 11,172

Comox was founded in the mid-1800s, taking its name from the Salish word *Koumuckthay,* meaning "land of plenty." Once an important port for ships of the Royal Navy, the east coast village became the home of a Royal Air Force base in 1942. CFB Comox maintains search-and-rescue operations, maritime patrols and support of naval and air force defense.

COMOX AIR FORCE MUSEUM is e. on Ryan Rd. following signs to CFB Comox main entrance. Museum displays outline the history of the base and West Coast aviation. Two squadrons continue to fly Cormorant helicopters and Buffalo and Aurora aircraft. Nearby, a heritage aircraft park displays vintage aircraft. Canada's flight pioneers are recognized in a videotape presentation.

On weekends visitors may view a Spitfire that is being restored. A comprehensive aviation library also is on site. **Time:** Allow 30 minutes minimum. **Hours:** Museum Tues.-Sun. 10-4. Heritage aircraft park daily 10-4, May-Sept. Closed Jan. 1 and Dec.

25-26. **Cost:** Donations. Heritage aircraft park free. **Phone:** (250) 339-8162.

FILBERG HERITAGE LODGE AND PARK is at 61 Filberg Rd. The 1929 heritage lodge and outbuildings stand on 4 hectares (9 acres) of landscaped grounds on Comox Bay. The timber lodge is restored and furnished in period. Rare and exotic trees, rhododendrons and herb gardens adorn the park, which offers 1-hour concerts most Sundays at 2 in July and August. A petting farm is available from mid-June to mid-August.

Pets are not permitted. **Time:** Allow 1 hour minimum. **Hours:** Lodge open Tues.-Fri. 10-3, Apr.-Sept.; phone for winter hours. Park open daily 8-dusk. Closed Jan. 1, second Mon. in Oct. and Dec. 25-26. **Cost:** Lodge by donations. Park free; admission is charged during special events. **Phone:** (250) 339-2715. 🏕

COOMBS (F-10) pop. 1,327

Coombs retains the atmosphere of a quaint village settled around 1910. The Coombs General Store, which has operated continuously since the settlement days, and the Old Country Market, which is unusual for the goats that are kept on the roof in summer, are two landmarks.

The town is on Vancouver Island, midway between Little Qualicum Falls Provincial Park *(see Recreation Chart)* and Englishman River Falls Provincial Park *(see Recreation Chart)*, where there are many recreational opportunities.

VANCOUVER ISLAND BUTTERFLY WORLD & ORCHID GARDENS is 1 km (.6 mi.) w. on Hwy. 4A at 1080 Winchester Rd. A walk-through tropical garden contains more than 30 species of free-flying butterflies; the insect's life cycle is portrayed through displays.

Other exhibits include birds in an outdoor aviary, a Japanese water garden with exotic fish, an orchid garden with some 800 orchids, a turtle pond, a petting zoo in the summer and Big Bug Jungle—an insectary housing large live jungle insects. An indoor water garden displays hundreds of orchids from around the world set amidst waterfalls and ponds.

Time: Allow 30 minutes minimum. **Hours:** Daily 10-5, May-Sept.; 10-4, Mar.-Apr. and in Oct. **Cost:** $11; $10 (ages 65+); $6 (ages 12-18); $5 (ages 3-12). Phone ahead to confirm prices. **Phone:** (250) 248-7026.

COQUITLAM—*see Vancouver p. 179.*

COURTENAY (F-10)
pop. 18,304, elev. 25 m/82′

Courtenay was established in the late 1860s when settlers began a major farming community near the Comox Valley. Known for a garden called the Mile of Flowers, the town is now a year-round recreation area with good skiing and sailing nearby.

The 1989 Puntledge River discovery of the fossilized intact skull of a 14-metre-long (46-ft.) elasmosaur, a long-necked Cretaceous marine reptile 80

million years old, brought Courtenay to the attention of the world of paleontology.

Courtenay is the terminus of the Powell River Ferry, which makes round-trip excursions to the mainland.

Comox Valley Visitor Centre: 2040 Cliffe Ave., Courtenay, BC, Canada V9N 2L3. **Phone:** (250) 334-3234 or (888) 357-4471.

COURTENAY MUSEUM is at 207 Fourth St., downtown at jct. Fourth St. and Cliffe Ave. Permanent exhibits, enhanced by audiovisuals, focus on native history, exploration, agriculture, logging and pioneer life. A reconstruction of an elasmosaur is displayed along with locally excavated fossil evidence from the age of dinosaurs. The museum has archival material pertaining to the nearby Comox Valley. Guided fossil discovery tours are available.

Time: Allow 1 hour minimum. **Hours:** Mon.-Sat. 10-5, Sun. noon-4, Victoria Day-Labour Day; Tues.-Sat. 10-5, rest of year. Closed Jan. 1, Good Friday, Victoria Day, Labour Day and Dec. 25. **Cost:** Donations. **Phone:** (250) 334-0686.

PUNTLEDGE HATCHERY is 3 km (1.9 mi.) w. on Lake Trail Rd., then 2 km (1.2 mi.) n. on Powerhouse Rd. following signs. The hatchery nurtures and releases several varieties of salmon and steelhead trout into the Puntledge River. Photographic displays outline the species' various stages of development. **Hours:** Daily 8-4; closed statutory holidays. **Cost:** Free. **Phone:** (250) 703-0907.

RECREATIONAL ACTIVITIES
Skiing
• **Mt. Washington Alpine Resort** is 31 km (19 mi.) n.w. on the Strathcona Pkwy. Other activities are available. **Hours:** Daily 9-3:30, Dec. 1 to mid-Apr. Phone ahead to confirm schedule. **Phone:** (250) 338-1386 or (888) 231-1499.

CRANBROOK (C-11)
pop. 18,476, elev. 940 m/3,083′

Cranbrook is the key city of the eastern Kootenays and the center of many circle tours. Nearby lakes, rivers and mountains provide such recreational opportunities as swimming, fishing, hiking, hunting and skiing. A scenic portion of Hwy. 93 runs north from Cranbrook into Alberta to the junction with Hwy. 16 in Jasper.

Cranbrook Chamber of Commerce: 2279 Cranbrook St. N. (Hwy. 3/95), P.O. Box 84, Cranbrook, BC, Canada V1C 4H6. **Phone:** (250) 426-5914 or (800) 222-6174.

Self-guiding tours: Information about driving and walking tours is available from the chamber of commerce.

CANADIAN MUSEUM OF RAIL TRAVEL is at 57 Van Horne St. (Hwy. 3/95). The museum restores and preserves vintage Canadian Pacific Railway passenger train sets, including cars from the luxury

Trans-Canada Limited. The lifestyle of rail travel is reflected in trains from 1880 to 1955, including cars of state, business and royalty. On the grounds is the original three-story café from the Canadian Pacific Railway's Royal Alexandra Hotel of Winnipeg. Several guided tours are available and can be taken in various combinations.

Time: Allow 1 hour, 30 minutes minimum. **Hours:** Museum open daily 9:45-6, late Apr. to mid-Oct.; Tues.-Sat. 10-5, rest of year. Guided tours are given daily every 45 minutes. Last tour begins 45 minutes before closing. **Cost:** Guided tours $3-$18; $2.55-$16.15 (ages 65+); $1.50-$9.65 (students with ID); 75c-$4.35 (ages 0-4); $8.65-$54.45 (family). **Phone:** (250) 489-3918 to verify tour schedule and rates.

GAMBLING ESTABLISHMENTS

• **Casino of the Rockies** is at 7777 Mission Rd. **Hours:** Sun.-Thurs. 10 a.m.-midnight, Fri.-Sat. and holidays 10 a.m.-2 a.m. Closed Dec. 25. **Phone:** (250) 417-2772.

CRESTON (D-11)
pop. 4,826, elev. 636 m/2,086′

The unusual Kutenai canoe, which has a bow and stern that both meet the waterline, was used by Indians in the area around Creston in pre-pioneer days. The only other place such a canoe has been found is the Amur River region in southeastern Russia. The canoe's use in this area supports the theory that Asians migrated to North America over a frozen Bering Strait.

In the 1930s about 8,100 hectares (20,000 acres) of land were reclaimed from the Kootenay Delta for agriculture. The Creston Valley floor is now quilted with a variety of seed and root crops, grains and fruit orchards. Other Creston industries include forestry, dairying and brewing.

The Columbia Brewing Co., 1220 Erickson St., offers narrated tours of its facilities mid-May to mid-October. Complimentary beer is available at the end of the tour; phone (250) 428-9344. Free guided tours of a candlemaking factory are offered year-round at Kootenay Candles, 1511 Northwest Blvd.; phone (250) 428-9785 or (866) 572-9785.

Summit Creek Park, 9 kilometres (6 mi.) west, offers camping, natural history programs and hiking along the old Dewdney Trail, which carried gold seekers from Hope to the Wild Horse goldfields in the 1860s. Mountain Stream Trout Farm and Recreation Area, 7 kilometres (4 mi.) north, features nature trails and ponds stocked with fish for catching and barbecuing on the premises.

Creston Visitor Centre: 121 Northwest Blvd., Creston, BC, Canada V0B 1G0. **Phone:** (250) 428-4342 or (866) 528-4342.

CRESTON MUSEUM is at 219 Devon St. via Hwy. 3A N. The 1957 Stone House, which has four stone fireplaces and walls more than one-third metre (1 ft.) thick, contains more than 10,000 pioneer and Indian artifacts, including a replica of a Kutenai Indian canoe and early agricultural tools. A schoolroom exhibit can be seen in the restored Kingsgate Schoolhouse on the museum grounds.

Time: Allow 1 hour minimum. **Hours:** Daily 10-5, mid-June to mid-Aug.; Mon.-Sat. 10-3:30, mid-May to mid-June and mid-Aug. to mid-Sept.; by appointment rest of year. **Cost:** $3; $2 (ages 6-16); $8 (family). **Phone:** (250) 428-9262.

CRESTON VALLEY WILDLIFE MANAGEMENT AREA is 13 km (6 mi.) w. on Hwy. 3. The 7,000-hectare (17,297-acre) area permits hiking, seasonal camping, bicycling, hunting, canoeing and picnicking in a managed waterfowl habitat. A variety of programs and canoe trips originate at the Interpretation Centre, which houses natural history displays and a theater. *See Recreation Chart.*

Hours: Wildlilfe management area open year-round. Interpretation Centre open Tues.-Sat. 9-5, May-Oct. **Cost:** $3; $2 (ages 0-11); $9 (family, six to nine people). **Phone:** (250) 402-6908.

CULTUS LAKE (I-12)
pop. 637, elev. 45 m/150′

Cultus Lake Provincial Park, 11 kilometres (7 mi.) southwest of Chilliwack off Hwy. 1, is a popular recreational area and offers camping, boating, fishing, horseback riding and hiking *(see Recreation Chart)*. Cultus Lake Waterpark, Hwy. 1 exit 119A, has giant waterslides, twisting tunnels, pools and inner tube rides; phone (604) 858-7241 for more information.

CUMBERLAND (F-10) pop. 2,737

Cumberland's origins are rooted in the rigors of coal mining. From 1888 until the last of its nine mines closed in 1966, the village produced some 25 million tons of high-grade coal. The lucrative enterprise solidified Cumberland's economy and contributed to its multi-ethnic mix, drawing miners from locations as diverse as England, Scotland, Italy, China and Japan. The village and many of its streets were named for the mining region in England known as Cumbria.

Nestled in the foothills of the Beaufort Mountains and a stone's throw from Comox Lake, Cumberland offers ample snow skiing, hiking, fishing and boating opportunities.

Cumberland Visitor Centre: 2680 Dunsmuir, P.O. Box 250, Cumberland, BC, Canada V0R 1S0. **Phone:** (250) 336-8313 or (866) 301-4636.

CUMBERLAND MUSEUM & ARCHIVES is off Hwy. 19 Cumberland exit, 2 km (1.2 mi.) w. on Cumberland Rd./4th St., then just w. to jct. 1st St. and Dunsmuir Ave. Visitors can walk through a replica of a coal mine and view exhibits about Cumberland's mining history. Outdoor heritage tours are offered.

Time: Allow 30 minutes minimum. **Hours:** Daily 9-5, July 1-Labour Day; Mon.-Fri. 9-4, Sat. 10-4, rest of year. **Cost:** $4; $3 (ages 60+); $2 (ages 13-18); $10 (family). Tours $2. **Phone:** (250) 336-2445.

DAWSON CREEK (D-6)
pop. 10,994, elev. 655 m/2,148′

Named for George Mercer Dawson of the Geological Survey of Canada, Dawson Creek was settled in 1912. Growth accelerated during World War II, as this was the southern terminus of the Alaska Highway. The highway was then called the Alcan Military Highway, and it served as a supply road to bases in Alaska. The Mile Zero Cairn, which marks the start of the Alaska Highway, and the Zero Milepost are in the center of town. Alpine skiing, camping, hiking and fishing are popular recreational activities.

Dawson Creek Visitor's Centre: 10201 10th St., Dawson Creek, BC, Canada V1G 3T5. **Phone:** (250) 782-9595 or (866) 645-3022.

DAWSON CREEK STATION MUSEUM is at 900 Alaska Ave. Artifacts, fossils and mounted animals and birds from the Peace River region are displayed. Highlights include an early 1900s railway caboose and a 1930s grain elevator as well as an art gallery and a video presentation about construction of the Alaska Highway.

Hours: Daily 8-5:30, Victoria Day-Labour Day; Tues.-Sat. 10-5, rest of year. Closed Jan. 1, Good Friday, Nov. 11 and Dec. 25-26. **Cost:** $2; $5 (family). **Phone:** (250) 782-5408.

WALTER WRIGHT PIONEER VILLAGE is just w. of jct. Hwy. 97N (Alaska Hwy.) and Hwy. 97S (Hart Hwy.). The complex of pioneer buildings includes a log schoolhouse, log cabin, general store, smithy and two churches. All contain period furnishings.

An extensive collection of farm machinery and implements also is featured as well as nine flower gardens, a memorial rose garden and a lake for swimming. **Time:** Allow 1 hour minimum. **Hours:** Daily 10-5, Victoria Day-Labour Day. **Cost:** $2; $5 (family). **Phone:** (250) 782-7144. 🍴

DELTA—*see Vancouver p. 179.*

DUNCAN (H-10) pop. 4,986, elev. 15 m/49′

Founded in 1887 as Alderlea, Duncan was renamed in 1912 in honor of farmer William Duncan, who gave his land for the original townsite. Settlers were attracted by the promise of copper and coal on nearby Mount Sicker, where abandoned mines and original homesteads still can be seen. The growth of the logging and farming industries brought increasing numbers to Duncan and the Cowichan Valley.

The area around Duncan is known for the handspun woolen sweaters produced by the Cowichan Indians. West on Hwy. 18 is the Cowichan Valley Demonstration Forest with scenic viewpoints and signs describing forest management practices and ecology. More than 80 totem poles dot the town of Duncan.

Duncan-Cowichan Chamber of Commerce: 381A Trans-Canada Hwy., Duncan, BC, Canada V9L 3R5. **Phone:** (250) 746-4636 or (888) 303-3337.

Shopping areas: Whippletree Junction, a group of shops and boutiques with late 1800s storefronts, is 5 kilometres (3 mi.) south on the Trans-Canada Highway.

BC FOREST DISCOVERY CENTRE is 1.5 km (1 mi.) n. off Hwy. 1 to 2892 Drinkwater Rd. The site has more than 40 hectares (99 acres) of forest and interactive displays and videotapes depicting British Columbia's forestry heritage, management practices and renewal efforts. In addition to a logging museum there are Douglas fir trees, forestry equipment and an old-time logging camp. A nature trail and a ride on a logging train are available July through August; a Christmas train ride and related events take place in late November and December.

Hours: Daily 10-5, June 1-Labour Day; Thurs.-Mon. 10-4:30, Easter-May 31 and day after Labour Day-Oct. 14; phone ahead for Christmas schedule. **Cost:** $14; $12 (ages 13-18 and 65+); $9 (ages 5-12); $50 (family). Christmas train $5. **Phone:** (250) 715-1113 or (866) 715-1113.

QUW'UTSUN' CULTURAL AND CONFERENCE CENTRE is 1 blk. w. of Hwy. 1 at 200 Cowichan Way. The 2.4-hectare (6-acre) site consists of a living-history museum and a gallery dedicated to the preservation and dissemination of the culture of the Northwest Coast Indians. Exhibits include numerous totem poles and historical artifacts as well as the Comeakin longhouse and Khenipsen Carving House. Interpretive tours, craft demonstrations and a film presentation also are featured.

Time: Allow 1 hour minimum. **Hours:** Tues.-Sat. 10:30-3:30, June 1 to mid-Sept. Guided tours are offered on the hour; multimedia presentations begin on the half-hour. Closed statutory holidays. **Cost:** $15; $12 (ages 12-18 and 55+); $8 (ages 5-11). Rates may vary; phone ahead. **Phone:** (250) 746-8119 or (877) 746-8119. 🍴

ERRINGTON (G-10)

NORTH ISLAND WILDLIFE RECOVERY ASSOCIATION is .7 km (.4 mi.) e. on Grafton Ave., then .4 km (.25 mi.) n. to 1240 Leffler Rd. Bald eagles, owls, hawks, swans and black bears are among the animals that can be viewed at this 3-hectare (8-acre) rehabilitation facility. An eagle flight cage houses eagles waiting to be released into the wild.

A nature museum, wildlife learning center, nature trails and a release pond are on the grounds. **Time:** Allow 30 minutes minimum. **Hours:** Daily 9-5, mid-Mar. through Dec. 31. **Cost:** $5; $3 (ages 3-12). **Phone:** (250) 248-8534. 🏧

FAIRMONT HOT SPRINGS (B-12)
pop. 489, elev. 810 m/2,657′

At the north end of Columbia Lake, Fairmont Hot Springs were discovered about 1840. This popular resort area offers four hot mineral springs with temperatures averaging 35 to 45 C (95 to 113 F). Water sports and alpine and cross-country skiing also are available. *See Recreation Chart and the AAA/CAA Western Canada & Alaska CampBook.*

RECREATIONAL ACTIVITIES

Skiing

- **Fairmont Hot Springs Resort** is on 5225 Fairmont Resort Rd. Other activities are available. **Hours:** Skiing daily 9:30-4, mid-Dec. to early Apr. **Phone:** (250) 345-6000 or (800) 663-4979.

FERNIE (C-12) pop. 4,217; elev. 1,005 m/3,297′

At the foot of Trinity Mountain in the British Columbia Rockies, Fernie is a year-round recreation center. The many surrounding lakes and mountains provide opportunities for boating, fishing, hiking, camping and skiing. Mount Fernie Provincial Park is 4.8 kilometres (3 mi.) east *(see Recreation Chart and the AAA/CAA Western Canada & Alaska CampBook).* Prentice and Rotary parks are downtown.

Fernie Chamber of Commerce: 102 Hwy. 3, Fernie, BC, Canada V0B 1M5. **Phone:** (250) 423-6868 or (877) 433-7643.

RECREATIONAL ACTIVITIES

Skiing

- **Fernie Alpine Resort** is 5 km (3 mi.) s.w. off Hwy. 3 at 5339 Fernie Ski Hill Rd. Other activities are offered. **Hours:** Daily 8-5, early Dec.-early Apr. **Phone:** (250) 423-4655 or (800) 258-7669.

White-water Rafting

- **Mountain High River Adventures Inc.** collects passengers at Riverside Mountain Lodge at 100 Riverside Way. Other activities are offered. **Hours:** Daily 8-8, Victoria Day-Sept. 30. **Phone:** (250) 423-5008 or (877) 423-4555.

FORT LANGLEY (H-11) elev. 12 m/39′

BRITISH COLUMBIA FARM MACHINERY AND AGRICULTURAL MUSEUM is at 9131 King St. This complex of buildings features artifacts and exhibits devoted to the development of farm machinery in British Columbia. Included are a hand-wrought plow, a threshing machine, carriages and buckboards, and a Tiger-Moth airplane used for crop dusting. A research library also is available.

Time: Allow 30 minutes minimum. **Hours:** Daily 10-4, Apr. 1-second Mon. in Oct. **Cost:** $4; $2 (ages 6-18 and 55+); $1 (ages 0-5). **Phone:** (604) 888-2273.

LANGLEY CENTENNIAL MUSEUM is at 9135 King St. Regional artifacts reflect the lifestyle of early explorers, fur traders and First Nations peoples. Re-created period rooms include a parlor, a kitchen and a general store. Displays also feature wood carvings, stone artifacts and baskets from the Coast Salish culture. Changing exhibits focus on art, science and Canadian and world history.

Hours: Mon.-Sat. 10-4:45, Sun. 1-4:45; closed Jan. 1, Good Friday, Easter Monday, Thanksgiving and Nov. 11. **Cost:** Donations. **Phone:** (604) 888-3922.

FORT LANGLEY NATIONAL HISTORIC SITE OF CANADA (I-11)

Fort Langley National Historic Site of Canada is 6.5 kilometres (4 mi.) north of Langley off Hwy. 1 at 23433 Mavis Ave. On the bank of the Fraser River, the 19th-century Hudson's Bay Company trading post was an important supply link in the company's network of fur trading forts west of the Rockies. British Columbia was proclaimed a colony at the site in 1858.

The site preserves an original 1840 storehouse and reconstructed wooden buildings, including a cooperage and blacksmith's shop and a log palisade. Interpreters in period costumes demonstrate fur-trading activities daily. A visitor center displays contemporary exhibits. Special events are presented throughout the year.

Picnicking is permitted. Allow 1 hour minimum. Daily 9-8, July-Aug.; 10-5, rest of year. Closed Jan. 1 and Dec. 25-26. Admission $7.80; $6.55 (ages 65+); $3.90 (ages 6-16); $19.60 (family). Phone (604) 513-4777.

FORT NELSON (B-5)
pop. 4,514, elev. 405 m/1,350′

Originally a fur-trading post, Fort Nelson thrived with the building of the Alaska Highway. during World War II. Nearby mountains, lakes, parks, forests and diverse wildlife populations make Fort Nelson a destination for adventurous tourists, anglers and hunters.

Fort Nelson Visitor Centre: 5430 50th Ave. N., Fort Nelson, BC, Canada V0C 1R0. **Phone:** (250) 774-6400.

FORT NELSON HERITAGE MUSEUM is w. on Hwy. 97. An albino moose is among the stuffed animals displayed at the museum, which chronicles the history of Fort Nelson. Exhibits include vintage cars, photographs of the construction of the Alaska Highway and a trapper's log cabin.

Time: Allow 30 minutes minimum. **Hours:** Daily 8:30-7:30, June-Aug.; 9-6, mid-May through May 31 and Sept. 1 to mid-Sept. Closed July 1 for morning parade. **Cost:** $5; $3 (ages 5-16 and senior citizens); $10 (family). **Phone:** (250) 774-3536.

FORT RODD HILL AND FISGARD LIGHTHOUSE NATIONAL HISTORIC SITES—*see Victoria p. 201.*

FORT ST. JAMES (E-4)
pop. 1,355, elev. 680 m/2,230′

Established in 1806 by Simon Fraser and John Stuart, the fur-trading post of Fort St. James became the capital of New Caledonia in 1821. Furs from outlying New Caledonia posts were brought overland to Fort St. James by dog sled and then shipped south during the spring thaw to the coast by canoe and horse.

During this time George Simpson, governor of the Hudson's Bay Co.'s vast empire, visited the fort. Determined to impress the Carrier Indians, Simpson organized a flamboyant procession complete with flute, bugle and bagpipe players in Highland dress, accompanied by a dog with a music box around its neck. Thereafter, the awe-struck Indians reverently referred to Simpson as the "great chief whose dog sings."

A Roman Catholic mission was founded at the fort in 1843. Services continue to be held in Our Lady of Good Hope Church, which was built in 1873 and is one of the oldest churches in British Columbia.

Mining activity supplemented the capital's trapping enterprises after the discovery of gold in the Omineca region in 1869. Interest in mining rekindled during World War II when the Pinchi Mine a few kilometres north yielded more mercury than any other mine in the British Commonwealth.

A lack of highways and railways prompted Fort St. James to pioneer bush flying as a means of transportation; it has served as an air base since the earliest days of charter flight.

The north shore of Stuart Lake, 16 kilometres (10 mi.) west, features some of the earliest signs of habitation in the form of prehistoric rock paintings just above the high-water mark. Although Fort St. James has emerged from relative wilderness, its surrounding evergreen forests continue to be among the best big-game hunting areas in the province. Alpine skiing is available nearby.

Fort St. James Visitor Centre: 115 Douglas Ave., P.O. Box 1164, Fort St. James, BC, Canada V0J 1P0. **Phone:** (250) 996-7023.

FORT ST. JAMES NATIONAL HISTORIC SITE OF CANADA is 2 blks. w. of Hwy. 27. Established on the southern shore of Stuart Lake by the North West Co. in 1806, Fort St. James contains one of the largest groups of original wooden buildings from Canada's fur trade. A massive fur warehouse is a noted example of Red River framing. The fully restored Hudson's Bay Co. post on the site served as a hub of commerce between fur traders and the First Nations peoples—and as the capital of New Caledonia, now central British Columbia.

The visitor center provides pictorial displays, artifacts and an audiovisual presentation. Changing exhibits also are offered seasonally. Interpreters in period costume provide living-history demonstrations throughout the day. **Time:** Allow 2 hours minimum. **Hours:** Daily 9-5, Victoria Day-Sept. 30; by appointment rest of year. **Cost:** $7.80; $6.55 (ages 66+); $3.90 (ages 6-16); $19.60 (family). Prices may vary; phone to confirm. **Phone:** (250) 996-7191. ⓣ

FORT ST. JOHN (D-5)
pop. 16,034, elev. 695 m/2,280′

One of the oldest European settlements in the province, Fort St. John was established in 1793 as a fur-trading outpost called Rocky Mountain Fort. Residents engage in gas and oil exploration as well as the lumber industry and cattle ranching. There are coalfields to the south and west.

Recreational activities include fishing for Arctic grayling and gray trout in nearby Charlie Lake (see Recreation Chart and the AAA/CAA Western Canada & Alaska CampBook), canoeing the rapids of the Peace River, skiing, and hunting for mountain caribou, mountain goats and black bears in the Rocky Mountain foothills. Floatplanes operating out of Charlie Lake provide access to the wilderness surrounding Fort St. John, and Hwy. 29 provides scenic driving to Chetwynd.

Fort St. John Visitor Centre: 9523-100th St., Fort St. John, BC, Canada V1J 4N4. **Phone:** (250) 785-3033 or (877) 785-6037.

FORT STEELE (C-12) elev. 771 m/2,529′

Founded during the 1864 Kootenay gold rush, Fort Steele, then known as Galbraith's Ferry, became the site of the first North West Mounted Police west of the Rockies. In 1888 the settlement's name was changed to honor police superintendent Samuel Steele, who peacefully settled tensions between European settlers and the Ktunaxa people.

As a result of the mining boom of the 1890s the town became a thriving center of trade, transportation, communication and social activity, with a population of more than 2,000. In 1898 the British Columbia Southern Railroad bypassed Fort Steele in favor of Cranbrook, 16 kilometres (10 mi.) southwest, and the town began its decline. At the end of World War II Fort Steele had fewer than 50 residents.

FORT STEELE HERITAGE TOWN is 3 km (1.9 mi.) s.w. at 9851 Hwy. 93/95. The 11-hectare (27-acre) site preserves an 1890s boomtown. More than 60 restored, reconstructed or original buildings include an operating bakery, restaurant, tinsmith shop, blacksmith shop and newspaper office. Street dramas and demonstrations such as quilting, horse farming and ice cream making help re-create life in the era.

Fort Steele's Clydesdales give wagon rides daily mid-June through Labour Day and perform a six-horse hitch show on July 1. Live entertainment is presented in the Wild Horse Theatre late June through Labour Day. Steam train rides are available during this time. A visitor reception center contains exhibits about the town's history.

Hours: Grounds open daily 9:30-6, July 1-day before Labour Day; 9:30-5, May-June and Labour Day-second Mon. in Oct.; 10-4, rest of year. Last admission 1 hour before closing. Programs, including street skits depicting daily life of the late 1890s, are presented daily 9:30-5:30, late June-Labour Day.

Closed Dec. 25-26. **Cost:** $5; free (ages 0-5). **Phone:** (250) 417-6000.

GALIANO ISLAND—*see Gulf Islands p. 123.*

GIBSONS (G-11) pop. 4,182

SUNSHINE COAST MUSEUM & ARCHIVES is at 716 Winn Rd. Two floors of exhibits explain the history of the Sunshine Coast and its inhabitants. The main floor features displays about the area's maritime past; the upper floor recounts information about the First Nations peoples and pioneers as well as natural history and industries. **Time:** Allow 1 hour minimum. **Hours:** Tues.-Sat. 10:30-4:30; closed statutory holidays. **Cost:** Donations. **Phone:** (604) 886-8232.

GLACIER NATIONAL PARK OF CANADA (A-10)

Elevations in the park range from 500 metres (1,640 ft.) at Revelstoke to 3,390 metres (11,121 ft.) at Mount Dawson. Refer to CAA/AAA maps for additional elevation information.

West of the Rockies in the southeast, Glacier National Park of Canada and its smaller counterpart Mount Revelstoke National Park of Canada *(see place listing p. 131)* encompass portions of the rugged Columbia Mountains. The 1,350 square kilometres (521 sq. mi.) of hard rock terrain present a jagged profile of angular mountains with narrow steep-walled valleys. The steep mountain slopes and enormous snowfall make this region susceptible to avalanches.

Rogers Pass in the heart of the park became the scene of a pitched 19th-century battle between the railroad engineers and these mountains. Sheer walls, numerous slide areas and severe weather proved almost insurmountable obstacles to the completion of Canada's first transcontinental railroad. Some of the largest railroad trestles then known were built to carry the line across raging streams to the summit of this pass across the Selkirks.

From there the tracks crossed to the southern wall of the valley on several loops to avoid the numerous avalanche slopes and the steep downgrade. Despite the ingenuity of its engineers, the new railroad had to be abandoned to the devastating winter forces that closed the pass the first year of construction. Avalanches attaining speeds of up to 325 kilometres (202 mi.) per hour tore up sections of the new track and left other sections buried under tons of snow.

Thirty-one snowsheds were built to shield the track, but even this was not enough. In 1910, 58 men were killed by an avalanche as they were clearing snow from an earlier slide. This incident, mounting costs and the dangerous grades of this section convinced the railroad to tunnel under Mount MacDonald.

The Trans-Canada Highway met similar obstacles as it crossed the pass, but the use of mobile howitzers to dislodge potential slides and other methods of controlling avalanches have held the road's position in the pass. Evidence of the struggle to build the railroad is visible from the road and the park's various campgrounds.

Several short trails follow the railroad's progress, winding past the ruins of Glacier House, a 19th-century resort hotel, remains of former snow sheds and the stone pillars that once supported the railroad trestles.

History is only part of the park's attractions. Twelve percent of the park is covered perpetually by snow and ice; more than 400 glaciers are scattered throughout the park. The contrast of the deep green forests and meadows with the glacial whites of these crags makes the park especially scenic.

Towering above the richly wooded valleys, the 3,297-metre (10,817-ft.) Mount Sir Donald rises to the east of the campgrounds, with Eagle and Uto peaks to the north. Day-hiking trails lead toward the Illecillewaet and Asulkan glaciers.

General Information and Activities

The park is open all year, but winter conditions are rigorous. Illecillewaet campground, the center of the park's best ski touring area, and Beaver River picnic area offer limited winter skiing. During the summer some of the popular activities are camping, hiking and mountaineering.

From Illecillewaet campground interpreters lead evening strolls and campfire talks as well as summer hikes that pass through the different life zones of the park's flora and fauna.

In addition, an extensive network of challenging day-hiking trails leads to such attractions as the Illecillewaet and Asulkan glaciers; Mount Abbott, with several fine viewpoints; Mount Tupper; and the Rogers group of peaks.

Grizzly and black bears are common in Glacier National Park of Canada; be cautious and make noise frequently as you hike. Climbers and overnight hikers may register at Rogers Pass Centre before and after every trip. Topographical maps and a hiker's guide also are available. Park use permits can be purchased at the welcome stations and the Rogers Pass Centre. *See Recreation Chart and the AAA/CAA Western Canada & Alaska CampBook.*

ADMISSION to the park is $6.90; $5.90 (ages 65+); $3.45 (ages 6-16); $17.30 (all occupants of a private vehicle with up to seven people).

PETS are permitted in the park provided they are on a leash at all times.

ADDRESS inquiries to the Superintendent, Glacier and Mount Revelstoke National Parks of Canada, P.O. Box 350, Revelstoke, BC, Canada V0E 2S0; phone (250) 837-7500.

ROGERS PASS CENTRE is 1.3 km (.8 mi.) e. of the Rogers Pass summit. Modeled after the snowsheds that once protected the railroad from avalanches, the visitor center includes a theater, an exhibit hall with railway models and displays about natural history. **Time:** Allow 30 minutes minimum. **Hours:** Daily 7:30 a.m.-8 p.m., mid-June through Labour Day; daily 8-4, day after Labour Day-Oct. 31 and Dec. 1 to mid-June; Thurs.-Mon. 8-4, rest of year. Phone ahead to confirm schedule. **Cost:** Free. **Phone:** (250) 814-5232.

GOLDEN (A-10) pop. 3,811, elev. 785 m/2,575′

On the Trans-Canada Highway at the confluence of the Columbia and Kicking Horse rivers, Golden is near Glacier *(see place listing p. 121)* and Yoho national parks of Canada *(see place listing p. 206)* as well as Banff National Park of Canada *(see place listing in Alberta p. 39)*. The community also is an outfitting point for sports enthusiasts.

The Golden and District Museum is at 11th Avenue and 13th Street. The museum is housed in a restored one-room schoolhouse and contains local historical items.

Kicking Horse Country Chamber of Commerce: 500 10th Ave. N., P.O. Box 1320, Golden, BC, Canada V0A 1H0. **Phone:** (250) 344-7125 or (800) 622-4653.

RECREATIONAL ACTIVITIES
White-water Rafting

• **Alpine Rafting Co.** is at 1416 Goldenview Rd. **Hours:** Trips depart daily 8 a.m.-9 p.m., mid-May to early Sept. **Phone:** (250) 344-6778 or (888) 599-5299.

• **Glacier Raft Company** is at 612 N. 7th St. **Hours:** Trips depart daily at 10 and 1, Victoria Day-Labour Day. **Phone:** (250) 344-6521.

• **Wild Water Adventures** is 25 km (15 mi.) s.e. on Hwy. 1. **Hours:** Trips are offered twice daily (weather permitting), mid-May to mid-Sept. **Phone:** (403) 522-2211 or (888) 647-6444.

GOLD RIVER (H-2)
pop. 1,362, elev. 122 m/400′

At the joining of the Gold and Heber rivers, the town of Gold River was built in 6 months in 1965 for employees of a pulp mill. The town, with its beautiful untamed countryside, has become popular with fishermen, photographers, hikers and campers.

The MV *Uchuck III* departs from the dock on Hwy. 28. The full-day and overnight cruises explore Tahsis, Nootka Sound and Friendly Cove, where Capt. James Cook met Chief Maquinna and the Nootka Indians when he landed on Vancouver Island in 1778; phone (250) 283-2418 for the tourist information center or (250) 283-2207 for the municipal office during off-season.

GRAND FORKS (D-9) pop. 4,036

Settlement at the confluence of the Kettle and Granby rivers began in the late 1800s when copper, gold and silver were discovered in the area. After 20 years of prosperity Grand Forks suffered reverses when the local copper smelter, said to be the largest

in the British Empire, closed due to faltering copper prices. The logging industry and seed growing operations later restored stability to the community.

The downtown Boundary District contains preserved historic homes, stores and civic buildings from the settlement period. It is flanked on the south and east by rivers, on the west by 5th Avenue and on the north by 75th Avenue. A walking tour map is available at the Boundary Museum *(see attraction listing)*.

Chamber of Commerce of the City of Grand Forks: 524 Central Ave., P.O. Box 2140, Grand Forks, BC, Canada V0H 1H0. **Phone:** (250) 442-5835.

BOUNDARY MUSEUM is 2 km (1.2 mi.) w. on Hwy. 3, then 1 km (.6 mi.) n. on Reservoir Rd., following signs. The museum depicts the area's history from the late 1800s. Artifacts, maps and photographs show the lifestyles of the Doukhobor and First Nations cultures. Other exhibits include a scale model and display of Grand Forks' Chinatown in the 1900s, a wildlife exhibit and a 1929 fire truck.

Hours: Daily 10-4, June-Sept.; Mon.-Fri. 10-4, rest of year. Guided tours are available by appointment outside of regular hours. Phone ahead to confirm schedule. **Cost:** $4; $2 (ages 60+); free (ages 0-11 with paying adult); $7 (family). Phone ahead to confirm rates. **Phone:** (250) 442-3737.

GULF ISLANDS (G-10)

Separated from the San Juan Islands in Washington only by an international boundary, the almost 200 islands of various shapes and sizes that make up the Gulf Islands nestle against the southeast coast of Vancouver Island. Formed by a series of moving land masses beginning about 100 million years ago, today's Gulf Islands are the result of a mass collision of land that produced the long ridges of sandstone, conglomerate and shale that constitute the islands' geology.

The area was discovered by Capt. George Vancouver while on a quest to find a northwest passage to the Orient in 1792. Erroneously named Gulf of Georgia by Vancouver, the water separating Vancouver Island from the southwestern portion of British Columbia was later correctly termed the Strait of Georgia. The islands, however, retained the designation Gulf Islands.

The area features a climate that is sunnier and milder than that found on the nearby mainland. The quiet waters promote a much quieter lifestyle as well, and the islands are a haven from the frantic pace of nearby cities. Each island, though similar in many respects, has its own distinct identity. Easily reached from the mainland, they have become popular weekend retreats offering varying degrees of amenities and activities. Artists and professionals have joined the population of local fishermen who relish the peaceful lifestyle created by the sparkling waters, cliffs, winding roads and parks.

The main components of the southern Gulf Islands are Galiano, Mayne, North and South Pender,

Salt Spring and Saturna islands. Although they can be explored by automobile, the best way to experience the islands is by bicycle or foot. The Islands Trust, a governmental agency, is charged with preserving and protecting the islands and waters in the Strait of Georgia.

BC Ferries provides year-round service to the main islands from Tsawwassen, south of Vancouver, and Swartz Bay, near Victoria. Vehicle reservations are recommended for travel between the mainland and the islands, but are not available for travel between Vancouver Island and the Gulf Islands or for inter-island travel. It is advisable to make reservations as far in advance as possible for summer and holiday travel. For schedule information and reservations phone (250) 386-3431 from the Victoria area and outside British Columbia or (888) 223-3779 from elsewhere in the province. Air service also is available.

Galiano Island (G-10) pop. 1,258

Named after Spanish explorer Dionisio Alcala Galiano, Galiano Island is a long narrow island that is a haven for bird watchers and naturalists. Bicycling, horseback riding, kayaking, fishing, sailing, diving, swimming and hiking are popular recreational activities. The efforts of hikers and cyclists are rewarded with grand vistas and viewpoints. Mount Galiano provides climbers with eye-catching views of the southern Gulf Islands and the Olympic Mountains.

Montague Harbour Marine Provincial Park has 3,000-year-old Indian middens; camping facilities are available at the park as well as at Dionisio Point Provincial Park *(see Recreation Chart and the AAA/ CAA Western Canada & Alaska CampBook)*. The Descanso Bay Regional Park offers 30 camping sites *(see Recreation Chart)*.

Galiano Island Chamber of Commerce: P.O. Box 73, Galiano Island, BC, Canada V0N 1P0. **Phone:** (250) 539-2233.

Mayne Island (H-10) pop. 1,112

Although visited by the Spanish in the 1790s, it was not until the 1850s that British Capt. George Richards surveyed and mapped the area. Capt. Richards named Mayne Island after his lieutenant, Richard Charles Mayne. During the gold rush of the mid-1800s the island, halfway between Victoria and the mouth of the Fraser River, was a stopping point for miners heading for the riches to be found at the gold fields along the river.

The island is known as a haven for artists and artisans. Small and sparsely settled, Mayne offers quiet beaches and hiking trails; wildflowers; a landscape heavy with trees; seals, sea lions, salmon and sole offshore; and a large variety of birds, from tiny hummingbirds to soaring bald eagles.

Mayne Island Community Chamber of Commerce: P.O. Box 2, Mayne Island, BC, Canada V0N 2J0.

Pender Islands (H-10)

The Penders, consisting of North and South Pender islands, are connected by a one-lane wooden bridge that spans the canal linking Bedwell and Browning harbors. An archeological dig conducted at the time the bridge was built found evidence of island occupation dating back 4,000 years.

The island's 20 public ocean access points and many coves allow ample opportunities for swimming and picnicking. Hiking, boating, fishing, golfing, bicycling, kayaking and scuba diving are other available recreational activities. Roadside stands offer locally grown produce. The view from the summit of Mount Norman is worth the climb.

Quadra Island (E-10)

Old totem poles are found within the Indian reservation on Quadra Island, which is reached by a 15-minute ferry ride from Campbell River *(see place listing p. 113)*.

RECREATIONAL ACTIVITIES
Scuba Diving

- **Abyssal Dive Charters** departs from Quadra Island. Other activities are available. **Hours:** Daily 7:30 a.m.-10:30 p.m. **Phone:** (250) 285-2420 or (800) 499-2297.

Salt Spring Island (H-10) pop. 9,780

Originally called Chuan Island, then Admiral Island, Salt Spring Island is the largest of the Gulf Island group and a popular spot for yachting, cycling, fishing and golfing. Bicycle and kayak rentals are available.

Although it is one of the most developed of the islands, it retains a rural feel. Mount Maxwell Park has a scenic drive leading to 610-metre (2,001-ft.) Baynes Peak. Ruckle Provincial Park *(see Recreation Chart)* offers 7 kilometres (4.3 mi.) of shoreline and has walking trails; bicycling, fishing, kayaking and picnicking are permitted.

The island also features popular Saturday farmers markets and arts and crafts, and is home to many fine artists such as Robert Bateman and Carol Evans. Ganges is the island's commercial hub.

Ferries operate daily from the island's three ferry terminals—between Swartz Bay and Fulford Harbour, between Crofton and Vesuvius Bay and between Long Harbour (the largest of the terminals) and Tsawwassen. For schedules and information phone BC Ferries, (250) 386-3431 from the Victoria area or outside British Columbia, or (888) 223-3779 from elsewhere in the province.

Salt Spring Island Visitor InfoCentre: 121 Lower Ganges Rd., Salt Spring Island, BC, Canada V8K 2T1. **Phone:** (250) 537-5252 or (866) 216-2936.

Saturna Island (H-10) pop. 359

Saturna Island—remote, rugged and sparsely populated—is probably the least visited of the Gulf

Islands. Mountain biking is one of the best ways to see the island. Its bays, beaches and tidal pools offer glimpses of many varieties of marine life. The southernmost of the Gulf Islands, Saturna offers hiking, bicycling and boating opportunities. There is no camping available and lodging is limited.

GULF ISLANDS NATIONAL PARK RESERVE OF CANADA (G-10)

Elevations in the park range from sea level to 401 metres (1,316 ft.) at Mt. Warburton Pike on Saturna Island. Refer to CAA/AAA maps for additional elevation information.

Gulf Islands National Park Reserve of Canada protects an island landscape of rocky headlands, forested hills and shorelines studded with colorful tide pools. The park encompasses areas of lands scattered over fifteen larger islands and includes many smaller islets and reefs. Waters adjacent to park lands, extending 200 metres (650 ft.) seaward, also are under Parks Canada management.

The park shares the larger populated islands of Mayne, Saturna and the Penders with communities that offer a range of tourist amenities. Facilities and services inside the national park reserve are currently limited. The populated larger islands are accessible by vehicle, bicycle and BC Ferries from Vancouver and Victoria. The smaller islands are accessible by only boat or kayak. Water taxis also operate in several areas. Many local tour operators offer such recreational opportunities as cycling, kayaking, scuba diving, whale-watching or hiking. Comfortable, sturdy shoes and water are recommended for all hiking excursions.

The islands are a haven for various wildlife, including such endangered species as the anatum peregrine falcon, the sharp-tailed snake, Townsend's big-eared bat and the western meadowlark. The southern Gulf Islands are home to the endangered Garry Oak ecosystem. Various shorebirds, waterfowl, great blue herons, seals and sea lions also inhabit the area.

For more information contact the Gulf Islands National Park Reserve of Canada InfoCentre, 2220 Harbour Rd., Sidney, BC, Canada V8L 2P6; phone (250) 654-4000. *See Recreation Chart.*

GWAII HAANAS NATIONAL PARK RESERVE AND HAIDA HERITAGE SITE (F-1)

Elevations in the park range from sea level along Kunghit and Moresby islands to 1,123 metres (696 ft.) at Mount de la Touche. Refer to CAA/AAA maps for additional elevation information.

Off the British Columbia coast west of Prince Rupert, Gwaii Haanas National Park Reserve and Haida Heritage Site is in the southern part of the Queen Charlotte Islands (*see place listing p. 151*), a remote island chain. The Queen Charlotte Islands also are known as the Haida Gwaii Islands. This protected area is jointly managed by the Government of Canada and the Council of the Haida Nation.

The 1,470 square kilometres (912 sq. mi.) of Gwaii Haanas National Park Reserve and Haida Heritage Site offer a rich and fascinating diversity of flora, sea creatures and wildlife. Remnants of native village sites on the 138 islands capture the history of the Haida. Haida Gwaii Watchmen basecamps have been established at major sites of cultural significance. Watchmen provide site security and protection of the cultural features.

Access to the park reserve is challenging: The only way to and around Gwaii Haanas is by air or sea. Solo travel is recommended only for the experienced outdoor traveler. Licensed tour operators provide a variety of excursions. Sea kayaking, sailboat and powerboat charters are the most popular ways to tour Gwaii Haanas. There are no maintained trails or designated campsites, and only limited visitor facilities are provided within the park reserve.

The Queen Charlotte Islands can be reached by air from Vancouver and Prince Rupert. BC Ferries also provides year-round service between the islands and Prince Rupert. Arrangements for ferry transportation should be made well in advance and reservations are highly recommended; phone (250) 386-3431 from the Victoria area and outside British Columbia or (888) 223-3779 from elsewhere in the province.

Single-day admission $19.60; $16.60 (ages 65+); $9.80 (ages 6-16); $49 (family, up to seven people). Reservations are required to visit the reserve May through September. Regulations allow for no more than 12 people on shore in one place at one time.

Note: All visitors must participate in one 60-minute orientation session offered daily at visitor centers in Sandspit and Queen Charlotte; phone (250) 559-8818 to guarantee a place. For more information write to Gwaii Haanas National Park Reserve and Haida Heritage Site, P.O. Box 37, Queen Charlotte, BC, Canada V0T 1S0 or phone (250) 559-8818, (877) 559-8818 or TTY (250) 559-8139.

HAGENSBORG (F-3) pop. 248, elev. 495′

SNOOTLI HATCHERY is 4 km (2.5 mi.) w. on Hwy. 20, following signs. The hatchery raises Chinook, Chum, Coho and Sockeye salmon as well as Steelhead trout for release into local rivers. **Time:** Allow 30 minutes minimum. **Hours:** Mon.-Fri. 8-4. Guided tours are available 8:30-3:30, June-Sept. **Cost:** Free. **Phone:** (250) 982-2214.

HARRISON HOT SPRINGS (C-7)
pop. 1,573, elev. 11 m/36′

At the foot of Harrison Lake, Harrison Hot Springs (*see Recreation Chart*) is a well-known health and vacation resort with two mineral springs and a sandy beach on the lakeshore. Strong area winds make this a favorite spot for windsurfing. The surrounding mountains are known as Sasquatch country, where sightings of the legendary apelike creature twice the size of a man have been reported dozens of times.

More likely to be found in the mountains are mutton-fat jades, garnets, agates, fossils and gold; the area is renowned among rock hounds.

Harrison Hot Springs Visitor InfoCentre: 499 Hot Springs Rd., P.O. Box 255, Harrison Hot Springs, BC, Canada V0M 1K0. **Phone:** (604) 796-5581.

HARRISON MILLS (D-7)
pop. 209, elev. 11 m/36'

KILBY HISTORIC SITE is 1.6 km (.9 mi.) s. of Hwy. 7 at 215 Kilby Rd. Costumed interpreters conduct tours of this 2-hectare (5-acre) living-history site, once the heart of a thriving community of lumber mills. The 1906 General Store contains forgotten foodstuffs, a wood stove and the traditional checkerboard. Other highlights include the Heritage Post Office, the Manchester House Hotel and animals of the Waterloo Farm.

Hours: Daily 11-5, June-Aug.; Thurs.-Mon. 11-4, Apr.-May and Sept.-Oct. **Cost:** $9; $8 (ages 66+); $7 (ages 6-18). **Phone:** (604) 796-9576. Ⓣ

HAZELTON (D-3) pop. 293, elev. 306 m/1,004'

A showplace of Indian culture, Hazelton originally was called Git-an-maks, meaning "where people fish by torchlight." European settlers arriving in 1872 renamed the area Hazelton, after the profusion of hazelnut trees covering the fertile farmland.

Considered holy by the Gitxsan Indian community, the forest land within a 64.4-kilometre (40-mi.) radius of Hazelton has the province's greatest concentration of standing totem poles, many portrayed in paintings by British Columbia artist Emily Carr.

'KSAN HISTORICAL VILLAGE & MUSEUM is 5 km (3 mi.) s. on Hwy. 62. The Gitxsan Indian village consists of seven tribal houses. The 'Ksan Museum, the Frog House of the Stone Age, the Wolf House or Feast House, the Eagle House, the Fireweed House, the studio, the 'Ksan Shop, and the carving shed and workshop are decorated with paintings, carved interior poles and painted scenes in classic West Coast Indian style.

Tours: Guided tours are available. **Hours:** Daily 9-5:30, May-Oct.; Mon.-Fri. 10-4:30, rest of year. **Cost:** $2. Tour $10; $8.50 (ages 6-18 and 65+). **Phone:** (250) 842-5544 or (877) 842-5518.

HOPE (C-7) pop. 6,185, elev. 39 m/127'

At the entrance to the Fraser River Valley, Hope dates from 1848 when the Hudson's Bay Co. established a fort. The town developed rapidly, especially during the gold rush of 1858. The 1859 Anglican Christ Church is one of the province's oldest churches.

From Hope the Trans-Canada Highway leads north to Fraser Canyon. Kawkawa Lake (see Recreation

Chart), Lake of the Woods, Mount Hope, Mount Ogilvie and Skagit Valley (see Recreation Chart) are just some of the nearby places that offer year-round recreational opportunities.

The result of the 1965 Hope Slide is evident about 16 kilometres (10 mi.) east beside Hwy. 3. A plaque at the edge of the present roadway explains the collapse of the side of Johnson Peak, which buried the highway under 45 metres (148 ft.) of rubble.

The Hope Museum, inside the Hope Visitor InfoCentre, portrays the town's history through native artifacts and historical settings; phone (604) 869-2021. Hope was the location of several films, including "Rambo: First Blood," "Shoot to Kill" with Sidney Poitier, and Disney's "Far From Home: The Adventures of Yellow Dog."

The Hope Arts Gallery, 349 Fort St., features the work of more than 20 artists; phone (604) 869-2408. More art can be found scattered throughout downtown Hope. Wood carvings in such shapes as a gold prospector with his horse to a bald eagle holding a salmon in his talons were created from dying trees with a chainsaw; most are on the grounds of Memorial Park. Brochures about the more than two dozen carvings can be picked up at the Hope Visitor InfoCentre.

Hope Visitor InfoCentre: 919 Water Ave., P.O. Box 370, Hope, BC, Canada V0X 1L0. **Phone:** (604) 869-2021.

E.C. MANNING PROVINCIAL PARK is e. on Hwy. 3. The mountain park includes the Hope-Princeton Hwy. (Hwy. 3), a 134-kilometre (83-mi.) ride that climbs from near sea level at Hope to the 1,346-metre (4,416-ft.) summit of Allison Pass. Blackwall Road off Hwy. 3 leads to Cascade Lookout and offers access to a subalpine meadow.

Recreational activities include hiking, camping, canoeing, bird-watching, cross-country skiing, mountain biking and horseback riding. See Recreation Chart and the AAA/CAA Western Canada & Alaska CampBook. **Hours:** The park is open daily 24 hours. Campgrounds are open May-Oct. **Cost:** Park free. Camping $14-$22 per night. **Phone:** (250) 840-8822 or (800) 330-3321.

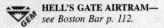 **HELL'S GATE AIRTRAM—** see Boston Bar p. 112.

OTHELLO-QUINTETTE TUNNELS are off Hwy. 3 exit 170 in Coquihalla Canyon Provincial Park; take 6th St. 1 blk. n. to Kawkawa Lake Rd., then 5 km (3 mi.) e. to Tunnels Rd. Five tunnels were built 1911-16 to complete a railroad through Coquihalla Canyon. The Coquihalla River zigzags through the canyon, presenting a challenge to engineer Andrew McCulloch, who used dynamite to blast through the canyon walls to create the narrow tunnels.

The railway ceased operations in 1959; wooden walkways now bridge the river's serpentine course between the tunnels and allow close-up views of the rushing waters.

Note: Wear shoes with good traction, as the gravel path through the tunnels may be wet and slippery. A flashlight is recommended for visibility. **Time:** Allow 1 hour, 30 minutes minimum. **Hours:** Daily dawn-dusk, Apr.-Oct. **Cost:** Free. **Parking:** $1 per hour, $3 per day. **Phone:** (604) 476-9069. 🚻

HUDSON'S HOPE (D-4)

pop. 1,012, elev. 520 m/1,706′

Hudson's Hope is one of the oldest settlements in the province: Only two communities on Vancouver Island have been continuously occupied from earlier dates. First discovered in 1793 by Alexander Mackenzie, the area was the site of a small fur-trading post built in 1805. In 1900 the post was moved to the present site of Hudson's Hope on the north side of the Peace River, where it flourished as a center of trade for the Hudson's Bay Co.

Hudson's Hope is an important supplier of hydroelectricity; its two dams generate about 38 percent of the hydropower used in British Columbia. The dams also are major recreation centers for the area.

Hudson's Hope Visitor Centre: 9555 Beattie Dr., P.O. Box 330, Hudson's Hope, BC, Canada V0C 1V0. **Phone:** (250) 783-9154 May-Oct., or (250) 783-9901 rest of year.

HUDSON'S HOPE MUSEUM is at 9510 Beattie Dr. Housed in a 1942 Hudson's Bay Co. store, the museum contains local artifacts and a collection of prehistoric items including ichthyosaur fossils and tracks. Outbuildings include an active log church built in 1938, a trapper's cabin, a fur cache and a pioneer house. A steam boiler and other antique machines are displayed on the grounds. Children can have fun at the Dino Dig and Walking in the Footsteps of the Dinos exhibits.

Hours: Daily 9:30-5:30, May-Sept.; Mon.-Fri. 10-4, in Dec.; Mon.-Wed. 1-4, rest of year. Closed Easter Monday and Dec. 23-31. **Cost:** Donations. **Phone:** (250) 783-5735.

◥ᴳᴱᴹ **PEACE CANYON DAM** is 4 km (2.5 mi.) s. on Hwy. 29. Completed in 1980, the dam is 50 metres (165 ft.) high and 533 metres (1,750 ft.) long. It reuses water that has generated electricity at the W.A.C. Bennett Dam, 23 kilometres (14 mi.) upstream on the Peace River. Nearby recreational facilities include a campground, picnic facilities and a boat launch to Dinosaur Lake, the dam's reservoir. **Hours:** Daily 8-4, mid-May through Labour Day.

Peace Canyon Dam Visitor Centre is next to the powerhouse. Exhibits reflect the area's natural history, its pioneer past and the Peace Canyon Project. Highlights include a replica of the stern-wheeler SS *Peace River,* a large-scale model of a generating unit, displays about the damming of the Peace River, and mammoth tusks found during excavation. Visitors can view the project's central control system, walk across the dam or visit the observation area on the main floor.

Guided tours of the visitor center are available. **Hours:** Daily 8-4, May 1-Labour Day; Mon.-Fri. 8-4, rest of year. Closed Jan. 1, Easter, second Mon. in Oct., Nov. 11 and Dec. 25-26. **Cost:** Free. **Phone:** (250) 783-7418.

◥ᴳᴱᴹ **W.A.C. BENNETT DAM** is 21 km (13 mi.) w. on Canyon Dr. following signs. A major hydroelectric project on the Peace River, the dam was completed in 1967 to produce electrical power for British Columbia. It is 183 metres (600 ft.) high, 2 kilometres (1.2 mi.) long and .8 kilometre (.5 mi.) thick at the base. Backup water from the dam forms 164,600-hectare (406,727-acre) Williston Lake, British Columbia's largest lake. Its shoreline stretches for 1,770 kilometres (1,100 mi.).

W.A.C. Bennett Dam Visitor Centre is about 1 km (.6 mi.) s.e. of the dam. Photographs and artifacts chronicle the history and geology of the region and the construction of the dam and powerhouse. A participatory exhibit demonstrates the generation of electricity and magnetism. Underground bus tours into the powerhouse and manifold chambers are available. A 40-minute multimedia presentation also is offered in the theater.

Note: Cameras, purses and bags are not permitted on the tour. **Hours:** Visitor center daily 10-6, Victoria Day-Labour Day. Underground powerhouse tours are available 10:30-4:30. Last tour begins at 4:30. Phone ahead to confirm times for tours. **Cost:** Visitor center free. Tour $5; $3 (ages 7-17 and 55+); $12 (family, two adults and two children). Reservations are required for the tour. **Phone:** (250) 783-5048 or (888) 333-6667. 🍴

INVERMERE (B-11) pop. 3,002

Nestled in the "Valley of a Thousand Peaks" between the Rocky and Purcell mountain ranges, Invermere's bucolic location on Lake Windermere's north shore makes it the ideal spot for summer recreation, including hiking, camping, fishing, boating and sailboarding. Hang gliders frequently take flight off nearby Mount Swansea.

Birds of a different feather fly freely at Wilmer National Wildlife Area, about 5 kilometres (3 mi.) north of town; bring your binoculars to peep at songbirds, woodpeckers, waterfowl and birds of prey as well as four-legged creatures including deer, elk, muskrats and beavers.

Roam down Main Street in Invermere's downtown, where flowers bloom in abundance and small-town charm pervades the boutiques, antique shops and cafés. Take in a first-run flick at the 1952 Toby Theatre; it also hosts a film festival from September through June.

Columbia Valley Chamber of Commerce: 651 Hwy. 93/95, P.O. Box 1019, Invermere, BC, Canada V0A 1K0. **Phone:** (250) 342-2844.

WINDERMERE VALLEY MUSEUM is at 622 Third St. Pioneer artifacts and local archives are displayed in a complex in a small park. The six log outbuildings have thematic displays. **Time:** Allow 1 hour minimum. **Hours:** Tues.-Sat. 9:30-4, July-Aug.; Mon.-Fri. 1-4 in June and Sept. Phone ahead to confirm schedule. **Cost:** Donations. **Phone:** (250) 342-9769.

KALEDEN—*see Okanagan Valley p. 139.*

KAMLOOPS (B-8)
pop. 80,376, elev. 345 m/1,131′

Founded in 1812 as a North West Co. depot, Kamloops later was a Hudson's Bay Co. post. Developed where the north and south branches of the Thompson River converge to form Kamloops Lake, Kamloops was named after an Indian word, *cumcloups,* or "the meeting of the waters." During the gold rush of the 1860s the Overlanders reached the city by rafting down the North Thompson.

Since the Cariboo's gold supply disappeared in the 1860s, Kamloops has developed as a center of cattle and sheep ranching.

Kamloops Heritage Railway, at #6-510 Lorne St., operates *The Spirit of Kamloops.* The restored steam locomotive 2141, with its hayrack cars and heritage coach, departs the Canadian National Railway station and carries passengers on a sightseeing tour, passing St. Joseph's Church along the way; phone (250) 374-2141.

Area lakes offer good fishing; Kamloops trout are known to jump a few feet in the air after being hooked. Outdoor enthusiasts also enjoy golfing, nature trails, boating, kayaking, hiking and mountain biking.

Kamloops Visitor Centre: 1290 W. Trans-Canada Hwy., Kamloops, BC, Canada V2C 6R3. **Phone:** (250) 372-3377. *See color ad.*

Self-guiding tours: Kamloops is the site of several historical attractions, including the provincial courthouse and several old houses and churches. Self-guiding tour brochures are available from Kamloops Museum and Archives.

BRITISH COLUMBIA WILDLIFE PARK is 17 km (10 mi.) e. on Hwy. 1 to 9077 Dallas Dr. Sixty-five species of local and endangered wildlife, including grizzly bears, timber wolves, cougars, moose, snakes and birds of prey live in natural habitats at this 50-hectare (120-acre) park. Highlights include interpretive talks, animal encounters, a children's play area and splash park, and seasonal miniature train. Discovery Centre features interactive displays. Wildlights, a holiday light display, is offered in December and January.

Hours: Park open daily 9:30-5, May-Sept.; daily 9:30-4, Mar.-Apr. and Oct. 1-early Nov.; Sat.-Sun. 9:30-4, rest of year. Train departs daily 9-5, June-Sept.; 9:30-4, Mar. 15-May 31 and in Oct.; 5-9, Dec. 14-Jan. 6. Closed Dec. 25. **Cost:** $12.95; $11.95 (ages 13-16 and 65+); $9.95 (ages 3-12). Train $1. Admission may vary; phone ahead. **Phone:** (250) 573-3242.

KAMLOOPS ART GALLERY is at 465 Victoria St. Works by regional, national and international contemporary and First Nations artists are featured. Exhibits change monthly and include paintings, sculptures, prints, drawings, photographs, video art and First Nations art.

Time: Allow 30 minutes minimum. **Hours:** Mon.-Wed. and Fri.-Sat. 10-5, Thurs. 10-9, Sun. noon-4; closed statutory holidays. **Cost:** $5; $3 (couples ages 62+); $3 (ages 62+ and students with ID); $8 (family); donations (Thurs. after 5). Admission may vary for certain exhibits; phone ahead. **Phone:** (250) 377-2400.

KAMLOOPS MUSEUM AND ARCHIVES is at 207 Seymour St. The area's history is portrayed in displays of Indian culture, fly-fishing, a reconstructed Hudson's Bay Co. fur-trading cabin, pioneer and Victorian artifacts and tableaux, transportation items, natural history specimens and the Life of the Secwepemc exhibit. A children's museum and rocks and minerals geology gallery are available. The archives has collections of photographs and manuscripts.

Tours: Guided tours are available. **Time:** Allow 1 hour minimum. **Hours:** Tues.-Sat. 9:30-4:30 (also Thurs. 4:30-7:30). Closed major holidays. **Cost:** Donations. **Phone:** (250) 828-3576.

ST. JOSEPH'S CHURCH is n. on Mount Paul Way, then w. to end of Chilcotin St. Constructed by Roman Catholic missionaries and the Kamloops Indian

Band in the late 19th century, the church has been meticulously renovated. The building's elaborate gilded altar and its many period religious artifacts also have been restored. **Time:** Allow 30 minutes minimum. **Hours:** Wed.-Sat. 12:30-7:30, July 1-Labour Day. Phone ahead to confirm schedule. **Cost:** Donations. **Phone:** (250) 374-7323.

SECWEPEMC MUSEUM AND HERITAGE PARK is at 200-355 Yellowhead Hwy. The 5-hectare (12-acre) park interprets the history and culture of the Secwepemc, or Shuswap, Nation. A walking trail leads through the archeological remains of a 2,000-year-old Shuswap winter village, pit house reconstructions and a summer village. The park also features a museum and ethnobotanical gardens.

Time: Allow 1 hour minimum. **Hours:** Daily 8-4, June 15-Labour Day; Mon.-Fri. 8-4, rest of year. Closed first week in Jan. and the last week in Dec. **Cost:** $7; $5 (ages 60+); $4 (ages 7-17 and students with ID). **Phone:** (250) 828-9749.

GAMBLING ESTABLISHMENTS

- **Lake City Casino** is at 540 Victoria St. **Hours:** Daily 10 a.m.-4 a.m., June-Oct.; 10 a.m.-2 a.m., rest of year. **Phone:** (250) 372-3336.

KASLO (C-11) pop. 1,072, elev. 588 m/1,929′

Kaslo began as a mill site in 1888. Following large silver strikes in 1893 the town quickly expanded to city proportions. A village once again, Kaslo is a distribution center for the Lardeau Valley.

Duncan Dam, 42 kilometres (26 mi.) north, was the first of the three dams constructed by B.C. Hydro in accordance with the Columbia River Treaty, ratified by British Columbia and the United States in 1964. Southwest of the dam is the Kokanee Spawning Channel, built to compensate for the loss of natural spawning areas resulting from the dam's construction. The 3.2-kilometre (2-mi.) channel, one of the longest in the world, is said to be the first constructed for freshwater fish.

SS MOYIE NATIONAL HISTORIC SITE is 1 blk. n. off Hwy. 31 at 324 Front St., following signs. Considered the world's oldest intact passenger sternwheeler, the *Moyie* operated on Kootenay Lake 1898-1957, hauling travelers and freight from Nelson to northern destinations along the shore. It is the last active commercial stern-wheeler in the province and contains artifacts, antiques, a model of Kaslo Harbor, a railway display and a photograph exhibit relating to the history of the vessel and its crew.

Time: Allow 30 minutes minimum. **Hours:** Daily 9-5, mid-June to mid-Oct.; Fri.-Mon. 9-5, rest of year. **Cost:** $7; $5 (ages 65+ and students with ID); $3 (ages 6-12); $18 (family). **Phone:** (250) 353-2525.

KELOWNA—see Okanagan Valley p. 139.

KEREMEOS (D-8) pop. 1,289, elev. 1,356′

The rich soil and desert climate of the Similkameen Valley drew early settlers, who planted the first fruit trees there in 1880. Today Keremeos is considered one of the best fruit-growing regions in British Columbia. Cherries, apples, grapes, peaches and apricots are among the area's bounties.

Keremeos Visitor Centre: 417 7th Ave., Keremeos, BC, Canada V0X 1N0. **Phone:** (250) 499-5225.

THE GRIST MILL AT KEREMEOS is 1.5 km (.9 mi.) n.e. on Hwy. 3A, then .8 km (.5 mi.) e. on Upper Bench Rd. Demonstrations of the principles of milling and restoration are offered at this 1877 flour mill, which features a working waterwheel and flume. A visitor center provides a schedule of living-history presentations for the Apple House Theatre and the summer kitchen. On the grounds are Victorian-era gardens, an heirloom apple orchard, heritage wheat fields and a tearoom.

Time: Allow 1 hour minimum. **Hours:** Mill and tearoom Sat.-Sun. 10-5, June-Sept. Gardens daily 10-5, June-Sept. **Cost:** $5; $4 (ages 5-17 and 65+). **Phone:** (250) 499-2888.

KIMBERLEY (C-11)
pop. 6,139, elev. 1,113 m/3,651′

Kimberley is a winter sports center with a Bavarian theme and a pedestrian mall—the Platzl—complete with wandering minstrels and a huge cuckoo clock. The Kimberley Community Gardens present colorful views June through October.

Built on the slopes of Sullivan and North Star hills, Kimberley is one of Canada's highest cities. It is perhaps best known as the site of the Sullivan Mine, one of the world's largest underground silver, lead and zinc mines. The mine closed in 2001 after 92 years of production, yielding more than $20 billion in ore.

In keeping with the Bavarian theme, the city presents the Kimberley Old Time Accordion Championships for a week each year in early July.

Kimberley Visitor Centre: 270 Kimberley Ave., Kimberley, BC, Canada V1A 3N3. **Phone:** (250) 427-3666 or (866) 913-3666.

KIMBERLEY HERITAGE MUSEUM is in the Platzl at 105 Spokane St. Permanent and changing exhibits depict local history and the legacy of mining in the area. Archives are available for research by request. **Hours:** Tues.-Sat. 9-4:30, July-Aug.; Mon.-Fri. 1-4, rest of year. Closed holidays and Dec. 15-31. **Cost:** Donations. **Phone:** (250) 427-7510.

KIMBERLEY'S UNDERGROUND MINING RAILWAY departs the lower train station, 2 blks. n.w. of the Platzle. The railway offers narrated 1-hour train rides, transporting passengers through the Mark Creek Valley on a narrow-gauge mine track. Interactive mining displays are offered in an underground tunnel.

Hours: Daily 11-3, July 1-Labour Day; Sat.-Sun. 11-3, Victoria Day-June 30. Phone ahead to confirm schedule. **Cost:** $15; $12 (ages 13-18 and 60+); $7 (ages 4-12). **Phone:** (250) 427-0022.

RECREATIONAL ACTIVITIES
Skiing
- **Kimberley Alpine Resort** is above town via Gerry Sorenson Way to 301 North Star Blvd. Other activities are offered. **Hours:** Daily 9-4, Dec. 1 to mid-Apr. **Phone:** (250) 427-4881 or (800) 258-7669.

KITIMAT (E-2) pop. 8,987, elev. 130 m/426′

Kitimat is a planned city built in the early 1950s by Alcan Smelters and Chemicals Ltd. The company chose the wilderness site for a new plant because of the area's deepwater harbor, flat land and hydroelectric plant.

Kitimat Chamber of Commerce: 2109 Forest Ave., P.O. Box 214, Kitimat, BC, Canada V8C 2G7. **Phone:** (250) 632-6294 or (800) 664-6554.

◆ KOOTENAY NATIONAL PARK OF CANADA (B-12)

Elevations in the park range from 918 metres (3,011 ft.) at the park entrance to 3,424 metres (11,235 ft.) at Deltaform Mountain. Refer to CAA/AAA maps for additional elevation information.

Straddling the Banff-Windermere Highway (Hwy. 93) as it travels down the western slope of the Rocky Mountains, Kootenay National Park of Canada encompasses 1,406 square kilometres (543 sq. mi.). Following the Vermilion and Kootenay river valleys, this slender 94-kilometre-long (63-mi.) park embraces several significant geologic features; Kootenay National Park of Canada, a World Heritage Site, is representative of the Rocky Mountain landscape.

Extensive faults created two of the park's significant and different features. Radium Hot Springs at the park's southern end resulted from rainwater and runoff being vaporized deep underground. The steam then returned to the surface via the earth's fissures and condensed in these springs, which were popularized by health buffs at the turn of the 20th century.

At the other end of the park are the Paint Pots, cold springs with a spiritual significance rather than physical. The exit holes, formed by the deposits of the iron-laden water, resemble earthen pots; Blackfoot, Stoney and Kootenay Indians once used the bright bronze mud to stain their bodies, decorate their tepees and draw rock paintings once visible near Sinclair Canyon.

Less dramatic are the topographical differences in the park. The Brisco and Stanford ranges intercept much of the coastal moisture bound for the park's southern region, but to the north, beyond Kootenay Crossing, the climate becomes much damper.

The dry southern climate offers winter shelter for animals migrating from the north and provides good grazing conditions for herds of bighorn sheep. Bears, moose, mountain goats and elk are common. Trails ranging from short hikes to overnight treks explore the park's wealth of evergreen forests, alpine meadows, glaciers and lakes.

General Information and Activities

Although the park is open all year, its three main campgrounds are open only from early May to late September. Winter camping is available at Dolly Varden campground. Information about self-guiding walks, trails, features and facilities can be obtained from information centers in the village of Radium Hot Springs and at Vermilion Crossing from Victoria Day weekend through Labour Day and at the gateway or park headquarters during the rest of the year.

Nonmotorized watercraft are permitted on all lakes and rivers in the park. Climbers can register at the information centers, and back-country campers must obtain a wilderness pass. *See Recreation Chart and the AAA/CAA Western Canada & Alaska CampBook.*

ADMISSION to the park is $9.80; $8.30 (ages 65+); $4.90 (ages 6-16); $19.60 (all occupants of a private vehicle with up to seven people).

PETS must be leashed at all times. Pets are permitted in the back-country overnight.

ADDRESS inquiries to the Superintendent, Kootenay National Park of Canada, Box 220, Radium Hot Springs, BC, Canada V0A 1M0; phone (250) 343-6783 or (800) 748-7275.

Points of Interest

MARBLE CANYON is n. of McLeod Meadows along the Vermilion River and 90 m (295 ft.) from the road. The walls of gray limestone and quartzite laced with a stratum of white and gray dolomite make this one of the most beautiful canyons in the park. Tokumm Creek has cut a sheer, narrow cleft to the depth of about 39 metres (128 ft.).

A self-guiding trail follows the top edge of the canyon and leads to a waterfall. Interpretive signs describe the power of water in shaping the canyon's features. **Time:** Allow 30 minutes minimum.

RADIUM HOT SPRINGS is just n. of the w. entrance to Kootenay National Park of Canada. Water temperatures range from 35 to 47 C (95 to 117 F). There is a hot pool, a cool pool and a 372-square-metre (4,000-sq.-ft.) day spa. Iron oxide also colors the towering sandstone cliffs, giving a perpetual sunset quality. *See Recreation Chart.*

Hours: Pools open daily 9 a.m.-11 p.m., mid-May to mid-Oct.; Sun.-Thurs. noon-9, Fri.-Sat. noon-10, rest of year. **Cost:** $6.30; $5.40 (ages 3-17 and 65+); $19.10 (family, two adults and two children; each additional child $3.40). **Phone:** (250) 347-9485 or (800) 767-1611.

LADYSMITH (G-10)
pop. 6,587, elev. 40 m/131′

On the 49th parallel, Ladysmith is noted for its scenic position between mountain and sea. Founded during the Boer War, Ladysmith was named for a sister city in South Africa. Transfer Beach Park offers a playground, picnic tables and a swimming area watched by lifeguards.

Ladysmith & District Chamber of Commerce:
626 1st Ave., Unit 102, P.O. Box 598, Ladysmith,
BC, Canada V9G 1A4. **Phone:** (250) 245-2112.

LAKE COWICHAN (G-10) pop. 2,948

KAATZA STATION MUSEUM AND ARCHIVES is
at 125 S. Shore Rd. Housed in the renovated Esquimalt and Nanaimo railway station, the museum
features murals, exhibits, photographs and archives
pertaining to various industries as well as pioneer
life in the area. **Time:** Allow 30 minutes minimum.
Hours: Daily 10-4, Mother's Day-Labour Day
weekend; Mon.-Fri. 9-4, Jan. 16-day before Mother's Day and day after Labour Day weekend-Dec.
14. Phone ahead to confirm schedule. **Cost:** $2; free
(ages 0-18). **Phone:** (250) 749-6142.

LANGLEY — *see Vancouver p. 179.*

LILLOOET (B-7) pop. 2,324, elev. 290 m/951'

Lillooet, on the Fraser River, marked the first leg
of the Cariboo Waggon Road and was therefore
sometimes referred to as "Mile 0." The trail reached
north to such destinations as 100 Mile House and
150 Mile House, named for their distances from the
start of the trail. In 1859, during the Cariboo Gold
Rush, the 15,000 inhabitants of Lillooet made it the
most populous city north of San Francisco and west
of Chicago. The surrounding area now is of particular interest to rockhounds.

LILLOOET MUSEUM AND VISITOR CENTRE is
at 790 Main St. Displays in the former Anglican
church include local pioneer relics, farm equipment,
Indian artifacts, Chinese utensils and late 19th-
century rooms. The museum houses the newspaper
equipment collection of Margaret "Ma" Murray,
Lillooet's beloved publisher. **Hours:** Daily 9-5, July-
Aug.; Tues.-Sat. 10-4, mid-Apr. through June 30 and
Sept.-Oct. **Cost:** Donations. **Phone:** (250) 256-4308.

MIYAZAKI HOUSE is at 643 Russell Ln., near jct.
Main St. and 6th Ave., following signs. Originally
owned by Caspar and Cerise Phair, the late 19th-
century house was built in the same architectural style
as Mrs. Phair's family home in Ireland. In the 1940s
Dr. Masajiro Miyazaki and his family purchased the
house. Visitors will learn about this family's history,
including a period when the doctor treated residents of
a local Japanese internment camp.

Tours: Guided tours are available. **Time:** Allow
30 minutes minimum. **Hours:** Tues.-Sat. 10-4:30,
June-Aug.; by appointment rest of year. **Cost:** Donations. **Phone:** (250) 256-6808, or (250) 256-4289
for tour appointments.

LYTTON (B-7) pop. 235, elev. 199 m/650'

At the junction of the Thompson and Fraser rivers, Lytton derives its livelihood from its location.
Indians harvested tons of salmon from this river
junction. Their trail along the Fraser became a major
route to the gold fields, with Lytton as a base of
supplies. This community calls itself the Rafting

Capital of Canada and claims some of the warmest
weather in the country.

Lytton & District Chamber of Commerce: 400
Fraser St., P.O. Box 460, Lytton, BC, Canada V0K
1Z0. **Phone:** (250) 455-2523.

RECREATIONAL ACTIVITIES

White-water Rafting

- **Kumsheen Rafting Resort** is 6 km (4 mi.) n.e.
  on Trans-Canada Hwy. Other activities are offered. **Hours:** Trips operate daily 8-8, May-Sept.
  Phone: (250) 455-2296 or (800) 663-6667.

MAPLE RIDGE — *see Vancouver p. 179.*

MAYNE ISLAND — *see Gulf Islands p. 123.*

MERRITT (C-7) pop. 6,998, elev. 858 m/2,814'

Merritt is known for its many lakes. Of particular
interest is Nicola Lake, a large warm-water lake 10
kilometres (6 mi.) north of town. Recreational activities include swimming, fishing, sailing, water skiing
and windsurfing. Monck Provincial Park, on the west
side of the lake, offers camping and picnic facilities.

Merritt Visitor Centre: 2202 Voght St., P.O. Box
1105, Merritt, BC, Canada V1K 1B8. **Phone:** (250)
378-0349.

NICOLA VALLEY MUSEUM & ARCHIVES is off
Coldwater Ave. at 1675 Tutill Ct. The history of the
region is chronicled in exhibits about mining, logging and ranching. Indian and pioneer artifacts are
displayed, along with photographs depicting the
lives of early settlers.

Time: Allow 30 minutes minimum. **Hours:** Mon.
10-3, Tues.-Sat. 9-5, July-Aug.; Mon.-Fri. 10-3, rest
of year. Closed holidays and Dec. 20-Jan. 3. Phone
ahead to confirm schedule. **Cost:** Donations. **Phone:**
(250) 378-4145.

MISSION — *see Vancouver p. 180.*

MORICETOWN (D-3) elev. 411 m/1,348'

Moricetown is a Wet'suwet'en community that
still practices the traditional hereditary system of
governance. Originally known as Kyah Wiget, it
was once the largest village of the Bulkley River
Carrier tribe, a settlement built some 4,000 years
ago. The town later took the name of Father A.G.
Morice, a missionary who lived among the Carrier
Indians in the late 19th century.

MORICETOWN CANYON is off Hwy. 16 and
Telkawa High Rd. The Bulkley River plunges
through this narrow gorge in a series of waterfalls.
The canyon was vital to First Nations tribes, whose
diet depended on salmon. Visitors can view fish ladders that help five species of salmon reach their annual spawning grounds. During the summer
Wet'suwet'en Indians still can be seen gaffing
salmon as the fish fight their way upstream. **Time:**
Allow 1 hour minimum.

MOUNT REVELSTOKE NATIONAL PARK OF CANADA (A-9)

Elevations in the park range from 760 metres (2,493 ft.) at the bottom of Mount Revelstoke to 1,920 metres (6,300 ft.) at the Mount Revelstoke summit at Balsam Lake. Refer to CAA/AAA maps for additional elevation information.

On the west edge of the Selkirk Range in southeastern British Columbia, Mount Revelstoke National Park of Canada is 260 square kilometres (100 sq. mi.) of sharp peaks, heavily timbered slopes and flowering meadows. The Selkirk Mountains, flanked on the east by the Purcell Range and on the west by the Monashee Range, are distinguished by their height and geologic complexity.

Erosion by glaciers and the heavy rainfall of the region have carved the rock of the Selkirks into jagged forms. Complementing the park's dense green forests and lush wildflower meadows are glacier-fed streams and lakes as well as the deep snows that blanket the slopes until late June.

Deer inhabit the lower slopes; black and grizzly bears and mountain caribou also may be seen in the park. Most mountain species of birds are represented, including fox sparrows, hermit thrushes and northern hawk owls.

The Trans-Canada Highway (Hwy. 1) passes through the southeastern portion of the park for 13 kilometres (8 mi.) and parallels its southern boundary for 18 kilometres (11 mi.).

General Information and Activities

The park is open all year. Visitor facilities and accommodations are available in Revelstoke at the western entrance. A park pass must be purchased at the park kiosk at Rogers Pass Centre.

From Hwy. 1, a 26-kilometre (16-mi.) hard surface road that is open only in summer leads to the summit of Mount Revelstoke, which provides an excellent panoramic view. Along its length are several viewpoints; many wildflowers bloom in August. Picnic areas are available at Monashee, the 8-kilometre (5-mi.) viewpoint on this road, and at Balsam Lake, 1 kilometre (.6 mi.) from the summit. Other picnic areas and nature trails are along the Trans-Canada Highway.

Recreation includes subalpine hiking, mountain climbing and fishing. More than 44 kilometres (27 mi.) of hiking trails lead to such sites as Miller and Jade lakes. Climbers and hikers traveling off park trails may register with a park warden before and after each trip. Fishing is by permit, available at the park administrative office in Revelstoke. *See Recreation Chart.*

ADMISSION to the park is $6.90; $5.90 (ages 65+); $3.45 (ages 6-16); $17.30 (all occupants of a private vehicle with up to seven people).

PETS are permitted in the park provided they are on leashes at all times.

ADDRESS inquiries to the Superintendent, Mount Revelstoke and Glacier National Parks of Canada, P.O. Box 350, Revelstoke, BC, Canada V0E 2S0; phone (250) 837-7500.

NAKUSP (B-10) pop. 1,524, elev. 914 m/2,998'

Nakusp, on the shore of Upper Arrow Lake between the Selkirk and Monashee mountain ranges, is named for an Indian word meaning "bay of quiet waters." Arrow Lake, part of the Columbia River system, is a popular destination for trout and salmon fishing. Heli-skiing is among the many winter activities offered in the area.

Nakusp Chamber of Commerce: 92 6th Ave. N.W., P.O. Box 387, Nakusp, BC, Canada V0G 1R0. **Phone:** (250) 265-4234, or (800) 909-8819 within British Columbia.

NAKUSP HOT SPRINGS is 12 km (7 mi.) n. on Nakusp Hot Springs Rd. Several mineral baths are sheltered by an outdoor cedar structure. The temperature of the pools varies from 36 to 41 C (97-107 F). *See Recreation Chart.*

Hours: Daily 11:30-9:30. Phone ahead to confirm schedule. **Cost:** One swim $8.57; $7.62 (ages 6-17 and 60+); $29 (family, two adults and two children; each additional child $5). Day pass $12.50; $11.50 (ages 6-17 and 60+); $38 (family, two adults and two children; each additional child $5). **Phone:** (250) 265-4528 or (866) 999-4528. 🍴 🎆 🔼

NANAIMO (G-10) pop. 78,692, elev. 30 m/98'

Some 120 kilometres (75 mi.) north of Victoria, Nanaimo began as a Hudson's Bay Co. outpost called Colvilletown, established for miners brought from England and Scotland to mine coal. A thriving forest and marine products industry replaced coal's influence, and the economy of contemporary Nanaimo is centered around technology, service, manufacturing, tourism and recreation.

Offshore islands and nearby mountains and lakes provide a variety of recreational opportunities including hiking, swimming, camping and picnicking. Charter companies offer wildlife tours year-round to view animals such as the area's bald eagles and sea lions.

For a touch of wilderness in the middle of the city, check out Bowen Park, on the Millstone River just north of downtown. This 36-hectare (89-acre) expanse provides an outlet for a variety of activities. Trails wind through forests of fir, hemlock, cedar and maple, and kids enjoy the 4-H barnyard open July through August. A rhododendron grove, a nature center, duck pond, picnic shelters, swimming pool and sports fields complete the complex. In winter, tobogganers take to the park's big hills.

Exotic trees provide a setting for picnicking at Harmac Arboretum, 11 kilometres (7 mi.) south at Harmac Pulp Mill and Duke Point roads. Newcastle Island *(see Recreation Chart and the AAA/CAA Western Canada & Alaska CampBook)* is a marine provincial park accessible by a 10-minute ferry ride from Maffeo-Sutton Park on the harborfront. Automobiles are not permitted; the ferry operates daily every 20 minutes in spring and summer.

In addition to the ferry, salmon sport fishing, scuba diving, windsurfing and sailing are also available from Nanaimo's natural harbor. An intertidal park with three lighted water curtains and a 4-kilometre (2.5-mi.) walkway along the seawall graces Nanaimo's waterfront. St. Jean's Custom Cannery is one of three factories where fishing enthusiasts can have their catch canned or smoked.

On a landscaped hillside, Vancouver Island University offers views of the city and harbor below and also is the site of Nanaimo Art Gallery *(see attraction listing)*. Visitors interested in prehistoric art can see First Nations sandstone carvings at Petroglyph Park, 3.25 kilometres (2 mi.) south on scenic Hwy. 1. Other cultural endeavors can be enjoyed at The Port Theatre, an 800-seat performing arts center at 125 Front St. that hosts local, national and international events; phone (250) 754-8550 for ticket information.

Nanaimo is accessible from the mainland by BC Ferries, which sails from Horseshoe Bay to Departure Bay and from Tsawwassen to Duke Point, 8 kilometres (5 mi.) south of Nanaimo. For more information phone (888) 223-3779.

Tourism Nanaimo: 2290 Bowen Rd., Nanaimo, BC, Canada V9T 3K7. **Phone:** (250) 756-0106 or (800) 663-7337. *See color ad.*

NANAIMO ART GALLERY is on the Vancouver Island University campus at 900 Fifth St. Two galleries display local, regional and national exhibits; the second gallery is downtown at 150 Commercial St. New exhibits are installed frequently.

Time: Allow 1 hour minimum. **Hours:** Campus gallery Mon.-Fri. 10-5, Sat. noon-4. Downtown gallery Tues.-Sat. 10:30-5:30. Closed major holidays. **Cost:** Donations. **Phone:** (250) 740-6350 for the Fifth Street gallery, or (250) 754-1750 for the Commercial Street gallery.

NANAIMO MUSEUM is at 100 Museum Way in the Vancouver Island Conference Centre. Nanaimo's history is explored through exhibits depicting life for the city's earliest settlers, its days as a 19th-century mining center and its transition into the 21st century. Visitors can discover stories about the Snunéymuxw First Nation and check out a replica coal mine to feel what it was like to be an underground miner.

Hours: Daily 10-5, Victoria Day weekend-Labour Day; Tues.-Sat. 10-5, rest of year. Closed winter holidays. Phone ahead to confirm schedule. **Cost:** $3; $2 (ages 6-18, ages 55+ and students with ID). **Phone:** (250) 753-1821.

The Bastion is on Front St. across from the Coast Bastion Inn. The small fort was built in 1853 to protect early settlers. A display shows how the bastion was used in the 1860s. A noon ceremonial cannon firing is conducted by staff dressed in period costumes. **Hours:** Daily 10-3, Victoria Day weekend-Labour Day weekend; by appointment rest of year. **Cost:** Donations. **Phone:** (250) 753-1821.

GAMBLING ESTABLISHMENTS

- **Great Canadian Casinos Nanaimo** is at 620 Terminal Ave. **Hours:** Mon.-Thurs. 11 a.m.-midnight, Fri. 11 a.m.-2 a.m., Sat. 10 a.m.-2 a.m., Sun. 10 a.m.-midnight. **Phone:** (250) 753-3033.

RECREATIONAL ACTIVITIES
Bungee Jumping

- **Wildplay Element Park** is at 35 Nanaimo River Rd. Other activities are offered. **Hours:** Daily 10-6, Victoria Day-Labour Day; Fri.-Mon. 10-6, rest of year. Phone ahead to confirm schedule. **Phone:** (250) 753-5867 or (888) 668-7874.

Hiking

- **Tracks Outdoor Adventures** meets passengers at pre-arranged pick-up points. Other activities are

available. **Hours:** Daily 9-5. **Phone:** (250) 754-8732 or (877) 898-8732.

NELSON (C-11) pop. 9,298, elev. 535 m/1,755'

An old iron and silver mining town, Nelson was settled by prospectors in the late 1880s. With the depletion of its mines, the town turned to logging, sawmilling and area trade. However, the legacy of the bonanza days lives on in the more than 350 heritage sites. Most of Nelson's historic commercial buildings are open to the public, but homes are private and closed to visitors.

Nearby parks, lakes, streams and mountains offer all types of summer and winter recreation. Kokanee Creek and Kokanee Glacier provincial parks (*see Recreation Chart and the AAA/CAA Western Canada & Alaska CampBook*) are 19 kilometres (12 mi.) northeast on Hwy. 3A.

Nelson Chamber of Commerce: 225 Hall St., Nelson, BC, Canada V1L 5X4. **Phone:** (250) 352-3433 or (877) 663-5706.

Self-guiding tours: Maps detailing walking and driving tours are available from the chamber of commerce.

INTERNATIONAL SELKIRK LOOP is a 405-kilometre (280-mi.) scenic byway through southeastern British Columbia and adjoining parts of Washington and Idaho. From Nelson the main route follows Hwy. 6 south to the U.S. border at Nelway. The other leg of the loop heads east on Hwy. 3A to Balfour, where what is said to be the world's longest free ferry service transports vehicles and passengers across Kootenay Lake. Hwy. 3A continues south along the lake's east shore to Creston, where Hwy. 21 connects with the U.S. border at Rykerts.

One 166-kilometre (103-mi.) side route follows Hwys. 3A, 6 and 22 from Nelson to Castlegar and Trail, then Hwy. 3B and 3 from Rossland to Salmo. Another 217-kilometre (135-mi.) side route connects Nelson with Slocan Lake via Hwys. 3A and 6, then continues east from New Denver to Kaslo on Hwy. 31, completing the loop back to Nelson following Hwys. 31 and 3A.

Scenic highlights of the loop include Kootenay Lake, thick coniferous forests, snowcapped peaks and the lush Creston Valley. Museums, historic mining towns, heritage architecture, crafts villages and seasonal produce stands beckon travelers.

Recreational activities abound, including golf, fishing, boating, swimming, hunting, camping, hiking, mountain biking, horseback riding, skiing and snowmobiling. You also can tour a gold mine and soak in a hot spring.

Towns with attraction listings on the loop and its side routes include Ainsworth Hot Springs, Boswell, Castlegar, Creston, Kaslo, Nelson, New Denver, Rossland, Sandon and Trail.

Chambers of commerce and visitor centers on the loop provide maps and more information, or contact the International Selkirk Loop, P.O. Box 920, Bonners Ferry, ID 83805. **Phone:** (208) 267-0822 or (888) 823-2626.

TOUCHSTONES NELSON: MUSEUM OF ART AND HISTORY is at s.e. corner of jct. Vernon and Ward sts. at 502 Vernon St. This renovated building features permanent visual and interactive exhibitions which examine the area's cultural, developmental and economic history. The Shawn Lamb Archives houses a thorough collection of materials relating to the region's diversified origins. Temporary exhibits and galleries also are available and change monthly.

Hours: Daily 10-5, June 15-Labour Day weekend; Tues.-Wed. and Sat. 10-5, Thurs. 10-8, Sun. noon-5, rest of year. Closed major holidays. **Cost:** $10; $6 (ages 60+ and college students with ID); $4 (ages 7-18); $25 (family). **Phone:** (250) 352-9813.

RECREATIONAL ACTIVITIES

Skiing

- **Whitewater Winter Resort** is 20 km (12 mi.) s. off Hwy. 6. **Hours:** Daily 9-3:30, early Dec.-early Apr. **Phone:** (250) 354-4944 or (800) 666-9420.

NEW DENVER (C-10)
pop. 512, elev. 555 m/1,850'

In 1891 prospectors poured into the area; New Denver sprang up as a supply point on the shores of Slocan Lake. Here goods and passengers switched from rail to lake stern-wheelers. The town also provided a more sedate environment to raise a family and conduct business than the rowdy mining camps of the so-called Silvery Slocan.

The Kohan Reflection Garden, at the foot of First Avenue, honors the Japanese-Canadians interned here during World War II. Shacks that formerly housed internees can still be seen around town. The Silvery Slocan Historical Society Museum, housed in the 1897 former Bank of Montreal Building on Sixth Avenue, contains artifacts and exhibits about the town's history; phone (250) 358-2316.

NIKKEI INTERNMENT MEMORIAL CENTRE is at 306 Josephine St. Dedicated to remembering the Japanese internment experience during World War II, the center commemorates the 22,000 Nikkei (people of Japanese descent) removed from their British Columbia homes and relocated to camps. Exhibits include a typical two-family shack, an outhouse and a peace garden. Tribute also is paid to the first generation of Japanese who arrived in Canada in 1877.

Guided tours are available; phone ahead. **Time:** Allow 30 minutes minimum. **Hours:** Daily 9:30-5, Victoria Day-Aug. 31. **Cost:** $6; $4 (ages 60+ and students with ID); free (ages 0-5); $12 (family). **Phone:** (250) 358-7288.

NEW WESTMINSTER—see Vancouver p. 180.

NORTH VANCOUVER—see Vancouver p. 181.

OKANAGAN CENTRE—
see Okanagan Valley p. 140.

OKANAGAN FALLS—
see Okanagan Valley p. 141.

Okanagan Valley

It's one thing to read about a place; it's quite another to experience it in person. Evocatively written guides and glossy photo books can pique the curiosity and whet the appetite of almost any traveler, but when it comes down to it you really need to get out of the armchair and go. This is certainly true of the Okanagan (oh-ka-NOG-an) Valley; in a province almost embarrassingly gifted with scenic riches, it still manages to stand out.

British Columbia—like much of Canada—is notable for its sheer ruggedness: lofty mountains, expansive forests, rushing rivers. The valley, in contrast, is an anomaly; it could almost be Italy or some other sun-kissed land. The sun does indeed shine warmly, and the azure sky is huge. Tawny bluffs rise from the shores of steel-blue lakes. Scraggly pine trees and compact mounds of silvery gray sagebrush cloak hillsides. Parts of the Okanagan are arid enough to meet the meteorological criteria of a desert, but irrigation has transformed it into one of the most productive fruit- and vegetable-growing regions in North America.

A Land Created by Glaciers

This long, narrow valley was shaped over time by glacial movement. Layers of ice more than a mile thick began retreating some 10,000 years ago, scraping the surface of the land and leaving behind deposits of sediment. Flowing mountain rivers caused innumerable cycles of flooding and erosion. All this water action contributed to a slow but steady accumulation of nutrient-rich soils that over time formed fertile deltas, setting the stage for the valley's eventual blossoming as an agricultural powerhouse.

Impressive mountains, with some peaks topping 3,000 metres (9,800 ft.), flank both sides of the Okanagan Valley—the Monashee range to the east, the Cascades to the west. The mountain systems in this part of North America are oriented in a north-south direction paralleling the Pacific coast, and the intervening valleys follow suit. The entire area is part of the vast Interior Plateau, an uplifted section of the Earth's crust that covers much of British Columbia's southern interior.

One of the Okanagan Valley's many virtues is its topographical variety—everything from desert to grassland to forest. The northern end is wetter and greener, with a panorama of snowcapped mountains rising off in the distance. As you head south into the heart of the valley the trees become more scattered; ponderosa pines speckling the hills are replaced by shrubs like antelope bush and hardy plants like

Okanagan Lake / © Don Weixl / age fotostock

bunch grass (so named because it grows in individual clumps or tufts rather than forming a uniform carpet), both of which are adapted to a drier climate.

Farther south the Okanagan verges on true desert. In and around Osoyoos the landscape is austere; towering cliffs and bare hillsides flaunt a palette of browns, beiges and grays, and the grasses and other low-growing plants are buffeted by persistent dry winds. The desert plants and animals that inhabit this arid environment are found nowhere else in Canada; the far southern end of the Okanagan Valley lies just above the northernmost reach of the Sonoran Desert, which extends south all the way into Mexico. This also is the country's warmest region, with relatively mild winters, hot summers and abundant sunshine, an ideal combination for irrigation-assisted agriculture.

Between Osoyoos to the east and Princeton to the west is the Similkameen Valley, nestled between steep rocky hills and threaded by the Similkameen River. Although a geographically separate region, it shares the southern Okanagan Valley's dramatic scenery and climatological characteristics. Similkameen country is known for its cattle ranches, horse farms and fruit orchards, and bills itself variously as the "Fruit Stand Capital of Canada" and "BC's Garden of Eden" in an attempt to step out of the better-known Okanagan's shadow.

Hwy. 3, also called the Crowsnest Highway, meanders along the province's southern border from Hope east to the Alberta border. Between Keremeos and Osoyoos the highway traverses an area that climatologists classify as a mid-altitude steppe, although it certainly *looks* like a desert. Away from the sweep of the ever-present irrigation sprinklers,

Okanagan Centre / © Wave Royalty Free / age fotostock

this little portion of extreme southern British Columbia—known as Canada's "pocket desert"—is home to sagebrush, prickly pear cactus, Western rattlesnakes and even the odd scorpion, all of which thrive in these desert-like conditions.

The bracing beauty of the Similkameen countryside is particularly evident in the vicinity of Hedley, a small village about 76 kilometres (47 mi.) west of Osoyoos on Hwy. 3. Here the waters of Hedley Creek rush into the Similkameen River. Stemwinder Mountain looms to the west, Nickel Plate Mountain to the east. Marbled cliffs rise up on both sides of the highway (the Similkameen Indians named this area Sna-za-ist, meaning "the striped rock place"). Notes of color are supplied by a bright blue sky, the deep green of flourishing fruit trees and (in season) the gold and purple hues of ripening apricots, peaches, plums and grapes.

About 9 kilometres (5.5 mi.) west of Osoyoos is Spotted Lake, which gets its name from one of the world's highest concentrations of magnesium sulfate, calcium, sodium sulfates and other minerals. In summer much of the lake's water evaporates and the minerals crystallize into circles on the surface that can be white, pale yellow, green or blue, depending on the mineral composition. The lake is on private land, but you can view it from the highway.

The Okanagan Valley's distinguishing feature, in fact, is its chain of long, narrow lakes that stretch from north to south. Created by receding glaciers, they are kept fresh and full by snowmelt and runoff from the mountains that flank both sides of the valley. The largest is Okanagan Lake, which stretches north to south for some 111 kilometres (69 mi.) while averaging just 5 kilometres (3 mi.) wide. Skaha, Vaseux and Osoyoos lakes continue the chain

to the south. To the east of Okanagan Lake are Kalamalka and Wood lakes; just north is little Swan Lake.

Cattle, Gold, Fruit and Wine

These valleys were first inhabited by the Okanagan Indians, an Interior Salish First Nations tribe. They hunted wild game, fished salmon runs, foraged for roots and berries and traded with other nations. The first European arrivals were fur traders searching for accessible routes to transport their goods to the Pacific. In the early 19th century they ventured north from Fort Okanogan, a Pacific Fur Co. trading post at the confluence of the Okanagan and Columbia rivers in present-day Washington state. Fur caravans were soon heading in and out of the valley region.

When the Oregon Treaty designated the 49th parallel as the border between the United States and the Canadian territory, Osoyoos became a port of entry, and vast herds of cattle were trailed through customs to supply food for miners who panned for

Destination Okanagan Valley

*N*ature has blessed the Okanagan Valley with fertile soil and sunny weather. Irrigation has transformed this delightfully scenic region into an agricultural wonderland known for its bounteous harvests of apples, apricots, peaches and other fruit.

*T*he Okanagan's picturesque hills also are striped with orderly rows of grapevines; this is British Columbia's premier wine-producing region, and dozens of small wineries are tucked into pastoral rural settings.

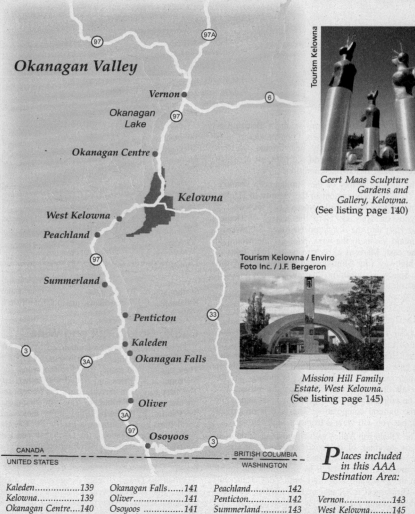

Okanagan Valley

Vernon

Okanagan Lake

Okanagan Centre

Kelowna

West Kelowna

Peachland

Summerland

Penticton

Kaleden

Okanagan Falls

Oliver

Osoyoos

CANADA
UNITED STATES

BRITISH COLUMBIA
WASHINGTON

Tourism Kelowna

Geert Maas Sculpture Gardens and Gallery, Kelowna. (See listing page 140)

Tourism Kelowna / Enviro Foto Inc. / J.F. Bergeron

Mission Hill Family Estate, West Kelowna. (See listing page 145)

*P*laces included in this AAA Destination Area:

placer gold along the Similkameen River. The bunch grass that grew along the river valley provided abundant forage, and ranches began to be established.

Father Charles Pandosy, an Oblate priest, founded a mission in 1859 on the eastern shore of Okanagan Lake. He and his followers endured a harsh first winter—they were forced to shoot their horses for food—but went on to build other missions in the Okanagan Valley, where Father Pandosy instructed the native people in European agricultural techniques in addition to performing baptisms, marriages and funerals.

The discovery of gold on the Fraser River in 1858 resulted in a full-fledged gold rush. British Columbia's southern interior was further opened up with the building of the Caribou Road (now Hwy. 97) and the Dewdney Trail (now Hwy. 3). By the late 19th century the Okanagan and Similkameen valleys were buzzing with gold camps and boom towns that began to spring up along the shores of the region's lakes.

The fruit industry that today is a hallmark of the Okanagan began with difficulty. Apple orchards were planted as early as 1892, but it wasn't until the 1920s that fruit crops proved economically successful. The valley's warm temperatures and long growing season—besides providing Canadians with approximately one-third of their apples—nurtures verdant orchards of apricots, cherries, peaches, pears and plums.

Commercial grape plantings near Kelowna supplied the Okanagan's first wineries. The local wine industry has grown exponentially since the introduction of large-scale irrigation, and almost all of British Columbia's wine comes from the Okanagan region. The diversity of growing conditions—from the hot, sandy desert soils of the south to the deep topsoil and clay of the cooler north, plus distinct microclimates created by the valley's lakes—help ensure a diversity of wines.

Vineyards at the southern end of the valley produce such vintages as Chardonnay, Merlot, Cabernet Sauvignon, Pinot Gris and Pinot Noir, while vineyards in the central and northern valley specialize in Pinot Blanc, Riesling and Gewürztraminer wines. Some grapes are left to freeze on the vine to produce icewine, a rich, sweet dessert wine. One of the Okanagan's most picturesque sights is orderly rows of grapevines, often covering a hillside that overlooks a deep blue lake.

Hwy. 97, which runs the length of British Columbia from the U.S. border just south of Osoyoos north to Watson Lake at the Yukon Territory border, is the principal route through the Okanagan Valley. From Osoyoos it travels north to Penticton, then follows the western shore of Okanagan Lake before crossing the lake on a floating bridge (the largest in the country) that is scheduled to be replaced with an overhead bridge.

Okanagan Lake is said to be the home of Ogopogo, the best known of Canada's unexplained lake

Kelowna Land and Orchard Co., Kelowna / © AAA / Ron Willis

creatures. Sightings of the mythical beast—most often described as 5 to 6 metres (15 to 20 ft.) long, shaped like a log and with a head resembling that of a horse or goat—date back as far as 1872. Indians believed that Ogopogo's home was small, barren Rattlesnake Island; they claimed that the island's rocky beaches were sometimes strewn with animal parts, presumably dinner remains, and when crossing the lake during bad weather always took along a small animal that would be thrown overboard in order to appease the monster. Interestingly, there are similarities between Okanagan Lake and Scotland's Loch Ness, home of the famed Loch Ness Monster; both bodies of water are long and narrow, and both lie at about the same latitude.

East of the lake Hwy. 97 winds north to Enderby, the unofficial northern end of the valley, before continuing on toward Sicamous. But whether you proceed from south to north or north to south, this 211-kilometre (131 mi.) journey through the heart of the Okanagan is utterly delightful. One minute the highway is running tantalizingly close to a sparkling lakeshore; the next it's in the shadow of a soaring, sagebrush-dotted bluff or looking down on checkerboard farmland. Each bend and turn reveals a new view, and each one is lovely. The scenery alone would be more than enough to recommend this drive, even if you didn't make a single stop.

Year-Round Fun

But of course you *will* want to stop, because this is Canada's No. 1 year-round recreation destination. Dozens of parks ring Okanagan Lake, offering myriad opportunities for hiking, backpacking, mountain biking and camping. Bear Creek Provincial Park, about 9 kilometres (6 mi.) west of Kelowna off Hwy. 97, has miles of hiking trails to explore, all beginning from a common trailhead at the park entrance. Bear Creek runs through the bottom of a tree-walled canyon, and the trails above wind past ponderosa pine, Douglas fir, juniper and prickly pear cactus that frame expansive lake views.

The lakes are, of course, ideal for water recreation, whether it's sailing, paddle boating, water skiing, jet skiing, kayaking, canoeing or freshwater fishing. Okanagan Lake is ringed with sandy beaches and sheltered coves, and numerous marina facilities provide equipment rentals.

For a northern Okanagan getaway head out to Kalamalka Lake Provincial Park, about 8 kilometres (5 mi.) southeast of Vernon off Hwy. 6. Kalamalka is known as a "marl lake," a process that begins when the water warms, forming calcium carbonate and limestone crystals that reflect sunlight. The water's distinctive blue-green color is often shot through with ribbons of deep blue, earning it the nickname "lake of a thousand colors." This largely undeveloped park encompasses rolling grasslands and forested ridges where Douglas fir and lodgepole pine grow; a paved trail leads to secluded beaches. Wildlife ranges from mule deer and minks to bobcats and western painted turtles. Bird-watching is rewarding, and the spring wildflower display is spectacular.

Nearly 40 golf courses are scattered from Vernon south to Osoyoos, with many of them concentrated around Kelowna. Due to the mild climate most courses open as early as March, and golfers frequently play into November. And this being the Okanagan, it's only natural that water and fruit trees figure into course layouts; the grounds of the Kelowna Springs Golf Club include seven spring-fed lakes, while fairways at the Harvest Golf Club are set in the midst of a huge hillside apple orchard and have prime views of Okanagan Lake.

Kelowna is the Okanagan Valley's largest city and a big summer vacation destination. Water sports—sailing, kayaking, windsurfing, fishing—rule the summer calendar, but downtown Kelowna also offers museums, art galleries, pretty lakeside parks, all kinds of restaurants and a lively nightlife. It makes a convenient base for touring the many small wineries in the vicinity.

Breezy Penticton has the best of both worlds: the north end of town fronts the southern tip of Okanagan Lake, while the south end brushes up against the north shore of Skaha Lake. Lakeside beaches give the city a summery feel, and families flock to Penticton's amusement centers, go-cart tracks, miniature golf course and waterslides. Stroll along Front Street, the original business corridor, which is lined with restaurants and funky little shops.

Situated between Swan, Kalamalka and Okanagan lakes, Vernon started out as a camp on the Okanagan Valley trail during the fur trade years; by the turn of the 20th century it was a bustling ranching center. Downtown Vernon truly earns the description "quaint": The tree-lined, flower-filled streets are packed with historic old buildings and specialty stores selling everything from Victorian crafts to homemade jams. Be sure to search out the 27 outdoor murals—some up to 91 metres (300 ft.) long—that depict Okanagan history, folklore and landscapes.

Just a stone's throw from the U.S. border, Osoyoos (oh-SOY-yoos) means, in the local Inkaneep native dialect, "where the water narrows"—a reference to its location spanning a narrow portion of Osoyoos Lake. Vineyards and orchards abound in the surrounding countryside, and the lake is one of Canada's warmest. Stroll along one of the lakeside parks in town while watching windsurfers and parasailing enthusiasts do their thing under sunny summer skies, and it's not that hard to believe you've happened onto some undiscovered Mediterranean resort.

The Okanagan Valley has something to offer regardless of the season. Downhill and cross-country skiers, snowboarders and other winter sports enthusiasts can choose from four ski resorts: Silver Star Mountain Resort, north of Vernon; Big White Ski Resort near Kelowna; Crystal Mountain resort near West Kelowna; and Apex Mountain Resort, southwest of Penticton.

Spring and summer are seasons to experience the valley's agricultural bounty. In the spring fruit trees are in full glorious bloom. Spring into early summer also is the time when wildflowers make their appearance in the Okanagan's wilderness parks.

Harvest time for the region's famous fruits and vegetables begins in late June and lasts until mid-October. If you're here in the summer or fall stop at one of the ubiquitous roadside fruit stands, which seem almost as plentiful as the trees themselves. Cherries are first in the fruit parade, ripening from late June through mid-July. Peaches appear from mid-July through September; pears in August and September; plums in September; and apples from August through October.

Practically every town in the valley has a farmers market, and you'll want to check out every single one. In addition to all sorts of fruit, the markets offer tomatoes, pumpkins, squash, asparagus, organic preserves, homemade pies, artisanal cheeses, honey, herbs, flowers—just about everything. Most are open April or May through October.

Grapes are harvested September through mid-October, an ideal time to go winery hopping. Most of the Okanagan's roughly 100 wineries can be visited, many have an intriguing history to share, and practically all of them enjoy a picturesque rural setting. Before hitting the tasting bars, pick up information and maps at any local visitor center.

So when should you plan a trip? Come to think of it, just about *any* time is right.

Destinations in this region listed under their own names are Kaleden, Kelowna, Okanagan Centre, Okanagan Falls, Oliver, Osoyoos, Peachland, Penticton, Summerland, Vernon and West Kelowna.

KALEDEN (C-9) pop. 1,289

DOMINION RADIO ASTROPHYSICAL OBSERVATORY is at 717 White Lake Rd. The site features radio telescopes used to study the universe. A self-guiding tour includes a 26-metre (85-ft.) parabolic antenna and an array of more sophisticated, computer-linked, 9-metre (30-ft.) antennae.

Since automobile ignitions cause radio interference, visitors are asked to leave their vehicles at the road and walk the 600 metres (.4 mi.) to the facility. **Time:** Allow 30 minutes minimum. **Hours:** Visitor center daily 10-5, Easter weekend-second Mon. in Oct.; Mon.-Fri. 10-4:30, rest of year. Guided tours are given Sat.-Sun. 2-5, July-Aug. **Cost:** Free. **Phone:** (250) 493-2277 or (250) 490-4355.

KELOWNA (C-9)
pop. 106,707, elev. 420 m/1,387'

Kelowna is the center of a fruit and vineyard region around Lake Okanagan, from which one-third of all apples harvested in Canada are shipped. The lake also is known for its legendary monster, the Ogopogo, a Loch Ness type beast reportedly 9 to 21 metres (30-69 ft.) long with a head resembling that of a horse, goat or sheep.

The Kelowna Community Theatre stages productions during fall and winter; phone (250) 763-9018. The Okanagan Symphony Orchestra is another prominent cultural feature; phone (250) 763-7544.

Recreation in the area includes water sports, fishing and golf. City Park on Lake Okanagan is the city's largest park, with a beach, tennis courts and a children's water park. The *Kelowna Princess II* sets sail from the park's lakefront (end of Bernard Street). Departures are subject to weather conditions; for information and sailing times phone (250) 869-6696.

The fall grape harvest is celebrated for 10 days in early October at the ⚘ Okanagan Fall Wine Festival. Wine and food lovers congregate to take in more than 165 events that take place throughout the Okanagan Valley.

Kelowna Visitor Centre: 544 Harvey Ave., Kelowna, BC, Canada V1Y 6C9. **Phone:** (250) 861-1515 or (800) 663-4345. *See color ad.*

B.C. ORCHARD INDUSTRY MUSEUM is at 1304 Ellis St. Housed in the historic Laurel Packing House, the museum explores the Okanagan's roots in the orchard industry. A 15-metre (50-ft.) model train layout is displayed. Other displays explain fruit production from planting to processing and preserving. The Apple Tree Activities Centre is available for children. **Time:** Allow 30 minutes minimum. **Hours:** Mon.-Fri. 10-5, Sat. 10-4. Closed Jan. 1 and Dec. 25-26. **Cost:** Donations. **Phone:** (250) 763-0433.

The BC Wine Museum & VQA Wine Shop is at 1304 Ellis St. Housed in a converted 1917 packing

house, the museum displays machines used for pressing and bottling as well as exhibits featuring the history of wine production in the area. Wine tastings are offered. Guided tours are available by appointment. **Hours:** Open Mon.-Fri. 10-6, Sat. 10-5, Sun. and holidays 11-5. Closed Jan. 1 and Dec. 25-26. **Cost:** Donations. **Phone:** (250) 868-0441.

ELYSIUM GARDENS is at 2834 Belgo Rd. The site covers 3 acres and includes organically grown perennial gardens and a Japanese garden. Featured are herb gardens, cut flower and kitchen gardens, xeriscape gardens, ornamental grasses and rock and scree beds. Dependent on the season, visitors will discover peonies, roses, primroses, tulips, day lilies and hydrangeas in full, fragrant bloom. Mountains and countryside views provide a backdrop for the gardens.

Time: Allow 1 hour minimum. **Hours:** Tues.-Sun. and holidays 9-5, Mar. 31-Sept. 30. **Cost:** $8.50; $4 (students with ID); free (ages 0-11); $18 (family). **Phone:** (250) 491-1368.

GEERT MAAS SCULPTURE GARDENS AND GALLERY is 10 km (6.2 mi.) n. on Hwy. 97N, then 2 km (1.2 mi.) w. on Sexsmith Rd. to 250 Reynolds Rd. Maas' semi-abstract sculptures of bronze, aluminum, stainless steel, stoneware and mixed media are exhibited in the gallery and in the .4-hectare (1-acre) sculpture garden. The complex contains one of the largest collections of bronze sculptures in Canada.

Medallions, paintings, etchings and reliefs can be seen in the permanent collection; changing exhibits also are offered. Time: Allow 1 hour minimum. **Hours:** Mon.-Sat. 10-5, May 1-Oct. 1; by appointment rest of year. Phone ahead to confirm schedule. **Cost:** Donations. **Phone:** (250) 860-7012.

KELOWNA LAND AND ORCHARD CO. is 3 km (1.9 mi.) s. on Gordon Rd., 4 km (2.5 mi.) e. on K.L.O. Rd., then 1 km (.6 mi.) n. on E. Kelowna Rd. to 3002 Dunster Rd. The working orchard offers visitors a chance to see techniques of the past as well as farm animals and current technologies used in growing apples. Self-guiding walking tours and guided covered hay-wagon tours of the orchard are available. Juice samples are included. A cidermaking facility also is on site.

Allow 30 minutes minimum for the walking tour, 1 hour minimum for the wagon tour. **Hours:** Grounds open daily 8-5. Guided wagon tours depart daily, Easter weekend-Oct. 31; by appointment, Nov.-Dec. Phone ahead for tour times. **Cost:** Self-guiding tours free. Guided tours $7.50; $5 (ages 8-16). **Phone:** (250) 763-1091. ⏱

OKANAGAN HERITAGE MUSEUM is at 470 Queensway Ave. Natural history displays offer a glimpse back into the history and settlement of the Okanagan Valley. The museum features a natural history gallery as well as rotating special exhibitions that explore regional and contemporary themes.

Hours: Daily 10-5. Closed Jan. 1 and Dec. 25-26. **Cost:** Donations. **Phone:** (250) 763-2417.

OKANAGAN MILITARY MUSEUM is at 1424 Ellis St. between Queensway and Doyle Ave. Permanent exhibits focus on the contributions of Okanagan Valley residents in the military. Items from the Boer War, World War I, World War II and others are on display. A reference library holds books on military history, and volunteer veterans are on-site to answer questions. **Time:** Allow 30 minutes minimum. **Hours:** Tues.-Sat. 10-4, June-Sept.; Tues., Thurs. and Sat. 10-4, rest of year. **Cost:** Donations. **Phone:** (250) 763-9292.

GAMBLING ESTABLISHMENTS

* **Lake City Casino** is at 1310 Water St. **Hours:** Daily 10 a.m.-4 a.m., June-Oct.; 10 a.m.-2 a.m., rest of year. **Phone:** (250) 860-9467.

RECREATIONAL ACTIVITIES

Skiing

* **Big White Ski Resort** is 54 km (34 mi.) e. on Hwy. 33 at 5315 Big White Rd. **Hours:** Daily 8:45-3:30 (also Tues.-Sat. 5-8), early Dec. to mid-Apr. **Phone:** (250) 765-3101 or (800) 663-6882.

WINERIES

* **CedarCreek Estate Winery** is 12 km (7 mi.) s. at 5445 Lakeshore Rd., following signs. **Hours:** Tastings daily 10-6, May-Oct.; 11-5, rest of year. Tours are given daily at 11, 1 and 3, May-Oct. Closed Jan. 1 and Dec. 25-26. **Phone:** (250) 764-8866, or (800) 730-9463 in Canada.

* **Quails' Gate Estate Winery** is at 3303 Boucherie Rd. at jct. Sunnyside Rd. **Hours:** Tastings daily 9:30-7, late June-Labour Day and Oct. 1-11; 10-7, late Apr.-late June and day after Labour Day-Sept. 30; 10-6, rest of year. Tours are given daily on the hour 11-4, late June-Labour Day and Oct. 1-11; daily at 11, 1 and 3, late Apr.-late June and day after Labour Day-Sept. 30. Phone ahead to confirm schedule. **Phone:** (250) 769-4451 or (800) 420-9463.

* **Summerhill Pyramid Organic Winery** is at 4870 Chute Rd. **Hours:** Daily 9-9. Tours are given on the hour. **Phone:** (250) 764-8000 or (800) 667-3538.

OKANAGAN CENTRE (C-8)
elev. 344 m/1,129'

WINERIES

* **Gray Monk Estate Winery** is at 1055 Camp Rd. **Hours:** Tastings daily 9-9, July-Aug.; daily 10-5, mid-Mar. through June 30 and Sept.-Oct.; Mon.-Sat. 11-5, Sun. noon-4, rest of year. Tours are given daily on the hour 11-4, Apr.-Oct.; daily at 2 in Mar. and Nov.-Dec.; Mon.-Sat. at 2, rest of year. Closed Jan. 1 and Dec. 25-26. **Phone:** (250) 766-3168 or (800) 663-4205.

OKANAGAN FALLS (C-9)

WINERIES

- **Hawthorne Mountain Vineyards** is 5 km (3 mi.) s.w. on Green Lake Rd. **Hours:** Daily 9-5, May-Oct.; 9-4, rest of year. Guided tours are given daily at 11, 1 and 3, May-Oct. Closed major holidays. **Phone:** (250) 497-8267.

OLIVER (D-9) pop. 4,370, elev. 307 m/1,007′

The northern tip of the American Great Basin Desert, which extends to Mexico, begins at Oliver. Irrigation begun in the 1920s converted the once desertlike valley floor and arid hillsides surrounding the town into productive orchards and vineyards. Abundant sunshine and little rain provide ideal conditions for growing wine grapes.

The area's climate also promotes numerous recreational activities. An 18-kilometre (11-mi.) paved bicycle trail travels through Oliver's rolling hills and along the Okanagan River. The valley lakes and streams offer boating and fishing. Vaseux Lake and Inkaneep provincial parks *(see Recreation Chart)* are nearby, as are Bear and Madden lakes, known for excellent trout fishing.

The Fairview Townsite, 3 kilometres (1.9 mi.) west on Fairview Road, formerly was the site of an 1880s boomtown. The town disappeared along with the gold in 1906; plaques at the site provide historical information.

Oliver Visitor Centre: 36205 93rd St., P.O. Box 460, Oliver, BC, Canada V0H 1T0. **Phone:** (250) 498-6321 or (866) 498-6321.

WINERIES

- **Inniskillin Okanagan Vineyards** is 5 km (3 mi.) s. on Hwy. 97 to Rd. 11W. **Hours:** Tastings daily 10-5, Apr.-Oct.; 10-4, rest of year. Tours are given daily, Apr.-Oct.; by appointment rest of year. Closed Jan. 1 and Dec. 24-26. **Phone:** (250) 498-6663 or (800) 498-6211.

OSOYOOS (D-9)
pop. 4,752, elev. 335 m/1,099′

From Osoyoos on the east side of Osoyoos Lake, an area of desert sand extends 48 kilometres (30 mi.) north to Skaha Lake and 24 kilometres (15 mi.) west along the Similkameen River. The area's similarity to Spain in climate and terrain inspired the citizens to adopt an Iberian style in their buildings. Despite its arid surroundings, Osoyoos has 19 kilometres (12 mi.) of sandy beach lining one of Canada's warmest freshwater lakes.

Man-made recreational facilities include the Wild Rapids on East Lakeshore Drive, with three large waterslides, five giant hot tubs and two minislides. Skiing is available nearby.

A heavy concentration of minerals, including evaporated copper, silver, gold and sulfate and Epsom salts, can be found at Spotted Lake, west on

Crowsnest Hwy. 3, which provides 446 kilometres (277 mi.) of scenic driving all the way to Hope.

Osoyoos & District Chamber of Commerce: 7610 Veterans Way, P.O. Box 227, Osoyoos, BC, Canada V0H 1V0. **Phone:** (250) 495-7142.

NK'MIP DESERT CULTURAL CENTRE is at 1000 Rancher Creek Rd. Visitors will experience a desert ecosystem and the traditions of the Okanagan people through interactive exhibits, artifacts, a re-created Okanagan village and self-guiding walking trails. The Village Trail is 1.4 kilometres (.9 mi.) long and has interpretive signs, benches and ramadas; the Loop Trail is 2 kilometres (1.2 mi.) and includes several uphill segments.

Tours: Guided tours are available. **Time:** Allow 1 hour minimum. **Hours:** Daily 9:30-4:30, mid-May to mid-Oct.; Tues.-Sat. 9:30-4, mid-Oct. through Oct. 31. **Cost:** $12; $8 (ages 6-18); $11 (ages 65+ and students with ID); $36 (family, two adults and two or more children). **Phone:** (250) 495-7901 or (888) 495-8555.

OSOYOOS DESERT CENTRE is 2.9 km (1.9 mi.) n. of jct. hwys. 3 and 97, then 1.2 km (.7 mi.) w. to 14580 146th Ave. The 26.8-hectare (66-acre) ecological, interpretive and education center is within the northern outpost of the Great Basin Desert, part of the vast Sonoran Desert that extends from Washington south into Mexico.

In addition to hands-on exhibits and a native plant demonstration garden, the center offers narrated 60-minute guided tours on a 1.5-kilometre (1-mi.) boardwalk trail that allow visitors to learn about rare, threatened and endangered plant and animal species. Night tours offer a greater chance to catch a glimpse of the nocturnal animals that live in this harsh environment.

Pets are not permitted. **Time:** Allow 1 hour, 30 minutes minimum. **Hours:** Open daily 9:30-4:30, mid-May to mid-Sept.; 10-2, late Apr. to mid-May and mid-Sept. to early Oct. Guided tours depart at 10, noon and 2, mid-May to mid-Sept. Hours may vary; phone ahead to confirm and to inquire about summer night tours. **Cost:** $7; $6 (ages 13-17 and 65+); $5 (ages 6-12); $16 (family). **Phone:** (250) 495-2470, or (877) 899-0897 in British Columbia.

OSOYOOS MUSEUM & ARCHIVES is in Gyro Community Park at 19 Park Pl. The museum houses children's art from the Inkameep Day School Art Collection—art and photographs created 1931-43 under the guidance of Anthony Walsh, the teacher and principal who based his teaching on the importance of art in education. Exhibits also include a butterfly collection, a Victorian parlor, First Nations artifacts, pioneer and agricultural artifacts, and an 1892 log building that served as a customs house, jail, school, residence and government office over the years.

Time: Allow 1 hour minimum. **Hours:** Daily 10-4, July-Aug.; Tues.-Fri. 10-2, mid-Jan. through

June 30 and Sept. 1 to mid-Dec. Last admission is 30 minutes before closing. Phone ahead to confirm schedule. **Cost:** $5; $2 (ages 6-14); $10 (family). **Phone:** (250) 495-2582.

WINERIES

- **Nk'Mip Cellars** is at 1400 Rancher Creek Rd. **Hours:** Tastings daily 9-5, May-Oct.; 10-4, rest of year. Tours daily at 11, 1 and 3. **Phone:** (250) 495-2985.

PEACHLAND (C-8)
pop. 4,883, elev. 366 m/1,200'

Peachland's rolling green countryside is a prosperous fruit growing, farming, lumber producing and mining area. The mining of molybdenum and copper from the Brenda Mines complex in the hills above Hwy. 97 spurred significant growth during the 1970s.

Nearby mountains, rivers and lakes, including Okanagan Lake (see Recreation Chart), offer abundant opportunities for skiing, hiking, fishing and water sports.

HARDY FALLS REGIONAL PARK is off Hwy. 97 via Hardy Rd. This tucked-away little jewel of a park has a paved walking trail that runs along the wall of a steep-banked canyon. At the end of the trail a lovely little waterfall tumbles down a rocky hillside into the waters of Deep Creek. Bright red kokanee salmon provide a brilliant show of color in early September as they return to their spawning grounds to lay their eggs. **Time:** Allow 30 minutes minimum. **Hours:** Daily dawn-dusk. **Cost:** Free.

PENTICTON (C-9)
pop. 31,909, elev. 345 m/1,131'

The first orchards in Okanagan Valley were planted by the Oblates at Okanagan Mission 1860-61, and the fruits, especially peaches, became a staple of the area. Tom Ellis established the first cattle ranch in 1865 and it was an empire when he sold it for a hefty sum in 1905; by 1909 orchards had replaced cattle in the agricultural economy. Today Penticton's fruit industry combines with tourism and lumber industries to keep the community strong.

Okanagan and Skaha lakes, at opposite ends of the city, offer ample expanses of shoreline for recreational pursuits. A popular summer activity is floating down the 8-kilometre (5-mi.) river channel from the mouth of Okanagan Lake (see Recreation Chart and the AAA/CAA Western Canada & Alaska CampBook) to Skaha Lake. The channel has rest and picnic areas and is paralleled by a bicycle path and a jogging trail. The Casabella Princess, a 48-passenger paddlewheeler departing from Penticton Marina, takes passengers on a 1-hour cruise of the south end of Okanagan Lake; phone (250) 492-4090.

Penticton Visitor Centre: 553 Railway St., Penticton, BC, Canada V2A 8S3. **Phone:** (250) 493-4055 or (800) 663-5052.

OKANAGAN INLAND MARINE HERITAGE PARK & SS SICAMOUS RESTORATION SOCIETY is on Okanagan Lake Beach at 1099 Lakeshore Dr. Featured on-site is the Sicamous, the last steam-powered stern-wheeler to operate on Okanagan Lake. Visitors can experience what once was a major means of transportation in the area. Also on view is the 1914 tugboat SS Naramata; it is one of only two tugs from the steam era that has survived in the province.

Time: Allow 30 minutes minimum. **Hours:** Tues.-Sat. 10-6, Sun. 10-4. Phone ahead to confirm schedule. **Cost:** $5; $2 (ages 5-12). **Phone:** (250) 492-0403 or (866) 492-0403.

PENTICTON ART GALLERY is at 199 Marina Way. Four exhibition halls and an art loft comprise the facility on the shore of Okanagan Lake, where works by professional local, provincial and nationally known artists are displayed. **Time:** Allow 30 minutes minimum. **Hours:** Tues.-Fri. 10-5, Sat.-Sun. noon-5; closed statutory holidays and Dec. 24-Jan. 1. **Cost:** $2; free (ages 0-19). **Phone:** (250) 493-2928.

PENTICTON MUSEUM is at 785 Main St. Displays describe the natural and social histories of the southern Okanagan Valley. A historic transportation exhibit about the Kettle Valley Railway is available along with an exhibit about the Canadian military.

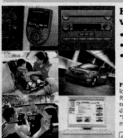

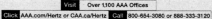

Summer programs include cemetery walks, heritage tours and children's activities. **Time:** Allow 1 hour minimum. **Hours:** Tues.-Sat. 10-5. Closed major holidays. **Cost:** Donations. **Phone:** (250) 490-2451.

GAMBLING ESTABLISHMENTS

• **Lake City Casino** is at 21 Lakeshore Dr. W. **Hours:** Daily 10 a.m.-2 a.m. **Phone:** (250) 487-1280.

RECREATIONAL ACTIVITIES

Skiing

• **Apex Mountain Resort** is 32 km (20 mi.) w. off Green Mountain Rd. Other activities are available. **Hours:** Daily 9-3:30, mid-Nov. through Mar. 30. **Phone:** (250) 292-8222 or (877) 777-2739.

WINERIES

• **Hillside Estate Winery** is 3 km (2 mi.) n. of jct. McMillan Ave. and Naramata Rd. at 1350 Naramata Rd. **Hours:** Tastings and self-guiding tours daily 10-6, May 1 to mid-Oct.; 11-4, in Apr.; by appointment rest of year. **Phone:** (250) 493-6274 or (888) 923-9463.

SUMMERLAND (C-9)
pop. 10,713, elev. 454 m/1,489'

Surrounded by lush orchards and vineyards, Summerland depends on fruit cultivation as its main industry. Overlooking Okanagan Lake *(see Recreation Chart and the AAA/CAA Western Canada & Alaska CampBook)*, the first commercial orchard in the Okanagan Valley was planted in 1890. Fruit stands are still the best way to sample the region's bountiful produce.

Summerland also was the first town on the lake to employ electricity as an energy source; it was generated by a small hydroelectric plant built on the lakeshore in 1905. These and other historical landmarks are the focus of Summerland Museum on Wharton Street; phone (250) 494-9395.

Giants Head Park on 910-metre (2,986-ft.) Giants Head Mountain offers picnic facilities and views of Summerland, the valley below and Okanagan Lake.

Many beaches, including Sunoka, Peach Orchard *(see the AAA/CAA Western Canada & Alaska CampBook)*, Powell and Rotary, line the shores of Okanagan Lake. Also of interest is the Summerland Trout Hatchery, 13405 Lakeshore Drive S., where rainbow, brook and Kokanee trout are raised; phone (250) 494-0491.

Summerland Visitor Centre: 15600 Hwy. 97, P.O. Box 130, Summerland, BC, Canada V0H 1Z0. **Phone:** (250) 494-2686.

KETTLE VALLEY STEAM RAILWAY is 5 km (3 mi.) w. on Prairie Valley Rd. to 18404 Bathville Rd. Passengers take a 1-hour, 45-minute narrated tour on the only preserved portion of the original Kettle Valley Railway Line, which ran from Midway to Hope.

Hours: The train departs from Prairie Valley Station Thurs.-Mon. at 10:30 and 1:30, July-Aug.; Sat.-Mon. at 10:30 and 1:30, mid-May through June 30

and Sept. 1-second Mon. in Oct. **Cost:** $20.95; $20 (ages 65+); $17 (ages 13-18); $13 (ages 3-12). Fares may vary; phone ahead. **Phone:** (250) 494-8422 or (877) 494-8424.

NIXDORF CLASSIC CARS, INC. is at 15809 Logie Rd. An inventory of more than 100 restored vehicles dating from 1936 to 1970 is rotated so that no fewer than half reside in the facility at one time. The cars, all of which are two-door hardtops or convertibles, may also be rented for chauffeured wine tours. **Time:** Allow 1 hour minimum. **Hours:** Daily 9-5, May 1-Oct. 6; by appointment rest of year. **Cost:** $10; $5 (ages 0-14). **Phone:** (250) 494-4111.

SUMMERLAND ORNAMENTAL GARDENS is s. on Hwy. 97 to 4200 Hwy. 97 on the grounds of Pacific Agri-Foods Research Centre. Established in 1916, the 300-hectare (741-acre) site specializes in xeriscape landscaping, the use of drought-tolerant plants. English gardens, roses, meadow plants and wetland plants also are cultivated. A butterfly and hummingbird garden is featured. **Time:** Allow 1 hour minimum. **Hours:** Daily 8-dusk, May-Sept.; weather permitting rest of year. **Cost:** Donations. **Phone:** (250) 494-6385. 🚗

WINERIES

• **Dirty Laundry Vineyard** is at 7311 Fiske St. **Hours:** Daily 10-5, May-Oct.; Mon.-Fri. 11-4, rest of year. **Phone:** (250) 494-8815.

• **Sumac Ridge Estate Winery** is 1 km (.6 mi.) n. at 17403 Hwy. 97. **Hours:** Tastings daily 9:30-6, late June-day before Labour Day; 10-6, Labour Day-second Mon. in Oct.; 10-5, rest of year (10-3, Dec. 31). Tours are given daily at 11, 1 and 3, May-Oct.; by availability, mid-Jan. through Apr. 30 and Nov. 1-late Dec. Closed Jan. 1 and Dec. 25-26. **Phone:** (250) 494-0451.

VERNON (B-9) pop. 33,494, elev. 383 m/1,256'

At the confluence of five valleys and bounded by three lakes, Vernon is an important shipping and trading center for the Okanagan region. The town's history is portrayed in 26 large murals painted on downtown buildings. On Hwy. 97 at 25th Avenue, Polson Park encompasses a Japanese garden, a Chinese tea house, a floral clock made of 3,500 plants and a children's water park.

Boating, fishing, hiking, mountain biking and golf are popular in summer; winter activities include skiing, dogsledding and snowshoeing. Several recreational opportunities are available at nearby Ellison Provincial Park *(see Recreation Chart and the AAA/CAA Western Canada & Alaska CampBook)* and Kalamalka Lake Provincial Park *(see attraction listing and Recreation Chart)*.

Silver Star Provincial Park offers mountain biking tours from late June to mid-September. A chairlift to the top of Silver Star Mountain operates daily, July 1 to mid-September.

For relaxation, the Kalamalka Lake viewpoint, 5 kilometres (3 mi.) south of 25th Avenue on Hwy. 97, provides an excellent view of the lake.

Tourism Greater Vernon: 701 Hwy. 97S, Vernon, BC, Canada V1B 3W4. **Phone:** (250) 542-1415 or (800) 665-0795.

ATLANTIS WATERSLIDES LTD. is 8 km (5 mi.) n. on Hwy. 97A at Pleasant Valley Rd. The water park has a slide with 10 flumes of varying lengths and slopes, a giant hot tub, miniature golf and a picnic area. **Time:** Allow 2 hours, 30 minutes minimum. **Hours:** Daily 10-7, July 1 to mid-Aug.; 10-6, mid-Aug. through Labour Day; 11-5, in June (weather permitting). **Cost:** $21; $15 (ages 4-12); $10 (ages 65+); $58 (family, two adults and two children). **Phone:** (250) 549-4121. 🍴

GREATER VERNON MUSEUM AND ARCHIVES is at 3009 32nd Ave. Exhibits include local and natural history items, Indian artifacts and period costumes and furniture. The Allan Brooks Gallery features works by the artist and naturalist. Archives and a research facility also are on the premises. **Time:** Allow 1 hour minimum. **Hours:** Tues.-Sat. 10-5. Closed major holidays. **Cost:** Donations. **Phone:** (250) 542-3142.

HISTORIC O'KEEFE RANCH is at 9380 Hwy 97N. One of the earliest cattle empires in the Okanagan Valley, the 1867 O'Keefe homestead includes a dozen restored structures. Guided tours are offered of the family's Victorian mansion. Other buildings include a log house, a church, a general store, a blacksmith shop, a cowboy bunk house, barns and tool sheds. A museum depicts the family's history and the ranching way of life.

Time: Allow 1 hour, 30 minutes minimum. **Hours:** Daily 9-6, July-Aug.; 9-5, May-June and Sept.-Oct. **Cost:** $12; $11 (ages 65+); $10 (ages 6-18); $30 (family). Prices may vary; phone ahead. **Phone:** (250) 542-7868. 🍴 🎒

KALAMALKA LAKE PROVINCIAL PARK is 8 km (5 mi.) s. off Hwy. 6. Largely undeveloped, the parkland protects an environment of north Okanagan grassland interspersed with stands of ponderosa pine and Douglas fir.

A paved trail winds down to the beaches at Jade and Juniper bays, popular swimming spots in summer. Other hiking trails crisscross the park, which provides refuge for a variety of mammals (white-tailed deer, coyotes, red foxes), birds, reptiles and other wildlife. Take in the panoramic vistas from the viewing platform atop Rattlesnake Point. *See Recreation Chart.* **Hours:** Daily dawn-dusk. **Cost:** Free. **Parking:** Day-use $1 per hour; $3 per day. **Phone:** (250) 545-9943.

OKANAGAN SCIENCE CENTRE is at 2704 Hwy. 6 in Polson Park. Housed in one of the oldest brick schoolhouses in British Columbia, the center features hands-on exhibits focusing on such topics as rocks, fossils, illusions, recycling and the environment. **Time:** Allow 1 hour minimum. **Hours:** Mon.-Fri. 10-5, Sat.-Sun. 11-5, July 1-Labour Day; Tues.-Fri. 10-5, Sat. 11-5, rest of year. **Cost:** $7; $4 (ages 3-18 and 60+). **Phone:** (250) 545-3644.

PLANET BEE HONEY FARM, 1 km (.6 mi.) w. on 5th Ave. from jct. Hwy. 97, just n. on 41st St., then w. to 5011 Bella Vista Rd., provides a variety of tours at several apiaries. Visitors may witness the complex societal structure and diligent work habits of more than 10,000 bees in indoor and outdoor observatories. The Inside the Hive tour allows visitors to don gear and explore a working hive. Free taste samples of honey are available from a selection of global sources.

Time: Allow 30 minutes minimum. **Hours:** Mon.-Sat. 8-7, Sun. 10-6, July-Aug.; Mon.-Sat. 8:30-5:30, Sun. 10-5:30, rest of year. Closed Dec. 25. Guided tour hours vary; phone ahead. **Cost:** Free. Guided tours $5-$12; $3-$4.50 (ages 4-10); $20 (family). **Phone:** (250) 542-8088 or (877) 233-9675. 🎒

VERNON PUBLIC ART GALLERY is at 3228 31st Ave. on the ground level of the Parkade Bldg. Three exhibition rooms feature works of regional and nationally known artists. Free gallery tours are available upon request. **Time:** Allow 30 minutes minimum. **Hours:** Mon.-Fri. 10-5, Sat. 11-4; closed statutory holidays. **Cost:** Free. **Phone:** (250) 545-3173.

GAMBLING ESTABLISHMENTS

- **Lake City Casino** is at 4801 27th St. **Hours:** Daily 10 a.m.-2 a.m. Phone ahead to confirm schedule. **Phone:** (250) 545-3505.

RECREATIONAL ACTIVITIES

Skiing

- **Silver Star Mountain Resort** is 22 km (15 mi.) n.e. on Silver Star Rd. **Hours:** Daily 8-4:30, mid-Nov. to mid-Apr. Other activities are available. **Phone:** (250) 542-0224 for information, or (800) 663-4431 for reservations.

WEST KELOWNA (C-9)

pop. 28,793, elev. 411 m/1,348′

West Kelowna (formerly known as Westbank) was a link on the fur-trading route from the north-central part of the province, called New Caledonia, to the Columbia River. In the early 1860s fortune seekers en route to the Cariboo gold mines followed the old trail through the Okanagan Valley.

Ideal climatic conditions in the Okanagan Valley nurture the city's many orchards and vineyards. Vacationers also are drawn by the favorable weather in the valley. Downhill and cross-country skiing in the surrounding countryside are popular in winter.

Westbank Visitor Centre: 2375 Pamela Rd., Unit 4, West Kelowna, BC, Canada V4T 2H9. **Phone:** (250) 768-3378 or (866) 768-3378.

WINERIES

- **Mission Hill Family Estate** is 4.5 km (3 mi.) e. off Hwy. 97 via Boucherie Rd. to 1730 Mission Hill Rd. **Hours:** Daily 10-6, July 4-Sept. 5; 10-5, May 1-July 3 and Sept. 6-Oct. 15; 11-5, Oct. 16-Nov. 30; 11-4, rest of year. **Phone:** (250) 768-6448.

Penticton Art Gallery, Penticton / © AAA / Ron Willis

This ends listings for the Okanagan Valley.
The following page resumes the alphabetical listings of cities in British Columbia.

OLIVER—*see Okanagan Valley p. 141.*

OSOYOOS—*see Okanagan Valley p. 141.*

▼ PACIFIC RIM NATIONAL PARK RESERVE OF CANADA (I-3)

Elevations in the park range from sea level along the Long Beach area to 140 metres (459 ft.) at Radar Hill. Refer to CAA/AAA maps for additional elevation information.

On the west coast of Vancouver Island, Pacific Rim National Park Reserve of Canada consists of three geographically distinct sections with different entry points: the Long Beach unit between Ucluelet and Tofino; the Broken Group Island unit, a cluster of islands in Barkley Sound; and the 75-kilometre-long (47-mi.) West Coast Trail unit between Bamfield and Port Renfrew.

Numerous contrasts exist in the 510-square-kilometre (197-sq.-mi.) reserve, which has sandy beaches, tranquil estuaries and lakes, rugged headlands, dense rain forests and rocky islands. Wildflowers nurtured by the area's moist and temperate climate thrive in an immense old-growth rain forest.

A stopping place for geese and ducks during their yearly migrations, the shoreline zone also accommodates colonies of sea birds and wildlife. Each spring some 20,000 gray whales migrate through the reserve's waters.

General Information and Activities

The reserve is open all year, although many facilities are seasonal. The Long Beach area, about 16 kilometres (10 mi.) west of the junction of Hwy. 4 and the Ucluelet highway, has 19 kilometres (12 mi.) of sandy beach and shoreline which are popular year-round with surfers and beachwalkers; wheelchair-accessible trails are available. Long Beach Information Centre, open mid-March to mid-October, is on Hwy. 4 inside the park boundary. There are self-guiding nature trails in the surrounding rain forest and other interpretive programs. The Wickaninnish Interpretive Centre features displays and films chronicling marine life of the Pacific.

The Broken Group Islands, accessible only by boat, offer pristine wilderness spread over a 100-island cluster in the center of Barkley Sound. Eagles and sea lions are abundant, while varied sea life and sunken ships create a diver's paradise. Camping is available in designated areas on eight islands.

The West Coast Trail, which had its beginnings as an avenue of rescue for shipwrecked sailors, follows the national park's rugged coastline between Port Renfrew and Bamfield. The trail is open to experienced hikers only and offers spectacular coastal scenery along its challenging path. Remnants of former settlements and shipwrecks can be seen along the shoreline.

The West Coast Trail Information and Registration Centres at Pachena Bay near Bamfield and at Port Renfrew are open May through September. Reservations to hike the trail may be made for June 15 through September 15; phone (800) 435-5622. *See Recreation Chart and the AAA/CAA Western Canada & Alaska CampBook.*

ADMISSION to the Long Beach area is $6.90; $5.90 (senior citizens); $3.45 (ages 6-16); $17.30 (family (up to seven people). Camping fee at Long Beach is $16-$25 per person per night. Camping fee at other designated sites is $9 per person per night. West Coast Trail use permit $110; reservation fee $25 (non-refundable). Ferry fee $15.

ADDRESS inquiries to the Superintendent, Pacific Rim National Park Reserve of Canada, P.O. Box 280, Ucluelet, BC, Canada V0R 3A0; phone (250) 726-7721, or (250) 726-4212 June 1 to mid-Sept.

PARKSVILLE (G-10)
pop. 10,993, elev. 80 m/262'

With its 1.6-kilometre-long (1-mi.) sandy beach on the Strait of Georgia, Parksville is a popular summer resort. Nearby Englishman and Little Qualicum rivers and parks, with scenic waterfalls, provide many opportunities for recreation, as do other area lakes, streams, mountains and parks. Rathtrevor Beach Provincial Park offers a beach, camping and picnicking. *See Recreation Chart and the AAA/CAA Western Canada & Alaska CampBook.*

Artistic endeavors in sand are the main focus of the ▼ Parksville Beach Festival. Elaborate sand sculptures compete for prizes each August, and attendees can also enjoy fireworks, children's activities and a volleyball tournament.

Parksville & District Chamber of Commerce: 1275 E. Island Hwy.; P.O. Box 99, Parksville, BC, Canada V9P 2G3. **Phone:** (250) 248-3613.

CRAIG HERITAGE PARK, MUSEUM & ARCHIVES is 4 km (2.5 mi.) s. at 1245 E. Island Hwy. The collection of historic buildings includes a church, a log house, a fire station, a turn-of-the-20th-century schoolhouse and two 19th-century post offices. Exhibits inside the buildings depict local history.

Time: Allow 30 minutes minimum. **Hours:** Daily 10-4, mid-May through Sept. 30. **Cost:** $5; $4 (ages 12-18, ages 60+ and students with ID); $6 (family). **Phone:** (250) 248-6966.

PEACHLAND—*see Okanagan Valley p. 142.*

PENDER ISLANDS—
see Gulf Islands p. 123.

PENTICTON—*see Okanagan Valley p. 142.*

PORT ALBERNI (F-10)
pop. 17,743, elev. 60 m/197'

A deepwater port and important fishing and lumber shipping center, Port Alberni was discovered in 1791 by Don Pedro Alberni, a Spanish sea captain.

Industry began in 1860 when nine workmen arriving on the schooner *Meg Merrilees* built a sawmill on the harbor's edge.

Port Alberni's harbor remains the city's focal point, enhanced by the Alberni Harbour Quay at the foot of Argyle Street. The facility includes shops, an arts and crafts outlet and the MV *Lady Rose* office. From the 1912 CPR Train Station, a logging locomotive takes visitors on a 35-minute journey along the waterfront to McLean Mill National Historic Site *(see attraction listing).*

Surrounded by mountains, lakes and forests, the city is a good base for naturalists and outdoors enthusiasts. Alpine and cross-country skiing are available nearby. Sproat Lake Provincial Park *(see Recreation Chart and the AAA/CAA Western Canada & Alaska CampBook)* features Indian carvings of mythological beasts. There are hundreds of giant Douglas firs, many that date from the late 12th century, at Cathedral Grove in MacMillan Provincial Park, 16 kilometres (10 mi.) east.

The region's natural wonders are protected by the Martin Mars Water Bombers based at Sproat Lake. Designed to combat forest fires, these huge aircraft carry 6,000 imperial gallons (7,206 U.S. gallons) of water.

Port Alberni Visitor Centre: 2533 Port Alberni Hwy., Port Alberni, BC, Canada V9Y 8P2. **Phone:** (250) 724-6535.

ALBERNI VALLEY MUSEUM is at 4255 Wallace St. in the Echo Centre building. Collections in this community museum communicate the history of the area and include Nuu Chah Nulth basketry, folk art, apparel, textiles, household implements, woodworking tools, medical equipment, war medals and 17,000 historic photographs.

Visitors also can see displays about the area's industrial past in logging, fishing, mining and farming. An exhibit about the West Coast Trail tells of its early uses as a telegraph line and a rescue trail for shipwrecked sailors. **Time:** Allow 30 minutes minimum. **Hours:** Tues.-Sat. 10-5 (also Thurs. 5-8). Closed major holidays. **Cost:** Donations. **Phone:** (250) 723-2181.

MARITIME DISCOVERY CENTRE is on the waterfront at 2750 Harbour Rd. The area's maritime history is documented at this museum, which was built from a coastal lighthouse. Highlights include an exhibit about the 1964 tidal wave. Traveling exhibits also are featured. **Time:** Allow 30 minutes minimum. **Hours:** Daily 10-5, July-Aug. **Cost:** Donations. **Phone:** (250) 723-6164.

McLEAN MILL NATIONAL HISTORIC SITE is 6 km (10 mi.) w. on Beaver Creek Rd., then 3 km (1.8 mi.) n. to 5633 Smith Rd., following signs. The 13-hectare (32-acre) site preserves a working 1926 steam sawmill that was operated by the R.B. McLean family until 1965. Thirty structures from the early days of British Columbia's forest industry include the camp where loggers and mill employees lived and worked. Interactive guided tours and stage shows and sawmill demonstrations are given Thursday through Monday.

Time: Allow 1 hour, 30 minutes minimum. **Hours:** Daily 10-4, mid-June through Labour Day. Phone ahead to confirm schedule. **Cost:** Mill and train tours $29.95; $22.50 (ages 13-18, ages 60+ and students with ID); $9.75 (ages 5-12). Rates may vary; phone ahead. Reservations are recommended. **Phone:** (250) 723-1376. [T]

Alberni Pacific Railway departs from the CPR Station at Argyle and Kingsway sts. Passengers embark upon a 35-minute train ride to McLean Mill National Historic Site. **Hours:** Trips depart Thurs.-Mon. at 10 and 2, mid-June through Labour Day. Last train leaves the mill at 5. Phone ahead to confirm schedule. **Cost:** Round-trip fare (includes mill admission) $29; $21.75 (students with ID and senior citizens); $9.75 (ages 5-12); $75 (family). Rates may vary; phone ahead. **Phone:** (250) 723-1376.

MV *LADY ROSE* MARINE SERVICES docks at the Argyle Pier in the Alberni Harbour Quay at the foot of Argyle St. The packet freighter takes visitors on an all-day cruise. The MV *Lady Rose* and her sister ship, the MV *Frances Barkley,* deliver mail and cargo to isolated villages, fishing resorts and camps. The freighters sail down the Alberni Inlet to Bamfield, Ucluelet and the Broken Group Islands.

Sensible shoes and a sweater or light jacket are advisable. **Hours:** Departures to Bamfield Tues., Thurs. and Sat.-Sun. at 8 a.m., July-Sept.; Tues., Thurs. and Sat. at 8 a.m., rest of year. Sailings to Ucluelet and Broken Group Islands Mon., Wed. and Fri. at 8 a.m., early June to mid-Sept. Phone ahead to confirm schedule.

Cost: Bamfield trip $66; $33 (ages 8-15). Ucluelet trip $72; $36 (ages 8-15). Fares may vary; phone ahead. All children must be accompanied by an adult. Reservations are recommended in summer. **Phone:** (250) 723-8313, or (800) 663-7192 Apr.-Sept. [T]

ROBERTSON CREEK FISH HATCHERY is 5 km (3 mi.) w. on Hwy. 4, then 7 km (4 mi.) n.w. on Great Central Lake Rd. The hatchery has an annual output of 8 million chinook and 800,000 coho salmon and 150,000 steelhead trout. Displays explain fish breeding process from incubation through release. Facilities include outdoor rearing ponds and raceways. **Hours:** Daily 8:30-3:30. Closed Dec. 25. **Cost:** Free. **Phone:** (250) 724-6521.

PORT COQUITLAM—*see Vancouver p. 183.*

PORT EDWARD (E-2) pop. 577

Port Edward, on the Tsimpsean Peninsula, was named after King Edward VI. The town was founded in 1908 and incorporated in 1966.

The river of mists, as the Indians called the Skeena River, bursts through the Coast Range and empties into the Pacific Ocean near Port Edward. The river provides the community's major commodity, fish, which is processed by local canneries. Salmon and steelhead trout, besides being economic staples, also offer a recreational challenge to anglers. Because of the area's proximity to luxuriant rain forests, mountain ranges and the river, sporting types also will find ample opportunities for canoeing, kayaking, camping, hunting and hiking.

NORTH PACIFIC CANNERY HISTORIC SITE & MUSEUM is 10 km (6 mi.) s. of Hwy. 16 at 1889 Skeena Dr. For almost 100 years (1889-1980) this cannery, one of more than 200 such businesses operating along the West Coast at the industry's peak, processed and canned salmon from the Skeena River. The Northern Pacific Cannery is said to be the oldest remaining untouched example of this manufacturing culture.

Operations in the more remote areas, such as this one, were virtual cities in themselves, incorporating machine and wood shops and residences for the cannery workers. Built directly on the water, visitors can see the peeling paint on many of the 30 restored buildings in the cannery (the oldest built in 1885) and hear the squeaking sounds of the wooden boards on the boardwalk.

The village includes the main cannery, reduction plant, staff housing and mess house. Artifacts of the fishing industry, such as boats, tools and machinery original to the shops as well as some of the workers' personal items are displayed throughout the complex. Guided tours feature a working canning line, and a live historical presentation is offered.

Tours: Guided tours are available. **Time:** Allow 1 hour minimum. **Hours:** Daily 10-4, July-Aug.; Tues.-Sat. 10-4, May-June and in Sept. Tours are given at 10:30, 1:30 and 2:30. **Cost:** $12; $9 (ages 65+); $6 (ages 6-18); $2 (ages 0-5). **Phone:** (250) 628-3538. 🍴

PORT McNEILL (H-2)
pop. 2,623, elev. 15 m/49'

In the scenic, untamed wilderness of northern Vancouver Island, Port McNeill occupies a rich lumber and fishing region popular with adventurous hikers, campers, spelunkers, fishermen and other sports enthusiasts.

Of interest to rock collectors and geologists are several nearby natural phenomena, including the Vanishing River, which plunges underground into a maze of caves and tunnels; the Devil's Bath, a huge rock bowl continuously filled by an underground spring; and the Eternal Fountain, which gushes from a rock crevice and then disappears underground again. All are reached by logging roads that are accessible only in summer.

An inter-island ferry operates a shuttle service between Port McNeill, Sointula and Alert Bay (see place listing p. 111).

Port McNeill & District Chamber of Commerce & Tourist Bureau: 1594 Beach Dr., P.O. Box 129, Port McNeill, BC, Canada V0N 2R0. **Phone:** (250) 956-3131 or (888) 956-3131.

PORT MOODY—see Vancouver p. 183.

POUCE COUPE (D-5)
pop. 739, elev. 652 m/2,139'

The village of Pouce Coupe is referred to as the gateway to Peace country because it is one of the first communities travelers will see when entering British Columbia from Alberta.

POUCE COUPE MUSEUM is at 5006 49th Ave. Pioneer artifacts are housed in the former Northern Alberta Railway station. **Hours:** Daily 8-5, May-Aug; by appointment rest of year. **Cost:** Donations. **Phone:** (250) 786-5555, or (250) 786-5794 for an appointment in the off-season.

POWELL RIVER (F-11)
pop. 12,957, elev. 55 m/180'

Rich forests and abundant water brought the founders of the Powell River Company to the area in the early 1900s. The townsite is one of the oldest company-built communities in western Canada.

Separated from the mainland by Jervis Inlet, the area offers year-round recreation including freshwater and saltwater fishing, scuba diving, boating, kayaking, hiking and bicycling. The Powell Forest Canoe Route connects eight lakes around the Upper Sunshine Coast region with camping areas along the scenic circuit.

A panorama of the Strait of Malaspina unfolds from the Mount Valentine viewpoint, reached by a rock stairway in the heart of town. Bald eagles can be observed at any time of year, especially in late fall when they are attracted by salmon spawning in channels and small streams. Also of interest are Sliammon Fish Hatchery and Powell River Salmon Society Spawning Channel.

Guided 2-hour tours of the Catalyst Paper Mill are offered through the visitor center. Part of the tour is outdoors; appropriate dress and low-heeled, closed footwear are advised. For information and reservations phone (877) 817-8669.

Powell River Visitor Centre: 4871 Joyce Ave., Unit 111, Powell River, BC, Canada V8A 5P4. **Phone:** (604) 485-4701 or (877) 817-8669.

INLAND LAKE PROVINCIAL PARK is 12 km (7 mi.) n. on Inland Lake Rd. In a semi-remote area with abundant and varied wildlife, the park offers wheelchair-accessible facilities for camping, hiking and fishing.

A 13-kilometre-long (8-mi.) circuit of crushed limestone with minimal grades has eight picnic and rest areas and six fishing wharves. Amenities include cabins exclusively for use by the physically impaired, and wheelchair-accessible outhouses. See Recreation Chart. **Hours:** Site open for day use daily 7 a.m.-10 p.m., Apr.-Oct. Phone ahead to confirm schedule. **Cost:** Free. **Phone:** (604) 487-4168.

POWELL RIVER HISTORICAL MUSEUM & ARCHIVES ASSOCIATION is on Marine Ave. across from Willingdon Beach. The museum houses artifacts, archival material and displays about the area's history. A children's treasure hunt is featured. **Time:** Allow 30 minutes minimum. **Hours:** Daily 9-4:30, mid-June through Aug. 31; Mon.-Fri. 9-4:30, rest of year. Closed major holidays. **Cost:** $2; $1 (ages 6-12). **Phone:** (604) 485-2222.

PRINCE GEORGE (E-5)
pop. 70,981, elev. 691 m/2,267'

At the confluence of the Nechako and Fraser rivers, the area was visited in 1793 by Alexander Mackenzie in his trek down the Fraser to the Pacific. In 1807 it became the site for Simon Fraser's North West Co. fort. Fraser's canoe brigades soon gave way to paddlewheelers and then railroads, which converged on this important northern crossroads. Prince George remains a major transportation and trade center, a role enhanced by a thriving forest industry.

Despite its urban transformation, the city has retained much of its natural heritage in its 116 parks. Of interest are Fort George Park, which contains a replica of Fraser's trading post; Connaught Park's manicured gardens and scenic views; and Cottonwood Island Park, which includes the Prince George Railway & Forestry Museum and its collection of railroad artifacts and cars.

Prince George blends its pastoral features with such cultural centers as Studio 2880 and Vanier Hall. Studio 2880, home to six craft guilds, is the site of craft markets and special events throughout the year. Concerts by the Prince George Symphony and by visiting performers are held in Vanier Hall.

These cultural amenities coexist with the more rugged recreational opportunities available in the wilderness that surrounds the city. Nearby lakes, rivers and mountains present an array of activities ranging from rugged back-country hikes and fishing to skiing and ice skating.

Tourism Prince George: 101-1300 First Ave., Prince George, BC, Canada V2L 2Y3. **Phone:** (250) 562-3700 or (800) 668-7646.

THE EXPLORATION PLACE is at the end of 20th Ave. at 333 Becott Pl. in Fort George Park. Fort George's history and development are explored through such topics as transportation, lumber and the First Nations culture. The Children's Gallery houses life-size dinosaur sculptures, skeletons and a dig pit. The Explorations Gallery features live animals and interactive computers. A SimEx virtual motion theater offers three rides daily. A steam locomotive ride is offered on weekends and holidays.

Time: Allow 1 hour minimum. **Hours:** Daily 10-5, day after Victoria Day-Labour Day; Wed.-Sun. 10-5, rest of year. Closed Jan. 1 and Dec. 25-26. **Cost:** Museum $8.95; $6.95 (ages 60+ and students with ID); $5.95 (ages 3-11); $20.95 (family, two adults and up to four children ages 0-18). Combination ticket with movie ride $10.95; $9.95 (ages 60+ and students with ID); $8.95 (ages 2-12); $29.95 (family, two adults and up to four children ages 0-18). Train rides $1. **Phone:** (250) 562-1612 or (866) 562-1612.

HUBLE HOMESTEAD HISTORIC SITE is 40 km (25 mi.) n. on Mitchell Rd. The site features several replicas of historic buildings as well as the original homestead of Al and Annie Huble. Along with his business partner Ed Seebach, Huble was instrumental in establishing a community within the Giscome Portage area. **Tours:** Guided tours are available. **Time:** Allow 1 hour minimum. **Hours:** Daily 10-5, Victoria Day weekend-Labour Day weekend. **Cost:** Donations. **Phone:** (250) 564-7033.

PRINCE GEORGE RAILWAY & FORESTRY MUSEUM is at 850 River Rd. The museum houses one of the largest collection of railway-related artifacts in British Columbia. Items, circa 1899-1960s, include a wooden snow plow, locomotives, box cars and cabooses.

Time: Allow 1 hour minimum. **Hours:** Daily 10-5, Victoria Day weekend-Labour Day weekend; Tues.-Sat. 11-4, rest of year. Closed Jan. 1-2, Thanksgiving and Dec. 25-31. Phone ahead to confirm schedule. **Cost:** $6; $5 (students and senior citizens); $3 (ages 5-12); $15 (family, two adults and two children). **Phone:** (250) 563-7351. ⌸

PRINCE RUPERT (E-2)
pop. 12,815, elev. 50 m/164'

At the turn of the 20th century Prince Rupert existed only in the imagination of Charles Hays, manager of the Grand Trunk Pacific Railway. Hays died with the sinking of the SS *Titanic,* but the Grand Trunk Pacific Railway carried out his intention to build a port to rival Vancouver on this rugged, uninhabited island bordered by a natural harbor. The new site was expected to be successful because it was closer to the Far East than Vancouver and would provide an outlet for the untapped resources of Canada's far north.

Prince Rupert has fulfilled that potential and is now one of Canada's major seaports. It is the southernmost port of the Alaska Ferry System, the northern terminus of the British Columbia Ferry Corp. and the western terminus of the Canadian National Railway. Cruise ships en route to coastal glaciers and fjords also stop at Prince Rupert's harbor, said to be the world's third largest natural ice-free deep-sea harbor.

Before the coming of the railroad the northern coast was home to the Tsimpsean and Haida, cultures whose ancestors inhabited the area for almost 5,000 years. Both are renowned for their stylized artworks, the most familiar of which are totem poles. Many of these graceful monuments are shown in such city parks as Service Park, the colorful terraced Sunken Gardens, and Roosevelt Park with its sweeping views of the Pacific.

On the waterfront, Kwinitsa Railway Station is a relic of the modern era. Restored and moved from its original location, Kwinitsa is one of the last of the Grand Trunk Pacific Railway stations; inside are exhibits about the railroad's history.

Just beyond the city, climate and soil have stunted and twisted lodgepole pines into a natural bonsai garden at Oliver Lake Provincial Park. Another interesting phenomenon is Butze Rapids, a series of reversing rapids between Wainwright and Morse basins that rival the reversing falls at Saint John, New Brunswick. A dramatic view of the rapids occurs during a falling tide and can be seen from a viewing point on Hwy. 16, which offers scenic driving east to Terrace (see place listing p. 155).

Guided tours are offered during the summer by Farwest Bus Lines Ltd., 225 Second Ave. W. Trans-Provincial Airlines and Northcoast Air Services offer flight tours of the region.

Prince Rupert Visitor Information Centre: 215 Cow Bay Rd., Suite 100, Prince Rupert, BC, Canada V8J 1A2. **Phone:** (250) 624-5637 or (800) 667-1994.

Self-guiding tours: A walking tour that includes sunken gardens, the harbor, sections of the downtown area and various attractions is detailed on maps and brochures available from the visitor bureau at the Museum of Northern British Columbia (see attraction listing).

MUSEUM OF NORTHERN BRITISH COLUMBIA is at 100 First Ave. W. and McBride St. Models, maps, graphic displays and an ethnological collection explain pioneer history and the lifestyles of the coastal First Nations groups from prehistoric times through their contacts with Europeans. Changing exhibits are displayed in the art gallery. Of interest are an early 20th-century steamroller and a modern First Nations carving shed with local artists on site.

Hours: Mon.-Sat. 9-8, June-Aug.; 9-5, rest of year. Closed Jan. 1 and Dec. 25-26. **Cost:** $5; $3 (students with ID); $2 (ages 6-12); $1 (ages 0-5); $10 (family). **Phone:** (250) 624-3207.

PRINCETON (C-8) pop. 2,677

Named "Vermilion Forks" by fur traders in the early 1800s, Princeton developed as a ranching and mining outpost in the foothills of the Cascade Mountains. In 1860 the town was renamed to honor a visit by the Prince of Wales. Revitalized downtown storefronts boast murals and facades in keeping with Princeton's Western heritage.

Princeton & District Chamber of Commerce: 105 Hwy. 3E, P.O. Box 540, Princeton, BC, Canada V0X 1W0. **Phone:** (250) 295-3103.

Self-guiding tours: Maps detailing walking tours are available from the chamber of commerce.

PRINCETON MUSEUM AND ARCHIVES is at 167 Vermilion Ave. The collection includes fossils and minerals, aboriginal baskets, lace and textiles, antique cooking utensils, mining tools and equipment, a large butterfly collection and a stagecoach. **Hours:** Daily 9-7, July-Aug.; 9-5, Apr.-June and Sept.-Oct. **Cost:** Donations. **Phone:** (250) 295-7588 or (866) 582-7632.

QUADRA ISLAND—see Gulf Islands p. 123.

QUALICUM BEACH (F-10)
pop. 6,921, elev. 9 m/30'

A popular resort and arts community, Qualicum Beach is known for its white sand beaches. Nearby Little Qualicum Falls (see Recreation Chart), Englishman River Falls (see Recreation Chart) and Horne Lake Caves provincial parks also present abundant recreational opportunities. Salmon and trout are raised at fish hatcheries on the Big and Little Qualicum rivers.

Qualicum Beach Visitor Information Centre: 2711 W. Island Hwy., Qualicum Beach, BC, Canada V9K 2C4. **Phone:** (250) 752-9532.

BIG QUALICUM HATCHERY is 12 km (7 mi.) n. on Hwy. 19A, then e. on Kenmuir Rd., following signs. Millions of chum, coho and chinook salmon are hatched here each year as part of the country's efforts to restore its salmon population. Steelhead and cutthroat trout also are raised. Visitors can see holding ponds, rearing channels and incubation units. Hiking trails are available. **Time:** Allow 30 minutes minimum. **Hours:** Daily dawn-dusk. **Cost:** Donations. **Phone:** (250) 757-8412.

HORNE LAKE CAVES is 15 km (9 mi.) n. on Hwy. 19 to exit 75 (Horne Lake Rd.), then 14 km (9 mi.) w. on a gravel rd., following signs to the parking lot. A part of the Horne Lake Caves Provincial Park, the cave system is considered to be one of the best in Canada. Tours are guided and highlights include crystal formations, ancient fossils and a waterfall.

The 1.5-hour Family Cavern Tour teaches about the geology and history of the caves. The interpretive tour starts with a 25-minute walk to the entrance. Once inside the cave, visitors explore the easy passages; no crawling or maneuvering in tight spaces is necessary.

Other 3-, 4-, and 5-hour tours also are offered. Self-guiding exploration is available in Horne Lake Main and Lower caves year-round. A helmet and two sources of light are required. Helmets may be rented for $5 each during the summer only.

Note: The caves are mostly undeveloped and do not provide lighting. Floors are rocky and uneven; children ages 0-4 and visitors with mobility issues could encounter difficulty walking. Warm clothing and comfortable boots or shoes are highly recommended, as the caves remain cool even in hot weather. Cameras are permitted. **Time:** Allow 1 hour, 30 minutes minimum.

Hours: Tours require a minimum of three people. Family Cavern Tour is given on a first-come, first-served basis daily on the hour 10-5, late June-Labour Day; by appointment rest of year. Last tour leaves at closing. Closed Jan. 1 and Dec. 25. **Cost:** Family Cavern Tour $17; $15 (ages 0-11). **Phone:** (250) 248-7829 for reservations, or (250) 757-8687 for tour information.

MILNER GARDENS AND WOODLAND, 2179 W. Island Hwy., comprises 24 hectares (60 acres) of

Douglas fir woodland and 4 hectares (10 acres) of garden surrounding a gabled heritage house. Visitors may view the dining, sitting and drawing rooms as well as the library. Historical photos, artifacts and keepsakes of visits by members of the Royal family also are displayed.

Time: Allow 1 hour minimum. **Hours:** Daily 10-5, May 1-Labour Day; Thurs.-Sun. and Mon. holidays 10-5 in Apr. and day after Labour Day to mid-Oct. **Cost:** $10; $6 (students with ID); free (ages 0-12 when accompanied by an adult). **Phone:** (250) 752-6153.

QUALICUM BEACH HISTORICAL & MUSEUM SOCIETY is at 587 Beach Rd. Two floors of exhibits highlight the history of Qualicum Beach and Canada. Included in the displays are murals, a diorama of a 1930s kitchen and a paleontology collection. The 1929 Powerhouse building also is on site and houses a variety of historical items. **Time:** Allow 30 minutes minimum. **Hours:** Tues.-Sat. 11-4, late May to mid-Sept. **Cost:** Donations. **Phone:** (250) 752-5533.

QUEEN CHARLOTTE ISLANDS (E-1)

The Queen Charlotte Islands were occupied by Haida Indians when Spanish sea captain Juan Pérez sighted the archipelago in 1774. A seafaring and artistic people, the Haida traded sea otter pelts with European traders during the early 1800s. By the late 19th century, however, the Haida had to vacate many of their ancestral villages to escape a devastating smallpox epidemic.

Only a fraction of their original number still inhabit the island—at Haida, near Masset, and Skidegate, near Queen Charlotte City. Continuing their cultural traditions, they carve elaborate works of art from argillite, a black slatelike stone found only in mountain deposits off the coast.

A group of about 150 islands forming an elongated triangle, the Queen Charlotte Islands stretch 250 kilometres (157 mi.) from north to south, 90 kilometres (56 mi.) off the coast of British Columbia. Characterized by fog and low clouds, these islands also are known as the Misty Islands. The towns are small and decidedly rural; the entire population of the Queen Charlotte Islands is about 5,000.

The largest of the islands is Graham. In the north on its broad and flat eastern side are most of the archipelago's communities—Masset, Old Masset, Port Clements, Queen Charlotte City, Skidegate, and Tlell—which are linked by a paved road. An airport is at Masset as well as at Sandspit, on the northeastern tip of Moresby Island.

A temperate marine climate supports dense coniferous forests, which, as the basis of the islands' economy, have been logged extensively. The fish and shellfish in the coastal waters supply the islands' important commercial fishing industry.

Visitors are attracted by the pristine wilderness, the hunting and fishing prospects, kayaking and hiking opportunities, and the handicrafts and art of the Haida. Wildlife is abundant; tiny Sitka deer and bald eagles frequent the shores, and seals, porpoises and whales often appear in the inlets. Bird-watching is a popular activity.

Points of interest include Naikoon Provincial Park (see Recreation Chart) on Graham Island, the remote Haida village sites, the Delkatla Wildlife Sanctuary in Masset, the Haida Heritage Centre at Kaay Llnagaay (see attraction listing p. 154) in Skidegate and the various carving sheds in Skidegate and Old Masset.

Permission to visit Haida unoccupied village sites must be obtained from Band Council offices; phone (250) 559-8225.

The Queen Charlotte Islands can be reached by air from Prince Rupert and Vancouver and by ferry from Prince Rupert. Phone BC Ferries at (888) 223-3779 for ferry reservations. Kayak rentals, fishing charters and various guided boat and land tours are available.

Queen Charlotte Visitor Centre: 3220 Wharf St., P.O. Box 819, Queen Charlotte, BC, Canada V0T 1S0. **Phone:** (250) 559-8316.

QUESNEL (F-4) pop. 9,326, elev. 545 m/1,788′

Discovery of gold in the surrounding area in the 1860s contributed to Quesnel's growth. The city is the center of a popular hunting and fishing region at the junction of the Fraser and Quesnel rivers. Lumber, pulp and plywood manufacturing, tourism, cattle ranching and mining are the city's primary sources of income.

East of the city on Hwy. 26 is a historic remnant of the gold rush days, Barkerville Historic Town (see place listing p. 112), a restored boomtown of that era. Just beyond Barkerville is Bowron Lake Provincial Park (see Recreation Chart and the AAA/CAA Western Canada & Alaska CampBook), which has a 116-kilometre (72-mi.) canoe circuit of interconnecting lakes. Alpine skiing is available nearby.

Quesnel Visitor Centre: 703 Carson Ave., Quesnel, BC, Canada V2J 2B6. **Phone:** (250) 992-8716 or (800) 992-4922.

COTTONWOOD HOUSE HISTORIC SITE is 28 km (17 mi.) e. on Hwy. 26. Cottonwood was built 1864-65 as a roadhouse for travelers on the Cariboo Wagon Road en route to the gold fields of Barkerville. The 11-hectare (26-acre) site includes a double barn, stable, animals, guesthouse, outbuildings and antique machinery. Costumed interpreters provide tours of Cottonwood House and wagon rides. A walking trail winds along the river.

Hours: Daily 10-5, mid-May through Labour Day. **Cost:** $4.50 (includes wagon ride); $3.50 (ages 60+); $2 (ages 12-18 and students with ID). **Phone:** (250) 992-2071.

QUESNEL & DISTRICT MUSEUM AND ARCHIVES is .7 km (.5 mi.) s. on Hwy. 97 at 705 Carson Ave. Marking the area's history from the days of Alexander Mackenzie's explorations and the 1862 gold rush, the museum includes exhibits about pioneer life, a hands-on area for children, items from the *Titanic*, Chinese artifacts from the gold rush, a doll that is said to be haunted and an archives.

Time: Allow 1 hour minimum. **Hours:** Daily 9-6, Victoria Day-Labour Day; Tues.-Sat. 9-4:30, rest of year. Closed statutory holidays. **Cost:** $3; $1.50 (ages 13-17). **Phone:** (250) 992-9580.

RADIUM HOT SPRINGS (B-11)
pop. 735, elev. 805 m/2,641'

Renowned for its mineral hot springs *(see Kootenay National Park of Canada p. 129 and Recreation Chart)*, Radium Hot Springs also is a popular departure point for scenic and white-water river excursions. More than 10 golf courses are in the vicinity.

RECREATIONAL ACTIVITIES
Skiing
• **Panorama Mountain Village** is 12 km (7.5 mi.) w. on Hwy. 95. Other activities are offered. **Hours:** Daily 9-4, Dec.-Apr. **Phone:** (250) 342-6941 or (800) 663-2929.

White-water Rafting
• **Kootenay River Runners** is at 4987 Hwy. 93. **Hours:** Daily 8 a.m.-10 p.m., early June to mid-Sept. **Phone:** (250) 347-9210 or (800) 599-4399.

REVELSTOKE (B-10)
pop. 7,230, elev. 440 m/1,433'

Revelstoke is at the western end of Rogers Pass, the section of the Trans-Canada Highway that traverses Glacier National Park of Canada *(see place listing p. 121)*. Rogers Pass is one of the world's most scenic mountain roads. Downhill skiing is available nearby.

Revelstoke Chamber of Commerce: 204 Campbell Ave., P.O. Box 490, Revelstoke, BC, Canada V0E 2S0. **Phone:** (250) 837-5345.

CANYON HOT SPRINGS is 35.5 km (22 mi.) e. on Hwy. 1. Bathers can dip in a pool of 40 C (104 F) mineral waters or swim in a pool that is 30 C (86 F). *See Recreation Chart.*

Hours: Daily 9 a.m.-10 p.m., July-Aug.; 9-9, May-June and in Sept. Phone ahead to confirm schedule. **Cost:** Day passes $12.50; $10.50 (ages 5-14 and 60+); $32 (family pass, two adults and two children). Single swim $8.50; $7 (ages 5-14 and 60+); $23 (family, two adults and two children). Rates may vary; phone ahead. **Phone:** (250) 837-2420. 🍴 🏕

ENCHANTED FOREST is 32 km (20 mi.) w. on Hwy. 1 to 7060 Trans-Canada Hwy. More than 350 handmade figurines include Old World fairy folk, dragons and dungeons in a natural forest setting with giant cedars, a stump house, a fish pond and a towering tree house that is reputedly one of the province's tallest. Swamp boat rides and a wetland boardwalk including lush vegetation, beaver dams and spawning salmon beds also are offered.

Hours: Daily 8-8, July-Aug.; 10-5, May-June and Sept. 1-second Mon. in Oct. (weather permitting). **Cost:** $9; $7 (ages 3-15). **Phone:** (250) 837-9477 or (866) 944-9744. 🏕

REVELSTOKE RAILWAY MUSEUM is at 719 Track St. W. off Victoria Rd. The building of the Canadian Pacific Railway is traced with artifacts, photographs and original equipment. One of the company's largest steam locomotives is displayed beside a restored 1929 solarium car inside the museum, while the yard features such rolling stock as a caboose, a snow plow and a flange car. A diesel cabin simulator allows visitors to experience the feeling of driving a train.

Time: Allow 30 minutes minimum. **Hours:** Daily 9-8, July-Aug.; daily 9-5, May-June and Sept.-Oct.; Thurs.-Tues. 9-5, Mar.-Apr.; Fri.-Tues. 11-4, rest of year. **Cost:** $8; $6 (ages 60+); $4 (ages 7-16); $16 (family). **Phone:** (250) 837-6060.

THREE VALLEY GAP HERITAGE GHOST TOWN is 19 km (12 mi.) w. on Hwy. 1. Near the original site of the 19th-century lumber and mining town of Three Valley are more than 40 relocated buildings including a hotel, a general store, a church, two schoolhouses, a saloon and many examples of handcrafted log buildings. An exhibit chronicles the history of steam, transportation and communication. Live performances of a musical stage show take place most nights May through September.

Hours: Guided 1-hour tours depart daily 9-5, mid-Apr. through Sept. 30. Phone ahead to confirm schedule. **Cost:** $12; $10 (ages 65+); $7 (ages 12-17); $5 (ages 6-11). An additional fee is charged for the stage show. Reservations are required. **Phone:** (250) 837-2109 or (888) 667-2109.

RECREATIONAL ACTIVITIES
Ziplines
• **SkyTrek Adventure Park Ltd.** is 32 km (20 mi.) w. on Hwy. 1 to 7060 Trans-Canada Hwy. **Hours:** Daily 10-6, mid-May to mid-Oct. **Phone:** (250) 837-9477 or (866) 944-9744.

RICHMOND—*see Vancouver p. 184.*

ROSSLAND (D-10)
pop. 3,278, elev. 1,039 m/3,408'

The 1890 gold rush on Red Mountain spurred the growth of Rossland from a prospectors' camp to a bustling town with 42 saloons, 17 law firms, four breweries and two distilleries. The area's vast mineral wealth, which supported a booming mining industry for 40 years, produced more than 6 million tons of ore valued at about $125 million.

Fishing, swimming and canoeing are available at Nancy Greene Provincial Park, 26 kilometres (16 mi.) northwest at hwys. 3 and 3B. *See Recreation Chart and the AAA/CAA Western Canada & Alaska CampBook.*

Rossland Chamber of Commerce: 2197 Columbia Ave., P.O. Box 1385, Rossland, BC, Canada V0G 1Y0. **Phone:** (250) 362-5666.

ROSSLAND HISTORICAL MUSEUM AND ARCHIVES is at jct. hwys. 3B and 22. Guided underground mine tours enter the historic Le Roi gold mine. The museum has mining artifacts and rock and mineral samples. There also are outdoor exhibits. Gold panning is offered. Articles in the archives chronicle the history of Rossland and the nearby mining area.

Time: Allow 2 hours minimum. **Hours:** Daily 9-5, mid-May to mid-Sept. Last mine tour departs 90 minutes before closing. **Cost:** Museum $5; $4 (ages 60+); $3 (students with ID); $1.50 (ages 6-13). Mine tours (museum included) $10; $8 (ages 60+); $5 (students with ID); $3 (ages 6-13); $28 (family). **Phone:** (250) 362-7722 or (888) 448-7444.

RECREATIONAL ACTIVITIES

Skiing

- **Red Mountain Ski Area** is 3 km (1.5 mi.) n. on Hwy. 3B at 4300 Red Mountain Rd. **Hours:** Daily 7:30-4:30, Dec. 1-Apr. 6. **Phone:** (250) 362-7384 or (800) 663-0105.

SAANICHTON—*see Victoria p. 201.*

SALMON ARM (B-9)
pop. 16,012, elev. 415 m/1,364'

R.J. HANEY HERITAGE VILLAGE & MUSEUM is 2 mi. e. on Hwy. 1, then just s. on Hwy. 97B. The village grew around the Haney House, built in 1910. Among the buildings in the community, all built in the early 20th century, are Salmon Arm's first gas station, a blacksmith shop, a Methodist church, a fire station and a schoolhouse.

In addition, the Beamish Building contains what is said to be Western Canada's largest collection of records and cylinders. A small museum, which changes displays every 2 years, focuses on local Shuswap history, and a 3-kilometre (2-mi.) nature walk, a tea house and a dinner theater also are on the property.

Guided tours of the Haney House are available. **Time:** Allow 1 hour minimum. **Hours:** Complex open Wed.-Sun. 10-5, mid-May through Sept. 30. Dinner theater Wed.-Thurs. and Sun., July-Aug. Museum only open rest of year; phone ahead for schedule. **Cost:** Donations. Guided tour of the Haney House $2.50. Reservations are required for the dinner theater. **Phone:** (250) 832-5243. 🍴 🚻

SALT SPRING ISLAND—
see Gulf Islands p. 123.

SANDON (C-10)

The remnants of one of western Canada's greatest mining towns nestle in the deep, wooded ravine of Carpenter Creek, high in the Selkirk Mountains. Pioneer prospectors Eli Carpenter and Jack Seaton

discovered rich deposits of silver-lead ore here in 1891, triggering a rush. At its peak in the late 1890s, Sandon had over 5,000 residents, 29 hotels, 28 saloons, three breweries, theaters, an opera house, a school and a hospital.

Fire destroyed the central business district on May 3, 1900. The town was quickly rebuilt, channeling Carpenter Creek into a flume and converting its former course into the main street. The 1900s, however, ushered in a long decline. Rising metal prices during World War I briefly renewed prosperity, but the town disincorporated in 1920.

During World War II Sandon housed nearly 1,000 Japanese-Canadians, relocated from the Pacific coast, but by the early 1950s fewer than 200 residents remained. Much of the town remained intact until a major flood devastated the canyon in 1955.

Since the 1970s, volunteers have worked to preserve and restore the old mining town and to protect its heritage from souvenir hunters. Visitors are welcome to wander Sandon's scattered remnants. An old locomotive and other railroad rolling stock idle on a restored section of track. A steep gravel road (a high clearance vehicle is required) leads from the far end of town to Idaho Peak, where a short trail accesses a panoramic view. Galena Trail and K & S Railgrade Trail follow the former railroad routes. The Sandon Museum acts as a visitor center.

SANDON MUSEUM is in the former Slocan Mercantile Block in the center of town. Built in 1900, the museum was the only brick edifice ever erected in Sandon. It served as a general store and during World War II housed Japanese-Canadian internees.

The museum contains a large treasure trove of artifacts from the town's mining past, including historical archives, photos, maps and mining equipment. The basement contains grave markers from the local cemetery, moved to protect them from vandals. Videos portray the history of Sandon. **Time:** Allow 30 minutes minimum. **Hours:** Daily 10-5, June-Sept. **Cost:** $4; $3 (ages 12-18 and 65+). **Phone:** (250) 358-7920.

SATURNA ISLAND—
see Gulf Islands p. 123.

SECHELT (G-11) pop. 8,454

CHAPMAN CREEK HATCHERY is at 4381 Parkway Dr. Visitors learn about the life-cycle of Pacific salmon. Throughout the facility, interpretive signs communicate the history of the hatchery and its function. **Time:** Allow 1 hour minimum. **Hours:** Daily 9-3:30. **Cost:** Donations. **Phone:** (604) 885-4136. 🚻

SICAMOUS (B-9)
pop. 2,676, elev. 352 m/1,155'

Flanked by Mara and Shuswap lakes, Sicamous has abundant recreational opportunities, including swimming, fishing, boating and other water sports. Full- and half-day cruises on Shuswap Lake (*see*

Recreation Chart) and 2- and 3-hour evening excursions on Mara Lake depart from the public wharf at the foot of Finlayson Street. Houseboats, which can be rented, are a popular way of touring the arms of Shuswap Lake.

At nearby Adams River almost 10 million scarlet sockeye salmon bury their eggs each October; it is one of the largest spawning grounds in the country. Several spawning grounds can be seen at Roderick Haig-Brown Provincial Park, 85 kilometres (53 mi.) northwest off Hwy. 1.

Sicamous Visitor Centre: 110 Finlayson St., P.O. Box 346, Sicamous, BC, Canada V0E 2V0. **Phone:** (250) 836-3313.

SIDNEY—*see Victoria p. 201.*

SKIDEGATE (E-1) pop. 781

HAIDA HERITAGE CENTRE AT KAAY LLNAGAAY is just n. of the BC Ferries terminal on Second Beach Rd. The center, on the site of the old Haida seaside village of Kaay Llnagaay, celebrates the relationship of the Haida people with the land and examines, through audiovisuals and interactive displays, Haida art, history and culture.

Traditional totem poles representing the 14 clans front the facility; three ancient poles are inside. A canoe house, a performing house and a carving shed also may be seen. The Haida Gwaii Museum includes exhibits about plants and wildlife as well as the Haida's belief in the natural and supernatural. A collection of argillite carvings and contemporary art is showcased.

Tours: Guided tours are available. **Time:** Allow 1 hour minimum. **Hours:** Daily 10-6, mid-June to mid-Sept.; Mon.-Sat. 10-6, May 1 to mid-June; Tues.-Sat. 10-5, rest of year. Closed holidays during the off-season. **Cost:** $12 (includes the heritage center and Haida Gwaii Museum); $9 (students ages 13-18 with ID); $5 (ages 6-12); $50 (family, up to six people). Guided tours $6; $5 (students with ID); $3 (ages 6-12). **Phone:** (250) 559-7885. 🏛

SMITHERS (E-3)
pop. 5,217, elev. 520 m/1,706′

Named for A.W. Smithers, one-time chairman of the Grand Trunk Pacific Railway, Smithers owes its location to railway construction crews who in 1913 selected the scenic spot at the base of Hudson Bay Mountain. It became a village in 1921 and officially a town in 1967. Today it is a distribution and supply center for local farms, mills and mines. Murals adorn many buildings within its alpine-style Main Street district.

Smithers is popular as a year-round skiing center thanks to 2,652-metre (8,700-ft.) Hudson Bay Mountain. The town also is a convenient starting point for fossil hunting, fishing, mountain climbing and trail riding.

Smithers Visitor Centre: 1411 Court St., P.O. Box 2379, Smithers, BC, Canada V0J 2N0. **Phone:** (250) 847-5072 or (800) 542-6673.

Self-guiding tours: Information about driving and walking tours is available at the chamber of commerce.

ADAMS IGLOO WILDLIFE MUSEUM is 10 km (6 mi.) w. on Hwy. 16. Mounted animals and birds native to British Columbia are displayed inside an igloo. **Time:** Allow 30 minutes minimum. **Hours:** Mon.-Sat. 9-6. **Cost:** $5; $3 (ages 6-18). **Phone:** (250) 847-3188.

SOOKE—*see Victoria p. 201.*

SPARWOOD (C-12)
pop. 3,618, elev. 1,143 m/3,750′

Once known as a mining town, Sparwood offers guided tours of the Elkview Coal Mine during summer. Popular area recreational activities include fly fishing, white-water rafting, hiking and mountain biking.

Sparwood Visitor Centre: 141A Aspen Dr., P.O. Box 1448, Sparwood, BC, Canada V0B 2G0. **Phone:** (250) 425-2423 or (877) 485-8185.

SQUAMISH (G-11) pop. 14,949, elev. 5 m/16′

Overshadowed by Stawamus Chief Mountain and other snowcapped peaks, Squamish was named for the Indian word meaning "mother of the wind." It is a popular stopover for tourists and recreation seekers. Rock climbing and windsurfing are popular activities.

Picnic facilities are available 3 kilometres (1.9 mi.) south at Shannon Falls, and camping facilities are available at Alice Lake Provincial Park *(see Recreation Chart and the AAA/CAA Western Canada & Alaska CampBook)* 13 kilometres (8 mi.) to the north.

Squamish Visitor Centre: 102-38551 Loggers Ln., Squamish, BC, Canada V8B 0H2. **Phone:** (604) 815-4994 or (866) 333-2010.

GARIBALDI PROVINCIAL PARK is accessible by trail from Hwy. 99 or the British Columbia Railway. The 194,650-hectare (480,980-acre) park is a pristine wilderness of peaks, glaciers, meadows, lakes and streams.

Access to the Garibaldi Lake/Black Tusk Area is by a 7-kilometre (5-mi.) trail off Hwy. 99, about 37 kilometres (23 mi.) north of Squamish. A gravel road leads 16 kilometres (10 mi.) to the base camp parking lot, where a trail follows Paul Ridge 11 kilometres (7 mi.) to the Diamond Head Area. Glacier-fed Cheakamus Lake lies at an elevation of less than 914 metres (2,999 ft.). *See Recreation Chart.* **Hours:** The park is open all year. **Cost:** Free. **Parking:** $3 per day. **Phone:** (604) 582-5200 for more information.

GLACIER AIR TOURS—*see Brackendale p. 113.*

WEST COAST RAILWAY HERITAGE PARK is 1 km (.6 mi.) w. off Hwy. 99 on Industrial Way, n. on Queensway Rd. to 39645 Government Rd. This outdoor museum is said to be home to western Canada's largest collection of heritage railway equipment. It features more than 60 railway heritage pieces dating to the early 1900s. Displays include steam and diesel locomotives, including a Royal Hudson locomotive; a sleeping car; caboose; bunk cars; a business car; and a new roundhouse.

A restoration exhibit demonstrates the process of restoring old railway cars. Visitors can ride a miniature train around the property on a 7.5-gauge track.

Time: Allow 30 minutes minimum. **Hours:** Daily 10-5. Miniature train operates daily 11-3. Closed Jan. 1 and Dec. 25. **Cost:** $15; $8.50 (ages 6-18 and 60+); $32 (family, two adults and three children). Miniature railway rides $2. **Phone:** (604) 898-9336 or (800) 722-1233. 🎫

SUMMERLAND—see Okanagan Valley p. 143.

SUN PEAKS (B-8)

The resort community of Sun Peaks nestles amid firs and aspen at the base of Tod Mountain and Mount Morrisey in central British Columbia. The core of the village, 31 kilometres (19 mi.) east of Hwy. 5 at Heffley Creek, consists of three- to five-story alpine motif buildings clustered along pedestrian walkways.

With nearly 1,497 hectares (3,700 acres) of terrain, Sun Peaks is reportedly the third largest ski area in Canada, offering both alpine and Nordic skiing as well as a tube park, ice skating, sleigh rides, snowmobiling and dog sledding. Summer activities include golf, tennis, hiking, mountain biking, kayaking, canoeing, fishing and trail rides.

RECREATIONAL ACTIVITIES

Skiing

- **Sun Peaks Resort** is 54 km (32 mi.) n. on Hwy. 5 at 1280 Alpine Rd. Other activities are available. **Hours:** Daily 8:30-3:30, mid-Nov. to mid-Apr. Phone ahead to confirm schedule. **Phone:** (250) 578-7222 or (800) 807-3257.

SUNSHINE COAST (H-4)

Lining the western edge of the British Columbia mainland, the Sunshine Coast offers a wide variety of marine and land habitats, from coastal rain forests and rocky beaches to an alpine wilderness with peaks reaching 2,500 metres (8,000 ft.).

Powell River (see place listing p. 148), with more than 100 regional dive sites, exceptionally clear water and deep ocean currents, is called the "Dive Capital of Canada." Desolation Sound's warm, sheltered waters also contribute to the destination's popularity with scuba divers and kayakers. Sechelt (see place listing p. 153) is known for its rich artisan community, while Gibsons (see place listing p. 121) is home to up to 200 bird species throughout the year.

SURREY—see Vancouver p. 186.

TELEGRAPH COVE (H-3)

The bay community served as the northern terminus of the telegraph line along the coast of Vancouver Island and later became a logging and salmon fishing area. Whale watching, fishing and camping are popular during the summer.

STUBBS ISLAND WHALE WATCHING departs from the end of the #24 boardwalk. For excursions on the Johnstone Strait, vessels are equipped with underwater microphones for listening to whale vocalizations. Multiday tours also are available.

Warm clothing is recommended. **Time:** Allow 3 hours, 30 minutes minimum. **Hours:** Daily departures mid-June to early Oct. Phone ahead to confirm schedule. **Cost:** Mid-day fare $94; $84 (ages 1-12 and 65+). Morning and evening fare $84. Reservations are required. **Phone:** (250) 928-3185 or (800) 665-3066.

WHALE INTERPRETIVE CENTRE is at the end of the boardwalk. Interpreters provide hands-on presentations and share information about and promote awareness of the marine environment. Exhibits include whale skeletons and artifacts. An educational video about marine-life also is featured. **Time:** Allow 45 minutes minimum. **Hours:** Daily 9-7, May-Sept. **Cost:** Donations. **Phone:** (250) 928-3129.

TERRACE (E-2) pop. 11,320, elev. 215 m/705'

On the banks of the Skeena River, Terrace is a major producer of forest products. The area provides excellent recreational opportunities ranging from hiking on a variety of trails to fishing in nearby rivers and creeks. Among the region's wildlife is a rare species of black bear, the white Kermodei. Native to the area, it is the city's symbol.

Among the most popular recreation areas are Lakelse Lake Provincial Park *(see Recreation Chart and the AAA/CAA Western Canada & Alaska CampBook)*; Lakelse River, a tributary of the Skeena River that harbors record-size salmon; and Williams Creek, which teems with spawning sockeye each August.

Several places of natural interest are nearby. At the eastern entrance to the city is Ferry Island, a park with hiking trails, swimming and camping *(see Recreation Chart).* About 20 kilometres (12 mi.) south of Terrace is Mount Layton Hot Springs Resort, which has waterslides and a pool filled with natural hot spring mineral water. Hwy. 16 offers a scenic drive west along the Skeena River to Prince Rupert.

Terrace Visitor Centre: 4511 Keith Ave., Terrace, BC, Canada V8G 1K1. **Phone:** (250) 635-4944 or (800) 499-1637.

HERITAGE PARK MUSEUM is at 4702 Kerby Ave. Historic buildings depict the history of pioneers in the region. The structures contain more than 4,000 artifacts pertaining to the life of settlers to the area 1890-1950. **Tours:** Guided tours are available. **Time:** Allow 1 hour minimum. **Hours:** Daily 10-5, July-Aug.; Mon.-Fri. 10-5, mid-May through June 30; by appointment rest of year. **Cost:** $5; $3 (ages 6-17, ages 55+ and students with ID); $15 (family). **Phone:** (250) 635-4546.

NISGA'A MEMORIAL LAVA BED PROVINCIAL PARK is 100 km (62 mi.) n. on Kalum Lake Dr. (Nisga'a Hwy.); the first 70 km (44 mi.) is paved. Drivers should watch for logging trucks.

Miles of lava beds were formed by a volcanic eruption some 250 years ago that destroyed two Nisga'a tribal villages, causing 2,000 deaths. The valley floor resembles the moon's surface. Interpretive trails provide easy access through the park. The New Aiyansh Indian Village, 16 kilometres (10 mi.) north, features totem poles, a tribal council hall and a Nisga'a Lisims government building. Guided hiking tours to the volcanic cone are available. *See Recreation Chart.*

Hours: Park daily dawn-dusk, May 1 to mid-Oct. Visitor center daily 10-6, June 1-early Sept. Guided hiking tours of the volcanic cone are offered Sat. at 10, mid-June through Aug. 31. **Cost:** Park free. Visitor center $2; free (ages 0-12). Guided hiking tour $40; $30 (ages 13-19); $25 (ages 7-12). Ages 0-6 are not permitted on the hiking tour. **Phone:** (250) 798-2466. 🎣 🏕

TOFINO (I-3) pop. 1,655

A fishing and resort village with sandy beaches, Tofino is on the western side of Vancouver Island at the end of Hwy. 4. The area was the site of Fort Defiance, where Boston fur trader Robert Gray and his men spent the winter of 1791. The fort was stripped and abandoned the next spring, and all that remains are scattered bricks and ruins.

Near Clayoquot Sound and the northern end of Pacific Rim National Park Reserve of Canada, the town's shoreline and waters are popular with scuba divers and beachcombers. In the spring whales often can be seen migrating along the coast. The Whale Centre and Museum at 411 Campbell St. exhibits scientific and artistic displays, photographs and artifacts depicting past and present whale encounters.

Several companies, including Adventures Pacific, (250) 725-2811; Jamie's Whaling Station, (250) 725-3919; Remote Passages, (250) 725-3330; and Sea Trek Tours and Expeditions, (250) 725-4412, offer whale-watching excursions on Clayoquot Sound. Tours lasting up to 2.5 hours may afford sightings of sea lions, porpoises and eagles. Combination whale-watching and hot springs cruises that last approximately 6.5 hours also are available.

Tofino-Long Beach Visitor Centre: 1426 Pacific Rim Hwy., P.O. Box 249, Tofino, BC, Canada V0R 2Z0. **Phone:** (250) 725-3414.

TOFINO BOTANICAL GARDENS is at 1084 Pacific Rim Hwy. This site consists of 5 hectares (12 acres) of gardens that include a children's garden, a medicinal herb garden, 1,000-year-old cedar trees, an orchard and a berry patch, and a bird-watching area. An old homestead also is on the grounds. Pets and smoking are not permitted. **Time:** Allow 1 hour minimum. **Hours:** Daily 9-dusk. **Cost:** $10; $6 (students); free (ages 0-12). **Phone:** (250) 725-1220. 🍴

TRAIL (D-10) pop. 7,237, elev. 430 m/1,410′

At City Hall a sculptured screen titled "City of Lead and Zinc" illustrates how Trail's mineral and industrial strength steadily developed since the discovery of gold and copper in the area about 1890. Hydroelectric dams along the Kootenay River power extensive mining and smelting operations, dominated by Teck Cominco Ltd. Enjoy free concerts at Gyro Park, 1090 Charles Lakes Dr., on Thursday evenings in July and August.

Trail and District Chamber of Commerce and Visitor Centre: 1199 Bay Ave., Suite 200, Trail, BC, Canada V1R 4A4. **Phone:** (250) 368-3144, or (877) 636-9569 within British Columbia.

Self-guiding tours: Brochures for walking tours are available at the chamber of commerce.

TECK TRAIL OPERATIONS INTERPRETIVE CENTRE is downtown at 1199 Bay Ave., Suite 200. The center has hands-on science exhibits that explain the processes of smelting and refining and how metals affect our everyday life. Tours of one of the largest lead-zinc smelters in the world depart from the interpretive center.

Long pants, long-sleeved shirts and closed shoes are required for the tours; cameras and video equipment are prohibited. Individuals with pacemakers should not attend. Full mobility is required on the plant portion of the tour. All visitors must provide heir own transportation to and from the interpretive center to the plant. **Time:** Allow 2 hours minimum.

Hours: Center open daily 9-5, July-Aug.; Mon.-Fri. 9-5, rest of year. Tours depart Mon.-Fri. at 10. July-Aug.; by appointment rest of year. Closed major holidays. **Cost:** Free. Ages 0-11 are not permitted on tours. **Phone:** (250) 368-3144.

UCLUELET (I-3) pop. 1,487

On Barkley Sound, Ucluelet was named for an Indian word meaning "safe harbor." Charter boats for salmon fishing, whale watching, skin diving and nature excursions are available; phone the chamber of commerce. The MV *Lady Rose* makes round trips between Port Alberni and Ucluelet June through September *(see attraction listing in Port Alberni p. 147).* He Tin Kis Park allows visitors to experience a Canadian rain forest and follow a boardwalk trail that leads to the ocean. The 5-kilometre (3-mi.) Wild Pacific Trail passes a lighthouse en route to cliffside ocean views.

Ucluelet Visitor Centre: 2791 Pacific Rim Hwy., Ucluelet, BC, Canada V0R 3A0. **Phone:** (250) 726-4600.

VALEMOUNT (F-5)
pop. 1,195, elev. 792 m/2,600′

Valemount, the valley in the mountains, offers many activities for outdoor enthusiasts. The village, where the Rocky, Cariboo and Monashee mountain ranges meet, is popular for both summer and winter pursuits, including hiking, rafting, skiing and snowmobiling. The area is rich with birds and other wildlife. Off Hwy. 16 is Mount Terry Fox Provincial Park. A viewing area affords vistas of the peak named for the late athlete.

Valemount Visitor and Interpretive Centre: 735 Cranberry Lake Rd., P.O. Box 146, Valemount, BC, Canada V0E 2Z0. **Phone:** (250) 566-4435, or (250) 566-9893 May-Sept.

GEORGE HICKS REGIONAL PARK is off Hwy. 5 at 785 Cranberry Lake Rd. The site offers a bird's-eye view of Chinook salmon as they near the end of a 1,280-kilometre (768-mi.) upstream trip from mid-August to mid-September. **Hours:** Daily mid-May to mid-Sept. **Cost:** Donations. **Phone:** (250) 566-9893.

MOUNT ROBSON PROVINCIAL PARK is on Hwy. 16. Mount Robson, at 3,954 metres (12,972 ft.) is the highest peak in the Canadian Rockies. Other park highlights include glacier-fed lakes, valleys, canyons, waterfalls, rivers and streams. More than 180 species of birds reside here along with deer, moose, bears, elk and caribou. Fishing, camping, horseback riding and hiking are just a few of the outdoor activities to be enjoyed.

Scenic views abound on the many walking and hiking trails. A visitor center is at the Mount Robson viewpoint. *See Recreation Chart and the AAA/CAA Western Canada & Alaska CampBook.* **Hours:** Park open daily 24 hours. Visitor center open May-Sept. **Cost:** Donations. **Phone:** (250) 566-4325.

ROBSON HELIMAGIC INC. tours depart from the Yellowhead Helicopters hangar, 5 km (3 mi.) n. on Hwy. 5 to 3010 Selwyn Rd. Helicopters take passengers on 12-36 minute tours of the Valemount and Mount Robson areas, providing breathtaking views of glaciers, snow-covered mountains, alpine meadows, valleys, waterfalls, lakes and rivers.

Heli-skiing, heli-snowshoeing and heli-snowboarding also are offered in winter. Summer activities are available. **Hours:** Daily 7-7, mid-May through Sept. 30; phone ahead for schedule rest of year. **Cost:** $99-$219. **Phone:** (250) 566-4700 or (877) 454-4700.

R.W. STARRATT WILDLIFE SANCTUARY is 1 km (.6 mi.) s. on Hwy. 5. The refuge is home to a variety of songbirds, waterfowl and other animals. Informational signs line a trail to two viewing platforms. **Time:** Allow 30 minutes minimum. **Hours:** Daily 9-9, July-Aug.; 9-8, mid-June through June 30; 10-6, June 1 to mid-June; 9-5, Sept. 1-Labour Day; 10-5, late May-May 31 and day after Labour Day-Sept. 30; 10-4, early May to mid-May. Phone ahead to confirm schedule. **Cost:** Free. **Phone:** (250) 566-4846.

Vancouver

City Population: 578,041
Elevation: 3 m/10 ft.

Editor's Picks:

Find more AAA top picks at AAA.com

Raimund Koch / Getty Images

Picture yourself hiking along a wide, bark-mulched trail through an old-growth forest of towering Western red cedar, Douglas fir and Western hemlock. These evergreen giants form a lacy canopy penetrated here and there by shafts of sunlight, but even on a warm, sunny summer day there's deep shade and it feels refreshingly cool. Salmonberry, huckleberry, bog buckbean and other native plants grow together in one luxurious tangle. A woodsy, pleasantly earthy aroma hangs in the air. Squirrels scamper across the path and then pause for a moment, tails flicking nervously. A raccoon ambles by, giving you an inquisitive look. Chickadees and towhees twitter. A goose honks in the distance. You suddenly stop and ask yourself, "Wait a minute—am I really in a city?" That question is answered within minutes, when you emerge from Stanley Park to the hustle and bustle of Georgia Street.

You're not only in a city; you're smack in the middle of Canada's third largest metropolitan area. There's no denying the beauty of this natural setting, with vistas of green coastal mountains and the deep blue Strait of Georgia tailor-made to grace the front of a postcard. And then there's downtown, which is really something of a marvel: skyscrapers, dense commercial development, human hubbub and quiet, tree-lined residential streets all coexisting harmoniously in one tightly packed urban cityscape. If that pocket description sounds a little bit like San Francisco, well, it's an apt comparison—but there really is no place like Vancouver.

No doubt the southwestern British Columbia wilderness impressed Capt. George Vancouver. An officer in the British Royal Navy, he sailed into Burrard Inlet on June 13, 1792, while searching for the Northwest Passage, the sea route that connects the Atlantic and Pacific oceans. Vancouver named the inlet after his friend Sir Harry Burrard, a member of Parliament, while the city and the large island that lies between the mainland and the Pacific both bear his name.

Tall timber and a rail line spurred initial growth. A sawmill was established in 1863, and it wasn't long before a wild and woolly settlement sprang up on the peninsula lying between the Fraser River and Burrard Inlet. Vancouver was incorporated in 1886, quite a young city given its present-day status. A Canadian Pacific Railway passenger train arrived the following year—the city was chosen as the end of the line due to its natural harbor facilities—showering exuberant spectators with soot and cinders. By the 1890s trans-Pacific shipping inaugurated Vancouver as a major world port, and the future was looking rosy indeed.

Getting There — starting on p. 162

Getting Around — starting on p. 162

What To See — starting on p. 163

What To Do — starting on p. 171

Where To Stay — starting on p. 600

Where To Dine — starting on p. 623

Essential Experiences — visit AAA.com

Editor's Event Picks — visit AAA.com

That era produced some colorful characters. Chief among them was one John Deighton, aka "Gassy Jack," a saloon owner who set up shop in Gastown, the city's oldest section and a popular tourist hangout. The name is a reference not to excessive flatulence but to Deighton's vaunted reputation for tall-tale bluster. His likeness stands at the circle where Water, Alexander, Powell and Carrall streets converge, and having your picture snapped in front of the old salt is a prime Vancouver photo op.

Standing across the circle from Jack is another legacy of the early days, the Hotel Europe. Commissioned by Italian business magnate Angelo Calori, this six-story landmark on Powell Street, built in 1908, is designed in the style of Manhattan's famous Flatiron Building. Stand directly across from the front entrance to fully appreciate its triangular shape and rounded contours. It couldn't be more different in appearance from nearby Canada Place, a waterfront facility topped with billowing white tent-frame sails that houses the Vancouver Convention and Exhibition Centre, the Pan Pacific Vancouver hotel, the IMAX Theatre at Canada Place and the Vancouver Port Authority terminal from which luxury cruise ships depart for Alaska.

Downtown Vancouver, in fact, is an architectural smorgasbord. Well-heeled Yaletown and Coal Harbour bristle with glittering, glass-walled high-rise condos. The polished brass doors and elevator walls of the Marine Building, on Burrard Street, are inlaid with hardwoods and depictions of marine creatures—sea horses, crabs, snails—while the Art Deco exterior flaunts more animal and plant designs. It's a favorite for film and TV shoots.

Mandarin and Cantonese are the mother tongues in almost one-third of this city's homes, and only

© Vancouver Lookout at Harbour Centre

San Francisco's Chinatown is bigger than Vancouver's. The Millennium Gate at Pender and Taylor streets is a symbolic entryway incorporating both eastern and western symbols. Between 1890 and 1920 Asian immigrants settled on back streets like Shanghai Alley off Pender Street; wall panels tell the story of their lives. And holding out your arms is almost enough to embrace the pencil-thin Sam Kee Building at 8 Pender St., which is a mere 6 feet wide.

Vancouver looks downright subtropical in a country most people equate with snow and cold weather. Winters are mild and wet, summers sunny and dry—in other words, vegetation-friendly climatic conditions. The magnificent spread of conifers in Stanley Park qualifies as an example of temperate rain forest. Throughout the city are blooming magnolias, azaleas and rhododendrons, flowering Japanese cherry trees, graceful Japanese maples and striking exotics like the scaly-leafed monkey puzzle tree, a native of Chile and Argentina. You'll even see palms and banana plants. This is Canada?

Destination Vancouver

*T*he nuances of cosmopolitan Vancouver's multiple cultures are revealed through the arts, in neighborhood preservation and by observing the lifestyle enjoyed by residents.

*Y*ou'll find ambience in green spaces and historic places; at galleries and gardens; and on beaches, bays and gap-spanning bridges.

© Rudy Sulgan / age fotostock

Capilano Suspension Bridge, North Vancouver. (See listing page 182)

Grouse Mountain Resorts Ltd.

Grouse Mountain, North Vancouver. (See listing page 182)

© Chris Howes / Wild Places Photography / Alamy

Vancouver Aquarium Marine Science Centre. (See listing page 168)

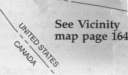

See Downtown map page 165

Vancouver

West Vancouver

North Vancouver

Port Moody

Burnaby

Port Coquitlam

Coquitlam

Maple Ridge

New Westminster

Richmond

Delta

Surrey

Mission

Langley

Aldergrove

See Vicinity map page 164

UNITED STATES
CANADA

BRITISH COLUMBIA
WASHINGTON

*P*laces included in this AAA Destination City:

© Allan Baxter / age fotostock

Science World at TELUS World of Science, Vancouver. (See listing page 167)

The Informed Traveler

Sales Tax: British Columbia's provincial sales tax is 7 percent. A 5 percent Goods and Services Tax (GST) also is levied, and there is a room tax of 10 percent on lodgings in the Vancouver area. This tax structure will be in effect until July 1, 2010, when the province will change to a harmonized sales tax, creating a single tax of 12 percent. The separate lodgings tax will be discontinued, and hotel accommodations will be subject to the harmonized tax.

WHOM TO CALL

Emergency: 911

Police (non-emergency): (604) 717-3321

Time and Temperature: (604) 664-9010

Hospitals: Mount Saint Joseph Hospital, (604) 874-1141; St. Paul's Hospital, (604) 682-2344; Vancouver General Hospital, (604) 875-4111.

WHERE TO LOOK

Newspapers

The two major daily newspapers, both published in the morning, are the *Province* and the *Vancouver Sun*.

Radio

Vancouver radio stations CBU-AM (690), CBU-FM (105.7), CHQM-FM (103.5), CKCL-FM (104.9), CKLG-FM (96.9) and CKWX-AM (1130) have news and weather reports.

Visitor Information

Vancouver Tourist InfoCentre: 200 Burrard St., Plaza Level, Vancouver, BC, Canada V6C 3L6. **Phone:** (604) 683-2000.

Maps, lodging reservations and literature about attractions as well as tickets for tours are available at the Vancouver Tourist InfoCentre which is open daily 8:30-6, Victoria Day weekend to mid-Sept.; Mon.-Sat. 8:30-5, rest of year.

TRANSPORTATION

Air Travel

Vancouver International Airport, in Richmond, is reached via Granville Street and the Arthur Lang Bridge, then Sea Island Way, which leads into Grant McConachie Way. Vancouver Airporter buses run every 20 minutes 8:55 a.m.-9:25 p.m. One-way bus service departs most major downtown hotels every 30 minutes. The fare is $13.50, round trip $21; phone (604) 946-8866 or (800) 668-3141. Taxis average $26 one-way.

Rental Cars

Hertz, at 1128 Seymour St., offers discounts to AAA and CAA members; phone (604) 606-4711, (800) 263-0600 in Canada, or (800) 654-3131 in North America. Additional agencies are listed in the telephone directory.

Rail Service

The Via Rail passenger train terminal is at 1150 Station St.; phone (888) 842-7245 in Canada or in the United States.

Buses

The bus terminal is at 1150 Station St.; phone (604) 482-8747 or (800) 661-8747.

Taxis

Fares start at $2.75, plus $1.50 per kilometre (.6 mi.). Companies include Black Top, (604) 731-1111; MacLure's, (604) 731-9211; Yellow Cab, (604) 681-1111; and Vancouver Taxi, (604) 255-5111.

Public Transport

Translink offers bus service as well as Sea-Bus and SkyTrain service. *See Public Transportation for details.*

Boats

BC Ferries links Vancouver Island with the rest of the province. Nanaimo and Sunshine Coast ferries leave from Horseshoe Bay, 21 kilometres (13 mi.) west of the city in West Vancouver. From Tsawwassen south of Vancouver automobile/passenger ferries make frequent trips to the southern Gulf Islands, Nanaimo and Swartz Bay, north of Victoria; Vancouver-Victoria bus service is available on most sailings.

For schedules phone the British Columbia Automobile Association, (604) 268-5555, British Columbia Ferries Information Centre, (250) 386-3431 outside British Columbia, (888) 223-3779 in British Columbia, or Tourism Vancouver, (604) 683-2000.

Just as Vancouver is a cosmopolitan blend of cultures, Vancouverites themselves represent a melting pot of nationalities. The original inhabitants of coastal British Columbia were the First Nations peoples, and their descendants live in urban areas as well as reserve communities located within ancestral territories, in each case keeping vibrant ceremonial and artistic traditions alive. Diversity is the keynote, whether preserved in street names like Barclay and Granville or neighborhoods like Greektown and Little India (Punjabi Market), and especially evident in the faces seen and languages heard on practically every corner.

And of course everyone will be watching when Vancouver and Whistler host the 2010 Olympic Winter Games, with Opening Ceremonies on Feb. 12, 2010, signaling the start of Olympic and Paralympic events. Not bad for a former lumber town, eh?

Getting There

By Car

Hwy. 1 and hwys. 1A and 7 are the major east-west routes to Vancouver. To reach downtown on the Trans-Canada Highway, use the First Avenue exit or continue to Hastings Street.

Hwy. 99 to S.W. Marine West becomes the major downtown artery, Granville Street. Before becoming a city street, Hwy. 99 begins its journey as I-5 at the Mexican border and crosses through California and the Pacific Northwest.

Getting Around

Street System

All streets and avenues in downtown Vancouver are named; many are one-way. Outside the business section, east-west avenues are numbered beginning with First Avenue, and north-south streets are named. Addresses begin at Ontario-Carrall streets for all east-west numbering and at Powell-Dundas streets for all north-south numbering.

The downtown peninsula is connected to western Vancouver by the Burrard, Granville and Cambie bridges and to North Vancouver and West Vancouver by the Lions Gate and the Iron Workers Memorial (Second Narrows) bridges.

Rush hours are 6-9:30 a.m. and 3-6:30 p.m. Right turns on red are permitted after a stop, unless otherwise posted; drivers must yield to pedestrians and vehicles in the intersection and to city buses pulling into traffic.

Parking

On-street parking, controlled by meter, is restricted on many thoroughfares during rush hours; violators' cars will be towed. Off-street parking is available in lots and garages at rates ranging from $1.25 per half-hour to $11 or more per day. Parking in a school zone between 8 and 5 on any school day is strictly prohibited unless otherwise posted.

Public Transportation

Translink offers bus service to points throughout Vancouver and to all suburban areas; it also offers

Burnaby / © Eero Sorila

SeaBus and SkyTrain service as well as the West Coast Express commuter rail.

SeaBus service conveys commuters between North Vancouver and the city of Vancouver, connecting with the bus system at the foot of Granville Street.

SkyTrain, Vancouver's rapid transit system, runs from Waterfront Station through downtown Vancouver to the suburbs of Burnaby and New Westminster and across the Fraser River to the suburb of Surrey.

SkyTrain's newest line, the Canada Line, began operation August 2009 connecting downtown, Richmond and Sea Island (Vancouver International Airport). In addition to stations in those locations, it also includes an underground tunnel running south from downtown's Waterfront Station; park-and-ride facilities; bus exchanges; and elevated guideways. The 19-kilometre (12-mi.) line includes stops at Vancouver City Centre, Olympic Village, Broadway-City Hall, Marine Drive, Vancouver International Airport and four Richmond locations. The train ride from downtown to the airport takes 26 minutes.

Trains operate every 5 minutes Mon.-Fri. 5:30 a.m.-midnight, Sat. 6:50 a.m.-12:30 a.m., Sun. 7:50 a.m.-11:30 p.m. Fares are the same for any Translink service. A 1-zone fare Monday through Friday until 6:30 p.m. is $2.50, a 2-zone fare is $3.75 and a 3-zone fare is $5; for ages 5-13 and 65+ a 1-zone fare is $1.75, a 2-zone fare is $2.50 and a 3-zone fare is $3.50. The fare for weekdays after 6:30 p.m. and Saturday, Sunday and holidays for all zones is $2.50; for ages 5-13 and 65+ the fare for all zones is $1.75.

Every SkyTrain station has information panels. A 1-day pass, available from SkyTrain and SeaBus ticket machines, Safeway food stores and 7-11 stores, costs $9; for ages 5-13 and 65+ the cost is $7. If you pay by cash on buses, exact change is required. Phone (604) 953-3333 Mon.-Sat. 6 a.m.-12:30 a.m., Sun. and holidays 8 a.m.-11 p.m. for more information.

Aquabus Ltd., (604) 689-5858, provides ferry service between Granville Island, Hornby Street, Yaletown, Stamps Landing and Science World at TELUS World of Science daily 7 a.m.-8 p.m. Times vary according to destination. Fare ranges from $4-$6. The Aquabus from Granville Island to Hornby Street is equipped to carry bicycles for an extra 50c.

Daily bus service between Vancouver International Airport and Whistler is provided by Whistler Skylynx. Passengers can be picked up and dropped off at major Vancouver and Whistler lodgings; reservations are required. Phone (604) 662-7575 or (800) 661-1725 for information.

What To See

B.C. SPORTS HALL OF FAME AND MUSEUM is at jct. Beatty and Robson sts., Gate A of the B.C. Place Stadium. The history of sports in British Columbia is traced from First Nations traditions to modern Olympic games. Honorees include amateur and professional teams, athletes, journalists and sports pioneers. Interactive galleries provide opportunities for running, climbing, throwing, riding and rowing. Rotating exhibits, a sports library and a stadium tour also are featured.

Hours: Daily 10-5. **Cost:** $10; $8 (ages 5-17, ages 65+ and students with ID); $25 (family). Half-price to B.C. Place Stadium or General Motors Place ticket-holders. **Phone:** (604) 687-5520.

BLOEDEL CONSERVATORY—
see Queen Elizabeth Park p. 166.

CHINATOWN—*see Shopping p. 175.*

CHRIST CHURCH CATHEDRAL is at 690 Burrard St. One of Vancouver's oldest stone churches, the cathedral was completed in 1895. In addition to stone, it also is constructed of old-growth wood. Its 37 English and Canadian stained-glass windows are highlights. **Tours:** Guided tours are available. **Hours:** Mon.-Fri. 10-4. **Cost:** Donations. **Phone:** (604) 682-3848.

DR. SUN YAT-SEN CLASSICAL CHINESE GARDEN is at 578 Carrall St. What this walled garden lacks in size it more than makes up for in serene beauty. Located next to the Chinese Cultural Centre in the heart of Chinatown, it's a delightful respite from the surrounding hustle and bustle. Modeled after private gardens in the city of Suzhou, the garden embodies the Taoist philosophy of yin and yang, where every element—light, texture, vegetation—is balanced.

The architecture of the pavilions, covered walkways, terraces and viewing platforms evokes Ming Dynasty classical design. Rocks and water are integral elements, while trees and plants—from pine trees and bamboo to graceful weeping willows and winter-flowering plum trees—all have symbolic connotations. The Jade Water Pavilion is graced with beautiful woodwork. Two of the garden's most intriguing elements are the 43 leak windows (each one has a different lattice pattern) and the groupings of Tai Hu rocks, interestingly shaped stones from China's Lake Tai that lend themselves to all sorts of artistic interpretations.

Visitors can walk through the garden on their own, but the guided tour offers historical perspective and encourages you to reflect on the design elements in different ways. Afterward, take a stroll through the adjacent public park, where pathways wind through clumps of bamboo and other plantings.

Art and horticultural exhibits and demonstrations also are offered. Festivals and concerts are featured throughout the year. **Time:** Allow 1 hour minimum. **Hours:** Daily 9:30-7, June 15-Aug. 31; 10-6, May 1-June 14 and in Sept.; 10-4:30, rest of year. Closed Jan. 1 and Dec. 25. **Cost:** $10 (includes guided tour and tea); $9 (ages 65+); $8 (ages 5-17 and students with ID). **Phone:** (604) 662-3207. *See color ad p. 167.*

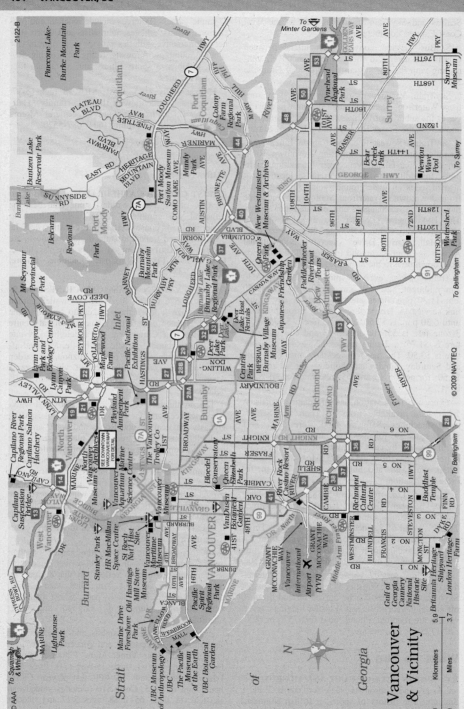

Vancouver & Vicinity

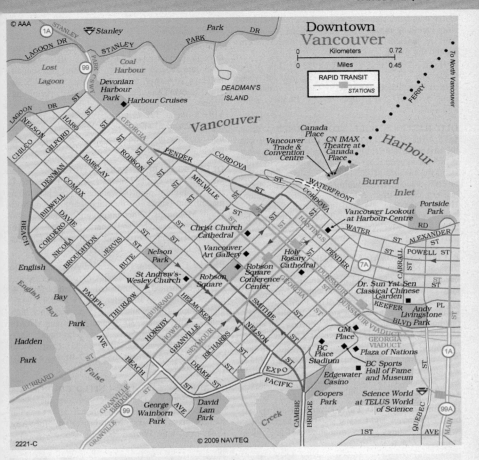

© AAA

Downtown Vancouver

2221-C

© 2009 NAVTEQ

HOLY ROSARY CATHEDRAL is at 646 Richards St. between Dunsmuir and W. Georgia sts. The church has stained-glass windows and eight bells hung in the rare English ringing style. **Hours:** Cathedral open Mon.-Sat. 6:30-6, Sun. 7:30 a.m.-9 p.m. Bell ringing Sun. at 10:30, Tues. at 7:30 p.m. **Cost:** Free. **Phone:** (604) 682-6774.

H.R. MacMILLAN SPACE CENTRE is at 1100 Chestnut St. in Vanier Park. The Virtual Voyages motion simulator is among the interactive exhibits and games featured at the center. The Planetarium Star Theatre and Ground-Station Canada present laser light shows and programs dealing with astronomy, solar history and space explorations.

Time: Allow 1 hour, 30 minutes minimum. **Hours:** Daily 10-5, late June-Labour Day; Tues.-Sun. 10-5, rest of year. Laser shows Fri.-Sat. at 9:15 p.m. and 10:30 p.m. Show times may vary; phone for schedule. Closed Dec. 25. **Cost:** $15; $10.75 (ages 5-18, ages 65+ and students with ID); $7

(ages 0-4 with simulator ride); free (ages 0-4 without simulator ride). Laser light show $9.35. Admission may vary depending on shows. **Phone:** (604) 738-7827.

IMAX THEATRE AT CANADA PLACE is at 201-999 Canada Pl. Various IMAX films are presented on a screen five stories tall. Three-dimensional movies are shown periodically. **Note:** The theater will be closed through mid-March 2010 due to the Olympics. **Time:** Allow 1 hour minimum. **Hours:** Daily on the hour 11-10. **Cost:** $12; $11 (ages 3-12 and 65+). **Phone:** (604) 682-4629 or (800) 582-4629.

MUSEUM OF VANCOUVER, on the s.w. end of Burrard St. in Vanier Park at 1100 Chestnut St., is reportedly Canada's largest civic museum with a collection of more than 100,000 objects. Permanent exhibits tell the city's stories from the early 1900s to the late 1970s and are complemented by contemporary groundbreaking exhibits. Devoted to the art, natural history, anthropology and history of the lower mainland, the museum displays regional artifacts including pieces from First Nations peoples as well as ancient and contemporary objects from around the world.

Hours: Daily 10-5 (also Thurs. 5-8), July-Aug.; Tues.-Sun. 10-5, (also Thurs. 5-9), rest of year. Closed Dec. 25. **Cost:** $11; $9 (ages 65+ and students with ID); $7 (ages 5-17). **Phone:** (604) 736-4431.

OLD HASTINGS MILL STORE MUSEUM is at 1575 Alma St. in Hastings Mill Park. The mill was the first industrial facility on the south shore of what is now Vancouver. One of the few buildings to withstand the ravages of the 1886 fire, it contains relics of early Vancouver, including native basketry and a hansom cab. **Time:** Allow 30 minutes minimum. **Hours:** Tues.-Sun. 1-4, mid-June to mid-Sept.; Sat.-Sun. 1-4, rest of year. Guided tours are offered by appointment Mar.-Nov. **Cost:** Donations. **Phone:** (604) 734-1212.

PACIFIC NATIONAL EXHIBITION is on E. Hastings St. between Renfrew and Cassiar sts. The site occupies 58 hectares (144 acres) and is home to Pacific Coliseum, a tradeshow and entertainment complex, and a skateboard park. The Pacific National Exhibition Fair is an end of summer highlight. Various trade and hobby shows, rock concerts and sporting events are scheduled throughout the year.

Hours: Fair daily 11 a.m.-midnight, mid- to late Aug. through Labour Day. Last admission 1 hour, 30 minutes before closing. **Cost:** Fair admission $15; $6 (ages 65+). Rates may vary; phone ahead. **Phone:** (604) 253-2311. ⑪

Playland Amusement Park is on E. Hastings St. between Renfrew and Cassiar sts. The 4-hectare (10-acre) park features games, miniature golf and rides, including a large wooden roller coaster and three "extreme rides."

Hours: Daily 11 a.m.-midnight, mid-Aug. through Labour Day; Mon.-Thurs. 10-7, Fri.-Sun. 10-8, late June to mid-Aug.; Sat.-Sun. and statutory holidays 10-6, Apr. 1-late June; Sat.-Sun. 10-6, day after Labour Day-Sept. 30 (weather permitting). Phone ahead to confirm schedule. **Cost:** $29.95; $19.95 (under 122 centimetres or 48 in. tall); free (ages 0-2 and 61+). $12.95 (parents when accompanied by a paying child ages 0-12). Rates may vary; phone ahead. **Phone:** (604) 253-2311.

QUEEN ELIZABETH PARK is off Cambie St. and W. 33rd Ave. On 167-metre (548-ft.) Little Mountain, the highest point in Vancouver, the park offers magnificent views of the city, harbor and North Shore Mountains. Other highlights include an arboretum; rose, sunken and quarry gardens; dancing fountains; tennis courts; and pitch and putt greens. **Hours:** Daily 24 hours. **Cost:** Free.

Bloedel Conservatory is at 33rd Ave. and Cambie St. Climatically varied species of plants grow in a climate-controlled, illuminated triodetic dome 43 metres (141 ft.) in diameter and 21 metres (70 ft.) high. Tropical birds and a fish pond are other highlights. **Time:** Allow 30 minutes minimum. **Hours:** Mon.-Fri. 9-8, Sat.-Sun. 10-9, May-Sept.; daily 10-5, rest of year. Closed Dec. 25. **Cost:** $4.80; $3.35 (ages 13-18 and 65+); $2.40 (ages 6-12). **Phone:** (604) 257-8584.

ST. ANDREW'S-WESLEY UNITED CHURCH is at 1022 Nelson St. The Gothic structure includes a large collection of British, French and Canadian stained glass. **Hours:** Mon.-Fri. 10-4, July-Aug. **Cost:** Donations. **Phone:** (604) 683-4574.

SCIENCE WORLD AT TELUS WORLD OF SCIENCE, 1455 Quebec St., features hands-on exhibits and demonstrations that explain scientific phenomena. The Eureka Gallery explores such themes as water, air, motion and invention. The Science Theatre features a variety of high-definition video shows throughout the day. The Centre Stage presents science demonstrations daily. Human performance and nature are the subjects of additional galleries. The Kidspace Gallery features activities for children ages 2 through 6. Also of interest is the OMNIMAX Theater that presents nature and science films.

Time: Allow 2 hours minimum. **Hours:** Daily 10-6, late June-Labour Day; Mon.-Fri. 10-5, Sat.-Sun. and holidays 10-6, rest of year. Closed during the Olympics, Labour Day and Dec. 25. **Cost:** Exhibits and Science Theatre $18.75; $15.50 (ages 13-18, ages 65+ and students with ID); $13.25 (ages 4-12); $71.50 (family). Parking $3-$7. Rates may vary; phone ahead. **Phone:** (604) 443-7443 or (604) 443-7440.

STANLEY PARK shares the peninsula where the city's business district is located.

Vancouver's first City Council made a momentous decision in 1886, when it petitioned the government to lease 405 hectares (1,000 acres) of largely logged-over land for public and recreation purposes. The result of this wise move was the creation of North America's third largest urban park—a cool, lush evergreen oasis right at downtown's doorstep.

Named for Lord Stanley, Governor General of Canada when the park officially opened in 1888, Stanley Park was once land hunted and foraged by the Musqueam and Squamish First Nations peoples. And a large part of what makes it such a special place is the lush West Coast rain forest growth. One of the park's great pleasures, in fact, is exploring the network of bark-mulched trails that wind through Douglas fir, western hemlock and western red cedar trees. These giants create a hushed environment of subdued light and cool air that is all the more remarkable given such close proximity to downtown's hurly-burly.

Such a magnificent setting, of course, offers plenty of inspiring views. For example, follow Prospect Point Trail, an invigorating uphill trek, to Prospect Point at the northern tip of the peninsula; from this elevated perspective the vista of Burrard Inlet, the Lions Gate Bridge, the North Shore and the mountains beyond is a stunner. For a more relaxed jaunt, amble along Stanley Park Drive, the seawall that encircles the peninsula. The route totals about 10 kilometres (6 mi.), and you'll be gazing out over water essentially the entire time. There are separate lanes for walkers and cyclists/roller bladers.

There are other ways to enjoy nature. Walk to Beaver Lake, a body of water that is in the process of shrinking as it transitions from lake to bog (and

may in time lose its watery aspects completely and become a meadow). Its surface is covered with yellow water lilies in summer. Or take a spin around Lost Lagoon, off the Georgia Street entrance to the park. This man-made body of water (created when the Stanley Park Causeway was built in 1916) provides a nesting ground for ducks, swans and Canada geese. The lagoon also is located on the Pacific Flyway, which makes it a favorite haunt of bird watchers as well as one of the park's most popular strolls.

Standing near the Brockton Oval (where you can watch a cricket match), just in from the seawall, are eight totem poles. They make a distinctive photo op, and you can learn about their history by reading the interpretive panels. You'll also want to take a ride in a horse-drawn carriage *(see sub-attraction listing)*; breathing in the scent of the cedar trees while listening to the gentle clip-clop of a Clydesdale's hooves is an eminently relaxing way to tour the park.

There are free tennis courts near Lost Lagoon and the Beach Avenue entrance. The Second Beach Pool has English Bay as a backdrop. An 18-hole pitch-and-putt golf course also is located at Second Beach. At low tide, explore the rocky shoreline along Second and Third beaches. For kids there are three playgrounds—at Lumbermen's Arch, Second Beach and near the park's Rose Garden—as well as the Children's Farmyard and a miniature steam train.

Shows take place at the open-air Malkin Bowl/ Theatre Under the Stars in July and August. A park information booth is just inside the Georgia Street entrance, next to the seawall. A free shuttle travels between the most popular destinations in summer; shuttles depart from the miniature railway parking lot.

Hours: Park open daily 24 hours. Information booth open 10-5, June 15-Sept. 15; 10-4, May 1-June 14 and Sept. 16-second Mon. in Oct. Booth hours may vary; phone ahead. Children's farmyard daily 11-4, steam train daily 10:30-5, June 27-day after Labour Day and during the holiday season; daily 11-4, rest of year (weather permitting). Shuttle daily 10-6:30, July 1-Labour Day. **Cost:** Park is free. Farmyard and steam train each $5.50; $4 (ages 13-18); $3.75 (ages 65+); $2.75 (ages 2-12); a family rate is available. Rates and schedules may vary;

phone ahead. **Phone:** (604) 681-6728, or (604) 257-8531 for steam train information. 🏦 🚂

Stanley Park Horse-drawn Tours depart from beside the information booth on Park Dr. off the Georgia St. entrance. The narrated, 1-hour tour highlights the park's points of interest. **Hours:** Tours depart daily every 20-30 minutes 9:30-5:30, July 1-Labour Day; 9:40-5, Apr.-June and day after Labour Day-Sept. 30; 9:40-4, Mar. 15-31 and in Oct. **Cost:** $28; $26 (ages 13-18, ages 65+ and students with ID); $15 (ages 3-12). **Phone:** (604) 681-5115 or (888) 681-5110.

🔷GEM **Vancouver Aquarium Marine Science Centre** is at 845 Avison Way. More than 70,000 marine animals are exhibited, with emphasis on such diverse habitats as the Canadian Arctic, the Amazon Rain Forest and the Pacific Northwest. Sharks, moray eels and colorful fish populate the Tropic Zone, while the Strait of Georgia exhibit features divers interacting with marine life. Programs allowing animal encounters with sea lions, seals, otters and beluga whales are available for an additional fee.

Walk the BC Hydro Salmon Stream in Stanley Park to learn about a salmon's incredible life journey. Other highlights include daily whale and dolphin shows, shark dives and sea otter feedings as well as exhibits that feature sea lions and harbor seals.

Time: Allow 2 hours minimum. **Hours:** Daily 9:30-7, late June-Labour Day; 9:30-5, rest of year. **Cost:** $22; $17 (ages 13-18, ages 65+ and students with ID); $14 (ages 4-12). Prices may vary during the peak of summer; phone ahead. **Phone:** (604) 659-3474. *See color ad p. 167.* 🏦

UNIVERSITY OF BRITISH COLUMBIA is on Point Grey. Encompassing 2,470 hectares (6,103 acres) overlooking the Strait of Georgia, the university is the largest in the province.

The Pacific Museum of the Earth is just off the West Mall of the university on the main floor of the Earth and Ocean Science Building at 6339 Stores Rd. A highlight of the 30,000-piece mineral and fossil collection is an 80 million-year-old Lambeosaurus dinosaur. Also featured are a 2-metre-long (7-ft.)

amethyst tube and a large sedimentary structure. **Time:** Allow 30 minutes minimum. **Hours:** Mon.-Fri. 9-5; closed statutory holidays, Jan. 1-2 and Dec. 18-31. **Cost:** Donations. **Phone:** (604) 822-6992.

UBC Botanical Garden is at 6804 S.W. Marine Dr. More than 10,000 plants from around the world are cultivated on 28 hectares (69 acres). Themed gardens include Asian, alpine, perennial, food, medicinal and native plantings. Nitobe Memorial Garden, one of the most accurately represented Japanese gardens in North America, features a tea garden and stroll garden with seasonal displays of irises, Japanese maples and flowering cherries.

Pets are not permitted. **Time:** Allow 1 hour minimum. **Hours:** Main garden open Mon.-Fri. 9-5. Nitobe Memorial Garden open daily 9-5, mid-Mar. to mid-Oct.; Mon.-Fri. 10-2:30, rest of year. **Cost:** Main garden $8; $6 (ages 13-17, senior citizens and non-UBC students with ID). Nitobe Memorial Garden $6; $5 (senior citizens); $3 (non-UBC students); $2 (ages 13-17). **Phone:** (604) 822-9666.

UBC Museum of Anthropology is at 6393 N.W. Marine Dr. on the Point Grey Cliffs. Traditional post and beam construction is utilized in this concrete and glass building designed by Canadian architect Arthur Erickson. The Great Hall, the main exhibition area, has soaring glass walls that let in natural light. It provides a striking setting for a major collection of Northwest Coast First Nations artwork, which includes totem poles, house posts, carved figures, feast dishes and other objects.

The Rotunda features one of the museum's highlights, "The Raven and the First Men" by Canadian artist Bill Reid. Reid, whose mother was a Haida, developed an interest in tribal folklore, and this carving—fashioned from a single block of laminated yellow cedar—powerfully depicts a Haida human creation myth. Four accompanying display cases contain more of Reid's works in gold, silver and argillite, a fine-grained sedimentary rock frequently used in Haida carvings.

In marked contrast to the often-monumental scale of the First Nations art is the 600-piece collection of 15th to 19th-century European ceramics—stoneware, lead-glazed earthenware and tin-glazed ware—on display in the Koerner Ceramics Gallery.

Time: Allow 1 hour minimum. **Hours:** Daily 10-5 (also Tues. 5-9), Victoria Day-second Mon. in Oct.; Tues.-Sun. 10-5 (also Tues. 5-9), rest of year. Closed Dec. 25-26. **Cost:** $14; $12 (ages 6-18, ages 65+ and students with ID); $35 (family). **Phone:** (604) 822-5087.

▼ VANCOUVER AQUARIUM MARINE SCIENCE CENTRE—*see Stanley Park p. 168.*

VANCOUVER ART GALLERY is downtown at 750 Hornby St. One of the largest art museums in Western Canada occupies a turn-of-the-20th-century building that originally was intended to serve as a provincial courthouse. Its stately exterior, however, is a contrast to much of the art inside, which tends

to reflect the creative energy and hip, progressive style that the city itself embodies.

While major historical figures are given their due, the focus of the gallery's changing thematic exhibitions is on contemporary artists and works that veer toward the cutting edge. The inspiration for the mixed-media installations can be anything from anime and Japanese manga (comics) to the artist's own body. In summer, the Gallery Café's outdoor patio is an airy space where you can relax over a bite to eat in the midst of downtown's bustle.

Time: Allow 1 hour minimum. **Hours:** Daily 10-5:30 (also Tues. and Thurs. 5:30-9). Closed Jan. 1, Dec. 25 and during the Olympics. **Cost:** $17; $13 (ages 65+); $12 (students with ID); $7 (ages 5-12); $50 (family, two adults and two children); donations (Tues. 5-9). Rates may vary; phone ahead. **Phone:** (604) 662-4719. *See color ad p. 167.*

VANCOUVER LOOKOUT AT HARBOUR CENTRE is at 555 W. Hastings St. Two glass elevators ascend the outside of this tower, which is crowned with an observation deck that offers a spectacular panoramic view of the city and outlying districts. Hourly guided tours point out the city's landmarks. The complex includes a revolving restaurant and a shopping mall.

Time: Allow 30 minutes minimum. **Hours:** Skylift elevator runs daily 8:30 a.m.-10:30 p.m., late Apr. to mid-Oct.; 9-9, rest of year. **Cost:** $15; $12 (ages 60+); $9 (ages 13-18); $5 (ages 6-12). Rates may vary; phone ahead. **Phone:** (604) 689-0421. *See color ad p. 167.*

VANCOUVER MARITIME MUSEUM is at 1905 Ogden Ave. at n. foot of Chestnut and Cypress sts. Discover the rich maritime traditions of the Pacific Coast. Model ships, naval uniforms and other artifacts relate to man's interaction with the sea. Historic vessels are displayed outside in the harbor. Tour the circa 1944 *St. Roch*, Canada's celebrated RCMP schooner. The Alcan Children's Maritime Discovery Centre features hands-on activities to introduce youngsters to ships and pirates of the sea.

Time: Allow 1 hour minimum. **Hours:** Daily 10-5, Victoria Day-Labour Day; Tues.-Sun. 10-5, rest of year. **Cost:** Museum (including the *St. Roch* National Historic Site) $10; $7.50 (ages 6-18 and 65+); $25 (family). **Phone:** (604) 257-8300.

***St. Roch* National Historic Site** is next to the Vancouver Maritime Museum. The supply ship was built in 1928 for the Royal Canadian Mounted Police Arctic patrol. During World War II the *St. Roch* became the first vessel to travel from the Pacific to the Atlantic via the treacherous Northwest Passage in the Arctic; it completed the round trip in 1944. After the war, the schooner reached its destination via the Panama Canal, becoming the first ship to circumnavigate the North American continent. Preserved in dry dock, the vessel is displayed as it appeared in 1944.

Time: Allow 1 hour minimum. **Hours:** Daily 10-5, Victoria Day-Labour Day; Mon.-Sat. 10-5,

Sun. noon-5, rest of year. **Cost:** Included in the admission for the Vancouver Maritime Museum. **Phone:** (604) 257-8300.

 VANDUSEN BOTANICAL GARDEN is at 5251 Oak St. (between Oak and Granville sts.) at W. 37th Ave. One benefit of Vancouver's benevolent maritime climate is that it creates a favorable environment for gardening, and the plant collections at VanDusen Botanical Garden offer spectacular proof. The 22-hectare (55-acre) site, once owned by the Canadian Pacific Railway and logged at the turn of the 20th century, was nurtured into a garden in the early 1970s in order to prevent the land from being developed for housing.

This is a botanical garden, as much scientifically organized and carefully labeled as it is visually pleasing. Trees, shrubs and perennials dominate the plantings, and there's something beautiful to see regardless of the season. Camellias, cherry trees, azaleas, magnolias and rhododendrons bloom from March through May. The Rose Garden begins flowering in June. Late July and August find flowering summer annuals and perennials at their peak. Japanese maples flaunt crimson fall foliage from September into October. And during the winter months, 140 different kinds of hollies along the Holly Trail are bright with berries.

Special gardens include the Perennial Garden, the Canadian Heritage Garden (where there is a lovely Korean Pavilion built from red cedar posts), the peaceful retreat that is the Meditation Garden, and the dark-leaved plants in the intriguing Black Garden. Rocks and water are integral elements as well, and the lakes and ponds are lovely spots to stop and reflect. Kids can puzzle their way around the hedges that form the Elizabethan Maze.

Time: Allow 1 hour, 30 minutes minimum. **Hours:** Daily 9-9, June-Aug.; 10-8, in May; 10-7, in Sept.; 10-6, in Apr.; 10-5 in Mar. and Oct.; 10-4, rest of year. Closed Dec. 25. **Cost:** Apr.-Sept. $8.85; $6.50 (ages 13-18 and 65+); $4.70 (ages 6-12); $20.30 (family, two adults and two children ages 6-18). Admission rest of year $6.50; $4.70 (ages 13-18 and 65+); $3.40 (ages 6-12); $13.50 (family, two adults and two children ages 6-18). **Phone:** (604) 878-9274. 〔ｌ〕

GAMBLING ESTABLISHMENTS

- **Edgewater Casino** is at 750 Pacific Blvd. S. **Hours:** Daily 24 hours. **Phone:** (604) 687-3343, ext. 305.

What To Do

Sightseeing

Opportunities to watch bustling harbor activities are available at several vantage points in Vancouver. Seaplanes, barges, tugboats, cargo ships, ferries and the SeaBus can be observed from Granville Square at the foot of Granville Street; from Canada Place at the foot of Howe St.; from Lonsdale Quay at the foot of Lonsdale Ave.; and from Stanley Park. Fine views of the city, sea and mountains are available at CypressBowl, Simon Fraser University atop Burnaby Mountain, Grouse Mountain and Queen Elizabeth Park.

Boat Tours

HARBOUR CRUISES departs from the n. foot of Denman St., next to Stanley Park. Scenic 75-minute harbor tours are offered aboard an authentic paddlewheeler. Lunch, dinner and carol ship cruises also are available.

Hours: Harbor tours board daily at 11:30, 1 and 2:30, mid-May to mid-Sept.; at 2:30, April 15 to mid-May and mid-Sept. through Oct. 31. **Cost:** Harbor tours $29.95; $24.95 (ages 12-17 and 60+); $10 (ages 5-11). Schedule and fares may vary; phone ahead. **Phone:** (604) 688-7246 or (800) 663-1500. *See color ad.*

Bus Tours

West Coast City and Nature Sightseeing Ltd. features sightseeing trips of the city and its surrounding natural areas in 12- to 30-passenger minibuses. Full-day trips to Victoria and the Whistler resort area also are available; phone (604) 451-1600 or (877) 451-1777.

Industrial Tours

Tours are available of the Vancouver Post Office, (604) 662-5715, 349 W. Georgia St. Reservations are required.

Plane Tours

Another way to see Vancouver and its surroundings is by air. Harbour Air offers flights lasting from 35 minutes to 1.25 hours; departure is from downtown on Coal Harbour Road, one block west of Canada Place. Fares vary, and reservations are required; phone (604) 274-1277.

Train Tours

Rocky Mountaineer Vacations offers scenic, 2-day, all daylight, narrated rail tours between Vancouver or Whistler, British Columbia, and Banff, Calgary, or Jasper, Alberta. Westbound or eastbound departures are offered mid-April to mid-October, with winter rail trips available in December. On-board meals and snacks as well as accommodations in Kamloops or Quesnel are included. A 3-hour trip on the Whistler Mountaineer also is available and runs between Vancouver and Whistler May through October. Phone (604) 606-7245 or (877) 460-3200 or (888) 687-7245 for information about Whistler trips.

Trolley Tours

Trolley tours provide a look at the city at a relaxed pace. The Downtown Historic Railway, comprised of two electric interurban railcars, skirts False Creek between Science World at TELUS World of

Science and Granville Island and runs from mid-May to mid-October; phone (604) 665-3903.

THE VANCOUVER TROLLEY CO. departs from many downtown accommodations and attractions. Narrated tours highlight Vancouver's major attractions. Passengers may board, depart or reboard at any stop on the route. A Grouse Mountain sunset tour also is available.

Note: There will be limited service during the period of the Olympic Games. **Time:** Allow 2 hours minimum. **Hours:** Daily 9-5. A 4-hour sunset tour leaves for Grouse Mountain at 6:15, mid-June to mid-Sept. **Cost:** One-day hop-on, hop-off fare $29.52; $26.67 (ages 13-18 and 65+); $15.24 (ages 4-12). Two-day hop-on, hop-off trolley fare $36.19; $33.33 (ages 13-18 and 65+); $19.05 (ages 4-12). Sunset tour $70; $67 (ages 65+); $60 (ages 13-18); $40 (ages 4-12). Combination tickets are available. **Phone:** (604) 801-5515 or (888) 451-5581. *See color ad p. 172.*

Sports and Recreation

Vancouver offers such a diversity of recreational opportunities that anyone with a yen for variety can ski on Grouse Mountain in the morning, golf on the banks of the Fraser River in the afternoon, fish for salmon in Horseshoe Bay at dusk and top off the day with a dip in English Bay.

Vancouver's park system has tennis courts, swimming pools, putting greens, golf courses, lawn bowling greens, hiking paths and a comprehensive bike route. For park information phone the Vancouver Park Board at (604) 257-8400.

Swimming is available along English Bay, which is bordered by beaches from West Point Grey to Stanley Park. Beaches are easily accessible from Northwest Marine Drive in West Point Grey, Point Grey Road in Vancouver West and from Beach Avenue downtown.

White-water rafting is available April through September on the nearby Chilliwack River and a little farther afield on the Lillooet, Fraser and Thompson rivers. Vancouver rafting companies offering day trips as well as multiday trips include REO Rafting Adventure Resort, (604) 461-7238 or (800) 736-7238, and Kumsheen Rafting Resort, (250) 455-2296 or (800) 663-6667. Lotus Land Tours offers **sea kayaking** trips on Indian Arm and **whale-watching** tours from Steveston; phone (604) 684-4922 or (800) 528-3531.

Winter visitors with a penchant for **skiing** can tackle the challenging slopes of Grouse Mountain or Mount Seymour Park in North Vancouver. East of Vancouver are Hemlock Valley and Manning Park ski resorts, offering both downhill and cross-country treks. Cypress Provincial Park in West Vancouver also has cross-country and downhill skiing *(see attraction listing p. 188 and Recreation Chart).* Skiers

can head north of Vancouver to Whistler and Black-comb Mountains; site of the 2010 Olympic and Paralympic Winter Games.

When the waters sparkle from the summer sun, Vancouver becomes a **boating** paradise. For visitors without a boat, several companies have craft for hourly or daily rental. For charter yachts phone Harbour Cruises, (604) 688-7246, or Westin Bayshore Yacht Charters, (604) 250-8008. For **fishing** charters and boat rentals phone Sewell's Ltd., (604) 921-3474, at Horseshoe Bay.

Vancouver residents love spectator sports, especially **football, hockey** and **soccer.** The B.C. Lions of the Canadian Football League play before capacity crowds in B.C. Place Stadium. The Canucks of the National Hockey League compete in General Motors Place. For football and hockey ticket information phone TicketMaster, (604) 280-4444. **Baseball** is played by the Vancouver Canadians at Nat Bailey Stadium; phone (604) 872-5232 for schedule and ticket information. Indoor **lacrosse** can be enjoyed at Bill Copeland Sports Centre in Burnaby, (604) 291-1261; and at Queens Park Arena, (604) 777-5111, in New Westminster.

Thoroughbred racing with pari-mutuel betting is held at Hastings Park Race Course on the grounds of the Pacific National Exhibition; phone (604) 254-1631 (see attraction listing p. 166).

Note: Policies concerning admittance of children to pari-mutuel betting facilities vary. Phone for information.

Shopping

When you set out on a Vancouver shopping expedition be sure to bring along the AAA street map, because you're definitely going to want to hang out in every one of this town's cool and distinctively different urban neighborhoods.

The West End is as good a starting point as any. Denman Street anchors this area of leafy blocks and old apartment buildings backed up by downtown's office high-rises, with English Bay and Stanley Park at its doorstep. Sidewalk restaurants and cafes, specialty shops and the 30-odd stores of Denman Place Mall fill the six blocks of Denman between Davie and Robson streets.

Yaletown, reached via Davie Street, is the *de rigueur* downtown residential address for successful young professionals (just look at all those glass-walled condo towers). This former 19th-century rail yard district has morphed into an uber-stylish urban enclave; the industrial brick warehouses of yore are now hip clothing boutiques and designer furniture outlets.

Multilevel Chintz & Company (950 Homer St.) has a dazzling assemblage of interior design furnishings and accessories; browsing here is sensory overload. Art galleries are concentrated along Homer and Mainland streets; the Coastal Peoples Fine Arts Gallery (1024 Mainland St.) has an excellent collection of Northwest Coast Native artwork. Yaletown's many dog owners shop for trendy canine accessories at The Dog & Hydrant (1146 Pacific Blvd.).

Robson Street, however, is downtown's shopping central. Stand at the intersection of Robson and Burrard on any given day and it's a sea of shopping bag-toting humanity. From Burrard up to Jervis Street Robson offers an uninterrupted stretch of window gazing: men's and women's fashions and accessories, shoes, jewelry, eyewear, gifts, chocolates, cosmetics and luggage, plus more restaurants than you can shake a stick at. For high-quality outdoor wear go to Roots, a popular Canadian chain. There are two locations, one for adults (1001 Robson St.) and one for kids (1153 Robson St.).

Very touristy but always enjoyable Gastown, the oldest section of the city, runs for several blocks along Water Street. The atmosphere is turn-of-the-20th-century renovated, with handsome brick buildings and white-globed lamp posts bedecked with flowery hanging baskets. There are lots of art galleries, antique shops and places to buy Canadian souvenirs. But Gastown isn't all about maple candy or a moose in a can; trendy home furnishings stores like Koolhaus (1 Water St.) sell sleekly contemporary furniture by well-known Canadian and international designers.

There's a Coastal Peoples Fine Arts Gallery here as well (312 Water St.). Visit the Jeffrey Boone Gallery (1 E. Cordova St.) and the Canvas Gallery (99 Powell St.), which is associated with a popular Gastown nightspot, the Canvas Lounge. Urbanity (207 Abbott St.) sells beautiful knit sweaters, coats and blankets. There also are specialty shops like Button Button (422 W. Cordova St.), with buttons in all shapes and sizes from around the world, and Kites on Clouds (201 Water St.), which stocks cool windsocks and mobiles as well as kites.

Walk a few blocks down Carrall Street into Chinatown (see attraction listing), another neighborhood made for sidewalk exploration. You'll probably look rather than buy, since most of the businesses are where residents do their shopping. The produce and food markets lining Keefer and Main streets are fascinating, with unusual vegetables and bins full of dried fish, mushrooms and other foodstuffs. You'll also find a couple of jewelry shops selling bead necklaces and various trinkets.

Note: While the main thoroughfares in Gastown and Chinatown are fun to visit during the day, use big-city common sense regarding any encounters with panhandlers and street people, and avoid wandering around side streets after dark.

Downtown certainly isn't the only place to shop. In Kitsilano, along the south shore of English Bay, the blocks of West 4th Avenue between Fir and Larch streets are filled with grocers, wine shops and stores selling fashions, sportswear and sports gear from bikes to skis to snowboards.

Also within "Kits," the 10-block stretch of Granville Street between 6th and 16th avenues—dubbed South Granville—is where old-money families do their shopping; think expensive clothing boutiques, upscale furniture retailers and a plethora of home accessories stores like 18 Karat, 3039

Granville St. (at 14th Avenue W.) and Chachkas 2423 Granville St.).

Much more down to earth is Commercial Drive, east of Kitsilano via Broadway E. From Venables Street south to Broadway is one of Vancouver's funkiest shopping experiences. Most of the shops and businesses are owner-operated; chains are few, which means that it's really fun to explore. Hit "the Drive" on a Saturday or Sunday afternoon. The heart of Commercial Drive is between Venables Street and 6th Avenue E. Books, CDs, vintage clothing and unusual gifts are all good bets.

Punjabi Market, in South Vancouver's Sunset neighborhood, is a small commercial district (along Main Street between 48th and 51st avenues) that serves the city's Indo-Canadian community and draws tourists as well. Restaurants and Indian businesses (grocers, sweet and spice shops, jewelry and fabric stores, Hindi video rentals) line Main Street. Several store windows feature mannequins outfitted in flowing, multicolored saris. Pick up some incense or a silk scarf.

You could easily spend an entire day doing Granville Island, but shoppers and foodies should focus on the Granville Island Public Market. The big building is crammed with vendors: produce, meat, seafood, baked goods, coffee and a head-spinning array of specialty foods. Take advantage of fresh B.C. salmon, artisanal cheeses and ripe, regionally grown fruit. Have lunch here, too; takeaway fast food counters offer Asian, Mexican, Indian, sushi, pizza and just about everything else.

There also are plenty of shops outside the market selling regionally produced art, food, jewelry, clothing, kids' toys and the like. And don't drive—it's much easier to take the False Creek Ferry. It's a 10-minute ride to Granville Island from the Aquatic Centre dock just off Beach Drive in the West End (ferries also depart from the dock at the foot of Davie Street in Yaletown).

Another popular destination is the Lonsdale Quay Market, at the foot of Lonsdale Avenue in North Vancouver. The lower level is a fresh market with vendors selling produce, seafood, baked goods and delicatessen items; specialty boutiques are on the upper level. Get a crab roll, fish and chips or a panini sandwich from one of the numerous stands at the international food bar and enjoy it outside on the dock, which has a great view of downtown and the harbor (don't feed the seagulls; they'll snitch a bite at any opportunity). There's a parkade for market customers (2 hours of free parking with proof of purchase, $1.50 per additional hour), but it often fills up; you also can take the Seabus, which shuttles between the downtown and North Vancouver terminals every 15 minutes.

Malls? Vancouver has several, if that's your shopping thing. Downtown, upscale Pacific Centre (corner of Georgia and Howe streets) is anchored by Sears and tony Holt Renfrew; other stores offer men's and ladies' wear, casual clothing, fashion accessories, shoes, electronics, sporting goods, handbags and cosmetics. On the North Shore, Park Royal (on either side of Marine Drive, just west of Taylor Way and the Lions Gate Bridge) consists of two enclosed malls with more than 280 stores and restaurants, plus The Village, specialty shops and cafés in an open-air setting.

For a true mega-mall experience, head to Burnaby and Metropolis at Metrotown, off Kingsway (Hwy. 1A/99A) between McKay and Nelson avenues. It's the province's largest shopping center, with The Bay (outfitters for the Canadian Olympic team), Sears and more than 450 other stores on three sprawling levels. Expect the usual chains and specialty outlets—everything from Absolute Dollar to Zellers—plus a food court and the latest box-office biggies at Famous Players SilverCity. Parking (plenty of it) is free.

CHINATOWN centers on E. Pender St. between Carrall and Gore sts. The second largest area of its kind in North America, Chinatown is lined with elaborately carved and gilded shops displaying jade, bamboo, rattan, brassware, silk and brocade. Sidewalk markets feature Oriental produce. Even the phone booths are topped with pagoda roofs.

The Chinese Cultural Centre Museum & Archives, 555 Columbia St., has some displays and photographs on its second floor relating to the history of the Chinese in British Columbia. During Chinese New Year the streets resound with the din of drums and fireworks. **Phone:** (604) 658-8850 for the Chinese Cultural Centre Museum & Archives.

Nightlife

Hip, cosmopolitan Vancouver has a buzzing nightlife, with plenty of spots where the young and beautiful congregate—and there are even a few options for the rest of us. Among the latter are several sophisticated hotel lounges where you can relax over drinks in a quiet, elegant atmosphere. The bar inside Yew, the restaurant at the Four Seasons Hotel Vancouver (downtown at 791 W. Georgia St.) is a lovely place to put a capper on a busy day. A 40-foot ceiling makes this a breathtakingly lofty space, warmed by wood-paneled walls and a big sandstone fireplace. The bar is open until midnight Sun.-Wed., 1 a.m. Thurs.-Sat.

Bacchus Piano Lounge, in The Wedgewood Hotel & Spa (downtown at 845 Hornby St.), is an equally elegant spot to enjoy a glass of B.C. wine or a martini in surroundings that exude luxury—subdued lighting, antique furniture and vases of fresh flowers, with a softly tinkling piano in the background. There's dancing Thursday through Saturday evenings. Do dress up.

Opus Bar, in the Opus Hotel (350 Davie St. at Hamilton Street) is a cool, sleek lounge in hot-to-trot Yaletown. The decor is stylish with a capital "S": designer furniture, iridescent mood lighting, shimmer screens and live video feeds that allow you to keep an eye on the action at the bar and in the lounge. DJs spin dance music for a fashionably dressed, upwardly mobile crowd.

Baby boomers will feel right at home in The Cascade Room, 2616 Main St. (a block south of Broadway). This restaurant and bar is a transplanted bit of British pub culture: Lampshades feature Queen Victoria's likeness, and a large glass panel advises patrons to "Keep calm and carry on"—a World War II slogan uttered by stiff-upper-lip Brits. Slide into one of the horseshoe-shaped booths for a cocktail, a beer or a pint of lager.

Granville Street is hopping with nightclubs, all with reasonable cover charges. Thirty-somethings hang out at Republic, (958 Granville St.). A bar runs almost the full length of the dance floor on the main level; a lounge with a glass-enclosed patio overlooking the Granville street scene is upstairs. DJs play music that varies from hip-hop, house and electro to dance mix mashups and reggae. The Caprice (967 Granville St.) has a lounge with an outdoor patio and TV screens showing sporting events. Special event nights augment DJ music (Wednesday through Saturday) that tends toward Top 40, R&B and dance hits.

The Roxy (932 Granville St.) draws a young, ready-to-party crowd with house bands pumping out rock and Top 40 and bartenders who put on their own show. If you don't feel like dancing, watch TV or play pool. It's open until 3 a.m. nightly. More sophisticated is Au Bar (674 Seymour St.), which has a New York feel—candlelit tables, intimate seating areas, two bars and a VIP lounge. There's usually a long line of very attractive people waiting to get in, and it's known to attract Hollywood types who are in town for on-location filming.

Touristy Gastown throngs with nightspots. The Steamworks Pub & Brewery (375 Water St.) is named for the Gastown steam line that runs through the premises. The hoist of choice here is beer (brewed onsite), from signature Lions Gate lager and Cascadia cream ale to such concoctions as Heroica oatmeal stout and sour cherry ale. Coffee drinkers will appreciate the Steamworks Grand, a combo of espresso and stout. The basement looks like a Bavarian-style drinking hall, while upstairs the atmosphere is clubbier, with leather chairs and windows overlooking the harbor.

In contrast, The Modern (7 Alexander St.) is an ultra-contemporary dance club replete with smoked glass and mirrors at every turn, the better to check out the scene as you sip a custom cocktail. The emphasis is on music, and the club books both Canadian and international DJ talent to provide hot dance mixes for cool kids. Cool kids also hang at Celebrities (1022 Davie St.) in Davie Village. Visiting DJs like Boy George take advantage of state-of-the-art sound and lighting, and the dance floor is invariably packed with chiseled, often shirtless young men. It's open every night but Monday.

Live music venues are plentiful. Richard's on Richards (1036 Richards St.) in Yaletown has shows several nights a week, a mix of hip-hoppers, world music artists and of-the-moment buzz bands like Crystal Antlers. It's also a nightclub with a huge dance floor, a circular balcony and several bars. The Commodore Ballroom (868 Granville St.) is an old-time dance hall that books everything from gospel choirs to death metal quadruple bills. This is the place to see up-and-coming bands as well as established acts that don't sell out arenas. The dance floor is in front of the stage and table seating is limited; arrive early unless you don't mind standing in the back of the room.

For a mellow evening, make it O'Doul's Restaurant & Bar (1300 Robson St. at Jervis, in the Listel Hotel). The West Coast cuisine is expertly prepared, the wine list is outstanding and live music is provided by the city's top jazz names. Solo artists perform Sunday through Wednesday, ensembles Thursday through Saturday. The music starts at 9 p.m.

If you want to hear blues in Vancouver, you go to the Yale Hotel (1300 Granville St., just south of Davie Street). This tavern has a lot of history—it was once a Canadian Pacific Railroad bunkhouse and then a hostelry with a reputation for wild nights—just the place, in other words, for musicians to get down and do their thing. Big names like Johnny Winter and Buckwheat Zydeco come through regularly, but there's plenty of local talent on tap, too. The Yale's weekend blues jams (Sat.-Sun. 3-7, no cover) are a tradition.

And here's a beautifully simple suggestion. On a balmy summer evening, head down to English Bay Beach (just off Beach Avenue at the south end of Denman Street). First, stop and get an ice cream cone or something from Starbucks (there's one at the corner of Davie and Denman). Then sit on a beach log or a bench, or stroll along the seawall promenade, and watch the sun set over the bay and the mountains rising beyond the North Shore, turning the water a pale luminescent blue or perhaps streaking the clouds fiery orange or crimson. It's just you and nature—plus the company of similar-minded souls.

Note: The *Georgia Straight*, a news and entertainment weekly that comes out on Thursday, has extensive arts and entertainment listings for greater Vancouver.

Performing Arts

The Centre in Vancouver for Performing Arts, 777 Homer St., is a premier facility for theater, dance and music; phone (604) 602-0616 for event information. The Queen Elizabeth Theatre at the intersection of Hamilton and Georgia streets, (604) 665-3050, is home to Ballet British Columbia, (604) 732-5003, and the Vancouver Opera Association, (604) 683-0222. The adjacent Vancouver Playhouse presents professional theater, recitals and chamber music; phone (604) 873-3311. The Vancouver Symphony Orchestra performs at the Orpheum Theatre, Smithe and Granville streets; phone (604) 876-3434 for ticket information.

Other prominent metropolitan theaters presenting dramatic productions include the Arts Club Theatre, on Johnston Street on Granville Island, (604) 687-1644; the Metro Theatre, 1370 S.W. Marine Dr.,

The Thrill of Victory

The eyes of the world truly will be on British Columbia as Vancouver and Whistler host the 2010 Olympic Winter Games. The Opening Ceremonies signal the start of 17 days of Olympic Games events (Feb. 12-28, 2010) and 10 days of Paralympic Games events (Mar. 12-21, 2010).

The Vancouver Organizing Committee for the 2010 Olympic and Paralympic Winter Games (VANOC) is responsible for the ambitious agenda of planning, organizing, financing and staging the XXI Olympic Winter Games and the X Paralympic Winter Games. The numbers are impressive: more than 80 countries participating in the Olympic Winter Games; more than 40 countries participating in the Paralympic Winter Games; some 6,850 participating athletes and officials; and an estimated global television audience of some 3 billion people.

Locations where Vancouver 2010 Olympic and Paralympic Winter Games events stretch from the shores of the city of Richmond north to the snow-covered mountain peaks framing the year-round recreational mecca of Whistler—a distance of 120 kilometres (about 75 miles). All sites are within a 2-hour drive of downtown Vancouver.

The Opening and Closing Ceremonies for the Olympic Winter Games and the Opening Ceremony for the Paralympic Winter Games will be held at BC Place in downtown Vancouver. Featuring the largest air-supported stadium roof in North America, this enclosed venue allows games organizers to take advantage of state-of-the-art lighting, projection, sound and special effects technologies. Nightly Victory Ceremonies presentations will take place at an outdoor plaza in Whistler's town center. In addition to honoring the day's medal winners, the plaza will be the site of the Paralympic Winter Games Closing Ceremony.

2010 Winter Games competition venues are spread among four locations. In downtown Vancouver, events will take place at Canada Hockey Place, home of the NHL Vancouver Canucks. Other venues include Pacific Coliseum, about 5 kilometres (3 miles) east of downtown; UBC Thunderbird Arena, on the University of British Columbia campus; and at the Vancouver Olympic/Paralympic Centre, south of downtown near Queen Elizabeth Park.

In Whistler, Whistler Creekside—well known for its challenging downhill runs—is the setting for Olympic and Paralympic alpine skiing events. The Whistler Sliding Centre on Blackcomb Mountain hosts the bobsleigh, luge and skeleton competitions. Whistler Olympic/Paralympic Park in Callaghan Valley encompasses a core area with three stadiums as well as 15 kilometres (9 miles) of competition trails for cross-country skiing and biathlon.

Freestyle skiing and snowboard competitions take place on Cypress Mountain in the district of West Vancouver. One of British Columbia's most popular skiing areas, the mountain offers spectacular views of downtown Vancouver and its harbor. Speed skaters take to the ice at the Richmond Oval, on the banks of the Fraser River across from Vancouver International Airport.

More information about the 2010 Winter Games can be found online at vancouver2010.com. In Whistler, visitors can speak with knowledgeable staff at the Vancouver 2010 Information Centre at 4365 Blackcomb Way. The center is open daily 11-5.

(604) 266-7191; Studio 58, 100 W. 49th Ave., (604) 323-5227; and the Vancouver East Cultural Centre, 1895 Venables St., (604) 251-1363.

During the summer concerts and musicals are presented in Stanley Park's Malkin Bowl. Kitsilano Showboat at Kitsilano Beach presents an outdoor variety show Monday, Wednesday and Friday at 7:30 p.m. during July and August (weather permitting). For more information phone (604) 734-7332.

Concerts in such genres as classical, country, pop and rock are presented year-round at the Pacific Coliseum, 100 N. Renfrew St., (604) 253-2311, and General Motors Place, 800 Griffiths Way, (604) 899-7444.

The daily papers carry listings of cultural events, as do weekly and monthly magazines. Ticket outlets include Ticketmaster Head Office, 1304 Hornby St.; and Ticketmaster, Pacific Centre Mall, 700 W. Georgia St.

Special Events

Life in a city where your office is only 25 minutes from a ski slope is worth celebrating, and the residents of Vancouver celebrate their setting throughout the year. New Year's Day sees the Polar Bear Swim at English Bay; the event draws many swimmers and hundreds of spectators. February brings the Chinese New Year and with it the ♥ Vancouver Chinese New Year Parade, with colorful entries marching through Chinatown in a splendid celebration of the Chinese lunar year.

The Vancouver Children's Festival in May ushers in summer, while cultural entertainment sails in with the Canadian International Dragon Boat Festival in mid-June. The Vancouver Folk Music Festival draws fans from as far away as Los Angeles for concerts during mid-July. HSBC Celebration of Light features 4 nights of fireworks displays and is held at English Bay the last week of July and the first week in August.

For 2 weeks in early August and staged in 10 venues throughout the city, MusicFest Vancouver runs the gamut in musical offerings including classical, opera, jazz and chamber music. Virtually all facets of life and work in British Columbia are celebrated in the Pacific National Exhibition, held at the Exhibition Grounds from late August through Labour Day. In late September and early October the Oktoberfest is held at the Exhibition Grounds, where the revelry continues into the wee hours.

The Christmas season begins with the Christmas Carol Ships, which lead a flotilla of private watercraft decorated with Christmas lights around the harbor in mid-December. Bright Nights in Stanley Park, a 20-year-old holiday tradition, turns the forest, the train and the Children's Farmyard into a wonderland with more than a million lights and animated displays. More information about events is available from your CAA or AAA club.

The Vancouver Vicinity

ALDERGROVE (H-11)
pop. 12,363, elev. 61 m/200′

A small town on the Lower Fraser Valley's southern side, Aldergrove is near the Fraser River and the Canada-United States border. Dairy, chicken, strawberry and raspberry farms dot the surrounding area. Just northeast of Aldergrove, Bradner grows about 400 varieties of daffodils.

GREATER VANCOUVER ZOO is at 5048 264th St. The 48-hectare (120-acre) zoo is devoted to the preservation of endangered species. More than 600 animals represent 135 species from around the world, including hippopotami, monkeys, giraffes and tigers. A narrated train ride takes passengers around the zoo's perimeter; a bus tour travels through the North American Wilds exhibit.

Time: Allow 2 hours minimum. **Hours:** Daily 9-7, May-Sept.; 9-4, rest of year. **Cost:** $18; $14 (ages 4-15 and 65+); $60 (family, two adults and two children). Train ride $5. Parking $4. Rates may vary; phone ahead. **Phone:** (604) 856-6825. Ⓣ 🅿

BURNABY (H-11)
pop. 202,799, elev. 40 m/130′

Burnaby is more than just a suburban, bedroom community of hills, ridges, valleys, plain, and stunning views; it is an urban center which is home to

Simon Fraser University and the British Columbia Institute of Technology.

DEER LAKE PARK is 14.5 km (9 mi.) s.e. at 6450 Deer Lake Ave. at Canada Way. The park contains the Century Gardens, with its distinctive rhododendron display and rose gardens. The Shadbolt Centre for the Arts offers community arts programs as well as theater and dance performances in its James Cowan Theatre. Several walking trails provide scenic views throughout the park. **Hours:** Daily 24 hours. **Cost:** Free. **Phone:** (604) 294-7450 or (604) 291-6864.

Burnaby Village Museum & Carousel is off Hwy. 1 Kensington Ave. S. exit to 6501 Deer Lake Ave. The 4-hectare (10-acre) village re-creates the sights and sounds of an 1890-1925 settlement in lower mainland British Columbia. Costumed townspeople welcome visitors to more than 30 shops and homes, including a printshop and schoolhouse. A restored 1912 Parker carousel is on the site. The Heritage Christmas celebration from late November to early January features carolers, entertainment, crafts and a chat with Father Christmas.

Time: Allow 1 hour minimum. **Hours:** Tues.-Sun. 11-4:30, May 1-Labour Day; daily noon-4, Mar. 8-14. Hours vary Nov. 20-Jan. 2. Closed Dec.

24-25. **Cost:** $11.66; $8.77 (ages 13-18 and 65+); $5.82 (ages 6-12). Carousel ride $1.89. Prices and schedule may vary; phone ahead. **Phone:** (604) 293-6500. ⊞

RECREATIONAL ACTIVITIES

Boating

• **Deer Lake Boat Rentals** is at 5435 Sperling Ave. **Hours:** Daily 10-8, mid-June through Labour Day; Mon.-Fri. by appointment, Sat.-Sun. 10-8, Apr. 1 to mid-June; Mon.-Fri. by appointment, Sat.-Sun. 10-7, day after Labour Day-second Mon. in Oct. **Phone:** (604) 839-3949.

COQUITLAM (H-11)
pop. 114,565, elev. 137 m/449′

Named for a type of landlocked salmon, Coquitlam borders Pitt Lake and encompasses Burke Mountain. Recreational opportunities, including swimming, canoeing, hiking and fishing, are available throughout the area.

Nearby parks and lakes include Mundy Park, 4 kilometres (2.5 mi.) south off Mariner Way; Belcarra Park, 15 kilometres (9 mi.) northwest off Ioco and Bedwell Bay roads; Buntzen Lake, 12 kilometres (7 mi.) northwest off East and Sunnyside roads; Minnekhada Regional Park, 13 kilometres (8 mi.) northeast off Victoria Drive and Quarry Road; Town Centre Park and Lafarge Lake, on Pinetree Way just north of Lougheed Highway; and Burke Mountain, 11 kilometres (7 mi.) northeast off Coast Meridian and Harper roads.

Visitor InfoCentre/Tri-cities Chamber of Commerce: 1209 Pinetree Way, Coquitlam, BC, Canada V3B 7Y3. **Phone:** (604) 464-2716.

DELTA (H-11) pop. 96,723, elev. 10 m/33′

Delta, composed of the three distinct communities of Ladner, Tsawwassen and North Delta, is an amalgam of commerce, fisheries, industry, farmland, beaches and suburban residences. The warm-water beaches on Boundary Bay and Tsawwassen are popular spots for swimming and sunbathing. Other recreational opportunities in the area include fishing for salmon and boating on the Fraser River and the Strait of Georgia.

Delta Chamber of Commerce: 6201 60th Ave., Delta, BC, Canada V4K 4E2. **Phone:** (604) 946-4232.

DELTA MUSEUM AND ARCHIVES is at 4858 Delta St. The museum houses marine, fishing and farming exhibits, pioneer and First Nations displays, reconstructed rooms of a late Victorian household and an early 1900s Delta street scene. **Time:** Allow 1 hour minimum. **Hours:** Museum open Tues.-Sat. 10-4:30. Archives open Tues.-Fri. 10-4, Sat. 12:30-4:30; closed Nov. 11 and Dec. 25. **Cost:** Donations. **Phone:** (604) 946-9322.

REIFEL MIGRATORY BIRD SANCTUARY is at 5191 Robertson Rd. on Westham Island. More than 286 species of birds have been observed at the refuge, which comprises 344 hectares (850 acres). This major bird-watching area offers superb observation from 7 kilometres (4 mi.) of trails bordering sloughs and ponds. Bird sightings reach their peak in November and nesting activity is in April and May. **Time:** Allow 1 hour minimum. **Hours:** Daily 9-4. **Cost:** $4; $2 (ages 2-14 and 60+). Bird seed 50c per bag. **Phone:** (604) 946-6980.

LANGLEY (H-11) pop. 23,606, elev. 10 m/33′

Langley, the site of a Hudson's Bay Co. fort built in 1840 *(see Fort Langley National Historic Site of Canada p. 119)*, is in an important farming region. Orchards, strawberry and raspberry farms, horse ranches and dairy, chicken and mink farms make a patchwork of the countryside.

Greater Langley Chamber of Commerce-Langley: Unit One, 5761 Glover Rd., Langley, BC, Canada V3A 8M8. **Phone:** (604) 530-6656.

CANADIAN MUSEUM OF FLIGHT is at Hangar 3, 5333 216th St., at the Langley Airport. The museum features a collection of more than 25 aircraft; some restored. Aircraft include a Handley-Page Hampden Bomber, helicopters and jets. The aircraft and artifacts displayed represent Canada's aviation history 1909 to the present day. A collection of other aviation memorabilia as well as a children's activity center is available.

Time: Allow 30 minutes minimum. **Hours:** Daily 10-4; closed Jan. 1 and Dec. 25-26. **Cost:** $7.55; $5 (ages 6-15 and 60+); $17 (family, two adults and up to five children). **Phone:** (604) 532-0035.

GAMBLING ESTABLISHMENTS

• **Cascades Langley City** is at 20393 Fraser Hwy. **Hours:** Daily 24 hours. **Phone:** (604) 530-2211.

WINERIES

• **Domaine de Chaberton Estate Winery** is at 1064 216th St. **Hours:** Tastings are given daily 10-5:30. Tours are offered at 2 and 4, Feb.-Nov.; at 3, rest of year (weather permitting). Closed Jan. 1 and Dec. 25-26. **Phone:** (604) 530-1736.

MAPLE RIDGE (H-12)
pop. 68,949, elev. 30 m/98′

Maple Ridge lies on the north shore of the Fraser River, with the Coast Mountains to the north and the Stave and Pitt Rivers forming its east and west boundaries. Snow-capped peaks overlook this Fraser Valley community.

The Fraser River Heritage Walk, which starts at Port Haney Wharf, passes many of the town's notable spots. The Haney House at 11612 224th St. was built in 1876 and contains many furnishings and artifacts owned by three generations of the Haney family; phone (604) 463-1377. Displays at Maple Ridge Museum, 22520 116th Ave., reflect the history and geography of the area; phone (604) 463-5311.

Kanaka Creek Regional Park *(see Recreation Chart)* offers hiking and horseback riding trails as well as canoeing, kayaking, fishing and picnic facilities. A fish hatchery is on the grounds. Phone (604) 530-4983. Maple Ridge also has a large per capita horse population and an extensive riding trail system.

Tourism Maple Ridge and Pitt Meadows: 12492 Harris Rd., Pitt Meadows, BC, Canada V3Y 2J4. **Phone:** (604) 460-8300 or (877) 465-8300.

UBC MALCOLM KNAPP RESEARCH FOREST is n. at 14500 Silver Valley Rd. Trails of various lengths lead visitors on tours through the forest, a research facility of the University of British Columbia. Bicycles, motorbikes, pets and horses are not permitted. **Hours:** Forest daily dawn-dusk. Office open Mon.-Fri. 8-4. **Cost:** Free. **Phone:** (604) 463-8148.

MISSION (H-12) pop. 34,505, elev. 55 m/180′

Mission developed from a Roman Catholic mission built in 1861 to serve Indian tribes. The site became a popular stopping place for trappers, settlers and other river travelers.

The Fraser River provides opportunities for swimming, fishing, boating and water sports; its sandbars are good for rockhounds in search of agates, jades and garnets. Motocross and boat races are held at Mission Raceway from March through October.

Mission Regional Chamber of Commerce: 34033 Lougheed Hwy., Mission, BC, Canada V2V 5X8. **Phone:** (604) 826-6914.

FRASER RIVER SAFARI departs from the harborfront at 7057 Mershon St. at jct. Harbour Ave. A 3-hour narrated cruise along the Fraser River in a fully covered jet boat comes complete with scenic mountain views; possible sightings of bears, seals, deer and birds; and entertaining folklore about First Nations legends, fur traders, gold miners and Sasquatch. A stop is made at Kilby Historic Site in Harrison Mills *(see attraction listing p. 125).*

Time: Allow 3 hours, 30 minutes minimum. **Hours:** Trips depart daily at 9:30 and 2, July-Sept.; at 10, rest of year. Closed Dec. 25. **Cost:** $110; $90 (senior citizens); $70 (ages 5-15); $300 (family, two adults and two children). Reservations are required. **Phone:** (604) 826-7361 or (866) 348-6877.

MISSION MUSEUM is downtown at 33201 Second Ave. at jct. Welton St. The museum, in a 1907 prefabricated building shipped to Mission to serve as the Canadian Bank of Commerce, was also the town's library before becoming a museum. The building now houses a parlor and a kitchen reminiscent of the 1920s and permanent exhibits about the First Nations people and the history of the city. A themed exhibit changes each year.

Time: Allow 30 minutes minimum. **Hours:** Tues.-Sat. 1-4, June-Aug.; Thurs. 10-noon and 1-4,

Fri. 1-4, rest of year. **Cost:** $2; $1 (ages 2-12); $5 (family). **Phone:** (604) 826-1011.

POWER HOUSE AT STAVE FALLS is 1.3 km (.8 mi.) w. on Ferndale Ave. from jct. Stave Lake St. and Ferndale Ave., then 12.9 km (8 mi.) n.w. on Dewdney Trunk Rd. to 31338 Dewdney Trunk Rd. Through interactive science games and historic displays, the facility tells the story of how power helped build British Columbia. Within a 50-seat theater, visitors may start their self-guiding tour with a 9-minute video that introduces life in the early 1900s. On display are generators and turbines within a 1912 generating station.

Time: Allow 1 hour minimum. **Hours:** Daily 10-5, Mar. 15-Oct. 31. **Cost:** $6; $5 (ages 6-8 and ages 55+); $15 (family, two adults and two children). **Phone:** (604) 462-1222.

WESTMINSTER ABBEY is 1.5 km (.9 mi.) e., .7 km (.5 mi.) n. of Hwy. 7 to 34224 Dewdney Trunk Rd. The Seminary of Christ the King is managed by Benedictine monks. Of interest are the view and architecture. Modest dress is required. **Time:** Allow 30 minutes minimum. **Hours:** Mon.-Sat. 1:30-4:30, Sun. 2-4:30. Grounds open daily 8-8. **Cost:** Donations. **Phone:** (604) 826-8975.

XÁ:YTEM LONGHOUSE INTERPRETIVE CENTRE is at 35087 Lougheed Hwy. (Hwy. 7). Xá:ytem (pronounced HAY-tum) is said to be British Columbia's oldest known dwelling site. It is evidence of one of many large villages that were once inhabited by the ancestors of today's Stó:lō people. Of note is a replica of a *skumel,* or underground pithouse, and the "Rock"—a physical manifestation of Stó:lō spirituality. Among the items housed at the cedar longhouse are artifacts found at the site.

Tours: Guided tours are available. **Time:** Allow 1 hour minimum. **Hours:** Mon.-Sat. 9-4:30. Closed Jan. 1 and Dec. 22-31. Phone ahead to confirm schedule. **Cost:** $12; $10 (ages 55+ and students with ID); $8 (ages 6-12). **Phone:** (604) 820-9725.

NEW WESTMINSTER (H-11)
pop. 58,549, elev. 75 m/246′

The oldest incorporated city in Western Canada, New Westminster—also known as the Royal City—was named by Queen Victoria. Transformed into a boomtown by the lure of gold in 1857, it plunged into a depression when the gold rush subsided in the late 1860s. The city was the provincial capital until 1868.

New Westminster also is known for its architecture. Parts of the city were built by the Royal Engineers, sent in 1855 to keep order in the new crown colony. Former members of this organization later formed the New Westminster Regiment, whose history is recounted in the Museum of the Royal Westminster Regiment at Sixth Street and Queens Avenue; phone (604) 526-5116.

Other places of interest include old houses, many of which survived a devastating fire in 1898. The houses can be toured in May. Tickets must be purchased in advance; for information phone the New Westminster Hyack Festival Association at (604) 522-6894.

Westminster Quay Public Market, on the waterfront, maintains a tradition started in 1892 when farmers, hunters and settlers came to barter for goods. Fresh meat, baked goods, produce and local crafts can be purchased daily.

Antique Alley, on historic Front Street, is known for its heritage buildings housing stores featuring an array of antiques and collectibles.

Also of interest is *Sampson V* Maritime Museum aboard the stern-wheeler berthed on the Fraser River at the foot of Tenth Street. The stern-wheeler, the last steam-powered paddlewheeler to operate on the Fraser, can be toured; phone (604) 522-6894. The Canadian Lacrosse Hall of Fame, which celebrates Canada's national summer sport, is at 65 E. Sixth Ave. at junction McBride Boulevard; phone (604) 527-4640.

New Westminster Chamber of Commerce: 601 Queens Ave., New Westminster, BC, Canada V3M 1L1. **Phone:** (604) 521-7781 or (604) 526-1905.

JAPANESE FRIENDSHIP GARDEN is next to City Hall at 511 Royal Ave. Waterfalls, pathways and flowering trees and shrubs adorn the garden, which features 100 Yoshino cherry trees, a gift from the city of Moriguchi, Japan. **Time:** Allow 1 hour, 30 minutes minimum. **Hours:** Daily dawn-dusk. **Cost:** Free. **Phone:** (604) 527-4567.

NEW WESTMINSTER MUSEUM AND ARCHIVES is at 302 Royal Ave. This 1864 mansion was built in the San Francisco Gothic Revival style for Capt. William Irving, a pioneer of the riverboat trade on the Fraser River. Furnished in period, the 14-room residence is bedecked in Victorian Christmas decor during December. The adjacent museum features artifacts, local history displays and an 1876 coach built to carry the governor general of Canada to the Cariboo goldfields.

Time: Allow 1 hour minimum. **Hours:** Museum Wed.-Sun. noon-5, May-Aug.; noon-4, rest of year. Mansion and archives Wed.-Sun. noon-5, May-Aug.; Sat.-Sun. noon-4, rest of year. Closed major holidays. Phone ahead to confirm schedule. **Cost:** Donations. **Phone:** (604) 527-4640.

PADDLEWHEELER RIVERBOAT TOURS departs from the boardwalk of the New Westminster Quay Public Market at 139-810 Quayside Dr. Narrated sightseeing tours of various lengths are offered aboard an authentic paddlewheeler. The MV *Native* is a replica of a late 19th-century riverboat that carried passengers on the historic Gold Rush Trail via the Fraser River. Evening entertainment cruises also are available.

Hours: Cruises depart daily year-round. Phone ahead to confirm schedule. **Cost:** Fare $49.95-$89.95; $44.95-$79.95 (ages 60+); $29.95-$59.95

(ages 6-12). Some fares may include meals. Reservations are required. **Phone:** (604) 525-4465 or (877) 825-1302.

QUEENS PARK is at 6th St. and McBride Blvd. in the center of town. The park includes a Salish totem pole, a picnic area, tennis courts, botanical gardens, nature trails, a stadium, an arena and a band shell in which concerts are presented in July and August. Splash pools, playgrounds and a petting zoo are open in summer. In Centennial Lodge, the Art Gallery in the Park features works by emerging and established artists.

Time: Allow 1 hour, 30 minutes minimum. **Hours:** Park open daily dawn-dusk. Art gallery daily 1-5, July-Aug.; Tues.-Sun. 1-5, rest of year. Splash pools daily 10-7, Victoria Day weekend-Labour Day weekend; Sat.-Sun. 10-7, day after Labour Day weekend-Sept. 30. Petting zoo daily 10-5:30, June-Aug. **Cost:** Donations. **Phone:** (604) 527-4567 for the park, or (604) 525-3244 for the gallery.

NORTH VANCOUVER (G-11)
pop. 44,303, elev. 99 m/325′

North Vancouver is a city, and it's also a district. All visitors really need to know, however, is that this North Shore destination is definitely worth checking out.

Lumbering and shipbuilding were important early on, and by the early 20th century the town across Burrard Inlet from Vancouver had incorporated. Today there are no discernible distinctions among the various municipalities that make up the North Shore. The city of North Vancouver does have its own impressive skyline, easily visible from the downtown Vancouver waterfront, while the district of North Vancouver is a bit of a hodgepodge, with pockets of industry and commercial development mixed in with parks and green spaces. It's also the location of Grouse Mountain and the Capilano Suspension Bridge *(see attraction listings)*, two of the North Shore's most popular tourist attractions.

From Vancouver, take either the Lions Gate Bridge or the Ironworkers Memorial Second Narrows Crossing (Hwy. 1) to North Vancouver. (The bridge's name honors 27 workers who were killed when several spans collapsed during construction.) But the most scenic approach is aboard TransLink's SeaBus, with terminals on Vancouver's downtown waterfront (near Canada Place) and in North Vancouver next to the Lonsdale Quay Market. These 400-passenger catamaran ferries make the one-way trip across Burrard Inlet in about 12 minutes. Ferries depart both terminals every 15 minutes Mon.-Fri. 6 a.m.-6:30 p.m., Sat. 10:15-6:45, Sun. 11:15-6:45. TransLink's fare system allows passengers to travel freely between buses, the SeaBus and the SkyTrain rapid transit system. For additional schedule and fare information phone (604) 953-3333.

If you arrive via the SeaBus, the first place you must explore is the Lonsdale Quay Market. It's a classic Vancouver fresh market with an abundance of vendors selling fruit, veggies, flowers, seafood and baked goods, plus yummy soups, sauces and other specialty items. You'll be hard pressed to decide on something to go from one of the international food bars—the choices are many and tempting, from noodle stir fries to seafood chowder—but once the decision is made, eat outside on the deck so you can watch the ferry boats come and go with downtown Vancouver as a backdrop. A farmers market sets up on the East Plaza at the Quay Saturdays from 10 to 3, May 10-Oct. 25. Organic farmers, bakers, jam and salsa makers and crafters all peddle their wares.

If peace and quiet is what you're seeking, head to Cates Park. From Vancouver, take the first exit off the Second Narrows bridge, following the signs for Deep Cove; then proceed east on Dollarton Highway about 8 kilometres (5 mi.) to the park entrance (on the right). There are grassy areas, a playground for kids and a pebble-sand beach. Watch the boats heading from Burrard Inlet into Indian Arm, check out the totem pole and First Nations canoe, hike a waterfront trail through stands of Douglas fir and big-leaf maple, or stretch out and take a nap under one of the huge cedar trees near the parking lot.

From Cates Park, get back on Dollarton Highway and continue north a couple of kilometres to the residential community of Deep Cove. The cove in question is a natural indentation of Indian Arm, a fiord-like extension of Burrard Inlet. In the 18th century First Nations tribes traveled up and down Indian Arm hunting and fishing, and lumbering was an important industry in this area in the first half of the 20th century.

What strikes you immediately about Deep Cove is how incredibly picturesque it is. Gallant Avenue is a quaint 2 blocks of eateries (fish and chips followed by a cone from Orca's Favourite Ice Cream makes a nice lunch combo), a shop or three and the Deep Cove Cultural Centre, which includes the Seymour Art Gallery and the Deep Cove Stage Society's community theater. The street ends at nicely landscaped Panorama Park, bright with flower beds in the summer. Walk down the stairs to the beach and then out onto the pier.

Sheltered, serene Deep Cove harbor will take your breath away. Trees frame the cove on both sides. Rising beyond the water to the left are the thickly forested slopes of Mount Seymour Provincial Park *(see attraction listing and Recreation Chart)*. The wooded hillsides to the right are speckled with houses that undoubtedly have views to die for. Across Indian Arm loom the Coast Mountains, dark masses in the distance. Sailboats bob on the cove's tranquil surface. Kayakers slice through the water. Canoeists paddle gracefully. It's quite an enchanting vista, one you'll likely end up gazing out on all afternoon.

CAPILANO SALMON HATCHERY is at 4500 Capilano Park Rd. Self-guiding tours allow visitors to view this architecturally acclaimed facility. Displays trace the development of coho, chinook and steelhead salmon. Live adult salmon may be seen in the fish ladder July through November. Scenic picnic areas are available. **Time:** Allow 30 minutes minimum. **Hours:** Daily 8-8, June-Sept.; 8-4, rest of year. **Cost:** Free. **Phone:** (604) 666-1790. 🅿️

CAPILANO SUSPENSION BRIDGE is off Hwy. 1 exit 14, then 2 km (1.2 mi.) n. to 3735 Capilano Rd. The swinging 137-metre-long (450-ft.) footbridge spans a 70-metre-deep (230-ft.) densely wooded gorge above the Capilano River. George Grant Mackay, a Scottish civil engineer, built the original bridge in 1889 from hemp rope and cedar planks; the fourth structure on the site is reinforced with steel cables and concrete.

The site features gardens; a totem park; Treetops Adventure, a series of suspension bridges; and a story center that displays artifacts of the bridge. The Living Forest includes interactive displays and naturalist exhibits which guide visitors through a West Coast rain forest. Artisans sculpt totem poles and masks in the Big House. First Nations dancers perform and costumed guides offer tours of the park and nature trails daily May through October.

Wheelchairs are not permitted on bridge. **Time:** Allow 1 hour minimum. **Hours:** Daily 8:30-8, May 30-Labour Day; 10-9, Jan. 1-2 and Dec. 5-31; 9-7, May 2-29 and day after Labour Day-Oct. 3; 9-6, Mar. 14-May 1 and Oct. 4-Nov. 1; 9-5, rest of year. Closed Dec. 25. Phone ahead to confirm schedule. **Cost:** $29.95; $27.95 (ages 65+); $23.75 (students with ID); $18.75 (ages 13-16); $10 (ages 6-12). **Phone:** (604) 985-7474 or (877) 985-7474. *See color ad p. 166 & p. 167.* 🍴

GROUSE MOUNTAIN is at 6400 Nancy Greene Way. From a height of 1,100 metres (4,100 ft.), the summit offers a panorama of the city. On clear nights floodlit buildings and twinkling lights are reflected in the still harbor. Skiing, snowshoeing, snowboarding, ice skating and sleigh rides are possible in the winter while helicopter tours are popular in the summer. Sports events and shows take place year-round. An aerial tramway operates all year to the chalet.

Each hour, Theatre in the Sky shows the film "Born to Fly," which provides an eagle's view of southwestern British Columbia. The Grouse Mountain Refuge for Endangered Wildlife is home to two orphaned grizzly bears and a pack of gray wolves. Also offered are a guided Eco Walk, a lumberjack show and a Birds in Motion demonstration. Grouse Grind, a grueling climb up the mountain, is popular with locals. Or, you can experience the beauty of the area from above on the Air Grouse zipline.

Daily bus service to the tramway is available. **Time:** Allow 1 hour minimum. **Hours:** Grouse Mountain open daily 9 a.m.-10 p.m. **Cost:** $37.95; $35.95 (ages 65+); $22.95 (ages 13-18); $13.95 (ages 5-12). Fares may vary; phone ahead. **Phone:** (604) 980-9311. 🍴 🅿️

LYNN CANYON ECOLOGY CENTRE is off Lynn Valley Rd. to the end of Peters Rd., following signs to 3663 Park Rd. The center is in a municipal park that features paths, natural streams and rivers and a 50-metre-high (166-ft.) suspension bridge spanning a waterfall and the canyon. The ecology center offers films, interactive displays and nature programs.

Hours: Park open daily dawn-dusk; closed Jan. 1 and Dec. 25-26. Ecology center open daily 10-5, June-Sept. **Cost:** Donations. **Phone:** (604) 990-3755. Ⓣ

MAPLEWOOD FARM is at 405 Seymour River Pl. This park-farm specializes in the display of domestic farm animals and birds. Visitors may pet the inhabitants of Goathill and Rabbitat and view a cow-milking demonstration. Pony rides are available daily in July and August and on weekends (weather permitting) the rest of the year.

Time: Allow 1 hour minimum. **Hours:** Daily 10-4, Apr. 1-Oct. 31; Tues.-Sun. 10-4, rest of year. Cow-milking demonstrations daily at 1:15. Closed Dec. 25. **Cost:** $5.25; $3 (ages 19 months-16 years and 55+). **Phone:** (604) 929-5610.

MOUNT SEYMOUR PROVINCIAL PARK is 24 km (15 mi.) n.e. The scenic area of 3,508 hectares (8,668 acres) is on the slopes of 1,433-metre (4,701-ft.) Mount Seymour. A good highway goes to the 1,006-metre (3,330-ft.) level. Hiking trails and downhill skiing are available in season. *See Recreation Chart.* **Hours:** Daily 7 a.m.-11 p.m. **Cost:** Free. **Parking:** $1 per hour or $3 per day. **Phone:** (604) 986-2261. 🅰

NORTH VANCOUVER MUSEUM AND ARCHIVES is in Presentation House at 209 W. Fourth St. The museum's artifacts and photographs document the community's growth from pioneer days. Documentary and photographic collections are housed in the archives at 3203 Institute Rd. Temporary exhibits are available.

Time: Allow 1 hour minimum. **Hours:** Museum open Tues.-Sun. noon-5. Archives open Tues.-Sat. noon-5. Complex closed Dec. 25-Jan. 1. **Cost:** Donations. **Phone:** (604) 990-3700.

PARK & TILFORD GARDENS is at jct. Cotton Rd. and Brooksbank Ave. at 440-333 Brooksbank Ave. The 1.2-hectare (3-acre) botanical site consists of eight interconnected theme gardens. A variety of both native and exotic floral arrangements leads through arboreal displays and to aviaries, where visitors may see parrots and other tropical birds.

An aromatic blend of plant and flower enclosures composes the Rose Garden, home to 24 varieties of plant life and more than 250 rose plants. **Tours:** Guided tours are available. **Time:** Allow 1 hour minimum. **Hours:** Daily 9:30-dusk. **Cost:** Free. **Phone:** (604) 984-8200.

ROCKWOOD ADVENTURES departs from downtown hotels. Half- and full-day guided nature walks are offered to area ecological destinations including

Lynn Canyon, a rain forest in Capilano River Canyon, a coastal forest at Burrard Inlet and Mount Gardner on Bowen Island. All trips include a snack or lunch.

Hours: Half-day tours depart daily at 9. **Cost:** $85; $78 (ages 12-25 and senior citizens); $60 (ages 4-11). Rate may vary depending on tour. Reservations are required. **Phone:** (604) 741-0802 or (888) 236-6606.

RECREATIONAL ACTIVITIES

Kayaking

- **Takaya Tours** depart from off Hwy. 1 exit 23A to Main St. (becomes Dollarton Hwy.), then 3.3 mi. e. to Cates Park docks, following signs. Shuttle transportation is available. **Hours:** Daily 9-8, May-Oct. **Phone:** (604) 904-7410 or (604) 936-0236.

PORT COQUITLAM (H-11)
pop. 52,687, elev. 10 m/33'

Port Coquitlam is bordered by the Pitt and Fraser rivers to the east and south and mountains to the north. The rivers were coveted fishing grounds, and in fact, Coquitlam is derived from the Salish word *kwayhquitlum*, which means "red fish in the river," referring to the annual salmon spawning run. Before the 1800s, the area was occupied by the ancestors of the Kwayhquitlum First Nations tribe. With the arrival of the first European settlers, Port Coquitlam began its growth as a farming and logging community.

Opportunities for recreational activities abound. The 29-kilometre (18-mi.) PoCo Trail passes through wooded areas and runs alongside the Pitt River, providing plenty of opportunities to observe waterfowl and other wildlife; the Pitt Dikes can be seen from the trail. Activities such as hiking, jogging, bicycling and horseback riding also can be enjoyed.

PORT MOODY (H-11)
pop. 27,512, elev. 10 m/33'

Port Moody once was the terminus of the Canadian Pacific Railway—the first train from Montréal to the Pacific arrived July 4, 1886. A year later the line was extended 20 kilometres (12 mi.) west to Vancouver. Rocky Point Park on Burrard Inlet offers picnicking, swimming, boating and nature trails.

PORT MOODY STATION MUSEUM is at 2734 Murray St. The museum displays community and railway artifacts and historical information about Port Moody in a former Canadian Pacific Railway depot with working and living areas restored to their early 1900s appearance. A heritage garden, typical of Canadian Pacific Railway stations 1882-1912, is on the grounds. A restored 1921 sleeper car also is on site.

Hours: Daily 10-5, Victoria Day-Labour Day; Wed.-Sun. noon-4, rest of year. Closed Jan. 1 and Dec. 25-26. **Cost:** $2. **Phone:** (604) 939-1648.

RICHMOND (H-11) pop. 174,461, elev. 5 m/16′

On an island at the mouth of the Fraser River, Richmond first was settled in 1879. The town grew and prospered with its farming, fishing and water-borne trade industries. Today, Richmond's major industries include aviation, berry farming, high technology and manufacturing.

Golden Village, in central Richmond, affords visitors the opportunity to experience the Asian culture through shopping, dining and festivals.

The Richmond Nature Park, 44 hectares (109 acres) at 11851 Westminster Hwy., has a bird pond, beehive displays, mounted birds, a quaking bog and plants identified by markers. A naturalist conducts hour-long tours of the park on Sunday.

Steveston, tucked away in Richmond's southwest corner, is a bit of a contradiction. It has a historic past, but it's also a residential neighborhood. Commercial fishing was once this area's lifeblood, but today you're just as likely to sample fish that's battered and sharing a plate with a pile of fries at a local restaurant as you are seeing one freshly caught. And while weather-beaten buildings hint at a hard-scrabble past, there's also a Starbucks.

Sitting at the confluence of two major bodies of water—the Strait of Georgia and the Fraser River—Steveston's first flush of success was as a salmon canning center. The Fraser's south arm was a fertile fishing ground, and a settlement grew up around this favored coastal location in the 1880s. Salmon turned Steveston into a classic turn-of-the-20th-century boom town: It became one of the busiest fishing ports in the world, with windjammers loading up canned salmon bound for far-flung markets.

The town was boisterous with a capital "B." Saloons and gambling dens thrived, and on Saturday nights crowds of sailors, First Nations peoples and European, Chinese and Japanese immigrants—most of them fishermen and cannery workers—thronged the boardwalks. In the years leading up to World War I eager boosters dubbed Steveston "Salmonopolis," but the boom was not to last. The internment during World War II of Japanese-Canadian citizens, who made up a large part of the town's population, struck a serious blow. The canning industry slowly declined, finally coming to an end by the early 1990s. You can learn more about this aspect of town history at the Gulf of Georgia Cannery National Historic Site *(see attraction listing)*.

Steveston, still an active fishing port that to a large degree has retained its salty character, makes a good day trip. From downtown Vancouver it's about a 30-minute drive. Take Granville Street south to Hwy. 99 (via 70th Avenue W.), then take Hwy. 99 south to exit 32 (Steveston Highway) and turn right (west). Summer, when the weather is usually sunny and a couple of annual festivals are on tap, is the time to go; during the chilly, rainy winter months many restaurants and attractions reduce their hours.

So what do you do? For starters, just explore where your feet take you. Follow the planked wooden boardwalk along the shore of Cannery Channel; interpretive panels provide background about Steveston's fishing and canning past. Have your picture taken sitting on a bench in the garden outside the Prickly Pear Garden Centre (on No. 1 Road, just off Bayview Street). In addition to lovely hanging flower baskets, the large, emerald-green leaves of a banana tree will have you scratching your head and reminding yourself that yes, you are in Canada.

Tramp around Garry Point Park (at the end of Moncton Street). Fronting the Strait of Georgia, it's basically undeveloped and has a wild and wind-swept look. Sunsets over the water can be showstoppers here, and the flat, open spaces bring out kite

flyers. Stop at the Fisherman's Memorial, which takes the shape of a giant net-mending needle and is inscribed with a poem, "Spawning Cycle":

These spring days grow longer
Until the dark comes closing
What tides disclose they again conceal
We're out to fish until again
It's time to be ashore
Because the geese go by
I'll be here with you
'Till it's time to be alone: the way out,
The way back, and all ways this one.

Stroll the boardwalk along bustling Fisherman's Wharf, where seiners, trawlers and other vessels cruise in and out of the harbor. Depending on the season, some of the boats docked along the boardwalk sell fresh catches of salmon, cod, octopus and prawns.

The Steveston Museum, 3811 Moncton St., resembles a one-room country schoolhouse with its red-and-yellow clapboard exterior and steep gabled roof. This former Northern Bank building has a general store layout with displays of late 19th-century furniture and office equipment. It's also a working post office. Phone (604) 271-6868.

For lunch, it really has to be fish and chips. And there's a choice: Dave's Fish & Chips (3460 Moncton St.) or Pajo's (two locations—on the wharf at the corner of Bayview Street and 3rd Avenue, and a takeout stand in the large administrative building at Garry Point Park). Although the menus at both include such non-fishy items as burgers, do the right thing and order fish and chips (aficionados will go for the halibut over cod or salmon). Mushy peas are a veddy British accompaniment.

The big event of the year is the Steveston Salmon Festival, held on July 1 in conjunction with Canada Day. Floats, marching bands, vintage vehicles and local community groups are part of a big parade that begins at 10 a.m. There's a craft fair, an art show, a Japanese cultural show, carnival rides and a midway, martial arts demonstrations and a youth festival. The main attraction, though, is a salmon barbecue; hundreds of filets are grilled to succulent perfection over open fire pits.

Summer in Steveston can get crowded, especially on nice sunny weekends. But there are several free parking lots in town, plenty of parking at Garry Point Park, and street parking if you're lucky enough to snag a space.

Tourism Richmond: 11980 Deas Thruway, Richmond, BC, Canada V6W 1L1. **Phone:** (604) 271-8280 or (877) 247-0777. *See color ad p. 184.*

BRITANNIA HERITAGE SHIPYARD is at 5180 Westwater Dr. at the foot of Railway Ave. The site contains 10 buildings that were once part of a late 1880s fishing village which included canneries, boatyards and homes. Four buildings are open for touring; visitors can view displays about maritime history and watch as old wooden boats are restored. **Time:** Allow 30 minutes minimum. **Hours:** Daily 10-6, May-Sept.; Sat. 10-4, Sun. noon-4, rest of year. **Cost:** Free. **Phone:** (604) 718-8050.

BUDDHIST TEMPLE is at 9160 Steveston Hwy. This working temple offers visitors tranquility through its classical Chinese garden, ponds, small waterfalls and gazebos. A courtyard features bonsai plants and a striking ceramic mural. The temple houses Chinese artifacts that reveal the artisans' skill in sculpture, painting, carpentry and embroidery. Also on site is the Seven Buddha Mural; at 22 metres (73 ft.) long it is said to be the only Buddhist mural of this size in the world. **Time:** Allow 1 hour minimum. **Hours:** Daily 9:30-5:30. **Cost:** Donations. **Phone:** (604) 274-2822.

 GULF OF GEORGIA CANNERY NATIONAL HISTORIC SITE is at 12138 Fourth Ave. in Steveston Village. The 1894 salmon cannery has been restored to serve as an interpretive center for Canada's West Coast fishing industry. Interactive video presentations, guided tours of the plant and replicated 1900-50 canning line, and equipment demonstrations are offered. Every 30 minutes the Boiler House Theatre presents a film about the West Coast fishing industry.

Hours: Mon.-Sat. 10-5, Sun. 11-5, May 2-Labour Day; Mon. and Thurs.-Sat. 10-5, Sun. 11-5, day after Labour Day-second Mon. in Oct. **Cost:** $7.43; $6.24 (ages 65+); $3.71 (ages 6-16). **Phone:** (604) 664-9009.

LONDON HERITAGE FARM is at 6511 Dyke Rd. The restored 1880s farmhouse, furnished in period, is the former residence of Charles and Henrietta London and their family. **Time:** Allow 1 hour minimum. **Hours:** Mon.-Fri. 10-4, Sat.-Sun. 10-5, July-Aug.; Sat.-Sun. noon-5, Feb.-June and Sept.-Dec. **Cost:** Donations. **Phone:** (604) 271-5220. 🅰️

RICHMOND CULTURAL CENTRE is off Granville St. at 7700 Minoru Gate. Home to the Richmond Arts Centre, Archives, Museum and Art Gallery, the center presents programs and events in art, music, drama and dance. The gallery features works from local artists and traveling exhibits. The museum depicts Richmond's history through early household items, personal effects and articles relating to the area's agriculture, dairying, fishing and transportation. Archives preserve public and community records, which are available for research.

Time: Allow 1 hour minimum. **Hours:** Museum open Mon.-Fri. 9 a.m.-9:30 p.m.; Sat.-Sun. 10-5. Art gallery open Mon.-Fri. 10-6, Sat.-Sun. 10-5. Archives open Mon.-Thurs. 9-4:30. Closed major holidays. Phone ahead to confirm schedule. **Cost:** Free. **Phone:** (604) 276-4000.

STEVESTON SEABREEZE ADVENTURES is at 12551 #1 Rd., Bldg. 43. A narrated whale-watching tour departs from historic Steveston village and transits the Fraser River Delta, Strait of Georgia and Gulf Islands. Hydrophones are used to listen to the whales vocalizing. The scenic trip affords passengers an opportunity to view other marine animals and wildlife.

Time: Allow 3 hours minimum. **Hours:** Departures daily at 9 and 2, mid-June to early Sept.; at 11, early Apr. to mid-June and early Sept.-late Oct. **Cost:** $105 (includes water/coffee and a snack); $95 (students with ID and senior citizens); $69 (ages 4-12). Reservations are recommended. **Phone:** (604) 272-7200.

VANCOUVER WHALE WATCH is at 210-12240 Second Ave. A 40-passenger, semi-covered vessel transports visitors through the Fraser River Delta, Strait of Georgia and Gulf Islands. Led by a naturalist, the narrated tour focuses on killer whales. Hydrophones are used to listen to the whales communicating. Other wildlife such as porpoises, sea lions, seals and eagles also may be seen. Binoculars are provided on loan.

Time: Allow 3 hours minimum. **Hours:** Departures daily at 9 and 2, mid-June to early Sept.; at 11, early Apr. to mid-June and early Sept.-late Oct. **Cost:** $105 (includes water and a snack); $95 (students with ID and senior citizens); $69 (ages 4-12). Reservations are recommended. **Phone:** (604) 274-9565.

GAMBLING ESTABLISHMENTS

- **River Rock Casino Resort** is at 8811 River Rd. **Hours:** Daily 24 hours. **Phone:** (604) 273-1895 or (877) 473-2818. *See color ad p. 657.*

SURREY (H-11) pop. 347,825, elev. 80 m/262′

Surrey's sights are popular with nature buffs. Bear Creek Park features a garden area that includes rhododendrons, azaleas, ornamental grasses and bulb displays. A shoreline walk extends from Crescent Beach to Peace Arch Park. Walkers can observe tide pools, dig for clams or watch the myriad native birds.

Surrey Regional Chamber of Commerce: 14439 104th Ave., Suite 101, Surrey, BC, Canada V3R 1M1. **Phone:** (604) 581-7130 or (866) 848-7130.

HISTORIC STEWART FARM is at 13723 Crescent Rd. Costumed guides offer tours of an 1890s farmhouse that has been restored to represent Victorian rural life. The site includes a pole barn, heritage gardens, an orchard and walking trails along the Nicomekl River. Demonstrations, and seasonal special events and programs also are featured. **Time:** Allow 30 minutes minimum. **Hours:** Tues.-Fri. 10-4, Sat.-Sun. noon-4, Mar. 1 to mid-Dec.; closed statutory holidays. **Cost:** Donations. **Phone:** (604) 592-6956. 🅿️

NEWTON WAVE POOL is at 13730 72nd Ave. The indoor aquatic center houses, in addition to the wave pool, two water slides, an interactive water fortress and a three-station water cannon platform. The complex also includes an exercise, a steam and 465-square-metre (5,000-sq.-ft.) weight room as well as a whirlpool.

Hours: Mon.-Sat. 8 a.m.-9 p.m., Sun 8-8. Phone ahead for leisure swim times. **Cost:** $5.25; $4 (students ages 19+ with ID and ages 60+); $2.75 (ages 2-18). **Phone:** (604) 501-5540.

SURREY MUSEUM is at 17710-56A Ave. Interactive exhibits and a 42-seat theater portray the history of Surrey. A textile library and weaving studio are featured on-site. Changing exhibits are offered. Also on the grounds is the Anderson cabin, the oldest remaining pioneer-era structure in Surrey. The cabin was built in 1872 by Eric Anderson, a Swedish immigrant and one of the first settlers in the area. **Time:** Allow 1 hour minimum. **Hours:** Tues.-Thurs. 10-6, Fri.-Sat. 10-5, early Feb.-Dec. 23. Closed statutory holidays. **Cost:** Donations. **Phone:** (604) 592-6956.

WEST VANCOUVER (G-11) pop. 42,131

If you're not a Vancouverite—or you're unfamiliar with British Columbia's Lower Mainland—you might think that the North Shore is simply one more spectacularly scenic backdrop to a city already blessed with loads of scenic allure. And you would be wrong. The North Shore is not only uncommonly beautiful; it's also teeming with things to do.

The city and district of North Vancouver are east of the Lions Gate Bridge; the district of West Vancouver spreads along the northern shore of Burrard Inlet from the bridge west to Horseshoe Bay. There's no manufacturing or industry here; "West Van" is primarily residential. It's also affluent, and there are many gorgeous and expensive homes tucked away on winding little streets or perched high on hillsides. All of West Vancouver is situated on slopes of the Coast Mountains, which means that most of these homes enjoy enviable vistas of water, trees, mountains or all three.

The Lions Gate Bridge, which connects Stanley Park and the North Shore, is the gateway to West Vancouver. This suspension bridge crosses the first narrows of Burrard Inlet, which accounts for its official name, the First Narrows Bridge; "lions gate" is a reference to two mountains known as the Lions.

Construction of the 1,795-metre (5,890-ft.) span began in 1937, and the bridge opened to traffic in 1938. It's similar in appearance to San Francisco's Golden Gate Bridge (although bright green rather than bright orange). Another similarity it shares with Golden Gate is the view from the bridge—it's gorgeous whether you're coming or going. The Guinness family (of beer fame), who for a time owned land on the North Shore, purchased decorative white lights for the bridge in 1986 as a gift to Vancouver, turning it into a distinctive nighttime landmark.

Marine Drive is West Vancouver's main thoroughfare. It runs from the bridge west to Horseshoe Bay, usually within sight of water, passing lovely neighborhoods and commercial blocks packed with shops and restaurants. Ambleside, between 11th and 23rd streets, is one of West Vancouver's oldest neighborhoods. The Centennial Seawalk in Ambleside Park is a breezy waterfront promenade that's a favorite spot for walkers, joggers or anyone who loves to gaze out onto the water and contemplate the awesome views of the bridge and Stanley Park. There's a long, sandy beach and a concession stand where you can grab a cheeseburger or an ice cream cone.

Ambleside also has art galleries and antique shops. The Silk Purse Gallery, 1570 Argyle Ave. (on the waterfront near John Lawson Park), is a comfy old cottage that used to be a haven for honeymooners. It's now home to the West Vancouver Community Arts Council, which presents rotating art exhibits and a series of summer concerts; for ticket information phone (604) 925-7292. Local artists exhibit at the Ferry Building Gallery, a lovingly restored heritage building at 1414 Argyle Ave.

Dundarave is another exceedingly picturesque little seaside community. Stroll along the water once again at Dundarave Park, at the foot of 25th Street, with Cypress Mountain looming in the distance. Old-fashioned lamp posts are installed on Marine Drive between 23rd and 25th streets, flowers cascade from hanging baskets, and the 2 blocks are filled with eateries and specialty shops. It's a nice area to spend an hour or two. Have lunch at the Red Lion Bar & Grill (2427 Marine Dr.), a classic British-style pub—think dark wood walls, stained glass and several fireplaces when the weather's nippy—or stop for coffee and a muffin at Delaney's Coffee House.

Marine Drive presses on to Caulfeild (yes, that spelling is correct), an exclusive residential community of narrow, precipitously winding streets and expensive homes shielded by tall privacy hedges. Almost every bend and curve of the road offers a brief, tantalizing water view. Walking the trails in Lighthouse Park (see attraction listing), a protected stand of old growth coastal forest, is well worth your time.

Past the Lighthouse Park turnoff Marine Drive winds north toward Horseshoe Bay. Side streets lead to tucked-away little green spaces like Kew Park (accessed via Kew Cliff Road and Seaside Place). The multimillion-dollar homes along Kew Cliff Road have stunning views of the Strait of Georgia. A bit farther north Marine Drive winds around Fisherman's Cove, bristling with the masts of pleasure craft moored at the West Vancouver Yacht Club.

Follow the signs to Horseshoe Bay, the North Shore's western bookend. This is where ferries depart for Vancouver Island and the Lower Mainland's "Sunshine Coast." The little community is another North Shore jewel. Take Nelson Avenue off Marine Drive, which leads to the ferry terminal and marina. BC Ferries chug in and out of port while sea gulls wheel overhead. Tree-covered slopes frame Horseshoe Bay, houses perch high above the water and the Coast Mountains loom in the distance. Charming really doesn't begin to describe it.

"Downtown" Horseshoe Bay has just a couple of streets, which makes it perfect for strolling. Browse a few art galleries. Lean against a dock piling and watch the waterfront activity. Get fish and chips or an oyster burger from one of the takeout restaurants on Bay Street and take your feast to Horseshoe Bay Park, where there's a little gravel beach, two totem poles and a massive cast-bronze propeller that came off a whaling ship. Listen to the gulls and breathe in the sea air. Now *this* is an afternoon outing.

Backtrack to Marine Drive and turn right instead of left (which will take you back to Hwy. 99). Stay on Marine Drive and you'll reach Whytecliff Marine Park *(see Recreation Chart).* Designated Canada's first salt water Marine Protected Area (MPA) in 1993, it's located at the entrance to Howe Sound and is known for excellent scuba diving. Seals frolic along this rugged stretch of coastline, and there's a pebbly beach to explore. Or just relax at the park's observation pavilion and—you guessed it—admire the view.

CYPRESS PROVINCIAL PARK is off Trans-Canada Hwy. exit 8, then w. following signs. The park encompasses 3,012 hectares (7,443 acres) of mountains, lakes and forests. Winter offers skiing and other snow-related activates, while summer features bird-watching and a wide range of hiking and nature trails. *See Recreation Chart.* **Hours:** Daily 24 hours. **Cost:** Free. **Phone:** (604) 924-2200. ⊞

LIGHTHOUSE PARK is off Marine Dr. (watch for the park sign at the turnoff), then a short distance s.

via Beacon Ln. to the parking area. Capt. George Vancouver sailed past the rocky peninsula at the entrance to Burrard Inlet in 1792 and named the site Point Atkinson. Today this lush remnant of old growth coastal forest is a peaceful haven and wonderful place to hike. The lofty Douglas firs and other conifers are up to 500 years old.

Several kilometres of trails crisscross the park; to get to the Point Atkinson Lighthouse take the Beacon Lane Trail south from the parking area. It's about a 15-minute walk to a viewpoint with an expansive vista (on clear days) of the lighthouse (a working one and therefore closed to the public), the inlet and downtown Vancouver on the opposite shore. From the lighthouse viewpoint, short East Beach Trail leads down to the rugged, rocky beach along Starboat Cove.

The group of buildings near the lighthouse were barracks during World War II, when a number of B.C. light stations were used for surveillance purposes. **Time:** Allow 30 minutes minimum. **Hours:** Daily dawn-dusk. **Cost:** Free. **Phone:** (604) 925-7000.

SEWELLS MARINA is off Trans-Canada Hwy. at Horseshoe Bay Ferry Terminal, following signs to village. Points of interest on the 2-hour high-speed Sea Safari tour of coastal British Columbia may include Bowyer Island, Pam Rocks—birthing ground to seal pups in July—Ragged Island and The Strait of Georgia. **Hours:** Tours depart daily at 10, 1 and 4, Apr.-Oct. **Cost:** $73; $57 (ages 65+ and students with ID); $43 (ages 5-12). **Phone:** (604) 921-3474.

**This ends listings for the Vancouver Vicinity.
The following resumes the alphabetical listings of cities in British Columbia.**

VANDERHOOF (E-4)
pop. 4,064, elev. 915 m/2,050'

When the last spike of the railroad was driven in 1914, the Grand Trunk Pacific Development Company offered land for sale. The decision of where to put the new settlement in the wilderness was decided by Herbert Vanderhoof, a railroad employee, and a town was built in just a few weeks. The site, unfortunately, was a poor choice, as the land flooded every spring. In 1919 the townspeople moved to higher ground on the opposite side of the tracks.

Mr. Vanderhoof's legacy to the town is its name, Dutch for "of the farm." The name is fitting, as farming has always been an economic mainstay in the area.

Vanderhoof District Chamber of Commerce: 2353 Burrard Ave., P.O. Box 126, Vanderhoof, BC,

Canada V0J 3A0. **Phone:** (250) 567-2124 or (800) 752-4094.

VANDERHOOF COMMUNITY MUSEUM is w. on Hwy. 16 to 478 W. First St. The collection of reconstructed buildings depicts rural agriculture in the 1920s. Among the buildings restored and open are the 1914 Board of Trade Building, a café, a police office, a 1914 jail cell and a home typical of those built in the area by early Mennonite settlers. In the town square are examples of farm machines and equipment. **Time:** Allow 30 minutes minimum. **Hours:** Daily 10-4, Victoria Day weekend-Labour Day. **Cost:** Donations. **Phone:** (250) 567-2991. ⊞

VERNON—*see Okanagan Valley p. 143.*

Victoria

City Population: 78,057
Elevation: 17m/56 ft.

Editor's Picks:

Inner Harbour / © Jon Arnold Images
Danita Delimont Stock Photography

"To realize Victoria," Rudyard Kipling wrote, "you must take all that the eye admires in Bournemouth, Torquay, the Isle of Wight, the Happy Valley at Hong Kong, the Doon, Sorrento, Camp's Bay, add reminiscences of the Thousand Islands and arrange the whole around the Bay of Naples with some Himalayas for the background."

Yet the capital of British Columbia remains quintessentially British. Along with its tearooms, double-decker buses, horse-drawn tallyho carriages and shops that sell china and woolens, Victoria proudly claims another, much older culture. Totem poles can be seen throughout local parks, reflecting the city's dual heritage.

Regarded as Canada's gentlest city, Victoria has uncluttered streets, gardens that bloom year-round and hotels that have been serving high tea for decades. Sharing a passion for gardening, Victoria residents tend their prim English gardens. The city's innumerable flower beds and hanging baskets, nurtured by its mild climate, bloom in bright displays while the rest of Canada shivers.

The heart of the city curves around the stone-walled Inner Harbour, alive with bobbing pleasure craft, fishing boats and coastal shipping vessels. Facing the harbor are the Parliament Buildings and the block-long, ivy-covered Empress Hotel.

Emily Carr, a native of Victoria, devoted her artistic career to capturing on canvas the brilliant totem poles carved by the vanishing Indian civilizations of the Pacific coast. Like those she found in deserted Indian villages, the fanciful totems in Thunderbird Park evoke the highly developed ancient culture that dominated the area long before Victoria was settled in the mid-19th century.

Fort Victoria was built by Hudson's Bay Co. in 1843. Six years later Vancouver Island became a crown colony, and as British Columbia's only port, it became a passage to the Cariboo goldfields on the mainland in 1858. Violence around Bastion Square was so commonplace during this rowdy boomtown period that the *Victoria Gazette* reported no deaths "from natural causes in the city during the last 30 days." Local politicians supposedly settled their debates with fist fights on Government Street.

After the gold fever broke, Victoria began to assume its characteristic cool reserve. Lured by modest land prices, English settlers developed their queen's namesake city into a thriving government and commercial center. In 1868 Victoria became the capital of the newly joined crown colonies of Vancouver Island and British Columbia.

Since commercial supremacy passed to Vancouver after the completion of the Canadian Pacific Railway, Victoria has adopted a slower pace with few heavy industries. Victoria's harbor is a center for commercial trade. Lumber and fishing also contribute to the bustle of this port. The dry dock at the Canadian Forces Base-Pacific Command is one of the world's largest.

The city's strong tourism industry is buoyed by the continuous stream of travelers who come by

Government House Gardens / Tourism Victoria
© Deddeda Stemler

ferry from Washington and throughout British Columbia.

Whether or not Victoria is more British than Britain remains an ongoing debate among Victoria's residents. Few would contest, however, that nature's blessings have endowed the city with ample charm in its own right. No one understood this better than its native Indians, whose awesome totems continue to speak the land's wonder.

Getting There

By Car

Victoria is the western terminus of the 7,760-kilometre (4,850-mi.) Trans-Canada Highway. The highway traverses the mainland to Horseshoe Bay in West Vancouver and resumes at the Nanaimo ferry terminal. It then proceeds south along the island's eastern shore to Victoria. Hwy. 17, the other major artery into the city, connects Victoria with the ferry terminals at Swartz Bay and Sidney on the Saanich Peninsula.

By Boat

Several ferry systems connect Vancouver Island and Victoria with mainland Canada and the United States. The most direct route is the Tsawwassen-Swartz Bay automobile/passenger ferry service used by the intercity buses between Vancouver and Victoria. British Columbia Ferries also connects Nanaimo, 111 kilometres (69 mi.) north of Victoria, to Horseshoe Bay in West Vancouver. Phone (250) 386-3431 outside British Columbia or (888) 223-3779 within British Columbia for ferry information or reservations.

Ferries linking the southern end of the island and Victoria with the United States include Black Ball Transport Inc., (250) 386-2202, from Port Angeles, Wash.; and Washington State Ferries, (206) 464-6400, from Anacortes, Wash., to Sidney. Reservations are available for the Anacortes, Wash., to Sidney route; phone 1 day in advance to determine estimated waiting time. Victoria Express provides fast passenger ferry service from Port Angeles, Wash., and to Friday Harbor in Washington's San Juan Islands; phone (250) 361-9144. Victoria/San Juan Cruises has seasonal passenger boat service to Friday Harbor and Bellingham, Wash.; phone (800) 443-4552.

Connecting Seattle and Victoria is the high-speed passenger ferry, the *Victoria Clipper;* phone (250) 382-8100 or (800) 888-2535.

Departing from the north end of the island at Port Hardy, British Columbia Ferries' vessels voyage through the Inside Passage to Prince Rupert, where they connect with the Alaska State Ferry system. Information can be obtained from British Columbia Ferries, 1112 Fort St., Victoria, BC, Canada V8V

Destination Victoria

*T*he British legacy is indelibly stamped on the city. Here you will find massive stone castles, palatial government buildings, quaint cottages and gardens that bloom almost all year.

*B*ut look closer—another culture has left its mark: Native Indian icons are displayed with equal prominence throughout Victoria.

Thunderbird Park, Victoria.
(See listing page 198)

Tourism Victoria

Tourism Victoria / © Mike Clausen

Beacon Hill Park, Victoria.
(See listing page 194)

Hatley Park National Historic Site, Victoria.
(See listing page 196)

Tourism Victoria
© Nick Redding

BRITISH COLUMBIA
WASHINGTON

Sidney

Saanichton

Brentwood Bay

14

17

Sooke

View Royal

See Downtown map page 195

Victoria

CANADA
UNITED STATES

Tourism Victoria
© Brian Young

Fisgard Lighthouse, Victoria.
(See mention page 201)

*P*laces included in this AAA Destination City:

The Informed Traveler

Sales Tax: British Columbia's provincial sales tax is 7 percent. A 5 percent Goods and Services Tax (GST) also is levied, and there is a room tax of 10 percent on lodgings in the Victoria area. This tax structure will be in effect until July 1, 2010, when the province will change to a harmonized sales tax, creating a single tax of 12 percent. The separate lodgings tax will be discontinued, and hotel accommodations will be subject to the harmonized tax.

WHOM TO CALL

Emergency: 911

Police (non-emergency): (250) 995-7654

Hospitals: Gorge Road Hospital, (250) 995-4700; Royal Jubilee Hospital, (250) 370-8000.

WHERE TO LOOK

Newspapers

Victoria's daily paper is the *Times-Colonist,* which is distributed in the morning.

Radio

Victoria radio stations CBC (90.5 FM), CIOC (98.5 FM), CFUV (102 FM) and C-FAX (1070 AM) have news and weather reports.

Visitor Information

Tourism Victoria Visitor Information Centre: 812 Wharf St., Victoria, BC, Canada V8W 1T3. **Phone:** (250) 953-2033 or (800) 663-3883.

The center provides maps and brochures outlining various self-guiding walking and driving tours. The center is open daily 8:30-6:30, mid-May to mid-Sept.; 9-5, rest of year.

TRANSPORTATION

Air Travel

Victoria International Airport is 22 kilometres (12 mi.) north on Hwy. 17 (Patricia Bay Highway). Air Canada makes frequent flights to Victoria from Vancouver and Seattle. International air connections are made in Vancouver.

Airport Bus Service runs between the airport and downtown hotels; phone (250) 386-2525. Fare $15; free (ages 0-4).

Rental Cars

Auto rental agencies include Hertz, 1640 Electra Blvd. and 2634 Douglas St., which offers discounts to AAA and CAA members; phone (250) 656-2312 or (250) 360-2822, or (800) 263-0600 in Canada, or (800) 654-3080 out of Canada. Additional agencies are listed in the telephone directory.

Rail Service

From its depot at 450 Pandora Ave., Via Rail has weekday passenger service between Victoria and Courtenay; phone (888) 842-7245 in Canada or in the United States.

Buses

Pacific Coach Lines, 700 Douglas St., provides daily bus service between Vancouver and Victoria via British Columbia Ferry. The vessels transport buses and personal vehicles; phone (604) 662-7575.

Island Coach Lines provides bus transportation between Victoria and Campbell River; Nanaimo; Port Alberni; Port Hardy; and Port McNeill. For information phone (250) 385-4411.

Taxis

Taxis charge $2.85 minimum plus $1.45 per kilometre (.6 mi.). Companies include Blue Bird Cabs, (250) 382-4235; Empress Taxi, (250) 381-2222; and Victoria Taxi, (250) 383-7111.

Public Transport

BC Transit provides bus service for Greater Victoria. Buses serve the downtown area 6:30 a.m.-midnight. Fare $2.25; senior citizens, students and children $1.40. Buses run frequently between downtown and the ferry terminal. For route information phone (250) 382-6161.

Boats

Several ferry systems make connections with mainland Canada and the United States. *See Getting There By Boat for details.*

4V2; phone (250) 386-3431 outside British Columbia or (888) 223-3779 within British Columbia.

Getting Around

Street System

Most traffic activity is on Wharf, Government and Belleville streets, which embrace the Inner Harbour. Ferries arrive from Port Angeles, Wash., all year and from Seattle in summer. The main east-west streets are Yates, Fort and Johnson. Pandora Avenue, renamed Oak Bay Avenue in midtown, crosses the city from the Inner Harbour to Oak Bay.

Major north-south thoroughfares are Blanshard Street (Hwy. 17) and Douglas Street (Hwy. 1), which begins at Victoria's southern coast along the Juan de Fuca Strait. Dallas Road borders the shore and continues as Beach Drive along Victoria's eastern coast. Many Victoria streets are one-way.

Parking

On-street parking is controlled by meters and posted restrictions Mon.-Sat. 9-6. Vehicles parked on specially posted blocks are subject to towing during rush hours. Downtown off-street parking is available in civic parkades and shopping center lots.

What To See

ART GALLERY OF GREATER VICTORIA is at 1040 Moss St. The gallery presents contemporary, historical and Asian exhibitions, including a permanent Emily Carr exhibition.

Hours: Mon.-Sat. 10-5 (also Thurs. 5-9), Sun. noon-5, Victoria Day to mid-Sept.; Tues.-Sat. 10-5 (also Thurs. 5-9), rest of year. Closed Good Friday, Nov. 11 and Dec. 25. **Cost:** $12; $10 (ages 65+ and students with ID); $2 (ages 6-17); $26 (family, two adults and four children under 18); donations (first Tues. of each month). Admission may increase for special exhibits. **Phone:** (250) 384-4171.

BASTION SQUARE overlooks the harbor. James Douglas established Fort Victoria on this site in 1843. Restored and preserved buildings from the 19th-century boom days surround a courtyard plaza.

BEACON HILL PARK is at Douglas and Dallas sts. The 74-hectare (183-acre) park features attractive flowerbeds, small lakes, playing fields and lawns that slope to the sea, and a totem pole carved by Chief Mungo Martin. **Hours:** Daily dawn-dusk. **Cost:** Free.

 **BUTCHART GARDENS—** see Brentwood Bay p. 200.

CANADIAN FORCES BASE ESQUIMALT NAVAL & MILITARY MUSEUM is 6 km (4 mi.) w. on Esquimalt Rd., then n. on Admirals Rd. to the main gate at Naden. Historic artifacts, documents and photographs relate to the naval and military heritage of the area.

Swan Lake-Christmas Hill Nature Sanctuary / © Don Johnston / age fotostock

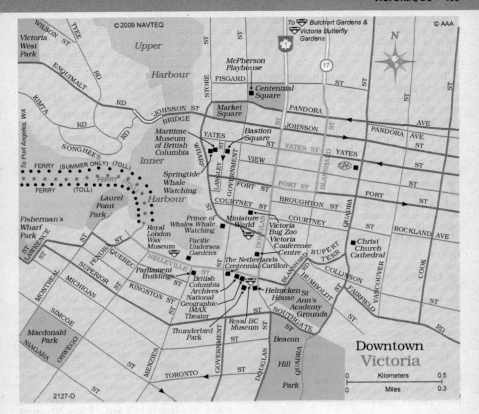

© 2009 NAVTEQ

Victoria
West
Park

Upper

Harbour

McPherson
Playhouse

FISGARD

To Butchart Gardens &
Victoria Butterfly
Gardens

© AAA

N

WILSON ST
TYEE ST
ESQUIMALT RD
KIMTA RD
SONGHEES RD
STORE ST

Centennial
Square

17

JOHNSON ST
BRIDGE

Market
Square

PANDORA

JOHNSON

PANDORA   AVE

AVE

ST

Maritime
Museum
of British
Columbia

YATES

Bastion
Square   ST

YATES ST

YATES

ST

BLANSHARD

To Port Angeles, WA

Inner

WHARF

VIEW

ST

ST

FERRY (SUMMER ONLY) (TOLL)

Springtide
Whale
Watching

LANGLEY

GOVERNMENT

FORT   ST

FORT ST

FORT

ST

FERRY   (TOLL)

Harbour

COURTNEY   ST

BROUGHTON   ST

QUADRA

ROCKLAND   AVE

Laurel
Point
Park

Royal
London
Wax
Museum

Prince of
Whales Whale
Watching

Pacific
Undersea
Gardens

Miniature
World

Victoria
Bug Zoo

COURTNEY

ST

Christ
Church
Cathedral

ST

COOK

Fisherman's
Wharf
Park

PENDRAY
QUEBEC

BELLEVILLE

Parliament
Buildings

KINGSTON   ST

British
Columbia
Archives
National
Geographic
IMAX
Theater

The Netherlands
Centennial Carillon

DOUGLAS

BLANSHARD

Victoria
Conference
Centre

RUPERT
TERR

HUMBOLDT

COLLINSON

FAIRFIELD

VANCOUVER

Helmcken
House   St
Ann's
Academy
Grounds

Thunderbird
Park

Royal BC
Museum

Beacon

SOUTHGATE

LAWRENCE
SUPERIOR
MICHIGAN
MONTREAL
SIMCOE
NIAGARA
OSWEGO
MENZIES
GOVERNMENT
DOUGLAS
QUADRA

Macdonald
Park

TORONTO

Hill

Park

RD

Downtown
Victoria

0   Kilometers   0.5

0   Miles   0.3

2127-D

Photo ID is required. **Time:** Allow 1 hour minimum. **Hours:** Daily 10-3:30, June-Aug.; Mon.-Fri. 10-3:30, rest of year. Closed statutory holidays. **Cost:** $2; $1 (children, students with ID and senior citizens); $5 (family). **Phone:** (250) 363-4312 or (250) 363-5655.

Esquimalt Navy Base Summer Bus Tour departs from the Canadian Forces Base Esquimalt Naval & Military Museum. A 1-hour tour of the base also passes the harbor, where navy warships can be seen. Photo ID is required. **Hours:** Mon.-Fri. 8-3, July-Aug. **Cost:** Free. **Phone:** (250) 363-7060.

CENTRE OF THE UNIVERSE is at 5071 W. Saanich Rd. Housed within the Dominion Astrophysical Observatory, this interpretive center affords visitors a glimpse into the world of astronomy. The facility offers interactive exhibits, theater presentations and a look at the constellations in the Starlab Planetarium. Visitors may tour the 1.8-metre (5-ft.) Plaskett Telescope.

Tours: Guided tours are available. **Time:** Allow 1 hour, 30 minutes minimum. **Hours:** Tues.-Sat. 3:30-11:30, Victoria Day-Labour Day; Tues.-Thurs. 1-4:30, Fri.-Sat. 3-11, day after Labour Day-Sept. 30; Tues.-Fri. 1-4:30, Sat. 10-4:30, Mar. 1-day before Victoria Day; Sat. 10-4:30, rest of year. Closed

Jan. 1-2 and Dec. 24-31. Phone ahead to confirm schedule. **Cost:** $12; $10 (ages 13-18 and 65+); $7 (ages 4-12); free (ages 0-3 when accompanied by a parent); $31 (family, two adults and three children). **Phone:** (250) 363-8262.

CHRIST CHURCH CATHEDRAL is at 911 Quadra St., between Burdett and Rockland sts. The Anglican-Episcopal cathedral is reminiscent of the great Gothic churches of the Middle Ages. Originally founded in 1856, the present cathedral is the third church built on this site. Started in the late 1920s and completed in 1986, it is one of Canada's largest cathedrals. The bells are replicas of those at Westminster Abbey in London, England. A labyrinth is on the grounds. **Hours:** Daily 8:45-5:15. **Cost:** Donations. **Phone:** (250) 383-2714.

CRAIGDARROCH CASTLE is at 1050 Joan Crescent St. The sandstone mansion was built in the late 1880s for Robert Dunsmuir, a Scottish immigrant who attained wealth and fame through politics and coal mining. Dunsmuir died before the 39-room castle was completed. The building later served as a military hospital, a college and a music conservatory.

Visitors can appreciate the castle's stained-glass windows, intricate woodwork, ceiling murals and

Victorian furnishings. There are numerous staircases, but no elevators. A self-guiding tour includes four floors of the castle and an 87-step climb to the tower, which offers stunning views of Victoria, the Strait and the Olympic Mountains.

Time: Allow 1 hour minimum. **Hours:** Daily 9-7, June 15-Labour Day; 10-4:30, rest of year. Closed Jan. 1 and Dec. 25-26. **Cost:** $13.75; $12.75 (ages 65+); $8.75 (ages 13-18 and students with ID); $5 (ages 6-12). **Phone:** (250) 592-5323. ⌂

EMILY CARR HOUSE is at 207 Government St. Built in 1864 a few blocks from the harbor, the house was the birthplace of artist and writer Emily Carr. The Victorian residence has been restored to the ambiance the Carr family experienced in the 1870s. Family possessions, including some of Carr's early pottery, are displayed. **Hours:** Tues.-Sat. 11-4, May-Sept. Last admission is at closing. **Cost:** $6; $5 (ages 6-18, students with ID and senior citizens); $15 (family). **Phone:** (250) 383-5843.

GLENDALE GARDENS & WOODLAND is off Hwy. 17 West Saanich/Quadra exit, then w. to Beaver Lake Rd., following signs to 505 Quayle Rd. Two hectares (5 acres) of educational gardens feature more than 10,000 plant varieties and sculptures. Highlights of the developing site include the Winter Garden and the Takata Japanese Garden. The surrounding 36 hectares (90 acres) include forests, wetlands and a haven for migratory birds.

Time: Allow 1 hour minimum. **Hours:** Mon.-Fri. 8-8, Sat.-Sun. 8-6, May-Sept.; daily 9-4, rest of year. Closed Jan. 1 and Dec. 24-26 and 31. **Cost:** $10; $7.50 (ages 60+ and students with ID); free (ages 0-15). **Phone:** (250) 479-6162. ⌂

GOVERNMENT HOUSE GARDENS is at 1401 Rockland Ave. The grounds in front of the lieutenant governor's residence consist of 5.7 hectares (14 acres) of formal gardens, featuring perennials, herbs, roses, irises, azaleas, rhododendrons and other floral varieties. The property behind the house, a terraced rock garden, covers a 9-hectare (22-acre) rare Garry oak woodland that is native to southeast Vancouver Island. **Hours:** Formal gardens daily dawn-dusk. **Cost:** Free. **Phone:** (250) 387-2080. ⌂

HATLEY PARK NATIONAL HISTORIC SITE is at 2005 Sooke Rd. The 216.5-hectare (565-acre) Hatley Park estate offers a variety of hands-on, educational visitor experiences. With its preserved old-growth forests, heritage gardens and spectacular vistas that overlook the Esquimalt Lagoon and the Juan de Fuca Strait, the centerpiece of this magnificent site is a 40-room Edwardian home built in 1908.

The Hatley Park Museum, part of the historic site, has exhibits reflecting the estate's days as home to the Dunsmuir family who built it, its days as Royal Roads Military College and its current use as the home of Royal Roads University.

Hours: Grounds open daily 10-8, early June-Labour Day; 10-3, rest of year. Museum daily 10-7,

early June-Labour Day; 10-4, rest of year. Guided tours of Hatley Castle are available daily 10-3:15, early June-Labour Day; 11-2:30, rest of year. **Cost:** Grounds and museum free. Hatley Castle tours (includes heritage gardens) May-Sept. $7-$17. Castle tours rest of year $5-$15. Heritage gardens admission May-Sept. $6-$9. Gardens rest of year $3-$4.50. **Phone:** (250) 391-2666 or (866) 241-0674.

LEGISLATIVE ASSEMBLY OF BRITISH COLUMBIA overlooks the Inner Harbour and yacht basin. The seat of British Columbia's legislature, the buildings have elaborately carved facades and are surrounded by 5 hectares (12 acres) of lawns, gardens, fountains and statues of dignitaries. The rooms have mosaic tile floors, rotundas, stained-glass windows, woodcarvings and murals.

Guided tours, conducted in several languages, are offered. Self-guiding tours also are available; a booklet can be picked up at the tour desk. **Hours:** Guided tours are given Mon.-Thurs. every 30 minutes 9-5, Fri.-Sun. 9-7, mid-May through Labour Day; Mon.-Fri. 9-4, rest of year. Phone the tour office to confirm times. **Cost:** Free. **Phone:** (250) 387-3046 for the tour office or (250) 382-1400.

MARITIME MUSEUM OF BRITISH COLUMBIA is at 28 Bastion Sq. The Pacific Northwest's maritime heritage is presented through ship models, figureheads, ships' tools and naval uniforms. Also featured is the 1860 *Tilikum*, an 11-metre (36-ft.) dugout canoe converted to a schooner, which sailed from Victoria to England 1901-04. The museum's 1889 building features one of the oldest operating birdcage elevators in North America.

Time: Allow 1 hour minimum. **Hours:** Daily 9:30-5, mid-June to mid-Sept.; 9:30-4:30, rest of year. Closed Dec. 25. **Cost:** $10; $8 (ages 65+ and students with ID); $5 (ages 6-11); $25 (family). **Phone:** (250) 385-4222.

◆ GEM **MINIATURE WORLD** is in The Fairmont Empress hotel at 649 Humboldt St. Animation, lighting and sound effects enhance more than 80 highly detailed miniature scenes. Displays include a circus, two of the world's largest dollhouses, a Swiss Family Robinson tree house and a futuristic space diorama. Scenes illustrate historic battles, fairy tales, nursery rhymes, "Gulliver's Travels" and novels by Charles Dickens. The Great Canadian Railway exhibit re-creates rail transportation in late 19th-century Canada.

Time: Allow 1 hour minimum. **Hours:** Daily 9-9, mid-May through Sept. 1; 9-5, rest of year. Closed Dec. 25. **Cost:** $13.05; $12.40 (senior citizens); $10.05 (ages 12-17); $8.05 (ages 5-11). **Phone:** (250) 385-9731.

PACIFIC UNDERSEA GARDENS is at 490 Belleville St. An observation room on the sea bottom allows visitors to view native marine life through large underwater windows. **Hours:** Daily 9-8, July-Aug.; 9-7, Apr.-June; 9-5, rest of year. **Cost:** $9.75; $8.75 (ages 65+); $7.75 (ages 12-17); $5.75 (ages 5-11). **Phone:** (250) 382-5717.

POINT ELLICE HOUSE is at 2616 Pleasant St. Built in 1861, the rambling Italianate residence contains many of its original furnishings. Lawns and a restored 19th-century garden surround the house. Self-guiding audiotapes are available.

Time: Allow 30 minutes minimum. **Hours:** Daily 11-5, mid-June through Labour Day; Thurs.-Mon. 11-4, May 1 to mid-June. Schedule varies rest of year; phone ahead. **Cost:** $6; $4 (ages 13-18); $3 (ages 6-12). Tour and tea $23; $12 (ages 6-12). **Phone:** (250) 380-6506. 🍴

PRINCE OF WHALES WHALE WATCHING is at 812 Wharf St. Narrated tours by a marine biologist provide passengers with information about marine life while sitting below cover on board the 19-metre (62-ft.) *Ocean Magic* cruiser. High-speed open-boat tours also are available.

Time: Allow 2 hours, 30 minutes minimum. **Hours:** *Ocean Magic* departures daily at 9, 12:15 and 3:30, May-Oct. Passengers should arrive 30 minutes prior to departure. **Cost:** $95; $85 (ages 13-18 and senior citizens); $75 (ages 5-12). Reservations are required. **Phone:** (250) 383-4882 or (888) 383-4884.

ROYAL BC MUSEUM is on the Inner Harbour at 675 Belleville St. Two floors of displays reflect the human and natural history of British Columbia. An early 1900s frontier town has a theater with silent movies, a saloon, shops and a hotel. The Natural History Gallery showcases the Living Land, Living Sea exhibit with a coastal rain forest display highlighted by live plants and tidal-pool animals as well as a climate change exhibit which explores the province's future climate. The First Peoples Gallery includes an exhibit focusing on the historic Nisga'a agreement and the present-day Nisga'a community, and Haida argillite carvings.

The on-site National Geographic IMAX Theatre offers films to complement the natural and human history theme of the museum as well as other exciting IMAX footage. Special exhibits are featured periodically.

Hours: Museum open daily 9-5. Theater open daily 10-8. Theater schedule varies; phone ahead. Closed Jan. 1 and Dec. 25. **Cost:** Museum $15; $9.50 (ages 6-18, ages 65+ and students ages 19+ with ID); $37.50 (family, two adults and two children). Combination ticket (Museum and IMAX Theatre) $35; $27 (students with ID); $26 (ages 65+); $25 (ages 6-18); $5 (ages 0-5); $108 (family, two adults and two children). Admission may increase for special exhibits. **Phone:** (250) 356-7226 or (888) 447-7977.

British Columbia Archives is at 655 Belleville St. Extensive public and private records are available to those conducting historical, genealogical or other research. Gardens containing native plants surround

the building. **Hours:** The archives are open to the public Mon.-Fri. 10-4. Closed holidays and 1 week in early May. **Cost:** Free. **Phone:** (250) 387-1952.

Helmcken House is next to the Royal BC Museum, in Thunderbird Park. One of the oldest houses in British Columbia still on its original site, the 1852 log structure was the home of John Sebastian Helmcken, a surgeon for Hudson's Bay Co. at Fort Victoria and a Father of Confederation. The restored house displays many original furnishings and a fine collection of period medical instruments.

Time: Allow 30 minutes minimum. **Hours:** Daily noon-4, June 1-Labour Day; by appointment rest of year. Phone ahead to confirm schedule. **Cost:** Free. **Phone:** (250) 356-7226.

The Netherlands Centennial Carillon is at the corner of Government and Belleville sts. The largest carillon in Canada houses 62 bells donated by British Columbians of Dutch origin in celebration of the 1967 Canadian Confederation Centennial and in recognition of Canada's role in the liberation of the Netherlands during World War II.

Hours: Carillon chimes ring hourly. Recitals are held Sat.-Sun. at 3, July-Aug.; Sun. at 3, Apr.-June and Sept.-Dec. Phone ahead to confirm schedule. **Cost:** Free. **Phone:** (250) 356-7226 or (888) 447-7977.

Thunderbird Park is at the corner of Douglas and Belleville sts. on the grounds of the Royal BC Museum. The park's collection of Northwest Coast totem poles was established in 1940, and re-carved via the Totem Restoration Program 1950-1990, when the originals began to decay beyond repair. A new Kwakwaka'wakw pole was carved and raised in 2000. **Hours:** Park open daily dawn-dusk. **Cost:** Free. **Phone:** (250) 356-7226 or (888) 447-7977.

ROYAL LONDON WAX MUSEUM is at 470 Belleville in the Inner Harbour opposite the Legislative Assembly buildings. Housed in the former steamship terminal, the museum features some 300 wax figures in more than 50 scenes. Included are Albert Einstein, Mother Teresa, Martin Luther King, Prince William and Princess Diana. Storytelling guides provide historical background about each figure. Themed exhibits include Royalty Row, Storybook Land, Martyrs of Hope, The Galaxy of Stars and The Chamber of Horrors.

A special exhibit with commentary, The Crown Jewels Theatre, displays replicas of the crown jewels of England. Frozen in Time, a multimedia theater presentation, focuses on the search for the Northwest Passage.

Time: Allow 1 hour minimum. **Hours:** Daily 9-8, May-Aug.; 10-5, rest of year. Closed Dec. 25. **Cost:** $12; $11 (ages 65+); $9.50 (ages 13-19 and military with ID); $6 (ages 6-12); $35 (family). **Phone:** (250) 388-4461 or (877) 929-3228.

SPRINGTIDE WHALE TOURS is at 1207 Wharf St. Depending on the season and in addition to killer whales, visitors also may encounter sea lions; seals; porpoises; humpback, grey and minke whales as well as a variety of birds. Tours are given on a 19-metre (61-ft.) motor yacht as well as on high-speed, open Zodiacs. A harbor tour is available year-round.

Time: Allow 3 hours minimum. **Hours:** Whale-watch tours are given daily at 10 and 2, Apr.-Oct. Other times are available; phone for schedule. **Cost:** Whale-watch tour $99; $95 (ages 65+); $79 (ages 13-18 and students with ID); $69 (ages 3-12). **Phone:** (250) 384-4444 or (800) 470-3474.

UNIVERSITY OF VICTORIA is on McKenzie Ave. at Gordon Head Rd. The 160-hectare (395-acre) campus includes the Mystic Vale Ecological Protection Area, several totems carved by local artists and Finnerty Gardens, known for its collection of more than 200 rhododendron species.

Guided tours of the campus are available; the meeting point is the University Centre. A self-guiding walking tour brochure is available from the MacPherson Library loans desk.

Hours: Guided tours are given Mon.-Sat. at 1, May-Aug.; Mon.-Fri. at 1, rest of year. Closed Jan. 1, Good Friday, Easter Monday, Victoria Day and Dec. 25-31. **Cost:** Free. Reservations are required for tours. **Parking:** $1 per hour. **Phone:** (250) 721-8949.

VICTORIA BUG ZOO is at 631 Courtney St. More than 50 species of tropical insects and spiders from around the world are on display. Highlights include a leaf-cutter ant farm and the giant African millipede. For the more adventurous, the zoo also provides the opportunity for and an environment conducive to a safe bug-handling experience.

Tours: Guided tours are available. **Time:** Allow 30 minutes minimum. **Hours:** Mon.-Sat. 10-6, Sun. 11-6, late June-Aug. 31; Mon.-Sat. 10-5, Sun. 11-5, rest of year. Closed Jan. 1 and Dec. 25. **Cost:** $8; $7 (senior citizens); $6 (ages 13-19); $5 (ages 3-12). **Phone:** (250) 384-2847.

What To Do

Sightseeing

Boat Tours

Sightseers using Victoria as a base for their travels can explore the Gulf Islands and Vancouver by ferry from Swartz Bay, north of Victoria via Hwy. 17; for schedule and toll phone the British Columbia Ferry Service at (250) 386-3431.

Opportunities for whale watching are offered by several boating companies, the oldest of which is Seacoast Expeditions, 146 Kingston St.; phone (250) 383-2254.

Bus and Carriage Tours

Guided tours of the city in red double-decker buses from London enhance Victoria's British atmosphere. Many of these tour operators are found along Belleville and Menzies streets by the harbor.

SAVE Gray Line, 4196 Glanford Ave., (250) 388-6539 or (800) 663-8390, conducts bus tours.

Narrated horse-drawn carriage tours of the city are offered by several companies, including Black Beauty Line Ltd., phone (250) 507-0789; Tallyho, phone (250) 383-5067; and Victoria Carriage Tours, phone (250) 383-2207. All tours leave from the corner of Belleville and Menzies streets.

Driving Tours

The Greater Victoria Visitors Information Centre has information about such scenic routes as Marine Drive along the shoreline, a trip to Sooke Harbour on the west coast and the Malahat Drive, which runs along the east coast and reaches an elevation of 381 metres (1,250 ft.). The trip to Butchart Gardens is one of the most popular drives, following Hwy. 17 and Hwy. 17A through the rural communities and pastoral valleys of the Saanich Peninsula.

Walking Tours

Victoria is the perfect size for visitors keen on walking. A favorite thoroughfare of strollers and shoppers is Government Street, graced by banners and five-globe Victorian lampposts supporting baskets of geraniums and petunias.

Sports and Recreation

The English spirit still is manifest in such games as **lawn bowling** at the corner of Belleville and Douglas streets and **cricket** at Beacon Hill Park. Any notion, however, that Victoria's sports are too staid is dispelled quickly by a **box lacrosse** game. This offspring of the Indian game of *baggataway* is a rough-and-tumble version of field lacrosse confined to a smaller, enclosed area. Canada's Parliament designated boxla, as it also is called, the national sport in 1867. The game is played from April to August at Memorial Arena, 1925 Blanshard.

All-star **wrestling** and **ice hockey,** two other spectator sports that hardly could be considered sedate, also are held at the arena.

Water sports have obvious appeal in this island city. The wide variety of game fish around southern Vancouver Island includes rockfish, lingcod, sole and flounder; fishing licenses are required. Surf **fishing** often yields rewarding catches of salmon and black sea bass. Clamming and oyster harvesting are popular activities on any of the Gulf Islands, which are accessible by ferry from Swartz Bay.

Oak Bay Marina, 1327 Beach Dr., offers fishing charters at an hourly rate. Fishing equipment, a tackle shop and marine store are available; phone (250) 598-3369. Other nearby marinas include Anglers Anchorage Marina, 933 Marchant, Brentwood Bay; North Saanich Marina, 1949 Marina Way, Sidney; and the West Bay Marina, 453 Head St.

Boating is enjoyed in the Strait of Georgia and the Saanich Inlet. Uplands Park on Oak Bay is equipped with boat ramps. Fine beaches border Dallas Road and Beach Drive.

With its scenic coastal location and balmy climate, Victoria offers excellent playing conditions for **golf.** On a peninsula jutting into the Juan de Fuca Strait, Victoria Golf Club is open to members of other clubs.

Other golf clubs include Ardmore (nine holes), 930 Ardmore Dr., North Saanich; Cedar Hill (18 holes), 1400 Derby Rd.; Cordova Bay (18 holes), 5333 Cordova Bay Rd.; Glen Meadows (18 holes), 1050 McTavish Rd.; Green Acres (nine holes), 3970 Metchosin Rd.; Henderson Park (nine holes), 2291 Cedar Hill Crossroad; Mount Douglas (nine holes), 4225 Blenkinsop Rd.; Olympic View Golf Course (18 holes), 643 Latoria Rd.; Prospect Lake (nine holes), 4633 Prospect Lake Rd.; and Royal Oak Golf Club (nine holes), 540 Marsett Pl.

Many parks are scattered throughout Victoria and its surrounding municipalities of Oak Bay, Saanich and Esquimalt. Some offer **swimming,** such as Elk/Beaver Lake Park, Island View Beach Park, Mount Work Park, Thetis Lake Park and Willows Beach Park. Swimmers also might wish to try the Crystal Pool in Central Park.

Hiking, nature and horse trails are found at several parks. For more information contact Victoria Downtown Park; phone (250) 361-0600. Bamberton Provincial Park *(see Recreation Chart and the AAA/CAA Western Canada & Alaska CampBook)* offers developed recreational facilities, including **camping.**

Swan Lake-Christmas Hill Nature Sanctuary, 6.5 kilometres (4 mi.) north via the Patricia Bay Highway, can be explored by hiking trails and floating walkways weaving through the area. Excellent views of Victoria and the sea are at Mount Douglas, Mount Tolmie and Beacon Hill Park.

Shopping

Lined with shops carrying English tweeds and fine china, Government Street maintains Victoria's heritage as a trading post of the British Empire. Such shops as E.A. Morris Tobacconist have distinguished Government Street since the 19th century. Established in 1833, Rogers' Chocolate Shop is a Victoria institution that counts British royalty in its clientele. The Rogers' factory, behind the store at 913 Government St., still produces its renowned bittersweet chocolate according to a guarded recipe.

Shoppers determined to bring home something other than a few extra pounds might want to explore the craft and specialty shops in the renovated squares and malls off Government Street. More than 30 quaint stores and restaurants in revitalized old buildings highlight Market Square, bounded by Johnson, Pandora and Store streets.

Trounce Alley, in the downtown core, is a hideaway of eclectic shops. Shops of mid-19th-century architecture display modern items in Bastion Square, once a hangout for prospectors and drifters. An attractive shopping arcade is in Centennial Square off Douglas Street. Nootka Court between Courtney and Humboldt streets contains small arts and crafts shops.

Popular items available in Victoria include hand-woven woolens from Ireland and England, hand-knit Cowichan Indian sweaters, Eskimo jade sculpture and Northwest Indian masks and prints. The Bay department stores, 1150 and 3125 Douglas St., sell authentic Cowichan sweaters. Also in Victoria are Hillside Shopping Centre, 1644 Hillside Rd.; Mayfair Shopping Centre, 3147 Douglas St.; and Sears, 3190 Shelbourne St.

In keeping with its Victorian image, Victoria has more than 50 antique shops. Many are found along Government and Fort streets and Oak Bay Avenue.

Performing Arts

McPherson Playhouse in Centennial Square is the center of Vancouver Island's regional and professional theater. The restored old theater regularly presents noontime concerts and musical comedy productions in the evening; phone (250) 386-6121 or (888) 717-6121. The Pacific Opera Victoria, (250) 385-0222, performs at the Royal Theatre.

The Royal Theatre on Broughton Street is also the home of the Victoria Symphony Orchestra, (250) 385-6515, which offers a pop and masterworks series September through May. The Victoria Conservatory of Music sometimes offers performances; phone (250) 386-5311.

Comedy revues and music hall shows also are staged frequently at the Belfry, (250) 385-6815, 1291 Gladstone, and the Royal Theatre, (250) 386-6121, 805 Broughton. The University of Victoria Auditorium on Finnerty Road also presents various cultural events; phone (250) 721-8480. Butchart Gardens mounts musical stage shows during the summer. Kaleidoscope Theatre, an open-air theater

at the Inner Harbour, also offers summer productions.

Top-name entertainers, rock groups and other performers draw large audiences to Memorial Arena, 1925 Blanshard. A carillon at the Parliament Buildings can be heard daily at 3 during the summer. The Royal BC Museum's National Geographic IMAX Theatre offers big-screen films complementing the museum's natural and human history themes; phone (250) 356-7226.

Special Events

As a city of traditions, Victoria celebrates many events and festivals year after year. Victoria Day, a Canadian national holiday, launches a week of festivities highlighted by a parade. The weekend following Victoria Day features the classic Swiftsure Race, which has drawn an armada of more than 450 sailboats from all over the world since 1930. The Highland Games take place in mid-May.

The performing arts provide a theme for the Victoria Harbour Festival the last week in May. Witness thousands of colorful paper lanterns, acrobats, musicians and costumed performers on the last day of July at the Luminara Victoria, a festival of lights held in Beacon Hill Park. Boating enthusiasts will enjoy the Classic Boat Festival at Inner Harbour from late August to early September.

Autumn shows off its best colors along the rural Saanich Peninsula, where the Saanich Fair has been held in early September for more than a century. Fall's lower temperatures provide an energy boost for several major sports events, including the Victoria Open PGA Tournament Players Series and the Royal Victoria Marathon.

The Victoria Vicinity

BRENTWOOD BAY (H-10)

BUTCHART GARDENS is 2 km (1.2 mi.) s. on W. Saanich Rd., then w. to 800 Benvenuto Ave. The 22-hectare (55-acre) site contains the Rose Garden, Japanese Garden, Italian Garden, as well as the Star Pond and Ross Fountain. The Sunken Garden was created by the Butcharts on the site of their depleted limestone quarry.

The spring season brings azaleas, tulips, daffodils and other delicate blossoms. Breathtaking roses, annuals and perennials bloom in summer, while bursts of colorful foliage appear in autumn; subtle colored lighting illuminates the gardens June 15 through September 15.

July through August, nightly entertainment is offered with fireworks displays Saturday nights. The sparkle of holiday lights and decorations complement the colorful berries on shrubs and trees from Dec. 1 to Jan. 6 during Christmas at Butcharts. An

outdoor skating rink, with skate rental, also is available in Waterwheel Square.

Time: Allow 2 hours minimum. **Hours:** Gardens open daily at 9; (at 1 on Dec. 25). Closing times vary depending on the season; phone ahead. **Cost:** June 15-Sept. 30, $29.50; $14.75 (ages 13-17); $3 (ages 5-12). Admission Mar. 21-June 14, $27.50; $13.75 (ages 13-17); $2 (ages 5-12). Admission Jan. 1-6 and in Dec. $24.75; $12.50 (ages 13-17); $3 (ages 5-12). Admission in Oct. $24.75; $12.50 (ages 13-17); $2 (ages 5-12). Admission Jan. 15-Mar. 20, $22; $11 (ages 13-17); $2 (ages 5-12). Admission in Nov. $19; $9.50 (ages 13-17); $2 (ages 5-12). Admission rest of year $16.25; $8.25 (ages 13-17); $2.00 (ages 5-12). **Phone:** (250) 652-5256 or (888) 824-7313. [T]

VICTORIA BUTTERFLY GARDENS is 2 km (1.2 mi.) s. at jct. Saanich and Keating Cross rds. to 1461 Benvenuto Ave. This 1,110-square-metre (12,000-sq.-ft.) indoor tropical garden was designed specifically for the housing and breeding of more than 35 exotic butterfly and moth species. Guided tours and a videotape explain the transformations the butterflies undergo during their life cycle. More than 300 pupae are imported each week and displayed in the Emerging Room.

Up to 2,000 butterflies—from the 1.3-centimetre-long (.5-in.) Glasswing to the 30.5-centimetre-long (1-ft.) Atlas Moth—fly free among tropical plants and flowers, including an orchid exhibit and a carnivorous bog. Water falls into a stream that is home to fish, tropical ducks and such rare birds as the South African turacos.

Time: Allow 1 hour minimum. **Hours:** Daily 9-5:30, May 1-Labour Day; 9:30-4:30, Mar.-Apr. and day after Labour Day-Oct. 31; 10-4, first weekend in Jan., in Feb. and Nov.-Dec. Phone ahead to confirm schedule. **Cost:** All-day admission $12.50; $11.50 (ages 13-18, ages 65+ and students with ID); $6.50 (ages 5-12). **Phone:** (250) 652-3822 or (877) 722-0272. ⓣ

FORT RODD HILL AND FISGARD LIGHTHOUSE NATIONAL HISTORIC SITES (I-10)

Fourteen kilometres (9 mi.) west of Victoria via Hwy. 1A, Fort Rodd Hill was a coastal artillery fort 1895-1956. Of interest are the loophole walls, underground magazines, artillery stores, command posts, barracks and gun and searchlight emplacements. Audiotape and videotape presentations, along with period rooms, depict life at the fort. The 1860 Fisgard Lighthouse, restored to its 1873 appearance, was the first built on this part of the coast. Still operational, the lighthouse has two floors of historical exhibits. A nature trail follows the paths formerly used by soldiers. Historical exhibits also are featured. Picnic facilities are available.

Note: The lighthouse is closed for renovation; reopening is planned for April 2010. Allow 1 hour, 30 minutes minimum. Park open daily 10-5:30, Feb. 15-Oct. 31; 9-4:30, rest of year. Exhibits daily 10-5, Mar.-Oct.; 9-4, rest of year. Closed Dec. 25. Admission (includes fort and lighthouse) $3.90; $3.40 (ages 65+); $1.90 (ages 6-16). Phone (250) 478-5849.

SAANICHTON (H-9) elev. 58 m/194′

HERITAGE ACRES (SAANICH HISTORICAL ARTIFACTS SOCIETY) is off Hwy. 17, e. on Island View Dr., then n. to 7321 Lochside Dr. The society is dedicated to maintaining artifacts from the area's rural past on 12 hectares (29 acres) of parkland. A museum exhibits historic household items, furnishings and farm equipment. Also part of the complex are a blacksmith's shop, a sawmill, nature trails and a one-room log cabin. Rides are offered aboard model trains.

Time: Allow 30 minutes minimum. **Hours:** Daily 9-4, mid-June to mid-Sept.; 9-noon, rest of year. Closed Dec. 25. **Cost:** Donations. Admission is charged during events. **Phone:** (250) 652-5522. ⊞

SIDNEY (H-10) pop. 11,315, elev. 9 m/30′

Salish Indians were the earliest known inhabitants of the area now called Sidney. Incorporated into a town in 1967, Sidney is known for its fishing and waterfront activity. Picnicking, beachcombing and camping are popular at Sidney Spit Marine Provincial Park *(see the AAA/CAA Western Canada & Alaska CampBook)*.

Saanich Peninsula Chamber of Commerce: 201-2453 Beacon Ave., P.O. Box 2014, Sidney, BC, Canada V8L 1X7. **Phone:** (250) 656-3616.

BRITISH COLUMBIA AVIATION MUSEUM is at Victoria Airport at 1910 Norseman Rd. Displays of memorabilia and aircraft include World War II planes and bush planes, a model plane exhibit, photographs and aircraft engines. **Tours:** Guided tours are available. **Time:** Allow 1 hour minimum. **Hours:** Daily 10-4 May-Sept.; 11-3, rest of year. Closed Jan. 1 and Dec. 25. **Cost:** $7; $5 (ages 66+); $3 (ages 13-18). **Phone:** (250) 655-3300.

MINERAL WORLD is at 9891 Seaport Pl. An interpretive center offers hands-on exhibits that use minerals, crystals and fossils to demonstrate principles of earth science. Visitors may search for semiprecious gemstones and pan for gold in the Scratch Patch.

Time: Allow 30 minutes minimum. **Hours:** Daily 9-9, July-Aug.; Mon.-Fri. 9:30-6, Sun. 11-5:30 in June and Sept.; Mon.-Fri. 9:30-5:30, Sun. 11-5, rest of year. Closed Dec. 25. **Cost:** Interpretive center free. Panning for gold, gemstones and shells $6-$10; panning for gold only $3. **Phone:** (250) 655-4367.

SHAW OCEAN DISCOVERY CENTRE is at 9811 Seaport Pl. The main concentration of this aquarium and marine education centre is the Salish Sea ecosystem. Visitors can examine plankton; see fish, invertebrates and plant life in aquarium habitats; and get up-close to some of the sea creatures in touch pools. **Time:** Allow 1 hour minimum. **Hours:** Daily 10-6, June-July; 10-5, rest of year. Phone ahead to confirm schedule. **Cost:** $12; $6 (ages 6-17). **Phone:** (250) 656-7511.

SIDNEY MUSEUM & ARCHIVES is at 2423 Beacon Ave. The early lives of Sidney and North Saanich pioneers are portrayed through photographs and artifacts. **Time:** Allow 1 hour minimum. **Hours:** Daily 10-4; closed Jan 1 and Dec. 25-26. **Cost:** Donations. **Phone:** (250) 655-6355.

SOOKE (H-9) pop. 9,704, elev. 38 m/125′

A natural harbor off the Juan de Fuca Strait, Sooke was discovered and claimed by the Spanish in 1790. The area, soon traded to the British by treaty, was named after a local Indian tribe, T'Sooke. It is a popular fishing site and the center of a large forest industry. A scenic portion of Hwy. 14 runs 43 kilometres (27 mi.) east from Sooke to Victoria.

Sooke Travel InfoCentre: 2070 Phillips Rd., Box 774, Sooke, BC, Canada V9Z 0Y3. **Phone:** (250) 642-6351 or (866) 888-4748.

SOOKE REGION MUSEUM & VISITOR CENTRE is 1 km (.6 mi.) e. on Hwy. 14 at 2070 Phillips Rd. Exhibits about First Nations peoples, early settlers and industrialization illustrate the history and economy of the west coast region. The 1870 Moss Cottage depicts late 19th-century family life, and visitors can see a 1910 lighthouse relocated from Cape Scott on Vancouver Island's northern tip. Documentary films are shown. In the summer salmon barbecues are scheduled; reservations are required.

Tours: Guided tours are available. **Time:** Allow 30 minutes minimum. **Hours:** Daily 9-5. Closed Jan. 1 and Dec. 25. **Cost:** Museum by donations. Moss Cottage $2; $1 (ages 0-12 and students with

ID). Lighthouse tours $3; $1.50 (ages 0-12 and students with ID). Hours and rates may vary; phone ahead. **Phone:** (250) 642-6351 or (866) 888-4748.

VIEW ROYAL (H-9) pop. 8,768, elev. 22 m/72'

CRAIGFLOWER NATIONAL HISTORIC SITE is at 110 Island Hwy. at jct. Admirals Rd. Built in 1856 by the Hudson's Bay Co. on an original homestead, the farmhouse is a fine example of early Georgian architecture. The heavy oak door reinforced with iron studs is a reminder of the British class system. A kitchen garden complements the atmosphere. The schoolhouse, said to be the oldest in western Canada, was built by the Craigflower farmhouse workers for their children.

Time: Allow 30 minutes minimum. **Hours:** Daily 10-4, May-Sept.; by reservation rest of year. **Cost:** $6; $4 (ages 6-18 and 65+). **Phone:** (250) 386-1606.

Craigdarroch Castle / © Eero Sorila

This ends listings for the Victoria Vicinity.
The following page resumes the alphabetical listings of cities in British Columbia.

VIEW ROYAL—*see Victoria p. 202.*

WARDNER (D-12)

KOOTENAY TROUT HATCHERY is 8 km (5 mi.) n. on the e. side of the Kootenay River at 4522 Fenwick Rd. The facility raises 3 million trout annually. An aquarium contains fish species raised at the hatchery, including the rare white sturgeon. Displays explain fish raising. An outside moat holds large rainbow trout. **Time:** Allow 30 minutes minimum. **Hours:** Mon.-Fri. 8-4, May 1-Labour Day; 8-3:30, rest of year. **Cost:** Donations. **Phone:** (250) 429-3214.

WEST KELOWNA—*see Okanagan Valley p. 145.*

WEST VANCOUVER—*see Vancouver p. 187.*

WHISTLER (G-12)
pop. 9,248, elev. 640 m/2,009′

Whistler would be a special place even without the whole enchilada it offers when it comes to winter sports. It would be special without the superb system of hiking and mountain biking trails that provide outdoor activity when the sun is warm and the snow isn't swirling. And it would be special without the amenities—all sorts of lodgings from basic to luxury, plenty of restaurants (and a few of culinary distinction), a nice selection of specialty shops, evening entertainment from mild to wild—that combine to create this covers-every-base active vacation destination.

The reason why has a lot to do with an old adage: location, location, location. About 2 hours north of Vancouver, Whistler snuggles in a Coast Mountains valley amid a cluster of shimmering small lakes, the reflection of forested slopes etched on their surfaces. Rivers rush through steep-walled canyons. Waterfalls plunge. The stark white of glacier ice contrasts with the black of mountain peaks, framed against a brilliantly blue sky. The wilderness is rugged and unspoiled, the air bracingly fresh. Given such a spectacular setting, it's easy to see why it has become one of Canada's best all-season resorts.

Of course Whistler will be in the world spotlight during the Olympic Winter Games Feb. 12-28, 2010, and the Paralympic Winter Games Mar. 12-21, 2010. National partners along with the Vancouver Organizing Committee (VANOC) include the Lil'wat, Musqueam, Squamish and Tsleil-Waututh First Nations tribes.

Alpine skiing events take place on the challenging downhill runs of Whistler Creekside; the bobsleigh, luge and skeleton competitions happen at the Whistler Sliding Centre on Blackcomb Mountain. Callaghan Valley's approximately 15 kilometres (9 miles) of competition trails is the location for cross-country skiing and biathlon events. Three stadiums are on hand to hold throngs of cheering spectators. Nightly Victory Ceremonies presentations take place at Whistler Village Square, which also will be the

site of the Paralympic Winter Games Closing Ceremony.

But Whistler is a pretty exciting place even without all the Olympics hoopla, and getting there is part of the fun. From Vancouver, the major road link is the Sea-to-Sky Highway (Hwy. 99). The approximately 2-hour drive offers a full plate of scenic views as the highway climbs from a coastal rain forest environment in the vicinity of Horseshoe Bay to the rugged mountain landscapes around Whistler. Between Horseshoe Bay and Squamish the road runs along the eastern edge of Howe Sound, punctuated by a series of fiords. From a distance, islands in the bay look like plump green mounds floating on water that is invitingly blue in sunny weather and brooding gray on overcast days.

Just south of Squamish water is left behind as the highway veers inland. If you want to take a break or need to make a pit stop before reaching Whistler, there are gas stations and a scattering of fast-food outlets at the intersection of Hwy. 99 and Cleveland Road. Past Squamish, Hwy. 99 twists and turns around tree-covered granite crags and sheer rock faces that rise almost straight up from the side of the road. Be sure to pull off and stop at the designated viewpoints; great views are guaranteed.

Note: The major road link between Vancouver and Whistler, the Sea-to-Sky Highway has undergone a widening and safety improvement project to accommodate the influx of Winter Olympics visitors. It's always a good idea to check road conditions before heading to Whistler; for information and traffic updates phone (877) 472-3399.

Whistler has no grand entrance; there are just two primary access roads off Hwy. 99 (Village Gate Drive and Lorimer Road). Whistler Village may seem small, but it's compact. Sitting at the base of Whistler Mountain's ski runs, this is where lots of hotels, restaurants and shops are concentrated. Blackcomb Way divides Whistler Village from the Upper Village, which lies at the base of Blackcomb Mountain's ski runs. Distinctions are pretty much a moot point, although the Upper Village tends to have more upscale accommodations and Whistler Village a livelier scene after dark.

You can walk between the two villages in about 5 minutes along Fitzsimmons Trail, which crosses burbling Fitzsimmons Creek via a covered bridge. Branching off Fitzsimmons Trail is Bridge Meadows Trail, a pleasant walk through the woods that follows the creek and ends up near the new Squamish Lil'wat Cultural Centre *(see attraction listing).* Pick up a copy of the tear-off Whistler walking map at your hotel's front desk, fold it up and stash it in your pocket.

Whistler Mountain and Blackcomb Mountain are Whistler's twin peaks. Each mountain has more than 1,524 metres (5,000 ft.) of vertical rise and more than 100 marked runs that are serviced by multiple lifts; together they offer more than 3,238 hectares (8,000 acres) of ski-worthy terrain. Challenge your thighs on downhill runs, negotiate spectacular alpine bowls or embark on a cross-country trek through deep powder. You can even ski on a glacier. There are lessons and instruction for every skill level, all sorts of equipment rentals and a variety of ski packages to choose from. If skiing doesn't strike your fancy, go snowshoeing, snowboarding, ice skating or snowmobiling. And if you're not the active sort, sit back and relax under a comfy blanket with a mug of hot chocolate on a Blackcomb Mountain sleigh ride. Even active sorts would enjoy this.

North America's first gondola connecting two mountain peaks, the Peak 2 Peak Gondola opened at Whistler-Blackcomb Resort in December 2008. The gondola's passenger cabins travel the 4.4-kilometre (2.7-mi.) distance between the two towers at the summit of Whistler and Blackcomb mountains in 11 minutes, allowing skiers to take advantage of cruising both mountains in the same day. Each gondola cabin holds up to 28 people, and two of them feature glass floors for a dizzying bird's-eye view of Fitzsimmons Valley 435 metres (1,427 ft.) below. Purchase of a regular lift ticket includes gondola transportation.

But Whistler isn't just about winter sports. Summer is prime time for hiking, mountain biking, windsurfing and canoeing, among other activities. Ski lifts take hikers up the two mountains to explore trails free of snow, but if you'd rather go down a different path, walk to Lost Lake. It takes about 30 minutes to get there from Whistler Village (trail access is off Lorimer Road), a good jaunt if you want to leave the hustle and bustle behind for an afternoon.

This tranquil lake is surrounded by Lost Lake Park's evergreen forests, with lovely views of mountains in the distance. The shallow water makes for good swimming on warm days. Numerous hiking trails crisscross this wooded area. There's no parking at the lake, but free shuttle bus service departs from the Gondola Transit Exchange on Blackcomb Way in July and August.

Walkers, hikers, cyclists and inline skaters all take advantage of the paved Valley Trail, which wends its way for some 30.5 kilometres (19 mi.) around the greater Whistler area, connecting parks, residential neighborhoods and the villages. It's a popular commuter biking route.

Adrenaline junkies head to Whistler Mountain Bike Park, a lift-accessed mountain biking haven. The terrain here covers the bases from gently banked trails through a lush coastal forest environment to single-track trails twisting in a series of tight turns to death-defying descents down the side of steep rock faces (which sounds a bit like skiing on wheels). Access is by lift tickets or park passes; bikes and accessories can be rented. The park is open from mid-May to mid-October.

More exhilarating thrills come by way of Ziptrek Ecotours. The Bear Tour (Ziptrek's original adventure, and the one to try if you're a zipline neophyte) propels riders along steel cables connected by a network of suspension bridges and boardwalks. You'll see vistas of temperate rain forest in the valley between Whistler and Blackcomb mountains from a giddy aerial perspective and at speeds up to 80 kilometres (50 mi.) per hour. The tours operate year-round in all weather conditions; reservations are highly advised. For additional information phone (604) 935-0001 or (866) 935-0001.

With four championship courses, Whistler's got some very good golf. The Whistler Golf Club, (604) 932-3280 or (800) 376-1777, is the first course in Canada designed by Arnold Palmer. Robert Trent Jones Jr. was the course architect for the Fairmont Chateau Whistler Golf Club, (877) 938-2092, at The Fairmont Chateau Whistler. The Golden Bear designed the Nicklaus North Golf Course, (604) 938-9898 or (800) 386-9898. Big Sky Golf and Country Club, (604) 894-6106 or (800) 668-7900, is near Pemberton, about a 25-minute drive north of Whistler. With a Bob Cupp-designed layout along the Green River, you can be assured that water will come into play.

For pure sightseeing fun, take the Whistler Village Gondola up Whistler Mountain. The bird's-eye views of alpine lakes, meadows full of wildflowers (in summertime) and mountain slopes from the enclosed gondola are breathtaking. The ride up takes about 25 minutes. Once at the top, hike backcountry trails or have a leisurely lunch at the Roundhouse Lodge, a cool 1,850 metres (6,069 ft.) above sea level, while taking in the scenery all around you. More intrepid souls can continue ascending on the Peak Chair to the 2,182-metre (7,160-ft.) level, where a 360-degree panorama of the Coast Mountains awaits.

And what do you do après skiing or otherwise testing your physical endurance? You stroll around Whistler Village. It's pedestrian-only, it's done in the style of a German mountain village, and it's *cute*. In winter the atmosphere is all woolen caps, puffy ski parkas and oversize mittens; summer brings out the hanging flower baskets and umbrella-shaded tables for outdoor cafe dining. Mogul's Coffee House, next to the drugstore at Village Square, is a funky little place to hang out for a spell.

Four large day-use lots between the two villages offer free parking. Whistler and Valley Express (WAVE) public buses operated by BC Transit provide service to the greater area. Various bus lines serve the resort; shuttle lines 5 and 6 are the most useful if you're staying in or near Whistler Village. The fare is $2; $1.50 (ages 65+ and students); free (ages 0-6). Exact change is required. WaveCards that are good for multiple rides can be purchased at the Whistler Visitor Centre, 4320 Gateway Dr. (in Whistler Village).

Tourism Whistler: 4230 Gateway Dr., Whistler, BC V0N 1B4. **Phone:** (604) 935-3357 or (877) 991-9988.

The Vancouver 2010 Information Centre, 4365 Blackcomb Way, has lots of Olympics-related information and staff members who can answer your questions. The center is open daily 11-5.

Shopping areas: With all kinds of specialty boutiques and eateries, Whistler Village is where it's at. Whistler's Marketplace (entrance off Lorimer Road) is the main shopping center. It has a ski lodge ambiance and retailers like the Escape Route, which carries a full lineup of outdoor recreation wear and accessories—body wear, head wear, hand wear, footwear, snowshoes, backpacks, you name it. Let kids loose in the Great Glass Elevator Candy Shop and its head-turning display of sweets. It just may be enough to drive you to the more adult-oriented Upper Village Market, where you can stock up on gourmet groceries (they'll also deliver to your hotel room).

Also in the Upper Village is Snowflake (in The Fairmont Chateau Whistler), with a selection of Canadian-designed fur and leather jackets, cashmere sweaters, scarves, shawls, boots and accessories for women. Bring lots of money. Back in Whistler Village, New Agers will want to waft into The Oracle (on Main Street) and check out the jewelry, candles, incense and gifts. Tarot card and palm readings are given, or you can give in to a relaxing reiki massage.

The Whistler Village Art Gallery exhibits contemporary paintings, sculpture and art and has two locations, in the Four Seasons Resort Whistler and at the Hilton Whistler Resort & Spa's Gallery Row. Also at the Hilton is the Black Tusk Gallery, which has a collection of masks, sculptures, totems and other objects created by Northwest Coast First Nations artists. Mountain Galleries at the Fairmont, in The Fairmont Chateau Whistler, exhibits museum-quality work—paintings, glass pieces, bronze sculptures, stone carvings—by respected Canadian artists.

About an hour south of Whistler on Hwy. 99 in Britannia Beach is the CRS Trading Post. The wood and soapstone carvings, silver jewelry, spirit masks, jade pieces, handcrafted walking sticks, moccasins and other items are created by British Columbia First Nations artists. Look for the rocks displaying hand-painted scenes by well-known local artist Ken Skoda. It's a good stop on your way back down Hwy. 99.

Nightlife: Whistler's a family-oriented kind of place, but that doesn't mean it lacks hotspots for those itching to get down and *party*. Maxx Fish, below the Amsterdam Cafe in Village Square, has plush booths and plasma-screen TVs, plus a light show choreographed to the slammin' beats cooked up by resident and visiting DJs. A similar uninhibited mood and young, good-looking crowd prevails at Tommy Africa's, not far away on Gateway Drive next to the taxi loop.

Garfinkels, on Main Street in Whistler Village, throws club night bashes on different days of the week; locals and visitors alike flock to "Happy Thursdays," and Saturday is another big party night. The music is DJ dance mixes, augmented by occasional live hip-hop shows. "Garf's" also has VIP hosts and table service, so reservations are a good idea; phone (604) 932-2323. Also in the village is

Buffalo Bills, a high-energy nightspot that packs 'em in with drink specials, a huge dance floor and a mix of mainstream and classic rock.

The Savage Beagle, in Whistler Village near Starbucks, has two levels: a relatively sedate upstairs lounge serving all sorts of cocktails, fresh-squeezed juice martinis and wines by the glass, and a downstairs dance floor where DJs pump up the volume. The après-ski crowd hangs out here.

On the other hand, if crowded clubs and ear-splitting music isn't your cup of tea, you could catch a movie at the Village 8 Cinemas in Whistler Village. Or better yet, pick up a to-go pie at Avalanche Pizza (locals say it's the best in town) and chill out in your room, because you just might want to save your energy for the slopes.

BLACKCOMB SLEIGH RIDES depart from Base II on Blackcomb Mountain, at the end of Glacier Dr. Fifty- to 60-minute scenic sleigh rides through Blackcomb's wooded countryside stop at a warming cabin for a cup of hot chocolate. Lunch, dinner and other sleigh ride options also are available. Carriage rides replace the sleigh rides in summer.

Hours: One-hour Blackcomb trips depart daily on the hour 5-8, late Nov.-Mar. 31. Carriage rides are available late June-Labour Day. **Cost:** Fare $55; $45 (ages 13-17); $35 (ages 3-12). **Phone:** (604) 932-8765.

SQUAMISH LIL'WAT CULTURAL CENTRE is at 4584 Blackcomb Way, just s. of Whistler's Upper Village. Conceived as a joint venture between the Squamish and Lil'wat First Nations, this facility is a showcase meant to share and preserve the culture and heritage of these two peoples. The spectacular building, with its rounded contours, was constructed to resemble a traditional Squamish longhouse and a Lil'wat *istken* (an earthen dwelling with a fire pit). Whistler and Blackcomb mountains are on view from the outdoor deck.

Inside, the Great Hall has soaring 22-foot ceilings, cedar wood walls and beautiful polished stone floors inlaid with different patterns. Among the exhibits are two Squamish canoes, traditional clothing and regalia, wall weavings, textiles and baskets. Visitors can watch artists at work and learn how to make a craft. Make sure you see the 15-minute film "Where Rivers, Mountains and People Meet," which provides some fascinating historical and cultural context to what is on display.

Parking is available in Day Lot 4 adjacent to the center. **Time:** Allow 1 hour minimum. **Hours:** Daily 9:30-5; winter and holiday hours are subject to change. **Cost:** $18; $13.50 (college students with ID); $11 (ages 13-18); $8 (ages 6-12). **Phone:** (866) 441-7522. ⓘ

WHISTLER AIR SERVICES is 3 km (1.9 mi.) n. on Hwy. 99, following signs. The company offers 30-minute to 2-hour floatplane tours over glaciers, ice caps or alpine lakes. **Hours:** Trips depart daily Apr.-Nov. (weather permitting). **Cost:** $135-$249; half-price (ages 0-11 with two adults). Reservations are required. **Phone:** (604) 932-6615 or (888) 806-2299.

RECREATIONAL ACTIVITIES
Mountain Biking

- **Whistler Mountain Bike Park** is at the base of Whistler Mountain. Other activities are offered. **Hours:** Daily 10-8, June 1-early Sept.; 10-5, early Sept.-early Oct. **Phone:** (604) 932-3434 or (866) 218-9690.

Skiing

- **Whistler/Blackcomb Mountain** is on Hwy. 99. Other activities are offered. **Hours:** Whistler daily mid-Nov. to mid-Apr. Blackcomb mid-Nov. to early June. **Phone:** (604) 932-3141 or (800) 766-0449.

White-water Rafting

- **Canadian Outback Adventures** departs from various locations in Whistler. Other activities are available. **Hours:** Tours daily 9-5, May-Sept. Shuttles depart at 7:30, 10:15 and 1. **Phone:** (604) 921-7250 or (800) 565-8735.

- **Whistler River Adventures** departs from 4165 Springs Ln. at the base of the Whistler Mountain gondola in Whistler Village. Other activities are offered. **Hours:** Trips depart daily 8-8, mid-May through Labour Day. **Phone:** (604) 932-3532 or (888) 932-3532.

Ziplines

- **WildPlay Element Park Whistler** is at 4293 Mountain Square, Unit 218. Other activities are offered. **Hours:** Daily 9-5:30, June-Sept.; 10-4, rest of year. Phone ahead to confirm schedule. **Phone:** (604) 932-4086 or (888) 297-2222.

WILLIAMS LAKE (G-5) pop. 10,744

The rush for gold brought prospectors to the heart of the Cariboo in the 1860s, but it was the 1920s Canadian Railway push that put Williams Lake on the map. Cattle ranching and timber production now are the economic mainstays. Twenty kilometres (12 mi.) north of Williams Lake, Bull Mountain Trails offers 30 kilometres (19 mi.) of trails for cross-country skiing, hiking and mountain biking.

Williams Lake and District Chamber of Commerce: 1660 S. Broadway, Williams Lake, BC, Canada V2G 2W4. **Phone:** (250) 392-5025 or (877) 967-5253.

MUSEUM OF THE CARIBOO CHILCOTIN is at 113 N. Fourth Ave. Highlights include the BC Cowboys Hall of Fame and displays portraying the ranching and rodeo history of the Cariboo Chilcotin region. Artifacts and photographs depict the lifestyles of cowboys and ranchers as well as First Nations peoples. **Time:** Allow 30 minutes minimum. **Hours:** Mon.-Sat. 10-4, June-Aug.; Tues.-Sat. 11-4, rest of year. Closed Jan. 1, Good Friday and Dec. 25. **Cost:** $2; free (ages 0-12). **Phone:** (250) 392-7404.

SCOUT ISLAND NATURE CENTER is off Hwy. 97 just e. of jct. Hwy. 20, s. on McKenzie Ave., then e.

on Borland Rd. Nature trails lead to views of Williams Lake. The island and marsh are prime nesting grounds for migratory birds. A nature house offers interactive displays, a marsh aquarium and a beehive. A viewing platform on the roof provides a vista of the marsh and valley. Walking trails, interpretive signs and an arboretum are on-site.

Hours: Grounds daily 8-dusk. Nature house Mon.-Wed. 9-5, Thurs.-Fri. 9-6, Sat.-Sun. 1-4, May-Aug. Phone ahead to confirm schedule. **Cost:** Donations. **Phone:** (250) 398-8532.

YALE (C-7) pop. 186

Settled at the southern entrance to Fraser Canyon, Yale was a major steamship port during the gold rush. The town was established in 1848 as a Hudson's Bay Co. fort, taking its name from the commander of Fort Langley. After gold was discovered on Hill's Bar in 1858, Yale's population swelled to 30,000. In later years the number dwindled to 200. Several buildings from the mid-1800s still stand, and a pioneer cemetery contains Victorian monuments to early settlers.

The Alexandra Suspension Bridge, 22 kilometres (14 mi.) north of town, was constructed in 1863 to ferry miners across the Fraser River. From the bridge, which was rebuilt in 1926 with the original foundations, the original wagon road to the Cariboo goldfields is visible. A hiking trail leading to the nearby Spirit Caves offers views of the canyon.

YALE HISTORIC SITE is at 31187 Douglas St. The museum displays artifacts about mining, paddlewheelers, the Canadian Pacific Railway, early settlers and the First Nations. The Church of St. John the Divine has served the area since it was built in 1863. Guided walking tours of the old townsite are offered in the summer. Gold panning instructions and trips also are available.

Hours: Daily 10-5, early May-Sept. 30. **Cost:** Museum $5; $4.50 (ages 65+); $3 (ages 6-18); $14 (family, two adults and two children ages 0-17). **Phone:** (604) 863-2324. 🍴

RECREATIONAL ACTIVITIES
White-water Rafting

- **Fraser River Raft Expeditions** is 1 km (.6 mi.) w. on Hwy. 1. **Hours:** Daily mid-May to late Sept. Departure times vary with trip. **Phone:** (604) 863-2336 or (800) 363-7238.

▼ YOHO NATIONAL PARK OF CANADA (A-11)

> Elevations in the park range from 1,098 metres (3,600 ft.) at the West Gate of the park to 3,562 metres (11,686 ft.) on Mount Goodsir at the South Tower. Refer to CAA/AAA maps for additional elevation information.

Reached by hwys. 1 and 93, Yoho National Park of Canada covers 1,310 square kilometres (507 sq.

mi.) just west of the Great Divide and Banff National Park of Canada. The word *yoho* is an exclamation of wonder or astonishment in the language of the Cree Indians.

In 1884 the Canadian Pacific Railway laid tracks through Kicking Horse Pass, discovered by Sir James Hector during his search for the best transportation route through the Rockies. The Trans-Canada Highway later was built along this same route.

Open mid-June through September as weather permits, the 13-kilometre-long (7.8-mi.) Yoho Valley Road winds up a narrow valley between high, wooded mountain slopes. Takakkaw Falls ("magnificent" in the Cree language) drops 380 metres (1,265 ft.) in all, its highest sheer fall being 254 metres (833 ft.), making it one of the highest falls in Canada.

Other sights in the park include Natural Bridge, Emerald Lake, Wapta Falls and the Spiral Tunnels of the Canadian Pacific Railway. The lower Spiral Tunnel can be viewed from the Trans-Canada Highway, 7 kilometres (4 mi.) east of Field. The upper Spiral Tunnel can be viewed from the Yoho Valley Road.

The park also contains the Burgess Shale fossil beds, which have preserved fossils of more than 120 species, including rare soft-bodied creatures dating back 515 million years to the Cambrian period. Specimens from the beds are displayed at the park's visitor information center.

General Information and Activities

Although the park is open all year, most facilities and interpretive programs operate only during July and August. However, a park information center on Hwy. 1 at Field is open year-round. The Trans-Canada Highway traverses the park and provides access to most of its roads and trails.

Access to the Burgess Shale fossil beds is limited to guided tours during July and August; fees range from $25-$70. Full-day round trips cover 19 kilometres (12 mi.) and are considered strenuous. Reservations are required; phone (800) 343-3006 Mon.-Fri. 10-3 in season.

There are several campgrounds in the park. Prices range from $16-$30 for sites and $7.90 for firewood. A wilderness pass is required to stay overnight in the backcountry. Passes are $9 per person each night and are available from the visitor information center.

Hiking trails range from nature walks to extended back-country trips; travelers on overnight outings should register at the visitor information center or with a park warden. Fishing, particularly rewarding to those in search of char and many other varieties of trout, requires a $29.70 annual permit, or an $8.90 1-day permit.

Horses, canoes and rowboats are available for rent at Emerald Lake. Winter activities include cross-country skiing, snowshoeing, ice climbing, back-country ski touring and winter camping. *See the Recreation Chart and the AAA/CAA Western Canada & Alaska CampBook.*

ADMISSION to the park is $8.90; $7.65 (ages 65+); $4.45 (ages 6-16); $17.80 (all occupants of a private vehicle with up to seven people).

ADDRESS inquiries to the Superintendent, Yoho National Park of Canada, P.O. Box 99, Field, BC, Canada V0A 1G0; phone (250) 343-6783.

Manitoba

Location is Everything
Winnipeg's position at the junction of two rivers led to its prominence as a trading post

Nature Made
Lakes, forests, rolling prairies and subarctic tundra are part of Manitoba's landscape

Polar Bears and Beluga Whales
Churchill is the place for viewing these magnificent creatures of the wild

The Water's Fine
Myriad lakes and rivers are popular with anglers, canoeists and boaters

Interpretive Sites
Manitoba's history is remembered at restored forts and trading posts

Whiteshell Provincial Park, Falcon Lake / © Dave Reede / age fotostock

Waves pound a rock-strewn shore at the narrows of Lake Manitoba, producing a noise oddly like a beating drum. To the Cree Indians, this sound was the great spirit Manitou, whose name was given to the lake and, in 1870, the entire province.

From clear water lapping in giant lakes—Winnipeg, Winnipegosis and Manitoba—to the rustling sigh of wind across golden seas of wheat, the great spirit of this province speaks with many voices and conveys many moods.

It echoes in the plaintive cry of migrating geese winging south and the hoarse chuffing of a protective mother polar bear herding her cubs along Hudson Bay's icy shore.

The spirit sings within a chorus of steel wheels as trains carry freight across the prairies from west to east and back again. It proclaims itself in the bustling streets of Winnipeg, where sundry languages—French, English, Ukrainian, Chinese and others—blend into a rich, evocative murmur, and laughs amid the joyous din of the city's various celebrations.

Even the silence deep within Manitoba's immense evergreen forests seems heavy with something left unsaid.

A province this vast has a lot to say; make the journey and let it speak to you.

An Unearthly Resplendence

Look north into the night sky. There. See it? A faint glow high above the horizon. . .

Watch as an arc of yellow light gradually forms. As it drifts upward, shimmering yellow-green streamers rise from it, rippling like a breeze-blown curtain. New arcs appear lined with bright amber streaks that curl like wisps of smoke. Eventually the swirls of color fade and darkness returns, ending your encounter with the aurora borealis.

In Manitoba you won't have to wait long for a repeat performance. This far north you can count on basking in the aurora's eerie luminescence nearly 90 nights a year. Even citizens of Winnipeg, the capital, are often treated to this celestial light show, despite living in the province's extreme south.

Gem of the Prairies

Sky-obscuring pollution may be the bane of many cities, but Winnipeg's clean air isn't likely to spoil your auroral view. And while multihued lights dance overhead, visitors to the "Gem of the Prairies" can enjoy an equally colorful cultural spectrum spread out before them. Home to more than half of all Manitobans, Winnipeg is a city of surprising diversity; the Ellice-Sargent neighborhood alone boasts 43 resident nationalities. Here it's not unusual to find a German butcher shop sandwiched between an Italian clothing store and a Vietnamese restaurant, all within a few steps of a Portuguese cafe.

Finding the cuisine you crave is a snap in this polyglot town. For Italian, follow your nose to the source of the garlic-tinged scents wafting from Corydon Avenue, Winnipeg's Little Italy. Here you'll find delicious pastas galore—from agnolotti to tufoli—and a table at a sidewalk bistro is perfect for people-watching while you nibble on a biscotti.

Those desiring a bit of Gallic flavor should saunter over to St. Boniface, home to Canada's largest French community west of the province of Québec. Restaurants serving French dishes are easy to find here, especially along Provencher Boulevard. And in winter St. Boniface comes alive during Le Festival du Voyageur, when Winnipegers turn out to celebrate the *joie de vivre* of the French fur traders who explored the area.

Red northern lights were once regarded as omens of war. If so, the skies must have shone red fairly often during the 18th century

Manitoba Historical Timeline

Capt. Thomas Button winters at Port Nelson on Hudson Bay and claims the land for England.
1612

Travel Manitoba

Henry Kelsey of the Hudson's Bay Co. spends 2 years exploring the province to find new sources of fur.
1690-92

1738
French fur-trader Pierre Gaultier de la Vérendrye arrives at the site now known as Winnipeg.

The Red River Colony, Manitoba's first permanent settlement, is established with a land grant from the Hudson's Bay Co.
1812

1869-70
The Métis, native people of mixed European and Indian ancestry, are led by Louis Riel in the Red River Rebellion to protect their language and property rights.

as conflicts escalated between French *voyageurs* and their English rivals. During this strife-ridden period, Fort Rouge—site of modern Winnipeg—was established where the Red and Assiniboine rivers meet.

Now known as The Forks, this riverfront area is a park where you can take a tree-shaded stroll past splashing fountains and vibrantly hued flower beds. During warm weather, people flock to the numerous festivals held here, including Winnipeg's International Children's Festival in early June.

Nearby, The Manitoba Museum invites visitors to take a whirlwind tour of the entire province by way of seven main galleries. And to learn more about auroras, stop by the museum's planetarium.

The Great White North

Follow your compass farther north and the chances of seeing Mother Nature's silent fireworks multiply. The northern lights not only occur more frequently in Manitoba's subarctic areas, but are brighter, too. In towns like Churchill, the lights are a major attraction.

But the real stars in this small community are its big, furry neighbors: polar bears. Sightings of the great white animals are common in October, when they migrate onto rapidly freezing Hudson Bay to fish, and late June, when thawing ice forces a return to shore.

The best way to meet these deceptively cuddly looking carnivores is safely ensconced in a specially designed, balloon-tired tundra vehicle. Climb aboard one for an unforgettable in-the-wild encounter. And when you're ready to thaw out, visit Churchill's Eskimo Museum, which is filled with ancient Inuit tools and other artifacts, as well as the recent, burnished wildlife sculptures carved in serpentine that are prized by international collectors.

Well-acquainted with the aurora's haunting glow, the Inuits crafted stories as elaborate as their carvings to explain what they saw. According to one tale, the lights are torches lit by spirits to guide those who will follow across the narrow bridge to heaven.

But you don't have to study Inuit mythology to appreciate the northern lights' otherworldly beauty, nor must you understand the scientific principles behind the phenomenon. All you really need to know is that the skies in Manitoba are perfect for admiring them.

Manitoba becomes the fifth Canadian province.
1870

Manitoba's boundary is extended north to Hudson Bay.
1912

Manitoba's French speakers win an important victory when the Supreme Court rules that all provincial laws passed since 1870 are invalid because they were written only in English.
1986

1900-13
Manitoba's grain production increases dramatically, and Winnipeg becomes the trade center for the prairie region.

© PhotoDisc

1997
More than 25,000 residents between the U.S. border and Winnipeg are forced to evacuate as Red River flood waters surge north.

1999
The Pan Am Games are held in Winnipeg.

Recreation

The overwhelming bulk of Manitoba's populace resides in a thin strip just above the U.S. border, which leaves a vast region of unspoiled territory farther north that's prime for exploration.

Much of the province's outdoor fun involves its 100,000 lakes and the many rivers that link them.

Colorful sails glide across the surface of Lake Winnipeg as **windsurfing** enthusiasts take advantage of breezy days. Put in at Grand Beach Provincial Park, at the far southeast end of the lake. **Canoeing** down the Grass River, near the junction of hwys. 10 and 39, gives you the opportunity to see the beauty of the northern frontier.

Manitoba's lakes are home to dozens of species of fish, including walleye, northern pike, smallmouth bass, trout, arctic grayling, sturgeon and channel catfish. Fly-in fishing—at such isolated spots as Aikens and Dogskin lakes, northeast of Bissett in Atikaki Provincial Park; Gods Lake, Gods River, Knee Lake, and Island Lake, all in northeast Manitoba; and Big Sand, Egenolf, and Nueltin lakes in the northwest region—attracts anglers of all skill levels. Contact Manitoba Conservation for information about licensing and regulations; phone (204) 945-6784.

Chilling Out

When the lakes freeze over, **ice fishing** and **ice skating** warm up as favored pursuits. Smooth blankets of snow—at such places as Assiniboine Park in Winnipeg—are irresistible for **snowshoeing** and **cross-country skiing.**

Many adventurers, too, have a hard time resisting the many **snowmobiling** trails that criss-cross the province. Kick up some powder in Duck Mountain and Turtle Mountain provincial parks.

Although **downhill skiing** is hard to come by in a province that's known mostly for its lowlands, skiers can take on 21 runs at Asessippi and Winter Park ski areas.

For **tobogganing** fun, head for the slides at Kildonan Park in Winnipeg.

Riding Mountain National Park of Canada rises from the flat prairie to provide a wealth of opportunity for activity. Self-guiding **hiking** trails range from the easy Beach Ridges Trail to the difficult Bald Hill Trail, named for the barren hill towering over scores of lush, green trees. Most memorable is the grueling but beautiful Ochre River Trail, which entices both trekkers and cross-country skiers.

The park's Clear Lake Trail is a challenging **cycling** route that traverses part of an unmaintained Indian reserve. Before tackling the entire 25-kilometre (16-mile) trail, obtain permission from the reserve; phone (204) 625-2004. **Mountain bikers** favor the exhilarating J.E.T. Trail, which rewards risk-takers with great views from the ridge. The multiuse Central Trail, the longest at 73 kilometres (45 miles), is especially popular for **horseback riding.**

Taking A Dive

Even **scuba divers** can indulge their passion in the crystal waters of Clear Lake. Register with the park before heading to facilities at Glen Beag day-use area. Divers also frequent West Hawk Lake, Manitoba's deepest. Formed by a meteorite, the lake is near the eastern entrance to Whiteshell Provincial Park.

Cree for "white bear," Wapusk National Park of Canada fittingly lives up to its name as a hot spot for polar bear viewing.

Black bears, whitetail deer, caribou and moose are among the big game species that contribute to the province's excellent rifle and bow **hunting** reputation.

An abundance of specimens draws **rockhounders** to Flin Flon, Souris, Thompson and Bissett, a former gold-mining town northwest of Nopiming Provincial Park. Contact the Deputy Office of Government Services for maps and information about rocks and minerals; phone (204) 945-1119.

Recreational Activities

Throughout the TourBook, you may notice a Recreational Activities heading with bulleted listings of recreation-oriented establishments listed underneath. Similar operations also may be mentioned in Destination City recreation sections. Since normal AAA inspection criteria cannot be applied, these establishments are presented only for information. Age, height and weight restrictions may apply. Reservations often are recommended and sometimes are required. Addresses and/or phone numbers are provided so visitors can contact the attraction for additional information.

Fast Facts

POPULATION: 1,148,401.

AREA: 552,370 sq km (213,270 sq mi); ranks 8th.

CAPITAL: Winnipeg.

HIGHEST POINT: 831 m/2,727 ft., Baldy Mountain.

LOWEST POINT: Sea level, Churchill.

TIME ZONE(S): Central. DST.

TEEN DRIVING LAWS: No more than one passenger is permitted unless a supervising licensed driver is seated in the front passenger seat. Driving is not permitted midnight-5 a.m. The minimum age for an unrestricted driver's license is 17 years, 6 months.

MINIMUM AGE FOR GAMBLING: 18.

SEAT BELT/CHILD RESTRAINT LAWS: Seat belts are required for driver and all passengers age 18 and older. Children ages 5 until 18 and over 23 kg. (50 lbs.) are required to be in a child restraint or seat belt; child restraints are required for under age 5 and under 23 kg. (50 lbs.).

HELMETS FOR MOTORCYCLISTS: Required for all riders.

RADAR DETECTORS: Not permitted.

FIREARMS LAWS: By federal law, all nonresidents entering Canada with a firearm must declare their weapon in writing and pay a fee of $25 (Canadian). Contact the Canadian Firearms Centre at (800) 731-4000 to receive a declaration form or for additional information.

HOLIDAYS: Jan. 1; Louis Riel Day (3rd Mon. in Feb.); Good Friday; Easter; Easter Monday; Victoria Day, May 24 (if a Mon.) or the closest prior Mon.; Canada Day, July 1; Civic Holiday, Aug. (1st Mon.); Labour Day, Sept. (1st Mon.); Thanksgiving, Oct. (2nd Mon.); Remembrance Day, Nov. 11; Christmas, Dec. 25; Boxing Day, Dec. 26.

TAXES: In addition to Manitoba's provincial sales tax of 7 percent, there is a national 5 percent Goods and Services Tax (GST).

INFORMATION CENTERS: Free travel literature and information are available at the following locations: Canada/United States border, Hwy. 75 at Emerson (daily 9 a.m.-7 p.m., mid-May through Labour Day.; Thurs.-Mon. 9-5, rest of year); Manitoba/Ontario boundary, Hwy. 1E just east of West Hawk Lake (daily 9 a.m.-7 p.m., mid-May through Labour Day; Wed.-Sun. 9-5, day after Labour Day to mid-Oct.); Manitoba/Saskatchewan boundaries on Hwy. 1W west of Kirkella, and Hwy. 16W near Russell (daily 9 a.m.-7 p.m., mid-May through Labour Day); and the Explore Manitoba Centre at The Forks National Historic Site of Canada in Winnipeg (daily 10-6).

FURTHER INFORMATION FOR VISITORS:

Travel Manitoba
155 Carlton St., 7th Floor
Winnipeg, MB, Canada R3C 3H8
(204) 927-7800
(800) 665-0040
See color ad p. 219

Explore Manitoba Centre
The Forks National Historic Site of Canada
401-25 Forks Market Rd.
Winnipeg, MB, Canada R3C 4S8
(204) 983-6757
(888) 773-8888

RECREATION INFORMATION:

Manitoba Conservation
Parks and Natural Areas
200 Saulteaux Crescent
Winnipeg, MB, Canada R3J 3W3
(204) 945-6784
(800) 214-6497

ALCOHOL CONSUMPTION: Legal age 18.

SPECIAL REGULATIONS: Dogs and cats transported from the United States must have proof of rabies vaccination.

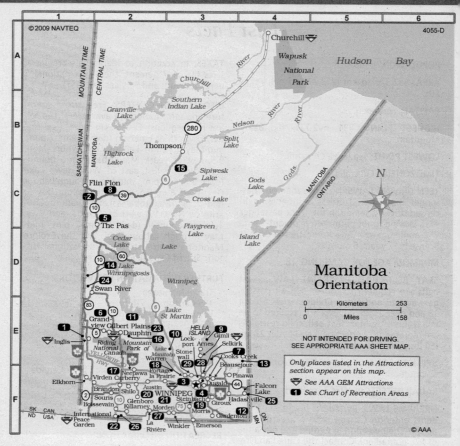

RECREATION AREAS

	MAP LOCATION	CAMPING	PICNICKING	HIKING TRAILS	BOATING	BOAT RAMP	BOAT RENTAL	FISHING	SWIMMING	PETS ON LEASH	BICYCLE TRAILS	WINTER SPORTS	VISITOR CENTER	LODGE/CABINS	FOOD SERVICE
NATIONAL PARKS *(See place listings)*															
Riding Mountain (E-2) 2,978 square kilometres. Backpacking, cross-country skiing, golf, hiking, horseback riding, scuba diving, tennis, water skiing, wind surfing; boat cruises, paddleboats.		•	•	•	•	•	•	•	•	•	•	•	•	•	•
Wapusk (A-5) 11,475 square kilometres. Polar bear viewing.										•					
PROVINCIAL															
Asessippi (E-1) 2,330 hectares 13 km from Shellmouth Dam on Hwy. 83. Fishing, snowmobiling; nature trail.	**1**	•	•	•	•	•	•	•	•	•			•		•	•
Bakers Narrows (C-1) 145 hectares 27 km s. of Flin Flon on Hwy. 10. Board sailing, canoeing; playground, wildlife watching.	**2**	•	•	•	•	•	•	•	•	•				•	•
Beaudry (F-3) 939 hectares 10 km w. of Winnipeg on Roblin Blvd./Hwy. 241.	**3**		•	•				•		•	•	•			
Birds Hill (F-3) 3,550 hectares 24 km n.e. of Winnipeg on Hwy. 59. Cross-country skiing, horseback riding, snowmobiling; interpretive programs, playground, wildlife watching.	**4**	•	•					•	•	•	•	•	•		
Clearwater Lake (C-2) 59,265 hectares 19 km n. of The Pas on Hwy. 10, then 2.5 km e. on Hwy. 287. Cross-country skiing, snowmobiling; interpretive trail.	**5**	•	•	•	•	•	•	•	•	•		•		•	•
Duck Mountain (E-2) 142,430 hectares 56 km n. of Roblin off Hwy. 83. Canoeing, cross-country skiing, snowmobiling.	**6**	•	•	•	•	•	•	•	•	•		•	•	•	•
Grand Beach (E-4) 2,490 hectares 80 km n.e. of Winnipeg on Hwy. 59, then 6 km w. on Hwy 12. Cross-country skiing, sailing, snowmobiling, tennis, windsurfing; interpretive programs, sand beaches.	**7**	•	•	•	•	•		•	•	•	•	•	•	•	•
Grass River (C-2) 228,018 hectares at Cranberry Portage off Hwy. 10. Canoeing; interpretive trail.	**8**	•	•	•	•	•	•	•	•	•		•		•	
Hecla/Grindstone (E-3) 108,440 hectares 165 km n. of Winnipeg via Hwy. 8. Cross-country skiing, golf, sailing, snowmobiling, tennis, windsurfing; interpretive programs. *(See Hecla Island p. 226)*	**9**	•	•	•	•	•	•	•	•	•	•	•	•	•	•
Lundar Beach (E-3) 23 hectares 18 km w. of Lundar on Hwy. 419.	**10**	•	•	•				•	•	•			•		
Manipogo (E-2) 61 hectares 47 km n. of Dauphin on Hwy. 20. Board sailing; playground, wildlife watching.	**11**	•	•	•	•			•	•	•					•
Moose Lake (F-4) 956 hectares 30 km n.e. of Sprague on Hwy. 308. Board sailing, canoeing, snowmobiling; playground, wildlife watching.	**12**	•	•		•	•		•	•	•			•	•	•
Nopiming (E-4) 142,910 hectares 70 km n.e. of Lac du Bonnet. Canoeing; interpretive trail.	**13**	•	•	•	•	•		•	•	•				•	•
North Steeprock Lake (D-1) 13 hectares 3 km n. of Birch River on Hwy. 10, then 40 km w. on Hwy. 365.	**14**	•	•		•	•		•	•	•					
Paint Lake (C-3) 8,848 hectares 32 km s. of Thompson on Hwy. 6. Canoeing, cross-country skiing, ice skating, snowmobiling, to-bogganing, windsurfing.	**15**	•	•	•	•	•	•	•	•	•		•	•	•	•
Rainbow Beach (E-2) 52 hectares 17 km e. of Dauphin on Hwy. 20. Board sailing, golfing; playground, wildlife watching.	**16**	•	•	•	•			•	•	•	•				
Rivers (F-2) 37 hectares 14 km n. of Brandon on Hwy. 10, then 26 km w. on Hwy. 25. Playground.	**17**	•	•	•	•	•		•	•	•					
St. Ambroise Beach (F-2) 46 hectares 47 km w. of Winnipeg on Hwy. 1, then 35 km n. on Hwy. 430. Windsurfing; interpretive trail.	**18**	•	•		•	•		•	•	•					

RECREATION AREAS

	Map Location	Camping	Picnicking	Hiking Trails	Boating	Boat Ramp	Boat Rental	Fishing	Swimming	Pets on Leash	Bicycle Trails	Winter Sports	Visitor Center	Lodge/Cabins	Food Service
St. Malo (F-3) 148 hectares 64 km s. of Winnipeg on Hwy. 59. Motorized boats not allowed.	**19**	•	•	•	•			•	•	•	•		•		•
Spruce Woods (F-2) 26,950 hectares 20 km s.e. of Carberry on Hwy. 5. Canoeing, cross-country skiing, ice skating, snowmobiling, tobogganing; horseback riding trails, interpretive programs. *(See Carberry p. 221)*	**20**	•	•	•	•			•	•	•	•	•	•	•	•
Stephenfield (F-2) 94 hectares 10 km w. of Carman on Hwy. 245. Board sailing, golfing; playground.	**21**	•	•	•	•			•	•	•	•				•
Turtle Mountain (F-2) 18,570 hectares 23 km s. of Boissevain off Hwy. 10. Cross-country skiing, ice skating, snowmobiling, tobogganing; interpretive trail, horse trails. *(See Boissevain p. 220)*	**22**	•	•	•	•	•		•	•	•	•	•			
Watchorn (E-2) 10 hectares 11 km w. of Moosehorn on Hwy. 237. Playground.	**23**	•	•		•			•	•	•					
Whitefish Lake (D-1) 24 hectares 13 km n. of Swan River, then 28 km w. on Hwy. 279. Playground.	**24**	•	•		•			•	•	•					
Whiteshell (F-4) 272,090 hectares off Hwy. 1 at Falcon Lake, near the Ontario border. Cross-country skiing, downhill skiing, golf, horseback riding, sailing, snowmobiling, tennis, tobogganing, windsurfing; interpretive programs, museum. *(See Falcon Lake p. 224)*	**25**	•	•	•	•	•	•	•	•	•	•	•	•	•	•
William Lake (F-2) 199 hectares 7 km e. of Horton, then 8 km s. Amphitheater, playground.	**26**	•	•		•			•	•	•					
OTHER															
Kildonan (F-3) 40 hectares at 2021 Main St. in Winnipeg. Cross-country skiing, ice skating, tobogganing; pool. *(See Winnipeg p. 240)*			•	•	•					•	•	•			•
La Barriere (F-3) 21 hectares 6 km s. of jct. Waverley St. and Perimeter Hwy. in Winnipeg. Canoeing, cross-country skiing, naturalist-guided hikes, snowshoeing.			•	•				•		•	•	•			
Lake Minnewasta (F-2) 125 hectares 2 km w. of Morden on Hwy. 3, then 1 km s. on Hwy. 434.	**27**	•	•	•	•	•		•	•	•	•	•			
Selkirk Park (E-3) 81 hectares on the banks of the Red River at Eveline St. in Selkirk. Cross-country skiing, ice fishing; bird sanctuary.	**28**	•	•		•	•		•	•						•
Stonewall Quarry (F-3) 30 hectares 4 blks. n. on Main St. in Stonewall. Nature programs. Cross-country skiing, ice skating, tobogganing. *(See Stonewall p. 230)*	**29**	•	•	•					•			•	•		•

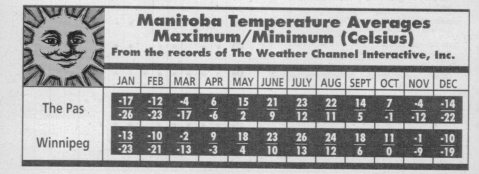

Manitoba Temperature Averages
Maximum/Minimum (Celsius)
From the records of The Weather Channel Interactive, Inc.

	JAN	FEB	MAR	APR	MAY	JUNE	JULY	AUG	SEPT	OCT	NOV	DEC
The Pas	-17 / -26	-12 / -23	-4 / -17	6 / -6	15 / 2	21 / 9	23 / 12	22 / 11	14 / 5	7 / -1	-4 / -12	-14 / -22
Winnipeg	-13 / -23	-10 / -21	-2 / -13	9 / -3	18 / 4	23 / 10	26 / 13	24 / 12	18 / 6	11 / 0	-1 / -9	-10 / -19

Points of Interest

ARNES (E-3) elev. 225 m/739′

An old fishing village, Arnes today offers sandy beaches, a marina and a nine-hole golf course. A monument to writer and explorer Vilhjalmur Stefansson is inscribed "I know what I have experienced, and I know what it has meant to me," a statement from his autobiography. Born in 1879, Stefansson traveled by boat and dog sled across the Arctic, mapping large areas of the archipelago and collecting ethnological data from the central Arctic coast. He proved through his explorations that it was possible to live off the land in this forbidding area.

Lake Winnipeg Visitor Centre-Arnes: P.O. Box 1246, Gimli, MB, Canada R0C 1B0. **Phone:** (204) 642-7974.

AUSTIN (F-2) elev. 262 m/860′

MANITOBA AGRICULTURAL MUSEUM, 2.5 km (1.6 mi.) s. of Hwy. 1 on Hwy. 34, displays a large

collection of steam engines, gasoline tractors, farm equipment and artifacts of pioneer farmers. The location also is home of the Manitoba Amateur Radio Museum. **Hours:** Daily 9-5, mid-May through Sept. 30. **Cost:** $5; $4 (students with ID and senior citizens); free (ages 0-5); $15 (family). **Phone:** (204) 637-2354.

Homesteaders' Village, at the museum, depicts pioneer life in the late 19th century through furnished buildings of the period. Included are log cabins, an 1883 schoolhouse, two churches, a printing office, blacksmith's shop, grain elevator, pioneer-style store and gristmill. **Hours:** Daily 9-5, mid-May through Sept. 30. **Cost:** included with Manitoba Agricultural Museum.

BEAUSEJOUR (E-3)
pop. 2,823, elev. 247 m/810′

Just 46 kilometres (29 mi.) northeast of Winnipeg, Beausejour is on one of the main roads to Whiteshell Provincial Park *(see attraction listing p. 224).* Nature enthusiasts take advantage of the walking, hiking and cross-country ski trails available at Wally Chryplywy Nature Park on First Street.

Beausejour and District Chamber of Commerce: P.O. Box 224, Beausejour, MB, Canada R0E 0C0. **Phone:** (204) 268-3502 or (204) 268-7550.

BROKEN BEAU HISTORICAL SOCIETY PIONEER VILLAGE MUSEUM, 1 blk. n. of Park Ave. and Seventh St. N., features a reassembled pioneer village with a restored railroad station, a blacksmith shop, a school, an old church, a community hall, a general store, a tailor's shop, a harness shop and a house, as well as pioneer artifacts and farm implements. **Time:** Allow 1 hour minimum. **Hours:** Mon.-Fri. 8:30-4:30, Sat.-Sun. and holidays 1-5, July-Aug.; by appointment rest of year. **Cost:** $5; free (ages 0-12). **Phone:** (204) 268-1318.

BOISSEVAIN (F-1) pop. 1,497

Nearby Turtle Mountain Provincial Park *(see Recreation Chart)* is named for the western painted turtle, which lives in the park's many shallow lakes. The park is the year-round home of a large number of waterfowl and of migratory birds in spring and fall. A wildlife center also is available.

As a connection to the park, the town has adopted as its symbol an 8.5-metre-tall (28-ft.) statue known as Tommy Turtle, which can be seen beside the visitor center on Hwy. 10.

An outdoor art gallery throughout the town depicts area history by way of more than 20 colorful wall-size murals, including a large scene painted on a grain elevator in downtown Boissevain. Scenic Hwy. 10 leads south to the North Dakota border and the International Peace Garden *(see place listing p. 226).*

Boissevain & District Tourism Office: P.O. Box 368, Boissevain, MB, Canada R0K 0E0. **Phone:** (204) 534-6303 or (800) 497-2393.

Self-guiding tours: Literature for a self-guiding walking tour of the city's historic buildings is available at the Boissevain Visitors Centre on Hwy. 10S.

BECKONING HILLS MUSEUM is at 425 Mill Rd. S. The museum exhibits pioneer artifacts, mementos such as uniforms from World Wars I and II, farming equipment, early photographs and items relating to culture, education and literature. **Time:** Allow 1 hour minimum. **Hours:** Daily 1-5, June-Sept.; other times by appointment. **Cost:** Donations. **Phone:** (204) 534-6544.

IRVIN GOODON INTERNATIONAL WILDLIFE MUSEUM is at 298 Mountain St. (Hwy. 10). Visitors can gain a better understanding of wildlife through the mounted animals displayed in natural-like dioramas. Each setting provides information about the animals and their behavior.

Tours: Guided tours are available. **Time:** Allow 30 minutes minimum. **Hours:** Daily 9-7, May-Oct.; by appointment rest of year. **Cost:** $7; $3 (ages 6-16). **Phone:** (204) 534-6662.

MONCUR GALLERY & MUSEUM, in the Civic Centre/Library Complex at 420 S. Railway St., contains 10,000 years of archeological history of early southwestern Manitoba. Included in the collection are projectile points, scrapers, ceremonial items and food preparation utensils. **Time:** Allow 30 minutes minimum. **Hours:** Tues.-Sat. 10-5. **Cost:** $3; $2 (ages 12-17). **Phone:** (204) 534-6478.

BRANDON (F-2)
pop. 41,511, elev. 409 m/1,300′

An agricultural and industrial center, Brandon is the second largest city in the province after Winnipeg and is known for its small-town warmth and big-city amenities.

The Riverbank Discovery Centre, in addition to providing information about Brandon and the surrounding region, is the starting point for the Assiniboine Riverbank Trail System, 17 kilometres (10.5 mi.) of trails that wind throughout Brandon, linking the downtown area with parks, picnic spots and sports venues. In summer the center is the site of a farmers market; in winter it hosts the Manitoba Hydro Power Smart Waterfall of Lights.

The Keystone Centre, with more than 3.5 hectares (9 acres) under one roof, plays host to some of Manitoba's larger events, concerts and sports competitions; phone (204) 726-3500. The Canada Games Sportsplex offers both winter and summer recreational activities. Built for the 1979 Canada Winter Games, the structure houses racquetball courts, an ice arena, Olympic-size swimming pool, indoor water slide and an outdoor running track; phone (204) 729-2475.

The Brandon Hills Wildlife Management Area, just a short drive south of the city on Hwy. 10 and east along Beresford Road, provides a setting for a variety of recreational pursuits such as hiking, mountain bicycling, cross-country skiing and bird-watching.

Regional Tourism Centre/Riverbank Discovery Centre: #1-545 Conservation Dr., Brandon, MB, Canada R7A 7L8. **Phone:** (204) 729-2141 or (888) 799-1111.

Self-guiding tours: A historical walking tour of the residential area between 10th and 18th streets offers interesting architecture and turn-of-the-20th-century homes; a booklet describing the tour is available for $3 from the tourism center.

ART GALLERY OF SOUTHWESTERN MANI-TOBA, 710 Rosser Ave. (entrance via the Town Centre Mall parkade), features changing exhibits with an emphasis on community-based art and contemporary works. Displays change every 6-7 weeks. Workshops and art classes are offered for a fee. **Time:** Allow 1 hour minimum. **Hours:** Mon.-Sat. 10-6 (also Thurs. 6-9 p.m., Sept.-June). Closed major holidays. **Cost:** Donations. **Phone:** (204) 727-1036.

COMMONWEALTH AIR TRAINING PLAN MUSEUM, in Hangar 1 at Brandon Airport, is dedicated to preserving the history of the British Commonwealth Air Training Plan of 1939-45. It has many of the aircraft used for training, photographs, artifacts and memorabilia. Three of the 11 aircraft displayed are in flying condition. A chapel has a book with names of more than 18,000 Canadian Air Force personnel who died during World War II.

Guided tours are available by appointment. **Hours:** Daily 10-4, May-Sept.; 1-4, rest of year. Closed Dec. 25. **Cost:** $6; $4 (ages 6-18). **Phone:** (204) 727-2444.

DALY HOUSE MUSEUM, 122 18th St., was built in 1882 as the home of Brandon's first mayor, Thomas Mayne Daly. It is furnished with late 19th-century upper middle-class pieces and houses photographs and artifacts that relate the city's history. Also featured are a general store and Brandon's old city hall council chambers. A research center on the third floor is available by appointment.

Tours: Guided tours are available. **Time:** Allow 1 hour minimum. **Hours:** Mon.-Sat. 10-noon and 1-5, Sun. 1-4, July-Aug.; Tues.-Sat. 10-noon and 1-5, rest of year. **Cost:** $5; $4 (ages 0-17 and 66+); $10 (family, two adults and two children). **Phone:** (204) 727-1722.

WESTMAN REPTILE GARDENS is 19 km (12 mi.) e. on PR 457 to the end of the road, 1.6 km (1 mi.) s. on Wagglesprings Rd. (gravel) to Thompson Rd., then just w. following signs. One of Canada's largest reptile exhibits, the museum has more than 300 displays. Visitors can see rattlesnakes, crocodiles, a giant tarantula, monitors and turtles. **Hours:** Mon.-Sat. 10-8, Sun. and holidays noon-5, Mar.-Oct. Tues.-Sat. noon-6, Sun. and holidays noon-5, rest of year. **Cost:** $5; $3 (ages 3-15). **Phone:** (204) 763-4030.

CARBERRY (F-2)

pop. 1,502, elev. 369 m/1,210'

The forests and sand dunes of nearby Spruce Woods Provincial Park *(see attraction listing)* inspired many of the works of artist, naturalist and writer Ernest Thompson Seton, including his stories "The Trail of the Sandhill Stag" and "Wild Animals I Have Known." He was appointed naturalist to the Manitoba government in 1892. A small highway park 15 kilometres (9 mi.) east of Carberry on Hwy. 1 has been dedicated to Seton.

Carberry Municipal Offices: P.O. Box 130, Carberry, MB, Canada R0K 0H0. **Phone:** (204) 834-6600.

CARBERRY PLAINS MUSEUM AND GINGER-BREAD HOUSE, at 520 James White Way, contains pioneer artifacts relating to the area, including period clothing, pictures and furniture as well as displays of original 19th-century art, a schoolroom, a church, a store, a bedroom and a kitchen. Military memorabilia from World Wars I and II also are displayed. **Time:** Allow 30 minutes minimum. **Hours:** Daily 1-6, June-Sept. **Cost:** $2; $1 (students with ID); $5 (family). **Phone:** (204) 834-6609, or (204) 834-2439 in the off-season.

THE SETON CENTRE, 116 Main St., features artwork and photographs depicting the life and philosophies of writer, artist, naturalist and early conservationist Ernest Thompson Seton. **Time:** Allow 30 minutes minimum. **Hours:** Mon.-Sat. 9-5, June-Aug.; by appointment rest of year. **Cost:** Donations. **Phone:** (204) 834-2509.

SPRUCE WOODS PROVINCIAL PARK is 25 km (16 mi.) s. on Hwy. 5. The 26,950-hectare (66,593-acre) park, a mosaic of geographic features, includes deciduous forests, creeping sand dunes, white spruce-covered sand hills, pots of quicksand and mixed grass prairie. The Assiniboine River winds through the park. Spirit Sands, rainwater trapped beneath the sandy surface that has emerged to create springs and quicksand, and Devil's Punch Bowl, a bowl-shaped depression, are highlights. *See Recreation Chart and Glenboro in the AAA/CAA Western Canada & Alaska CampBook.*

The Spirit Sands are remnants of an ancient river delta. This desertlike area is a 5-kilometre (3-mi.) tract of open sand dunes that tower 30 metres (98 ft.) above the surrounding prairie. The eerie blue-green pond color of The Devil's Punch Bowl, near the Spirit Sands, can be observed from several viewpoints; the depression was caused by the currents of an underground stream.

Spruce Woods is home to the western plains hognose snake; the northern prairie skink, Manitoba's only lizard; wapiti (elk); white-tailed deer; coyotes; and pin cushion and prickly pear cactuses.

An 8.6-kilometre (5.1-mi.) self-guiding trail leads through the dunes to the Punch Bowl, and a 4-kilometre (2.5-mi.) trail meanders through the Spirit Sands. Both trail entrances are located just north of the Assiniboine River off Hwy. 5. Interpretive signs along the trails provide insight into the cultural and natural surroundings.

Interpretive programs about park resources and natural and cultural history are offered. Every weekend May through September, family events, campfire and amphitheater programs and guided hikes are offered. Comfortable walking shoes, a hat and drinking water are recommended. **Time:** Allow 2 hours minimum. **Hours:** Park open daily 24 hours. **Cost:** Free. **Phone:** (204) 827-8850 May-Sept., or (204) 834-8800 rest of year.

Spirit Sands Wagon Outfitters, 27 km (17 mi.) s.e. on Hwy. 5 in Spruce Woods Provincial Park, offers 90-minute covered wagon rides through the Spirit Sands and Devil's Punch Bowl, providing views of sand dunes, cactuses, rare snakes and lizards, rolling grasslands and marshes. **Hours:** Trips depart daily mid-May through Labour Day. **Cost:** Fare $11; $7 (ages 3-16). **Phone:** (204) 827-2800 for wagon office, or (204) 526-2764 off-season.

CHURCHILL (A-4) pop. 923, elev. 29 m/100′

Churchill, on the shore of Hudson Bay, is Canada's northernmost subarctic sea port. It also is the site of the Hudson's Bay Co.'s Prince of Wales Fort National Historic Site of Canada *(see attraction listing)*, a partially restored ruin across from Churchill and Cape Merry Battery at the mouth of the Churchill River. Built over a period of 40 years during the 1700s to hold as many as 400 soldiers, the impressive stone fortress housed only 39 untrained men when three French warships mounted a surprise attack in 1782. The fort's governor wisely surrendered without engaging in battle.

After spending 3 unsuccessful days trying to demolish the 12-metre-thick (40-ft.) outer walls, the French abandoned the fort; it was never occupied again. The site is accessible by boat July through August (weather and tides permitting).

The area around Churchill holds an attraction for two giant mammals: the polar bear and the beluga whale. In fact the Churchill region is said to have the greatest concentration of accessible polar bears in the world. Having spent the winter hunting on the frozen bay, the bears come to shore south of Churchill as the ice melts, scatter along the coast and up to 50 kilometres (31 mi.) inland, and then return to the ice in autumn when the bay refreezes. Beluga whales are often sighted off the coast of Cape Merry during July and August.

Other natural features include flowers, arctic plant life, various wildlife and some 200 species of birds, which nest or pass through Churchill on their annual migrations. An excellent spot for bird-watching is Bird Cove, on the coast 16 kilometres (9 mi.) east of Churchill. The aurora borealis (northern lights) seen from Churchill during the fall and winter months are among the most brilliant in the world.

Churchill can be reached only by train or airplane. Via Rail Canada trains run from Winnipeg and Thompson to Churchill; phone (888) 842-7245. Calm Air offers flights from Winnipeg to Churchill; phone (800) 839-2256.

The Parks Canada Visitor Reception Centre offers information, interpretive displays and programs, historical exhibits and videotaped presentations June though November; by appointment rest of year. Phone (204) 675-8863.

Churchill Chamber of Commerce: P.O. Box 176, Churchill, MB. Canada R0B 0E0. **Phone:** (204) 675-2022 or (888) 389-2327.

CAPE MERRY NATIONAL HISTORIC SITE, accessible via the Cape Merry Centennial Pkwy., 3 km (1.9 mi.) w. to the e. shore of the Churchill River, is marked by a stone cannon battery built in 1746 to complement the defenses of the Prince of Wales Fort. An original cannon and powder magazine remain. A cairn commemorating Capt. Jens Munk, the first European to enter the Churchill River in 1619, is displayed. The cape offers views of harbor activity as well as whales, waterfowl and the Prince of Wales Fort.

Time: Allow 30 minutes minimum. **Hours:** Daily 24 hours. Parks Canada offers guided tours June-Aug. **Cost:** Free. **Phone:** (204) 675-8863.

 ESKIMO MUSEUM, 242 La Verendrye Ave., contains exhibits that depict the history and culture of the northern region of Canada. Founded in 1944 by Roman Catholic missionaries, it pays tribute to the creativity of the Canadian Inuits. Highlights of the museum are Inuit carvings in bone, ivory, stone and antler as well as wildlife specimens, artifacts, and tools dating from 1700 B.C. **Hours:** Mon. 1-5, Tues.-Sat. 9-noon and

© Mike Macri

1-5, June-Nov.; Mon.-Sat. 1-4:30, rest of year. Closed major holidays. **Cost:** Donations. **Phone:** (204) 675-2030.

FRONTIERS NORTH'S TUNDRA BUGGY ADVENTURE is at 124 Kelsey Blvd. Specially designed vehicles called Tundra Buggies carry guests on full-day fall tours across the tundra to view polar bears in the Churchill Wildlife Management Area. Half- and full-day summer wildlife and nature tours, also on Tundra Buggies, venture along area shorelines. Multiday beluga whale-watching and ecological boat tours off the coast of Cape Merry also are offered; phone for information.

Hours: Full-day Tundra Buggy tours are offered most days, early Oct. to mid-Nov. Half-day wildlife and nature tours are available Tues., Thurs. and Sat., early July-late Sept. Full-day wildlife and nature tours are offered Wed. and Fri., early July-late Sept. **Cost:** Tundra Buggy fare early Oct. to mid-Oct. $299; $219 (ages 0-11). Tundra Buggy fare mid-Oct. to mid-Nov. $399; $299 (ages 0-11). Half-day summer wildlife and nature tour fare $119; $89 (ages 0-11). Full-day summer wildlife and nature tour fare $169; $129 (ages 0-11). Reservations are required. **Phone:** (204) 675-2121 or (800) 663-9832. *See color ad p. 222.*

NORTH STAR TOURS, 203 La Verendrye St., conducts historical and land-based cultural tours of the Churchill area by bus. **Time:** Allow 4 hours minimum. **Hours:** Daily 8-1, mid-June to mid-Nov. **Cost:** Fare Oct. 1 to mid-Nov. $100; free (children). Fare mid-June through Sept. 30 $75; free (children). **Phone:** (204) 675-2356 or (800) 665-0690.

PRINCE OF WALES FORT NATIONAL HISTORIC SITE OF CANADA, at the mouth of the Churchill River, is accessible by boat only. A huge stone fortress built 1731-71 by the Hudson's Bay Co., the fort fell to the French without incident in 1782. Independent whale-watching boat tours, including those offered by Sea North Tours Ltd. *(see attraction listing)* and Lazy Bear Lodge, usually include the fort on their itineraries.

Time: Allow 2 hours minimum. **Hours:** Access is possible on the changing tides 6 hours daily, July-Aug. (weather permitting); by appointment in Sept. **Cost:** Boat fare (site admission included) $80-$86. **Phone:** (204) 675-8863 for Parks Canada historic site information, (204) 675-2195, (204) 675-2969 for the Lazy Bear Lodge, or (888) 348-7591 for Sea North Tours information.

SEA NORTH TOURS LTD., 39 Franklin St., offers boat tours to Prince of Wales Fort National Historic Site of Canada *(see attraction listing)* in craft ranging in size up to the 30-passenger *Sea North II*. This vessel is equipped with stereo hydrophones so that passengers can listen to the sounds made by the beluga whales that swim within feet of the boat. Tours also offer chances of sighting polar bears, ice formations and indigenous birds. Kayak tours and snorkeling also are available.

Time: Allow 3 hours minimum. **Hours:** Daily dawn-dusk (times may vary depending on tides), mid-June to late Aug. **Cost:** Fare $90; $45 (ages 0-11). **Phone:** (204) 675-2195 or (888) 348-7591.

YORK FACTORY NATIONAL HISTORIC SITE OF CANADA is 250 km (150 mi.) s.e. near the mouth of the Hayes River; access to the site is limited to charter plane or boat. The site was established by the Hudson's Bay Co. as part of a series of fur trading posts. The 1832 depot is the oldest wooden structure still standing on permafrost. Interpretive tours of the site feature reconstructed buildings containing area artifacts.

Visitors should contact Parks Canada for transportation and safety information. Facilities at the site are limited; camping is not permitted. **Time:** Allow 4 hours minimum. **Hours:** Daily 8-5, June 15-Sept. 1 (weather permitting). **Cost:** Free. Guided tour $7.80; free (ages 0-4). **Phone:** (204) 675-8863.

COOKS CREEK (E-3) elev. 238 m/780′

COOK'S CREEK HERITAGE MUSEUM, jct. Hwy. 212 and Sapton Rd., houses artifacts pertaining to the life of the early settlers from Poland, Ukraine and other eastern European countries. Highlights include religious artifacts, folk art, clothing, a blacksmith shop, pioneer houses furnished in period and farm machines. **Time:** Allow 1 hour minimum. **Hours:** Thurs.-Tues. 10-5, mid-May through Aug. 31. **Cost:** $3; $2 (ages 0-18 and 66+). **Phone:** (204) 444-4448.

IMMACULATE CONCEPTION CHURCH AND THE GROTTO OF OUR LADY OF LOURDES is 3 km (1.9 mi.) n. on Hwy. 212 (Cooks Creek Rd.) from jct. Hwy. 213 (Garvin Rd.). The Ukrainian Catholic church, built by Father Philip Ruh 1930-52, features onion domes and the Icon of Our Lady of Perpetual Help, a replica of the Miraculous Icon in Rome. The grotto adjacent to the church is a replica of the original Grotto of Lourdes in France.

Guided tours are available by appointment. **Time:** Allow 1 hour minimum. **Hours:** Sat.-Sun. and holidays noon-6, May-Sept. **Cost:** $1. **Phone:** (204) 444-2478.

DAUPHIN (E-2) pop. 7,906, elev. 293 m/960′

Dauphin (DAW-fin) lies in a fertile farming valley between Duck Mountain Provincial Park *(see Recreation Chart)* and Riding Mountain National Park of Canada *(see place listing p. 229)*. Lake Dauphin, 15 kilometres (9 mi.) east of Dauphin, offers fishing.

The nation's rich Ukrainian culture and heritage are celebrated each year during Canada's National Ukrainian Festival, a 3-day event held in early August. Ukrainian music, food and dance take center stage at Selo Ukraina, a heritage village 12 kilometres (7.5 mi.) south of Dauphin near Riding Mountain National Park of Canada.

Dauphin Economic Development: 100 Main St. S., Dauphin, MB, Canada R7N 1K3. **Phone:** (204) 622-3229 or (877) 566-5669.

FORT DAUPHIN MUSEUM, 140 Jackson St., is surrounded by a wooden palisade suggestive of an 18th-century fur trading fort of the North West Co. A trapper's cabin, schoolhouse, church, blacksmith shop, trading post and pioneer house inside the fort are furnished in the style of the early settlers. Archeological, fur trade and pioneer artifacts also are featured.

Time: Allow 1 hour minimum. **Hours:** Daily 9-5, July-Aug.; Mon.-Fri. 9-5, rest of year. **Cost:** $4; $3 (students with ID); free (ages 0-11 with adult). **Phone:** (204) 638-6630.

ELKHORN (F-1) pop. 461, elev. 526 m/1,700′

THE MANITOBA ANTIQUE AUTOMOBILE MUSEUM is on Hwy. 1W. The museum displays some 100 vintage automobiles dating from 1908 to the mid-1960s; several are in operating condition. Also exhibited are steam engines, gas tractors and other farm machinery as well as aboriginal, household and pioneer artifacts. **Time:** Allow 1 hour minimum. **Hours:** Daily 9-6, May-Sept. **Cost:** $7.50; $2 (ages 5-16). **Phone:** (204) 845-2604, or (204) 845-2161 Oct.-Apr.

EMERSON (F-3) pop. 689

Emerson was named after American poet Ralph Waldo Emerson. When Manitoba became a province in 1870, this town on the border of the United States and Canada was the site of the province's first customs house. The original log buildings still stand just north of the Customs Port of Entry.

In 1874 the North West Mounted Police, later renamed the Royal Canadian Mounted Police, organized at Fort Dufferin, thus beginning their career of maintaining law and order in the untamed western areas of Canada. A 5-metre (15-ft.) bronze statue of a North West Mounted Police Officer and his horse is located next to the Tourist Information Centre on Hwy. 75. The statue is a tribute to the members of the force who made the historic "Trek West" from Emerson to Fort McLeod, Alberta.

The Boundary Commission Trail provides 3 kilometres (1.9 mi.) of hiking along the Red River north to the Historic Fort Dufferin Site. At the fort are the remains of old buildings, grave sites and a memorial to the North West Mounted Police.

Town of Emerson: P.O. Box 340, Emerson, MB, Canada R0A 0L0. **Phone:** (204) 373-2002.

FALCON LAKE (F-4) elev. 305 m/1,001′

As it winds its way across the country, the Trans Canada Trail enters Manitoba from Ontario at West Hawk Lake in Whiteshell Provincial Park *(see attraction listing)*, crossing the park diagonally as it heads westward to Pinawa. Incorporating many existing trails and utilizing abandoned railway lines, the trail offers hikers a diverse sampling of the province's topography.

WHITESHELL PROVINCIAL PARK is accessible via an especially scenic stretch of Hwy. 1E. The park's four districts encompass both wilderness and developed resort areas, more than 200 lakes and 12 rivers.

Alfred Hole Goose Sanctuary, east of Rennie on Hwy. 44, is a nesting ground for giant Canada geese, which can be seen from the interpretive center's observation deck. Believed extinct 1930-60, the birds can be seen at close range from the interpretive center. The center contains exhibits and informative videotapes. Rocks found throughout the park are part of the Precambrian Shield, the oldest geological formation in the world. *See Recreation Chart and the AAA/CAA Western Canada & Alaska CampBook.*

Among the rivers in the four districts—Falcon Lake, Rennie, Seven Sisters and West Hawk Lake—is the Winnipeg River with numerous falls and rapids. West Hawk Lake, near the Ontario border, is one of the deepest lakes in Manitoba. It is thought that the lake was formed by a meteor more than 100 million years ago.

Near Betula Lake are the Bannock Point Petroforms-ceremonial Anishinabe boulder mosaics of snakes, turtles and geometric shapes. Along with its beauty and tranquility, the park is popular during the summer for interpretive programs, swimming, scuba diving, canoeing, lawn bowling, tennis, miniature golf, horseshoes, horseback riding, sailing, hiking and golfing; in winter it provides ample opportunities for cross-country and downhill skiing, snowmobiling and snowshoeing.

Hours: Park open daily 24 hours. An interpretive center at Whiteshell Fish Hatchery is open daily 9:30-4:30, June 1-Labour Day. One-hour tours of the center are given daily at 11 and 2. **Cost:** Free. **Phone:** (204) 349-2201 for the Falcon Lake District, (204) 348-4004 for the Seven Sisters District, (204) 349-2245 for the West Hawk Lake District, (204) 369-5246 for the Rennie District, or (204) 349-8204 for the interpretive center at the fish hatchery.

Whiteshell Natural History Museum is deep within Whiteshell Provincial Park near Seven Sisters Falls on PR 307 at Nutimik Lake, opposite the boat launch. Mounted animals within the log cabin museum depict the wildlife residing within the provincial park. Other exhibits include displays about the boreal forest, native peoples, wild rice, sturgeon and the Winnipeg River.

Time: Allow 30 minutes minimum. **Hours:** Daily 9-noon and 1-5, Victoria Day weekend-Labour Day weekend. **Cost:** Free. **Phone:** (204) 348-2846. 🎣

RECREATIONAL ACTIVITIES
Horseback Riding

- **Falcon Beach Riding Stables and Guest Ranch** is off Hwy. 1 Falcon Lake exit. **Hours:** Daily 9-5, July-Aug.; by appointment rest of year. **Phone:** (204) 349-2410, or (877) 949-2410 in Canada.

FLIN FLON (C-1)
pop. 5,836, elev. 304 m/1,000′

Flin Flon was founded in 1915 when Tom Creighton, one of six prospectors, discovered an ore body which led to the development of Flin Flon as a mining town.

The community owes its name to Josiah Flintabbatey Flonatin, the major character of "The Sunless City," a dime novel found in the area by the discoverers of the mineral deposits. Off Hwy. 10 is a humorous 7.5-metre (25-ft.) statue of Flintabbatey Flonatin ("Flinty" for short) designed by the American cartoonist Al Capp, of "L'il Abner" fame. A boardwalk around Ross Lake, a walking trail and a park also remember the city's namesake; the park features a smaller statue of Flinty.

The Flin Flon Station Museum, north on Hwy. 10A, is open seasonally and displays artifacts collected from mining, transportation and cultural sources; phone (204) 687-2946. Bordering Saskatchewan, Flin Flon is the northern terminus of the Manitoba stretch of scenic Hwy. 10.

Flin Flon and District Chamber of Commerce: 235-35 Main St., Flin Flon, MB, Canada R8A 1J7. **Phone:** (204) 687-4518.

GARDENTON (F-3) elev. 298 m/979'

Some of the earliest Ukrainian settlers in Manitoba came to Gardenton in 1896. St. Michael's Ukrainian Orthodox Historical Church, 4 kilometres (2.5 mi.) west, is purportedly North America's first Ukrainian Orthodox church; the church was built 1897-99. Lithographed icons from St. Petersburg, Moscow and Kiev ornament the sanctuary. A pilgrimage is held the third Sunday in August. Phone (204) 425-3595 for an appointment to tour the church.

The Ukrainian Museum contains articles of clothing and hand tools depicting life in the late 1800s and early 1900s, a one-room schoolhouse and a thatched roof house. Also in the area is a tallgrass prairie. For further information about the museum phone (204) 425-3072 in summer, or (204) 425-3501 rest of year.

GILBERT PLAINS (E-2) pop. 760

WASYL NEGRYCH PIONEER HOMESTEAD is 17.3 km (10.8 mi.) n. on PR 274, then 3.2 km (2 mi.) e. on Negrych Rd. (gravel). The homestead's 10 log buildings, built in 1899, are said to be the province's most complete set of period farmyard buildings and the oldest Ukrainian-style house in Manitoba. The buildings reflect the architectural style of the Carpathian Mountain region. **Time:** Allow 1 hour minimum. **Hours:** Daily 10-5, July-Aug. **Cost:** $5; $3 (students with ID); free (ages 0-5). **Phone:** (204) 548-2326.

GIMLI (E-3) pop. 1,891, elev. 220 m/723'

Established in 1875, Gimli was the site of Canada's first permanent Icelandic settlement, the largest outside Iceland. The town's name, derived from Norse mythology, means "home of the gods." A Viking statue designed by Gissur Eliasson and the oldest Icelandic cemetery in Canada testify to Gimli's Nordic heritage. Gimli is located on the western shore of Lake Winnipeg, one of the largest freshwater lakes in the world.

Lake Winnipeg Visitor Centre-Gimli: 108-84 1st Ave., Gimli, MB, Canada R0C 1B0. **Phone:** (204) 642-7974.

NEW ICELAND HERITAGE MUSEUM is at 94 1st Ave. Displayed in three buildings are exhibits that focus on the area's Icelandic roots, the fishing industry and Lake Winnipeg's natural history. Multimedia exhibits at the Waterfront Centre examine area history, while displays at the visitor center feature the fishing industry and the lake's natural history. A classroom typical of early 1900s rural Manitoba can be seen at the 1915 Gimli Public School.

Time: Allow 30 minutes minimum. **Hours:** Waterfront Centre daily 10-4, Victoria Day weekend-Labour Day; Mon.-Fri. 10-4, Sat.-Sun. 1-4, rest of year. Visitor center and school daily 10-4, Victoria Day weekend-Labour Day. **Cost:** $5; $4 (ages 61+ and students with ID); free (ages 0-6); $15 (family). **Phone:** (204) 642-4001.

GIROUX (F-3) elev. 271 m/888'

PHILIP'S MAGICAL PARADISE: MUSEUM OF MAGIC AND ILLUSION, 39 Municipal Rd. at jct. Hwy. 311, houses a variety of items donated by magicians from around the world. **Time:** Allow 30 minutes minimum. **Hours:** Mon.-Fri. 7 p.m.-9 p.m., Sat.-Sun. 1-6, mid-May to late Sept. **Cost:** Donations. **Phone:** (204) 326-1219.

GLENBORO (F-2) pop. 633, elev. 375 m/1,230'

Glenboro is known as the gateway to Spruce Woods Provincial Park (see Carberry p. 221) and the Manitoba Desert. At the junction of Hwys. 2 and 5 in Camel Park stands Sara the Camel, a 7-metre-high (24-ft.) symbol of the Spirit Sands. A portion of the SS Alpha, a steamship that ran aground on the Assiniboine River in 1885, also is displayed in the park.

Slightly northwest of Glenboro on Hwy. 2 is what is purported to be the last cable river ferry in southern Manitoba; phone (204) 827-2252.

GRANDVIEW (E-2)
pop. 839, elev. 434 m/1,425'

WATSON CROSSLEY COMMUNITY MUSEUM is on the w. side of town at the sports grounds on Railway Ave. The museum displays regional pioneer items including automobiles, horsedrawn equipment, tractors, farm machinery and other artifacts. A restored 1896 homesteader's cabin, a pioneer church with a free-standing bell tower, a rural schoolhouse and a three-story 1918 pioneer house are furnished in their respective periods.

Time: Allow 2 hours minimum. **Hours:** Daily 10-5, late June-early Sept.; by appointment rest of year. **Cost:** $4; $3 (ages 13-17). **Phone:** (204) 546-2040 late June-early Sept., (204) 546-2661, or (204) 546-2764 rest of year.

HADASHVILLE (F-3) elev. 297 m/975′

SANDILANDS FOREST CENTRE, about 2 km (1.2 mi.) s. of jct. Hwys. 1 and 11, tells visitors about forest conservation, reforestation and fire prevention. A train car used 1919-74 to promote the nationwide planting of trees is shown, an electronic display tests tree species knowledge and a museum has area plants and animals. The Old Beaver Dam Trail, reached by a suspension bridge over the Whitemouth River, penetrates aspen parkland and a boreal forest.

Guided tours of the center are available. **Time:** Allow 1 hour minimum. **Hours:** Thurs.-Mon. 10-5, July-Aug.; by appointment May-June and in Sept. Phone ahead to confirm schedule. **Cost:** Donations. Guided tours $3. Reservations are required for guided tours. **Phone:** (204) 453-5374.

HECLA ISLAND (E-4) elev. 210 m/690′

HECLA/GRINDSTONE PROVINCIAL PARK, 165 km (103 mi.) n. of Winnipeg, or 54 km (34 mi.) n. of Riverton, on Hwy. 8, is comprised of several islands in Lake Winnipeg, the largest of which is Hecla Island. The original settlers were Icelanders displaced from their homeland in 1876, fleeing poverty and Danish rule. Guided walks through the restored buildings of Hecla Village—a church, school, community hall, period house, dockside fish station, a tool display and a partially completed boarding house—are offered. *See Recreation Chart.*

Interpretive programs also are available, as are camping facilities, cabins, hiking trails, picnic areas, bicycling, fishing and swimming. For further information contact the Department of Conservation, P.O. Box 70, Riverton, MB, Canada R0C 2R0. **Hours:** Daily 24 hours. **Cost:** Free. **Phone:** (204) 279-2032 May-Sept., or (204) 378-2261 rest of year.

Grassy Narrows Marsh and Wildlife Viewing Tower, at Hecla/Grindstone Provincial Park, offers wildlife viewing from trails and boardwalks along the marsh as well as from towers along the trails. Some trails are designated bicycling trails. The marsh, a nesting area for Canada geese and other waterfowl, is named after the Narrows, a channel between Hecla Island and the mainland. The tower was built for viewing moose as they feed in the marsh. **Note:** Visitors should bring drinking water and wear comfortable walking shoes. **Hours:** Daily 24 hours. **Cost:** included with park fee.

Hecla Fish Station, at Hecla/Grindstone Provincial Park, is in an old ice house, or "fish station." The site provides a look at the commercial fishing industry of Lake Winnipeg through artifacts, wall plaques and a small museum. During fishing season visitors may view fishermen bringing in the day's catch. **Hours:** Daily 11:30-4:30, June 10-Aug. 30. **Cost:** Free.

Hecla Island Heritage Home Museum, at Hecla/Grindstone Provincial Park, depicts the lifestyle of an Icelandic family from the 1920s to the 1940s.

The restored 1928 house is furnished in period with items donated by descendants of the original owners and by other islanders. Walking tours are available. **Hours:** Wed.-Sun. 10-4, June 15-Aug. 30. **Cost:** Donations.

INGLIS (E-1)

 INGLIS GRAIN ELEVATORS NATIONAL HISTORIC SITE is along Railway Ave.

These five vintage grain elevators, once a common sight on western Canadian prairies, have been restored and are now the last remaining row of standard wooden grain elevators in Canada. Dating to the 1920s, similar rows of elevators, built by grain companies and agricultural cooperatives, once stood along rail lines in most small Canadian communities.

An interpretive center in the Paterson elevator explains the importance of these structures to the nation's agricultural history. Exhibits and displays complement a videotape presentation, which shows how the elevators operated, transporting wheat into storage bins. A walking tour of the grounds provides further insights into the development of Canada's grain industry.

Time: Allow 1 hour minimum. **Hours:** Mon.-Sat. 10-6, Sun. noon-5, July-Aug.; otherwise by appointment. **Cost:** $5; $3 (students with ID); free (ages 0-5). **Phone:** (204) 564-2243.

INTERNATIONAL PEACE GARDEN (F-1)

On US 281 and scenic Hwy. 10, the International Peace Garden consists of 586 hectares (1,451 acres) in Canada and an adjoining 360 hectares (888 acres) in North Dakota. Set among the lakes and streams of the wooded Turtle Mountains, the botanical garden and park commemorates the friendship between these two countries on the longest unfortified border in the world.

Centers of attraction include the Peace Tower, which represents people from the four corners of the world coming together for the common purpose of peace; an interpretive center depicting the history and development of the park; the Peace Chapel, which includes quotations etched in limestone walls; more than 150,000 annual flowers in the formal gardens that line the boundary; a floral clock; the Carillon Bell Tower, which chimes every 15 minutes; and a memorial cairn, constructed of steel salvaged from the destruction of the World Trade Center, commemorating the tragic events of September 11, 2001.

Other facilities include campgrounds, hiking and bicycling trails and picnic areas. Self-guiding walking and driving tours are available. Flowers are in full bloom mid-July to early September (weather permitting).

The International Music Camp Summer School of Fine Arts is held at the garden June through July. The Canadian Legion Sports Camp, held during July through August, attracts coaches and athletes from many countries.

Allow 1 hour minimum. The garden and port of entry offices are open daily 24 hours. Daily vehicle permits $10; season permits $25; pedestrian permits $5. Visitors are required to go through customs after leaving the garden. Phone (204) 534-2510 in Canada, (701) 263-4390 in the United States, or (888) 432-6733.

KILLARNEY (F-2)
pop. 2,199, elev. 495 m/1,625′

The area's resemblance to Ireland's Killarney Lakes prompted John Sidney O'Brien to change the name of the town of Oak Lake to Killarney. Green fire engines and a replica of the Blarney Stone are further evidence of the town's Irish heritage.

Killarney and District Chamber of Commerce: P.O. Box 809, Killarney, MB, Canada R0K 1G0. **Phone:** (204) 523-4202.

J.A.V. DAVID MUSEUM, 414 Williams Ave., displays Indian and pioneer artifacts, local memorabilia, quilts and collections of birds, butterflies and animals. Also featured are an early 1900s schoolroom, a Ninette Sanitorium display, a post office display and a country store. **Time:** Allow 1 hour minimum. **Hours:** Tues.-Sat. 10-5, July-Aug.; by appointment rest of year. Closed major holidays. **Cost:** $2; $1 (students); free (ages 0-10); $5 (family). **Phone:** (204) 523-7325.

LA RIVIÈRE (F-2)

ARCHIBALD HISTORICAL MUSEUM is 3 km (2 mi.) e. on Hwy. 3, then 6 km (4 mi.) n. on a dirt road, following signs. The museum consists of buildings moved to the site from neighboring areas. Two homes lived in by social activist and author Nellie McClung in the late 19th and early 20th centuries are included, both furnished in period, as are the mansard-roofed former CPR train station (with a 1913 wooden caboose in front), a house with tin siding and a three-story barn with a country store, tools, buggies, household artifacts and tractors.

Native artifacts and vintage cars, trucks and gas pumps also can be seen. **Time:** Allow 1 hour minimum. **Hours:** Fri.-Tues. noon-8, mid-May through Labour Day. Phone ahead to confirm schedule. **Cost:** $6; $2 (ages 5-11). **Phone:** (204) 242-2825.
⛐

LOCKPORT (E-3) elev. 313 m/1,000′

At Lockport Provincial Heritage Park *(see attraction listing)*, on Hwy. 44 just east of the Lockport bridge, is St. Andrews Lock and Dam. This rare structure on Canada's flat prairies was completed in 1910 to allow access and permit navigation on the Red River from Lake Winnipeg to the city of Winnipeg; it is purportedly the only lock and dam of its kind still standing in North America. Picnic sites and footpaths overlook the dam.

Red River North Tourism-Lockport: 18 Main St., 2nd floor, Selkirk, MB, Canada R1A 1P5. **Phone:** (204) 482-2022 or (800) 894-2621.

ST. ANDREW'S CHURCH is 2 km (1.2 mi.) s. on Hwy. 9, then e. on St. Andrews Rd. (Hwy. 410) to jct. River Rd. (Hwy. 238) at 374 River Rd. Designed by its first rector 1844-49, this stone Gothic-Revival Anglican church is the oldest house of worship in continuous use in western Canada. It retains many of its original fixtures, such as buffalo-hide-covered kneeling benches. The church's cemetery is adjacent. **Time:** Allow 30 minutes minimum. **Hours:** Tours Wed.-Sun. 9:30-5, mid-May through Labour Day. **Cost:** Donations. **Phone:** (204) 334-6405.

St. Andrew's Rectory National Historic Site of Canada is across from St. Andrew's Church. The two-story stone building, constructed in 1854 for the church's rectors, has exhibits on the ground floor about the building's architecture, the work of the early missionaries and life in the Red River Settlement. The building is home to the current church rector. **Hours:** Wed.-Sun. 9:30-5, mid-May through Labour Day. **Cost:** Donations. **Phone:** (204) 334-6405.

MORDEN (F-2) pop. 6,571, elev. 302 m/990′

Named after the area's first settler, Alvey Morden, the town grew almost overnight when the Canadian Pacific Railroad arrived in 1882. Located near the Boundary Commission-NWMP Trail in the Boundary Trail Heritage Region, Morden has a progressive industrial and business sector. Abundant recreational activities at Lake Minnewasta *(see Recreation Chart)* and Colert Beach include camping, swimming, fishing, water skiing, canoeing, sailing, bicycling and hiking in the summer. Winter activities include cross-country skiing, snowmobiling and ice fishing.

A mural on the corner of Stephen and Nelson streets is a re-creation of one of the earliest known photographs taken in the area. The scene depicts the supply train for Her Majesty's British North American Boundary Commission at Dead Horse Creek in June 1873.

Another mural, at the corner of Stephen and 7th streets, remembers the visit of Canada's first prime minister, Sir John A. MacDonald, to the town on July 15, 1886. The depiction features Sir John speaking from the rear of his railcar and Philip Locke presenting him with a bouquet of prairie flowers; a version of an Indian war dance also is depicted.

A third mural, at 306 N. Railway St., depicts the original uniform of the North West Mounted Police and provides a history of the force, now known as the Royal Canadian Mounted Police.

Morden and District Chamber of Commerce: 311 N. Railway St., Morden, MB, Canada R6M 1S9. **Phone:** (204) 822-5630.

Self-guiding tours: Heritage Series Brochures, available at the chamber of commerce, describe self-guiding walking tours of Morden's turn-of-the-20th-century homes and buildings.

CANADIAN FOSSIL DISCOVERY CENTRE is in the lower level of the recreation center at 111-B Gilmour St. Fossil displays chronicle regional paleontology and geology. Marine reptile fossils, such as mosasaurs and plesiosaurs, date from 80 million years ago when the Western Interior Seaway covered much of North America. A highlight of the exhibits is Bruce, a 43-foot mosasaur and said to be the largest discovered in Canada. The process of finding, excavating and displaying the fossils also is depicted. Fossil Dig Adventure Tours offer a chance to excavate fossils at a site nearby.

Time: Allow 1 hour minimum. **Hours:** Daily 10-5, May-Aug.; 1-5, rest of year. Closed Dec. 25. **Cost:** $6; $3 (ages 5-17); $12 (family, two adults and up to three children). A fee is charged for Fossil Dig. **Phone:** (204) 822-3406.

MORRIS (F-3) pop. 1,643, elev. 236 m/775′

Two rival fur-trading companies—the North West Co. and the Hudson's Bay Co.—set up shop on the Morris River in 1801. Not until 1874 did a permanent settlement take hold; incorporation took place in 1883. Both the town and the river on which it grew were named for Alexander Morris, the second lieutenant governor of Manitoba during the 1870s.

Morris & District Chamber of Commerce: P.O. Box 98, Morris, MB, Canada R0G 1K0. **Phone:** (204) 746-6275.

MORRIS & DISTRICT CENTENNIAL MUSEUM, on Main St. at jct. Hwys. 75 and 23, consists of two buildings. The main building is the original Carleton School, which contains pioneer era displays of farm tools and a laundry and dairy section. The second building contains five rooms featuring furniture and artifacts from the turn of the 20th century. A mural depicts the history of the Red River Valley. **Hours:** Daily noon-5, June-Sept. **Cost:** Donations. **Phone:** (204) 746-2169.

NEEPAWA (F-2) pop. 3,298, elev. 400 m/1,300′

Neepawa, whose name derives from a native word for plenty, is a service center for the surrounding grain and livestock farms on the fertile plains northwest of Winnipeg. This community of tree-lined streets, well-known as the birthplace of author Margaret Laurence, offers many pleasant diversions for residents and travelers alike, including Riverbend Park, a fitness trail and camping area.

The city calls itself the World Lily Capital. This claim is bolstered by the annual 🌸Neepawa & Area Lily Festival held the third week in July. More than 2,000 varieties of lilies are grown in the Neepawa area, and the community celebrates their beauty with live entertainment, music, street vendors and food kiosks, a quilt show, a parade, tours by bus and horse-drawn vehicles and a photography contest.

Neepawa and District Chamber of Commerce: 282 Hamilton St., P.O. Box 726, Neepawa, MB, Canada R0J 1H0. **Phone:** (204) 476-5292.

BEAUTIFUL PLAINS MUSEUM, 91 Hamilton St. W., is housed in a former CNR station. The museum features several rooms of historical items. A children's room contains antique toys and books, and a military room has uniforms and pictures of local residents involved in World Wars I and II. Other rooms include items dedicated to nature, stores, Masonic lodges, sports and vintage clothing. An extensive doll collection also is displayed.

Time: Allow 30 minutes minimum. **Hours:** Mon.-Fri. 9-5, Sat.-Sun. 1-5, July 1-early Sept.; Mon.-Fri. 9-5, late May-June 30. **Cost:** Donations. **Phone:** (204) 476-3896.

MARGARET LAURENCE HOME, 312 First Ave., contains photographs, memorabilia, autographed books and research materials of the award-winning Canadian author, born here in 1926. **Tours:** Guided tours are available. **Hours:** Daily 10-4, mid-May through Sept. 30; by appointment rest of year. **Cost:** $3; $2 (students); free (ages 0-12). **Phone:** (204) 476-3612.

PINAWA (F-3) pop. 1,450, elev. 282 m/925′

Named "Pinnawak," meaning calm waters, by the aboriginal people, Pinawa was first settled by families who operated one of the earliest hydroelectric power dams built between Sault Ste. Marie, Ontario, and the Rockies. The townsite was abandoned in 1951, and the historic site is now Pinawa Dam Provincial Heritage Park. The new Pinawa was built in 1963 when the Federal Crown Corp., Atomic Energy of Canada Limited (AECL) built its research center near the old townsite.

PORTAGE LA PRAIRIE (F-2)
pop. 12,728, elev. 332 m/1,100′

The city's name is derived from the prairie portage between the Red and Assiniboine rivers and Lake Manitoba. In the heart of the city at Crescent Road and Royal Road S. is Island Park. Surrounded by horseshoe-shaped Crescent Lake, this scenic park has a deer sanctuary, a large captive flock of Canada geese and offers opportunities for other bird-watching. Park features include exhibition grounds, seasonal harness racing, a golf course, an arboretum, tennis courts, picnic areas and bicycling and hiking trails.

Portage la Prairie City Hall, built in 1898, was designed by one of Canada's foremost architects, Thomas Fuller.

Portage and District Chamber of Commerce: 11 Second St. N.E., Portage la Prairie, MB, Canada R1N 1R8. **Phone:** (204) 857-7778.

FORT LA REINE MUSEUM, PIONEER VILLAGE AND TOURIST BUREAU is at jct. Hwys. 26 and 1A E. The central museum includes pioneer household articles and implements, a log fort, school, doctor's office, trading post, furnished homestead and church as well as railway, farming and military displays. Canadian railway official Sir William Van Horne's business car also is displayed. A tourist bureau is available.

Time: Allow 1 hour minimum. **Hours:** Mon.-Sat. 9-6, Sun. noon-6, mid-May to mid-Sept. **Cost:** $8; $6 (ages 60+); $3 (ages 6-12). **Phone:** (204) 857-3259.

RIDING MOUNTAIN NATIONAL PARK OF CANADA (E-2)

Elevations in the park range from 230 metres (755 ft.) at Henderson Creek in the northeastern area to 756 metres (2,480 ft.) at Bald Hill in the eastern side of the park. Refer to CAA/AAA maps for additional elevation information.

Accessible from the north and south via scenic Hwy. 10, or from the east via Hwy. 19, Riding Mountain National Park of Canada lies on the plateau of the Manitoba escarpment, 197 kilometres (123 mi.) north of the U.S. border and 259 kilometres (162 mi.) northwest of Winnipeg. This 2,978-square-kilometre (1,150-sq.-mi.) area is blanketed with forests, lakes and meadows. The park is home to elk, moose, deer, bears and a wide variety of birds and vegetation. Waterfowl and beavers populate the waterways, and a herd of bison grazes in a large enclosure near Lake Audy.

General Information and Activities

Although the park is open year-round, complete facilities are available only from mid-May to mid-October. The park also encompasses the historic resort town of Wasagaming on Clear Lake, which offers the amenities of a resort destination.

Recreational activities available within the park include tennis, golfing, lawn bowling, swimming, hiking, fishing, canoeing, sailing, cross-country skiing, horseback riding, bicycling, camping and snowshoeing. More than 400 kilometres (250 mi.) of hiking, bicycling and horseback trails lead to lakes, meadows and evergreen forests. Bicycle and boat rentals are available.

Several forms of recreation can be pursued nearby. Guides and outfitters offer horseback riding and wagon excursions along with other wilderness activities. There are boat launching facilities at Clear Lake. Snowshoeing and cross-country skiing are other popular activities. *See Recreation Chart and the AAA/CAA Western Canada & Alaska CampBook.*

ADMISSION is $7.80; $6.55 (ages 65+); $19.60 (family, up to seven people). Annual pass $39.20; $34.30 (ages 65+); $98.10 (family).

PETS are allowed in the park. Dogs must be leashed at all times.

ADDRESS inquiries to Visitor Information, Riding Mountain National Park of Canada, Wasagaming, MB, Canada R0J 2H0; phone (204) 848-7275 or (204) 848-7272.

VISITOR INFORMATION CENTRE OF WASAGAMING is on the s. shore of Clear Lake. The center maintains exhibits and displays about the natural and human history of the area. Interpretive programs include nature walks, campfires, theater programs and guided hikes. **Hours:** Daily 9:30-8, Victoria Day weekend-early Sept. **Cost:** Free. **Phone:** (204) 848-7275 or (204) 848-7272.

SELKIRK (E-3) pop. 9,515, elev. 231 m/800'

Selkirk's name honors Lord Selkirk, the Scottish philanthropist whose 1803 settlement in the Red River Valley to the south laid the foundation for Winnipeg. During the late 19th and early 20th centuries, Selkirk's position on the Red River made it a base for trade and communication with the more isolated settlements around Lake Winnipeg.

Chuck the Channel Catfish, a 9-metre (30-ft.) fiberglass statue, greets visitors on Main Street. The oversized catfish is an apt representation of the live version: Catfish weighing more than 9 kilograms (20 lbs.) abound in the Red River between Selkirk and Lockport.

St. Peter's Dynevor Church, 6.5 kilometres (4 mi.) northeast off Hwy. 59, was built in 1853. The original church, erected in 1836, was the center for Anglican missionary work among the Saulteaux Indians.

Red River North Tourism-Selkirk: 18 Main St., 2nd floor, Selkirk, MB, Canada R1A 1P5. **Phone:** (204) 482-2022 or (800) 894-2621.

LOWER FORT GARRY NATIONAL HISTORIC SITE OF CANADA, 5 km (3 mi.) s.

on Hwy. 9, is purportedly the oldest intact stone fur-trading post in North America. The 19th-century buildings are restored and furnished as they might have been in their early days. Costumed staff members perform tasks and re-enact events that re-create the early 1850s atmosphere of the fort in its heyday. The Visitor Reception Centre offers exhibits about the fort's history.

Time: Allow 2 hours minimum. **Hours:** Daily 9-5, mid-May through Labour Day. **Cost:** $7.80; $6.55 (ages 65+); $3.90 (ages 6-17); $19.60 (family, up to two adults and five children). **Phone:** (204) 785-6050 or (888) 773-8888.

MARINE MUSEUM OF MANITOBA, at the entrance to Selkirk Park at Eveline St. and Queen Ave., reflects Selkirk's nautical past through displays of outboard motors, tools used for early 1900s shipbuilding, two lighthouses and six restored ships. The 1897 passenger steamship SS *Keenora* houses nautical artifacts and photographs. Other displays include early 1900s underwater diving and a graphite exhibit representing the species of fish caught in Lake Winnipeg and the Red River.

Also displayed are the 1942 *Chickama II;* the 1944 MS *Northland Lady Canadian;* the CGS *Bradbury,* an ice-breaker steam vessel built in 1915; the MS *Peguis II,* a lake and river tug built in 1955; the *Joe Simpson,* a freighter built in 1963; and the 1952

Jackie S., the last all wood, white fish (gas boat) to sail Lake Winnipeg. **Time:** Allow 1 hour minimum. **Hours:** Mon.-Fri. 9-5, Sat.-Sun. and holidays 10-6, mid-May through Labour Day. **Cost:** $6.50; $5(ages 66+); $3 (ages 6-17). **Phone:** (204) 482-7761.

SHILO (F-2)

THE ROYAL REGIMENT OF CANADIAN ARTIL-LERY MUSEUM is on the Canadian Forces Base via Hwy. 340. This indoor-outdoor museum exhibits more than 10,000 articles of dress, technical instruments, ammunition, small arms, guns and World War II vehicles. Among the more than 150 pieces of major military equipment dating to 1796 are German, Russian and French guns.

Guided tours are available by appointment. **Time:** Allow 1 hour minimum. **Hours:** Mon.-Sat. 9-5, Sun. and holidays 10-5, Victoria Day-Labour Day; Mon.-Fri. 10-5, rest of year. **Cost:** $5; $3 (senior citizens and students with ID); free (ages 0-5). **Phone:** (204) 765-3000, ext. 3570.

SOURIS (F-2) pop. 1,772, elev. 396 m/1,300′

The free-swinging 177-metre (581-ft.) footbridge built in 1904 over the Souris (SIR-iss) River is considered the longest free-suspension foot bridge in Canada. The bridge was reconstructed after being destroyed by a flood in 1976. Victoria Park has more than 6 kilometres (4 mi.) of walking trails, a viewing tower and a bird sanctuary containing geese, peacocks and swans *(see the AAA/CAA Western Canada & Alaska CampBook).*

Rockhounding in nearby agate pits yields agate, dendrite, jasper, petrified wood and epidote; the area offers one of the largest varieties of semi-precious stones found in North America. Permits are required and cost $10 per private vehicle. Contact the Rock Shop, 8 First St. S., Souris, MB, Canada R0K 2C0; phone (204) 483-2561.

HILLCREST MUSEUM, Crescent Ave. and Sowden St. next to the swinging bridge, is a restored late 19th-century residence furnished with settler artifacts and antiques. Highlights include an agricultural display with a covered wagon, tractor and farm tools as well as a printing press, a collection of more than 5,000 butterflies and a caboose. **Time:** Allow 30 minutes minimum. **Hours:** Daily 10-6, July 1-Labour Day. **Cost:** $3; $2 (ages 0-15). **Phone:** (204) 483-2008.

STEINBACH (F-3)
pop. 11,066, elev. 261 m/900′

MENNONITE HERITAGE VILLAGE, 3 km (1.9 mi.) n. on Hwy. 12, centers on a replica of a Mennonite village with more than 20 completely furnished buildings that were moved to the site. On the 16-hectare (40-acre) grounds are a fruit garden, stock pens, a steam engine, gas tractors and other machinery. The village windmill is said to be the only one of its kind in Canada. A museum displays antiques and manuscripts.

Time: Allow 1 hour minimum. **Hours:** Mon.-Sat. 10-6, Sun. noon-6, July-Aug.; Mon.-Sat. 10-5, Sun. noon-5, May-June and in Sept.; Mon.-Fri. 10-4 or by appointment, rest of year. **Cost:** $10; $7 (ages 13-22 and 66+); $2 (ages 6-12); $20 (family). **Phone:** (204) 326-9661.

STONEWALL (E-3) pop. 4,376

Nobody knows for sure if Stonewall was named after founding father S.J. "Stonewall" Jackson or the limestone ridge on which the town is built. The name fits well, though, since limestone quarrying sustained the area's economy from the early 1880s until 1967. Stonewall's past is captured through the old stone buildings dotting its streets.

Stonewall and District Chamber of Commerce: P.O. Box 762, Stonewall, MB, Canada R0C 2Z0. **Phone:** (204) 467-8377.

OAK HAMMOCK MARSH INTERPRETIVE CENTRE is 13 km (8 mi.) e. on Hwy. 67, then 4 km (2.5 mi.) n. on Hwy. 220. This 3,600-hectare (9,000-acre) restored prairie wetland is home to more than 295 species of birds, 25 species of mammals and thousands of other plant and animal species. Scores of migrating birds and waterfowl can be seen in the spring and fall.

The area is a remnant of the historic St. Andrews Bog that once covered much of southern Manitoba's Interlake area. Hikers can explore 30 kilometres (19 mi.) of trails over a system of boardwalks and dikes. The interpretive center has displays, films and interpretive programs.

The center was designed to educate visitors about the important role wetland environments play in the Earth's ecology. There are daily marsh canoe excursions spring through fall and snowshoe walkabouts in the winter. **Time:** Allow 2 hours minimum. **Hours:** Area open daily 24 hours. Interpretive center open daily 10-dusk, Sept.-May; 10-8, rest of year. Closed Dec. 25. **Cost:** Interpretive center (includes guided tour of the center and the wetlands) $6; $5 (ages 56+); $4 (ages 3-17); $20 (family). **Phone:** (204) 467-3300 or (800) 665-3825. 🍴 🎡

STONEWALL QUARRY PARK, on the n. end of Main St., commemorates the important role limestone played in the town's development. The interpretive center has a museum, videotape presentations and exhibits; an observation tower affords a panorama of the area. Self-guiding tours around the 30-hectare (75 acre) grounds offer a closer look at kilns, fossil deposits in rock and wildlife. Kinsmen Lake has a sandy beach and swimming; tobogganing is a winter option. *See Recreation Chart.*

Note: The interpretive center was destroyed by fire, but the park remains open. The center is scheduled to re-open in spring 2011. **Tours:** Guided tours are available. Allow 1 hour minimum. **Hours:** Daily 11-5, May 1-Labour Day. Hours vary rest of year; phone ahead. **Cost:** Free. Lake area swimming $5.50; $4.50 (ages 66+ and students); free (ages 0-1). Reservations are required for guided tours. **Phone:** (204) 467-7980. ⊺ ⊼ ⬟

SWAN RIVER (D-2)
pop. 3,859, elev. 340 m/1,116′

During the last 13 years of the 18th century, control of the Swan River Valley was sought by both the North West Co. and the Hudson's Bay Co. Each company built fur-trading posts in the area, but by 1800 the concentrated trapping generated by the rivalry had depleted the number of fur-bearing animals. The Hudson's Bay Co. abandoned the area until the two companies joined in 1821.

The Swan River Valley, nestled between the Duck and Porcupine mountains, offers fishing, hunting, boating, camping, swimming and picnicking. Scenic Hwy. 10 passes just east of town.

Swan River Chamber of Commerce: P.O. Box 1540, Swan River, MB, Canada R0L 1Z0. **Phone:** (204) 734-3102.

SWAN VALLEY HISTORICAL MUSEUM, 1.5 km (1 mi.) n. on Hwy. 10, reflects life in Manitoba's pioneer era through artifacts and restored buildings. Highlights include two machine sheds, two log cabins, a CN railroad station, a telephone station, a blacksmith shop, a pioneer store, two churches and a 1900s one-room schoolhouse.

Time: Allow 1 hour minimum. **Hours:** Mon.-Fri. 9-5, Sat.-Sun. and holidays 1-5, May-Sept.; by appointment rest of year. **Cost:** $2; free (ages 0-11). **Phone:** (204) 734-3585 or (204) 734-2713.

THE PAS (C-2) pop. 5,589, elev. 274 m/900′

A cairn in Devon Park at The Pas (pronounced "the paw") honors Henry Kelsey, the first known European to see the northern prairies in 1690. It is rumored that the first wheat on the prairies was planted in the area in 1734.

Christ Church (Anglican), on Edwards Avenue, was founded in 1840 by Henry Budd, the first native Indian ordained to the Anglican ministry. The church contains hand-hewn furnishings made by ships' carpenters in 1847. Tours are offered by appointment; phone (204) 623-2119 or (204) 624-5433.

SAM WALLER MUSEUM is at 306 Fischer Ave. Housed in what is said to be northern Manitoba's oldest brick edifice, the museum originally was the town's Courthouse and Community building. On display are natural history exhibits, local historical materials and Indian and fur-trading artifacts. The basement features original jail cells and a children's discovery room. Historic walking tours of the downtown and riverfront areas also are offered.

Time: Allow 1 hour minimum. **Hours:** Daily 10-5, July-Aug.; 1-5, rest of year. Historic walking tours by appointment. Closed major holidays. **Cost:** $3; $1 (ages 56+ and students with ID); $6 (family). Admission Wed. by donation. **Phone:** (204) 623-3802.

Bison

The Europeans who explored Canada in the 18th century were awed by the throngs of huge furry cattle that swarmed across the plains. Then, as many as 60 million North American bison, or plains buffalo, roamed the Canadian flatlands. They were the main food source for the Plains Indians, who had mastered the art of harvesting bison for food and clothing: Scaring the animals into a stampede, the Indians then ran them into corrals, where the bison could be killed as they were needed.

Later, the Métis, people of French and Indian heritage, became expert bison hunters as well. Hides were transformed into heavy robes that became the fashion in Europe; tongues were cooked and prized as delicacies; and bison meat, dried and pounded and mixed with fat and sometimes berries, was used to make pemmican, a Canadian aboriginal food which was packed in bags and stored.

As the Europeans fought the Indians and each other, the bison fell victim to reckless slaughter, the repeating rifle and politics. Carcasses of animals killed solely for their tongues or hides littered the plains. When the white settlers realized they could starve the natives by killing the bison, they set fire to the plains, killing thousands of the animals and driving others into what is now the United States. By 1885 the bison faced extinction in Canada.

Around 1900 a handful of conservation-minded cattlemen convinced the Canadian government to protect the bison, and the killing stopped. Manitoba acknowledges its debt to the bison by placing its image on the province's crest.

THOMPSON (B-2)
pop. 13,446, elev. 206 m/675'

Thompson sprang up after the discovery of one of the world's largest nickel deposits and is a major mining, communications, transportation, medical and retailing center.

Lakes and rivers abound in this rugged, picturesque area. Paint Lake Provincial Recreation Park *(see Recreation Chart and the AAA/CAA Western Canada & Alaska CampBook)* is 32 kilometres (20 mi.) south on Hwy. 6.

Also south of Thompson on Hwy. 6 is the starting point for a 10 kilometre (6-mi.) hiking trail that will take you over a bridge to Kwasitchewan Falls, the highest waterfall in the province. Between Wabowden and Thompson, within Pisew Falls Provincial Park, is Pisew Falls, the second-highest waterfall in Manitoba accessible by road. A 1.3-kilometre (.8-mi.) trail leads from the highway through the dense foliage to a platform overlooking the 12.8-metre (42-ft.) falls. Twelve site plaques describe the flora and fauna of this boreal forest. Picnic facilities are available.

Thompson Spirit Way is a combination gravel and pavement path that offers 16 points of interest. Designed for bicycling or walking, the route starts at the Heritage North Museum and ends at Miles Hart Bridge. Though hiking boots are not required, it is essential to wear comfortable walking shoes. The route stretches for 2 kilometres (1 mi.) and highlights include an 86-foot-tall wolf mural that is said to be the largest lighted mural in the world as well as a restored Norseman floatplane. Display panels share information about the sites and vantage points present scenic views. Official Spirit Way guide books may be purchased from the museum or the chamber of commerce at 79 Selkirk Ave.; phone (204) 677-4155.

Thompson Chamber of Commerce: 79 Selkirk Ave., Thompson, MB, Canada R8N 1M2. **Phone:** (204) 677-4155 or (888) 307-0103.

HERITAGE NORTH MUSEUM, in a log cabin at jct. Princeton Dr. and Mystery Lake Rd., also serves as the tourist information center. Displayed are an assortment of stuffed and mounted animals native to the area, fossils, a mining exhibit, a woolly mammoth tusk found near Thompson, a boreal forest exhibit which includes a caribou-hide tepee, and changing exhibits. A second log building houses a mining exhibit. Archives are available.

Hours: Daily 9-5, in summer; Mon.-Sat. 1-5, rest of year. **Cost:** $3.25; $2 (ages 13-18 and 60+); $1 (ages 6-12). **Phone:** (204) 677-2216.

VIRDEN (F-2) pop. 3,010, elev. 439 m/1,440'

About 1,200 oil wells dot the landscape in and around Virden—the richest source of petroleum in Manitoba. The first oil-producing well was sunk in the 1950s in the Rosalee field northwest of Virden.

Many original fieldstone buildings, such as the 1892 St. Mary's Anglican Church at the corner of Queen Street and 9th Avenue, are still in use today. The site of Fort Montagne à la Bosse, built by the North West Co. in 1790, is northeast of Virden on the old Trans-Canada Highway. To help cool things off in the summer, the fairgrounds has a public pool and waterslides.

Virden and District Chamber of Commerce: P.O. Box 899, Virden, MB, Canada R0M 2C0. **Phone:** (204) 748-3955.

VIRDEN PIONEER HOME MUSEUM INC. is at 390 King St. W. The museum, in a large brick house, is a living memorial to the pioneers who came to the region. Built in 1888, it is furnished with family pieces donated by descendants of the pioneers. **Time:** Allow 30 minutes minimum. **Hours:** Mon.-Sat. 9-6, Sun. 1-6, May-Aug.; by appointment rest of year. **Cost:** $3; $1 (ages 0-16). **Phone:** (204) 748-1659 or (204) 748-3573.

WAPUSK NATIONAL PARK
OF CANADA (A-4)

Elevations in the park range from sea level along the Hudson Bay coastal areas to 94 metres (308 ft.) at Silcox Creek. Refer to CAA/AAA maps for additional elevation information.

South and east of Churchill on the shore of Hudson Bay, Wapusk (pronounced to rhyme with tusk) was established in 1996. The park consists of 11,475 square kilometres (7,119 sq. mi.). Translated from the Cree language, Wapusk means "white bear," a fitting name for a park that has an area where polar bears den and produce offspring.

Much of the national park, part of the Hudson Bay and James Bay lowlands, is a flat plain covered by an extensive layer of peat; a layer of permafrost lies underneath. The treeless tundra consists mainly of wetlands—lakes, streams, bogs and rivers.

Polar bears congregate in the northern part of the park near Churchill around October, as they wait for freezing weather and the time when they can return to the ice in search of seals, their main food. The females dig their dens, and their young are born in late November and in December. The area around Churchill *(see place listing p. 222)* is one of the world's best places for viewing polar bears in their native habitat. Specialized tundra vehicles take visitors for close-up encounters.

The park, along a migratory flyway, also is a popular spring and fall feeding spot for waterfowl and shorebirds, including such rare species as the king eider, Ross' gull and gyrfalcon. Many build their nests here on the coast of Hudson Bay during the summer.

Churchill, in a somewhat remote location in northern Manitoba, can be reached by air and rail from Winnipeg. Since Wapusk is a wilderness park, it has no roads or trails. In order to visit the park, it is necessary to be part of an organized tour group, and several commercial operators provide tours into the park by plane, helicopter or tundra vehicle. The park office can provide a list. Park admission is free. For additional information contact Wapusk National Park of Canada, P.O. Box 127, Churchill, MB, Canada R0B 0E0; phone (204) 675-8863.

WARREN (E-2) elev. 248 m/815′

V. GROSS' DOLL MUSEUM, on Hwy. 3W, 3 km (1.9 mi.) n. of jct. Hwys. 6 and 67, displays some 3,500 dolls, ranging from those of the late 1890s to the present. **Time:** Allow 30 minutes minimum.

Hours: Sun.-Fri. 10-5 (also Sat. and evenings by appointment), May-Oct.; by appointment rest of year. **Cost:** $4; free (ages 0-5). **Phone:** (204) 322-5346.

WINKLER (F-3) pop. 9,106, elev. 271 m/890′

PEMBINA THRESHERMAN'S MUSEUM, 5 km (3 mi.) w. on Hwy. 3, features guided tours through displays of agricultural machinery, tools and household items as well as a steam threshing unit and a working sawmill. **Time:** Allow 1 hour minimum. **Hours:** Mon.-Fri. 9-5, Sat.-Sun. and holidays 1-5, May-Sept. **Cost:** $7.50; free (ages 0-11). **Phone:** (204) 325-7497.

Winnipeg

City Population: 633,451
Elevation: 229 m/763 ft.

Editor's Picks:

Dalnavert Museum ....(see p. 237)
The Forks ....(see p. 238)
The Manitoba Museum ....(see p. 240)

Royal Canadian Mint / © Bilderbuch / age fotostock

The real estate agent's cry of "Location!" could have been invented in Winnipeg; the position of Manitoba's capital has determined both the city's past and present. Archeological evidence shows that Winnipeg has been an important place of settlement for more than 6,000 years.

The confluence of the Red River, which flows from south to north, and the Assiniboine River, whose eastward flowing waters were a main route of Western exploration, led to the founding of fur-trading posts in the early 18th century near the present site of Winnipeg. The fertile lands created by the rivers later drew farmers and other settlers.

Still later, the area's position south of the peaks of the Canadian Shield meant that roads and railroads were forced to converge at Winnipeg, making it the point through which the eastbound raw materials of the West and the westbound manufactured goods of the East passed. Profiting by the hydroelectric power generated from its rivers, the city emerged in the 20th century as a manufacturing center in its own right.

French Canadian explorer and trader Pierre Gaultier de la Vérendrye founded Fort Rouge at the confluence of the rivers in 1738. This fur-trading post was succeeded by Fort Gibraltar, built by the North West Co. in 1804, and Fort Garry, founded by the Hudson's Bay Co. in 1821. In the same year, Lord Selkirk brought a party of Scottish settlers to these fertile lands, a move that greatly disturbed the trappers and voyageurs who feared their livelihoods would be destroyed.

The small settlement managed to survive, and the shift from trapping and hunting to agriculture began. Because of aggressive Canadian advertising campaigns in Europe and a homestead policy similar to that being used to settle the plains of the United States, large numbers of immigrants began to flow into the area in the 1860s.

In 1873 the village that had grown about a half mile north of Fort Garry was incorporated and named for the Cree Indian words *win* ("muddy") and *nipee* ("water"). The railroad aided Winnipeg's growth still further: In 1876 the city began to ship wheat east, and when the Canadian Pacific Railway connected the coasts in 1885, freight and passengers began to flow through the city in both directions.

The diversity of today's Winnipeg mirrors the many nationalities who settled it, some drawn by agriculture, some by the railroad, some by industry. From countries throughout Great Britain and Europe they came, creating a cultural mix that is reflected in the city's skyline, which includes the neoclassical splendor of the Manitoba Legislative Building *(see attraction listing p. 240)*, the century-old buildings of Old Market Square and the rounded spires of the Ukrainian Greek Orthodox Cathedral.

The Golden Boy, sculpted by Charles Gardet of Paris, is a 5.25-metre-tall (17.2-ft.), 1,650-kilogram (3,638-lb.) statue sheathed in 24 karat gold leaf atop the dome of the Legislative Building. In many ways it symbolizes both the past and the future of the residents of Winnipeg. The statue was diverted on its journey from a French foundry during World War

Getting There — *starting on p. 235*

Getting Around — *starting on p. 235*

What To See — *starting on p. 237*

What To Do — *starting on p. 242*

Where To Stay — *starting on p. 721*

Where To Dine — *starting on p. 723*

Folkorama / Travel Manitoba

I, while the vessel that was carrying it served as a troop transport for 2 years.

After crossing the Atlantic many times, the golden immigrant was finally placed where he stands today, one hand holding aloft the torch of progress, the other cradling a symbolic sheaf of wheat. High above the city, he strides toward the increasingly important natural resources of the north, his color echoing the golden hue of the rolling fields of grain that brought the city below both population and prosperity.

Evidence has been uncovered through archeological digs that the current site of The Forks (see attraction listing p. 238) was a seasonal meeting place for aboriginal peoples more than 6,000 years ago. Tools, bones, footprints and pottery have been unearthed at the site located at the confluence of the Red and Assiniboine rivers.

Getting There

By Car

Forming a circle around Winnipeg is a perimeter highway. To the north of the Trans-Canada Highway, the major approach from the east and west, this perimeter road is designated Hwy. 101. To the south of the Trans-Canada Highway it is numbered Hwy. 100.

There are three major approaches to the perimeter highway: the Trans-Canada Highway, which approaches from both the east and west, and Hwy. 75, which approaches from the south. To the west of the city the Trans-Canada Highway is posted Hwy. 1W; from the east, Hwy. 1E.

Within the perimeter highway all three major approaches change designation: Hwy. 1W becomes Metro Rte. 85, Hwy. 1E becomes Metro Rte. 135, and Hwy. 75 becomes Metro Rte. 42.

Getting Around

Generally, rush hour in Winnipeg is from 7 to 9 a.m. and 3:30 to 5:30 p.m. As in most cities, stress can be alleviated if driving during rush hour is avoided. If driving during these times, be careful and be patient; the city's speed limit is 50 kilometres per hour (30 mph) unless otherwise posted.

Note the pedestrian crosswalks marked by pavement stripes and illuminated overhead signs. All vehicles must stop if the crosswalk is occupied by a pedestrian or if a pedestrian on the curb indicates an intention to cross. No vehicle may pass another that is stopped or slowing to yield to a pedestrian. Right turns on red are permitted after a stop, unless otherwise posted.

Street System

Winnipeg's streets are laid out in a number of grids, but each is oriented to a different compass direction. Visitors will find it easiest to orient themselves to the major thoroughfares, which have signs

The Informed Traveler

Sales Tax: Manitoba's provincial sales tax is 7 percent. A 5 percent Goods and Services Tax (GST) also is levied in Canada on most sales and services. There is no additional local sales tax or tax on hotel/motel rooms or car rentals.

WHOM TO CALL

Emergency: 911

Police (non-emergency): (204) 986-6222

Weather: (204) 983-2050

Hospitals: Concordia Hospital, (204) 667-1560; Health Sciences Centre, (204) 787-3661; St. Boniface General Hospital, (204) 233-8563; Seven Oaks General Hospital, (204) 632-7133; Victoria General Hospital, (204) 269-3570.

WHERE TO LOOK

Newspapers

Winnipeg has two daily newspapers, the *Free Press* and *The Sun,* both distributed in the morning.

Radio

The Canadian Broadcasting Corporation (CBC) has both AM (990) and FM (98.3) stations in Winnipeg as well as an AM (1050) station broadcasting in French.

Visitor Information

Destination Winnipeg: 259 Portage Ave., Winnipeg, MB, Canada R3B 2A9. **Phone:** (204) 943-1970 or (800) 665-0204.

Destination Winnipeg is open Mon.-Fri. 8:30-4:30. A second branch, at Winnipeg James Armstrong Richardson International Airport, is open daily 8 a.m.-9:45 p.m.; phone (204) 982-7543.

Travel Manitoba's Explore Manitoba Centre at The Forks: 21 Forks Market Rd., Winnipeg, MB, Canada R3C 4T7. **Phone:** (204) 927-7838 or (800) 665-0040. *See color ad p. 219.*

Explore Manitoba Centre is staffed with on-site travel counselors daily 9-6. The

telephones are manned daily 8:30-4:30. The 24-hour Forks Hot Line, (204) 957-7618, also provides information. The center features dioramas depicting the various regions of the province.

TRANSPORTATION

Air Travel

Winnipeg James Armstrong Richardson International Airport is about 8 kilometres (5 mi.) northwest of downtown off Metro Rte. 90. Daily bus service between the airport and downtown is provided by Winnipeg Transit between 5:51 a.m. and 12:44 a.m. The one-way fare is $2.30; passengers must have exact change. Phone 311 or (877) 311-4974 for information. Major hotels offer limousine service to and from the airport.

Rental Cars

Hertz, (204) 925-6600, (800) 263-0600 in Canada, or (800) 654-3080 out of Canada, offers discounts to AAA and CAA members. Winnipeg locations are at Winnipeg James Armstrong Richardson International Airport, 1577 Erin St. and 830 Waverly St.

Rail Service

The VIA Rail Canada depot is downtown at 123 Main St.; phone (888) 842-7245.

Taxis

Cab companies include Blueline, (204) 925-8888; Duffy's, (204) 925-0101; and Unicity, (204) 925-3131. Base fare is $3.30, plus a charge of 10c for each additional metre (3.28 ft.) or 14 seconds of metered waiting time.

Public Transport

Winnipeg Transit, the public bus system, serves downtown Winnipeg and its suburbs. Route maps and route information are available by phoning 311. The average bus fare is $2; riders must have exact change.

carrying the word "Route" and a number. Routes ending in even numbers designate north-south thoroughfares, and those ending in odd numbers designate major east-west arteries.

The primary north-south routes that cross the downtown area are 42, 52 and 62. The major east-west highways include 105, 115, 57 and 85. A good street map will enable drivers to see how the various grids of named streets connect with the main numbered routes.

Parking

Visitors will do best to park in a commercial lot, where rates average about $1.10 to $1.35 for the first hour and $1.10 to $1.60 for subsequent hours. Daily rates are about $4 to $10. Parking meters downtown cost $1 an hour, but most carry a 1- or 2-hour limit. Some parking in downtown is free in designated metered areas.

Parking is strictly controlled along major downtown streets. Cars parked between signs reading "No Parking Between" from 7 to 9 a.m. and 3:30 to 5:30 p.m. will be towed.

What To See

ASSINIBOINE PARK is at jct. Park Blvd. and Wellington Crescent; it also may be accessed from Portage Ave. via a footbridge over the Assiniboine River. The 153-hectare (378-acre) park has a zoo, miniature railway, duck pond, walking and biking paths, a conservatory, sculpture garden, a pavilion, Citizens Hall of Fame, gardens and an outdoor theater where concerts are held in summer. Tobogganing, cross-country skiing and ice skating are available in the winter. Winnipeg's only cricket tournaments are played in the park.

Assiniboine Forest, south of the park off Grant Avenue, is one of the largest urban nature parks in Canada. The 283-hectare (700-acre) forest of aspen and oak is home to more than 39 species of mammals, including deer and foxes, and more than 80 species of birds. The 1 kilometre (.6 mi.) Saginay Trail leads hikers to Eve Werier Pond, where a variety of waterfowl can be seen. **Hours:** Daily dawn-dusk. **Cost:** Free. **Phone:** (204) 986-7234.

Assiniboine Park Conservatory, in Assiniboine Park, features indoor gardens, changing floral and plant displays and art work by local artists. A tropical palm house contains orchids, ferns and banana plants. **Hours:** Daily 9-4:30 (also Sun.-Mon. 4:30-8, mid-Apr. to early Sept.). **Cost:** Donations. **Phone:** (204) 986-5537 or (877) 311-4974. ⟦¶⟧

Assiniboine Park Zoo, in Assiniboine Park, has more than 1,600 different animals in naturalistic settings. The zoo specializes in animals found in cooler climates from around the world as well as native North American species. Siberian tigers, snow leopards, polar bears, lynxes, elk, bison, and many other hardy species can be seen outside throughout the year. Large indoor facilities provide warm-weather viewing of many tropical animals.

Hours: Daily 9-6, Victoria Day-Labour Day; 10-4, rest of year. Closed mornings of Nov. 11 and Dec. 25. **Cost:** Mar.-Oct. $4.25; $4 (ages 65+); $2.75 (ages 13-17); $2.25 (ages 2-12); $15 (family, two adults and children ages 0-17 living in the same household). Rest of year $3.75; $3.50 (ages 65+); $2.25 (ages 13-17); $1.75 (ages 2-12); $12 (family, two adults and children ages 0-17 living in the same household). **Phone:** (204) 986-2327 or (877) 311-4974. ⟦¶⟧

Leo Mol Sculpture Garden, in Assiniboine Park, is said to be the first sculpture garden in North America dedicated to the works of a single artist. The garden and gallery feature bronze sculptures, porcelains, paintings and sketches by the Winnipeg artist. The gardens also are home to the Leo Mol Schoolhouse Studio. A reflecting pool and fountain are located in front of the gallery. **Hours:** Grounds open daily 6:30 a.m.-10 p.m. Gallery and studio open Tues.-Sun. 10-6, May-Aug.; Sat.-Sun. 11-5, in Sept. **Cost:** Donations. **Phone:** (204) 888-5466.

Pavilion Gallery Museum is in Assiniboine Park at 55 Pavilion Crescent. Housed in a restored 1929 pavilion, the museum contains a permanent collection featuring the work of three prominent artists: Ivan Eyre, Walter Phillips and Clarence Tillenius. **Time:** Allow 1 hour minimum. **Hours:** Tues.-Sun. 10-5, Victoria Day-Labour Day; Tues.-Sun. 11-5, rest of year. **Cost:** Free. **Phone:** (204) 888-5466.

COSTUME MUSEUM OF CANADA, 109 Pacific Ave., features a 35,000-piece collection of textiles, clothing and accessories dating from 1565. The museum's exhibitions are presented in a *tableau vivant,* or living-picture style; each year a new exhibition is displayed. A visual storage room offers a close-up view of accessories. Free audio tours are available.

Time: Allow 45 minutes minimum. **Hours:** Mon.-Sat. 10-5, Sun. noon-4. Closed major holidays. **Cost:** $5; $4.50 (senior citizens); $3.50 (students with ID); free (ages 0-5); $14 (family). **Phone:** (204) 989-0072.

DALNAVERT MUSEUM, .5 blk. s. of Broadway at 61 Carlton St., is the former home of Sir Hugh John Macdonald, prominent lawyer and politician. Built in 1895, it was one of the first houses in Winnipeg to have hot-water heating, electric lighting and indoor plumbing.

Named after the Scottish birthplace of Macdonald's grandmother, the red brick Queen Anne Revival-style house features stained glass windows and a wraparound porch. The restored house, which was saved from demolition, is opulently furnished with Victorian antiques. Guided tours provide a glimpse into the lifestyles of early 20th-century Winnipeg society.

The visitor center behind the museum has been designed to be a "green" building, incorporating reclaimed and recycled materials during its construction and utilizing geothermal energy to heat and cool the building.

Time: Allow 1 hour minimum. **Hours:** Guided tours are given Wed.-Fri. 10-5, Sat. 11-6, Sun. noon-4, July 1-Labour Day; Wed.-Fri. 11-4, Sat. 11-6, Sun. noon-4, rest of year. Closed major holidays. **Cost:** $5; $4 (ages 65+); $3 (ages 5-17); $12 (family, up to two adults and three children). **Phone:** (204) 943-2835.

THE FORKS, at the confluence of the Red and Assiniboine rivers, has been a meeting place for more than 6,000 years, beginning with the aboriginal peoples. By virtue of location the 23-hectare (56-acre) site evolved into the center of the European fur trade in the 1730s. Métis, natives and eventually European settlers created a community along the rivers. More than a century later, the area became a transportation center as the railways laid tracks of steel across the prairie.

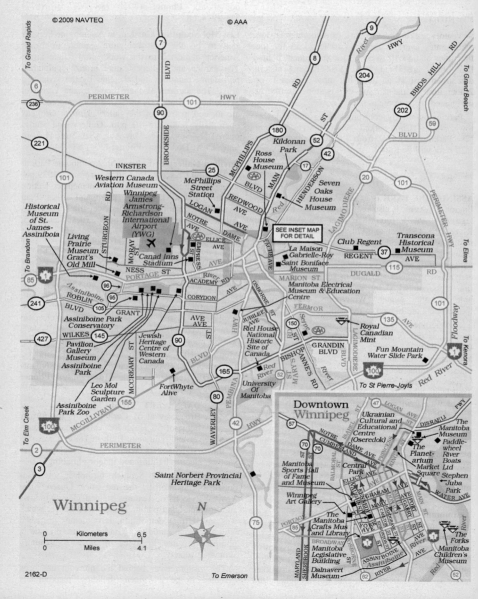

Now Winnipeg's main gathering spot, The Forks is a favorite place for shopping, dining and entertainment. The Riverwalk follows the water's edge from the Manitoba Legislature to The Forks through downtown Winnipeg, and the Wall Through Time chronicles area history from glacial Lake Agassiz to the present.

Canoes and "sea cycles" can be rented seasonally at The Forks Historic Port. Concerts and special events take place at The Forks throughout the year (see Special Events p. 244). Travel Manitoba's Explore Manitoba Centre at The Forks provides information about events and attractions throughout Manitoba and The Forks. **Phone:** (204) 957-7618 for an events hotline or (800) 665-0040.

The Forks Market is at the confluence of the Red and Assiniboine rivers. Housed in refurbished stable buildings, the market contains shops that offer jewelry and crafts; fresh, specialty and ethnic foods; produce; and baked goods. A six-story glass tower affords a view of the rivers and the downtown area. **Hours:** Mon.-Sat. 9:30-9, Sun. 9:30-6:30, July-Aug.; daily 9:30-6:30 (also Fri. 6:30-9 p.m.), rest of year. **Cost:** Free. **Phone:** (204) 942-6302.

The Forks National Historic Site of Canada, at the confluence of the Red and Assiniboine rivers, is a 3.5-hectare (9-acre) park that offers an outdoor playground and a riverside amphitheater with a view of historic St. Boniface. Interpretive programs and festivals are held Victoria Day through Labour Day. A variety of guided tours and theatrical presentations are available July through August. **Hours:** Daily 24 hours. **Cost:** Free. **Phone:** (204) 983-6757.

Johnston Terminal, in the heart of The Forks, is a renovated railway cold storage warehouse. The four-story structure now features shops, boutiques and restaurants. **Time:** Allow 1 hour minimum. **Hours:** Mon.-Fri. 10-9, Sat.-Sun. 10-6. **Cost:** Free. **Phone:** (204) 956-5593.

Manitoba Children's Museum, in the Kinsmen Building at 45 Forks Market Rd., is in western Canada's oldest train repair facility. The museum houses six galleries offering a wide variety of hands-on activities. At All Aboard children can pretend to be an engineer or conductor on the diesel train or Pullman car that are inside the museum.

They can climb into and slide down a 5-metre-tall (17-ft.) oak tree and see what life is like in a beaver lodge at The Tree & Me, or play with the latest technology in the Livewire gallery. They can be the star anchor in their own newscast at Our TV, then move on to Wonderworks and use child-size heavy equipment to design and build their own cities.

Time: Allow 1 hour minimum. **Hours:** Daily 9:30-6, July 1-Labour Day; Sun.-Thurs. 9:30-4:30, Fri.-Sat. 9:30-6, rest of year. Closed Easter, 4 days following Labour Day and Dec. 24-26. **Cost:** $7

(ages 2-17); $6.75 (adults); $6.25 (ages 65+). **Phone:** (204) 924-4000. 🅰

FORTWHYTE ALIVE is at 1961 McCreary Rd. Bison on their own prairie, deer, foxes, prairie dogs, waterfowl and songbirds can be seen at this 259-hectare (640-acre) nature and recreational center. There also are trails, floating boardwalks, birdfeeding stations, a bison-viewing mound, a family treehouse, fishing, boat and canoe rentals, snowshoeing, skating, tobogganing, a sod house, a tipi encampment and an interpretive center.

"Bison buggies" for touring some areas are available for rent. The interpretive center features the Aquarium of the Prairies, a climate exhibit, the Honeybee Observation Hive, and the Touch Museum. **Time:** Allow 1 hour minimum. **Hours:** Mon.-Fri. 9-8, Sat.-Sun. and holidays 9-5. Schedule varies summer and fall; phone for hours. Evening hours are extended Sept.-Oct. for viewing migrating Canada geese. Closed Dec. 25. **Cost:** $6; $5 (ages 55+); $4 (ages 3-17). **Phone:** (204) 989-8364. 🍽 🅰

FUN MOUNTAIN WATER SLIDE PARK, off Hwy. 1E on Murdock Rd., offers 10 waterslides, a swimming area, a hot tub, bumper boats, miniature golf and locker and changing facilities. **Hours:** Open daily at 10, June-Aug. (weather permitting). Closing hours vary; phone ahead. **Cost:** $15.50; $12.50 (ages 4-12); $7 (observers and ages 55+). Twilight rate $10.50. **Phone:** (204) 255-3910. 🍽 🅰

GRANT'S OLD MILL is at Portage Ave. and Booth Dr. This operational, reconstructed log flour mill—the original was built in 1829—marks the first use of water power in the Western provinces. **Tours:** Guided tours are available. **Time:** Allow 30 minutes minimum. **Hours:** Daily 10-6, mid-May through Labour Day. **Cost:** Donations. **Phone:** (204) 986-5613.

HISTORICAL MUSEUM OF ST. JAMES-ASSINIBOIA, 3180 Portage Ave., houses a collection of artifacts relating to the history of the St. James-Assiniboia area and a display building of pioneer activities. Guided interpretive tours through the mid-19th-century William Brown Red River Log House offer a glimpse of the pioneer lifestyle. **Time:** Allow 1 hour minimum. **Hours:** Daily 10-4:30, mid-May through Labour Day; Mon.-Fri. 10-5, rest of year. **Cost:** Donations. **Phone:** (204) 888-8706.

JEWISH HERITAGE CENTRE OF WESTERN CANADA, 123 Doncaster St., site of the Fort Osborne Barracks, shares the history, experiences, achievements and culture of Jewish people in Western Canada. The Corridor Museum exhibit depicts the settlement of Jews in Western Canada through artifacts, photographs and archival material. The Holocaust Education Centre features items from the Holocaust. Changing exhibits also are available.

Time: Allow 30 minutes minimum. **Hours:** Mon.-Thurs. 6:30 a.m.-10 p.m., Fri. 6:30 a.m.-7 p.m., Sat.

noon-6, Sun. 7-7. **Cost:** Donations. **Phone:** (204) 477-7460 for tours or appointments.

KILDONAN PARK is at 2021 Main St. In its 40 hectares (99 acres) along the Red River the park has some of the province's oldest and largest trees, flower and rock gardens, and a model of the witch's hut from "Hansel and Gretel."

Summer options include swimming; boating; bicycling; walking; in-line skating; and Rainbow Stage, Winnipeg's outdoor theater. Tobogganing, ice skating and cross-country skiing are winter sports *(see Recreation Chart)*. **Hours:** Daily 7-dusk. **Cost:** Free. **Phone:** (204) 986-7623. 🍴

LA MAISON GABRIELLE-ROY, 375 Deschambault St. in St. Boniface, is the birthplace and childhood home of Gabrielle Roy, one of Canada's most famous 20th-century authors, known for her works about the underprivileged and poverty-stricken. The 1905 house contains furnishings and artifacts indicative of the early 20th-century period when the author lived here. Tours are given in English and French.

Time: Allow 30 minutes minimum. **Hours:** Mon.-Fri. 10-5, Sat.-Sun. 1-5, June-Aug.; Wed.-Sun. 1-4, rest of year. Last tour begins 30 minutes before closing. Closed Jan. 1 and Dec. 25. **Cost:** $5; $3 (ages 65+ and students with ID); free (ages 0-5). **Phone:** (204) 231-3853 or (866) 808-8338.

LIVING PRAIRIE MUSEUM is at 2795 Ness Ave. This 12-hectare (30-acre) unplowed tract supports more than 160 native plant species and is a remnant of the prairie that once covered much of North America. An interpretive center features displays of plants and animals of the tall grass prairie. Nature talks and hikes are offered, and a self-guiding trail brochure is available.

Time: Allow 1 hour minimum. **Hours:** Interpretive center daily 10-5, July-Aug.; Sun. 10-5, May-June; by appointment rest of year. **Cost:** Donations. **Phone:** (204) 832-0167.

THE MANITOBA CRAFTS MUSEUM AND LIBRARY, downtown at 183 Kennedy St., has a permanent collection of approximately 5,000 traditional Manitoba crafts, including embroidery, knitting, quilting, weaving, lace, pottery, beadwork and basketry. The library has books, patterns and scrapbooks about many forms of craftwork. **Time:** Allow 30 minutes minimum. **Hours:** Tues.-Wed. 10-4, Sat. noon-4 or by appointment. Summer hours may vary; phone ahead. Closed major holidays. **Cost:** Donations. **Phone:** (204) 487-6117.

MANITOBA ELECTRICAL MUSEUM & EDUCATION CENTRE is 1 blk. w. of jct. Pembina Hwy. and Stafford St. at 680 Harrow St. The museum's six galleries tell the story of electricity in the province beginning in the 1870s.

Themed areas such as The Light Goes On 1882-1900, Energizing Manitoba 1900-1960 and Powering up the Farm 1942-1960 provide an idea of the museum's offerings. A yellow turbine runner from one of the oldest hydroelectric stations in Manitoba is outside the 1931 building. **Time:** Allow 1 hour minimum. **Hours:** Mon.-Thurs. 1-4. Closed major holidays. **Cost:** Free. **Phone:** (204) 477-7905.

MANITOBA LEGISLATIVE BUILDING, bordered by Broadway Ave., Kennedy and Osborne sts. and the Assiniboine River, reflects neoclassical design in native Tyndall limestone. The Italian marble grand staircase is guarded at its base by two life-size bronze bison, the emblems of Manitoba.

Atop the dome is Golden Boy by Parisian sculptor Charles Gardet. The torch, in the right hand, points to economic development and progress in the north; the sheaf of wheat in the left arm represents agriculture. This 5.25-metre-tall (17.2-ft.) statue weighs 1,650 kilograms (3,638 lbs.) and is sheathed in 24 karat gold leaf. The statue represents eternal youth and the province's spirit of enterprise. Plots on the site's 12 hectares (30 acres) contain flowers, foliage and ornamental plants. **Hours:** Guided tours are conducted daily on the hour 9-4, July 1-Labour Day; by appointment rest of year. Self-guiding tours are available daily 8-8, year-round. **Cost:** Free. **Phone:** (204) 945-5813.

◆ **THE MANITOBA MUSEUM,** Main St. and
GEM Rupert Ave., illustrates the relationship of
[SAVE] people and their environment in Manitoba's history. The Earth History Gallery shows geologic and organic evolution. the Arctic/Sub-Arctic Gallery explores Inuit culture and the zone's flora and fauna, and the Boreal Forest Gallery features a diorama of a granite cliff, waterfall, marsh, Cree family and a wandering moose. A bat cave, snake pit and a Ukrainian rye farm can be seen at the Parklands/Mixed Woods Gallery.

Visitors can see a replica of the ketch *Nonsuch;* the ship's 1668 voyage to Hudson Bay opened western Canada to commerce. The Hudson's Bay Company Gallery highlights fur trading and early exploration. A teepee and a sod house are part of the Grasslands Gallery, and the Urban Gallery shows a 1920s boom-town Winnipeg.

Time: Allow 1 hour minimum. **Hours:** Daily 10-5, Victoria Day-Labour Day; Tues.-Fri. 10-4, Sat.-Sun. and holidays 11-5, rest of year. **Cost:** $8; $6.50 (ages 3-17, ages 60+ and students with ID); $26.50 (family, up to six people with no more than two adults). Combination ticket including museum, The Planetarium and The Science Gallery $18.50; $13 (ages 3-17, ages 60+ and students with ID); $62 (family, up to six people with no more than two adults). **Phone:** (204) 956-2830 or (204) 943-3139.

The Planetarium, on the lower level of The Manitoba Museum, presents interactive and multimedia shows about our universe. **Time:** Allow 1 hour minimum. **Hours:** Shows are presented daily, Victoria Day-second Mon. in Oct.; Tues.-Sun., rest of year. Phone ahead to confirm schedule. **Cost:** $6.50; $5 (ages 3-17, ages 60+ and students with ID); $20 (family, up to six people with no more than two adults). Combination ticket including The Manitoba Museum, The Planetarium and The Science Gallery

$18.50; $13 (ages 3-17, ages 60+ and students with ID); $62 (family, up to six people with no more than two adults). **Phone:** (204) 956-2830, or (204) 943-3139 for show times.

The Science Gallery, on the lower level of The Manitoba Museum, has more than 100 hands-on exhibits. **Time:** Allow 1 hour minimum. **Hours:** Daily 10-5, July 1-Labour Day; Tues.-Fri. 10-4, Sat.-Sun. and holidays 11-5, rest of year. **Cost:** $7; $5.50 (ages 3-17, ages 60+ and students with ID); $22 (family, up to six people with no more than two adults). Combination ticket including The Manitoba Museum, The Planetarium and The Science Gallery $18.50; $13 (ages 3-17, ages 60+ and students with ID); $62 (family, up to six people with no more than two adults). **Phone:** (204) 956-2830 or (204) 943-3139.

MANITOBA SPORTS HALL OF FAME AND MUSEUM, on the fifth floor of The Bay, 450 Portage Ave., focuses on sports history and legendary athletes and teams. Interactive exhibits change every few months. **Time:** Allow 1 hour minimum. **Hours:** Tues.-Sat. 10-5, in summer; Wed.-Sat. 10-5, rest of year. Closed major holidays. **Cost:** Donations. **Phone:** (204) 774-0002.

RIEL HOUSE NATIONAL HISTORIC SITE OF CANADA, 330 River Rd., was the home of the mother of Louis Riel. Although this leader of the Métis and founder of the provisional government of Manitoba never lived in the house, his body lay in state for several days after his execution in 1885. The small log building with board siding is furnished in period.

The walkway to the house has signs explaining the history of the Métis and of the Riel family. **Time:** Allow 30 minutes minimum. **Hours:** Guided tours daily 10-6, mid-May through Labour Day. **Cost:** $3.90; $3.40 (ages 65+); $1.90 (ages 6-16). **Phone:** (204) 257-1783.

ROSS HOUSE MUSEUM, 140 Meade St. N. in Joe Zuken Heritage Park, was the first post office in western Canada in 1854. Displays reflect the life of the Ross family when their home served as the post office. **Time:** Allow 30 minutes minimum. **Hours:** Wed.-Sun. 10-4:30, June-Aug. **Cost:** Free. **Phone:** (204) 943-3958.

ROYAL CANADIAN MINT is at 520 Lagimodière Blvd. at jct. Trans-Canada Hwy. and Hwy. 59. This high-tech, high-volume manufacturing facility is considered one of the world's most modern mints; its high-speed coining presses can each strike 750 coins per minute. The Winnipeg Plant produces all of the circulation coinage for Canada as well as coinage for more than 60 foreign countries.

The building includes a landscaped interior courtyard and a glass tower overlooking the manufacturing plant. At the mint's interactive museum visitors can lift a gold bar worth more than $200,000.

Tours: Guided tours are available. **Hours:** Daily 9-5. Last tour begins 1 hour before closing. Phone ahead to confirm schedule. **Cost:** Museum free. Guided tour (Mon.-Fri.) $5; $3 (ages 4-15); $13 (family, two adults and up to four children). Guided tour (Sat.-Sun.) $3.50; $2 (ages 4-15); $10 (family, two adults and up to four children). **Phone:** (204) 983-6429.

SAINT BONIFACE MUSEUM, s.e. on Main St. (Hwy. 1), then n. to 494 Taché Ave., was built 1846-51 as the first convent and hospital in western Canada. Displays depict the Red River Settlement and early French and Métis Manitoba; an exhibit is dedicated to Louis Riel, leader of the Red River Resistance. Visitors also can view the nearby ruins of the cathedral as well as the cemetery where Riel is buried.

Time: Allow 30 minutes minimum. **Hours:** Mon.-Fri. 9-5 (also Thurs. 5-8), Sat.-Sun. and holidays noon-4, May-Sept.; Mon.-Fri. 9-5, Sun. noon-4, rest of year. Closed Dec. 24-25 and 31. **Cost:** $5; $3 (ages 61+, physically impaired and students with ID); free (ages 0-5); $12 (family). **Phone:** (204) 237-4500.

SAINT NORBERT PROVINCIAL HERITAGE PARK is at 40 Turnbull Dr. at the fork of the Red and La Salle rivers. Near the former village of St. Norbert, this 7-hectare (17-acre) park is rich in history and linked to Manitoba's entry into the Confederation. A restored 19th-century farmhouse and village house are decorated in period.

A walking trail with information about native inhabitants and Manitoba history and a house belonging to a member of Louis Riel's provisional government are available. Fishing is permitted. **Tours:** Guided tours are available. **Time:** Allow 1 hour minimum. **Hours:** Daily 10:30-5, Victoria Day-Labour Day. **Cost:** Donations. **Phone:** (204) 945-4236, or (204) 945-4375 Sept.-Apr. 🎣

SEVEN OAKS HOUSE MUSEUM, 1.5 blks. e. of Main St. off Rupertsland Blvd. and Jones St. in W. Kildonan, is said to be the oldest habitable house in Manitoba. This sturdy building, with its stone foundation, hand-hewn oak timbers, hand-split shingles and buffalo hair-bound plaster, was built 1851-53. The house displays belongings of the original occupants and other period furnishings. **Tours:** Guided tours are available. **Time:** Allow 30 minutes minimum. **Hours:** Daily 10-5, last weekend in May-Labour Day. **Cost:** Donations. **Phone:** (204) 339-7429.

TRANSCONA HISTORICAL MUSEUM is at 141 Regent Ave. W. In a 1925 bank building, the museum explores the origins of Transcona, a railroad town amalgamated into Winnipeg, and the accomplishments of its residents. In addition to displays about the town's railroad heritage, veterans and community leaders, there also are archeology and butterfly exhibits.

Time: Allow 30 minutes minimum. **Hours:** Mon.-Sat. 9-4, June-Aug.; Mon.-Fri. 10-4, Feb.-May and Sept.-Dec. Closed long holiday weekends. **Cost:** Donations. **Phone:** (204) 222-0423.

UKRAINIAN CULTURAL AND EDUCATIONAL CENTRE (OSEREDOK), 184 Alexander Ave. E., at Main St. and Disraeli Frwy., is dedicated to the preservation of Canadian-Ukrainian culture. Highlights include a museum, an art gallery, a library and archives. Interpretive exhibits relate to the Ukrainian heritage around the world and include a wide range of artifacts, from fine art to farm implements to rare 16th-century maps.

Guided tours are available by appointment. **Time:** Allow 30 minutes minimum. **Hours:** Mon.-Sat. 10-4; Sun. 1-4, July-Aug.; Mon.-Sat. 10-4, rest of year. **Cost:** Donations. **Phone:** (204) 942-0218.

WESTERN CANADA AVIATION MUSEUM, in an aircraft hangar off Ellice Ave. at 958 Ferry Rd., displays 23 vintage aircraft. All aspects of aviation are exhibited, from bush planes to commercial airliners to combat planes and homemade aircraft. Children can explore the interactive Skyways exhibit. Videotaped presentations about historical aircraft are offered. A research library and archives can be seen by appointment.

Guided tours are available by appointment. **Time:** Allow 1 hour minimum. **Hours:** Mon.-Fri. 9:30-4:30, Sat. 10-5, Sun. and holidays noon-5. Closed Jan. 1, Good Friday and Dec. 25-26. **Cost:** $7.50; $5 (students with ID and senior citizens); $3 (ages 3-12); $18 (family, two adults and three children). **Phone:** (204) 786-5503.

WINNIPEG ART GALLERY is at 300 Memorial Blvd. Eight galleries contain contemporary and historical works by Manitoba, Canadian and international artists. The Inuit art collection is reputed to be the largest public collection of contemporary Inuit art in the world. Guided tours are offered; reservations must be made 2 weeks in advance.

Time: Allow 1 hour minimum. **Hours:** Tues.-Sun. 11-5 (also Thurs. 5-9). **Cost:** $8; $6 (ages 60+ and students with ID); $4 (ages 6-12); $18 (family). **Phone:** (204) 786-6641, or (204) 789-1760 for recorded information. [T]

GAMBLING ESTABLISHMENTS

- **Club Regent** is at 1425 Regent Ave. **Hours:** Mon.-Sat. 10 a.m.-3 a.m., Sun. noon-3 a.m. Closed Easter, Nov. 11 and Dec. 24-25. **Phone:** (204) 957-2500. *See color ad p. 219.*

- **McPhillips Street Station** is at 484 McPhillips St. **Hours:** Mon.-Sat. 10 a.m.-3 a.m., Sun. noon-3 a.m. Closed Easter, Nov. 11 and Dec. 24-25. **Phone:** (204) 957-2500.

What To Do

Sightseeing

The intersection of Portage Avenue and Main Street, a few blocks from the juncture of Winnipeg's two rivers, has been the major crossroads since the city's earliest days and is a good place to start a sightseeing foray.

Although now part of Winnipeg, the early settlement of St. Boniface has retained its French Canadian identity. A monument honoring the explorer Pierre Gaultier de la Vérendrye is on Taché Avenue opposite St. Boniface Hospital. Also in St. Boniface is the grave of Louis Riel, leader of the Métis and of the provisional government 1869-70. The grave is at Taché and Cathedral avenues in the churchyard of the St. Boniface Basilica.

Boat Tours

PADDLEWHEEL RIVER BOATS LTD. departs from the Alexander Docks at jct. Alexander Ave. and Waterfront Dr. The company offers 2-hour daytime sightseeing tours of Winnipeg aboard the MS *Paddlewheel Queen* and MS *Paddlewheel Princess* as well as evening dinner and dance cruises on the Assiniboine and Red rivers.

Hours: Sightseeing cruise departs daily at 1, May-Oct. **Cost:** Sightseeing fare $16.75; $14.75 (ages 65+); $8.25 (ages 0-11). Reservations are recommended. **Phone:** (204) 942-4500 or (204) 944-8000. [T]

SPLASH DASH WATER BUS departs from the bottom of the river walk at The Forks. The boats provide 30-minute guided historical tours of a section of the Red and Assiniboine rivers. Points of interest are noted along the way. **Time:** Allow 30 minutes minimum. **Hours:** Departures every 15 minutes daily 10-dusk (weather permitting), mid-June through Aug. 31; noon-6, Sept.-Oct. **Cost:** Fare $10; $9 (ages 4-18 and 55+). **Phone:** (204) 783-6633.

Plane Tours

The Winnipeg Flying Club, (204) 338-7927, 16 kilometres (10 mi.) north of the perimeter on Hwy. 9 at St. Andrews Airport, offers scenic flights over Winnipeg, the Red River and the Lake Winnipeg area. Phone for information and reservations.

Train Tours

Antique rail cars pulled by a vintage locomotive take passengers on 2.5-hour trips departing from a 1910 station at Inkster Junction, 3 kilometres (1.9 mi.) west of Hwy. 90 and Inkster Boulevard. The Prairie Dog Central Railway makes stops at country markets in Grosse Isle and Warren. The scenic ride operates weekends May through September; phone (204) 832-5259.

Walking Tours

Guided walking tours of the 20-block Historic Winnipeg area near Portage Avenue and Main Street in the Exchange District are available June through Labour Day weekend. Departing from the Exchange District Information Booth on the east corner of King Street and Bannatyne in Old Market Square, these tours visit many of Manitoba's finest historical buildings; for schedule information phone (204) 942-6716.

Walking tours of the old St. Boniface area are available; phone (204) 233-8343 or (866) 808-8338 for information and reservations.

Sports and Recreation

Devotees of organized sports will find many opportunities to indulge themselves in Winnipeg. Canadians love **hockey**, and those who fancy flying sticks and flashing skates will find the American Hockey League's Manitoba Moose locking horns with their opponents downtown at the MTS Centre at Donald Street and Portage Avenue.

Football fans can watch the Canadian Football League's Winnipeg Blue Bombers playing at the Canad Inns Stadium from June to November. The Northern **Baseball** League's Winnipeg Goldeyes play at CanWest Global Park at The Forks from May to August.

To obtain additional information and tickets for sports and recreation events listed above, phone (204) 780-3333.

Sports car racing enthusiasts converge at the Red River Speedway, (204) 582-0527, on Hwy. 75, 4 kilometres (2.5 mi.) south of St. Norbert, from April through October (weather permitting).

Assiniboia Downs, 3975 Portage Ave. at the Perimeter Highway, offers **Thoroughbred racing** early May to mid-October. Simulcast races are offered year-round; phone (204) 885-3330.

Note: Policies concerning admittance of children to pari-mutuel betting facilities vary. Phone for information.

Other spectator sports include minor league hockey, **curling** and **ringette** games, held at municipal skating rinks, and **cricket** played in Assiniboine Park. Ringette, similar to hockey, is a popular women's sport developed in Canada.

There are 33 **golf** courses in Winnipeg. Nine-hole public courses include Crescent Drive, 781 Crescent Dr., (877) 311-4974, and Harbour View, 1867 Springfield Rd., (204) 222-2751. Among the 18-hole public courses are Kildonan Park, 2021 Main St., (877) 311-4974; Tuxedo, 400 Shaftesbury Blvd., (204) 888-2867; and Windsor Park, 10 Rue des Meurons, (877) 311-4974. John Blumberg, 4540 Portage Ave., (204) 986-3490, offers both nine- and 18-hole layouts.

Winnipeg has more than 280 **tennis** courts, some lighted for night matches. Many courts are at community centers. Championship matches are held during the summer at various locations throughout the city. **Squash, handball** and **racquetball** players can avail themselves of courts at a number of athletic clubs and local universities. For information contact Sport Manitoba; phone (204) 925-5600.

Fans of **bicycling** and **in-line skating** take to the marked paths in Winnipeg's city parks. Bicycle trails along less-traveled side streets in and around Winnipeg also have been established. **Cross-country skiing, tobogganing** and **ice skating** facilities are available at Assiniboine, Kildonan and St. Vital parks; facilities for ice skating also are found at numerous schools and community clubs.

Downhill skiing is available at Spring Hill Winter Park Ski Area, (204) 224-3051, near Birds Hill Provincial Park at the junction of Hwy. 59N at the Floodway; and Stony Mountain Winter Park, (204) 344-5977, 10 kilometres (6 mi.) north of the perimeter of Hwy. 7. Birds Hill Provincial Park, (204) 222-9151, also is a site for **snowmobiling** and cross-country skiing.

Swimming can be pursued all year in Winnipeg, where numerous indoor pools include those at four YM-YWCAs; phone (204) 947-3044. The Pan-Am Pool, 25 Poseidon Bay, is one of the largest indoor bodies of water in Canada and is open all year; phone (877) 311-4974.

Many recreational activities are available at the Harbour View Recreation Complex in the northeastern section of Winnipeg in Kil-Cona Park, 1867 Springfield Rd. At this 162-hectare (400-acre) park are facilities for **miniature golf, lawn bowling, shuffleboard** and **horseshoes** as well as tennis courts, a golf course, a driving range and pedal boats during the summer. Golf and tennis lessons are available April to October. Ice skating, tobogganing and cross-country skiing are available during the winter. Phone (204) 222-2766.

Shopping

The intersection of Portage Avenue and Main Street is a good starting point for a shopping excursion. Winnipeg Square and the underground Lombard Concourse offer shops ranging from boutiques to bookstores. Portage Avenue also is the site of the city's largest department stores. Portage Place connects The Bay (The Hudson's Bay Co.) to other department stores with an extensive system of skywalks.

Winnipeg has a historic area where shoppers can browse through merchandise of today amid structures of the past. The Forks Market *(see attraction listing p. 239)* is behind Union Station, off Main Street (near Portage and Main). The shops and restaurants are located in an indoor market with more than 80 vendors selling everything from fresh fish and baked goods to arts and crafts items. The Johnston Terminal *(see attraction listing p. 239)*, across from the market, offers specialty boutiques and eateries.

Shopping for Western wear and accessories is possible at such factory outlet stores as Canada West Boots, 1250 Fife St., or MWG Factory Outlet, 1147 Notre Dame Ave.

More than 125 shops and restaurants can be found at Osborne Village, between River and Wardlaw avenues 2 blocks south of the Manitoba Legislative

Building. Travelers in search of a truly representative souvenir may want to examine the native arts and crafts and western wear available at Winnipeg Outfitters Inc. at 250 McPhillips St.

Finally, visitors who like their shopping climate-controlled and under one roof can visit the malls at Cityplace, 333 St. Mary Ave. at Hargrave Street; Garden City, 2305 McPhillips St., with Sears and Winners as its anchor stores; Grant Park, 1120 Grant Ave., with Zellers; Kildonan Place, 1555 Regent Ave. W., with anchors Sears and Zellers; Polo Park, 1485 Portage Ave., which has The Bay and Sears for anchors; Portage Place, 393 Portage Ave.; or St. Vital Centre, 1225 St. Mary's Rd., with The Bay and Sears as its anchor stores.

Performing Arts

Canada's Royal Winnipeg Ballet, Winnipeg Symphony Orchestra and Manitoba Opera perform in Centennial Concert Hall, 555 Main St., opposite City Hall. The oldest company in Canada and the second oldest in North America, Canada's Royal Winnipeg Ballet is known for its versatile style and performs an eclectic mix of classical and contemporary ballets. At home performances are from October through May. For ticket information phone (204) 956-2792 or (800) 667-4792.

The Winnipeg Symphony Orchestra performs September to May and offers classical, contemporary and popular orchestral music; for concert information phone (204) 949-3999. The Manitoba Opera performs October through May; phone (204) 942-7479, or (204) 780-3333 for tickets.

Modern dance is presented by Winnipeg's Contemporary Dancers from December through April at the Centennial Concert Hall; for information phone (204) 452-0229.

Theater lovers can enjoy performances of the classics, comedies and modern dramas at the Manitoba Theatre Centre Mainstage, 174 Market St., from October to May; for general information or tickets phone (204) 942-6537. The MTC Warehouse Theatre, 140 Rupert Ave., (204) 942-6537, features alternative theater performances from November to April. The Lyric Theatre, just east of the Pavilion in Assiniboine Park, (204) 888-5466, is an outdoor theater showcasing drama festivals as well as performances by the Royal Winnipeg Ballet, the Winnipeg Symphony Orchestra and other musical groups.

For both adults and young people, the Prairie Theatre Exchange, at Portage Place, 393 Portage Ave., (204) 942-7291, or (204) 942-5483 for ticket information, presents a season of modern Canadian plays from October to April. Rainbow Stage in Kildonan Park offers musicals in a covered outdoor theater from July through August; phone (204) 989-5261 or (888) 989-0888. Celebrations Dinner Theatre, 1824 Pembina Hwy. in the Canad Inns Fort

Garry, combines an original, three-act musical comedy with a four-course dinner for a one-stop evening out; phone (204) 982-8282.

The IMAX Theatre, Portage Place, 393 Portage Ave. in downtown Winnipeg, features a five-and-one-half-story-high by 22-metre-wide (72-ft.) screen; phone (204) 956-4629 for information or (204) 780-7328 to reserve tickets.

A variety of theatrical productions for children of all ages is presented at The Forks by the Manitoba Theatre for Young People; for information phone (204) 942-8898.

The French Canadian heritage of St. Boniface, in the heart of the French district, is remembered through the support of the Centre Culturel Franco-Manitobain at 340 Provencher Blvd.; phone (204) 233-8972. The center is the home of such cultural groups as Le Cercle Molière theater company (Canada's oldest active theater group), the dance group L'Ensemble Folklorique de la Rivière Rouge, and the choral groups L'Alliance Chorale Manitoba and La Chorale des Intrépides; phone (204) 233-8053 for more information.

Special Events

Winnipeg's calendar of events, with more than 130 days of festivals, reflects more than 43 nationalities that have made the city home. The *joie de vivre* spirit of the French voyageurs is revived each February during ⛵ Le Festival du Voyageur, a 10-day-long celebration including winter sports, ice-sculpting contests, music and food. With the 18th-century fur trade as its theme, the event takes place in St. Boniface, Winnipeg's French quarter.

The city plays host to the 4-day Winnipeg International Children's Festival at The Forks in early June. Music, theater, dance and comedy performances are offered as well as hands-on workshops and evening shows.

The weeklong Jazz Winnipeg Festival in late June features jazz performers on an outdoor stage. The ⛵ Red River Exhibition, known locally as the "The Ex" is held during late June. The Ex's many rides, midway activities and games of chance as well as nightly concerts take place at Red River Exhibition Park off Perimeter Highway behind Assiniboia Downs.

In mid-July is the 10-day Winnipeg Fringe Festival, with various theater performances in the Exchange District. Mid-July also brings the 4-day ⛵ Winnipeg Folk Festival to nearby Birds Hill Provincial Park, where more than 200 concerts, children's activities, music workshops and food are highlighted.

Early August brings the 2-week ⛵ Folklorama multicultural celebration, Winnipeg's largest event and reputedly the largest multicultural festival of its kind.

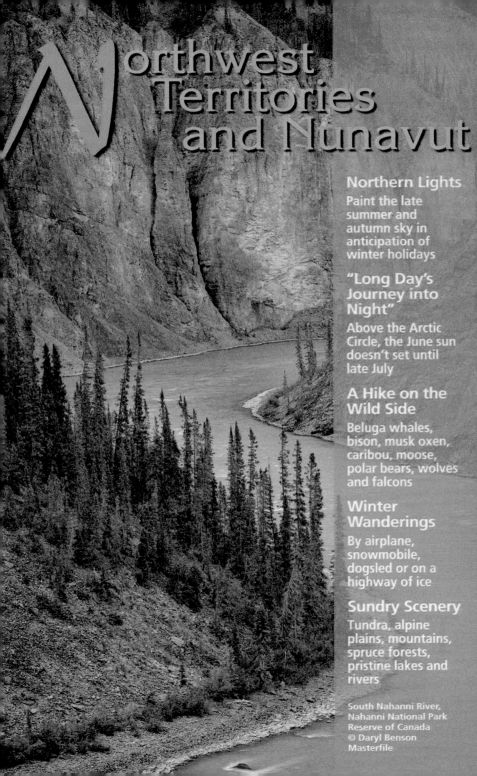

Northwest Territories and Nunavut

Northern Lights
Paint the late summer and autumn sky in anticipation of winter holidays

"Long Day's Journey into Night"
Above the Arctic Circle, the June sun doesn't set until late July

A Hike on the Wild Side
Beluga whales, bison, musk oxen, caribou, moose, polar bears, wolves and falcons

Winter Wanderings
By airplane, snowmobile, dogsled or on a highway of ice

Sundry Scenery
Tundra, alpine plains, mountains, spruce forests, pristine lakes and rivers

South Nahanni River, Nahanni National Park Reserve of Canada
© Daryl Benson
Masterfile

Auyuittug National Park of Canada, near Baffin Island, Nunavut / © J. David Andrews / Masterfile

Take a journey into northern Canada and you may be surprised at your options for enjoyment.

Residents joke that the four seasons in the Northwest Territories and Nunavut—June, July, August and winter—are a bit unlike seasons in the rest of the world. The absence of a "real" spring or fall leaves busy summers and extra-long winters.

Arrive in June, July or August and you can dip your toes in the Arctic Ocean and marvel at the wildflower-dotted tundra under a midnight sun.

Or visit during the 6 months of winter and you can choose from myriad activities that involve snow and ice: snowmobiling, building an igloo, ice fishing, riding on a paw-powered sled or simply driving on an "ice highway," made

of hard-packed snow piled on frozen lakes.

Celebrate the end of a long, dark winter by living it up at Inuvik's Sunrise Festival—held in January in honor of the sun's appearance after months of hiding.

Other diversions do not depend on snow or sun: Try a musk ox burger or dine on arctic char. Shop for such treasures as whalebone or soapstone carvings. Stay at a remote wilderness lodge and discover the specialized flora and fauna of the Arctic Circle. Learn about the traditions of the Inuit and Dene cultures. Set your sights on beluga whales or polar bears. See a shaggy musk-ox up close or listen to the roar of hooves from a migrating herd of caribou.

Whatever the season, the Northwest Territories and Nunavut invite you to refresh your senses in the north.

On April Fools' Day, 1999, in the eastern Northwest Territories, very few Inuit people were worried about such practical jokes as sugar in the salt shaker.

Instead the focus was on celebrating the birth of Nunavut, Canada's newest territory. On this night Inuit eyes were toward the heavens, watching as a grand display of colorful explosions lit up the black sky. Matching the glow of the fireworks were the sparks in the hearts of the Inuit, whose hopes are high for a bright future.

Twenty-four years after a separation was proposed, Nunavut (meaning "our land" in the Inuktitut language) officially seceded from the expansive Northwest Territories to form its own territory. A new line on the Canadian map allows its approximately 29,474 residents—85 percent of whom are Inuit—the chance to reclaim and govern what they have always believed to be their own.

Where the Streets Have No Name

Nunavut, a giant chunk of arctic earth stretching so far northeast it almost tickles the shores of Greenland, contains only one road within its nearly 2 million square kilometres (772,204 sq. mi.). Above the tree line it's a place where animals outnumber humans; where brightly colored rhododendron, lupines, yellow buttercups and mountain avens sprinkle treeless tundra; and where it may be easier to hook a trout for dinner than pick up a cheeseburger at a drive-thru.

The capital city of Iqaluit rests at the southern tip of mountainous Baffin Island, from which steep cliffs drop about 610 metres (2,001 ft.) to the sea. It's no surprise to see caribou wandering just outside the city limits along the Road to Nowhere. But don't worry; there are plenty of folks who can show you around, and during summer the midnight sun shines bright to light your way.

Even farther north is Quttinirpaaq National Park of Canada, which extends above the 80th parallel, just a snowball's throw from Santa's workshop. In this globe-top world of snow-capped peaks and glaciers, ice simply does not melt.

Despite the recent division of Nunavut and Northwest Territories, the two still share similar features. Take light, for example. During summer above the Arctic Circle, days have no end. A shining sun never dips below the horizon, and the sky is illuminated 24 hours a

---

Sir Martin Frobisher, searching for the Northwest Passage to the Orient, arrives.
1576

The Treaty of Paris grants Canada to the British.
1763

Alexander Mackenzie leads an expedition along a westward-flowing river, unearthing another route to the Arctic Ocean.

1789

1771
Hudson's Bay Co. explorer-trader Samuel Hearne arrives at Great Slave Lake.

NW Territories Historical Timeline

1850
Capt. Robert John Le Mesurier McClure discovers the Northwest Passage.

day. In winter the opposite occurs as days and nights melt together under a cold, dark sky.

Sound dismal and depressing? Well, picture the sight of a black sky pin-pricked with stars surrounding a full, glowing moon, its light sprawling across wide, snow-covered tundra and frozen lakes. On such a clear winter night the flat, stark-white landscape glistens and appears endless.

Bright Lights, Small Cities

The northern lights, or "aurora borealis," painting the winter sky are no less impressive. A faint glow slightly above the horizon serves as the show's opening act. When the lights rise, they resemble curtains in shades of red, lavender and green. Feather-shaped and stretching across the night sky, the lights ripple and curl, forming watercolor waves.

In the Northwest Territories you'll have a good chance to catch this dazzling display October through March. A spot void of city lights is best; try giant Great Slave Lake near Yellowknife. Frozen in winter, this fifth largest freshwater lake in North America provides a fine view of the vivid night sky.

Then visit Yellowknife, on the lake's north arm. Once glittering with gold, this former

1930s mining camp now flaunts its colorful past in Old Town, where shops and quaint neighborhoods nestle against the shore.

West of the city is Nahanni National Park Reserve of Canada, where Virginia Falls plummets 90 metres (295 ft.) into South Nahanni River. The falls, arguably more spectacular than Niagara, form a pool of eddies and perilous rapids surrounded by cliffs taller than Toronto's CN Tower.

Roads are in short supply here, but sparkling falls and rivers await you on scenic drives. Mackenzie Hwy., the Territories' only paved highway, crosses the Mackenzie River near Fort Providence. Continue east along the Waterfalls Route (Hwy. 1) to Sambaa Deh Falls Territorial Park, where trails lead to two cascades.

Some ice roads mid-December through April allow drives as far north as Tuktoyaktuk and Aklavik. Many motorists also choose to navigate the Dempster Hwy., which begins in Dawson City, Yukon Territory, and dead-ends at Inuvik, the continent's farthest point north accessible by road.

In fact visiting the lands north of the 60th parallel may be the brightest idea you've ever had.

Hudson's Bay Co. cedes the region to Canada.
1870

Northwest Territories divides into two territories; the eastern, Inuit-governed territory becomes Nunavut.
1999

A Soviet nuclear-powered satellite crashes into the Great Slave Lake area; debris is spread over 124,000 square kilometres.
1978

1920
Oil is discovered at Norman Wells.

Terry Parker/NWTT

1934
Gold is discovered at Yellowknife on Great Slave Lake.

1993
The Nunavut Land Claims Agreement, under which the Inuit give up any future aboriginal rights to their traditional land in return for the power to govern their own territory, is passed.

Recreation

Welcome to the top of the world. The vast Northwest Territories and Nunavut boast an area filled with wild rivers, icy seas, lofty mountains and Arctic tundra. Recreational diversions for both the adventure seeker and casual traveler are numerous.

Summer days, typically June through August, are long and surprisingly mild. With an average temperature of 21 C (70 F), visitors can enjoy the outdoors without the gear that winter demands. **Hikers** can check out a wide variety of topography, from steep mountain trails to Arctic tundra. The Canol Heritage Trail, en route to the Yukon, offers some challenging terrain.

Snowmobiling, snowshoeing, dogsledding and **cross-country skiing** are a way of life that has been known to extend into May—the warmer air and long days make this the perfect time for such outdoor pursuits. Recreational activities also can be combined with viewing the spectacular northern lights. Many outfitters offer snowmobile tours or flights to remote areas to observe this brilliant display. Hint: The best time for viewing these dancing lights is October through March.

Getting There is Half the Fun

Travel anywhere in the territories can include aircraft, boat, automobile, snowmobile, Inuit qomatiq (sled) and even dogsled. Of the Northwest Territories' four national parks, only Wood Buffalo can be reached by road. Nahanni's rugged beauty is accessible solely by air. Only the hardy recreationalist should fly to the extremely remote Aklavik, where craggy badlands include thousands of archeological sites. The newest park, Tuktut Nogait, is a hiker's paradise where float planes begin landing on the Homaday River in mid-June.

High in Canada's eastern Arctic is Nunavut's Baffin Island. Auyuittuq National Park of Canada, reached by dogsled in winter and boat in summer, draws avid hikers and **climbers** to its lofty peaks. The sheer cliffs and arctic fiords of Quttinirpaaq National Park of Canada (formerly Ellesmere Island National Park Reserve), the northernmost national park in North America, can be explored by guided tour; outfitters are available in Grise Fiord, Iqaluit and Resolute.

Land of Adventure

Water challenges come in varying degrees of difficulty. **Canoeing** and **kayaking** conditions depend on the weather. Arctic rivers, while dangerous, can offer the ultimate thrill if explored cautiously. Sea kayakers can flow beside towering icebergs, while the many rivers stemming off the meandering Mackenzie are a canoeist's dream. Paddlers will be dazzled by the breathtaking scenery on the Nahanni. Hoist your sails on Great Slave Lake, where the wind is just right for **sailing,** or if you are brave enough, **scuba dive** in the frigid waters. Slave River rapids await **whitewater rafting** enthusiasts.

Cold northern waters yield excellent **fishing.** Plenty of lakes, streams and rivers are full of prize catches, from the feisty arctic char to the fierce northern pike. Some of the territories' waters are ranked the best in the world for angling, including Great Slave, Great Bear and Murky lakes and the Stark and Snowdrift rivers. **Ice fishing** is another way to reel in the big one. Don't forget your fishing license.

The land's beauty, combined with unspoiled wilderness and vast game selections, makes **hunting** quite a rewarding experience. For the ultimate hunt, sports enthusiasts can track down one of the world's largest predators—the polar bear—by dogsled. Hunting for caribou or musk ox are additional options. Hunts are strictly controlled; licensed guides and permits are required.

For those who like to shoot with a camera, **wildlife viewing** is rewarding. **Bird-watchers** flock to the Mackenzie River delta, one of the world's biggest nesting grounds.

Whether you are seeking adventure for a few hours or several days, an outfitter will help. Northwest Territories Tourism, (867) 873-7200 or (800) 661-0788, or Nunavut Tourism, (866) 686-2888, can offer information about tour companies and outfitters.

Recreational Activities

Throughout the TourBook, you may notice a Recreational Activities heading with bulleted listings of recreation-oriented establishments listed underneath. Similar operations also may be mentioned in Destination City recreation sections. Since normal AAA inspection criteria cannot be applied, these establishments are presented only for information. Age, height and weight restrictions may apply. Reservations often are recommended and sometimes are required. Addresses and/or phone numbers are provided so visitors can contact the attraction for additional information.

Fast Facts

POPULATION: Northwest Territories 41,464. Nunavut 29,474.

AREA: Northwest Territories 1,140,835 sq km (440,479 sq mi); ranks 3rd. Nunavut 1,932,255 sq km (746,048 sq mi); ranks 1st.

CAPITAL: Yellowknife, Northwest Territories; Iqaluit, Nunavut.

HIGHEST POINT: 2,762 m/9,062 ft., Cirque of the Unclimbables Mountain in Nahanni National Park Reserve of Canada.

LOWEST POINT: Sea level, Beaufort Sea.

TIME ZONE(S): Mountain/Central/Eastern/Atlantic. DST.

TEEN DRIVING LAWS: Minimum age for an unrestricted driver's license is 17. Phone (867) 873-7406 for more information about Northwest Territories driver's license regulations.

SEAT BELT/CHILD RESTRAINT LAWS: Seat belts required for driver and all passengers 18 kg (40 lbs.) and over; children under 18 kg (40 lbs.) required to be in a child restraint.

HELMETS FOR MOTORCYCLISTS: Required for all riders.

RADAR DETECTORS: Not permitted.

FIREARMS LAWS: By federal law, all nonresidents entering Canada with a firearm must declare their weapon in writing and pay a fee of $25 (Canadian).

HOLIDAYS: Jan. 1; Good Friday; Easter Monday; Victoria Day, May 24 (if a Mon.) or the closest prior Mon.; Aboriginal Day, June 21; Canada Day, July 1; Nunavut Day, July 9; Civic Holiday, Aug. (1st Mon.); Labour Day, Sept. (1st Mon.); Thanksgiving, Oct. (2nd Mon.); Remembrance Day, Nov. 11; Christmas, Dec. 25; Boxing Day, Dec. 26.

TAXES: The Northwest Territories and Nunavut have no territorial sales tax. However, a 5 percent Goods and Service Tax (GST) is levied.

INFORMATION CENTERS: Territorial welcome centers in the Northwest Territories include an office on Hwy. 1 at the Alberta border (on the 60th parallel) near Enterprise; it is open 8:30-8:30, mid-May to mid-Sept. Dempster/Delta Visitor Information Centre at Km-post 77 on Hwy. 8 near Fort McPherson is open 9-8, mid-May to mid-Sept. The Western Arctic Regional Visitor Information Centre at the termination of the Dempster Hwy. in Inuvik is open daily 9-8, mid-May to mid-Sept. The Northern Frontier Visitor's Centre in Yellowknife is open daily 8:30-6, June-Sept.; Mon.-Fri. 8:30-5:30, Sat.-Sun. and holidays noon-4, rest of year. Phone (867) 873-4262 or (877) 881-4262.

In Nunavut the Unikkaarvik Visitor Centre in Iqaluit is open Mon.-Fri. 9-6, Sat.-Sun. 1-4, June-Aug.; Mon.-Fri. 9-6, rest of year. Phone (867) 979-4636 or (866) 686-2888.

FURTHER INFORMATION FOR VISITORS:

Northwest Territories Tourism
P.O. Box 610
Yellowknife, NT, Canada X1A 2N5
(867) 873-7200
(800) 661-0788

Nunavut Tourism
P.O. Box 1450
Iqaluit, NU, Canada X0A 0H0
(866) 686-2888

FISHING AND HUNTING REGULATIONS:

Northwest Territories Environment and
.Natural Resources
P.O. Box 1320
Yellowknife, NT, Canada X1A 2L9
(867) 873-7184
(800) 661-0788

FERRY AND ROAD INFORMATION: (867) 667-5196 (800) 661-0408 (valid only in Canada)

ALCOHOL CONSUMPTION: Legal age 19.

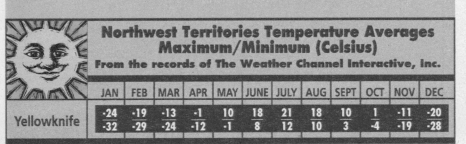

Northwest Territories Temperature Averages Maximum/Minimum (Celsius)

From the records of The Weather Channel Interactive, Inc.

	JAN	FEB	MAR	APR	MAY	JUNE	JULY	AUG	SEPT	OCT	NOV	DEC
Yellowknife	-24	-19	-13	-1	10	18	21	18	10	1	-11	-20
	-32	-29	-24	-12	-1	8	12	10	3	-4	-19	-28

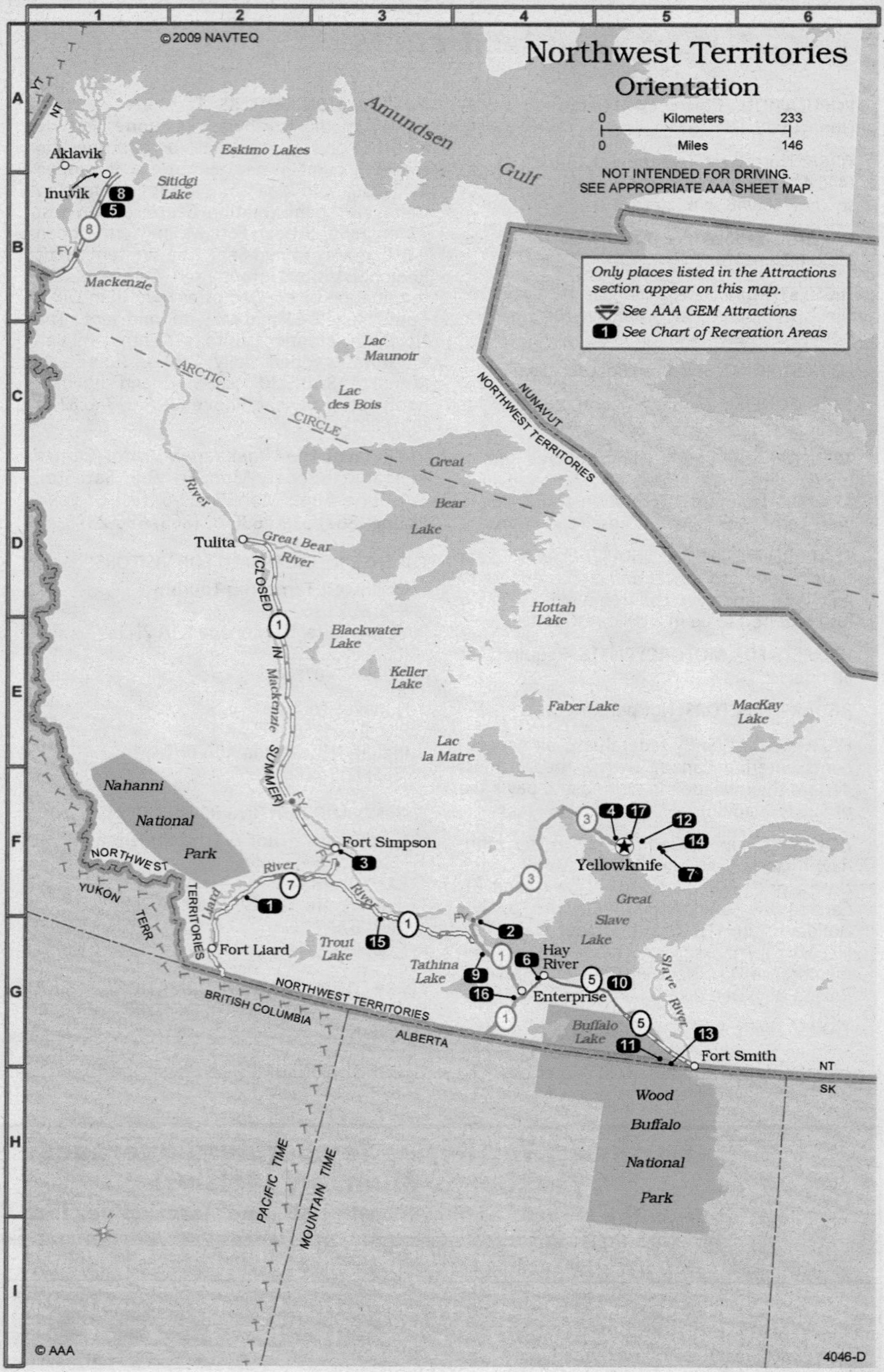

© 2009 NAVTEQ

Northwest Territories
Orientation

Kilometers
0   233
Miles
0   146

NOT INTENDED FOR DRIVING.
SEE APPROPRIATE AAA SHEET MAP.

Only places listed in the Attractions
section appear on this map.

See AAA GEM Attractions

See Chart of Recreation Areas

Amundsen

Gulf

NUNAVUT

NORTHWEST TERRITORIES

Eskimo Lakes

Aklavik

Inuvik

Sitidgi
Lake

Mackenzie

ARCTIC

CIRCLE

River

Lac
Maunoir

Lac
des Bois

Great

Bear

Lake

Hottah
Lake

Tulita

Great Bear
River

(CLOSED IN

Blackwater
Lake

Keller
Lake

Faber Lake

MacKay
Lake

Mackenzie

SUMMER)

Lac
la Matre

Nahanni

National

Park

NORTHWEST

YUKON

TERR

TERRITORIES

River

Fort Simpson

River

Fort Liard

Trout
Lake

Tathina
Lake

Yellowknife

Great

Slave

Lake

Slave River

Hay
River

Enterprise

Buffalo
Lake

Fort Smith

NT
SK

NORTHWEST TERRITORIES

BRITISH COLUMBIA

ALBERTA

Wood

Buffalo

National

Park

PACIFIC TIME

MOUNTAIN TIME

© AAA

4046-D

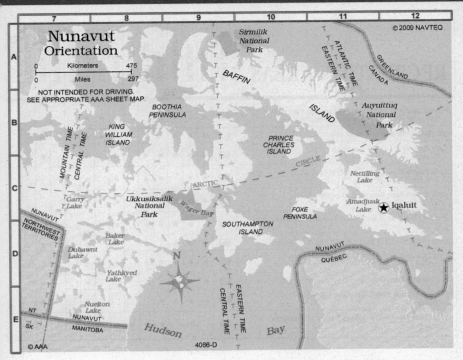

RECREATION AREAS

	MAP LOCATION	CAMPING	PICNICKING	HIKING TRAILS	BOATING	BOAT RAMP	BOAT RENTAL	FISHING	SWIMMING	PETS ON LEASH	BICYCLE TRAILS	WINTER SPORTS	VISITOR CENTER	LODGE/CABINS	FOOD SERVICE
NATIONAL PARKS *(See place listings)*															
Nahanni (F-1) 30,000 square kilometres 145 km w. of Fort Simpson. The park is not accessible by road; no motor boats allowed.		●	●	●	●			●	●	●			●		
Wood Buffalo (H-5) 44,807 square kilometres on Hwy. 5.		●	●	●	●			●	●	●			●	●	●
TERRITORIAL															
Blackstone (F-2) 1,430 hectares 166 km s. of Fort Simpson. on Hwy. 7 or 115 km n. of Fort Liard on Hwy. 7.	**❶**	●	●	●	●	●		●	●	●			●		
Fort Providence (G-4) 10 hectares at Fort Providence on Hwy. 3.	**❷**	●	●	●	●			●		●					
Fort Simpson (F-3) 18 hectares in Fort Simpson on Hwy. 1.	**❸**	●	●	●	●					●			●		
Fred Henne (F-5) 500 hectares on Hwy. 3 across from Yellowknife airport. Sailing. *(See Yellowknife p. 260)*	**❹**	●	●	●	●	●		●	●	●			●		●
Gwich'in Reserve (B-1) 8,800 hectares s. of Inuvik on Hwy. 8.	**❺**	●	●		●			●		●					
Hay River (G-4) 11 hectares on Vale Island in Hay River.	**❻**	●	●	●	●		●	●	●	●			●		

RECREATION AREAS

RECREATION AREAS	MAP LOCATION	CAMPING	PICNICKING	HIKING TRAILS	BOATING	BOAT RAMP	BOAT RENTAL	FISHING	SWIMMING	PETS ON LEASH	BICYCLE TRAILS	WINTER SPORTS	VISITOR CENTER	LODGE/CABINS	FOOD SERVICE
Hidden Lake (F-5) 1,950 hectares 45 km e. of Yellowknife along Hwy. 4. Scenic. Canoeing, golf; interpretive displays.	**7**	•		•	•			•	•	•					
Jak (B-1) 49 hectares s. of Inuvik on Hwy. 8.	**8**	•	•	•				•	•	•			•		
Lady Evelyn Falls (G-4) 5 hectares 6.5 km off Hwy. 1 near Kakisa.	**9**	•	•	•	•	•		•		•			•		
Little Buffalo River Crossing (G-5) 33 hectares off Hwy. 6, 30 km w. of Fort Resolution.	**10**	•	•		•	•		•		•					
Little Buffalo River Falls (G-5) 33 hectares off Hwy. 5, 50 km n.w. of Fort Smith.	**11**	•	•	•	•	•		•		•					
Prelude Lake (F-5) 95 hectares 29 km w. of Yellowknife on Hwy. 4. *(See Yellowknife p. 259)*	**12**	•	•	•	•	•	•	•	•	•			•	•	
Queen Elizabeth (G-5) 38 hectares off Hwy. 5 in Fort Smith.	**13**	•	•	•						•	•		•		
Reid Lake (F-5) 68 hectares 60 km e. of Yellowknife on Hwy. 4.	**14**	•	•	•	•			•	•	•					
Sambaa Deh Falls (G-3) s. of Fort Simpson on Hwy. 1.	**15**	•	•	•						•			•		
Twin Falls Gorge (G-4) 673 hectares at Km-post 75 on Hwy. 1.	**16**	•	•	•	•					•			•		
Yellowknife River (F-5) 2 hectares 9 km. e. of Yellowknife on Hwy. 4.	**17**		•		•	•	•	•		•					

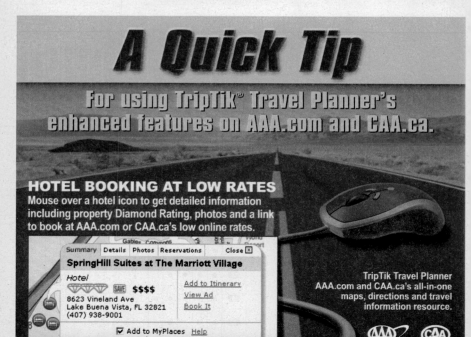

Points of Interest

AKLAVIK (A-1)

Aklavik, which means "the place of the Barrenland grizzly," was founded in 1912 as the Mackenzie River delta outpost of Hudson's Bay Co. A thriving company base in addition to a trading and trapping center, the town became the administrative center of the Western Arctic region.

However, since the community rested in the middle of the largest delta in Canada, it faced constant change as the powerful Mackenzie River built up new land and flooded the old. These conditions prevented the construction of major roads and airstrips. As a result, the newer town of Inuvik (see place listing p. 256) absorbed Aklavik's administrative role. There are no roads into Aklavik; it is accessible by air from Inuvik or by ice roads during winter.

Many Aklavik residents refuse to move. The descendants of the early traders and trappers work on oil rigs in the Beaufort Sea or trap muskrat in the delta, which is rich in wildlife. A museum, the original company store and restored log cabins serve as reminders of the past.

Just off Main Street is a tree stump in which Albert Johnson, the suspected "Mad Trapper of Rat River," carved his initials. The town also contains his grave. Johnson, who allegedly killed prospectors and trappers for the gold in their teeth, was shot in 1932 after one of the most intensive manhunts in Canadian history. Whether he actually was the "mad trapper" has been a subject explored in both books and film.

BAFFIN ISLAND

High in Nunavut's Eastern Arctic is Baffin Island, the homeland of the Inuit. It is a land of majestic fiords, icebergs, bountiful wildlife and the midnight sun, which shines until 3 a.m. from March to June. Although Baffin Island is not accessible by car, Iqaluit (see place listing p. 256), Nunavut's capital city, is served by two airlines.

Qaummaarviit Territorial Park, 12 kilometres (7 mi.) west of Iqaluit, can be reached by boat in summer or by dogsled and snowmobile in spring. An easy-to-follow trail links the island's ruins with signs depicting aspects of prehistoric life and culture.

Auyuittuq National Park of Canada, 32 kilometres (20 mi.) from Pangnirtung, is accessible by dogsled, snowmobile or boat. The park is notable for its fiords and glaciated valleys and mountains and for being the first national park established above the Arctic Circle. Polar bears, arctic foxes, caribou, seals, walruses, whales and narwhals inhabit the region.

Included in the approximately 40 bird species spotted in the park are the rare gyrfalcon and whistling swan. Remains of the 1,000-year-old Thule Eskimo culture have been found in Cumberland Sound. Hikers and mountain campers traversing Auyuittuq's Akshayuk Pass—commonly known as the "Pang Pass"—will find challenging trails, abundant wildlife and spectacular scenery.

Quttinirpaaq National Park of Canada (formerly known as Ellesmere Island National Park Reserve) is the most northerly land mass in Canada and contains 2,604-metre (8,544-ft.) Mount Barbeau, the highest mountain in eastern North America, and Lake Hazen, one of the largest lakes north of the Arctic Circle. The reserve is primarily a polar desert encompassing 39,500 square kilometres (15,250 sq. mi.) of mountain ranges, glaciers, ice shelves and fiords. Remains of buildings from European expeditions can be found on the rocky terrain. Outfitters in Grise Fiord, Iqaluit and Resolute Bay can arrange trips into the park.

Katannilik Territorial Park, between Kimmirut and Iqaluit, is rich with wildlife and unique flora. River tours, hiking and northern survival challenge even the hardiest adventurers. Information can be obtained from Nunavut Tourism; phone (866) 686-2888.

In spring and summer licensed guides from Angmarlik Visitors Centre lead expeditions into Kekerten Territorial Park, 50 kilometres (32 mi.) south of Pangnirtung; phone (867) 473-8737. Visitors can see remains of whale lookouts, blubber vats, whalers' houses and Inuit homes. A self-guiding trail connects dozens of ruins.

In the northeasternmost part of Baffin Island is Sirmilik National Park of Canada, approximately 22,000 square kilometres (8,494 sq. mi.) of rugged mountains, glaciers, ice fields, ocean fiords and coastal lowlands. In fact Sirmilik translates to "the place of glaciers." Pond Inlet, the closest community to the park, is 25 kilometres (16 mi.) south. Travel to the park—by boat, dogsled or snowmobile (depending on the season)—can be arranged through outfitters in Pond Inlet or Arctic Bay.

The park is accessible year-round, except in October and November when the ice freezes up and in July during ice break up. Popular with mountain climbers, Sirmilik is also a haven for bird-watchers. Colonies of seabirds, including thick-billed murres, black-legged kittiwakes and greater snow geese, inhabit Bylot Island. For additional information contact the park office in Pond Inlet; phone (867) 899-8092.

ENTERPRISE (G-4) pop. 100

Enterprise is the first Northwest Territories community encountered by travelers heading north on Mackenzie Hwy. A major service center for commercial traffic, the town is best known for its spectacular view of Hay River Gorge near the local Esso station.

Scenic 33-metre (108-ft.) Alexandra Falls and 15-metre (50-ft.) Louise Falls in Twin Falls Gorge Territorial Park (see Recreation Chart) are about 9 kilometres (6 mi.) south on Mackenzie Hwy. Camping and picnicking are permitted.

FORT LIARD (G-2) pop. 500

Fort Liard is in the Territories' southwest corner. Nearby archeological digs have revealed strata showing 9,000 years of human occupancy. Prior to 1807 Northwest Co. founded a post that was taken over by Hudson's Bay Co. in 1821 when the companies merged. An earnest fur trade continues.

The opening of Liard Hwy. in the early 1980s put the quiet village on the map. The community is characterized by lush growth and a relatively mild climate, despite its northern location. Bird-watchers will find many songbirds during spring and summer. A small lakefront campground is nearby.

Boat launching is possible on the Petitot and Liard rivers, where visitors can see interesting rock formations and fish for pickerel at the rivers' mouth. Fort Liard is a good jumping-off point for exploring the surrounding mountains and Nahanni National Park Reserve of Canada (see place listing p. 257). Chartered flights and a forestry office are available in town.

FORT SIMPSON (F-3) pop. 1,300

Established in 1804 at the fork of the Mackenzie and Liard rivers, Fort Simpson is the oldest continuously occupied trading post in the Mackenzie River Valley. Once a district headquarters for Hudson's Bay Co., the town developed into a center of river trade. Originally Fort of the Forks, the town was renamed to honor Thomas Simpson, first governor of the merged Northwest and Hudson's Bay companies.

Fort Simpson has always been a gathering place for people. It serves as a center for territorial government administration and oil and mining exploration. It also serves as a departure point for air, raft and canoe trips into Nahanni National Park Reserve of Canada (see place listing p. 257). A visitor center offers interpretive films, historical walking tours and a native crafts display; phone (867) 695-3182.

The Village of Fort Simpson Tourist Information Centre: P.O. Box 438, Fort Simpson, NT, Canada X0E 0N0. **Phone:** (867) 695-3182.

FORT SMITH (G-5) pop. 2,400

Initially a link in a strategic chain of 19th-century trading posts along the Mackenzie portage route to the Arctic, Fort Smith became an autonomous town in 1966. It is regional headquarters for the government of the Northwest Territories and contains several governmental offices. The town also is the site of the Thebacha Campus of Aurora College. Nearby Wood Buffalo National Park of Canada (see place listing p. 258) is home to one of the largest buffalo herds in the world.

Fort Smith Visitor Information Centre: 108 King St., P.O. Box 370, Fort Smith, NT, Canada X0E 0P0. **Phone:** (867) 872-3065 or (867) 872-8400.

NORTHERN LIFE MUSEUM is at 110 King St. The museum examines area history through collections of native artifacts, tools, crafts, manuscripts and paintings. Exhibits cover the history of the fur trade, aboriginal culture and the unique aspects of transportation in the north. Traveling exhibits from other Canadian museums are occasionally featured. **Hours:** Daily 10-7, late June-late Aug.; Mon.-Fri. 10-5, rest of year. **Cost:** Donations. **Phone:** (867) 872-2859.

HAY RIVER (G-4) pop. 3,600

Recent archeological finds show that the Slavey Dene have used the area around Hay River for thousands of years, but the first buildings did not appear until 1868 when Hudson's Bay Co. established a trading post. The town's strategic location prompts its occasional reference as the "Hub of the North."

Hay River is the southernmost port of the Mackenzie River system. During the 5-month shipping season barges, fishing boats and Coast Guard craft clog the protected river channels. The town serves as headquarters of the Great Slave Lake commercial fishing industry, which supplies the demand for Great Slave Lake whitefish. Dene Cultural Institute, on the Hay River Dene Reserve, is open for tours mid-May to mid-September. A visitor center on Mackenzie Hwy. is open 9-9, mid-May to mid-September; phone (867) 874-3180.

Hay River Chamber of Commerce: 10 Gagnier St., Suite K, Hay River, NT, Canada X0E 1G1. **Phone:** (867) 874-2565.

INUVIK (B-1) pop. 3,300

Inuvik, meaning "place of man," was erected in 1958 to replace nearby Aklavik (see place listing p. 255), which appeared to be sinking into the Mackenzie River delta. The town boomed in the 1970s as the center of the Beaufort Sea oil exploration, which since has shifted to other areas. As well as being the communications, commerce and government center for the Western Arctic, the town was the site of a Canadian Forces station until 1986.

Accessible via Dempster Hwy., Inuvik is one of the northernmost points on the North American continent that can be reached by public road. During June and most of July there are 24 hours of daylight. The town also serves as a departure point for plane trips to the Arctic Ocean and the Mackenzie River delta system.

Western Arctic Regional Visitors Centre: 2 Firth St., P.O. Box 1160, Bag Service #1, Inuvik, NT, Canada X0E 0T0. **Phone:** (867) 777-8600.

IQALUIT, NUNAVUT (C-12)

In 1576 British explorer Martin Frobisher arrived at Iqaluit's bay in present-day Nunavut and assumed that he had discovered the Northwest Passage. A discovery he had believed to be gold proved to be iron pyrite, or "fools gold." The Baffin Island town honored his memory in its name—Frobisher Bay—until 1987, when its name officially was changed back to the traditional Inuit name, Iqaluit (ih-KA-loo-it), which means "place of many fish."

Iqaluit, now the capital of Nunavut, began as a small trading post. During the 19th century European and American whalers frequented the bay waters hoping to supply their home ports with whalebone for women's corsets and blubber for lamp oil. Hiking opportunities are plentiful on the outskirts of town or through the nearby mountains. Inaccessible by car, Iqaluit can be reached by air from Calgary and Edmonton via Yellowknife, Winnipeg via Rankin Inlet, Montréal and Ottawa.

With the construction of the Distant Early Warning (DEW) Line in 1954, the town became an important defense site and a major refueling station for both commercial and military aircraft. Iqaluit is the largest community in Nunavut and the educational, administrative, transportation and economic center for the Baffin region. A focal point for Inuit art, the town boasts numerous galleries.

In 1971 the Astro Hill Complex, which includes retail stores, a hotel, movie theater, high-rise apartments, offices and a swimming pool, was completed using modular precast concrete units. Of architectural interest at the time, the complex was designed to withstand northern climatic extremes.

A kilometre northwest of Iqaluit is Sylvia Grinnell Territorial Park on the Sylvia Grinnell River. Visitors to the park can enjoy a picnic with a view of gentle waterfalls and can survey the tundra scenery from a platform overlooking the river. For more information, phone Iqaluit's Unikkaarvik Visitor Centre at (867) 979-4636.

Nunavut Tourism: P.O. Box 1450, Iqaluit, NU, Canada X0A 0H0. **Phone:** (866) 686-2888.

NUNATTA SUNAKKUTAANGIT is at 212 Sinaa. The museum's name translates to "things of the land." Exhibits of various art forms and artifacts, housed in a renovated Hudson's Bay Co. warehouse, focus on the Inuit culture of the Baffin region through displays. **Hours:** Daily 1-5, June-Aug.; Tues.-Sun. 1-5, rest of year. Closed July 1, Nov. 11 and Dec. 25. **Cost:** Donations. **Phone:** (867) 979-5537.

NAHANNI NATIONAL PARK RESERVE OF CANADA (F-1)

Elevations in the park range from 1,853 metres (6,079 ft.) at the South Nahanni River to 2,762 metres (9,062 ft.) in the Cirque of the Unclimbables in the park's northwest corner. Refer to CAA/AAA maps for additional elevation information.

About 145 kilometres (90 mi.) west of Fort Simpson and accessible only by air, the park uses Fort Liard and Fort Simpson in the Territories, Muncho Lake in British Columbia, and Watson Lake and Whitehorse in the Yukon Territory as its major supply and jumping-off points. Steeped in myth, mystery and adventure, Nahanni National Park Reserve

Permafrost

Permafrost, or permanently frozen ground, is a fact of life in most of the Northwest Territories and Nunavut. In his "Observations on Hudson's Bay 1743," James Isham wrote "the shortness of the summers is not sufficient to thaw the ice...therefore it gathers more and more every year." The permafrost layer is estimated to be as deep as 500 metres (1,640 ft.) in some areas.

Settlers found that attempts to build on the ice-filled ground were thwarted

© PhotoDisc

when heat from their structures melted the permafrost's top layer, causing foundations to crack and buildings to sink. Nearby Yukon Territory gold miners had to thaw and remove permafrost before they could extract the gold that lay beneath it.

In the 20th century Canadians began to work with permafrost. They found they could maintain its frozen state by insulating or preserving the top layer, making a surface strong enough to support any construction. Gravel pads 1 to 2 metres (4 to 6 ft.) thick were used beneath smaller structures; pilings driven into the permafrost elevated larger buildings, preventing heat from penetrating the ground beneath them. In some instances permafrost was excavated and replaced with various forms of fill.

In 1954 the Canadian government spent $34 million to build the new town of Inuvik on stilts. Pilings support buildings and connecting "utilidors," insulated corridors that house heating, water and sewage pipes.

Although the number of successful settlements built on top of permafrost is growing, mining is still a problem. To prevent shaft collapses resulting from a permafrost thaw, miners must shore open their holes with timbers or concrete.

of Canada covers more than 30,000 square kilometres (11,583 sq. mi.) of wilderness in the South Nahanni country.

Liard Hwy., linking Fort Nelson and Fort Simpson *(see place listing p. 256)*, passes Blackstone Territorial Park, east of Nahanni National Park Reserve of Canada, providing access to Liard River and Nahanni Butte, 30 kilometres (19 mi.) upriver.

A land of rivers, ragged peaks, more than 30 species of mammals and a waterfall twice the height of Niagara Falls, Nahanni National Park Reserve of Canada was created in 1972. It was placed on the UNESCO (United Nations Educational, Scientific and Cultural Organization) World Heritage list 6 years later and cited as an "exceptional natural site forming part of the heritage of mankind."

In the early 1900s the area received a reputation for myth and adventure. Gold prospectors, drawn by rumors of placer deposits, began to arrive. When the decapitated bodies of the two MacLeod brothers were found, stories of huge mountain men proliferated.

Although no real mountain men ever were seen, the park remains a place of rugged beauty with little development, including accommodations for visitors. Those who come to raft and canoe on the rivers and hike the forests, alpine tundra and canyons of Nahanni will find it a bracing experience. Travel by water is an excellent way to enjoy the park; however, it can be dangerous and should be attempted only by those experienced in canoeing and rafting. Reservations are required for river trips. Due to the trips' popularity, reservations should be made well in advance; phone the park office for information.

Less experienced river travelers should hire a licensed outfitter for guided river trips down the South Nahanni River. Tours pass Virginia Falls, where the South Nahanni River plunges more than 90 metres (295 ft.); the Gate, a 90-degree river bend below 213-metre (700-ft.) vertical cliffs; and hot springs such as those at First Canyon and Rabbitkettle. Visitors to Rabbitkettle **must** register at the warden's cabin and have park staff accompany them to the springs. Daytime air trips to Virginia Falls should be prearranged through an air charter company in Fort Simpson, Fort Liard, Watson Lake, Whitehorse or Muncho Lake.

Fishing for arctic grayling, lake and bull trout and northern pike is permitted with a national park fishing license (annual pass $34.30), which can be obtained at the Fort Simpson Administration Office or at the warden's cabin at Rabbitkettle Lake. All national park regulations apply. Firearms are not permitted.

Wildlife species include moose, beavers, woodland caribou, Dall sheep, grizzly and black bears, white-tailed deer and mountain goats. Visitors should take particular care when traveling in areas where they are likely to encounter bears.

The park is open year-round. The park administration office at Fort Simpson is open daily 8-noon and 1-5, mid-June to mid-Sept.; Mon.-Fri. 8:30-noon and 1-5, rest of year. Overnight visitors and those planning river rafting or canoe trips must register before entering the park and upon leaving.

One-day admission to the park is $24.50 per person. For route information, park regulations, weather conditions and park activities write to the Superintendent, Nahanni National Park Reserve of Canada, P.O. Box 348, Fort Simpson, NT, Canada X0E 0N0; phone (867) 695-3151. *See Recreation Chart.*

TULITA (D-2)

Because of the lack of roads on the frontier, most towns were founded along rivers. Originally called Fort Norman, Tulita was established in 1810 when Northwest Co. built a trading post at the confluence of the Great Bear and Mackenzie rivers. The town's name means "where two rivers meet."

Later years brought additional industries. In 1920 pitchblende—the chief ore-mineral source of uranium—was discovered, and the early 1980s brought the construction of the Wells-Zama oil pipeline.

Tulita is accessible via air service from Norman Wells. No all-weather roads lead into the comunity, but a winter road—open from late January to mid-March—connects Tulita to surrounding communities. Nearby is one of the Northwest Territories' oldest Anglican churches, built of squared logs in the 1860s. The restored church can be visited.

About 20 kilometres (12 mi.) away is a bed of low-grade coal that has been burning for centuries. Although the fire likely was ignited by lightning, Dene legend attributes it to a giant's campfire. During the summer the surface of the bed sometimes rises and the coals are exposed. Firefighters' attempts to extinguish the smoldering coals have failed.

Hamlet Office: P.O. Box 91, Tulita, NT, Canada X0E 0K0. **Phone:** (867) 588-4471.

WOOD BUFFALO NATIONAL PARK OF CANADA (H-5)

Elevations in the park range from 183 metres (600 ft.) at the Little Buffalo River to 945 metres (3,100 ft.) in the Caribou Mountains. Refer to CAA/AAA maps for additional elevation information.

Accessible by Hwy. 5, which connects with Mackenzie Hwy. at Hay River, Wood Buffalo National Park of Canada is the second largest park in the world. Covering about the same area as the states of Maryland and New Jersey combined, the national park straddles the border between the Northwest Territories and Alberta.

This vast subarctic wilderness contains such remarkable geological features as the Salt Plains, Alberta Plateau, the deltas and lowlands of the Peace and Athabasca rivers, and extensive gypsum karst formations. The park was established in 1922 to protect one of the world's largest free-roaming herds of wood bison; approximately 4,300 of these animals now live there. Moose, caribou, muskrats, beavers and black bears are among other park residents.

The Peace Athabasca Delta is an important stopover for North America's four major waterfowl flyways. A large variety of waterfowl as well as hawks, eagles and pelicans, are present for part of the year. The northeastern corner of the park is one of the last nesting grounds in the world for the endangered whooping crane. Some of the park's lakes and rivers contain pike, pickerel, trout, whitefish and goldeye. Wildflowers and berries abound in the rolling meadows.

The 508-kilometre (316-mi.) Fort Chipewyan Winter Road is open mid-December to mid-March (weather permitting). The road runs from Fort Mc-Murray, Alberta, to Fort Smith; part of the road is formed by ice. To check road conditions between Fort Chipewyan and Fort Smith, phone the park office or (867) 872-7962 for recorded information. To check road conditions between Fort Chipewyan and Fort McMurray, phone the Regional Municipality of Wood Buffalo at (780) 697-3600.

Visitors can see such magnificent snow-covered scenery as boreal forest, lakes and wide-open meadows. Before departure travelers should contact the park office for a list of driving regulations and recommended travel supplies.

Boating, picnicking and camping are permitted at Pine Lake. The park has hiking trails, which can be used for snowshoeing and cross-country skiing in winter. Contact the park for information about guided nature hikes and other interpretive events.

The park is open year-round; however, campgrounds and facilities are open Victoria Day weekend through Labour Day. The Fort Smith Visitor Reception Centre at 126 McDougal Rd. is open Mon.-Fri. 9-noon and 1-5, Sat.-Sun. 1-5, mid-June through Labour Day; Mon.-Fri. 9-noon and 1-5, rest of year. Phone (867) 872-7960, or TTY (867) 872-7961. The Fort Chipewyan Visitor Reception Centre on Mac-Kenzie Avenue is open Mon.-Fri. 8:30-noon and 1-5, Sat.-Sun. 1-5, mid-June through Labour Day; Mon.-Fri. 8:30-noon and 1-5, rest of year. Phone (780) 697-3662.

Admission to the park is free. For route information, road conditions or details about park activities contact the Superintendent, Wood Buffalo National Park of Canada, P.O. Box 750, Fort Smith, NT, Canada X0E 0P0; phone (867) 872-7900. *See Recreation Chart and the AAA/CAA Western Canada & Alaska CampBook.*

YELLOWKNIFE (F-5) pop. 18,700

Although the Dene hunted the Yellowknife region for thousands of years and Europeans explored it in 1771, a permanent settlement was not established until the discovery of gold in 1934. Taking the name of the copper knives carried by the Chipewyan Indians, the town is now the capital of the Northwest Territories and the site of a functioning gold mine and a booming diamond industry.

In 1967 Yellowknife replaced Ottawa as the seat of government for the Northwest Territories. Tours of the Legislative Assembly are available Mon.-Fri. at 10:30, 1:30 and 3:30, Sun. at 1:30, June-Aug.; Mon.-Fri. at 10:30, rest of year. Phone (867) 669-2200. On the northern shore of Great Slave Lake, this "metropolis" of the north lies less than 500 kilometres (311 mi.) from the Arctic Circle and is an excellent place to shop for Northern arts.

The city's historic Old Town retains the gold rush excitement of the 1930s with quaint restaurants, art galleries, shops, and boat, kayak, canoe and yacht rentals. Planes are available for sightseeing and fishing trips. The visitor center on 49th Street can provide information about rentals and excursions. The visitor center also is the starting point for guided tours of the Capital Park area, conducted in July and August.

Best viewed October through March, the aurora borealis, or northern lights, is produced when atomic particles from outside the atmosphere strike and excite atoms within the upper atmosphere. The lights sweep mysteriously across the clear night sky as luminescent curtains of red, green, pink and purple light in patterns called rayed bands. Guided viewing trips are available.

DID YOU KNOW

Summer daytime highs in Northwest Territories and Nunavut average about 21 C (70 F).

The scenic 71-kilometre (44-mi.) Ingraham Trail (Hwy. 4) to Tibbett Lake allows year-round access to several chains of lakes and streams. Seven boat launches and two campgrounds lie along the road. Prelude Nature Trail runs 3 kilometres (1.8 mi.)from Prelude Lake Territorial Park *(see Recreation Chart)* through the wilderness to several lookout points, while another trail leads to Cameron Falls.

Prospector's Trail is in Fred Henne Territorial Park *(see Recreation Chart)*, west near Long Lake.The 4-kilometre (2.5-mi.) loop points out the region's varied geological features and is of interest to rock hounds; sturdy footwear and insect repellent are necessary. Other hiking trails lead from Ingraham Trail; information and brochures are available at the visitor center.

Easily accessible area lakes include Prosperous, Pontoon, Prelude, Reid and Tibbett. Walsh Lake has good trout fishing, but is accessible only by going through Reid Lake.

The scenic portion of Hwy. 3 runs north from Mackenzie Bison Sanctuary to Edzo, then parallels the northern shore of Great Slave Lake. Driving anywhere in the area, or throughout the Northwest Territories, demands that a vehicle be in top mechanical condition.

Northern Frontier Regional Visitor Center: #4 4807 49th St., Yellowknife, NT, Canada X1A 3T5. **Phone:** (867) 873-4262 or (877) 881-4262.

Self-guiding tours: The visitor center provides brochures for a walking tour of Old Town and New Town.

BECK'S KENNELS DOGSLED TOURS is at 124 Curry Dr. Visitors are transported on a traditional dogsled ride around Grace Lake. Several other tours also are offered. **Note:** Though spare winter gear is provided, visitors should dress appropriately for cold outdoor weather. **Time:** Allow 30 minutes minimum. **Hours:** Daily 9-noon and 2-11:45, Nov. 16-Apr. 14; by appointment in summer. **Cost:** Fare $45; $22.50 (ages 0-12). Cash only. **Phone:** (867) 873-5603.

THE PRINCE OF WALES NORTHERN HERITAGE CENTRE is .4 km (.25 mi.) w. on Hwy. 4 at 4750 48th St. The center preserves area history through exhibits depicting aspects of Dene and Inuit cultures. Displays pertain to geology, archeology, exploration, fur trading, transportation, aviation and bush pilots, natural history, artwork and handicrafts. **Hours:** Daily 10:30-5:30, June-Aug.; Mon.-Fri. 10:30-5, Sat.-Sun. noon-5, rest of year. Closed Jan. 1 and Dec. 25. **Cost:** Donations. **Phone:** (867) 873-7551.

Saskatchewan

The Last Frontier

Rolling grasslands and evergreen forests create an unspoiled paradise

Big Muddy Badlands

Trace Butch Cassidy's Outlaw Trail through this colorfully rugged terrain

Call of the Wild

Whistling swans and white-tailed deer are among the many wilderness residents

Qu'Appelle Valley

The sun seems a little brighter as it shines upon this region's golden farmland

The Mounties

Explore the history of those who brought law and order to the Canadian West

Rural Saskatchewan
© John E. Marriott
age fotostock

Prince Albert National Park of Canada / © Mike Grandmaison / age fotostock

A visit to Saskatchewan is a perfect escape from the hustle and bustle.

Named after the Plains Cree term *kisiskatchewan,* meaning "the river that flows swiftly," Saskatchewan boasts more than just a great river with an unusual name.

Along country roads, you'll encounter prairies, mountains, grasslands and even sand dunes. While approximately half the province is covered in pine, white spruce and other trees, a good portion is blanketed with fields of wheat.

Look for signs marked with a barn symbol; they designate bed and breakfast inns and vacation farms, where you can take part in milking cows and—if you're lucky—enjoy

homemade berry preserves or baked goods.

Take a dip into one of more than 100,000 freshwater lakes, some of which can be found in the Qu'Appelle Valley. Nestled among the water holes in this region are resorts and golf courses with rolling fairways.

For history, head to towns that preserve the origin of the Mounted Police, the heritage of Métis culture or the rough-and-tumble cowboy lifestyle.

Or visit the Beaver Lodge Cabin on Ajawaan Lake in Prince Albert National Park of Canada, residence of naturalist author Grey Owl, who coined the now-popular belief that "you belong to nature, not it to you."

The hues of Saskatchewan's palette were determined both with and without man's help. Painted by nature and the history of the plains, vibrant gold, green and red are the prominent colors in the province's scheme.

Sheaves of Golden Wheat

Shimmering fields of grain, glinting gold in the sunlight, are probably the image most associated with Saskatchewan. Captured on innumerable postcards and snapshots, the plains seem to stretch to the horizon in a never-ending series of undulating waves, interrupted only by an occasional silo. And the fields are certainly productive—more than 50 percent of Canada's wheat crop comes from this land.

Proof of the grain's economic importance to the province is the three golden wheat sheaves on its coat of arms. Saskatchewan's flag provides further evidence; its lower half, a solid band of gold, represents the grain fields dominating the province's southern portion.

You can experience early 20th-century pioneer prairie life at Motherwell Homestead National Historic Site, near Abernethy. Costumed interpreters busily carry out typical daily tasks of the period at the 1912 farmstead of William Richard Motherwell, farmer, politician and agricultural innovator. Motherwell developed techniques enabling early settlers to overcome the region's dry soil and short growing season.

If a more modern approach to rural life appeals to you, spend a few days at one of Saskatchewan's vacation farms. Helping with chores can offset the pounds you might gain from the hearty meals provided by your hosts. More than 70 Saskatchewan families offer visitors a chance to experience what living on a farm is all about.

Landscapes of Green

Color Regina green—the city is known for having more than 350,000 trees. A particularly verdant section of town is Wascana Centre, a 930-hectare urban park that is truly the heart of Saskatchewan's capital.

The center, lining the rambling shoreline of Wascana Lake, is home to cultural and educational institutions as well as the architecturally impressive Legislative Building, the seat of provincial government. Works by Canadian artists grace the building's walls. Galleries at the nearby Royal Saskatchewan Museum are devoted to earth and life sciences and the First Nations people. Young guests will have fun

---

Henry Kelsey, an English fur trader, explores Saskatchewan.
1690

The first permanent settlement is built by the Hudson's Bay Company.
1774

The massacre of a band of Assiniboine First Nations by U.S. wolf-hunters prompts the creation of the Mounted Police.

Tourism Saskatchewan
Douglas E. Walker

1873

1870
Canada acquires present-day Saskatchewan as part of the Northwest Territories.

1885
Louis Riel leads the Métis tribe's battle for land rights in the Northwest Rebellion.

Saskatchewan Historical Timeline

visiting a robotic dinosaur and digging into the hands-on exhibits in the Paleo Pit.

Initially known as Pile-O-Bones (the translation of the Cree word *Oscana*), Regina's early name is a reference to the buffalo remains left behind when the site served as a hunters' camp. Its present name was adopted in honor of Queen Victoria—Regina being Latin for queen. And the good monarch's husband was not forgotten when provincial town names were assigned—the city of Prince Albert was named for Victoria's consort in 1886.

The nearly 1 million acres of nearby Prince Albert National Park of Canada encompass other shades of green, primarily those of aspens and evergreens. Its woodlands, boreal landscapes and grasslands form just a small portion of the forests covering half the province.

Within the park is the simple lakeside cabin of Grey Owl, the First Nations name assumed by Englishman Archibald Belaney. This early environmentalist, writer and lecturer, accepted into the Ojibwa tribe in the 1930s, was dedicated to the preservation of the Canadian wilderness and its wildlife. His gravesite is close by on a wooded hill.

Red Coats of the Canadian West

The Royal Canadian Mounted Police are immediately recognizable by their scarlet tunics. In fact, the route they took across the prairie in 1874 to establish law and order in western Canada is retraced along Hwy. 13, the Red Coat Trail. Many of their early posts are now national historic sites, including Fort Battleford, off Hwy. 4 near Battleford, and Fort Walsh, southwest of Maple Creek.

Regina is home to the RCMP's only training academy. Visitors are welcomed at the RCMP Heritage Centre, which tells the story of the force through interactive exhibits and the stirring sculptural procession "March of the Mounties." If your timing is right, you can watch the cadets drill at the Sergeant Major's Parade, usually held Monday through Friday at 12:45 p.m.

If you're in town in July or early August and truly want to be inspired by the colors of the province, try to catch the Sunset Retreat Ceremony. Culminating in the lowering of the Canadian flag at dusk, the golden glow cast by the fading sun seems a fitting background as the cadets, in traditional red jackets, proudly march against the backdrop of lush greenery bordering the parade grounds.

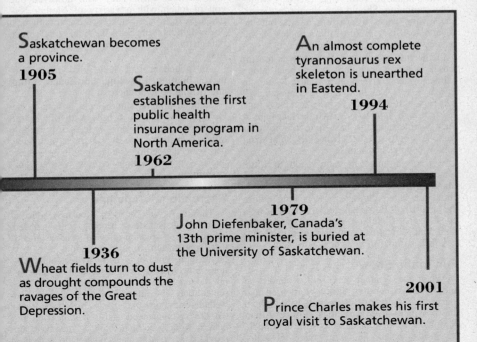

Saskatchewan becomes a province.
1905

Saskatchewan establishes the first public health insurance program in North America.
1962

An almost complete tyrannosaurus rex skeleton is unearthed in Eastend.
1994

1979
John Diefenbaker, Canada's 13th prime minister, is buried at the University of Saskatchewan.

1936
Wheat fields turn to dust as drought compounds the ravages of the Great Depression.

2001
Prince Charles makes his first royal visit to Saskatchewan.

Recreation

Contrary to popular belief, Saskatchewan is not all prairie. Even in the southern half, where farming is predominant, lakes and parks abound with recreational options.

Angling Heaven

With more than 100,000 lakes, rivers and streams to choose from, you're never really far from a good freshwater **fishing** spot. While northern pike, rainbow trout and walleye will take your bait at fishin' holes throughout the province, you'll have to head for northern waters to land trophy-size lake trout, Arctic grayling and other sport fish.

Lake Diefenbaker, south of Outlook, is a favorite fishing destination with both locals and visitors; this is the place to go if you're after walleye or northern pike. The Precambrian Shield, in the northern third of the province, is just about as good as it gets for anglers, with almost 40 percent of its area consisting of H_2O. Try Lac la Ronge if you're a trout fishing devotee. Outfitters will be happy to fly you to some of the more remote northern fishing lakes.

Tumbling east to west across the province north of the 55th parallel, the Churchill River provides some of North America's best whitewater **canoeing.** Should you choose to experience white water by **rafting,** check out the Clearwater River. Both of these bodies of water flow in northern Saskatchewan.

If the rush of white-water action is too intense, consider paddling your boat along calmer waters. The Bagwa Canoe Route, in Prince Albert National Park of Canada, will take you through several pristine lakes. Late May through September, when the lakes are at their warmest, is the best time to dip your oars. A bonus is the chance to sight bald eagles, ospreys and loons.

For the ultimate in calm, head to Little Manitou Lake, near the resort community of Manitou Beach. First Nations people knew about the lake's curative powers long before the arrival of European settlers. And there's no danger of sinking in these waters—the high concentration of minerals makes this impossible, so float to your heart's content.

Fun in the Snow

When the weather turns cold, bundle up and try **cross-country skiing.** Groomed and marked trails are easily accessible throughout the province—even in cities. Prince Albert National Park of Canada, almost in the middle of Saskatchewan, has more than 100 kilometres (60 mi.) of trails. Moose Mountain Provincial Park, north of Carlyle, adds another 50 kilometres (30 mi.) to explore, while the forests, lakes and valleys of Duck Mountain Provincial Park, east of Kamsack, provide a picturesque backdrop for cross-country excursions.

If you prefer to stay within city limits, the Meewasin Valley Trail follows the Saskatchewan River through the middle of Saskatoon, the province's largest city.

Snowmobiling enthusiasts love the thousands of kilometres of interconnected, groomed trails linking towns and parks along Canada's version of Route 66, in this case a cross-country snowmobile route. Popular put-in points include Hudson Bay, Nipawin, North Battleford and Yorkton. Trail permits are mandatory; phone Tourism Saskatchewan, (877) 237-2273, for a provincial snowmobile trail map.

Warm Weather Choices

When the weather turns warm, everyone flocks to Prince Albert National Park of Canada. You don't even need **hiking** boots on a few of the park's short trails. Boundary Bog, Mud Creek and Treebeard, all loop trails, traverse fairly level terrain and take no longer than an hour each. They will, however, put you in touch with a variety of Mother Nature's creations—a black spruce and tamarack bog; sightings of beavers, otters and great blue herons; and forests of aspens and balsam firs.

An abundance of lakes and trails also makes **boating, bicycling, horseback riding** and fishing popular choices.

Another popular summer playground is the Qu'Appelle Valley, a broad swath of land in southern Saskatchewan bordered by rolling hills. A chain of lakes and three provincial parks are the setting for resort villages where guests enjoy boating, **water skiing** and **swimming.**

Recreational Activities

Throughout the TourBook, you may notice a Recreational Activities heading with bulleted listings of recreation-oriented establishments listed underneath. Similar operations also may be mentioned in Destination City recreation sections. Since normal AAA inspection criteria cannot be applied, these establishments are presented only for information. Age, height and weight restrictions may apply. Reservations often are recommended and sometimes are required. Addresses and/or phone numbers are provided so visitors can contact the attraction for additional information.

Fast Facts

POPULATION: 978,933.

AREA: 651,036 sq km (251,365 sq mi); ranks 7th.

CAPITAL: Regina.

HIGHEST POINT: 1,392 m/4,566 ft., Cypress Hills.

LOWEST POINT: 65 m/213 ft., Lake Athabasca.

TIME ZONE(S): Central and Mountain.

TEEN DRIVING LAWS: Teens who have had a license less than 6 months may transport no more than one non-family member. Other passengers must be family members, all of whom must have a seat belt. The minimum age for an unrestricted license is 17 years, 6 months. Phone (800) 667-8015 for more information about Saskatchewan's driver's license regulations.

MINIMUM AGE FOR GAMBLING: 19.

SEAT BELT/CHILD RESTRAINT LAWS: Seat belts are required for the driver and all passengers 16+. Children under 16 and weighing more than 18 kilograms (40 lbs.) are required to wear a seat belt; child restraints are required for children weighing less than 18 kilograms.

HELMETS FOR MOTORCYCLISTS: Required for all riders.

RADAR DETECTORS: Permitted.

FIREARMS LAWS: By federal law, all nonresidents entering Canada with a firearm must declare their weapon in writing and pay a fee of $25 (Canadian). Contact the Canadian Firearms Centre at (800) 731-4000 for additional information or to receive a declaration form.

HOLIDAYS: Jan. 1; Family Day, Feb. (3rd Mon.); Good Friday; Victoria Day, May 24 (if a Mon.) or the closest prior Mon.; Canada Day, July 1; Saskatchewan Day, Aug. (1st Mon.); Labour Day, Sept. (1st Mon.); Thanksgiving, Oct. (2nd Mon.); Remembrance Day, Nov. 11; Christmas, Dec. 25; Boxing Day, Dec. 26.

TAXES: The federal Goods and Service Tax is 5 percent. Saskatchewan's provincial sales tax also is 5 percent.

INFORMATION CENTERS: Provincial welcome centers are along Hwy. 1 east of Fleming; at 1922 Park St. in Regina; near Maple Creek on Hwy. 1; Hwy. 16 at Langenburg and Lloydminster; and Hwy. 39 at North Portal. All information centers are open daily mid-May to early September except the center in Regina, which is open Mon.-Fri. 8-5.

FURTHER INFORMATION FOR VISITORS:
Tourism Saskatchewan
1922 Park St.
Regina, SK, Canada S4N 7M4
(306) 787-9600
(877) 237-2273
See color ad inside front cover

FISHING AND HUNTING REGULATIONS:
Saskatchewan Environment
3211 Albert St.
Regina, SK, Canada S4S 5W6
(306) 787-9037

ALCOHOL CONSUMPTION: Legal age 19.

Saskatchewan Temperature Averages Maximum/Minimum (Celsius)
From the records of The Weather Channel Interactive, Inc.

	JAN	FEB	MAR	APR	MAY	JUNE	JULY	AUG	SEPT	OCT	NOV	DEC
Prince Albert	-14	-9	-3	9	18	22	24	23	16	9	-3	-12
	-26	-22	-16	-4	3	8	11	9	3	-3	-13	-22
Regina	-11	-8	-1	10	18	23	26	26	18	12	0	-9
	-22	-18	-12	-3	4	9	12	11	4	-2	-11	-19

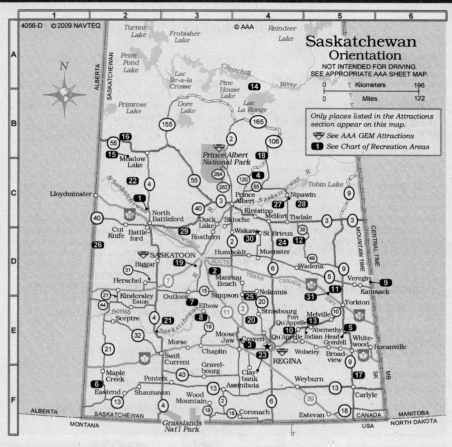

Saskatchewan
Orientation

NOT INTENDED FOR DRIVING.
SEE APPROPRIATE AAA SHEET MAP.

Only places listed in the Attractions
section appear on this map.
See AAA GEM Attractions
See Chart of Recreation Areas

4056-D ©2009 NAVTEQ   © AAA

RECREATION AREAS

	MAP LOCATION	CAMPING	PICNICKING	HIKING TRAILS	BOATING	BOAT RAMP	BOAT RENTAL	FISHING	SWIMMING	PETS ON LEASH	BICYCLE TRAILS	WINTER SPORTS	VISITOR CENTER	LODGE/CABINS	FOOD SERVICE
NATIONAL PARKS (See place listings)															
Grasslands 906 square kilometres.		●	●	●						●			●		
Prince Albert 3,875 square kilometres. Horse rental.		●	●	●	●	●	●	●	●	●	●	●	●	●	●
PROVINCIAL															
The Battlefords (C-2) 600 hectares 4.75 km n. of Cochin off Hwy. 4. Cross-country skiing, golf.	❶	●	●	●	●	●	●	●	●	●		●		●	●
Blackstrap (D-3) 530 hectares 8 km e. of Dundurn via Hwy. 211. Cross-country and downhill skiing; sailboard rental.	❷	●	●		●	●		●	●	●		●			●
Buffalo Pound (E-4) 1,930 hectares 19 km n. of Moose Jaw on Hwy. 2, then 13 km e. on Hwy. 202. Cross-country and downhill skiing, tennis; pool.	❸	●	●	●	●	●		●	●	●		●		●	
Candle Lake (C-4) 1,270 hectares 60 km n.e. of Prince Albert on hwys. 55 and 120. Cross-country skiing.	❹	●	●	●	●	●	●	●	●	●				●	●
Clearwater River 224,040 hectares 50 km n.e. of La Loche on Hwy. 955 (north of area shown on map). Canoeing.		●	●	●				●							
Crooked Lake (E-5) 190 hectares 30 km n. of Broadview on Hwy. 605. Golf.	❺	●	●	●	●	●	●	●	●					●	●
Cypress Hills (F-2) 18,410 hectares 30 km s. of Maple Creek on Hwy. 21. Cross-country skiing, golf, tennis; horse rental, pool. Five horsepower limit for boats. (See Elkwater, Alberta, p. 76).	❻	●	●	●	●		●	●	●	●	●	●	●	●	●
Danielson (E-3) 2,910 hectares on n. end of Lake Diefenbaker via hwys. 44, 45 or 219.	❼	●	●		●	●		●	●	●					
Douglas (E-3) 4,430 hectares 11 km s.e. of Elbow on Hwy. 19. Houseboat rental.	❽	●	●		●	●		●	●	●					
Duck Mountain (D-6) 26,160 hectares 25 km e. of Kamsack on Hwy. 57. Cross-country and downhill skiing, golf, tennis; horse rental.	❾	●	●	●	●	●	●	●	●	●		●		●	●
Echo Valley (E-4) 640 hectares 8 km w. of Fort Qu'Appelle off Hwy. 10. Cross-country skiing; horse rental.	❿	●	●	●	●	●		●	●	●		●		●	●
Good Spirit Lake (D-5) 1,900 hectares 24 km n.e. of Springside via Hwy. 47. Cross-country skiing, tennis.	⓫	●	●	●	●	●	●	●	●	●			●		●
Greenwater Lake (D-4) 20,720 hectares 38 km n. of Kelvington on Hwy. 38. Cross-country skiing, golf, tennis.	⓬	●	●	●	●	●	●	●	●	●		●		●	●
Katepwa Point (E-5) 8 hectares 10 km s.e. of Lebret on Hwy. 56.	⓭		●		●	●	●	●	●						
Lac la Ronge (A-4) 344,470 hectares 48.25 km n. of La Ronge on Hwy. 102. Cross-country skiing; houseboat rental.	⓮	●	●	●	●	●	●	●	●	●		●		●	●
Makwa Lake (B-2) 2,560 hectares n.w. of Loon Lake off Hwy. 26. Cross-country skiing; horse rental.	⓯	●	●	●		●	●		●	●	●				
Meadow Lake (B-2) 156,970 hectares 5 km n. of Goodsoil via Hwy. 26. Cross-country skiing, tennis; horse rental, sailboat rental.	⓰	●	●	●	●	●	●	●	●	●			●		●
Moose Mountain (F-5) 40,060 hectares 22.5 km n. of Carlyle on Hwy. 9. Cross-country skiing, golf (18 holes), tennis; horse rental.	⓱	●	●	●				●	●	●	●	●	●	●	●
Narrow Hills (B-4) 53,610 hectares 64.25 km n. of Smeaton on Hwy. 106. Canoeing, cross-country skiing, snowmobiling; playground.	⓲	●	●	●	●	●	●	●	●	●		●		●	
Pike Lake (D-3) 500 hectares 30.5 km s. of Saskatoon on Hwy. 60. Golf, tennis; pool. Ten horsepower limit for boats.	⓳	●	●		●	●	●	●	●				●		●

RECREATION AREAS

	MAP LOCATION	CAMPING	PICNICKING	HIKING TRAILS	BOATING	BOAT RAMP	BOAT RENTAL	FISHING	SWIMMING	PETS ON LEASH	BICYCLE TRAILS	WINTER SPORTS	VISITOR CENTER	LODGE/CABINS	FOOD SERVICE
Rowan's Ravine (E-4) 270 hectares 22.5 km w. of Bulyea on Hwy. 220.	20	•	•	•	•	•	•	•	•	•	•				•
Saskatchewan Landing (E-3) 5,600 hectares 45 km n. of Swift Current via Hwy. 4. Horse rental, windsurfing rental.	21	•	•	•	•	•	•	•	•	•			•	•	•
OTHER															
Bright Sand Lake (C-2) 648 hectares 27 km e. of St. Walburg off Hwy. 26 on a gravel road. Bird-watching, canoeing, cross-country skiing, golf, miniature golf, mountain biking, snowmobiling; beach, canoe rental, nature trails with interpretive signs, playground.	22	•	•	•	•	•	•	•	•	•	•	•	•	•	•
Dunnet (E-4) 50 hectares 7 km s. of Avonlea on Hwy. 334. Cross-country skiing, ice fishing, snowmobiling.	23	•	•	•	•	•			•	•	•	•			•
Kipabiskau (D-4) 16 hectares 35 km s.w. of Tisdale off Hwy. 3 or Hwy. 35. Cross-country skiing, ice fishing, snowmobiling; beach, canoe and kayak rental, nature trails, playground.	24	•	•	•	•	•	•	•	•	•	•			•	•
Last Mountain Lake (D-4) 65 hectares 20 km n.w. of Govan off Hwy. 20 on a gravel road. Bird-watching, ice fishing; pool. *(See Simpson p. 287)*	25	•	•	•				•	•	•	•			•	•
Macklin Lake (D-2) 154 hectares .4 km s. of Macklin on Hwy. 31. Golf; beach, playground, wildlife preserve.	26	•	•	•				•	•	•				•	•
Nipawin and District (C-4) 121 hectares 3 km n.w. of Nipawin on Hwy. 55. Cross-country skiing, golf, snowmobiling; petting zoo, playground, spray pool.	27	•	•	•	•	•	•	•	•	•	•	•		•	•
Pasquia (C-4) 65 hectares 12 km n. of Arborfield on Hwy. 23. Cross-country and downhill skiing, golf; Andy Jamault nature trail to the Pasquia paleontological site, pool.	28	•	•	•					•	•	•	•			•
Redberry Lake (D-3) 5,600 hectares 12.8 km e. of Hafford on Hwy. 40. Cross-country skiing, golf.	29	•	•	•	•	•		•	•	•	•		•	•	•
St. Brieux (D-4) 65 hectares 1 km w. of St. Brieux on Hwy. 368. Historic. Cross-country skiing, golf, miniature golf; beach, playground.	30	•	•	•	•	•		•	•	•	•	•			•
Whitesand (D-5) 49 hectares 9 km n.e. of Theodore off Hwy. 16. Golf, miniature golf; playground.	31	•	•	•	•	•		•		•	•				•

Points of Interest

ABERNETHY (E-5) pop. 197

In 1882, about 2 decades before he began his distinguished career in Canadian politics, William Richard Motherwell arrived in southeastern Saskatchewan from his Ontario birthplace and acquired a 64-hectare (160-acre) homestead grant near Abernethy. He farmed the land using several techniques of scientific agriculture then considered revolutionary.

Motherwell was later instrumental in launching the Territorial Grain Growers Association. His knowledge of the land groomed him for later roles as Saskatchewan's minister of agriculture 1905-18 and federal minister of agriculture during the 1920s.

MOTHERWELL HOMESTEAD NATIONAL HISTORIC SITE is 9 km (5 mi.) s. of jct. hwys. 10 and 22. The site commemorates William Richard Motherwell and his contributions to Canadian agriculture. Motherwell's farmstead, including 3 hectares (8 acres) of landscaped grounds, Ontarian-style barn and six-bedroom fieldstone house, have been restored to the pre-World War I era.

Tours: Guided tours are available. **Time:** Allow 1 hour minimum. **Hours:** Daily 9-5, Victoria Day-Labour Day. **Cost:** $7.80; $6.55 (ages 65+); $3.90 (ages 6-16); $19.60 (family). **Phone:** (306) 333-2116.

ASSINIBOIA (F-3) pop. 2,305

Assiniboia is an Ojibwa word meaning "one who cooks with stones." Southeast of town off Hwy. 2 is St. Victor Petroglyphs Provincial Historic Park, the site of a sandstone cliff etched with prehistoric First Nations carvings. The carvings at the top of the cliff depict human faces, footprints and animal tracks. Since they have faded with time, the designs are best seen late in the afternoon or on a cloudy day. There is a picnic site near the base of the cliff that is open June 1 through Labour Day. Phone (306) 694-3659 for more information.

The Prince of Wales Cultural and Recreation Centre, 201 3rd Ave. W., was built through volunteer effort; Charles, Prince of Wales turned the sod for the groundbreaking during a visit to Saskatchewan. It houses an auditorium where performing arts, trade shows and other events take place, and the Assiniboia & District Public Library, which presents monthly displays featuring the work of local artists in the Kay Cristo Room. The grounds feature xeriscaping, landscaping with plants that require little water. For information phone (306) 642-3634.

The Visitor Information Centre at 501 Hwy. 2N houses the Prentice African Safari Exhibit, a collection of 24 mounted animals hunted during three 1970s safaris.

ASSINIBOIA AND DISTRICT MUSEUM is at 506 3rd Ave. W. The museum depicts the growth of Assiniboia from 1912 to the present. A guided tour includes exhibits such as a collection of antique cars dating from 1916-50 as well as vintage heavy farm equipment. **Time:** Allow 30 minutes minimum. **Hours:** Daily 9-noon and 1-5, July-Aug.; Mon.-Fri. 9-11:30 and 1-4, rest of year. Closed major holidays. **Cost:** $4; $1 (ages 13-18). **Phone:** (306) 642-5353, or (306) 642-4216 after hours. ⛨

SHURNIAK ART GALLERY is at 122 3rd Ave. W. The gallery, which houses the private collection of international businessman William Shurniak, features paintings and sculptures by Canadian artists as well as art, furniture and rugs from China, Southeast Asia and Australia. Included in the collection are pieces by the Canadian artists known as the Group of Seven. **Hours:** Tues.-Sat. 10-4:30, Sun. 1-5; closed holiday weekends. **Cost:** Donations. **Phone:** (306) 642-5292. 🛈

BATOCHE (C-3)

Having had their lands in Manitoba's Red River Valley divided and bought out from under them by swelling numbers of homesteaders, the Métis—a people of mixed First Nations and French heritage—migrated to the area around Batoche, in the valley of the South Saskatchewan River, about 1870. Building a settlement along the riverbank, they farmed and hunted, but conflict arose with the Canadian government, which was bent on settling the country's western reaches. Although the Métis set up a provisional government to give voice to their concerns and petitioned for rights to the land, their requests were ignored.

Batoche National Historic Site *(see attraction listing)* chronicles the history behind the events that led to armed conflict in 1885. It also presents the culture and traditions of Métis descendants who continue to prosper in Saskatchewan today.

BATOCHE NATIONAL HISTORIC SITE is w. on Hwy. 225. The decisive battle of the Northwest Rebellion/Métis Resistance of 1885 was fought at this site, which covers 1,080 hectares (1,650 acres). Features include the ruins of a Batoche village, the St. Antoine de Padoue church, a rectory and a Visitor Reception Centre with an audiovisual presentation. There are interpretive signs and costumed interpreters at key locations throughout the park.

Hours: Daily 9-5, Victoria Day weekend to mid-Sept. **Cost:** $7.80; $6.55 (ages 65+); $3.90 (ages 6-16); $19.60 (family). **Phone:** (306) 423-6227 or (306) 423-6228.

BATTLEFORD (D-2) pop. 3,685

Once capital of the Northwest Territories, Battleford is one of Saskatchewan's oldest communities. As soon as the Canadian Pacific Railway began construction, citizens made plans for their town to become a western metropolis. But the railroad took a more southerly route, and in 1883 the capital was moved to Regina.

Battleford's hopes revived in 1905 when the Canadian Northern Railway proposed a westward route, but the line was built north of town on the other side of the Saskatchewan River, spawning the new town of North Battleford *(see place listing p. 280)*. Battleford and its sister city have continued to grow as the province's vast northwest region has become more developed.

FORT BATTLEFORD NATIONAL HISTORIC SITE is 2 km (1.2 mi.) off Hwy. 4. The North West Mounted Police district headquarters was established here in 1876 to enforce law and order. The fort became the site of armed confrontations between the First Nations and federal troops in 1885. Five buildings have been preserved; various illustrative exhibits are featured. Costumed staff members provide interpretive information. Historic weapons demonstrations are given, and historic trails also are on site. **Tours:** Guided tours are available. **Time:** Allow 1 hour, 30 minutes minimum. **Hours:** Daily 9-5, Victoria Day weekend-Labour Day. Tours are offered hourly beginning at 9:15. **Cost:** $7.80; $6.55 (ages 65+); $3.90 (ages 6-16); $19.60 (family). **Phone:** (306) 937-2621. 🎫

BIGGAR (D-2) pop. 2,033

Named after W.H. Biggar, General Counsel for the Grand Trunk Pacific Railroad, Biggar was incorporated as a village in 1909 and as a town in 1911. In 1910 the GTPR established a divisional point. A construction boom resulted, and so did an increase in population. The town became one of the home terminals where train crews changed: The station was one of the largest in the West. During the years that followed the population remained stable, and it wasn't until the 1950s that Biggar experienced renewed growth.

The name Sandra Schmirler is synonymous with Biggar. A three-time world curling champion (1993, 1994 and 1997) and 1998 Olympic gold medalist for the sport of curling, Schmirler was born and schooled in Biggar. Sandra Schmirler Olympic Gold Park was opened in her honor in 2000.

BIGGAR MUSEUM AND GALLERY is at 105 3rd Ave. W. Highlighting the story of settlement in Biggar, the museum features two outdoor murals; a plesiosaur diorama; the Earl of Saskesk exhibit; replicas of a CN railway station, the Hanson buck and a silent film theater; and a Ku Klux Klan exhibit. Also included is an art gallery. Changing exhibits are presented regularly in the museum and art gallery. **Time:** Allow 30 minutes minimum. **Hours:** Mon.-Sat. 9-5, Victoria Day weekend-Sept. 30; 1-5, rest of year. Closed major holidays. **Cost:** Donations. **Phone:** (306) 948-3451.

HOMESTEAD MUSEUM is 1.6 km (1 mi.) w. on Hwy. 51. The museum houses an early 20th-century wooden home, a replica of a sod house, a store with a barbershop, a school, a restored 1913 homestead with a collection of character dolls, a bunkhouse, a church, a barn and a general display building. **Time:** Allow 2 hours minimum. **Hours:** Mon.-Sat. 9-9, Sun. noon-9, Victoria Day weekend-second Mon. in Oct. **Cost:** Free. **Phone:** (306) 948-3427.

BROADVIEW (E-5) pop. 611

Broadview began as a division point on the Canadian Pacific Railway. A marker in a park on the west side of town marks the location of the original tracks laid in 1882. Also in town is a sanctuary for Canada geese.

Broadview Chamber of Commerce: P.O. Box 119, Broadview, SK, Canada S0G 0K0. **Phone:** (306) 696-2533.

BROADVIEW MUSEUM is 1 blk. s. of Hwy. 1 on N. Front St. A First Nations log house, an 1897 rural school and a Canadian Pacific Railroad station and caboose are displayed at the museum. Exhibits include First Nations and pioneer artifacts, old photographs, and maps of early homesteads and trails. **Hours:** Daily 9:30-5:30, June-Aug. **Cost:** Donations. **Phone:** (306) 696-3244.

CARLYLE (F-5) pop. 1,257

North of Carlyle is Moose Mountain Provincial Park *(see Recreation Chart and the AAA/CAA Western Canada & Alaska CampBook)*, which began as a resort beach on Lake Kenosee in 1906. The park is home to herds of moose and elk and is a nesting place for geese and other birds. There also are more than 450 beaver lodges.

Recreational facilities include an 18-hole golf course, hiking and equestrian trails, riding stables, a clubhouse and a swimming beach. Across from the entrance is Kenosee Superslide, a water park.

CANNINGTON MANOR PROVINCIAL HISTORIC PARK is e. on Hwy. 13 to Grid Rd. 603, then 2 km (1.2 mi.) n. on gravel roads. The village of Cannington Manor, founded in 1882, was an attempt to duplicate the upper-middle-class English way of life, including cricket matches and fox hunts. The museum and seven buildings contain antiques, artifacts and farming implements used by the settlers.

Guides in period costumes demonstrate activities typical of the settlement in the last 2 decades of the 19th century. **Hours:** Wed.-Mon. 10-5, Victoria Day-Labour Day. **Cost:** $4; $1 (students with ID); free (ages 0-5); $9 (family). **Phone:** (306) 577-2600 or (306) 739-5251. 🎫

CARLYLE RUSTY RELIC MUSEUM AND TOURIST INFORMATION CENTRE is at Railway Ave. and 3rd St. W. Housed in the former Canadian National Railway Station, the museum features historical items from the area. Thirteen rooms contain such exhibits as a dentistry collection, farm equipment,

World War II military uniforms, medical equipment, a restored kitchen and photographs.

A restored one-room schoolhouse and a tourist information center also are on the grounds. **Time:** Allow 1 hour minimum. **Hours:** Tues.-Sat. 10-5, June 1-Labour Day. **Cost:** Donations. **Phone:** (306) 453-2266.

GAMBLING ESTABLISHMENTS

- **Bear Claw Casino** is on Hwy. 9. **Hours:** Mon.-Thurs. 9 a.m.-1 a.m., Fri.-Sat. 9 a.m.-2 a.m., Sun. 10 a.m.-midnight. Closed Dec. 24-25. **Phone:** (306) 577-4577.

CHAPLIN (E-3) pop. 235, elev. 674 m/2,214'

CHAPLIN NATURE CENTRE is at the western approach to town via Hwy. 1. The center is in the midst of the Chaplin Lake area, which encompasses some 6,000 hectares (15,000 acres) of inland saline water. More than 30 species of shorebirds, some endangered, either rest and refuel here during migratory journeys or nest and raise their young in the summer, feasting on brine shrimp that teem in the salty, shallow water.

Guided bus tours are available; binoculars are provided. **Time:** Allow 1 hour, 30 minutes minimum. **Hours:** Daily 9-5, Victoria Day weekend-Labour Day. **Cost:** Center displays free. Guided tour $10; $5 (students with ID). Reservations are recommended. **Phone:** (306) 395-2770 or (877) 746-7273.

CLAYBANK (F-4) pop. 20

CLAYBANK BRICK PLANT NATIONAL HISTORIC SITE is 1 km (.6 mi.) e. on Hwy. 339. This plant is said to be North America's most intact early 20th-century brick factory and was active 1912-89. Visitors may tour the large site, which comprises more than 20 structures. The plant also is open on special event days to afford visitors an opportunity to see the brick-making process.

Time: Allow 1 hour minimum. **Hours:** Tours daily at 11:30, 1, 2:30 and 4, July-Aug.; by appointment rest of year. **Cost:** $8; $20 (family). **Phone:** (306) 868-4474. ⓘ ⊞

CORONACH (F-4) pop. 770

POPLAR RIVER POWER STATION AND STRIP MINE is 10 km (6 mi.) s.e. Bus tours lasting 2.5 hours depart from the information center at jct. Centre St. and Railway Ave. (Hwy. 18). Guides provide interpretive explanations during a walking tour of the power plant and the bus tour of the strip-mining site. Durable clothing and flat-heeled shoes are recommended. **Hours:** Tours are given daily at 9:30 and 1, Mar.-Dec. (weather permitting). **Cost:** Free. **Phone:** (306) 267-2078, or (306) 267-2157 Sat.-Sun.

CRAVEN (E-4) pop. 274

Last Mountain House Provincial Historic Park, 8 kilometres (5 mi.) north of town on Hwy. 20, preserves the site of a fur-trade outpost that operated 1869-71. Park interpreters offer guided tours of the site's three reconstructed buildings Thursday through Sunday, July 1-Labour Day; phone (306) 731-4409 or (306) 787-0731.

CUT KNIFE (D-2) pop. 532

In 1885 Cut Knife was the site of several First Nations uprisings that were inspired by the Métis rebellion (*see Batoche p. 271*). The Battle of Cut Knife Hill, between the Cree tribe led by Chief Poundmaker and the North West Mounted Police under Col. W.D. Otter, ended in the retreat of the Mounties to Battleford.

Poundmaker, who stopped his warriors from pursuing and ambushing Otter's troops, later surrendered to the authorities to help restore peace between the First Nations and settlers. A national historic plaque and a framework of tepee poles mark the chief's grave at the Poundmaker Reserve.

Dominating Cut Knife's horizon is the massive tomahawk in Tomahawk Park. The handle is a pipe 17 metres (57 ft.) long and weighs 3,928 kilograms (8,660 lbs.).

Cut Knife Chamber of Commerce: P.O. Box 504, Cut Knife, SK, Canada S0M 0N0. **Phone:** (306) 398-2363.

CLAYTON McLAIN MEMORIAL MUSEUM is 3 blks. w. on Hill Ave. in Tomahawk Park. First Nations artifacts, local historical records and articles used by early settlers are exhibited at the museum, which also includes several buildings depicting an early pioneer settlement. A trout pond is on the grounds. **Time:** Allow 1 hour minimum. **Hours:** Mon.-Sat. 9-5, Sun. 1-5, July-Aug.; by appointment rest of year. **Cost:** $2; $1 (ages 0-11); $5 (family). **Phone:** (306) 398-2345.

DUCK LAKE (C-3) pop. 610

The town of Duck Lake lies between the North Saskatchewan and South Saskatchewan rivers. The actual lake is a few kilometres west of town. A nearby cairn marks the site of the Battle of Duck Lake, in which the Métis First Nations defeated the North West Mounted Police on Mar. 26, 1885.

DUCK LAKE REGIONAL INTERPRETIVE CENTRE is at the jct. of hwys. 11 and 212. The center focuses on the historical contributions made by First Nations, Métis and pioneer populations in the area's development. A museum features collections ranging from traditional clothing to tools used in buffalo hunts. The history and cultures of the area are presented in a 15-minute video, and a tower provides panoramic views.

Time: Allow 30 minutes minimum. **Hours:** Daily 10-5:30, Victoria Day weekend-Labour Day weekend. **Cost:** $4.50; $3.50 (senior citizens); $2.50 (students with ID); free (ages 0-5); $12 (family). **Phone:** (306) 467-2057 or (866) 467-2057.

FORT CARLTON PROVINCIAL HISTORIC PARK
is 26 km (16 mi.) w. on Hwy. 212. The fort that
played a part in the settlement of north-central Saskatchewan has been reconstructed at the site, which
features three tepees depicting the Plains Cree culture as it existed 1860-70. A replica of the Hudson's
Bay Store is a museum of fur-trading history. The
visitor center is a reconstruction of the 1879 home
of the trading post overseer.
Time: Allow 30 minutes minimum. **Hours:** Daily
10-6, Victoria Day-Labour Day. **Cost:** $2.50; $1
(ages 6-17); free (ages 66+); $6 (family). **Phone:**
(306) 467-5205. [A]

EASTEND (F-2) pop. 471

EASTEND MUSEUM-CULTURAL CENTRE is
downtown at 306 Redcoat Dr. Items of local interest
are displayed, including early settler, business and
First Nations artifacts and a collection of dinosaur
bones found in the area. Adjoining the museum is a
rancher's restored log house dating from around
1911. **Time:** Allow 30 minutes minimum. **Hours:**
Daily 9-5, Victoria Day-Labour Day; by appointment rest of year. **Cost:** $3; free (ages 0-12).
Phone: (306) 295-3375.

T.REX DISCOVERY CENTRE is at 1 T-rex Dr. In
partnership with the Royal Saskatchewan Museum,
the center houses fossils and replicas of dinosaurs, a
98-seat theater and interpretive displays. Educational
activities also are offered. A nearly complete T-rex
skeleton was discovered in the area in 1991.
Tours: Guided tours are available. **Time:** Allow
1 hour minimum. **Hours:** Daily 9-9, Jul.-Aug.; 9-5
rest of year. **Cost:** $8.45; $7.95 (ages 65+); $6 (ages
6-18). **Phone:** (306) 295-4009.

ELBOW (E-3) pop. 294

ELBOW MUSEUM is at 239 Saskatchewan St. The
area's history is depicted from 1905 to the present.
Items displayed include arrowheads, photographs
and maps. A replica of a sod house, furnished in
pioneer style, also is on-site. The house reflects the
ingenuity of early settlers in surviving the harsh environment with a scarcity of building materials.
Time: Allow 30 minutes minimum. **Hours:** Daily
1-5, July-Aug.; by appointment rest of year. **Cost:**
Donations. **Phone:** (306) 854-2277.

ESTEVAN (F-4)
pop. 10,084, elev. 570 m/1,870′

Estevan, founded in 1892 just north of the Souris
River, is one of Saskatchewan's major centers for
coal and oil. The sun shines an average of 2,540
hours annually, making the town among the sunniest
spots in Canada.

Southeast of town off Hwy. 39 is Roche Percée, a
group of strangely eroded rock formations that were
once venerated by local First Nations. Although
most of the animals and initials carved on the rocks
can no longer be seen, the site is still supposedly
visited by spirits whose murmurs can be heard when
the wind blows.

On Hwy. 39 at 118 4th St. is the Estevan Art Gallery & Museum. The facility provides information
about local events and also presents changing exhibitions and occasional interpretive programs or
tours; phone (306) 634-7644.

The Wood End Building, next to the center, was
the 1893 barracks for the North West Mounted Police and contains artifacts that relate to the organization's early days. Also nearby is Eli Mandel Heritage Park, which contains an oil field display.

Tours to Shand Power Station and Luscar Boundary Mine can be arranged June through August
through the Estevan Tourism Booth; phone (306)
634-6044.

Estevan Chamber of Commerce: 303-1133 4th
St., Estevan, SK, Canada S4A 0W6. **Phone:** (306)
634-2828.

BOUNDARY DAM POWER STATION is 5 km (3
mi.) w. on Hwy. 18. This power station, which contains one of the largest lignite-burning plants in
Canada, utilizes southeast Saskatchewan's vast coal
reserves to produce more kilowatts than any other
dam in the province. Swimming and boating are
permitted. **Time:** Allow 2 hours minimum. **Hours:**
Guided tours are given Tues.-Sat. at 9 and 1, June-
Aug. Phone ahead to confirm schedule. **Cost:** Free.
Phone: (306) 634-6044.

RECREATIONAL ACTIVITIES
Recreational Complex
- **Souris Valley Aquatic and Leisure Center** is at
  701 Souris Ave., Estevan, SK, Canada S4A 2T1.
  Hours: Mon.-Fri. 6 a.m.-9:30 p.m., Sat. 8 a.m.-
  9:30 p.m., Sun. noon-9:30. **Phone:** (306)
  634-1888.

ESTON (E-2) pop. 971, elev. 682 m/2,240′

Founded in 1916, Eston is a major grain center;
more than one million bushels of grain are produced
annually.

PRAIRIE WEST HISTORICAL CENTRE is at 946
2nd St. S.E. The restored 1910 Evans house contains more than 3,000 artifacts that include period
furnishings and photographs, agricultural displays, a
homesteader shack and the Heritage Art Gallery. A
pioneer schoolroom is depicted at the Lovedale
school. A wildflower garden is on the grounds.
Time: Allow 30 minutes minimum. **Hours:** Mon.-
Sat. 9-noon and 1-5, Sun. 1-5, July-Aug.; daily
1:30-4:30, day after Victoria Day weekend-June 30;
by appointment rest of year. **Cost:** Free. **Phone:**
(306) 962-3772.

FORT QU'APPELLE (E-4) pop. 1,919

With the 1874 signing of Treaty Number IV, representatives of the Cree and Saulteaux First Nations
gave away their legal right to vast tracts of southern
Saskatchewan; near the center of Fort Qu'Appelle
(kwah-PELL) a cairn marks the site of the signing.
The fort for which the town is named was built in
1864 mainly for use as a trading post.

Fort Qu'Appelle is on the Qu'Appelle River in a broad valley of lush farmland. The area is known for the wide variety of berries growing on the moist, north-facing slopes. The dry, south-facing slopes are carpeted with wildflowers. Several kinds of hawks soar above this peaceful valley, and pelicans, herons, ducks and geese nest in the marshes. Near Fort Qu'Appelle the river widens into a chain of lakes.

The river's unusual name is the French translation of the Cree word *catabuysepu*, or "the river that calls." According to First Nations legend, the river was haunted by a spirit that could be heard crying as it moved up and down the water.

Also taking its name from this Cree expression is nearby Katepwa Point Provincial Park, a lakeside recreation area offering day-use facilities. Another provincial park, Echo Valley, is west of town. *See Recreation Chart and the AAA/CAA Western Canada & Alaska CampBook.*

Fort Qu'Appelle Chamber of Commerce: P.O. Box 1273, Fort Qu'Appelle, SK, Canada S0G 1S0.

FISH CULTURE STATION is 6 km (4 mi.) w. on Hwy. 210. The station raises such fish as northern pike, whitefish, walleye, sturgeon and rainbow, brown, lake, tiger and brook trout through their life cycle from the egg stage to adult, then distributes them to various lakes and rivers to bolster fish populations. **Tours:** Guided tours are available. **Time:** Allow 30 minutes minimum. **Hours:** Daily 9-noon and 1-4, May 1-Labour Day. **Cost:** Free. **Phone:** (306) 332-3200.

FORT QU'APPELLE MUSEUM is at Bay Ave. and 3rd St. A small log building remaining from the original 1864 Hudson's Bay Co. trading post adjoins a modern structure displaying relics of the past, First Nations crafts and a model of Fort Qu'Appelle. **Hours:** Daily 1-5, June 1-Labour Day; other times by appointment. **Cost:** $2; $1 (children); $5 (family). **Phone:** (306) 332-6033.

GRASSLANDS NATIONAL PARK (F-3)

Elevations in the park range from 747 metres (2,450 ft.) at the Frenchman River to 998 metres (3,275 ft.) at Horse Creek. Refer to CAA/AAA maps for additional elevation information.

Grasslands National Park of Canada encompasses the grasslands in two separate blocks between Val Marie and Killdeer in the southern part of the province. When completed, the park will preserve 900 square kilometres (350 sq. mi.) of Saskatchewan's original mixed-grass prairie, including such topographic features as buttes, badlands and coulees. Among the wildlife species found in the park are black-tailed prairie dogs, golden eagles, rattlesnakes, short-horned lizards, pronghorn antelopes, mule deer and most recently, reintroduced plains bison.

These grasslands also claim a rich history. The first recorded discovery of dinosaur remains in western Canada was made in the badlands in 1875.

Proof of early habitation includes remnants of tepee rings, ranch buildings, corrals and old homestead shacks.

Ranching operations exist in the area, and some of the proposed parkland is still under private ownership. Before entering the park, visitors are invited to contact or stop at the visitor center located in Val Marie, which offers park information, maps and permits as well as interpretive programs, guided hikes and special events. Park open year-round. Visitor center daily 8-5, Victoria Day weekend-Labour Day weekend; 8-noon and 1-4:30, Apr. 1-day before Victoria Day weekend and day after Labour Day weekend-Oct. 31. Write Grasslands National Park, P.O. Box 150, Val Marie, SK, Canada S0N 2T0; phone (306) 298-2257. *See Recreation Chart.*

GRAVELBOURG (F-3) pop. 1,089

CATHÉDRALE NOTRE-DAME DE L'ASSOMPTION is at 1st Ave. and Main St. The 1918 Cathedral of Our Lady of the Assumption is noted for the beauty of its interior murals, painted 1921-29 by founding pastor Monsignor Charles Maillard, as well as its stained-glass windows. Guided tours are available in English and French. **Hours:** Open daily 9-5, June-Aug.; by appointment rest of year. **Cost:** $5; $3 (ages 10-18). **Phone:** (306) 648-3322, or (306) 648-3105 to schedule a guided tour.

GRENFELL (E-5) pop. 947

Grenfell is about 124 kilometres (77 mi.) east of Regina at the junction of Hwys. 1 and 47. Hwy. 47 north from town leads to scenic Hwy. 247, which runs east along the northern shores of Crooked and Round lakes to the junction with Hwy. 9; from there, Hwy. 9 offers another scenic stretch of roadway south to Whitewood.

GRENFELL MUSEUM is at Wolseley Ave. and Stella St. Adare, the former home of the editor/publisher of Grenfell's first newspaper, is furnished in period. The 1904 house contains a brass bed, a wood-burning kitchen range, an icebox, a hand-operated vacuum cleaner and a dining table set with china. A separate building houses antiques, pioneer artifacts and military displays. **Time:** Allow 2 hours minimum. **Hours:** Fri.-Sun. 2-8, early July-Aug. 31; other times by appointment. **Cost:** Donations. **Phone:** (306) 697-2839.

HERSCHEL (D-2) pop. 30

ANCIENT ECHOES INTERPRETIVE CENTRE is on 1st Ave. The first part of this attraction—the interpretive center—depicts the area's natural history. Items include fossils, aboriginal artifacts and examples of taxidermy. The second part leads visitors on a guided tour, using their own vehicle, to 1,800-year-old petroglyphs located 3.2 kilometres (2 mi.) away. At the destination, a hiking trail reveals glacial ravines, freshwater springs and a variety of flora and fauna. A video of the hike is available for viewing.

Time: Allow 1 hour, 30 minutes minimum. **Hours:** Daily 9-5, May 15-Sept. 1; by appointment rest of year. **Cost:** Interpretive center $6; $5 (ages 5-12 and 65+). Guided tour to the petroglyphs $6; $5 (ages 5-12). Reservations are required for archeological site tours. **Phone:** (306) 377-2045. 🍴 🅰

HUMBOLDT (D-3) pop. 4,998

Humboldt is on Hwy. 5 about 111 kilometres (69 mi.) east of Saskatoon; the drive takes about 90 minutes. Named for author, explorer and scientist Baron Friedrich Heinrich Alexander von Humboldt, the town reveals its German heritage through architecture, festivals, downtown murals and folk art, a cottage industry. The Willkommen Centre has information about Humboldt's history and area sightseeing.

Annual events include Polkafest, celebrated the last weekend in May; the Summer Sizzler & Rodeo, held the last weekend in June; and Oktoberfest, which takes place the last Saturday in October.

Willkommen Centre/Humboldt Tourism: 601 Main St., P.O. Box 1598, Humboldt, SK, Canada S0K 2A0. **Phone:** (306) 682-3444 or (877) 277-6748.

HUMBOLDT AND DISTRICT MUSEUM AND GALLERY is at Main St. and Sixth Ave. Housed in a restored, early 20th-century post office (a national historic site), the museum features a Humboldt Telegraph Station exhibit, a Sports Hall of Fame and local history displays. It also showcases the work of regional artists. **Time:** Allow 30 minutes minimum. **Hours:** Tues.-Sat. 10-5, Sun. 1-5, July-Aug.; Tues.-Sat. 1-5, rest of year. **Cost:** Donations. **Phone:** (306) 682-5226.

INDIAN HEAD (E-5) pop. 1,634

INDIAN HEAD MUSEUM is at 610 Otterloo St. Housed in an old fire hall, this museum displays an extensive collection of artifacts dating back to the district's pioneer beginnings. Also on the grounds is an 1883 cottage that farm laborers lived in, as well as a 1926 school. A 1952 Pontiac in mint condition resides in a replicated 1930s village garage. A large assortment of farm machinery also is on display.

Guided tours are available by appointment. **Time:** Allow 1 hour minimum. **Hours:** Daily 1-4, July-Aug.; by appointment rest of year. **Cost:** $2; 50c (ages 12-19). **Phone:** (306) 695-3908.

PFRA SHELTERBELT CENTRE is 1.6 km (1 mi.) s. of jct. hwys. 1 and 56. A short, self-guiding nature trail and picnic areas are part of the Prairie Farm Rehabilitation Administration (PFRA). **Hours:** Outdoor areas open daily dawn-dusk. **Cost:** Free. **Phone:** (306) 695-2284.

KAMSACK (D-5) pop. 1,713

KAMSACK POWERHOUSE MUSEUM is 1.5 km (1 mi.) w. of Hwy. 5 to the Riverside Golf Course, following signs. Housed in a 1914 power plant, the museum features a 1914 generator, old farm equipment, household artifacts, a printing press, vintage clothing and replicas of an early 1900s doctor's office, hospital room, kitchen, bedroom and barbershop. **Hours:** Daily 1-5, June 1-Labour Day; by appointment rest of year. **Cost:** $3; free (ages 0-12). **Phone:** (306) 542-4415.

KINDERSLEY (D-2) pop. 4,412

Kindersley is a popular stop for bird-watchers. The surrounding region annually attracts thousands of migrating geese, more than 10 species of ducks, and a few whistling swans and whooping cranes. Kindersley celebrates the annual Goose Festival in September.

Kindersley Chamber of Commerce: 305 Main St., Box 1537, Kindersley, SK, Canada S0L 1S0. **Phone:** (306) 463-2320.

KINDERSLEY PLAINS MUSEUM is 1 km (.6 mi.) e. on Hwy. 7 to 903 11th Ave. Geological displays, First Nations artifacts and farming and military items are featured. **Tours:** Guided tours are available. **Time:** Allow 30 minutes minimum. **Hours:** Daily 9-5, May 13-Aug. 31. **Cost:** $5; $3 (ages 12-18); $10 (family). **Phone:** (306) 463-6620.

KINISTINO (C-4) pop. 643

One of the oldest purely agricultural settlements in the province, Kinistino takes its name from *kinistineaux,* meaning "they who were the first to arrive." The allusion refers to the Cree First Nations, who lived in the area before the arrival of homesteaders.

KINISTINO DISTRICT PIONEER MUSEUM is on Main St. The museum displays pioneer and aboriginal artifacts. **Time:** Allow 30 minutes minimum. **Hours:** Mon., Wed. and Fri. 1-7, July-Aug. **Cost:** Donations. **Phone:** (306) 864-2838.

LLOYDMINSTER (C-1)

Lloydminster is the province's only city with one foot planted in Saskatchewan and the other in Alberta. Four 31-metre-tall (100-ft.) border markers—shaped like the survey stakes used during the original survey of the border between the two provinces—represent four themes: oil and gas, agriculture, the Barr Colonists and native North Americans. The downtown monument, erected in 1994, denotes the city's bi-provincial status.

Many nearby lakes, regional parks and campgrounds offer opportunities for fishing, bird-watching and other pursuits. Other recreational opportunities include an 18-hole golf course and an aquatic leisure center with a wave pool and a water slide.

Summer events include Canada Day celebrations, which are held July 1 in Weaver Park; Colonial Days, a 4-day fair with a parade, agricultural exhibits and grandstand entertainment held in mid-July; and racing action at the Canadian Professional Chuckwagon Finals in mid-August.

Lloydminster Tourism: 4420 50th Ave., Lloydminster, AB, Canada T9V 0W2. **Phone:** (780) 871-8333 or (800) 825-6180.

BARR COLONY HERITAGE CULTURAL CENTRE is on Hwy. 16E at 45th Ave. This complex of museums, galleries and changing exhibits chronicles the history of one of North America's largest organized colonizations, led by Rev. Isaac Barr. It is next to Weaver Park, where the English colonists built their first settlement in 1903. The facilities and exhibits include The Richard Larsen Museum, The Fuchs Wildlife Exhibit, The Imhoff Art Collection and The Oilfield Technical Society Heavy Oil Science Centre.

Hours: Cultural center open Tues.-Sat. 9-8, Sun. noon-8, Mon. 9-5, Victoria Day weekend-Labour Day; Tues.-Sat. 9-5, rest of year. **Cost:** $6.75; $5.75 (students with ID and senior citizens); $4 (ages 6-12); $3 (ages 2-5). **Phone:** (306) 825-5655.

BORDER CITY PETTING ZOO is 8 km (5 mi.) e. on Hwy. 16. The zoo is home to such species as lions, wolves, bears, deer, exotic cattle, chickens, ducks, sheep, pigs and a large collection of reptiles including crocodiles and tortoises and the zoo's mascot Peanut, a royal ball python. One of the zoo's newest members is a black bear named Baloo. Visitors can take a ride in a covered wagon pulled by two Percherons.

Time: Allow 1 hour minimum. **Hours:** Daily 10:30-8, May-Sept. **Cost:** $6; $5 (ages 3-16). Wagon rides $2. **Phone:** (306) 825-4472. ⊞ ⊞

BUD MILLER ALL SEASONS PARK is at 2902 59th Ave. The park consists of 81 hectares (200 acres) of walking and bicycling trails, gardens, picnic areas, playgrounds, sports facilities and a skateboard park. Fishing, tennis, beach volleyball, lawn bowling and miniature golf are among the activities offered. An aquatic complex offers a wave pool, waterslide, whirlpool, steam room and sauna. Self-guiding interpretive trails are available.

Hours: Park open daily 7 a.m.-11 p.m. Aquatic complex hours vary with seasons and events; phone ahead. **Cost:** Park admission free. Aquatic complex $6.75; $5.75 (ages 13-17 and 60+); $4 (ages 6-12); $3 (ages 2-5); $20 (family). **Phone:** (780) 875-4497, (780) 875-4499 or (800) 825-6180. ⊞

MANITOU BEACH (D-3) pop. 233

The resort community of Manitou Beach is on the shore of Little Manitou Lake. The mineral waters of this lake were believed by the First Nations people to possess curative powers, and the sick of the tribe were brought for treatment long before Europeans knew of the land. Akin to the Dead Sea, the 19-kilometre-long (12-mi.) lake is three times saltier than the ocean and perfectly buoyant, allowing swimmers to float effortlessly. The village has a nine-hole golf course, spa hotel, convention center, mini-mall, tennis courts, drive-in movie theater, cross-country ski trails, an indoor heated mineral pool and a 212-site, full-service campground.

Along the lake lies Camp Easter Seal, which provides summer recreation for the physically impaired; visitors are welcome. At the east end of town on Hwy. 365 is Danceland, a dance hall with a 464-square-metre (5,000-sq.-ft.) maple hardwood dance floor. On Friday and Saturday evenings couples take to the floor for old-fashioned ballroom and rousing square dancing to live music; gospel shows take place on Sunday. For tourism information phone (866) 756-6665.

MAPLE CREEK (F-2) pop. 2,198

The town of Maple Creek was named by the Canadian Pacific Railway workers who spent the winter of 1882 on the banks of Maple Creek. Livestock, grain, tourism, natural gas and oil development provide the area with a stable economy. Maple Creek also has a golf course and campgrounds.

South of town on Hwy. 21 is Cypress Hills Interprovincial Park *(see attraction listing in Alberta p. 76, Recreation Chart and the AAA/CAA Western Canada & Alaska CampBook)*. The lofty hills are characterized by forest-covered buttes, plateaus and ridges interspersed with large areas of ranchland.

The Great Sand Hills region is located about 70 kilometres (44 mi.) north of Maple Creek via Hwy. 21. Occupying approximately 190,000 hectares (469,500 acres), this area in southwestern Saskatchewan is characterized by fragile native grasslands and open sand dunes, the largest some 25 metres (82 ft.) high. The dunes are fringed by small clumps of aspen, birch and willow trees, rose bushes, sagebrush and choke cherry. Subjected to strong winds blowing from the northwest, the dunes are moving east at a rate of almost 4 metres (13 ft.) per year.

Cypress Hills Regional Economic Development Authority: 114 Jasper St., P.O. Box 428, Maple Creek, SK, Canada S0N 1N0. **Phone:** (306) 662-4299.

FORT WALSH NATIONAL HISTORIC SITE is 55 km (34 mi.) s.w. on Hwy. 271. The site preserves an early North West Mounted Police fort. Reconstructed period buildings house exhibits of original post artifacts. Tours include trips to the site of the 1873 Cypress Hills massacre and the fort. Visitors also can bird-watch, walk a self-guiding nature trail and participate in geocaching. A bus trip around the park includes an interpretive commentary.

Time: Allow 2 hours minimum. **Hours:** Daily 9:30-5:30, Victoria Day weekend-Labour Day. **Cost:** $9.80; $8.30 (ages 66+); $4.90 (ages 6-16); $22 (family). **Phone:** (306) 662-3590.

THE JASPER CULTURAL AND HISTORICAL CENTRE is at 311 Jasper St. Several rooms of historical displays and art are housed in a 1913 two-story brick school building. Exhibits include ranching, railroad, rodeo and school memorabilia. **Time:** Allow 30 minutes minimum. **Hours:** Mon.-Fri. 9-5, Sat.-Sun. and holidays noon-4. **Cost:** $5; $2 (students with ID); $1 (ages 6-12); $10 (family). **Phone:** (306) 662-2434.

OLDTIMER'S MUSEUM is at 218 Jasper St. The museum contains collections of photographs, artifacts and archival material relating to the First Nations people, the North West Mounted Police, ranching and early settlement. **Hours:** Mon.-Sat. 9-5:30, Sun. 1-4, Victoria Day weekend-Labour Day. **Cost:** $5; $4 (students with ID); $2 (ages 0-11). **Phone:** (306) 662-2474.

MEADOW LAKE (B-2) pop. 4,771

Meadow Lake functions as a retail, service and distribution center for northwestern Saskatchewan's major industries as well as a shopping destination for communities in the region. Pastimes include fishing and hunting for big game, ducks and geese as well as snowmobiling, cross-country skiing and other recreational activities.

With 25 sparkling lakes, Meadow Lake Provincial Park *(see Recreation Chart and the AAA/CAA Western Canada & Alaska CampBook)* is a haven for fishing, swimming, boating and camping. The park offers hiking trails, beaches, interpretive and recreational programs, cabins, a miniature golf course and a 179-kilometre (111-mi.) canoe route stretching along the Waterhen and Beaver rivers. The town's recreational facilities include the Lions Regional Campground and RV Park, an aquatic center and an 18-hole golf course.

Of historical interest is Steele Narrows Provincial Historic Park, 72 kilometres (45 mi.) southwest via hwys. 304 and 26. The last armed conflict on Canadian soil occurred between Big Bear and his band of Cree First Nations and Maj. Sam Steele of the North West Mounted Police. The defeat of Big Bear on June 3, 1885, was the end of the Métis and First Nations rebellion that began in March 1885 *(see Batoche p. 271).*

Meadow Lake & District Chamber of Commerce: P.O. Box 1168, Meadow Lake, SK, Canada S9X 1Y8. **Phone:** (306) 236-4447.

MEADOW LAKE & DISTRICT INFORMATION CENTRE & MUSEUM is at Hwy. 4 and 9th Ave. W. Local pioneer artifacts and antiques are displayed. **Hours:** Mon.-Sat. 8-6, Sun. noon-6, Victoria Day-Labour Day; by appointment rest of year. **Cost:** Donations. **Phone:** (306) 236-3622.

MELFORT (C-4) pop. 5,192, elev. 457 m/1,500′

Known as the City of Northern Lights due to the visibility of the aurora borealis in the night sky for much of the year, Melfort is in the Carrot River Valley, an area known for its fertile black loam. Agriculture has been the major industry in the area since the days of early settlement in the late 19th century. Melfort was incorporated as a village in 1903, as a town in 1907 and as the province's twelfth city on Sept. 2, 1980.

Melfort & District Chamber of Commerce: Box 2002, Melfort, SK, Canada S0E 1A0. **Phone:** (306) 752-4636.

MELFORT & DISTRICT MUSEUM is at 401 Melfort St. W. Historic buildings include a 1912 power house, reconstructed log farmhouse, general store and post office, barbershop, schoolhouse, blacksmith shop and real estate office. The museum also features farm machinery, equipment and tools used in the development of the local agricultural industry.

Tours: Guided tours are available. **Time:** Allow 1 hour minimum. **Hours:** Mon.-Fri. 9-5, mid-May to early Sept. Closed major holidays. **Cost:** $4; $3 (ages 13-17); $2 (ages 6-12); $12 (family). **Phone:** (306) 752-5870.

MELVILLE (E-5) pop. 4,149, elev. 555 m/1,820′

Situated on the east-west main line of the Canadian National Railway and also on an important north-south line of that company, Melville is known as "The Rail Centre." It came to provincial prominence when it was selected as a major railway service center early in the 20th century. The railway is still the city's largest employer, and its facilities are essential in marketing agricultural products as well as potash from nearby Esterhazy.

Melville & District Chamber of Commerce: P.O. Box 429, Melville, SK, Canada S0A 2P0. **Phone:** (306) 728-4177.

MELVILLE HERITAGE MUSEUM is at 100 Heritage Dr. Formerly the Luther Academy, the restored 1913 building now houses this regional museum. Exhibits include artifacts from various churches and denominations; sports, recreation and railway exhibits; military memorabilia; and more than 100 original photographs depicting Melville's early 20th-century progress. The oldest artifact, a German pulpit Bible, dates to 1721. A chapel and library are here as well.

Tours: Guided tours are available. **Time:** Allow 1 hour minimum. **Hours:** Tues.-Sun. 10-noon and 1-4, mid-May to mid-Oct.; by appointment rest of year. **Cost:** $3; free (ages 0-12). **Phone:** (306) 728-2070.

MOOSE JAW (E-3)
pop. 32,132, elev. 542 m/1,778′

Moose Jaw's unusual name is probably derived from the big bend in Moose Jaw Creek. The First Nations called this creek *moosichappishannissippi,* or "the creek that bends like a moose's jaw." Another popular theory is that an early traveler through the area fixed his cart wheel with a moose's jawbone found in the vicinity. Today's visitors are greeted by "Mac," a 9-metre-tall (30-ft.) statue said to be the world's largest moose.

During Prohibition in the United States Moose Jaw was the home of an industrious band of bootleggers and American gangsters, earning the town the nickname "Little Chicago of the Prairies." Moose Jaw is an important western Canadian industrial city, and hard spring wheat also is grown in the area. The Canadian Forces base just south of the city is home to one of Canada's busiest airports and headquarters of the Snowbirds, the Canadian armed forces aerobatic team.

The Murals of Moose Jaw, painted on several downtown buildings, are a collection of more than 40 scenes depicting the town's history. Tours of the murals and heritage buildings can be arranged at Trudy's Gift Shop, in the lobby of the Temple Gardens Mineral Spa Resort Hotel, 24 Fairford St. E.; phone (306) 694-5055. The Yvette Moore Gallery, downtown at 76 Fairford St. W., exhibits the work of local artist Yvette Moore, whose paintings also can be seen in Moose Jaw hotels and businesses; phone (306) 693-7600.

A historic landmark south of town is Hwy. 2, once part of the Powder River Trail used by freighters and ranchers to reach Denver before the advent of the railroad. About 42 kilometres (26 mi.) north on Hwy. 2 is Buffalo Pound Provincial Park *(see Recreation Chart and the AAA/CAA Western Canada & Alaska CampBook)*, where 350 hectares (865 acres) are set aside as grazing land for a herd of buffaloes.

Wakamow Valley, in Moose Jaw, is a recreational development that includes Plaxton's Lake, North River Park, Kiwanis River Park, Kinsmen Wellesley Park, Connor Park and the Devonian Trail, a pedestrian and bicycle trail system. Visitors can enjoy picnicking, camping, bird-watching, hiking, jogging and bicycling.

Moose Jaw Chamber of Commerce: 88 Saskatchewan St. E., Box 1359, Moose Jaw, SK, Canada S6H 4R3. **Phone:** (306) 692-6414.

Self-guiding tours: Brochures outlining a self-guiding tour of some of downtown Moose Jaw's most significant historic sites are available at the Moose Jaw Art Museum and National Exhibits in Crescent Park *(see attraction listing)*.

CRESCENT PARK is at Fairford and Athabasca sts. An outdoor swimming pool, war memorial gardens and recreational facilities are contained on 11 hectares (27 acres). Free entertainment is presented Wednesday evenings July through August. The Moose Jaw Art Museum and National Exhibits, next to the public library, displays historical items of local, regional and national interest.

Hours: Museum open daily noon-5 (also Tues. and Thurs. 7-9 p.m.). Closed Good Friday, Easter and Dec. 25. Outdoor pool open daily 1-4 and 7-8:30, June 1-Labour Day. **Cost:** Museum free. Admission to pool $4.55; $3.55 (ages 13-17); $2.55 (ages 3-12); $9.75 (family). **Phone:** (306) 692-4471, or (306) 694-4500 for the pool.

MOOSE JAW TROLLEY COMPANY tours depart from the Tourism Moose Jaw Visitor Centre at jct. Hwy. 1 and Thatcher Dr. E. Visitors are led on a guided tour of the city's quaint streets and can experience its rich history while riding on board a replicated electric streetcar that operated 1911-32.

Time: Allow 1 hour minimum. **Hours:** Tours depart daily (weather permitting), May-Oct. Phone

ahead to confirm schedule. **Cost:** Fare $12; $10 (ages 65+); $7 (ages 13-17); $5 (ages 6-12). **Phone:** (306) 693-8537 or (306) 693-8097.

SUKANEN SHIP, PIONEER VILLAGE AND MUSEUM is 13 km (8 mi.) s. on Hwy. 2. The large, unfinished ship was built by Tom Sukanen, a Finnish settler who had planned to sail the boat home to his native country by way of the South Saskatchewan River, Hudson Bay, Greenland and Iceland. A village preserves an old post office, blacksmith shop, school, church, railroad station, a general store and the Diefenbaker homestead as well as a collection of antique tractors, trucks and cars.

Hours: Mon.-Sat. 9-5, Sun. noon-6, mid-May to mid-Sept. **Cost:** $6; $5 (students with ID and ages 66+); $2 (ages 8-12). **Phone:** (306) 693-7315.

TUNNELS OF MOOSE JAW is at 18 N. Main St. Two themed 50-minute tours take visitors under the streets of Moose Jaw. Miss Fanny and Gus are the guides for the Chicago Connection tour, which explores gangster Al Capone's bootlegging operation and the tunnels he is said to have used to escape American authorities. The Passage to Fortune tour depicts the story of early Chinese immigrants who came to build the Canadian Pacific Railway and their footsteps through adversity and persecution to eventual success.

Hours: Guided tours are offered Mon.-Sat. 10-5:30, Sun. noon-5:30, July-Aug.; daily 10-5:30, rest of year. Closed Dec. 25. Phone ahead to confirm schedule. **Cost:** Individual tour fare $14; $10.50 (ages 66+); $12 (ages 13-17); $7.50 (ages 5-12). Combination ticket $21; $17 (ages 66+); $16 (ages 13-17); $10 (ages 5-12). Reservations are recommended. **Phone:** (306) 693-5261.

SAVE **WESTERN DEVELOPMENT MUSEUM'S HISTORY OF TRANSPORTATION** is at 50 Diefenbaker Dr. Displays illustrate air, water, rail and land transportation. The museum also houses an observatory. The Snowbird Gallery contains aircraft and memorabilia from the Canadian armed forces aerobatic team. Trips aboard the Short Line, a miniature steam locomotive, are available on weekends.

Time: Allow 1 hour minimum. **Hours:** Museum open daily 9-5, Apr.-Dec.; Tues.-Sun. 9-5, rest of year. Train rides Sat.-Sun., Victoria Day-Labour Day (weather permitting). Closed Jan. 1 and Dec. 25-26. Phone ahead to confirm schedule. **Cost:** Museum $8.50; $7.50 (ages 65+); $5.75 (students with ID); $2 (ages 6-12); $18.50 (family). Train rides $2. **Phone:** (306) 693-5989. 🅰️

GAMBLING ESTABLISHMENTS

- **Casino Moose Jaw** is at 21 Fairford St. E. **Hours:** Sun.-Thurs. 9 a.m.-2 a.m., Fri.-Sat. 9 a.m.-3 a.m. Closed Dec. 25. **Phone:** (306) 694-3888.

RECREATIONAL ACTIVITIES
Recreational Complex

- **Kinsmen Sportsplex** is at 855 McDonald St. W., Moose Jaw, SK, Canada S6H 2W3. **Hours:** Daily

1-4 and 7-9, mid-Mar. to mid-Oct.; Sat. 2-3, Sun. 7-8, rest of year. Closed Jan. 1, Good Friday and Dec. 25. **Phone:** (306) 694-4483.

MORSE (E-3) pop. 236

MORSE MUSEUM & CULTURAL CENTRE is at 410 McKenzie St. Housed in a brick school built in 1912, the exhibits focus on the town's development from the time of the early settlers to the 1970s. The displays include nine themed rooms, a Victorian-style parlor and an art gallery featuring works by local, regional and provincial artists. Tea is served at the end of the guided tour.

Time: Allow 1 hour minimum. **Hours:** Mon.-Sat. 9-5, May-Oct.; Mon.-Fri. 9-5, rest of year. Closed major holidays. **Cost:** Donations. **Phone:** (306) 629-3230 or (306) 629-3861.

MUENSTER (D-4) pop. 342

ST. PETER'S ABBEY is 1 km (.6 mi.) e. off Muenster access rd. on Hwy. 5. A self-guiding walking tour of the abbey complex enables visitors to learn about monastic life. Brochures are available at Severin Hall. Sts. Peter and Paul Church, recreational facilities, a farm, gardens, an orchard, trails, print shop, workshops, a cemetery and a greenhouse are points of interest. **Time:** Allow 1 hour minimum. **Hours:** Daily 8-dusk. **Cost:** Free. **Phone:** (306) 682-1777.

ST. PETER'S CATHEDRAL is 1 km (.6 mi.) n. of Hwy. 5 on the Muenster access rd. The cathedral's walls and ceiling are lined with paintings by Berthold von Imhoff, who created the 80 life-size figures as a gift to the abbot of St. Peter's Abbey. **Time:** Allow 30 minutes minimum. **Hours:** Daily 9-9, May-Oct.; by appointment rest of year. **Cost:** Free. **Phone:** (306) 682-1777 or (306) 682-1789.

NIPAWIN (C-4) pop. 4,153

The Nipawin Hydroelectric Station, northwest of town, uses water impounded in Codette Lake by the Francois-Finlay Dam to generate 1.1 billion kilowatt hours of electricity annually. Guided tours of the facility are conducted by the chamber of commerce on Fridays, June through August; phone ahead to confirm tour availability. SaskPower also conducts tours, but requires 2 weeks' advance notice; phone (306) 862-3148.

Nipawin & District Chamber of Commerce: Box 177, Nipawin, SK, Canada S0E 1E0. **Phone:** (306) 862-5252.

LIVING FORESTRY MUSEUM is just w. on Hwy. 35N. The museum contains rotating exhibits that describe the history of the area. Several historic buildings have been relocated to the vicinity, including a sawmill, schoolhouse, shingle mill, church and the 1924 Hornseth House. Demonstrations of the saw and shingle mills and a steam engine are provided during the summer months. **Time:** Allow 1 hour minimum. **Hours:** Daily 9:30-4:30, May-Aug. **Cost:** $3; free (ages 0-12). **Phone:** (306) 862-9299.

NOKOMIS (D-4) pop. 404

First named Blakemore and then Blaikie by railroad officials, Nokomis began as the junction of the Old Grand Trunk Railway and the Canadian Provincial Railway. Arriving from England, Mrs. Thomas Halstead, the town's postmistress, was intrigued by the West and the romantic domain of the First Nations and chose the name Nokomis, from Henry Wadsworth Longfellow's poem "Hiawatha," for the young town.

NOKOMIS AND DISTRICT MUSEUM is at 3rd Ave. and Queen St. Housed in the former railway station, the museum features re-creations of a post office, schoolhouse, dentist's office, hospital room and equipment, hardware store, a garage with a 1930 Chevrolet and a church. Photographs, vintage clothing and antiques are displayed. Junction City 1907, behind the museum, is a replica of a small town. **Time:** Allow 1 hour minimum. **Hours:** Daily 10-5, June 1-Labour Day. **Cost:** $2; $5 (family). **Phone:** (306) 528-2979.

NORTH BATTLEFORD (C-2) pop. 13,190

On the bank of the North Saskatchewan River, North Battleford is a gateway to the province's northwest parkland area. Agriculture is the backbone of the area's economy, with farms producing cereal grains, oil seeds and hay crops as well as cattle, hogs, poultry and bison. Forestry, manufacturing and heavy crude oil development also are important industries.

The Battlefords Provincial Park *(see Recreation Chart and Cochin in the AAA/CAA Western Canada & Alaska CampBook)* is approximately 42 kilometres (26 mi.) north off Hwy. 4 and offers fishing, water skiing, boating and hiking trails. Cross-country skiing and ice fishing are popular winter activities at the park.

Battlefords Chamber of Commerce: Hwys. 16 and 40E, P.O. Box 1000, North Battleford, SK, Canada S9A 3E6. **Phone:** (306) 445-6226.

ALLEN SAPP GALLERY is at 1 Railway Ave. This award-winning public gallery features powerful and sensitive images of the Northern Plains Cree by renowned Cree artist Allen Sapp. Sapp's works capture the life and history of the Cree at the turn of the 20th century. Other exhibits include large-screen videos and historical artifacts.

Hours: Daily 11-5, June-Sept.; Wed.-Sun. noon-4, rest of year. **Cost:** Donations. **Phone:** (306) 445-1760.

THE CHAPEL GALLERY is at 891 99th St., just e. of S. Railway Ave., at the s. end of the Don Ross Centre. Formerly a chapel, the building was converted to an art gallery in 1986. The collection includes local, regional and provincial works; exhibits change regularly. **Tours:** Guided tours are available. **Time:** Allow 30 minutes minimum. **Hours:** Daily noon-5, June-Aug.; Wed.-Sun. noon-4, rest of year.

Closed Jan. 1 and Dec. 25. **Cost:** Donations. **Phone:** (306) 445-1757.

SAVE WESTERN DEVELOPMENT MUSEUM'S HERITAGE FARM AND VILLAGE is at jct. hwys. 16 and 40. The story of agriculture and pioneer life is the focus of the museum, which preserves a 1920s pioneer village and features the exhibit Winning the Prairie Gamble. A working farm offers demonstrations of early agricultural equipment and techniques.

Time: Allow 2 hours minimum. **Hours:** Daily 9-5, Apr.-Dec.; Tues.-Sun. 9-5, rest of year. Closed provincial holidays Oct.-May. **Cost:** (good for 2 consecutive days) $8.50; $7.50 (ages 65+); $5.75 (students with ID); $2 (ages 6-12); $18.50 (family). **Phone:** (306) 445-8033. ⊞

GAMBLING ESTABLISHMENTS

- **Gold Eagle Casino** is at 11902 Railway Ave. E. **Hours:** Thurs.-Sat. 9 a.m.-4 a.m., Sun.-Wed. 9 a.m.-3 a.m. Closed Dec. 24-25. **Phone:** (306) 446-3833 or (877) 446-3833.

OUTLOOK (D-3) pop. 1,938

Agriculture has traditionally sustained Outlook, where such crops as corn, potatoes, vegetables and sunflowers are grown. The town came upon its name in an unusual way. As two Canadian Pacific Railway officials stood quietly on the edge of an expansive valley, intensely watching the raging South Saskatchewan River gushing below them, the silence was broken when one uttered the words, "What a wonderful outlook!"

Outlook and District Regional Park, located along the South Saskatchewan River on the west edge of town, covers 40 hectares (100 acres) and features a golf course, swimming pool, campgrounds and hiking trails. Nature enthusiasts will especially appreciate the many species of birds as well as the venerable elm trees. Phone (306) 867-8846.

A large salt and pepper shaker collection is the highlight of the Outlook & District Heritage Museum, in the center of town at 100 Railway Ave. E. Skytrail, just northwest of the center of town following signs, is one of Canada's longest pedestrian bridges, spanning the South Saskatchewan River 46 metres (150 ft.) above the water and running for a distance of 914 metres (3,000 ft.). Side rails and a safe walking surface allow users to focus their attention on the views.

The South Saskatchewan River Project, on the South Saskatchewan and Qu'Appelle rivers, consists of two dams. Gardiner Dam, midway between Elbow and Outlook, is 5 kilometres (3 mi.) long, 64 metres (210 ft.) high and 1,615 metres (5,300 ft.) wide at its base. The impounded water forms Lake Diefenbaker, about 225 kilometres (140 mi.) long, up to 5 kilometres (3 mi.) wide and 56 metres (184 ft.) deep. The second, smaller structure is Qu'Appelle Dam. A visitor center at Gardiner Dam is open Victoria Day weekend-Labour Day; phone (306) 857-5500.

Town of Outlook: 400 Saskatchewan Ave., Box 518, Outlook, SK, Canada S0L 2N0. **Phone:** (306) 867-8663.

PONTEIX (F-2) pop. 531

NOTUKEU HERITAGE MUSEUM is at 110 Railway Ave. An extensive collection of First Nations artifacts, including arrowheads, is displayed. Guided tours are available in French or English. **Time:** Allow 30 minutes minimum. **Hours:** Mon.-Fri. 9-noon and 1-5, Sat.-Sun. by appointment. Closed major holidays. **Cost:** $3; $2 (ages 8-12); $10 (family). **Phone:** (306) 625-3340. ⊞

PRINCE ALBERT (C-4) pop. 34,138

The gateway to Saskatchewan's north country, Prince Albert is one of the province's oldest communities. Trapper Peter Pond built a trading post on the north side of the North Saskatchewan River in 1776. Credited with founding the town, the Rev. James Nisbet settled on the south shore in 1866.

The log Presbyterian church that Nisbet built that year is now in Kinsmen Park. A blockhouse next to the church dates from the Northwest Rebellion/Métis Resistance of 1885. The Prince Albert Historical Museum *(see attraction listing)* occupies the site of the church built by Nisbet.

Prince Albert Tourism & Convention Bureau: 3700 2nd Ave. W., Prince Albert, SK, Canada S6W 1A2. **Phone:** (306) 953-4386.

ART GALLERY OF PRINCE ALBERT is at 142 12th St. W., at jct. Hwy. 2N. The spacious gallery area displays paintings and other works, with a focus on contemporary art. Temporary exhibitions also are presented. **Time:** Allow 30 minutes minimum. **Hours:** Daily noon-5. Closed major holidays. **Cost:** Free. **Phone:** (306) 763-7080.

DIEFENBAKER HOUSE MUSEUM is at 246 19th St. W. The 1947-75 home of the Right Honourable John G. Diefenbaker contains furniture and other possessions of the prime minister of Canada 1957-63. **Time:** Allow 30 minutes minimum. **Hours:** Daily 10-6, Victoria Day-Labour Day. **Cost:** Donations. **Phone:** (306) 953-4863.

EVOLUTION OF EDUCATION MUSEUM is at the corner of Marquis Rd. and Hwy. 2 at 3700 2nd Ave. W. The one-room, 1920 schoolhouse was designed to provide maximum warmth and light, with all large windows on the building's east side and desks facing south. Exhibits relate to area education and include pencil boxes, Dick and Jane readers and chalk clamps once used to draw lines on a blackboard.

An interpreter is available to answer questions; a visitor information center also is in the building. **Time:** Allow 30 minutes minimum. **Hours:** Daily 10-6, Victoria Day weekend-Labour Day; by appointment rest of year. **Cost:** Free. **Phone:** (306) 763-3506.

LITTLE RED RIVER PARK is at the confluence of the North Saskatchewan and Little Red rivers on Hwy. 55. A scenic drive follows the north bank of the North Saskatchewan River. Winter sports are available. Swimming in the river is not recommended. **Cost:** Free. ⛻

PRINCE ALBERT HISTORICAL MUSEUM is at 10 River St. E. at Central Ave. The museum is housed in an old fire hall that overlooks the North Saskatchewan River. Featured is the first fire engine pumper used in the territory. Other displays include First Nations, fur trade and pioneer artifacts as well as a table and benches carved by the Rev. James Nisbet. A tearoom provides a view of the river. **Time:** Allow 1 hour minimum. **Hours:** Daily 10-6, Victoria Day-Labour Day weekend. **Cost:** $2; $1 (ages 6-12). **Phone:** (306) 764-2992.

ROTARY MUSEUM OF POLICE AND CORRECTIONS is at the corner of Marquis Rd. and Hwy. 2 at 3700 2nd Ave. W. Displays pertain to the Royal Canadian Mounted Police, local police, provincial police and corrections services. Exhibits include corporal punishment items, police uniforms and weapons. The museum is in a landscaped park with a visitor center; an interpreter is available to answer questions. **Time:** Allow 30 minutes minimum. **Hours:** Daily 10-6, Victoria Day weekend-Labour Day; by appointment rest of year. **Cost:** Free. **Phone:** (306) 922-3313.

GAMBLING ESTABLISHMENTS

- **Northern Lights Casino** is at 44 Marquis Rd. **Hours:** Thurs.-Sat. 9 a.m.-4 a.m., Sun.-Wed. 9 a.m.-3 a.m. Closed Dec. 25. **Phone:** (306) 764-4777.

◥ GEM PRINCE ALBERT NATIONAL PARK OF CANADA (B-3) pop. 200

Elevations in the park range from **488** metres (1,600 ft.) on the western side of the park to **724** metres (2,375 ft.) on the southern side of the park. Refer to CAA/AAA maps for additional elevation information.

The main entrance to Prince Albert National Park of Canada is 81 kilometres (50 mi.) north of the city of Prince Albert via hwys. 2 and 264.

The park covers 3,875 square kilometres (1,496 sq. mi.) of wilderness in central Saskatchewan. Its lakes, ponds, streams, bogs and rolling hills are a legacy of the glacial epoch. Notable are Sandy, Waskesiu, Kingsmere, Namekus, Crean and the Hanging Heart lakes. There also are several hundred smaller lakes and ponds and many sand beaches.

Heavy growths of conifers and several species of hardwoods surround the lakes, along with numerous shrubs and wildflowers. Fall foliage is especially colorful. Such wild animals as elk, deer, moose and bears are plentiful. A herd of bison roams the southwest corner of the park.

Early morning and evening provide the best chances of seeing wildlife along park roads, especially the Narrows and Kingsmere roads along Waskesiu Lake. Although some animals may seem tame, they are wild and should be observed only from a safe distance.

The park also preserves the legacy of Grey Owl. Born as Archibald Stansfeld Belaney, this controversial Englishman arrived in Canada in 1905. Adopted by the Ojibwa First Nations and later married into the tribe, Grey Owl turned his love of nature to the re-establishment of the region's beaver population, which had been decimated by hunters and trappers. For 7 years he lived at Beaver Lodge on Ajawaan Lake, where he continued his restoration and conservation efforts.

General Information and Activities

Although the park is open throughout the year, complete facilities are provided Victoria Day-Labour Day only. Information is available from the information bureau in the Waskesiu Lake Visitor Services Centre, 8 kilometres (5 mi.) from the park's main gate on Hwy. 264.

Roads traverse the park and lead to Waskesiu, Namekus, Sandy and the Hanging Heart lakes and to the Kingsmere River. Although no roads lead directly to Kingsmere and Crean lakes, access is possible by boat. A light railway with handcars assists in portaging around the unnavigable stretch of the Kingsmere River.

There are more than 100 kilometres (60 mi.) of hiking trails traversing the park. Some are suitable for day walks, while others require an overnight stop. Pamphlets outlining self-guiding tours are available for the Mud Creek and Boundary Bog nature trails. From the boat dock on the north shore of Kingsmere Lake a 3-kilometre (1.9-mi.) trail leads to the home and grave of Grey Owl.

Park facilities include boat launching and berthing areas at the Hanging Heart Lakes, the Narrows and the main marina on Waskesiu Lake. Boats, canoes and outboard motors can be rented at all three marinas; paddle-wheeler tours are offered daily in summer. There are bicycle rentals, tennis and volleyball courts and bowling greens at the Waskesiu Lake Visitor Services Centre.

Waskesiu Lake's 18-hole golf course ranks among the finest in Canada. A 150-kilometre (93-mi.) network of groomed cross-country ski trails is open in winter. Snowshoeing and ice fishing also are permitted. Fishing licenses are required and can be obtained at the park information center, park entrances and campground offices.

Park naturalists offer a free summer interpretive program that includes car caravans on park roadways and special daily events. Interpretive programs are regularly presented at the outdoor theaters at the Narrows and Beaver Glen campgrounds.

At the Waskesiu Lake Visitor Services Centre is the Park Nature Centre, which has natural history exhibits, a bookstore and a theater; the nature center is open in July and August. *See Recreation Chart and the AAA/CAA Western Canada & Alaska Camp-Book.*

ADMISSION to the park is $7.80 (per day); $6.80 (ages 66+); $3.90 (ages 6-16); $19.60 (per day per group of up to seven adults).

PETS (dogs and cats) are permitted in the park as long as they are on leashes.

ADDRESS inquiries to the Superintendent, Prince Albert National Park of Canada, P.O. Box 100, Waskesiu Lake, SK, Canada S0J 2Y0; phone (306) 663-4522.

REGINA (E-4) pop. 179,246, elev. 578 m/1,896′

First Nations people once used the banks of Wascana Creek for drying buffalo meat and cleaning and stretching the hides. Thus the area became known as *Oscana*, a Cree word meaning "pile of bones." In 1882 the Canadian Pacific Railway completed its track across the plains, and the settlement of Pile-O-Bones sprang up at the rail terminal on Wascana Creek.

The seat of government of the Northwest Territories and the headquarters of the North West Mounted Police were established the same year. A few years later Princess Louise, the wife of Canada's governor-general, renamed the city Regina (Latin for queen) to honor her mother, Queen Victoria. In 1905 Saskatchewan became a province, with Regina as its capital.

In the heart of downtown is City Centre, the site of such buildings as the municipal government offices and the public library. The Prairie History Room, which documents local history, and the Dunlop Art Gallery, which displays works by regional artists, are both housed in the library. A glockenspiel chimes at the corner of 12th Avenue and Scarth Street in tribute to the city's ethnic vitality.

The Globe Theatre in the old City Hall is the home of Regina's professional acting company. Another restored building is Union Station, a transportation hub in the early years of rail travel that is now occupied by Casino Regina. Guided historical tours explore parts of a tunnel system that once stretched beneath downtown streets and also offer a behind-the-scenes look at casino operations; under 19 are not permitted. For ticket information phone (800) 555-3189.

Following Wascana Creek for about 8 kilometres (5 mi.) is the Devonian Pathway, a paved bicycle trail that passes through six city parks and is used for jogging and walking as well as other activities; in winter it is groomed and lighted for cross-country skiing. The Condie Nature Refuge, just north of the city on Hwy. 11, offers nature trails that afford views of the refuge's grassland and marsh animals. For spectators the No. 1 sport is summer football, played by the Canadian Football League's Saskatchewan Roughriders at Mosaic Stadium at Taylor Field.

Regina Convention and Visitors Bureau: Hwy. 1E, P.O. Box 3355, Regina, SK, Canada S4P 3H1. **Phone:** (306) 789-5099 or (800) 661-5099.

Shopping areas: Regina's major shopping mall is Cornwall Centre, 2101 11th Ave. It has 87 stores, including The Bay and Sears. The specialty shops and eateries of Scarth Street Mall, downtown between 11th and 12th avenues, line a pedestrian-only street. The Cathedral Village shopping district, another downtown cluster of shops, is centered around 13th Avenue from Albert to Argyle streets and from Saskatchewan Drive to College Avenue.

GOVERNMENT HOUSE MUSEUM AND HERITAGE PROPERTY is at 4607 Dewdney Ave. This Italianate-style mansion was the home of the lieutenant governors of the Northwest Territories 1891-1905 and the lieutenant governors of Saskatchewan 1905-45. From 1945 to the mid-1970s the house served as a rest home for World War II veterans and as an adult education center.

Flanked by 2.5 hectares (6 acres) of gardens and orchards, the official residence has been restored to its Victorian elegance. Docents dressed in period conduct guided tours of the house. An interpretive center has hands-on exhibits and depicts the history of the province.

Time: Allow 1 hour minimum. **Hours:** Tues.-Sun. 10-4. Guided tours depart every 30 minutes. Closed Good Friday and Dec. 25. **Cost:** Free. **Phone:** (306) 787-5773.

HOLY ROSARY CATHEDRAL is at 3125 13th Ave., just w. of jct. Albert St. This Cruciform/Romanesque structure, built in 1912, features 43 stained-glass windows installed in 1951 by French artisan Andre Rault, who designed windows for more than 50 other Canadian churches. Their artistry is best appreciated on a sunny day. A Casavant pipe organ, known for its exceptional sound quality, plays during Sunday services.

Tours: Guided tours are available. **Time:** Allow 30 minutes minimum. **Hours:** Tues.-Fri. 9-1. The cathedral is kept locked for security purposes. Phone ahead to confirm schedule. **Cost:** Donations. **Phone:** (306) 565-0909.

REGINA PLAINS MUSEUM, on the second floor at 1835 Scarth St., features Saskatchewan artist Jacqueline Berting's sculpture "The Glass Wheatfield," consisting of 14,000 waist-high stalks of handcrafted glass. Also on display is a mural by aboriginal artist Sherry Farrell Racette. Rotating exhibitions focus on the city's history. **Hours:** Tues.-Fri. 10-4; Mon. 1-4. **Cost:** Free. **Phone:** (306) 780-9435.

RCMP HERITAGE CENTRE is on Dewdney Ave. at the entrance to the RCMP Academy, "Depot" Division. The center tells the story of the Royal Canadian Mounted Police (RCMP), created by an act of Parliament in 1873 to maintain law and order on the Canadian frontier and pave the way for westward settlement.

Stretching the length of the main exhibition hall, the sculptural procession "March of the Mounties" anchors the core exhibit areas; graphics trace Canada's geography from west to east and depict the historical evolution of the RCMP from its inception to the present day.

Interactive educational exhibits include Maintaining Law and Order in the West, which chronicles the force's late 19th-century efforts to suppress the whisky trade, establish amicable relations with Native tribes and ensure the safety of settlers and rail workers; Serving All of Canada, an overview of the RCMP's 20th-century evolution; and Cracking the Case, a hands-on look at the high-tech side of contemporary policing. The 27-minute multimedia presentation "Tour of Duty" is shown in the center's SGI CANADA Theatre.

Time: Allow 2 hours minimum. **Hours:** Daily 9-5 (also Tues. 5-10), Victoria Day-Labour Day; Tues.-Sun. 10-5, rest of year. A colorful Sergeant Major's Parade is usually held Mon.-Fri. at 12:45 p.m. (except Fri. preceding a holiday weekend). Sunset Ceremonies are held Tues. at 6:30 p.m., July 1-first week in Aug. Closed Dec. 25. **Cost:** $12; $10 (ages 13-17 and 65+); $6 (ages 6-12); $3 (ages 3-5). **Phone:** (306) 522-7333 or (866) 567-7267. ⑪

ST. PAUL'S CATHEDRAL is at 1861 McIntyre St. This Gothic Revival-style church is said to be the oldest in Regina; its cornerstone was laid in 1894. A columbarium (housing the ashes of the deceased) and museum are located under the church and are open by appointment; the museum houses books and artifacts dating to the 1600s. **Tours:** Guided tours are available. **Time:** Allow 30 minutes minimum. **Hours:** Mon.-Fri. 9-4. **Cost:** Donations. **Phone:** (306) 522-6439.

SASKATCHEWAN SPORTS HALL OF FAME is at 2205 Victoria Ave. Photographs, trophies, records and other memorabilia represent noted athletes and teams from Saskatchewan. **Hours:** Mon.-Fri. 9-5, Sat.-Sun. and holidays 1-5, Victoria Day-Labour Day; Mon.-Fri. 9-5, rest of year. **Cost:** Free. **Phone:** (306) 780-9232.

WASCANA CENTRE surrounds Wascana Lake. The 930-hectare (2,300-acre) park is the center of recreational and cultural activity in Regina and includes the Conexus Centre of the Arts, a performing arts venue. Wascana Place is both a departure point for sightseeing tours and a reservation office for special events. Ferry boat rides to the Willow Island picnic area are available. Wascana Waterfowl Park and Speakers' Corner also are in the area.

Hours: Wascana Place Mon.-Fri. 8-5:30, Sat.-Sun. 9-5:30, Victoria Day-Labour Day; Mon.-Fri. 8-4:30, rest of year. **Cost:** Ferry boat fare $5; $2 (ages 0-18). **Phone:** (306) 522-3661 daily 5-9 p.m. for reservation information.

Legislative Building (Capitol) is off Albert St. in Wascana Centre. Surrounded by 67 hectares (165 acres) of landscaped grounds, the imposing landmark is the seat of provincial government. Completed in 1912, the building reflects the architecture of the English Renaissance and Louis XIV of France.

The building houses several art galleries, including the Cumberland Gallery, a showcase for works of the Native Heritage Foundation of Canada. More than 34 different types of marble adorn the interior. On the east side of the building is Trafalgar Fountain, which was in London's Trafalgar Square 1845-1939.

Guided tours of the building are offered. Tours in French are available. **Time:** Allow 30 minutes minimum. **Hours:** Daily 8 a.m.-8:30 p.m., Victoria Day-Labour Day; 8-4:30, rest of year. Closed Jan. 1,

Good Friday and Dec. 25. Guided tours depart every 30 minutes. **Cost:** Free. **Phone:** (306) 787-5358.

MacKenzie Art Gallery is in the T.C. Douglas Building at the s.w. corner of Wascana Centre at Albert St. and 23rd Ave. A major exhibition center for Saskatchewan, it contains permanent and changing exhibits of Canadian and international art. **Tours:** Guided tours are available. **Time:** Allow 1 hour minimum. **Hours:** Mon.- Fri. 10-5:30 (also Fri. 5:30-9 p.m.), Sat.-Sun. and holidays noon-5:30. **Cost:** Donations. **Phone:** (306) 584-4250.

Royal Saskatchewan Museum is at College Ave. and Albert St. in Wascana Centre.

The Earth Sciences Gallery focuses on the geological and paleontological evolution of Saskatchewan and includes Canada's only resident robotic dinosaur. The Paleo Pit features hands-on exhibits. The First Nations Gallery portrays the culture and heritage of the province's aboriginal population through artwork and artifacts.

The Life Sciences Gallery explores Saskatchewan's natural history and current environmental issues. Exhibits depict life in a beaver pond, a Costa Rican rain forest and human actions that are disturbing the global ecosystem. **Time:** Allow 1 hour minimum. **Hours:** Daily 9-5:30, May 1-early Sept.; 9-4:30, rest of year. Closed Dec. 25. **Cost:** Donations. **Phone:** (306) 787-2815.

[SAVE] **Saskatchewan Science Centre** is on Winnipeg St. at Wascana Dr. in Wascana Centre. The Powerhouse of Discovery houses more than 100 permanent hands-on science exhibits and features live stage shows and demonstrations. Visitors who want to test their physical skills can tackle one of the tallest climbing walls in Canada. The 165-seat Kramer IMAX Theatre uses a five-story screen and four-way sound system to present science and nature films in a giant format.

Time: Allow 2 hours minimum. **Hours:** Mon.-Fri. 9-6, Sat.-Sun. and holidays 11-6. Hours for IMAX films vary. Phone ahead to confirm schedule. **Cost:** $8; $6 (ages 6-13 and 61+); $3.75 (ages 3-5). IMAX shows $7.50; $5.50 (ages 6-13 and 61+); $3.75 (ages 3-5). Combination tickets are available. **Phone:** (306) 522-4629, or (800) 667-6300 in Canada. [II]

GAMBLING ESTABLISHMENTS

- **Casino Regina** is at 1880 Saskatchewan Dr. **Hours:** Daily 9 a.m.-4 a.m. Closed Dec. 24-25. **Phone:** (306) 565-3000 or (800) 555-3189.

ROCANVILLE (E-5) pop. 869

ROCANVILLE AND DISTRICT MUSEUM is at Qu'Appelle Ave. and Saint Albert St. A variety of local artifacts include steam tractors, a train station, blacksmith shop and schoolhouse. **Time:** Allow 2 hours minimum. **Hours:** Wed.-Sun. 10-5, July-Aug.; by appointment rest of year. **Cost:** Donations. **Phone:** (306) 645-2113 or (306) 645-2164.

ROSTHERN (D-3) pop. 1,382

SEAGER WHEELER FARM is 7 km (4 mi.) e. on Hwy. 312, following signs. One of the most noted farmers in Canada, Wheeler won five international wheat championships 1911-18 and was a prominent educator in progressive agricultural techniques. The farm features restored buildings and equipment. Also on the grounds are English flower gardens, orchards, a 24-hectare (60-acre) bird sanctuary, a tearoom and a visitor center with interpretive displays.

Tours: Guided tours are available. **Time:** Allow 1 hour minimum. **Hours:** Tues.-Sun. 9-5 (also Thurs. 7-9 p.m.), May-Aug. **Cost:** $5; free (ages 0-12 when accompanied by an adult). Guided tour $1. **Phone:** (306) 232-5959. [⛺]

ST. BRIEUX (D-4)
pop. 492, elev. 547 m/1,797′

ST. BRIEUX MUSEUM is at 300 Barbier Dr., the main access road to the village. Originally a Roman Catholic rectory, it displays pioneer tools, furniture, period clothing and other artifacts and memorabilia related to the early 20th-century settlement of the St. Brieux district. **Tours:** Guided tours are available. **Hours:** Wed.-Sun. 1-4, Victoria Day-Aug. 31; by appointment rest of year. **Cost:** Guided tour fee $2; free (ages 0-18). **Phone:** (306) 275-2315.

SASKATOON (D-2)
pop. 202,425, elev. 487 m/1,598′

Saskatoon was founded in 1882 as a temperance colony under leader John Lake. According to legend a Cree brought Lake a handful of the purple berries that grew in abundance alongside the river. Lake was so taken with the fruit he named his settlement Saskatoon, after *misaskquatoomina*, the First Nations name for the wild berries. Today a slice of Saskatoon pie is a traditional treat recalling the city's past.

Straddling the South Saskatchewan River, Saskatoon is known as "The City of Bridges" because of the seven spans connecting its banks. It also is home to the University of Saskatchewan, which is building a reputation for research and development in science, medicine and agriculture. The Diefenbaker Canada Centre on campus showcases memorabilia of Canada's 13th prime minister.

The Local History Room on the second floor of the Frances Morrison Library, 311-23rd St. E., serves as a research facility for information that focuses on prairie history relating to Saskatoon in particular and western Canada in general. Collections include more than 60,000 historic photographs, thousands of books, pamphlets, maps, artifacts and periodicals. An art gallery is next to the room. Phone (306) 975-7558.

The Saskatchewan Railway Museum, 6 kilometres (4 mi.) west on Hwy. 7, then 2 kilometres (1.2 mi.) south on Hwy. 60, is operated by the Saskatchewan Railroad Historical Association and displays old railroad buildings and artifacts, including locomotives, cabooses and streetcars; phone (306) 382-9855 May through September.

TCU Place—Saskatoon's Art & Convention Centre, 35 22nd St., is home to the Saskatoon Symphony and the site of traveling shows throughout the year. The Meewasin Valley Centre, 402 3rd Ave. S., features interpretive displays pertaining to the area's history. Credit Union Centre features rock concerts, trade shows, and hockey and other sporting events. The facility is on the north side of the city next to hwys. 2 and 16.

The Meewasin Valley Trail, following the South Saskatchewan River through the heart of the city, has bicycle and jogging trails, picnic areas and playgrounds and provides opportunities for cross-country skiing and ice skating. Recreational activities are available at nearby Pike Lake and Blackstrap provincial parks *(see Recreation Chart and the AAA/ CAA Western Canada & Alaska CampBook)*.

Queen Elizabeth Power Station, 3 kilometres (1.9 mi.) south of the junction of 11th Street W. and Avenue H S. at 2211 Spadina Crescent W., is a thermal power station originally named the South Saskatchewan River Generating Station but renamed and commissioned in 1959 by Queen Elizabeth II. Guided tours are available with 24 hours' advance notice; phone (306) 934-7994.

Racing fans can enjoy horse racing at Marquis Downs, 503 Ruth St., from late May to early September. Races are held Fri.-Sat. 7-10 p.m.; phone (306) 242-6100. Drag racing heats up the Saskatchewan International Raceway, 13 kilometres (8 mi.) s. on Hwy. 11, from early May to mid-September; phone (306) 955-3724. Stock car racing takes place at the Auto Clearing Motor Speedway, north on Hwy. 12, from May through September; phone (306) 651-3278.

Note: Policies concerning admittance of children to pari-mutuel betting facilities vary. Phone for information.

Tourism Saskatoon: 101-202 4th Ave. N., Saskatoon, SK, Canada S7K 0K1. **Phone:** (306) 242-1206 or (800) 567-2444.

Shopping areas: Midtown Plaza, downtown at 1st Avenue and 21st Street, is a two-level mall with more than 130 shops, including anchor stores The Bay and Sears.

BEAVER CREEK CONSERVATION AREA is 13 km (8 mi.) s. on Hwy. 219 (Lorne Ave.). Self-guiding nature trails and interpretive displays are offered. **Time:** Allow 2 hours minimum. **Hours:** Daily 9-9, July-Aug.; daily 9-5, May-June; Mon.-Fri. 9-5, Sat.-Sun. and holidays noon-5, Sept.-Oct.; Mon.-Fri. 9-5, Sat.-Sun. noon-5, rest of year. **Cost:** Free. **Phone:** (306) 374-2474 or (306) 665-6887.

DIEFENBAKER CANADA CENTRE is at 101 Diefenbaker Pl. on the University of Saskatchewan campus. The archives and personal belongings of prime minister John Diefenbaker are housed at the center; his grave site is on the grounds. The museum also offers changing exhibits about Canadian history, art, politics, science, culture and current affairs.

Half-hour guided tours are available. **Hours:** Open Mon.-Fri. 9:30-4:30 (also Thurs. 4:30-8), Sat.-Sun. and holidays noon-4:30; closed Jan. 1, Good Friday, Nov. 11 and Dec. 25-26. **Cost:** $5; $3 (children and senior citizens); $12.50 (family, parents and dependent children). Guided tours $7; $5 (children and senior citizens); $15 (family, parents and dependent children). **Phone:** (306) 966-8384.

MENDEL ART GALLERY AND CIVIC CONSERVATORY is at 950 Spadina Crescent E. in a park between Queen and 25th sts. This attractive complex overlooks the South Saskatchewan River. In the art gallery are exhibitions of international, national and regional works, including historical and contemporary art. Visitors may view the display of tropical and native plants in the conservatory.

Programs and activities are presented in combination with each series of exhibitions. **Time:** Allow 30 minutes minimum. **Hours:** Daily 9-9. Complex closes at 5 on Dec. 24 and 31. Closed Dec. 25. **Cost:** Free. **Phone:** (306) 975-7610.

SASKATCHEWAN INDIAN CULTURAL CENTRE is at 120 33rd St. E. The center is dedicated to preserving First Nations cultures in Saskatchewan such as the Woodland, Swampy and Plains Cree; Dene; Nakawe; Dakota; Lakota; and Nakota. Exhibits include historic artifacts as well as contemporary arts and crafts. **Time:** Allow 30 minutes minimum. **Hours:** Mon.-Thurs. 8:30-5, Fri. 8:30-4. Tours are given by appointment. **Cost:** Free. **Phone:** (306) 373-9901 to schedule a guided tour.

SASKATOON FORESTRY FARM PARK AND ZOO is n.e. off Attridge Dr., following signs. Displayed in settings resembling their natural habitats are 350 species of birds and animals native to Saskatchewan and western Canada. The park offers a children's zoo, a reptile and tropical fish display, stocked fishing pond and nature walkways. The Kinsmen Express train provides a tour around the park and zoo.

Time: Allow 1 hour, 30 minutes minimum. **Hours:** Zoo and park open daily 9-9, Apr. 1-Labour Day; 10-4, rest of year. **Cost:** $7.90; $4.75 (ages 6-18); $15.80 (family). Fishing pond $2; $1 (ages 6-16). **Phone:** (306) 975-3382.

SHEARWATER BOAT CRUISES is off Spadina Crescent opposite Kinsmen Park, at the Mendel Art Gallery dock. Scenic 1-hour cruises aboard the *Saskatoon Princess* take in the downtown waterfront. The 49-passenger vessel is equipped with restrooms and a heated cabin and has a licensed bar. A dinner cruise is available Friday evening.

Hours: One-hour cruises depart daily at 1:30, 3, 4:30 and 7, Victoria Day weekend-Labour Day. Phone ahead to confirm schedule. **Cost:** One-hour cruise fare $17; $16 (ages 6-19 and 61+); $10 (ages 0-5). **Phone:** (888) 747-7572.

UKRAINIAN MUSEUM OF CANADA is at 910 Spadina Crescent E. Displays include folk and fine art, domestic and agricultural tools, and documents and photographs of Ukrainian immigrants. Two galleries feature changing exhibits. **Tours:** Guided tours are available. **Time:** Allow 30 minutes minimum. **Hours:** Tues.-Sat. 10-5, Sun. 1-5; closed Canadian holidays, Orthodox Christmas (early Jan.) and Good Friday. **Cost:** $4; $3 (ages 65+); $2 (ages 6-16). **Phone:** (306) 244-3800.

WANUSKEWIN HERITAGE PARK is 5 km (3.1 mi.) n. on Hwy. 11, 3 km (1.9 mi.) s. on Warman Rd., then 2 km (1.2 mi.) e. on Penner Rd., following signs. This 760-acre First Nations heritage park traces more than 6,000 years of area history. It showcases 19 sites representing the Northern Plains peoples, including summer and winter campsites, bison kill sites, tipi rings and a boulder alignment known as a medicine wheel.

The park's interpretive center contains a DVD theater and features state-of-the-art exhibits pertaining to Northern Plains culture. Self-guiding trails take visitors through the park, with interpretive signs explaining past uses of the land.

Time: Allow 2 hours minimum. **Hours:** Daily 9-8, Victoria Day-Labour Day; 9-5, rest of year. Closed Good Friday and Dec. 25-Jan. 1. **Cost:** $8.50; $7.50 (ages 65+); $6.50 (ages 6-18); $25 (family). **Phone:** (306) 931-6767 or (877) 547-6546.

SAVE **WESTERN DEVELOPMENT MUSEUM'S 1910 BOOMTOWN** is at 2610 Lorne Ave. This indoor representation of a typical prairie town features more than 30 buildings. Displays include transportation artifacts and vintage agricultural equipment. **Time:** Allow 2 hours minimum. **Hours:** Daily 9-5, Jan.-Apr.; Tues.-Sat. 9-4, rest of year. Museum closes at 3 on Dec. 24 and 31. Closed Jan. 1, second Mon. in Oct., Nov. 11 and Dec. 25-26. **Cost:** $8.50; $7.50 (ages 66+); $5.75 (students with ID); $2 (ages 6-12); $18.50 (family). **Phone:** (306) 931-1910.

GAMBLING ESTABLISHMENTS

• **Dakota Dunes Casino** is 24 km (15 mi.) s. on Hwy. 219. **Hours:** Sun.-Wed. 9 a.m.-3 a.m., Thurs.-Sat. 9 a.m.-4 a.m. **Phone:** (306) 667-6400.

SCEPTRE (E-2) pop. 99, elev. 671 m/2,200′

GREAT SANDHILLS MUSEUM is on Hwy. 32. Housed in a former school, the museum has rooms depicting early pioneer life in the community, including a boarding house, library, hospital, blacksmith shop, dentist's office, schoolhouse, general store display, barn and church. An interpretive center provides information about the great sandhills. **Time:** Allow 30 minutes minimum. **Hours:** Tues.-Sat. 10-noon and 12:30-4:30, Sun. 1-5, May 15-Sept. 2. **Cost:** $3; $2 (ages 6-18). **Phone:** (306) 623-4345.

SHAUNAVON (F-2) pop. 1,691

GRAND COTEAU HERITAGE AND CULTURAL CENTRE, 2 blks. n. of Third Ave. at 440 Centre St., houses a museum with displays depicting local and natural history. The building also mounts exhibitions of contemporary art and serves as a tourist information center. **Time:** Allow 30 minutes minimum. **Hours:** Mon.-Sat. 9-5, May 1-Oct. 1; Tues.-Sat. 1:30-5, rest of year. **Cost:** Free. **Phone:** (306) 297-3882.

SIMPSON (D-3) pop. 118

LAST MOUNTAIN LAKE SANCTUARY is at the n. end of Last Mountain Lake; access is via a grid road branching off Hwy. 2 (watch for signs). Said to be the oldest bird sanctuary in North America, the wildlife refuge was established in 1887 and covers 1,012 hectares (2,500 acres). The area's favorable habitats and location make it a haven for more than 280 species of birds.

Each year during May and between mid-August and mid-September more than 20,000 sandhill cranes stop at the sanctuary during their seasonal migration. There are two self-guiding nature trails and a self-guiding driving tour. *See Recreation Chart.* **Time:** Allow 1 hour minimum. **Hours:** Daily dawn-dusk. **Cost:** Free. **Phone:** (306) 836-2022.

STRASBOURG (E-4) pop. 732

STRASBOURG AND DISTRICT MUSEUM is at Mountain St. and Railway Ave. Nature displays, handicrafts and pioneer artifacts are exhibited. **Hours:** Tues.-Sat. 10-4, Sun. 1-5, July-Sept. **Cost:** Donations. **Phone:** (306) 725-3443.

SWIFT CURRENT (E-3) pop. 14,946

Once the site of transient First Nations and fur trader camps, Swift Current began as a North West Mounted Police encampment on Swift Current Creek in 1874. Soon after, the Canadian Pacific Railway built a depot, and the settlement became the freight terminus for western Canada. From this point goods were hauled by wagon on overland trails; deep ruts can still be seen on the old North Battleford Trail north of Swift Current.

With the turn of the 20th century came the farmers and ranchers whose trades formed the backbone of the city's economy. Oil was discovered in this area in 1952, and in the decades since Swift Current has not only developed into a business hub for the oil, gas and agricultural industries but has become the major health care center for southwestern Saskatchewan.

Swift Current Creek runs through town, and two nearby lakes offer recreational facilities. At Saskatchewan Landing Provincial Park *(see Recreation Chart),* a plaque marks the spot where pioneers once forded the South Saskatchewan River on their way into the wilds of the northern province. In the park's hills are several First Nations grave sites and tepee rings.

Doc's Heritage Village, 17th Avenue S.E. and S. Railway Street in Kinetic Exhibition Park, has a collection of buildings typical of early 20th-century prairie towns, including a blacksmith shop, church and school. Costumed staff are on hand to answer questions; phone (306) 773-2944.

Swift Current Chamber of Commerce: 885 6th Ave. N.E., Swift Current, SK, Canada S9H 2M9. **Phone:** (306) 773-7268.

Self-guiding tours: A brochure with details about a walking tour of historic buildings in downtown Swift Current is available at the Swift Current Museum and from downtown merchants.

ART GALLERY OF SWIFT CURRENT is at 411 Herbert St. E. This public art gallery offers exhibitions of local, provincial and national artwork. Cultural events and festivals are scheduled throughout the year. Guided tours are given upon request. **Hours:** Open Mon.-Thurs. 2-5 and 7-9 p.m., Fri.-Sat. 1-5, Sun. 1-4:30, Sept.-June; Mon.-Thurs. 2-5 and 7-9 p.m., Fri.-Sat. 1-5, rest of year. Closed major holidays and during exhibition changes. **Cost:** Free. **Phone:** (306) 778-2736.

SWIFT CURRENT MUSEUM is at 44 Robert St. W. Exhibits depict the natural and human history of southwest Saskatchewan. **Tours:** Guided tours are available. **Hours:** Open Mon.-Fri. 9-5, Sat.-Sun. 1-5, June-Aug.; Mon.-Fri. 9-5, rest of year. Closed major holidays. **Cost:** Free. **Phone:** (306) 778-2775.

GAMBLING ESTABLISHMENTS

- **Living Sky Casino** is at 1401 North Service Rd. E. **Hours:** Thurs.-Sat. 9 a.m.-4 a.m., Sun.-Wed. 9 a.m.-3 a.m. Closed Dec. 24-25. **Phone:** (306) 778-5759.

TISDALE (C-4) pop. 2,981

This rural community in northeastern Saskatchewan provides easy access to several provincial parks offering recreational activities from fishing and boating in summer to skiing in winter. A roadside attraction, claimed to be the world's largest honeybee, stands on the south side of Hwy. 3 in town.

Greville Jones Wildlife Sanctuary is reached by a gravel access road about 6.4 kilometres (4 mi.) southwest of Tisdale off Hwy. 3, following signs. The site of an old farmstead, it is a pleasant place for a summer picnic or hike along one of several nature trails.

Another scenic route is the Doghide River Trail, a system of walking, cycling and skiing trails that run along several sections of the riverbank. The trail can be accessed from the junction of Hwys. 3 and 35; proceed east .8 kilometre (.5 mi.), then north .5 kilometre (.3 mi.) and turn right into Kinsmen McKay Park.

TISDALE & DISTRICT MUSEUM, HERITAGE CENTRE AND DOGHIDE VILLAGE, at jct. Hwy. 3 and Heritage Rd. at the western approach to town, comprises three main areas. The Station houses a bee farming display, while Doghide Village features the furnished 1920 Pearse House, a log barn and

milk house and a fire hall complete with antique water wagon. The Heritage Centre contains the Dagg Collection of vintage automobiles, which range from standard Fords and Chevrolets to such unusual makes as Star, Whippet and Essex.

Tours: Guided tours are available. **Time:** Allow 30 minutes minimum. **Hours:** Daily 9-5, Victoria Day-Labour Day. **Cost:** $2; $5 (family). **Phone:** (306) 873-4999. ⊞

VEREGIN (D-5) pop. 65

Emigrating from Russia in 1899 due to persecution, the Doukhobors named their village after their theocratic leader, Peter Vasilovich Veregin. The Doukhobor way of life centers on communal living and renounces violence and war. Its followers do not eat meat or use alcohol or tobacco. The community flourished for 2 decades before a majority of the sect relocated to British Columbia. A prayer house built by Veregin and a machine shed are all that remain of the original Doukhobor colony.

NATIONAL DOUKHOBOR HERITAGE VILLAGE is across the tracks s. of Hwy. 5. The village is composed of the original Doukhobor prayer home and several reconstructed buildings typical of Veregin's Doukhobor dwellings at the turn of the 20th century. A museum displays Doukhobor handicrafts, clothing, hand tools, a collection of Leo Tolstoy's works and other artifacts.

Time: Allow 30 minutes minimum. **Hours:** Daily 10-6, mid-May to mid-Sept.; by appointment rest of year. **Cost:** $5; $3 (students with ID); $1 (ages 5-12). **Phone:** (306) 542-4441.

WADENA (D-4) pop. 1,315, elev. 488 m/1,600′

WADENA & DISTRICT MUSEUM is at 302 Main St. S. Housed in a 1904 train station, the museum preserves items relating to the history of the pioneers who settled the area in the early 20th century. Exhibits include antique farm equipment, a 1914 farm house, a country schoolhouse, church, general store, blacksmith shop and a Royal Canadian Mounted Police barracks. A caboose is adjacent to the station.

Time: Allow 30 minutes minimum. **Hours:** Tues.-Sat. 9-5, Sun. 10-5, mid-May through Labour Day. Closed major holidays. **Cost:** $5; $3 (ages 12-18); $2 (ages 5-11). **Phone:** (306) 338-3454.

WAKAW (D-4) pop. 864

WAKAW HERITAGE MUSEUM is in the center of town at 300 1st St. S. Exhibits include Ukrainian artworks and implements, mementos from both world wars, homestead displays and a wide assortment of items dating from the early to late 1900s. **Time:** Allow 1 hour minimum. **Hours:** Mon.-Fri. 1-4, Sat.-Sun. 10-4, July 1-Labour Day. **Cost:** Donations. **Phone:** (306) 233-4223.

John Diefenbaker's Law Office is off 1st St. S. at 3rd Ave. S. The site is a replica of the original office where the 13th prime minister of Canada practiced law 1919-25. Guides are available at the

Wakaw Heritage Museum. **Hours:** Mon.-Fri. 1-4, Sat.-Sun. 10-4, July 1-Labour Day. **Phone:** (306) 233-4223.

WEYBURN (F-4) pop. 9,433

Weyburn's name was coined in 1893 by Scottish railroad workers, who called this marshy area at the headwaters of the Souris River "wee burn." From these humble beginnings the town has grown into a major marketing center for the surrounding agricultural area. Weyburn is the southeastern terminus of scenic Hwy. 39, which continues to Moose Jaw.

The town was immortalized as "Crocus, Saskatchewan" in the works of W.O. Mitchell, who was born and reared in Weyburn and penned the book "Who Has Seen the Wind." A summary of Weyburn's history since its earliest days is depicted on the "Wheel of Progress" at the Weyburn Library. Between the spokes of the brass-rimmed mahogany wheel, which weighs 909 kilograms (2,000 lbs.) and has a diameter of 3.9 metres (13 ft.), are 10 mosaic panels showing highlights of the city's past.

Weyburn Chamber of Commerce: 405 Coteau Ave., Weyburn, SK, Canada S4H 3G5. **Phone:** (306) 842-4738.

SOO LINE HISTORICAL MUSEUM is e. on Hwy. 39 at 411 Industrial Ln. Local pioneer artifacts trace the area's early history. The museum houses more than 5,000 pieces of silver, glass and antique furniture dating 1750-1970. Donated by Charles Wilson, the exhibit is reputed to be one of the country's largest private collections. **Time:** Allow 30 minutes minimum. **Hours:** Mon.-Fri. 9-6, Sat.-Sun. 11-6, June-Aug.; Mon.-Fri. 1-5, rest of year. **Cost:** $5; $4 (students with ID); $2 (ages 2-11). **Phone:** (306) 842-2922.

WEYBURN HERITAGE VILLAGE is 1 km (.6 mi.) s. from jct. Hwys. 35 and 39, then 1 km (.6 mi.) e. on 10th Ave. S.E. This historical village has been replicated to depict community life from the turn of the 20th century to the 1940s. All the buildings have been restored. Farm machinery is on display and visitors also may view a one-room school, rural municipality office, country church and blacksmith shop.

Tours: Guided tours are available. **Time:** Allow 1 hour minimum. **Hours:** Daily 1-8, May-Aug. **Cost:** $3; $2 (ages 13-19); $1 (ages 5-12); $10 (family). **Phone:** (306) 842-6377. ⊞

WHITEWOOD (E-5) pop. 869

OLD GEORGE'S HIDDEN VILLAGE MUSEUM AND ANTIQUES is on Hwy. 1 just w. of town. On this 4.5-hectare (11-acre) property, a 30-room brick dwelling houses such collectibles as oil lamps, clocks, crocks and jugs, First Nations artifacts, antique bottles and spinning wheels. Hidden Village consists of 40 buildings representative of pioneer life, including four log cabins, a saloon, a trapper's cabin, a post office and a general store.

Tours: Guided tours are available. **Time:** Allow 1 hour minimum. **Hours:** Daily 10-6, mid-May to mid-Oct.; by appointment rest of year. **Cost:** $5; $1 (ages 0-11). **Phone:** (306) 735-2255.

WOLSELEY (E-4) pop. 782

Incorporated in 1898, Wolseley earned the nickname "The Town With the Swinging Bridge" when just such a contraption was built over man-made Fairly Lake in the center of town—itself created by damming Wolf Creek to provide the Canadian Pacific Railway with a badly needed reservoir for its steam engines. The bridge, which connected homes on the north side of the lake with the business section on the south side, has had a checkered history: It was destroyed by a storm in 1954, rebuilt 10 years later, collapsed in 1993 during repairs and reopened again in 2004 thanks to the fund-raising efforts of the Heritage Canada Foundation.

The Romanesque-style Town Hall & Opera House, at the corner of Richmond and Varennes streets, was completed in 1907. The two-tone brick building (brick was imported from Manitoba when the local supply ran out) housed the town's administrative offices, fire hall, library, jail cell and community hall—commonly known as an Opera House—where touring vaudeville, theatrical and opera companies would perform. The building was extensively refurbished in the early 1990s.

Wolseley & District Museum, 101 Blanchard St., has a collection of locally obtained artifacts reflecting life in the area circa 1880-1950. The exhibits, which include medical, real estate and lumber offices as well as clothing from the various eras, are displayed in a two-story 1901 boarding house. The original office of the Beaver Lumber Company, also filled with artifacts, has been moved to the museum site. Phone (306) 698-2360.

WOOD MOUNTAIN (F-3) pop. 100

RODEO RANCH MUSEUM is 8 km (5 mi.) s. on Hwy. 18 in Wood Mountain Regional Park. This museum features exhibits about local ranching, First Nations people and saddle making. An adjacent adobe and log building houses blacksmithing tools. A rodeo is held on the grounds during the second weekend in July.

Time: Allow 1 hour minimum. **Hours:** Daily 10-noon and 1-5, mid-May through Labour Day. **Cost:** $2; $1 (students with ID); free (ages 0-9 with adult). **Phone:** (306) 266-4953 or (306) 266-4205. ⊞ ▲

WOOD MOUNTAIN POST PROVINCIAL HISTORIC PARK is 8 km (5 mi.) s. on Hwy. 18. Two buildings are on the site of the North West Mounted Police post that stood 1874-1918; small stumps outline the rest of the post. Inside the buildings are displays about the Mounted Police, Sioux First Nations and local history. An interpretive staff is on duty to answer questions. **Time:** Allow 1 hour minimum. **Hours:** Thurs.-Mon. 10-5, June 1 to mid-Aug. **Cost:** Donations. **Phone:** (306) 266-5525.

YORKTON (E-5) pop. 15,038

In 1882 some 200 settlers from Ontario bought land in the Northwest Territories in what is now southeastern Saskatchewan. They called the community around their trading post York City. In 1890 the railroad arrived in the area 5 kilometres (3 mi.) to the south. The York City colonists relocated to be near the railroad and named the new settlement Yorkton. A plaque marks the site of York City; nearby are millstones from the original colony's gristmill.

Recreation is available at nearby Good Spirit Lake Provincial Park. The park, originally a Hudson's Bay Co. post in the 1880s, is noted for its miles of sandy beaches and fine dunes. *See Recreation Chart and the AAA/CAA Western Canada & Alaska CampBook.*

Tourism Yorkton Visitor Information Centre: Hwy. 9, Box 460, Yorkton, SK, Canada S3N 2W4. **Phone:** (306) 783-8707.

Self-guiding tours: The Yorkton Heritage Walking Tour affords visitors the opportunity to view gardens and historic buildings. The City Cemetery Walking Tour features the grave sites of many of the city's early pioneers. Materials outlining each tour are available at the information center.

GODFREY DEAN ART GALLERY is in the Godfrey Dean Cultural Centre at 49 Smith St. E. Assorted art forms are displayed, along with works by contemporary Canadian artists. Exhibits change monthly. **Hours:** Mon.-Fri. 11-5 (also Thurs. 6-9 p.m.), Sun. 1-4. Closed major holidays. **Cost:** Free. **Phone:** (306) 786-2992.

[SAVE] **WESTERN DEVELOPMENT MUSEUM'S STORY OF PEOPLE** is .4 km (.25 mi.) w. on Hwy. 16A. The museum focuses on the cultural roots of the settlers of western Canada. **Time:** Allow 1 hour minimum. **Hours:** Daily 9-5, May-Aug.; Mon.-Wed. 2-5, rest of year. **Cost:** $5; $4 (ages 65+); $3 (students with ID); $1 (ages 6-12); $10 (family). **Phone:** (306) 783-8361. ⛩

GAMBLING ESTABLISHMENTS

* **Painted Hand Casino** is at 510 Broadway St. W. **Hours:** Wed.-Sat. 9 a.m.-4 a.m., Sun.-Tues. 9 a.m.-3 a.m. Closed Dec. 25. **Phone:** (306) 786-6777.

Yukon Territory

A Panful of Nuggets

Miners still find gold a century after the great Klondike Gold Rush

Spirit of Adventure

Wild waterways, rugged mountains and unexplored wilderness await

All That Glitters

Black diamond jade, amber, topaz, malachite, obsidian and gold bejewel the territory

Lofty Mount Logan

Canada's highest peak rises from the icy Saint Elias Mountains

The Northern Lights

Aurora borealis offers nature's nightly light show

Off Dempster Hwy, near the Arctic Circle
John E. Marriott
Getty Images

Near Lowell Glacier, Kluane National Park and Reserve of Canada / © 2009 John Hyde / AlaskaStock

To find gleaming gifts of topaz in outcroppings of rock. To wander trails once trodden by miners and trappers. To cry "Mush!" behind a stalwart team of sturdy Alaskan huskies.

To do any of these is to begin to understand the majestic allure of the endless Yukon.

The roughly triangular territory is a land of adventure, a lonely wilderness, a rugged and pristine land of splendor and beauty.

Turbulent rivers of splashing white water weave through soaring mountain ranges. Soft blankets of white pull up snugly over a serene countryside.

The very essence of the sprawling territory is aptly captured in one moving stanza from poet Robert Service's homage, "The Spell of the Yukon":

There's gold, and
it's haunting and haunting;
It's luring me on as of old;
Yet it isn't the gold that I'm wanting
so much as just finding the gold.
It's the great, big, broad
land 'way up yonder,
It's the forests
where silence has lease;
It's the beauty
that thrills me with wonder,
It's the stillness
that fills me with peace.

"Thick between the flaky slabs, like cheese sandwiches"—this was how prospector George Washington Carmack described the gold he saw glimmering between rocks in Bonanza Creek near Dawson City on August 16, 1896.

On July 14, 1897, the steamship *Excelsior* arrived in San Francisco carrying a treasure worth more than $500,000; a few days later the *Portland* docked in Seattle with one ton of gold piled on its deck. News of these recently discovered riches spread like wildfire, and thousands of get-rich-quick hopefuls began to head for the wealth that lay in Yukon Territory.

Klondike or Bust

That following winter, some 100,000 prospectors began a long, arduous journey to the Yukon to seek their fortunes. While the rush only lasted about 5 years, history was left in its trampled tracks. Following the Yukon River from Marsh Lake, near British Columbia's border, to Dawson City, you can explore the past on a course pursued by gold diggers more than 100 years ago.

If stampeders survived the trek through Chilkoot Pass—a climb over frozen mountains with heavy packs full of supplies strapped to their backs—they crossed the border into the Yukon Territory at Bennett Lake.

The lake, surrounded by mighty peaks and woodlands, links to the Yukon River. Most fortune seekers waited out the harsh winter at the southern shore, which quickly transformed into a crowded tent city. Transients built boats, temporary shelter and a little log church out of timber hewn from the forest. In late May of 1898, the lake's ice broke and 7,000 handmade vessels headed across its waters, leaving memories of a bitter season behind.

Today, original miners' cabins still line Bennett Lake's northern shore at Carcross, a town chock full of gold rush history. The Caribou Hotel, built in 1898 to welcome gold rushers, is downtown, and graves of such early pioneers as Kate Carmack, Skookum Jim Mason and Tagish Charlie dot the city's cemetery.

From Carcross the gold route followed the Yukon River to Miles Canyon, just south of Whitehorse. Currents here were so dangerous that hundreds of boats capsized, and licensed

The Hudson's Bay Co. sets up trading posts in the Yukon.
1800

Yukon Territory becomes a provisional district of the Northwest Territories.
1895

Gold rush veteran Martha Black is elected to the House of Commons.
1935

1898-1904
More than $100 million in gold is mined in the region.

Government of Yukon

Yukon Territory Historical Timeline

1942
The Alaska Highway is constructed, creating a new overland transportation route.

guides were a must for piloting would-be miners with smaller vessels through the rocks and whirlpools.

Cheechakos, or newcomers, relied upon their own floating devices until stern-wheelers became a popular means of travel; by the early 1950s, more than 250 steamboats plied the Yukon. Boats were specifically designed for the river, employing flat bottoms that allowed for docking on sandbars. Nevertheless, many ran aground or were smashed by rapids or rocks on the Yukon's perilous waters.

A few stout vessels remain from this turbulent time. The restored steamer SS *Klondike II* resides in Whitehorse, while Dawson City is home to the dry-docked SS *Keno*.

The River to Riches

After stopping to relax and dry out in Whitehorse, miners pressed on, traversing Lake Laberge to enter a stretch of the Yukon called Thirty Mile. Due to swift currents and rocks, it was perhaps the most dangerous portion of the entire route. Historical sites along Thirty Mile—which is designated a Historic River—include abandoned Northwest Mounted Police posts, simple grave markers, woodcutters' cabins, telegraph stations, old log buildings and remains of beached paddle-wheelers. They all bring yesteryear into focus.

More dangerous eddies had to be negotiated at Five Finger Rapids, just outside Carmacks, before exhausted voyagers passed Fort Selkirk and reached Dawson City—the golden ticket.

Downtown Dawson City remains much as it was when prospectors arrived, thanks to codes requiring new buildings to sport fronts reminiscent of the gold rush era. And old buildings have been restored: Cancan dancing takes place at Diamond Tooth Gertie's Casino and the log cabins once inhabited by author Jack London and poet Robert Service remain as examples of gold rush housing. A 1912 dredge can be seen along a tributary of the Klondike, and placer mining still occurs at nearby creeks such as the Eldorado.

And don't forget to stop by where it all began—a brass plaque on Bonanza Creek Road marks the spot that caused a great many to risk life and limb for a golden nugget that promised a change of fate.

Yukon's capital is moved from Dawson City to Whitehorse.
1953

Government of Yukon

Kluane National Park is declared a Natural World Heritage Site.
1979

The Council for Yukon Indians and the Canadian and Yukon Territory governments sign an agreement stating the terms for final land claim settlements in the territory.
1993

1959
At a cost of $1 million, a large fish ladder is built at the Whitehorse Rapids for migrating chinook salmon.

1997
Yukon spends $37 million on mining exploration.

1999
Yukon signs an accord with the Vuntut Gwitchin people, thereby recognizing a First Nation tribe as a legitimate government for the first time in the territory's history.

Recreation

Through its pristine waterways, rugged mountains and unexplored wilderness, the Yukon evokes a spirit of adventure in visitors.

Highways to Adventure

There is no better place than the Chilkoot Trail to understand the challenges faced by early pilgrims—the gold-rush stampeders—coming into Yukon Territory. The Yukon's original inroad, with its trail head in Dyea, Alaska, affords today's experienced **hiking** enthusiasts a 53-kilometre (33-mi.), one-way walk through history that can take 3 to 5 days to complete.

Preparation—proper gear, provisions, permits and registration—is key to enjoying this demanding trip through boreal forests and over alpine tundra and snow-patched mountains. You must reserve a campsite for each night you plan to spend on the trail. The Trail Centre in Skagway, Alaska, is the official registration point and offers maps, safety tips and a few words about bears during the Chilkoot hiking season, May through early September. For information phone Parks Canada year-round at (800) 661-0486.

At trail's end in Bennett, British Columbia, reward yourself with a railroad ride back to Skagway aboard the White Pass & Yukon Route, which shuttles returning Chilkoot hikers regularly. Reservations are a must; phone (907) 983-2217 or (800) 343-7373. Another return option is to hop a bus at Log Cabin, British Columbia.

Camping in summer, June through mid-September, truly is a wilderness experience. While you won't have to chop firewood (it's there and it's free), you will have to pump your own water. Government campgrounds are spread throughout the Yukon roughly 81-121 kilometres (50-75 mi.) apart. Many are beside lakes, rivers or streams, where you might hook a few Arctic graylings for dinner. Of the 10 campgrounds along the Alaska Highway (Hwy. 1), Watson Lake is one of the first you'll find as you enter the Yukon from British Columbia; it has 55 campsites. Farther west bordering the Kluane region is Congdon Creek; with 78 campsites, it's one of the largest in the territory. Both areas offer **fishing, swimming** and hiking.

Take scenic Dempster Highway (Hwy. 5) from Dawson City to Rock River Campground, the northernmost public facility at Km-post 447. Congratulate yourself upon arriving: You've crossed the Continental Divide—twice—*and* the Arctic Circle! There is no well water for the 14 sites at Rock River,

so be sure to stock up on supplies in Dawson City or when you get to Eagle Plains—your last chance—at Km-post 371.

The Klondike Highway (Hwy. 2), open all year, is dotted with roadside respites for camping and **picnicking.** You also can camp just off the Robert Campbell and Silver Trail highways (Hwys. 4 and 11, respectively). Travelers can access daily road condition reports by dialing the Department of Highways and Public Works hotline; phone (877) 456-7623 within the Yukon or (867) 456-7623 outside the Yukon. Wherever the road leads, watch for wildlife, especially around viewing areas identified with a sign picturing binoculars.

The Other Extremes

With almost 7 months of winter (October through April), **snow skiing** is a way of life in the Yukon. Near Whitehorse, a chalet and night lighting attract cross-country skiers to Mount McIntyre's world-class trails, while Mount Sima, one of the largest ski areas in the Yukon, appeals to downhill skiers with its nine runs and one chairlift. **Snowboarding,** too, is a favorite at Mount Sima's snowpark. Power up a snowmobile and glide on groomed trails around Whitehorse, or venture over more rugged terrain out of Dawson City, said to be the **snowmobiling** capital of the Yukon.

The territory's rich "veins"—its wild rivers—yield excitement other than gold finds. Outfitters are available in Whitehorse to take you **kayaking** or **white-water rafting** on the Tatshenshini's class three and four rapids, or through Kluane National Park and Reserve of Canada on the Alsek, a designated heritage river. Many sections of the Yukon River, which once ushered fortune seekers north to the Klondike goldfields, are easily navigated by canoe. And there are tons more nuggets of adventure to be discovered in the Yukon Territory.

Recreational Activities

Throughout the TourBook, you may notice a Recreational Activities heading with bulleted listings of recreation-oriented establishments listed underneath. Similar operations also may be mentioned in Destination City recreation sections. Since normal AAA inspection criteria cannot be applied, these establishments are presented only for information. Age, height and weight restrictions may apply. Reservations often are recommended and sometimes are required. Addresses and/or phone numbers are provided so visitors can contact the attraction for additional information.

Fast Facts

POPULATION: 28,674.

AREA: 482,443 sq km (186,271 sq mi); ranks 9th.

CAPITAL: Whitehorse.

HIGHEST POINT: 5,959 m/19,545 ft., Mount Logan.

LOWEST POINT: Sea level, Beaufort Sea.

TIME ZONE(S): Pacific.

TEEN DRIVING LAWS: Driving is not permitted midnight-5 a.m. Minimum age for an unrestricted driver's license is 17 years, 6 months.

MINIMUM AGE FOR GAMBLING: 19.

SEAT BELT/CHILD RESTRAINT LAWS: Seat belts required for driver and all passengers ages 6 and older. Child restraints required for under age 7 and under 22 kg (48 lbs).

HELMETS FOR MOTORCYCLISTS: Required for all riders.

RADAR DETECTORS: Not permitted.

FIREARMS LAWS: By federal law, all nonresidents entering Canada with a firearm must declare their weapon in writing and pay a fee of $25 (Canadian). Contact the Canadian Firearms Centre at (800) 731-4000 to receive a declaration form or for additional information.

HOLIDAYS: Jan. 1; Heritage Day, Feb. 25; Good Friday; Easter Monday; Victoria Day, May 24 or the closest prior Mon.; Canada Day, July 1; Discovery Day, Aug. (3rd Mon.); Labour Day, Sept. (1st Mon.); Thanksgiving, Oct. (2nd Mon.); Remembrance Day, Nov. 11; Christmas, Dec. 25; Boxing Day, Dec. 26.

TAXES: The Yukon Territory has no territorial sales tax. The federal Goods and Services Tax (GST) is 5 percent.

FERRY SCHEDULES AND INFORMATION: The Department of Highways runs ferries along Dempster Hwy. and at Dawson City. Phone (867) 667-3710.

ROAD CONDITIONS: Through its Yukon Network the Canadian Broadcasting Corporation reports road conditions on the Alaska Hwy. and all other Yukon highways. Major participating stations, with their frequencies in kilohertz (kHz), are listed from south to north: Watson Lake, 990; Swift River, 970; Teslin, 940; Whitehorse, 570; Haines Junction, 860; Destruction Bay, 940; Beaver Creek, 690; Carmacks, 990; Mayo, 1230; Elsa, 560; Dawson City, 560; Faro, 105.1 FM; and Ross River, 990.

For changes on Yukon road conditions, phone (867) 456-7623, (877) 456-7623 or 511 within the Yukon Territory.

INFORMATION CENTERS: Territorial information centers in Beaver Creek, Carcross, Dawson City, Haines Junction, Watson Lake and Whitehorse are open 12 hours a day, mid-May to mid-Sept., with reduced hours early to mid-May and mid- to late Sept. The Whitehorse Visitor Information Centre also is open Mon.-Fri. 8:30-noon and 1-5, Sat. 10-2, in winter.

FURTHER INFORMATION FOR VISITORS:
Department of Tourism & Culture
P.O. Box 2703
Whitehorse, YT, Canada Y1A 2C6
(800) 661-0494

FISHING AND HUNTING REGULATIONS:
Yukon Government Fish and Wildlife
Branch
P.O. Box 2703 (V-5)
Whitehorse, YT, Canada Y1A 2C6
(867) 667-5715
(800) 661-0408, ext. 5715

ALCOHOL CONSUMPTION: Legal age 19.

Yukon Territories Temperature Averages
Maximum/Minimum (Celsius)
From the records of The Weather Channel Interactive, Inc.

	JAN	FEB	MAR	APR	MAY	JUNE	JULY	AUG	SEPT	OCT	NOV	DEC
Watson Lake	-19	-12	-3	6	13	19	21	19	13	4	-11	-18
	-30	-25	-18	-7	0	6	8	7	2	-5	-20	-28
Whitehorse	-14	-8	-2	6	12	18	20	18	12	4	-7	-12
	-23	-18	-13	-6	0	5	7	6	2	-3	-14	-20

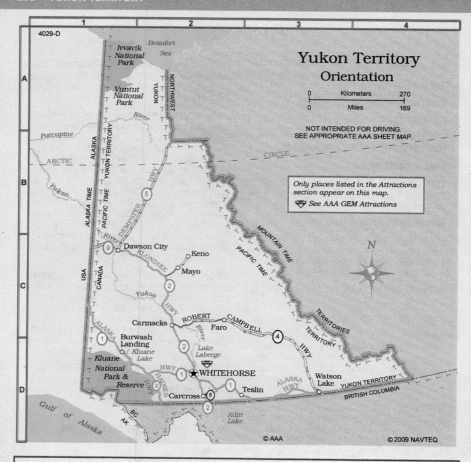

Yukon Territory
Orientation

NOT INTENDED FOR DRIVING.
SEE APPROPRIATE AAA SHEET MAP.

Only places listed in the Attractions
section appear on this map.
See AAA GEM Attractions

Points of Interest

BURWASH LANDING (D-1) pop. 73

In 1904, a year after gold was discovered in Fourth of July Creek, Morley Bones staked a discovery claim on Burwash Creek. Soon after the small community of Burwash sprang up around a trading post. Burwash Landing, with an airstrip and a resort, lies between the Kluane Lake and Kluane Game Sanctuary.

KLUANE MUSEUM OF NATURAL HISTORY is at Historic Mile 1093 on the Alaska Hwy. The museum contains a nature and taxidermy display, handmade First Nations crafts and costumes, a mineral and fossil collection and a large topographical map of the surrounding area. **Time:** Allow 1 hour minimum. **Hours:** Daily 9-7, May 15-Sept. 15. **Cost:** $3.95; $2.95 (ages 61+); $2.25 (ages 6-16); $9.75 (family). **Phone:** (867) 841-5561.

CARCROSS (D-2) pop. 331

Carcross, 74 kilometres (46 mi.) from Whitehorse on the S. Klondike Hwy., originally was called Caribou Crossing. The town's current name is a combination of the first syllable of each word. From this settlement George Carmack's party set out on the prospecting trip that began the gold rush of 1898. On July 29, 1900, the railroad's final spike was driven, marking the completion of the White Pass & Yukon Route, which linked Alaska and the Yukon Territory by rail.

Today the White Pass & Yukon Route (*see attraction listing in Alaska p. 358*) transports passengers between Carcross and Bennett, British Columbia; phone (907) 983-2217 or (800) 343-7373 for schedule and reservations.

Near the town's train depot is the "Duchess," a tiny locomotive that ran the 6.4-kilometre (4-mi.) line from Taku Arm on Tagish Lake to Atlin Lake in the early 1900s. It supposedly was the shortest and most expensive rail trip in the world—one-way fare was $2—and passengers had to sit on their baggage in the cramped compartment.

Recalling the feverish gold rush days is the Caribou Hotel. Regarded as the Yukon's oldest operating hotel, the historic building, which opened in 1898 to accommodate gold seekers heading north, is a Yukon Historic Site. **Note:** The hotel is currently closed for restoration.

The Carcross Visitor Information Centre on the Klondike Hwy. at Km-post 106 is in the historic White Pass & Yukon Route train depot. The center provides extensive information about Carcross, one of the Yukon's most picturesque areas; phone (867) 821-4431.

Just north of town along the Klondike Hwy. lies the Carcross Desert, considered the smallest desert in the world. The 260-hectare (650-acre) area was created by retreating glaciers that left a sandy lake bottom; today winds from Lake Bennett constantly shift the sand, limiting vegetation to such plants as kinnikinnick and lodgepole pine.

CARIBOU CROSSING TRADING POST is 3.2 km (2 mi.) n. on S. Klondike Hwy. to Km-post 109. At this 12-hectare (30-acre) park, visitors can view mounted animals in dioramas representing their natural habitats, explore an outdoor heritage area depicting the region's frontier days and climb to a lookout that provides a view of Lake Bennett, Carcross and surrounding mountains. The park includes a nature trail, petting farm and miniature golf.

Time: Allow 1 hour, 30 minutes minimum. **Hours:** Daily 9-5, mid-May to mid-Sept. **Cost:** $7.25; $5.25 (ages 3-12). Miniature golf tickets $12; $9 (ages 3-12). **Phone:** (867) 821-4055. 🍴

CARMACKS (C-2) pop. 425

Carmacks, named for George Washington Carmack, one of the discoverers of gold in the Klondike, was an important stopover point on the Overland Trail that linked Whitehorse and Dawson City before the Klondike Hwy. was built. Items from early travelers still can be found along the trail near town.

About 22 kilometres (14 mi.) north of Carmacks are the Five Fingers Rapids, which claimed the lives of many prospectors trying to reach Dawson City by way of the Yukon River.

TAGE CHO HUDAN INTERPRETIVE CENTRE is .4 km (.25 mi.) n. on the Klondike Hwy. The culture of the Northern Tutchone people, Yukon's oldest inhabitants, is explored through a collection of traditional tools and dioramas featuring a dugout, moose skin boats and moose skin clothing. Outside displays such as a pole house, a moose skin tanning camp and a winter moose skin home are featured. A garden with medicinal plants and a trail also are on-site.

Tours: Guided tours are available. **Time:** Allow 30 minutes minimum. **Hours:** Daily 9-6, mid-May to mid-Sept. **Cost:** Donations. **Phone:** (867) 863-5830. 🪧

DAWSON CITY (C-1) pop. 1,327

Dawson City was the center of the excitement caused by one of the world's most fabulous gold strikes. On Aug. 16, 1896, George Washington Carmack and his companions Skookum Jim and Tagish Charlie made the first strike on Bonanza Creek, a tributary of the Klondike River.

In the summer of 1897 miners from Dawson City arrived in Seattle and San Francisco with nearly $2 million as they carried word of the discovery to the United States, then in the midst of a depression. By the next spring more than 60,000 men and women had passed through Seattle and Alaska's Chilkoot and White passes on their way to the Klondike.

The Dawson settlement, which sprang up at the confluence of the Yukon and Klondike rivers, became a thriving city with some 30,000 inhabitants by the summer of 1898, making it the largest city west of Winnipeg and north of San Francisco.

All the creeks in the area had been staked by the spring of 1899. Hillside and bench claims were made, some yielding rich gold finds in the White Channel gravels. Between 1896 and 1904 Klondike creeks brought in more than $100 million in gold.

This period of Dawson City's history has been preserved by Rex Beach, Jack London, Robert W. Service and others who wrote colorful tales of personal experiences.

It was in Dawson City that London became acquainted with a large dog that he named Buck, a cross between a St. Bernard and a German shepherd that became the prototype for the dog in "Call of the Wild." Daily readings from the works of Jack London are given 10-6, mid-May to mid-Sept., at a replica of his cabin on Eighth Avenue at Firth Street. The cabin is part of the Jack London Interpretive Center, which features London's food cache and memorabilia related to his activities in the area.

Many historic buildings, some still in use, survive from the days when Dawson City was the gold capital of the world. The Midnight Sun and Eldorado hotels conjure memories of a lively past.

Harrington's Store, Princess Street and Third Avenue, has a free photographic exhibit titled "Dawson as They Saw It." The 1901 Post Office, King Street and Third Avenue, offers a visitor information exhibit; phone (867) 993-7200. Both are open June through September.

The SS *Keno*, in dry-dock on First Avenue between King and Queen streets, is typical of the stern-wheelers of the gold rush era. Built in 1922, it was one of the last riverboats to run between Dawson City and Whitehorse.

The summit of Midnight Dome, 7 kilometres (4 mi.) southeast via Front Street, offers a panorama of Dawson City, the Yukon and Klondike rivers and the gold fields. Many Dawson City pioneers are buried in cemeteries on the hillsides flanking the dome.

South on Bonanza Creek Road is the Discovery Claim, which started the great rush. Panning for gold is possible at several locations along the Klondike Hwy.: Claim 33, Guggieville RV Park, Dawson City RV Park, Gold Bottom Mines and Eureka Mines.

Yukon Queen River Cruises has one-way and round-trip cruises to Eagle, Alaska; for schedule and information phone (867) 993-5599.

The Dawson City Visitor Information Centre features exhibits about Klondike history and is open daily 8-8, mid-May to mid-Sept.; daily 10-6, early to mid-May and mid- to late Sept.

The town celebrates its gold mining heritage during Discovery Days Festival, a weeklong event held at various locations in mid-August.

Dawson City Visitor Information Centre: Front and King streets, Dawson City, YT, Canada Y0B 1G0. **Phone:** (867) 993-5566.

Self-guiding tours: A brochure describing walking tours of historic sites is available at the visitor information center.

BONANZA CREEK DISCOVERY CLAIM is 14.8 km (9.3 mi.) s. on Bonanza Creek Rd. Signs portray the story of gold mining along this famous creek. Discovery Claim #1 is the spot where gold first was discovered. A historical marker at Km-post 17.71 identifies the town of Grand Forks, which had a population of 5,000 during its prime. Dredge #4 at Km-post 12.3 was used to recover gold from creekbeds. **Hours:** A trailer with exhibits about the dredge is open daily 9-5, mid-June to mid-Sept. **Cost:** Free. **Phone:** (867) 993-7200.

DANOJA ZHO CULTURAL CENTRE is on Front St., across from the Dawson City Visitor Information Centre. Guided tours, exhibits, video presentations, dance performances and hands-on activities give visitors an interesting perspective into the culture of the Tr'ondek Hwech'in First Nations peoples. Displays include archeological artifacts, traditional costumes and reproduction tools. Special events also are featured. **Time:** Allow 30 minutes minimum. **Hours:** Daily 10-6, June-Sept. **Cost:** $5; $2.50 (ages 12-18). **Phone:** (867) 993-6768.

DAWSON CITY MUSEUM is on Fifth Ave. Gold rush items are displayed at the museum, which contains a smithy, a general store, an old miner's cabin, a saloon and Chilkoot Hall. First Nations artifacts and an outdoor transportation exhibit with locomotives from the Klondike Mines Railway also are featured. **Hours:** Daily 10-6, Victoria Day weekend-Labour Day; limited hours in May and day after Labour Day-Sept. 30. **Cost:** $7; $5 (senior citizens and students with ID); free (ages 0-6); $16 (family). **Phone:** (867) 993-5291.

SAVE **GRAY LINE YUKON TOURS,** 902 Front St., offers a variety of tours by bus, jeep and raft. The Ghosts of Dawson City walking and bus tour visits historic buildings, museums and Gold Dredge #4. **Hours:** Ghost tour departs daily at 9, late May-early Sept. Schedule varies for other tours. **Cost:** Ghost tour $36. Fares vary for other tours. **Phone:** (867) 993-5599 or (800) 544-2206.

ROBERT SERVICE CABIN is 1 blk. s. of Church St. on Eighth Ave. The restored 1898 log cabin of the Bard of the Yukon is furnished as it was 1909-12 when Service was a resident and wrote many of his ballads and poems. **Tours:** Guided tours are available. **Time:** Allow 30 minutes minimum. **Hours:** Daily 10-noon and 1-4:30, late May to mid-Sept. **Cost:** $6; free (children). Rates may vary; phone ahead. **Phone:** (867) 993-7200.

TOMBSTONE TERRITORIAL PARK is 71 km (44 mi.) n. of jct. Dempster and Klondike hwys. This park spans an area of more than 2,164 square kilometres (836 sq. mi.) and features a diversity of wildlife and bird species as well as a variety of vegetation. Although there are no established hiking trails within the park, there are accessible portions off the highway that offer short hikes and challenging backpacking and mountain climbing excursions. The park's Arctic Tundra environment creates a landscape with spectacular views. The interpretive center has natural history displays and provides interpretive programs and nature walks.

Note: When traveling to the park have enough gas and spare tires since there are no roadside services available until Eagle Plains, which is 369 kilometres (229 mi.) north of the Klondike Hwy. Once in the park, be aware that it is an isolated and potentially hazardous environment. Rough terrain, drastic weather changes and encounters with wildlife are factors to consider. **Time:** Allow 3 hours minimum. **Hours:** Interpretive center open daily 9-9, mid-June to mid-Sept. Park daily 9-dusk year-round. Phone ahead to confirm schedule. **Cost:** Free. **Phone:** (867) 667-5648.

GAMBLING ESTABLISHMENTS

- **Diamond Tooth Gertie's Casino**, Queen St. and Fourth Ave. **Hours:** Daily 7 p.m.-2 a.m., May 12-Sept. 17 (opens at 2 p.m. Sat.-Sun., mid-June through Labour Day). **Phone:** (867) 993-5575.

FARO (C-2) elev. 2,352′

CAMPBELL REGION INTERPRETIVE CENTRE is on Campbell Street. A spruce log building houses a permanent exhibit about the history, geology and wildlife of the Faro area. **Time:** Allow 1 hour minimum. **Hours:** Daily 8-6, June-Aug.; 10-5, May 5-31 and Sept. 1-29. **Cost:** Donations. **Phone:** (867) 994-2288.

IVVAVIK NATIONAL PARK OF CANADA (A-1)

Ivvavik National Park of Canada is in the extreme northwestern corner of the Yukon. Virtually untouched by humans, the Arctic wilderness is of great geologic interest; it is one of the few regions in Canada that contains areas never covered by glaciers.

Every spring it becomes the calving grounds of Porcupine caribou that arrive after a long, difficult migration from the south and west. The park provides an important nesting area for North American waterfowl and a home to grizzly, black and polar bears. The only access to the park is by air.

KENO (C-2) pop. 15, elev. 3,120′

In 1919, silver and lead ore were discovered in Keno Hill, and by 1920 Keno became a busy community with cabins, a stable and a hotel. The following year, the city was the center of a thriving

Sourdoughs and Cheechakos

To distinguish between the fortune seekers who entered the Yukon Territory during the 1897-98 Klondike Gold Rush, veterans of the '49 California Rush labeled the seasoned arrivals "Sourdoughs" and the greenhorns "Cheechakos" (CHE-cha-kos). Named after the staple bread of the frontier, Sourdoughs were prospectors who had survived a Yukon winter. The term Cheechako came from the Chinook Indian word for "new to come."

© PhotoDisc

Once off the steamer at Skagway, Alaska, these newcomers had to transport thousands of pounds of survival gear—the Northwest Mounted Police wisely required each prospector to bring a year's supply of food—over the precipitous Chilkoot Pass. After that they had to float their unwieldy cargo over the treacherous rapids of the Yukon River.

More obstacles awaited the greenhorns at the gold sites. By the time the Cheechakos arrived, much of the gold field already was depleted or staked. To make things worse, Cheechakos were often directed to the hills by unscrupulous Sourdoughs who knew the gold nuggets tended to settle in creek beds. Nonetheless, some did tap into a channel of an ancient gold-bearing stream on Cheechako Hill.

Those who had survived to see the ice melt were dubbed Sourdoughs; the graveyards of those who had not succeeded dotted the route all the way back to Skagway. As one cynical Sourdough put it: "We were SOUR on the Yukon and didn't have enough DOUGH to get out."

mining district. The town's name comes from the popular gambling game played at casinos. Today, Keno is home to artists who are inspired by the area's natural beauty.

No matter the season, outdoor recreational opportunities abound and include hiking, bicycling, cross-country skiing, snowmobiling, fishing and canoeing. The awe-inspiring northern lights may be seen from late August through April. A must-see is the often-photographed signpost at the top of Keno Hill, showing mileage to such cities as London, Paris and Rome. The 1,829-metre (6,000-ft.) hill also plays host to a breathtaking view.

Self-guiding tours: This historic walking tour starts from Tolmie Cabin on Duncan Creek Road and includes the Beer Bottle House, Keno City Mining Museum and All Saints Anglican Church. Brochures are available from the Keno City Mining Museum. Phone (867) 995-2792 or (867) 995-2730.

KENO CITY MINING MUSEUM is on Silver Tr. Hwy. Housed in a dance hall, the museum depicts the history of the local community and gold and silver mining through exhibits, photographs, equipment and tools. An interpretive center focuses on the history of alpine wildlife, including wildflowers, birds, butterflies and wild animals; several hiking trails begin at the center. **Time:** Allow 30 minutes minimum. **Hours:** Daily 10-6, mid-May to mid-Sept. **Cost:** $3.50; $2.50 (ages 66+); free (ages 0-12). **Phone:** (867) 995-2792.

KLUANE NATIONAL PARK AND RESERVE OF CANADA (D-1)

Elevations in the park range from 400 metres (1,300 ft.) in the Alsek River to 5,959 metres (19,545 ft.) at Mount Logan. Refer to CAA/AAA maps for additional elevation information.

Kluane (kloo-AH-nee) National Park and Reserve of Canada is bounded by the Haines (Hwy. 3) and Alaska (Hwy. 1) hwys. along its northeastern border. The park covers 22,015 square kilometres (8,500 sq. mi.) of wilderness.

Near its southeastern boundary was the Dalton Trail, a route used during the Klondike Rush of 1898. In 1904 a North West Mounted Police post was established on the south shore of Kluane Lake, and in 1942 the lake became a meeting place for crews building the Alaska Hwy.

During the building of the highway the wilderness area was preserved as the Kluane Game Sanctuary. In 1979 Kluane was declared a World Heritage Site for its impressive topographical features and its massive nonpolar ice fields.

The park is dominated by the Saint Elias Mountains, which run through the park in a southeasterly direction. Mount Logan, Canada's highest peak at 5,959 metres (19,545 ft.), and Mount St. Elias at 5,489 metres (18,008 ft.) dominate the range. The Saint Elias Mountains hold extensive ice fields that date from the last ice age and constitute the largest nonpolar glacier systems in the world.

An extensive network of glaciers, together with the ice fields, covers more than half of the park's area throughout the year. Notable are the Steele Glacier, which moves sporadically at a relatively rapid rate, and the Kaskawulsh and Lowell glaciers, which are flanked by moraines—accumulations of earth and stones carried and deposited by the glaciers. The movement and debris of the glaciers contribute to such park features as sand dunes and dust storms.

The park has a variety of flora. Such coniferous species as white spruce characterize the boreal forest of the river valleys. Lichens, dwarf birch trees and low shrubs distinguish the tundra uplands in the northern section, and colorful Arctic flowers cling to the crevices and ledges of the mountains. In the southeastern section, where the Pacific Ocean's moderating influence is felt in the climate, the vegetation is more luxuriant.

Arctic grayling, lake trout, northern pike and kokanee salmon are found in lakes and streams. Other park species include golden eagles, ptarmigans, Dall sheep, mountain goats, caribou, moose and wolves. Kluane has one of the largest populations of grizzly bears and subspecies of moose in the world.

General Information and Activities

The park is open all year, but access may be limited in the winter, depending on weather conditions. The Kluane National Park and Reserve of Canada headquarters, at Km-post 1635 in Haines Junction, is open year-round. The Sheep Mountain Visitor Centre at Km-post 1707 is open mid-May to early September.

The park primarily is a wilderness area, so there are no roads except on the eastern and northern perimeters, traversed by Hwy. 3 and Hwy. 1, respectively. Hiking is the most popular activity in the park, with approximately 250 kilometres (155 mi.) of hiking trails. Hiking is possible along a few old mining roads, creekside paths and marked trails. Some trails are self-guiding. All overnight hikers must register at one of the information centers or with a park warden before and after hikes.

Mountain climbing should be done only by well-trained climbers, who must obtain a climbing permit and register with the Warden Service before and after climbs.

Other recreational pursuits include fishing, backpacking, boating, cross-country skiing and ice fishing. All anglers within the park must obtain a national park fishing license, available at the park visitor centers and from area stores and lodges. Camping, fishing and picnic facilities are available at Kathleen Lake, 27 kilometres (17 mi.) south of Haines Junction.

During the summer the Kluane National Park and Reserve of Canada headquarters sponsors interpretive activities including campfire talks and guided walks. A relief map and an interactive computer touch screen are available. Information about recreational opportunities, sightseeing by small aircraft and other guided tours is available.

ADMISSION to the park is free.

PETS are permitted in the park if kept on a leash, but visitors are advised not to bring them.

ADDRESS inquiries about the park to Kluane National Park and Reserve of Canada, P.O. Box 5495, Haines Junction, YT, Canada Y0B 1L0; phone (867) 634-7250.

MAYO (C-2)

Mayo lies 53 kilometres (33 mi.) northeast of the Klondike Hwy. at the confluence of the Stewart and Mayo rivers. Both the town and the river were named for the pioneer prospector and trader Alfred Mayo. In the early 1900s Mayo Landing became a shipping point for the gold and silver that was mined farther north in Elsa.

Mayo Lake to the northeast provides excellent fishing. The summit of nearby 1,890-metre (6,200-ft.) Keno Mountain provides a scenic view of the mining village of Keno. This once bustling community has a mining museum.

Further details about the silver mining towns of Mayo, Elsa and Keno, known collectively as the Silver Trail, are available at the information booth at Stewart Crossing.

BINET HOUSE INTERPRETIVE CENTRE is at jct. Second Ave. and Centre St. The two-story building features exhibits that include a collection of historic photographs, artifacts and a 3-D relief map of the region identifying the location of mineral deposits. **Tours:** Guided tours are available. **Time:** Allow 30 minutes minimum. **Hours:** Daily 10-6, June-Aug. **Cost:** $2; free (ages 0-11). **Phone:** (867) 996-2926. ⒜

TESLIN (D-3) pop. 141

The Nisutlin Bay Bridge, the longest water span on the Alaska Hwy., crosses an arm of Teslin Lake at Teslin. The highway parallels the 116-kilometre (72-mi.) lake for about 55 kilometres (34 mi.), providing a scenic drive bordered on both sides by mountains. The area is noted for abundant game, and the fjord-like lake provides excellent fishing. The economy of the community depends heavily on hunting, fishing and trapping.

Teslin has one of the largest First Nations populations in the Yukon, with many of its residents descended from the coastal Tlingit tribe. The original First Nations settlement is reached by a loop road. In the old village are Catholic and Anglican missions as well as a Royal Canadian Mounted Police station.

GEORGE JOHNSTON MUSEUM is 1 km (.6 mi.) w. of the Alaska Hwy. at Km-post 296. George Johnston, a Tlingit Indian, recorded his culture through his camera. A selection of Johnston's work,

displays of the Tlingit tribe's rich and colorful history, Tlingit dancing costumes and pioneer items are exhibited. **Hours:** Daily 9-5, mid-May through Aug. 31. **Cost:** $5; $4 (ages 61+ and college students with ID); $3 (ages 6-17); $15 (family). **Phone:** (867) 390-2550.

TESLIN TLINGIT HERITAGE CENTRE is 4 km (2.5 mi.) w. on Hwy. 1. Totem poles, hand-carved masks, crafts, artifacts and photographs provide insight into the life and culture of the Teslin Tlingit people. **Time:** Allow 30 minutes minimum. **Hours:** Mon.-Sat. 9-5, Sun. 11-5, June-Aug. **Cost:** $4; $3 (ages 55+ and students with ID); $3 (ages 6-17); $15 (family). **Phone:** (867) 390-2532. ⒜

WATSON LAKE (D-3) pop. 1,251

At Km-post 1016.8 on the Alaska Hwy., Watson Lake is an important transportation, distribution and communication center for the southern Yukon. The town was named for Frank Watson, a trapper from England who settled there in 1898.

Watson Lake is known for the signpost collection that was begun by a homesick soldier during construction of the Alaska Hwy. in 1942. Over the years, tourists have continued adding signs showing the names of their hometowns, and now the collection includes more than 60,000 signs.

From Watson Lake the historic Robert Campbell Hwy. loops north and west through the wilderness of southeastern Yukon.

NORTHERN LIGHTS CENTRE is at 807 Frank Tr. Images of the aurora borealis are displayed in a planetarium-like dome theater. Narration details the myths and science behind the luminous phenomena. **Time:** Allow 1 hour minimum. **Hours:** Daily 12:30-9:30, mid-May to mid-Sept. **Cost:** $10; $9 (ages 66+ and students with ID); $6 (ages 6-12); $24 (family, two adults and three children). **Phone:** (867) 536-7827.

WATSON LAKE VISITOR INFORMATION CENTRE is at jct. Alaska and Robert Campbell hwys. A DVD presentation explains the history and hardship surrounding the construction of the Alaska Hwy. **Time:** Allow 30 minutes minimum. **Hours:** Daily 8-8, mid-May to mid-Sept.; daily 10-6, early to mid-May and mid- to late Sept. **Cost:** Free. **Phone:** (867) 536-7469.

WHITEHORSE (D-2)
pop. 20,461, elev. 689 m/2,260'

Whitehorse began during the Klondike gold rush when thousands of prospectors journeyed by ship to Skagway, Alaska, then climbed the rugged mountain passes to the headwaters of the Yukon River. They constructed nearly anything floatable for the more than 900-kilometre (559-mi.) trip to Dawson City via Whitehorse. Above Whitehorse many prospectors died in the dangerous Whitehorse Rapids.

When stern-wheeler service to Dawson became available, the trip from Whitehorse took 2.5 days;

the return trip against the current took 5 days. The first rails of the White Pass & Yukon Route were laid at Skagway in May 1898, and the line to Whitehorse opened in July 1900.

During World War II Canadian and United States Army personnel building the Alaska Hwy. moved to Whitehorse, which became the capital of the Yukon Territory in 1953.

Evolving into the transportation, communication and distribution center of the Yukon, Whitehorse also became the territorial headquarters of the Royal Canadian Mounted Police as well as the heart of the territorial government and federal departments.

Attractions on a much larger scale include Lake Laberge, the setting for Robert W. Service's "The Cremation of Sam McGee," and the Robert Lowe Suspension Bridge across Miles Canyon.

The Whitehorse Power Dam features one of the world's longest wooden fish ladders; the salmon, running in late July or early August, can be seen from viewing windows. Lake Schwatka, impounded by the power dam, was named after Frederick Schwatka, the first U.S. army lieutenant to navigate the entire length of the Yukon River.

Visible from the Alaska Hwy., 24 kilometres (15 mi.) south of Whitehorse, is Marsh Lake Lock, the northernmost lock in the Western Hemisphere. It is used by small craft navigating the upper Yukon River.

Guided tours of the town and surrounding area are available through Gray Line/Yukon (see attraction listing). Several companies provide Yukon River cruises, guided hikes, and canoe, boat and raft trips on area rivers. The Yukon Conservation Society gives guided nature walks in the summer.

The Swan Haven Interpretive Centre, on the shores of M'Clintock Bay, affords bird enthusiasts the opportunity to learn about migratory birds, in particular Trumpeter swans. The center is open Mon.-Fri. 5-8 p.m., Sat.-Sun. noon-7, Apr. 1-early May. Phone (867) 667-8291.

Whitehorse Visitor Information Centre, on Second Avenue and Lambert Street, features exhibits and audiovisual presentations about the Yukon. The center is open daily 8-8, mid-May to mid-Sept.; daily 10-6, early to mid-May and mid- to late Sept.; Mon.-Fri. 8:30-noon and 1-5, rest of year. Phone (867) 667-3084.

Whitehorse is the terminus for the 1,000-mile Yukon Quest International Sled Dog Race, which starts in Fairbanks, Alaska, and takes place over a two-week period from early to mid-February.

City of Whitehorse Tourism: 3128 Third Ave., Whitehorse, YT, Canada Y1A 1E7. **Phone:** (867) 668-8687. *See color ad.*

Self-guiding tours: Guidebooks and audio walking tours are available from the Yukon Historical and Museums Association, 3126 Third Ave., P.O. Box 4357, Whitehorse, YT, Canada Y1A 3T5; phone (867) 667-4704.

FRANTIC FOLLIES is presented in the Village Square room of the Westmark Whitehorse Hotel at 201 Wood St. The Gay '90s vaudeville revue has a cast of professional actors, dancers and musicians and recaptures the spirit and enthusiasm of the Klondike gold rush. The 1.7-hour family-style show includes music, comedy, magic, dancing and the poetry of Robert W. Service, Bard of the Yukon.

Hours: Performances are given nightly at 7 and 9:15, June 14-July 25; at 8:30, May 26-June 13 and June 26-Sept. 5. Phone ahead to confirm schedule. **Cost:** $19; $9.50 (ages 0-11). **Phone:** (867) 668-2042.

SAVE **GRAY LINE YUKON WHITEHORSE CITY TOUR** leaves from the Westmark Whitehorse Hotel, 201 Wood St. The narrated tour acquaints visitors with the city by calling upon such landmarks as the stern-wheeler SS *Klondike II*, the Whitehorse Power Dam and the Miles Canyon lookout. Other places of interest include museums, the longest wooden fish ladder in North America and a log skyscraper. **Hours:** Bus tours depart daily at 9, May 22-Sept. 9. **Cost:** Fare $25; $13 (ages 2-12). **Phone:** (867) 668-3225.

MacBRIDE MUSEUM OF YUKON HISTORY is at 1124 First Ave. The museum offers an in-depth look at the Yukon heritage with exhibits ranging from prehistoric mammals to the 1898 gold rush. Displays include Sam McGee's 1899 cabin, First Nations relics and sample minerals of the territory. On the grounds are an old steam locomotive, a sleigh wagon and a giant nugget of copper weighing about 1,170 kilograms (2,580 lbs.).

Hours: Daily 10-6, June 1-Labour Day; daily noon-4, Apr.-May; Mon.-Sat. 10-4, day after Labour Day-Sept. 30; Thurs.-Sat. noon-4, rest of year. **Cost:** $8; $7 (ages 61+); $4 (ages 6-12). **Phone:** (867) 667-2709.

OLD LOG CHURCH MUSEUM is at Third Ave. and Elliott St. Built in 1900, the church houses many missionary, First Nations and Inuit items as well as an audiovisual presentation about the history of the Anglican church in the Yukon. **Tours:** Guided tours are available. **Time:** Allow 30 minutes minimum. **Hours:** Daily 10-6, mid-May through Labour Day. **Cost:** $3; $2.50 (ages 56+ and students with ID); free (ages 0-11); $6 (family). **Phone:** (867) 668-2555.

THE SS *KLONDIKE II* NATIONAL HISTORIC SITE is next to the river at Second Ave. and Robert Campbell Bridge. One of the largest stern-wheelers on the Yukon River, the *Klondike II* ran its route 1937-55. The original *Klondike* struck a reef in 1936; a replacement was built the same year.

Tours are available. A videotape, "In the Days of the Riverboat," is presented prior to each tour. **Time:** Allow 30 minutes minimum. **Hours:** Daily 10-6, mid-May to mid-Sept. Last tour begins 30 minutes before closing. **Cost:** $6; free (ages 0-5). **Phone:** (867) 667-4511.

TAKHINI HOT SPRINGS is 10 km (6 mi.) w. off Klondike Hwy. at Km-post 10. Natural mineral hot spring pools are maintained at 36 degrees C (96.8 degrees F) for year-round swimming. Other activities include horseback riding, hiking, camping, climbing and cross-country skiing. **Hours:** Pool open daily 8 a.m.-10 p.m., July 1 to mid-Sept. **Cost:** $9.50; $7 (ages 65+); $6 (ages 5-18). **Phone:** (867) 633-2706.

WATERFRONT TROLLEY departs northbound from Rotary Peace Park and southbound from Spook Creek Station. Visitors may ride a restored narrow-gauge 1925 trolley originally from Portugal. The bright yellow car seats 24 passengers and travels along the waterfront in downtown Whitehorse, making stops along the way at Rotary Peace Park, the visitor center, White Pass Train Depot, Jarvis Street, Shipyards Park and Kishwoot. The conductor provides narration about the history of the waterfront and the White Pass & Yukon Railroad. **Time:** Allow 1 hour minimum. **Hours:** Trips depart on the hour 9-9 from Rotary Peace Park and on the half-hour 8:30 a.m.-8:55 p.m. from Spook Creek Station, mid-May to mid-Sept. **Cost:** Fare $2; free (ages 0-7). **Phone:** (867) 667-6355.

WHITEHORSE FISHWAY is at the end of Nisutlin Dr. via Lewes Blvd. Said to be the longest wooden fish ladder in the world, the fishway enables chinook salmon and other fish to bypass the Whitehorse Rapids Dam during their 3,000-kilometre (1,860-mi.) migration between the Bering Sea and their freshwater spawning grounds in southern Yukon. Underwater windows provide a close-up view of the migrating fish. **Time:** Allow 30 minutes minimum. **Hours:** Daily 9-9, June 1-early Sept. **Cost:** Donations. **Phone:** (867) 633-5965.

YUKON ARTS CENTRE is at 80 Range Rd. An art gallery features contemporary revolving exhibits and a theater presents concerts, dramas and musicals throughout the year. Phone for schedules and show information. **Time:** Allow 1 hour minimum. **Hours:** Tues.-Fri. noon-6, Sat.-Sun. noon-5. Closed major holidays. **Cost:** Donations. **Phone:** (867) 667-8578.

YUKON BERINGIA INTERPRETIVE CENTRE is 2 km (1.2 mi.) e. on the Alaska Hwy. to Km-post 1473 (mi. 914) by Whitehorse Airport. An area of the Yukon, Alaska and Siberia never covered by glaciers during the ice age, Beringia is believed to be the route traveled by the first people who entered the Americas from Asia.

Fossils, life-size animal and First Nations exhibits, interactive computer kiosks, and murals and dioramas of Beringia's landscape illustrate the area's history, geographical events and culture, from the ice age to the present. Highlights include fossils of woolly mammoths, scimitar cats, giant beavers, short-faced bears and steppe bison. A diorama depicts the Bluefish Caves, an important North American archeological site.

Hours: Daily 8:30-7, June-Aug.; 9-6, in May and Sept. Mon.-Sat. by appointment and Sun. 1-5, rest of year. Phone ahead to confirm schedule. **Cost:** $6; $5 (ages 56+); $25 (family). Combination ticket with Yukon Transportation Museum $9. **Phone:** (867) 667-8855.

YUKON HISTORICAL AND MUSEUMS ASSOCIATION GUIDED TOURS depart from the Donnenworth House, 3126 Third Ave. Guides in period costume describe the architecture, history and local color of Whitehorse on 1-hour walking tours. Historic structures include the 1901 telegraph office, the log church and rectory, the city fire station, the

Klondike Airways building, the Royal Canadian Mounted Police compound, the Mast house and Sam McGee's cabin.

Self-guiding walking tour brochures also are available. **Time:** Allow 1 hour minimum. **Hours:** Tours depart Mon.-Sat. at 9, 11, 1 and 3, June-Aug. **Cost:** $4; free (ages 0-11). Self-guiding walking tour brochure $8.95. **Phone:** (867) 667-4704.

YUKON RIVER CRUISE docks 3.2 km (2 mi.) s. of downtown at 68 Miles Canyon Rd. Two-hour narrated excursions of the Yukon River through Miles Canyon are offered aboard the MV *Schwatka*. The boat passes the remains of a wooden tramway built to carry freight around the rapids, the site of Canyon City and the ruins of the Camp McCrae laundry, which served 30,000 troops stationed nearby during the construction of the Alaska Hwy.

Gray Line/Yukon provides shuttle service to the departure site from downtown hotels. **Hours:** Cruises depart daily at 2 and 7, mid-June to mid-Aug.; at 2, early June to mid-June and mid Aug. to mid-Sept. Hours may vary; phone ahead. Shuttle departs hotels about 30 minutes before cruise time. **Cost:** Cruise fare $30; $15 (ages 6-12). A fee is charged for shuttle. Fare may vary; phone ahead. **Phone:** (867) 668-4716, (867) 668-3225 for the shuttle service, or (866) 417-7365 for reservations.

YUKON TRANSPORTATION MUSEUM is off Alaska Hwy. at Km-post 1475.7 by Whitehorse Airport. Exhibits highlight various modes of transportation, including snowshoes, dog sleds, stage coaches, boats, aircraft and military vehicles used during the construction of the Alaska Hwy. The *Queen of the Yukon*, the sister plane of Charles A. Lindbergh's *Spirit of St. Louis,* also is displayed.

Time: Allow 30 minutes minimum. **Hours:** Daily 10-6, mid-May through Aug. 31. Phone ahead to confirm schedule. **Cost:** $6; $5 (ages 56+); $4 (ages 13-17 and students with ID); $3 (ages 6-12). Combination ticket with Yukon Beringia Interpretive Centre $9. **Phone:** (867) 668-4792.

YUKON WILDLIFE PRESERVE is 40 km (25 mi.) n. on Takhini Hot Springs Rd. Guided 1-hour interpretive tours depart from the log gatehouse every 90 minutes. The more than 283-hectare (700-acre) site is home to 10 major species of Northern mammals, including moose, musk ox, mountain goat and caribou. **Time:** Allow 1 hour minimum. **Hours:** Daily 8-5, June-Sept. **Cost:** $22; $20 (senior citizens); $12 (ages 6-17); $55 (family, two adults and up to three children). **Phone:** (867) 633-2922.

RECREATIONAL ACTIVITIES
White-water Rafting
- **Tatshenshini Expeditions**, 17 Koidern Ave., Whitehorse, YT, Canada Y1A 3N7. **Hours:** Daily mid-June to early Sept. **Phone:** (867) 633-2742.

Alaska

Batter-up at Midnight
Fairbanks hosts late-night baseball as the Arctic Circle is blanketed with continuous sunshine

Dancing Northern Lights
Brilliant bands of yellow, green and red quietly jump across night skies

"The Mountain"
Mount McKinley, North America's tallest mountain, towers over Denali National Park and Preserve

Seward's Folly
Bought at just 2 cents per acre, Alaska surprised the world with its wealth of natural resources

Pacific Ring of Fire
Erupting volcanoes are commonplace in the Valley of Ten Thousand Smokes

Tongass National Forest, south of Juneau
© Mark Conlin
Larry Ulrich Stock

Kodiak Island / © Mark Conlin / Larry Ulrich Stock

While the sights of The Last Frontier can be described as splendid, its sounds are no less spectacular.

A breathy blow accompanied by a geyserlike spray of seawater alerts you to the presence of a humpback whale. It's hard to ignore the loud, slapping sound associated with tail lobbing or breaching—when a whale will throw itself completely out of the water and smack the sea upon return—and it's usually followed by hoots and hollers from observers.

Sea lions make music all their own. Their squawky barking can be heard as you approach a rock packed with the huge creatures.

Drop anchor in ice-filled waters to experience the most spectacular sounds: A popping noise similar to a firecracker

signals a calving, when ice separates from a glacier. As chunks detach and fall, a thunderous roar echoes against the mountains, followed by a crash as they hit the sea. The show ends with the soft hiss of settling water.

Alaskan sounds identify the state's history and culture: Drumbeats, clapping, rattle-shaking, foot-tapping and rhythmic chanting resonate from native performances. A sharp cry of "Mush!" or "All right!" from a musher gets a team of sled dogs moving; a command of "Come gee!" alerts the huskies to a right turn.

And just when a hush falls over The Great Land, the low hum of a floatplane is heard from the clouds, ready to take you to another adventure.

Totem poles—slender cedar logs with intricately carved and brightly painted bears, eagles, fish, whales, ravens or frogs—are true artistic works representing the history and customs of native Alaskans. Features of these poles give insight to the blessings of the 49th state.

When visiting Alaska, a stop at a totem pole park should be high on your list of things to do. To get the full effect, choose a tall, colorful totem and stand about 2 feet from it. After admiring the details, look up. Your first impression? Massive. At 85 feet tall and too big to hug, you may have to step back just to be able to catch a glimpse of the figure at the top of the pole. A glance at an Alaska state map also may elicit amazement—it's *huge,* and there's much to see and do.

Natives didn't call this state *Alyeska*—the Great Land—for nothing. It looms larger than life. There are approximately 3 million lakes, 3,000 rivers, 1,800 islands and 100,000 glaciers in Alaska's 586,000 square miles of untamed wilderness. And if that isn't enough, nine national parks and preserves and two expansive national forests total about 66 million acres of undisturbed land. Don't be upset when you find that little of this grandiose scenery fits nicely into your camera lens.

Tales from The Last Frontier

When examined in sequence, the array of symbolic figures on totem poles describe native tales. Likewise, Alaska's diversity is illustrated through its distinct natural features, which leave most anyone speechless. The state is home to towering Mount McKinley—so high that it's cloaked in clouds most of the time. Long, bright days are typical during the summer solstice, when the sun accompanies your every move and never completely disappears.

Options for excitement in The Land of the Midnight Sun seem endless. You can walk on an ice field and feel the crunch of ice under your boots; explore muted, willow-covered desert tundra; peer over chunky glaciers and sweeping mountain ranges from the seat of a helicopter; gaze at a sky painted with water-colored northern lights; enjoy a ride on a boat navigating through blue-green waters packed with bobbing icebergs; marvel at 25-foot-tall sand dunes; or board a bush plane to catch a glimpse of steam from an active volcano.

Library of Congress

U.S. Secretary of State William H. Seward purchases Alaska from Russia for less than 2 cents per acre; the unpopular deal becomes known as "Seward's Folly."

1867

Russian explorer Vitus Bering, sent by Peter the Great to explore the North Pacific, is the first European to set foot on Alaskan soil.

1725

A submarine cable links Seattle to Sitka and Sitka to Valdez, increasing communication between Alaska and the rest of the world.

1903

1880
"**S**eward's Folly" becomes a gold mine as vast deposits of precious metals are discovered in Juneau, followed by discoveries in Skagway in 1897, Nome in 1898 and Fairbanks in 1903.

Alaska Historical Timeline

Ernst Schneider/Alaska Dept. of Commerce

1942
Japan attacks Dutch Harbor and consequently occupies the Aleutian Islands for nearly a year during World War II.

Tribe members, ingenious at adapting to their variable and sometimes hostile surroundings, made the most of the state's natural offerings, which included the creatures portrayed in their art.

Salmon and orcas are just a couple of animals that appear on totems. Used for sustenance, they were often depicted in oral tales; today animals remain the focus of many pictures and the subjects of travelogues. Visitors relish the opportunity to snap a photograph of a moose cow nibbling grass alongside her twins or grizzly cubs wrestling under the protective watch of mama bear.

Affluent Alaska

For many residents Alaska's riches are liquid: The creation of the Trans-Alaska Pipeline made it possible to transport crude oil almost 800 miles from Prudhoe Bay south to Valdez. The pipeline, an amazing engineering feat crossing three mountain ranges and three fault lines, is able to withstand an earthquake measuring up to 8.5 on the Richter scale as well as temperatures as low as minus 80 F.

Oil isn't Alaska's only rich resource. Discoveries of gold in Fairbanks, Fort Yukon, Juneau, Nome, Skagway and Wrangell lured prospectors from the "Lower 48" to seek their fortune. Visit abandoned gold dredges, camps and mines scattered throughout the state and imagine the fervor that once pervaded these sites, many of which now serve as attractions.

And there was more money to be made. Russian trappers came in search of valuable sea otter pelts, placing the term "fur trade" in Alaskan history books. The first capital of Russian America, Kodiak is graced by the onion-shaped domes of a historic Russian Orthodox church.

But Alaska's native tribes have left the most enduring impact. Traditions of the Aleut, Alutiiq, Athabascan, Cup'ik, Haida, Inupiaq, Tlingit, Tsimshian and Yup'ik tribes can be appreciated through the acts of proud dancers and storytellers who keep family legacies alive. And artisans create soapstone and whalebone carvings, clothing adorned with intricate beading and baskets made from white birch bark—all coveted by visitors.

And totem poles, Alaska's silent, symbolic sentries, are just one reminder of what makes this land truly great.

A Good Friday earthquake destroys Anchorage, the Northwest Panhandle and Cook Inlet and sends a tsunami that wipes out the town of Valdez.
1964

International efforts to rescue two whales trapped in ice off the Barrow coast captures worldwide attention.
1988

Alaska Gov. Sarah Palin is the first woman to be on a Republican presidential ticket after Sen. John McCain names her his running mate for the 2008 presidential election.
2008

Alaska Dept. of Commerce

Alaska Dept. of Commerce

1968
"Black Gold" is discovered on Prudhoe Bay, spurring the construction of an 800-mile pipeline to transport the oil to an ice-free port at Valdez.

1989
The worst oil spill in U.S. history occurs when the *Exxon Valdez* spills some 11 million gallons of crude oil into Prince William Sound.

1977
Construction of the Trans-Alaska Pipeline is complete.

Recreation

In the Land of the Midnight Sun, it's a far better idea to set your itinerary by "sight" rather than time. While there are lots of activities to keep your blood pumping, most people visit Alaska for what there is to *see:* Chances for **wildlife viewing** are as plentiful as snowflakes during winter.

Oh, *Another* Bald Eagle?

This phrase, overheard on a small boat weaving through the watery inlets of the Tongass National Forest, testifies to the fact that Alaska has one of the largest bald eagle populations in the world. If you know what to look for—white dots on dark spruce tree branches—you may lose count of all these stately birds. They aren't difficult to spot at the Chilkat Bald Eagle Preserve near Haines; more than 3,500 visit the area to feed from October to February.

Many **wildlife cruises** headed for the Inside Passage depart from Juneau. Arm yourself with some good binoculars, a camera and a journal to record your sightings. Entries might include descriptions of huge, barking Steller sea lions lounging on top of each other; Dall's porpoises frolicking in a boat's wake; Sitka black- or white-tailed deer sipping from a stream; soaring peregrine falcons; or furry otters doing the backstroke.

Black bears fish for salmon in Anan Creek near Wrangell Island, and the west coast of Prince of Wales Island (near Ketchikan) is a great spot for watching tufted puffins. It's no "fluke" to see a whale tail—humpbacks often make appearances in Prince William Sound, and wherever there's an iceberg, you can be sure to find harbor seals resting upon floating ice chunks.

Day cruises depart from Seward and Whittier to explore Prince William Sound and Kenai Fjords National Park, home to sea mammals galore. Along the Kenai Peninsula, both humpback and beluga whales perform aquatic acrobatics near the Turnagain Arm. Nearby, Dall sheep can be seen grazing atop steep cliffs that grace Cook Inlet.

Looking for bears? The Kodiak National Wildlife Refuge is home to some 2,300 Kodiak bears, and Brooks Camp in Katmai National Park and Preserve safeguards one of the world's largest brown bear populations.

Grizzlies as well as caribou and moose roam the desertlike tundra of Denali National Park and Preserve; take a narrated bus tour into the interior to catch a glimpse. Near the park entrance, forest rangers give a demonstration of sled dogs at work, which is a howling good show. Even better, hang on tight for a **sled ride** pulled by Iditarod huskies in Seward.

And a View, Too

Seward Highway, connecting Seward and Anchorage, is Alaska's most traveled scenic byway, and it's easy to see why. Snaking along the coast of Turnagain Arm, scenes from the road include the lush Kenai Mountains, saltwater bays, jagged ridges and green alpine meadows. **Rock climbers** dangle from cliffs between Potters Marsh and Bird Creek.

As a matter of fact, any activity in Alaska includes a magnificent view: Try **rafting** in Denali on the Nenana River Gorge or **canoeing** near Admiralty Island National Monument. **Kayakers** also enjoy the Sarkar Lake Canoe Route in Tongass National Forest. Winter options include **cross-country skiing, dog sledding** or **snowmobiling** on the Twin Ridge or Upper Twin ski trails in Tongass National Forest, or **downhill skiing** at Mount Alyeska in Girdwood.

Want to stand on a glacier? **Hikers** in Kenai Fjords National Park follow rangers on **nature walks** to a nearby ice field. For a bit of history, try **bicycling** or **walking** the first mile of the original Iditarod Trail, now a paved beach path in Seward. Horseshoe Lake Trail provides a leisurely 1.5-mile walk through the woods of Denali National Park and Preserve.

Floatplane or **helicopter sightseeing** is an excellent way to see glaciers, ice fields, mountain ranges, waterfalls, lakes or stark tundra. Nearly every city has **flightseeing** tour operators.

A **fishing** charter from one of various harbors is a good way to hook steelhead, grayling or rainbow trout. **Sport fishing** yields red snapper or cod—and Resurrection Bay (near Seward), Sitka and Wrangell are home to world-class halibut and salmon.

Recreational Activities

Throughout the TourBook, you may notice a Recreational Activities heading with bulleted listings of recreation-oriented establishments listed underneath. Similar operations also may be mentioned in Destination City recreation sections. Since normal AAA inspection criteria cannot be applied, these establishments are presented only for information. Age, height and weight restrictions may apply. Reservations often are recommended and sometimes are required. Addresses and/or phone numbers are provided so visitors can contact the attraction for additional information.

Fast Facts

POPULATION: 626,932.

AREA: 586,412 square miles; ranks 1st.

CAPITAL: Juneau.

HIGHEST POINT: 20,320 ft., Mount McKinley.

LOWEST POINT: Sea level, Pacific Ocean.

TIME ZONE(S): Alaska for most of the state; Hawaii-Aleutian for the extreme western portion of the Aleutian Islands. DST.

TEEN DRIVING LAWS: Driving is not permitted 1 a.m.-5 a.m. No passengers, with the exception of family members, are permitted for the first 6 months. The minimum age for an unrestricted driver's license is 16 years and 6 months.

SEAT BELT/CHILD RESTRAINT LAWS: Seat belts are required for driver and all passengers 16 and older. Children ages 8 through 16 are required to be in a child restraint or seat belt; child restraints are required for children under the age of 8 unless at least 4 feet, 9 inches tall or weighing more than 65 pounds.

CELL PHONE RESTRICTIONS: All drivers are prohibited from text messaging while driving.

HELMETS FOR MOTORCYCLISTS: Required for drivers under 18 years old and all passengers.

RADAR DETECTORS: Permitted.

MOVE OVER LAW: Driver is required to slow down and vacate the lane nearest stopped police, fire and rescue vehicles using audible or flashing signals.

FIREARMS LAWS: Vary by state and/or county. Contact the Division of State Troopers, Headquarters, 5700 E. Tudor Rd., Dept. P, Anchorage, AK 99507; phone (907) 269-5511.

HOLIDAYS: Jan. 1; Martin Luther King Jr. Day, Jan. (3rd Mon.); Presidents Day, Feb. (3rd Mon.); Seward's Day, Mar. (last Mon.); Memorial Day, May (last Mon.); July 4; Labor Day, Sept. (1st Mon.); Columbus Day, Oct. (2nd Mon.); Alaska Day, Oct. 18; Veterans Day, Nov. 11; Thanksgiving; Christmas, Dec. 25.

TAXES: Alaska does not have a statewide sales tax, but cities and boroughs may levy a sales tax of up to 7 percent, plus special taxes on goods and services. A 10 percent tax is levied on rental cars.

INFORMATION CENTERS: Tourist literature and reports on highway and weather conditions are available at the Log Cabin Visitor Information Center, jct. F St. and 4th Ave. in Anchorage; the Fairbanks Visitor Information Center, 101 Dunkel St. in Fairbanks; the Southeast Alaska Discovery Center, 50 Main St. in Ketchikan; and the Tok Information Center, jct. SR 2 (Alaska Hwy.) and SR 1 in Tok.

FURTHER INFORMATION FOR VISITORS:
Alaska Travel Industry Association
2600 Cordova St., Suite 201
Anchorage, AK 99503
(907) 929-2842

FISHING AND HUNTING REGULATIONS:
Alaska Department of Fish and Game
1255 W. 8th St.
P.O. Box 115526
Juneau, AK 99811-5526
(907) 465-4180 (Division of Sport Fishing)
(907) 465-4190 (Division of Wildlife
Conservation)

ALASKA FERRY INFORMATION:
Alaska Marine Highway
6858 Glacier Hwy.
P.O. Box 112505
Juneau, AK 99811-2505
(907) 465-3941
(800) 642-0066

NATIONAL FOREST INFORMATION:
U.S. Forest Service
P.O. Box 21628
Juneau, AK 99802
(907) 586-8800
(877) 444-6777 (reservations)
TTY (907) 790-7444

NATIONAL PARK INFORMATION:
Alaska Public Lands Information Center
101 Dunkel St., Suite 110
Fairbanks, AK 99701
(907) 459-3730
(866) 869-6887
TTY (907) 456-0532

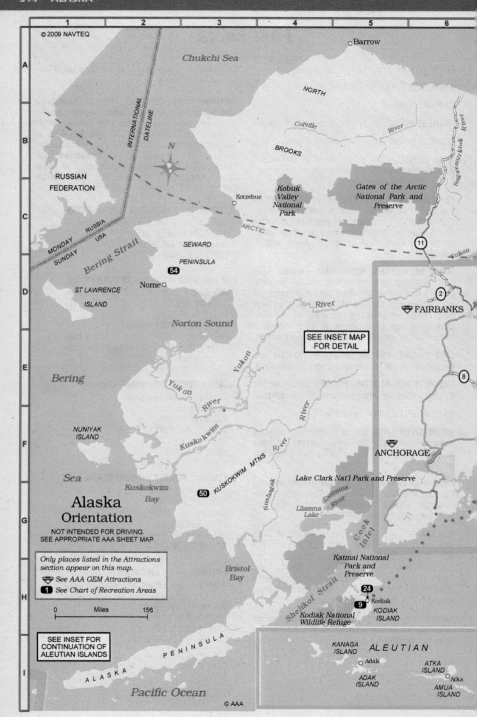

© 2009 NAVTEQ

Chukchi Sea

Barrow

NORTH

Colville

River

BROOKS

Kobuk Valley National Park

Gates of the Arctic National Park and Preserve

RUSSIAN FEDERATION

Kotzebue

ARCTIC

MONDAY RUSSIA USA SUNDAY

Bering Strait

SEWARD PENINSULA

54

ST LAWRENCE ISLAND

Nome

Norton Sound

11

Yukon

2 ▽ FAIRBANKS

Bering

Yukon River

River

SEE INSET MAP FOR DETAIL

8

Yukon River

Sea

NUNIYAK ISLAND

Kuskokwim River

KUSKOKWIM MTNS

50

Nushagak River

▽ ANCHORAGE

Lake Clark Nat'l Park and Preserve

Kuskokwim Bay

Lliamna Lake Dumina River

Cook Inlet

Alaska
Orientation

NOT INTENDED FOR DRIVING.
SEE APPROPRIATE AAA SHEET MAP.

Only places listed in the Attractions section appear on this map.
▽ See AAA GEM Attractions
❶ See Chart of Recreation Areas

Bristol Bay

Katmai National Park and Preserve

24

9 Kodiak

Shelikof Strait

Kodiak National Wildlife Refuge

KODIAK ISLAND

0   Miles   156

SEE INSET FOR CONTINUATION OF ALEUTIAN ISLANDS

PENINSULA

ALASKA

Pacific Ocean

© AAA

KANAGA ISLAND

ALEUTIAN

Adak

ADAK ISLAND

ATKA ISLAND

Atka

AMUA ISLAND

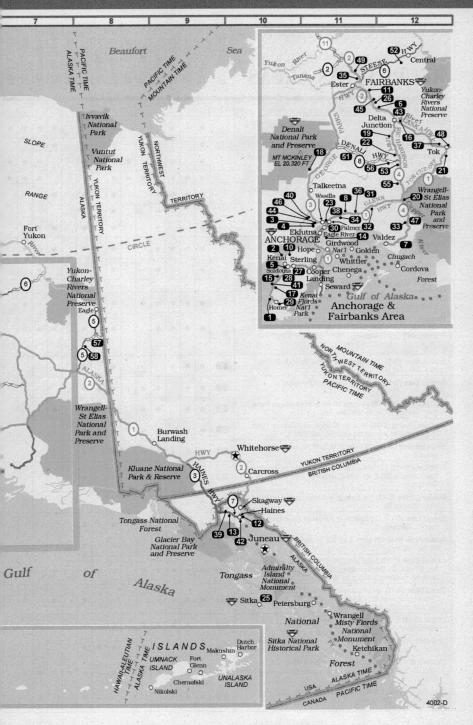

Anchorage & Fairbanks Area

RECREATION AREAS

	MAP LOCATION	CAMPING	PICNICKING	HIKING TRAILS	BOATING	BOAT RAMP	BOAT RENTAL	FISHING	SWIMMING	PETS ON LEASH	BICYCLE TRAILS	WINTER SPORTS	VISITOR CENTER	LODGE/CABINS	FOOD SERVICE
NATIONAL PARKS AND PRESERVES (See place listings)															
Denali (B-10) 6,028,203 acres. Cross-country skiing, dog mushing, snowmobiling, snowshoeing.		•	•	•				•		•		•	•	•	•
Gates of the Arctic (C-6) 8,500,000 acres. Bird watching.		•			•			•					•	•	
Glacier Bay (G-9) 3,283,168 acres. Bird watching, hunting, kayaking, rafting.		•		•	•	•	•	•		•			•	•	•
Katmai (G-5) 4,159,097 acres. Canoeing, hunting, kayaking.		•	•	•	•	•	•	•					•	•	•
Kenai Fjords (D-11) 600,000 acres. Cross-country skiing, kayaking, snowmobiling.		•	•	•				•		•			•	•	
Kobuk Valley (C-5) 1,710,000 acres. Sand dunes.		•		•	•			•							
Lake Clark (F-5) 4,000,000 acres. Bird watching, hunting, kayaking, rafting.		•						•		•				•	
Wrangell-St. Elias (C-12, F-8) 3,000,000 acres. Hunting, sea kayaking; all-terrain vehicle trails.		•	•	•				•		•				•	
Yukon-Charley Rivers (B-12, D-8) 500,000 acres. Historic. Hunting.		•		•										•	
NATIONAL FORESTS (See place listings)															
Chugach (D-12) 5,500,000 acres in south-central Alaska. Cross-country skiing, hunting, snowboarding, snowmobiling.		•	•	•	•	•		•		•	•	•	•	•	
Tongass (G-9) 17,000,000 acres in southeastern Alaska. Canoeing, cross-country and downhill skiing, ice skating, kayaking, snowboarding, snowmobiling.		•	•	•	•			•		•			•	•	
STATE															
Anchor River (D-10) 264 acres near Anchor Point on Sterling Hwy., Milepost 157.	**1**	•	•	•				•		•					
Bernice Lake (C-10) 152 acres 10 mi. n. of Kenai on N. Kenai Rd.	**2**	•	•		•	•		•	•	•					
Big Lake (North) (C-10) 19 acres 10 mi. w. of Wasilla on Parks Hwy., then 6 mi. s.w. on Big Lake Rd.	**3**	•	•		•	•		•	•	•					
Big Lake (South) (C-10) 16 acres 10 mi. w. of Wasilla on Parks Hwy., then 4 mi. s.w. on Big Lake Rd. and 2 mi. s.	**4**	•	•		•	•		•	•	•					
Bings Landing (D-10) 126 acres e. of Soldotna on Sterling Hwy., Milepost 79.	**5**	•	•	•	•	•		•	•	•					
Birch Lake (B-12) 191 acres n.e. of Delta Junction on Richardson Hwy., Milepost 305.5. Ice fishing, jet skiing, water skiing; ice fishing huts.	**6**	•	•		•	•		•	•	•					
Blueberry Lake (C-12) 192 acres e. of Valdez on Richardson Hwy., Milepost 23.	**7**	•	•					•	•						
Bonnie Lake (C-11) 129 acres e. of Palmer on Glenn Hwy., Milepost 83. Canoeing.	**8**	•			•	•		•	•	•					
Buskin River (H-5) 168 acres 4 mi. s.e. on Base-Town Rd. in Kodiak. Historic.	**9**	•	•	•				•		•					
Captain Cook (C-10) 3,466 acres 24 mi. n. of Kenai on N. Kenai Rd., Milepost 36. Beachcombing, berry picking (in season), bird watching, canoeing, hunting, ice fishing.	**10**	•	•	•	•	•		•	•	•			•		
Chena River (A-12) 254,000 acres 27 mi. e. of Fairbanks on Chena Hot Springs Rd. Canoeing, cross-country skiing, kayaking, rock climbing, snowmobiling.	**11**	•	•	•	•			•		•			•		•
Chilkat (G-10) 9,837 acres 7 mi. s. of Haines on Haines Hwy.	**12**	•	•	•	•			•		•				•	
Chilkoot Lake (G-10) 80 acres 11 mi. n. of Haines on Lutak Rd., Milepost 10.	**13**	•	•		•	•		•	•	•					
Chugach (C-11) 495,204 acres just e. of Eagle River on Glenn Hwy. Numerous access points. Rafting; horse rental. (See Eagle River p. 333)	**14**	•	•	•	•	•		•		•		•	•	•	•
Clam Gulch (D-10) 129 acres s. of Soldotna on Sterling Hwy., Milepost 117. Clam digging.	**15**	•	•					•		•					

RECREATION AREAS

Area	Map Location	Camping	Picnicking	Hiking Trails	Boating	Boat Ramp	Boat Rental	Fishing	Swimming	Pets on Leash	Bicycle Trails	Winter Sports	Visitor Center	Lodge/Cabins	Food Service
Clearwater (B-12) 27 acres 11 mi. s.e. of Delta Junction on Alaska Hwy., Milepost 1415, then 8 mi. n.e. on side road.	16	•			•	•		•		•					
Deep Creek (D-10) 155 acres near Ninilchik on Sterling Hwy., Milepost 137.3. Bird watching, clam digging.	17	•	•		•	•		•		•					
Denali (B-11) 324,240 acres n. of Talkeetna on Parks Hwy., Milepost 135-164.	18	•	•	•	•	•		•		•					
Donnelly Creek (B-11) 42 acres s. of Delta Junction on Richardson Hwy., Milepost 238.	19	•	•					•		•					
Dry Creek (C-12) 372 acres n. of Glennallen on Richardson Hwy., Milepost 117.5.	20	•	•					•		•					
Eagle Trail (B-12) 280 acres 16 mi. s. of Tok on Tok Cut-off, Milepost 109.5.	21	•	•	•						•					
Fielding Lake (B-11) 300 acres s. of Delta Junction on Richardson Hwy., Milepost 201.	22	•			•	•		•		•					
Finger Lake (C-11) 47 acres 4 mi. w. of Palmer on Palmer-Wasilla Rd., then 1 mi. n. and .5 mi. w.	23	•	•	•	•	•		•	•	•			•		
Fort Abercrombie (H-5) 183 acres 4.5 mi. s.e. of Kodiak on Miller Point. Historic. *(See Kodiak p. 349)*	24	•	•	•				•		•			•		
Halibut Point (H-10) 40 acres 4 mi. n.e. of Sitka on Halibut Rd. Beachcombing.	25		•	•				•		•					
Harding Lake (A-12) 169 acres .5 mi. n.e. from Milepost 321 on the Richardson Hwy. Canoeing, jet skiing.	26	•	•		•	•		•	•	•		•			
Izaak Walton (D-10) 8 acres e. of Soldotna off Glenn Hwy.	27	•	•		•			•		•					
Johnson Lake (D-10) 332 acres 16 mi. s. of Soldotna on Glenn Hwy.	28	•	•		•	•		•	•	•					
Kachemak Bay (D-10) 368,290 acres near Seldovia, at the end of Sterling Hwy., then by boat or plane across Kachemak Bay. Bird watching, kayaking.	29	•	•	•	•			•		•				•	
Kepler-Bradley Lakes (C-11) 344 acres e. of Palmer on Glenn Hwy., Milepost 36.4.	30		•	•				•		•					
Lake Louise (C-11) 90 acres n.w. of Glennallen on Glenn Hwy., Milepost 160.	31	•			•	•		•		•		•			
Little Nelchina (C-11) 22 acres s.e. of Glennallen on Glenn Hwy., Milepost 137.4.	32	•		•	•			•		•					
Little Tonsina (C-12) 103 acres near Copper Center on Richardson Hwy., Milepost 65.	33	•						•		•					
Long Lake (C-11) 480 acres 7 mi. e. of Sutton on Glenn Hwy.	34	•	•		•	•		•	•	•					
Lower Chatanika River (A-11) 120 acres n.w. of Fairbanks off SR 2, Milepost 9.	35	•	•		•	•		•		•					
Matanuska Glacier (C-11) 229 acres e. of Palmer on Glenn Hwy., Milepost 101.	36	•	•	•						•					
Moon Lake (B-12) 22 acres 18 mi. w. of Tok on Alaska Hwy., near Milepost 1332. Water skiing.	37	•	•		•			•	•	•					
Moose Creek (C-11) 40 acres near Palmer on Glenn Hwy., Milepost 54.4.	38	•	•	•						•					
Mosquito Lake (G-9) 10 acres 27.5 mi. w. of Haines on Haines Hwy., then 2.5 mi. on Mosquito Lake Rd.	39	•	•		•	•		•	•	•			•		
Nancy Lake, South (C-10) 22,685 acres 3.5 mi. s. of Willow on Parks Hwy., then 7 mi. w. on side road.	40	•	•	•	•	•		•		•			•	•	
Ninilchik (D-10) 97 acres n. of Homer on Sterling Hwy., Milepost 135. Clam digging.	41	•	•					•		•					
Portage Cove (G-10) 7 acres s. of Haines at 1 Beach Rd.	42	•	•					•		•					
Quartz Lake (B-12) 600 acres 2 mi. n.w. of Delta Junction on Alaska Hwy.	43	•	•		•	•		•	•	•		•		•	•
Rocky Lake (C-10) 48 acres 28 mi. w. of Palmer via Wasilla off Parks Hwy. at Milepost 3.5 of Big Lake Rd.	44	•	•		•	•		•		•					

RECREATION AREAS

	MAP LOCATION	CAMPING	PICNICKING	HIKING TRAILS	BOATING	BOAT RAMP	BOAT RENTAL	FISHING	SWIMMING	PETS ON LEASH	BICYCLE TRAILS	WINTER SPORTS	VISITOR CENTER	LODGE/CABINS	FOOD SERVICE
Salcha River (B-11) 61 acres s.e. of North Pole on Alaska Hwy., Milepost 323. Canoeing.	45	•	•		•	•		•		•				•	
South Rolly Lake (C-10) 200 acres just w. of Wasilla off Parks Hwy. at Milepost 6.5 of Nancy Lake Pkwy.	46	•	•		•	•		•	•	•			•		
Squirrel Creek (C-12) 350 acres near Copper Center on Richardson Hwy., Milepost 79.5.	47	•	•					•		•					
Tok River (B-12) 9 acres 5 mi. e. of Tok Junction on Alaska Hwy., Milepost 1309.	48	•			•	•		•	•	•			•		
Upper Chatanika River (A-11) 73 acres n.e. of Fairbanks off Steese Hwy.	49	•	•					•		•					
Wood-Tikchik (G-3) 1,600,000 acres n. of Dillingham.	50	•			•			•							
OTHER															
Brushkana (B-11) 15 acres 30 mi. e. of Cantwell on Denali Hwy., Milepost 104.	51	•	•					•		•					
Cripple Creek (A-12) 5 acres 50 mi. n.e. of Fairbanks on Steese Hwy., Milepost 60.	52	•	•					•		•					
Paxson Lake (B-12) 80 acres 10 mi. s. of Paxson on Richardson Hwy., Milepost 175.	53	•			•	•		•		•					
Salmon Lake (D-2) 20 acres 40 mi. n. of Nome.	54	•	•		•	•		•		•					
Sourdough (C-12) 140 acres 35 mi. n. of Glennallen on the Richardson Hwy., Milepost 148.	55	•	•		•	•		•		•					
Tangle Lakes (B-11) 100 acres 22 mi. w. of Paxson on Denali Hwy., Milepost 22.	56	•	•		•	•		•		•					
Walker Fork (E-8) 10 acres 80 mi. n.e. of Tok on Taylor Hwy., Milepost 82.	57	•	•	•				•		•					
West Fork (E-8) 10 acres 65 mi. n.e. of Tok on Taylor Hwy., Milepost 49.	58	•						•		•					

Alaska Temperature Averages
Maximum/Minimum (Fahrenheit)
From the records of The Weather Channel Interactive, Inc.

	JAN	FEB	MAR	APR	MAY	JUNE	JULY	AUG	SEPT	OCT	NOV	DEC
Anchorage	22 / 9	26 / 12	34 / 18	44 / 29	55 / 39	62 / 47	65 / 52	63 / 49	55 / 41	40 / 28	28 / 16	24 / 11
Barrow	-8 / -20	-10 / -22	-7 / -20	6 / -7	25 / 15	40 / 30	47 / 34	44 / 34	35 / 28	19 / 10	5 / -6	-5 / -16
Fairbanks	2 / -13	10 / -10	26 / 1	44 / 19	61 / 35	71 / 47	73 / 50	67 / 45	55 / 34	32 / 16	12 / -2	5 / -9
Juneau	31 / 21	34 / 24	39 / 28	48 / 33	56 / 40	62 / 46	64 / 49	63 / 48	56 / 44	47 / 38	38 / 29	33 / 24
Kotzebue	4 / -9	3 / -10	7 / -8	20 / 3	38 / 25	51 / 39	60 / 49	57 / 47	46 / 37	28 / 19	13 / 3	6 / -6
Nome	13 / -2	14 / -2	18 / 1	27 / 12	43 / 31	54 / 41	59 / 47	56 / 45	49 / 37	34 / 23	23 / 11	16 / 1

Points of Interest

ADMIRALTY ISLAND NATIONAL MONUMENT (H-10)

Accessible by floatplane from Juneau and Sitka or via ferries of the Alaska Marine Highway to Angoon, Admiralty Island is part of Tongass National Forest *(see place listing p. 360)*. Between the rocky beaches and high mountain peaks lie a million acres of coastal rain forests, freshwater lakes and streams, alpine meadows and dense thickets of wild currants and other berries.

Alaskan brown bears outnumber human beings, and the greatest concentration of bald eagles in North America nests along the coast. Beavers, martens, minks, river otters, Sitka black-tailed deer and weasels share the island with Vancouver Canada geese and trumpeter and whistling swans. Offshore are harbor seals, sea lions and whales.

Alaska
You know you want to

So what are you waiting for? AAA members save 10% on Alaska Railroad Vacation packages.

1-800-544-0552 • (907) 265-2494

AlaskaRailroad.com

Motorboating and sea kayaking are popular in protected saltwater bays, and a canoe portage trail connects nine interior lakes to bays on the east and west shores. Rustic cabins can be reserved, and campsites and open shelters are available on a first-come-first-served basis. Most of the island is a wilderness area; be prepared for rain and follow no-trace camping practices.

For more information write the U.S. Forest Service *(see Fast Facts)*, or phone (907) 586-8800 or TTY (907) 790-7444.

ANCHORAGE (C-10, F-5)
pop. 260,283, elev. 118′

Anchorage, on a high bluff enfolded by the two branches of Cook Inlet, lies as far west as the Hawaiian Islands and as far north as Helsinki, Finland. The tides in the inlet rise from 30 to 33 feet, and the surrounding mountains loom several thousand feet overhead. The protective mountain barrier and the proximity of the ocean afford Anchorage a surprisingly moderate climate, relative to most of Alaska.

Anchorage is Alaska's largest city and is home to almost half of the state's residents. While not a dazzling metropolis, each summer the city is beautifully decorated with almost 100,000 hanging flower baskets brimming with brightly-colored blooms.

Established in 1915 as the construction headquarters for the Alaska Railroad *(see attraction listing)*, it is the transportation and business center of south-central Alaska and a major winter recreation area. Anchorage's heritage as a road town is recalled by a number of historic buildings, notably the Pioneer Schoolhouse in Ben Crawford Memorial Park and two nearby one-room log cabins. As well, landmarks denote both Russian and American Indian heritage.

Anchorage suffered from the effects of the 1964 Good Friday earthquake, one of the strongest in history, which destroyed much of downtown. Earthquake Park, at the west end of Northern Lights Boulevard, has a walking trail and interpretive signs that provide information about the massive temblor. The park also provides a stunning vista of Cook Inlet.

The dramatic beauty of the nearby mountains, inlets and glaciers offers an easily accessible sampling

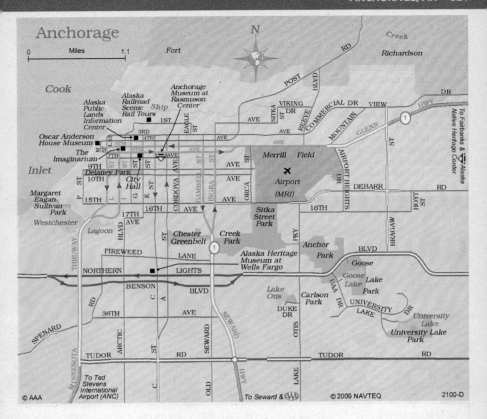

Anchorage

Miles

0   1.1

of Alaska's natural splendors. Two roads affording beautiful views link to Anchorage; scenic SR 1/9 extends south to Seward, and SR 1 extends north to Glennallen.

From Anchorage visitors also can take various sightseeing tours of the area, including the Kenai Peninsula and places of interest inaccessible by road. Trolley, flightseeing and other types of tours given by Anchorage City Trolley Tours depart daily May through September from 612 W. Fourth Ave. between F and G streets; phone (907) 276-5603. Among the more novel sightseeing trips are dog sled tours, which leave from the Alyeska Resort and Ski Area (see Girdwood p. 339) December through March.

The Park Connection offers twice-daily shuttle service from Anchorage to Denali National Park and Preserve and Seward mid-May to mid-September; phone (907) 344-8775.

One-hour float trips on the Matanuska River depart by van from Anchorage to the launch point. Panning for gold is available an hour from downtown. For a different perspective, try flightseeing—operators can be found at the airport and Lake Hood.

SAVE Gray Line of Alaska (see color ad p. 325 & p. 336) and Princess Tours offer a float adventure on Eagle River; tours to Barrow, Juneau, Kodiak Island,

Kotzebue, Matanuska Valley, Nome, Portage Glacier and Prudhoe Bay; fishing on the Kenai River; cruises on Prince William Sound to Columbia Glacier; and a city tour of Anchorage.

These agencies also offer 2-, 3- and 4-day round trips between Anchorage and Denali National Park and Preserve. The trips include travel in railway cars equipped with glass ceiling panels. These same three companies also offer longer excursions to the interior and cruises up the Inside Passage.

The Alaska Center for the Performing Arts Discovery Theatre, at 621 W. 6th Ave., presents a 40-minute, large-screen slide show called "AurorA" that displays a series of stunning images of the aurora borealis synchronized to classical music. Shows are offered daily late May through August; phone (907) 263-2900, or (907) 263-2787 for tickets.

Anchorage serves as the starting line for the 1,049-mile Iditarod Trail Race, which begins the first Saturday in March. The actual mileage of the race is 1,161 miles; however, 1,049 is often used as a symbolic figure because the distance is always more than 1,000 miles, and 49 was added to signify Alaska's rank as the 49th state. Dogs and mushers travel over the Alaska Range and across frozen Norton Bay, arriving in Nome nearly 2 weeks later.

The Bear & Raven Adventure Theater, 315 E St., offers "The Amazing Trail," a 30-minute multimedia presentation relating the history of the Iditarod race, which draws its inspiration from the mushers and nearly 150 sled dogs that delivered a diphtheria serum through blizzard conditions and nearly 700 miles away to Nome in 1925. Interactive sledding, ballooning and fishing exhibits interpret the trail experience, provide aerial views of the city and allow visitors to simulate the angling of a king salmon. The 15-minute "Those Amazing Bears" film includes footage of grizzly bears interacting with nature. The theater is open mid-May to mid-September as well as during the Iditarod; phone (907) 277-4545 for tickets.

Anchorage Convention and Visitors Bureau: 524 W. Fourth Ave., Anchorage, AK 99501-2212. **Phone:** (907) 276-4118, or (800) 478-1255 to request a visitors guide.

Self-guiding tours: A guide outlining a walking tour and driving tours north and south of the city is available at Log Cabin Visitor Information Center, Fourth Avenue and F Street; phone (907) 274-3531.

26 GLACIER CRUISE BY PHILLIPS CRUISES— *see Whittier p. 363.*

ALASKA AVIATION HERITAGE MUSEUM, on Lake Hood at 4721 Aircraft Dr., displays 24 vintage

aircraft and a flight simulator. Visitors also can observe restorations in progress. Memorabilia and photographs chronicle the history of civilian and military aviation in Alaska; films are shown continuously. **Time:** Allow 30 minutes minimum. **Hours:** Daily 9-5, mid-May to mid-Sept.; Wed.-Sun. 9-5, rest of year. Closed major holidays in winter. **Cost:** $10; $8 (ages 12-18 and 65+); $6 (ages 5-12); free (active military and veterans with ID). **Phone:** (907) 248-5325.

ALASKA BOTANICAL GARDEN is 3 mi. e. of New Seward Hwy. on Tudor Rd., then just s. to 4601 Campbell Airstrip Rd. Arctic horticulture is showcased in a 110-acre birch and spruce woodland replete with more than 1,100 varieties of perennials, 150 species of native Alaskan plants as well as herb and alpine rock gardens. The park includes a wildflower walk, a 1-mile interpretive nature trail and a creek where salmon spawn in the summer. The peak blooming season commences in late May and culminates in mid-September, occasionally lasting into October.

Time: Allow 1 hour, 30 minutes minimum. **Hours:** Daily 9-9. **Cost:** $5; $10 (family). **Phone:** (907) 770-3692.

ALASKA HERITAGE MUSEUM AT WELLS FARGO, at Northern Lights Blvd. and C St. in the Wells Fargo Bank Building, displays more than 900 Eskimo and other native artifacts, an extensive collection of walrus ivory carvings, traditional clothing

and paintings by Alaskan artists. The collection also includes a two-third scale stagecoach from the Gold Rush era. **Time:** Allow 30 minutes minimum. **Hours:** Mon.-Fri. noon-5 in summer; noon-4, rest of year. **Cost:** Free. **Phone:** (907) 265-2834.

ALASKA NATIVE HERITAGE CENTER is about 3 mi. e. on Glenn Hwy. to N. Muldoon Rd. exit, then 1 mi. e. on Heritage Center Dr. Situated on 26 wooded acres, the center presents information about the five regional, native groups that inhabit Alaska: the Aleut and Alutiiq; Athabascan; Eyak, Tlingit, Haida and Tsimshian; Inupiaq and St. Lawrence Island Yup'ik; and Yup'ik and Cup'ik cultures.

The main building offers the Gathering Place for storytelling, dance, native games and musical performances as well as a theater for cultural films. The Hall of Cultures exhibit is divided into five areas with changing multimedia displays about the ways of life of native cultures. Artisans create and display their crafts in adjacent studios.

Outside, five village sites surround Lake Tiulana, and site hosts are available to explain each dwelling, aspects of daily life and customs. **Time:** Allow 2 hours minimum. **Hours:** Daily 9-5, mid-May to mid-Sept. **Cost:** $24.95; $21.95 (ages 62+); $16.95 (ages 7-16); $71.50 (family, two adults and two children). Combination ticket with Anchorage Museum at Rasmuson Center $26. **Phone:** (907) 330-8000 or (800) 315-6608. *See color ad p. 322.*

ALASKA PUBLIC LANDS INFORMATION CENTER, 605 W. Fourth Ave., offers information about Alaska's state and federal public lands, including forests, parks and refuges. Exhibits include displays about Alaska's native culture, history and wildlife; films and interpretive programs are offered during the summer season. Visitors can plan their own trips with assistance from the staff as well as obtain free brochures and maps. State and federal passes also are available. **Hours:** Daily 9-5, June-Aug.; Mon.-Fri. 10-5, rest of year. Closed winter holidays. **Cost:** Free. **Phone:** (907) 644-3661, (866) 869-6887 or TTY (907) 271-2738.

ALASKA RAILROAD SCENIC RAIL TOURS departs from 411 W. First Ave. Narrated sightseeing tours on The Denali Star Train are offered northward between Anchorage and Fairbanks with stops at Wasilla, Talkeetna and Denali National Park and Preserve. The Glacier Discovery Train travels south from Anchorage to Whittier following the Turnagain Arm of Cook Inlet and stops at Girdwood and Portage. The Coastal Classic Train runs from Anchorage to Seward and offers a glimpse of wildlife and glaciers. Special winter routes also are available.

Domed cars with glass-covered viewing platforms allow for 180-degree views. Excursions and connections to air, rail and boat tours also are available. **Hours:** Trips depart daily, mid-May through mid-Sept.; trains depart Sat.-Sun., rest of year. Phone ahead to confirm schedule. **Cost:** One-way fares $49-$210 (an extra fee applies for first-class seating on northbound trains). Reservations are recommended. **Phone:** (907) 265-2494, (800) 544-0552 or TTY (907) 265-2620. *See color ad p. 319.*

ALASKA ZOO is 7.5 mi. s. on SR 1 (Seward Hwy.), then 2 mi. e. on O'Malley Rd.; a shuttle provides transportation from some local hotels during summer months. The grounds encompass a 25-acre wooded home to arctic, subarctic and Alaskan native animals, including Amur (Siberian) tigers, black and polar bears, seals, snow leopards, Tibetan yaks and wolves. Visitors may interact with selected animals during the 2-hour Discovery Tour. The Animal Encounter program allows visitors to work with animal handlers as they clean, feed and train the animals.

Time: Allow 1 hour, 30 minutes minimum. **Hours:** Daily 9-6 (also Tues. and Fri. 6-9), Memorial Day-Labor Day; 10-5, rest of year (weather permitting). Discovery Tour departs daily at noon, Memorial Day through mid-Sept. Closed Thanksgiving and Dec. 25. **Cost:** $12; $9 (ages 65+ and military with ID); $6 (ages 3-17). Zoo admission and guided grounds tour $15; $10 (ages 3-17). Zoo admission and Discovery Tour $25; $15 (ages 3-17). Animal Encounter $65; $30 (ages 0-11 with paid adult). Reservations are required for most tours. **Phone:** (907) 346-3242. ⓣ ⒜

ANCHORAGE MUSEUM AT RASMUSON CENTER, 625 C St., has exhibits focusing on the art, history and cultures of Alaska. The Alaska Gallery includes objects dating from prehistoric times through European exploration, Russian settlement, the gold rush era, World War II and statehood. Full-scale dioramas of an Athabascan tent; Yupik Eskimo, Tlingit and Aleut houses; a gold miner's cabin; an early Anchorage house; and Quonset huts (in use during World War II) provide insight to early Alaskan life.

In addition, a display about the Alaska Pipeline features a sample of the 4-foot-tall pipe. "Art of the Far North" contains drawings and paintings by Alaska's first explorers to current artists. Other highlights include summer films, a children's gallery and traveling exhibitions.

Time: Allow 1 hour minimum. **Hours:** Daily 9-6 (also Thurs. 6-9), late May to mid-Sept.; Tues.-Sat. 10-6, Sun. noon-6, rest of year. Closed Jan. 1, Thanksgiving and Dec. 25. **Cost:** $8; $7 (ages 65+, military and students with ID); by donation (ages 0-17). Combination ticket with Alaska Native Heritage Center $26. **Phone:** (907) 929-9200. ⓣ

ANCHORAGE TRAIL SYSTEM, found throughout and near the city, consists of 120 miles of paved trails and 300 miles of unpaved and wilderness trails. The 11-mile Tony Knowles Coastal Trail stretches from downtown and winds along the scenic coastline; Flattop Mountain is a popular 3-mile day hike with spectacular views of the Alaska Range and Anchorage; Williwaw Valley contains a 14-mile-long trail with views of emerald lakes, wildflowers and Dali sheep; Kincaid Park's 43-mile trail meanders throughout 1,400 acres and is popular with runners; and Turnagain Arm Trail is a pleasant 9-mile amble along Turnagain Arm. **Cost:** Free. **Phone:** (907) 276-4118.

THE IMAGINARIUM, Fifth Ave. and G St., is a hands-on science discovery center offering exhibits that explore nature, science and technology. Highlights include a marine wildlife area, reptile exhibits, a bubble lab and a planetarium. **Time:** Allow 1 hour minimum. **Hours:** Mon.-Sat. 10-6, Sun. noon-5. Closed Jan. 1, Easter, July 4, Thanksgiving and Dec. 25. **Cost:** $5.50; $5 (ages 2-12 and 66+). **Phone:** (907) 276-3179.

MAJOR MARINE TOURS—*see Whittier p. 363.*

OSCAR ANDERSON HOUSE MUSEUM, 420 M St. in Elderberry Park, was built by Swedish immigrant and businessman Oscar Anderson in 1915 on one of the first townsite lots in Anchorage. The small wood-frame house is restored and furnished in period and offers a fine view of Cook Inlet. An operational 1909 Hallet & Davis player piano is demonstrated during 45-minute guided tours. Swedish Christmas decorations and holiday traditions are featured during Swedish Christmas tours the first two weekends of December.

Time: Allow 1 hour minimum. **Hours:** Mon.-Fri. 1-5, June 1 to mid-Sept. **Cost:** $3; $1 (ages 5-12). **Phone:** (907) 274-2336.

PORTAGE GLACIER RECREATION AREA— *see Chugach National Forest p. 329.*

RENOWN TOURS—*see Seward p. 356.*

RUST'S FLYING SERVICE departs from the south shore of Lake Hood off International Airport Rd. at Anchorage International Airport. The service provides narrated sightseeing tours by seaplane of Denali National Park and Preserve, Knik Glacier, Mount McKinley and Prince William Sound. Tours to Brooks Falls and Redoubt Bay Lodge provide opportunities to view such wildlife as brown bears and marine animals. Glacier landings, river float trips and one-day and three-night fishing trips also are available.

Note: Departures require a minimum of 2 people. Singles are accommodated on a space-available basis. **Time:** Allow 1 hour, 30 minutes minimum. **Hours:** Daily by appointment, mid-May to mid-Sept.; Mon.-Fri. by appointment, rest of year. Closed Jan. 1, Thanksgiving and Dec. 25. **Cost:** Fare $100-$785. **Phone:** (907) 243-1595 or (800) 544-2299.

TRANS ARCTIC CIRCLE TREKS AND GLACIER BLUE TOURS—*see Fairbanks p. 338.*

DID YOU KNOW

Reindeer and caribous are the same animal—reindeer are domesticated.

BARROW (A-5) pop. 4,581, elev. 2′

The northernmost settlement in Alaska, Barrow is 340 miles north of the Arctic Circle on the edge of the omnipresent Arctic icepack. The sun does not go below the horizon for 82 days from early May to early August or rise above the horizon for 51 days between November and January. The town is reached by daily scheduled flights from Anchorage and Fairbanks. Husky sled dogs still are used, but snowmobiles have become more popular.

Barrow is one of the world's largest Eskimo settlements. Although to some extent the people continue to follow their old traditions, the trend is toward a more modern way of life: The North Slope oil discovery created great wealth in the area.

The Post-Rogers Memorial, at the airport, commemorates the deaths of Will Rogers and his pilot, Wiley Post, who were killed in a 1935 plane crash 12 miles down the coast.

CENTRAL (A-12) pop. 134

Named Central House in the 1890s, the mining community officially became known as Central in the 1930s following the completion of the nearby Steese Highway. The town's mining industry has experienced great fluctuation, reaching lows during and after World War II and peaking in the 1970s as gold rose in value.

An eight-mile trip southeast via the gravel Circle Hot Springs Road culminates at Circle Hot Springs. The town was discovered when George Crowe, a prospector on Deadwood Creek, wounded and trailed a moose across an unusually warm creek. Crowe traced the heat to the hot springs, which run 140 degrees Fahrenheit at the source.

The Circle District Historical Society Museum, Steese Highway Milepost 128, features artifacts, mining equipment and a miner's cabin; phone (907) 520-1893.

CHUGACH NATIONAL FOREST (D-12, G-6)

> Elevations in the forest range from sea level at the Pacific Ocean at Prince William Sound to 13,176 ft. at Mount Marcus Baker. Refer to AAA maps for additional elevation information.

Extending along the Gulf of Alaska from Cape Suckling to Seward, Chugach (CHEW-gatch) National Forest covers 5,500,000 acres, roughly as large as New Hampshire. It is second in size only to the Tongass National Forest *(see place listing p. 360)* and includes many of the islands and much of the land bordering Prince William Sound and the northeastern portion of the Kenai Peninsula.

Within the 700,000-acre Copper River Delta Wildlife Management Area just east of Cordova is one of the largest concentrations of trumpeter swans in North America. Also in abundance are dusky Canada geese, short-billed dowitchers, red-throated loons and green-winged teal. Prince William Sound has spectacular scenic opportunities with its 3,500 miles of coastline as well as dramatic tidewater glaciers and marine life that includes many species of whales.

Both saltwater and freshwater fishing are available in abundance in the forest. Halibut, red snapper, salmon and crabs are plentiful along the more than 3,500 miles of saltwater shoreline. Popular spots are Resurrection Bay at Seward and in Prince William Sound around Valdez and Cordova. Freshwater lakes and streams provide red salmon, Dolly Varden char and rainbow trout. A sportfishing license is required for all types of fishing within the forest.

For photographers and sport hunters, the forest offers a variety of big game, including black and brown bears, moose and Dall sheep. Hunting is subject to Alaska's fish and game management laws, seasons and bag limits.

Seward Highway offers 127 miles of scenic driving along saltwater bays, ice-blue glaciers and valleys dotted with native wildlife. The highway connects the cities of Anchorage and Seward. Bordering the forest on the northwest is SR 4; its scenic portion extends from Valdez to the junction of SR 10 west of Chitina. Portions of one of the most famous trails, The Historic Iditarod Trail, can be hiked, skied, dog sledded or explored on snowmobile.

In addition to 14 road-accessible campgrounds and 200 miles of hiking trails, the Forest Service operates 42 cabins in remote areas near lakes, bays and streams. Accessible by trail, boat or floatplane, the cabins are equipped with bunks, tables, chairs, wood or oil stoves and outdoor sanitary facilities, but no electricity.

The fee is $25-$45 per night per party. Reservations are required and can be made up to six months in advance. Further information also can be obtained from the Chugach National Forest, 3301 C St., Suite 300, Anchorage, AK 99503, phone (907) 743-9500, (877) 444-6777 for reservations or the U.S. Forest Service in Juneau *(see Fast Facts). Also see Recreation Chart and the AAA Western Canada & Alaska CampBook.*

ALASKA WILDLIFE CONSERVATION CENTER, Seward Hwy. Milepost 79, is a 140-acre, drive-through wild animal park. Among the animals to be seen are musk oxen, red foxes, lynx, buffaloes, Sitka blacktail deer, caribou, eagles, moose, reindeer, elk and bears. **Time:** Allow 30 minutes minimum. **Hours:** Daily 10-6, Mar. 1 to mid-May; 8-8, mid-May to mid-Sept.; 10-5, rest of year. Last admission is 30 minutes before closing. **Cost:** $10; $7.50 (ages 4-12, ages 65+ and active military with ID). The maximum fee is $30 per carload. Pets are not permitted. **Phone:** (907) 783-2025.

PORTAGE GLACIER CRUISES depart 1.5 mi. s. of the Begich-Boggs Visitor Center in the Portage Glacier Recreation Area *(see attraction listing).* A 1-hour narrated cruise aboard the *mv Ptarmigan* takes passengers to the face of Portage Glacier. Sections of the glacier "calving" or breaking away into the lake below often can be seen. The 200-passenger ship has a climate-controlled cabin with oversize windows and an open-air observation deck. Shuttle and tour packages from Anchorage also are available.

Inquire about weather policies. **Time:** Allow 1 hour, 30 minutes minimum. **Hours:** Cruises depart daily at 10:30, noon, 1:30, 3 and 4:30, mid-May to mid-Sept. **Cost:** Fare $29; $14.50 (ages 2-12). **Phone:** (907) 277-5581 or (800) 544-2206. *See color ad p. 325.*

PORTAGE GLACIER RECREATION AREA is 5.5 mi. e. from Milepost 79 of the Seward-Anchorage Hwy. Large icebergs calve off the face of the glacier into 650-foot-deep Portage Lake. An observation platform and a wayside exhibit are at the entrance to Williwaw Campground. Wayside exhibits also are available at Explorer Glacier. Iceworm safaris are offered. **Tours:** Guided tours are available. **Hours:** The road to and within the area is open all year. **Phone:** (907) 783-3242. 🍴 🎣

Begich-Boggs Visitor Center, off the Seward-Anchorage Hwy. on Portage Valley Rd., contains an observatory, orientation area, exhibit hall and learning center. A 20-minute film titled "Voices from the Ice" is shown every half hour. **Hours:** Daily 9-6, Memorial Day to late Sept.; hours vary rest of year. **Cost:** Visitor center and film $3; free (ages 0-15). **Phone:** (907) 783-2326.

COOPER LANDING (D-10) pop. 369

RECREATIONAL ACTIVITIES
Boating

- **Alaska Wildland Adventures** departs for Kenai River trips from the launch site on Sterling Hwy. (SR 1) Milepost 50.1. Other activities are offered. **Hours:** Daily May-Sept. **Phone:** (907) 783-2928 or (800) 334-8730.

CORDOVA (D-12) pop. 2,454, elev. 100'

Cordova is located on the eastern shores of Prince William Sound and is surrounded by the Chugach Mountain Range and the Chugach National Forest. The town can be reached by air from Juneau and Anchorage or via the Alaska Marine Highway from Valdez and Whittier. In the early 1900s, Cordova was the terminus of the Copper River Northwest Railroad that carried copper ore from the Kennecott Mines in McCarthy. Today the town's industry focuses on commercial fishing.

Cordova Chamber of Commerce: 404 First St., Cordova, AK 99574. **Phone:** (907) 424-7260.

RECREATIONAL ACTIVITIES
Kayaking

- **Cordova Coastal Outfitters** offers tours departing from Harbor Loop Rd. Lot 9 at the Cordova Harbor. Other activities are offered. **Hours:** Trips depart daily by appointment. **Phone:** (907) 424-7424.

DELTA JUNCTION (B-11) pop. 840

The official northern terminus of the Alaska Highway, Delta Junction is one of the state's strongest agricultural producers. The town offers panoramic views of the Alaska Range as well as the Trans-Alaska Pipeline, the Delta Bison Range and glaciers.

BIG DELTA STATE HISTORICAL PARK AND RIKA'S ROADHOUSE AND LANDING, at Milepost 275 on Richardson Hwy., is a restored 10-acre homestead with a museum, historic cabins, a roadhouse, a garden and livestock and poultry pens. **Tours:** Guided tours are available. **Hours:** Daily

9-5, May 15-Sept. 15; by appointment rest of year. **Cost:** Free. **Phone:** (907) 895-4201 May 15-Sept. 15, or (907) 895-4938 rest of year. [T]

DENALI NATIONAL PARK AND PRESERVE (B-10)

Elevations in the park and preserve range from 626 ft. at the northwest corner of the park at Chilcukabena Lake to the 20,320 ft. Mount McKinley. Refer to AAA maps for additional elevation information.

In the interior of Alaska, primitive and wild Denali National Park and Preserve covers 9,419 square miles and offers spectacular views of quiet lakes, snowcapped peaks and varicolored tundra. In addition to 20,320-foot Mount McKinley, the highest peak in North America, the park encompasses 17,400-foot Mount Foraker, 13,220-foot Silverthrone and 11,670-foot Mount Russell.

Mount McKinley, known to the early Athabascan Indians as Denali, "the high one," has two peaks: South Peak, the true summit, and 2 miles away, 19,470-foot North Peak. Most of the mountain is covered by ice and snow all year. Excellent views of Mount McKinley are possible along the park road (weather permitting); clouds hide the summit about 75 percent of the time in summer and 60 percent the rest of the year.

The park's many glaciers originate on the slopes of the Alaska Range. Muldrow Glacier, the largest northward-flowing glacier in Alaska, stretches from between Mount McKinley's twin peaks to within a few miles of the park road; it can be seen from several vantage points.

More than 167 species of birds and 39 kinds of mammals inhabit the park; grizzly bears, moose, Dall sheep, wolves and caribous are some of the larger mammals. Equally varied is the vegetation. The chief conifers are black and white spruce, while dwarf birch grow in thickets on the lower slopes and along the intermountain valleys. Low, boggy meadows are the habitat of stunted, twisted black spruce.

Above the river valleys, forests give way to vast stretches of wet tundra supporting shrubby plants and often underlain by permafrost. Dry alpine tundra blankets the slopes and ridges at the higher elevations.

General Information and Activities

From Anchorage and Fairbanks, the George Parks Highway (SR 3) provides access to the park all year, and SR 8 from Paxson is usually open from early June to mid-October. The park also is accessible from Anchorage or Fairbanks via the Alaska Railroad; there is daily service from late May to mid-September. Trains run northbound to Fairbanks on Saturday and southbound to Anchorage on Sunday the rest of the year. Charter flights are available from principal airports.

Denali Park Road, beginning at SR 3 at the park's eastern boundary, runs about 90 miles westward through the park, terminating at a partly abandoned mining town, Kantishna. Only the first 14.8 miles to Savage River are paved, and most of the road is narrow with many sharp curves. It is usually open from early June to mid-September. The George Parks Highway (SR 3) runs along the eastern border of the park and offers sweeping views of the park's alpine scenery from Willow to Nenana.

Private vehicles may be used only on the first 14.8 miles of Denali Park Road unless you have a registered campsite at Teklanika Campground. Transportation beyond Savage River or to Sanctuary, Igloo and Wonder Lake campgrounds is provided by

shuttle buses that operate to Toklat, Wonder Lake and other points in the park.

Fare for the shuttle varies with destination. Fare to Kantishna $46.70; $23.35 (ages 15-17). Fare to Wonder Lake $42.95; $21.50 (ages 15-17). Fare to Toklat and Polychrome $24.70; $12.35 (ages 15-17). Three- and 6-day trip passes are available; prices vary by destination. These fares do not include the $4 registration fee or the park admission fees.

More than half of the shuttle seats are available for telephone reservation; phone (907) 272-7275 or (800) 622-7275 in advance. The rest of the spaces can be reserved only in person within 2 days of departure. Buses depart approximately every half-hour beginning at 5 a.m. from the Wilderness Access Center near the entrance at Milepost 0.6 on Denali Park Road. The bus stops to view wildlife when conditions are safe. Shuttle buses also drop off and pick up passengers along the park road on a space-available basis. The center houses a small theater.

The Denali Visitor Center, Milepost 1.2 on Denali Park Road, contains an information desk, exhibits, a slide show and interpretive programs. It is open daily 8-6, late May to mid-September. The Eielson Visitor Center, Milepost 66 on Denali Park Road, displays "Seasons of Denali," a quilt by fabric artist Ree Nancarrow. The center is open daily 9-7, late May to mid-September.

The Murie Science and Learning Center, at Milepost 1.3 on Denali Park Road, is dedicated to research and education about America's eight northernmost national parks and offers field seminars and educational programs. It is open daily 9:30-5, late May to mid-September; 10-4, rest of year. Phone (907) 683-1269 or (888) 688-1269.

The Talkeetna Ranger Station, Milepost 98 on George Parks Highway (SR 3), also offers interpretive programs and is open daily 8-6, mid-April through Labor Day; Mon.-Fri. 8-4:30, rest of year. Phone (907) 733-2231.

To camp outside the established campgrounds, stop at the Wilderness Access Center for a backcountry permit. Reservations for all campgrounds may be made here.

Sled dog demonstrations are given by rangers at the park kennels, Milepost 3 on Denali Park Road. The 40-minute presentations are offered daily at 10, 2 and 4, June through August; phone ahead for availability. Ranger-naturalists also present various lectures, hikes and other activities daily at various campgrounds. Information about activities is available at the park Visitor Center and ranger stations, or pick up a copy of the park's informational newspaper, *Denali Alpenglow*.

Guided and self-guiding hikes are available along several nature trails with trailheads along the paved portion of the park road. Throughout the rest of the park, hiking is generally cross-country. The Spruce Forest Trail loop takes about 15 minutes, while the Morino Trail takes 30 minutes to complete. Backcountry permits are available from the Backcountry Information Center, adjacent to the Wilderness Access Center. Five- and 8-hour guided hikes depart from the Denali Visitor Center and range from $24-$74, depending on the tour.

Do not feed or disturb wildlife. Grizzly bears in particular can be dangerous; inquire at the Visitor Center about how to avoid close encounters with grizzlies. Firearms must be declared and made inoperative when you enter the park; hunting and shooting are forbidden.

Most fishing is poor in the park; only streams that are free of glacial silt are good fishing spots. No license is required within the national park; the daily creel limit is 10 fish, only two of which may be lake trout. An Alaska fishing license is required

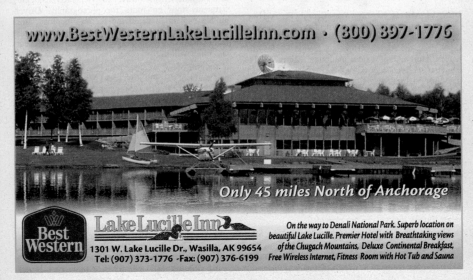

in the national preserve areas. Check at a ranger station for further information.

Temperatures during the park season can vary from 40 to 80 degrees Fahrenheit, with an average of 50 to 54 degrees June through August. Daylight generally lasts for more than 18 hours during the summer months.

A store near the park entrance contains supplies, but no gas is available; the store is open approximately 7 a.m.-9 p.m. during peak season, shorter hours at other times. A gas station north of the park entrance on George Parks Highway (SR 3) is open in the summer. Food and supplies also are available at Riley Creek campground just inside the park boundaries. *See Recreation Chart and the AAA Western Canada & Alaska CampBook.*

ADMISSION, valid for 7 days, is $10 per person or $20 per family.

PETS are permitted in the park only if they are leashed or otherwise physically restrained; they are not allowed on trails, shuttle buses or in the backcountry.

ADDRESS inquiries to the Superintendent, Denali National Park and Preserve, P.O. Box 9, Denali Park, AK 99755; phone (907) 683-2294 or (800) 622-7275 for reservations.

ALASKA CABIN NITE DINNER THEATRE is 1.7 mi. n. of the park entrance on George Parks Hwy. (SR 3) at Milepost 239. The theater presents a 1915-style dinner show that highlights Alaska's gold-mining history. A pre-show dinner is served family-style. **Time:** Allow 2 hours minimum. **Hours:** Shows daily at 5:30 and 8:30 p.m., mid-May to mid-Sept. **Cost:** $62; $31 (ages 0-11). Reservations are required. **Phone:** (907) 683-8200, or (800) 276-7234 for reservations. 🍴

DENALI AIR is 10 mi. s. on George Parks Hwy. (SR 3) at Milepost 229.5. Commentary about history, scenery and topography complements an hour-long flight along the Alaska Range and around Mount McKinley. **Time:** Allow 1 hour minimum. **Hours:** Flights depart every even hour daily 8-8 (weather permitting), mid-May to mid-Sept. **Cost:** Fare $350; $175 (ages 2-12). **Phone:** (907) 683-2261.

DENALI BACKCOUNTRY ADVENTURE departs from Denali Cabins, Milepost 229, George Parks Hwy. (SR 3), 9 mi. s. of park entrance. This narrated bus tour travels along the 95-mile Denali Park Road to Denali Backcountry Lodge in Kantishna. Along the route, the guide points out wildlife such as moose and caribou, and makes stops at various times for photography. The complete trip lasts 13 hours and includes either goldpanning or a guided nature walk to Fannie Quigley's historic pioneer cabin. Lunch and snacks are provided.

Allow a full day. **Hours:** Tours depart daily at 6:15 a.m., early June to mid-Sept. **Cost:** Fee $169 (plus $10 park entrance fee). **Phone:** (907) 376-1992 or (877) 233-6254. *See color ad p. 328, p. 330 & p. 774.*

DENALI WILDERNESS SAFARIS, at Milepost 216 on George Parks Hwy. (SR 3), offers 3-hour heated jet boat rides or 2-hour dog sled rides to a camp in the Alaskan "bush" country, where locals share their methods of hunting, prospecting and trapping. Gold panning opportunities are presented. Free transportation is provided from all area hotels. **Hours:** Wilderness trips depart daily at 8, 10, 2 and 6. **Cost:** Boat fare $119; $79 (ages 0-12). Dog sled $79; $59 (ages 0-12). Fees include a snack. Reservations are recommended. **Phone:** (907) 768-2550.

ERA HELICOPTERS FLIGHTSEEING TOURS is at 1 Glacier Way. The company offers a narrated 1- and 2-hour aerial tour of North America's highest mountain, Mount McKinley, as well as 75-minute glacier landing tours. Five-hour heli-hiking excursions also are available. Caribous, moose and Dall sheep can be seen in the valleys. Free transportation is provided from area hotels. **Hours:** Daily 7-7, May-Sept. **Cost:** Tours range from $235-$465. Tours subject to passenger minimums. **Phone:** (907) 248-4422 or (800) 843-1947.

NATURAL HISTORY TOUR, departing from area hotels, takes visitors on a bus tour across sections of the park where they can enjoy views of the Alaska Range from Mount McKinley to Mount Deborah. Driver-guides explain the region's natural history, unusual geological formations and local flora and fauna. A stop at the Wilderness Access Center allows time to view the film "Across Time and Tundra."

Hours: The 5-hour trip departs two times daily, mid-May to mid-Sept. Phone ahead to confirm schedule. **Cost:** Fare (includes park admission and a snack) $72.10; $41.50 (ages 0-14). **Phone:** (907) 272-7275 or (800) 622-7275.

TUNDRA WILDERNESS TOURS picks up visitors at local hotels. Buses travel to Toklat River, making frequent stops en route for photography. Driver-guides explain in detail the region's geology, flora and fauna on the 7- to 9-hour tours. Binoculars are recommended for spotting moose, caribou, bears and other wildlife.

Inquire about weather policies. **Hours:** Trips depart daily 5:30-7:30 a.m. and 1:30-3 p.m., mid-May to mid-Sept. **Cost:** Fare (includes park admission and a box lunch) $114.35; $63.10 (ages 0-14). Reservations are recommended. **Phone:** (907) 272-7275 or (800) 622-7275.

RECREATIONAL ACTIVITIES
White-water Rafting

- **Alaska Raft Adventures** departs from the McKinley Chalet at Milepost 238 on George Parks Hwy. (SR 3). **Hours:** Trips depart daily at 7:30, 1:30, 2 and 6. **Phone:** (907) 276-7234 or (800) 276-7234.

- **Denali Raft Adventures, Inc.** is .5 mi. n. of the park entrance at Milepost 238.6 on George Parks Hwy. (SR 3). **Hours:** Trips depart daily mid-May to mid-Sept.; check-in times vary depending on trip. **Phone:** (907) 683-2234 or (888) 683-2234.

EAGLE (D-8) pop. 129

Eagle was settled in 1897 by 28 miners who named the town after the bald eagles that nested on the nearby bluff. In 1899, the Army established Fort Egbert and within several years, some 37 military buildings were constructed. Founded along the Yukon River near the Canadian border, Eagle is the only planned town of the gold rush.

Eagle Historical Society: P.O. Box 23, Eagle, AK 99738. **Phone:** (907) 547-2325.

EAGLE MUSEUMS are all within 1 sq. mi. of town. Tours depart from the courthouse at First and Berry sts. Visitors can join a walking tour that includes six restored buildings, including Judge James Wickersham's original courthouse, the Army Mule Barn, Redman Lodge, Customs House, St. Paul's Log Church and the Waterwagon Shed. Each building contains memorabilia portraying the small town's history. **Time:** Allow 3 hours minimum. **Hours:** Tours depart daily at 9, Memorial Day-Labor Day. **Cost:** $7; free (ages 0-11). **Phone:** (907) 547-2325.

EAGLE RIVER (C-11)

CHUGACH STATE PARK is e. on Glenn Hwy. Wildlife populations flourish within the park's 700 square miles of mountains, rivers, lakes and glaciers, providing many opportunities for viewing moose and beavers as well as the occasional bear or wolf. Major areas are Eklutna Lake, Eagle River, Anchorage Hillside and Turnagain Arm. A number of recreational activities are available. The park's headquarters is in the historic Potter Section House, at Milepost 115 of the Seward Highway. *See Recreation Chart and the AAA Western Canada & Alaska CampBook.*

Hours: Headquarters open Mon.-Fri. 10-4:30. **Cost:** Free. **Parking:** $5 at many trailheads. **Phone:** (907) 345-5014. ▲

EAGLE RIVER NATURE CENTER is 12 mi. s.e. on Eagle River Rd. to its end at 32750 Eagle River Rd. The center sponsors interpretive programs including guided hikes along the four trails it maintains. A hands-on area allows visitors to touch antlers, bones, pelts and other collected items. **Time:** Allow 30 minutes minimum. **Hours:** Daily 10-5 (also Fri.-Sat. 5-7), June-Aug.; Fri.-Sun. 10-5, Oct.-Apr.; Tues.-Sun. 10-5, rest of year. Guided hikes depart at 1. **Cost:** Free. **Parking:** $5. **Phone:** (907) 694-2108.

EKLUTNA (C-10)

More than 150 years ago Russian missionaries came to Eklutna to convert the Athabascan Indians. Originally built in the 1830s, the St. Nicholas Russian Orthodox Church was reconstructed in the 1970s. The church is at the site of the former Eklutna Historical Park. Adjacent to the church is the Eklutna Cemetery, which dates to the 1650s and remains in use.

FAIRBANKS (A-11, D-6)
pop. 30,224, elev. 432'
See map page 334.

Fairbanks, near the geographical center of Alaska, is a major visitor center and the northern terminus of the Alaska Railroad. The military, transportation and market nucleus of the Alaskan interior, Fairbanks is a supply point for arctic oil operations and a departure point for airlines statewide.

In 1901 Capt. E.T. Barnette founded a trading post where Fairbanks now stands—a riverboat captain refused to ferry him any farther up the Chena River due to the low water level. Gold was discovered nearby a year later, and the first wave of prospectors flooded up the river. The settlement was named for Charles Warren Fairbanks of Indiana, a U.S. senator who later became vice president to Theodore Roosevelt.

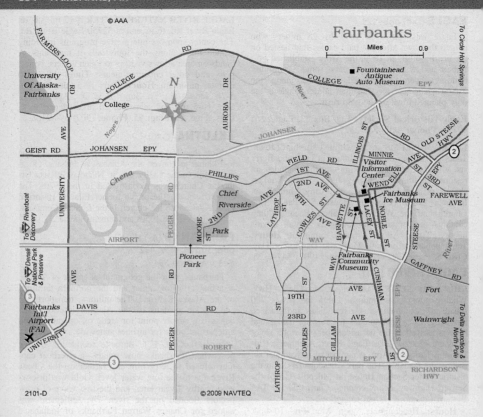

Fairbanks

The construction of the Alaska Highway and the influx of the military into Fairbanks heralded a second boom. And in 1968 the discovery of oil in Prudhoe Bay, 390 miles north, triggered a third wave of development.

Fairbanks offers a variety of winter sports and other activities, including aurora viewing, cross-country and downhill skiing, curling, ice hockey and dog mushing. The city's geographical location allows the semiprofessional Alaska Goldpanners baseball team to play its Midnight Sun Game at 10:30 p.m. on June 21 without using artificial lighting.

The Robert G. White Large Animal Research Station, 2220 Yankovich Rd., is a 134-acre facility offering .25-mile narrated outdoor walking tours of its grounds, allowing visitors to observe such animals as caribou, musk oxen and reindeer. Tours are conducted Memorial Day-Labor Day and regardless of weather conditions; visitors should dress appropriately. Phone (907) 474-7207 or (907) 474-5724.

Local sightseeing tours to Alaska's arctic zone and other remote places are available from Fairbanks. Using railway cars with skylights, SAVE Gray Line of Alaska and Princess Tours offer trips between Anchorage and Fairbanks via Denali National Park and Preserve. Canoes for trips on the Chena River can be rented from several outfitters.

Interesting drives include visits to Chena Hot Springs and the town of Ester. Abandoned gold dredges can be seen outside of Fairbanks along the roads to Chatanika and Ester. The Alaska Public Lands Information Center, at the Morris Thompson Cultural and Visitors Center at 101 Dunkel St., Suite 110, shows free movies and has information about public lands and parks; phone (907) 459-3730 or (866) 869-6887, or TTY (907) 456-0532.

Fairbanks Convention and Visitors Bureau: 101 Dunkel St., Suite 111, Fairbanks, AK 99701. **Phone:** (907) 456-5774 or (800) 327-5774. *See color ad p. 335.*

Self-guiding tours: Information about a historical walking tour is available from the Fairbanks Visitor Information Center.

EL DORADO GOLD MINE is 9 mi. n. off Steese Hwy. to Elliott Hwy. at Milepost 1.3. A 2-hour narrated trip aboard a replica of a Tanana Valley Railroad train passes through a permafrost tunnel into a working gold mine where mining techniques are demonstrated. Passengers have the opportunity to pan for gold.

Time: Allow 2 hours minimum. **Hours:** Tours depart Mon.-Fri. and Sun. at 9:45 and 3, Sat. at 3, mid-May to mid-Sept. **Cost:** Fare $34.95; $22.95 (ages 3-12). Rates may vary; phone ahead. Reservations are required. **Phone:** (907) 479-6673 or (866) 479-6673.

FAIRBANKS COMMUNITY MUSEUM is at 410 Cushman St. at jct. 5th St. Housed in the 1935 city hall building, the museum features the Deluge: The Flood of '67 exhibit, which relates the story of the disastrous 1967 flood that caused more than $80 million in damage to the area. Antique winter sports equipment, including a still-operable 1962 snowmobile, is displayed. Exhibits highlight the area's gold rush and dog mushing history and include a replica of a gold panner's home and such mushing equipment as vintage dog sleds.

Time: Allow 30 minutes minimum. **Hours:** Mon.-Fri. 10-4, May-Sept.; 11-3, Oct.-Mar. **Cost:** Donations. **Phone:** (907) 457-3669.

FAIRBANKS ICE MUSEUM, jct. 2nd Ave. and Lacey St. at 500 2nd Ave., showcases life-size ice sculptures viewable from either inside their glass-fronted display cases, which are kept at a frosty 20 degrees Fahrenheit, or from an indoor theatre. The 25-minute multimedia presentation "Freeze Frame" details the harvesting of ice blocks and their evolution into the finished products displayed at Ice Art,

an international ice-sculpting competition held each March in Fairbanks. Ice-carving demonstrations are offered during winter, the sculpting season's acme.

Hours: Daily 10-8, May-Sept.; by appointment rest of year. **Cost:** $12; $11 (ages 65+ and military with ID); $6 (ages 6-12). **Phone:** (907) 451-8222.

FOUNTAINHEAD ANTIQUE AUTO MUSEUM is off Johansen Expwy. exit 4 (College Rd.), just w. on College Rd., then .2 mi. n. on Margaret Ave.; the museum is at 212 Wedgewood Dr. on the grounds of the Wedgewood Resort. The museum's collection of more than 60 pristine working condition automobiles, which date from the turn of the 20th century to the late 1930s, includes the only surviving 1920 Argonne; a 1917 Owen-Magnetic M-25 Touring, a gas hybrid; and series of Fords and Packards.

Other exhibits include historical photographs and vintage clothing displays. One-hour guided tours of the vehicles, 50 of which are displayed at any given time, are offered.

Time: Allow 1 hour minimum. **Hours:** Sun.-Thurs. 11-10, Fri.-Sat. 11-6, June 1 to mid-Sept.; Sun. noon-6, in winter. Phone ahead to confirm schedule. **Cost:** $8; $5 (ages 6-12); $4 (Fountainhead Hotel guests). Guided tour $40. Reservations are required for guided tours. **Phone:** (907) 450-2100 or (800) 528-4916.

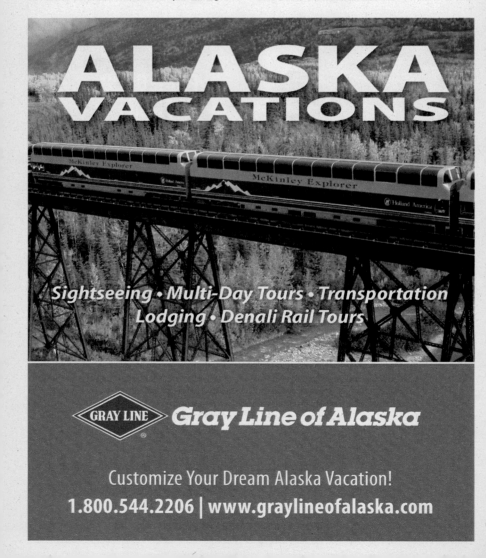

GOLD DREDGE NUMBER 8 is n. on SR 2 (Old Steese Hwy.) to Goldstream Rd., following signs. The five-deck, 250-foot-long ship was built in 1928 to ply Goldstream and Engineer creeks for the precious metal. Following a 90-minute tour, visitors can pan for gold and search for bison and mammoth bones. **CLOSURE INFORMATION:** The ship is closed for renovations with no scheduled reopening date. **Phone:** (907) 457-6058.

NORTHERN ALASKA TOUR COMPANY departs from the e. ramp of the Fairbanks International Airport. Tours highlight the natural and cultural aspects of Alaska's arctic region. Excursions, which last a full day to multiple days, explore the arctic circle by plane, or bus along the Dalton Highway. Other trips visit the Anaktuvuk Pass, Beaver Village, Brooks Range, Barrow and Nome. Guides offer insight along the route. **Time:** Allow 1 hour minimum. **Hours:** Tours depart daily, mid-May to mid-Sept.; Mon.-Sat., rest of year. Hours vary by trip. **Cost:** Fare $189-$989. **Phone:** (907) 474-8600 or (800) 474-1986. *See color ad p. 333.*

PIONEER PARK is at 2300 Airport Way. The pioneer theme park offers four museums; the Kitty Hensley and Wickersham houses, two restored early 20th-century dwellings; the renovated *S.S. Nenana*, one of the largest wooden sternwheelers ever constructed; Red & Roela's Carousel; and a train that travels and offers unique views of the park. Such activities as miniature golf are provided; bocce courts as well as horseshoe and volleyball areas also are on the premises. A revue show at The Palace Theatre and The Big Stampede show at Pioneer Hall also are offered.

Hours: Park open daily noon-8, Memorial Day-Labor Day. Train trips depart every 15 minutes from noon-7:45. Palace Theater show nightly at 8:15. Big Stampede shows are presented daily at 11:30, 1, 2:30, 4 and 5:30. **Cost:** Park free. Train ride $2; $1

(ages 4-13). Palace Theater show $18; $9 (ages 4-13). Big Stampede show $4; $2 (ages 4-13). A small fee is applicable at several of the attractions and museums. **Phone:** (907) 459-1087. [TI] [🍴]

 RIVERBOAT DISCOVERY, departing from a pier on Discovery Rd. off Airport Way, provides 3.5-hour trips on the Chena and Tanana rivers aboard the stern-wheeler *Discovery III*. Guides discuss area wildlife, history, anthropology, geology and customs. Views vary from wilderness to elegant houses, and the trip includes a guided walking tour of the Chena Indian village. **Hours:** Trips depart Mon.-Fri. at 8:45 and 2, Sat. at 8:45, Sun. at 2, late May to mid-Sept. **Cost:** Fare $54.95; $37.95 (ages 3-12). Reservations are required. **Phone:** (907) 479-6673 or (866) 479-6673.

TRANS ARCTIC CIRCLE TREKS AND GLACIER BLUE TOURS is at 4825 Glasgow Dr., with pick-up service available from area hotels and RV parks. This tour company offers a variety of guided excursions including day trips to the Arctic Circle and multi-day trips to the Arctic Ocean, Brooks Range, Prudhoe Bay and Point Barrow. Visitors on the 1-day tour can enjoy mountain scenery, a walk through alpine tundra and a hands-on Trans-Alaska Pipeline demonstration. Add-on land and air excursions are available.

Hours: One-day tour departs daily mid-May to mid-Sept. Other tours depart throughout the year. **Cost:** Fare for 1-day tour start at $169. Rates vary according to tour; phone ahead. Reservations are required. **Phone:** (907) 479-5451 or (800) 336-8735.

UNIVERSITY OF ALASKA MUSEUM OF THE NORTH, on the West Ridge of the University of Alaska campus, contains natural and cultural history exhibits. The Rose Berry Alaska Art Gallery is dedicated to Alaskan art. Also on display are an extensive gold collection and a steppe bison killed by a lion 36,000 years ago and preserved in the permafrost. "Dynamic Aurora," which explains the northern lights, and "Winter," which documents Alaska's longest season, are 50-minute multimedia presentations offered during summer months.

Time: Allow 30 minutes minimum. **Hours:** Daily 9-9, May 15-Sept. 15; Mon.-Sat. 9-5, rest of year. "Dynamic Aurora" daily at 10, 1, 3, 5 and 7:30, "Winter" daily at 11, 2 and 4 during summer months. Closed Jan. 1, Thanksgiving and Dec. 25. **Cost:** $10; $9 (ages 60+); $5 (ages 7-17). Multimedia shows $5. **Phone:** (907) 474-7505.

Student-guided Walking Tours of the University of Alaska Fairbanks depart from Signers' Hall. Tours of the campus last 1.5 to 2 hours. Comfortable shoes are recommended. Other activities include the Arctic Region Supercomputing tour; the International Arctic Research Center tour; the Geophysical Institute tour; and the Georgeson Botanical Garden tour. **Hours:** Mon.-Fri. at 10, June-Aug. Closed July 2-4. Reservations are required. **Phone:** (907) 474-7021 for campus tours, or (907) 474-7558 for all other tours.

DID YOU KNOW

Some sites in Alaska boast snow and ice year-round—even when the temperature soars to 80 degrees.

FORT YUKON (C-7) pop. 595

Just north of the Arctic Circle at a point where the Yukon River is almost 3 miles wide, the Athabascan Indian village of Fort Yukon was established as a trading post by the Hudson's Bay Co. in 1847. The village was an important port during the gold rush days, and the post office has remained popular for those who wish to mail from above the Arctic Circle.

Fort Yukon is reached by daily air service from Fairbanks. Visitors can see fish wheels in operation and purchase craftwork and fine furs. Temperatures have ranged as high as 100 degrees Fahrenheit in the summer and as low as minus 78 degrees Fahrenheit in winter.

GATES OF THE ARCTIC NATIONAL PARK AND PRESERVE (C-5)

Elevations in the park and preserve range from 300 ft. along the Kobuk River to 8,510 ft. at Mount Igikpak. Refer to AAA maps for additional elevation information.

Lying north of the Arctic Circle, Gates of the Arctic National Park and Preserve's 8.5 million acres features a raw, austere landscape of sparse vegetation and jagged spires. The rocky spine of the Brooks Range forms the park's backbone, and a boreal forest, or taiga, of spruce, birch and poplar meets the almost treeless tundra that rolls uninterrupted to the Arctic Ocean.

Despite being four times the size of Yellowstone National Park, Gates of the Arctic is a meager larder for the caribou, moose, wolves and bears that roam the park in search of food. Fortunately much of their arctic range is protected, as Gates of the Arctic is joined on either side by Noatak National Preserve and nearby Arctic National Wildlife Refuge.

It was a forester on leave, Bob Marshall, who, in exploring this uncharted region in the late 1930s, christened this land Gates of the Arctic. The term both describes and evokes the grandeur of this wilderness—the soaring immensity of sky and mountains, the burst of wildflowers in summer and the cyclical abundance of wildlife.

But as Marshall remarked, the greatest pleasure is its undeveloped and wild character, which gives the visitor the sense of being the first to visit the tundra foothills or one of the park's nameless peaks. Today a good way to enjoy the park is to follow Marshall's example and hike the park's rugged terrain, which offers challenging backpacking. A popular alternative is to canoe or raft the network of rivers and lakes.

Most visitors use various air charter services from Fairbanks and Bettles Field to reach the park's interior. The Dalton Highway skirts the park's eastern edge and is the only road that approaches the park. Because of Gates of the Arctic's fragile ecology, there are no park facilities, trails or campgrounds within the park. For trip planning assistance and a list of outfitters, guides and air taxi operators, write Gates of the Arctic National Park and Preserve, P.O. Box 30, Bettles, AK 99726; phone (907) 692-5494. *See Recreation Chart.*

GIRDWOOD (C-11) elev. 23'

Initially called Glacier City, Girdwood was established at the turn of the 20th century as a gold mining town. The community prospered until mine closures in the 1930s reduced it to a virtual ghost town. Misfortune struck again when the 1964 Good Friday earthquake caused massive destruction along the coast, forcing residents to move the town 2.5 miles inland to its present location. Today Girdwood thrives as a year-round recreation destination.

Girdwood is on Turnagain Arm, a fjord carved by glaciers and known for its dramatic bore tides, which can be 6 feet high and travel at speeds of up to 15 miles an hour. The town also is located at the base of 3,939-foot Mount Alyeska; a 60-passenger tramway ascends to the 2,300-foot level and offers a panorama of the valley and Turnagain Arm.

RECREATIONAL ACTIVITIES
Skiing
- **Alyeska Resort and Ski Area** is on SR 1 (Seward Hwy.). Other activities are offered. **Hours:** Mid-Nov. to mid-Apr., weather permitting. **Phone:** (907) 754-1111.

GLACIER BAY NATIONAL PARK AND PRESERVE (G-9)

Elevations in the park and preserve range from sea level at Glacier Bay to 15,320 ft. at Mount Fairweather. Refer to AAA maps for additional elevation information.

Stretching northward from Cross Sound to the Canadian border, Glacier Bay National Park is one of the most scenic spots in Alaska. In this 3,283,168-acre park, blue-white glaciers flow from the snow-clad peaks of the Fairweather Range to fiordlike inlets.

The park features 15,320-foot Mount Fairweather and Glacier Bay. The bay, about 65 miles long and 2.5 to 10 miles wide, was filled with ice 5,000 feet thick as recently as 200 years ago. The park contains some of the world's most impressive tidewater glaciers. Icebergs that crack off, or calve, from the nearly vertical ice cliffs dot the waters of the upper bay. Boaters are likely to encounter numerous harbor seals and an occasional whale.

This spectacular region is accessible only by plane or boat. Alaska Airlines offers flights from Juneau daily June through early September. A 10-mile road connects the park headquarters with the small community of Gustavus, where charter vessels and air and boat service to Juneau are available.

A boat tour of the bay departs from Glacier Bay Lodge each morning, late May to mid-September; phone (888) 229-8687.

Due to concern for the endangered humpback whale, permits are required from June through August for private vessels to enter Glacier Bay. An Alaska fishing license is required for fishing. Boaters should contact the National Park Service for current regulations; phone (907) 697-2627. For further information about the park contact the Superintendent, Glacier Bay National Park and Preserve, P.O. Box 140, Gustavus, AK 99826; phone (907) 697-2230. *See Recreation Chart.*

HAINES (G-10) pop. 1,811, elev. 66'

Haines lies in a spectacular setting on the Chilkat Peninsula near the northern end of Lynn Canal between the waters of the Inside Passage and the Chilkat River. The Alaska Marine Highway links Haines with Prince Rupert, British Columbia, and Bellingham, Wash., and enables visitors to connect with the Alaska Highway at Haines Junction, Milepost 1016, via SRs 7 and 4. For information about the Alaska Marine Highway phone (907) 766-2111 or (800) 642-0066, ext. 9604.

The 40-acre Kroschel Wildlife Park, 27 miles north on scenic Haines Highway, is home to reindeer, wolverines, bears, falcons and other native species. Reservations are required for tours; phone (907) 767-5464.

Nearby, from late October through February the 48,000-acre Chilkat Bald Eagle Preserve, between Mileposts 9 and 31 on Haines Highway, harbors one of the largest congregations of bald eagles in the world. More than 3,500 of the birds gather to feed on the salmon in the Chilkat River; sometimes as many as 30 eagles roost in a tree during this time. Use roadside pull-offs for viewing; stopping on the road is prohibited. Tour information is available at Haines Visitor Center.

Other interesting drives near Haines include Lutak Road, leading to Chilkoot Lake, and Mud Bay Road, which passes Pyramid Harbor and an old cannery with its salmon boats before approaching Chilkat State Park *(see Recreation Chart and the AAA Western Canada & Alaska CampBook).* Davidson and Rainbow glaciers also are visible from this route.

Buildings that once comprised Fort William H. Seward, the site of the first permanent Army post in Alaska, have been restored and contain inns, hotels and galleries. A historic area at the south end of Haines Highway, the fort also contains a replica of a tribal house. The old hospital houses carvers who use traditional Tlingit Indian methods. Phone (907) 766-2234 for fort information.

Fjord Express, (800) 320-0146, and Haines-Skagway Fast Ferry, (907) 766-2100 or (888) 766-2103, provide efficient transportation between Haines, Skagway and Juneau.

Haines Convention & Visitors Bureau: 122 Second Ave., P.O. Box 530, Haines, AK 99827. **Phone:** (907) 766-2234 or (800) 458-3579. *See color ad.*

Self-guiding tours: Brochures featuring walking tours of Haines and Fort William H. Seward are available from Haines Visitor Center and Hotel Halsingland.

CHILKAT BALD EAGLE PRESERVE FLOAT TRIPS, on Sawmill Rd., pass through the Bald Eagle Preserve on the Chilkat River and offer views of the Chilkat Mountains and bald eagles in their natural habitat. Transportation to and from the river is provided. Bring warm clothes, binoculars, camera, sunglasses and rain gear. Inquire about weather policies. **Hours:** The 4.5- to 5-hour float trip departs daily, May-Sept. Phone ahead to confirm schedule.

Cost: Fare $89; $62 (ages 7-14). Reservations are recommended. **Phone:** (907) 766-2491.

CHILKOOT LAKE TOURS, 1069 Haines Hwy., offers sightseeing and fishing cruises of Chilkoot Lake. Brown bears, bald eagles and spawning salmon often are seen. Inquire about weather policies. **Time:** Allow 3 hours minimum. **Hours:** Daily at 9 and 2, May 1-Sept. 15; other times by appointment. Phone ahead to confirm schedule. **Cost:** Fare for sightseeing cruise $85; fishing cruise $99. **Phone:** (907) 766-2891.

SHELDON MUSEUM AND CULTURAL CENTER, on Main St. above the boat harbor, allows visitors to experience the art and culture of the Tlingit native people and to learn about the early pioneer history of Haines Mission, the Porcupine gold rush and Fort Seward, a frontier army post. **Time:** Allow 1 hour, 30 minutes minimum. **Hours:** Mon.-Fri. 10-5, Sat.-Sun. 1-4, mid-May to mid-Sept.; Mon.-Sat. 1-4, rest of year. **Cost:** $3; free (ages 0-12). **Phone:** (907) 766-2366.

RECREATIONAL ACTIVITIES
Bicycling

- **Sockeye Cycle Co.,** 24 Portage St., offers rental bikes and guided biking tours. **Hours:** Trips depart daily by appointment. Bike rentals are available Mon.-Sat. 10-5, Apr.-Sept. **Phone:** (907) 766-2869 or (877) 292-4154.

HOMER (D-10) pop. 3,946, elev. 67′

Homer Pennock landed a party of gold and coal prospectors in the schooner *Excelsior* in 1896 and established Homer. Gold was not found, but an abundance of coal was and the settlement remained.

Healthy fishing and tourism industries support Homer's economy. Kachemak Bay, a 30-mile arm of lower Cook Inlet, provides a usually ice-free deep-water harbor for Homer. A small boat harbor has launching facilities and charter boats. Charter planes are available in town for hunting, fishing, wildlife viewing and sightseeing expeditions. Cross-country skiing is popular in winter. The city is linked by daily air service with Anchorage, and by the Alaska Marine Highway with Seward, Kodiak and Seldovia.

Skyline Drive, accessible from West and East Hill roads, follows the rim of the plateau behind the town and offers access to ski slopes and views of the bay, Homer Spit and the Kenai Mountains. Chartered bush flights afford panoramas of the bay, open coal seams and Harding Icefield to the southeast.

Homer Chamber of Commerce: 201 Sterling Hwy., Homer, AK 99603. **Phone:** (907) 235-7740.

ALASKA ISLANDS & OCEAN VISITOR CENTER is at 95 Sterling Hwy. The center presents an overview of the area through interpretive exhibits about Kachemak Bay; local estuaries; research ships; and the seabird and marine inhabitants of the Alaska Maritime National Wildlife Refuge. Outdoor nature trails link the 60-acre site with Bishop's Beach Park on Kachemak Bay. Naturalist-led tours are offered, and a short movie about the Aleutian Islands is shown.

Time: Allow 2 hours minimum. **Hours:** Daily 9-6, Memorial Day-Labor Day; hours vary rest of year. Closed major holidays. **Cost:** Donations. **Phone:** (907) 235-6961.

PRATT MUSEUM is .5 blks. n. of Pioneer Ave. at 3779 Bartlett St. Highlights at the community museum include a botanical garden; a homestead cabin; a marine gallery; fishing boat models; sea birds and marine mammals; a forest trail; an exhibit detailing the impact of the *Exxon Valdez* oil spill; and native artifacts. Alaskan art from the Kenai Peninsula also is exhibited. Remote cameras provide visitors live images of seabirds and local wildlife.

Time: Allow 1 hour minimum. **Hours:** Daily 10-6, Memorial Day-Labor Day; Tues.-Sun. noon-5, mid-Sept. to mid-May. Closed Jan. 1, Thanksgiving and Dec. 25. **Cost:** $8; $6 (ages 66+); $4 (ages 6-18); $25 (family, two adults and children). **Phone:** (907) 235-8635.

RECREATIONAL ACTIVITIES
Fishing

- **Homer Ocean Charters** is at Cannery Row boardwalk on Homer Spit Rd. **Hours:** Trips depart daily by appointment. **Phone:** (907) 235-6212 or (800) 426-6212.

HOPE (C-10) pop. 137, elev. 32′

RECREATIONAL ACTIVITIES
White-water Rafting

- **Chugach Outdoor Center** departs from Milepost 7.5, Hope Hwy. Other activities are offered. **Hours:** Trips depart daily at 9 and 2, May-Sept. **Phone:** (907) 277-7238 or (866) 277-7238.

JUNEAU (G-10) pop. 30,711, elev. 12′

See map page 342.

Juneau, Alaska's capital city, lies along the beautiful Gastineau Channel at the foot of snowcapped mounts Roberts and Juneau. The borough of Juneau covers 3,108 square miles of towering mountains, islands, saltwater bays, forested valleys and residential flatlands. Its road system extends from Thane, 6 miles southeast of downtown, northwest to Echo Cove at Milepost 40.2 on the Glacier Highway. The city is accessible by air or by sea.

When Joe Juneau and Richard Harris discovered gold in 1880, they started the first rush in American Alaska. At one time the Alaska-Juneau and Treadwell mines were producing about 20,000 tons of ore daily. Not until 1944, when the low price of gold and the high cost of extraction rendered it impractical, did mining operations cease.

The Alaska State Capitol, Fourth and Main streets, offers free 30-minute tours in summer. The State Office Building, one block west of the capitol at 333 Willoughby Ave., contains a century-old totem pole and a Kimball Theatre pipe organ equipped

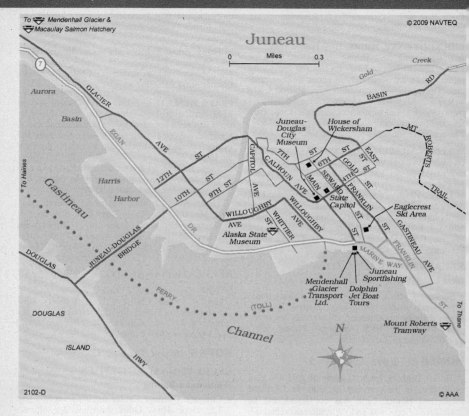

To Mendenhall Glacier & Macaulay Salmon Hatchery

Juneau

with such accessories as a glockenspiel, sleigh bells and bird whistles. Free concerts are held Friday at noon in the eighth-floor atrium. Also on the eighth floor, a terrace affords panoramas of the harbor and the surrounding mountains.

Tours of one of the oldest churches in southeastern Alaska are available mid-May to mid-September. Built in 1894, St. Nicholas Russian Orthodox Church is at Fifth and Gold streets. The Shrine of St. Therese, near Milepost 23 on the Glacier Highway, is a stone chapel on an island connected to shore by a gravel causeway.

There are many ways to tour Juneau. Nearby hiking trails, which vary in length and difficulty, lead to fishing spots, scenic mountain areas, old mine ruins and points near Mendenhall Glacier. Bus tours circle points of interest in Juneau and visit Mendenhall Glacier and the log Chapel-by-the-Lake at Auke Lake. Tours depart from the cruise ship docks during the summer. Visitors also can charter boats for sightseeing or fishing.

A good way to see the ice field is to take a charter flight. Companies that offer flightseeing tours from Juneau are Alaska Fly 'n' Fish Charters, (907) 790-2120; Alaska Seaplane Service, (907) 789-3331; Ward Air, (907) 789-9150; and Wings of Alaska,

(907) 789-0790. Helicopter tours, float trips, gold-panning excursions and several tours of nearby and more distant points of interest are available through SAVE Gray Line of Alaska, (907) 586-3773; and Princess Tours, (907) 463-3900.

Salmon bakes are held at Thane Ore House daily in summer; phone (907) 586-3442.

Juneau Convention and Visitors Bureau: 101 Egan Dr., Juneau, AK 99801. **Phone:** (907) 586-2201 or (888) 581-2201.

Self-guiding tours: Free walking tour maps of the historical and governmental districts are available at the Juneau Convention and Visitors Bureau.

ALASKA STATE MUSEUM, w. of Egan Dr. at 395 Whittier St., chronicles the state's history and preserves and exhibits Tlingit and Athabascan Indian, Eskimo and Aleut culture. Wildlife and mining displays, Russian-American historical exhibits and art of Alaska are featured. Highlights include a bald eagle nesting tree.

Guided tours are available in summer. **Time:** Allow 1 hour minimum. **Hours:** Daily 8:30-5:30, mid-May to mid-Sept.; Tues.-Sat. 10-4, rest of the

Closed Memorial Day, July 4 and Labor Day. **Cost:** Mid-May to mid-Sept. $5; free (ages 0-18). Rest of year $3; free (ages 0-18 and first Fri. of Oct.-Apr. 4:30-7). **Phone:** (907) 465-2901.

DOLPHIN JET BOAT TOURS provides pick-up downtown at the tram parking area. Three-hour tours on a jet boat offer the opportunity to view humpback and killer whales, porpoises, sea lions, seals and eagles. Other tours are available. **Hours:** Tours depart daily at 9, 11, 1, 3 and 5, May 1-Sept. 20. **Cost:** Fare $110; $90 (ages 2-12). **Phone:** (907) 463-3422 or (800) 719-3422.

ERA HELICOPTERS FLIGHTSEEING TOURS depart from the North Douglas Heliport. Narrated, 1-hour tours offer views of the capital city, abandoned mines and four glaciers in the Juneau Icefield. Highlights include a glacier landing to explore the blue ice. A 1.75-hour flight to visit dog sled camps near Anchorage also is available. **Time:** Allow 2 hours minimum. **Hours:** Daily 8-7, May-Sept. **Cost:** Fare $279-$479. Flights require a minimum of four passengers. **Phone:** (907) 586-2030 or (800) 843-1947.

FOREST SERVICE INFORMATION CENTER is at 8510 Mendenhall Loop Rd. Trail guides, maps, current conditions and recreation and cabin reservation information about Tongass National Forest and Glacier Bay National Park are available. **Hours:** Mon.-Fri. 8-5. **Cost:** Free. **Phone:** (907) 586-8800.

GLACIER GARDENS RAINFOREST ADVENTURE is at 7600 Glacier Hwy. A motorized shuttle takes passengers up Thunder Mountain through botanical gardens nestled in a lush Alaskan rain forest. Guests travel past streams, ponds, waterfalls and such flora as rhododendrons, Japanese maples and ferns. A scenic overlook at the 580-foot marker offers a spectacular view of the Mendenhall Valley and Chilkat Mountains. **Time:** Allow 1 hour minimum. **Hours:** Daily 9-6, May-Sept. **Cost:** $21.95; $15.95 (ages 6-12). **Phone:** (907) 790-3377.

HOUSE OF WICKERSHAM, 213 Seventh St., was the residence of Judge James Wickersham, noted Alaskan statesman, historian and pioneer judge. Built 1898-99 on "Chicken Ridge," this large Victorian house offers panoramic views of Gastineau Channel. Wherever the judge traveled in Alaska he collected ivory pieces, basketry and carvings, which are on display.

Hours: Tues.-Sat. 10-4, mid-May to late Sept.; by appointment rest of year. **Cost:** Donations. **Phone:** (907) 586-9001.

JUNEAU-DOUGLAS CITY MUSEUM is at Fourth and Main sts. Visitors can view exhibits about the area's early gold mining days, Tlingit culture and life in the Juneau-Douglas areas. Special exhibits about the greater Juneau area change annually. A relief map of the city's topography and a video presentation titled "Juneau: City Built on Gold" are

other features. Guided 1-hour walking tours or free maps outlining a historic self-guided walking tour are available.

Hours: Mon.-Fri. 9-5, Sat.-Sun. 10-5, May-Sept.; Tues.-Sat. 10-4 and by appointment, rest of year. Guided walking tours depart Tues., Thurs., and Sat. at 1:30, mid-May to mid-Sept. Closed July 4 and winter holidays. **Cost:** $4; free (ages 0-18). Guided tours $10; $7 (ages 0-18). **Phone:** (907) 586-3572.

MACAULAY SALMON HATCHERY is at 2697 Channel Dr. During 10- to 15-minute presentations, tour guides explain hatchery processes, beginning with the imprinting of young salmon to ensure a return at the end of their lifespan and concluding with egg retrieval. In May-June, visitors may observe the juvenile salmon pre-release; from mid-June through October, the returning salmon may be seen in their outdoor holding tanks where they are separated and prepared for egg harvesting. Indoor aquariums contain more than 100 species of southeast Alaska sea life, including anemones, crabs and octopi. Visitors may feel such animals as starfish in touch tanks.

Tours: Guided tours are available. **Time:** Allow 30 minutes minimum. **Hours:** Mon.-Fri. 10-5, Sat.-Sun. 8-5, May-Sept.; by appointment rest of year. **Cost:** $3.25; $1.75 (ages 3-12). **Phone:** (907) 463-4810 or (877) 463-2486.

MENDENHALL GLACIER, 13 mi. n.w. via SR 7 and Mendenhall Loop Rd., is an impressive river of blue ice, 13 miles long and 1.5 miles wide at its widest point. The glacier is fed by the 1,500-square-mile Juneau Icefield, part of the Tongass National Forest *(see place listing p. 360).*

Trails on either side of the glacial valley afford scenic views. To the east are Mendenhall Lake and Nugget Creek Falls; the west trail ascends above the glacier. Camping and picnic facilities are available at Mendenhall Lake. An easily traversable .5-mile nature trail begins near the visitor center; brochures are available.

The Steep Creek viewing platform near the visitor center parking lot is a good vantage point from which to see spawning sockeye salmon mid-July through mid-September. The salmon run attracts bald eagles and black bears mid-September through November.

Mendenhall Glacier Visitor Center, at the end of Glacial Spur Rd., contains a model depicting glacier dynamics, dioramas and display cases that interpret five evolving ecosystems at the glacier and a naturalistic salmon-filled stream that tumbles over rocks. A film is shown three times every hour during the summer, otherwise by request. Interpretive talks and nature hikes also are offered. **Hours:** Daily 8-7:30, May-Sept.; Thurs.-Sun. 10-4, rest of year. Closed winter holidays. **Cost:** May-Sept. $3; free (ages 0-15 and rest of year). **Phone:** (907) 789-0097 or (907) 789-6640.

MENDENHALL GLACIER TRANSPORT LTD., departing from the cruise ship dock downtown, provides sightseeing excursions of Juneau by bus. The tour stops at the Chapel by the Lake and Mendenhall Glacier. Other tours are available. **Time:** Allow 2 hours, 30 minutes minimum. **Hours:** Daily 9-3:30, May-Sept. **Cost:** Fare $27. **Phone:** (907) 789-5460. *See color ad p. 343.*

MOUNT ROBERTS TRAMWAY, 490 S. Franklin St. on the cruise ship dock, offers a 6-minute ride to the 1,800-foot level of Mount Roberts. At the top, visitors can stop at the nature center, see a live bald eagle displayed by the Juneau Raptor Center, take wildlife or nature walks and view the spectacular scenery. "Seeing Daylight," a movie about Alaska's native Tlingit, is presented in the Chilkat Theater. Other tours are available. **Time:** Allow 1 hour, 30 minutes minimum. **Hours:** Mon.-Fri. 8-9; Sat.-Sun. 9-9, May-Sept. **Cost:** Fare $27; $13.50 (ages 6-12). **Phone:** (907) 463-3412 or (888) 461-8726. *See color ad p. 787.*

TAKU GLACIER LODGE FLIGHTSEEING ADVENTURE departs from the wharf near the cruise ship docks. A Wings Airways floatplane takes passengers to a 1923 fishing and hunting lodge in the Taku River Valley for a salmon feast. Aerial views include mountains, Taku Inlet, waterfalls and five glaciers. Walking trails explore the area surrounding the historic lodge, which is across the river from the

Hole-in-the-Wall Glacier. **Time:** Allow 3 hours minimum. **Hours:** Trips depart daily at 9, 11, 1 and 3, May-Sept. **Cost:** Fare $260; $220 (ages 0-11). **Phone:** (907) 586-6275.

RECREATIONAL ACTIVITIES

Fishing

- **Juneau Sportfishing** offers round-trip transportation from local hotels and ships. Half, full and multiple day tours are available. **Hours:** Trips depart daily. **Phone:** (907) 586-1887.

- **Salmon Guaranteed Charters**, 4510 Prospect Way, Juneau, AK 99801. **Hours:** Daily May-Oct. **Phone:** (907) 364-3474.

Skiing

- **Eaglecrest Ski Area** is 12 mi. n.w. off the N. Douglas Hwy. **Hours:** Thurs.-Mon. 9-4, Dec.-Mar. (also Thurs. 4-9, early Jan. to mid-Mar.). **Phone:** (907) 790-2000.

KATMAI NATIONAL PARK AND PRESERVE (G-5)

Elevations in the park and preserve range from sea level at the Shelikof Strait to 7,606 ft. at Mount Dennison. Refer to AAA maps for additional elevation information.

On the northern portion of the Alaska Peninsula, 4.1-million-acre Katmai National Park and Preserve displays an outstanding example of volcanism. In 1912 one of the greatest volcanic explosions in recorded history turned a nameless green valley into what became known as the Valley of Ten Thousand Smokes. For more than 45 years the eruption was attributed to Mount Katmai, but recent studies indicate that the source was a new volcanic vent called Novarupta, some 6 miles distant.

During or shortly after the eruption, the peak of Mount Katmai collapsed, forming a caldera that subsequently filled with water. Molten material released from Novarupta and surrounding vents flowed down the valley, and thousands of holes from which smoke and gases arose formed as gases and vaporized surface water percolated through the volcanic deposits. These fumaroles, which gave the valley its name, lasted only about 20 years.

Although nearly all of the "smokes" have died out, steam columns from nearby volcanoes sometimes can be seen. By air it is possible to see the jade-green lake in the crater of Mount Katmai and to circle over still-active mounts Trident, Mageik and Martin.

In addition to its superlative scenery—large lakes, rivers, glaciers and active volcanoes—the park is noted for its abundant wildlife. The most prominent mammal is the Alaskan brown bear, the world's largest carnivore, averaging 500 pounds with some reaching 1,200 pounds. It is recommended that visitors maintain at least 50 yards from individual bears

Mountains of Ice

Glaciers—blue-white in color, with long frozen tongues reaching into the water—cover more than 75,000 square miles in the United States, and most are found in Alaska.

If you've explored the waters of the Inside Passage or Prince William Sound, you've certainly seen them.

But how is a glacier formed? Here are the basics: Glaciers are created when more snow falls each winter than melts the following summer. As areas receive snowfall year after year, new snow layers create pressure on existing layers of snow and ice. This creates firn, small granules of compacted snow. Firn from previous years is buried and turns to ice through  crystallization. The process continues, increasing the pressure on the ice field until air diminishes, and solid crystalline ice is formed.

As the layers of snow, firn and ice thicken, the lower ice can no longer support the weight of the mass, and it moves downward, smoothing surrounding mountain walls and floors and leaving grooves in a U-shaped valley.

You may be wondering why glacial ice is blue. It's actually not. Glacial ice is so concentrated that it absorbs all colors in the light spectrum except blue, which is reflected back at the viewer—making the ice *appear* blue. The lack of oxygen in the ice causes it to melt much more slowly than ice created in your freezer.

Some of the more popular glaciers to visit are Columbia, Exit, Hubbard, LeConte, Mendenhall and Portage. But while you're gazing at these giant frozen wonders, keep in mind that almost 90 percent of an iceberg is below water!

and 100 yards from sows with young. Visitors also should make noises while walking or hiking.

Katmai National Park can be reached only by boat or plane. A boat ramp is at Lake Camp, 10 miles by dirt road from King Salmon. Commercial airlines serve King Salmon, 35 miles from Brooks Camp. Amphibious aircraft make daily scheduled flights between King Salmon and Brooks Camp. Bush planes can be chartered.

Daily 1-hour tours to the Valley of Ten Thousand Smokes begin at Brooks Camp at 8:30 a.m. Fare $96 (with bag lunch); $88 (no lunch); $51 (one way). Departures require a minimum of 2 people. Other tours are available; for more information phone Katmailand, Inc., (800) 544-0551. For further information about the park contact the Superintendent, Katmai National Park and Preserve, P.O. Box 7, King Salmon, AK 99613; phone (907) 246-3305. *See Recreation Chart.*

KENAI (D-10) pop. 6,942, elev. 86′

Established as Fort St. Nicholas by Russian fur traders in 1791, Kenai (KEEN-eye) is one of the oldest permanent settlements in Alaska. Until 1953 the town grew under a squatters' rights policy. Kenai is the closest settlement to the south-central region's most promising oil-development fields and is the site of major petrochemical plants.

Kenai's Russian Orthodox Church, established in 1894, contains religious and art objects brought from Russia in 1841.

A popular, colorful pastime during the summer months in Kenai is berry picking. Such berries as Alaska blueberries (a smaller version of its common cousin), nagoonberries (reddish purple in color), cloudberries and salmonberries (both peach in color), crowberries (black in color), northern red currants, wild raspberries and cranberries grow on the peninsula.

Kenai Visitors and Convention Bureau: 11471 Kenai Spur Hwy., Kenai, AK 99611. **Phone:** (907) 283-1991.

KENAI NATIONAL WILDLIFE REFUGE— *see Soldotna p. 359.*

KENAI VISITORS & CULTURAL CENTER, 11471 Kenai Spur Hwy., offers visitor information as well as displays about Kenai's history and culture. Exhibit rooms showcase Dena'ina Athabascan art and artifacts, Russian relics and educational displays describing Alaskan wildlife. The center also hosts traveling and temporary exhibitions of photography, art, crafts, native culture and Alaska history throughout the year.

Time: Allow 30 minutes minimum. **Hours:** Mon.-Fri. 9-7, Sat.-Sun. 10-6, mid-May to mid-Sept.; Mon.-Fri. 9-5, Sat. 11-4, rest of year. **Cost:** $5; free (ages 0-18). **Phone:** (907) 283-1991.

KENAI FJORDS NATIONAL PARK (D-11)

Elevations in the park range from sea level at Nuka Bay to 6,400 ft. at a peak on the Harding Icefield. Refer to AAA maps for additional elevation information.

On the southeastern side of the Kenai Peninsula, Kenai Fjords National Park covers more than 600,000 acres. Access to the park is by private vehicle, plane or boat from Seward. Air charters also are available from other communities on the Kenai Peninsula. Scheduled bus service is available between Seward and Anchorage. Several tour companies offer trips to Exit Glacier and boat trips to the fjords.

The park encompasses a coastal mountain range that includes most of Harding Icefield, one of the four largest ice fields in the United States. A remnant of the ice age, it blankets all but the top of the Kenai Mountains. Along the coast is the rugged shoreline of the glacier-carved Kenai Fjords. Seals, porpoises, whales and sea otters are some of the 23 marine mammal species that inhabit the coastal waters.

Exit Glacier is the most accessible of the glaciers that flow from Harding Icefield. Three miles north of Seward via the Seward Highway and Exit Glacier Road, the glacier is reached by a .7-mile trail that begins at the Exit Glacier parking area; guided tours depart daily at 10, 2 and 4, mid-May to mid-September. A strenuous 7-mile round-trip journey from the base of Exit Glacier to Harding Icefield departs from the visitor center at 9, July through August. Bald eagles, bears, moose, mountain goats and Steller sea lions inhabit the area.

Picnicking and backcountry camping are permitted; a 12-site walk-in tent campground and three rustic cabins are available. Winter activities at Exit Glacier include skiing, snowmobiling, snowshoeing and dog sledding. Boat and air charters provide access to the coast during the summer.

Both park headquarters and a visitor center are in Seward. Park headquarters is at 500 Adams St., Suite 103, and the visitor center is at 1212 4th Ave. next to the harbormaster's office. Slide shows, exhibits and information about ranger-conducted activities are available.

Headquarters and visitor center open daily 9-5, Memorial Day-Labor Day; Mon.-Fri. 8-5, rest of year. Admission to Exit Glacier is $5 per vehicle. For information write the Superintendent, Kenai Fjords National Park, P.O. Box 1727, Seward, AK 99664; phone (907) 224-7500 or (907) 224-2132 for recorded information. *See Recreation Chart.*

KETCHIKAN (I-11) pop. 7,922

Alaska's southernmost city sits on stilts at the base of the Tongass National Forest (*see place listing p. 360*). On Revillagigedo Island, separated from the mainland by Behm Canal, Ketchikan claims to be the salmon capital of the world. An average annual rainfall of 156 to 162 inches makes it the wettest community in North America. The city's economic base relies on fishing, canning, mineral exploration, tourism and logging and cold-storage operations.

The town is populated with native culture and contains the largest concentration of Tlingit (KLINK-it), Haida (HY-dah), and Tsimshian (SIMP-shee-ane) people in Alaska. This heritage can be seen in the many totem poles that populate the area. Totem poles—tall cedar logs carved with eagles, ravens, wolves, bears, whales and other figures—depict stories or designate clans or lineage, and Ketchikan is reputed to contain the most in the world.

Creek Street is a relic of Ketchikan's rough-and-tumble past. Built on stilts over Ketchikan Creek, the street was once the site of a thriving red-light district. Highlights include art galleries, shops and a museum. The creek is a spawning ground for salmon.

SAVE Gray Line of Alaska, (907) 225-2404, and Princess Tours, (800) 774-6237, are among the companies that offer tours of the city. Ketchikan Visitors Center can provide a more complete list. Charter aircraft, boats, rental cars, buses and taxis are available at the Ketchikan Visitors Bureau, the airport and the ferry terminal.

Southeast Alaska Discovery Center: 50 Main St., Ketchikan, AK 99901. **Phone:** (907) 228-6220 or TTY (907) 228-6237.

Self-guiding tours: Information about a 2-hour walking tour of downtown is provided at the Ketchikan Visitors Bureau, 131 Front St., Ketchikan, AK 99901; phone (907) 225-6166 or (800) 770-3300.

Shopping areas: The Creek Street boardwalk area in downtown contains a number of specialty shops and boutiques.

BERING SEA CRAB FISHERMEN'S TOUR departs from the Main Cruise Ships dock at the Front St. pier. This 3.5-hour excursion on the waters of the Metlakatla Indian Community is conducted on the *Aleutian Ballad* — a vessel featured in the TV show "Deadliest Catch" — and offers passengers a first-hand look at the king crab fishing industry and its techniques. As the tour proceeds, passengers are regaled with tales of life at sea and educated about the state's fishing history and the variety of fishing vessels used. A heated and sheltered amphitheater allows passengers to observe the ship's crew as it unloads 700-pound crab pots.

Often seen among the ship's catch are such sea creatures as octopi, prawns, sharks and wolf eels; many animals are placed in an on-deck tank for observation and photo opportunities prior to release back into the sea. Such local wildlife as bald eagles, sea lions, seals and humpback whales may be seen during the tour.

Note: Prior to boarding, potential passengers should seek to locate a tour representative on the dock at least 30 minutes before the scheduled departure time. Those unable to locate a representative at least 15 minutes prior to departure may proceed to the *Aleutian Ballad* at the Berth 3 Tender Float. Passengers should dress in comfortable and warm layers of clothing. Each passenger should be of sufficient age and capacity to remain in the ship's passenger-designated zones and outside its working areas as well as be able to navigate the ship's aisles and stairs. Limited storage space is available. Photo ID is required. **Time:** Allow 3 hours, 30 minutes minimum.

Hours: Tours depart twice per day Mon. and Wed.-Fri. (departure times vary) and once per day Tues. (departure time varies), Sat. at 11 and Sun. at 8, May 1 to mid-Sept. The schedule is designed to accommodate passengers; phone ahead to verify departure times. **Cost:** Fare $159; $99 (ages 5-12). Children ages 0-4 are not permitted on the tour. **Phone:** (360) 642-4935 or (888) 239-3816. [T]

CLASSIC TOURS picks up passengers at the downtown cruise ship dock or local accommodation. Up to five passengers may ride in a restored 1955 Chevy driven by a retired schoolteacher clad in a poodle skirt and saddle shoes. Two narrated tours focus on the natural and cultural history of Ketchikan. The 2-hour Totem Tour includes visits to Saxman Totem Pole Park and the Creek Street boardwalk area. The 3-hour Totems and Eagles Tour also includes a visit to the rainforest, a bald eagle's nest and a king salmon site (in season). Wildlife viewing is possible. Private tours can be arranged.

Hours: Daily 8-6, early May-Sept. 30. **Cost:** Fare $139 (3-hour tour); $109 (2-hour tour). Fare includes admission to area museums and parks. Reservations are recommended. **Phone:** (907) 225-3091.

DEER MOUNTAIN TRIBAL HATCHERY AND EAGLE CENTER, .5 mi. n.e. at 1158 Salmon Rd. across the bridge from the Totem Heritage Center, raises king (chinook) and coho (silver) salmon, and steelhead and rainbow trout. Bald eagles also are featured in a landscaped enclosure. **Time:** Allow 30 minutes minimum. **Hours:** Daily 8-4:30, May-Sept. **Cost:** Guided tour $10; $5 (ages 0-11). **Phone:** (907) 228-5530.

SAXMAN NATIVE VILLAGE, 2.5 mi. s. on S. Tongass Hwy., is a Tlingit (KLINK-it) Indian village of about 350 residents. The totem park contains 30 totem poles, and master carvers can be seen at work in the carving center. A 2-hour guided tour also includes the Beaver Tribal House, the Old School House and Cape Fox Dancers performances.

Time: Allow 30 minutes minimum. **Hours:** Daily 8-5, mid-May through Sept. 30; hours vary rest of year. Cape Fox Dancers performance schedule varies; phone ahead. **Cost:** Free. Self-guided tour $3. Guided tour $35; $17.50 (ages 0-11). **Phone:** (907) 225-4846, ext. 100.

TONGASS HISTORICAL MUSEUM, 629 Dock St. in Ketchikan's Centennial Building, displays pioneer items as well as art and artifacts from northwest cultures. Historical and changing exhibits are offered. **Time:** Allow 30 minutes minimum. **Hours:** Daily 8-5, May-Sept.; Wed.-Fri. 1-5, Sat. 10-4, Sun. 1-4, rest of year. Closed winter holidays. **Cost:** May-Sept. $2; rest of year free. **Phone:** (907) 225-5600.

TOTEM BIGHT STATE HISTORICAL PARK, 10 mi. n. on N. Tongass Hwy., displays 14 poles by Haida and Tlingit clans and a model of a Tlingit clan house. The site is reached by a short trail through a forest from the parking area. A brochure describes typical totem characters and gives insight to the art of totem carving. More totem poles are in Saxman Native Village, 2.5 miles south on S. Tongass Highway. **Time:** Allow 30 minutes minimum. **Hours:** Daily 6 a.m.-10 p.m. **Cost:** $3. **Phone:** (907) 247-8574.

TOTEM HERITAGE CENTER, 601 Deermount St., displays original 19th-century totem poles retrieved from native villages and emphasizes traditional Tlingit, Haida and Tsimshian art. **Tours:** Guided tours are available. **Time:** Allow 30 minutes minimum. **Hours:** Daily 8-5, May-Sept.; Mon.-Fri. 1-5 and during classes, rest of year. Closed winter holidays. **Cost:** May-Sept. $5; rest of year free. **Phone:** (907) 225-5900.

KLONDIKE GOLD RUSH NATIONAL HISTORICAL PARK—*see Skagway p. 358.*

KOBUK VALLEY NATIONAL PARK (C-4)

Elevations in the park range from 100 ft. at the point where the Kobuk River flows out of the southwest corner of the park to 4,700 ft. in the Brooks Range, which forms the park's northern border. Refer to AAA maps for additional elevation information.

Some 25 miles north of the Arctic Circle, Kobuk Valley National Park covers 1,710,000 acres in the heart of the arctic wildlands, where the boreal forest gives way to the frozen tundra. The broad Kobuk Valley is enclosed almost completely by the Baird Mountains to the north and the Waring Mountains to the south. Traversing the valley from east to west, the wide and placid Kobuk River offers good fishing and idyllic float trips. The swifter Salmon River, a designated Wild and Scenic River, flows south from the Baird Mountains.

Preserved within the park are the 25-square-mile Great Kobuk Sand Dunes, the largest active dunes in the Arctic. Created by the grinding action of ancient glaciers, the sand was carried by wind and water to a wide area south of the Kobuk River. The 100-foot dunes are accessible by a difficult hike from the river along Kavet Creek.

Home to seminomadic tribes for more than 12,500 years, the region still supports the native Inupiats; they are granted by law the right to continue subsistence hunting, trapping and other practices. Important to their survival is North America's largest caribou herd, numbering some 500,000. Many can be seen crossing the Kobuk River in September during their migration southward.

Other wildlife common to the region include moose, grizzly and black bears, wolves, red foxes, lynxes, wolverines and martens. Golden eagles can be seen in the northern latitudes; other birds include sandhill cranes, arctic loons, American golden plovers and arctic terns.

The park attracts experienced backpackers, campers and river travelers. Though the park is open year-round, the elements limit most visits to June through September. Fishing is good when the rivers are clear of silt; catches include salmon, pike, arctic char, whitefish and grayling. An Alaska fishing license is required. Hunting is not permitted, but it is legal to carry a firearm for protection from bears.

Access to the region is by daily commercial flights from Anchorage and Fairbanks to Kotzebue *(see place listing p. 349),* where connections to the villages of Kiana and Ambler can be made. Air taxi service into the park is available from Kotzebue, Kiana and Ambler. There are no facilities, services, trails or campgrounds in the park; a ranger station near Onion Portage is open June through September. The park headquarters in Kotzebue is open late May through September.

Due to its location, the area is subject to harsh weather and high winds. It is advisable to carry protection against hypothermia, mosquitoes and biting flies.

For trip planning assistance and a list of authorized outfitters, guides and air taxi operators, write the Superintendent, Western Arctic National Parklands, P.O. Box 1029, Kotzebue, AK 99752; phone (907) 442-3760 in summer, or (907) 442-3890. *See Recreation Chart.*

KODIAK (H-5) pop. 6,334

A Russian explorer-trader's quest for sea otter pelts led to the European settlement of Kodiak Island in 1784. The community of Kodiak was established about 1792 when Alexander Baranov moved his headquarters from the original 1784 settlement at Three Saints Bay, making Kodiak the first capital of Russian America. The blue, onion-shaped domes of the Holy Resurrection Russian Orthodox Church recall the days when the Russian Empire in the North Pacific was administered from Kodiak.

One of the oldest communities in Alaska, Kodiak also is a leading commercial fishing port. The town is on the northeastern tip of Kodiak Island, which is home to the Kodiak brown bear.

Kodiak was nearly destroyed twice; in June 1912, an eruption from Mount Novarupta covered the town with ash. On Good Friday in 1964 an earthquake in south central Alaska created tsunamis that enveloped the islands. Citizens found refuge on nearby Pillar Mountain and returned with the task of rebuilding the city.

Kodiak can be reached by air service from Anchorage or by the Alaska Marine Highway, a passenger/vehicle ferry, from Homer and Seward. Reservations are required well in advance for the ferry; write Alaska Marine Highway, P.O. Box 703, Kodiak, AK 99615, or phone (907) 486-3800 or (800) 526-6731.

Kodiak Island Convention and Visitors Bureau: 100 Marine Way, Suite 200, Kodiak, AK 99615. **Phone:** (907) 486-4782 or (800) 789-4782.

BARANOV MUSEUM, in the Erskine House on the harbor front, has collections of early Russian and Alaskan artifacts as well as American household furnishings from the early 20th century. The building, which dates from 1808, was used by Alexander Baranov as a warehouse for storing furs. Original log construction methods can be examined inside. **Time:** Allow 1 hour minimum. **Hours:** Mon.-Sat. 10-4, Sun. noon-4, Memorial Day-Labor Day; Tues.-Sat. 10-3, rest of year. Closed major holidays. **Cost:** $3; free (ages 0-11). **Phone:** (907) 486-5920.

FORT ABERCROMBIE STATE HISTORICAL PARK, 4.5 mi. n.e. on Miller Point, is a World War II fortification. The 183-acre park offers a view of the rocky coastline and nearby islands. Interpretive programs are given, and hiking trails are available. World War II artifacts remain; the visitor center offers natural-history displays and information about Alaska's participation in World War II. Tidal pools are within walking distance of the visitor center. *See Recreation Chart and the AAA Western Canada & Alaska CampBook.*

Hours: Daily 24 hours. **Cost:** Free. **Phone:** (907) 486-6339. 🅰

KODIAK ALUTIIQ DANCERS perform at 312 W. Marine Way. Traditional Alutiiq dances are performed by elaborately costumed dancers, who express cultural and spiritual values that have survived for thousands of years. Narration is provided. **Time:** Allow 30 minutes minimum. **Hours:** Performances daily at 3:30, June-Sept.; by appointment rest of year. Closed major holidays. Phone ahead to confirm schedule. **Cost:** $12; $10 (ages 55+); $7 (ages 0-8). Reservations are recommended. **Phone:** (907) 486-4449.

KODIAK LABORATORY AQUARIUM & TOUCH TANK at the Kodiak Fisheries Research Center at 301 Research Ct. The 3,500-gallon aquarium displays specimens collected from Kodiak Island's waters, including crabs, mollusks and other invertebrates as well as such echinoderms as anemones, sea cucumbers and starfish. A touch tank allows visitors to interact with selected intertidal organisms.

Time: Allow 30 minutes minimum. **Hours:** Mon.-Fri. 8-4:30. Closed major holidays. **Cost:** Free. **Phone:** (907) 481-1800.

KODIAK NATIONAL WILDLIFE REFUGE occupies the southwestern two-thirds of Kodiak Island and 50,000 acres on Ban Island and the northwestern tip of Afognak Island. The 1,865,000 acres were set aside to preserve the habitat of the Kodiak bear, some of which weigh up to 1,500 pounds. Among other inhabitants are Sitka black-tailed deer, sea lions, sea otters and bald eagles. The refuge is accessible only by plane and boat. Cabins and a number of recreational activities are available. **Cost:** Free. **Phone:** (907) 487-2600 or (888) 408-3514.

Visitor Center, 402 Center St., offers displays, videotapes, audiovisual presentations and information about the refuge. **Time:** Allow 1 hour minimum. **Hours:** Daily 9-5, Memorial Day-Labor Day; Tues.-Sat. 10-5, rest of year. Closed major holidays. **Cost:** Free. **Phone:** (907) 487-2626.

KODIAK TOURS depart from the lobby of the Best Western Kodiak Inn. Custom narrated historic tours of the island are tailored to the interests of the visitor. The U.S. Coast Guard Base, Cannery Row, boat harbors, Fisheries Research Center and Pillar Mountain are among the sites. The tour stops to view the island's wildlife and scenery. Half-day tours last 4 hours, while full-day tours last 8 hours.

Inquire about weather policies. **Hours:** Full-day tours depart daily at 9. Half-day tours depart daily at 9 and 1. **Cost:** Full-day fare (includes all attraction admission fees) $95. Half-day fare $55. Reservations are required. **Phone:** (907) 486-3920.

KOTZEBUE (C-3) pop. 3,082, elev. 20′

Kotzebue, on the Baldwin Peninsula, sits on glacial moraine on the eastern edge of Kotzebue Sound. It was named after Otto Von Kotzebue, a German sailor exploring for Russia around 1818. Inhabited by the Kikiktagruk Inupiat Eskimos since the early 19th century, the area later became a seasonal trading center for the various Eskimo tribes due to its position at the confluence of the Noatak and Kobuk rivers. Its establishment as a permanent city began in 1899 with a Quaker mission.

Kotzebue is situated 33 miles above the Arctic Circle in the treeless tundra; the sun rises each year in early June and remains above the horizon for only 38 days. A spectacular ice breakup takes place for 2 weeks between mid-May and mid-June.

The second-largest Eskimo village in Alaska, Kotzebue is reached only by daily air service from Anchorage, Nome and Fairbanks. Arrangements for bush plane flights over the surrounding tundra and to the Kobuk River for hunting and fishing expeditions can be made at the airport. Short air and boat excursions to most of the surrounding villages also are available through independent operators. Nana Museum of the Arctic, near the airport, offers a slide show and a tour.

LAKE CLARK NATIONAL PARK AND PRESERVE (F-5)

Elevations in the park and preserve range from sea level along Cook Inlet to 10,197 ft. at Mount Redoubt. Refer to AAA maps for additional elevation information.

West of Cook Inlet, Lake Clark National Park and Preserve is an almost 4-million-acre mountainous crossroads where ice and fire meet. The Pacific crust grinds beneath the North American plate, creating the Chigmit Mountains, a jagged array of spires and two steaming volcanoes, Mount Redoubt and Mount Iliamna. Mount Redoubt, the more active, last erupted in December 1989; it continues to emit steam and, less frequently, ash.

Covered by massive ice fields, the seemingly impenetrable Chigmit Mountains are formed by the linkage of two great ranges, the Alaska and the Aleutian. Together the ranges divide the park into distinct areas: the eastern flank's coastal plain bordering Cook Inlet and the lake and tundra region on the western flank. Lake Clark, 50 miles long, juts in from the southwest.

Moisture abounds along the park's coastal area, which is characterized by rocky cliffs along its southern portion, giving way to tidal marshes and grasslands in the north. In contrast to the luxuriant alder thickets and Sitka spruce along Cook Inlet, lakes, boreal forests and rolling tundra highlands distinguish the park's western landscape.

Numerous glacier-fed rivers and creeks are channeled through Lake Clark, creating one of the richest sockeye salmon spawning grounds in the world. The park was created primarily to protect this fruitful breeding area.

Although the park is open all year, most people visit during the peak of the summer season, late June through August. Even in summer months, weather conditions vary in the interior; it is advisable to bring protection against insects as well as clothing for sunny, wet or freezing weather. Visitors should outfit themselves in Kenai, Homer or Anchorage, as the communities closer to the park have limited supplies.

For anglers the rivers and lakes on the park's western side provide a variety of trophy-size fish, including salmon, arctic grayling and trout. A 2- to 3-mile trail to Tanalian Falls and Kontrashibuna Lake is accessible from Port Alsworth, near Lake Clark. The open foothills are ideal for backpacking. River-running also is popular on the Mulchatna, Tlikakila and Chilikadrotna rivers, all federally designated wild and scenic rivers.

As there are no roads in the park, access is almost exclusively by air. Most travelers charter aircraft; the closest airport is south of the park in Iliamna. A 1- to 2-hour flight from Anchorage, Homer or Kenai will provide access to most points within the park and preserve.

The National Park Service facility is at Port Alsworth and contains a visitor center with displays regarding natural history topics. The center is open Mon.-Fri. 8-5 (also Sat. 8-5, June-Aug.); phone (907) 781-2106. While there are minimal National Park facilities—staffed patrol cabins at Telaquana Lake, Twin Lakes, Crescent Lake and Chinitna Bay—there are a number of private lodges and cabins in the park.

For information about accommodations as well as a list of outfitters and maps, write the Superintendent, Lake Clark National Park and Preserve, 4230 University Dr., Suite 311, Anchorage, AK 99508; phone (907) 644-3626. *See Recreation Chart.*

MISTY FIORDS NATIONAL MONUMENT (H-11)

East of Ketchikan and within the Tongass National Forest *(see place listing p. 360),* Misty Fiords National Monument covers about 3,580 square miles of wilderness. The area is accessible by float plane from Ketchikan and other communities near the national forest. An information center and cruises to the monument are available in Ketchikan *(see place listing p. 346).*

Behm Canal, a deep inlet of the Pacific Ocean, leads to the interior of the monument, where rock walls that rise 3,000 feet surround Walker Cove and Rudyerd Bay. Geological features include mineral springs, 237-foot-tall New Eddystone Rock, 3,150-foot-tall Punchbowl Face, lava flows, five major rivers and hundreds of small streams. The region receives more than 120 inches of precipitation each year. Bald eagles, brown and black bears, wolves and mountain goats inhabit the area; whales, porpoises, seals and sea lions can be sighted in Behm Canal or in the ocean nearby.

Recreational activities include backpacking, picnicking, bird watching, hunting, fishing and crabbing. Rustic cabins are available for $25-$45 per day; reservations may be made by calling Reserve America, (877) 444-6777. Four free Adirondack-type shelters are available on a first-come, first-served basis. For further information contact the Southeast Alaska Discovery Center, 50 Main St., Ketchikan, AK 99901; phone (907) 228-6220, or TTY (907) 228-6237.

NOME (D-2) pop. 3,505, elev. 13′

Placer gold washed from the hillsides to the beaches at Nome lured thousands to the remote shores of the Bering Sea in 1898. At the height of the gold rush, 20,000 people lived in Nome, once the largest settlement in Alaska.

On the Seward Peninsula, Nome is the judicial and commercial center of northwestern Alaska and the main supply point for nearby mining districts and Eskimo villages. The city is accessible daily by plane from Anchorage. Regularly scheduled and charter flights are available to various Eskimo villages.

Cruise ships serve Nome during the summer, and rental cars provide visitors with opportunities for self-guiding trips to nearby villages.

When a diphtheria epidemic threatened the town in 1925, the necessary serum was delivered by dog team. The annual Iditarod Trail Race commemorates this emergency mission. The race, which begins in Anchorage *(see place listing p. 320)* the first Saturday in March, encompasses treacherous climbs, river passages and bone-chilling blizzards. Mushers cross the finish line in Nome after traveling roughly 1,160 miles, exhausted but invigorated by cheers from supporters lining the chute on Front Street.

One of the activities during the final week of the race is the Bering Sea Ice Classic, a six-hole golf tournament played on frozen Norton Sound.

The Midnight Sun Festival celebrates the summer solstice, the longest day of the year with almost 24 hours of sunlight. The mid-June festival lasts several days and includes a parade and The Nome River Raft Race.

Nome Convention and Visitors Bureau: P.O. Box 240 H-P, Nome, AK 99762. **Phone:** (907) 443-6624.

CARRIE M. McLAIN MEMORIAL MUSEUM is at 223 Front St. The museum showcases the history of the Nome gold rush, the lifestyles of Bering Strait Eskimos and the early days of sled dog racing. **Hours:** Daily 9:30-5:30, June-Sept.; Tues.-Sat. noon-5:30, rest of year. Closed major holidays. Phone ahead to confirm schedule. **Cost:** Donations. **Phone:** (907) 443-6630.

PALMER (C-11) pop. 4,533, elev. 240'

The peaks of the Chugach and Talkeetna mountains rise above Palmer, a city surrounded by the lush pastures and dairy and vegetable farms of the fertile Matanuska Valley, where cabbages can grow to weigh more than 70 pounds. A drive to Wasilla *(see place listing p. 362)* provides a good view of the valley and its farms. The Matanuska Agricultural Experimental Farm, 7 miles southwest, is operated by the University of Alaska Fairbanks' School of Natural Resources and Agricultural Sciences and welcomes visitors.

Palmer lies near the intersection of the Glenn and George Parks highways (SRs 1 and 3), both of which are scenic highways. An interesting drive is along a narrow, rough, winding road that follows Willow Creek through formerly rich gold areas. The road crosses Hatcher Pass en route to Willow.

The Palmer Visitor and Information Center, 550 S. Alaska St., Suite 101, contains a historical museum featuring items from the city's pioneer era. The 2-acre Agricultural Showcase Garden is on the center's grounds and features a variety of perennials; phone (907) 745-2880.

Mat-Su Convention & Visitors Bureau: Milepost 35.5, George Parks Hwy. (SR 3), 7744 E. Visitors View Ct., Palmer, AK 99645. **Phone:** (907) 746-5000.

INDEPENDENCE MINE STATE HISTORICAL PARK, 19 mi. n. on Hatcher Pass Rd., is a 761-acre park in the 221,000-acre Hatcher Pass region. The

Stories in Cedar

The art of totem pole carving in Alaska originated with the Tlingit, Haida and Tsimshian native tribes. Abundant food supplies along the Inside Passage allowed the natives the leisure time necessary to develop their elaborate craft.

Cedar totem poles served many purposes. Each figure on the pole represented an element in a story, and together the figures recorded the legends and histories of the

tribes, who have no written language.

Genealogy poles, erected in front of an owner's house, identified a clan, told a family story or conveyed the family's status. Crests (usually in the shapes of eagles or ravens) denoted the clans of the husband and wife. Mortuary poles included a compartment for the ashes of a deceased clan member or chief and were carved in honor of that individual. Shame poles were created to chastise someone who wronged the clan or village—the pole remained standing until the debt was repaid tenfold. Other totem poles conveyed mythological or legendary stories, or commemorated a notable event, such as a birth or a good deed.

Colors were limited to natural pigments made from salmon eggs or hematite. Black was the primary color; red was used for secondary elements; and blue-green was used for highlighting.

An intimate knowledge of native traditions is necessary to fully interpret the totem poles, but there are common figures that are relatively easy to identify: the raven, a symbol of the creator, who changes form at will; the eagle, representing peace and friendship; the killer whale, a symbol of strength; and the beaver, bear and wolf.

The Last Great Race

To commemorate the 1925 event in which 20 mushers relayed serum to Nome to save children who contracted diphtheria, the first Iditarod Race took place on Mar. 3, 1973.

Beginning in Anchorage and culminating in Nome, the race trail covers some 1,160 miles of rugged terrain, takes between 9-17 days to complete and can reach temperatures of minus 60 F.

In preparation for the great race, the trail is broken and marked with reflector tape, and checkpoints are chosen where teams stop to eat and rest. Since it's not feasible for mushers to carry

© PhotoDisc

all of their provisions in their sleds, the bulk of food and supplies is shipped to the checkpoints prior to the race.

To aid in endurance, dogs ingest 5,000 calories or more each day, gobbling such delicacies as moose, caribou or even seal meat. Concern for the dogs' health is strong: Booties are worn for paw protection, and about 25 veterinarians man the checkpoints to examine each dog.

While teams may begin the race with as many as 16 dogs, some drop from the race. "Dropped dogs"—dogs that do not finish the race due to dehydration, flu or fatigue—are carried to the nearest checkpoint and flown back to Anchorage. A musher must finish the race with at least five dogs.

Teams travel at night as well as during the day, and dogs rest about 10-12 hours per 24-hour period. But mushers don't enjoy that luxury: Responsible for feeding and caring for the dogs (including changing their booties every 100 miles), they rarely sleep more than 2 hours per night.

The goal? Nome's Burled Arch on Front Street. At this finish line, teams are greeted by cheering crowds and the sounding of the city's fire siren.

park preserves 15 buildings and numerous artifacts from its heyday as a gold boom town in the 1930s and 1940s. The history of the mine is chronicled in a museum and at the visitor center. Walking trails lead visitors past many of the mine camp's buildings, including bunkhouses, warehouses, the commissary and mess halls.

Tours: Guided tours are available. **Hours:** Park open daily. Visitor center open daily 11-6, June 15-Labor Day. Tours are given daily at 1 and 3. **Cost:** $5 per private vehicle. Tour $5. **Phone:** (907) 745-2827 or (907) 745-3975.

MUSK OX FARM, 2 mi. n. at Milepost 50 on Glenn Hwy., is said to be the only musk ox domestication project in the world. The shaggy creatures are valued for their fine underwool called "qiviut." Eskimos knit the hair, eight times warmer by weight than wool, into hats and scarves. Hands-on exhibits are available. Guided tours offer insight into the animal's history and behavior and allow observation from fenced walkways.

Hours: Daily 10-6, mid-May to late Sept. **Cost:** $8; $7 (ages 65+ and military with ID); $6 (ages 5-12). **Phone:** (907) 745-4151. 🚿

PETERSBURG (H-10) pop. 3,224, elev. 28′

Petersburg, at the north end of Mitkof Island, is an Alaska Marine Highway port. In 1897 Norwegian Peter Buschmann decided to build a cannery on Mitkof Island at the head of picturesque Wrangell Narrows. The facility at the north end of Nordic Drive was completed in 1900 and packed 32,750 cases of salmon during its first production year. Now Petersburg Fisheries, the firm is a pioneer in Alaska's expanding bottom-fishing and salmon industries.

Nicknamed "Little Norway," Petersburg boasts brightly painted wooden houses decorated with hand-painted floral designs, a traditional craft called rosemaling.

Among the nearby points of interest is LeConte Glacier, the southernmost of its kind in the northern hemisphere; just south of Petersburg; it can be reached via chartered plane, helicopter or boat. In nearby Frederick Sound whale-watching is popular; the area is home to orca and humpback whales as well as other sea mammals.

Petersburg Visitor Information Center: First and Fram sts., P.O. Box 649, Petersburg, AK 99833. **Phone:** (907) 772-4636 or (866) 484-4700.

CLAUSEN MEMORIAL MUSEUM, 203 Fram St., features exhibits about commercial fishing and canning, a dugout Tlingit Indian canoe, tools and artifacts. A "Fisk" fountain and a 126.5-pound king salmon, said to be a world record catch, also are on display. **Tours:** Guided tours are available. **Hours:** Mon.-Sat. 10-5, May 1-Sept. 4; Tues.-Sat. 10-2, Sept. 5-Dec. 23. Winter hours may vary; phone ahead. Closed major holidays. **Cost:** $3; free (ages 0-11). **Phone:** (907) 772-3598.

SEWARD (D-11) pop. 2,830, elev. 70′

Named for William H. Seward, who negotiated the purchase of Alaska, Seward is an ice-free port in a setting of great beauty. At the northeast end of a bay named Resurrection by Russians who arrived in its waters on Easter, the city is surrounded by lush, tall mountains and ice fields.

Charter boats and planes can be hired for fishing, hunting and sightseeing trips. Seward is the southern terminus of the Seward Highway, a national scenic byway extending north to Anchorage through an alpine terrain of glaciers and lakes. Seward also is the main access point to Kenai Fjords National Park

(*see place listing p. 346*), which includes Exit Glacier, one of the few accessible glaciers.

Seward Community Library, 238 5th Ave., shows movies and slides of the havoc wreaked by the 1964 Good Friday earthquake. Phone (907) 224-4082 for information and reservations.

Seward Chamber of Commerce: P.O. Box 749, Seward, AK 99664. **Phone:** (907) 224-8051.

Self-guiding tours: Information about a walking tour is available at the chamber of commerce's visitor information center, 2001 Seward Hwy.; phone (907) 224-8051 for details.

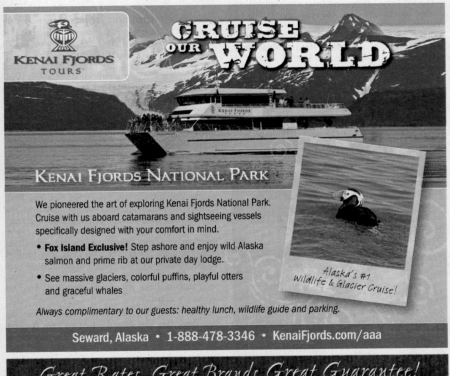

KENAI FJORDS TOURS

CRUISE OUR WORLD

KENAI FJORDS NATIONAL PARK

We pioneered the art of exploring Kenai Fjords National Park. Cruise with us aboard catamarans and sightseeing vessels specifically designed with your comfort in mind.

- **Fox Island Exclusive!** Step ashore and enjoy wild Alaska salmon and prime rib at our private day lodge.

- See massive glaciers, colorful puffins, playful otters and graceful whales

Alaska's #1 Wildlife & Glacier Cruise!

Always complimentary to our guests: healthy lunch, wildlife guide and parking.

Seward, Alaska • 1-888-478-3346 • KenaiFjords.com/aaa

ALASKA SEALIFE CENTER, on Seward Hwy. (SR 9) at Milepost 0, is dedicated to understanding and maintaining the integrity of Alaska's marine ecosystem through research, rehabilitation, conservation and public education. Highlights include Steller sea lions, harbor seals, Giant Pacific octopus and a sea bird habitat that allows visitors to get up close to puffins, kittiwakes and other Alaskan avian wonders.

Exhibits also include a jellyfish display, the hands-on Discovery touch pool and the Lifecycles of Pacific Salmon, which examines the life stages of all five species of Pacific Salmon. More than 300 of the fish may be observed in 2,200- to 6,000-gallon tanks.

Guided behind-the-scenes tours are available, including marine mammal, octopus and puffin encounters. Reservations for behind-the-scenes and encounter tours are recommended. **Time:** Allow 1 hour, 30 minutes minimum. **Hours:** Mon.-Thurs. 9-6:30, Fri.-Sun. 8-6:30, May 1-Sept. 15; daily 10-5, rest of year. Behind-the-scenes tours depart daily at 10, 1 and 3, May 1-Sept. 15; daily at 1, rest of year. Marine mammal encounter tours depart daily at 11 and 3. Puffin encounter tours depart daily at 11 and 2. Octopus encounter tours depart daily at 1. Closed Thanksgiving and Dec. 25. **Cost:** $20; $15 (ages 12-17 and college students with ID); $10 (ages 4-11). Behind-the-scenes tours $15; $10 (ages 4-17). Marine mammal, puffin and octopus encounter tours

$79; $59 (ages 12-17); $39 (ages 4-11). **Phone:** (907) 224-6300, (888) 378-2525 for reservations or (800) 224-2525.

GODWIN GLACIER DOG SLED TOURS offers excursions departing from the Seward Airport off Seward Hwy. Beginning with a helicopter flight to Godwin Glacier, the guided tour includes a 2.5-mile dog sled ride traversing the glacier's ancient snowfield. During the round-trip flight, passengers may spot mountain goats, bears, moose and eagles. Other tours are available. **Time:** Allow 2 hours minimum. **Hours:** Tours depart daily on the hour 8-6, May 27 to late Sept. (weather permitting). **Cost:** Fare $450; $420 (ages 0-12). **Phone:** (907) 224-8239 or (888) 989-8239.

IDIDARIDE SLED DOG TOURS is off Seward Hwy. (SR 9) Milepost 3.6, 1 mi. w. on Exit Glacier Rd., .4 mi. n. on Old Exit Glacier Rd. (gravel road) following signs. An Iditarod champion offers a summer version of a sled dog ride aboard a wheeled sled during a 2-mile trip through Box Canyon. Visitors can tour the dog kennel to socialize with the husky puppies and witness a sled dog training demonstration.

Time: Allow 1 hour, 30 minutes minimum. **Hours:** Daily 8-8, May-Sept. **Cost:** $59; $29 (ages 2-11). **Phone:** (907) 224-8607 or (800) 478-3139.

KENAI FJORDS TOURS depart from the Seward Small Boat Harbor. The company offers glacier and wildlife cruises into the waters that surround Kenai Fjords National Park. Cruises also explore Resurrection Bay and the northwestern fjords, where active tidewater glaciers are a highlight. A variety of marine mammals can be seen; gray whales often are spotted on whale-watching tours. Six-hour Kenai Fjords National Park tours; 9.5-hour Northwestern Fjords tours; 4- and 5-hour Resurrection Bay wildlife tours and Fox Island Salmon Bake cruises, which last 4, 5 or 8.5 hours, are available.

Inquire about weather policies. **Hours:** Tours depart daily, late Mar.-Oct. 31. Kenai Fjords National Park tours depart at 8, 10, 11:30 and 3. Northwestern Fjords tours depart at 9. Resurrection Bay wildlife tours depart at noon and 5:30. Salmon bake cruises depart at 9 and noon. **Cost:** Park tour $139-$159; $69.50-$79.50 (ages 2-11). Fjord tour $169; $84.50 (ages 2-11). Bay tour $79-$89; $39.50-$44.50 (ages 2-11). Salmon bake cruise $129-$189. Reservations are recommended. **Phone:** (907) 224-8068 or (877) 777-4051. *See color ad p. 353.*

MAJOR MARINE TOURS depart from the Seward Small Boat Harbor, 1 blk. e. of Seward Hwy. Narrated glacier and wildlife sightseeing cruises visit Kenai Fjords National Park. Passengers may spot bald eagles, otters, porpoises, puffins, sea lions and whales.

Inquire about weather policies Full-day cruise not recommended for infants and toddlers. **Hours:**

Cruises depart daily, early May to late Sept. Half-day cruise departs at 12:30, full-day cruise departs at 11:45. **Cost:** Half-day fare $77; $38 (ages 2-11). Full-day fare $150; $75 (ages 2-11). **Phone:** (907) 274-7300 or (800) 764-7300. *See color ad p. 323 & p. 354.* 🍴

RENOWN TOURS depart from the Seward Small Boat Harbor. Six-hour catamaran cruises into Kenai Fjords National Park, 3-hour Resurrection Bay cruises and 4-hour Gray Whale-watching cruises are guided by local, experienced captains. In addition to glaciers, humpback whales, orcas, sea otters, Steller sea lions, Dall's porpoises, bald eagles and puffins may be spotted.

Hours: National park cruise departs daily at 11:30, May-Sept. Resurrection Bay cruise departs daily at noon, May-Sept (also 3:30, June-Aug.). Gray Whale cruise departs daily at noon, Apr.-May. Check-in is 30 minutes before departure. **Cost:** National park cruise $149; $74 (ages 3-11). Resurrection Bay and Gray Whale cruises $69; $35 (ages 3-11). Reservations are recommended. **Phone:** (907) 224-3806 or (888) 514-8687.

SCENIC MOUNTAIN AIR (FLIGHTSEEING) operates wheeled planes from Seward Airport and float planes from Trail Lake in Moose Pass. Sights on the varied tours include Harding Icefield, Kenai Fjords and wildlife. Fly-in fishing tours also are available. **Hours:** Flights depart daily 8 a.m.-7 p.m., May 1-Sept. 15 (weather permitting). **Cost:** Fares $99-$229, depending on length of tour. **Phone:** (907) 288-3646.

SEWARD MUSEUM, 336 Third Ave., is operated by the Resurrection Bay Historical Society and has exhibits about the main events in Seward's history. A collection of native baskets and ivory carvings is displayed. **Hours:** Daily 10-5, Memorial Day-Labor Day; otherwise varies. **Cost:** $3. **Phone:** (907) 224-3902.

RECREATIONAL ACTIVITIES

Kayaking

- **Sunny Cove Sea Kayaking** offers tours departing 2 mi. from downtown at Lowell's Point on Resurrection Bay, and from Seward Small Boat Harbor traveling to Fox Island. Other activities are offered. **Hours:** Daily 7:30-7, May-Sept.; by appointment, rest of year. Closed winter holidays. **Phone:** (907) 224-8810, or (800) 770-9119 for reservations.

SITKA (H-10) pop. 8,835

Surrounded by high peaks and small wooded islands, historic Sitka is accessible by air or the Alaska Marine Highway.

In 1804 Russians led by Alexander Baranov established a settlement on the site of an ancient Tlingit (KLINK-it) village; that settlement became the capital of Russian America. Originally named New Archangel, it was a thriving port of nearly 3,000 when San Francisco was just a mission village. Castle Hill marks the site of Baranov's headquarters and commemorates the 1867 ceremony that transferred ownership of Alaska from Russia to the United States. St. Michael's Cathedral, a restored Russian church with an onion-shaped dome, contains a collection of religious icons and artwork; phone (907) 747-8120.

The colorfully costumed New Archangel Dancers perform Russian dances in the Harrigan Centennial Hall auditorium during summer when large ships are in port; phone (907) 747-5516. Performances by the Sheet'ka Kwaán Naa Kahidi Native Dancers are given at the Tribal Community House on Katlian Street; phone (907) 747-7290.

For cruise ship and ferry passengers, Sitka Tours offers a short bus tour of Sitka, which includes guide service and round-trip transportation from the port. Boat tours to view wildlife and the surrounding area also are available.

Sitka Convention and Visitors Bureau: P.O. Box 1226, Sitka, AK 99835. **Phone:** (907) 747-5940 or (800) 557-4852.

◆GEM **ALASKA RAPTOR CENTER,** .8 mi. e. of Lake St. at 1000 Raptor Way, is home to 25 "raptors in residence," including bald and golden eagles, hawks, falcons and owls. The 17-acre rehabilitation center, surrounded by muskeg, mountains and the Indian River, provides medical treatment to more than 100 eagles and other birds of prey each year. A stage presentation, a videotape, live demonstrations of birds in flight training and a .25-mile nature trail are available.

Raptors unable to be released into the wild help educate visitors and travel to schools nationwide to raise awareness of wild birds and their habitats. Feathers, bones, photographs and a national map indicating where birds have been released are displayed. Visitors can view raptors in their natural habitats outside the center as well as in the clinic's treatment room and recuperation areas.

Tours: Guided tours are available. **Time:** Allow 1 hour, 30 minutes minimum. **Hours:** Daily 8-4, May-Sept. **Cost:** $12; $6 (ages 0-12). **Phone:** (907) 747-8662 or (800) 643-9425.

ISABEL MILLER MUSEUM is in Harrigan Centennial Building. The museum features exhibits depicting the history of Sitka, including the area's earliest inhabitants and the legacy of World War II. Displays illustrate the lifestyles of the Tlingit along with the town's Russian, Finish, Asian and American settlers. An 8-square-foot diorama shows Sitka as it appeared in 1867, the year Alaska was transferred to the United States from Russia.

Time: Allow 30 minutes minimum. **Hours:** Mon.-Tues. 8:30-4:30, Sat.-Sun. 10-4, early May to late Sept.; Tues.-Sat. 10-4, rest of year. Phone ahead to confirm schedule. **Cost:** $2; free (ages 0-18). **Phone:** (907) 747-6455.

SHELDON JACKSON MUSEUM is at 104 College Dr. Housed in one of the first concrete structures built in Alaska, it is reputed to be the oldest continuing museum in Alaska. Displays of Eskimo, Aleut and Northwest Coast and Athabaskan Indian artifacts include pelts, sleds, kayaks, ceremonial masks, and tools and utensils of wood, bone and ivory.

Time: Allow 30 minutes minimum. **Hours:** Daily 9-5, mid-May to mid-Sept.; Tues.-Sat. 10-4, rest of year. Closed major holidays. **Cost:** mid-May to mid-Sept. $4; rest of year $3; free (ages 0-18). **Phone:** (907) 747-8981.

SITKA NATIONAL HISTORICAL PARK (I-10)

Near downtown Sitka on Lincoln Street, this urban park commemorates the Battle of Sitka, fought in 1804 between the Kiksadi Tlingit Indians and the fur hunters and Aleut natives of the Russian-American Co. The battle marked the last major resistance by Alaskan natives to European domination. The 113-acre park preserves the Tlingit fort site, the battlefield and the 1842 Russian Bishop's House.

A fine collection of Tlingit (KLINK-it) and Haida (HY-dah) totem poles, some more than a century old, is displayed along a 2-mile trail through the park's temperate rain forest and coastal intertidal area. During August and September visitors may view salmon spawning in the Indian River.

The visitor center contains exhibits and audiovisual presentations about the area's Tlingit Indian heritage as well as its Russian legacy. Within the visitor center skilled native artisans demonstrate traditional crafts at the Southeast Alaska Indian Cultural Center, which is open daily.

Visitor center open daily 8-5, mid-May through Sept. 30; Mon.-Sat. 8-5, rest of year. Closed winter holidays. Park free. Visitor center $4. Address inquiries to the Superintendent, Sitka National Historical Park, 103 Monastery St., Sitka, AK 99835; phone (907) 747-0110.

THE RUSSIAN BISHOP'S HOUSE, 501 Lincoln St. across from Crescent Harbor, is a two-story log structure completed in 1843. It is one of the last surviving colonial Russian buildings in North America. Restored to its 1853 appearance, the building reflects the influence of the Russian Orthodox Church and the traders of the Russian-American Co., who made Sitka the capital of colonial Russian America.

Time: Allow 30 minutes minimum. **Hours:** Daily and holidays 8-5, mid-May to late Sept.; by appointment rest of year. **Cost:** $4; free (ages 0-11). **Phone:** (907) 747-0110.

SKAGWAY (G-10) pop. 862, elev. 2′

During the icy winter of 1897-98 hordes of enthusiastic would-be prospectors who had heard of the Klondike gold strike swarmed ashore at Dyea. They assembled their gear and began the trek over treacherous mountains and down raging rivers to the Klondike. Within 3 months of the first gold strike, the settlement at Skagway grew from one cabin into a thriving city of more than 20,000 people. But the gold rush ended suddenly, and those who had come to Skagway moved on.

The notorious outlaw Jefferson R. "Soapy" Smith and Frank Reid, who represented the outraged citizenry, shot it out in a battle that cost both men their lives. Gold Rush Cemetery, 1.5 miles from town, contains the graves of both "Soapy" Smith and Frank Reid.

A stop on many summer cruises along the Inside Passage, Skagway is the northern terminus of the Alaska Marine Highway. Sightseeing opportunities include visits to Reid Falls and flower gardens; tours of the city and the harbor; flightseeing tours to Glacier Bay, gold rush trails and the Juneau Ice Cap; bus excursions to Dyea and Carcross, Yukon Territory; and hiking trips to AB Mountain and the Dewey Lakes.

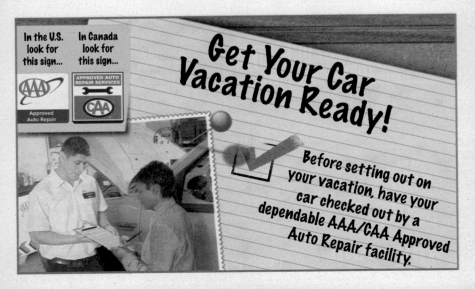

SAVE Gray Line of Alaska offers historical points-of-interest tours daily; phone (907) 983-2241 or (800) 544-2206.

Skagway Convention & Visitors Bureau: P.O. Box 1029, Skagway, AK 99840. **Phone:** (907) 983-2854 or (888) 762-1898.

THE DAYS OF '98 SHOW WITH SOAPY SMITH, presented at Eagles' Hall, 6th Ave. and Broadway, includes a stage show with original songs, a cancan line, a historic shoot-out and mock gambling. **Hours:** Mock gambling nightly at 7. Stage shows daily at 10:30, 12:30, 2:30 and 8, mid-May to late Sept. **Cost:** Shows $18; $10 (ages 3-15). **Phone:** (907) 983-2545, or (808) 328-9132 Oct.-Apr.

JEWELL GARDENS & GLASSWORKS is 1.5 mi. n. on Klondike Hwy. Once the site of a late 19th-century vegetable farm known best for its rhubarb, the gardens feature such spectacular flowers as begonias, delphiniums, lilacs, nasturtiums and poppies. The mountains along the Lynn Canal serve as a backdrop to the site, which also is home to organic herb and vegetable gardens and a greenhouse. At the glassblowing theater, visitors may observe daily demonstrations.

Time: Allow 3 hours minimum. **Hours:** Daily 9-5, early May-late Sept. **Cost:** $12; $6 (ages 0-12). **Phone:** (907) 983-2111.

GEM **KLONDIKE GOLD RUSH NATIONAL HISTORICAL PARK** includes the Skagway Historic District and Chilkoot and White Pass trails, over which each prospector was required to haul nearly a ton of supplies during the gold rush of 1897-98. It was during this stampede that Skagway's population boomed from 5 to more than 10,000.

The park visitor center is in the original White Pass and Yukon Route Railroad Depot, one of Alaska's oldest. At Broadway and Second Avenue, it contains exhibits and interpretive programs about the era. Two films are shown: an orientation film about the gold rush, and a film about hiking the Chilkoot Trail. Walking tours led by a park ranger explore the Skagway Historic District, where many restored buildings represent a colorful history. The Chilkoot Trail Center provides information about day hikes and backpacking on the Chilkoot Trail.

Hours: Visitor center exhibits daily 8-6, early May-late Sept.; 8-5, rest of year. Orientation film is shown on the hour at 8, 9 and 11-5. Walking tours depart the visitor center daily on the hour 9-11 and at 2 and 3, early May-late Sept. Trail center daily 8-5, June-Labor Day weekend. **Cost:** Visitor and trail centers free. Walking tours free. Fees apply and reservations are recommended for Chilkoot Trail backpacking. **Phone:** (907) 983-2921 for the visitor center, (907) 983-9234 for trail information June-Aug., or (800) 661-0486 for trail information rest of year.

SKAGWAY MUSEUM is at Seventh Ave. and Spring St. in the McCabe College Building. Displays pertain to Alaskan history and native cultures, including a Tlingit war canoe, photographs, documents, gold rush relics and native artifacts. **Hours:** Mon.-Fri. 9-5, Sat. 10-5, Sun. 10-3, May-Sept.; hours vary, rest of year. **Cost:** $2; $1 (senior citizens and students with ID); free (ages 0-12). **Phone:** (907) 983-2420.

GEM **WHITE PASS & YUKON ROUTE** is at Second Ave. and Spring St. A vintage train chugs across mountain rivers and chasms during fully narrated narrow-gauge rides. The rail line was built in 1898 to carry people and supplies to the Klondike gold rush. Passengers travel round-trip in a period parlor car to the summit of White Pass or Fraser Meadows, past granite gulches, cascading waterfalls and spectacular scenery. A narrator tells the story of the stampede north into the gold

fields through some of the most rugged terrain in the United States and Canada.

The 3-hour White Pass summit excursion rises from tidewater elevations to 2,865 feet in 20 miles. The 4-hour summit excursion to Fraser Meadows rises from tidewater elevation to 3,000 feet in 26 miles. One-way excursions to Lake Bennett in British Columbia and Carcross in Yukon Territory as well as to Fraser, British Columbia also are available.

Hours: Ticket office open daily 7:30-4:30, May-Sept. White Pass excursions depart Mon.-Thurs. at 8:15, 12:45 and 4:30, Fri.-Sun. at 8:15 and 12:45 (weather permitting), early May-late Sept. Fraser Meadows excursions depart Fri.-Sat. at noon, mid-May to mid-Sept. **Cost:** White Pass fare $103; $51.50 (ages 3-12). Fraser Meadows fare $133; $66.50 (ages 3-12). Reservations are required. **Phone:** (800) 343-7373. *See color ad p. 358.*

SOLDOTNA (D-10) pop. 3,759

Soldotna's location on the Kenai Peninsula at the junction of Sterling and Kenai Spur highways has ensured its steady growth since homesteading began in 1947. World War II veterans were among the first homesteaders; they were given a 90-day preference right in choosing and filing for land.

The area is rich with opportunities for year-round recreation—hiking, fishing, camping, canoeing and ice fishing are favored activities. Nearby Kenai River yields record catches of salmon and rainbow trout.

Soldotna Chamber of Commerce and Visitor Information Center: 44790 Sterling Hwy., Soldotna, AK 99669. **Phone:** (907) 262-9814 or (907) 262-1337.

KENAI NATIONAL WILDLIFE REFUGE, with its headquarters in Soldotna, covers about 1,920,000 acres. The refuge was established in 1941 by President Franklin D. Roosevelt to preserve the area's large moose population. Other wildlife include Dall sheep, coyotes, black bears and bald eagles. Fishing and hunting are subject to state and federal regulations. Boat ramps, trails and camping are available. *See the AAA Western Canada & Alaska CampBook.*

Hours: The refuge is open all year, except when roads are impassable. **Phone:** (907) 262-7021 or TTY (907) 260-2803.

Visitor Center, 1 mi. s.e. of the Kenai River Bridge on Ski Hill Rd., exhibits wildlife dioramas and presents films. **Hours:** Mon.-Fri. 8-4:30, Sat.-Sun. 9-5, June 1-Labor Day; Mon.-Fri. 8-4:30, Sat.-Sun. 10-5, rest of year.

STERLING (D-10) pop. 4,705, elev. 198′

RECREATIONAL ACTIVITIES
Fishing

• **Great Alaska International Adventure.** 33881 Sterling Hwy., Sterling, AK 99672. Other activities are offered. **Hours:** Trips are offered mid-May through Sept. 30. **Phone:** (907) 262-4515, mid-Apr. to late Sept., or (800) 544-2261, rest of year.

TALKEETNA (C-11) pop. 772, elev. 355′

Situated at the confluence of the Talkeetna, Susitna and Chulitna rivers, Talkeetna takes its name from the Tanaina Indian word for "river of plenty." The village was an important supply station for gold prospectors from the late 1800s to 1940, but is now a popular staging area for outdoors enthusiasts.

Self-guiding tours: A map of a downtown walking tour is available at Talkeetna Historical Society Museum *(see attraction listing)* and the visitor center next to Village Park on Main Street.

K-2 AVIATION is at Talkeetna State Airport off Talkeetna Spur Rd. Flightseeing tours of varying types and lengths include the 1-hour McKinley Experience, which offers views of Mount McKinley and Ruth Glacier; the 75-minute McKinley Climber & Summit Tour to the mountain's summit; the McKinley Flyer Tour, which lasts 75 minutes and offers views of the mountain range's south side; and the 90-minute Denali Grand Tour, which encircles the mountain and offers views of Kahiltna and Ruth glaciers. Glacier landings are available for an additional fee.

Note: A fuel surcharge of 5 percent is added to the cost of each trip. **Hours:** Daily 7 a.m.-9 p.m., mid-May to late-Sept.; Mon.-Fri. 8:30-4, rest of year (weather permitting). **Cost:** McKinley Experience fare $190; $265 (with glacier landing). McKinley Flyer Tour fare $235; $310 (with glacier landing). Denali Grand Tour fare $280; $355 (with glacier landing). McKinley Climber & Summit Tour fare $295. Reservations are recommended. **Phone:** (907) 733-2291 or (800) 764-2291.

MAHAY'S RIVERBOAT SERVICE departs from Milepost 14 on Talkeetna Spur Rd. The company offers three excursions: a 2-hour, 20-mile Wilderness Jetboat Adventure; a 3.5-hour, 50-mile three-river tour on the Chulitna, Susitna and Talkeetna rivers; and a 5-hour Devil's Canyon tour. Tours offer a leisurely .25-mile nature walk to a native Indian encampment and a view into the lives of turn-of-the-century trappers.

Time: Allow 2 hours minimum. **Hours:** Office open daily 7 a.m.-9 p.m., mid-May to mid-Sept. Wilderness Jetboat Adventure departs daily at 8:45, noon, 2:30 and 6:30, mid-May to mid-Sept. Three-river tour departs daily at 3:15, mid-May to mid-Sept. Canyon tour departs daily at 9:30, mid-May to mid-Sept. **Cost:** Wilderness Jetboat Adventure $65; $32.50 (ages 0-5). Three-river tour $110; $55 (ages 0-5). Canyon tour $155; $75.50 (ages 0-12). **Phone:** (907) 733-2223 or (800) 736-2210.

MUSEUM OF NORTHERN ADVENTURE, on Main St. across from the post office, recounts the eras, lore and natural history of northern Alaska through dioramas, life-size wax figures, sound effects, photographs and newspaper articles. A trophy room contains big game and other wildlife taxidermy. **Time:** Allow 30 minutes minimum. **Hours:** Daily

10-6, May 1 to mid-Sept. **Cost:** $2; $1 (ages 0-11 and 65+); $5 (family). **Phone:** (907) 733-3999.

TALKEETNA AERO SERVICES/FLY DENALI departs from Talkeetna State Airport, off Talkeetna Spur Rd., and Healy Denali Airport. Passengers are treated to views of Mt. McKinley, Denali National Park and Preserve or the Kahiltna Glacier from 20,000 feet as well as glacier landings on Mt. McKinley. Flights from Anchorage and Talkeetna to Denali National Park and Preserve are available. **Time:** Allow 2 hours minimum. **Hours:** Daily 7 a.m.-8 p.m., mid-May to mid-Sept.; 9-5, rest of year (weather permitting). **Cost:** Fare $250-$425 (depending on tour). **Phone:** (907) 733-2899 or (888) 733-2899.

TALKEETNA AIR TAXI, at Talkeetna State Airport off Talkeetna Spur Rd., offers three flightseeing tours: a 1-hour South Face McKinley Tour, with views of Ruth Gorge; a 75-minute McKinley Base Camp Tour, which circles over Kahiltna Glacier; and a 90-minute Grand Denali Tour, which offers views of active gold mines, Kahiltna base camp and Wickersham Wall. Other activities such as mountain climbing, glacier landings and support and wilderness tours also are offered. **Hours:** Daily 7 a.m.-10 p.m., May-Sept.; 9-4, rest of year (weather permitting). Phone ahead to confirm schedule. **Cost:** South Face McKinley Tour fare May-Sept. $190; $265 (with glacier landing). McKinley Base Camp Tour fare May-Sept. $235; $310 (with glacier landing). Grand Denali Tour fare May-Sept. $280; $355-$ (with glacier landing). Call ahead for winter rates. **Phone:** (907) 733-2218 or (800) 533-2219.

TALKEETNA HISTORICAL SOCIETY MUSEUM, in five buildings at the corner of First Alley and Village Airstrip Rd., displays a wealth of local history memorabilia within re-creations of a log cabin, a one-room schoolhouse, a railroad depot and section house. Of interest is a large-scale model of Mount McKinley and the surrounding area.

Time: Allow 30 minutes minimum. **Hours:** Daily 10-6, May-Sept.; by appointment rest of year. Phone ahead to confirm schedule. **Cost:** $3; free (ages 0-11 and students with ID). **Phone:** (907) 733-2487.

TOK (B-12) pop. 1,393

On the Alaska Highway 93 miles from the Canadian border, Tok is a trade center for nearby Athabascan villages. Some claim that Tok's name derives from the native word meaning "peace crossing"; others say Tok was the name of a survey crew's dog.

A center for dog breeding, training and mushing, Tok claims the title "Dog Capital of Alaska."

Tok Chamber of Commerce: P.O. Box 389, Tok, AK 99780. **Phone:** (907) 883-5775.

ALASKA PUBLIC LANDS INFORMATION CENTER, Milepost 1314 on Alaska Hwy., includes displays, state and federal information, a trip planning room and interpretive programs. **Hours:** Daily 8-7,

Memorial Day-Labor Day; Mon.-Fri. 8-5, rest of year. **Cost:** Free. **Phone:** (907) 883-5666 or (907) 883-5667.

TETLIN NATIONAL WILDLIFE REFUGE is in e. central Alaska, directly s. of the Alaska Hwy. and n. of Wrangell-St. Elias National Park and Preserve; the visitor center is at Milepost 1229 on Alaska Hwy. The gateway to Alaska, the refuge occupies 730,000 acres along a major bird migration corridor. At least 115 of the 186 bird species stay to nest. Black and grizzly bears, moose, wolves and caribou are year-round residents. A visitor center, containing an observation deck and wildlife exhibit, is built in a log trapper's cabin style with a sod roof.

Recreational activities include bird-watching, canoeing, fishing, hiking and hunting. The refuge operates three cabins and two seasonal, public campgrounds. **Hours:** Refuge open daily 24 hours. Visitor center open daily 8-4:30, May 15-Sept. 15. **Cost:** Free. **Phone:** (907) 883-5312. ▲

TONGASS NATIONAL FOREST (G-8)

Elevations in the forest range from sea level at the Pacific Ocean to 10,290 ft. at Mount Ratz. Refer to AAA maps for additional elevation information.

In southeastern Alaska, Tongass National Forest covers about 17 million acres, making it the largest national forest. In 1907 Teddy Roosevelt created the forest, taking the name from the "Tongass" clan of Tlingit Indians that lived along the southern edge of the forest's present-day boundaries. It boasts more than 5 million acres of preserved wilderness, including Misty Fiords National Monument *(see place listing p. 350)* and Admiralty Island National Monument *(see place listing p. 319).*

Consisting mostly of islands, the forest also includes a mountainous mainland strip deeply cleft by rock-walled fiords, bays, inlets and channels with glaciers, ice fields and waterfalls. The abundant wildlife includes trumpeter swans, bald eagles and Alaskan brown (grizzly) and black bears. Licenses are required for hunting and fishing.

The largest island within the National Forest and one of the largest islands in the United States is Prince of Wales Island. Long inlets and deep bays mark its 1,000-mile coastline, while U-shaped valleys and low mountains rising up to 3,800 feet distinguish its interior. Thanks to a moist climate, a dense forest of spruce and hemlock blankets the landscape.

One of the most interesting features of the island is its caves, including El Capitan, a large limestone cave system with 11,000 feet of mapped passages. Grizzly bear bones more than 12,000 years old have been found inside. The Forest Service provides free 2-hour tours of El Capitan from mid-May to early September; reservations are required. Access to the cave entrance is via a steep 1,300-foot-long trail and visitors need to bring their own equipment for the tour, including flashlights and sturdy footgear. The underground temperature is a constant 40 degrees Fahrenheit. Phone (907) 828-3304 for information and reservations.

The Forest Service provides cabins at several locations within Tongass National Forest. Many rental cabins are near lakes and streams or high in alpine meadows. Although a few can be reached by boat or trail, most are accessible only by charter plane from Craig, Hoonah, Juneau, Ketchikan, Petersburg, Sitka, Wrangell and Yakutat. Charter planes seating two to five people cost about $325-$550 an hour.

A $25-$45 per-party, per-night fee is charged for cabins. There is a 7-night limit May through September; a 10-night limit the rest of the year. Cabin permits are necessary and can be requested up to 180 days prior to use; full payment is required at the time the reservation is made. Forest information centers with exhibits, films and cabin reservation information are in Juneau *(see place listing p. 341)*, Ketchikan *(see place listing p. 346)* and Petersburg *(see place listing p. 352)*.

For further information write Southeast Alaska Discovery Center, 50 Main St., Ketchikan, AK 99901; phone (907) 228-6220, TTY (907) 228-6237, or (877) 444-6777 for camping reservations. *See Recreation Chart and the AAA Western Canada & Alaska CampBook.*

 **MENDENHALL GLACIER—**
see Juneau p. 344.

VALDEZ (C-11) pop. 4,036, elev. 15′

Called the "Switzerland of Alaska," Valdez (val-DEEZ) is ringed by snowcapped mountains. As the northernmost ice-free port, the town was established in 1898 as an outfitting point for miners taking the hazardous pack trail over Valdez Glacier to the northern gold fields.

In addition to the gold rush, Valdez's rich history includes the 5-minute, 9.2-magnitude Good Friday earthquake in 1964; construction of the Trans-Alaska Pipeline and Marine Terminal in the 1970s; and the 1989 *Exxon Valdez* oil spill and cleanup.

Access into Valdez is by scheduled air service, ferry or via the scenic Richardson Highway. Near Milepost 16 are Bridal Veil and Horsetail falls and the Historic 1899 Trans-Alaska Military Trail & Wagon Road. Thompson Pass, Milepost 26, offers a spectacular view of the Chugach Mountains, valley rivers and historic Keystone Canyon. At Milepost 29 is Worthington Glacier State Park, which has walking trails.

Nearby glaciers in Prince William Sound include Mears, Shoup and Columbia, the second largest tidewater glacier in North America. Cruises are available to Mears and Columbia.

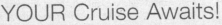

Valdez Convention and Visitors Bureau: 200 Chenega St., P.O. Box 1603, Valdez, AK 99686. **Phone:** (907) 835-2984.

MAXINE & JESSE WHITNEY MUSEUM is on the grounds of Prince William Sound Community College at 303 Lowe St. The museum's collection of Alaskan native art, artifacts, beadwork, dolls and furs comprises one of the largest of its kind. Its pieces were collected over more than 50 years of travel to Alaskan villages by Jesse Whitney and wife Maxine after the couple moved to Alaska in 1947. The Paul Kulik History of Transportation Collection features to-scale vehicle models made of Eskimo ivory and that interpret the state's aviation history.

Time: Allow 30 minutes minimum. **Hours:** Daily 9-7, May 1-Labor Day; by appointment rest of year. **Cost:** $5; $4 (senior citizens and military with ID); $3 (ages 0-11). **Phone:** (907) 834-1690 or (800) 478-8800.

STAN STEPHENS GLACIER & WILDLIFE CRUISES departs from 112 N. Harbor Dr., 3 blks. e. of jct. Richardson Hwy. and Meals St. The outfit offers 7- and 9-hour narrated sightseeing cruises on Prince William Sound to Columbia and Meares glaciers. Along the way, guests might glimpse bald eagles, Dall's porpoises, black bears, sea otters, Steller sea lions, puffins, mountain goats and humpback, minke and orca whales. A narrator details area history and information about the Trans-Alaska Pipeline. A light meal is included.

Hours: Columbia Glacier trips depart daily at noon, mid-May to mid-Sept. Columbia and Meares glaciers trips depart daily at 10, early June through Aug. 31. Phone ahead to confirm schedule. **Cost:** Fare $112-$147; $56-$73 (ages 3-12). Reservations are recommended. **Phone:** (907) 835-4731 or (866) 867-1297. *See color ad p. 361.*

VALDEZ MUSEUM & HISTORICAL ARCHIVE is at 217 Egan Dr. The museum documents the complete history of Valdez. Interpretive exhibits explain the impact of the gold rush, the 1964 earthquake, the construction of the Trans-Alaska Pipeline and the 1989 *Exxon Valdez* oil spill. The Remembering Old Valdez exhibit, 436 S. Hazelet Ave., focuses on the years 1957-67. A 1907 Ahrens fire truck and a Fresnel lighthouse lens also are featured.

Time: Allow 30 minutes minimum. **Hours:** Museum daily 9-5, mid-May to early Sept.; Mon.-Sat. 1-5, rest of year. Remembering Old Valdez daily 9-5, mid-May to early-Sept.; by appointment rest of year. **Cost:** $6; $5.50 (ages 60+); $5 (ages 13-17). **Phone:** (907) 835-2764.

WORTHINGTON GLACIER, about 30 mi. e. on the Richardson Hwy., is Alaska's most accessible glacier. Milepost 28.7 provides an excellent viewpoint; a road leads to the glacier. The Moraine Trail leads to a viewing platform. Camping at the foot of the glacier is permitted.

RECREATIONAL ACTIVITIES
Kayaking
- **Anadyr Adventures** departs from 225 N. Harbor Dr. **Hours:** Daily 8 a.m.-10 p.m., May-Oct.; call

ahead for specific excursion times and dates. **Phone:** (907) 835-2814.

WASILLA (C-11) pop. 5,469

Founded in 1917 with the construction of the Alaska Railroad, the community of Wasilla is contiguous to the junction of SRs 1 and 3, both of which are scenic highways, and rests in the Matanuska-Susitna Valley. The area's name originates from that of a respected Indian chief and has varying interpretations; some believe the word is defined as "breath of air" in the Dena'ina Athabascan Indian dialect, while others attribute it to a variation of the Russian word for the name William, "Vasili."

Gold miners from nearby Knik and Willow Creek flocked to Wasilla in the early 1900s due to its proximity to the gold fields and newly constructed railroad. With the advent of Anchorage in 1915 and Wasilla's founding two years later, Knik and other neighboring communities were rapidly abandoned. Mining in Wasilla played an integral role through much of World War II and the mid-20th century; a handful of the area's mines, which once numbered more than 50, remain active to this day.

The Dorothy G. Page Museum, 323 N. Main St., contains historical artifacts and relates the heritage of Wasilla, Knik and Willow Creek. The museum is open year-round; phone (907) 373-9071. Adjoining the museum is the Old Wasilla Town Site, which preserves Wasilla's first school, two log cabins, a smithy and the town's first public bath.

In August 2008, former Alaska Gov. Sarah Palin, who served two terms as mayor of Wasilla 1996-2002, was chosen by Arizona Sen. John McCain as his running mate in the November presidential election. Her GOP nomination set several precedents as Palin became the first Alaskan and only the second woman—and the first woman as a Republican—to appear on a major party's presidential ticket.

Greater Wasilla Chamber of Commerce: 415 E. Railroad Ave., Wasilla, AK 99654. **Phone:** (907) 376-1299.

MUSEUM OF ALASKA TRANSPORTATION AND INDUSTRY, Milepost 47 on George Parks Hwy. (SR 3), displays various items relating to Alaska's transportation and industrial history. Fifteen acres of outdoor exhibits include aircraft, boats, tractors, dog sleds, snowmobiles, farm implements, railroad cars, fire trucks, antique automobiles and memorabilia from early railroading days. Also featured are aviation photographs, vintage farm equipment and engines.

Hours: Daily 10-5, May-Sept. **Cost:** $8; $5 (ages 3-17, ages 65+ and military with ID); $18 (family). **Phone:** (907) 376-1211. ⊞

WHITTIER (D-11) pop. 1,658

Nearly surrounded by mountains and perched at the edge of beautiful Prince William Sound, Whittier remained relatively isolated until June 2000 when a

2.5-mile railroad tunnel was converted to accommodate automobile traffic. The unusual Anton Anderson Memorial Tunnel is a single-lane combination highway and railway that enables cars and trains to take turns passing through the tunnel. Because the tunnel has only one lane, the direction of traffic alternates, ceasing altogether while trains travel through.

Phone (877) 611-2586 for the tunnel's traffic schedule. Tunnel information also is broadcast by radio on 530 AM in Whittier and 1610 AM in Portage and Bear Valley. A toll of $12 per car is charged at the tunnel's western entrance; toll increases with size of vehicle.

26 GLACIER CRUISE BY PHILLIPS CRUISES departs from the port of Whittier. Cruises explore the calm, protected waters of Prince William Sound. Passengers aboard the company's high-speed catamaran can see tidewater glaciers plus an array of wildlife on this 4.5-hour tour.

Hours: Cruises depart daily at 1 early May-Sept. 30. **Cost:** Fare $139; $79 (ages 2-11). Bus or rail service is offered from Anchorage at an additional cost. Reservations are recommended. **Phone:** (907) 276-8023 or (800) 544-0529. *See color ad p. 326.*

MAJOR MARINE TOURS depart from the marina day-cruise dock. A 5-hour sightseeing cruise narrated by a Chugach forest ranger takes passengers to see spectacular 1,700-foot-tall active tidewater glaciers and picturesque waterfalls in Prince William Sound. Eagles, otters and shorebirds may be spotted.

Inquire about weather policies. **Time:** Allow 5 hours minimum. **Hours:** Departures daily at 1:15, mid-May to mid-Sept. **Cost:** Fare $107; $53 (ages 2-11). Rates may vary; phone ahead. Reservations are recommended. **Phone:** (907) 274-7300 or (800) 764-7300. *See color ad p. 354.* 🍴

PRINCE WILLIAM SOUND CRUISES AND TOURS, departing from the foot of Pier 1 at the Whittier Boat Harbor, offers two cruises. The 4-hour Glacier Adventure Cruise brings passengers close to two active tidewater glaciers and waterfalls. The 6-hour Wilderness Explorer Glacier Cruise plies the calm waters of Prince William Sound, passes glaciers in Esther Passage, Harriman Fjord and Barry Arm, and stops at a working fish hatchery. Both trips include lunch and opportunities for spotting wildlife.

Time: Allow 4 hours minimum. **Hours:** Glacier Adventure Cruise departs daily at 1:30, early June-early Sept. Wilderness Explorer Glacier Cruise departs daily at 11, mid-May to mid-Sept. **Cost:** Glacier Adventure Cruise $109; $54.50 (ages 2-11). Wilderness Explorer Glacier Cruise $139; $69.50 (ages 2-11). **Phone:** (907) 777-2805 or (877) 777-2805. *See color ad.*

RECREATIONAL ACTIVITIES

Kayaking

- **Alaska Sea Kayakers** depart from the Whittier Boat Harbor. **Hours:** Daily 8-7, May-Sept. **Phone:** (907) 472-2534 or (877) 472-2534.

WRANGELL (H-11) pop. 2,308, elev. 37′

Petroglyphs pecked into shale rock and elaborately carved totem poles, cedar monuments of the Stikine (STIK-een) and Tlingit (KLINK-it) Indians, are interesting aspects of Wrangell. Although European and American explorers visited the area in the late 1700s, Russians began trading here by 1811 and established a redoubt in Wrangell in 1834. The only Alaskan town to have existed under Russian, British and American rule, it also survived three gold rushes—In 1861, 1872 and 1898 the lure of riches brought a rush of miners and settlers.

Petroglyphs can be seen on a beach at the north end of Wrangell Island. Of undetermined age, some carvings face the water, others the shore or sky. They are best viewed at low tide. Nearby Anan Creek allows the opportunity to observe sea lions and seals and watch black bear fish for salmon.

Other attractions include the nine totem poles (some are replicas carved by the Civilian Conservation Corps in the late 1930s) on Shakes Island in Wrangell Harbor, as well as the four totem poles in Kiksadi Totem Park at Front and Episcopal streets. Artifacts are displayed in Chief Shakes Tribal House, also on the island. A large concentration of bald eagles gather in Wrangell from January to mid-April waiting for smelt to run up the Stikine River.

Wrangell Chamber of Commerce: 224 Front St., P.O. Box 49, Wrangell, AK 99929. **Phone:** (907) 874-3901 or (800) 367-9745.

WRANGELL MUSEUM is at 296 Outer Dr. The collection describes the colorful history of the Wrangell area. Of note are four beautiful Tlingit houseposts—carved in the 1700s, they are believed to be the oldest in existence. A variety of displays detail early Russian and English settlement and the city's role in the 1861 Stikine gold rush. Spruceroot and cedarbark baskets, beadwork, stone tools and other artifacts crafted by Alaskan natives are shown.

Time: Allow 30 minutes minimum. **Hours:** Mon.-Sat. 10-5, May-Sept.; Tues.-Sat. 1-5, rest of year. Closed major holidays. **Cost:** $5; $3 (ages 65+); $2 (ages 6-12); $12 (family). **Phone:** (907) 874-3770.

WRANGELL-ST. ELIAS NATIONAL PARK AND PRESERVE (C-12, F-8)

Elevations in the park and preserve range from sea level at the Gulf of Alaska to 18,008 ft. at Mount St. Elias. Refer to AAA maps for additional elevation information.

In south central Alaska bordering Canada's Yukon Territory, Wrangell-St. Elias National Park and Preserve is the country's largest national park. It is a place of overpowering dimensions, embracing an area larger than Massachusetts, Rhode Island and Connecticut combined; glaciers five times the size of Manhattan; and nine of the 16 highest peaks in North America.

In this 13-million-acre park, the collision of two continental plates has produced some of the world's highest coastal ranges. Forming a barrier along the Gulf of Alaska are the Chugach Mountains, and paralleling them to the north are the Wrangell Mountains.

Between these two ranges are the St. Elias Mountains, extending like the stem of the letter "Y" into Canada's Kluane National Park. Atop these towering peaks are ice fields so immense that they act as a natural cooling system, affecting areas as far south as Chicago and the Central Plains.

As imposing as its ice fields are, it was another commodity traded by the Ahtna Dene or "people of the Copper River" that caught the world's attention. These and other tribes forged tools of locally mined copper. The first person of European descent to verify the source of the copper trading was Lt. Henry Allen, who in 1885 explored much of Alaska's interior.

Fifteen years later two miners discovered the malachite cliffs above the Kennicott Glacier, which became one of the world's richest sources of copper. The subsequent founding of the Kennecott Mine became one of the most significant events in Alaska's history: The great wealth and development it spawned affected not only Alaska but the entire nation. Currently the ruined mine is all that remains of this immense enterprise. Information about the history and current renovation efforts of the Kennecott Mines National Historic Landmark may be obtained at the Kennecott Visitor Center; phone (907) 554-1105.

Legacies of the Kennecott Mine and the Yukon gold fields are some of the area's roads, which provide limited access to the park. One of Alaska's oldest roadways is the Richardson Highway, which was completed in 1919 and was the first all-Alaska route to the Yukon gold fields. Both the Richardson and Glenn highways follow the curve of the park's western boundary and offer several spectacular views of 12,010-foot Mount Drum, 14,163-foot Mount Wrangell and 16,237-foot Mount Sanford.

Two other roads penetrate the park's interior—the Chitina-McCarthy and the Nabesna. Both of these gravel roads offer good views of the mountains and are convenient jumping-off places for hiking and river-running. The 60-mile McCarthy Road follows an abandoned railroad bed. Visitors should allow a minimum of 3 hours to drive between Chitina and McCarthy. Before using either of these routes, check with the ranger stations in Slana and Chitina.

The park's headquarters and visitor center, 3 miles north of Copper Center on Richardson Highway at Milepost 106.8, provides trip-planning assistance and information about park activities. Fishing, hiking, rafting and wildlife- viewing, especially of the park's large population of Dall sheep, are just some of the activities pursued in the park; phone (907) 822-7250.

On the southeastern edge of the park and accessible only by sea is Hubbard Glacier on Disenchantment Bay. In 1986 this vast, active tidewater glacier advanced so quickly that for several months it blocked the entrance to Russell Fjord behind a dam of ice, briefly turning it into a lake.

For more information write the Superintendent, Wrangell-St. Elias National Park and Preserve, P.O. Box 439, Copper Center, AK 99573; phone (907) 822-5234. *See Recreation Chart.*

YUKON-CHARLEY RIVERS NATIONAL PRESERVE (A-12, D-7)

Elevations in the preserve range from 600 ft. on the Yukon River where it leaves the preserve near Circle to 6,435 ft. in the Cirque Lakes area on the Charley River drainage. Refer to AAA maps for additional elevation information.

Near the Canadian border in east central Alaska, more than 140 miles of the Yukon River and the entire watershed of the Charley River are encompassed within the 2.5 million acres of the Yukon-Charley Rivers National Preserve. John McPhee remarked in his book "Coming into the Country" that New Jersey could easily fit into this vast emptiness between Eagle and Circle.

Although only 10 year-round residents now live within the preserve's boundaries, it was not always so sparsely populated. During the gold rush, the Yukon—a summer waterway and winter highway—was thronged with people who briefly transformed such communities as Circle and Dawson City, Canada into the "Paris of the North." This rough-and-tumble gold rush region was the grist of Robert Service's poetry and Jack London's stories.

Now quiet has returned, and where riverboats once departed from Eagle, river runners make the 5- to 7-day float down the river to Circle. One of the pleasures of this trip is the opportunity to see Peregrine falcons, a threatened species that makes its home in the bluffs along the river. Hikers can catch a glimpse of caribou and Dall sheep in the preserve's upland regions and moose in the lowlands.

The Taylor and Steese highways are the primary summer access routes to the national preserve, terminating respectively in Eagle and Circle just outside the preserve's boundaries. The scenic portion of the Taylor Highway from Chicken to Eagle runs through mountains, rolling tundra and river valleys. Most people, however, reach the park by boat or float on the Yukon River and its tributaries.

The preserve has no roads and no established trails or maintained public airstrips. Seven public-use cabins are available on a first-come, first-served basis. Food service, basic supplies, lodgings and charter boat and air service are available during the summer months in nearby Eagle and Circle. A list of authorized guides can be obtained from the preserve headquarters and visitor center in Eagle.

In addition, the Bureau of Land Management administers Fort Egbert and a campground in Eagle (see the AAA Western Canada & Alaska CampBook). A visitor center, open Mon.-Fri. 8-5, Memorial Day-Labor Day, can be contacted at P.O. Box 167, Eagle, AK 99738; phone (907) 547-2233. For more information write the Superintendent, Yukon-Charley Rivers National Preserve, P.O. Box 74718, Fairbanks, AK 99707-4718. See Recreation Chart.

The Alaska Highway

On March 9, 1942, the U.S. Army Corps of Engineers began bulldozing its way through mountains and forests to create a direct land route linking the United States to the Alaska Territory. The Alaska Highway originated as an emergency passage for American troops during World War II following the Japanese occupation of the Aleutian Islands, which extend southwestward from the Alaska Peninsula.

Alaska Dept. of Commerce

More than 11,000 troops worked on the road, and American Indians, trappers and prospectors were hired to help. Canada supplied the right of way and materials in exchange for use of the road following the war. The workers built 133 log and pontoon bridges and dug more than 8,000 culverts. Despite untold hardships and the worst winter in recorded history, the highway was completed in just 8 months. In 1943 the highway became public, and for the next 7 years more than 70 companies and 16,000 civilian workers labored to turn it into a year-round, all-weather road.

The 1,523-mile Alaska Highway takes its travelers on a wilderness tour starting at Dawson Creek, British Columbia, through the Yukon Territory and on through Delta Junction to Fairbanks. The scenery is picture perfect, with an abundance of spruce forests, magnificent mountain passes, lakes, rivers and glacial ice formations. Bears, moose and other wildlife can appear at any time.

The road is maintained daily, but be aware that conditions often change depending on the weather. Take your time, drive with your headlights on and drive defensively. Always be alert for bumps and holes in the road. Gas, food and lodging are conveniently found every 20 to 50 miles.

America on the Move is made possible by generous support from General Motors Corporation, AAA, State Farm Companies Foundation, The History Channel, United States Congress, U.S. Department of Transportation, Exxon Mobil, American Public Transportation Association, American Road & Transportation Builders Association, Association of American Railroads, National Asphalt Pavement Association, The UPS Foundation.

No matter the Disney destination,
the smiles are always the same.

Let a AAA/CAA Travel professional help you get there.

A Disney vacation can take you to the world's greatest Theme Parks, *Walt Disney World* Resort in Florida and *Disneyland* Resort in California, and much, much more. Chart a course for magic on *Disney Cruise Line*, featuring fun for every member of the family. Or immerse your family in the stories of some of the world's greatest destinations with *Adventures by Disney*. A brand-new way for you to travel the globe.

Whatever you choose, make sure you book through your AAA/CAA Travel professional to receive exclusive benefits.

Where dreams come true

DISNEYLAND® • WALT DISNEY WORLD® • DISNEY CRUISE LINE® • ADVENTURES BY DISNEY

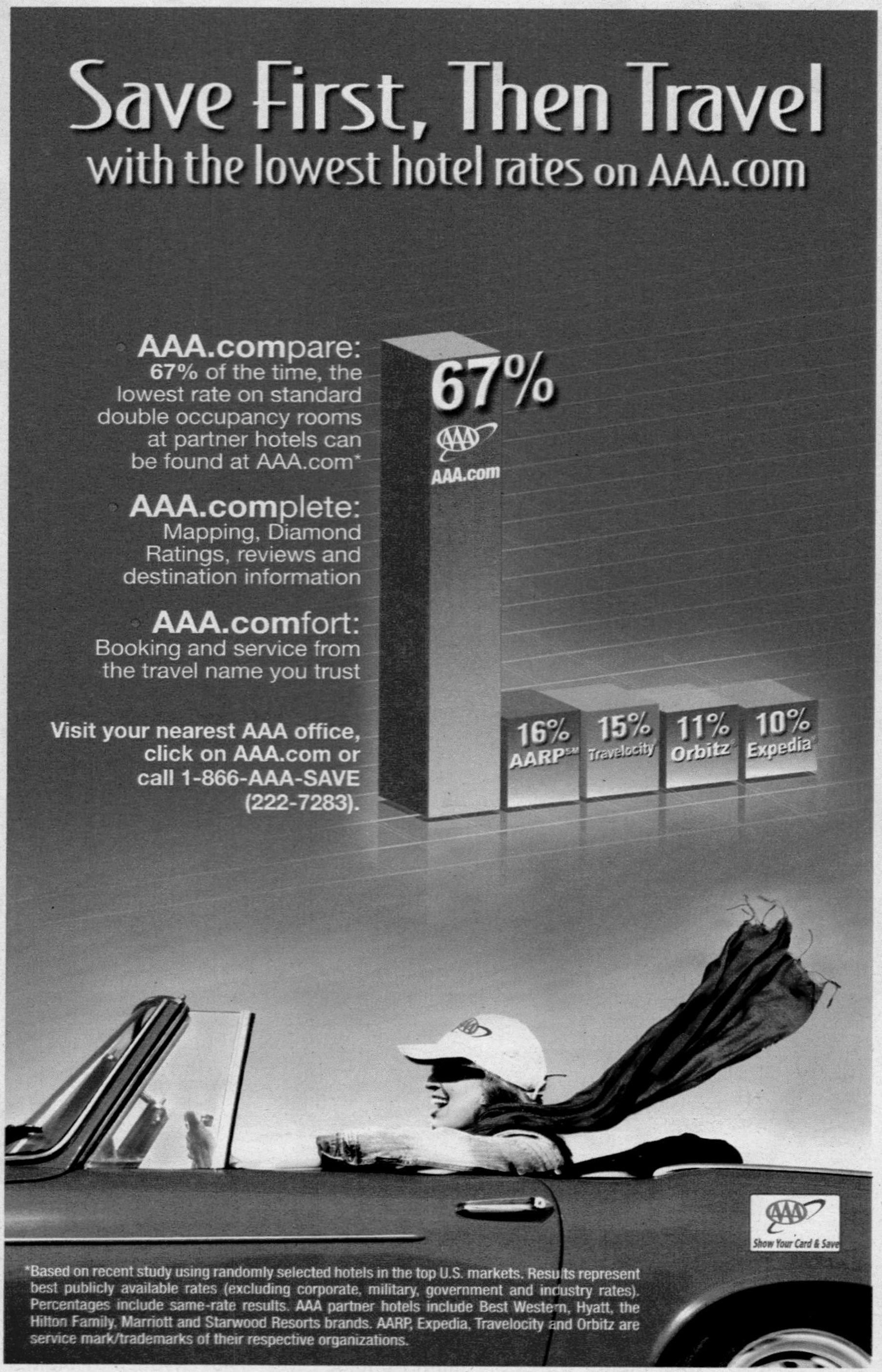

Save First, Then Travel
with the lowest hotel rates on AAA.com

AAA.compare:
67% of the time, the lowest rate on standard double occupancy rooms at partner hotels can be found at AAA.com*

AAA.complete:
Mapping, Diamond Ratings, reviews and destination information

AAA.comfort:
Booking and service from the travel name you trust

Visit your nearest AAA office, click on AAA.com or call 1-866-AAA-SAVE (222-7283).

67%
AAA.com

16% AARP℠

15% Travelocity

11% Orbitz

10% Expedia

Show Your Card & Save

*Based on recent study using randomly selected hotels in the top U.S. markets. Results represent best publicly available rates (excluding corporate, military, government and industry rates). Percentages include same-rate results. AAA partner hotels include Best Western, Hyatt, the Hilton Family, Marriott and Starwood Resorts brands. AARP, Expedia, Travelocity and Orbitz are service mark/trademarks of their respective organizations.

Alberta

Athabasca River, Jasper
National Park of Canada
© Daryl Benson
Masterfile

AIRDRIE—See Calgary p. 428.

Banff

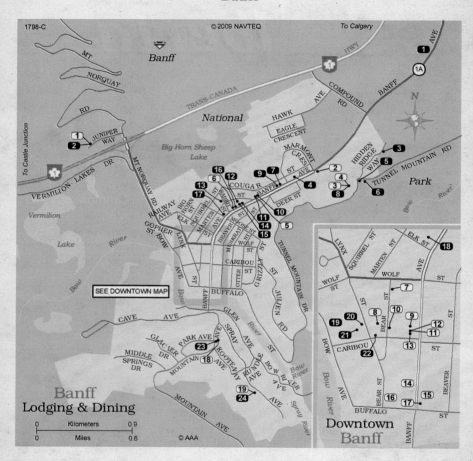

1798-C   © 2009 NAVTEQ

To Calgary

Banff National

Banff Lodging & Dining

| Kilometers | 0 | 0.9 |
| Miles | 0 | 0.6 |

© AAA

Downtown Banff

This index helps you "spot" where approved lodgings and restaurants are located on the corresponding detailed maps. Lodging daily rate range is for comparison only and show the property's high season. Restaurant rate range is a combination of lunch and/or dinner. Turn to the listing page for more detailed rate information and consult display ads for special promotions.

BANFF

Map Page	OA	Lodgings	Diamond Rated	High Season	Page
❶ / above		Banff Rocky Mountain Resort	▽▽▽	$170-$385	375
❷ / above		The Juniper	▽▽▽	$119-$339	382
❸ / above		Hidden Ridge Resort - see color ad p 374	▽▽▽	Rates not provided	381
❹ / above	CAA	**Rundlestone Lodge**	▽▽▽	$115-$401 SAVE	382
❺ / above	CAA	**Douglas Fir Resort & Chalets** - see color ad p 378	▽▽▽	$117-$459 SAVE	377
❻ / above		Tunnel Mountain Resort	▽▽	$233-$294	382
❼ / above		Banff Caribou Lodge - see color ad p 374	▽▽	$149-$475	374

BANFF (cont'd)

Map Page	OA	Lodgings (cont'd)	Diamond Rated	High Season	Page
8 / p. 372		Buffalo Mountain Lodge	◇◇◇	$169-$339	376
9 / p. 372		Charlton's Cedar Court - see color ad p 377	◇◇◇	$95-$235	376
10 / p. 372		The Fox Hotel & Suites - see color ad p 374	◇◇◇	$214-$739	379
11 / p. 372		Delta Banff Royal Canadian Lodge - see color ad p 378	◇◇◇	$139-$335	376
12 / p. 372	CAA	**Best Western Siding 29 Lodge**	◇◇◇	$100-$400 [SAVE]	375
13 / p. 372		Buffaloberry Bed and Breakfast	◇◇◇	$250-$325	376
14 / p. 372	CAA	**Irwin's Mountain Inn**	◇◇	$89-$165 [SAVE]	381
15 / p. 372	CAA	**Red Carpet Inn**	◇◇	$89-$159 [SAVE]	382
16 / p. 372	CAA	**High Country Inn**	◇◇◇	$104-$294 [SAVE]	381
17 / p. 372	CAA	**Banff Aspen Lodge**	◇◇	$119-$241 [SAVE]	374
18 / p. 372		Banff Ptarmigan Inn - see color ad p 374	◇◇	$159-$329	374
19 / p. 372	CAA	**Bow View Lodge**	◇◇	$99-$299 [SAVE]	375
20 / p. 372		Banff Park Lodge Resort Hotel & Conference Centre - see color ad p 375	◇◇◇	$149-$399	374
21 / p. 372		Homestead Inn	◇	Rates not provided	381
22 / p. 372	CAA	**Brewster's Mountain Lodge**	◇◇	$117-$401 [SAVE]	376
23 / p. 372	CAA	**The Rimrock Resort Hotel**	◇◇◇◇	$225-$685 [SAVE]	382
24 / p. 372	CAA	**The Fairmont Banff Springs**	◇◇◇◇	Rates not provided [SAVE]	379

Map Page	OA	Restaurants	Diamond Rated	Cuisine	Meal Range	Page
1 / p. 372	CAA	**Muk a Muk Bistro & Lounge**	◇◇	Canadian	$14-$37	385
2 / p. 372		Bumper's The Beef House	◇◇	Steak	$13-$40	384
3 / p. 372		Sleeping Buffalo Dining Room	◇◇◇	Regional Canadian	$14-$38	385
4 / p. 372		Cilantro Mountain Cafe	◇◇	California	$14-$15	384
5 / p. 372		The Evergreen	◇◇◇	International	$10-$37	384
6 / p. 372	CAA	**Ticino Swiss-Italian Restaurant**	◇◇◇	Swiss	$17-$38	385
7 / p. 372		St. James's Gate Olde Irish Pub	◇◇	Irish	$11-$28	385
8 / p. 372		Saltlik A Rare Steakhouse	◇◇◇	Steak	$10-$30	385
9 / p. 372		Giorgio's Trattoria	◇◇	Italian	$15-$40	384
10 / p. 372		Coyotes Deli & Grill	◇◇	Regional Canadian	$8-$29	384
11 / p. 372	CAA	**Silver Dragon Restaurant Banff**	◇◇	Chinese	$10-$24	385
12 / p. 372		Sukiyaki House	◇◇	Japanese	$10-$36	385
13 / p. 372		Grizzly House	◇◇	Fondue	$12-$50	384
14 / p. 372	CAA	**The Maple Leaf Grille & Spirits**	◇◇◇	Canadian	$12-$50	385
15 / p. 372		Tommy's Neighbourhood Pub	◇	American	$7-$13	385
16 / p. 372	CAA	**Le Beaujolais**	◇◇◇◇	French	$55-$95	384
17 / p. 372		Fuze Finer Dining	◇◇◇	International	$28-$39	384
18 / p. 372	CAA	**Eden**	◇◇◇◇◇	French	$95-$150	384
19 / p. 372	CAA	**The Banffshire Club**	◇◇◇◇	Continental	$28-$49	384

BANFF pop. 6,700 (See map and index starting on p. 372)

BANFF ASPEN LODGE

Book great rates at AAA.com

Phone: (403)762-4401 **17**

Hotel
$119-$241 All Year

Address: 401 Banff Ave T1L 1A9 **Location:** Between Moose and Rabbit sts. **Facility:** Smoke free premises. 89 units. 68 one- and 21 two-bedroom standard units. 3 stories, interior/exterior corridors. **Parking:** on-site, winter plug-ins. **Terms:** 2 night minimum stay - seasonal and/or weekends, cancellation fee imposed. **Amenities:** voice mail, irons, hair dryers. **Leisure Activities:** sauna, whirlpools, steamroom, ski locker, outdoor fireplace. **Guest Services:** valet and coin laundry, area transportation (fee)-ski hills, wireless Internet. **Business Services:** meeting rooms, PC (fee). **Free Special Amenities:** expanded continental breakfast.

BANFF CARIBOU LODGE

Book great rates at AAA.com

Phone: (403)762-5887 **7**

Hotel
$149-$475 All Year

Address: 521 Banff Ave T1L 1A4 **Location:** Trans-Canada Hwy 1, exit Banff (Minnewanka Loop), 2.1 mi (3.5 km) sw. Opposite Rotary Park. **Facility:** Smoke free premises. 195 one-bedroom standard units, some with whirlpools. 4 stories, interior corridors. **Parking:** on-site. **Terms:** check-in 4 pm, 3 day cancellation notice-fee imposed. **Amenities:** high-speed Internet, voice mail, irons, hair dryers. *Some:* DVD players. **Leisure Activities:** whirlpool, steamroom, exercise room, spa. **Guest Services:** valet and coin laundry, area transportation (fee), wireless Internet. **Business Services:** meeting rooms, PC (fee). *(See color ad below)*

BANFF PARK LODGE RESORT HOTEL & CONFERENCE CENTRE

Book great rates at AAA.com

Phone: (403)762-4433 **20**

Hotel
$149-$399 All Year

Address: 222 Lynx St T1L 1K5 **Location:** Between Caribou and Wolf sts; downtown. **Facility:** Smoke free premises. 211 units. 208 one-bedroom standard units, some with whirlpools. 3 one-bedroom suites with whirlpools. 3 stories, interior corridors. **Parking:** on-site (fee) and valet. **Terms:** check-in 4 pm, 3 day cancellation notice-fee imposed. **Amenities:** voice mail, safes, irons, hair dryers. *Some:* DVD players, high-speed Internet (fee). **Pool(s):** heated indoor. **Leisure Activities:** whirlpool, steamroom, hiking trails. **Guest Services:** valet and coin laundry, area transportation (fee), wireless Internet. **Business Services:** conference facilities, PC (fee). *(See color ad p 375)*

BANFF PTARMIGAN INN

Book at AAA.com

Phone: (403)762-2207 **18**

Hotel
$159-$329 All Year

Address: 337 Banff Ave T1L 1B1 **Location:** Between Moose and Elk sts. **Facility:** Smoke free premises. 134 one-bedroom standard units, some with whirlpools. 2-3 stories, interior corridors. **Parking:** on-site, winter plug-ins. **Terms:** check-in 4 pm, 3 day cancellation notice-fee imposed. **Amenities:** irons, hair dryers. **Leisure Activities:** sauna, whirlpools, steamroom, limited exercise equipment. *Fee:* massage. **Guest Services:** valet laundry, area transportation (fee), wireless Internet. **Business Services:** meeting rooms, PC (fee). *(See color ad below)*

(See map and index starting on p. 372)

BANFF ROCKY MOUNTAIN RESORT   *Book at AAA.com*   **Phone:** (403)762-5531

Resort Condominium
$170-$385 3/1-1/2

Address: 1029 Banff Ave T1L 1A2 **Location:** Banff Ave and Tunnel Mountain Rd; just s of Trans-Canada Hwy 1. **Facility:** Just outside of downtown, this condo-style resort is nestled at the base of the Rundle and Cascade mountains; all rooms have gas fireplaces. Smoke free premises. 171 units. 54 one-bedroom standard units, some with kitchens. 54 one- and 63 two-bedroom suites, some with kitchens and/or whirlpools. 2 stories (no elevator), exterior corridors. **Parking:** on-site, winter plug-ins. **Terms:** open 3/1-1/2, check-in 5 pm, 3 day cancellation notice-fee imposed. **Amenities:** voice mail, irons, hair dryers. *Fee:* video games, high-speed Internet. **Pool(s):** heated indoor. **Leisure Activities:** sauna, whirlpools, 2 tennis courts, recreation programs, playground, exercise room, basketball. *Fee:* bicycles, massage. **Guest Services:** valet and coin laundry, area transportation, wireless Internet. **Business Services:** meeting rooms, PC (fee).

BEST WESTERN SIDING 29 LODGE   *Book great rates at AAA.com*   **Phone:** (403)762-5575

Hotel
$100-$400 All Year

Address: 453 Marten St T1L 1B3 **Location:** 0.6 mi (1 km) ne, just off Banff Ave. Located in a residential area. **Facility:** Smoke free premises. 56 units. 53 one- and 2 two-bedroom standard units, some with kitchens and/or whirlpools. 1 one-bedroom suite with whirlpool. 3 stories, interior corridors. **Parking:** on-site. **Terms:** check-in 4 pm. **Amenities:** high-speed Internet, irons, hair dryers. **Pool(s):** heated indoor. **Leisure Activities:** whirlpool. **Guest Services:** wireless Internet. **Business Services:** PC. **Free Special Amenities:** local telephone calls and high-speed Internet.

AAA Benefit:
Members save up to 20%, plus 10% bonus points with rewards program.

BOW VIEW LODGE   *Book great rates at AAA.com*   **Phone:** (403)762-2261

Motel
$99-$299 All Year

Address: 228 Bow Ave T1L 1A5 **Location:** Between Lynx St and Bow Ave; on Wolf St. **Facility:** Smoke free premises. 58 units. 55 one- and 3 two-bedroom standard units. 3 stories, interior corridors. **Parking:** on-site, winter plug-ins. **Terms:** check-in 4 pm, 3 day cancellation notice-fee imposed. **Amenities:** voice mail, hair dryers. *Some:* irons. **Guest Services:** wireless Internet. **Business Services:** PC (fee).

FREE room upgrade and preferred room (each subject to availability with advance reservations)

(See map and index starting on p. 372)

BREWSTER'S MOUNTAIN LODGE

Book great rates at AAA.com

Phone: (403)762-2900

Hotel
$117-$401 All Year

Address: 208 Caribou St T1L 1C1 **Location:** Just w off Banff Ave; downtown. **Facility:** Smoke free premises. 77 one-bedroom standard units, some with whirlpools. 3 stories, interior corridors. **Parking:** on-site (fee). **Terms:** check-in 4 pm, 3 day cancellation notice-fee imposed. **Amenities:** voice mail, irons, hair dryers. **Leisure Activities:** sauna, whirlpool, exercise room. **Guest Services:** valet and coin laundry, area transportation (fee)-ski hills, wireless Internet. **Business Services:** meeting rooms, PC (fee). 🗙 🗙 🗙 📺 / SOME UNITS 🖫

FREE continental breakfast and high-speed Internet

BUFFALOBERRY BED AND BREAKFAST

Phone: (403)762-3750 🔢

Bed & Breakfast
$250-$325 All Year

Address: 417 Marten St T1L 1G5 **Location:** Just e of jct Rabbit St. Located in a residential area. **Facility:** Each room at this B&B offers its own unique, attractive decor, and secure underground parking is available. Smoke free premises. 4 one-bedroom standard units. 2 stories, interior corridors. *Bath:* combo or shower only. **Parking:** on-site. **Terms:** check-in 4 pm, 21 day cancellation notice-fee imposed. **Amenities:** DVD players, high-speed Internet, hair dryers. **Guest Services:** wireless Internet. ASK 🗙 🗙 🎞

BUFFALO MOUNTAIN LODGE

Phone: 403/762-2400 🔢

Hotel
$169-$339 All Year

Address: 700 Tunnel Mountain Rd T1L 1B3 **Location:** Jct Banff Ave and Wolf St, 1 mi (1.6 km) ne. Located in a secluded area. **Facility:** Smoke free premises. 108 units. 92 one-bedroom standard units, some with efficiencies. 16 one-bedroom suites with efficiencies. 2 stories (no elevator), exterior corridors. **Parking:** on-site, winter plug-ins. **Terms:** check-in 4 pm, 3 day cancellation notice-fee imposed. **Amenities:** video library, high-speed Internet, voice mail, irons, hair dryers. *Some:* DVD players. **Dining:** Cilantro Mountain Cafe, Sleeping Buffalo Dining Room, see separate listings. **Leisure Activities:** whirlpool, steamroom, exercise room. **Guest Services:** valet laundry, area transportation (fee), wireless Internet. **Business Services:** conference facilities, business center. ECO ASK 🍴 🍸 🗙 🗙 🗙 📺 / SOME UNITS 🖫 🖾

CASTLE MOUNTAIN CHALETS

Book at AAA.com

Phone: (403)762-3868

Cabin
$150-$345 All Year

Address: Bow Valley Pkwy (Hwy 1A) T1L 1B5 **Location:** 20 mi (32 km) w on Trans-Canada Hwy 1, jct Castle, 0.6 mi (1 km) ne on Hwy 1A (Bow Valley Pkwy). **Facility:** Smoke free premises. 22 cabins. 1 story, exterior corridors. *Bath:* combo or shower only. **Parking:** on-site, winter plug-ins. **Terms:** office hours 7 am-10 pm, 2 night minimum stay - weekends, 14 day cancellation notice-fee imposed. **Amenities:** video library (fee), DVD players, hair dryers. **Leisure Activities:** whirlpool, cross country skiing, recreation programs, rental bicycles, limited exercise equipment. **Guest Services:** coin laundry, wireless Internet. **Business Services:** meeting rooms, PC. ASK 🗙 🗙 🗙 🎞 🍽 🖫 📺 / SOME UNITS FEE 🐾 🖾

CHARLTON'S CEDAR COURT

Book great rates at AAA.com

Phone: (403)762-4485 🔢

Motel
$95-$235 All Year

Address: 513 Banff Ave T1L 1B4 **Location:** On Banff Ave, just w of Marmot Cres. **Facility:** Smoke free premises. 57 units. 41 one- and 16 two-bedroom standard units, some with efficiencies. 2-3 stories, exterior corridors. *Bath:* combo or shower only. **Parking:** on-site, winter plug-ins. **Terms:** office hours 7 am-11 pm, check-in 4 pm, 3 day cancellation notice-fee imposed. **Amenities:** video games (fee), voice mail, irons, hair dryers. **Pool(s):** heated indoor. **Leisure Activities:** whirlpool, steamroom. **Guest Services:** valet laundry, area transportation, wireless Internet. **Business Services:** PC. *(See color ad p 377)* ASK 🍴 🔽 🗙 🎞 🖫 📺 / SOME UNITS 🖾

DELTA BANFF ROYAL CANADIAN LODGE

Book great rates at AAA.com

Phone: (403)762-3307 🔢

Hotel
$139-$335 All Year

Address: 459 Banff Ave T1L 1B4 **Location:** 0.6 mi (1 km) ne. **Facility:** Smoke free premises. 99 one-bedroom standard units, some with whirlpools. 3 stories, interior corridors. **Parking:** on-site and valet. **Terms:** check-in 4 pm, 5 day cancellation notice-fee imposed. **Amenities:** video games (fee), high-speed Internet, voice mail, safes, irons, hair dryers. **Dining:** The Evergreen, see separate listing. **Pool(s):** heated indoor. **Leisure Activities:** whirlpool, steamroom, exercise room, massage. **Guest Services:** valet laundry, area transportation, wireless Internet. **Business Services:** meeting rooms, PC. *(See color ad p 378)* ECO ASK 🍴 24 🍸 🔽 🗙 🗙 🎞 📺 / SOME UNITS 🖫

(See map and index starting on p. 372)

DOUGLAS FIR RESORT & CHALETS *Book great rates at AAA.com* Phone: (403)762-5591 **5**

Condominium
$117-$459 All Year

Address: 525 Tunnel Mountain Rd T1L 1B2 **Location:** Jct Banff Ave and Wolf St, 1 mi (1.6 km) ne. Located in a secluded area. **Facility:** On a wooded hillside with scenic mountain views, the resort offers a mix of chalets and condos perfect for longer visits. Smoke free premises. 133 units. 57 one-bedroom standard units with kitchens, some with whirlpools. 65 one-, 1 two- and 1 three-bedroom suites with kitchens, some with whirlpools. 9 cottages. 2-3 stories, interior/exterior corridors. **Parking:** on-site, winter plug-ins. **Terms:** check-in 4 pm, cancellation fee imposed. **Amenities:** dual phone lines, voice mail, safes, irons, hair dryers. *Some:* DVD players. **Pool(s):** heated indoor. **Leisure Activities:** saunas, whirlpools, steamroom, waterslide, tennis court, playground, exercise room. **Guest Services:** coin laundry, area transportation-downtown shuttle, wireless Internet. **Business Services:** PC. **Free Special Amenities:** local telephone calls and high-speed Internet. *(See color ad p 378)*

(See map and index starting on p. 372)

▼ See AAA listing p 376 ▼

▼ See AAA listing p 377 ▼

(See map and index starting on p. 372)

THE FAIRMONT BANFF SPRINGS *Book great rates at AAA.com* Phone: 403/762-2211

Historic Resort Hotel

Rates not provided

Address: 405 Spray Ave T1L 1J4 **Location:** Just s on Banff Ave over the bridge, 0.3 mi (0.5 km) e. **Facility:** With a distinctive design that brings to mind a castle, this engaging hotel offers guest rooms that range from compact to extravagant suites. Smoke free premises. 768 units. 718 one-bedroom standard units, some with whirlpools. 50 one-bedroom suites, some with whirlpools. 3-9 stories, interior corridors. **Parking:** on-site (fee) and valet, winter plug-ins. **Terms:** check-in 4 pm. **Amenities:** voice mail, safes, irons, hair dryers. *Fee:* video games, high-speed Internet. *Some:* CD players. **Dining:** 9 restaurants, also, The Banffshire Club, see separate listing. **Pool(s):** heated outdoor, heated indoor. **Leisure Activities:** saunas, whirlpools, steamrooms, 5 tennis courts, ice skating, recreation programs, audio visual theatre, hiking trails, jogging, spa. *Fee:* golf-27 holes, tobogganing, bowling, bicycles, horseback riding. **Guest Services:** valet laundry, wireless Internet, beauty salon. **Business Services:** conference facilities, business center.

THE FOX HOTEL & SUITES *Book at AAA.com* Phone: (403)760-8500 10

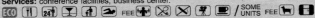

Hotel

$214-$739 All Year

Address: 461 Banff Ave T1L 1B1 **Location:** Just w of Fox St. **Facility:** Smoke free premises. 116 units. 61 one-bedroom standard units. 49 one- and 6 two-bedroom suites. 4 stories, exterior corridors. **Parking:** on-site. **Terms:** check-in 4 pm, 3 day cancellation notice-fee imposed. **Amenities:** high-speed Internet, voice mail, safes, irons, hair dryers. *Some:* DVD players. **Leisure Activities:** whirlpool. **Guest Services:** coin laundry, wireless Internet. **Business Services:** meeting rooms, PC (fee). *(See color ad p 374)*

▼ See AAA listing p 432 ▼

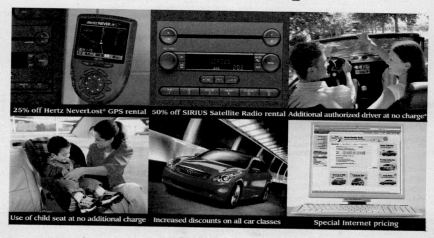

(See map and index starting on p. 372)

HIDDEN RIDGE RESORT *Book at AAA.com* Phone: 403/762-3544 **3**

Condominium
Rates not provided

Address: 901 Hidden Ridge Way T1L 1B7 **Location:** 1.5 mi (2.4 km) ne at Tunnel Mountain Rd. **Facility:** Set above the Banff townsite and between downtown and the Hoodoos, property guests will enjoy renovated rooms and an inviting hot tub. Smoke free premises. 107 units. 64 one- and 43 two-bedroom suites with kitchens, some with whirlpools. 2-4 stories (no elevator), exterior corridors. **Parking:** on-site, winter plug-ins. **Terms:** check-in 4 pm. **Amenities:** video library, DVD players, irons, hair dryers. *Some:* video games, CD players. **Leisure Activities:** sauna, whirlpools. **Guest Services:** coin laundry, area transportation, wireless Internet. **Business Services:** PC (fee).
(See color ad p 374) 🛎️ ✕ 🗄️ 📷 🖥️ / SOME UNITS FEE 🐕 🗝️

HIGH COUNTRY INN *Book great rates at AAA.com* Phone: (403)762-2236 **16**

(AAA) (SAVE)
Hotel
$104-$294 All Year

Address: 419 Banff Ave T1L 1A7 **Location:** Between Beaver and Rabbit sts. **Facility:** Smoke free premises. 70 units. 62 one-bedroom standard units, some with whirlpools. 7 one- and 1 two-bedroom suites. 3 stories, interior corridors. *Bath:* combo or shower only. **Parking:** on-site, winter plug-ins. **Terms:** check-in 4 pm, cancellation fee imposed. **Amenities:** voice mail, irons, hair dryers. *Some: Fee:* DVD players, video games. **Dining:** Ticino Swiss-Italian Restaurant, see separate listing. **Pool(s):** heated indoor. **Leisure Activities:** sauna, whirlpools, ski storage. **Guest Services:** valet and coin laundry, area transportation (fee)-ski areas, wireless Internet. **Business Services:** meeting rooms, PC (fee). **Free Special Amenities:** continental breakfast and high-speed Internet.
🌿 🛎️ 🏊 ✕ ✕ 🗄️ 🖥️ / SOME UNITS 📷

HOMESTEAD INN Phone: 403/762-4471 **21**

Motel
Rates not provided

Address: 217 Lynx St T1L 1A7 **Location:** Banff Ave, just w on Caribou St, then just n; downtown. **Facility:** Smoke free premises. 27 one-bedroom standard units. 3 stories (no elevator), exterior corridors. **Parking:** on-site, winter plug-ins. **Terms:** office hours 7 am-11 pm. **Amenities:** hair dryers. *Some:* irons. **Guest Services:** area transportation (fee), wireless Internet. 🛎️ ✕ 🗝️ 🗄️ 🖥️

IRWIN'S MOUNTAIN INN *Book great rates at AAA.com* Phone: (403)762-4566 **14**

(AAA) (SAVE)
Hotel
$89-$165 3/1-9/30
$79-$149 10/1-2/28

Address: 429 Banff Ave T1L 1B2 **Location:** N of Rabbit St. **Facility:** Smoke free premises. 65 units. 59 one- and 6 two-bedroom standard units, some with whirlpools. 3 stories, interior corridors. **Parking:** on-site, winter plug-ins. **Terms:** check-in 4 pm. **Amenities:** voice mail, hair dryers. **Leisure Activities:** sauna, whirlpool, ski lockers, exercise room. **Guest Services:** area transportation (fee)-ski areas, wireless Internet. **Business Services:** meeting rooms, PC (fee). **Free Special Amenities:** high-speed Internet. 🛎️ ✕ ✕ 🖥️ / SOME UNITS FEE 🐕 🗄️ 📷

▼ See AAA listing p 382 ▼

(See map and index starting on p. 372)

JOHNSTON CANYON RESORT

Phone: (403)762-2971

Cabin

$149-$314 6/19-10/11
$119-$268 5/21-6/18

Address: Hwy 1A T1L 1A9 **Location:** 15 mi (24 km) nw on Hwy 1A (Bow Valley Pkwy). Located at Johnston Canyon. **Facility:** Smoke free premises. 42 cabins. 1 story, exterior corridors. *Bath:* combo or shower only. **Parking:** on-site. **Terms:** open 5/21-10/11, office hours 8 am-10 pm, check-in 4 pm, 3 day cancellation notice. **Amenities:** video library (fee). **Dining:** 2 restaurants. **Leisure Activities:** tennis court, barbecue area, hiking trails. *(See color ad p 381)*

THE JUNIPER *Book at AAA.com*

Phone: (403)762-2281 [2]

Hotel
$119-$339 All Year

Address: 1 Juniper Way T1L 1E1 **Location:** Trans-Canada Hwy 1, exit Mt. Norquay Rd, just n **Facility:** Smoke free premises. 52 units. 50 one-bedroom standard units, some with kitchens and/o whirlpools. 2 cabins. 3 stories (no elevator), interior corridors. *Bath:* combo or shower only. **Parking** on-site, winter plug-ins. **Terms:** check-in 4 pm, 3 day cancellation notice-fee imposed. **Amenities:** CD players, high-speed Internet, voice mail, irons, hair dryers. *Some:* DVD players, safes. **Dining:** Muk a Muk Bistro & Lounge, see separate listing. **Leisure Activities:** whirlpool. **Guest Services:** wireless Internet. **Business Services:** meeting rooms, PC (fee).

RED CARPET INN *Book great rates at AAA.com*

Phone: (403)762-4184 [15]

Hotel
$89-$159 3/1-9/30
$79-$149 10/1-2/28

Address: 425 Banff Ave T1L 1B6 **Location:** Between Beaver and Rabbit sts. **Facility:** Smoke free premises. 52 one-bedroom standard units, some with whirlpools. 3 stories, interior/exterior corridors. **Parking:** on-site, winter plug-ins. **Terms:** check-in 4 pm. **Amenities:** safes, hair dryers. *Some:* irons. **Leisure Activities:** whirlpool. **Guest Services:** valet laundry, area transportation (fee)-ski shuttle, wireless Internet. **Business Services:** PC (fee). **Free Special Amenities:** continental breakfast and high-speed Internet.

THE RIMROCK RESORT HOTEL *Book great rates at AAA.com*

Phone: (403)762-3356 [23]

Hotel
$225-$685 All Year

Address: 300 Mountain Ave T1L 1J2 **Location:** 2.4 mi (4 km) s via Sulphur Mountain Rd; adjacent to Upper Hot Springs Pool. Located in a quiet secluded area. **Facility:** Tucked in the mountains just on the outskirts of town, this luxurious resort hotel features elegant rooms and upscale dining. Smoke free premises. 348 units. 330 one-bedroom standard units. 18 one-bedroom suites. 9 stories, interior corridors. **Parking:** on-site and valet, winter plug-ins. **Terms:** check-in 4 pm, 3 day cancellation notice-fee imposed. **Amenities:** video games (fee), dual phone lines, voice mail, irons, hair dryers. *Some:* safes. **Dining:** Eden, see separate listing, entertainment. **Pool(s):** heated indoor. **Leisure Activities:** sauna, whirlpool, steamrooms, ice skating, hiking trails, spa, aerobics, sports court. **Guest Services:** valet laundry, area transportation-downtown, wireless Internet. **Business Services:** conference facilities, business center. **Free Special Amenities:** local telephone calls.

RUNDLESTONE LODGE *Book great rates at AAA.com*

Phone: (403)762-2201 [4]

Hotel
$115-$401 All Year

Address: 537 Banff Ave T1L 1A6 **Location:** Trans-Canada Hwy 1, exit Banff Ave, 2 mi (3.4 km) sw. **Facility:** 96 units. 94 one-bedroom standard units, some with efficiencies and/or whirlpools. 2 two-bedroom suites with kitchens and/or whirlpools. 3 stories, interior corridors. **Parking:** on-site. **Terms:** check-in 4 pm, cancellation fee imposed. **Amenities:** high-speed Internet, hair dryers. *Some:* DVD players. **Pool(s):** heated indoor. **Leisure Activities:** whirlpool, ski locker, exercise room. **Guest Services:** valet and coin laundry, wireless Internet. **Business Services:** meeting rooms, PC (fee). **Free Special Amenities:** high-speed Internet.

TUNNEL MOUNTAIN RESORT *Book at AAA.com*

Phone: (403)762-4515 [6]

Condominium
$233-$294 1/7-2/28
$195-$294 3/1-1/6

Address: 502 Tunnel Mountain Rd T1L 1B1 **Location:** Jct Banff Ave and Wolf St, 1 mi (1.6 km) ne. Located in a secluded area. **Facility:** Smoke free premises. 94 units. 24 one-bedroom standard units with whirlpools. 15 one- and 55 two-bedroom suites with kitchens, some with whirlpools. 2 stories, exterior corridors. **Parking:** on-site, winter plug-ins. **Terms:** check-in 4 pm, 3 day cancellation notice-fee imposed. **Amenities:** voice mail, hair dryers. *Some:* DVD players, dual phone lines, safes, irons. **Pool(s):** heated indoor. **Leisure Activities:** sauna, whirlpools, steamroom, playground, exercise room. **Guest Services:** valet and coin laundry, wireless Internet. **Business Services:** PC (fee).

(See map and index starting on p. 372)

—— WHERE TO DINE ——

THE BANFFSHIRE CLUB

Phone: 403/762-6860   (1)

Continental
$28-$49

Reminiscent of a castle dining room, this restaurant is beautiful and elegant, complete with a ston fireplace, original stone walls and dark wood accents. Accomplished servers provide a wonderful dinir experience, and a talented team of chefs serve up offerings with a very good variety of local and region menu items with some exotic treats such as Quebec foie gras or sweetbreads and lobster arugula pack Guests will also find a fantastic cheese cart and an extensive wine cellar. Dressy casual. **Bar:** Full ba **Reservations:** required. **Hours:** Open 3/1-11/2 & 12/1-2/28; 6 pm-10 pm. Closed: Sun & Mo **Address:** 405 Spray Ave T1L 1J4 **Location:** Just s on Banff Ave over the bridge, 0.3 mi (0.5 km) e; in Th Fairmont Banff Springs. **Parking:** on-site and valet.

BUMPER'S THE BEEF HOUSE

Phone: 403/762-2622   (2)

Steak
$13-$40

Established in 1975, the restaurant occupies an A-frame building. The decor is a blend of the Old West an a mountain chalet, with the loft-lounge overlooking the dining room. Patrons can enjoy the all-you-can-ea salad bar with each entree. Although the succulent hamburgers are a favorite, the menu also features prim rib and steaks, all served by the friendly staff. Casual dress. **Bar:** Full bar. **Reservations:** accepte **Hours:** 5 pm-9:30 pm. Closed: 12/24, 12/25; also 12/1-12/15. **Address:** 603 Banff Ave T1L 1A **Location:** 0.8 mi (1.2 km) ne on Banff Ave at Marmot St; in Bumper's Inn. **Parking:** on-site.

CILANTRO MOUNTAIN CAFE

Phone: 403/760-4488   (4)

California
$14-$15

This seasonal restaurant treats patrons to fine, friendly service in a casual atmosphere. However, the food– an eclectic mix of designer wood-fired pizzas, pasta dishes and fantastic desserts, all relying heavily o regional ingredients—is anything but casual. On summer days, locals often congregate on the patio. Casua dress. **Bar:** Beer & wine. **Hours:** Open 3/1-9/30 & 12/10-2/28; 5 pm-10 pm; hours vary in winter. Closec Mon & Tues. **Address:** 700 Tunnel Mountain Rd T1L 1B3 **Location:** Jct Banff Ave and Wolf St, 1 mi (1. km) ne; in Buffalo Mountain Lodge. **Parking:** on-site. Ⓜ

COYOTES DELI & GRILL

Phone: 403/762-3963   (10)

Regional
Canadian
$8-$29

Set in a relaxed yet lively deli-bistro, Coyotes focuses on contemporary Southwest cuisine with an accent on creativity and color. A large open kitchen allows you to watch your food being prepared. Casual dress. **Bar** Full bar. **Reservations:** suggested, for dinner. **Hours:** 7:30 am-4 & 5-10 pm. Closed: 12/25. **Address:** 20(Caribou St T1L 1A2 **Location:** Just w of Banff Ave; centre. **Parking:** street.

EDEN   *Menu on AAA.com*

Phone: 403/762-1840   (18)

French
$95-$150

Tastes, textures, creativity and imagination mingle to produce an exquisite meal from beginning to end. A touch of something magical is evident at the intimate restaurant, where hours pass unnoticed as diners unwind in plush wingback chairs, gazing out at the spectacular Rocky Mountains and Banff cityscape Attentive staff ensure wine and water glasses never sit unattended. The dining climax hits with the entrée which arrives enclosed in caloches and are removed in perfect synchronism without a millisecond o difference. Dressy casual. **Bar:** Full bar. **Reservations:** suggested. **Hours:** 6 pm-10 pm. Closed: Mon & Tues. **Address:** 100 Mountain Ave T1L 1J2 **Location:** 2.4 mi (4 km) s via Sulphur Mountain Rd; adjacent tc Upper Hot Springs Pool; in The Rimrock Resort Hotel. **Parking:** on-site and valet.

THE EVERGREEN

Phone: 403/762-3307   (5)

International
$10-$37

An open-concept kitchen, innovative Continental menu and comfortable yet elegant ambience make the restaurant a popular choice. Dishes highlight fresh local and regional ingredients. This place is within eas walking distance of the town center. Casual dress. **Bar:** Full bar. **Reservations:** suggested. **Hours:** 6:3(am-10 pm. **Address:** 459 Banff Ave T1L 1B4 **Location:** 0.6 mi (1 km) ne; in Delta Banff Royal Canadiar Lodge. **Parking:** valet and street.

FUZE FINER DINING

Phone: 403/760-0853   (17)

International
$28-$39

This chic, sexy restaurant has distinctive display cases filled with wines that professionally trained sommeliers know well. Global dishes integrate the accents and ingredients of France, Asia and India Casual dress. **Bar:** Full bar. **Reservations:** suggested. **Hours:** 5:30 pm-9 pm. Closed major holidays **Address:** 110 Banff Ave, 2nd Floor T1L 1C9 **Location:** Centre; 2nd floor of Clock Tower Village Mall **Parking:** street.

GIORGIO'S TRATTORIA

Phone: 403/762-5114   (9)

Italian
$15-$40

This downtown restaurant's Southern and Mediterranean decor offers a warm, relaxed ambience. The dishes include fresh pasta made in house, meat and seafood specialties, and pizza cooked in a traditional wood-burning oven. Casual dress. **Bar:** Full bar. **Reservations:** suggested. **Hours:** 5 pm-10 pm; hours vary off season. **Address:** 219 Banff Ave T0L 0C0 **Location:** Centre. **Parking:** street.

GRIZZLY HOUSE

Phone: 403/762-4055   (13)

Fondue
$12-$50

The eclectic, rustic downtown restaurant treats patrons to a distinctive fondue experience. Hot rock fondues are particularly memorable, and beef, buffalo, chicken, ostrich, rattlesnake, lobster and shark are among meats available for dipping. Finish the meal with a decadent chocolate fondue: The bustling atmosphere is fun and lively, and there are phones at every table. Casual dress. **Bar:** Full bar. **Reservations:** suggested. **Hours:** 11:30 am-midnight. **Address:** 207 Banff Ave T1L 1B4 **Location:** Between Caribou and Wolf sts. **Parking:** street. Ⓜ

LE BEAUJOLAIS   *Menu on AAA.com*

Phone: 403/762-2712   (16)

French
$55-$95

Guests ascend the stairs to the elegant dining room, which overlooks one of the main streets. The restaurant offers an experience, not just a meal. Professional servers ensure a memorable event from beginning to end. The cuisine, a harmony of traditional elements prepared with a contemporary flair, is available as a prix fixe menu or a la carte. The wine list is among the most impressive in town. Dressy casual. **Bar:** Full bar. **Reservations:** suggested. **Hours:** 6 pm-10 pm. **Address:** 212 Buffalo St T1L 1B5 **Location:** Northwest corner of Banff Ave and Buffalo St; upstairs; near bridge. **Parking:** street.

(See map and index starting on p. 372)

THE MAPLE LEAF GRILLE & SPIRITS

Phone: 403/760-7680 (14)

Canadian
$12-$50

The restaurant is a favorite for a truly Canadian experience, both in food and decor. The cozy, rock-and-wood interior displays Canadian art, as well as a canoe on the ceiling and snowshoes on the walls. The chef creates artistic regional dishes, using organic, free-range, locally grown ingredients when possible. Among selections are preparations of elk, venison, salmon and char, all made to complement the season. Dressy casual. **Bar:** Full bar. **Reservations:** suggested. **Hours:** 11 am-10 pm. **Closed:** for lunch 12/25. **Address:** 137 Banff Ave T1L 1C8 **Location:** Corner of Banff Ave and Caribou St. **Parking:** street.
CALL M

MUK A MUK BISTRO & LOUNGE   *Menu on AAA.com*

Phone: 403/763-6205 (1)

Canadian
$14-$37

Offering an unparalleled view of Mt. Rundle, the Vermillion Lakes and the Banff town site, this upscale restaurant with its semi-open kitchen features a creative Canadian menu and a variety of Native dishes designed to be shared. Casual dress. **Bar:** Full bar. **Reservations:** suggested. **Hours:** 8 am-9 pm. **Address:** 1 Juniper Way T1L 1E1 **Location:** Trans-Canada Hwy 1, exit Mt. Norquay Rd, just n; in The Juniper. **Parking:** on-site. CALL M

ST. JAMES'S GATE OLDE IRISH PUB

Phone: 403/762-9355 (7)

Irish
$11-$28

For a casual place to kick back in the typical Irish way, look no further. The modern-day version of a rustic pub serves traditional food, such as shepherd's pie, steak and Guinness pie. Lamb stew is a fantastic, hearty choice, served with a chunk of soda bread. Guests can savor a pint of locally brewed beer or try some of the ales from overseas. Also on hand is an impressive selection of single-malt scotches, local and imported draft beers and cigars. Casual dress. Entertainment. **Bar:** Full bar. **Reservations:** not accepted. **Hours:** 11 am-11 pm. **Address:** 207 Wolf St T1L 1C2 **Location:** Just w of Banff Ave; centre. **Parking:** street.

SALTLIK A RARE STEAKHOUSE

Phone: 403/762-2467 (8)

Steak
$10-$30

True to its name, the restaurant truly is a "rare steak house" and a superb place. From the moment guests ascend the stairs to the upscale, contemporary dining room, they're impressed by the atmosphere. Also praiseworthy are the incredibly friendly, attentive servers, who take the time to explain the different cuts of meat and accompanying sauces. All entrees are a la carte, and the side orders are large enough to share. Casual dress. **Bar:** Full bar. **Reservations:** not accepted. **Hours:** 11 am-11 pm. **Closed:** 12/25. **Address:** 221 Bear St T1L 1B3 **Location:** Jct Caribou and Bear sts. **Parking:** street. CALL M

SILVER DRAGON RESTAURANT BANFF

Phone: 403/762-3939 (11)

Chinese
$10-$24

Two flights up from street level, the restaurant is a definite stop for those who crave Chinese food. Dishes of seafood, pork, noodles and beef are certain to satisfy any appetite. Patrons discover a contemporary decor, complete with a fish tank that the kids will enjoy. Casual dress. **Bar:** Full bar. **Reservations:** accepted. **Hours:** 11:30 am-10 pm. **Address:** 211 Banff Ave T1L 1E4 **Location:** Centre. **Parking:** street. CALL M

SLEEPING BUFFALO DINING ROOM

Phone: 403/760-4484 (3)

Regional
Canadian
$14-$38

You'll appreciate the casual elegance in this restaurant's mountain setting. Its Rocky Mountain cuisine features wild-game meat, robust flavors and an excellent wine list. After-dinner drinks and a cigar menu are offered fireside in the lounge. Casual dress. **Bar:** Full bar. **Reservations:** suggested. **Hours:** 7 am-10 pm. **Address:** 700 Tunnel Mountain Rd T1L 1B3 **Location:** Jct Banff Ave and Wolf St, 1 mi (1.6 km) ne; in Buffalo Mountain Lodge. **Parking:** on-site.

SUKIYAKI HOUSE

Phone: 403/762-2002 (12)

Japanese
$10-$36

Diners who crave sushi might try the modest eatery, upstairs along the city's main avenue. The traditional sushi house decor includes an open-concept sushi bar, where guests can choose from love boat platters, varied sushi and sashimi and traditional miso soup. Casual dress. **Bar:** Full bar. **Reservations:** suggested. **Hours:** 4:30 pm-10 pm; also noon-2:30 pm 6/1-9/30. **Closed:** 12/24, 12/25. **Address:** 211 Banff Ave T1L 1B8 **Location:** In Park Avenue Mall, 2nd Floor; downtown. **Parking:** street.

TICINO SWISS-ITALIAN RESTAURANT

Phone: 403/762-3848 (6)

Swiss
$17-$38

Set amongst the spectacular mountain peaks of Banff, this Swiss restaurant, which has been serving customers for over 30 years, has developed a solid reputation with locals and repeat visitors alike for its contemporary "Cucina Nostrana." Using local ingredients, whenever possible, the restaurant also features a number of traditional Swiss dishes including Medallions of Venison, roasted duck breasts and their famous fondues including a superb chocolate fondue for desert. Casual dress. **Bar:** Full bar. **Reservations:** suggested. **Hours:** Open 3/1-11/8 & 12/8-2/28; 5:30 pm-10 pm. **Address:** 415 Banff Ave T1L 1B5 **Location:** Between Beaver and Rabbit sts; in High Country Inn. **Parking:** on-site.

TOMMY'S NEIGHBOURHOOD PUB

Phone: 403/762-8888 (15)

American
$7-$13

After a day on the ski hills or hiking in the mountains, the restaurant is a good stop for a great burger and a pint of ale. Locals frequent the place not only for its food but also for its casual, pub-style atmosphere. Menu offerings also include soups, salads and sandwiches. Guests can settle into a booth or belly up to the bar for great conversation and good times. Casual dress. **Bar:** Full bar. **Hours:** 11 am-11 pm. **Closed:** 12/25. **Address:** 120 Banff Ave T1L 1A4 **Location:** Downtown. **Parking:** street.

BEAVER MINES pop. 71

ASPEN GROVE B & B

Bed & Breakfast
$95 All Year

Phone: 403/627-2928

Address: Range Rd 2-5 T0K 1W0 **Location:** Hwy 6, 11.8 mi (19 km) w on SR 507, 4.3 mi (7 km) s or SR 744, then 1.2 mi (2 km) w; Hwy 3, 12.5 mi (20 km) s on SR 744, then 1.2 mi (2 km) w at Buckhorn Rd. **Facility:** Nestled in a spectacular mountain setting, the upscale B&B offers sweeping views and proximity to skiing. Smoke free premises. 4 one-bedroom standard units. 2 stories (no elevator) interior corridors. **Bath:** combo or shower only. **Parking:** on-site, winter plug-ins. **Terms:** 2 night minimum stay - seasonal and/or weekends, 7 day cancellation notice-fee imposed. **Amenities:** Some hair dryers. **Leisure Activities:** fishing, hiking trails. *Fee:* horseback riding. **Guest Services:** TV in common area, coin laundry, wireless Internet. **Business Services:** meeting rooms.

BROOKS pop. 12,498

BROOKS SUPER 8

Hotel
$120-$125 All Year

Phone: 403/363-0080

Address: 115 Fifteenth Ave W T1R 1C4 **Location:** Just s off Trans-Canada Hwy 1. **Facility:** 94 units 89 one-bedroom standard units, some with efficiencies and/or whirlpools. 5 one-bedroom suites. 3 stories, interior/exterior corridors. *Bath:* combo or shower only. **Parking:** on-site, winter plug-ins **Terms:** 5 day cancellation notice. **Amenities:** high-speed Internet, voice mail, safes, irons, hair dryers *Some:* DVD players, video games (fee). **Pool(s):** heated indoor. **Leisure Activities:** whirlpool waterslide, exercise room. **Guest Services:** coin laundry, wireless Internet. **Business Services** meeting rooms. **Free Special Amenities:** expanded continental breakfast and high-speed Internet.

HERITAGE INN   *Book at AAA.com*

Hotel
$109-$169 1/1-2/28
$105-$160 3/1-12/31

Phone: (403)362-6666

Address: 1217 2nd St W T1R 1P7 **Location:** Trans-Canada Hwy 1, exit Hwy 873, 0.5 mi (0.8 km) s. **Facility:** 106 units. 103 one-bedroom standard units. 3 one-bedroom suites, some with efficiencies. 2 stories (no elevator), interior corridors. **Parking:** on-site, winter plug-ins. **Amenities:** voice mail. **Leisure Activities:** sauna, whirlpool. **Guest Services:** valet and coin laundry, wireless Internet. **Business Services:** meeting rooms.

HERITAGE INN & SUITES

Hotel
Rates not provided

Phone: 403/362-8579

Address: 1239 2nd St W T1R 1B8 **Location:** Trans-Canada Hwy 1, exit Hwy 873, 0.5 mi (0.8 km) s. **Facility:** 61 units. 52 one- and 6 two-bedroom standard units, some with whirlpools. 2 one- and 1 two-bedroom suites, some with efficiencies and/or whirlpools. 3 stories, interior corridors. *Bath:* combo or shower only. **Parking:** on-site, winter plug-ins. **Amenities:** high-speed Internet, voice mail, irons, hair dryers. *Some:* DVD players, CD players. **Pool(s):** heated indoor. **Leisure Activities:** whirlpool, exercise room. **Guest Services:** valet and coin laundry, wireless Internet. **Business Services:** meeting rooms, PC (fee).

LAKEVIEW INNS & SUITES   *Book great rates at AAA.com*

Hotel
$119-$179 All Year

Phone: (403)362-7440

Address: 1307 2nd St W T1R 1P7 **Location:** Trans-Canada Hwy 1, exit Hwy 873, 0.5 mi (0.8 km) s. **Facility:** 77 units. 62 one-bedroom standard units, some with whirlpools. 15 one-bedroom suites. 3 stories, interior corridors. **Parking:** on-site, winter plug-ins. **Terms:** cancellation fee imposed. **Amenities:** DVD players, dual phone lines, irons, hair dryers. **Pool(s):** heated indoor. **Leisure Activities:** whirlpool, exercise room. *Fee:* game room. **Guest Services:** valet and coin laundry, wireless Internet. **Business Services:** meeting rooms, PC. **Free Special Amenities:** expanded continental breakfast and local telephone calls.

—— WHERE TO DINE ——

O'SHEA'S EATERY & ALE HOUSE

Canadian
$10-$25

Phone: 403/501-5656

This attractive, Irish theme restaurant offers up an expanded pub menu as well as a good variety of salads, pastas, chicken, ribs, fish and steaks. The kitchen also cooks up such classic Irish favorites as fish and chips, shepherd's pie and Guinness beef stew. Casual dress. **Bar:** Full bar. **Hours:** 11 am-10 pm, Fri & Sat-11 pm. Closed: 12/25. **Address:** 119 15th Ave W T1R 1C3 **Location:** On Trans-Canada Hwy 1, 0.3 mi (0.4 km) w of jct Hwy 3; access 7th St SW. **Parking:** on-site.

Destination Calgary

pop. 988,193

A versatile city with an abundance of theaters and shopping malls, Calgary seems to have something for everyone.

Y ou can attend a horse show, join in a rousing celebration of the Wild West or browse through unique marketplaces. Want to ride down a rushing river? Calgary won't leave you high and dry.

Travel Alberta

Spruce Meadows, Calgary.
(See mention page 56)

Tourism Calgary

Pengrowth Saddledome,
Calgary.
(See mention
page 56)

Taste of Calgary.

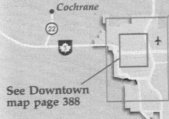

Tourism Calgary

See Vicinity
map page 392

Airdrie

Cochrane

See Downtown
map page 388

Calgary

Strathmore

Okotoks

P laces included in this
AAA Destination City:

Travel Alberta

Stephen Avenue Walk, Calgary.
(See mention page 56)

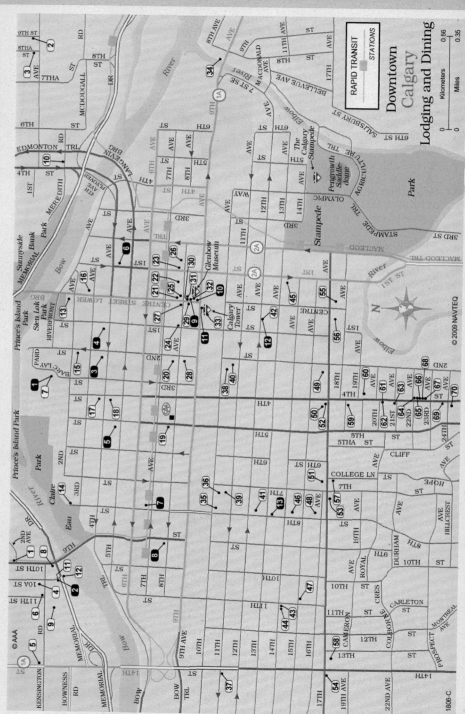

Downtown
Calgary
Lodging and Dining

Downtown Calgary

This index helps you "spot" where approved lodgings and restaurants are located on the corresponding detailed maps. Lodging daily rate range is for comparison only and show the property's high season. Restaurant rate range is a combination of lunch and/or dinner. Turn to the listing page for more detailed rate information and consult display ads for special promotions.

DOWNTOWN CALGARY

Map Page	OA	Lodgings	Diamond Rated	High Season	Page
1 / p. 388	AAA	**Sheraton Suites Calgary Eau Claire**	4 diamonds	Rates not provided SAVE	401
2 / p. 388	AAA	**Kensington Riverside Inn**	3 diamonds	$259-$429 SAVE	400
3 / p. 388	AAA	**The Westin Calgary**	4 diamonds	$139-$489 SAVE	401
4 / p. 388	AAA	**International Hotel of Calgary**	3 diamonds	$149-$499 SAVE	399
5 / p. 388		5 Calgary Downtown Suites	2 diamonds	$89-$269	397
6 / p. 388	AAA	**Delta Bow Valley** - see color ad p 399	3 diamonds	$119-$399 SAVE	398
7 / p. 388		Sandman Hotel Downtown Calgary	3 diamonds	$149-$218	400
8 / p. 388		Holiday Inn Express Hotel & Suites Calgary Downtown - see color ad on insert	3 diamonds	Rates not provided	399
9 / p. 388	AAA	**Hyatt Regency Calgary**	4 diamonds	$149-$489 SAVE	399
10 / p. 388	AAA	**Calgary Marriott Hotel** - see color ad p 398	3 diamonds	$209-$249 SAVE	398
11 / p. 388		The Fairmont Palliser	4 diamonds	$149-$449	398
12 / p. 388	AAA	**Hotel Arts**	3 diamonds	$149-$319 SAVE	399
13 / p. 388	AAA	**Best Western Suites Downtown** - see color ad p 397	2 diamonds	$150-$320 SAVE	397

Map Page	OA	Restaurants	Diamond Rated	Cuisine	Meal Range	Page
1 / p. 388		Broken Plate Kitchen & Bar	2 diamonds	Greek	$10-$32	402
2 / p. 388		La Brezza	2 diamonds	Italian	$9-$25	405
3 / p. 388	AAA	**La Dolce Vita Ristorante Italiano**	3 diamonds	Italian	$9-$40	405
4 / p. 388		Charly Chan's Rice House	2 diamonds	Szechuan	$8-$16	403
5 / p. 388		Sultan's Tent	2 diamonds	Traditional Moroccan	$17-$26	408
6 / p. 388		Maurya	2 diamonds	Eastern Indian	$14-$16	406
7 / p. 388		Barclay's	3 diamonds	International	$12-$35	401
8 / p. 388		Julio's Barrio Mexican Restaurant	2 diamonds	Mexican	$12-$21	405
9 / p. 388		Pulcinella	2 diamonds	Pizza	$12-$24	407
10 / p. 388	AAA	**Il Sogno**	4 diamonds	Italian	$12-$36	404
11 / p. 388		The Chef's Table	3 diamonds	Canadian	$36-$43	403
12 / p. 388		Muse Restaurant & Lounge	3 diamonds	International	$25-$40	406
13 / p. 388		Sakana Grill	2 diamonds	Japanese	$13-$20	408
14 / p. 388		The Belvedere	3 diamonds	Continental	$18-$45	402
15 / p. 388		Don Quijote	2 diamonds	Spanish	$12-$26	403
16 / p. 388	AAA	**Silver Dragon Restaurant**	2 diamonds	Chinese	$6-$17	408
17 / p. 388	AAA	**Caesar's Steakhouse**	3 diamonds	Steak	$15-$70	402

Map Page	OA	Restaurants (cont'd)	Diamond Rated	Cuisine	Meal Range	Page
18 / p. 388		The Glory Of India	◆◆	Indian	$17-$22	404
19 / p. 388		Chicago Chophouse	◆◆◆	Steak	$20-$49	403
20 / p. 388		Metropolitan Grill	◆◆◆	Canadian	$13-$38	406
21 / p. 388	CAA	**Catch Oyster Bar**	◆◆◆	Seafood	$18-$28	402
22 / p. 388	CAA	**Centini Restaurant and Lounge**	◆◆◆	Italian	$18-$52	402
23 / p. 388	CAA	**Teatro**	◆◆◆	New Italian	$15-$49	409
24 / p. 388		Murrieta's Westcoast Grill	◆◆◆	Western Pacific Rim	$10-$35	406
25 / p. 388		Thomson's Restaurant	◆◆◆	Canadian	$13-$36	409
26 / p. 388		River Cafe	◆◆◆	Regional Canadian	$16-$50	408
27 / p. 388		Tribune Restaurant	◆◆◆	Continental	$12-$50	409
28 / p. 388		The Orchid Room Fusion Cuisine	◆◆	Vietnamese	$16-$23	407
29 / p. 388		Divino Wine & Cheese Bistro	◆◆◆	International	$12-$35	403
30 / p. 388		Saltlik, A Rare Steakhouse	◆◆◆	Steak	$12-$40	408
31 / p. 388		Avenue Diner	◆◆	Canadian	$10-$18	401
32 / p. 388	CAA	**Catch Dining Room**	◆◆◆◆	Seafood	$18-$50	402
33 / p. 388		The Rimrock Dining Room	◆◆◆	Continental	$17-$50	408
34 / p. 388		Deane House Historic Site Restaurant at Fort Calgary	◆◆	Canadian	$8-$17	403
35 / p. 388		Bonterra Trattoria	◆◆◆	New Italian	$12-$38	402
36 / p. 388		The Holy Grill	◆	Deli	$8-$13	404
37 / p. 388		Pegasus	◆◆	Greek	$12-$24	407
38 / p. 388		Thai Sa-On Restaurant	◆◆	Thai	$11-$18	409
39 / p. 388		The King & I	◆◆◆	Thai	$8-$32	405
40 / p. 388		Vintage Chophouse & Tavern	◆◆◆	Steak	$10-$50	409
41 / p. 388		Gnocchi's Ristorante	◆◆◆	Italian	$10-$25	404
42 / p. 388		Saint Germain	◆◆◆	French	$8-$38	408
43 / p. 388		Galaxie Diner	◆	Canadian	$8-$15	404
44 / p. 388		Palace of Eats	◆	Sandwiches	$10-$13	407
45 / p. 388		Manuel Latruwe Belgian Patisserie & Bread Shop	◆◆	Breads/Pastries	$3-$20	406
46 / p. 388		Ric's Grill	◆◆◆	Steak	$10-$39	407
47 / p. 388		Good Earth Coffeehouse & Bakery	◆	Deli	$5-$8	404
48 / p. 388		Steeps The Urban Teahouse	◆	Deli	$5-$6	408
49 / p. 388		Cilantro	◆◆◆	California	$12-$42	403
50 / p. 388		El Sombrero Restaurant	◆◆	Mexican	$11-$20	404
51 / p. 388		Nellie's Kitchen	◆	Canadian	$4-$9	406
52 / p. 388		The Living Room	◆◆◆	Canadian	$14-$43	405
53 / p. 388		Manies Greek Cuisine	◆◆	Greek	$8-$22	405

Map Page	OA	Restaurants (cont'd)	Diamond Rated	Cuisine	Meal Range	Page
54 / p. 388		Moti Mahal	♦♦	Northern Indian	$10-$17	406
55 / p. 388		Da Paolo Ristorante	♦♦♦	Italian	$14-$35	403
56 / p. 388	CAA	**La Chaumiere Restaurant**	♦♦♦♦	French	$13-$37	405
57 / p. 388		Brava Bistro	♦♦♦	Canadian	$14-$32	402
58 / p. 388		Codo Vietnamese Restaurant	♦♦	Vietnamese	$8-$10	403
59 / p. 388		Hana Sushi	♦♦	Japanese	$7-$20	404
60 / p. 388		Peking Dragon	♦♦	Chinese	$9-$20	407
61 / p. 388		Le Chien Chaud	♦	Hot Dog	$6-$8	405
62 / p. 388		Fleur de Sel	♦♦	New French	$12-$37	404
63 / p. 388		Ouzo Greek Taverna	♦♦	Greek	$9-$28	407
64 / p. 388		Sushi Kawa	♦♦	Japanese	$6-$20	408
65 / p. 388		Aida's	♦♦	Lebanese	$5-$21	401
66 / p. 388		Bistro Twenty Two Ten	♦♦♦	Canadian	$12-$29	402
67 / p. 388		Mercato	♦♦	Italian	$15-$44	406
68 / p. 388		Purple Perk	♦	Coffee/Tea	$8	407
69 / p. 388		The Joyce on 4th Irish Pub	♦♦	Irish	$7-$18	405
70 / p. 388		Wildwood	♦♦♦	Regional Canadian	$10-$40	409

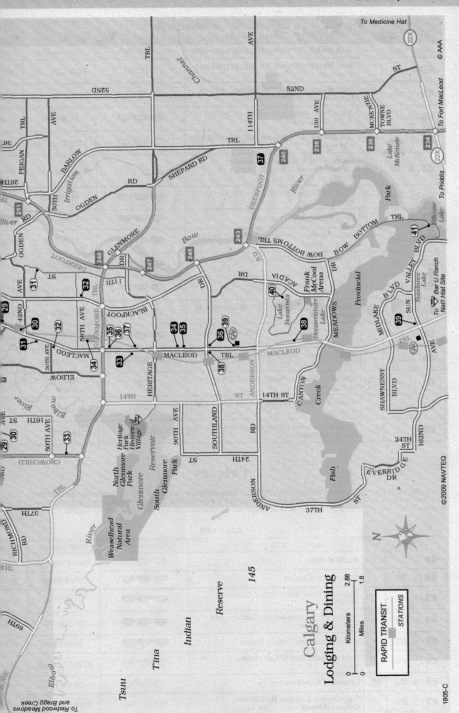

Calgary
Lodging & Dining

✈ Airport Accommodations

Map Page	OA	CALGARY INTERNATIONAL AIRPORT	Diamond Rated	High Season	Pag
19 / p. 392	CAA	**Best Western Airport Inn, 6.2 mi (10 km) s of airport**	◆◆	$135-$220 SAVE	410
6 / p. 392	CAA	**Best Western Port O'Call Hotel, 3.8 mi (6 km) s of airport**	◆◆◆	$129-$199 SAVE	411
27 / p. 392		Coast Plaza Hotel & Conference Centre, 7.4 mi (12 km) s of airport	◆◆◆	$129-$334	413
11 / p. 392	CAA	**Comfort Inn & Suites-Airport, 4.9 mi (8 km) s of airport**	◆◆◆	$129-$299 SAVE	413
8 / p. 392	CAA	**Country Inn & Suites By Carlson, Calgary-Airport, 4.1 mi (6.5 km) s of airport**	◆◆◆	$139-$229 SAVE	414
16 / p. 392		Days Inn Calgary Airport, 4.9 mi (8 km) s of airport	◆◆◆	$150-$190	415
2 / p. 392		Delta Calgary Airport, at airport	◆◆◆	$149-$329	415
13 / p. 392		Executive Royal Inn North Calgary, 5 mi (8.2 km) s of airport	◆◆◆	$130-$325	416
5 / p. 392		Hilton Garden Inn-Calgary Airport, 4.2 mi (7 km) s of airport	◆◆◆	$109-$299	417
26 / p. 392		Holiday Inn Calgary-Airport, 6.2 mi (10 km) s of airport	◆◆◆	$139-$259	417
7 / p. 392	CAA	**Lakeview Signature Inn, 3.7 mi (6 km) s of airport**	◆◆◆	$139-$309 SAVE	419
24 / p. 392		Radisson Hotel Calgary Airport, 6.2 mi (10 km) s of airport	◆◆◆	Rates not provided	420
3 / p. 392		Sandman Hotel Suites & Spa Calgary Airport, 4.3 mi (7 km) s of airport	◆◆◆	$129-$199	420
10 / p. 392	CAA	**Sheraton Cavalier Hotel, 4.6 mi (7.5 km) s of airport**	◆◆◆	Rates not provided SAVE	421
12 / p. 392	CAA	**Super 8 Calgary Airport, 3 mi (4.8 km) s of airport**	◆◆	$119-$289 SAVE	421
14 / p. 392	CAA	**Travelodge Hotel Calgary Airport, 4.9 mi (8 km) s of airport**	◆◆	$119-$179 SAVE	421

Calgary

This index helps you "spot" where approved lodgings and restaurants are located on the corresponding detailed maps. Lodgi
daily rate range is for comparison only and show the property's high season. Restaurant rate range is a combination of lun
and/or dinner. Turn to the listing page for more detailed rate information and consult display ads for special promotions.

CALGARY

Map Page	OA	Lodgings	Diamond Rated	High Season	Page
1 / p. 392	CAA	**Acclaim Hotel** - see color ad p 410	◆◆◆	$169-$189 SAVE	409
2 / p. 392		Delta Calgary Airport	◆◆◆	$149-$329	415
3 / p. 392		Sandman Hotel Suites & Spa Calgary Airport	◆◆◆	$129-$199	420
4 / p. 392		Holiday Inn Express Airport Calgary - see color ad on insert	◆◆◆	$150-$170	419
5 / p. 392		Hilton Garden Inn-Calgary Airport	◆◆◆	$109-$299	417
6 / p. 392	CAA	**Best Western Port O'Call Hotel** - see color ad p 412	◆◆◆	$129-$199 SAVE	411
7 / p. 392	CAA	**Lakeview Signature Inn**	◆◆◆	$139-$309 SAVE	419
8 / p. 392	CAA	**Country Inn & Suites By Carlson, Calgary-Airport** - see color ad p 415	◆◆◆	$139-$229 SAVE	414

CALGARY (cont'd)

Map Page	OA	Lodgings (cont'd)	Diamond Rated	High Season	Page
9 / p. 392	CAA	**Four Points by Sheraton Hotel and Suites, Calgary West** - see color ad p 417	◆◆ ◆◆ ◆◆	$99-$349 SAVE	416
10 / p. 392	CAA	**Sheraton Cavalier Hotel**	◆◆ ◆◆ ◆◆	Rates not provided SAVE	421
11 / p. 392	CAA	**Comfort Inn & Suites-Airport** - see color ad p 414	◆◆ ◆◆ ◆◆	$129-$299 SAVE	413
12 / p. 392	CAA	**Super 8 Calgary Airport**	◆◆ ◆◆	$119-$289 SAVE	421
13 / p. 392		Executive Royal Inn North Calgary	◆◆ ◆◆ ◆◆	$130-$325	416
14 / p. 392	CAA	**Travelodge Hotel Calgary Airport**	◆◆ ◆◆	$119-$179 SAVE	421
15 / p. 392	CAA	**Staybridge Suites Calgary Airport** - see color ad on insert	◆◆ ◆◆ ◆◆	$153-$243 SAVE	421
16 / p. 392		Days Inn Calgary Airport	◆◆ ◆◆ ◆◆	$150-$190	415
17 / p. 392	CAA	**Comfort Inn & Suites-Motel Village** - see color ad p 414	◆◆ ◆◆ ◆◆	$119-$449 SAVE	413
18 / p. 392	CAA	**Quality Inn University** - see color ad p 420	◆◆ ◆◆ ◆◆	$99-$169 SAVE	420
19 / p. 392	CAA	**Best Western Airport Inn** - see color ad p 411	◆◆ ◆◆	$135-$220 SAVE	410
20 / p. 392	CAA	**Best Western Village Park Inn** - see color ad p 413	◆◆ ◆◆	$120-$180 SAVE	411
21 / p. 392	CAA	**Econo Lodge Inn & Suites University** - see color ad p 416	◆◆ ◆◆	$89-$169 SAVE	415
22 / p. 392	CAA	**Hampton Inn & Suites by Hilton Calgary NW** - see color ad p 418	◆◆ ◆◆ ◆◆	Rates not provided SAVE	417
23 / p. 392	CAA	**Travelodge Calgary University**	◆◆ ◆◆	$98-$199 SAVE	421
24 / p. 392		Radisson Hotel Calgary Airport	◆◆ ◆◆ ◆◆	Rates not provided	420
25 / p. 392	CAA	**Econo Lodge Motel Village**	◆◆ ◆◆	$89-$149 SAVE	416
26 / p. 392		Holiday Inn Calgary-Airport - see color ad on insert	◆◆ ◆◆ ◆◆	$139-$259	417
27 / p. 392		Coast Plaza Hotel & Conference Centre	◆◆ ◆◆ ◆◆	$129-$334	413
28 / p. 392	CAA	**Calgary Westways Guest House**	◆◆ ◆◆ ◆◆	$99-$180 SAVE	412
29 / p. 392	CAA	**Best Western Calgary Centre Inn**	◆◆ ◆◆ ◆◆	$159-$249 SAVE	410
30 / p. 392	CAA	**Holiday Inn Calgary-MacLeod Trail South** - see color ad p 419	◆◆ ◆◆ ◆◆	$129-$159 SAVE	418
31 / p. 392	CAA	**Comfort Inn & Suites-South** - see color ad p 414	◆◆ ◆◆ ◆◆	$100-$160 SAVE	414
32 / p. 392		Blackfoot Inn	◆◆ ◆◆ ◆◆	$169-$335	412
33 / p. 392	CAA	**Econo Lodge South**	◆◆ ◆◆	$89-$129 SAVE	416
34 / p. 392	CAA	**Carriage House Inn**	◆◆ ◆◆ ◆◆	$149-$229 SAVE	412
35 / p. 392	CAA	**Travelodge Calgary Macleod Trail**	◆◆ ◆◆	$119-$179 SAVE	421
36 / p. 392		Delta Calgary South	◆◆ ◆◆ ◆◆	$109-$369	415
37 / p. 392	CAA	**Service Plus Inn & Suites Calgary**	◆◆ ◆◆ ◆◆	$159 SAVE	420
38 / p. 392		Holiday Inn Express Hotel & Suites Calgary-South - see color ad on insert	◆◆ ◆◆ ◆◆	$129-$259	419
39 / p. 392		Wingate by Wyndham Calgary	◆◆ ◆◆ ◆◆	$149-$259	423

Map Page	OA	Restaurants	Diamond Rated	Cuisine	Meal Range	Page
1 / p. 392		Buffet Yangtze	◆◆	Chinese	$11-$19	424
2 / p. 392		Captain Scott's Fish & Chips	◆◆	Seafood	$7-$15	424
3 / p. 392		Alberta King of Subs	◆◆	Canadian	$5-$13	423

Map Page	OA	Restaurants (cont'd)	Diamond Rated	Cuisine	Meal Range	Page
④ / p. 392		Jamesons Restaurant & Bar	◈◈	Western Canadian	$10-$19	425
⑤ / p. 392	CAA	**Nick's Steakhouse & Pizza**	◈◈	Steak	$8-$30	426
⑥ / p. 392		Carver's Steakhouse	◈◈◈	Steak	$25-$47	424
⑦ / p. 392		Misai Japanese Restaurant	◈◈	Japanese	$9-$15	426
⑧ / p. 392		Thai Boat	◈◈	Thai	$8-$13	428
⑨ / p. 392		Clay Oven	◈◈	Eastern Indian	$12-$20	424
⑩ / p. 392		Samosa Grill	◈◈	Eastern Indian	$14-$16	427
⑪ / p. 392		Big T's BBQ	◈◈	Barbecue	$10-$35	423
⑫ / p. 392		Lina's Italian Market	◈	Deli	$5-$10	426
⑬ / p. 392		Jamesons Irish Pub	◈◈	Irish	$8-$15	425
⑭ / p. 392		The Cheesecake Cafe	◈◈	Canadian	$10-$26	424
⑮ / p. 392		Gus's Cafe & Pizzeria	◈◈	Pizza	$5-$15	425
⑯ / p. 392		Santorini Greek Taverna	◈◈	Greek	$14-$30	427
⑰ / p. 392		Forbidden City Seafood & Dim Sum Restaurant	◈◈	Chinese	$4-$20	425
⑱ / p. 392		Open Range	◈◈	Canadian	$21-$36	426
⑲ / p. 392		Boogie's Burgers	◈	American	$5-$15	423
⑳ / p. 392		Diner Deluxe	◈◈	Canadian	$7-$22	425
㉑ / p. 392		Heartland Cafe	◈	Deli	$5-$13	425
㉒ / p. 392		Rouge	◈◈◈	French	$30-$44	427
㉓ / p. 392		Sugo Caffe Italia	◈◈◈	Italian	$15-$39	428
㉔ / p. 392		Kane's Harley Diner	◈	Canadian	$7-$22	426
㉕ / p. 392		Spolumbo's Deli	◈	Deli	$6-$10	428
㉖ / p. 392		Capo Restaurant	◈◈◈	New Italian	$16-$44	424
㉗ / p. 392		Crete Souvlaki	◈	Greek	$5-$9	424
㉘ / p. 392		Rajdoot Restaurant	◈◈	Indian	$11-$27	427
㉙ / p. 392		Belmont Diner	◈	Canadian	$9-$12	423
㉚ / p. 392		Nellie's in the Loop	◈◈	Canadian	$8-$13	426
㉛ / p. 392		Rocky's Burgers	◈	Canadian	$3-$6	427
㉜ / p. 392		Boyd's Seafood Restaurant	◈◈	Seafood	$10-$37	423
㉝ / p. 392	CAA	**Pfanntastic Pannenkoek Haus**	◈◈	Dutch	$7-$13	427
㉞ / p. 392		Bagolac Saigon Restaurant	◈◈	Vietnamese	$6-$12	423
㉟ / p. 392		Open Sesame	◈◈	Asian	$9-$22	427
㊱ / p. 392		Smuggler's Inn	◈◈	Steak	$12-$32	428
㊲ / p. 392		The Cheesecake Cafe	◈◈	Canadian	$10-$26	424
㊳ / p. 392		Emperor Buffet & Restaurant	◈	Chinese	$8-$14	425
㊴ / p. 392		Broken Plate Kitchen & Bar	◈◈	Greek	$10-$32	423
㊵ / p. 392		Newport Grill on Lake Bonavista	◈◈◈	Continental	$14-$40	426
㊶ / p. 392		The Ranche Restaurant	◈◈◈	Regional Canadian	$15-$40	427

OWNTOWN CALGARY (See map and index starting on p. 388)

CALGARY DOWNTOWN SUITES   *Book at AAA.com*   Phone: (403)263-0520   **5**

Extended Stay
Hotel
$89-$269 All Year

Address: 618 5th Ave SW T2P 0M7 **Location:** Corner of 5th Ave SW and 5th St SW. **Facility:** 302 units. 42 one-bedroom standard units with kitchens. 194 one- and 66 two-bedroom suites with kitchens. 28 stories, interior corridors. **Parking:** on-site, winter plug-ins. **Terms:** cancellation fee imposed. **Amenities:** video games (fee), high-speed Internet, voice mail, irons, hair dryers. *Some:* fax. **Pool(s):** heated outdoor. **Leisure Activities:** sauna, steamroom, exercise room, spa. **Guest Services:** valet and coin laundry, wireless Internet. **Business Services:** meeting rooms, business center.

BEST WESTERN SUITES DOWNTOWN   *Book great rates at AAA.com*   Phone: (403)228-6900   **13**

Hotel
$150-$320 All Year

Address: 1330 8th St SW T2R 1B6 **Location:** Corner of 8th St and 13th Ave SW. **Facility:** Smoke free premises. 123 units. 82 one-bedroom standard units, some with efficiencies and/or whirlpools. 17 one- and 24 two-bedroom suites, some with kitchens and/or whirlpools. 16 stories, interior corridors. **Parking:** on-site, winter plug-ins. **Terms:** cancellation fee imposed. **Amenities:** high-speed Internet, voice mail, irons, hair dryers. *Some:* DVD players. **Leisure Activities:** sauna, exercise room. **Guest Services:** valet and coin laundry, wireless Internet. **Business Services:** meeting rooms, PC. *(See color ad below)*

AAA Benefit:
Members save up to 20%, plus 10% bonus points with rewards program.

FREE continental breakfast and high-speed Internet

▼ See AAA listing above ▼

"Suite Lifestyle in Downtown Calgary"

- Free Parking, Local Calls
- Aeroplan Points
- Fitness Centre and Sauna
- Free High Speed Internet Access
- Kitchenettes, Jacuzzi Rooms
- Business Centre and Meeting Rooms
- Free Newspaper

Approved

Free Deluxe Continental Breakfast Buffet

Best Western

www.bestwesternsuitescalgary.com

TOLL FREE RESERVATIONS 1-800-981-2555
1330 8th Street SW • Calgary, AB T2R 1B6

(See map and index starting on p. 388)

CALGARY MARRIOTT HOTEL   *Book great rates at AAA.com*   Phone: (403)266-7331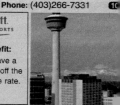

CAA SAVE
▽▼▽▼▽▼
Hotel
$209-$249 All Year

Address: 110 9th Ave SE T2G 5A6 **Location:** Jct 9th Ave and Centre St; adjacent to Telus Convention Centre. Located across from Calgary Tower. **Facility:** Smoke free premises. 384 units. 374 one-bedroom standard units. 10 one-bedroom suites. 22 stories, interior corridors. *Bath:* combo or shower only. **Parking:** on-site (fee) and valet, winter plug-ins. **Terms:** cancellation fee imposed. **Amenities:** voice mail, irons, hair dryers. *Fee:* video games, high-speed Internet. **Pool(s):** heated indoor. **Leisure Activities:** whirlpool, exercise room. **Guest Services:** valet laundry, wireless Internet. **Business Services:** meeting rooms, business center. *(See color ad below)*

Marriott HOTELS & RESORTS

AAA Benefit:
Members save a minimum 5% off the best available rate.

DELTA BOW VALLEY   *Book great rates at AAA.com*   Phone: (403)266-1980

CAA SAVE
▽▼▽▼▽▼
Hotel
$119-$399 All Year

Address: 209 4th Ave SE T2G 0C6 **Location:** 1st St SE and 4th Ave SE. **Facility:** Smoke free premises. 394 one-bedroom standard units, some with whirlpools. 25 stories, interior corridors. *Bath:* combo or shower only. **Parking:** on-site (fee) and valet. **Terms:** cancellation fee imposed. **Amenities:** dual phone lines, voice mail, irons, hair dryers. *Fee:* video games, high-speed Internet. **Pool(s):** heated indoor. **Leisure Activities:** saunas, whirlpool, exercise room. **Guest Services:** valet laundry, wireless Internet. **Business Services:** conference facilities, business center. *(See color ad p 399)*

THE FAIRMONT PALLISER   *Book at AAA.com*   Phone: (403)262-1234

▽▼▽▼ ▽▼▽▼
Historic Hotel
$149-$449 All Year

Address: 133 9th Ave SW T2P 2M3 **Location:** 9th Ave SW and 1st St SW. **Facility:** A sense of history and nostalgia reigns at this grand hotel, which features an imperial theme throughout its luxurious and upscale guest rooms. 405 units. 385 one-bedroom standard units. 20 one-bedroom suites. 12 stories, interior corridors. **Parking:** on-site (fee) and valet, winter plug-ins. **Terms:** check-in 4 pm. **Amenities:** dual phone lines, voice mail, honor bars, irons, hair dryers. *Fee:* video games, high-speed Internet. *Some:* DVD players, CD players, safes. **Dining:** The Rimrock Dining Room, see separate listing. **Pool(s):** heated indoor. **Leisure Activities:** whirlpool, steamroom. *Fee:* massage, esthetics. **Guest Services:** valet laundry, beauty salon. **Business Services:** conference facilities, business center.

▼ *See AAA listing above* ▼

(See map and index starting on p. 388)

HOLIDAY INN EXPRESS HOTEL & SUITES CALGARY DOWNTOWN   *Book at AAA.com*

Hotel
Rates not provided

Phone: 403/269-8262   **8**

Address: 1020 8th Ave SW T2P 1J2 **Location:** At 10th St SW. **Facility:** 56 units. 49 one-bedroom standard units. 7 one-bedroom suites with whirlpools. 9 stories, interior corridors. **Parking:** on-site, winter plug-ins. **Amenities:** high-speed Internet, dual phone lines, voice mail, irons, hair dryers. **Leisure Activities:** exercise room. **Guest Services:** valet and coin laundry, wireless Internet. **Business Services:** meeting rooms, PC. *(See color ad on insert)*

HOTEL ARTS   *Book great rates at AAA.com*

CAA SAVE

Hotel
$149-$319 1/1-2/28
$139-$309 3/1-12/31

Phone: (403)266-4611   **12**

Address: 119 12th Ave SW T2R 0G8 **Location:** At 1st St SW; centre. **Facility:** Smoke free premises. 175 one-bedroom standard units, some with whirlpools. 11 stories, interior corridors. *Bath:* combo or shower only. **Parking:** on-site, winter plug-ins. **Terms:** cancellation fee imposed. **Amenities:** high-speed Internet (fee), voice mail, irons, hair dryers. **Dining:** Saint Germain, see separate listing. **Pool(s):** heated outdoor. **Leisure Activities:** exercise room. **Guest Services:** valet laundry, wireless Internet. **Business Services:** meeting rooms, business center. **Free Special Amenities:** local telephone calls and high-speed Internet.

HYATT REGENCY CALGARY   *Book great rates at AAA.com*

CAA SAVE

Hotel
$149-$489 All Year

Phone: (403)717-1234   **9**

Address: 700 Centre St SE T2G 5P6 **Location:** Corner of Centre St and 7th Ave SW. Adjacent to Telus Convention Centre. **Facility:** Featuring a Canadian theme throughout, this downtown hotel with a luxurious ambience offers attentive service, upscale rooms and a new spa. 355 units. 342 one-bedroom standard units, some with whirlpools. 22 stories, interior corridors. *Bath:* combo or shower only. **Parking:** on-site (fee) and valet. **Terms:** cancellation fee imposed. **Amenities:** high-speed Internet (fee), dual phone lines, voice mail, safes, honor bars, irons, hair dryers. *Some:* DVD players, CD players. **Dining:** Thomson's Restaurant, see separate listing. **Pool(s):** heated indoor. **Leisure Activities:** whirlpool, steamroom, exercise room, spa. **Guest Services:** valet laundry, wireless Internet. **Business Services:** conference facilities, business center. **Free Special Amenities:** local telephone calls and newspaper.

> **HYATT**
> HOTELS & RESORTS
>
> **AAA Benefit:**
> Ask for the AAA rate
> and save 10%.

INTERNATIONAL HOTEL OF CALGARY   *Book great rates at AAA.com*

CAA SAVE

Hotel
$149-$499 3/1-7/11 &
7/16-2/28

Phone: (403)265-9600   **4**

Address: 220 4th Ave SW T2P 0H5 **Location:** Corner of 4th Ave and 2nd St SW. **Facility:** Smoke free premises. 248 units. 98 one-bedroom standard units. 120 one- and 30 two-bedroom suites. 35 stories, interior corridors. **Parking:** on-site and valet. **Terms:** open 3/1-7/11 & 7/16-2/28, cancellation fee imposed. **Amenities:** voice mail, safes, irons, hair dryers. *Fee:* video games, high-speed Internet. *Some:* CD players. **Pool(s):** heated indoor. **Leisure Activities:** whirlpool, exercise room. *Fee:* massage. **Guest Services:** airport transportation (fee)-Calgary International Airport, area transportation-downtown shuttle, wireless Internet, barber shop. **Business Services:** meeting rooms, business center. **Free Special Amenities:** full breakfast and newspaper.

▼ *See AAA listing p 398* ▼

(See map and index starting on p. 388)

KENSINGTON RIVERSIDE INN *Book great rates at AAA.com* Phone: (403)228-4442 **2**

CAA SAVE

▼▼▼▼

Bed & Breakfast
$259-$429 All Year

Address: 1126 Memorial Dr NW T2N 3E3 **Location:** Just w of 10th St NW. Located in Kensington area. **Facility:** Upscale and exquisite, the inn features original artwork, gourmet breakfasts and well-equipped guest rooms that are ideal for business travelers. Smoke free premises. 19 one-bedroom standard units, some with whirlpools. 2 stories, interior corridors. **Parking:** on-site. **Terms:** 2-3 night minimum stay - seasonal, 3 day cancellation notice-fee imposed. **Amenities:** CD players, high-speed Internet, voice mail, irons, hair dryers. *Some:* DVD players. **Dining:** The Chef's Table, see separate listing. **Leisure Activities:** jogging. **Guest Services:** valet laundry, wireless Internet. **Business Services:** meeting rooms.

SANDMAN HOTEL DOWNTOWN CALGARY *Book at AAA.com* Phone: (403)237-8626 **7**

▼▼▼

Hotel
$149-$218 All Year

Address: 888 7th Ave SW T2P 3J3 **Location:** Corner of 7th Ave SW and 8th St SW. **Facility:** 301 one-bedroom standard units. 23 stories, interior corridors. **Terms:** cancellation fee imposed. **Amenities:** video games (fee), high-speed Internet, dual phone lines, voice mail, irons, hair dryers. **Dining:** Moxie's Classic Grill, see separate listing. **Pool(s):** heated indoor. **Leisure Activities:** whirlpool, exercise room. **Guest Services:** valet laundry, wireless Internet. **Business Services:** meeting rooms, business center.

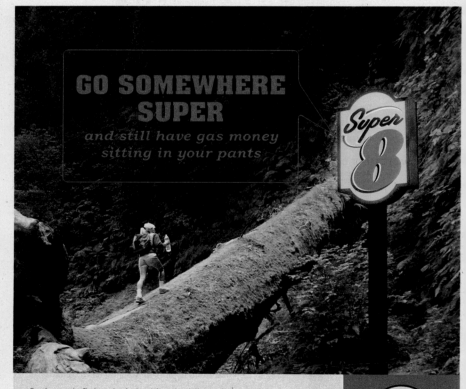

(See map and index starting on p. 388)

SHERATON SUITES CALGARY EAU CLAIRE   *Book great rates at AAA.com*   Phone: 403/266-7200

Hotel
Rates not provided

Address: 255 Barclay Parade SW T2P 5C2 **Location:** At 3rd St SW and 2nd Ave SW. **Facility:** Set along the river's edge, and with a prime location next to the Eau Claire market, this all-suite hotel offers upscale rooms and attentive service. Smoke free premises. 323 units. 313 one- and 10 two-bedroom suites, some with whirlpools. 15 stories, interior corridors. *Bath:* combo or shower only. **Parking:** on-site (fee) and valet. **Amenities:** high-speed Internet (fee), dual phone lines, voice mail, honor bars, irons, hair dryers. *Some:* DVD players, CD players, fax, safes. **Dining:** 2 restaurants, also, Barclay's, see separate listing. **Pool(s):** heated indoor. **Leisure Activities:** sauna, whirlpool, waterslide, jogging, exercise room. *Fee:* massage. **Guest Services:** valet and coin laundry, wireless Internet. **Business Services:** conference facilities, PC (fee). **Free Special Amenities:** newspaper.

AAA Benefit:
Members get up to 15% off, plus Starwood Preferred Guest® bonuses.

THE WESTIN CALGARY   *Book great rates at AAA.com*   Phone: (403)266-1611   [3]

Hotel
$139-$489 All Year

Address: 320 4th Ave SW T2P 2S6 **Location:** Corner of 4th Ave SW and 3rd St. **Facility:** The upscale hotel's newly renovated lobby is inviting with a contemporary refinement; guest rooms offer a spacious desk area. Smoke free premises. 525 units. 469 one-bedroom standard units. 56 one-bedroom suites. 20 stories, interior corridors. *Bath:* combo or shower only. **Parking:** on-site (fee) and valet. **Amenities:** dual phone lines, voice mail, safes, honor bars, irons, hair dryers. *Fee:* video games, high-speed Internet. **Dining:** 2 restaurants. **Pool(s):** heated indoor. **Leisure Activities:** saunas, whirlpool, exercise room, spa services. **Guest Services:** valet laundry, wireless Internet. **Business Services:** conference facilities, business center.

WESTIN
HOTELS & RESORTS

AAA Benefit:
Enjoy up to 15% off your next stay, plus Starwood Preferred Guest® bonuses.

——— WHERE TO DINE ———

AIDA'S   Phone: 403/541-1189   [65]

Lebanese
$5-$21

Hearty portions of tasty, traditional Lebanese food await patrons of the cozy, bistro-style restaurant. A taste of Lebanon infuses such dishes as falafel and flavorful tabbouleh salad. Save room for dessert, particularly the delicious layali loubnan, a Lebanese version of tiramisu. Casual dress. **Bar:** Full bar. **Reservations:** suggested, weekends. **Hours:** 11 am-10 pm, Mon-9 pm. Closed major holidays; also Sun. **Address:** 2208 4th St SW T2S 1W9 **Location:** At 4th St and 23rd Ave. **Parking:** street.

AVENUE DINER   Phone: 403/263-2673   [31]

Canadian
$10-$18

The quiet but welcoming exterior overlooking the Stephen Street pedestrian mall hints at things to come. Inside this comfortable and slightly upscale restaurant, tables near the back, which look over to the open kitchen, are in high demand. The menu is limited to breakfast and lunch items, and the kitchen uses some of the finest quality and local ingredients in its creative twists on standard French toast and fried egg sandwiches. Casual dress. **Bar:** Full bar. **Reservations:** not accepted. **Hours:** 7 am-3 pm, Sat & Sun from 8 am. Closed: 12/25. **Address:** 105 8th Ave SW T2P 1B4 **Location:** Jct Centre St S; along Stephen Ave walk. **Parking:** street.

BARCLAY'S   Phone: 403/517-6666   [7]

International
$12-$35

Patrons can choose from the regular a la carte menu or share selections from the new fondue menu. The casually upscale eatery offers fine service and good value for the dollar. Casual dress. **Bar:** Full bar. **Reservations:** suggested. **Hours:** 6 am-10 pm, Fri & Sat-11 pm; seasonal hours vary. Closed major holidays. **Address:** 255 Barclay Parade SW T2P 5C2 **Location:** At 3rd St SW and 2nd Ave SW; in Sheraton Suites Calgary Eau Claire. **Parking:** on-site (fee) and valet.

(See map and index starting on p. 388)

THE BELVEDERE
Phone: 403/265-9595 **14**

Continental
$18-$45

New York meets Calgary at the upscale, intimate restaurant, tucked amid the shops and restaurants of Stephen Avenue. The decor is all New York, a long, narrow space with exposed brick walls, mirrors, walnut trim and exposed lighting. The menu changes every few months but might list such innovative creations as gingered ahi tuna, venison or duck. The romantic setting is fitting for special occasions, and the plush lounge at the entrance is the perfect relaxing spot for an after-work cocktail. Dressy casual. **Bar:** Full bar **Reservations:** suggested. **Hours:** 11:30 am-2 & 5-10 pm, Sat from 5 pm. Closed major holidays; also Sun **Address:** 107 8th St SW T2P 1B4 **Location:** Just e of 1st St SW. **Parking:** street. CALL M

BISTRO TWENTY TWO TEN
Phone: 403/228-4528 **66**

Canadian
$12-$29

In a small storefront along the Fourth Avenue strip, the simple space has off-white wood-plank walls and floors, exposed brick and a century-old tin ceiling. French influences are evident in contemporary Canadian dishes, such as duck two ways with seared sliced duck breast and confit leg with maple-orange glaze; flat-bread pizzas, such as buffalo pepperoni, smoked mozzarella and portobello mushrooms; and roasted pork stuffed with figs and drizzled with pear sauce. Service is friendly but casual. Casual dress. **Bar:** Full bar. **Reservations:** accepted. **Hours:** 11 am-2 & 5-10 pm, Sat from 10 am, Sun 10 am-2 pm. Closed major holidays; also Mon. **Address:** 2210 4th St SW T2S 1W9 **Location:** Just n of 22nd Ave. **Parking:** street. CALL M

BONTERRA TRATTORIA
Phone: 403/262-8480 **35**

New Italian
$12-$38

For an upscale Italian dining experience, look no further than this restaurant. Sumptuous smells waft from the open concept kitchen, where contemporary Italian dishes are created. The romantic dining room is a great place for a special occasion, and in the summer a garden oasis patio awaits in the back. With an extensive wine list, and superb professional service, this is one fine place for a great meal. Casual dress. **Bar:** Full bar. **Reservations:** suggested. **Hours:** 11:30 am-2:30 & 5-10 pm, Fri-11 pm, Sat 5 pm-11 pm, Sun 5 pm-9 pm. Closed major holidays. **Address:** 1016 8th St SW T2R 1K2 **Location:** 10th Ave and 8th St SW. **Parking:** on-site.

BRAVA BISTRO
Phone: 403/228-1854 **57**

Canadian
$14-$32

Old World inspiration combines with New World ingredients at the upscale, trendy addition to the dining options on 17th Avenue. The restaurant is an ideal place for a first date or special occasion. Artistic and creative dishes—ranging from risotto with squash and duck confit to linguine with saffron and seafood—emphasize freshness, simplicity and seasonality. Diners can complete their meal with a selection from the award-winning wine list. Dressy casual. **Bar:** Full bar. **Reservations:** suggested. **Hours:** 11:30 am-10 pm, Fri & Sat-10:30 pm, Sun 5 pm-10 pm. Closed: 12/24-12/26. **Address:** 723 17th Ave SW T2S 0B6 **Location:** Just e of 7th St. **Parking:** on-site and street.

BROKEN PLATE KITCHEN & BAR
Phone: 403/283-6300 **1**

Greek
$10-$32

On the main street of the trendy Kensington neighborhood, this small chain restaurant is one of three in the city. Offering a wide selection of Greek standards, the comfortable restaurant reflects plenty of blue and white accents and shows how its name came about via the occasional broken plate. Casual dress. **Bar:** Full bar. **Reservations:** accepted. **Hours:** 11:30 am-10 pm, Fri & Sat-11 pm, Sun 5 pm-10 pm. Closed major holidays. **Address:** 302 10th St NW T2N 1V8 **Location:** 0.6 mi (1 km) n of Memorial Dr. **Parking:** street.

CAESAR'S STEAKHOUSE
Phone: 403/264-1222 **17**

Steak
$15-$70

One of the city's original steakhouses, the dark, dimly lit restaurant speaks to years gone by, with professionally dressed servers, intimate corners and a booming lunch business. A trip to the West is not complete without a stop at this popular restaurant. An extensive selection of Alberta AAA beef is prepared to the diner's liking from the glassed-in barbecue area. The place buzzes at lunch, as many corporate-types nosh on a Caesar salad alongside their steak. Dressy casual. **Bar:** Full bar. **Reservations:** suggested. **Hours:** 11 am-2 & 4:30-midnight, Sat from 4:30 pm. Closed major holidays; also Sun. **Address:** 512 4th Ave SW T2P 0J6 **Location:** Just e of 5th St. **Parking:** valet and street.

CATCH DINING ROOM
Phone: 403/206-0000 **32**

Seafood
$18-$50

There are three levels to this restaurant. On the first floor, you'll find a fun, casual oyster bar. On the third level, an atrium and nestled in the middle, a stunning, upscale dining room, with lofty ceilings, warm wood tones, and exquisite table presentations. If you have a craving for seafood, this is the place to go. With an impressive selection of seafood from around the world, including Alaskan sablefish, Atlantic halibut cheeks, and Pacific salmon, seafood lovers will be in heaven. Dressy casual. **Bar:** Full bar. **Reservations:** suggested. **Hours:** 11:30 am-2 & 5:30-9:30 pm, Sat from 5:30 pm. Closed major holidays; also Sun. **Address:** 100 8th Ave SE T2P 1B3 **Location:** Corner of 8th Ave SE (Stephen Ave) and Centre St SE; second level. **Parking:** street.

CATCH OYSTER BAR
Menu on AAA.com   Phone: 403/206-0000 **21**

Seafood
$18-$28

Down the stairs from Catch, which offers a more upscale experience, the oyster bar is more casual yet still boasts the same fine food. The bustling, nautical place prepares an extensive selection of fresh seafood, flown in each day. Guests can enjoy not only oysters but also other distinctive choices, including salmon, traditional fish and chips and the catch of the day. Casual dress. **Bar:** Full bar. **Reservations:** suggested. **Hours:** 11:30 am-9:30 pm, Sat from 5 pm. Closed major holidays; also Sun. **Address:** 100 8th Ave SE T2P 1B3 **Location:** Corner of 8th Ave SE (Stephen Ave) and Centre St SE; main level. **Parking:** street.

CENTINI RESTAURANT AND LOUNGE
Phone: 403/269-1600 **22**

CAA
Italian
$18-$52

While the dining room at Centini is decidedly upscale, the atmosphere remains quite informal. An excellent selection of wines, cognacs and aged scotches complements items on seasonal menus, which feature new Italian cuisines incorporating Asian and French influences combined with more local ingredients. Must-try entrees include the fresh Italian truffles, which find their way onto the menu in the fall. The restaurant validates underground parking. Dressy casual. **Bar:** Full bar. **Reservations:** suggested. **Hours:** 11 am-11 pm, Fri-midnight, Sat 5 pm-midnight. Closed major holidays; also Sun. **Address:** 160 8th Ave SE T2G 0K6 **Location:** Corner of 8th Ave SE (Stephen Ave) and 1st St SE; in Telus Convention Centre. **Parking:** street. CALL M

(See map and index starting on p. 388)

CHARLY CHAN'S RICE HOUSE
Phone: 403/283-6165   **4**

Szechuan
$8-$16

In the heart of Kensington nestled just below street level, the simple restaurant serves Szechuan food. Dishes are hearty and tasty, and the service is pleasant and friendly. Those seeking good value on the dollar will like this place. Casual dress. **Bar:** Full bar. **Reservations:** accepted. **Hours:** 11 am-11 pm, Fri & Sat-midnight. Closed: 12/25. **Address:** 1140 Kensington Rd NW T2N 3P3 **Location:** From 10th St NW, just w at Kensington Rd. **Parking:** on-site (fee) and street.

THE CHEF'S TABLE
Phone: 403/228-4442   **11**

Canadian
$36-$43

Located in the heart of trendy Kensington, the tiny, intimate restaurant is new to the Calgary dining scene. The open-kitchen concept gives some real insight into the inner workings of the kitchen. Meals are beautifully presented, not to mention delicious. The chef's five-course tasting menu changes bi-weekly, and a la carte offerings feature house-smoked organic salmon and Black Angus beef. Guests can relax in a contemporary lounge to enjoy a fireplace and original artwork. Dressy casual. **Bar:** Full bar. **Reservations:** suggested. **Hours:** 7 am-10 & 5-9 pm, Sat 8 am-noon & 5-9 pm, Sun 8 am-noon. Closed major holidays. **Address:** 1126 Memorial Dr NW T2N 3E3 **Location:** Just w of 10th St NW; in Kensington Riverside Inn. **Parking:** on-site. CALL &M

CHICAGO CHOPHOUSE
Phone: 403/265-3000   **19**

Steak
$20-$49

Guests can see and be seen at the ultra-modern, contemporary steakhouse, in the heart of the city. Efficient, professional servers help make this place popular with the business crowd at lunchtime. The menu blends a wide selection of top-quality cuts of beef with sandwiches and meal-size salads. The chic, lofty interior has an open-concept kitchen, and the selection of by-the-glass wines is one of the best in the city. Casual dress. **Bar:** Full bar. **Reservations:** suggested. **Hours:** 11:30 am-11 pm, Fri-11:30 pm, Sat 5 pm-11:30 pm. Closed major holidays; also Sun. **Address:** 604 8th Ave SW T2P 1G4 **Location:** Corner of 8th Ave SW and 5th St SW. **Parking:** street. CALL &M

CILANTRO
Phone: 403/229-1177   **49**

California
$12-$42

The dark wood interior and lovely stained-glass windows combine to create an intimate atmosphere in the small dining room, where guests can enjoy an interesting selection of California-inspired cuisine. Good choices include melt-in-the-mouth sea bass, various pastas and salads and any of the delectable desserts. Service is professional and friendly. Casual dress. **Bar:** Full bar. **Reservations:** suggested. **Hours:** 11 am-10 pm, Fri-11 pm, Sat 5 pm-11 pm, Sun 5 pm-10 pm. Closed major holidays; also Mon. **Address:** 338 17th Ave SW T2S 0A8 **Location:** Just e of 4th St SW. **Parking:** on-site and street.

CODO VIETNAMESE RESTAURANT
Phone: 403/228-7798   **58**

Vietnamese
$8-$10

A favorite among locals, this simple restaurant is one of the city's best-kept secrets. Huge portions of fresh Vietnamese food mean great value for the dollar. Representative of traditional fare are spring rolls, vermicelli rice dishes and a variety of curries. Although it can often be busy, especially on weekends, the restaurant's service is quick and attentive. Casual dress. **Bar:** Full bar. **Reservations:** accepted, except for weekends. **Hours:** 11 am-10 pm, Fri & Sat-11 pm. Closed major holidays. **Address:** 1411 17th Ave SW T2T 0L4 **Location:** Just e of jct 14th St and 17th Ave SW. **Parking:** street.

DA PAOLO RISTORANTE
Phone: 403/228-5556   **55**

Italian
$14-$35

The popular restaurant serves traditional fare with a warm, welcoming attitude. Dozens of fresh pasta and seafood dishes are complemented by chicken and veal entrees. The wine list includes well-chosen Italian selections. Formal service is the standard, and chef/owner Paulo often exits the kitchen to make an appearance. Casual dress. **Bar:** Full bar. **Reservations:** suggested. **Hours:** 11:30 am-2 & 5-close, Sat from 5 pm. Closed major holidays; also Sun. **Address:** 121 17th Ave SE T2G 1H3 **Location:** Just w on 17th Ave SE from MacLeod Tr S (which becomes Hwy 2A S). **Parking:** on-site.

DEANE HOUSE HISTORIC SITE RESTAURANT AT FORT CALGARY
Phone: 403/269-7747   **34**

Canadian
$8-$17

The glassed-in, veranda dining room offers a lovely view of the Elbow River. Menu offerings include fresh scones, homemade soup, eggs Benedict, French toast, quiche, bacon and eggs and gingerbread cake. Friendly servers work quickly. On Friday from 6:30 pm to 10:30 pm, the Mystery from History dinner theater takes the stage. Casual dress. **Bar:** Full bar. **Reservations:** suggested. **Hours:** 11 am-3 pm, Sat & Sun from 10 am. Closed: 12/23-1/2. **Address:** 806 9th Ave SE T2P 2M5 **Location:** Corner of 8th St. **Parking:** on-site. **Historic** CALL &M

DIVINO WINE & CHEESE BISTRO
Phone: 403/410-5555   **29**

International
$12-$35

There's more than just wine and cheese at this upscale bistro, and the variety makes it a good reason to come. Cheese from around the world, including Alberta varieties, is paired with fresh artisan bread. Those in the mood for something more can expect decadent, beautiful food, ranging from mushroom risotto appetizers to roasted halibut to lobster cannelloni. Professional service completes the experience. Casual dress. **Bar:** Full bar. **Reservations:** suggested. **Hours:** 11:30 am-10 pm, Fri & Sat-11 pm. Closed major holidays; also Sun. **Address:** 113 8th Ave SW T2P 1B4 **Location:** On 8th Ave (Stephen Ave). **Parking:** street. CALL &M

DON QUIJOTE
Phone: 403/205-4244   **15**

Spanish
$12-$26

The restaurant is a great place to have tapas and dance the salsa. Focusing on the seafood of the Spanish ports, it relies heavily on the tradition of butter, garlic and lemon. For a decadent finish, try the rich custard-filled cake soaked in cinzano. Dressy casual. **Entertainment. Bar:** Full bar. **Reservations:** suggested. **Hours:** 11:30 am-2 & 5-10 pm. Closed major holidays; also for dinner Mon. **Address:** 309 2nd Ave SW T2P 0C5 **Location:** Across from Eau Claire Market. **Parking:** street.

EARLS RESTAURANT
Phone: 403/265-3275

Canadian
$10-$35

Offering an experience that falls between fast food and fine dining, the fun, relaxed restaurant prepares great food at a great price. Choices range from juicy burgers, hearty sandwiches, fresh salads, wings and pizza to full entrees of steak, chops and seafood. Made-from-scratch soups and assorted breads, as well as a nice choice of wines and beers, round out the offerings. This is a fitting spot for impromptu get-togethers and festive occasions. Casual dress. **Bar:** Full bar. **Hours:** 11 am-11 pm, Fri & Sat-1 am. Closed: 12/25. **Address:** 315 8th Ave SW, A1, Level 1 T2P 1C4 **Location:** In Bankers Hall. **Parking:** street.

(See map and index starting on p. 388)

EARLS RESTAURANT

Canadian
$10-$35

Phone: 403/228-4141

Offering an experience that falls between fast food and fine dining, the fun, relaxed restaurant prepares great food at a great price. Choices range from juicy burgers, hearty sandwiches, fresh salads, wings and pizza to full entrees of steak, chops and seafood. Made-from-scratch soups and assorted breads, as well as a nice choice of wines and beers, round out the offerings. This is a fitting spot for impromptu get-togethers and festive occasions. Casual dress. **Bar:** Full bar. **Reservations:** not accepted. **Hours:** 11 am-midnight, Fri & Sat-1 am. Closed: 12/25; also for dinner 12/24. **Address:** 2401 4th St SW T2S 1X5 **Location:** Corner of 4th St SW and 24th Ave. **Parking:** on-site (fee) and street. CALL

EL SOMBRERO RESTAURANT

Mexican
$11-$20

Phone: 403/228-0332 50

A taste of Mexico awaits at this cozy bistro-style restaurant, one staircase up from street level in the trendy 17th Avenue district. A guitarist adds ambience to the evening, strumming and singing in the background as guests enjoy hearty Mexican fare. Casual dress. **Bar:** Full bar. **Reservations:** accepted. **Hours:** 4 pm-10 pm, Fri & Sat-11 pm, Sun-9 pm. Closed: 12/25, 12/26. **Address:** 520 17th Ave SW T2S 0B1 **Location:** Between 5th and 4th sts SW; upper level. **Parking:** street.

FLEUR DE SEL

New French
$12-$37

Phone: 403/228-9764 62

Elegantly funky is a good descriptor for the atmosphere at this small brasserie. A favorite with locals, this spot serves nouveau French cuisine and fine wines. A memorable experience encompasses more than just creative, sophisticated food. Jazz music fills the dining room, and the open concept warehouse pipes have been boldly painted in primary colors to contrast with a red brick accent wall. Efficient, friendly service awaits, and the owner often appears to chat with guests. Casual dress. **Bar:** Full bar. **Reservations:** suggested. **Hours:** 11 am-2 & 5-close, Sat-Mon from 5 pm. Closed: 1/1, 12/25. **Address:** 2015 4th St SW, #2 T2S 1W6 **Location:** 4th St and 21st Ave SW; in Tivoli Theatre Building. **Parking:** street.

GALAXIE DINER

Canadian
$8-$15

Phone: 403/228-0001 43

Decorated with a few Elvis posters, the unassuming diner often has locals waiting in lengthy lines on the weekend, all vying for a spot at one of the few crowded tiny tables. It would be fair to say the atmosphere is intimate, very intimate, but it's the simple, uncomplicated and uncluttered home cooking and comfort foods that pack customers in. All-day breakfasts along with burgers, sandwiches and thick milkshakes complete the menu. Cash only. Casual dress. **Reservations:** not accepted. **Hours:** 7 am-3 pm, Sat & Sun-4 pm. Closed: 12/25. **Address:** 1413 11th St SW T3C 0M9 **Location:** Just n of 17th Ave SW. **Parking:** street.

THE GLORY OF INDIA

Indian
$17-$22

Phone: 403/263-8804 18

This casual Indian restaurant serves tasty portions of traditional Indian cuisine. The lunch buffet is popular, and reservations are recommended. A la carte dinner items are best enjoyed with several people to allow for sampling of the varied dishes, including ali goobi, lamb and beef curries and chicken tikka. Casual dress. **Bar:** Full bar. **Reservations:** accepted. **Hours:** 11:30 am-2 & 5-10 pm, Sat from 5 pm. Closed major holidays; also Sun. **Address:** 515 4th Ave SW T2P 0J8 **Location:** Jct 5th St and 4th Ave SW; on ground floor of apartment building. **Parking:** street.

GNOCCHI'S RISTORANTE

Italian
$10-$25

Phone: 403/262-2887 41

An elegant, upscale dining room awaits guests of this bistro, which prepares a wide array of traditional Italian cuisine that's a cut above the standard family Italian restaurant. Hearty portions of minestrone soup, pasta, veal and fish include gorgeous fresh vegetables, and the namesake gnocchi is served eight ways, each prepared with a secret recipe. It's a must-try. Casual dress. **Bar:** Full bar. **Reservations:** suggested. **Hours:** 11:30 am-2:30 & 5-9 pm, Fri & Sat-10:30 pm. Closed major holidays; also Sun. **Address:** 1238 8th St SW T2R 1A9 **Location:** Corner of 8th St SW and 13th Ave SW. **Parking:** on-site.

GOOD EARTH COFFEEHOUSE & BAKERY

Deli
$5-$8

Phone: 403/228-9543 47

One of several locations in Calgary, the casual restaurant offers a variety of take-out items, including garden salads and soups. Also on the menu are sweet and savory baked goods, freshly made sandwiches and a limited selection of hot entrées that can be enjoyed over a lingering cup of coffee at one of the comfortable tables. Casual dress. **Reservations:** not accepted. **Hours:** 6:30 am-10 pm, Sun 8 am-8 pm. Closed: 12/25. **Address:** 1502 11th St SW T3C 0M9 **Location:** Just n of 17th Ave. **Parking:** street.

HANA SUSHI

Japanese
$7-$20

Phone: 403/229-1499 59

The small, traditional restaurant is a great spot for good sushi at a great value. In addition to a wide variety of sushi and sashimi, the menu lists full dinners that include miso soup, salad and a selection of sushi. Casual dress. **Bar:** Full bar. **Reservations:** suggested. **Hours:** 11:30 am-2 & 5-10 pm. Closed major holidays; also Sun. **Address:** 1803 4th St SW T2S 1W2 **Location:** Corner of 18th Ave SW. **Parking:** street.

THE HOLY GRILL

Deli
$8-$13

Phone: 403/261-9759 36

The casual restaurant serves exciting and interesting soups, sandwiches and salads that are made to order while guests wait. Casual dress. **Reservations:** not accepted. **Hours:** 7:30 am-4 pm, Sat from 10 am. Closed major holidays; also Sun. **Address:** 827 10th Ave SW T2R 0B4 **Location:** Jct 8th St SW; across from MEC. **Parking:** street.

IL SOGNO   *Menu on AAA.com*

Italian
$12-$36

Phone: 403/232-8901 10

Italian for "the dream," Il Sogno is a simply elegant restaurant with an upscale decor and sumptuous Italian food. Classically prepared and beautifully presented dishes on the seasonally inspired menu incorporate the finest regional and imported Italian products, including exotic house-made pastas, Alberta rabbit, Quebec foie gras, Alberta beef and fresh fish and other seafood. The building originally was a rooming house, and the owners have maintained the history and integrity in the decor. Dressy casual. **Bar:** Full bar. **Reservations:** suggested. **Hours:** 11:30 am-2 & 5-close, Sat from 5 pm. Closed major holidays; also Sun. **Address:** 24 4th St NE T2E 3R7 **Location:** Just n of Memorial Dr; at Meredith Rd and 4th St NE. **Parking:** on-site. **Historic**

(See map and index starting on p. 388)

JOEY RESTAURANTS

Phone: 403/263-6336

Mediterranean
$10-$32

The cuisine blends Mediterranean and Asian cooking styles and emphasizes finger foods for sharing. Those who aren't big fans of tapas can consider full meal offerings centered on steaks and chops. Casual dress. **Bar:** Full bar. **Reservations:** not accepted. **Hours:** 11 am-1 am, Sun-midnight. Closed: 12/25. **Address:** 200 Barclay Parade SW T2P 4R5 **Location:** At 208 Eau Claire Market. **Parking:** on-site.

THE JOYCE ON 4TH IRISH PUB

Phone: 403/541-9168 69

Irish
$7-$18

A wide selection of ales and whiskeys complements traditional fare, including boxty, an Irish dish made with a potato pancake and various fillings, and Guinness and beef pie. Saturday visitors can expect live music and Celtic dancers. The rich decor incorporates oversized couches and a long bar. The mood is lively and upbeat. Casual dress. **Bar:** Full bar. **Reservations:** accepted. **Hours:** 11 am-1 am, Fri-2 am, Sat 9 am-2 am, Sun 9 am-11 pm. Closed: 12/25. **Address:** 506 24th Ave SW T2S 0K4 **Location:** Jct 24th Ave SW and 4th St SW. **Parking:** on-site. CALL 🚹Ⓜ

JULIO'S BARRIO MEXICAN RESTAURANT

Phone: 403/203-3066 8

Mexican
$12-$21

This upbeat, casual and boisterous restaurant is a fun place to visit for hearty helpings of Mexican cuisine. Casual dress. **Bar:** Full bar. **Reservations:** accepted. **Hours:** 11:30 am-11 pm, Fri & Sat-midnight; Sun-Thurs to 10 pm 9/5-5/20. Closed major holidays; also for dinner 12/24. **Address:** 101 10th St NW T2N 1V4 **Location:** Corner of Memorial Dr. **Parking:** on-site (fee) and street. CALL 🚹Ⓜ

THE KING & I

Phone: 403/264-7241 39

Thai
$8-$32

Experience a taste of Thailand in an upscale, contemporary atmosphere. Here, modern furnishings and decor set the scene for authentic, tasty Thai dishes. The menu features a wide variety of appetizers, including calamari and fresh spring rolls. Diners should arrive with an appetite, as main dishes are heaping, with options varying from traditional pad thai to a number of curry dishes. Casual dress. **Bar:** Full bar. **Reservations:** suggested. **Hours:** 11:30 am-10:30 pm, Fri-11:30 am, Sat 4:30 pm-11:30 pm, Sun 4:30 pm-9:30 pm. Closed major holidays. **Address:** 822 11th Ave SW T2R 0E5 **Location:** Corner of 11th Ave SW and 8th St SW. **Parking:** street.

LA BREZZA

Phone: 403/262-6230 2

Italian
$9-$25

In a small house, the setting enhances a warm, relaxed atmosphere, topped by funky lighting crisscrossing the ceiling. Whether for a first date or a reunion with old friends, the restaurant's eclectic atmosphere, refined service and creative Italian cuisine will create a lingering memory. Casual dress. **Bar:** Full bar. **Reservations:** suggested. **Hours:** 11:30 am-2:30 & 5:30-10:30 pm, Sat & Sun from 5 pm. Closed major holidays. **Address:** 990 1st Ave NE T2E 4J9 **Location:** At 9th St NE; in Bridgeland. **Parking:** on-site.

LA CHAUMIERE RESTAURANT

Phone: 403/228-5690 56

French
$13-$37

This upscale restaurant's impressive, almost château-like building has a peaked roof and elegant exterior, making it an ideal spot for fine French dining. From the moment patrons cross the threshold over polished granite floors into an exquisitely appointed dining room, they will experience professional service. Donned in black and white, servers begin by pulling out chairs and end with a polite "adieu." A French accent can be heard in the dining room. Semi-formal attire. **Bar:** Full bar. **Reservations:** suggested. **Hours:** 11:45 am-2 & 5:45-10 pm, Sat from 5:30 pm. Closed major holidays; also Sun. **Address:** 139 17th Ave SW T2S 0A1 **Location:** Corner of 1st St SW and 17th Ave SW. **Parking:** on-site.

LA DOLCE VITA RISTORANTE ITALIANO

Phone: 403/263-3445 3

Italian
$9-$40

In the city's "Little Italy" area, the restaurant boasts stucco yellow walls, hardwood floors and colorful art upstairs, amid an upbeat atmosphere. Downstairs is more intimate, with a rich color scheme and formal table settings. The menu features large appetizers, including sumptuous salmon salad, mussels or scampi. Mouthwatering veal options as well as homemade pastas satisfy hearty appetites. Formally attired servers provide brisk service during the lunch rush but are more attentive at dinner. Semi-formal attire. **Bar:** Full bar. **Reservations:** suggested. **Hours:** 11:30 am-2 & 5:30-10:30 pm, Sat 5:30 pm-11 pm. Closed major holidays; also Sun. **Address:** 916 1st Ave NE T2E 0C5 **Location:** At 9th St NE; in Bridgeland. **Parking:** street.

LE CHIEN CHAUD

Phone: 403/229-3041 61

Hot Dog
$6-$8

Chilean, Mexican, French, Mediterranean, Italian and Ukrainian dogs can all be found here at this gourmet, quick-serve hot dog joint. Casual dress. **Reservations:** not accepted. **Hours:** 11 am-8 pm, Sun noon-5 pm. Closed major holidays. **Address:** 2015 4th St SW, #3 T2S 1W6 **Location:** Jct 20th Ave. **Parking:** street.

THE LIVING ROOM

Phone: 403/228-9830 52

Canadian
$14-$43

The contemporary restaurant serves imaginative Canadian fare, including a five-course menu surprise. As the name suggests, the decor—including oversize couchlike chairs—contributes to a cozy and comfortable dining environment. Casual dress. **Bar:** Full bar. **Reservations:** suggested. **Hours:** 11:30 am-2 & 5-midnight, Sat & Sun from 5 pm. Closed major holidays. **Address:** 514 17th Ave SW T5W 4X6 **Location:** Just e of 5th St SW. **Parking:** on-site and street.

MANIES GREEK CUISINE

Phone: 403/228-9207 53

Greek
$8-$22

Attractive framed photographs of Greece adorn the walls of this casual, family-run restaurant. Friendly staff circulate through the dining room with plates of traditional Greek food, such as the souvlaki pita, lamb chops and moussaka, as well as oven-baked thick-crust pizzas. Casual dress. **Bar:** Full bar. **Reservations:** accepted. **Hours:** 11 am-midnight. Closed: 12/25. **Address:** 819 17th Ave SW T2T 0A1 **Location:** Between 8th and 7th sts SW. **Parking:** street.

(See map and index starting on p. 388)

MANUEL LATRUWE BELGIAN PATISSERIE & BREAD SHOP

Phone: 403/261-1092 (45)

Breads/Pastries
$3-$20

Elegance and refinement characterize the upscale bakery, which features the divine dessert creations of Manuel Latruwe. The display case is filled with gorgeous mousses, cheesecakes, tarts and pastries as well as artisan breads. Although there are three small cafe tables, most people, including business folks en route to work and skiers headed to the mountains, get their selections to go. Ice creams and sorbets also are concocted here. Casual dress. **Reservations:** accepted. **Hours:** 7:30 am-5 pm. Closed major holidays; also Sun & Mon. **Address:** 1333 1st St SE T2G 5L1 **Location:** At 13th Ave. **Parking:** on-site. CALL

MAURYA

Phone: 403/270-3133 (6)

Eastern Indian
$14-$16

Excellent, tasty East Indian cuisine awaits at Maurya, tucked away in the heart of the shopping area in trendy Kensington. The menu specializes in tandoori and includes many vegetarian dishes. Mint or coriander sauces are served atop of crispy pakoras and samosas. An extensive lunch buffet has more than a dozen items, and diners often linger in this relaxing, simple ambience. Efficient servers ensure refills keep coming. Casual dress. **Bar:** Full bar. **Reservations:** suggested. **Hours:** 11:30 am-2 & 5-10 pm, Fri & Sat-11 pm. Closed major holidays. **Address:** 1204 Kensington Rd NW T2N 3P5 **Location:** At 12th St NW. **Parking:** street.

MERCATO

Phone: 403/263-5535 (67)

Italian
$15-$44

The aromatic restaurant takes up half of an Italian grocery store stocked with typical assortments of delicatessen meats, cheeses, olive oils, dried pastas and produce. Bar stools overlook the open kitchen, and small bowls of marinated green and black olives adorn every stylishly set table. The lunch-only menu consists of choices ranging from a formaggi appetizer to bistecca, a Fiorentina-style rib-eye steak with grilled lemons and first-press Fontodi olive oil. Casual dress. **Bar:** Full bar. **Reservations:** suggested. **Hours:** 11:30 am-2 & 5-9 pm, Thurs-Sat to 10 pm. Closed: 1/1, 10/11, 12/25. **Address:** 2224 4th St SW T2S 1W9 **Location:** Just s of 22nd Ave SW. **Parking:** street. CALL

METROPOLITAN GRILL

Phone: 403/263-5432 (20)

Canadian
$13-$38

Across from Banker's Hall, the Stephen Street location is the place to be for a power lunch. The upscale restaurant is known for its creative takes on classic comfort food, ranging from lobster macaroni and cheese to great AAA Alberta steaks. Casual dress. **Bar:** Full bar. **Hours:** 11 am-10 pm, Fri & Sat-1 am. Closed major holidays. **Address:** 318 8th Ave SW T2P 1C4 **Location:** In TD Square. **Parking:** street.

MOTI MAHAL

Phone: 403/228-9990 (54)

Northern Indian
$10-$17

Based on the cuisine of Northern India, the varied menu lists such dishes as buttery masalas, curries and the specialty chicken tikka with spicy yogurt and tomato sauce. Tapestries hang around the dining room, creating a royal environment. Casual dress. **Bar:** Full bar. **Reservations:** suggested. **Hours:** 11:30 am-1:30 & 5:30-9 pm, Thurs-9:30 pm, Fri-10:30 pm, Sat 5:30 pm-10:30 pm. Closed major holidays. **Address:** 1805 14th St SW T2T 3P1 **Location:** Just s of jct 17th Ave SW and 14th St SW; in small strip mall. **Parking:** on-site. CALL

MOXIE'S CLASSIC GRILL

Phone: 403/234-7507

Canadian
$10-$30

This sleek, funky and popular restaurant presents an extensive menu of creatively prepared dishes, including pizza, pasta, rice, noodles, signature salads and burgers. Other menus include one for children and one for Sunday brunch. Lending to the upbeat, stylish decor are dark wood appointments and river rock fireplaces. Casual dress. **Bar:** Full bar. **Reservations:** not accepted. **Hours:** 6 am-midnight. **Address:** 888 7th Ave SW T2P 3J3 **Location:** Corner of 7th Ave SW and 8th St SW; in Sandman Hotel Downtown Calgary. **Parking:** on-site (fee).

MURRIETA'S WESTCOAST GRILL

Phone: 403/269-7707 (24)

Western Pacific Rim
$10-$35

The lively, airy dining room buzzes with sounds from the open-concept kitchen amid animated conversations. The bustling restaurant has an energy and liveliness that makes it a popular spot for a gathering of friends. For a more intimate experience, smaller areas are tucked away from the main dining room. Among offerings are mussels, ahi tuna, salmon and various pasta dishes. Casual dress. **Bar:** Full bar. **Reservations:** suggested. **Hours:** 11 am-11 pm, Sun 4 pm-10 pm. Closed major holidays. **Address:** 200-808 1st St SW T2P 1M9 **Location:** Corner of 8th Ave SW and 1st St SW; 2nd Floor. **Parking:** street. CALL

MUSE RESTAURANT & LOUNGE

Phone: 403/670-6873 (12)

International
$25-$40

As one of the city's best newer restaurants, the establishment presents a dazzling, innovative menu. The decor sets the scene for an upscale evening. The chef emphasizes regional items in the imaginative dishes. Desserts are delicious. Dressy casual. **Bar:** Full bar. **Reservations:** suggested. **Hours:** 5 pm-10 pm, Fri & Sat-11 pm. Closed major holidays; also Mon. **Address:** 107-10A St NW T2N 4M7 **Location:** From Memorial Dr, just n on 10th St, just w on Kensington Rd, then just s at 10A St NW. **Parking:** street.

NELLIE'S KITCHEN

Phone: 403/244-4616 (51)

Canadian
$4-$9

Particularly popular on weekends, the bustling, cozy diner is a favorite for its fabulous, home-cooked breakfasts. Served all day, they range from omelets to French toast to fluffy pancakes. Moist, homemade banana bread is well worth a splurge, and the appropriately named Belly Buster includes three eggs any style, toast, hashbrowns and a choice of meat, French toast or pancakes. The menu does list some lunch options. Friendly, chatty servers deliver breakfast quickly. Casual dress. **Reservations:** not accepted. **Hours:** 7:30 am-3:30 pm. Closed: 12/25. **Address:** 738B 17th Ave SW T2S 0B7 **Location:** Corner of 7th St and 17th Ave SW. **Parking:** street.

(See map and index starting on p. 388)

THE ORCHID ROOM FUSION CUISINE

Phone: 403/263-4457

Vietnamese
$16-$23

A combination of Vietnamese and French cuisine makes for an eclectic menu with an accent on healthy choices. Colorful plate presentations include banana leaves, yellow daisies and orchids. Among choices are many unusual vegan dishes. The cozy setting has an open annex. Casual dress. **Bar:** Full bar. **Reservations:** suggested, for lunch. **Hours:** 10 am-6 pm, Thurs & Fri-8 pm, Sat 11 am-5 pm. Closed major holidays; also Sun. **Address:** 315 8th Ave SW T2P 4K1 **Location:** Corner of 2nd St SW; in Bankers Hall, 2nd Floor. **Parking:** on-site (fee) and street.

ORIENTAL PHOENIX

Phone: 403/262-3633

Vietnamese
$9-$14

Traditional Vietnamese food is served simply, but the service and decor is anything but. Upscale and sleek, the modern dining room is a busy place at lunch and around the dinner hour. Guests can sample tasty food in fine surroundings characterized by bold, contemporary colors and art. Among the varied choices are salad rolls, rice vermicelli dishes and noodle soups. Semi-formal attire. **Bar:** Full bar. **Reservations:** accepted. **Hours:** 11 am-8:30 pm, Fri-9:30 pm, Sat 5 pm-8:30 pm. Closed major holidays; also Sun & 2 weeks during Christmas. **Address:** 401 9th Ave SW, #105 T2P 3C5 **Location:** Jct 4th St SW; in Gulf Canada Square. **Parking:** street.

OUZO GREEK TAVERNA

Phone: 403/229-1400

Greek
$9-$28

One of the newer additions to the Fourth Street restaurant scene, the family-owned Greek restaurant serves hearty, delicious fare prepared in the traditional sense. This spot is popular with locals for its large seasonal patio, healthy portions and friendly service. Casual dress. **Bar:** Full bar. **Reservations:** suggested. **Hours:** 11:30 am-9 pm, Fri & Sat-10 pm. Closed major holidays. **Address:** 2005 B 4th St SW T2S 1W6 **Location:** Corner of 20th Ave and 4th St SW. **Parking:** street.

PALACE OF EATS

Phone: 403/244-6602

Sandwiches
$10-$13

The funky, table-free eatery takes its name from a restaurant that stood in downtown Calgary from 1920 to the mid-'60s. A true gem, this place specializes in Montreal-style bagels, creamy milkshakes and hand-sliced, stacked Montreal smoked meat sandwiches on Winnipeg rye. Check out the original mahogany paneling and benches, which give the restaurant an antique feel. Casual dress. **Reservations:** not accepted. **Hours:** 11 am-4 pm. Closed major holidays. **Address:** 1411 11th St SW T2R 1G7 **Location:** Just n of 17th Ave SW. **Parking:** street.

PEGASUS

Phone: 403/229-1231

Greek
$12-$24

A favorite among the locals, the homelike, traditional restaurant features a wide selection of Greek dishes, such as souvlaki and moussaka. Patrons who visit on the weekend may enjoy traditional Greek dancing and entertainment. Casual dress. **Bar:** Full bar. **Reservations:** suggested. **Hours:** 11:30 am-2 & 5-10 pm, Fri-11 pm, Sat 5 pm-11 pm, Sun 5 pm-10 pm. Closed: 1/1, 12/24-12/26. **Address:** 1101 14th St SW T3C 1C2 **Location:** At 11th Ave SW. **Parking:** on-site.

PEKING DRAGON

Phone: 403/228-1205

Chinese
$9-$20

A popular spot with the locals, this casual Chinese restaurant prepares traditional selections and offers fine, friendly service. Among choices are egg rolls, Peking duck and egg foo yong. Casual dress. **Bar:** Full bar. **Reservations:** accepted. **Hours:** 11 am-10 pm, Fri-11 pm, Sat 4:30 pm-11 pm, Sun 4:30 pm-10 pm. Closed major holidays. **Address:** 1904 4th St SW T2S 1W3 **Location:** At 19th Ave SW. **Parking:** on-site.

PULCINELLA

Phone: 403/283-7793

Pizza
$12-$24

The restaurant is a member of an Italian organization dedicated to preserving Naples-style pizza. An apple wood-burning oven imported from Italy cooks the 18 varieties of thin-crust pizza, in addition to a few additional choices, such as polenta lasagna and arancini rice balls stuffed with mozzarella and tomato sauce. The cheerful spot displays an impressive number of white mosaic tiles and back-lit black and white photographs featuring street scenes around a Naples pizzeria. Casual dress. **Bar:** Full bar. **Reservations:** accepted. **Hours:** 11:30 am-11 pm, Fri & Sat-midnight, Sun-10 pm. Closed major holidays. **Address:** 1147 Kensington Crescent NW T2N 1X7 **Location:** 0.3 mi (0.4 km) e of jct 14th St NW. **Parking:** street.

PURPLE PERK

Phone: 403/244-1300

Coffee/Tea
$8

This is more than just a coffee shop. In addition to great coffee, guests will find a variety of freshly made wraps and panini, soup, salads and such pastas as lasagna and macaroni and cheese. Delicious homemade squares, cookies, muffins and other desserts round out the choices. Seats are inside or streetside, where diners can watch the action along trendy 4th Street. Casual dress. **Reservations:** not accepted. **Hours:** 7 am-10 pm. Closed: 12/25. **Address:** 2212 4th St SW T2S 1W9 **Location:** Between 22nd and 23rd aves SW. **Parking:** street.

RIC'S GRILL

Phone: 403/269-7427

Steak
$10-$39

"Funky and modern" describes the decor and the food at the upscale steakhouse, which bustles with activity. Steaks are well worth it, but then again, so are the salmon, chicken and pasta dishes. A wide variety of distinctive appetizers rounds out the menu. Servers are friendly and attentive. Dressy casual. **Bar:** Full bar. **Reservations:** suggested. **Hours:** 11 am-10 pm, Fri & Sat-midnight, Sun 4 pm-10 pm. Closed: 12/25. **Address:** 1436 8th St SW T2R 1R7 **Location:** Just n of jct 17th Ave SW. **Parking:** on-site (fee) and street.

(See map and index starting on p. 388)

THE RIMROCK DINING ROOM

Continental
$17-$50

Phone: 403/260-1219   33

The fine dining room has an upscale and elegant Western flair complete with an original wall mural, leather tooled pillars and a heritage fireplace. The establishment has a reputation for delivering high-quality, locally farmed, organic beef and bison as well as delicious fish, pork, lamb and chicken choices. Patrons celebrating anniversaries or other special occasions are treated by attentive servers. Dressy casual. **Bar:** Full bar. **Reservations:** suggested. **Hours:** 6:30 am-1:30 & 5:30-9 pm, Sat 6:30 am-11 & 5:30-9 pm, Sun 6:30-11 am. **Address:** 133 9th Ave SW T2P 2M3 **Location:** 9th Ave SW and 1st St SW; in The Fairmont Palliser. **Parking:** on-site (fee).

RIVER CAFE

Regional
Canadian
$16-$50

Phone: 403-261-7670   26

In the heart of Prince's Island Park, the enchanting, tree house-like restaurant features natural wood accents and a large fireplace. Dining at the River Cafe is like visiting a friend's place for dinner, except that a menu incorporates Canadian Rocky Mountain cuisine. During summer, seating is available on the patio, and in winter, the atmosphere is cozy inside. Servers are friendly and casual, and guests are welcome to linger. Casual dress. **Bar:** Full bar. **Reservations:** suggested. **Hours:** Open 3/1-12/31 & 2/1-2/28; 11 am-11 pm, Sat & Sun from 10 am. Closed: 12/25. **Address:** 200 Barclay Parade SW T2G 0K7 **Location:** On Prince's Island; on Bow River. **Parking:** no self-parking. CALL &M

SAINT GERMAIN

French
$8-$38

Phone: 403/290-1322   42

The restaurant has an elegant, contemporary decor, the highlight of which is a floor-to-ceiling, glassed-in wine cellar. A modern, French-inspired menu tries to utilize as much local products as possible and features such items as beef bourguignonne, High Country bison, Sunworks Farm chicken and whole trout. Casual dress. **Bar:** Full bar. **Reservations:** suggested. **Hours:** 11:30 am-2 & 5-10 pm, Fri-11 pm, Sat 5 pm-11 pm, Sun & Mon 5 pm-10 pm. Closed major holidays. **Address:** 115 12th Ave SW T2R 0G8 **Location:** At 1st St SW; centre; in Hotel Arts. **Parking:** street.

SAKANA GRILL

Japanese
$13-$20

Phone: 403/290-1118   13

Near the Eau Claire market, the bustling Japanese restaurant has many distinctive features, including a sushi bar, teppanyaki grill and private dining rooms. Business folks frequent the place at lunch time, grabbing seats at the sushi bar and making selections from the boat that floats by. Fantastic sushi and sashimi options offer exceptional value for the dollar. Casual dress. **Bar:** Full bar. **Reservations:** suggested. **Hours:** 11 am-11 pm. Closed: 1/1, 12/25. **Address:** 116 2nd Ave SW T2P 0B9 **Location:** Corner of 1st St and 2nd Ave SW; in Chinatown. **Parking:** on-site (fee) and street.

SALTLIK, A RARE STEAKHOUSE

Steak
$12-$40

Phone: 403/537-1160   30

True to its name, the restaurant truly is a "rare steak house" and a superb place. From the moment guests ascend the stairs to the upscale, contemporary dining room, they're impressed by the atmosphere. Also praiseworthy are the incredibly friendly, attentive servers, who take the time to explain the different cuts of meat and accompanying sauces. All entrees are a la carte, and the side orders are large enough to share. Casual dress. **Bar:** Full bar. **Reservations:** suggested. **Hours:** 11 am-11 pm, Sat from 5 pm, Sun 5 pm-10 pm. Closed: 12/25, 12/26. **Address:** 101 8th Ave SW T6E 1H1 **Location:** Corner of 8th Ave SW and 1st St SW. **Parking:** street. CALL &M

SILVER DRAGON RESTAURANT   *Menu on AAA.com*

Chinese
$6-$17

Phone: 403/264-5326   16

The restaurant specializes in Cantonese and Szechuan cuisine, including excellent ginger beef. A delicious dim sum selection is served each day. The contemporary decor comprises nouveau Oriental artwork. Servers are cordial. Casual dress. **Bar:** Full bar. **Reservations:** suggested. **Hours:** 10 am-midnight, Fri & Sat-2 am, Sun 9:30 am-10 pm. **Address:** 106 3rd Ave SE T2G 0B6 **Location:** In Chinatown. **Parking:** street.

STEEPS THE URBAN TEAHOUSE

Deli
$5-$6

Phone: 403/209-0076   48

The teahouse lures those who yearn for a pot of tea. It's a little-known fact that the Americanization of tea involved the creation of the tea bag, but loose teas—150 types, ranging from the rare and exotic to more common varieties—are the preference at the urban spot. Guests can take their time choosing from one of the many tins, which can be paired with soup and a sandwich, a samosa or wrap or one of the homemade desserts. Casual dress. **Reservations:** not accepted. **Hours:** 9 am-11 pm, Fri & Sat-midnight. Closed major holidays. **Address:** 880 16th Ave SW T2T 0A3 **Location:** At 8th St SW; in Mount Royal Shops. **Parking:** street. CALL &M

SULTAN'S TENT

Traditional
Moroccan
$17-$26

Phone: 403/244-2333   5

Eating is a communal event at this cozy Moroccan restaurant. Representative of the food are such delicacies as couscous, merguez, lamb, a five-course sultan's feast and other traditional dishes. And the traditional method of eating such creations is with the hands. The decor, inspired by the Berber culture of North Africa, offers intimate, tent-style seating. Casual dress. **Bar:** Full bar. **Reservations:** suggested. **Hours:** 5 pm-11 pm. Closed major holidays; also Sun & Mon. **Address:** 4 14th St NW T2N 1Z4 **Location:** Just n of Kensington Rd NW. **Parking:** on-site.

SUSHI KAWA

Japanese
$6-$20

Phone: 403/802-0058   64

Fourth Street is a popular area for sushi restaurants, but what sets this one apart is the incredible and imaginative variety of appetizers and sushi platters. Patrons might try a vegetable sushi bowl—fresh vegetables atop sushi rice. Sushi pizzas, vegetable gyozas and an incredible variety of other appetizers are pictured on the colorful menu, making decisions difficult. Sumo wrestling often is shown on the large-screen TV, and the decor is simple and contemporary. Casual dress. **Bar:** Full bar. **Reservations:** suggested. **Hours:** 11:30 am-2 & 5-9:30 pm, Thurs & Fri-10 pm, Sat noon-2:30 & 4:30-9:30 pm. Closed major holidays. **Address:** 2204 4th St SW T2S 1W9 **Location:** Jct 4th St SW and 22nd Ave. **Parking:** street.

(See map and index starting on p. 388)

TEATRO

New Italian
$15-$49

Phone: 403/290-1012 (23)

Located in the theater district, the upscale Italian trattoria is a great place to dine before a show, on a special occasion or for a first date. Featured several times on the Food Network, the chef surprises and delights diners with many inventive creations. The seafood, pasta and meat dishes are exquisite. Dressy casual. **Bar:** Full bar. **Reservations:** suggested. **Hours:** 11:30 am-10:30 pm. Closed major holidays. **Address:** 200 8th Ave SE T2G 0K7 **Location:** Corner of 8th Ave SE and 1st St SE. **Parking:** street. CALL

THAI SA-ON RESTAURANT

Thai
$11-$18

Phone: 403/264-3526 (38)

Decorative presentation and good use of spices and condiments characterize offerings of well-prepared cuisine, including many vegetarian items. The quiet, casual ambience is enhanced by music and artwork from Thailand. Casual dress. **Bar:** Full bar. **Reservations:** suggested. **Hours:** 11:30 am-2 & 5-10 pm, Fri & Sat-10:30 pm. Closed major holidays; also Sun. **Address:** 351 10th Ave SW T2R 0A5 **Location:** At 4th St SW; behind Gulf Canada Parkade. **Parking:** street.

THOMSON'S RESTAURANT

Canadian
$13-$36

Phone: 403/537-4449 (25)

The restaurant presents a varied menu of seafood, steaks and other regional meats. Guests can expect casual yet attentive service in the upscale dining room. A sumptuous breakfast buffet in addition to an a la carte menu is offered along with a Sunday brunch. Casual dress. **Bar:** Full bar. **Reservations:** suggested. **Hours:** 6:30 am-1:30 & 5-11 pm. **Address:** 700 Centre St SE T2G 5P6 **Location:** Corner of Centre St and 7th Ave SW; in Hyatt Regency Calgary. **Parking:** on-site. CALL

TRIBUNE RESTAURANT

Continental
$12-$50

Phone: 403/269-3160 (27)

It's easy to walk right by the attractive restaurant, which is on the Stephen Avenue walkway beside a large bookstore. However, it's wise to keep focused to find the dimly lit entrance, where you'll encounter stone walls, dark wood accents and a large U-shaped bar on the first floor and a comfortably upscale restaurant on the lower level. Well-prepared standards include burgers, steaks and a modest choice of seafood. Service is proficient and, despite the unexpected visible tattoo, professional. Dressy casual. **Bar:** Full bar. **Reservations:** suggested. **Hours:** 11 am-10 pm, Sat from 4 pm. Closed major holidays; also Sun. **Address:** 118 8th Ave SW (Stephen Ave) T2E 0P5 **Location:** Just w of Centre Ave; centre. **Parking:** street. CALL

VINTAGE CHOPHOUSE & TAVERN

Steak
$10-$50

Phone: 403/262-7262 (40)

An upscale, elegant experience awaits at the fine steakhouse set in a historic building. Inside, however, the atmosphere is anything but historic. A large lounge caters to the after-work crowd, and the dining room allows for a more leisurely, romantic meal. Steaks feature prominently on the menu, but diners also will find salmon, pasta dishes and ribs. Finely executed service, including tableside preparation of Caesar salad, adds to the overall experience. Dressy casual. Entertainment. **Bar:** Full bar. **Reservations:** suggested. **Hours:** 11 am-close, Sat & Sun from 5 pm. Closed: 12/25. **Address:** 322 11th Ave SW T2R 0C5 **Location:** Corner of 3rd St and 11th Ave SW. **Parking:** street. CALL

WILDWOOD

Regional Canadian
$10-$40

Phone: 403/228-0100 (70)

Rocky Mountain cuisine is the specialty at the upscale brew pub and dining room. Upstairs, diners enter into a beautiful loft-like dining room done in rich, warm tones and where sounds and smells float from the open-concept kitchen. The food, including Arctic char, flat breads and chicken, is beautiful and imaginative. Guests can expect to enjoy some regional dishes in a warm, cozy atmosphere. Casual dress. **Bar:** Full bar. **Reservations:** suggested, weekends. **Hours:** 11:30 am-2 & 5-10 pm, Fri & Sat-11 pm, Sun 5 pm-9 pm. Closed: 1/1, 12/24, 12/25. **Address:** 2417 4th St SW T2S 1X5 **Location:** Corner of 4th St SW and 25th Ave. **Parking:** on-site and street. CALL

CALGARY pop. 988,193   (See map and index starting on p. 392-395)

ACCLAIM HOTEL

Hotel
$169-$189 5/1-2/28
$149-$169 3/1-4/30

Book great rates at AAA.com

Phone: (403)291-8000 ①

Address: 123 Freeport Blvd NE T3N 0A3 **Location:** 1 mi (1.6 km) n of Calgary International Airport on Barlow Tr. **Facility:** Smoke free premises. 123 one-bedroom standard units. 4 stories, interior corridors. *Bath:* combo or shower only. **Parking:** on-site. **Terms:** check-in 4 pm, cancellation fee imposed. **Amenities:** video library, DVD players, high-speed Internet, dual phone lines, voice mail, safes, irons, hair dryers. **Leisure Activities:** whirlpools, exercise room. **Guest Services:** valet laundry, airport transportation-Calgary International Airport, area transportation-Crossiron Mills Mall in Balzac, wireless Internet. **Business Services:** conference facilities. *(See color ad p 410)*

ECO CALL

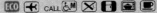

FREE expanded continental breakfast and high-speed Internet

(See map and index starting on p. 392)

BEST WESTERN AIRPORT INN   *Book great rates at AAA.com*   Phone: (403)250-5015

Hotel
$135-$220 All Year

Address: 1947 18th Ave NE T2E 7T8 **Location:** 0.6 mi (1 km) e of jct Hwy 2 (Deerfoot Tr) and 16th Ave NE (Trans-Canada Hwy 1), just n on 19th St NE, then just w on 19th Ave NE. **Facility:** Smoke free premises. 76 one-bedroom standard units, some with whirlpools. 3 stories, interior corridors. **Parking:** on-site, winter plug-ins. **Amenities:** voice mail, irons, hair dryers. *Some:* high-speed Internet. **Pool(s):** heated indoor. **Leisure Activities:** whirlpool, exercise room. **Guest Services:** valet and coin laundry, airport transportation-Calgary International Airport, wireless Internet. **Business Services:** PC (fee). *(See color ad p 411)*

AAA Benefit:
Members save up to 20%, plus 10% bonus points with rewards program.

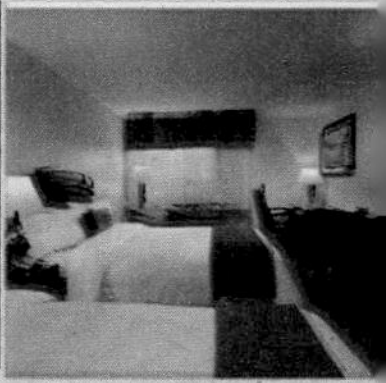

FREE expanded continental breakfast and high-speed Internet

BEST WESTERN CALGARY CENTRE INN   *Book great rates at AAA.com*   Phone: (403)287-3900

Hotel
$159-$249 3/1-9/7
$149-$239 9/8-2/28

Address: 3630 MacLeod Tr S T2G 2P9 **Location:** East side of Hwy 2A (MacLeod Tr) at 36th Ave SE. **Facility:** 71 units. 69 one-bedroom standard units, some with whirlpools. 2 one-bedroom suites with whirlpools. 4 stories, interior corridors. **Parking:** on-site, winter plug-ins. **Amenities:** high-speed Internet, voice mail, irons, hair dryers. *Some:* dual phone lines. **Pool(s):** heated indoor. **Leisure Activities:** whirlpool, exercise room. **Guest Services:** valet and coin laundry, wireless Internet. **Business Services:** PC. **Free Special Amenities: continental breakfast and high-speed Internet.**

AAA Benefit:
Members save up to 20%, plus 10% bonus points with rewards program.

▼ See AAA listing p 409 ▼

SLEEP WITH SOMEONE NEW

➤ Convenient to Calgary Int'l airport
➤ Easy access to main thoroughfares
➤ 7 mins. from Crossiron Mills Mall

Rates include: Breakfast, Movies, Internet, Parking, Airport Shuttle

Acclaim
HOTEL

www.acclaimhotel.ca   1-866-955-0008

See map and index starting on p. 392)

BEST WESTERN PORT O'CALL HOTEL

 Book great rates at AAA.com

Phone: (403)291-4600 **6**

Hotel
$129-$199 All Year

Address: 1935 McKnight Blvd NE T2E 6V4
Location: 1.6 mi (2.5 km) ne of jct Hwy 2
(Deerfoot Tr); at 19th St NE. **Facility:** 201 units.
198 one-bedroom standard units, some with
whirlpools. 3 one-bedroom suites with
whirlpools. 6-7 stories, interior corridors. *Bath:*
combo or shower only. **Parking:** on-site. **Terms:**
cancellation fee imposed. **Amenities:** voice mail,
irons, hair dryers. *Some:* high-speed Internet,
dual phone lines, safes. **Dining:** 2 restaurants.
Pool(s): heated indoor. **Leisure Activities:**
whirlpool, steamrooms, exercise room.
Fee: massage. **Guest Services:** valet laundry, airport transportation (fee)-Calgary International
Airport, wireless Internet. **Business Services:** conference facilities, PC. *(See color ad p 412)*

AAA Benefit:
Members save up to
20%, plus 10%
bonus points with
rewards program.

FREE local telephone calls and high-speed Internet

BEST WESTERN VILLAGE PARK INN

 Book great rates at AAA.com

Phone: (403)289-0241 **20**

Hotel
$120-$180 3/1-10/1
$110-$140 10/2-2/28

Address: 1804 Crowchild Tr NW T2M 3Y7
Location: Just ne of jct Trans-Canada Hwy 1
and Crowchild Tr. Located in Motel Village.
Facility: Smoke free premises. 159 units. 156
one-bedroom standard units. 3 one-bedroom
suites with whirlpools. 5 stories, interior
corridors. **Parking:** on-site. **Terms:** cancellation
fee imposed. **Amenities:** video games (fee),
voice mail, irons, hair dryers. *Some:* DVD
players, CD players, safes. **Pool(s):** heated
indoor. **Leisure Activities:** whirlpool. **Guest
Services:** valet and coin laundry, wireless
Internet. **Business Services:** meeting rooms, PC. *(See color ad p 413)*

AAA Benefit:
Members save up to
20%, plus 10%
bonus points with
rewards program.

FREE local telephone calls and high-speed Internet

▼ See AAA listing p 410 ▼

Home Away from Home

- Complimentary Hot Breakfast Buffet
- Fitness Center • Pool • Hot Tub
- Complimentary Airport Shuttle
- Room Service
- Complimentary High Speed Internet
- Award Winning Thai Restaurant

Best Western Airport Inn

1947 18th Avenue NE, Calgary, AB T2E 7T8

403.250.5015

1.877.499.5015

www.bestwesternairportinncalgary.com

Airport Inn

(See map and index starting on p. 392)

BLACKFOOT INN *Book at AAA.com* **Phone:** (403)252-2253

Hotel
$169-$335 All Year

Address: 5940 Blackfoot Tr SE T2H 2B5 **Location:** At 58th Ave SE; access to property from 58th Av only. **Facility:** 200 units. 199 one-bedroom standard units. 1 one-bedroom suite. 7 stories, interic corridors. *Bath:* combo or shower only. **Parking:** on-site, winter plug-ins. **Terms:** cancellation fe imposed. **Amenities:** video games (fee), high-speed Internet, voice mail, irons, hair dryers. *Som* DVD players, CD players, fax, safes. **Pool(s):** heated outdoor. **Leisure Activities:** whirlpoo steamroom, exercise room. **Guest Services:** valet laundry, wireless Internet. **Business Services** conference facilities, business center.

ASK CALL / SOME UNITS FEE

CALGARY WESTWAYS GUEST HOUSE *Book great rates at AAA.com* **Phone:** (403)229-1758

CAA SAVE

Historic Bed & Breakfast
$99-$180 3/1-10/31
$99-$150 11/1-2/28

Address: 216 25th Ave SW T2S 0L1 **Location:** 1.1 mi (1.7 km) s on Hwy 2A (MacLeod Tr S), the just w. Located in a residential area. **Facility:** This unassuming 1912 house offers a variety of upscal lodgings ranging from smaller original units to deluxe, spacious rooms. Smoke free premises. 5 one bedroom standard units, some with whirlpools. 3 stories (no elevator), interior corridors. *Bath:* comb or shower only. **Parking:** on-site, winter plug-ins. **Terms:** 2 night minimum stay - seasonal, 4 da cancellation notice-fee imposed. **Amenities:** video library, DVD players, CD players, high-spee Internet, voice mail, irons, hair dryers. **Leisure Activities:** bicycles. **Guest Services:** complimentar laundry, wireless Internet. *Fee:* airport transportation-Calgary International Airport, area transportatior downtown. **Business Services:** PC. **Free Special Amenities: full breakfast and high-spee Internet.**

FEE / SOME UNITS FEE

CARRIAGE HOUSE INN *Book great rates at AAA.com* **Phone:** (403)253-1101

CAA SAVE

Hotel
$149-$229 All Year

Address: 9030 MacLeod Tr S T2H 0M4 **Location:** On Hwy 2A (MacLeod Tr); corner of 90th Ave SW **Facility:** Smoke free premises. 157 units. 151 one-bedroom standard units. 6 one-bedroom suites wit whirlpools. 4-10 stories, interior corridors. *Bath:* combo or shower only. **Parking:** on-site, winter plug ins. **Terms:** check-in 4 pm. **Amenities:** high-speed Internet, voice mail, irons, hair dryers. *Some:* du phone lines. **Dining:** 3 restaurants. **Pool(s):** heated outdoor. **Leisure Activities:** saunas, whirlpoo exercise room. *Fee:* massage. **Guest Services:** valet laundry, wireless Internet. **Business Services** conference facilities, business center. **Free Special Amenities: full breakfast and high-spee Internet.**

ECO / SOME UNITS FEE

▼ See AAA listing p 411 ▼

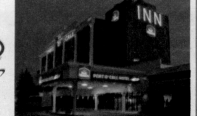

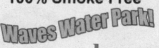

See map and index starting on p. 392)

COAST PLAZA HOTEL & CONFERENCE CENTRE *Book at AAA.com* Phone: (403)248-8888 27

Hotel
$129-$334 All Year

Address: 1316 33rd St NE T2A 6B6 **Location:** Just s of jct 16th Ave (Trans-Canada Hwy 1) and 36th St NE, just w on 12th Ave NE. Adjacent to Pacific Place Mall. **Facility:** 248 units. 245 one-bedroom standard units. 3 one-bedroom suites with whirlpools. 6-12 stories, interior corridors. *Bath:* combo or shower only. **Parking:** on-site (fee) and valet, winter plug-ins. **Terms:** cancellation fee imposed. **Amenities:** video games (fee), high-speed Internet, voice mail, irons, hair dryers. **Pool(s):** heated indoor. **Leisure Activities:** sauna, whirlpool, exercise room. **Guest Services:** valet laundry, wireless Internet. **Business Services:** conference facilities, business center.

COMFORT INN & SUITES-AIRPORT *Book great rates at AAA.com* Phone: (403)735-1966 11

Hotel
$129-$299 3/1-9/30
$119-$189 10/1-2/28

Address: 3111 26th St NE T1Y 7E4 **Location:** Just se of jct 32nd Ave NE and Barlow Tr NE. **Facility:** Smoke free premises. 74 units. 56 one-bedroom standard units, some with whirlpools. 18 one-bedroom suites. 4 stories, interior corridors. **Parking:** on-site, winter plug-ins. **Terms:** cancellation fee imposed. **Amenities:** high-speed Internet, voice mail, safes (fee), irons, hair dryers. **Pool(s):** heated indoor. **Leisure Activities:** whirlpool, steamroom, waterslide, limited exercise equipment. **Guest Services:** valet and coin laundry, airport transportation-Calgary International Airport, wireless Internet. **Business Services:** PC. **Free Special Amenities: expanded continental breakfast and high-speed Internet.** *(See color ad p 414)*

COMFORT INN & SUITES-MOTEL VILLAGE *Book great rates at AAA.com* Phone: (403)289-2581 17

Hotel
$119-$449 All Year

Address: 2369 Banff Tr NW T2M 4L2 **Location:** Just n of jct Trans-Canada Hwy 1 and Crowchild Tr. Located in Motel Village. **Facility:** Smoke free premises. 82 units. 58 one-bedroom standard units, some with whirlpools. 24 one-bedroom suites. 4 stories, interior corridors. **Parking:** on-site, winter plug-ins. **Terms:** cancellation fee imposed. **Amenities:** high-speed Internet, voice mail, irons, hair dryers. **Pool(s):** heated indoor. **Leisure Activities:** whirlpool, waterslide, limited exercise equipment. **Guest Services:** valet and coin laundry, wireless Internet. **Business Services:** meeting rooms, PC (fee). **Free Special Amenities: continental breakfast and high-speed Internet.** *(See color ad p 414)*

▼ See AAA listing p 411 ▼

Now That's *Refreshing*

Take the surprise out of hotel and restaurant visits. Let the simple, reliable AAA/CAA Diamond Ratings guide your decisions.

(See map and index starting on p. 392)

COMFORT INN & SUITES-SOUTH   *Book great rates at AAA.com*   Phone: (403)287-7070   [3]

CAA SAVE

Hotel
$100-$160 3/1-9/30
$100-$120 10/1-2/28

Address: 4611 MacLeod Tr SW T2G 0A6 **Location:** Hwy 2A (MacLeod Tr), w on 45th Ave. **Facility:** 93 units. 68 one-bedroom standard units, some with whirlpools. 25 one-bedroom suites. 4 stories, interior corridors. **Parking:** on-site, winter plug-ins. **Terms:** cancellation fee imposed. **Amenities:** video games (fee), high-speed Internet, voice mail, safes, irons, hair dryers. **Pool(s):** heated indoor. **Leisure Activities:** whirlpool, waterslide, limited exercise equipment. **Guest Services:** valet and coin laundry, wireless Internet. **Business Services:** meeting rooms, business center. **Free Special Amenities: continental breakfast and high-speed Internet.** *(See color ad below)*

COUNTRY INN & SUITES BY CARLSON,
CALGARY-AIRPORT   *Book great rates at AAA.com*   Phone: (403)250-1800   [8]

CAA SAVE

Hotel
$139-$229 All Year

Address: 2481 39th Ave NE T2E 8V8 **Location:** Barlow Tr and 39th Ave NE; access via 37th Ave. **Facility:** Smoke free premises. 106 units. 50 one-bedroom standard units, some with whirlpools. 56 one-bedroom suites. 3 stories, interior corridors. *Bath:* combo or shower only. **Parking:** on-site, winter plug-ins. **Amenities:** high-speed Internet, dual phone lines, voice mail, irons, hair dryers. **Pool(s):** heated indoor. **Leisure Activities:** whirlpool, exercise room. **Guest Services:** valet and coin laundry, airport transportation-Calgary International Airport, wireless Internet. **Business Services:** meeting rooms. *(See color ad p 415)*

FREE expanded continental breakfast and high-speed Internet

(See map and index starting on p. 392)

DAYS INN CALGARY AIRPORT   *Book at AAA.com*   Phone: (403)250-3297   🔟6️⃣

▼▼▼▼
Hotel
$150-$190 All Year

Address: 2799 Sunridge Way NE T1Y 7K7 **Location:** Barlow Tr, just e of Sunridge Way NE. **Facility:** 76 units. 70 one-bedroom standard units, some with whirlpools. 6 one-bedroom suites with whirlpools. 4 stories, interior corridors. **Parking:** on-site, winter plug-ins. **Terms:** check-in 4 pm, 3 day cancellation notice-fee imposed. **Amenities:** voice mail, irons, hair dryers. *Some:* high-speed Internet. **Pool(s):** heated indoor. **Leisure Activities:** whirlpool, waterslide, exercise room. **Guest Services:** valet and coin laundry, wireless Internet. **Business Services:** PC (fee).

ECO ASK FEE ✈ 🍴 🏊 ✕ 🎥 🔌 📻 💻 / SOME UNITS ✕

DELTA CALGARY AIRPORT   *Book at AAA.com*   Phone: (403)291-2600   2️⃣

▼▼▼▼
Hotel
$149-$329 6/1-2/28
$149-$289 3/1-5/31

Address: 2001 Airport Rd NE T2E 6Z8 **Location:** At Calgary International Airport. **Facility:** Smoke free premises. 296 units. 284 one-bedroom standard units. 12 one-bedroom suites, some with whirlpools. 3-8 stories, interior corridors. **Parking:** on-site (fee) and valet. **Amenities:** voice mail, irons, hair dryers. *Fee:* video games, high-speed Internet. **Pool(s):** heated indoor. **Leisure Activities:** whirlpool, exercise room. **Guest Services:** valet laundry. **Business Services:** conference facilities, business center.

ECO ASK 🍴 🍸 CALL 📶 🏊 ✕ 🔌 📻 💻 / SOME UNITS FEE 🐾

DELTA CALGARY SOUTH   *Book at AAA.com*   Phone: (403)278-5050   3️⃣6️⃣

▼▼▼▼
Hotel
$109-$369 3/1-10/31
$89-$349 11/1-2/28

Address: 135 Southland Dr SE T2J 5X5 **Location:** On Hwy 2A (MacLeod Tr); corner of Southland Dr. **Facility:** Smoke free premises. 252 units. 249 one-bedroom standard units. 3 one-bedroom suites with whirlpools. 3-8 stories, interior corridors. **Bath:** combo or shower only. **Parking:** on-site, winter plug-ins. **Terms:** cancellation fee imposed. **Amenities:** video games (fee), voice mail, irons, hair dryers. **Pool(s):** 2 heated indoor. **Leisure Activities:** whirlpools, waterslide, exercise room. **Guest Services:** valet laundry, wireless Internet. **Business Services:** conference facilities, business center.

ECO ASK 🍴 🍸 CALL 📶 🏊 ✕ ✕ 🔌 📻 💻 / SOME UNITS FEE 🐾

ECONO LODGE INN & SUITES UNIVERSITY   *Book great rates at AAA.com*   Phone: (403)289-1921   2️⃣1️⃣

CAA SAVE
▼▼▼
Motel
$89-$169 6/1-2/28
$79-$149 3/1-5/31

Address: 2231 Banff Tr NW T2M 4L2 **Location:** Just n of jct 16th Ave NW (Trans-Canada Hwy 1) and Banff Tr NW. Located in Motel Village. **Facility:** 82 units. 78 one- and 4 two-bedroom standard units, some with efficiencies or kitchens. 2-5 stories, interior/exterior corridors. **Parking:** on-site, winter plug-ins. **Terms:** cancellation fee imposed. **Amenities:** high-speed Internet, voice mail, irons, hair dryers. **Pool(s):** heated indoor. **Leisure Activities:** whirlpool, exercise room. **Guest Services:** coin laundry, wireless Internet. *(See color ad p 416)*

🍴 🏊 🔌 📻 💻 / SOME UNITS ✕

FREE continental breakfast and high-speed Internet

(See map and index starting on p. 392)

ECONO LODGE MOTEL VILLAGE   *Book great rates at AAA.com*   Phone: (403)289-2561   **25**

Motel
$89-$149 6/1-2/28
$69-$129 3/1-5/31

Address: 2440 16th Ave NW T2M 0M5 **Location:** Jct 16th Ave NW (Trans-Canada Hwy 1) and Banff Tr NW. Located in Motel Village. **Facility:** 56 units. 55 one-bedroom standard units, some with efficiencies. 1 two-bedroom suite with efficiency. 2 stories (no elevator), interior/exterior corridors. **Parking:** on-site, winter plug-ins. **Terms:** cancellation fee imposed. **Amenities:** irons, hair dryers. **Leisure Activities:** sauna, limited exercise equipment. **Guest Services:** valet and coin laundry. **Free Special Amenities: continental breakfast and high-speed Internet.**

ECONO LODGE SOUTH   *Book great rates at AAA.com*   Phone: (403)252-4401   **33**

Motel
$89-$129 All Year

Address: 7505 MacLeod Tr SW T2H 0L8 **Location:** Corner of Hwy 2A (MacLeod Tr) and 75th Ave. **Facility:** 73 units. 71 one-bedroom standard units, some with efficiencies or kitchens. 2 one-bedroom suites with efficiencies. 2 stories (no elevator), interior/exterior corridors. **Parking:** on-site, winter plug-ins. **Terms:** cancellation fee imposed. **Amenities:** voice mail, irons, hair dryers. **Pool(s):** heated indoor. **Leisure Activities:** whirlpool, limited exercise equipment. **Guest Services:** valet and coin laundry, wireless Internet. **Business Services:** meeting rooms, PC. **Free Special Amenities: continental breakfast and high-speed Internet.**

EXECUTIVE ROYAL INN NORTH CALGARY   *Book at AAA.com*   Phone: (403)291-2003   **13**

Hotel
$130-$325 All Year

Address: 2828 23rd St NE T2E 8T4 **Location:** Barlow Tr NE, just w; at 27th Ave NE. **Facility:** Smoke free premises. 201 units. 191 one-bedroom standard units. 10 one-bedroom suites with whirlpools. 6 stories, interior corridors. **Parking:** on-site, winter plug-ins. **Terms:** check-in 4 pm, cancellation fee imposed. **Amenities:** video games (fee), high-speed Internet, dual phone lines, voice mail, irons, hair dryers. **Leisure Activities:** whirlpools, steamrooms, exercise room. **Guest Services:** valet laundry, wireless Internet. **Business Services:** conference facilities, business center.

FOUR POINTS BY SHERATON HOTEL AND SUITES, CALGARY WEST   *Book great rates at AAA.com*   Phone: (403)288-4441   **9**

Hotel
$99-$349 All Year

Address: 8220 Bowridge Cres NW T3B 2V1 **Location:** Opposite Canada Olympic Park. **Facility:** Smoke free premises. 150 units. 78 one-bedroom standard units, some with whirlpools. 72 one-bedroom suites. 4 stories, interior corridors. **Parking:** on-site, winter plug-ins. **Terms:** cancellation fee imposed. **Amenities:** high-speed Internet, dual phone lines, voice mail, safes, irons, hair dryers. **Pool(s):** heated indoor. **Leisure Activities:** whirlpool, waterslide, exercise room, spa. **Guest Services:** valet and coin laundry, wireless Internet, beauty salon. **Business Services:** conference facilities, business center. *(See color ad p 417)*

FOUR POINTS
BY SHERATON

AAA Benefit:
Members get up to 15% off, plus Starwood Preferred Guest® bonuses.

▼ See AAA listing p 415 ▼

(See map and index starting on p. 392)

HAMPTON INN & SUITES BY HILTON CALGARY
NW *Book great rates at AAA.com* Phone: 403/289-9800 **22**

Hotel
Rates not provided

Address: 2231 Banff Tr NW T2M 4L2 **Location:** Just n of jct 16th Ave NW (Trans-Canada Hwy 1). **Facility:** Smoke free premises. 96 units. 72 one-bedroom standard units, some with whirlpools. 24 one-bedroom suites with efficiencies. 4 stories, interior corridors. **Parking:** on-site, winter plug-ins. **Amenities:** DVD players, high-speed Internet, voice mail, irons, hair dryers. **Pool(s):** heated indoor. **Leisure Activities:** whirlpool, waterslide, exercise room. **Guest Services:** valet and coin laundry, wireless Internet. **Business Services:** meeting rooms, business center. *(See color ad p 418)*

AAA Benefit:
Members save up to 10% everyday!

FREE expanded continental breakfast and high-speed Internet

HILTON GARDEN INN-CALGARY AIRPORT *Book great rates at AAA.com* Phone: (403)717-1999 **5**

Hotel
$109-$299 All Year

Address: 2335 Pegasus Rd NE T2E 8C3 **Location:** Jct Barlow Tr and McKnight Blvd, just w, n on 19th St NE, then just e. **Facility:** 135 units. 131 one-bedroom standard units. 4 one-bedroom suites with whirlpools. 5 stories, interior corridors. **Parking:** on-site, winter plug-ins. **Terms:** 1-7 night minimum stay, cancellation fee imposed. **Amenities:** high-speed Internet, dual phone lines, voice mail, irons, hair dryers. **Pool(s):** heated indoor. **Leisure Activities:** whirlpool, exercise room. **Guest Services:** valet and coin laundry, area transportation, wireless Internet. **Business Services:** meeting rooms, business center.

AAA Benefit:
Members save 5% or more everyday!

HOLIDAY INN CALGARY-AIRPORT *Book at AAA.com* Phone: (403)230-1999 **26**

Hotel
$139-$259 All Year

Address: 1250 McKinnon Dr NE T2E 7T7 **Location:** 0.6 mi (1 km) e of jct Hwy 2 (Deerfoot Tr) and 16th Ave NE (Trans-Canada Hwy 1). **Facility:** Smoke free premises. 168 one-bedroom standard units, some with whirlpools. 5 stories, interior corridors. **Parking:** on-site, winter plug-ins. **Terms:** cancellation fee imposed. **Amenities:** video games (fee), high-speed Internet, voice mail, irons, hair dryers. **Pool(s):** heated indoor. **Leisure Activities:** whirlpool, exercise room. **Guest Services:** valet and coin laundry, wireless Internet. **Business Services:** meeting rooms, PC. *(See color ad on insert)*

▼ See AAA listing p 416 ▼

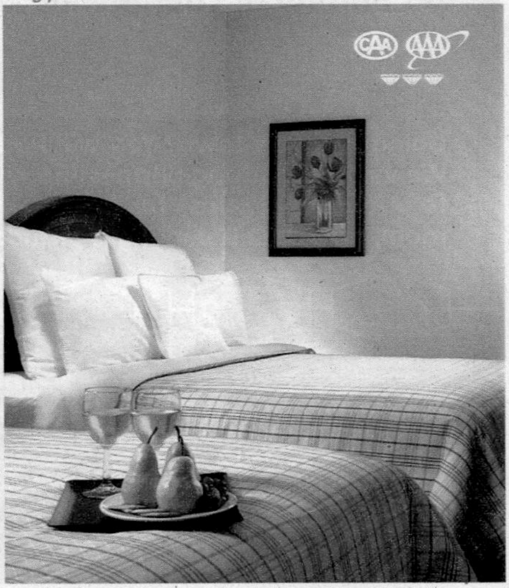

(See map and index starting on p. 392)

HOLIDAY INN CALGARY-MACLEOD TRAIL SOUTH   *Book great rates at AAA.com*   Phone: (403)287-2700

Hotel
$129-$159 All Year

Address: 4206 MacLeod Tr S T2G 2R7 **Location:** Corner of 42nd Ave SW and MacLeod Tr S. **Facility:** Smoke free premises. 150 one-bedroom standard units. 4 stories, interior corridors. *Bath:* combo or shower only. **Parking:** on-site, winter plug-ins. **Terms:** cancellation fee imposed. **Amenities:** high-speed Internet, voice mail, irons, hair dryers. **Pool(s):** heated indoor. **Leisure Activities:** exercise room. **Guest Services:** valet and coin laundry. **Business Services:** conference facilities, PC. *(See color ad p 419)*

▼ See AAA listing p 417 ▼

A friendly place. A great value.
Courtesy of your friends at Hampton, Calgary, Alberta

10% *
Off Published Rates

Going to a new town? You will find a friend in Hampton. We value our strong partnership with AAA and are delighted to offer special rates* for AAA members. Indoor pool, hot tub, exercise room, breakfast & parking is included.

100% Hampton GUARANTEE

we love having you here.®

Hampton Inn & Suites by Hilton

Friendly Service   Free Hot Breakfast   Cozy Hampton Bed   100% Satisfaction Guarantee

Hampton Inn & Suites by Hilton Calgary NW
2231 Banff Tr NW
Calgary, AB T2M 4L2
403-289-9800 • 1-888-432-6777 • www.hampton.com

The Hilton Family
©2009 Hilton Hotels Corporation

Approved

(See map and index starting on p. 392)

HOLIDAY INN EXPRESS AIRPORT CALGARY *Book at AAA.com* **Phone:** (403)769-1888 **4**

Hotel

$150-$170 3/1-9/30
$125-$150 10/1-2/28

Address: 45 Hopewell Way NE T3J 4V7 **Location:** Jct Barlow Tr NE and McKnight Blvd NE, just n, then just e. Located in an industrial area. **Facility:** Smoke free premises. 101 units. 83 one-bedroom standard units, some with whirlpools. 17 one- and 1 two-bedroom suites. 4 stories, interior corridors. *Bath:* combo or shower only. **Parking:** on-site, winter plug-ins. **Terms:** check-in 4 pm, cancellation fee imposed. **Amenities:** high-speed Internet, voice mail, irons, hair dryers. **Pool(s):** heated indoor. **Leisure Activities:** whirlpool, waterslide, exercise room. **Guest Services:** valet and coin laundry, wireless Internet. **Business Services:** meeting rooms, business center. ***(See color ad on insert)***

ASK

HOLIDAY INN EXPRESS HOTEL & SUITES CALGARY-SOUTH *Book at AAA.com* **Phone:** (403)225-3000 **38**

Hotel

$129-$259 All Year

Address: 12025 Lake Fraser Dr SE (MacLeod Tr S) T2J 7G5 **Location:** Hwy 2 (Deerfoot Tr), exit Anderson Rd W, just s on MacLeod Tr, just e on Lake Fraser Gate, then 0.4 mi (0.7 km) n. **Facility:** 106 units. 63 one-bedroom standard units. 43 one-bedroom suites, some with whirlpools. 4 stories, interior corridors. **Parking:** on-site, winter plug-ins. **Terms:** check-in 4 pm, 3 day cancellation notice-fee imposed. **Amenities:** video games (fee), high-speed Internet, dual phone lines, voice mail, irons, hair dryers. **Pool(s):** heated indoor. **Leisure Activities:** whirlpool, waterslide, exercise room. **Guest Services:** valet and coin laundry, wireless Internet. **Business Services:** meeting rooms, PC. ***(See color ad on insert)*** ASK / SOME UNITS FEE

LAKEVIEW SIGNATURE INN *Book great rates at AAA.com* **Phone:** (403)735-3336 **7**

CAA SAVE

Hotel

$139-$309 All Year

Address: 2622 39th Ave NE T1Y 7J9 **Location:** Barlow Tr NE, just e. **Facility:** Smoke free premises. 120 units. 48 one-bedroom standard units, some with efficiencies or kitchens. 48 one- and 24 two-bedroom suites, some with efficiencies or kitchens. 4 stories, interior corridors. *Bath:* combo or shower only. **Parking:** on-site, winter plug-ins. **Terms:** cancellation fee imposed. **Amenities:** CD players, high-speed Internet, dual phone lines, voice mail, irons, hair dryers. **Pool(s):** heated indoor. **Leisure Activities:** whirlpool, limited exercise equipment, sports court. **Guest Services:** valet and coin laundry, airport transportation-Calgary International Airport, area transportation-within 3 km. **Business Services:** meeting rooms, PC. **Free Special Amenities: expanded continental breakfast and local telephone calls.**

ECO CALL / SOME UNITS FEE

▼ *See AAA listing p 418* ▼

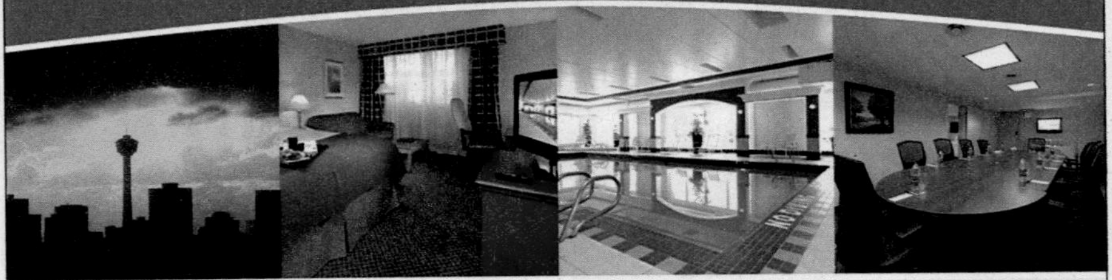

(See map and index starting on p. 392)

QUALITY INN UNIVERSITY   *Book great rates at AAA.com*   Phone: (403)289-1973   **18**

CAA SAVE

Hotel
$99-$169 All Year

Address: 2359 Banff Tr NW T2M 4L2 **Location:** Just n of jct Trans-Canada Hwy 1 and Crowchild Tr. Located in Motel Village. **Facility:** Smoke free premises. 105 units. 104 one-bedroom standard units, some with whirlpools. 1 one-bedroom suite with whirlpool. 2 stories, interior/exterior corridors. *Bath:* combo or shower only. **Parking:** on-site, winter plug-ins. **Terms:** check-in 4 pm, cancellation fee imposed. **Amenities:** voice mail, safes, irons, hair dryers. **Pool(s):** heated indoor. **Leisure Activities:** exercise room, spa. *Fee:* game room. **Guest Services:** valet and coin laundry, wireless Internet. **Business Services:** meeting rooms, business center. *(See color ad below)*

FREE continental breakfast and high-speed Internet

RADISSON HOTEL CALGARY AIRPORT   *Book at AAA.com*   Phone: 403/291-4666   **24**

Hotel
Rates not provided

Address: 2120 16th Ave NE T2E 1L4 **Location:** Just e of jct 16th Ave NE (Trans-Canada Hwy 1) and Hwy 2 (Deerfoot Tr). **Facility:** Smoke free premises. 185 units. 177 one-bedroom standard units, some with whirlpools. 8 one-bedroom suites. 10 stories, interior corridors. *Bath:* combo or shower only. **Parking:** on-site, winter plug-ins. **Amenities:** high-speed Internet, dual phone lines, voice mail, irons, hair dryers. **Pool(s):** heated indoor. **Leisure Activities:** whirlpool, exercise room. **Guest Services:** valet laundry, wireless Internet. **Business Services:** conference facilities, PC (fee).

SANDMAN HOTEL SUITES & SPA CALGARY
AIRPORT   *Book at AAA.com*   Phone: (403)219-2475   **3**

Hotel
$129-$199 All Year

Address: 25 Hopewell Way NE T3J 4V7 **Location:** Just n of jct Barlow Tr and McKnight Blvd. **Facility:** 177 units. 113 one-bedroom standard units. 64 one-bedroom suites, some with whirlpools. 4 stories (no elevator), interior corridors. **Parking:** on-site, winter plug-ins. **Terms:** check-in 4 pm. **Amenities:** video games (fee), high-speed Internet, dual phone lines, voice mail, irons, hair dryers. **Pool(s):** heated indoor. **Leisure Activities:** whirlpool, exercise room. **Guest Services:** valet laundry, wireless Internet. **Business Services:** meeting rooms, PC (fee).

SERVICE PLUS INN & SUITES CALGARY   *Book great rates at AAA.com*   Phone: (403)256-5352   **37**

CAA SAVE

Hotel
$159 All Year

Address: 3503 114th Ave SE T2Z 3X2 **Location:** South end of Barlow Tr, just w. Located in an industrial area. **Facility:** Smoke free premises. 139 units. 127 one- and 12 two-bedroom standard units, some with whirlpools. 4 stories, interior corridors. *Bath:* combo or shower only. **Parking:** on-site, winter plug-ins. **Amenities:** high-speed Internet, voice mail, irons, hair dryers. **Pool(s):** heated indoor. **Leisure Activities:** whirlpool, waterslide, exercise room. **Guest Services:** valet laundry, area transportation-Deerfoot Casino, wireless Internet. **Business Services:** meeting rooms. **Free Special Amenities:** expanded continental breakfast and high-speed Internet.

▼ *See AAA listing above* ▼

(See map and index starting on p. 392)

SHERATON CAVALIER HOTEL   *Book great rates at AAA.com*   Phone: 403/291-0107   **10**

Hotel
Rates not provided

Address: 2620 32nd Ave NE T1Y 6B8 **Location:** Barlow Tr at 32nd Ave NE. **Facility:** Smoke free premises. 306 units. 286 one-bedroom standard units. 20 one-bedroom suites with whirlpools. 7 stories, interior corridors. **Parking:** on-site and valet, winter plug-ins. **Amenities:** dual phone lines, voice mail, honor bars, irons, hair dryers. *Fee:* video games, high-speed Internet. *Some:* fax. **Dining:** Carver's Steakhouse, see separate listing. **Pool(s):** heated indoor. **Leisure Activities:** sauna, whirlpools, waterslide, exercise room. **Guest Services:** valet laundry, airport transportation (fee)-Calgary International Airport, wireless Internet. **Business Services:** conference facilities, business center. **Free Special Amenities:** newspaper.

⑤ Sheraton
HOTELS & RESORTS
AAA Benefit:
Members get up to
15% off, plus
Starwood Preferred
Guest® bonuses.

ⒺⒸⓄ FEE ✈ 🍴 24 🍸 🏊 🏋 ✕ 🎮 💻 / SOME UNITS 🐾

STAYBRIDGE SUITES CALGARY AIRPORT   *Book great rates at AAA.com*   Phone: (403)204-7829   **15**

Extended Stay
Hotel
$153-$243 All Year

Address: 2825 Sunridge Way NE T1Y 7K7 **Location:** Trans-Canada Hwy 1, exit Barlow Tr NE, just n, then just e. **Facility:** Smoke free premises. 96 units. 49 one-bedroom standard units with efficiencies. 36 one- and 11 two-bedroom suites with efficiencies. 4 stories, interior corridors. *Bath:* combo or shower only. **Parking:** on-site, winter plug-ins. **Terms:** cancellation fee imposed. **Amenities:** video library, DVD players, high-speed Internet, dual phone lines, voice mail, irons, hair dryers. **Pool(s):** heated indoor. **Leisure Activities:** whirlpool, waterslide, exercise room, sports court. **Guest Services:** complimentary and valet laundry, airport transportation (fee)-Calgary International Airport, wireless Internet. **Business Services:** meeting rooms, business center. **Free Special Amenities:** expanded continental breakfast and high-speed Internet.** *(See color ad on insert)*

FEE ✈ CALL 🎬 🏊 ✕ 🎮 🖥 🍴 💻

SUPER 8 CALGARY AIRPORT   *Book great rates at AAA.com*   Phone: (403)291-9888   **12**

Hotel
$119-$289 3/1-9/30
$109-$179 10/1-2/28

Address: 3030 Barlow Tr NE T1Y 1A2 **Location:** Corner of 32nd Ave and Barlow Tr NE. **Facility:** Smoke free premises. 61 one-bedroom standard units. 4 stories, interior corridors. **Parking:** on-site, winter plug-ins. **Terms:** cancellation fee imposed. **Amenities:** safes (fee), irons, hair dryers. **Guest Services:** coin laundry, airport transportation-Calgary International Airport, wireless Internet. ✈ 🍴 ✕ 🎮 🖥

FREE continental breakfast and high-speed Internet

TRAVELODGE CALGARY MACLEOD TRAIL   *Book great rates at AAA.com*   Phone: (403)253-7070   **35**

Hotel
$119-$179 All Year

Address: 9206 MacLeod Tr S T2J 0P5 **Location:** On MacLeod Tr; just s of 90th Ave SW. **Facility:** 254 units. 253 one-bedroom standard units. 1 one-bedroom suite. 6 stories, interior corridors. *Bath:* combo or shower only. **Parking:** on-site, winter plug-ins. **Amenities:** video games (fee), voice mail, irons, hair dryers. *Some:* high-speed Internet. **Dining:** entertainment. **Pool(s):** heated indoor. **Leisure Activities:** whirlpool, limited exercise equipment. **Guest Services:** coin laundry, wireless Internet. **Business Services:** meeting rooms, PC (fee).

ⒺⒸⓄ 🍴 🍸 🏊 🎮 💻 / SOME UNITS FEE 🐾 ✕ 🍴 🖥

TRAVELODGE CALGARY UNIVERSITY   *Book great rates at AAA.com*   Phone: (403)289-6600   **23**

Hotel
$98-$199 All Year

Address: 2227 Banff Tr NW T2M 4L2 **Location:** 16th Ave NW (Trans-Canada Hwy 1) and Banff Tr NW. Located in Motel Village across from McMahon Stadium. **Facility:** 64 one-bedroom standard units. 3 stories, interior corridors. *Bath:* combo or shower only. **Parking:** on-site, winter plug-ins. **Amenities:** dual phone lines, voice mail, irons, hair dryers. **Pool(s):** heated outdoor. **Leisure Activities:** exercise room. **Guest Services:** valet laundry, wireless Internet. **Business Services:** meeting rooms, PC (fee). **Free Special Amenities:** expanded continental breakfast and high-speed Internet. 🍴 🏊 🎮 🍴 🖥 💻 / SOME UNITS FEE 🐾 ✕

TRAVELODGE HOTEL CALGARY AIRPORT   *Book great rates at AAA.com*   Phone: (403)291-1260   **14**

Hotel
$119-$179 All Year

Address: 2750 Sunridge Blvd NE T1Y 3C2 **Location:** Just se of jct 32nd Ave NE and Barlow Tr NE. **Facility:** 203 one-bedroom standard units. 6 stories, interior corridors. **Parking:** on-site (fee), winter plug-ins. **Amenities:** video games (fee), voice mail, irons, hair dryers. *Some:* high-speed Internet. **Pool(s):** heated indoor. **Leisure Activities:** whirlpool, exercise room. **Guest Services:** valet and coin laundry, airport transportation-Calgary International Airport, wireless Internet. **Business Services:** meeting rooms, PC (fee).

ⒺⒸⓄ ✈ 🍴 🍸 🎬 🏊 🎮 💻 / SOME UNITS FEE 🐾 ✕ 🍴 🖥

At 100 kph (60 mph), if you reach
down to change the radio station
you can travel the length
of a football field.

Stay Focused
Keep your mind on the road.

(See map and index starting on p. 392)

WINGATE BY WYNDHAM CALGARY   *Book at AAA.com*   **Phone:** (403)514-0099

Hotel
$149-$259 All Year

Address: 400 Midpark Way SE T2X 3S4 **Location:** Hwy 2A (MacLeod Tr), 0.3 mi (0.5 km) e on Sun Valley Blvd SE, just n on Midpark Blvd SE, then just s. **Facility:** 103 units. 87 one-bedroom standard units, some with whirlpools. 16 one-bedroom suites, some with whirlpools. 4 stories, interior corridors. *Bath:* combo or shower only. **Parking:** on-site, winter plug-ins. **Terms:** 4 day cancellation notice-fee imposed. **Amenities:** video games (fee), high-speed Internet, dual phone lines, voice mail, safes, irons, hair dryers. **Pool(s):** heated indoor. **Leisure Activities:** whirlpool, waterslide, exercise room. **Guest Services:** valet and coin laundry, wireless Internet. **Business Services:** meeting rooms, business center.

—— WHERE TO DINE ——

ALBERTA KING OF SUBS   **Phone:** 403/293-5809   ③

Canadian
$5-$13

Montreal-style smoked-meat sandwiches and hot grilled subs are specialties at the strip mall eatery, which has only nine tables and a counter. French fries, coleslaw and sugar pie also are on the menu. Service is friendly and polite. Casual dress. **Bar:** Beer only. **Reservations:** not accepted. **Hours:** 10 am-9 pm, Thurs-Sat to 10 pm. Closed: 1/1, 4/4, 12/25. **Address:** 7196 Temple Dr NE, #22 T1Y 4E8 **Location:** McKnight Blvd and 52nd St NE, just s on 52nd St NE. **Parking:** on-site.

BAGOLAC SAIGON RESTAURANT   **Phone:** 403/252-5588   ㉞

Vietnamese
$6-$12

Upscale decor awaits at this fancy Vietnamese restaurant, where a mixture of Thai and Vietnamese dishes coexist on the menu. The selection is so outstanding that you may have a hard time selecting. It is best to order a variety of dishes to truly experience the tastes and flavors of this cuisine, starting with salad rolls, a traditional bun or noodle soup. Casual dress. **Bar:** Full bar. **Hours:** 11 am-9 pm, Fri & Sat-9:30 pm. Closed major holidays; also Sun. **Address:** 6130 1A St SW, #8 T2H 0G3 **Location:** Just e off MacLeod Tr; near Chinook Centre. **Parking:** on-site.

BEARS DEN   **Phone:** 403/241-7611

Regional
Canadian
$25-$74

A bit of a drive from downtown, this bunker-looking complex at the edge of the city limits offers a number of surprises. The restaurant follows in the tradition of legendary steakhouses with a rich and warmly luxurious set of dining rooms reminiscent of an old gentleman's club. Accents include dark wood paneling, hand-crafted relief murals and beautiful fireplaces. In addition to preparing some of the finest cuts of AAA Alberta beef, this place also puts together satisfying non-steak dishes. Dressy casual. **Bar:** Full bar. **Reservations:** suggested. **Hours:** 5 pm-10 pm, Fri & Sat-midnight. Closed major holidays; also Mon. **Address:** 254028 Bearspaw Rd NW T3L 2P7 **Location:** 1.2 mi (2 km) w of jct Stoney Tr; along Hwy 1A (Crowchild Tr). **Parking:** on-site.

BELMONT DINER   **Phone:** 403/242-6782   ㉙

Canadian
$9-$12

Diners in search of a hearty breakfast need look no further than this Marda Loop diner. At lunchtime, sandwiches and milkshakes are popular choices. Casual dress. **Reservations:** not accepted. **Hours:** 7 am-3 pm, Sat & Sun-4 pm. Closed: 12/25. **Address:** 2008 33rd Ave SW T2T 1Z6 **Location:** At 33rd Ave and 20th St; in Marda Loop. **Parking:** street.

BIG T'S BBQ   **Phone:** 403/284-5959   ⑪

Barbecue
$10-$35

Southern barbecue at its messiest is the name of the game at this casual restaurant, where enormous portions will satisfy even the hungriest diner. Casual dress. **Bar:** Full bar. **Reservations:** accepted. **Hours:** 11 am-11 pm. Closed: 12/25. **Address:** 2138 Crowchild Tr NW T2M 3Y7 **Location:** Jct 23 Ave NW; across from McMann Stadium. **Parking:** on-site.

BOOGIE'S BURGERS   **Phone:** 403/230-7070   ⑲

American
$5-$15

A favorite neighborhood haunt, this burger joint whips up creamy milkshakes, huge burgers and crispy fries. Guests can grab a seat at the counter, or in the summer, enjoy a shake at a picnic table. Seating is at a premium at this popular diner, which features vintage photos and decor. Expect fast, friendly service from the South African owners, who holler out orders or prepare them in rapid time for take-out. Those with hearty appetites should try the half-pound, homemade, charbroiled burger. Casual dress. **Bar:** Beer & wine. **Hours:** 11 am-9 pm, Sat-8 pm. Closed major holidays; also Sun. **Address:** 908 Edmonton Tr NE T2E 3K1 **Location:** Corner of 8th Ave NE. **Parking:** on-site.

BOYD'S SEAFOOD RESTAURANT   **Phone:** 403/253-7575   ㉜

Seafood
$10-$37

A long and varied menu of seafood is presented at this casual family restaurant, which transports guests to the east coast of Nova Scotia for a taste of the maritime. Fish and chips, mussels, Alaskan halibut, clams and more are dished in heaping portions. Most selections are flown in fresh daily, and there is something for everyone. This place offers a great value for the dollar. Service is friendly. Casual dress. **Bar:** Full bar. **Reservations:** suggested. **Hours:** 11:30 am-9 pm, Fri & Sat-10 pm. Closed major holidays. **Address:** 5211 MacLeod Tr S T2H 0J3 **Location:** Corner of 50th and MacLeod Tr. **Parking:** on-site.

BROKEN PLATE KITCHEN & BAR   **Phone:** 403/225-9650   ㊴

Greek
$10-$32

While guests are not encouraged to actually throw plates on to the ground after eating, it is not unusual to throw hands up in the air and shout "opa!" after enjoying Greek dishes made from fresh and authentic ingredients. One of three Calgary locations, the restaurant seems to have been imported directly from Greece. While service can be a little relaxed, the menu is serious about showcasing both comfortable and traditional selections. Casual dress. **Bar:** Full bar. **Reservations:** accepted. **Hours:** 11:30 am-11 pm, Fri & Sat-11 pm, Sun 5 pm-10 pm. Closed major holidays. **Address:** 590-10816 MacLeod Tr SE T2J 5N8 **Location:** Just n of Anderson Rd; west side of Willow Park Shopping Plaza. **Parking:** on-site.

(See map and index starting on p. 392)

BUFFET YANGTZE

Chinese
$11-$19

Phone: 403-275-3337 ①

In the Deerfoot Crossing outlet mall, this unassuming restaurant is a bit of a drive from most hotels, especially during rush hour. However, the navigation skills that come in handy on the Deerfoot Expressway also prove useful in negotiating the vast Chinese buffet. Food is refreshed regularly for the hungry patrons who loyally frequent this place. Casual dress. **Bar:** Full bar. **Hours:** 11 am-10 pm. **Address:** 901 64th Ave NW T2E 7P4 **Location:** At north entrance of Deerfoot Mall. **Parking:** on-site.

CACTUS CLUB CAFE

International
$10-$32

Phone: 403-255-1088

This bustling, casual restaurant serves huge burgers, sandwiches, pasta, salads, soups, quesadillas, fajitas, vegetarian dishes, steak, ribs, chicken and fish. Featured are certified Angus beef and fresh wild British Columbia salmon. The thick and creamy milk shakes come highly recommended. Casual dress. **Bar:** Full bar. **Reservations:** accepted. **Hours:** 11 am-midnight, Fri & Sat-1 am. Closed: 12/25. **Address:** 7010 MacLeod Tr SE T2H 0L3 **Location:** Jct Glenmore Tr SW, just s. **Parking:** on-site. CALL ♿M

CACTUS CLUB CAFE

International
$10-$32

Phone: 403-250-1120

This bustling, casual restaurant serves huge burgers, sandwiches, pasta, salads, soups, quesadillas, fajitas, vegetarian dishes, steak, ribs, chicken and fish. Featured are certified Angus beef and fresh wild British Columbia salmon. The thick and creamy milk shakes come highly recommended. Casual dress. **Bar:** Full bar. **Reservations:** accepted. **Hours:** 11 am-midnight. Closed: 12/25. **Address:** 2612 39th Ave NE T1Y 7S9 **Location:** Barlow Tr at 39th Ave NE. **Parking:** on-site. CALL ♿M

CAPO RESTAURANT

New Italian
$16-$44

Phone: 403-264-2276 ㉖

Under the direction of respected chef Giuseppe Di Gennaro, the kitchen precisely executes dishes with clear flavors. The signature entree of roasted pheasant breast, Muscat wine and rosemary reduction with morel mushrooms and parsnip puree stands out. Reservations are all but a must at the small restaurant, which is just east of downtown in the Inglewood district. The most notable design features are the huge hanging blue-white globes that light the room, leather banquettes and trendy artwork. Dressy casual. **Bar:** Full bar. **Reservations:** suggested. **Hours:** 5:30 pm-10 pm, Wed-Fri also 11:30 am-2 pm. Closed major holidays; also Sun. **Address:** 1420 9th Ave SE, Suite 4 T2G 0T5 **Location:** Just e of 12th St SE; in Inglewood. **Parking:** street. CALL ♿M

CAPTAIN SCOTT'S FISH & CHIPS

Seafood
$7-$15

Phone: 408-280-0009 ②

With its location in the far northeast of landlocked Calgary, Captain Scott's does a pretty good imitation of an East Coast fish and chips shop. While the fish isn't wrapped in newspaper for take-out, most guests regardless enjoy a good selection of deep-fried fish with a tasty batter in the modest, nautically themed restaurant. Casual dress. **Bar:** Beer only. **Reservations:** not accepted. **Hours:** 11 am-8:30 pm, Sat from 3 pm, Sun 3 pm-7:30 pm. Closed major holidays; also Mon. **Address:** 55 Castleridge Blvd NE, #76 T3J 1Y9 **Location:** Jct 52nd St NE (Falconridge Blvd NE) and McKnight Blvd NE; in Castleridge Plaza. **Parking:** on-site.

CARVER'S STEAKHOUSE

Steak
$25-$47

Phone: 403/250-6327 ⑥

One of Calgary's finest steak houses, this formal, contemporary restaurant is the place to go for made-to-order, mouthwatering steaks. Don't overlook the decadent desserts. Casual dress. **Bar:** Full bar. **Reservations:** suggested. **Hours:** 5:30 pm-10:30 pm, Sun 5 pm-9 pm. Closed major holidays. **Address:** 2620 32nd Ave NE T1Y 6B8 **Location:** Barlow Tr at 32nd Ave NE; in Sheraton Cavalier Hotel. **Parking:** on-site and valet.

THE CHEESECAKE CAFE

Canadian
$10-$26

Phone: 403/255-7443 ㊲

As might be expected, cheesecake is the cafe's signature item, and lip-smacking varieties are made on the premises. A huge dessert display case greets guests upon arrival. Offerings on the extensive lunch and dinner menu range from sandwiches and entree salads to pasta, pizza and seafood selections. It takes a while to get through the menu. Casual dress. **Bar:** Full bar. **Reservations:** accepted, except weekends. **Hours:** 11 am-11 pm, Fri & Sat-midnight, Sun 10 am-11 pm; Sunday brunch. Closed major holidays. **Address:** 7600 MacLeod Tr SE T2H 0L9 **Location:** Just s of jct Glenmore Tr. **Parking:** on-site.

THE CHEESECAKE CAFE

Canadian
$10-$26

Phone: 403/280-7798 ⑭

As might be expected, cheesecake is the cafe's signature item, and lip-smacking varieties are made on the premises. A huge dessert display case greets guests upon arrival. Offerings on the extensive lunch and dinner menu range from sandwiches and entree salads to pasta, pizza and seafood selections. It takes a while to get through the menu. Casual dress. **Bar:** Full bar. **Reservations:** accepted, except weekends. **Hours:** 11 am-11 pm, Fri & Sat-midnight, Sun 10 am-11 pm; Sunday brunch. Closed: 12/24, 12/25. **Address:** 2121 36th St NE T1Y 5S3 **Location:** Just n of jct 16th Ave; adjacent to Sunridge Shopping Centre. **Parking:** on-site.

CLAY OVEN

Eastern Indian
$12-$20

Phone: 403/250-2161 ⑨

This Indian restaurant is one of Calgary's favorite; of course, many of the dishes come from the namesake clay oven. Casual dress. **Bar:** Full bar. **Reservations:** suggested. **Hours:** 11:30 am-2 & 5-8:30 pm, Fri-9:30 pm, Sat 5 pm-9:30 pm. Closed major holidays; also Sun. **Address:** 3132 26th St NE, #349 T1Y 6Z1 **Location:** Just n of 32nd Ave; in small strip plaza. **Parking:** on-site. CALL ♿M

CRETE SOUVLAKI

Greek
$5-$9

Phone: 403/246-4777 ㉗

Fast, fresh and cheap are all words to describe the distinctive restaurant. Heaping portions of Greek food are dished at the quick-serve eatery, which is attached to the OK gas station on 17th Avenue. Most people get their food to go, but there are a few tables available. Casual dress. **Reservations:** accepted. **Hours:** 10 am-10 pm, Sat from 11 am, Sun 11 am-8 pm. Closed major holidays. **Address:** 2623 17th Ave SW T3E 0A5 **Location:** Jct 26th St SW. **Parking:** on-site.

(See map and index starting on p. 392)

DINER DELUXE
Phone: 403/276-5499   (20)

Canadian
$7-$22

Everything old is new again, and such is the case at this funky retro diner, where all-day breakfasts are made with gourmet and specialty ingredients. The nostalgic atmosphere is complete with '50s-style Formica countertops, boldly colored vinyl chairs, tall milkshakes and hearty burgers. Friendly servers are quick and knowledgeable and offer great detail about the various dishes. Casual dress. **Bar:** Full bar. **Hours:** 7:30 am-9:30 pm, Sat 8 am-3 & 5-9:30 pm, Sun 8 am-3 pm. Closed: 12/25. **Address:** 804 Edmonton Tr NE T2E 3J6 **Location:** Corner of Edmonton Tr NE and 7th Ave NE. **Parking:** street.

EARLS RESTAURANT
Phone: 403/289-2566

Canadian
$10-$35

Offering an experience that falls between fast food and fine dining, the fun, relaxed restaurant prepares great food at a great price. Choices range from juicy burgers, hearty sandwiches, fresh salads, wings and pizza to full entrees of steak, chops and seafood. Made-from-scratch soups and assorted breads, as well as a nice choice of wines and beers, round out the offerings. This is a fitting spot for impromptu get-togethers and festive occasions. Casual dress. **Bar:** Full bar. **Hours:** 11 am-11 pm, Fri & Sat-midnight. Closed: 12/25. **Address:** 1110 16th Ave NW T2M 0K8 **Location:** Jct 11th St NW. **Parking:** on-site.

EARLS RESTAURANT
Phone: 403/291-6700

Canadian
$10-$35

Offering an experience that falls between fast food and fine dining, the fun, relaxed restaurant prepares great food at a great price. Choices range from juicy burgers, hearty sandwiches, fresh salads, wings and pizza to full entrees of steak, chops and seafood. Made-from-scratch soups and assorted breads, as well as a nice choice of wines and beers, round out the offerings. This is a fitting spot for impromptu get-togethers and festive occasions. Casual dress. **Bar:** Full bar. **Hours:** 11 am-midnight, Fri & Sat-1 am. Closed major holidays. **Address:** 3030 23rd St NE T2E 8R7 **Location:** Jct 32nd Ave NE and Barlow Tr NE. **Parking:** on-site.

EMPEROR BUFFET & RESTAURANT
Phone: 403/252-8250   (38)

Chinese
$8-$14

Overlooking the parking lot of a strip mall, this second-floor restaurant isn't known for its views. However, the owners of this attractive buffet restaurant have garnered extensive experience in various restaurants in Calgary's Chinatown and bring their touches to this place's extensive spread of Chinese and Western dishes. Casual dress. **Bar:** Full bar. **Hours:** 11 am-2 & 4:30-9 pm. **Address:** 9737 MacLeod Tr SW, 100 T2J 0P6 **Location:** Jct Southland Dr at Southland Crossing. **Parking:** on-site.

FORBIDDEN CITY SEAFOOD & DIM SUM RESTAURANT
Phone: 403/250-1848   (17)

Chinese
$4-$20

The large, contemporary restaurant serves all the classic Chinese dishes, and lunch is extremely busy thanks to the dim sum offerings. Best enjoyed with a group of people, dim sum includes dozens of items, from steamed shrimp dumplings and crepes to fried rice dishes. Service is quick and efficient, and the atmosphere is bustling. Casual dress. **Bar:** Full bar. **Reservations:** not accepted. **Hours:** 10 am-10 pm, Fri & Sat-11 pm. **Address:** 220 Pacific Pl, 999 36th St NE T2A 7X6 **Location:** 16th Ave NE (Trans-Canada Hwy 1), exit 36th St E, just s; in Pacific Place Shopping Plaza. **Parking:** on-site.

GUS'S CAFE & PIZZERIA
Phone: 403/282-4005   (15)

Pizza
$5-$15

Ideally located just off Trans-Canada Highway 1 and near the hospital, this family-run restaurant serves simply good food. Though the specialty is pizza, a variety of other items line the menu, including soups, salads and sandwiches. Service is quick and prompt, the owner often sits to chat with regulars. Casual dress. **Bar:** Full bar. **Reservations:** suggested. **Hours:** 9 am-10 pm, Sat 4 pm-10 pm. Closed major holidays; also Sun. **Address:** 1620 29th St NW, #180 T2W 4L7 **Location:** 16th Ave (Trans-Canada Hwy 1), just s at 29th St NW. **Parking:** on-site.

HEARTLAND CAFE
Phone: 403/270-4541   (21)

Deli
$5-$13

In a heritage building in the trendy Kensington neighborhood, the cafe is a few blocks away from the neighborhood's crowded, noisy heart. In a dining room marked by exposed brick walls and hardwood floors, patrons sip coffee as they nosh on excellent scones and sandwiches. It's a good place to get away from the crowds. Casual dress. **Reservations:** not accepted. **Hours:** 8 am-8 pm, Sun-Tues to 5 pm. Closed major holidays. **Address:** 940 2nd Ave NW T2M 0E7 **Location:** Just n of Memorial Dr NW; in Kensington. **Parking:** street.

JAMESONS IRISH PUB
Phone: 403/285-1608   (13)

Irish
$8-$15

Just across from Sunridge Mall, the Irish pub welcomes travelers from around the globe. The restaurant offers a lively atmosphere, friendly service and live entertainment, as well as an extensive menu of both pub and Irish favorites. The selection of on-tap Irish beers is excellent. Casual dress. **Bar:** Full bar. **Reservations:** accepted. **Hours:** 11 am-midnight. Closed major holidays. **Address:** 3575 20th Ave NE T1Y 6R3 **Location:** Jct 36th St NE; across from Sunridge Mall. **Parking:** on-site.

JAMESONS RESTAURANT & BAR
Phone: 403/220-9888   (4)

Western Canadian
$10-$19

This casual and lively restaurant and Irish pub presents a menu of comfort foods, including fish and chips, corned beef sandwiches, shepherd's pie, burgers, wraps and Philly cheese melts. Also offered are chicken teriyaki noodles, maple-glazed salmon, pasta dishes, steaks, baby back ribs, fried pickles, calamari and thin-crust pizzas. Guests may sit at tables in the center pub area or off to the sides in comfortable booths. Breakfast is served late on weekends. Casual dress. **Bar:** Full bar. **Reservations:** suggested. **Hours:** 11 am-1 am, Sat & Sun from 10 am. Closed: 12/25. **Address:** 17-3802 Brentwood Rd NW T2L 1K8 **Location:** Just nw of Crowchild Tr and 32nd Ave NW; in Brentwood Village Mall. **Parking:** on-site.

JOEY RESTAURANTS
Phone: 403/692-6626

Mediterranean
$12-$35

The cuisine blends Mediterranean and Asian cooking styles and emphasizes finger foods for sharing. Those who aren't big fans of tapas can consider full meal offerings centered on steaks and chops. Casual dress. **Bar:** Full bar. **Reservations:** not accepted. **Hours:** 11 am-1 am. Closed: 12/25. **Address:** 6455 MacLeod Tr SW, 100A T2H 0K8 **Location:** At Chinook Centre Mall. **Parking:** on-site.

(See map and index starting on p. 392)

JOEY RESTAURANTS

Phone: 403/547-5639

Mediterranean
$12-$35

The cuisine blends Mediterranean and Asian cooking styles and emphasizes finger foods for sharing. Those who aren't big fans of tapas can consider full meal offerings centered on steaks and chops. Casual dress. **Bar:** Full bar. **Reservations:** not accepted. **Hours:** 11:30 am-2 am. Closed: 12/25. **Address:** 50 Crowfoot Way NW T3G 4C8 **Location:** Just nw of Nose Hill Dr NW and Ranchlands Blvd NW. **Parking:** on-site.

JOEY RESTAURANTS

Phone: 403/219-8465

Mediterranean
$12-$35

The cuisine blends Mediterranean and Asian cooking styles and emphasizes finger foods for sharing. Those who aren't big fans of tapas can consider full meal offerings centered on steaks and chops. Casual dress. **Bar:** Full bar. **Reservations:** not accepted. **Hours:** 11:30 am-1 am. Closed: 12/25. **Address:** 3026 23rd St NE T2E 8R7 **Location:** At Barlow Tr, just w of 26th St NE. **Parking:** on-site.

KANE'S HARLEY DINER

Phone: 403/269-7311   [24]

Canadian
$7-$22

Orange and brown retro decor sets the scene at the popular diner in the town's heart. Guests seat themselves in booths and admire Harley motorcycles as they peruse the menu, which is laden with comfort foods. Among choices are grilled cheese and ham sandwiches, poutine, hearty hamburgers and even liver and onions. Breakfast is served all day, and service always comes with a smile. Casual dress. **Bar:** Full bar. **Reservations:** accepted. **Hours:** 8 am-3 pm, Sat & Sun-4 pm. Closed major holidays. **Address:** 1209 9th Ave SE T2G 3E8 **Location:** 9th Ave SE at 12th St; in Inglewood. **Parking:** street. CALL

LINA'S ITALIAN MARKET

Phone: 403/277-9166   [12]

Deli
$5-$10

The family-owned, coffee bar-style restaurant has been an area landmark for many years. Inside, find eight tables and over-the-counter ordering. Big food comes at small prices. On the menu are homemade pizzas, pasta dishes, soups, salads and Italian pastries. Check out the family-size tiramisu in the cooler. Service is casual and friendly, and guests are often surprised to find that the polite person behind the counter is the owner. Casual dress. **Bar:** Full bar. **Reservations:** not accepted. **Hours:** 9 am-7 pm, Sat & Sun-5 pm. Closed major holidays. **Address:** 2202 Centre St NE T2E 2T4 **Location:** 0.3 mi (0.5 km) n of jct 16th Ave (Trans-Canada Hwy 1). **Parking:** on-site.

MISAI JAPANESE RESTAURANT

Phone: 403/250-1688   [7]

Japanese
$9-$15

Traditional decor awaits at the Northeast establishment, which is near many hotels and not far from the airport. In fact, the restaurant offers shuttle service to and from local hotels. Japanese art decorates individual booths, as well as rooms, in the dark-wood interior. The selection of sushi, sashimi, tempura and stir-fries offers good value for the dollar. Casual dress. **Bar:** Full bar. **Reservations:** suggested. **Hours:** 11 am-2 & 5-9 pm, Fri & Sat-10:30 pm, Sun 5 pm-9 pm. Closed: for dinner on holidays. **Address:** #7 1915-32 Ave NE T2E 7C8 **Location:** From Barlow Tr, 0.6 mi (1 km) w at 32nd Ave. **Parking:** on-site. CALL

MOXIE'S CLASSIC GRILL

Phone: 403/291-4636

Canadian
$10-$30

This sleek, funky and popular restaurant presents an extensive menu of creatively prepared dishes, including pizza, pasta, rice, noodles, signature salads and burgers. Other menus include one for children and one for Sunday brunch. Lending to the upbeat, stylish decor are dark wood appointments and river rock fireplaces. Casual dress. **Bar:** Full bar. **Hours:** 6 am-midnight. Closed: 12/24, 12/25. **Address:** 29 Hopewell Way NE T3J 4V7 **Location:** Just n of jct Barlow Tr and McKnight Blvd; adjacent to Sandman Hotel Suites & Spa Calgary Airport. **Parking:** on-site.

NELLIE'S IN THE LOOP

Phone: 403/802-2174   [30]

Canadian
$8-$13

This Marda Loop outpost of the Nellie's chain is particularly popular on weekends. Not surprisingly, the bustling, cozy diner is a favorite for its fabulous home-cooked breakfasts, which are available all day. In addition to omelets, French toast and pancakes, the menu also lists some lunch options. The moist and tasty homemade banana bread is well worth the indulgence. Friendly, chatty servers keep things moving swiftly. Casual dress. **Reservations:** not accepted. **Hours:** 7 am-3 pm, Sat & Sun 8 am-4 pm. Closed: 12/25. **Address:** 2015 33rd Ave SW T2T 1Z5 **Location:** 0.6 mi (1 km) e of jct Crowchild Tr SW; in Marda Loop. **Parking:** street.

NEWPORT GRILL ON LAKE BONAVISTA

Phone: 403/271-6711   [40]

Continental
$14-$40

Lovely views of Lake Bonavista can be had from almost every table at the upscale restaurant. Among interesting and eclectic entrees are preparations of salmon, linguine and buffalo. Formerly called the Inn on Lake Bonavista, the restaurant has undergone a complete renovation and now boasts good food in fine surroundings. Casual dress. **Bar:** Full bar. **Reservations:** suggested. **Hours:** 11:30 am-2 & from 5 pm, Sun from 11 am. Closed major holidays. **Address:** 205-747 Lake Bonavista Dr SE T2J 0N2 **Location:** 6.7 mi (11.2 km) se via MacLeod Tr, 0.5 mi (0.8 km) e on Anderson Rd to Bonaventure Dr, just s to Lake Bonavista Dr, then 0.7 mi (1.2 km) e to Lake Bonavista Shopping Centre. **Parking:** on-site.

CALL

NICK'S STEAKHOUSE & PIZZA

Phone: 403/282-9278   [5]

Steak
$8-$30

A favorite with families, the restaurant has been a local fixture for more than 20 years. Steaks are grilled to perfection, and pizza is prepared with a variety of unusual toppings. The cozy decor and simple menu suit the tastes of all kinds of patrons, and food is presented exactly as requested. Casual dress. **Bar:** Full bar. **Reservations:** accepted. **Hours:** 11 am-midnight. Closed: 12/24, 12/25. **Address:** 2430 Crowchild Tr NW T2M 4N5 **Location:** Just nw of Motel Village. **Parking:** on-site.

OPEN RANGE

Phone: 403/277-3408   [18]

Canadian
$21-$36

With an elegant feel, this Western-theme restaurant serves up a variety of meat dishes, including venison osso buco, Alberta beef and braised Alberta lamb shank. Such fish as steelhead trout and salmon please a lighter palate. Casual dress. **Bar:** Full bar. **Reservations:** suggested. **Hours:** 5 pm-10 pm, Thurs-Sat to 10:30 pm. Closed: 12/25. **Address:** 1114 Edmonton Tr NE T2E 3K4 **Location:** Just n on Edmonton Tr; at 11th St NE. **Parking:** street.

(See map and index starting on p. 392)

OPEN SESAME

Asian
$9-$22

Phone: 403/259-0123 ③⑤

Guests must descend the stairs to discover this restaurant's treasures. The Pan Asian noodle house features a do-it-yourself stir-fry station, as well as a full menu. Made-to-order dishes include sumptuous pot sticker appetizers and varied stir-fried noodle preparations. The rich decor of mahogany woods and dark, intimate corners sets the stage for a memorable meal. Casual dress. **Bar:** Full bar. **Reservations:** suggested. **Hours:** 11:30 am-10 pm, Fri & Sat-11 pm, Sun 4:30 pm-10 pm. Closed: 12/25. **Address:** 6920 MacLeod Tr S T2H 0L3 **Location:** Just s of Hwy 8 (Glenmore Tr). **Parking:** on-site.

ORIENTAL PHOENIX

Vietnamese
$8-$15

Phone: 403/253-8383

Traditional Vietnamese food is served simply, but the service and decor is anything but. Upscale and sleek, the modern dining room is a busy place at lunch and around the dinner hour. Guests can sample tasty food in fine surroundings characterized by bold, contemporary colors and art. Among the varied choices are salad rolls, rice vermicelli dishes and noodle soups. Semi-formal attire. **Bar:** Full bar. **Hours:** 11 am-8:30 pm, Fri-9:30 pm, Sat noon-9:30 pm. Closed major holidays; also Sun & 2 weeks during Christmas. **Address:** 104 58th Ave SW, #80 T2H 0N7 **Location:** Jct MacLeod Tr SW, just e. **Parking:** on-site.

CALL ⑤M

PFANNTASTIC PANNENKOEK HAUS   *Menu on AAA.com*

Dutch
$7-$13

Phone: 403/243-7757 ③③

The restaurant prepares 75 varieties of meal-size Dutch crepes served with various toppings. A savory selection for dinner and a sweet choice for dessert make for a tasty meal. Diners should come with an appetite since servings are huge. Soups and salads are also offered. Super friendly, efficient servers tend to recommend their favorite pannenkoek, and they'll also help you with pronunciation! Casual dress. **Bar:** Full bar. **Reservations:** accepted, except Sun. **Hours:** 10 am-8 pm, Sat from 8 am, Sun 8 am-3 pm. Closed: Mon & Tues. **Address:** 2439 54th Ave SW T3E 1M4 **Location:** Just ne of jct Hwy 8 (Glenmore Tr) and Crowchild Tr; in small strip mall. **Parking:** on-site.

RAJDOOT RESTAURANT
Indian
$11-$27

Phone: 403/245-0181 ②⑧

The casual Indian restaurant lures locals and celebrities alike for its fantastic all-you-can-eat lunch buffet. Casual dress. **Bar:** Full bar. **Reservations:** suggested. **Hours:** 11:30 am-2 & 5-10 pm, Fri-11 pm, Sat 5 pm-11 pm, Sun 5 pm-10 pm. Closed: 12/25. **Address:** 2424 4th St SW T2S 2T4 **Location:** 4th St at 24th Ave SW. **Parking:** on-site and street.

THE RANCHE RESTAURANT

Regional
Canadian
$15-$40

Phone: 403/225-3939 ④①

Originally built more than 100 years ago as a wealthy gent's mansion that lapsed into disuse, the house has been restored to its former grandeur. Creative, well-executed preparations draw on a variety of prairie ingredients and flavors. In a park in the southern part of Calgary, the restaurant offers a superb setting and experience. Casual dress. **Bar:** Full bar. **Reservations:** required. **Hours:** 5 pm-9 pm; Sunday brunch 10:30 am-2 pm. Closed major holidays. **Address:** 9005 15979 Bow Bottom Tr SE T2P 0Y8 **Location:** Off Bow Bottom Tr; in Fish Creek Provincial Park. **Parking:** on-site. **Historic**

RICKY'S ALL DAY GRILL

Continental
$10-$25

Phone: 403/571-3220

The comfortable eatery, which employs friendly servers, presents a varied menu that includes pasta dishes, wraps, omelets, stir-fry preparations and burgers. Portions are generous. Children's and senior selections are offered. Guests can request seating in a booth or at a table. Casual dress. **Bar:** Full bar. **Reservations:** accepted, except weekends. **Hours:** 6 am-10 pm, Sun from 7 am. Closed: 1/1, 12/25. **Address:** 3321 20th Ave NE T1Y 7A8 **Location:** Just w of 36th St NE; across from Sunridge Mall. **Parking:** on-site. CALL ⑤M

ROCKY'S BURGERS

Canadian
$3-$6

Phone: 403/243-0405 ③①

Inside an old transit bus in an industrial section of the city are some of the best hamburgers in the province. Hand-made beef burgers, hand-cut fries and creamy milkshakes make this spot popular and distinctive. Plus, the food is cheap. Casual dress. **Reservations:** not accepted. **Hours:** 10 am-3 pm; hours may vary. Closed major holidays; also Sat & Sun. **Address:** 4645 12th St SE T3E 4R7 **Location:** From MacLeod Tr, 1.2 mi (2 km) e at 46th Ave to 12th St. **Parking:** on-site. AC

ROUGE

French
$30-$44

Phone: 403/531-2767 ②②

In a residential area near the zoo, the historic house has been converted into a quaint restaurant featuring contemporary French cuisine. Seasonally inspired dishes range from ricotta ravioli to salmon and specialty soups. Each dish is a work of art, and servers are highly attentive. The home maintains its historic roots with Victorian decor in each of its small dining rooms. Casual dress. **Bar:** Full bar. **Reservations:** suggested. **Hours:** 11:30 am-2 & 5-10 pm, Sat from 5:30 pm; from 5 pm 9/1-6/30. Closed major holidays; also Sun. **Address:** 1240 8th Ave SE T2G 0M7 **Location:** Corner of 12th St and 8th Ave SE. **Parking:** on-site. **Historic** CALL ⑤M AC

SAMOSA GRILL

Eastern Indian
$14-$16

Phone: 403/250-2515 ①⓪

This second floor walk-up restaurant offers a unique mix of East Indian and East African dishes. Surrounded by lots of greenery and African tribal masks, diners will enjoy tasty and exotic dishes such as the house specialties of crispy samosas and tandoori chicken. The buffet offers a good value. Casual dress. **Bar:** Full bar. **Reservations:** accepted. **Hours:** 11:30 am-2:30 & 5-9:30 pm, Fri & Sat-10:30 pm. Closed major holidays. **Address:** 210-3393 26th Ave NE T1Y 6L4 **Location:** Jct 36th St NE; across from Peter Longhead Hospital. **Parking:** on-site.

SANTORINI GREEK TAVERNA
Greek
$14-$30

Phone: 403/276-8363 ①⑥

Hearty Greek food, friendly service and a bustling, festive atmosphere define the cozy taverna, which makes guests feel as though they've stepped into small town in Greece. The menu features traditional dishes, including mouthwatering moussaka, sumptuous souvlaki and spanakopita. Save some room for bougatsa, a distinctive custard dessert. Casual dress. **Bar:** Full bar. **Reservations:** suggested, weekends. **Hours:** 11 am-10 pm, Sun from 4 pm. Closed: major holidays, 12/26; also Mon. **Address:** 1502 Centre St N T2E 2R9 **Location:** Just s of 16th Ave and Centre St N. **Parking:** on-site.

(See map and index starting on p. 392)

SMUGGLER'S INN

Phase: 403/253-5355 (36)

Steak
$12-$32

One of the city's oldest steak and prime rib houses, this place lets guests sample the all-you-can-eat soup and salad bar with any entree. The menu centers on steak, prime rib and chicken. The dark, cozy interior is a favorite with the business-lunch crowd. Casual dress. **Bar:** Full bar. **Reservations:** suggested. **Hours:** 11 am-10 pm, Sun 9:30 am-2 & 4:30-10 pm. Closed: 12/25. **Address:** 6920 MacLeod Tr T2H 0L3 **Location:** Just s of Glenmore Tr; attached to Open Sesame. **Parking:** on-site.

SPOLUMBO'S DELI

Phone: 403/264-6452 (25)

Deli
$6-$10

Owned by a group of former Canadian Football League Stampeders players, this bustling, energetic deli serves varied meats, including outstanding, high-quality sausage. This is a popular place at lunch, when patrons order at the counter and have their basket of food delivered to them. Casual dress. **Bar:** Beer & wine. **Reservations:** not accepted. **Hours:** 8 am-5:30 pm. Closed major holidays; also Sun. **Address:** 1308 9th Ave SE T2G 0T3 **Location:** Corner of 9th Ave SE and 13th St SE; in Inglewood. **Parking:** on-site.
CALL

SUGO CAFFE ITALIA

Phone: 403/263-1115 (23)

Italian
$15-$39

In the funky Inglewood area, the upscale Italian eatery has a cozy decor to complement its innovative menu. Although the ingredients are not classically Italian, guests still can find daily selections of pasta and traditionally prepared food. The service is fine, and the atmosphere is casually elegant. Casual dress. **Bar:** Full bar. **Reservations:** suggested. **Hours:** 11 am-2 & 5-11 pm. Closed: major holidays, 12/26; also for lunch Sun & Mon. **Address:** 1214 9th Ave SE T2G 0S9 **Location:** Corner of 9th Ave SE and 12th St; in Inglewood. **Parking:** street. CALL

THAI BOAT

Phone: 403/291-9887 (8)

Thai
$8-$13

The restaurant is a must-stop for folks staying out by the airport. A sister property to Thai SaOn downtown, this place displays casual Thai decor inside, but the food—an array of traditional items—is anything but casual. Thai salad rolls wow the taste buds. This place is affordable and enjoyable at lunch, and the service is friendly and efficient. Casual dress. **Bar:** Full bar. **Reservations:** suggested. **Hours:** 11 am-2 & 5-10 pm, Fri-11 pm, Sat 5 pm-11 pm. Closed major holidays; also Sun. **Address:** 2323 32 Ave NE, #108 T2E 6Z3 **Location:** Just w of Barlow Tr at 32nd Ave. **Parking:** on-site. CALL

WHITE SPOT

Phone: 403/278-8212

Canadian
$8-$24

Open for three meals a day, the popular casual restaurant prepares offerings such as sandwiches and burgers, fresh salads, pastas and stir-fries, fish and chips, chargrilled sirloin steaks and chicken, in addition to a selection of yummy desserts. Casual dress. **Bar:** Full bar. **Reservations:** accepted, except weekends. **Hours:** 8 am-10 pm, Fri & Sat-11 pm. Closed: 12/25. **Address:** 10440 MacLeod Tr SE T2J 0P8 **Location:** 0.3 mi (0.5 km) s of jct Southland Dr SE. **Parking:** on-site.

The Calgary Vicinity

AIRDRIE pop. 28,927

BEST WESTERN REGENCY INN   *Book great rates at AAA.com*

Phone: (403)948-3838

Hotel
$121-$159 All Year

Address: 121 Edmonton Tr SE T4B 1S2 **Location:** Hwy 2, exit Airdrie/Irricona, just w, then just s. **Facility:** Smoke free premises. 57 units. 56 one-bedroom standard units. 1 one-bedroom suite. 3 stories, interior/exterior corridors. **Parking:** on-site, winter plug-ins. **Amenities:** voice mail, irons, hair dryers. **Leisure Activities:** exercise room. **Guest Services:** valet and coin laundry, wireless Internet. **Business Services:** PC (fee).

AAA Benefit:
Members save up to 20%, plus 10% bonus points with rewards program.

FREE local telephone calls and high-speed Internet

HOLIDAY INN EXPRESS HOTEL & SUITES
AIRDRIE-CALGARY NORTH   *Book at AAA.com*

Phone: (403)912-1952

Hotel
$129-$179 All Year

Address: 64 E Lake Ave NE T4A 2G8 **Location:** Hwy 2, exit E Lake Crescent, 0.6 mi (1 km) n. **Facility:** Smoke free premises. 79 one-bedroom standard units, some with whirlpools. 4 stories, interior corridors. *Bath:* combo or shower only. **Parking:** on-site. **Amenities:** high-speed Internet, voice mail, irons, hair dryers. **Pool(s):** heated indoor. **Leisure Activities:** whirlpool, waterslide, exercise room. **Guest Services:** valet and coin laundry, wireless Internet. **Business Services:** meeting rooms, PC.

RAMADA INN & SUITES

Book great rates at AAA.com   Phone: 403/945-1288

Hotel
Rates not provided

Address: 191 E Lake Crescent T4A 2H7 **Location:** Hwy 2, exit E Airdrie. **Facility:** 59 units. 41 one-bedroom standard units, some with kitchens. 16 one- and 2 two-bedroom suites, some with kitchens and/or whirlpools. 4 stories, interior corridors. *Bath:* combo or shower only. **Parking:** on-site, winter plug-ins. **Amenities:** high-speed Internet, voice mail, irons, hair dryers. **Pool(s):** heated indoor. **Leisure Activities:** whirlpool, waterslide, exercise room. **Guest Services:** valet and coin laundry, wireless Internet. **Business Services:** meeting rooms, PC (fee). **Free Special Amenities: continental breakfast and high-speed Internet.**

SUPER 8 AIRDRIE

Book at AAA.com   Phone: (403)948-4188

Hotel
$109-$155 All Year

Address: 815 E Lake Blvd T4A 2G4 **Location:** Hwy 2, exit E Airdrie, 0.5 mi (0.8 km) e on Hwy 587 E. **Facility:** Smoke free premises. 49 units. 47 one- and 2 two-bedroom standard units. 3 stories, interior corridors. **Parking:** on-site, winter plug-ins. **Amenities:** hair dryers. **Guest Services:** coin laundry, wireless Internet.

——— WHERE TO DINE ———

SMITTY'S

Phone: 403/945-1225

International
$7-$20

The family-oriented restaurant satisfies patrons with its ever-popular all-day breakfast items, as well as tasty and wholesome soups and salads at lunchtime. A relaxed mood characterizes the dining space. Casual dress. **Reservations:** not accepted. **Hours:** 6 am-9 pm. Closed major holidays. **Address:** 191 E Lake Crescent T4A 1H3 **Location:** Hwy 2, exit E Lake Crescent; beside Ramada Inn & Suites. **Parking:** on-site.

COCHRANE pop. 13,760

BEST WESTERN HARVEST COUNTRY INN

Book great rates at AAA.com   Phone: (403)932-1410

Hotel
$90-$160 All Year

Address: 11 West Side Dr T4C 1M1 **Location:** Jct Hwy 1A, 0.3 mi (0.5 km) s on Hwy 22; just e on Quigley Dr, then just s. **Facility:** Smoke free premises. 48 one-bedroom standard units, some with whirlpools. 3 stories (no elevator), interior/exterior corridors. **Parking:** on-site, winter plug-ins. **Amenities:** high-speed Internet, voice mail, irons, hair dryers. **Leisure Activities:** exercise room. **Guest Services:** valet and coin laundry, wireless Internet. **Business Services:** meeting rooms, PC (fee). **Free Special Amenities: expanded continental breakfast and local telephone calls.**

AAA Benefit:
Members save up to 20%, plus 10% bonus points with rewards program.

DAYS INN & SUITES COCHRANE

Phone: 403/932-5588

Hotel
$109-$169 3/1-9/15
$99-$139 9/16-2/28

Address: 5 West Side Dr T4C 1M1 **Location:** Jct Hwy 1A, 0.3 mi (0.5 km) s on Hwy 22, just e on Quigley Dr, then just s. **Facility:** 61 units. 55 one-bedroom standard units, some with efficiencies, kitchens and/or whirlpools. 6 one-bedroom suites. 4 stories, interior corridors. *Bath:* combo or shower only. **Parking:** on-site, winter plug-ins. **Terms:** check-in 4 pm, cancellation fee imposed. **Amenities:** high-speed Internet, voice mail, irons, hair dryers. **Pool(s):** heated indoor. **Leisure Activities:** exercise room. **Guest Services:** valet and coin laundry, wireless Internet. **Business Services:** meeting rooms, PC.

SUPER 8-COCHRANE

Book at AAA.com   Phone: (403)932-6355

Hotel
$143-$181 All Year

Address: 10 West Side Dr T4C 1M1 **Location:** Jct Hwy 1A, 0.3 mi (0.5 km) s on Hwy 22, just e on Quigley Dr, then just s. **Facility:** 72 units. 71 one- and 1 two-bedroom standard units, some with efficiencies and/or whirlpools. 4 stories, interior corridors. *Bath:* combo or shower only. **Parking:** on-site, winter plug-ins. **Amenities:** high-speed Internet, voice mail, irons, hair dryers. *Some:* DVD players, video games (fee). **Pool(s):** heated indoor. **Leisure Activities:** whirlpool, waterslide, exercise room. **Guest Services:** valet and coin laundry, wireless Internet. **Business Services:** meeting rooms, PC (fee).

——— WHERE TO DINE ———

BLUE DOG CAFE

Phone: 403/932-4282

Cajun
$10-$26

With a touch of jazz and a taste of funk, the eclectic cafe offers an intimate, memorable dining experience in this small town. The dining room has a mere 15 tables. On the menu are Cajun specialty dishes, including jambalaya and catfish. Casual dress. **Bar:** Full bar. **Reservations:** suggested. **Hours:** 11 am-10 pm. Closed: 1/1, 12/24-12/26; also Mon. **Address:** 110 Third Ave W T0L 0W0 **Location:** Hwy 1A, 2 blks w. **Parking:** on-site.

HQ COFFEE & PIE EMPORIUM

Phone: 403/932-2111

Canadian
$11-$18

A cozy, country atmosphere awaits patrons at this restaurant, known throughout the province for its "splurgeworthy" homemade pies, of which there are usually more than 45 varieties. Homemade comfort foods range from quiches to soups to sandwiches. Also available is an extensive breakfast menu. Casual dress. **Bar:** Full bar. **Reservations:** accepted. **Hours:** 10 am-5 pm. Closed: 1/1, 12/24, 12/25. **Address:** 216 1st St W T4C 1B3 **Location:** Downtown. **Parking:** on-site.

PRAIRIE SMOKE RESTAURANT

Phone: 403/932-9001

▼▼ ▼▼
Canadian
$8-$24

Located a few steps away from the hotels, this stylish restaurant offers diners a comfortable setting to enjoy its extensive menu. Featuring Alberta beef, many items ranging from steaks, shish kebabs, shrimps and chicken are charbroiled to order. The restaurant also offers a full range of hamburgers and chicken dishes. Casual dress. **Bar:** Full bar. **Reservations:** suggested. **Hours:** 11 am-10 pm. Closed: 1/1, 12/24, 12/25. **Address:** 19 Westside Dr T4C 1M1 **Location:** Hwy 1A, 0.6 mi (1 km) sw on Hwy 22. **Parking:** on-site.

OKOTOKS pop. 17,145

LAKEVIEW INNS & SUITES   *Book great rates at AAA.com*

Phone: (403)938-7400

ⓒⒶⒶ SAVE
▼▼ ▼▼
Hotel
$129-$149 All Year

Address: 22 Southridge Dr T1S 1N1 **Location:** Hwy 2, exit 2A, 2.5 mi (4 km) s to Southridge Dr. **Facility:** 64 units. 41 one-bedroom standard units. 23 one-bedroom suites, some with whirlpools. 2 stories, interior corridors. **Parking:** on-site, winter plug-ins. **Terms:** 14 day cancellation notice-fee imposed. **Amenities:** video library, DVD players, voice mail, irons, hair dryers. *Some:* high-speed Internet. **Leisure Activities:** exercise room. **Guest Services:** coin laundry, wireless Internet. **Business Services:** meeting rooms, PC. **Free Special Amenities: continental breakfast and local telephone calls.** 〔ECO〕 🛗 🖫 🖥 📷 🖵 /SOME UNITS FEE 🐾 ✕

STRATHMORE pop. 10,225

BEST WESTERN STRATHMORE INN   *Book great rates at AAA.com*

Phone: (403)934-5777

ⓒⒶⒶ SAVE
▼▼ ▼▼
Hotel
$110-$131 All Year

Address: 550 Hwy 1 T1P 1M6 **Location:** Trans-Canada Hwy 1, jct SR 817; centre. **Facility:** Smoke free premises. 81 units. 54 one- and 14 two-bedroom standard units. 11 one- and 2 two-bedroom suites, some with whirlpools. 3 stories (no elevator), interior corridors. **Parking:** on-site, winter plug-ins. **Terms:** check-in 4 pm. **Amenities:** high-speed Internet (fee), voice mail, irons, hair dryers. *Some:* DVD players. **Pool(s):** heated indoor. **Leisure Activities:** whirlpool, barbecue area, exercise room. **Guest Services:** complimentary laundry, wireless Internet. **Business Services:** meeting rooms, PC. **Free Special Amenities: expanded continental breakfast and room upgrade (subject to availability with advance reservations).**

🛗 🖘 ✕ ✕ 🖫 🖥 🖵 /SOME UNITS FEE 🐾

> **AAA Benefit:**
> Members save up to 20%, plus 10% bonus points with rewards program.

HOLIDAY INN EXPRESS HOTEL & SUITES   *Book at AAA.com*

Phone: (403)934-1134

▼▼▼
Hotel
$140-$150 7/1-2/28
$135-$145 3/1-6/30

Address: 400 Ranch Market T1P 0B2 **Location:** Trans-Canada Hwy 1, just n at Lakeside Blvd (Centre St). **Facility:** Smoke free premises. 102 one-bedroom standard units, some with whirlpools. 4 stories, interior corridors. **Bath:** combo or shower only. **Parking:** on-site. **Amenities:** high-speed Internet, voice mail, irons, hair dryers. **Pool(s):** heated indoor. **Leisure Activities:** whirlpool, waterslide, exercise room. **Guest Services:** complimentary laundry, wireless Internet. **Business Services:** meeting rooms, PC.

ASK CALL 🔊🖳 🖘 ✕ ✕ 🎥 🖫 🖥 🖵 /SOME UNITS FEE 🐾

TRAVELODGE STRATHMORE   *Book at AAA.com*

Phone: (403)901-0000

▼▼▼▼
Hotel
$134-$144 6/1-2/28
$119-$126 3/1-5/31

Address: 350 Ridge Rd T1P 1B5 **Location:** Just n of Trans-Canada Hwy 1 at Ridge Rd. **Facility:** 121 units. 116 one-bedroom standard units, some with kitchens and/or whirlpools. 2 one- and 3 two-bedroom suites, some with whirlpools. 3 stories, interior corridors. **Parking:** on-site, winter plug-ins. **Terms:** check-in 4 pm, cancellation fee imposed. **Amenities:** high-speed Internet, voice mail, irons, hair dryers. *Some:* DVD players. **Pool(s):** heated indoor. **Leisure Activities:** whirlpool, waterslide, exercise room. **Guest Services:** valet and coin laundry. **Business Services:** conference facilities, business center. ASK 🛗 🖘 ✕ 🎥 🖫 🖥 🖵 /SOME UNITS FEE 🐾 ✕

—————— **WHERE TO DINE** ——————

STRATHMORE STATION RESTAURANT & PUB

Phone: 403/934-0000

ⓒⒶⒶ
▼▼ ▼▼
Canadian
$8-$22

Families and groups alike will enjoy the nostalgia of the Strathmore Station, which has a medley of comfort foods, including pizza, steak, pasta and oversize salads. Railway enthusiasts will enjoy the train decor, complete with black-and-white photos from the railway days, large colorful murals and a special caboose dining car. Casual dress. **Bar:** Full bar. **Reservations:** accepted. **Hours:** 10 am-11 pm. Closed: 12/25. **Address:** 380 Ridge Rd T1P 1B5 **Location:** Trans-Canada Hwy 1, just w of jct SR 817. **Parking:** on-site.

This ends listings for the Calgary Vicinity.
The following page resumes the alphabetical listings of cities in Alberta.

CAMROSE pop. 15,620

NORSEMEN INN

Hotel
$99-$129 All Year

Phone: 780/672-9171

Address: 6505 48th Ave T4V 3K3 **Location:** Hwy 13 (48th Ave) at 65th St; west end of town. **Facility:** Smoke free premises. 76 one-bedroom standard units, some with whirlpools. 4 stories, interior corridors. *Bath:* combo or shower only. **Parking:** on-site, winter plug-ins. **Amenities:** high-speed Internet, irons, hair dryers. **Leisure Activities:** *Fee:* game room. **Guest Services:** valet laundry, wireless Internet. **Business Services:** conference facilities, PC (fee).

ASK ▯ ⊻ ✕ ▤ ▤ ▤ ▯ / SOME UNITS FEE 🐾

R & R INN AND SUITES CAMROSE

Hotel
$85-$114 All Year

Phone: 780/672-2292

Address: 6508 48th Ave (Hwy 13) T4V 3A3 **Location:** Hwy 13 (48th Ave) at 66th St; west end of town. **Facility:** 45 one-bedroom standard units, some with whirlpools. 2 stories (no elevator), interior/exterior corridors. **Parking:** on-site, winter plug-ins. **Terms:** cancellation fee imposed. **Amenities:** high-speed Internet, voice mail, hair dryers. *Some:* irons. **Leisure Activities:** sauna, whirlpool. **Guest Services:** coin laundry. **Business Services:** meeting rooms, PC (fee).

ASK ▯ ▤ ▤ ▤ ▤ ▯ / SOME UNITS ✕

——— **WHERE TO DINE** ———

MONTE CARLO RESTAURANT

Steak
$9-$33

Phone: 780/672-1040

One of the most popular places in town, the restaurant draws flocks of locals for lunch. Among menu choices are steaks, pizzas, pasta dishes and entree-size salads. Service is fast and friendly, and the atmosphere is casual. Casual dress. **Bar:** Full bar. **Reservations:** accepted. **Hours:** 11 am-9 pm, Fri-10 pm, Sat 11:30 am-10 pm, Sun 11:30 am-8 pm, Mon 11 am-8 pm. Closed major holidays. **Address:** 4907 48th Ave T4V 0J4 **Location:** Corner of 49th St and Hwy 13 (48th Ave). **Parking:** on-site.

CANMORE pop. 12,039

BANFF BOUNDARY LODGE *Book great rates at AAA.com*

Condominium
$89-$239 All Year

Phone: (403)678-9555

Address: 1000 Harvie Heights Rd T1W 2W2 **Location:** Trans-Canada Hwy 1, exit 86, just n. **Facility:** Smoke free premises. 42 units. 14 one- and 28 two-bedroom suites with kitchens. 1-2 stories (no elevator), exterior corridors. **Parking:** on-site, winter plug-ins. **Terms:** office hours 8 am-8 pm, check-in 4 pm, 3 day cancellation notice-fee imposed. **Amenities:** video library (fee), hair dryers. **Leisure Activities:** whirlpool, picnic area with gas barbecue. **Guest Services:** coin laundry, wireless Internet. **Business Services:** meeting rooms, PC (fee).

✕ ▤ ▤ ▤ ▯ / SOME UNITS FEE 🐾

BEST WESTERN POCATERRA INN *Book great rates at AAA.com*

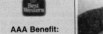

Hotel
$120-$210 All Year

Phone: (403)678-4334

Address: 1725 Mountain Ave T1W 2W1 **Location:** Trans-Canada Hwy 1, exit 86, 1.3 mi (2.1 km) e. **Facility:** Smoke free premises. 83 units. 81 one-bedroom standard units, some with whirlpools. 2 one-bedroom suites with whirlpools. 4 stories, interior corridors. **Parking:** on-site, winter plug-ins. **Terms:** check-in 4 pm, cancellation fee imposed. **Amenities:** dual phone lines, voice mail, irons, hair dryers. **Pool(s):** heated indoor. **Leisure Activities:** sauna, whirlpool, steamroom, waterslide, exercise room. **Guest Services:** valet and coin laundry, wireless Internet. **Business Services:** meeting rooms, business center.

AAA Benefit:
Members save up to 20%, plus 10% bonus points with rewards program.

▯ CALL ▤M 🐕 ✕ ✕ ▤ ▤ ▤ ▤ ▯ / SOME UNITS FEE 🐾

FREE continental breakfast and local telephone calls

BOW VALLEY MOTEL

Motel
$90-$130 All Year

Phone: 403/678-5085

Address: 610 8th St T1W 2B5 **Location:** Trans-Canada Hwy 1, exit 89, 1.1 mi (1.8 km) se. **Facility:** Smoke free premises. 25 one-bedroom standard units, some with efficiencies. 1-3 stories (no elevator), exterior corridors. **Parking:** on-site, winter plug-ins. **Terms:** office hours 8 am-11 pm, cancellation fee imposed. **Amenities:** voice mail, hair dryers. **Leisure Activities:** whirlpool. **Guest Services:** coin laundry, wireless Internet.

ASK ▯ ✕ ▤ ▯ / SOME UNITS ▤

CANADIAN ROCKIES CHALETS *Book great rates at AAA.com*

Condominium
$79-$275 All Year

Phone: (403)678-3799

Address: 1206 Bow Valley Tr T1W 1N6 **Location:** Trans-Canada Hwy 1, exit 89, 0.9 mi (1.5 km) se. **Facility:** Smoke free premises. 40 units. 20 two- and 20 three-bedroom suites with kitchens. 3 stories (no elevator), exterior corridors. **Parking:** on-site, winter plug-ins. **Terms:** check-in 4 pm, 3 day cancellation notice-fee imposed. **Amenities:** video library (fee), DVD players, high-speed Internet, voice mail, hair dryers. *Some:* irons. **Leisure Activities:** whirlpool, barbecues. **Guest Services:** wireless Internet. **Business Services:** meeting rooms, PC.

▯ ✕ ▤ ▤ ▤ ▤ ▯ / SOME UNITS FEE 🐾

CANMORE INN & SUITES   *Book at AAA.com*   Phone: (403)609-4656

Hotel
$79-$262 All Year

Address: 1402 Bow Valley Tr T1W 1N5 **Location:** Trans-Canada Hwy 1, exit 89, 1 mi (1.7 km) se. Located next to railway tracks. **Facility:** Smoke free premises. 189 units. 187 one-bedroom standard units, some with efficiencies and/or whirlpools. 1 one- and 1 two-bedroom suites with kitchens and whirlpools. 3 stories, interior corridors. *Bath:* combo or shower only. **Parking:** on-site, winter plug-ins. **Terms:** check-in 4 pm, cancellation fee imposed. **Amenities:** voice mail, safes, irons, hair dryers. **Pool(s):** heated indoor. **Leisure Activities:** whirlpool, waterslide, exercise room. **Guest Services:** valet and coin laundry, wireless Internet. **Business Services:** meeting rooms, PC (fee).

ECONO LODGE CANMORE   *Book great rates at AAA.com*   Phone: (403)678-5488

(AAA) (SAVE)

Hotel
$120-$150 5/14-2/28
$90-$120 3/1-5/13

Address: 1602 2nd Ave T1W 1M8 **Location:** Trans-Canada Hwy 1, exit 89, 1.3 mi (2.1 km) e. **Facility:** Smoke free premises. 61 one-bedroom standard units, some with efficiencies. 2 stories (no elevator), interior corridors. **Parking:** on-site, winter plug-ins. **Terms:** check-in 4 pm. **Amenities:** voice mail, irons, hair dryers. *Some:* DVD players. **Dining:** Chez Francois, see separate listing. **Leisure Activities:** whirlpool, limited exercise equipment. **Guest Services:** wireless Internet. **Business Services:** meeting rooms, PC.

FREE continental breakfast

FALCON CREST LODGE   *Book great rates at AAA.com*   Phone: (403)678-6150

(AAA) (SAVE)

Condominium
$159-$329 All Year

Address: 190 Kananaskis Way T1W 3K5 **Location:** Trans-Canada Hwy 1, exit 89, 1.2 mi (2 km) s. **Facility:** Units in this family-friendly property feature a comfortable contemporary decor with fireplaces and in-suite laundry facilities. Smoke free premises. 68 units. 18 one-bedroom standard units with efficiencies. 42 one- and 8 two-bedroom suites with kitchens. 4 stories, interior corridors. **Parking:** on-site. **Terms:** 3 day cancellation notice-fee imposed. **Amenities:** DVD players, irons, hair dryers. **Leisure Activities:** whirlpools, limited exercise equipment. **Guest Services:** complimentary laundry, wireless Internet. **Business Services:** PC (fee). *(See color ad p 379)*

FIRE MOUNTAIN LODGE   *Book at AAA.com*   Phone: (403)609-9949

Condominium
$180-$440 All Year

Address: 121 Kananaskis Way T1W 2X2 **Location:** Trans-Canada Hwy 1, exit 89, 1 mi (1.6 km) s. **Facility:** Smoke free premises. 24 units. 19 two- and 5 three-bedroom suites with kitchens. 2 stories (no elevator), exterior corridors. **Parking:** on-site. **Terms:** off-site registration, 1-2 night minimum stay - seasonal and/or weekends. **Amenities:** DVD players, voice mail, irons, hair dryers. **Leisure Activities:** whirlpool, exercise room. **Guest Services:** complimentary and valet laundry, wireless Internet.

HOTEL OF THE ROCKIES   *Book great rates at AAA.com*   Phone: (403)609-4422

(AAA) (SAVE)

Hotel
$110-$300 All Year

Address: #1 Silver Tip Tr T1W 2Z7 **Location:** Trans-Canada Hwy 1, exit 89, just s. **Facility:** Smoke free premises. 99 units. 94 one-bedroom standard units, some with whirlpools. 5 one-bedroom suites. 3 stories, interior corridors. *Bath:* combo or shower only. **Parking:** on-site, winter plug-ins. **Amenities:** video games (fee), voice mail, irons, hair dryers. **Leisure Activities:** whirlpool, hiking trails, exercise room. **Business Services:** meeting rooms, PC. **Free Special Amenities:** local telephone calls and high-speed Internet.

THE LADY MACDONALD COUNTRY INN   Phone: (403)678-3665

(AAA) (SAVE)

Country Inn
$110-$250 All Year

Address: 1201 Bow Valley Tr T1W 1P5 **Location:** Trans-Canada Hwy 1, exit 89, 1 mi (1.6 km) sw. **Facility:** A retreat-like ambiance enhances the upscale country inn, which features individually decorated rooms and a Victorian-style dining room. Smoke free premises. 12 units. 11 one- and 1 two-bedroom standard units, some with whirlpools. 2 stories (no elevator), interior corridors. *Bath:* combo or shower only. **Parking:** on-site, winter plug-ins. **Terms:** office hours 7:30 am-7:30 pm. **Amenities:** voice mail, hair dryers. **Leisure Activities:** *Fee:* massage. **Guest Services:** wireless Internet. **Free Special Amenities:** full breakfast and high-speed Internet.

THE LODGES AT CANMORE   *Book at AAA.com*   Phone: (403)678-9350

Condominium
$132-$385 All Year

Address: 107 Montane Rd T1W 3J2 **Location:** Trans-Canada Hwy 1, exit 86, 0.5 mi (0.8 km) s. **Facility:** Smoke free premises. 54 units. 8 one-bedroom standard units with kitchens. 16 one- and 30 two-bedroom suites with kitchens. 3 stories, interior corridors. **Parking:** on-site. **Terms:** check-in 4 pm. **Amenities:** DVD players, CD players, voice mail, irons, hair dryers. **Pool(s):** heated outdoor. **Leisure Activities:** whirlpools, exercise room. **Guest Services:** complimentary and valet laundry, wireless Internet, indoor heated parking. **Business Services:** meeting rooms, PC (fee).

MYSTIC SPRINGS CHALETS & HOT POOLS *Book at AAA.com* Phone: (403)609-0333

Condominium
$180-$380 All Year

Address: 140 Kananaskis Way T1W 2X2 **Location:** Trans-Canada Hwy 1, exit 89, 1.1 mi (1.8 km) s. **Facility:** Featuring an outdoor saltwater pool, a barbecue area and upscale accommodations, this property offers amenities from martini glasses to DVD players. Smoke free premises. 44 two-bedroom suites with kitchens. 2 stories (no elevator), exterior corridors. **Parking:** on-site. **Terms:** office hours 7 am-11 pm, check-in 4 pm. **Amenities:** DVD players, CD players, high-speed Internet, voice mail, irons, hair dryers. **Pool(s):** heated outdoor. **Leisure Activities:** whirlpool, limited exercise equipment. *Fee:* massage. **Guest Services:** valet and coin laundry. **Business Services:** meeting rooms.

QUALITY RESORT-CHATEAU CANMORE *Book great rates at AAA.com* Phone: (403)678-6699

Hotel
$150-$200 6/14-2/28
$125-$155 3/1-6/13

Address: 1720 Bow Valley Tr T1W 2X3 **Location:** Trans-Canada Hwy 1, exit 86, 0.5 mi (0.8 km) s. **Facility:** Smoke free premises. 93 units. 26 one-bedroom standard units, some with whirlpools. 67 one-bedroom suites. 4 stories, interior/exterior corridors. **Parking:** on-site, winter plug-ins. **Terms:** check-in 4 pm, cancellation fee imposed. **Amenities:** video library (fee), voice mail, irons, hair dryers. *Some:* DVD players. **Pool(s):** heated indoor. **Leisure Activities:** sauna, whirlpool, hot tub, lighted tennis court, exercise room, spa. **Guest Services:** valet and coin laundry, wireless Internet, tanning facilities. **Business Services:** meeting rooms, business center. **Free Special Amenities:** local telephone calls and newspaper.

RADISSON HOTEL & CONFERENCE CENTRE *Book great rates at AAA.com* Phone: 403/678-3625

Hotel
Rates not provided

Address: 511 Bow Valley Tr T1W 1N7 **Location:** Trans-Canada Hwy 1, exit 89, 1.4 mi (0.8 km) s. **Facility:** Smoke free premises. 224 units. 214 one-bedroom standard units, some with efficiencies. 2 one- and 2 two-bedroom suites, some with kitchens and/or whirlpools. 2-3 stories, interior/exterior corridors. *Bath:* combo or shower only. **Parking:** on-site, winter plug-ins. **Terms:** check-in 4 pm. **Amenities:** high-speed Internet, voice mail, irons, hair dryers. **Pool(s):** heated indoor. **Leisure Activities:** whirlpool, steamroom, picnic area, playground, exercise room. **Guest Services:** valet and coin laundry, wireless Internet. **Business Services:** conference facilities, PC (fee).

ROCKY MOUNTAIN SKI LODGE Phone: (403)678-5445

Motel
$119-$209 All Year

Address: 1711 Bow Valley Tr T1W 2T8 **Location:** Trans-Canada Hwy 1, exit 86, 0.5 mi (0.8 km) s. Located in a commercial area. **Facility:** Smoke free premises. 82 units. 40 one-bedroom standard units, some with efficiencies. 40 one- and 2 two-bedroom suites. 1-2 stories (no elevator), exterior corridors. **Parking:** on-site, winter plug-ins. **Terms:** office hours 7 am-11 pm, cancellation fee imposed. **Amenities:** voice mail, hair dryers. *Some:* DVD players. **Leisure Activities:** sauna, whirlpool, wax room, ski & bike storage, playground. **Guest Services:** coin laundry, wireless Internet. **Business Services:** meeting rooms, PC.

FREE newspaper and high-speed Internet

RUNDLE MOUNTAIN LODGE Phone: 403/678-5322

Motel
$75-$210 All Year

Address: 1723 Bow Valley Tr T1W 1L7 **Location:** Trans-Canada Hwy 1, exit 86, 0.5 mi (0.8 km) s. **Facility:** Smoke free premises. 61 units. 47 one- and 6 two-bedroom standard units, some with efficiencies, kitchens and/or whirlpools. 6 one- and 2 two-bedroom suites with kitchens. 1-2 stories (no elevator), exterior corridors. **Parking:** on-site, winter plug-ins. **Terms:** office hours 7 am-11 pm, check-in 4 pm, 7 day cancellation notice-fee imposed. **Amenities:** *Some:* DVD players, hair dryers. **Pool(s):** heated indoor. **Leisure Activities:** whirlpool, playground. **Guest Services:** coin laundry, wireless Internet. **Business Services:** meeting rooms.

WINDTOWER LODGE & SUITES *Book at AAA.com* Phone: (403)609-6600

Condominium
$149-$429 All Year

Address: 160 Kananaskis Way T1W 3E2 **Location:** Trans-Canada Hwy 1, exit 89, 1.1 mi (1.8 km) s. **Facility:** Smoke free premises. 105 units. 49 one-bedroom standard units. 56 one-bedroom suites with kitchens. 2 stories, interior corridors. *Bath:* combo or shower only. **Parking:** on-site (fee) and street. **Terms:** check-in 4 pm, 2 night minimum stay - seasonal, 3 day cancellation notice-fee imposed. **Amenities:** voice mail, hair dryers. *Some:* irons. **Leisure Activities:** whirlpool, putting green, exercise room. **Guest Services:** wireless Internet. **Business Services:** meeting rooms, PC (fee).

—— WHERE TO DINE ——

BEAMER'S COFFEE BAR Phone: 403/678-3988

Coffee/Tea
$3-$10

In a convenient spot, the contemporary coffeehouse draws both locals and those en route to the ski hills. Among healthy offerings are magnificent muffins, soups, breakfast bagels and, of course, Beamer's coffee. Big boy sandwiches are built on the premises with fresh, multigrain bread and a choice of toppings. For those with a sweet tooth, the display case features some tempting choices. Casual dress. **Reservations:** not accepted. **Hours:** 6 am-6 pm. Closed: 12/25. **Address:** 1702A Bow Valley Tr T1W 1N5 **Location:** Trans-Canada Hwy 1, exit 86, 0.5 mi (0.8 km) s. **Parking:** on-site.

CHEF'S STUDIO JAPAN

Japanese
$14-$28

Phone: 403/609-838:

If you're craving sushi, this restaurant is a treat. Its location, between two art galleries, appears to hav inspired the chef, who utilizes fresh, high-quality ingredients to create Japanese works of art. Casual dress **Bar:** Full bar. **Reservations:** suggested. **Hours:** 5:30 pm-10:30 pm. Closed: 1/1, 12/25; also Tues **Address:** 108-709 8th (Main) St T1W 2B2 **Location:** Between 6th and 7th aves; down a small lanewa behind Bank of Montreal; downtown. **Parking:** on-site and street.

CHEZ FRANCOIS

French
$8-$40

Phone: 403/678-611

This fine-dining establishment features classic French cuisine, seafood and pasta. This is a popular plac with locals. Casual dress. **Bar:** Full bar. **Reservations:** suggested. **Hours:** 7 am-2 & 5-10 pm **Address:** 1602 2nd Ave T1W 1P7 **Location:** Trans-Canada Hwy 1, exit 89, 1.3 mi (2.1 km) e; in Canmor Mountain Lodge. **Parking:** on-site. CALL ♿M

CRAIG'S WAY STATION

Canadian
$7-$15

Phone: 403/678-265(

Well suited for family dining, this casual diner offers great mountain views through large windows and coz seating in front of a stone fireplace. Popular comfort foods include fresh beef burgers, clam chowder, club c Western Denver sandwiches, Salisbury steak with onions and mushrooms, the 10-ounce "rustler" Albert steak, veal cutlets, chicken fettuccine and stir-fries. Steak and eggs, blueberry pancakes and othe breakfast items are served all day, and kids can order from the children's menu. Casual dress. **Bar:** Beer & wine. **Reservations:** not accepted. **Hours:** 6 am-10 pm. Closed: 12/25. **Address:** 1727 Mountain Ave T1V 2W1 **Location:** 3.6 mi (5.8 km) e of Banff National Park east gate on Hwy 1A (Bow Valley Tr). **Parking** on-site.

CRAZYWEED KITCHEN

Canadian
$10-$36

Phone: 403/609-253(

This contemporary bistro features a high ceiling and sleek upscale design. The menu highlights a variety c innovative food pairings in such dishes as Alaskan sablefish, wood-oven roasted sockeye salmon, Tha grilled chicken, red curry seafood bowl, 12-ounce Sterling rib-eye steaks and fettuccine. The youthfu waitstaff provide friendly and proficient service. Casual dress. **Bar:** Full bar. **Reservations:** accepted, fo dinner. **Hours:** noon-3 & 6-close. Closed: 1/1, 12/25, 12/26. **Address:** 1600 Railway Ave T1W 1P(**Location:** Centre. **Parking:** on-site.

THE GRIZZLY PAW BREWING COMPANY

Canadian
$8-$28

Phone: 403/678-998:

A taste of local ales awaits at the popular brew pub, where beer is made on site. The menu features a variety of hearty pub food, ranging from hamburgers to fish and chips, jalapeno poppers, soups and salads For a casual meal, this is a popular spot. Casual dress. **Bar:** Full bar. **Reservations:** not accepted **Hours:** 11 am-10 pm, Fri & Sat-11 pm. Closed: 12/25. **Address:** 622 Main St T1W 2B: **Location:** Downtown. **Parking:** on-site.

LUNA BLUE RESTAURANT

Italian
$8-$20

Phone: 403/609-322

Almost every pasta dish on the extensive menu contains fresh pasta made locally every day. On the mai drag, the casual eatery serves hearty and healthy options in a cozy environment. Casual dress. **Bar:** Fu bar. **Reservations:** suggested. **Hours:** noon-3 & 5-9 pm, Fri & Sat-10 pm, Mon-Wed 5 pm-9 pm. Closed 12/25; also Sun. **Address:** 107-721 Main St T1W 2B2 **Location:** Jct 7th Ave; downtown. **Parking:** street.

MURRIETA'S BAR & GRILL

Western Pacific
Rim
$11-$39

Phone: 403/609-950(

Upstairs from street level, the classy, upbeat restaurant boasts West Coast cuisine, including a variety o sandwiches and salads at lunch and heartier dishes at dinner. Reservations are recommended at the popular spot in this mountain town, especially for the dinner hour. Lending to the restaurant's atmospher are cozy mountain decor, wooden accents, a lounge and a fireplace. Casual dress. **Bar:** Full bar **Reservations:** suggested. **Hours:** 11 am-10 pm. **Address:** 200, 737 Main St T1W 2B2 **Location:** Corner o 7th and Main sts; on 2nd level; downtown. **Parking:** street.

PATRINOS STEAKHOUSE & PUB

Canadian
$11-$27

Phone: 403/678-406(

The simple, family-run, roadside restaurant features a good selection of comfort foods, ranging from pizza and pasta to steaks. Guests can eat in the casual dining room or grab something in the lounge next doo Expect friendly, attentive service. Casual dress. **Bar:** Full bar. **Reservations:** suggested. **Hours:** 11 am-1 pm, Sun from 10 am. Closed: 12/25. **Address:** 1602 Bow Valley Tr T1W 1N5 **Location:** At 15th St **Parking:** on-site. CALL ♿M

QUARRY BISTRO

Provincial French
$13-$32

Phone: 403/678-608(

Along the city's main street, the restaurant displays simple, contemporary and chic decor. A collection o locally and seasonally inspired dishes, the menu is rooted in the classic French and Italian Provincial style Choices might include macaroni and cheese, dry-aged Alberta beef and organically raised rainbow trout chicken and bison. The popular brunch menu may feature creative preparations of French toast, egg-bage sandwiches and cheese frittata. Servers willingly share wine descriptions. Casual dress. **Bar:** Full bar **Reservations:** suggested. **Hours:** 11:30 am-3 & 5-10 pm, Sat & Sun from 9 am; Saturday & Sunday brunch; seasonal hours may vary. Closed major holidays; also Wed. **Address:** 718 Main St T1W 2B(**Location:** Downtown. **Parking:** street.

RAILWAY DELI

Deli
$7-$14

Phone: 403/678-363

Serving breakfast and lunch, this cafeteria-style deli offers a varied menu of traditional morning meals to lunch specials of fresh soup, assorted meat and veggie pies, quiche, rotisserie chicken, sandwiches burgers and schnitzel. Although the cafeteria closes after lunch, the delicatessen remains open and offers the perfect spot to grab cheeses, bread, sausage, pastries and pies, and frozen soups and stews to take back to the hotel or to make up a picnic lunch. Casual dress. **Bar:** Beer & wine. **Reservations:** no accepted. **Hours:** 9 am-3 pm, Sat-7 pm. Closed major holidays; also Sun & Mon. **Address:** 702 Bow Valley Tr, Unit 101 T1W 2H4 **Location:** Trans-Canada Hwy 1, exit 89, 0.7 mi (1.1 km) s. **Parking:** on-site.

CALL ♿M

ROCKY MOUNTAIN FLATBREAD COMPANY

Phone: 403/609-5508

◆◆ ◆◆
Pizza
$12-$30

The comfortable, casual restaurant offers diners a wide selection of thin-crust pizzas, fresh soup and pasta and home-baked desserts, many of which are cooked in the hand-built masonry oven. The menu features many organic and oceanwise ingredients and has initiatives in place to help support the environment. Casual dress. **Bar:** Full bar. **Reservations:** accepted. **Hours:** Open 7/1-9/1; 5 pm-9 pm. Closed major holidays; also Mon & Tues. **Address:** 838 10th St, Unit 101 T1W 2A8 **Location:** Corner of 8th Ave and 10th St; downtown. **Parking:** on-site and street.

SAGE BISTRO

Phone: 403/678-4878

◆◆ ◆◆
Canadian
$16-$30

On its own by the gas station, this log cabin would be easy to drive by. Inside this rustic space, the kitchen elevates Canadian comfort food to new levels by using local products, including produce and game. Casual dress. **Bar:** Full bar. **Reservations:** suggested. **Hours:** Open 3/1-10/31 & 11/27-2/28; 5 pm-9 pm, Fri-10 pm, Sat 9 am-10 pm, Sun 9 am-9 pm. Closed: 12/25; also Wed. **Address:** 1712 Bow Valley Tr T1W 1P2 **Location:** 3.1 mi (5.2 km) e of Banff National Park east gate on Hwy 1A (Bow Valley Tr); jct 17th St. **Parking:** on-site.

TAPAS RESTAURANT

Phone: 403/609-0583

◆◆◆ ◆◆◆
Mediterranean
$8-$20

Diners should come in groups to sample and savor the widest variety of memorable tapas preparations. Drawing on influences from both Spain and Portugal, selections are mouthwatering. Delicious favorites include fiery sweet potato tapas, eggplant and paella for two. The casual spot is popular with locals and visitors alike for its comfortable surroundings and superb food. Casual dress. **Bar:** Full bar. **Reservations:** suggested. **Hours:** 11 am-11 pm; from 5 pm in winter. Closed major holidays. **Address:** 633 10th St T1W 2A2 **Location:** Downtown; next to Paintbox Lodge. **Parking:** street. CALL ⌖M

THE TROUGH DINING CO.

Phone: 403/678-2820

◆◆◆ ◆◆◆
Canadian
$24-$38

Don't be duped by the name as this small but warm, welcoming and inviting restaurant offers imaginative Canadian cuisine incorporating fresh local and regional ingredients into outstanding dishes such as the Unpredictable Caesar Salad or Asian Valbella Pork Tenderloin. Service is unfussy but highly competent and don't be surprised to see some extra treats served along with your menu choices. Casual dress. **Bar:** Full bar. **Reservations:** suggested. **Hours:** 6 pm-9 pm, Fri & Sat from 5:30 pm; from 5:30 pm 7/1-8/31. Closed major holidays; also Tues. **Address:** 725 9th St T1W 2V7 **Location:** Downtown; on Walk of Champions. **Parking:** street.

CARDSTON pop. 3,452

SOUTH COUNTRY INN

Phone: 403/653-8000

◆◆◆ ◆◆
Hotel
$73-$135 All Year

Address: 404 Main St T0K 0K0 **Location:** On Hwy 2; centre. **Facility:** Smoke free premises. 45 units. 40 one- and 5 two-bedroom standard units, some with whirlpools. 2 stories (no elevator), interior corridors. **Parking:** on-site, winter plug-ins. **Amenities:** hair dryers. Some: irons. **Pool(s):** indoor. **Leisure Activities:** whirlpool. **Guest Services:** coin laundry, wireless Internet, tanning facilities. **Business Services:** meeting rooms. ASK ⑪ 🕭 ✕ / SOME UNITS 🖥

------ **WHERE TO DINE** ------

THE COBBLESTONE MANOR DINING ROOM

Phone: 403/653-2701

◆◆ ◆◆
Canadian
$11-$38

This little restaurant is located in a historic house listed as one of National Geographic's Crowns of the Continent. Completed in 1926, the restaurant has three rooms with distinct decor featuring hardwoods from around the world, accented by Tiffany glass. A simple menu lists such dinner entrees as maple chicken breast, wild Canadian salmon and Alberta beef, all at very reasonable prices. Casual dress. **Reservations:** suggested. **Hours:** 7 am-9 pm; from 11:30 am 9/15-6/15. Closed: 1/1, 12/25; also Sun. **Address:** 173 7th Ave W T0K 0K0 **Location:** Hwy 5 (1st Ave), 0.7 mi (1.1 km) s on Main St, then just w. **Parking:** on-site. **Classic Historic**

PIZZAS & CREAM

Phone: 403/653-4143

◆◆
Pizza
$6-$9

A play on words, the retro diner's name aptly describes its food: pizza and ice cream. Whimsical, nostalgic memorabilia ranges from Trivial Pursuit to Lite Brite to roller skates and pop bottles. Guests seat themselves in a red and silver booth and phone orders to the front counter (no prank calls, please!). Piping-hot pizza delivered atop an old-fashioned pizza stand tastes great with a frothy milkshake. Casual dress. **Reservations:** accepted. **Hours:** noon-10 pm, Fri & Sat-11 pm. Closed major holidays; also Sun. **Address:** 325 Main St T0K 0K0 **Location:** Downtown. **Parking:** street.

CLAIRMONT pop. 1,508

RAMADA INN & SUITES   *Book great rates at AAA.com*

Phone: (780)814-7448

CAA SAVE

Hotel
$149-$349 All Year

Address: 7201 99th St T0H 0W0 **Location:** Jct Hwy 43 and 2, 0.7 mi (0.4 km) n, then just e, 0.7 mi (0.4 km) s. **Facility:** 98 units. 70 one-bedroom standard units. 28 one-bedroom suites, some with whirlpools. 4 stories, interior corridors. **Parking:** on-site, winter plug-ins. **Terms:** cancellation fee imposed. **Amenities:** high-speed Internet, voice mail, irons, hair dryers. **Leisure Activities:** whirlpool, exercise room. **Guest Services:** valet and coin laundry, wireless Internet. **Business Services:** meeting rooms, PC. **Free Special Amenities:** early check-in/late check-out and high-speed Internet.

CLARESHOLM pop. 3,700

BLUEBIRD MOTEL

Phone: 403/625-3395

Motel
$84-$94 All Year

Address: 5505 1st St W T0L 0T0 **Location:** 0.3 mi (0.5 km) n on Hwy 2. **Facility:** Smoke free premises. 22 units. 14 one-bedroom standard units, some with efficiencies or kitchens. 7 one- and 1 two-bedroom suites, some with efficiencies or kitchens. 1 story, exterior corridors. *Bath:* combo or shower only. **Parking:** on-site, winter plug-ins. **Terms:** office hours 7 am-11 pm. **Amenities:** high-speed Internet, voice mail, hair dryers. *Some:* irons.

MOTEL 6 CLARESHOLM   *Book great rates at AAA.com*

Phone: 403/625-4646

Hotel
Rates not provided

Address: 11 Alberta Rd (Hwy 2) T0L 0T0 **Location:** North end of town. **Facility:** 69 one-bedroom standard units. 3 stories, interior corridors. *Bath:* combo or shower only. **Parking:** on-site, winter plug-ins. **Amenities:** high-speed Internet. **Guest Services:** coin laundry, wireless Internet. *(See color ad below)*

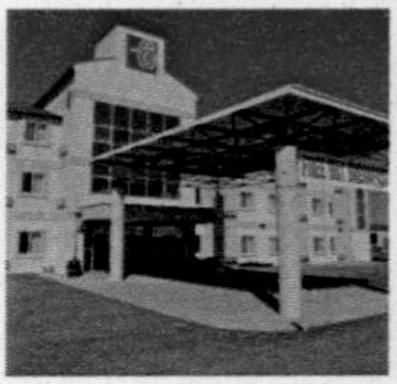

COCHRANE—See Calgary p. 429.

COLD LAKE pop. 11,991

BEST WESTERN COLD LAKE INN   *Book great rates at AAA.com*

Phone: 780/594-4888

CAA SAVE

Hotel
Rates not provided

Address: 4815 52nd St T9M 1P1 **Location:** Corner of 55th Ave (Hwy 25 and 55) and 52nd St; south end of city. **Facility:** Smoke free premises. 88 units. 85 one-bedroom standard units, some with whirlpools. 3 one-bedroom suites. 2-3 stories, interior/exterior corridors. **Parking:** on-site, winter plug-ins. **Amenities:** high-speed Internet, voice mail, irons, hair dryers. **Leisure Activities:** whirlpool, exercise room. **Guest Services:** valet laundry, wireless Internet. **Business Services:** meeting rooms, PC. **Free Special Amenities:** local telephone calls and high-speed Internet.

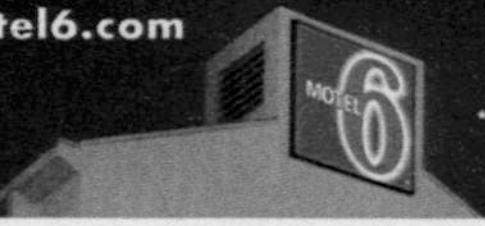

AAA Benefit:
Members save up to 20%, plus 10% bonus points with rewards program.

DEAD MAN'S FLATS

COPPERSTONE RESORT HOTEL   *Book great rates at AAA.com*

Phone: (403)678-0303

Condominium
$129-$279 All Year

Address: 250 2nd Ave T1W 2W4 **Location:** Trans-Canada Hwy 1, exit 98, just n on 2nd St, then just e. **Facility:** Spacious and upscale suites feature granite kitchen countertops, an electric fireplace, flat-screen TV, stereo system and private balcony. Smoke free premises. 70 units. 25 one- and 45 two-bedroom suites with kitchens. 2-3 stories, interior corridors. **Parking:** on-site. **Terms:** 3 day cancellation notice-fee imposed. **Amenities:** DVD players, CD players, voice mail, irons, hair dryers. **Leisure Activities:** whirlpool, exercise room. *Fee:* pool table. **Guest Services:** complimentary laundry, wireless Internet. *(See color ad p 377)*

DRAYTON VALLEY pop. 6,893

DRAYTON VALLEY RAMADA INN   *Book at AAA.com*

Phone: (780)514-7861

Hotel
$124-$133 All Year

Address: 2051 50th St T7A 1S5 **Location:** Just n on Hwy 39; south end of town. **Facility:** Smoke free premises. 82 units. 70 one-bedroom standard units, some with efficiencies. 12 one-bedroom suites, some with whirlpools. 4 stories, interior/exterior corridors. **Parking:** on-site, winter plug-ins. **Amenities:** DVD players, high-speed Internet, voice mail, irons, hair dryers. **Pool(s):** heated indoor. **Leisure Activities:** whirlpool, waterslide, exercise room. **Guest Services:** valet and coin laundry, wireless Internet. **Business Services:** meeting rooms, PC (fee).

HOLIDAY INN EXPRESS HOTEL & SUITES   *Book great rates at AAA.com*

Phone: (780)515-9888

Hotel
$109-$169 All Year

Address: 5001 Brougham Dr T7A 0A1 **Location:** Hwy 22, exit Drayton Valley, 1.5 mi (2.4 km) n; east end of town. **Facility:** 96 units. 89 one-bedroom standard units, some with whirlpools. 7 one-bedroom suites. 3 stories, interior corridors. **Parking:** on-site, winter plug-ins. **Terms:** cancellation fee imposed. **Amenities:** high-speed Internet, dual phone lines, voice mail, irons, hair dryers. **Leisure Activities:** whirlpool, exercise room. **Guest Services:** valet and coin laundry, wireless Internet. **Business Services:** meeting rooms, PC. **Free Special Amenities:** expanded continental breakfast and high-speed Internet. *(See color ad on insert)*

LAKEVIEW INNS & SUITES   *Book great rates at AAA.com*

Phone: (780)542-3200

Hotel
$113-$150 All Year

Address: 4302 50th St T7A 1M4 **Location:** Hwy 22, exit Drayton Valley, 1.5 mi (2.4 km) n; east end of town. **Facility:** 91 units. 82 one-bedroom standard units, some with whirlpools. 9 one-bedroom suites. 3 stories (no elevator), interior corridors. **Parking:** on-site, winter plug-ins. **Amenities:** video library, DVD players, high-speed Internet, irons, hair dryers. **Leisure Activities:** sauna, whirlpool, exercise room. **Guest Services:** coin laundry, wireless Internet. **Business Services:** meeting rooms, PC. **Free Special Amenities:** expanded continental breakfast and local telephone calls.

—— WHERE TO DINE ——

FLUIDS BAR & GRILL

Phone: 780/621-3341

Canadian
$11-$28

The establishment might look like an Irish pub but the food is anything but typical, except for the Guinness battered halibut and classic burger. For starters, try the smoked chicken and asparagus risotto followed by spicy chorizo pasta, bouillabaisse or lamb tenderloin. Service is casual and efficient. Casual dress. **Bar:** Full bar. **Reservations:** accepted. **Hours:** 11 am-10 pm. Closed major holidays; also Sun. **Address:** 5-5505 50th St T7A 1W2 **Location:** Hwy 22, just se; in strip mall. **Parking:** on-site.

DRUMHELLER pop. 7,932

BEST WESTERN JURASSIC INN *Book great rates at AAA.com*

Phone: (403)823-7700

Hotel
$126-$180 All Year

Address: 1103 Hwy 9 S T0J 0Y0 **Location:** Hwy 9, southeast access to town. **Facility:** 48 units. 45 one-bedroom standard units, some with efficiencies. 3 one-bedroom suites with efficiencies, some with whirlpools. 2 stories (no elevator), interior/exterior corridors. **Parking:** on-site, winter plug-ins. **Amenities:** voice mail, irons, hair dryers. *Some:* DVD players. **Leisure Activities:** whirlpool, steamroom, exercise room. **Guest Services:** valet and coin laundry, wireless Internet. **Business Services:** meeting rooms, PC (fee). **Free Special Amenities:** local telephone calls and high-speed Internet.

AAA Benefit:
Members save up to 20%, plus 10% bonus points with rewards program.

INN AND SPA AT HEARTWOOD

Phone: 403/823-6495

Boutique
Hotel
$99-$280 All Year

Address: 320 N Railway Ave E T0J 0Y4 **Location:** Downtown. **Facility:** Classic old-fashioned touches distinguish this commercial-district inn, skillfully renovated to modern standards. Smoke free premises. 10 units. 8 one-bedroom standard units with whirlpools. 1 house and 1 cottage. 2 stories (no elevator), interior/exterior corridors. **Parking:** on-site, winter plug-ins. **Terms:** office hours 8 am-11 pm, check-in 4 pm, 2 night minimum stay - weekends, age restrictions may apply, 3 day cancellation notice. **Amenities:** video library, irons, hair dryers. *Some:* DVD players (fee). **Leisure Activities:** spa. **Guest Services:** wireless Internet.

FREE local telephone calls and high-speed Internet

RAMADA INN & SUITES *Book at AAA.com*

Phone: 403/823-2028

Hotel
Rates not provided

Address: 680 2nd St SE T0J 0Y0 **Location:** Off Hwy 9. **Facility:** 74 units. 68 one-bedroom standard units, some with whirlpools. 6 one-bedroom suites. 4 stories, interior/exterior corridors. *Bath:* combo or shower only. **Parking:** on-site, winter plug-ins. **Amenities:** high-speed Internet, voice mail, irons, hair dryers. **Pool(s):** heated indoor. **Leisure Activities:** whirlpool, waterslide, exercise room. **Guest Services:** coin laundry, wireless Internet. **Business Services:** meeting rooms, business center.

SUPER 8 *Book at AAA.com*

Phone: (403)823-8887

Hotel
$139-$250 All Year

Address: 600-680 2nd St SE T0J 0Y0 **Location:** Off Hwy 9. **Facility:** 72 units. 69 one-bedroom standard units, some with efficiencies, kitchens and/or whirlpools. 3 one-bedroom suites. 2 stories, interior/exterior corridors. **Parking:** on-site, winter plug-ins. **Terms:** cancellation fee imposed. **Amenities:** voice mail, irons, hair dryers. *Some:* DVD players, high-speed Internet. **Pool(s):** heated indoor. **Leisure Activities:** whirlpool, waterslide, exercise room. **Guest Services:** valet and coin laundry, wireless Internet.

TASTE THE PAST BED & BREAKFAST

Phone: 403/823-5889

Historic Bed
& Breakfast
$115 All Year

Address: 281 2nd St W T0J 0Y0 **Location:** Hwy 9, exit 2nd St W; centre. **Facility:** Built by a coal baron in 1910, this large home features a working 1930s billiards table in the lounge area. Smoke free premises. 3 one-bedroom standard units. 3 stories (no elevator), interior corridors. *Bath:* combo or shower only. **Parking:** on-site, winter plug-ins. **Terms:** check-in 4 pm, 7 day cancellation notice-fee imposed. **Guest Services:** TV in common area.

——— WHERE TO DINE ———

CAFE ITALIANO

Phone: 403/823-4443

Coffee/Tea
$4-$8

The small downtown cafe is best known for its panini and dessert offerings, not to mention a good cup of coffee and lively bantering between the owner and locals. Casual dress. **Reservations:** accepted. **Hours:** 7 am-5 pm. Closed major holidays. **Address:** 35 3rd Ave W T0J 0Y0 **Location:** Downtown. **Parking:** street.

SIZZLING HOUSE

Phone: 403/823-8098

Chinese
$7-$16

This is the place for Chinese food with Thai and Szechuan twists. The decor is simple, the service is friendly, and the food is delicious. The lunch buffet is a great value, but diners also can opt to order a la carte from the menu. Casual dress. **Bar:** Full bar. **Hours:** 11 am-9 pm, Fri & Sat-10 pm. Closed: 12/25, 12/26; also Tues. **Address:** 160 Centre St T0J 0Y0 **Location:** Downtown. **Parking:** street.

THE WHISTLING KETTLE

Phone: 403/823-9997

Coffee/Tea
$4-$9

This simple café serves homemade soups and sandwiches with assorted teas. Casual dress. **Reservations:** suggested. **Hours:** Open 3/1-12/24; 7:30 am-4 pm. **Address:** 109 Centre St T0J 0Y0 **Location:** Downtown; across from Tourist Information Centre. **Parking:** street.

Earn extra rewards when you book the **"Bonus CAA Package"** rate **IKCA1**.
Receive your choice* of **1,000** BONUS Priority Club® Points, or **200** BONUS Aeroplan® Miles, or **25** BONUS AIR MILES®† reward miles when you stay at participating hotels.

InterContinental Hotels & Resorts	Crowne Plaza Hotels & Resorts	hotel Indigo	Holiday Inn	Holiday Inn Express	Staybridge Suites	Candlewood Suites
◆	▲	❖	■	⌘	❍	ɷ

Alberta
- ■ 67 Street (Red Deer)
- ⌘ Airport-Calgary
- ⌘ Calgary
- ■ Calgary Airport
- ❍ Calgary Airport
- ⌘ Calgary South
- ⌘ Drayton Valley
- ■ Edmonton Convention Center/SE
- ⌘ Edmonton Downtown
- ⌘ Slave Lake
- ■ West Edmonton

British Columbia
- ⌘ Kelowna
- ⌘ Langley
- ■ North Vancouver
- ⌘ Riverport Richmond
- ■ Vancouver Airport- Richmond
- ■ Vancouver Centre (Broadway)
- ■ Vancouver Downtown
- ⌘ Vancouver Metrotown (Burnaby)
- ⌘ Vernon
- ■ West Kelowna

Manitoba
- ■ Winnipeg-Downtown

New Brunswick
- ⌘ Dieppe Airport
- ▲ Fredericton-Lord Beaverbrook
- ⌘ Moncton
- ▲ Moncton Downtown
- ⌘ Saint John Harbourside

Newfoundland
- ■ St. John's-Govt. Center
- ■ Stephenville

Nova Scotia
- ⌘ Halifax Airport
- ⌘ Halifax (Bedford)
- ■ Halifax Harbourview
- ⌘ Stellarton-New Glasgow
- ■ Truro

Ontario
- ⌘ 1000 Islands-Gananoque
- ⌘ Barrie
- ⌘ Brampton
- ⌘ Brockville
- ■ Burlington Hotel and Conf. Centre
- ■ Cambridge-Hespeler Galt
- ⌘ Dryden
- ■ Fort Erie/Niagara Conv. Centre
- ❍ Guelph
- ■ Guelph Hotel & Conference Ctr.
- ❍ Hamilton-Downtown
- ⌘ Hamilton-Stoney Creek
- ⌘ Huntsville
- ■ Kingston-Waterfront
- ■ Kitchener-Waterloo Conf. Ctr.
- ■ London
- ❍ London
- ■ Mississauga
- ■ Mississauga Toronto West
- ■ Niagara Falls By The Falls
- ⌘ North Bay
- ■ Oakville @ Bronte
- ❍ Oakville-Burlington
- ■ Oakville Centre
- ■ Oshawa Whitby Conf. Centre
- ⌘ Ottawa Airport
- ❖ Ottawa Downtown City Center
- ■ Ottawa-Downtown
- ■ Peterborough Waterfront
- ■ St.Catharines North (Opening Q3 2010)
- ■ Sarnia Hotel and Conf. Centre
- ▲ Toronto Airport
- ❖ Toronto Airport
- ⌘ Toronto-Airport Area/Dixie Rd.
- ◆ Toronto Centre
- ■ Toronto Airport-East
- ■ Toronto-Brampton Conf. Centre
- ■ Toronto International Airport
- ■ Toronto-Markham
- ⌘ Toronto-Markham
- ❍ Toronto-Mississauga
- ■ Toronto Yorkdale
- ⌘ Vaughan Southwest
- ■ Windsor (Ambassador Bridge)
- ■ Windsor Downtown

Prince Edward Island
- ⌘ Charlottetown

Quebec
- ■ Gatineau-Ottawa Plz. Chaudiere
- ◆ Montreal
- ■ Montreal Airport
- ▲ Montreal Airport
- ⌘ Montreal Airport
- ■ Montreal-Longueuil
- ■ Montreal-Midtown
- ■ Montreal Downtown (Centre-Ville)
- ⌘ Montreal Downtown (Centre-Ville)
- ɷ Montreal Downtown (Centre-Ville)
- ⌘ St.Jean-Sur-Richelieu

aeroplan | PRIORITY CLUB REWARDS It's easier. Enjoy. | AIR MILES

PRIORITY CLUB REWARDS

InterContinental Hotels & Resorts | Crowne Plaza Hotels & Resorts | hotel Indigo | Holiday Inn | Holiday Inn Express | Staybridge Suites | Candlewood Suites

Offer valid from March 1st, 2010 to February 28th, 2011. Must be a Priority Club® Rewards member to participate in this promotion. Bonus points or miles will be awarded on every qualifying stay at participating IHG hotels in Canada at the promotional rate code IKCA1. For complete promotional details and Priority Club Rewards Terms and Conditions, please visit www.offers.ihg.com. ® Aeroplan is a registered trademark of Aeroplan Canada Inc. ®† Trademarks of AIR MILES® International Trading B.V. used under license by LoyaltyOne, Inc. and InterContinental Hotels Group. © 2009 InterContinental Hotels Group. All rights reserved. Most hotels are independently owned and/or operated.

Destination Edmonton
pop. 730,372

*E*dmonton, nicknamed "Gateway to the North," was once a place for gold miners to stop and gather provisions for their rough journey into the icy Klondike.

*D*isappointed prospectors who eventually returned to help build Edmonton indeed struck gold: Today the shining city is a mecca of culture and recreation, with its lovely theaters, parks and gardens.

Travel Alberta

Ukrainian Cultural Heritage Village, Edmonton.
(See listing page 71)

Old Strathcona dining, Edmonton.
(See mention page 73)

Travel Alberta

Travel Alberta

The Saskatchewan River, Edmonton.
(See mention page 90)

Travel Alberta

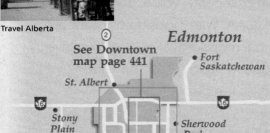

Edmonton

② **See Downtown map page 441**

• *Fort Saskatchewan*

St. Albert •

⑯

• *Stony Plain*

⑯

• *Sherwood Park*

⑥⓪ ②①⑥ ⑭

See Vicinity map page 444

⑲

✈ • *Nisku*

• *Leduc*
②

②①

William Hawrelak Park, Edmonton.
(See mention page 73)

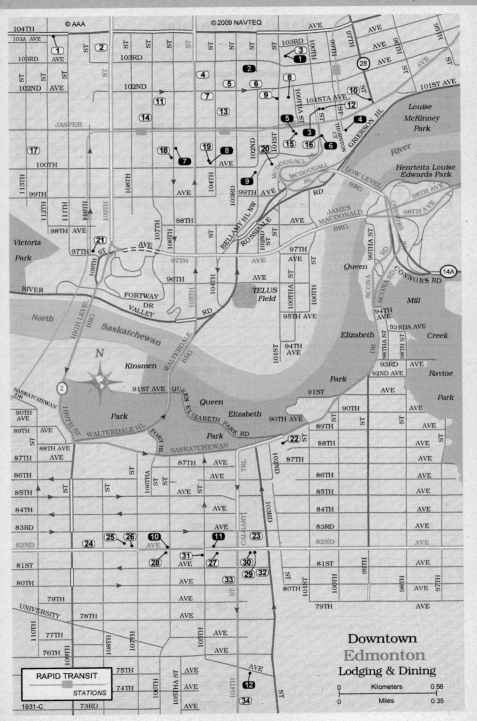

© AAA © 2009 NAVTEQ

Downtown
Edmonton
Lodging & Dining

RAPID TRANSIT
STATIONS

1931-C

Downtown Edmonton

This index helps you "spot" where approved lodgings and restaurants are located on the corresponding detailed maps. Lodging daily rate range is for comparison only and show the property's high season. Restaurant rate range is a combination of lunch and/or dinner. Turn to the listing page for more detailed rate information and consult display ads for special promotions.

DOWNTOWN EDMONTON

Map Page	OA	Lodgings	Diamond Rated	High Season	Page
1 / p. 441		The Sutton Place Hotel Edmonton	◈◈◈	$235-$395	449
2 / p. 441		Delta Edmonton Centre Suite Hotel	◈◈◈	$99-$379	448
3 / p. 441	CAA	**The Westin Edmonton**	◈◈◈	$119-$499 [SAVE]	449
4 / p. 441		Courtyard by Marriott Edmonton	◈◈◈	$206-$252	448
5 / p. 441	CAA	**Union Bank Inn**	◈◈◈	$209-$409 [SAVE]	449
6 / p. 441	CAA	**The Fairmont Hotel Macdonald**	◈◈◈◈	Rates not provided [SAVE]	448
7 / p. 441	CAA	**Days Inn Downtown Edmonton**	◈◈	$109-$169 [SAVE]	448
8 / p. 441	CAA	**Holiday Inn Express Edmonton-Downtown** - see color ad on insert	◈◈◈	$149-$189 [SAVE]	448
9 / p. 441		Coast Edmonton House	◈◈	Rates not provided	448
10 / p. 441		Varscona Hotel on Whyte	◈◈◈	$160-$350	449
11 / p. 441		Metterra Hotel on Whyte	◈◈◈	Rates not provided	448
12 / p. 441		Days Inn Edmonton South	◈◈◈	$126-$180	448

Map Page	OA	Restaurants	Diamond Rated	Cuisine	Meal Range	Page
(1) / p. 441		Wild Tangerine	◈◈◈	Asian	$13-$30	452
(2) / p. 441		Mikado	◈◈	Japanese	$10-$20	452
(3) / p. 441		Capitals Restaurant	◈◈◈	Canadian	$12-$30	450
(4) / p. 441		Characters	◈◈◈	Canadian	$16-$40	450
(5) / p. 441		The Creperie	◈◈	French	$10-$30	450
(6) / p. 441		L'azia	◈◈◈	International	$10-$38	451
(7) / p. 441		Ric's Grill	◈◈◈	Steak	$12-$37	452
(8) / p. 441		Bistro Praha	◈◈	Czechoslovakian	$9-$30	449
(9) / p. 441		Lux steakhouse & bar	◈◈◈	Steak	$14-$46	451
(10) / p. 441		Hardware Grill	◈◈◈	Regional Canadian	$30-$52	451
(11) / p. 441		Khazana	◈◈	Indian	$10-$20	451
(12) / p. 441		Pradera Cafe	◈◈◈	Canadian	$15-$35	452
(13) / p. 441		Blue Plate Diner	◈◈	Fusion	$8-$20	450
(14) / p. 441	CAA	**Doan's Restaurant**	◈◈	Vietnamese	$8-$17	450
(15) / p. 441		Madison's Grill	◈◈◈	Continental	$11-$42	452
(16) / p. 441	CAA	**The Harvest Room**	◈◈◈	Canadian	$18-$48	451
(17) / p. 441		Bua Thai Restaurant	◈◈	Thai	$9-$18	450
(18) / p. 441		Cafe Select	◈◈◈	Continental	$8-$25	450

Map Page	OA	Restaurants (cont'd)	Diamond Rated	Cuisine	Meal Range	Page
⑲ / p. 441		The Free Press Bistro	◈◈	Deli	$10-$26	451
⑳ / p. 441		La Ronde Revolving Restaurant	◈◈◈	Canadian	$29-$39	451
㉑ / p. 441		The Copper Pot Restaurant	◈◈◈	International	$12-$38	450
㉒ / p. 441		New Asian Village	◈◈◈	Eastern Indian	$11-$27	452
㉓ / p. 441		Packrat Louie's Kitchen & Bar	◈◈◈	Continental	$12-$44	452
㉔ / p. 441		Cafe Mosaics	◈	Vegetarian	$11-$13	450
㉕ / p. 441		Tokyo Noodle Shop	◈◈	Japanese	$8-$20	452
㉖ / p. 441		The King & I	◈◈	Thai	$10-$24	451
㉗ / p. 441		Yiannis Taverna	◈◈	Greek	$8-$22	453
㉘ / p. 441		O'Byrne's Irish Pub	◈	Irish	$8-$15	452
㉙ / p. 441		Flavours Modern Bistro	◈◈◈	Canadian	$11-$29	451
㉚ / p. 441		Block 1912	◈	Coffee/Tea	$8-$12	449
㉛ / p. 441		Chianti	◈◈	Italian	$8-$22	450
㉜ / p. 441		Von's Steak & Fish House	◈◈◈	Steak	$23-$40	452
㉝ / p. 441		Bee-Bell Health Bakery	◈	Breads/Pastries	$2-$9	449
㉞ / p. 441		Billingsgate Seafood Market Lighthouse Cafe	◈◈	Seafood	$8-$40	449

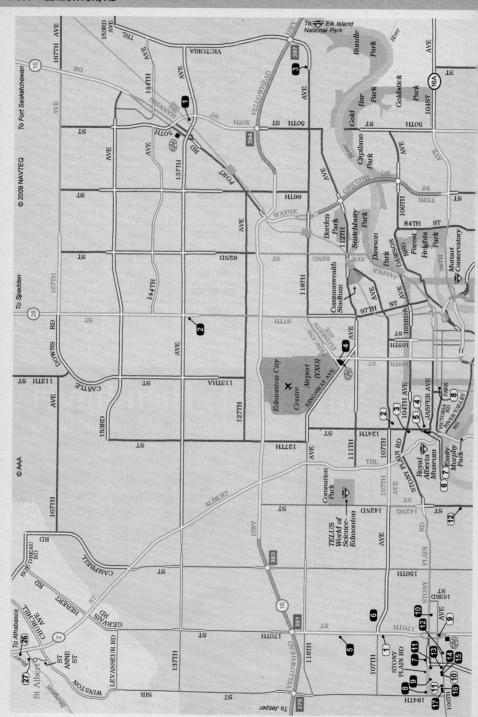

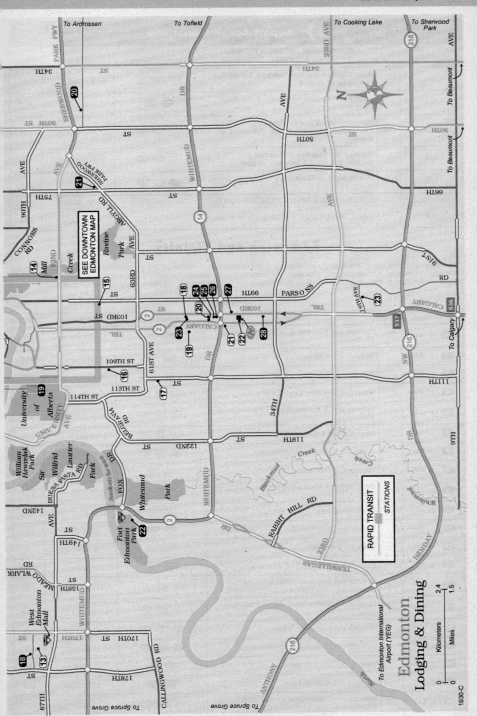

Edmonton
Lodging & Dining

1930-C

✈ Airport Accommodations

Map Page	OA	EDMONTON INTERNATIONAL AIRPORT	Diamond Rated	High Season	Page
N/A	ⒶⒶ	**Best Western Denham Inn and Suites, 5 mi (8 km) se of airport**	◈◈◈	$150-$156 SAVE	464
N/A		Edmonton International Airport-Super 8, 3.8 mi (6 km) se of airport	◈◈	$125	465
N/A	ⒶⒶ	**Hampton Inn & Suites Edmonton International Airport, 2.3 mi (3.8 km) e of airport**	◈◈	$149-$159 SAVE	465
N/A	ⒶⒶ	**Holiday Inn Express Edmonton Int'l Airport, 2.3 mi (3.7 km) e of airport**	◈◈	$151-$230 SAVE	465
N/A		Quality Inn & Suites-Airport, 2.3 mi (3.7 km) e of airport	◈◈◈	$110-$120	465
Map Page	OA	**EDMONTON MUNICIPAL AIRPORT**	Diamond Rated	High Season	Page
N/A		Holiday Inn & Suites, 3 mi (5 km) e of airport		Rates not provided	533

Edmonton and Vicinity

This index helps you "spot" where approved lodgings and restaurants are located on the corresponding detailed maps. Lodging daily rate range is for comparison only and show the property's high season. Restaurant rate range is a combination of lunch and/or dinner. Turn to the listing page for more detailed rate information and consult display ads for special promotions.

EDMONTON

Map Page	OA	Lodgings	Diamond Rated	High Season	Page
❶ / p. 444	ⒶⒶ	**Holiday Inn Express & Suites Edmonton North**	◈◈	$139-$229 SAVE	458
❷ / p. 444		Rosslyn Inn & Suites	◈◈	$117-$159	459
❸ / p. 444	ⒶⒶ	**Travelodge Edmonton East**	◈◈	$89-$139 SAVE	460
❹ / p. 444	ⒶⒶ	**Best Western City Centre Inn**	◈◈◈	$149-$179 SAVE	453
❺ / p. 444	ⒶⒶ	**Holiday Inn & Suites, West Edmonton** - see color ad on insert	◈◈◈	$139-$249 SAVE	457
❻ / p. 444	ⒶⒶ	**Mayfield Inn & Suites at West Edmonton**	◈◈◈	$150-$225 SAVE	458
❼ / p. 444		Hilton Garden Inn-West Edmonton	◈◈◈	$139-$219	457
❽ / p. 444	ⒶⒶ	**Travelodge Edmonton West**	◈◈	$109-$159 SAVE	460
❾ / p. 444	ⒶⒶ	**Best Western Westwood Inn** - see color ad p 454	◈◈◈	$109-$189 SAVE	454
❿ / p. 444	ⒶⒶ	**Continental Inn**	◈◈	$110-$145 SAVE	455
⓫ / p. 444		Quality Inn West Harvest	◈◈	$105-$199	459
⓬ / p. 444	ⒶⒶ	**Comfort Inn West**	◈◈	$99-$159 SAVE	454
⓭ / p. 444		Executive Royal Inn West Edmonton	◈◈	$120	456
⓮ / p. 444	ⒶⒶ	**Holiday Inn Express Hotel & Suites Edmonton** - see color ad p 458	◈◈◈	$149-$189 SAVE	458
⓯ / p. 444	ⒶⒶ	**Days Inn & Suites West Edmonton** - see color ad p 455	◈◈◈	$149-$189 SAVE	455
⓰ / p. 444		Wingate Inn Edmonton West	◈◈◈	$139-$160	460
⓱ / p. 444		Hampton Inn & Suites Edmonton West	◈◈◈	$159-$189	456
⓲ / p. 444		West Edmonton Mall Inn	◈◈	$149	460
⓳ / p. 444		Campus Tower Suite Hotel	◈◈	$125-$245	454
⓴ / p. 444	ⒶⒶ	**Holiday Inn Convention Centre (S.E. Edmonton)** - see color ad on insert	◈◈◈	$109-$229 SAVE	457

EDMONTON (cont'd)

Map Page	OA	Lodgings (cont'd)	Diamond Rated	High Season	Page
21 / p. 444	ⒶⒶ	Four Points by Sheraton Edmonton South - see color ad p 457	◆◆◆	Rates not provided SAVE	456
22 / p. 444		Hotel Selkirk	◆◆◆	Rates not provided	458
23 / p. 444	ⒶⒶ	Best Western Cedar Park Inn - see color ad p 453	◆◆	$99-$189 SAVE	453
24 / p. 444		Travelodge Edmonton South	◆◆	$109-$159	460
25 / p. 444	ⒶⒶ	Radisson Hotel Edmonton South	◆◆◆	$165-$200 SAVE	459
26 / p. 444		Delta Edmonton South Hotel and Conference Centre	◆◆◆	Rates not provided	455
27 / p. 444	ⒶⒶ	Sawridge Inn Edmonton South - see color ad p 459	◆◆◆	$129-$159 SAVE	459
28 / p. 444		Super 8 Edmonton South	◆◆	Rates not provided	460

Map Page	OA	Restaurants	Diamond Rated	Cuisine	Meal Range	Page
1 / p. 444		Fife N' Dekel	◆	Deli	$6-$10	461
2 / p. 444		The Blue Pear	◆◆◆	French	$85	460
3 / p. 444		The Dish Bistro	◆◆	International	$12-$16	461
4 / p. 444		Glenora Bistro	◆◆◆	Canadian	$11-$29	461
5 / p. 444		Urban Diner	◆◆	Canadian	$8-$15	463
6 / p. 444		La Favorite Pastry Shop	◆	Breads/Pastries	$4-$8	462
7 / p. 444		Manor Cafe	◆◆	International	$12-$34	462
8 / p. 444		Il Pasticcio Trattoria	◆◆	Italian	$12-$35	461
9 / p. 444		The Cheesecake Cafe	◆◆	American	$10-$25	461
10 / p. 444		ConYac's Bar & Grill	◆◆	Canadian	$9-$25	461
11 / p. 444		Homefire Bar & Grill	◆◆	Canadian	$14-$32	461
12 / p. 444		Delux Burger Bar	◆◆	American	$9-$20	461
13 / p. 444		T & T Supermarket Cafe	◆	Chinese	$5-$7	463
14 / p. 444		Unheardof Restaurant	◆◆◆	Canadian	$34-$43	463
15 / p. 444		Barb & Ernie's	◆	German	$8-$25	460
16 / p. 444		Parkallen Restaurant	◆◆	Lebanese	$9-$34	462
17 / p. 444		Jack's Grill	◆◆◆	Regional Canadian	$28-$43	461
18 / p. 444		Seasons Grill - see color ad p 453	◆◆	Canadian	$11-$25	463
19 / p. 444		Lemongrass Cafe	◆◆	Vietnamese	$6-$19	462
20 / p. 444		Koutouki Taverna	◆◆	Greek	$20-$35	462
21 / p. 444		Tom Goodchilds Moose Factory	◆◆	Steak	$11-$50	463
22 / p. 444		Century Grill	◆◆◆	Northern Pacific Rim	$17-$41	460
23 / p. 444		OPM Asian Bistro & Lounge	◆◆	Asian	$13-$20	462

ST. ALBERT

Map Page	OA	Restaurants	Diamond Rated	Cuisine	Meal Range	Page
26 / p. 444		River House Grill	◆◆◆	Canadian	$19-$34	466
27 / p. 444		Ric's Grill	◆◆◆	Steak	$9-$30	465

DOWNTOWN EDMONTON   (See map and index starting on p. 441)

COAST EDMONTON HOUSE   *Book at AAA.com*   Phone: 780/420-4000   [9]

Condominium
Rates not provided

Address: 10205 100th Ave T5J 4B5 **Location:** Just se of jct 102nd St and 100th Ave. **Facility:** 305 units. 289 one- and 16 two-bedroom suites, some with efficiencies or kitchens. 35 stories, interior corridors. **Parking:** on-site, winter plug-ins. **Amenities:** voice mail, irons, hair dryers. *Some:* high-speed Internet. **Pool(s):** heated indoor. **Leisure Activities:** exercise room. **Guest Services:** valet and coin laundry, area transportation, wireless Internet. **Business Services:** meeting rooms.

COURTYARD BY MARRIOTT EDMONTON   *Book great rates at AAA.com*   Phone: (780)423-9999   [4]

Hotel
$206-$252 All Year

Address: 1 Thornton Ct T5J 2E7 **Location:** Just off Jasper Ave; between 99th and 97th sts. **Facility:** Smoke free premises. 177 units. 172 one-bedroom standard units, some with whirlpools. 5 one-bedroom suites. 11 stories, interior corridors. *Bath:* combo or shower only. **Parking:** on-site (fee) and valet. **Terms:** cancellation fee imposed. **Amenities:** high-speed Internet, dual phone lines, voice mail, irons, hair dryers. **Leisure Activities:** exercise room. **Guest Services:** valet and coin laundry, wireless Internet. **Business Services:** meeting rooms, PC.

COURTYARD Marriott

AAA Benefit:
Members save a minimum 5% off the best available rate.

DAYS INN DOWNTOWN EDMONTON   *Book great rates at AAA.com*   Phone: (780)423-1925   [7]

(AAA) (SAVE)
Hotel
$109-$169 All Year

Address: 10041 106th St T5J 1G3 **Location:** Just s of Jasper Ave. **Facility:** Smoke free premises. 76 one-bedroom standard units. 4 stories, interior corridors. **Parking:** on-site, winter plug-ins. **Amenities:** irons, hair dryers. **Leisure Activities:** exercise room. **Guest Services:** valet and coin laundry, airport transportation (fee)-Edmonton International Airport, wireless Internet. **Business Services:** meeting rooms, PC. **Free Special Amenities:** room upgrade (subject to availability with advance reservations) and high-speed Internet.

DAYS INN EDMONTON SOUTH   *Book at AAA.com*   Phone: (780)430-0011   [12]

Hotel
$126-$180 All Year

Address: 10333 University Ave T6E 6N3 **Location:** Just s of Whyte Ave; between 103rd and 104th sts. **Facility:** Smoke free premises. 85 one-bedroom standard units, some with whirlpools. 4 stories, interior corridors. *Bath:* combo or shower only. **Parking:** on-site, winter plug-ins. **Amenities:** high-speed Internet, voice mail, irons, hair dryers. **Guest Services:** valet and coin laundry, wireless Internet. **Business Services:** business center.

DELTA EDMONTON CENTRE SUITE HOTEL   *Book at AAA.com*   Phone: (780)429-3900   [2]

Hotel
$99-$379 All Year

Address: 10222 102nd St T5J 4C5 **Location:** At 102nd St at 103rd Ave. Attached to a shopping centre. **Facility:** Smoke free premises. 169 units. 63 one-bedroom standard units with whirlpools. 106 one-bedroom suites with whirlpools. 7 stories, interior corridors. **Parking:** on-site (fee) and valet, winter plug-ins. **Terms:** cancellation fee imposed. **Amenities:** video games (fee), high-speed Internet, dual phone lines, voice mail, irons, hair dryers. **Leisure Activities:** whirlpool, steamroom, exercise room. **Guest Services:** valet and coin laundry, wireless Internet. **Business Services:** conference facilities, business center.

THE FAIRMONT HOTEL MACDONALD   *Book great rates at AAA.com*   Phone: 780/424-5181   [6]

(AAA) (SAVE)
Historic Hotel
Rates not provided

Address: 10065 100th St T5J 0N6 **Location:** Just s of Jasper Ave. **Facility:** Perched atop the river valley, this historic hotel with a majestic ambience offers attentive service and upscale rooms, some with a view. 199 units. 190 one-bedroom standard units, some with whirlpools. 9 stories, interior corridors. **Parking:** on-site (fee) and valet, winter plug-ins. **Amenities:** CD players, voice mail, honor bars, irons, hair dryers. *Fee:* video games, high-speed Internet. *Some:* DVD players, dual phone lines, safes. **Dining:** The Harvest Room, see separate listing. **Pool(s):** heated indoor. **Leisure Activities:** sauna, whirlpool, steamroom, 2 squash courts. *Fee:* massage. **Guest Services:** valet laundry, airport transportation (fee)-Edmonton International Airport, wireless Internet. **Business Services:** conference facilities, business center. **Free Special Amenities:** newspaper.

HOLIDAY INN EXPRESS EDMONTON-DOWNTOWN   *Book great rates at AAA.com*   Phone: (780)423-2450   [8]

(AAA) (SAVE)
Hotel
$149-$189 All Year

Address: 10010 104th St T5J 0Z1 **Location:** Corner of 100th Ave; centre. **Facility:** Smoke free premises. 140 one-bedroom standard units. 7 stories, interior corridors. **Parking:** on-site (fee). **Terms:** check-in 4 pm, cancellation fee imposed. **Amenities:** video games (fee), high-speed Internet, dual phone lines, voice mail, irons, hair dryers. *Some:* CD players. **Dining:** The Free Press Bistro, see separate listing. **Pool(s):** heated indoor. **Leisure Activities:** whirlpool, steamrooms, exercise room. **Guest Services:** valet and coin laundry, airport transportation (fee)-Edmonton International Airport, wireless Internet, beauty salon. **Business Services:** conference facilities, business center. **Free Special Amenities:** expanded continental breakfast and high-speed Internet.
(See color ad on insert)

METTERRA HOTEL ON WHYTE   *Book at AAA.com*   Phone: 780/465-8150   [11]

Hotel
Rates not provided

Address: 10454 82nd Ave (Whyte Ave) T6E 4Z7 **Location:** Just e of 105th St. **Facility:** Smoke free premises. 98 units. 92 one-bedroom standard units. 6 one-bedroom suites with whirlpools. 8 stories, interior corridors. *Bath:* combo or shower only. **Parking:** valet and street. **Amenities:** video library, CD players, high-speed Internet, voice mail, irons, hair dryers. *Some:* DVD players, safes. **Leisure Activities:** exercise room. **Guest Services:** valet laundry, wireless Internet. **Business Services:** meeting rooms, PC.

(See map and index starting on p. 441)

THE SUTTON PLACE HOTEL EDMONTON   *Book at AAA.com*   **Phone:** (780)428-7111   1

Hotel
$235-$395 All Year

Address: 10235 101st St T5J 3E9 **Location:** 102nd Ave at 101st St. **Facility:** Smoke free premises. 313 one-bedroom standard units. 26 stories, interior corridors. **Parking:** on-site (fee) and valet. **Terms:** cancellation fee imposed. **Amenities:** dual phone lines, voice mail, irons, hair dryers. *Some:* CD players, high-speed Internet, safes. **Dining:** Capitals Restaurant, see separate listing. **Pool(s):** heated indoor. **Leisure Activities:** saunas, whirlpool. **Guest Services:** valet laundry, wireless Internet. **Business Services:** conference facilities, PC (fee).

ASK FEE 🖥 🍽 🍸 🏊 FEE ✚ ✕ 📷 💻 / SOME UNITS FEE 🐾 🚻

UNION BANK INN   *Book great rates at AAA.com*   **Phone:** (780)423-3600   5

(CAA) SAVE

Hotel
$209-$409 All Year

Address: 10053 Jasper Ave T5J 1S5 **Location:** Corner of 101st St. **Facility:** Smoke free premises. 34 units. 33 one-bedroom standard units, some with whirlpools. 1 one-bedroom suite with whirlpool. 3-5 stories, interior corridors. **Parking:** on-site. **Terms:** cancellation fee imposed. **Amenities:** high-speed Internet, voice mail, safes, irons, hair dryers. *Some:* DVD players. **Dining:** Madison's Grill, see separate listing. **Leisure Activities:** limited exercise equipment. **Guest Services:** valet laundry, airport transportation (fee)-Edmonton International Airport. **Business Services:** meeting rooms, PC. **Free Special Amenities: full breakfast and high-speed Internet.**

FEE 🖥 🍽 🍸 ✕ 📷 💻 / SOME UNITS 🚻

VARSCONA HOTEL ON WHYTE   *Book at AAA.com*   **Phone:** (780)434-6111   10

Hotel
$160-$350 All Year

Address: 8208 106th St T6E 6R9 **Location:** Corner of 82nd Ave (Whyte Ave) and 106th St. **Facility:** Smoke free premises. 89 units. 85 one-bedroom standard units. 4 one-bedroom suites. 6 stories, interior corridors. **Bath:** combo or shower only. **Parking:** on-site and valet, winter plug-ins. **Terms:** cancellation fee imposed. **Amenities:** CD players, high-speed Internet, voice mail, irons, hair dryers. *Some:* DVD players, dual phone lines. **Leisure Activities:** exercise room. **Guest Services:** valet laundry, wireless Internet. **Business Services:** meeting rooms, PC.

ECO ASK 🍽 🍸 ✕ 🚻 💻 / SOME UNITS FEE 🐾 📷

THE WESTIN EDMONTON   *Book great rates at AAA.com*   **Phone:** (780)426-3636   3

(CAA) SAVE

Hotel
$119-$499 All Year

Address: 10135 100th St T5J 0N7 **Location:** 101st Ave at 100th St. **Facility:** Smoke free premises. 413 units. 402 one-bedroom standard units. 8 one- and 3 two-bedroom suites. 20 stories, interior corridors. **Parking:** on-site (fee) and valet. **Amenities:** video games (fee), dual phone lines, voice mail, safes, honor bars, irons, hair dryers. *Some:* high-speed Internet. **Dining:** Pradera Cafe, see separate listing. **Pool(s):** heated indoor. **Leisure Activities:** saunas, whirlpool, exercise room. **Guest Services:** valet laundry, airport transportation (fee)-Edmonton International Airport, wireless Internet. **Business Services:** conference facilities, business center.

WESTIN
HOTELS & RESORTS

AAA Benefit:
Enjoy up to 15% off your next stay, plus Starwood Preferred Guest® bonuses.

ECO FEE 🖥 🍽 24 🍸 🏊 ✕ ✕ 📷 💻 / SOME UNITS 🐾

—— **WHERE TO DINE** ——

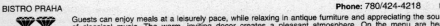

BEE-BELL HEALTH BAKERY   **Phone:** 780/439-3247   33

Breads/Pastries
$2-$9

Although there are no places to sit and eat, the bakery is a favorite for those planning a picnic in the park or a festival outing. Patrons step up to the counter to order a variety of breads, quiches and delectable desserts. Casual dress. **Reservations:** not accepted. **Hours:** 9 am-5:30 pm, Sat from 8 am. Closed major holidays; also Sun. **Address:** 10416 80th Ave T6E 5T7 **Location:** E at 80th Ave to 104th St. **Parking:** street.

BILLINGSGATE SEAFOOD MARKET LIGHTHOUSE CAFE   **Phone:** 780/433-0091   34

Seafood
$8-$40

Patrons walk past displays of fresh seafood to the lively, bright restaurant, where seafood lovers indulge in jewels from the ocean. Fresh halibut, salmon, trout and a catch of the day are sure to delight, as does traditional fish and chips. Desserts made on the premises are well worth saving room for. The cafe-style restaurant bustles at lunchtime, and a distinctive East Coast flair characterizes the decor. Casual dress. **Bar:** Full bar. **Reservations:** suggested. **Hours:** 11:30 am-9 pm, Fri & Sat-10 pm, Sun-8 pm. Closed: 12/25. **Address:** 7331 104th St T6E 4B9 **Location:** Corner of 73rd Ave and 104th St. **Parking:** on-site.

BISTRO PRAHA   **Phone:** 780/424-4218   8

Czechoslovakian
$9-$30

Guests can enjoy meals at a leisurely pace, while relaxing in antique furniture and appreciating the sounds of classical music. The warm, inviting decor creates a pleasant atmosphere. On the menu are hearty portions of steak tartare, various schnitzels and a selection of crepes for dessert. Casual dress. **Bar:** Full bar. **Reservations:** suggested. **Hours:** 11 am-1 am, Sat noon-2 am, Sun 4 pm-midnight. Closed major holidays. **Address:** 10168 100A St T5J 0R6 **Location:** Just n of Jasper Ave. **Parking:** street.

BLOCK 1912   **Phone:** 780/433-6575   30

Coffee/Tea
$8-$12

There's a bit of an interesting mix to the decor of this European feeling room, and it could be the decidedly Indian artwork that hangs on the walls. Primarily a coffee shop, the large space is perfectly placed as a pit stop among the shops of Whyte Avenue. Offerings include a decent selection of sandwiches, made-in-house gelato and freshly baked sweet and savory baked goods. Casual dress. **Bar:** Full bar. **Reservations:** not accepted. **Hours:** 9 am-10 pm, Fri & Sat 10 am-11 pm, Sun 10 am-10 pm. Closed: 1/1, 12/25. **Address:** 10361 82nd Ave NW T6E 1Z9 **Location:** Jct Calgary Tr NW; on historic Whyte Ave. **Parking:** street.

(See map and index starting on p. 441)

BLUE PLATE DINER
Phone: 780/429-0740 ⑬

Fusion
$8-$20

In the heart of downtown, the diner displays comfortable yet eclectic decor, which includes exposed brick walls and bright paint, and is as far from a classic diner as it gets. Offering an ever-changing menu, the kitchen produces a good selection of vegetarian dishes, as well as a variety of creative takes on down-home comfort food. Casual dress. **Bar:** Full bar. **Reservations:** suggested. **Hours:** 11 am-10 pm, Sat & Sun from 9 am. Closed major holidays. **Address:** 10145 104th St T5J 0Z9 **Location:** Just s of Jasper Ave. **Parking:** street.

BUA THAI RESTAURANT
Phone: 780/482-2277 ⑰

Thai
$9-$18

For fantastic Thai food, diners need look no further than this family-run restaurant just south of Jasper Avenue. Because locals frequent this place, it's a good idea to make a reservation. Dishes range from pad thai to various curries, and all are sure to please. Casual dress. **Bar:** Full bar. **Reservations:** suggested. **Hours:** 11 am-2 & 5-9 pm, Thurs & Fri-9:30 pm, Sat 5 pm-9:30 pm. Closed major holidays; also Sun. **Address:** 10049 113th St NW T5K 1N9 **Location:** Just s of Jasper Ave at 113th St. **Parking:** on-site.

CAFE MOSAICS
Phone: 780/433-9702 ㉔

Vegetarian
$11-$13

An eclectic and funky respite for vegetarians, the small cafe is along trendy Whyte Avenue. Home-cooked meals, including a large selection of vegetarian entrees, are served in a cozy setting. Whether a hearty bowl of soup, a distinctive pizza or an entree-size spinach salad, the servings are large and a good value for the dollar. This place is nice for spending hours catching up with a friend over a cup of coffee. Casual dress. **Bar:** Full bar. **Reservations:** not accepted. **Hours:** 9 am-9 pm, Sun 11 am-2:30 pm. Closed major holidays. **Address:** 10844 82nd Ave T6E 2B3 **Location:** 82nd Ave (Whyte Ave), just e of 109th St. **Parking:** street.

CAFE SELECT
Phone: 780/428-1629 ⑱

Continental
$8-$25

Patrons unwind in a comfortable, intimate atmosphere while contemplating a menu of traditional favorites, such as rack of lamb and beef tenderloin as well as lighter fare ranging from salads to fondue. Patio dining is available in season. Whether in a hurry or prepared for a long, lingering meal, expect appropriate service. The wait staff is fast, friendly, cordial and unobtrusive. Dressy casual. **Bar:** Full bar **Reservations:** suggested. **Hours:** 11:30 am-midnight, Fri-2 am, Sat 5 pm-2 am, Sun 5 pm-midnight. Closed: 1/1, 12/24, 12/25. **Address:** 10018 106th St T5J 1G1 **Location:** Just s of Jasper Ave. **Parking:** street.

CAPITALS RESTAURANT
Phone: 780/428-7111 ③

Canadian
$12-$30

The upscale restaurant prepares selections of regional cuisine. Service is fine and friendly. Casual dress. **Bar:** Full bar. **Reservations:** suggested. **Hours:** 6-10:30 am, 11:30-2:30 & 5:30-11 pm. **Address:** 10235 101st St T5J 3E9 **Location:** 102nd Ave at 101st St; in The Sutton Place Hotel, Edmonton. **Parking:** on-site (fee) and valet. CALL

CHARACTERS
Phone: 780/421-4100 ④

Canadian
$16-$40

Polished hardwood floors, brick walls and a glimmering open-concept kitchen set the tone for this fresh contemporary restaurant. The seasonally inspired menu changes, but can include a variety of offerings including duck, lamb, Alberta pork and beef. An impressive wine list will ensure a memorable experience. Dressy casual. **Bar:** Full bar. **Reservations:** suggested. **Hours:** 11:30 am-2 & 5:30-10 pm, Sat from 5:30 pm, Mon 11 am-2 pm. Closed major holidays; also Sun. **Address:** 10257 105th St T5J 1E3 **Location:** Just n of jct 102nd Ave and 105th St. **Parking:** on-site. CALL

CHIANTI
Phone: 780/439-9829 ㉛

Italian
$8-$22

In a former post office building on trendy Whyte Avenue, the lively, long-established restaurant serves entrees of pasta, veal, seafood and chicken, and most menu items can be served in half portions. This place is ideal for large gatherings or an evening out in a festive atmosphere. When busy, service might suffer a bit, but expect friendly, knowledgeable assistance in general. Casual dress. **Bar:** Full bar. **Reservations:** accepted. **Hours:** 11 am-11 pm. Closed: 1/1, 12/25. **Address:** 10501 82nd Ave NW T6E 2A3 **Location:** Corner of 105th St. **Parking:** street.

THE COPPER POT RESTAURANT
Phone: 780/452-7800 ㉑

International
$12-$38

Near the legislative buildings and overlooking the river valley, the intimate restaurant is tucked away on the ground floor of an office tower. The innovative and eclectic menu lists several pasta dishes, Alberta bison and seafood selections, all plated in hearty portions. Service is relaxed yet professional. Casual dress. **Bar:** Full bar. **Reservations:** suggested. **Hours:** 11 am-10 pm, Sat from 4 pm. Closed: 1/1, 12/25; also Sun & Mon. **Address:** 101-9707 110th St T5K 2L9 **Location:** From 109th St, just w at 97th Ave (one way street), then just n. **Parking:** on-site.

THE CREPERIE
Phone: 780/420-6656 ⑤

French
$10-$30

Patrons can prepare themselves for delectable French cuisine—including outstanding stuffed crepes—in the cozy restaurant, just below street level. Menu options, such as seafood and vegetarian dishes, are varied enough to tempt any palate. Casual dress. **Bar:** Full bar. **Reservations:** suggested. **Hours:** 11:30 am-9 pm, Fri-10 pm, Sat 5 pm-10 pm, Sun 5 pm-9 pm. Closed: 12/25, 12/26; also Mon. **Address:** 10220 103rd St T5J 0Y8 **Location:** Just n of 102nd Ave. **Parking:** on-site (fee) and street.

DOAN'S RESTAURANT
Phone: 780/424-3034 ⑭

Vietnamese
$8-$17

Visitors to the simple, neatly furnished and spacious dining room can enjoy classic Vietnamese dishes, such as hearty rice and noodle soup. Several meat dishes are expertly spiced by the restaurant's signature sauces. Casual dress. **Bar:** Full bar. **Reservations:** suggested. **Hours:** 11 am-10 pm, Fri & Sat-11 pm. Closed: 12/25. **Address:** 10130 107th St NW T5J 1J4 **Location:** Just n of Jasper Ave at 107th St. **Parking:** on-site.

(See map and index starting on p. 441)

FLAVOURS MODERN BISTRO
Phone: 780/439-9604 29

Canadian
$11-$29

Located on trendy Whyte Avenue, this enticing, family-owned bistro features an exposed brick wall along one length of the long, narrow room and mirrored walls along the other. Wood floors and jewel tones complete the picture. The chef favors organic and local products and serves up some flavorable creations featuring items like bison and lamb. Save room for the fabulous desserts, like triple chocolate bread pudding. Casual dress. **Bar:** Full bar. **Reservations:** suggested. **Hours:** 11 am-10 pm, Fri & Sat-11 pm, Sun 11 am-3 pm. Closed major holidays. **Address:** 10354 Whyte Ave NW T6E 1Z8 **Location:** On 82nd Ave (Whyte Ave); between 103rd and 104th sts NW. **Parking:** street.

THE FREE PRESS BISTRO
Phone: 780/497-7784 19

Deli
$10-$26

On the back end of the Holiday Inn Express hotel, this quiet and casual restaurant seems miles away from the hustle and bustle of nearby Jasper Avenue. Offerings include a good selection of paninis and in-house-made soups. A throwback to the days when newspapers were the kings of media, this place imports syrups for its delicious egg custards directly from New York. Casual dress. **Bar:** Full bar. **Reservations:** suggested, for lunch. **Hours:** 11 am-9 pm. Closed major holidays; also Sat & Sun. **Address:** 10014 104th St, #80 T5J 0Z1 **Location:** Corner of 100th Ave; centre; in Holiday Inn Express Edmonton-Downtown. **Parking:** street.

HARDWARE GRILL
Phone: 780/423-0969 10

Regional
Canadian
$30-$52

Superb service, fine surroundings and a wonderful menu combine to create a truly memorable dining experience in the former hardware store. The warehouse-like dining room is open and airy, and there are hints of history throughout. Representative of seasonally-inspired Canadian cuisine are such choices as mocha-crusted bacon-wrapped elk, applewood smoked Kurobuta pork loin and cedar-planked salmon. The grand finale is exceptional desserts, including warm gingerbread cake. Dressy casual. **Bar:** Full bar. **Reservations:** suggested. **Hours:** 5 pm-9:30 pm, Fri & Sat-10:30 pm. Closed major holidays; also Sun. **Address:** 9698 Jasper Ave T5H 3V5 **Location:** Corner of 97th St. **Parking:** street.

THE HARVEST ROOM
Phone: 780/424-5181 16

Canadian
$18-$48

The atmosphere is warm and vibrant in the elegant surroundings of this restaurant. Views of the North Saskatchewan River are beautiful. Creative Canadian Prairie cuisine is prepared in the open-concept kitchen. Among tempting entrees are preparations of Alberta beef and venison. Professional, upscale service complements the delicious, upscale food presentations. Dressy casual. **Bar:** Full bar. **Reservations:** suggested. **Hours:** 6:30 am-2 & 5:30-10 pm, Sat & Sun from 7 am. **Address:** 10065 100th St T5J 0N6 **Location:** Just s of Jasper Ave; in The Fairmont Hotel Macdonald. **Parking:** valet. CALL ⬤M

JOEY RESTAURANTS
Phone: 780/420-1996

Mediterranean
$10-$29

The cuisine blends Mediterranean and Asian cooking styles and emphasizes finger foods for sharing. Those who aren't big fans of tapas can consider full meal offerings centered on steaks and chops. Casual dress. **Bar:** Full bar. **Hours:** 11 am-1 am. Closed: 12/25. **Address:** 11228 Jasper Ave T5K 2V2 **Location:** At 112th St NW. **Parking:** on-site.

KHAZANA
Phone: 780/702-0330 11

Indian
$10-$20

Khazana's features an authentic, tasty tandoori cuisine of papadams, fresh naan bread, peshawari kebab (lamb), boti kebab (prime beef) and murgh tandoori (chicken). The inviting, upscale decor includes original artwork from New Delhi, and costumed servers take the time to explain every course of the meal, from the appetizer to the palette cleanser at the finale. Casual dress. **Bar:** Full bar. **Reservations:** suggested. **Hours:** 11:30 am-2 & 5-9:30 pm, Fri-10:30 pm, Sat 5 pm-10:30 pm, Sun 5 pm-9:30 pm. Closed major holidays. **Address:** 10177 107 St T5J 1J5 **Location:** Corner of 102nd Ave. **Parking:** street.

THE KING & I
Phone: 780/433-2222 26

Thai
$10-$24

Zesty vegetarian, meat, seafood and poultry dishes provide sensational, savory variety at the pleasant southside curry house, just off Whyte Avenue. Steaming regional Thai curries are an aromatic, tasty choice to enjoy with friends. Thai art and comfy, padded booths and chairs create a comfortable atmosphere in which to enjoy zesty vegetarian, meat, seafood and poultry dishes with sensational, savory variety. Friendly and unobtrusive, servers are helpful to the first-timer. Casual dress. **Bar:** Full bar. **Reservations:** suggested. **Hours:** 11:30 am-10:30 pm, Fri-11:30 pm, Sat 4:30 pm-11:30 pm. Closed: major holidays, 12/26; also Sun. **Address:** 8208 107th St T6E 6P4 **Location:** Corner of 107th St, just n of 82nd Ave (Whyte Ave). **Parking:** street. CALL ⬤M

LA RONDE REVOLVING RESTAURANT
Phone: 780/420-8366 20

Canadian
$29-$39

The revolving rooftop restaurant offers a panoramic view of the city. The atmosphere is elegant, yet casual, and classic European cuisine reflects Asian influences. Prix fixe selections cater to couples and include aperitifs and champagnes. Dressy casual. **Bar:** Full bar. **Reservations:** suggested. **Hours:** 5:30 pm-10 pm; Sunday brunch 10:30 am-2 pm. **Address:** 10111 Bellamy Hill T5J 1N7 **Location:** Jct 101st St, MacDonald Dr and Bellamy Hill; in Crowne Plaza Edmonton-Chateau Lacombe. **Parking:** on-site. CALL ⬤M

L'AZIA
Phone: 780/990-0188 6

International
$10-$38

Inside a downtown shopping center, the restaurant entices hordes of office workers on their lunch hours. Upscale Asian fusion dishes exhibit creative and unusual twists on the foods of China, Korea, Thailand and Vietnam. Dressy casual. **Bar:** Full bar. **Reservations:** suggested. **Hours:** 11 am-10 pm, Fri & Sat-midnight. Closed major holidays. **Address:** 10200 102nd Ave T5J 4B7 **Location:** Centre; in Edmonton City Centre; beside the Bay. **Parking:** on-site (fee). CALL ⬤M

LUX STEAKHOUSE & BAR
Phone: 780/424-0400 9

Steak
$14-$46

In the heart of downtown, this contemporary restaurant features Alberta prime-aged, AAA beef along with salmon, chicken and lamb. A good range of appetizers, decadent side dishes like truffle lobster mac and cheese, and house-made desserts complete the menu. Popular for after work revelry, the restaurant features a lounge with a long, New York-style bar. **Bar:** Full bar. **Reservations:** suggested. **Hours:** 11:30 am-2:30 & 5-10 pm, Fri-11 pm, Sat 5 pm-11 pm. Closed major holidays; also Sun. **Address:** 10155 101st St, Commerce Place T5J 4G8 **Location:** Just n of Jasper Ave at 101st St. **Parking:** on-site (fee).

(See map and index starting on p. 441)

MADISON'S GRILL   Phone: 780/401-2222   ⓕ⑮

Continental
$11-$42

The popular, trendy restaurant features food flavored with contemporary touches. Patrons can tempt their taste buds with crab cakes prepared in tempura batter. Among the wide selection of main courses are preparations of halibut, snapper and lamb chops. After dinner, guests can relax in the small library lounge with a sumptuous dessert. Dressy casual. **Bar:** Full bar. **Reservations:** suggested. **Hours:** 7 am-10 pm, Fri-11 pm, Sat 8 am-11 pm, Sun 8 am-9 pm. **Address:** 10053 Jasper Ave T5J 1S5 **Location:** Corner of 101st St; in Union Bank Inn. **Parking:** on-site and street.

MIKADO   Phone: 780/425-8096   ②

Japanese
$10-$20

The eatery is a hot spot for sushi in the capital city. As they enter, patrons are greeted with a warm towel and a friendly smile. The bright, contemporary dining room offers a variety of seating options—in private dining rooms, in the main restaurant or at the sushi bar. The chef is a master, creating a wide variety of sushi and sashimi. Casual dress. **Bar:** Full bar. **Reservations:** suggested. **Hours:** 11 am-10 pm, Fri & Sat-11 pm, Sun 4 pm-9 pm. **Closed:** 12/25. **Address:** 10350 109th St T5J 4X9 **Location:** Jct 103rd Ave and 109th St; in shopping plaza. **Parking:** on-site. CALL 🅼

NEW ASIAN VILLAGE   Phone: 780/433-3804   ㉒

Eastern Indian
$11-$27

East Indian cuisine is served in a cozy maharajah room or in the main dining room, which affords views of the city. Sounds of Indian music and scents of curry pique the senses, arousing an appetite for dishes such as tasty tandoori chicken, goat, lamb and vegetarian specialties. Servers are happy to offer advice about spices and specialties. Casual dress. **Bar:** Full bar. **Reservations:** suggested. **Hours:** 11 am-2:30 & 5-10 pm, Fri-11 pm, Sat 5 pm-11 pm, Sun 5 pm-10 pm. **Closed:** 12/25. **Address:** 10143 Saskatchewan Dr TZE 1V6 **Location:** From 109th St, just e. **Parking:** on-site. CALL 🅼

O'BYRNE'S IRISH PUB   Phone: 780/414-6766   ㉘

Irish
$8-$15

In a trendy area, the Irish pub welcomes travelers from around the globe. The restaurant offers a lively atmosphere, friendly service and live entertainment, as well as an all-day Irish breakfast and an excellent selection of Irish beers on tap. Casual dress. Entertainment. **Bar:** Full bar. **Reservations:** accepted. **Hours:** 11 am-midnight. **Closed:** 12/24, 12/25. **Address:** 10616 82nd Ave (Whyte Ave) T6E 2A7 **Location:** Corner of 106th St. **Parking:** on-site (fee) and street.

PACKRAT LOUIE'S KITCHEN & BAR   Phone: 780/433-0123   ㉓

Continental
$12-$44

In the heart of Old Strathcona, the bistro-style restaurant prepares fresh market cuisine. Guests can choose from pizza made in a wood-burning oven, organic chicken breasts or fresh fish and weekly specials. Dessert is a must. The Swiss owner is known for his fine desserts and Swiss chocolate truffles. Casual dress. **Bar:** Full bar. **Reservations:** suggested. **Hours:** 11:30 am-10 pm, Fri & Sat-11 pm. Closed major holidays; also Sun. **Address:** 10335 83rd Ave T6E 2C6 **Location:** Jct 103rd St and 83rd Ave, just 1 blk n of Jasper Ave. **Parking:** on-site.

PRADERA CAFE   Phone: 780/493-8994   ⑫

Canadian
$15-$35

The elegant dining room invites diners to peruse an excellent menu, which blends international influences with regional ingredients and offers some unique twists. Diners are sure to enjoy the signature zesty bread dip along with some classic offerings including salmon and Alberta beef. Service is professional and friendly. Casual dress. **Bar:** Full bar. **Reservations:** suggested. **Hours:** 6:30 am-10 pm, Sat & Sun from 7 am. **Address:** 10135 100th St T5J 0N7 **Location:** 101st St at 100th St; in The Westin Edmonton. **Parking:** on-site (fee) and valet.

RIC'S GRILL   Phone: 780/429-4333   ⑦

Steak
$12-$37

"Funky and modern" describes the decor and the food at the upscale steakhouse, which bustles with activity. Steaks are well worth it, but then again, so are the salmon, chicken and pasta dishes. A wide variety of distinctive appetizers rounds out the menu. Servers are friendly and attentive. Casual dress. **Bar:** Full bar. **Reservations:** suggested. **Hours:** 11 am-10 pm, Fri-11 pm, Sat & Sun 4 pm-10 pm. Closed major holidays. **Address:** 10190 104th St T5J 1A7 **Location:** Corner of 104th St and 102nd Ave; in historic Metals Building. **Parking:** street. **Historic** CALL 🅼

TOKYO NOODLE SHOP   Phone: 780/430-0838   ㉕

Japanese
$8-$20

The popular restaurant gives diners a choice of good, affordable sushi selections. Casual dress. **Bar:** Full bar. **Reservations:** accepted. **Hours:** 11:30 am-10 pm, Thurs-Sat to 2 am. **Closed:** 12/25. **Address:** 10736 82nd Ave T6E 6P4 **Location:** On 82nd Ave (Whyte Ave) at 107th St. **Parking:** street.

VON'S STEAK & FISH HOUSE   Phone: 780/439-0041   ㉜

Steak
$23-$40

In Strathcona, an old part of town south of the river, the restaurant offers casual dining in a subdued, intimate atmosphere. The dining room sports wood beams and a large river stone fireplace. Beef and seafood are mainstays on a menu of choices that display Louisiana and Mediterranean influences. Casual dress. **Bar:** Full bar. **Reservations:** suggested. **Hours:** 4:30 pm-10 pm. Closed: 1/1, 12/24, 12/25. **Address:** 10309 81st Ave T6E 1X3 **Location:** Just s of 82nd Ave (Whyte Ave) at 103rd St. **Parking:** street.

WILD TANGERINE   Phone: 780/429-3131   ①

Asian
$13-$30

Across from Grant McEwan College and a bevy of new condominium developments, the hip and colorful restaurant nurtures a cozy atmosphere amid its limited number of tables. Traditional Asian cuisine is overhauled in a decidedly playful and contemporary manner in reasonably priced creations such as shrimp lollipops with wasabi yogurt and five-spice octopus salad with peppers, taro, lotus root and citrus dressing. Service is friendly. Casual dress. **Bar:** Full bar. **Reservations:** accepted. **Hours:** 11:30 am-10 pm, Sat from 5 pm. Closed major holidays; also Sun. **Address:** 10383 112 St T5K 1M9 **Location:** Jct 104 Ave; at Coinfield Shopping Center. **Parking:** on-site. CALL 🅼

(See map and index starting on p. 441)

YIANNIS TAVERNA   Phone: 780/433-6768   ㉗

Greek
$8-$22

The lively, traditional restaurant is reminiscent of a cozy tavern in Greece, complete with a quaint sidewalk patio. Music, art and atmosphere combine to provide an enjoyable experience. Weekend entertainment features the hasapiko dance, belly dancing at 8:30 pm and later in the evening, the Zorba dance, in which patrons are encouraged to participate. Service is friendly, efficient and, at times, laced with Greek phrases. Casual dress. **Bar:** Full bar. **Reservations:** suggested. **Hours:** 11:30 am-10 pm, Fri & Sat-midnight, Sun & Mon 5 pm-10 pm. Closed: 1/1, 4/4, 12/24, 12/25. **Address:** 10444 82nd Ave NW (Whyte Ave) T6E 2A2 **Location:** Corner of 104th St. **Parking:** street. CALL 🅜

EDMONTON pop. 730,372 (See map and index starting on p. 444)

BEST WESTERN CEDAR PARK INN   *Book great rates at AAA.com*   Phone: (780)434-7411   ㉓

Hotel
$99-$189 All Year

Address: 5116 Gateway Blvd T6H 2H4 **Location:** Hwy 2 (Gateway Blvd) at 51st Ave. **Facility:** 195 units. 192 one-bedroom standard units, some with whirlpools. 3 one-bedroom suites, some with whirlpools. 5 stories, interior corridors. **Parking:** on-site, winter plug-ins. **Terms:** cancellation fee imposed. **Amenities:** video games (fee), voice mail, irons, hair dryers. *Some:* CD players, safes. **Dining:** Seasons Grill, see separate listing. **Pool(s):** heated indoor. **Leisure Activities:** exercise room. **Guest Services:** valet laundry, wireless Internet. **Business Services:** meeting rooms, PC. *(See color ad below)*

AAA Benefit:
Members save up to 20%, plus 10% bonus points with rewards program.

🍽 🍸 CALL 🅜 🏊 ✈ 🚪 💻 /SOME UNITS FEE 🛏 ✕ 🖥

FREE local telephone calls and high-speed Internet

BEST WESTERN CITY CENTRE INN   *Book great rates at AAA.com*   Phone: (780)479-2042   ❹

CAA SAVE
Hotel
$149-$179 All Year

Address: 11310 109th St T5G 2T7 **Location:** From Kingsway Ave NW, just n. **Facility:** 109 units. 103 one-bedroom standard units, some with whirlpools. 5 one- and 1 two-bedroom suites. 2 stories, interior/exterior corridors. **Parking:** on-site, winter plug-ins. **Amenities:** high-speed Internet, voice mail, irons, hair dryers. **Pool(s):** heated indoor. **Leisure Activities:** whirlpool, waterslide, exercise room. **Guest Services:** valet and coin laundry, airport transportation (fee)-Edmonton International Airport, wireless Internet. **Business Services:** meeting rooms, PC. **Free Special Amenities:** local telephone calls and high-speed Internet.

AAA Benefit:
Members save up to 20%, plus 10% bonus points with rewards program.

FEE ✈ 🍽 24 🍸 🏊 ✕ ✈ 💻 🖥 /SOME UNITS ✕ 🖥

▼ *See AAA listing above* ▼

(See map and index starting on p. 444)

BEST WESTERN SOUTH EDMONTON INN & SUITES　　Phone: 780/801-3580

fyi
Hotel
$129-$149 All Year

Too new to rate, opening scheduled for October 2009. **Address:** 1204 101st St T6X 0P1 **Location:** Hwy 2, exit 1. **Amenities:** 105 units, coffeemakers, microwaves, refrigerators, pool.

AAA Benefit:
Members save up to 20%, plus 10% bonus points with rewards program.

BEST WESTERN WESTWOOD INN　　*Book great rates at AAA.com*　　Phone: (780)483-7770　　⑨

CAA SAVE
▼▼▼▼▼
Hotel
$109-$189 All Year

Address: 18035 Stony Plain Rd T5S 1B2 **Location:** Hwy 16A (Stony Plain Rd) at 180th St. **Facility:** 171 one-bedroom standard units, some with whirlpools. 3-6 stories, interior corridors. **Parking:** on-site, winter plug-ins. **Terms:** cancellation fee imposed. **Amenities:** video games (fee), voice mail, safes, irons, hair dryers. *Some:* high-speed Internet. **Pool(s):** heated indoor. **Leisure Activities:** exercise room. *Fee:* game room. **Guest Services:** valet laundry, wireless Internet. **Business Services:** conference facilities, business center. *(See color ad below)*

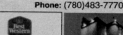

AAA Benefit:
Members save up to 20%, plus 10% bonus points with rewards program.

FREE local telephone calls and high-speed Internet

CAMPUS TOWER SUITE HOTEL　　*Book at AAA.com*　　Phone: (780)439-6060　　⑲

◆◆ ◆◆
Hotel
$125-$245 All Year

Address: 11145 87th Ave T6G 0Y1 **Location:** At 111th St and 87th Ave. Located near University and Hospital campuses. **Facility:** Smoke free premises. 90 units. 9 one-bedroom standard units, some with efficiencies or kitchens. 72 one- and 9 two-bedroom suites, some with efficiencies or kitchens. 16 stories, interior corridors. **Parking:** on-site, winter plug-ins. **Terms:** check-in 4 pm, cancellation fee imposed. **Amenities:** voice mail, irons, hair dryers. *Some:* CD players, high-speed Internet, dual phone lines. **Leisure Activities:** exercise room. **Guest Services:** valet and coin laundry, wireless Internet. **Business Services:** meeting rooms. *Fee:* administrative services, PC.

COMFORT INN WEST　　*Book great rates at AAA.com*　　Phone: (780)484-4415　　⑫

CAA SAVE
▼▼ ▼▼
Hotel
$99-$159 All Year

Address: 17610 100th Ave T5S 1S9 **Location:** At 176th St. **Facility:** 100 one-bedroom standard units. 2 stories (no elevator), interior corridors. **Parking:** on-site, winter plug-ins. **Terms:** cancellation fee imposed. **Amenities:** voice mail, irons, hair dryers. **Guest Services:** valet and coin laundry, wireless Internet. **Business Services:** meeting rooms, PC (fee).

▼ *See AAA listing above* ▼

(See map and index starting on p. 444)

CONTINENTAL INN

Hotel
$110-$145 All Year

Phone: (780)484-7751 ⑩

Address: 16625 Stony Plain Rd T5P 4A8 **Location:** On Hwy 16A (Stony Plain Rd) at 166th St. **Facility:** 100 one-bedroom standard units, some with whirlpools. 6 stories, interior corridors. **Parking:** on-site, winter plug-ins. **Terms:** 6 day cancellation notice-fee imposed. **Amenities:** high-speed Internet (fee), voice mail, hair dryers. *Some:* irons. **Dining:** 2 restaurants. **Leisure Activities:** exercise room. **Guest Services:** valet and coin laundry, wireless Internet. **Business Services:** meeting rooms, PC (fee). **Free Special Amenities:** local telephone calls and high-speed Internet.

DAYS INN & SUITES WEST EDMONTON

Book great rates at AAA.com

Hotel
$149-$189 All Year

Phone: (780)444-4440 ⑮

Address: 10010 179A St T5S 2T1 **Location:** From Anthony Henday Dr, 1.2 mi (2 km) e. **Facility:** Smoke free premises. 108 units. 84 one-bedroom standard units. 24 one-bedroom suites with efficiencies, some with whirlpools. 4 stories, interior corridors. **Parking:** on-site, winter plug-ins. **Terms:** check-in 4 pm, cancellation fee imposed. **Amenities:** video games (fee), high-speed Internet, dual phone lines, voice mail, irons, hair dryers. *Some:* CD players. **Dining:** ConYac's Bar & Grill, see separate listing. **Pool(s):** heated indoor. **Leisure Activities:** whirlpool, exercise room. **Guest Services:** valet and coin laundry, airport transportation (fee)-Edmonton International Airport, wireless Internet. **Business Services:** meeting rooms, PC. **Free Special Amenities:** local telephone calls and high-speed Internet. *(See color ad below)*

DELTA EDMONTON SOUTH HOTEL AND CONFERENCE CENTRE

Book at AAA.com

Hotel
Rates not provided

Phone: 780/434-6415 ㉖

Address: 4404 Gateway Blvd T6H 5C2 **Location:** Jct Calgary Tr (Hwy 2) and Whitemud Dr. **Facility:** Smoke free premises. 237 units. 233 one-bedroom standard units, some with whirlpools. 4 one-bedroom suites with whirlpools. 11 stories, interior corridors. **Parking:** on-site and valet, winter plug-ins. **Amenities:** high-speed Internet (fee), voice mail, irons, hair dryers. *Some:* DVD players. **Pool(s):** heated indoor. **Leisure Activities:** whirlpool, exercise room. **Guest Services:** valet laundry. **Business Services:** conference facilities, business center.

EDMONTON MARRIOTT AT RIVER CREE RESORT

Book great rates at AAA.com

Hotel
$188-$230 All Year

Phone: (780)484-2121

AAA Benefit: Members save a minimum 5% off the best available rate.

Address: 300 E Lapotac Blvd T7X 3Y3 **Location:** 1 mi (1.6 km) w of jct Hwy 216 (Anthony Henday Dr) and Whitemud Dr W. **Facility:** Located on the western outskirts of Edmonton and ten minutes of West Edmonton Mall, the hotel offers spacious guest rooms with contemporary decor. Smoke free premises. 249 units. 239 one-bedroom standard units. 10 one-bedroom suites. 9 stories, interior corridors. *Bath:* combo or shower only. **Parking:** on-site. **Terms:** check-in 4 pm, cancellation fee imposed. **Amenities:** high-speed Internet (fee), voice mail, irons, hair dryers. **Dining:** 3 restaurants, also, Sage Restaurant, see separate listing. **Pool(s):** heated indoor. **Leisure Activities:** whirlpool, hockey rinks, exercise room. **Guest Services:** valet laundry, area transportation-West Edmonton Mall. **Business Services:** conference facilities, business center. *(See color ad p 456)*

FREE newspaper

(See map and index starting on p. 444)

EXECUTIVE ROYAL INN WEST EDMONTON   *Book at AAA.com*   **Phone:** (780)484-6000   **13**

Hotel
$120 All Year

Address: 10010 178th St T5S 1T3 **Location:** Corner of 178th St and 100th Ave. **Facility:** Smoke free premises. 235 units. 230 one-bedroom standard units, some with whirlpools. 5 one-bedroom suites with whirlpools. 4 stories, interior corridors. *Bath:* combo or shower only. **Parking:** on-site, winter plug-ins. **Terms:** check-in 4 pm. **Amenities:** video games (fee), voice mail, irons, hair dryers. *Some:* high-speed Internet. **Leisure Activities:** whirlpools, exercise room. **Guest Services:** valet laundry, area transportation (fee), wireless Internet. **Business Services:** conference facilities, PC.

ECO ASK FEE 🚭 ▥ ▦ ✕ 🎥 ▤ / SOME UNITS FEE 🐕 ▢

FOUR POINTS BY SHERATON EDMONTON SOUTH   *Book great rates at AAA.com*   **Phone:** 780/465-7931   **21**

CAA SAVE
Hotel
Rates not provided

Address: 7230 Argyll Rd T6C 4A6 **Location:** Hwy 2 (Gateway Blvd), 2.3 mi (3.7 km) e at 63rd Ave (which becomes Argyll Rd); at 75th St. **Facility:** Smoke free premises. 139 units. 109 one-bedroom standard units, some with whirlpools. 30 one-bedroom suites. 7 stories, interior corridors. **Parking:** on-site, winter plug-ins. **Amenities:** high-speed Internet, voice mail, irons, hair dryers. **Pool(s):** heated indoor. **Leisure Activities:** whirlpool, exercise room. **Guest Services:** valet laundry, wireless Internet. **Business Services:** conference facilities, business center. *(See color ad p 457)*

FOUR POINTS BY SHERATON

AAA Benefit:
Members get up to 15% off, plus Starwood Preferred Guest® bonuses.

▥ ▦ CALL 🏋M 🏊 ✕ 🎥 ▤ / SOME UNITS FEE 🐕 ▢ ▦

FREE room upgrade (subject to availability with advance reservations) and high-speed Internet

---

HAMPTON INN & SUITES EDMONTON WEST   *Book great rates at AAA.com*   **Phone:** (780)484-7280   **17**

Hotel
$159-$189 All Year

Address: 18304 100th Ave T5S 2V2 **Location:** From Anthony Henday Dr, 0.8 mi (1.3 km) e. **Facility:** Smoke free premises. 103 one-bedroom standard units. 5 stories, interior corridors. *Bath:* combo or shower only. **Parking:** on-site, winter plug-ins. **Terms:** check-in 4 pm, 1-7 night minimum stay, cancellation fee imposed. **Amenities:** high-speed Internet, voice mail, safes, irons, hair dryers. **Pool(s):** heated indoor. **Leisure Activities:** whirlpool, exercise room. **Guest Services:** valet and coin laundry, wireless Internet. **Business Services:** meeting rooms, business center.

AAA Benefit:
Members save up to 10% everyday!

FEE 🚭 ▥ CALL 🏋M 🏊 ✕ ▤ / SOME UNITS ▢ ▦

▼ See AAA listing p 455 ▼

(See map and index starting on p. 444)

HILTON GARDEN INN-WEST EDMONTON *Book great rates at AAA.com* **Phone:** (780)443-2233 **7**

Hotel
$139-$219 All Year

Address: 17610 Stony Plain Rd T5S 1A2 **Location:** From 176th St, just w. **Facility:** Smoke free premises. 160 units. 155 one-bedroom standard units. 5 one-bedroom suites with whirlpools. 6 stories, interior corridors. **Parking:** on-site, winter plug-ins. **Terms:** check-in 4 pm, 1-7 night minimum stay, cancellation fee imposed. **Amenities:** video games (fee), high-speed Internet, dual phone lines, voice mail, safes, irons, hair dryers. **Pool(s):** heated indoor. **Leisure Activities:** whirlpool, exercise room. **Guest Services:** valet and coin laundry, wireless Internet. **Business Services:** meeting rooms, business center.

CALL

Hilton Garden Inn

AAA Benefit:
Members save 5% or more everyday!

HOLIDAY INN & SUITES, WEST EDMONTON *Book great rates at AAA.com* **Phone:** (780)444-3110 **5**

CAA SAVE

Hotel
$139-$249 All Year

Address: 11330 170th St T5S 2X1 **Location:** Between 114th and 113th aves. **Facility:** Smoke free premises. 112 units. 96 one-bedroom standard units, some with whirlpools. 16 one-bedroom suites. 4 stories, interior corridors. *Bath:* combo or shower only. **Parking:** on-site, winter plug-ins. **Amenities:** high-speed Internet, dual phone lines, voice mail, irons, hair dryers. **Pool(s):** heated indoor. **Leisure Activities:** whirlpool, exercise room. **Guest Services:** valet and coin laundry, wireless Internet. **Business Services:** meeting rooms, PC. **Free Special Amenities: local telephone calls and high-speed Internet.** *(See color ad on insert)*

CALL / SOME UNITS

HOLIDAY INN CONVENTION CENTRE (S.E. EDMONTON) *Book great rates at AAA.com* **Phone:** (780)468-5400 **20**

CAA SAVE

Hotel
$109-$229 All Year

Address: 4520 76th Ave T6B 0A5 **Location:** Hwy 14, just s via 50th St exit, then just e. **Facility:** 93 one-bedroom standard units, some with whirlpools. 6 stories, interior corridors. **Parking:** on-site, winter plug-ins. **Amenities:** dual phone lines, voice mail, irons, hair dryers. *Fee:* video games, high-speed Internet. **Pool(s):** heated indoor. **Leisure Activities:** whirlpool, steamroom, exercise room. **Guest Services:** valet laundry, wireless Internet. **Business Services:** conference facilities, PC. **Free Special Amenities: newspaper and high-speed Internet.** *(See color ad on insert)*

/ SOME UNITS

▼ *See AAA listing p 456* ▼

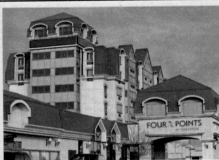

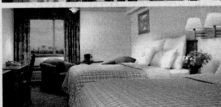

(See map and index starting on p. 444)

HOLIDAY INN EXPRESS & SUITES EDMONTON NORTH

Hotel
$139-$229 All Year

Phone: 780/476-9898 **1**

Address: 13742 50th St NW T5A 4Y3 **Location:** Hwy 16 (Yellowhead Tr); 1 mi (1.6 km) n on 50th St (SR 15). **Facility:** Smoke free premises. 95 units. 56 one-bedroom standard units, some with whirlpools. 39 one-bedroom suites. 6 stories, interior corridors. *Bath:* combo or shower only. **Parking:** on-site, winter plug-ins. **Terms:** cancellation fee imposed. **Amenities:** high-speed Internet, voice mail, irons, hair dryers. **Pool(s):** heated indoor. **Leisure Activities:** whirlpool. **Business Services:** PC (fee). **Free Special Amenities:** expanded continental breakfast and high-speed Internet.

HOLIDAY INN EXPRESS HOTEL & SUITES EDMONTON *Book great rates at AAA.com*

Hotel
$149-$189 All Year

Phone: (780)483-4000 **14**

Address: 10017 179A St T5S 2L4 **Location:** On 100th Ave, just w of 178th St. **Facility:** 102 units. 68 one-bedroom standard units, some with whirlpools. 34 one-bedroom suites, some with whirlpools. 4 stories, interior corridors. **Parking:** on-site, winter plug-ins. **Terms:** check-in 4 pm, cancellation fee imposed. **Amenities:** video games (fee), dual phone lines, voice mail, irons, hair dryers. **Pool(s):** heated indoor. **Leisure Activities:** whirlpool, steamroom, exercise room. *Fee:* game room. **Guest Services:** valet and coin laundry, airport transportation (fee)-Edmonton International Airport, wireless Internet. **Business Services:** meeting rooms, PC. *(See color ad below)*

FREE expanded continental breakfast and high-speed Internet

HOTEL SELKIRK

Hotel
Rates not provided

Phone: 780/496-7227 **22**

Address: 7000 143rd St T5J 2R7 **Location:** From Whitemud Dr, exit Fox Dr, follow signs for Fort Edmonton. Located in Fort Edmonton Park. **Facility:** Smoke free premises. 28 units. 26 one-bedroom standard units. 2 one-bedroom suites. 2 stories, interior corridors. **Parking:** on-site and valet. **Terms:** open 5/16-9/1, office hours 7 am-11 pm, check-in 4 pm. **Amenities:** voice mail, hair dryers. *Some:* irons. **Leisure Activities:** hiking trails. **Guest Services:** wireless Internet.

MAYFIELD INN & SUITES AT WEST EDMONTON *Book great rates at AAA.com*

Hotel
$150-$225 All Year

Phone: (780)484-0821 **6**

Address: 16615 109th Ave T5P 4K8 **Location:** 1 mi (1.6 km) n of jct Hwy 2 (170th St) and 16A (Stony Plain Rd). **Facility:** Smoke free premises. 327 units. 219 one-bedroom standard units, some with kitchens and/or whirlpools. 108 one-bedroom suites, some with whirlpools. 10 stories, interior corridors. **Parking:** on-site, winter plug-ins. **Terms:** cancellation fee imposed. **Amenities:** video games (fee), high-speed Internet, voice mail, irons, hair dryers. *Some:* DVD players, dual phone lines, safes. **Dining:** 2 restaurants, nightclub. **Pool(s):** heated indoor. **Leisure Activities:** saunas, whirlpool, steamroom, racquetball courts, 5 squash courts, spa. *Fee:* esthetics. **Guest Services:** valet and coin laundry. **Business Services:** conference facilities, business center. **Free Special Amenities:** local telephone calls and high-speed Internet.

(See map and index starting on p. 444)

QUALITY INN WEST HARVEST *Book at AAA.com*   Phone: (780)484-8000   11

◊◊◊
Hotel
$105-$199 All Year

Address: 17803 Stony Plain Rd NW T5S 1B4 **Location:** Hwy 16A (Stony Plain Rd) at 178th St. **Facility:** Smoke free premises. 159 one-bedroom standard units, some with whirlpools. 3 stories, interior corridors. *Bath:* combo or shower only. **Parking:** on-site, winter plug-ins. **Terms:** check-in 4 pm, cancellation fee imposed. **Amenities:** video games (fee), voice mail, irons, hair dryers. *Some:* high-speed Internet. **Guest Services:** valet parking, wireless Internet. **Business Services:** meeting rooms, PC. ASK ⊣⊢ ⧓ ⊠ ⚟ ⊑ / SOME UNITS FEE ⊨ ⊟ ⊡

RADISSON HOTEL EDMONTON SOUTH *Book great rates at AAA.com*   Phone: (780)437-6010   25

(CAA) SAVE
◊◊◊
Hotel
$165-$200 All Year

Address: 4440 Gateway Blvd NW T6H 5C2 **Location:** Between Whitemud Dr and 45th Ave. **Facility:** 235 units. 223 one-bedroom standard units. 12 one-bedroom suites, some with whirlpools. 4 stories, interior corridors. **Parking:** on-site, winter plug-ins. **Terms:** cancellation fee imposed. **Amenities:** video games, high-speed Internet, voice mail, irons, hair dryers. **Pool(s):** heated indoor. **Leisure Activities:** sauna, whirlpool, steamroom, aerobics, indoor track, massage, sports court. **Guest Services:** valet and coin laundry, airport transportation (fee)-Edmonton International Airport. **Business Services:** PC. **Free Special Amenities:** local telephone calls and high-speed Internet.

ECO FEE ⊣⊢ ⧓ ⊠ ⚟ ⊑ / SOME UNITS FEE ⊨ ⊠ ⊟ ⊡

ROSSLYN INN & SUITES *Book at AAA.com*   Phone: (780)476-6241   2

◊◊◊
Hotel
$117-$159 All Year

Address: 13620 97th St T5E 4E2 **Location:** Hwy 16 (Yellowhead Tr), exit 97th St, 1 mi (1.6 km) n. **Facility:** Smoke free premises. 93 units. 77 one-bedroom standard units, some with whirlpools. 16 one-bedroom suites. 2-5 stories, interior corridors. *Bath:* combo or shower only. **Parking:** on-site, winter plug-ins. **Terms:** cancellation fee imposed. **Amenities:** video games (fee), voice mail, irons, hair dryers. *Some:* high-speed Internet. **Leisure Activities:** exercise room. **Guest Services:** valet and coin laundry, wireless Internet. **Business Services:** meeting rooms, PC (fee).

ECO ASK ⊣⊢ ⧓ ⊠ ⚟ ⊑ / SOME UNITS FEE ⊨ ⊟ ⊡

SAWRIDGE INN EDMONTON SOUTH *Book great rates at AAA.com*   Phone: (780)438-1222   27

(CAA) SAVE
◊◊◊
Hotel
$129-$159 All Year

Address: 4235 Gateway Blvd T6J 5H2 **Location:** Just s of Whitemud Dr. **Facility:** 136 units. 109 one- and 14 two-bedroom standard units, some with whirlpools. 13 one-bedroom suites. 5 stories, interior corridors. *Bath:* combo or shower only. **Parking:** on-site, winter plug-ins. **Terms:** 14 day cancellation notice. **Amenities:** video games (fee), high-speed Internet, dual phone lines, voice mail, irons, hair dryers. **Leisure Activities:** whirlpools, steamroom, exercise room. **Guest Services:** valet laundry, airport transportation-Edmonton International Airport, area transportation-West Edmonton Mall, wireless Internet, beauty salon. **Business Services:** conference facilities. *(See color ad below)*

⊣⊢ ⧓ ⊠ ⚟ ⊑ / SOME UNITS FEE ⊨ ⊠ ⊟ ⊡

(See map and index starting on p. 444)

SUPER 8 EDMONTON SOUTH   *Book at AAA.com*   Phone: 780/433-8688   2

▽▽▽
Hotel
Rates not provided

Address: 3610 Gateway Blvd T6J 7H8 **Location:** Jct 36th Ave. **Facility:** Smoke free premises. 10 units. 69 one-bedroom standard units, some with whirlpools. 35 one-bedroom suites. 4 stories, interic corridors. *Bath:* combo or shower only. **Parking:** on-site, winter plug-ins. **Amenities:** high-spee Internet, voice mail, irons, hair dryers. **Pool(s):** heated indoor. **Leisure Activities:** whirlpoo waterslide. **Guest Services:** valet and coin laundry, wireless Internet.

FEE ⬅ 🍴 CALL 🄼 🏊 ✕ 🖥 💻 / SOME UNITS FEE 🐾 📷

TRAVELODGE EDMONTON EAST   *Book great rates at AAA.com*   Phone: (780)474-0456   3

CAA SAVE
▽▽ ▽▽
Hotel
$89-$139 All Year

Address: 3414 118th Ave T5W 0Z4 **Location:** 5 mi (8 km) e of Capilano Dr, 0.6 mi (1 km) s from V Hwy 16 (Yellowhead Tr), exit Victoria Tr. **Facility:** 86 one-bedroom standard units. 2 stories (n elevator), interior corridors. **Parking:** on-site, winter plug-ins. **Amenities:** voice mail, hair dryer *Some:* irons. **Dining:** 2 restaurants. **Guest Services:** wireless Internet, barber shop. **Busines Services:** meeting rooms, PC (fee). **Free Special Amenities: expanded continental breakfast an high-speed Internet.**

🍴 🍷 🖥 💻 / SOME UNITS FEE 🐾 ✕

TRAVELODGE EDMONTON SOUTH   *Book at AAA.com*   Phone: (780)436-9770   2

▽▽ ▽▽
Hotel
$109-$159 All Year

Address: 10320 45th Ave S T6H 5K3 **Location:** Jct Calgary Tr (Hwy 2) and 45th Ave, just n c Whitemud Dr. **Facility:** 219 one-bedroom standard units. 3 stories, interior corridors. **Parking:** on-sit winter plug-ins. **Amenities:** video games (fee), voice mail, irons, hair dryers. *Some:* high-spee Internet. **Pool(s):** heated indoor. **Leisure Activities:** whirlpool, limited exercise equipment. **Gue Services:** valet and coin laundry, wireless Internet. **Business Services:** PC (fee).

ECO ASK 🍴 🏊 🎥 💻 / SOME UNITS FEE 🐾 ✕ 🖥 📷

TRAVELODGE EDMONTON WEST   *Book great rates at AAA.com*   Phone: (780)483-6031   6

CAA SAVE
▽▽ ▽▽
Hotel
$109-$159 All Year

Address: 18320 Stony Plain Rd T5S 1A7 **Location:** Hwy 16A (Stony Plain Rd) at 184th S **Facility:** 220 one-bedroom standard units. 5 stories, interior corridors. **Parking:** on-site **Amenities:** video games (fee), voice mail, irons, hair dryers. *Some:* high-speed Interne **Pool(s):** heated indoor. **Leisure Activities:** whirlpool, waterslide. *Fee:* game room. **Guest Services** valet and coin laundry, wireless Internet. **Business Services:** meeting rooms.

ECO 🍴 🏊 ✕ 🎥 💻 / SOME UNITS FEE 🐾 ✕ 🖥 📷

WEST EDMONTON MALL INN   *Book at AAA.com*   Phone: (780)444-9378   18

▽▽ ▽▽
Hotel
$149 All Year

Address: 17504 90th Ave T5T 6L6 **Location:** Whitemud Dr, exit 170th St N, just w. Located next t the mall. **Facility:** 88 one-bedroom standard units. 3 stories, interior corridors. **Parking:** on-site, winte plug-ins. **Terms:** check-in 4 pm, cancellation fee imposed. **Amenities:** high-speed Internet (fee), voic mail, hair dryers. *Some:* irons. **Guest Services:** valet laundry, wireless Internet. **Business Services** meeting rooms. ASK 🍴 CALL 🄼 🎥 🖥 💻 / SOME UNITS FEE 🐾 ✕ 📷

WINGATE INN EDMONTON WEST   *Book at AAA.com*   Phone: (780)443-1000   16

▽▽▽
Hotel
$139-$160 All Year

Address: 18220 100th Ave T5S 2V2 **Location:** From Anthony Henday Dr, 0.9 mi (1.5 km) e at 182n St. **Facility:** 105 units. 101 one-bedroom standard units. 4 one-bedroom suites, some with whirlpools 4 stories, interior corridors. **Parking:** on-site, winter plug-ins. **Terms:** cancellation fee impose **Amenities:** video games (fee), high-speed Internet, dual phone lines, voice mail, safes, irons, ha dryers. **Pool(s):** heated indoor. **Leisure Activities:** whirlpool, waterslide, exercise room. **Gues Services:** valet and coin laundry, wireless Internet. **Business Services:** meeting rooms, busines center. ASK 🍴 🏊 ✕ 🎥 🖥 📷 💻 / SOME UNITS FEE 🐾 ✕

—— WHERE TO DINE ——

BARB & ERNIE'S   Phone: 780/433-3242   15

German
$8-$25

Ask any local for a favorite breakfast place, and this is often mentioned. Lunch and dinner are popular a well. Ernie himself often greets guests as they enter. Among the homey restaurant's pleasing array c Bavarian dishes are sauerkraut and sausages. Casual dress. **Bar:** Full bar. **Reservations:** accepted **Hours:** 7 am-7:30 pm, Sat 8 am-8 pm, Sun 8 am-3 pm. Closed major holidays; also Mon. **Address:** 990 72nd Ave NW T6E 0Z3 **Location:** 99th St S, w at 72nd Ave. **Parking:** on-site.

THE BLUE PEAR   Phone: 780/482-7178   2

French
$85

The name of the upscale restaurant is derived from its previous name, D'Anjou. After ringing the doorbel guests enter a small dining room, where there are but 12 tables amid serene, simple decor. Featurin French cooking techniques and regional ingredients, the five-course prix fixe menu changes monthly Representative of typical menu fare are veal osso buco with saffron risotto or butter-poached Australian Ba lobster layered in herb lasagna. Servers are well-versed in food and wine pairings. Dressy casual. **Bar:** Fu bar. **Reservations:** required. **Hours:** 5 pm-9 pm. Closed major holidays; also Mon & Tues. **Address:** 1064 123rd St T5N 1P3 **Location:** Southeast corner of 123rd St and 7th Ave. **Parking:** on-site. CALL 🄼

CENTURY GRILL   Phone: 780/431-0303   2

Northern Pacific
Rim
$17-$41

Chic and contemporary, the upscale restaurant features a lovely open-concept dining room with black an gray decor. Patrons can dine in the restaurant or the more casual lounge. Creative cuisine boldly pair varied tastes and sensations. The menu focuses heavily on regional ingredients and also exhibits Californian flair. Casual dress. **Bar:** Full bar. **Reservations:** suggested. **Hours:** 11 am-2 & 5-10 pm, Fri Sat-11 pm, Sun-10 pm. Closed major holidays. **Address:** 3975 Calgary Tr T6J 6S6 **Location:** Calgary Tr a at 39th Ave. **Parking:** on-site. CALL 🄼

(See map and index starting on p. 444)

THE CHEESECAKE CAFE

Phone: 780/486-0440   **9**

American
$10-$25

As might be expected, cheesecake is the signature item, and it's worth saving room for one of the lip-smacking varieties made on the premises. A huge dessert display case greets guests upon arrival. Offerings on the extensive lunch and dinner menu range from sandwiches and entree salads to pasta, pizza and seafood selections. It takes a while to get through the menu. Casual dress. **Bar:** Full bar. **Reservations:** not accepted. **Hours:** 11 am-10 pm, Fri & Sat-11 pm, Sun 10 am-10 pm. Closed: 12/24. **Address:** 17011 100th Ave T5S 1T9 **Location:** Jct 100th Ave and 170th St. **Parking:** on-site. CALL 👍M

CONYAC'S BAR & GRILL

Phone: 780/483-2255   **10**

Canadian
$9-$25

As far as hotel restaurants go, this place doesn't fit into the conventional mold. Seats and booths in the comfortably decorated dining room are designed to be comfortable for longer visits. While the menu does not take any risks, diners will find all of the classic dishes to be solidly executed and tasty. Casual dress. **Bar:** Full bar. **Reservations:** accepted. **Hours:** 6:30 am-10 pm. **Address:** 10010 179A St T5S 2T1 **Location:** From Anthony Henday Dr, 1.2 mi (2 km) e; in Days Inn & Suites West Edmonton. **Parking:** on-site. CALL 👍M

DELUX BURGER BAR

Phone: 780/420-0101   **12**

American
$9-$20

Burgers almost seem out of place at this upbeat and stylish space, but the menu lists several gourmet varieties, such as the Black Angus-infused burger, in addition to lobster nachos, sweet potato fries and the signature deluxe donuts. Casual dress. **Bar:** Full bar. **Reservations:** not accepted. **Hours:** 11 am-11 pm, Fri & Sat-2 am. Closed major holidays. **Address:** 9682 142 St T5N 4B2 **Location:** Jct 97 Ave NW; in shopping plaza. **Parking:** on-site.

THE DISH BISTRO

Phone: 780/488-6181   **3**

International
$12-$16

In the art district, the little bistro is a cozy place for a healthy, quick bite or quaint, leisurely meal. Among interesting creations are curried egg sandwiches, crab cakes and sumptuous pastas. The dining room has original artwork, hardwood floors and large, street-view windows. Casual dress. **Bar:** Full bar. **Reservations:** suggested. **Hours:** 11 am-9 pm. Closed major holidays; also Sun. **Address:** 12417 Stony Plain Rd T5N 3N3 **Location:** Just w of jct Hwy 16A (Stony Plain Rd) and 124th St. **Parking:** street.

FIFE N' DEKEL

Phone: 780/489-6436   **1**

Deli
$6-$10

Quick, healthy lunch options are plentiful at the cafeteria-style eatery. Guests order at the counter and watch their sandwich being made. In addition to such sandwiches as roasted turkey, beef, ham and vegetarian, the menu lists soups, salads and tempting selections from a dessert case full of sumptuous options. Because this place draws a good crowd at lunch, patrons should arrive early to avoid lines. Casual dress. **Reservations:** not accepted. **Hours:** 7 am-4:30 pm, Sat 10:30 am-3 pm. Closed major holidays; also Sun. **Address:** 10646 170th St T5S 1P3 **Location:** At 106th Ave; in industrial shopping plaza; on west side of road. **Parking:** on-site.

GLENORA BISTRO

Phone: 780/482-3531   **4**

Canadian
$11-$29

On the ground floor of a bed and breakfast, this European-feeling restaurant serves up food that's anything but quaint. Taking a contemporary international approach, the chef sources out the best of local and seasonal ingredients to create classic dishes that have clean, distinct and exciting flavors and truly express what good food is all about. Casual dress. **Bar:** Full bar. **Reservations:** accepted. **Hours:** 7 am-10 pm, Sat & Sun from 8 am. Closed major holidays. **Address:** 10139 124th St T5N 1P5 **Location:** At 124th St; in Glenora Bed & Breakfast Inn. **Parking:** street.

HOMEFIRE BAR & GRILL

Phone: 780/489-8086   **11**

Canadian
$14-$32

This upscale yet comfortable restaurant features a large central fireplace that serves to remind guests that this place specializes in forno-style dishes. In addition to oven-baked pasta, pizzas, rotisserie chicken and other comfort foods, the menu also takes a few detours into Vietnamese and Thai cooking. Casual dress. **Bar:** Full bar. **Reservations:** suggested, weekends. **Hours:** 11 am-10 pm, Fri & Sat-11 pm. Closed: 12/25. **Address:** 18210 100th Ave T5S 2V2 **Location:** Jct 184th St and 100th Ave; next to Wingate Inn Edmonton West. **Parking:** on-site. CALL 👍M

IL PASTICCIO TRATTORIA

Phone: 780/488-9543   **8**

Italian
$12-$35

Just a block south of Jasper Avenue, the funky little trattoria nurtures a cozy atmosphere, complete with an open kitchen where diners can watch the chefs toss homemade pasta and put together traditional Italian meat dishes. Boldly painted walls and black tablecloths set the scene. Servers are prompt and friendly. Casual dress. **Bar:** Full bar. **Reservations:** accepted. **Hours:** 11 am-2 & 5-10 pm, Sat from 5 pm, Sun 5 pm-9 pm. Closed major holidays. **Address:** 11520 100th Ave T5K 0J7 **Location:** Corner of 116th St and 100th Ave. **Parking:** on-site (fee).

JACK'S GRILL

Phone: 780/434-1113   **17**

Regional
Canadian
$28-$43

The chef is an architect who builds unusual, inventive cuisine with fresh ingredients, bold flavors and French and West Coast influences. The relaxed, casual atmosphere sustains a feel of upscale elegance. Regardless of whether diners choose seating in the dining room or on the seasonal patio, they can expect flawless, professional service. The owner himself often checks on his guests. Dressy casual. **Bar:** Full bar. **Reservations:** suggested. **Hours:** 5 pm-10 pm. Closed major holidays; also Sun & 1st week of Jan. **Address:** 5842 111th St T6H 3G1 **Location:** Whitemud Dr, exit 111th St, 0.5 mi (0.8 km) n, then just w on 57th Ave; in strip mall. **Parking:** on-site. CALL 👍M

JOEY RESTAURANTS

Phone: 780/465-1880

Mediterranean
$10-$29

The cuisine blends Mediterranean and Asian cooking styles and emphasizes finger foods for sharing. Those who aren't big fans of tapas can consider full meal offerings centered on steaks and chops. **Bar:** Full bar. **Hours:** 11:30 am-1 am. Closed: 12/25. **Address:** 9911 19th Ave NW T6N 1M4 **Location:** South Edmonton Commons. **Parking:** on-site.

(See map and index starting on p. 444)

KOUTOUKI TAVERNA　　　　　　　　　　　　Phone: 780/432-3660　〔20〕

Greek
$20-$35

This restaurant served as a set in the Food Network Canada TV series "The Family Restaurant," a behind-the-scenes drama about the ongoing antics of a local restaurateur and his Greek family. Cool, comfortable decor is reflective of Greece, with many white and blue accents, terra cotta tiles and fake grape-covered arbors hanging from the ceilings. Not surprisingly, the menu is typical Greek, listing such favorites as souvlaki, moussaka and roasted lamb. Belly dancers occasionally perform. Casual dress. **Bar:** Full bar. **Reservations:** suggested. **Hours:** 4:30 pm-10 pm. Closed: 12/25. **Address:** 10310 45 Ave T6H 5K3 **Location:** Jct Gateway Blvd NW; just n of Whitemud Dr. **Parking:** on-site. CALL 🅼

LA FAVORITE PASTRY SHOP　　　　　　　　　Phone: 780/482-7024　〔6〕

Breads/Pastries
$4-$8

Opening into a bookstore, the pastry shop generates the smells of chocolate and sugar that tend to waft through both. The cute little chocolate shop has several small tables and chairs at which to enjoy a fresh cup of coffee and a slice (or more) of any of the beautiful cakes the store makes fresh each day. Casual dress. **Reservations:** not accepted. **Hours:** 10 am-5:30 pm, Sun noon-4 pm. Closed major holidays. **Address:** 12431 102nd Ave NW T5N 0M2 **Location:** Just w of jct 124th St W. **Parking:** on-site.

LEMONGRASS CAFE　　　　　　　　　　　　Phone: 780/413-0088　〔19〕

Vietnamese
$6-$19

This restaurant has a deceptively unassuming exterior. Just behind the doors is a bright, cheerful, airy cafe offering exciting, fresh, healthy entrees. Traditional Vietnamese fare includes salad rolls, curries and the house specialty: spiced salmon wrapped in banana leaf with vermicelli. Guests can finish off the meal with a single malt scotch or innovative dessert. Casual dress. **Bar:** Full bar. **Reservations:** suggested, weekends. **Hours:** 11 am-9 pm, Fri & Sat-10 pm, Sun 4 pm-9 pm. Closed major holidays. **Address:** 10417 51st Ave T6H 0K4 **Location:** Just w of 104th St on Allard Way; in small strip mall. **Parking:** on-site.

MANOR CAFE　　　　　　　　　　　　　　　Phone: 780/482-7577　〔7〕

International
$12-$34

The cafe occupies the beautifully restored home of one of Alberta's former attorney generals. Decor is charming, warm and intimate, with a casual feel. The bistro-style menu includes progressive and innovative international dishes. Casual dress. **Bar:** Full bar. **Reservations:** suggested. **Hours:** 11 am-4 & 5-10 pm, Fri & Sat-midnight, Sun 11 am-2 & 5-9 pm; Sunday brunch. Closed major holidays. **Address:** 10109 125th St T5N 1S7 **Location:** Just s of 102nd Ave. **Parking:** on-site. CALL 🅼

MOXIE'S CLASSIC GRILL　　　　　　　　　　Phone: 780/484-204●

Canadian
$10-$30

This sleek, funky and popular restaurant presents an extensive menu of creatively prepared dishes including pizza, pasta, rice, noodles, signature salads and burgers. Other menus include one for children and one for Sunday brunch. Lending to the upbeat, stylish decor are dark wood appointments and river rock fireplaces. Casual dress. **Bar:** Full bar. **Hours:** 11 am-midnight. Closed major holidays. **Address:** 1710 100th Ave NW T5S 2GS **Location:** Jct 170th St NW and 100th Ave NW. **Parking:** on-site. CALL 🅼

MOXIE'S CLASSIC GRILL　　　　　　　　　　Phone: 780/484-666●

Canadian
$10-$30

This sleek, funky and popular restaurant presents an extensive menu of creatively prepared dishes including pizza, pasta, rice, noodles, signature salads and burgers. Other menus include one for children and one for Sunday brunch. Lending to the upbeat, stylish decor are dark wood appointments and river rock fireplaces. Casual dress. **Bar:** Full bar. **Reservations:** not accepted. **Hours:** 11 am-11 pm, Sat from 10 am. Closed: 12/25. **Address:** 1670 8882-170th St T5T 4M2 **Location:** In West Edmonton Mall; in Bourbon Street District. **Parking:** on-site.

OPM ASIAN BISTRO & LOUNGE　　　　　　　Phone: 780/989-5898　〔23〕

Asian
$13-$20

In among the retail outlets and big box stores, this sleek Asian-inspired bistro is a popular gathering spot for those looking for creative interpretations of nouveau Asian cuisine. Casual dress. **Bar:** Full bar. **Hours:** 11 am-midnight, Sun & Mon-11 pm. Closed: 12/25. **Address:** 1820 99th St T6N 1M5 **Location:** On south side of South Edmonton Commons. **Parking:** on-site.

PARKALLEN RESTAURANT　　　　　　　　　Phone: 780/436-8080　〔18〕

Lebanese
$9-$34

A popular spot with the locals, the family-run restaurant is considered to be one of the city's best ethnic restaurants. The menu centers on selections of traditional Lebanese fare, including fatouche salad, baba ghanoush and marinated kebabs. Those not in the mood for Lebanese cuisine also can try award-winning pizza. The wine list is extensive. The casually elegant dining room displays traditional art. Servers are friendly and knowledgeable. Casual dress. **Bar:** Full bar. **Reservations:** suggested. **Hours:** 11 am-2 & 5-10 pm, Fri & Sat 10 am-2 & 5-11 pm. Closed: 12/24, 12/25. **Address:** 7018 109th St NW T6H 3C● **Location:** Corner of 70th Ave and 109th St. **Parking:** on-site.

RICKY'S ALL DAY GRILL　　　　　　　　　　Phone: 780/486-710●

Continental
$8-$23

The comfortable eatery, which employs friendly servers, presents a varied menu that includes pasta dishes, wraps, omelets, stir-fry preparations and burgers. Portions are generous. Children's and senior selections are offered. Guests can request seating in a booth or at a table. Casual dress. **Bar:** Full bar. **Reservations:** accepted, after 4 pm. **Hours:** 7 am-9 pm, Fri & Sat-10 pm. Closed: 12/25. **Address:** 991● 170th St T5P 4S2 **Location:** Just s of jct 100th Ave NW. **Parking:** on-site. CALL 🅼

ROYAL FORK BUFFET RESTAURANT　　　　　Phone: 780/484-702●

American
$11-$15

The Royal Fork features buffet-style dining with a wide variety of freshly made choices, including sugar-free desserts. Families can be fed for an excellent value. Dinner prices are in effect starting at 4 pm Monday through Saturday and all day on Sunday and major holidays. Casual dress. **Reservations:** not accepted. **Hours:** 11 am-8:30 pm, Fri & Sat-9 pm, Sun 10 am-8 pm; Sunday brunch. Closed: 12/25. **Address:** 1506 Stony Plain Rd NW T5P 4W1 **Location:** Hwy 16A (Stony Plain Rd) at 150th St. **Parking:** on-site.

(See map and index starting on p. 444)

SAGE RESTAURANT

Phone: 780/930-2626

Steak
$25-$45

Just off the casino floor, this cool, trendy restaurant has a large curved oyster bar just inside its entrance, slightly upscale tables, a fireplace and private dining areas. Designed for the high roller, the menu is expensive and includes freshly baked bread still warm from the oven, fried calamari, gulf shrimp and rock cod appetizer, big-eye tuna carpaccio, Canadian Prime bone-in rib-eye and lamb porterhouse. Friendly servers are attentive without being overbearing. Casual dress. **Bar:** Full bar. **Reservations:** suggested. **Hours:** 5 pm-10 pm. Closed: 12/25; also Mon. **Address:** 300 E Lapotac Blvd T7X 3Y3 **Location:** 1 mi (1.6 km) w of jct Hwy 216 (Anthony Henday Dr) and Whitemud Dr W; in Edmonton Marriott at River Cree Resort. **Parking:** on-site.

SEASONS GRILL

Phone: 780/437-7011 ⑱

Canadian
$11-$25

The recently renovated restaurant lets patrons peruse a seasonally inspired menu amid cozy, contemporary surroundings. Ranging from prime rib to sole, the menu variety is surprising and delightful. Casual dress. **Bar:** Full bar. **Reservations:** suggested. **Hours:** 6:30 am-10 pm, Sat & Sun from 7 am. **Address:** 5116 Gateway Blvd T6H 2H4 **Location:** Hwy 2 (Gateway Blvd) at 51st Ave; in Best Western Cedar Park Inn. **Parking:** on-site. *(See color ad p 453)* CALL &M

T & T SUPERMARKET CAFE

Phone: 780/483-6638 ⑬

Chinese
$5-$7

Inside the main entrance of an Asian grocery store, the cafe is tucked away from the crowds that wander the corridors. Quality meats, produce, noodles and typical Asian ingredients combine in dishes that line up cafeteria style. Among choices are curried chicken with Chinese broccoli, braised ribs, Shanghai noodles, chicken feet and varied seafood preparations. The seating area is small. Casual dress. **Reservations:** not accepted. **Hours:** 9 am-9:30 pm. **Address:** 2580-8882 170th St T5T 4M2 **Location:** In West Edmonton Mall; 2nd Floor above Bourbon St. **Parking:** on-site. CALL &M

TOM GOODCHILDS MOOSE FACTORY

Phone: 780/437-5616 ㉑

Steak
$11-$50

The restaurant doesn't look big from the outside, but inside the formal yet comfortable dining area, guests have the choice of being seated in one of several differently decorated rooms. Tuxedoed servers have a casual edge that makes everyone feel at home. Known for its steaks, the menu is a carnivore's dream come true. Casual dress. **Bar:** Full bar. **Reservations:** accepted. **Hours:** 11 am-10 pm, Fri & Sat-10:30 pm, Sun 10 am-2 & 4-10 pm; Sunday brunch. Closed major holidays. **Address:** 4810 Calgary Tr S T6H 5H5 **Location:** Just n of Whitemud Dr NW. **Parking:** on-site. CALL &M

UNHEARDOF RESTAURANT

Phone: 780/432-0480 ⑭

Canadian
$34-$43

In an old house along the east end of Whyte Avenue, this cozy eatery draws patrons for its fine food and splendid service. Food made from regional ingredients is offered from a prix fixe menu or a la carte. The wine list is fantastic. This place is a favorite for special occasions. Casual dress. **Bar:** Full bar. **Reservations:** suggested. **Hours:** 5:30 pm-close. Closed major holidays; also Mon. **Address:** 9602 82nd Ave T6C 1A1 **Location:** Corner of 82nd Ave (Whyte Ave) and 96th St. **Parking:** street.

URBAN DINER

Phone: 780/488-7274 ⑤

Canadian
$8-$15

We should be so lucky as to have such a classic neighborhood restaurant in our neck of the woods. While there is a definite upscale diner feel to this place, the kitchen presents a tight little menu of comfort food and regularly, sometimes daily, changing specials. Using top-notch ingredients, much of them sourced locally, the chefs displays their talents in the partially open kitchen and evoke clean and distinct flavors from even the simplest of dishes. Casual dress. **Bar:** Full bar. **Reservations:** not accepted. **Hours:** 11 am-9 pm, Sat from 9 am, Sun 9 am-3 pm. Closed: 1/1, 12/25; also Mon. **Address:** 12427 102nd Ave T5N 0M2 **Location:** Just w of jct 124th St W. **Parking:** on-site. CALL &M

WHITE SPOT

Phone: 780/432-9153

Canadian
$9-$23

Open for three meals a day, the popular casual restaurant prepares offerings such as sandwiches and burgers, fresh salads, pastas and stir-fries, fish and chips, chargrilled sirloin steaks and chicken, in addition to a selection of yummy desserts. Casual dress. **Bar:** Full bar. **Reservations:** accepted. **Hours:** 7:30 am-10 pm, Fri & Sat-11 pm. Closed: 12/25. **Address:** 3921 Calgary Tr T6J 5M8 **Location:** Just s of jct Whitemud Dr NW. **Parking:** on-site.

The Edmonton Vicinity

FORT SASKATCHEWAN pop. 14,957

LAKEVIEW INNS & SUITES   *Book great rates at AAA.com*   **Phone:** (780)998-7888

Hotel
$125-$179 All Year

Address: 10115 88th Ave T8L 2T1 **Location:** Just w of Hwy 15/21 and 101st St. **Facility:** 69 one bedroom standard units, some with whirlpools. 4 stories, interior corridors. **Parking:** on-site, winter plug-ins. **Terms:** cancellation fee imposed. **Amenities:** video library, DVD players, dual phone lines irons, hair dryers. *Some:* high-speed Internet. **Leisure Activities:** exercise room. **Guest Services** coin laundry, wireless Internet. **Business Services:** meeting rooms. **Free Special Amenities** continental breakfast and local telephone calls.

SUPER 8 HOTEL-FORT SASKATCHEWAN   *Book at AAA.com*   **Phone:** 780/998-2898

Hotel
Rates not provided

Address: 8750 84th St T8L 4P5 **Location:** Just e of jct Hwy 15/21. **Facility:** 87 units. 80 one- and two-bedroom standard units, some with whirlpools. 3 stories, interior corridors. *Bath:* combo or shower only. **Parking:** on-site, winter plug-ins. **Amenities:** high-speed Internet, hair dryers. *Some:* irons **Pool(s):** heated indoor. **Leisure Activities:** whirlpool, limited exercise equipment. **Guest Services** coin laundry, wireless Internet. **Business Services:** PC (fee).

LEDUC pop. 16,967

BEST WESTERN DENHAM INN AND SUITES   *Book great rates at AAA.com*   **Phone:** (780)986-2241

Hotel
$150-$156 All Year

Address: 5207 50th Ave T9E 6V3 **Location:** Hwy 2, exit Leduc/City Centre, just e. **Facility:** 95 one-bedroom standard units, some with whirlpools. 2-5 stories, interior corridors. **Terms:** check-in 4 pm. **Amenities:** video games (fee), high-speed Internet, voice mail, irons, hair dryers. *Some:* CD players. **Leisure Activities:** whirlpool, exercise room. **Guest Services:** valet and coin laundry, airport transportation-Edmonton International Airport, wireless Internet. **Business Services:** meeting rooms, PC. *(See color ad below)*

AAA Benefit:
Members save up to 20%, plus 10% bonus points with rewards program.

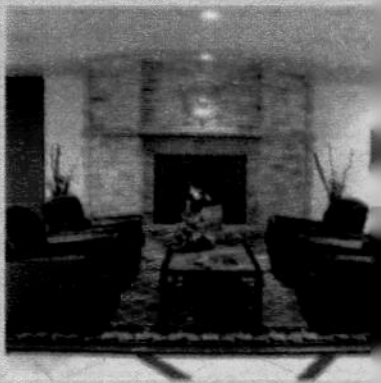

FREE continental breakfast and high-speed Internet

▼ *See AAA listing above* ▼

EDMONTON INTERNATIONAL AIRPORT-SUPER 8   *Book at AAA.com*   Phone: (780)986-8898

Hotel
$125 All Year

Address: 8004 Sparrow Crescent T9E 7G1 **Location:** Hwy 2, exit N Sector Leduc. **Facility:** Smoke free premises. 64 units. 53 one-bedroom standard units. 11 one-bedroom suites, some with whirlpools. 4 stories, interior corridors. **Parking:** on-site, winter plug-ins. **Amenities:** high-speed Internet, hair dryers. **Guest Services:** coin laundry, wireless Internet. **Business Services:** PC (fee).

HAMPTON INN & SUITES EDMONTON INTERNATIONAL AIRPORT   *Book great rates at AAA.com*   Phone: 780/980-9775

Hotel
Rates not provided

Address: 3914 84th Ave T9E 7G1 **Location:** Hwy 2, exit Edmonton International Airport, just e. **Facility:** 110 one-bedroom standard units, some with whirlpools. 4 stories, interior corridors. *Bath:* combo or shower only. **Parking:** on-site, winter plug-ins. **Amenities:** high-speed Internet, voice mail, irons, hair dryers. **Pool(s):** heated indoor. **Leisure Activities:** whirlpool, exercise room. **Guest Services:** valet and coin laundry, airport transportation-Edmonton International Airport, wireless Internet. **Business Services:** PC.

AAA Benefit:
Members save up to 10% everyday!

FREE expanded continental breakfast and high-speed Internet

------ **WHERE TO DINE** ------

RUTH'S DELI   Phone: 780/986-0433

Deli
$5-$9

The delicatessen appeals to hurried diners looking for a quick, healthy bite to eat. Guests can get a sandwich and soup to go or eat in at one of the small dinner tables. Patrons should check out the sandwich board for daily specials before ordering at the counter. Meals are ready in minutes. Casual dress. **Reservations:** not accepted. **Hours:** 8 am-5 pm, Fri-3 pm. Closed major holidays; also Sat & Sun. **Address:** 26-5201 50th St T9E 6T4 **Location:** Just n at 50th St; in City Centre Mall. **Parking:** on-site.

ZAMBELLIS RESTAURANT   Phone: 780/980-9669

International
$8-$33

Although it's described as a steak and pizza place, the restaurant presents a much more diverse menu. Greek food is a highlight, as are child- and senior-size portions. The large, bustling dining room features an open-concept kitchen and small sports lounge. Expect generous portions and friendly service. Casual dress. **Bar:** Full bar. **Hours:** 11 am-10 pm. Closed major holidays. **Address:** 6210 50th St T9E 7G9 **Location:** Hwy 2, exit Leduc Business Centre (50th St). **Parking:** on-site.

NISKU

HOLIDAY INN EXPRESS EDMONTON INT'L AIRPORT   *Book great rates at AAA.com*   Phone: (780)955-1000

Hotel
$151-$230 All Year

Address: 1102 4th St T9E 8E2 **Location:** Hwy 2, exit Edmonton International Airport/Nisku Business Park (10th Ave), 0.5 mi (0.9 km) e. **Facility:** Smoke free premises. 120 units. 118 one-bedroom standard units, some with whirlpools. 2 one-bedroom suites with whirlpools. 4 stories, interior corridors. *Bath:* combo or shower only. **Parking:** on-site, winter plug-ins. **Amenities:** high-speed Internet, dual phone lines, voice mail, irons, hair dryers. **Pool(s):** heated indoor. **Leisure Activities:** whirlpool, waterslide, exercise room. **Guest Services:** valet and coin laundry, airport transportation-Edmonton International Airport, wireless Internet. **Business Services:** meeting rooms, PC (fee). **Free Special Amenities:** expanded continental breakfast and high-speed Internet.

QUALITY INN & SUITES-AIRPORT   *Book at AAA.com*   Phone: (780)955-3001

Hotel
$110-$120 All Year

Address: 501 11th Ave T9E 7N5 **Location:** Hwy 2, exit Edmonton International Airport/Nisku Business Park (10th Ave), 0.8 mi (1.3 km) e. **Facility:** 73 units. 64 one-bedroom standard units, some with whirlpools. 9 one-bedroom suites. 2-4 stories (no elevator), interior corridors. **Parking:** on-site, winter plug-ins. **Terms:** cancellation fee imposed. **Amenities:** voice mail, irons, hair dryers. *Some:* high-speed Internet. **Leisure Activities:** exercise room. **Guest Services:** valet laundry, wireless Internet. **Business Services:** meeting rooms, PC.

ST. ALBERT pop. 57,719 (See map and index starting on p. 444)

------ **WHERE TO DINE** ------

RIC'S GRILL   Phone: 780/460-6602   (27)

Steak
$9-$30

"Funky and modern" describes the decor and the food at the upscale steakhouse, which bustles with activity. Steaks are well worth it, but then again, so are the salmon, chicken and pasta dishes. A wide variety of distinctive appetizers rounds out the menu. Servers are friendly and attentive. Dressy casual. **Bar:** Full bar. **Reservations:** accepted. **Hours:** 11:30 am-10 pm, Fri-11 pm, Sat 4:30 pm-11 pm, Sun 4:30 pm-9 pm. Closed major holidays. **Address:** 24 Perron St T8N 1E7 **Location:** Hwy 2 N, just e at St. Anne St; corner of St. Anne and Perron sts. **Parking:** on-site.

(See map and index starting on p. 444)

RIVER HOUSE GRILL

Canadian
$19-$34

Phone: 780/458-2232   (26)

In a picturesque converted Victorian Red house on the banks of the Sturgeon River, the friendly, intimate spot makes a real effort to use local, fresh ingredients in interesting dishes that mix flavors but never in an overpowering way. Hardwood floors and art on the walls enhance the dining area, which abuts a scenic patio. A wine list that includes a good choice of by-the-glass options complements creative presentations of local fish, lamb, chicken and Prime Alberta beef. Dressy casual. **Reservations:** suggested. **Hours:** 5 pm-9 pm, Fri-10 pm, Sat & Sun 4:30 pm-8 pm. Closed major holidays; also Mon. **Address:** 8 Mission Ave T8N 1H4 **Location:** Jct Hwy 2 (St. Albert Rd); downtown. **Parking:** on-site.

SHERWOOD PARK

COAST EDMONTON EAST HOTEL   *Book at AAA.com*

Hotel
Rates not provided

Phone: 780/464-4900

Address: 2100 Premier Way T8H 2G4 **Location:** Hwy 16, exit Broadmoor Blvd, 0.6 mi (1 km) sw. Located next to Millennium Place Recreation Centre. **Facility:** Smoke free premises. 258 units. 242 one- and 14 two-bedroom standard units, some with whirlpools. 2 one-bedroom suites. 5 stories, interior corridors. *Bath:* combo or shower only. **Parking:** on-site, winter plug-ins. **Terms:** check-in 4 pm. **Amenities:** high-speed Internet, dual phone lines, voice mail, irons, hair dryers. **Leisure Activities:** exercise room. **Guest Services:** valet and coin laundry. **Business Services:** conference facilities, business center. 🌱 🍽 ⛉ ✕ 📷 🔌 💻 🖥 / SOME UNITS 🗑

FRANKLIN'S INN

CAA SAVE

Hotel
$129-$169 All Year

Phone: (780)467-1234

Address: 2016 Sherwood Dr T8A 3X3 **Location:** At Granada Blvd. Located next to a shopping complex. **Facility:** 40 one-bedroom standard units, some with whirlpools. 3 stories, interior corridors. **Parking:** on-site, winter plug-ins. **Terms:** 3 day cancellation notice. **Amenities:** voice mail, hair dryers. *Some:* irons. **Leisure Activities:** *Fee:* esthetics. **Guest Services:** valet laundry, wireless Internet, beauty salon. **Business Services:** conference facilities. **Free Special Amenities: full breakfast and high-speed Internet.** 🍽 ⛉ 📷 🔌 🖥 💻 / SOME UNITS FEE 🐾 ✕

HOLIDAY INN EXPRESS   *Book great rates at AAA.com*

CAA SAVE

Hotel
$143-$159 All Year

Phone: (780)417-3388

Address: 11 Portage Ln T8H 2R7 **Location:** Hwy 16, exit Broadmoor Blvd, 0.6 mi (1 km) s. **Facility:** Smoke free premises. 90 one-bedroom standard units, some with whirlpools. 4 stories, interior corridors. *Bath:* combo or shower only. **Parking:** on-site. **Terms:** check-in 4 pm. **Amenities:** high-speed Internet, voice mail, irons, hair dryers. *Some:* CD players. **Leisure Activities:** whirlpool, exercise room. **Guest Services:** valet laundry, wireless Internet. **Business Services:** meeting rooms, PC. **Free Special Amenities: expanded continental breakfast and high-speed Internet.** 🌱 🍽 ✕ 📷 🔌 🖥 / SOME UNITS 🗑

RAMADA LIMITED-EDMONTON EAST/SHERWOOD PARK   *Book at AAA.com*

Hotel
Rates not provided

Phone: 780/467-6727

Address: 30 Broadway Blvd T8H 2A2 **Location:** Hwy 16, exit Broadmoor Blvd, 1.2 mi (2 km) s. **Facility:** Smoke free premises. 63 one-bedroom standard units. 4 stories, interior corridors. **Parking:** on-site, winter plug-ins. **Amenities:** voice mail, irons, hair dryers. **Leisure Activities:** exercise room. **Guest Services:** valet and coin laundry, wireless Internet. **Business Services:** meeting rooms. 🍽 ✕ 🔌 🖥 / SOME UNITS FEE 🐾 🗑

ROADKING INNS

Hotel
Rates not provided

Phone: 780/464-1000

Address: 26 Strathmoor Dr T8H 2B6 **Location:** Hwy 16, exit Broadmoor Blvd, just sw. Located next to a truck stop facility. **Facility:** 88 one-bedroom standard units. 2 stories, interior corridors. **Parking:** on-site. **Amenities:** video games (fee), voice mail, irons, hair dryers. **Guest Services:** coin laundry, wireless Internet. **Business Services:** meeting rooms. 🍽 ⛉ 📷 🔌 🖥 💻 / SOME UNITS FEE 🐾 ✕

─────── **WHERE TO DINE** ───────

JOEY RESTAURANTS

Mediterranean
$12-$35

Phone: 780/449-1161

The cuisine blends Mediterranean and Asian cooking styles and emphasizes finger foods for sharing. Those who aren't big fans of tapas can consider full meal offerings centered on steaks and chops. Casual dress. **Bar:** Full bar. **Reservations:** not accepted. **Hours:** 11 am-1 am. Closed: 12/25. **Address:** 360-222 Baseline Rd T8H 1S8 **Location:** Between 17th St NE and Sherwood Dr. **Parking:** on-site.

SORRENTINO'S BISTRO BAR

Italian
$8-$30

Phone: 780/449-1384

Italian ambience and cuisine await at the cozy restaurant, which prepares pizza, calzones and, of course, pasta dishes. There are daily specials, and the service is friendly and attentive. Casual dress. **Bar:** Full bar. **Reservations:** suggested. **Hours:** 11 am-2 & 5-10 pm, Fri 11 am-2 & 4-11 pm, Sat & Sun 4 pm-11 pm. Closed: 1/1, 12/25. **Address:** 1020 Sherwood Dr T8A 2G4 **Location:** Hwy 16, exit Broadmoor Blvd S, 3.1 mi (5 km) to Wye Rd; northeast corner of Sherwood Dr and Wye Rd. **Parking:** on-site.

THE SOUP & SANDWICH CO.

Phone: 780/467-8530

Deli
$5-$6

Crowds often line out the front door in this cozy little restaurant, which seems lost in the generic-looking commercial plaza near the Holiday Inn Express. Patrons get good value for the dollar in the varied homemade soups, made-to-order sandwiches and hot, freshly made daily entrees. Casual dress. **Reservations:** not accepted. **Hours:** 8 am-2:30 pm. Closed major holidays; also Sat & Sun. **Address:** 2833 Broadmoor Blvd, #144 T8H 2H3 **Location:** Hwy 16, exit Broadmoor Blvd, 0.6 mi (1 km) s. **Parking:** on-site.

SUMO SUMO SUSHI BAR & GRILL

Phone: 780/416-7866

Sushi
$8-$15

In a small shopping plaza, this gem of a restaurant appeals to those with sumo appetites but who don't want to pay sumo prices. A wonderful selection of traditional and nouveau sushi is available, as is a teppanyaki bar. Locals frequent this place. Casual dress. **Bar:** Full bar. **Reservations:** suggested, on weekends. **Hours:** 11:30 am-9 pm, Fri & Sat-9:30 pm, Sun noon-9 pm. Closed: 12/25. **Address:** #390, 222 Baseline Rd T8H 1S8 **Location:** Corner of Baseline Rd and Broadmoor Blvd; in Baseline Village Shopping Plaza. **Parking:** on-site. CALL 🔊M

VICKY'S RESTAURANT

Phone: 780/417-1750

International
$7-$35

A well-known spot in the Sherwood Park community, the family-run restaurant has been serving excellent homemade food for many years. Patrons can choose from such Greek specialties as spanakopita and souvlaki or try one of the other International dishes. A visit is not complete without a trip to the restroom, where an eclectic mix of interesting trinkets is on display. Casual dress. **Bar:** Full bar. **Reservations:** suggested. **Hours:** 11 am-2:30 & 4:30-10 pm, Sat from 4 pm. Closed major holidays; also Sun. **Address:** #86, 993 Fir St T8A 4N5 **Location:** Corner of Broadmoor Blvd and Wye Rd; accessible from Broadmoor Blvd. **Parking:** on-site. CALL 🔊M

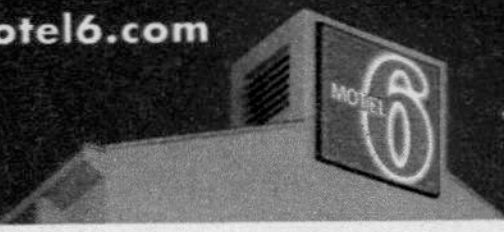

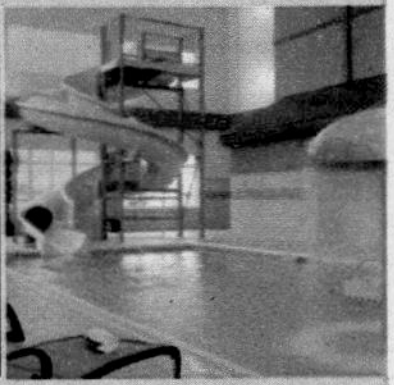

STONY PLAIN pop. 12,363

▼ See AAA listing p 468 ▼

MOTEL 6 STONY PLAIN   *Book great rates at AAA.com*    **Phone:** (780)968-5123

Hotel
$75-$91 All Year

Address: 66 Boulder Blvd T7Z 1V7 **Location:** Just off Hwy 16A (Township Rd 530). **Facility:** Smoke free premises. 78 units. 76 one-bedroom standard units. 2 one-bedroom suites with kitchens. 2 stories, interior corridors. **Parking:** on-site, winter plug-ins. **Amenities:** high-speed Internet, voice mail. *Some:* irons, hair dryers. **Guest Services:** coin laundry. *(See color ad p 467)*

RAMADA INN & SUITES   *Book at AAA.com*   **Phone:** (780)963-0222

Hotel
$90-$180 All Year

Address: 3301 43rd Ave T7Z 1L1 **Location:** Hwy 16A (Township Rd 530), just s on S Park Dr, then just e. **Facility:** 88 units. 77 one- and 11 two-bedroom standard units, some with efficiencies, kitchens and/or whirlpools. 2 stories (no elevator), interior/exterior corridors. **Parking:** on-site, winter plug-ins. **Terms:** check-in 4 pm, cancellation fee imposed. **Amenities:** irons, hair dryers. **Pool(s):** heated indoor. **Leisure Activities:** sauna, whirlpool. **Guest Services:** valet and coin laundry, wireless Internet. **Business Services:** meeting rooms, PC.

Santa Maria, Deep Sea Adventure, West Edmonton Mall / Travel Alberta

This ends listings for the Edmonton Vicinity.
The following page resumes the alphabetical listings of cities in Alberta.

EDSON pop. 8,098

BEST WESTERN HIGH ROAD INN   *Book great rates at AAA.com*

Phone: (780)712-2378

CAA SAVE
Hotel
$109-$129 All Year

AAA Benefit:
Members save up to
20%, plus 10%
bonus points with
rewards program.

Address: 300 52nd St T7E 1V8 **Location:** On 2nd Ave; centre. **Facility:** 114 units. 107 one-bedroom standard units. 7 one-bedroom suites, some with whirlpools. 4 stories, interior corridors. **Parking:** on-site, winter plug-ins. **Amenities:** high-speed Internet, voice mail, irons, hair dryers. *Some:* dual phone lines. **Pool(s):** heated indoor. **Leisure Activities:** whirlpool, waterslide, exercise room. **Guest Services:** valet laundry. **Business Services:** meeting rooms, business center. **Free Special Amenities:** local telephone calls and high-speed Internet.

EDSON COMFORT INN & SUITES   *Book at AAA.com*

Phone: (780)723-7303

Hotel
$80 All Year

Address: 5517 4th Ave T1E 1L6 **Location:** Hwy 16, west end of town. **Facility:** 40 units. 37 one- and 3 two-bedroom standard units, some with kitchens. 4 stories, interior corridors. *Bath:* combo or shower only. **Parking:** on-site, winter plug-ins. **Amenities:** high-speed Internet, voice mail, irons, hair dryers. **Leisure Activities:** exercise room. **Guest Services:** valet and coin laundry, wireless Internet. **Business Services:** PC.

GUEST HOUSE INN & SUITES

Phone: 780/723-4486

CAA SAVE
Motel
$101-$124 All Year

Address: 4411 4th Ave T7E 1B8 **Location:** 0.6 mi (1 km) e on Hwy 16. **Facility:** 108 units. 89 one-bedroom standard units, some with kitchens and/or whirlpools. 18 one- and 1 two-bedroom suites with kitchens. 1-3 stories (no elevator), interior/exterior corridors. **Parking:** on-site, winter plug-ins. **Terms:** cancellation fee imposed. **Amenities:** high-speed Internet, voice mail, hair dryers. *Some:* irons. **Leisure Activities:** sauna, steamroom, exercise room. **Guest Services:** coin laundry, wireless Internet. **Business Services:** meeting rooms, PC. **Free Special Amenities:** full breakfast and high-speed Internet.

LAKEVIEW INNS & SUITES   *Book great rates at AAA.com*

Phone: (780)723-2500

CAA SAVE
Hotel
$120 All Year

Address: 4300 2nd Ave T7E 1B8 **Location:** 0.6 mi (1.1 km) e on Hwy 16. **Facility:** 45 one-bedroom standard units. 2 stories (no elevator), interior corridors. **Parking:** on-site, winter plug-ins. **Terms:** cancellation fee imposed. **Amenities:** video library, DVD players, irons, hair dryers. *Some:* high-speed Internet. **Guest Services:** coin laundry, wireless Internet. **Business Services:** PC. **Free Special Amenities:** continental breakfast and local telephone calls.

—— WHERE TO DINE ——

MOUNTAIN PIZZA & STEAK HOUSE

Phone: 780/723-3900

Steak
$7-$27

This casual, busy restaurant has been a popular spot for more than 30 years. Inside the pyramid-shaped building is a stained wooden roof with a skylight and a large fig tree as the focal point. Tourists from around the world return to sample the top-secret, spiced steaks. Also featured is shish kebabs, Italian veal and chicken dishes and, of course, pizza. Leave room for a slice of homemade carrot cake or cheesecake. Casual dress. **Bar:** Full bar. **Reservations:** suggested. **Hours:** 11 am-11 pm, Sun-10 pm. Closed: 12/25, 12/26. **Address:** 5102 4th Ave T7E 1T8 **Location:** Hwy 16 (westbound) at 51st St. **Parking:** on-site.

FORT MACLEOD pop. 3,072

SUNSET MOTEL

Phone: 403/553-4448

CAA SAVE
Motel
$72-$80 All Year

Address: 104 Hwy 3 W T0L 0Z0 **Location:** 0.6 mi (1 km) w on Hwy 2 and 3. **Facility:** 22 units. 13 one- and 8 two-bedroom standard units, some with kitchens. 1 three-bedroom suite with kitchen. 1 story, exterior corridors. *Bath:* combo or shower only. **Parking:** on-site, winter plug-ins. **Terms:** office hours 7 am-11 pm. **Amenities:** high-speed Internet. **Free Special Amenities:** continental breakfast and local telephone calls.

—— WHERE TO DINE ——

JOHNNY'S RESTAURANT

Phone: 403/553-3939

Chinese
$7-$23

The highly trained chef/owner prepares an extensive selection of Western and Chinese dishes. Fresh ingredients, generous portions and good value make this a gem of a place. All members of the family take part in serving and exhibit unsurpassed friendliness. Entrees include selections of salmon, veal, prawns, ribs and steak as well as fresh pasta and lighter sandwiches. An old-fashioned sign serves as a beacon to this downtown restaurant, which is quite popular with the locals. Casual dress. **Bar:** Full bar. **Reservations:** suggested. **Hours:** 10 am-9 pm, Sun 11 am-8 pm. Closed: 1/1, 12/25. **Address:** 225 24th St (Main St) T0L 0Z0 **Location:** Centre; next to Empress Theatre. **Parking:** street.

FORT MCMURRAY pop. 47,705

ADVANTAGE WEST INNS & SUITES   *Book at AAA.com*

Phone: 780/713-4111

Hotel
Rates not provided

Address: 200 Parent Way T9H 5E6 **Location:** 3.1 mi (5 km) s on Hwy 63 (Sakitaww Tr). **Facility:** Smoke free premises. 83 one-bedroom standard units. 4 stories, interior corridors. **Parking:** on-site, winter plug-ins. **Amenities:** video library (fee), DVD players, CD players, high-speed Internet, voice mail, irons, hair dryers. **Leisure Activities:** exercise room. **Guest Services:** coin laundry. **Business Services:** meeting rooms, PC (fee).

CLEARWATER SUITE HOTEL   *Book at AAA.com*   Phone: 780/799-7676

▼◆▼◆▼
Hotel
Rates not provided

Address: 4 Haineault St T9H 1L6 **Location:** Hwy 63 (Sakitawaw Tr), just n on Hardin St, just e on Franklin Ave, then just s. **Facility:** Smoke free premises. 150 units. 33 one-bedroom standard units with efficiencies. 117 one-bedroom suites with efficiencies. 4 stories, interior corridors. **Parking:** on-site, winter plug-ins. **Amenities:** high-speed Internet, voice mail, irons, hair dryers. **Leisure Activities:** sauna, whirlpool, steamroom, exercise room, spa. **Guest Services:** complimentary laundry. **Business Services:** business center. 🛬 🍴 🍽 ⛷ ⊠ 🐾 🎦 🖥 📷 💻 / SOME UNITS FEE 🐕

FRANKLIN SUITE HOTEL   *Book at AAA.com*   Phone: 780/788-2199

▼◆▼◆▼
Hotel
Rates not provided

Address: 10030 Franklin Ave T9H 0A5 **Location:** Hwy 63 (Sakitawaw Tr), just n on Morrison St, then just w. **Facility:** Smoke free premises. 75 one-bedroom standard units. 5 stories, interior corridors. **Parking:** on-site, winter plug-ins. **Amenities:** high-speed Internet, voice mail, irons, hair dryers. **Leisure Activities:** exercise room. **Guest Services:** valet and coin laundry, wireless Internet. **Business Services:** meeting rooms, business center. 🛬 🍴 ⊠ 🎦 🖥 📷 💻

MERIT HOTEL   *Book at AAA.com*   Phone: (780)714-9444

▼◆▼◆▼
Hotel
$189-$289 All Year

Address: 8200 Franklin Ave T9H 2H9 **Location:** Hwy 63 (Sakitawaw Tr), 0.6 mi (1 km) se. **Facility:** 92 units. 62 one-bedroom standard units, some with whirlpools. 30 one-bedroom suites. 3 stories, interior corridors. **Parking:** on-site. **Amenities:** high-speed Internet, dual phone lines, voice mail, irons, hair dryers. **Pool(s):** heated indoor. **Leisure Activities:** whirlpool, exercise room. **Guest Services:** valet laundry, wireless Internet. **Business Services:** meeting rooms, PC (fee).

(ASK) 🛬 🍴 🍽 🏊 🖥 📷 💻 / SOME UNITS ⊠

RADISSON HOTEL & SUITES   *Book at AAA.com*   Phone: (780)743-2400

▼◆▼◆▼
Hotel
$199-$319 All Year

Address: 435 Gregoire Dr T9H 4K7 **Location:** Hwy 63 (Sakitawaw Tr), 0.6 mi (1 km) n. **Facility:** 134 units. 123 one-bedroom standard units. 11 one-bedroom suites, some with whirlpools. 5 stories, interior corridors. **Bath:** combo or shower only. **Parking:** on-site. **Terms:** cancellation fee imposed. **Amenities:** high-speed Internet, voice mail, safes, irons, hair dryers. *Some:* dual phone lines. **Pool(s):** heated indoor. **Leisure Activities:** whirlpool, waterslide, exercise room. **Guest Services:** coin laundry, wireless Internet. **Business Services:** meeting rooms.

(ECO) (ASK) 🍴 CALL 🚹 🏊 ⊠ 🖥 💻 / SOME UNITS ⊠ 🖥 📷

SUPER 8   *Book at AAA.com*   Phone: (780)799-8450

▼◆▼ ▼◆▼
Hotel
$165-$215 All Year

Address: 321 Sakitawaw Tr T9H 5E7 **Location:** Just w of Hwy 63 (Sakitawaw Tr), 3.1 mi (5 km) s. **Facility:** 100 one-bedroom standard units, some with whirlpools. 2 stories (no elevator), interior corridors. **Parking:** on-site, winter plug-ins. **Terms:** cancellation fee imposed. **Amenities:** high-speed Internet, voice mail, irons, hair dryers. **Leisure Activities:** whirlpool, exercise room. **Guest Services:** coin laundry, wireless Internet. **Business Services:** meeting rooms, PC.

(ECO) (ASK) 🍴 🎦 🖥 📷 💻 / SOME UNITS ⊠

─────── **WHERE TO DINE** ───────

THE FISH PLACE   Phone: 780/791-4040

▼◆▼ ▼◆▼
Seafood
$12-$40

A well-known fact about Fort McMurray is that the largest population of Newfoundlanders outside of Newfoundland is found here. As a result, the superb fish restaurant was established to accommodate that population. Seven days a week, the nautical, cozy restaurant is busy serving seafood and evening specials. Seafood lovers looking for a hearty meal with speedy service should look no further. Casual dress. **Bar:** Full bar. **Reservations:** suggested. **Hours:** 11 am-11 pm, Sun-10 pm. Closed major holidays. **Address:** 412 Thickwood Blvd T9K 1P1 **Location:** Hwy 63 (Sakitawaw Tr), exit Thickwood Blvd, 1 mi (1.8 km) w; in small shopping plaza. **Parking:** on-site.

FORT SASKATCHEWAN—See Edmonton p. 464.

GRANDE CACHE pop. 3,783

BEST WESTERN GRANDE MOUNTAIN GETAWAYS & HOTEL   *Book great rates at AAA.com*   Phone: (780)827-3303

(CAA) (SAVE)
▼◆▼◆▼
Hotel
$140-$190 All Year

Address: 9901 100th St T0E 0Y0 **Location:** Hwy 40 (100th St); south end of town. **Facility:** 145 units. 105 one-bedroom standard units, some with whirlpools. 40 one-bedroom suites. 3 stories, interior corridors. **Parking:** on-site, winter plug-ins. **Amenities:** irons, hair dryers. *Some:* high-speed Internet. **Leisure Activities:** saunas, whirlpool, exercise room. **Guest Services:** coin laundry, wireless Internet. **Business Services:** meeting rooms, PC. **Free Special Amenities:** local telephone calls and high-speed Internet.

🍴 🍽 CALL 🚹 ⊠ 🎦 🖥 📷 💻 / SOME UNITS FEE 🐕 ⊠

AAA Benefit:
Members save up to 20%, plus 10% bonus points with rewards program.

GRANDE PRAIRIE pop. 47,076

BEST WESTERN GRANDE PRAIRIE HOTEL & SUITES   *Book great rates at AAA.com*

Hotel
$130-$160 All Year

Phone: (780)402-2378

Address: 10745 117th Ave T8V 7N6 **Location:** Corner of Hwy 43 (100th Ave) and 117th Ave. **Facility:** 100 units. 63 one-bedroom standard units, some with whirlpools. 37 one-bedroom suites. 4 stories, interior corridors. **Parking:** on-site, winter plug-ins. **Amenities:** video games (fee), high-speed Internet, dual phone lines, voice mail, irons, hair dryers. **Pool(s):** heated indoor. **Leisure Activities:** whirlpool, exercise room. **Guest Services:** airport transportation-Grande Prairie Airport, wireless Internet, tanning facilities. **Business Services:** meeting rooms, PC. **Free Special Amenities: expanded continental breakfast and high-speed Internet.**

AAA Benefit:
Members save up to 20%, plus 10% bonus points with rewards program.

GRANDE PRAIRIE INN   *Book at AAA.com*

Hotel
$99-$149 All Year

Phone: (780)532-5221

Address: 11633 Clairmont Rd T8V 3Y4 **Location:** Jct Hwy 43 (100th Ave) and 116th Ave. **Facility:** 204 units. 197 one-bedroom standard units, some with whirlpools. 7 one-bedroom suites. 5-6 stories, interior corridors. **Parking:** on-site, winter plug-ins. **Amenities:** voice mail, hair dryers. *Some:* safes, irons. **Pool(s):** heated indoor. **Leisure Activities:** whirlpool, steamroom, exercise room, massage. **Guest Services:** valet laundry, wireless Internet, beauty salon. **Business Services:** conference facilities, PC.

MOTEL 6 GRANDE PRAIRIE   *Book great rates at AAA.com*

Hotel
Rates not provided

Phone: 780/830-7744

Address: 15402 101st St T8V 0P7 **Location:** Jct Hwy 2 and 43 (100th Ave), just s. **Facility:** 132 one-bedroom standard units. 4 stories, interior corridors. *Bath:* combo or shower only. **Parking:** on-site, winter plug-ins. **Amenities:** high-speed Internet, voice mail. *Some:* irons, hair dryers. **Guest Services:** valet and coin laundry. *(See color ad below)*

PODOLLAN INN & SPA   *Book at AAA.com*

Hotel
$149-$199 All Year

Phone: (780)830-2000

Address: 10612 99th Ave T8V 8E8 **Location:** Jct Hwy 43 (100th Ave) and 40 (108th St), just e. **Facility:** 108 units. 68 one-bedroom standard units, some with whirlpools. 40 one-bedroom suites. 4 stories, interior corridors. *Bath:* some combo, shower or tub only. **Parking:** on-site. **Amenities:** high-speed Internet, dual phone lines, voice mail, irons, hair dryers. **Dining:** Jax Grill & Lounge, see separate listing. **Leisure Activities:** spa. **Guest Services:** valet laundry, wireless Internet. **Business Services:** meeting rooms.

▼ *See AAA listing above* ▼

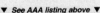

POMEROY INN & SUITES, GRANDE PRAIRIE

Phone: 780/831-2999

Hotel
$150-$160 All Year

Address: 11710 102nd St T8V 7S7 **Location:** 102nd St at 117th Ave. **Facility:** 152 units. 81 one-bedroom standard units, some with kitchens and/or whirlpools. 68 one- and 3 two-bedroom suites, some with kitchens. 3-4 stories, interior corridors. *Bath:* combo or shower only. **Parking:** on-site, winter plug-ins. **Terms:** cancellation fee imposed. **Amenities:** high-speed Internet, voice mail, irons, hair dryers. **Pool(s):** heated indoor. **Leisure Activities:** whirlpool, waterslide, exercise room. **Guest Services:** valet and coin laundry, airport transportation-Grand Prairie Airport, wireless Internet. **Business Services:** meeting rooms, PC. **Free Special Amenities: expanded continental breakfast and room upgrade (subject to availability with advance reservations).**

QUALITY HOTEL & CONFERENCE CENTRE GRANDE PRAIRIE *Book great rates at AAA.com*

Phone: (780)539-6000

Hotel
$90-$135 All Year

Address: 11201 100th Ave T8V 5M6 **Location:** 1.8 mi (2.9 km) w on Hwy 2. **Facility:** 102 units. 98 one-bedroom standard units. 4 one-bedroom suites with efficiencies. 10 stories, interior corridors. **Parking:** on-site, winter plug-ins. **Amenities:** video games (fee), high-speed Internet, voice mail, irons, hair dryers. **Leisure Activities:** exercise room. **Guest Services:** valet laundry, airport transportation-Grand Prairie Airport. **Business Services:** conference facilities, PC. **Free Special Amenities: full breakfast and high-speed Internet.**

SERVICE PLUS INNS AND SUITES *Book at AAA.com*

Phone: (780)538-3900

Hotel
$159-$300 All Year

Address: 10810 107A Ave T8V 7A9 **Location:** 1.4 mi (2.2 km) w on Hwy 2, just n. Adjacent to a casino. **Facility:** 123 units. 120 one- and 3 two-bedroom standard units, some with whirlpools. 4 stories, interior corridors. *Bath:* combo or shower only. **Parking:** on-site, winter plug-ins. **Amenities:** video games (fee), voice mail, irons, hair dryers. *Some:* fax. **Pool(s):** heated indoor. **Leisure Activities:** whirlpool, waterslide, limited exercise equipment. **Guest Services:** valet laundry, wireless Internet. **Business Services:** meeting rooms, PC.

STANFORD INN

Phone: (780)539-5678

Hotel
$99-$120 All Year

Address: 11401 100th Ave T8V 5M6 **Location:** 1.8 mi (2.8 km) w on Hwy 2. **Facility:** 203 units. 203 one-bedroom standard units, some with efficiencies, kitchens and/or whirlpools. 1 two-bedroom suite with kitchen and whirlpool. 2 stories (no elevator), interior/exterior corridors. **Parking:** on-site, winter plug-ins. **Terms:** cancellation fee imposed. **Amenities:** video library, voice mail, irons, hair dryers. *Some:* high-speed Internet. **Leisure Activities:** steamroom, exercise room. **Guest Services:** coin laundry, wireless Internet. **Business Services:** meeting rooms, PC (fee).

STONEBRIDGE HOTEL *Book at AAA.com*

Phone: 780/539-5561

Hotel
Rates not provided

Address: 12102 100th St T8V 5P1 **Location:** 100th St at 121st Ave. **Facility:** 126 units. 125 one-bedroom standard units, some with whirlpools. 1 one-bedroom suite with whirlpool. 3 stories, interior corridors. **Parking:** on-site, winter plug-ins. **Amenities:** video library, DVD players, voice mail, irons, hair dryers. *Some:* high-speed Internet. **Leisure Activities:** exercise room. **Guest Services:** valet laundry, wireless Internet. **Business Services:** meeting rooms, PC.

SUPER 8 *Book at AAA.com*

Phone: 780/532-8288

Hotel
Rates not provided

Address: 10050 116th Ave T8V 4K5 **Location:** 102nd St at 117th Ave. **Facility:** 149 units. 89 one-bedroom standard units, some with whirlpools. 50 one- and 10 two-bedroom suites. 4 stories, interior corridors. **Parking:** on-site, winter plug-ins. **Amenities:** video games (fee), voice mail, irons, hair dryers. **Pool(s):** heated indoor. **Leisure Activities:** whirlpool, waterslide, exercise room. **Guest Services:** valet and coin laundry, wireless Internet.

—— WHERE TO DINE ——

ACROPOLIS

Phone: 780/538-4424

Greek
$22-$33

A taste of Greece is found at the downtown eatery, where diners find fare ranging from spanakopita and souvlaki to moussaka and baklava. Portions are not skimpy and are served by friendly, attentive staff members. Casual dress. **Bar:** Full bar. **Reservations:** suggested. **Hours:** 4:30 pm-10 pm. Closed major holidays; also Sun & Mon. **Address:** 10011 101st Ave T8V 0X9 **Location:** Corner of 100th St and 101st Ave; downtown. **Parking:** street.

JAKE'S DOWN SOUTH

Phone: 780/532-5667

Cajun
$7-$27

Using the term "down south" while so far north may seem an anomaly, but this place offers Cajun and Mexican flavors mixed with Canadian favorites with some zesty twists. Friendly, efficient servers deliver such appetizers as crawfish spring rolls and gator crostini. The menu offers a selection of po' boys, burgers and steaks, along with other entrees featuring catfish, jambalaya or curried coconut shrimp. A simple, open decor features abstract, Southern wall murals. Casual dress. **Bar:** Full bar. **Reservations:** accepted. **Hours:** 11 am-10 pm, Fri-11 pm, Sat 10 am-11 pm, Sun 10 am-10 pm. Closed: 12/25. **Address:** 10702 108A St T8V 7A9 **Location:** Just n on 108th St. **Parking:** on-site. CALL

JAX GRILL & LOUNGE

Phone: 780/830-2000

International
$11-$27

Cushy banquettes and high-top tables enhance the intimate and stylish setting at this lounge. The menu features items from around the world: Tangy Indian butter chicken, Mexican enchiladas and a European entrée with cabbage rolls, perogies and sausage. Steaks, burgers, Alaskan halibut, ahi tuna and pasta dishes also share space on the menu. The must-try sweet potato fries are delicious. Casual dress. **Bar:** Full bar. **Reservations:** suggested. **Hours:** 11 am-11 pm. Closed: 1/1, 12/25. **Address:** 10612 99th Ave T8V 8E8 **Location:** Jct Hwy 43 (100th Ave) and 40 (108th St), just e; in Podollan Inn & Spa. **Parking:** on-site.

CALL

JEFFERY'S CAFE CO.

Phone: 780/830-0140

Canadian
$8-$15

Prepared using fresh-made breads, this little café's gourmet sandwiches will definitely lighten up the day, as do the surrounding windows. Select from such toppings as pesto, teriyaki or curry chicken; smoked turkey; or Italian meatballs. Patrons will also find intriguing salads, hearty soups and pasta or rich dishes on the menu. The sinfully delicious desserts are a must-have. Casual dress. **Reservations:** suggested, for lunch. **Hours:** 7:30 am-8 pm, Sat 9 am-5 pm. Closed major holidays; also Sun. **Address:** 10605 Westside Dr T8V 8E6 **Location:** Jct Hwy 43 and 40, just s, then just e. **Parking:** on-site. CALL 🖳M

TITO'S BISTRO & CAFE

Phone: 780/539-4881

Lebanese
$8-$13

Homemade and healthy choices line the menu at this cafeteria-style restaurant. Select from such choices as sandwich-style beef and chicken shawarma, the full-meal deal with rice and a salad, donairs, souvlaki, Greek salad and an array of pastries and desserts. The less adventurous diner might opt for a sandwich, burger or classic breakfast offering. Tuesday is open-mike night so don't forget the guitar. Casual dress. **Reservations:** not accepted. **Hours:** 7 am-8 pm, Fri & Sat-9 pm, Sun noon-6 pm. **Address:** 101-10006 101st Ave T8V 0Y1 **Location:** Corner of 100th St and 101st Ave; downtown. **Parking:** on-site.

GRIMSHAW pop. 2,537

POMEROY INN & SUITES   *Book at AAA.com*

Phone: 780/332-2000

Extended Stay
Hotel
Rates not provided

Address: 4311 51st St T0H 1W0 **Location:** Hwy 2, south end of town. **Facility:** 62 units. 26 one-bedroom standard units, some with kitchens. 36 one-bedroom suites with kitchens. 3 stories, interior corridors. *Bath:* combo or shower only. **Parking:** on-site, winter plug-ins. **Amenities:** high-speed Internet, voice mail, irons, hair dryers. **Pool(s):** heated indoor. **Leisure Activities:** whirlpool, waterslide, exercise room. **Guest Services:** valet and coin laundry, wireless Internet. **Business Services:** meeting rooms, business center. 🏊 ✕ 📠 💻 / SOME UNITS FEE 🐾 ✕ 🖥

HANNA pop. 2,847

SUPER 8 HANNA   *Book at AAA.com*

Phone: (403)854-2400

Hotel
$130-$140 All Year

Address: 113 Palliser Tr T0J 1P0 **Location:** Hwy 9, just n. **Facility:** 63 units. 61 one-bedroom standard units, some with efficiencies. 2 one-bedroom suites with efficiencies and whirlpools. 2 stories (no elevator), interior/exterior corridors. **Parking:** on-site, winter plug-ins. **Amenities:** voice mail, irons, hair dryers. *Some:* DVD players, high-speed Internet. **Pool(s):** heated indoor. **Leisure Activities:** exercise room. **Guest Services:** coin laundry, wireless Internet. **Business Services:** meeting rooms.
ECO ASK 🍽 🏊 🎥 🖥 📠 💻 / SOME UNITS FEE 🐾 ✕

HIGH LEVEL pop. 3,887

SUPER 8 HIGH LEVEL

Phone: 780/841-3448

Hotel
Rates not provided

Address: 9502 114th Ave T0H 1Z0 **Location:** Hwy 35, just se, south end of town. **Facility:** 81 units. 73 one-bedroom standard units. 8 one-bedroom suites. 4 stories, interior/exterior corridors. **Parking:** on-site, winter plug-ins. **Amenities:** video games (fee), high-speed Internet, dual phone lines, voice mail, irons, hair dryers. **Pool(s):** heated indoor/outdoor. **Leisure Activities:** whirlpool, waterslide, exercise room. **Guest Services:** valet and coin laundry. **Business Services:** PC.
✈ 🍽 CALL 🖳M 🏊 ✕ 🎥 🖥 📠 💻 / SOME UNITS FEE 🐾 ✕

HIGH PRAIRIE pop. 2,750

POMEROY INN & SUITES HIGH PRAIRIE   *Book at AAA.com*

Phone: (780)523-2398

Hotel
$159-$169 5/1-2/28
$149-$159 3/1-4/30

Address: 3905 51st Ave T0G 1E0 **Location:** Hwy 2, just n; east end of town. **Facility:** 91 units. 85 one-bedroom standard units, some with kitchens. 6 one-bedroom suites with kitchens. 4 stories, interior/exterior corridors. **Parking:** on-site, winter plug-ins. **Amenities:** high-speed Internet, voice mail, irons, hair dryers. *Some:* DVD players. **Pool(s):** heated indoor. **Leisure Activities:** whirlpool, waterslide, exercise room. **Guest Services:** valet and coin laundry, wireless Internet. **Business Services:** business center. ASK 🍽 🍸 🏊 ✕ 🖥 📠 💻 / SOME UNITS FEE 🐾 ✕

HIGH RIVER pop. 10,716

HERITAGE INN   *Book at AAA.com*

Phone: (403)652-3834

Hotel
$129-$249 1/1-2/28
$124-$245 3/1-12/31

Address: 1104 11th Ave SE T1V 1M4 **Location:** Trans-Canada Hwy 2, exit 23, 0.5 mi (0.8 km) w of Hwy 2. **Facility:** 73 units. 72 one-bedroom standard units, some with whirlpools. 1 one-bedroom suite with whirlpool. 2 stories (no elevator), interior corridors. **Parking:** on-site, winter plug-ins. **Amenities:** irons, hair dryers. *Some:* DVD players, high-speed Internet. **Pool(s):** heated indoor. **Leisure Activities:** whirlpool. **Guest Services:** wireless Internet. **Business Services:** meeting rooms.
ASK 🍽 🍸 🏊 🖥 💻 / SOME UNITS FEE 🐾 ✕

SUPER 8   *Book at AAA.com*

Phone: 403/652-4448

Hotel
Rates not provided

Address: 1601 13th Ave SE T1V 2B1 **Location:** Trans-Canada Hwy 2, exit High River, just w. **Facility:** 60 one-bedroom standard units, some with efficiencies and/or whirlpools. 3 stories, interior corridors. *Bath:* combo or shower only. **Parking:** on-site, winter plug-ins. **Amenities:** high-speed Internet, voice mail, irons, hair dryers. *Some:* DVD players, video games. **Pool(s):** heated indoor. **Leisure Activities:** whirlpool, waterslide, exercise room. **Guest Services:** coin laundry, wireless Internet. **Business Services:** meeting rooms.
🍽 🏊 ✕ 🖥 📠 💻 / SOME UNITS FEE 🐾 ✕

—— **WHERE TO DINE** ——

WHISTLESTOP CAFE   Phone: 403/652-7026

Canadian
$9-$10

Simple, well-prepared food is one of the reasons to come to the distinctive eatery. Its location in a 1947 Canadian Pacific rail coach car, complete with CP memorabilia, is another. On the menu is a wide variety of comfort foods, including sandwiches, quiche, quesadillas and fried green tomatoes. The dessert selection is extensive. Guests can enjoy lunch or afternoon tea and imagine the car swaying gently along the tracks as it did long ago. Casual dress. **Hours:** 10 am-4 pm, Sun-3 pm. Closed major holidays; also Mon. **Address:** 406 1st St SW T1V 1S2 **Location:** 0.6 mi (1 km) n at 3rd Ave; next to museum. **Parking:** on-site.

HINTON pop. 9,738

BEST WESTERN WHITE WOLF INN   *Book great rates at AAA.com*   Phone: 780/865-7777

Hotel
Rates not provided

Address: 828 Carmichael Ln T7V 1T1 **Location:** At west end of town; just off Hwy 16. **Facility:** 42 units. 40 one-bedroom standard units, some with whirlpools. 2 one-bedroom suites with efficiencies. 2 stories (no elevator), exterior corridors. **Parking:** on-site, winter plug-ins. **Terms:** check-in 4 pm. **Amenities:** irons, hair dryers. *Some:* high-speed Internet. **Leisure Activities:** whirlpool, interpretive trail, limited exercise equipment. **Guest Services:** valet laundry, wireless Internet. **Business Services:** PC. **Free Special Amenities: local telephone calls and high-speed Internet.**

AAA Benefit:
Members save up to 20%, plus 10% bonus points with rewards program.

HOLIDAY INN EXPRESS   *Book great rates at AAA.com*   Phone: (780)865-2048

Hotel
$125-$173 All Year

Address: 462 Smith St T7V 2A1 **Location:** 1.2 mi (2 km) e on Hwy 16. **Facility:** 99 units. 98 one-bedroom standard units. 1 one-bedroom suite with whirlpool. 4 stories, interior corridors. *Bath:* combo or shower only. **Parking:** on-site, winter plug-ins. **Amenities:** high-speed Internet, voice mail, irons, hair dryers. **Pool(s):** heated indoor. **Leisure Activities:** sauna, whirlpool, waterslide, exercise room. **Guest Services:** valet and coin laundry, wireless Internet. **Business Services:** meeting rooms, PC (fee). **Free Special Amenities: full breakfast and high-speed Internet.**

HOLIDAY INN HINTON   *Book great rates at AAA.com*   Phone: (780)865-3321

Hotel
$129-$139 All Year

Address: 393 Gregg Ave, #306 T7V 1N1 **Location:** 0.3 mi (0.5 km) w on Hwy 16. **Facility:** 104 units. 102 one-bedroom standard units. 1 one- and 1 two-bedroom suites, some with whirlpools. 2 stories (no elevator), interior corridors. **Parking:** on-site, winter plug-ins. **Amenities:** video games (fee), voice mail, irons, hair dryers. *Some:* high-speed Internet. **Pool(s):** heated indoor. **Leisure Activities:** sauna, whirlpool, waterslide, exercise room. **Guest Services:** valet and coin laundry, wireless Internet. **Business Services:** meeting rooms, PC (fee). **Free Special Amenities: newspaper and high-speed Internet.**

LAKEVIEW INNS & SUITES   *Book great rates at AAA.com*   Phone: (780)865-2575

Hotel
$120-$140 All Year

Address: 500 Smith St T7V 2A1 **Location:** 1.1 mi (1.7 km) e on Hwy 16. **Facility:** 55 units. 46 one-bedroom standard units. 9 one-bedroom suites, some with kitchens and/or whirlpools. 2 stories (no elevator), interior/exterior corridors. *Bath:* combo or shower only. **Parking:** on-site, winter plug-ins. **Amenities:** video library, DVD players, voice mail, irons, hair dryers. **Leisure Activities:** whirlpool, limited exercise equipment. **Guest Services:** coin laundry, wireless Internet. **Business Services:** meeting rooms, PC (fee). **Free Special Amenities: expanded continental breakfast and local telephone calls.**

OVERLANDER MOUNTAIN LODGE   Phone: (780)866-2330

Country Inn
$139-$239 3/1-12/31
$139-$199 2/1-2/28

Address: Hwy 16 T7V 1X5 **Location:** Hwy 16, 15 mi (24 km) w; just outside Jasper National Park gates. **Facility:** Smoke free premises. 40 units. 24 one-bedroom standard units, some with kitchens and/or whirlpools. 11 one-bedroom suites. 5 cottages. 1-2 stories (no elevator), interior/exterior corridors. **Parking:** on-site, winter plug-ins. **Terms:** open 3/1-12/31 & 2/1-2/28, office hours 7 am-11 pm, check-in 4 pm, 3 day cancellation notice-fee imposed. **Amenities:** hair dryers. *Some:* irons. **Dining:** Stone Peak Restaurant & Lounge, see separate listing. **Leisure Activities:** hiking trails. **Guest Services:** wireless Internet. **Business Services:** meeting rooms. **Free Special Amenities: newspaper and high-speed Internet.**

SUPER 8   *Book at AAA.com*   Phone: 780/817-2228

Hotel
Rates not provided

Address: 284 Smith St T7V 2A1 **Location:** 1 mi (1.6 km) e on Hwy 16. **Facility:** 48 units. 46 one-bedroom standard units. 2 one-bedroom suites. 2 stories (no elevator), interior corridors. **Parking:** on-site, winter plug-ins. **Amenities:** hair dryers. *Some:* irons. **Pool(s):** heated indoor. **Leisure Activities:** whirlpool. **Guest Services:** coin laundry, wireless Internet. **Business Services:** PC.

—— **WHERE TO DINE** ——

L & W FAMILY RESTAURANT   Phone: 780/865-4892

Canadian
$7-$17

Ask any local in town for a good place to eat, and the diner-style restaurant is mentioned time and time again. Guests order at the counter and pick up their food when their number is called. Among offerings are Greek specialties, such as souvlaki and spanakopita, and hamburgers, pizzas and steaks, which are served in ample portions. Casual dress. **Bar:** Full bar. **Reservations:** accepted. **Hours:** 10:30 am-11 pm. Closed: 1/1, 12/24-12/26. **Address:** 414 Carmichael Ln T7V 1X7 **Location:** West end of city on Hwy 16; across from Holiday Inn Hinton. **Parking:** on-site.

SMITTY'S

International
$7-$20

Phone: 780/865-6151

The family-oriented restaurant satisfies patrons with its ever-popular all-day breakfast items, as well as tasty and wholesome soups and salads at lunchtime. A relaxed mood characterizes the dining space. Casual dress. **Reservations:** not accepted. **Hours:** 5:30 am-10 pm. Closed major holidays. **Address:** 445 Gregg Ave T7V 1X8 **Location:** 0.4 mi (0.7 km) w on Hwy 16. **Parking:** on-site. CALL 👐Ⓜ

STONE PEAK RESTAURANT & LOUNGE   *Menu on AAA.com*

ⒸⒶⒶ

International
$8-$44

Phone: 780/866-2330

Just outside of town, the restaurant is worth the drive. Diners can enjoy seasonally inspired cuisine in the log interior, which features a cozy decor. Chocolate pecan pie, created from a recipe so secret that the chef won't allow his staff to see him make it, is a great way to finish a fine meal. The cozy surroundings afford views of the mountains in the distance. Casual dress. **Bar:** Full bar. **Reservations:** suggested. **Hours:** 7 am-9:30 pm; 7 am-10:30 & 5-9 pm 10/10-6/15. Closed: 12/25, 12/26; also 1/1-1/31. **Address:** Hwy 16 T7V 1X5 **Location:** Hwy 16, 15 mi (24 km) w; just outside Jasper National Park gates; in Overlander Mountain Lodge. **Parking:** on-site.

INNISFAIL pop. 7,316

BEST WESTERN INNISFAIL INN   *Book great rates at AAA.com*

ⒸⒶⒶ SAVE

Hotel
$100-$160 All Year

Address: 5010 40th Ave T4G 1Z1 **Location:** Hwy 2, exit Hwy 54 (Innisfail/Caroline), just w. **Facility:** Smoke free premises. 66 one-bedroom standard units, some with whirlpools. 3 stories, interior corridors. *Bath:* combo or shower only. **Parking:** on-site, winter plug-ins. **Amenities:** high-speed Internet, voice mail, irons, hair dryers. **Pool(s):** heated indoor. **Leisure Activities:** whirlpool, exercise room. **Guest Services:** valet and coin laundry, wireless Internet. **Business Services:** business center.

AAA Benefit:
Members save up to 20%, plus 10% bonus points with rewards program.

Phone: (403)227-4405

🍽 CALL 👐Ⓜ 🛥 ❌ 📷 🗄 💻 📺

FREE expanded continental breakfast and high-speed Internet

JASPER pop. 4,265

ALPINE VILLAGE

Cabin
$180-$320 6/11-10/11
$110-$260 5/1-6/10

Phone: 780/852-3285

Address: Hwy 93A T0E 1E0 **Location:** Jct Hwy 16 and 93, 0.9 mi (1.4 km) s on Hwy 93, then just n. **Facility:** These upscale cabins, which range in size and decor, are in a wooded, riverfront setting outside of town; a 16-foot outdoor hot tub is on site. Smoke free premises. 47 units. 12 one-bedroom standard units. 35 cabins. 1 story, exterior corridors. *Bath:* combo or shower only. **Parking:** on-site. **Terms:** open 5/1-10/11, office hours 8 am-10 pm, check-in 4 pm, 14 day cancellation notice-fee imposed. **Amenities:** hair dryers. *Some:* DVD players (fee). **Leisure Activities:** bocci, board games, hiking trails, playground. **Guest Services:** valet laundry. *(See color ad below)*

AMETHYST LODGE

Hotel
$85-$285 All Year

Book great rates at AAA.com

Phone: (780)852-3394

Address: 200 Connaught Dr T0E 1E0 **Location:** 0.3 mi (0.5 km) e. **Facility:** Smoke free premises. 97 units. 91 one-bedroom standard units. 6 one-bedroom suites. 3 stories, interior/exterior corridors. **Parking:** on-site, winter plug-ins. **Terms:** check-in 4 pm, cancellation fee imposed. **Amenities:** voice mail, hair dryers. *Some:* irons. **Leisure Activities:** whirlpools. **Guest Services:** valet laundry, area transportation-train station, wireless Internet. **Business Services:** meeting rooms, PC. **Free Special Amenities:** local telephone calls and high-speed Internet.

BECKER'S CHALETS

Cabin
$135-$190 5/2-10/13

Phone: 780/852-3779

Address: Hwy 93 S T0E 1E0 **Location:** 4.3 mi (6.8 km) s. Located in a quiet rustic area. **Facility:** Smoke free premises. 118 units. 5 one-bedroom standard units. 52 one-, 14 two- and 2 three-bedroom suites with kitchens. 45 cabins. 2 stories (no elevator), exterior corridors. *Bath:* combo or shower only. **Parking:** on-site. **Terms:** open 5/2-10/13, office hours 7 am-11 pm, 7 day cancellation notice. **Amenities:** irons, hair dryers. **Leisure Activities:** fishing, hiking trails, playground. **Guest Services:** coin laundry, wireless Internet. *(See color ad p 477)*

BEST WESTERN JASPER INN & SUITES   *Book great rates at AAA.com*   **Phone:** (780)852-4461

Hotel
$110-$246 All Year

AAA Benefit:
Members save up to
20%, plus 10%
bonus points with
rewards program.

Address: 98 Geikie St T0E 1E0 **Location:** Corner of Geikie and Bonhomme sts. Located in a residential area. **Facility:** Smoke free premises. 143 units. 93 one- and 26 two-bedroom standard units, some with kitchens and/or whirlpools. 24 one-bedroom suites with kitchens. 2-3 stories (no elevator), interior/exterior corridors. **Parking:** on-site, winter plug-ins. **Terms:** check-in 4 pm, 3 day cancellation notice-fee imposed. **Amenities:** voice mail, irons, hair dryers. *Some:* DVD players. **Pool(s):** heated indoor. **Leisure Activities:** sauna, whirlpool, steamroom, ski lockers. **Guest Services:** coin laundry, wireless Internet. **Business Services:** meeting rooms, PC. *(See color ad p 478)*

FREE local telephone calls and high-speed Internet

CHATEAU JASPER   *Book great rates at AAA.com*   **Phone:** (780)852-5644

Hotel
$109-$295 All Year

Address: 96 Geikie St T0E 1E0 **Location:** Corner of Juniper and Geikie sts. Located in a residential area. **Facility:** 119 one-bedroom standard units, some with whirlpools. 3 stories, interior corridors. **Parking:** on-site, winter plug-ins. **Terms:** check-in 4 pm, cancellation fee imposed. **Amenities:** voice mail, safes, irons, hair dryers. **Pool(s):** heated indoor. **Leisure Activities:** whirlpool, exercise room. **Guest Services:** valet laundry, area transportation-train & bus station, wireless Internet. **Business Services:** conference facilities. **Free Special Amenities: local telephone calls and high-speed Internet.**

THE COAST PYRAMID LAKE RESORT   *Book great rates at AAA.com*   **Phone:** (780)852-4900

Hotel
$161-$368 4/22-10/31

Address: Pyramid Lake Rd T0E 1E0 **Location:** Jct Connaught Dr and Cedar St, 3.8 mi (6 km) nw via Pyramid Lake Rd. Located in a quiet area. **Facility:** Smoke free premises. 62 units. 40 one-bedroom standard units. 20 one- and 2 two-bedroom suites with efficiencies. 2 stories (no elevator), exterior corridors. **Parking:** on-site, winter plug-ins. **Terms:** open 4/22-10/31, 2-3 night minimum stay - weekends, 3 day cancellation notice. **Amenities:** voice mail, hair dryers. **Dining:** The Pines, see separate listing. **Leisure Activities:** whirlpool, steamroom, rental boats, rental canoes, rental paddleboats, boat dock, rental bicycles, hiking trails, exercise room. *Fee:* fishing, 2 person kayaks, barbecue patio. **Guest Services:** wireless Internet. **Business Services:** meeting rooms, business center. *(See color ad p 479)*

FREE local telephone calls and high-speed Internet

▼ See AAA listing p 476 ▼

THE FAIRMONT JASPER PARK LODGE

Book great rates at AAA.com

Phone: (780)852-3301

Resort
Hotel
$229-$499 All Year

Address: Lodge Rd T0E 1E0 **Location:** 3 mi (4.8 km) ne via Hwy 16; 2 mi (3.2 km) se off highway via Maligne Rd, follow signs. **Facility:** It's said that at one time, Marilyn Monroe frequented this resort set along two lakes just outside of town; activities and scenic grounds await. Smoke free premises. 446 units. 331 one-bedroom standard units. 115 one-bedroom suites, some with whirlpools. 1-2 stories (no elevator), exterior corridors. **Parking:** on-site and valet, winter plug-ins. **Terms:** check-in 4 pm, 3 day cancellation notice-fee imposed. **Amenities:** video games (fee), voice mail, irons, hair dryers. *Some:* CD players, high-speed Internet (fee), dual phone lines, safes. **Dining:** 5 restaurants, also, The Edith Cavell, The Moose's Nook Northern Grill, see separate listings, entertainment. **Pool(s):** heated outdoor. **Leisure Activities:** saunas, whirlpool, steamroom, rental boats, rental canoes, rental paddleboats, 4 tennis courts, cross country skiing, ice skating, tobogganing, recreation programs, Kids Club, rental bicycles, hiking trails, playground, exercise room, horseshoes, shuffleboard. *Fee:* fishing, guided fishing trips, white-water rafting, canoe rides, golf-18 holes, wagon rides, snowshoeing, canyon tours, guided mountain hikes, trail rides, horseback riding, massage, game room. **Guest Services:** valet laundry, wireless Internet. *Fee:* airport transportation-Edmonton, Calgary & Hinton airports, area transportation-ski hills. **Business Services:** conference facilities, business center.

JASPER HOUSE BUNGALOWS

Phone: 780/852-4535

Cabin
$160-$265 6/10-10/15
$75-$150 5/1-6/9

Address: Hwy 93 S T0E 1E0 **Location:** 2.5 mi (4 km) s on Hwy 93. Located in a quiet rustic area. **Facility:** Smoke free premises. 56 cabins. 1 story, exterior corridors. *Bath:* combo or shower only. **Parking:** on-site. **Terms:** open 5/1-10/15, office hours 8 am-10 pm, 7 day cancellation notice. **Amenities:** hair dryers. **Leisure Activities:** hiking trails, horseshoes. **Guest Services:** coin laundry, wireless Internet. **Business Services:** PC (fee).

▼ *See AAA listing p 477* ▼

Experience our year round playground in Jasper National Park!

- 10 minutes walking distance to the heart of Jasper

- Inn Restaurant & Terrace; a local favorite

- Indoor pool, jacuzzi, sauna & steam room

- Choose from a variety of family suites

Show Your Card & Save

Best Western Jasper Inn & Suites

98 Geikie St. • Jasper, AB T0E 1E0

780.852.4461 | 1.800.661.1933

bestwesternjasperinn.com

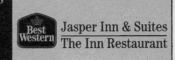

Jasper Inn & Suites
The Inn Restaurant

LOBSTICK LODGE

(AAA) (SAVE)

▼▼▼▼

Hotel
$99-$255 All Year

Book great rates at AAA.com   Phone: (780)852-4431

Address: 94 Geikie St T0E 1E0 **Location:** Corner of Geikie and Juniper sts. **Facility:** 139 units. 98 one-bedroom standard units, some with kitchens. 41 one-bedroom suites with kitchens. 3 stories, interior corridors. *Bath:* combo or shower only. **Parking:** on-site, winter plug-ins. **Terms:** check-in 4 pm, cancellation fee imposed. **Amenities:** voice mail, irons, hair dryers. **Pool(s):** heated indoor. **Leisure Activities:** sauna, whirlpools, sun deck, exercise room. **Guest Services:** valet and coin laundry, area transportation-train station, wireless Internet. **Business Services:** meeting rooms, PC. **Free Special Amenities:** local telephone calls and high-speed Internet.

(icons)

MALIGNE LODGE

▼▼▼▼

Motel
$99-$400 All Year

Book at AAA.com   Phone: (780)852-3143

Address: 900 Connaught Dr T0E 1E0 **Location:** 0.6 mi (1 km) sw. **Facility:** Smoke free premises. 98 units. 79 one-bedroom standard units. 19 two-bedroom suites with kitchens, some with whirlpools. 2 stories (no elevator), interior/exterior corridors. **Parking:** on-site, winter plug-ins. **Terms:** check-in 4 pm, 3 day cancellation notice-fee imposed. **Amenities:** voice mail, hair dryers. **Pool(s):** heated indoor. **Leisure Activities:** saunas, whirlpool, limited exercise equipment. **Guest Services:** coin laundry, wireless Internet. **Business Services:** PC.

(icons)

MARMOT LODGE

(AAA) (SAVE)

▼▼▼▼

Motel
$89-$255 All Year

Book great rates at AAA.com   Phone: (780)852-4471

Address: 86 Connaught Dr T0E 1E0 **Location:** 1 mi (1.6 km) ne. **Facility:** Smoke free premises. 107 units. 81 one-bedroom standard units, some with kitchens. 25 one- and 1 two-bedroom suites with kitchens, some with whirlpools. 2 stories (no elevator), exterior corridors. *Bath:* combo or shower only. **Parking:** on-site, winter plug-ins. **Terms:** check-in 4 pm, cancellation fee imposed. **Amenities:** voice mail, hair dryers. *Some:* irons. **Pool(s):** heated indoor. **Leisure Activities:** sauna, whirlpools. **Guest Services:** coin laundry, area transportation-train station, wireless Internet. **Business Services:** meeting rooms. **Free Special Amenities:** local telephone calls and high-speed Internet.

(icons)

▼ See AAA listing p 477 ▼

MOUNT ROBSON INN   *Book great rates at AAA.com*   Phone: (780)852-3327

Motel
$114-$339 All Year

Address: 902 Connaught Dr T0E 1E0 **Location:** 0.6 mi (1 km) sw. **Facility:** 80 units. 74 one-bedroom standard units, some with whirlpools. 6 one-bedroom suites. 2 stories (no elevator), exterior corridors. **Parking:** on-site, winter plug-ins. **Terms:** check-in 4 pm, cancellation fee imposed. **Amenities:** hair dryers. *Some:* video games, irons. **Leisure Activities:** whirlpools. **Guest Services:** coin laundry, area transportation-train station, wireless Internet. **Business Services:** PC (fee). *(See color ad below)*

FREE local telephone calls and high-speed Internet

PARK PLACE INN   Phone: 780/852-9770

Hotel
$129-$265 All Year

Address: 623 Patricia St T0E 1E0 **Location:** Downtown. **Facility:** Smoke free premises. 14 units. 12 one-bedroom standard units, some with whirlpools. 2 one-bedroom suites with whirlpools. 2 stories, interior corridors. **Parking:** on-site. **Terms:** check-in 4 pm, 5 day cancellation notice. **Amenities:** hair dryers. **Guest Services:** wireless Internet. **Free Special Amenities:** local telephone calls and high-speed Internet.

─── ▼ *See AAA listing above* ▼ ───

·Mount Robson Inn·

www.MountRobsonInn.com
Reservations: **1.800.587.3327**

Kids Suites · Executive Suites · Free Wi-Fi · Outdoor Whirlpools
Refrigerators · Fully Air Conditioned · Microwaves

902 Connaught Dr. info@**MountRobsonInn**.com **780.852.3327**

PATRICIA LAKE BUNGALOWS

Cabin
$87-$325 5/2-10/15

Phone: 780/852-3560

Address: Pyramid Lake Rd T0E 1E0 **Location:** 3 mi (4.8 km) nw via Pyramid Lake Rd. **Facility:** Smoke free premises. 49 units. 5 one-bedroom standard units. 16 one- and 8 two-bedroom suites, some with kitchens. 20 cabins. 1 story, exterior corridors. *Bath:* combo or shower only. **Parking:** on-site. **Terms:** open 5/2-10/15, office hours 8 am-10 pm, check-in 4 pm, 7 day cancellation notice. **Amenities:** hair dryers. *Some:* DVD players, irons. **Leisure Activities:** whirlpool, rental boats, rental canoes, rental paddleboats, boat dock, fishing, rental bicycles, playground. **Guest Services:** coin laundry. **Business Services:** PC (fee).

THE SAWRIDGE INN AND CONFERENCE CENTRE

Book great rates at AAA.com

CAA SAVE

Hotel
$112-$282 All Year

Phone: (780)852-5111

Address: 82 Connaught Dr T0E 1E0 **Location:** 1.1 mi (1.7 km) e. **Facility:** Smoke free premises. 153 units. 149 one-bedroom standard units. 4 one-bedroom suites with whirlpools. 3 stories, interior corridors. *Bath:* combo or shower only. **Parking:** on-site, winter plug-ins. **Terms:** check-in 4 pm, 3 day cancellation notice-fee imposed. **Amenities:** video games (fee), voice mail, irons, hair dryers. *Some:* CD players, high-speed Internet. **Dining:** nightclub. **Pool(s):** heated indoor. **Leisure Activities:** sauna, whirlpools, recreation programs in summer, exercise room, spa. **Guest Services:** valet and coin laundry, area transportation-downtown, wireless Internet. **Business Services:** conference facilities, PC. *(See color ad below)*

FREE local telephone calls and high-speed Internet

SUNWAPTA FALLS RESORT

Book great rates at AAA.com

CAA SAVE

Cabin
$89-$395 5/8-10/15

Phone: (780)852-4852

Address: Hwy 93 T0E 1E0 **Location:** 34.7 mi (55 km) s on Icefields Pkwy (Hwy 93). Located in a quiet secluded setting. **Facility:** Smoke free premises. 53 one-bedroom standard units. 1-2 stories (no elevator), exterior corridors. **Parking:** on-site. **Terms:** open 5/8-10/15, check-in 4 pm, 7 day cancellation notice-fee imposed. **Amenities:** *Some:* irons, hair dryers. **Leisure Activities:** rental bicycles, hiking trails. *Fee:* fishing, fishing equipment, whitewater rafting. **Guest Services:** wireless Internet. **Business Services:** meeting rooms, PC. *(See color ad p 482)*

FREE local telephone calls and early check-in/late check-out

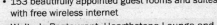

TONQUIN INN   *Book at AAA.com*   Phone: (780)852-4987

Motel
$135-$400 3/1-12/31
$140-$300 1/1-2/28

Address: 100 Juniper St T0E 1E0 **Location:** Corner of Juniper and Geikie sts. **Facility:** Smoke free premises. 137 units. 107 one- and 20 two-bedroom standard units, some with kitchens. 4 one- and 6 two-bedroom suites with kitchens. 2-3 stories, interior/exterior corridors. **Parking:** on-site, winter plug-ins. **Terms:** check-in 4 pm, 3 day cancellation notice. **Amenities:** voice mail, hair dryers. *Some:* irons. **Pool(s):** heated indoor. **Leisure Activities:** saunas, whirlpools, exercise room. **Guest Services:** coin laundry, wireless Internet. **Business Services:** meeting rooms.

—— WHERE TO DINE ——

ANDY'S BISTRO   Phone: 780/852-4559

International
$22-$40

Sharing an entranceway with one of the best wine stores in town, the bistro boasts a great wine list with many available by the glass. Soft candlelight and a wine cellar-style decor adorn the bistro. Swiss-born-and-trained chef Andy is respected by local chefs for his robust fare with clean, distinct flavors. The menu changes often, sometimes daily, to feature local, in-season ingredients such as wild game, organic fruits, vegetables and herbs that are often procured from nearby farms. Casual dress. **Bar:** Full bar. **Reservations:** suggested. **Hours:** 5 pm-9 pm. Closed: 12/23-12/26. **Address:** 606 Patricia St T0E 1E0 **Location:** Centre. **Parking:** street.

BEAR'S PAW BAKERY   Phone: 780/852-3233

Breads/Pastries
$2-$10

Guests can savor the aroma of freshly baked goods at the cozy hideaway bakery. Eyes feast on European-style pastries, artisan breads and Vienna pastries. Beware: Standing too long in front of the display case will cause mouths to water. Representative of the many temptations are trail cookies, Bear's Paw cinnamon buns, carrot cake and date squares. Only one table is available, so most patrons grab a sweet and a cup of coffee and head out into the mountain air. Casual dress. **Reservations:** not accepted. **Hours:** Open 3/1-10/31 & 12/1-2/28; 6 am-6 pm. Closed: 1/1, 12/25. **Address:** 4 Cedar Ave T0E 1E0 **Location:** Just w off Connaught Dr at Cedar Ave. **Parking:** street.

BECKER'S GOURMET RESTAURANT   Phone: 780/852-3535

Continental
$18-$40

Along the river just south of the city, the restaurant is a favorite among Jasper residents. The dining room's warm oak and fir decor is distinctly Canadian and, set against the backdrop of the river, provides an idyllic setting. Regionally inspired Continental cuisine ranges from salmon and scallops to beef tenderloin and lamb. Casual dress. **Bar:** Full bar. **Reservations:** suggested. **Hours:** Open 5/4-10/13; 8 am-11 & 5:30-9 pm. **Address:** Hwy 93 T0E 1E0 **Location:** On Hwy 93, 4.3 mi (6.8 km) s. **Parking:** on-site.

CAFE MONDO   Phone: 780/852-9676

Deli
$6-$12

Under the same ownership as the former Truffles and Trout, this casual eatery has a subtle European feel that just begs customers to sit and relax for a while. A good variety of baked goods, soups and sandwiches can be enjoyed with a freshly made cup of coffee or cold beverage. Casual dress. **Reservations:** not accepted. **Hours:** 8 am-9 pm; to 8 pm in winter. Closed: 12/25. **Address:** 616 Patricia St T0E 1E0 **Location:** Centre. **Parking:** street.

THE EDITH CAVELL   Phone: 780/852-6052

Canadian
$38-$49

Views of Lac Beauvert and Mount Edith Cavell and the rich, mahogany woodwork of the elegant dining room set the scene for a truly enchanting experience. The restaurant's delightful, complex nouvelle cuisine draws inspiration from the Northwest. Among delicacies are preparations of Arctic char, salmon and venison. In season, guests can savor a weekly changing tasting menu. Dressy casual. Entertainment. **Bar:** Full bar. **Reservations:** suggested. **Hours:** Open 5/1-10/11 & 12/19-1/1; 6 pm-9 pm. **Address:** Lodge Rd T0E 1E0 **Location:** 3 mi (4.8 km) ne via Hwy 16; 2 mi (3.2 km) se off highway via Maligne Rd, follow signs; in The Fairmont Jasper Park Lodge. **Parking:** on-site and valet.

FIDDLE RIVER RESTAURANT   Phone: 780/852-3032

Canadian
$20-$38

An ever-changing seafood menu is the highlight of the casual yet cozy restaurant, upstairs from street level. Fresh is the operative word, and patrons might find salmon, trout, sole, king crab, cod or blackened shrimp on the menu. For a view of the mountains, request a window seat. Service is friendly and attentive. Casual dress. **Bar:** Full bar. **Reservations:** suggested. **Hours:** 5 pm-10 pm. Closed: 12/25, 12/26. **Address:** 620 Connaught Dr T0E 1E0 **Location:** At Hazel Ave; upstairs. **Parking:** street.

JASPER BREWING CO   Phone: 780/852-4111

International
$8-$25

Great food with a local flavor and an international flair, accompanied by the local brew, makes for a good night out. Casual dress. **Bar:** Full bar. **Reservations:** not accepted. **Hours:** 11:30 am-midnight. Closed: 12/25. **Address:** 624 Connaught Dr T0E 1E0 **Location:** Centre. **Parking:** street.

JASPER PIZZA PLACE   Phone: 780/852-3225

Pizza
$10-$17

Those looking for pizza need search no further. Thick crusted pies are available with unusual toppings, such as spinach, barbecue chicken and artichokes. At night, the wood-fired oven gets going and the menu lists even more exotic combinations. In additional to pizza, the menu lists casual noodle and pasta dishes, burgers, wraps, salads and steak and chicken entrées. The rooftop patio is popular during the summer. Casual dress. **Bar:** Full bar. **Reservations:** not accepted. **Hours:** 11 am-10 pm; from 3 pm 9/15-5/15. Closed: 12/25; also 2 weeks in Nov. **Address:** 402 Connaught Dr T0E 1E0 **Location:** Centre. **Parking:** street.

KAROUZO'S STEAKHOUSE

Phone: 780/852-4640

Steak
$8-$50

On the main street leading into town, the family-run steak and seafood restaurant features a wide variety of entrees, including some pasta dishes. Casual dress. **Bar:** Full bar. **Reservations:** accepted. **Hours:** Open 3/15-10/10; 11 am-10 pm. **Address:** 628 Connaught Dr T0E 1E0 **Location:** Between Spruce and Hazel aves. **Parking:** street.

LA FIESTA

Phone: 780/852-0404

Mexican
$9-$31

A fusion of Mexican and Spanish cuisines awaits in the cozy restaurant boasting friendly, casual service. Daily-made soups complement the more-Mexican-than-Spanish menu, but a definite modern twist is evident in all the dishes. Burgers and wraps are standard lunch fare, but guests will find more serious dishes at dinner. Adobe-spiced mahi mahi as well as crab and ancho chili burritos are enticing. Since the chef creates everything from scratch, diners enjoy each bite. Casual dress. **Bar:** Full bar. **Reservations:** suggested. **Hours:** noon-11 pm. Closed: 12/25; also Sun in winter. **Address:** 504 Patricia St T0E 1E0 **Location:** Between Elm and Miette aves; across from Information Centre. **Parking:** street.

L & W FAMILY RESTAURANT

Phone: 780/852-4114

International
$8-$23

Those looking for good value for the dollar will find this family-run restaurant a good choice. The restaurant overflows with an abundance of huge, rubber plants and other greenery, and a menu lists something for everyone. Guests have their choice of Greek dishes, burgers, pizza and sandwiches. Casual dress. **Bar:** Full bar. **Hours:** 11 am-midnight. Closed: 12/25. **Location:** Corner of Hazel Ave and Patricia St. **Parking:** street.

THE MOOSE'S NOOK NORTHERN GRILL

Phone: 780/852-6052

Regional
Canadian
$28-$42

CALL

This "nook" of a restaurant is casual, but the food is anything but. Representative of creative, inventive regional cuisine are Alberta beef and pork entrees, seasonal greens and tempting desserts. The service and ambience are upscale without being pretentious and laid-back yet classy. This spot shouldn't be missed for those looking for a taste of Canada. Casual dress. Entertainment. **Bar:** Full bar. **Reservations:** suggested. **Hours:** 6 pm-9 pm. **Address:** Lodge Rd T0E 1E0 **Location:** 3 mi (4.8 km) ne via Hwy 16; 2 mi (3.2 km) se off highway via Maligne Rd, follow signs; in The Fairmont Jasper Park Lodge. **Parking:** on-site and valet.

PAPA GEORGE'S RESTAURANT

Phone: 780/852-3351

Continental
$9-$42

Open since 1925, the restaurant is one of the oldest restaurants in town but continues to produce hearty yet innovative food using free-range Alberta meats, local wild mushrooms and seasonal vegetables. With a comfortable, open space dotted with historical Jasper pictures and a beautiful quartzite fireplace and large picture windows overlooking local mountain ranges, the restaurant is a popular gathering spot for groups and families. Casual dress. **Bar:** Full bar. **Reservations:** suggested. **Hours:** 7 am-2:30 & 5-10 pm. **Address:** 404 Connaught Dr T0E 1E0 **Location:** Centre; in Astoria Hotel. **Parking:** on-site.

PATRICIA STREET DELI

Phone: 780/852-4814

Deli
$8-$18

It would be easy to walk past the small, unassuming entrance to the subtly decorated delicatessen. However, it's worth seeking this place out for freshly made sandwiches, which can be eaten at one of the limited tables or in a multitude of green spaces within a short walk. Casual dress. **Reservations:** not accepted. **Hours:** 10 am-6 pm; seasonal hours may vary. Closed: 12/25. **Address:** 606 Patricia St T0E 1E0 **Location:** Centre. **Parking:** street.

THE PINES

Phone: 780/852-3810

Canadian
$10-$38

With wood beams overhead and lovely views of the lake, this cozy yet upscale dining room makes guests feel as though they are dining in a lodge. Each preparation of regional cuisine is an artistic creation. The atmosphere and service are sure to please. Casual dress. **Bar:** Full bar. **Reservations:** suggested. **Hours:** Open 4/22-10/30; 6:30 am-10 pm. **Location:** Jct Connaught Dr and Cedar St, 3.8 mi (6 km) nw via Pyramid Lake Rd; in The Coast Pyramid Lake Resort. **Parking:** on-site. *(See color ad p 479)*

SOFT ROCK CAFE

Phone: 780/852-5850

Deli
$4-$12

While the café may look a little rough at times—what with the scuffed hardwood floors, scratched tables and understated decor—few patrons come for the decor. The food is what brings skiers and families out for oversize portions of fabulously rustic grub: Fluffy omelets, pancakes and sinful, home-baked goods. The place is more or less self-service; diners place an order at the counter and wait for their name to be called, though every now and then someone will bring food to the table. Casual dress. **Bar:** Full bar. **Reservations:** not accepted. **Hours:** 7:30 am-10 pm; 7 am-4 pm in winter. Closed: 12/25. **Address:** 632 Connaught Dr T0E 1E0 **Location:** Just n of Hazel Ave. **Parking:** street.

SOMETHING ELSE RESTAURANT

Phone: 780/852-3850

Greek
$11-$28

The menu lists large portions of lamb and chicken dishes and pizza. Preparations show a tasty mix of International flavor. The staff provides friendly, cheerful and prompt service in a modest, casual atmosphere. Casual dress. **Bar:** Full bar. **Reservations:** accepted. **Hours:** 11 am-11 pm. Closed: 12/25. **Address:** 621 Patricia St T0E 1E0 **Location:** Just w of Connaught Dr; centre. **Parking:** on-site.

TREELINE RESTAURANT

Phone: 780/852-3093

Canadian
$6-$18

A spectacular view of five mountain ranges, lakes and the town awaits above the treeline atop the Jasper Tramway (additional fee) in this self-serve cafeteria. Almost everything on the menu is prepared fresh and includes soups, sandwiches, spaghetti, burgers and hot dogs. The evening menu expands to include entrées such as crab stuffed salmon, steak sandwich and fish and chips. Casual dress. **Bar:** Beer & wine. **Reservations:** accepted. **Hours:** Open 4/30-10/12; 10 am-5 pm; 9:30 am-6:30 pm 5/15-6/24; 9 am-8 pm 6/25-8/28. **Location:** 1.8 mi (3 km) s on Hwy 93, 2.5 mi (4 km) w at Whistlers Campground; tram ride to restaurant for an additional charge. **Parking:** on-site.

VILLA CARUSO

Phone: 780/852-3920

Steak
$11-$37

Established in 1977, the longstanding steakhouse sits above street level but is accessible via elevator. The spacious lodge-like setting has wood beams and hardwood floors, and guests seated near the windows are treated to a great view of the mountains. Alberta beef is the house specialty, but other Canadian specialties, including salmon, also find their way onto the menu. Casual dress. **Bar:** Full bar. **Reservations:** suggested. **Hours:** 11 am-midnight; 3 pm-11 pm 11/1-4/30. Closed major holidays. **Address:** 640 Connaught Dr T0E 1E0 **Location:** Connaught Dr and Hazel Ave; 2nd level. **Parking:** street.

KANANASKIS pop. 429

DELTA LODGE AT KANANASKIS   *Book great rates at AAA.com*

Phone: (403)591-7711

Resort
Hotel
$139-$309 All Year

Address: Kananaskis Village T0L 2H0 **Location:** Trans-Canada Hwy 1, 14.7 mi (23.5 km) s on Hwy 40 (Kananaskis Tr), then 1.8 mi (3 km) on Kananaskis Village access road, follow signs. Located in a quiet area. **Facility:** This attractive resort, nestled in a tranquil mountain village, is near recreation areas and offers a mix of room styles. Smoke free premises. 412 units. 370 one- and 14 two-bedroom standard units, some with whirlpools. 28 one-bedroom suites, some with whirlpools. 3 stories, interior corridors. **Parking:** on-site (fee) and valet, winter plug-ins. **Terms:** check-in 4 pm, 3 day cancellation notice-fee imposed. **Amenities:** video games (fee), high-speed Internet, voice mail, irons, hair dryers. *Some:* CD players, safes. **Dining:** The Fireweed Grill, see separate listing. **Pool(s):** heated indoor. **Leisure Activities:** sauna, whirlpool, steamroom, 6 lighted tennis courts, cross country skiing, ice skating, tobogganing, recreation programs, rental bicycles, hiking trails, playground, sports court. *Fee:* horseback riding, massage, game room. **Guest Services:** valet and coin laundry, area transportation, wireless Internet. **Business Services:** conference facilities, business center. *(See color ad below)*

(ASK) FEE ⊕ ⓘ ⓘ ⓘ ⓘ ⓘ ⓘ ⓘ ⓘ ⓘ / SOME UNITS FEE ⓘ ⓘ

—— WHERE TO DINE ——

THE FIREWEED GRILL

Canadian
$14-$40

Phone: 403/591-7711

This comfortably casual restaurant is a popular pick for both hotel guests and day-trippers. Casual dress. **Bar:** Full bar. **Hours:** 7-11 am, 11:30-2 & 5:30-10 pm. **Address:** Kananaskis Village T0L 2H0 **Location:** Trans-Canada Hwy 1, 14.7 mi (23.5 km) s on Hwy 40 (Kananaskis Tr), then 1.8 mi (3 km) on Kananaskis Village access road, follow signs; in Delta Lodge at Kananaskis. **Parking:** on-site (fee) and valet. *(See color ad p 485)* CALL 🔒M

LAKE LOUISE

THE FAIRMONT CHATEAU LAKE LOUISE   *Book great rates at AAA.com*

Phone: (403)522-3511

Historic Retro Hotel
$279-$2123 All Year

Address: 111 Lake Louise Dr T0L 1E0 **Location:** 1.8 mi (3 km) up the hill from the village. **Facility:** Surrounded by mountains and set alongside Lake Louise, this property features a grand lobby and some rooms with views of Victoria Glacier. 563 units. 537 one-bedroom standard units, some with whirlpools. 26 one-bedroom suites, some with whirlpools. 8 stories, interior corridors. **Parking:** on-site (fee) and valet. winter plug-ins. **Terms:** check-in 4 pm, 3 day cancellation notice-fee imposed. **Amenities:** high-speed Internet (fee), voice mail, safes, irons, hair dryers. *Some:* CD players, dual phone lines. **Dining:** 7 restaurants, also, Chateau Deli, Fairview Dining Room, see separate listings. **Pool(s):** heated indoor. **Leisure Activities:** whirlpool, steamroom, rental canoes, recreation programs, hiking trails, exercise room, spa. *Fee:* cross country skiing, ice skating, horseback riding. **Guest Services:** valet laundry, airport transportation (fee)-Calgary International Airport, area transportation-ski hill, wireless Internet, beauty salon. **Business Services:** conference facilities, business center.

ECO FEE ✈ 🍴 24h 🍸 🏋 ⚓ ✕ 🎥 💻 / SOME UNITS FEE 🐾 ✕ 🐕 🔌 🖨

LAKE LOUISE INN   *Book at AAA.com*

Phone: (403)522-3791

Hotel
$98-$431 All Year

Address: 210 Village Rd T0L 1E0 **Location:** Just w of 4-way stop. **Facility:** Smoke free premises. 247 units. 219 one-bedroom standard units, some with efficiencies. 18 one- and 10 two-bedroom suites with efficiencies. 2-3 stories, interior/exterior corridors. **Parking:** on-site, winter plug-ins. **Terms:** check-in 4 pm, 7 day cancellation notice-fee imposed. **Amenities:** voice mail, hair dryers. *Some:* irons. **Dining:** Legends, see separate listing. **Pool(s):** heated indoor. **Leisure Activities:** whirlpools, steamroom, ice skating, recreation programs, exercise room. *Fee:* massage. **Guest Services:** coin laundry, area transportation, wireless Internet. **Business Services:** meeting rooms, PC (fee).

(ASK) 🍴 🍸 🏋 ⚓ ✕ ✕ 💻 / SOME UNITS FEE 🐾 🐕 🔌 🖨

MOUNTAINEER LODGE

Phone: (403)522-3844

Hotel
$109-$339 5/21-10/15

Address: 101 Village Rd T0L 1E0 **Location:** Just e of 4-way stop. **Facility:** Smoke free premises. 78 units. 74 one- and 4 two-bedroom standard units. 2 stories (no elevator), interior/exterior corridors. *Bath:* combo or shower only. **Parking:** on-site. **Terms:** open 5/21-10/15, office hours 7 am-midnight, check-in 4 pm, 7 day cancellation notice-fee imposed. **Amenities:** irons, hair dryers. **Leisure Activities:** whirlpool, steamroom. **Guest Services:** wireless Internet. **Business Services:** PC (fee).

(ASK) 🍴+ ✕ 🐕 🔌 💻 / SOME UNITS 🔌 🖨

POST HOTEL & SPA

Phone: (403)522-3989

Hotel
$320-$715 11/24-2/28
$250-$715 3/1-10/11

Address: 200 Pipestone Rd T0L 1E0 **Location:** Just w of main intersection; in village. **Facility:** Mountain decor, luxurious bathrooms, upscale rooms and fine service await at this cozy hotel, located in the heart of Lake Louise village. Designated smoking area. 96 units. 65 one-bedroom standard units with whirlpools. 27 one-bedroom suites with whirlpools. 4 cabins. 3 stories, interior corridors. **Parking:** on-site and valet, winter plug-ins. **Terms:** open 3/1-10/11 & 11/24-2/28, check-in 3:30 pm, 14 day cancellation notice. **Amenities:** video library, voice mail, safes, hair dryers. *Some:* DVD players, irons. **Dining:** Post Hotel Dining Room, see separate listing. **Pool(s):** heated indoor. **Leisure Activities:** whirlpool, steamroom, exercise room, spa. **Guest Services:** valet laundry, wireless Internet. **Business Services:** meeting rooms, PC.

🍴 🍸 🏋 ⚓ ✕ ✕ / SOME UNITS 🐕 🔌 🖨 💻

—— WHERE TO DINE ——

CHATEAU DELI

Deli
$9-$16

Phone: 403/522-3511

Long lines are not uncommon at this delicatessen, which is open 24 hours. Selections from the limited wine list complement custom-made sandwiches and hot entrees. Desserts have good eye appeal. Casual dress. **Bar:** Wine only. **Hours:** 24 hours. **Address:** 111 Lake Louise Dr T0L 1E0 **Location:** 1.8 mi (3 km) up the hill from the village; in The Fairmont Chateau Lake Louise. **Parking:** on-site (fee) and valet. CALL 🔒M

FAIRVIEW DINING ROOM
Phone: 403/522-1818

Canadian
$25-$37

Ask for a seat by the oversized windows and be rewarded with commanding views of Lake Louise and the Victoria Glacier. From start to finish, diners can expect professional and knowledgeable service amid exquisite surroundings. The menu explores a diverse selection of Canadian cuisine, ranging from venison to organic chicken, and decadent desserts. A trip to Lake Louise would be remiss without a meal in this elegant restaurant. Dressy casual. **Bar:** Full bar. **Reservations:** required. **Hours:** 6 pm-9 pm; hours may vary off season. **Address:** 111 Lake Louise Dr T0L 1E0 **Location:** 1.8 mi (3 km) up the hill from the village; in The Fairmont Chateau Lake Louise. **Parking:** on-site (fee) and valet. **Historic**

LAGGAN'S MOUNTAIN BAKERY & DELI
Phone: 403/522-2017

Deli
$6-$7

One of the few village restaurants not located in a hotel, the very popular bakery serves an extensive range of baked goods and freshly made sandwiches, as well as several soups of the day. Casual dress. **Reservations:** not accepted. **Hours:** 6 am-6 pm. Closed: 1/1, 12/25. **Address:** 101 Lake Louise Dr T0L 1E0 **Location:** Centre; in Samson Mall. **Parking:** on-site.

LAKE LOUISE STATION
Phone: 403/522-2600

Canadian
$15-$34

This restaurant is located in a beautifully restored heritage railway station that includes a 1925 dining car. The progressive Continental cuisine offers lasagna, chicken, pork ribs, stuffed halibut, salmon, rack of lamb and even build-your-own pizza. Casual dress. **Bar:** Full bar. **Reservations:** suggested. **Hours:** 11:30 am-9:30 & 5-9 pm; seasonal hours may vary. Closed: 12/25; also 10/15-11/15. **Address:** 200 Sentinel Rd T0L 1E0 **Location:** From 4-way stop, just s via underpass, 0.6 mi (1 km) w. **Parking:** on-site.

LEGENDS
Phone: 403/522-3791

Canadian
$8-$36

This casual dining room features a river stone fireplace and hanging banners of Rocky Mountain historical characters. Well-prepared meals include AAA beef, pork tenderloin and chicken. Casual dress. **Bar:** Full bar. **Reservations:** suggested. **Hours:** 6 am-9 pm; seasonal hours vary. **Address:** 210 Village Rd T0L 1E0 **Location:** Just w of 4-way stop; in Lake Louise Inn. **Parking:** on-site.

MOUNT FAIRVIEW DINING ROOM
Phone: 403/552-4202

Regional
Canadian
$16-$40

This restaurant is tucked behind the lounge of a historic hotel deep in the heart of the Rockies. With windows on three sides, every seat affords commanding views of the mountains and the nearby Chateau hotel. An extraordinary wine list includes selections perfectly matched to the creative and artistic food, which blends the best seasonal and local ingredients. This place is well known for its preparations of game, most of which is raised in a ranch outside of Calgary. Casual dress. **Bar:** Full bar. **Reservations:** suggested. **Hours:** Open 3/1-10/19 & 12/3-2/28; 7 am-11 & 6-10:30 pm. **Address:** 80 Lake Louise Dr T0L 1E0 **Location:** 1.8 mi (3 km) up hill from village; in Deer Lodge Hotel. **Parking:** on-site.

POST HOTEL DINING ROOM
Phone: 403/522-3989

Continental
$14-$54

Delicious food lends to the restaurant's exceptional reputation. European classics are wonderfully flavorful and colorfully presented. A less extensive menu is offered at lunch. A cigar room is available. Dressy casual. **Bar:** Full bar. **Reservations:** suggested, for dinner. **Hours:** Open 3/1-10/17 & 11/26-2/28; 7-11 am, 11:30-2 & 5-10 pm. **Address:** 200 Pipestone Rd T0L 1E0 **Location:** Just w of main intersection; in village; in Post Hotel & Spa. **Parking:** on-site.

LEDUC—See Edmonton p. 464.

LETHBRIDGE pop. 74,637

BEST WESTERN HEIDELBERG INN

Phone: (403)329-0555

AAA Benefit:
Members save up to 20%, plus 10% bonus points with rewards program.

Hotel
$130-$140 All Year

Address: 1303 Mayor Magrath Dr S T1K 2R1 **Location:** Hwy 3 (Crowsnest Tr), exit Mayor Magrath Dr S, 1.8 mi (2 km) s. **Facility:** 65 one-bedroom standard units. 9 stories, interior corridors. **Parking:** on-site, winter plug-ins. **Amenities:** video library (fee), voice mail, irons, hair dryers. *Some:* DVD players, high-speed Internet, dual phone lines. **Leisure Activities:** sauna, exercise room. **Guest Services:** valet laundry, wireless Internet. **Business Services:** meeting rooms, PC. **Free Special Amenities:** newspaper and high-speed Internet.

COMFORT INN
Book at AAA.com
Phone: 403/320-8874

Hotel
Rates not provided

Address: 3226 Fairway Plaza Rd S T1K 7T5 **Location:** Hwy 3 (Crowsnest Tr), exit Mayor Magrath Dr S, 1.8 mi (3 km) s, then just e on 24th Ave. **Facility:** 58 one-bedroom standard units. 4 stories, interior corridors. *Bath:* combo or shower only. **Parking:** on-site, winter plug-ins. **Amenities:** high-speed Internet, voice mail, irons, hair dryers. **Pool(s):** heated indoor. **Leisure Activities:** whirlpool, exercise room. **Guest Services:** valet and coin laundry, wireless Internet. **Business Services:** PC.

DAYS INN LETHBRIDGE

Book at AAA.com Phone: (403)327-6000

Hotel
$105-$185 All Year

Address: 100 3rd Ave S T1J 4L2 **Location:** Corner of 3rd Ave and Scenic Dr; centre. **Facility:** 87 units. 85 one-bedroom standard units, some with whirlpools. 2 one-bedroom suites. 2 stories (no elevator), interior/exterior corridors. **Parking:** on-site, winter plug-ins. **Terms:** cancellation fee imposed. **Amenities:** hair dryers. *Some:* DVD players, irons. **Pool(s):** heated indoor. **Leisure Activities:** whirlpool, waterslide. **Guest Services:** coin laundry, wireless Internet. **Business Services:** PC (fee).

HOLIDAY INN EXPRESS HOTEL & SUITES LETHBRIDGE

Book great rates at AAA.com Phone: 403/394-9292

CAA SAVE

Hotel
Rates not provided

Address: 120 Stafford Dr S T1J 4W4 **Location:** Hwy 3 (Crowsnest Tr), exit Stafford Dr, just s; downtown. **Facility:** 102 units. 82 one-bedroom standard units, some with whirlpools. 20 one-bedroom suites. 4 stories, interior corridors. **Parking:** on-site, winter plug-ins. **Amenities:** high-speed Internet, dual phone lines, voice mail, irons, hair dryers. **Pool(s):** heated indoor. **Leisure Activities:** whirlpool, waterslide, limited exercise equipment. **Guest Services:** valet and coin laundry, wireless Internet. **Business Services:** meeting rooms, PC. **Free Special Amenities:** expanded continental breakfast and high-speed Internet.

LETHBRIDGE LODGE HOTEL AND CONFERENCE CENTRE

Book great rates at AAA.com Phone: (403)328-1123

CAA SAVE

Hotel
$119-$199 All Year

Address: 320 Scenic Dr T1J 4B4 **Location:** Scenic Dr at 4th Ave S; centre. **Facility:** Smoke free premises. 190 units. 154 one-bedroom standard units. 36 one-bedroom suites, some with whirlpools. 4 stories, interior corridors. **Parking:** on-site, winter plug-ins. **Terms:** check-in 4 pm, cancellation fee imposed. **Amenities:** high-speed Internet, voice mail, irons, hair dryers. **Dining:** nightclub. **Pool(s):** heated indoor. **Leisure Activities:** whirlpool, exercise room. **Guest Services:** valet laundry. **Business Services:** conference facilities, PC. **Free Special Amenities:** local telephone calls and high-speed Internet.

PEPPER TREE INN

Phone: (403)328-4436

CAA SAVE

Motel
$65-$120 3/1-10/31
$55-$100 11/1-2/28

Address: 1142 Mayor Magrath Dr S T1K 2P8 **Location:** Hwy 3 (Crowsnest Tr), exit Mayor Magrath Dr S, then 1 mi (1.7 km) s. **Facility:** 56 one-bedroom standard units, some with efficiencies. 2 stories (no elevator), exterior corridors. **Parking:** on-site, winter plug-ins. **Amenities:** video library (fee), DVD players, voice mail. *Some:* irons, hair dryers. **Pool(s):** outdoor. **Leisure Activities:** whirlpool. **Guest Services:** coin laundry, wireless Internet. **Free Special Amenities:** local telephone calls and high-speed Internet.

PREMIER INN & SUITES

Book great rates at AAA.com Phone: (403)380-6677

CAA SAVE

Hotel
$90-$130 3/1-9/30
$80-$115 10/1-2/28

Address: 2225 Mayor Magrath Dr S T1K 7M1 **Location:** Hwy 3 (Crowsnest Tr), exit Mayor Magrath Dr S, 1.8 mi (3 km) s, then just e on 22nd St. **Facility:** Smoke free premises. 50 units. 44 one- and 6 two-bedroom standard units. 4 stories, interior corridors. *Bath:* combo or shower only. **Parking:** on-site, winter plug-ins. **Terms:** cancellation fee imposed. **Amenities:** high-speed Internet, hair dryers. **Leisure Activities:** whirlpool, exercise room. **Guest Services:** coin laundry. **Business Services:** PC. **Free Special Amenities:** continental breakfast and high-speed Internet.

QUALITY INN & SUITES

Book great rates at AAA.com Phone: (403)331-6440

CAA SAVE

Hotel
$99-$115 All Year

Address: 4040 2nd Ave S T1J 3Z2 **Location:** Hwy 3 (Crowsnest Tr), just s on WT Hill Blvd, then just e. **Facility:** 60 one-bedroom standard units, some with whirlpools. 4 stories, interior corridors. *Bath:* combo or shower only. **Parking:** on-site, winter plug-ins. **Amenities:** high-speed Internet, voice mail, irons, hair dryers. **Pool(s):** heated indoor. **Leisure Activities:** whirlpool, waterslide, exercise room. **Guest Services:** valet and coin laundry, wireless Internet. **Business Services:** meeting rooms, business center. **Free Special Amenities:** room upgrade (subject to availability with advance reservations) and high-speed Internet.

RAMADA LETHBRIDGE

Book at AAA.com Phone: (403)380-5050

Hotel
$140-$160 All Year

Address: 2375 Mayor Magrath Dr S T1K 7M1 **Location:** Hwy 3 (Crowsnest Tr), exit Mayor Magrath Dr S, 1.8 mi (3 km) s, then just e on 22nd St. **Facility:** Smoke free premises. 119 units. 97 one- and 10 two-bedroom standard units. 12 one-bedroom suites, some with whirlpools. 4 stories, interior corridors. **Parking:** on-site, winter plug-ins. **Terms:** check-in 4 pm, cancellation fee imposed. **Amenities:** video games (fee), dual phone lines, voice mail, irons, hair dryers. **Pool(s):** heated indoor. **Leisure Activities:** whirlpool, waterslide, exercise room. *Fee:* game room. **Guest Services:** valet and coin laundry, wireless Internet. **Business Services:** conference facilities, PC.

SANDMAN HOTEL LETHBRIDGE

Book at AAA.com Phone: (403)328-1111

Hotel
$109-$159 All Year

Address: 421 Mayor Magrath Dr S T1J 3L8 **Location:** Hwy 3 (Crowsnest Tr), exit Mayor Magrath Dr, just s. **Facility:** 139 units. 137 one-bedroom standard units, some with whirlpools. 2 one-bedroom suites. 8 stories, interior corridors. **Parking:** on-site, winter plug-ins. **Terms:** check-in 4 pm, cancellation fee imposed. **Amenities:** high-speed Internet, irons, hair dryers. **Pool(s):** heated indoor. **Leisure Activities:** limited exercise equipment. **Guest Services:** valet laundry. **Business Services:** conference facilities, business center.

360 INSPIRED CUISINE

Phone: 403/329-3609

Canadian
$10-$30

While chic and contemporary, the restaurant manages to maintain an intimate atmosphere. The chef serves up some truly inspiring cuisine at reasonable prices. The menu includes everything from chicken, salmon, bison and AAA beef to ahi tuna with superlative vinaigrettes and sauces. Dressy casual. **Bar:** Full bar. **Reservations:** suggested. **Hours:** 11:30 am-10 pm. Closed major holidays; also Sun. **Address:** 100 5th St S T1J 2B2 **Location:** Corner of 5th St S and 1st Ave S. **Parking:** street.

THE CHEESECAKE CAFE

Phone: 403/394-2253

American
$10-$26

As might be expected, cheesecake is the signature item, and it's worth saving room for one of the lip-smacking varieties made on the premises. A huge dessert display case greets guests upon arrival. Offerings on the extensive lunch and dinner menu range from sandwiches and entree salads to pasta, pizza and seafood selections. It takes a while to get through the menu. Casual dress. **Bar:** Full bar. **Reservations:** accepted, except weekends. **Hours:** 11 am-11 pm, Fri & Sat-midnight, Sun 10 am-11 pm; Sunday brunch. Closed: 12/24, 12/25. **Address:** 904 2nd Ave S T1J 0C6 **Location:** At Stafford Dr and 2nd Ave S; downtown. **Parking:** on-site.

COCO PAZZO

Phone: 403/329-8979

Italian
$8-$30

The cozy Italian cafe has a fun, casual atmosphere. Finely tuned, guest-oriented service enhances the meals, which range from wood-fired-oven pizzas and fresh pasta to seafood and other nicely prepared meat and poultry dishes. Casual dress. **Bar:** Full bar. **Hours:** 11:30 am-10 pm, Fri & Sat-11 pm, Sun 4:30 pm-9 pm. Closed: 1/1, 12/25, 12/26. **Address:** 1264 3rd Ave S T1J 0J9 **Location:** Corner of 12th St. **Parking:** on-site.

DIONYSIOS MEDITERRANEAN GRILL

Phone: 403/320-6554

International
$13-$30

The restaurant's décor has an astonishing collection of bits and pieces from Greece, India and the Mediterranean and has an eclectic menu to match. You'll find everything from souvlaki, butter chicken, Moroccan sole, Italian pastas and unique steaks sharing menu space. Service is casual and friendly, and patrons can partake in the plate smashing pit, just don't use the food plates. Casual dress. **Bar:** Full bar. **Reservations:** suggested. **Hours:** 5 pm-9 pm, Fri & Sat-10 pm, Sun-9 pm. Closed major holidays; also Mon. **Address:** 635 13th St N T1H 2S9 **Location:** Between 7th and 6th aves N. **Parking:** on-site.

LA MEZZA LUNA

Phone: 403/327-3067

Italian
$9-$26

A great place for families, the casual restaurant serves a wide range of pizzas and steaks as well as other dishes, including large sandwiches, oversize salads and nachos. Patrons get great value for the dollar, and there's something for everyone. Casual dress. **Bar:** Full bar. **Reservations:** suggested. **Hours:** 11 am-midnight, Fri & Sat-1 am. Closed: 12/25. **Address:** 2433 Fairway Plaza Rd S T1K 6Z2 **Location:** Mayor Magrath Dr, exit Scenic Dr northbound to Fairway Plaza; southeast end of town. **Parking:** on-site.

PENNY COFFEE HOUSE

Phone: 403/320-5282

Deli
$7-$10

Street signs and local artwork cover the walls of this local coffee shop, which features a wide range of soups, salads and sandwiches. Many of the pastries are made on the premises. Casual dress. **Reservations:** not accepted. **Hours:** 7:30 am-9 pm, Sat-7 pm, Sun 9 am-5 pm. Closed: 1/1, 12/25. **Address:** 331 5th St S T1J 2B4 **Location:** Jct 3rd Ave; centre. **Parking:** street.

STREATSIDE EATERY

Phone: 403/328-8085

Canadian
$11-$29

A favorite among the locals, the casual downtown eatery prepares homemade comfort food from fresh ingredients. Although this place is known for its quiche of the day, guests can also try entree-size salads and sandwiches. The red brick interior and outdoor patio contribute to a pleasant atmosphere. Casual dress. **Bar:** Full bar. **Hours:** 11 am-9 pm, Thurs-Sat to 10 pm, Sun-8 pm. Closed major holidays. **Address:** 317 8th St S T1J 2J5 **Location:** At 3rd Ave and 8th St; downtown. **Parking:** street.

TREATS EATERY

Phone: 403/380-4880

American
$12-$25

Although the fun, casual establishment has an unusual Western theme, it doesn't offer Western-style dishes. On the menu are deli-style burgers, sandwiches and quiche, as well as health-conscious dishes and more elaborate dinner items. Casual dress. **Bar:** Full bar. **Reservations:** suggested. **Hours:** 11 am-9 pm, Fri & Sat-10 pm, Sun noon-9 pm. Closed: 1/1, 12/25. **Address:** 1104 Mayor Magrath Dr T1K 2P9 **Location:** 2 mi (3.2 km) se on Hwy 4 and 5, exit Mayor Magrath Dr, at 10th Ave S. **Parking:** on-site.

LLOYDMINSTER pop. 15,910—See also nearby SK city of LLOYDMINSTER.

BEST WESTERN WAYSIDE INN & SUITES

Book great rates at AAA.com

Phone: (780)875-4404

Hotel
$139-$279 All Year

Address: 5411 44th St T9V 0A9 **Location:** 0.5 mi (0.8 km) w on Hwy 16 from jct Hwy 17. **Facility:** 127 units. 95 one-bedroom standard units. 32 one-bedroom suites, some with whirlpools. 6 stories, interior corridors. **Parking:** on-site, winter plug-ins. **Amenities:** high-speed Internet, voice mail, irons, hair dryers. **Pool(s):** heated indoor. **Leisure Activities:** exercise room. **Guest Services:** valet laundry, wireless Internet. **Business Services:** conference facilities, administrative services (fee), PC. **Free Special Amenities:** local telephone calls and high-speed Internet.

HOLIDAY INN HOTEL & SUITES   *Book great rates at AAA.com*   Phone: (780)870-5050

Hotel
$123-$143 All Year

Address: 5612 44th St T9V 0B6 **Location:** Jct Hwy 16 and 17, 0.6 mi (1 km) w. **Facility:** 100 units. 84 one-bedroom standard units. 16 one-bedroom suites, some with whirlpools. 4 stories, interior corridors. *Bath:* combo or shower only. **Parking:** on-site, winter plug-ins. **Terms:** check-in 4 pm, cancellation fee imposed. **Amenities:** high-speed Internet, dual phone lines, voice mail, irons, hair dryers. **Pool(s):** heated outdoor. **Leisure Activities:** whirlpool, exercise room. **Business Services:** meeting rooms, PC. **Free Special Amenities: local telephone calls and high-speed Internet.**

WEST HARVEST EXPRESS   *Book at AAA.com*   Phone: (780)875-8884

Hotel
$135-$145 All Year

Address: 1402 50th Ave T9V 2K5 **Location:** Hwy 16, 1.9 mi (3.1 km) s. **Facility:** Smoke free premises. 80 units. 72 one-bedroom standard units. 6 one- and 2 two-bedroom suites, some with efficiencies and/or whirlpools. 4 stories, interior corridors. *Bath:* combo or shower only. **Parking:** on-site, winter plug-ins. **Terms:** check-in 4 pm, cancellation fee imposed. **Amenities:** high-speed Internet, voice mail, irons, hair dryers. **Guest Services:** valet and coin laundry, wireless Internet. **Business Services:** PC.

WEST HARVEST INN   *Book at AAA.com*   Phone: (780)875-6113

Hotel
$129-$169 All Year

Address: 5620 44th St T9V 0B6 **Location:** Jct Hwy 16 and 17, 0.6 mi (1 km) w. **Facility:** Smoke free premises. 97 one-bedroom standard units, some with whirlpools. 2 stories (no elevator), interior/exterior corridors. **Parking:** on-site, winter plug-ins. **Terms:** check-in 4 pm. **Amenities:** high-speed Internet, voice mail, irons, hair dryers. **Leisure Activities:** steamrooms, exercise room. **Guest Services:** valet and coin laundry, wireless Internet. **Business Services:** meeting rooms, PC (fee).

——— WHERE TO DINE ———

MR BILL'S FAMILY RESTAURANT   Phone: 780/875-3388

Continental
$9-$45

In a border town that features predominantly chain eateries, the excellent family restaurant serves burgers, sandwiches, pasta and a few Greek dishes. For a delicious, hearty lunch, try the avgolemono soup; it's superb. Popular with locals, the spot offers fast, friendly service. Trendy decor comprises turquoise walls, wooden accents, some interesting lighting techniques and both table and booth seating. Casual dress. **Bar:** Full bar. **Reservations:** suggested. **Hours:** 10 am-10 pm. Closed major holidays; also Sun. **Address:** 5405 44th St, Suite 10 T9V 0A9 **Location:** Corner of Hwy 16 and 54th Ave; in strip mall. **Parking:** on-site.

SPIRO'S   Phone: 780/875-4241

Mediterranean
$8-$23

A great place to take a family for a meal, the steak and pizza house has something for everyone on its menu. In addition to the requisites, this place serves sandwiches and some Greek dishes. Casual dress. **Bar:** Full bar. **Reservations:** suggested. **Hours:** 11 am-9 pm, Sun from 4 pm. Closed: 1/1, 12/25, 12/26; also Mon. **Address:** 3425 50th Ave T9V 0Y1 **Location:** Hwy 16, 1.9 mi (3.1 km) s. **Parking:** on-site.

MEDICINE HAT pop. 56,997

BEST WESTERN INN   *Book great rates at AAA.com*   Phone: (403)527-3700

Hotel
$105-$250 All Year

Address: 722 Redcliff Dr T1A 5E3 **Location:** On Trans-Canada Hwy 1, 0.3 mi (0.4 km) w of jct Hwy 3, access 7th St SW. **Facility:** 122 units. 115 one-bedroom standard units, some with efficiencies and/or whirlpools. 7 one-bedroom suites, some with efficiencies and/or whirlpools. 2 stories (no elevator), interior/exterior corridors. **Parking:** on-site, winter plug-ins. **Amenities:** video games (fee), voice mail, irons, hair dryers. *Some:* high-speed Internet, dual phone lines. **Pool(s):** 2 heated indoor. **Leisure Activities:** sauna, whirlpools, exercise room. **Guest Services:** valet and coin laundry, airport transportation-Medicine Hat Municipal Airport, wireless Internet. **Business Services:** meeting rooms, administrative services (fee), PC. **Free Special Amenities: continental breakfast and high-speed Internet.**

AAA Benefit:
Members save up to 20%, plus 10% bonus points with rewards program.

COMFORT INN & SUITES   *Book great rates at AAA.com*   Phone: (403)504-1700

Hotel
$99-$189 All Year

Address: 2317 Trans-Canada Way SE T1B 4E9 **Location:** Trans-Canada Hwy 1, just n on Dunmore Rd, then just w. Opposite Medicine Hat Mall. **Facility:** 100 units. 71 one-bedroom standard units, some with whirlpools. 29 one-bedroom suites, some with whirlpools. 3 stories, interior corridors. **Parking:** on-site, winter plug-ins. **Terms:** check-in 4 pm, 3 day cancellation notice. **Amenities:** high-speed Internet, voice mail, irons, hair dryers. **Pool(s):** heated indoor. **Leisure Activities:** whirlpool, exercise room. **Guest Services:** valet and coin laundry, wireless Internet. **Business Services:** meeting rooms, PC. **Free Special Amenities: continental breakfast and high-speed Internet.**

DAYS INN-MEDICINE HAT   *Book at AAA.com*   Phone: (403)580-3297

Hotel
$130-$150 6/1-2/28
$120-$145 3/1-5/31

Address: 24 Strachan Ct SE T1B 4R7 **Location:** Trans-Canada Hwy 1, exit Dunmore Rd, just sw. **Facility:** 76 units. 61 one-bedroom standard units, some with whirlpools. 15 one-bedroom suites, some with whirlpools. 4 stories, interior corridors. **Parking:** on-site, winter plug-ins. **Terms:** check-in 4 pm. **Amenities:** voice mail, irons, hair dryers. *Some:* video games, high-speed Internet. **Pool(s):** heated indoor. **Leisure Activities:** whirlpool, waterslide. **Guest Services:** valet and coin laundry, wireless Internet. **Business Services:** PC.

HOLIDAY INN EXPRESS HOTEL & SUITES   *Book at AAA.com*   **Phone: (403)504-5151**

Hotel
$145-$309 All Year

Address: 9 Strachan Bay SE T1B 4Y2 **Location:** Trans-Canada Hwy 1, just s on Dunmore Rd, then just e; east end of city. **Facility:** 93 units. 89 one- and 3 two-bedroom standard units, some with kitchens and/or whirlpools. 1 one-bedroom suite with kitchen. 4 stories, interior corridors. *Bath:* combo or shower only. **Parking:** on-site, winter plug-ins. **Amenities:** high-speed Internet, voice mail, irons, hair dryers. *Some:* DVD players. **Pool(s):** heated indoor. **Leisure Activities:** whirlpool, waterslide, exercise room. **Guest Services:** valet and coin laundry, wireless Internet. **Business Services:** meeting rooms, PC.

MEDICINE HAT LODGE RESORT, CASINO & SPA   *Book at AAA.com*   **Phone: (403)529-2222**

Hotel
$149-$174 1/1-2/28
$139-$169 3/1-12/31

Address: 1051 Ross Glen Dr SE T1B 3T8 **Location:** Trans-Canada Hwy 1, just n on Dunmore Rd. **Facility:** A variety of rooms are offered at this casino hotel, including some poolside units. Children will enjoy the indoor waterslides. Smoke free premises. 221 units. 187 one-bedroom standard units, some with whirlpools. 34 one-bedroom suites, some with whirlpools. 4 stories, interior corridors. *Bath:* combo or shower only. **Parking:** on-site, winter plug-ins. **Terms:** check-in 4 pm. **Amenities:** video games (fee), voice mail, irons, hair dryers. *Some:* high-speed Internet, safes. **Dining:** M Grill, see separate listing. **Pool(s):** heated indoor. **Leisure Activities:** whirlpool, waterslide, exercise room, spa. *Fee:* game room. **Guest Services:** valet and coin laundry, wireless Internet, beauty salon. **Business Services:** conference facilities, administrative services (fee), PC.

MOTEL 6-MEDICINE HAT #5700   *Book great rates at AAA.com*   **Phone: (403)527-1749**

Hotel
$85-$95 All Year

Address: 20 Strachan Ct SE T1B 4R7 **Location:** Trans-Canada Hwy 1, just s on Dunmore Rd, then just w; southeast end of city. **Facility:** 79 one-bedroom standard units. 3 stories, interior corridors. *Bath:* combo or shower only. **Parking:** on-site, winter plug-ins. **Terms:** check-in 4 pm. **Amenities:** *Some:* irons, hair dryers. **Guest Services:** coin laundry, wireless Internet. **Business Services:** PC (fee). *(See color ad below)*

SUPER 8   *Book at AAA.com*   **Phone: (403)528-8888**

Hotel
$87-$149 All Year

Address: 1280 Trans-Canada Way SE T1B 1J5 **Location:** Trans-Canada Hwy 1 at 13th Ave SE; just n off Trans-Canada Hwy 1. **Facility:** 70 units. 69 one-bedroom standard units, some with kitchens. 1 one-bedroom suite with kitchen. 2-3 stories (no elevator), interior/exterior corridors. **Parking:** on-site, winter plug-ins. **Terms:** check-in 4 pm, cancellation fee imposed. **Amenities:** voice mail, hair dryers. **Pool(s):** heated indoor. **Leisure Activities:** whirlpool, limited exercise equipment. **Guest Services:** valet laundry, wireless Internet. **Business Services:** PC.

—— WHERE TO DINE ——

BEEFEATER STEAKHOUSE
Phone: 403/526-6925

Steak
$9-$40

Patrons appreciate the good value they receive at the restaurant, which offers relaxed dining in an attractive library-like setting. The menu specializes in prime rib and seafood, with a nice selection of sandwiches at lunch. Service is efficient. Casual dress. **Bar:** Full bar. **Reservations:** suggested. **Hours:** 11 am-10 pm, Sat from 4:30 pm, Sun 4:30 pm-9 pm. Closed: 12/24-12/26. **Address:** 3286 13th Ave SE T1B 1H8 **Location:** 2.2 mi (3.6 km) se; just n off Trans-Canada Hwy 1; in Imperial Inn. **Parking:** on-site.

DEVINE GRILL
Phone: 403/580-5510

Canadian
$9-$34

As the name hints, the cuisine here is divine. Using fresh ingredients from local and Canadian merchants, the kitchen staff create a globally-inspired, innovative menu. Start the experience with the house-cured, smoked wild salmon followed by Deerview Farms venison or wild Pacific halibut. The lunch fare is a little simpler but no less delicious with the addition of flatbreads and sandwiches. The popular patio also offers a special menu. Casual dress. **Bar:** Full bar. **Reservations:** suggested. **Hours:** 11 am-2:30 & 5-9 pm, Sat from 5 pm; 11 am-9 pm 5/15-9/30. Closed major holidays; also Sun. **Address:** 579 3rd St SE T1A 0H7 **Location:** Between 5th and 6th aves; downtown. **Parking:** street. CALL ⓛⓜ

THE GARAGE PUB AND EATERY
Phone: 403/580-2588

Canadian
$6-$12

Located in an old gas station, the funky diner has a great collection of vintage gas and air pumps, auto and gas memorabilia and, of course, a jukebox. All the classic pub food is featured, including burgers, but fresh-made wraps and sandwiches are the way to go. Make sure you try some hubcaps (hot, seasoned potato chips), but diners won't be able to tempt a sweet tooth, as there are no desserts. In the summer there is a great patio on which to unwind. This spot caters to those 18 and older. Casual dress. **Bar:** Full bar. **Reservations:** accepted. **Hours:** 11 am-11 pm. Closed: 1/1, 12/25. **Address:** 710 Gershaw Dr SW T1A 5C8 **Location:** On Trans-Canada Hwy 1, just e of jct Hwy 3 (Crowsnest Tr). **Parking:** on-site.

HAT'S RESTAURANT
Phone: 403/529-9739

Chinese
$7-$15

Locals claim the wonderful Chinese restaurant as a favorite for its flavorful, reasonably priced food. Traditional foods line the all-you-can-eat buffet, as well as the a la carte menu. Also offered is a smattering of Western cuisine. Friendly servers keep drinks full and tables cleared. Casual dress. **Bar:** Full bar. **Reservations:** suggested, weekends. **Hours:** 4 pm-10 pm, Fri & Sat-11 pm. Closed major holidays. **Address:** 1701 Dunmore Rd SE T1A 1Z8 **Location:** Jct 19th Ave SE; in Crestwood Shopping Centre. **Parking:** on-site.

MAD HATTER COFFEE ROASTERY
Phone: 403/529-2344

Coffee/Tea
$3-$5

This downtown spot takes its coffee seriously, as evidenced by the coffee roaster set in the middle of the space. A limited variety of baked goods are available at the front counter. Local musicians are sometimes on hand to serenade you while you sip your brew or loose leaf tea. Casual dress. **Reservations:** not accepted. **Hours:** 7 am-5:30 pm, Sat from 8 am, Sun 10 am-5 pm. Closed major holidays. **Address:** 513 3rd St SE T1A 0H2 **Location:** Jct 5th Ave; downtown. **Parking:** street.

M GRILL
Phone: 403/529-2222

Continental
$18-$37

The varied menu includes preparations of pasta, seafood, veal and Alberta beef. The restaurant's elegant garden setting lends to a casual, relaxed atmosphere. Service is efficient and friendly. Dressy casual. **Bar:** Full bar. **Reservations:** accepted. **Hours:** 4 pm-10 pm. **Address:** 1051 Ross Glen Dr SE T1B 3T8 **Location:** Trans-Canada Hwy 1, just n on Dunmore Rd; in Medicine Hat Lodge Resort, Casino & Spa. **Parking:** on-site.

THAI ORCHID ROOM
Phone: 403/580-8210

Thai
$10-$18

The restaurant, which boasts a contemporary decor, prides itself on the use of the finest and freshest ingredients available. While not an extensive menu, the dishes are well made and seasoned to taste along with vibrantly colored vegetables and housemade sauces. Servers are smartly clad and friendly. Casual dress. **Bar:** Full bar. **Reservations:** accepted. **Hours:** 11 am-9 pm, Sat 4:30 pm-10 pm, Sun noon-9 pm. Closed major holidays; also Mon & 12/24-1/2. **Address:** #3-36 Strachan Ct SE T1B 4R7 **Location:** Trans-Canada Hwy 1, just s on Dunmore Rd, then just w. **Parking:** on-site. CALL ⓛⓜ

MOUNTAIN VIEW pop. 20

ROCKY RIDGE COUNTRY LODGE
Phone: 403/653-2350

Bed & Breakfast
$60-$225 All Year

Address: 523 2nd St N T0K 1N0 **Location:** Just n of Village Church, follow signs. **Facility:** Smoke free premises. 7 units. 6 one-bedroom standard units. 1 cabin. 2 stories (no elevator), interior corridors. *Bath:* some shared or private, combo or shower only. **Parking:** on-site, winter plug-ins. **Terms:** 7 day cancellation notice. **Amenities:** hair dryers. **Leisure Activities:** sauna, whirlpool, game room. **Guest Services:** TV in common area, wireless Internet. ⊠ ⊠ Ⓦ Ⓩ / SOME UNITS Ⓚ

NISKU—See Edmonton p. 465.

OKOTOKS—See Calgary p. 430.

OLDS pop. 7,248

BEST WESTERN OF OLDS   *Book great rates at AAA.com*

Phone: (403)556-5900

Hotel
$120 All Year

Address: 4520 46th St T4H 1P7 **Location:** Hwy 2, exit 340B (Olds, Sundre), 3 mi (5 km) w. **Facility:** 41 units. 38 one-bedroom standard units. 3 one-bedroom suites with efficiencies, some with whirlpools. 2 stories (no elevator), interior corridors. *Bath:* combo or shower only. **Parking:** on-site, winter plug-ins. **Amenities:** irons, hair dryers. *Some:* high-speed Internet. **Pool(s):** heated indoor/outdoor. **Leisure Activities:** whirlpool, exercise room. **Guest Services:** complimentary laundry, wireless Internet. **Business Services:** PC. **Free Special Amenities: continental breakfast and high-speed Internet.**

AAA Benefit:
Members save up to 20%, plus 10% bonus points with rewards program.

PINCHER CREEK pop. 3,625

HERITAGE INN   *Book at AAA.com*

Phone: (403)627-5000

Hotel
$125-$289 7/1-2/28
$120-$269 3/1-6/30

Address: 919 Waterton Ave (Hwy 6) T0K 1W0 **Location:** Hwy 3 (Crowsnest Tr), 1.3 mi (2.1 km) s, follow Hwy 6 (Waterton Ave) e, then 1.6 mi (2.6 km) s. **Facility:** 78 units. 74 one-bedroom standard units. 3 one- and 1 two-bedroom suites, some with efficiencies and/or whirlpools. 2 stories, interior corridors. **Parking:** on-site, winter plug-ins. **Amenities:** irons. *Some:* high-speed Internet, hair dryers. **Pool(s):** heated indoor. **Leisure Activities:** sauna, whirlpool, exercise room. **Guest Services:** coin laundry, wireless Internet. **Business Services:** conference facilities.

RAMADA INN & SUITES   *Book at AAA.com*

Phone: (403)627-3777

Hotel
$150-$250 All Year

Address: 1132 Table Mountain St T0K 1W0 **Location:** Hwy 3 (Crowsnest Tr), 1.3 mi (2.1 km) s on Hwy 6. **Facility:** Smoke free premises. 78 units. 73 one-bedroom standard units, some with efficiencies and/or whirlpools. 5 one-bedroom suites. 3 stories, interior/exterior corridors. *Bath:* combo or shower only. **Parking:** on-site, winter plug-ins. **Terms:** cancellation fee imposed. **Amenities:** high-speed Internet, voice mail, irons, hair dryers. *Some:* DVD players. **Pool(s):** heated outdoor. **Leisure Activities:** whirlpool, waterslide, exercise room. **Guest Services:** valet and coin laundry, wireless Internet. **Business Services:** meeting rooms, PC (fee).

———— WHERE TO DINE ————

SWISS ALPINE RESTAURANT

Phone: 403/627-5079

Continental
$8-$22

This popular restaurant features Swiss croute, crepes, lamb, Alberta beef, sandwiches, pasta and stir-fry dishes, which are prepared with fresh ingredients and a Swiss flair. Sunday night has a prime rib special. The rustic dining room displays art for sale. Casual dress. **Bar:** Full bar. **Reservations:** suggested, in summer. **Hours:** 11 am-10 pm. Closed: 1/1, 12/25; also Sun & Mon. **Address:** 988 Main St T0K 1W0 **Location:** Jct Hwy 6 and Main St. **Parking:** on-site.

RED DEER pop. 82,772

BEST WESTERN RED DEER INN & SUITES   *Book great rates at AAA.com*

Phone: (403)346-3555

Hotel
$105-$150 All Year

Address: 6839 66th St T4P 3T5 **Location:** Hwy 2, exit 67th St, just e. **Facility:** 92 units. 86 one- and 6 two-bedroom standard units, some with whirlpools. 4 stories, interior corridors. *Bath:* combo or shower only. **Parking:** on-site. **Amenities:** high-speed Internet, voice mail, irons, hair dryers. **Pool(s):** heated indoor. **Leisure Activities:** whirlpool. **Guest Services:** valet and coin laundry, wireless Internet. **Business Services:** PC. **Free Special Amenities: full breakfast and early check-in/late check-out.**

AAA Benefit:
Members save up to 20%, plus 10% bonus points with rewards program.

CAPRI HOTEL TRADE & CONVENTION CENTRE   *Book great rates at AAA.com*

Phone: (403)346-2091

Hotel
$109-$149 All Year

Address: 3310 50th Ave T4N 3X9 **Location:** Hwy 2, exit 394 (Gaetz Ave), 1.8 mi (2.9 km) n. **Facility:** 220 units. 196 one-bedroom standard units. 16 one- and 8 two-bedroom suites, some with whirlpools. 2-14 stories, interior corridors. **Parking:** on-site, winter plug-ins. **Terms:** cancellation fee imposed. **Amenities:** video games (fee), voice mail, irons, hair dryers. *Some:* high-speed Internet (fee). **Dining:** 4 restaurants. **Pool(s):** heated outdoor. **Leisure Activities:** sauna, whirlpool, exercise room. *Fee:* massage. **Guest Services:** valet laundry, area transportation (fee), wireless Internet, beauty salon. **Business Services:** conference facilities, business center.

COMFORT INN & SUITES   *Book great rates at AAA.com*

Phone: (403)348-0025

Hotel
$105-$159 All Year

Address: 6846 66th St T4P 3T5 **Location:** Hwy 2, exit 67th St, just e. Located in a commercial area. **Facility:** 88 units. 82 one-bedroom standard units, some with whirlpools. 6 one-bedroom suites. 4 stories, interior corridors. *Bath:* combo or shower only. **Parking:** on-site, winter plug-ins. **Amenities:** high-speed Internet, voice mail, irons, hair dryers. **Pool(s):** heated indoor. **Leisure Activities:** whirlpool, waterslide, exercise room. **Guest Services:** valet and coin laundry. **Business Services:** meeting rooms, business center. **Free Special Amenities: continental breakfast and high-speed Internet.**

DAYS INN RED DEER *Book at AAA.com* **Phone: (403)340-3297**

Hotel
$104-$144 All Year

Address: 1000-5001 19th St T4R 3R1 **Location:** Hwy 2, exit 394 (Gaetz Ave), just w. **Facility:** 76 units. 66 one-bedroom standard units, some with whirlpools. 10 one-bedroom suites. 4 stories (no elevator), interior corridors. *Bath:* combo or shower only. **Parking:** on-site, winter plug-ins. **Terms:** check-in 4 pm, cancellation fee imposed. **Amenities:** high-speed Internet, voice mail, irons, hair dryers. *Some:* DVD players, video games, CD players. **Pool(s):** heated indoor. **Leisure Activities:** whirlpool, waterslide, exercise room. **Guest Services:** coin laundry. **Business Services:** PC.

HOLIDAY INN 67TH STREET *Book great rates at AAA.com* **Phone: (403)342-6567**

(CAA) (SAVE)

Hotel
$109-$119 All Year

Address: 6500 67th St T4P 1A2 **Location:** Hwy 2, exit 67th St, 0.5 mi (0.8 km) e. **Facility:** 142 units. 136 one-bedroom standard units, some with whirlpools. 6 one-bedroom suites, some with whirlpools. 4 stories, interior corridors. *Bath:* combo or shower only. **Parking:** on-site, winter plug-ins. **Amenities:** video games (fee), high-speed Internet, dual phone lines, voice mail, irons, hair dryers. **Pool(s):** heated indoor. **Leisure Activities:** sauna, whirlpool, game room. *Fee:* massage. **Guest Services:** coin laundry, wireless Internet, tanning facilities. **Business Services:** conference facilities, business center. **Free Special Amenities: expanded continental breakfast and local telephone calls.** *(See color ad on insert)*

HOLIDAY INN EXPRESS RED DEER *Book great rates at AAA.com* **Phone: (403)343-2112**

(CAA) (SAVE)

Hotel
$119-$139 All Year

Address: 2803 50th Ave T4R 1H1 **Location:** Hwy 2, exit 394 (Gaetz Ave), 1.8 mi (2.9 km) n. **Facility:** 91 one-bedroom standard units, some with whirlpools. 2 stories, interior corridors. **Parking:** on-site, winter plug-ins. **Amenities:** video games (fee), high-speed Internet, voice mail, irons, hair dryers. *Some:* high-speed Internet. **Pool(s):** heated indoor. **Leisure Activities:** sauna, whirlpool, exercise room. **Guest Services:** valet and coin laundry, wireless Internet. **Business Services:** PC (fee). **Free Special Amenities: full breakfast and high-speed Internet.** *(See color ad on insert)*

MOTEL 6 - RED DEER *Book great rates at AAA.com* **Phone: (403)340-1749**

Hotel
$65-$85 All Year

Address: 900-5001 19th St T4R 3R1 **Location:** Hwy 2, exit 394 (Gaetz Ave), just w; in Southpointe Common Shopping District. Located in a commercial area. **Facility:** 79 one-bedroom standard units. 3 stories, interior corridors. *Bath:* combo or shower only. **Parking:** on-site, winter plug-ins. **Amenities:** high-speed Internet, voice mail. *Some:* irons, hair dryers. **Guest Services:** coin laundry. **Business Services:** PC. *(See color ad below)*

RED DEER RAMADA INN *Book at AAA.com* **Phone: (403)358-7722**

Hotel
$129 All Year

Address: 4217 50th Ave T4N 3Z4 **Location:** At 42nd St; centre. **Facility:** Smoke free premises. 86 units. 62 one-bedroom standard units, some with whirlpools. 24 one-bedroom suites. 4 stories, interior corridors. **Parking:** on-site, winter plug-ins. **Terms:** cancellation fee imposed. **Amenities:** voice mail, irons, hair dryers. **Leisure Activities:** limited exercise equipment. **Guest Services:** coin laundry, wireless Internet. **Business Services:** PC (fee).

SANDMAN HOTEL RED DEER   *Book at AAA.com*   Phone: (403)343-7400

Hotel
$119-$214 All Year

Address: 2818 Gaetz Ave T4R 1M4 **Location:** Hwy 2, exit 394 (Gaetz Ave), 1.6 mi (2.6 km) n. **Facility:** 143 units. 94 one-bedroom standard units, some with whirlpools. 49 one-bedroom suites. 4 stories, interior corridors. **Parking:** on-site, winter plug-ins. **Terms:** check-in 4 pm, cancellation fee imposed. **Amenities:** high-speed Internet, dual phone lines, voice mail, irons, hair dryers. **Pool(s):** heated indoor. **Leisure Activities:** whirlpool, exercise room. **Guest Services:** valet laundry, wireless Internet. **Business Services:** meeting rooms, business center.

────── **WHERE TO DINE** ──────

EARLS RESTAURANT   Phone: 403/342-4055

Canadian
$10-$28

Offering an experience that falls between fast food and fine dining, the fun, relaxed restaurant prepares great food at a great price. Choices range from juicy burgers, hearty sandwiches, fresh salads, wings and pizza to full entrees of steak, chops and seafood. Made-from-scratch soups and assorted breads, as well as a nice choice of wines and beers, round out the offerings. This is a fitting spot for impromptu get-togethers and festive occasions. Casual dress. **Bar:** Full bar. **Hours:** 11:30 am-11 pm, Fri & Sat-midnight. Closed: 12/25. **Address:** 2111 Gaetz Ave T4R 1Z4 **Location:** Hwy 2, exit 394 (Gaetz Ave), 0.9 mi (1.4 km) n. **Parking:** on-site.

MOHAVE GRILL   Phone: 403/340-3463

Southwestern
$10-$28

Diners will find mainly Mexican food at the funky, festive restaurant, just off the highway. However, the eclectic menu takes some chances by delving into Cajun, Southwestern and Jamaican influences. Each dish is sure to please, and the servings are plentiful. Casual dress. **Reservations:** accepted. **Hours:** 11 am-11 pm, Sun-10 pm. Closed: 12/25. **Address:** 6608 Orr Dr T4P 3T5 **Location:** Hwy 2, exit 67th St, 0.3 mi (0.5 km) e; next to Service Plus Inns & Suites. **Parking:** on-site.

REDSTONE GRILL   Phone: 403/342-4980

Canadian
$9-$43

Contemporary and comfortable, the restaurant features a sleek design and a menu to match. Service is friendly, and servers like to take care of you. Food is tasty, and menu highlights include rack of lamb, sea bass, salmon and AAA beef. Live music is featured some evenings. Casual dress. **Bar:** Full bar. **Reservations:** suggested. **Hours:** 11:30 am-11 pm, Sun 5 pm-10 pm. Closed: 1/1, 10/11, 12/25. **Address:** #107, 5018 45th St T4N 1K9 **Location:** Hwy 2, exit 394 (Gaetz Ave), 2.5 mi (4 km) n, then just w. **Parking:** on-site.

RUSTY PELICAN   Phone: 403/347-1414

Continental
$8-$29

Ask any local for a great place to eat, and this place is mentioned often. The large, loft-like dining room creates a casual atmosphere, and most tables feature a large umbrella. Many entrees amid the menu's eclectic array exhibit Asian influences. Among selections are lettuce wraps, sumptuous salmon, pasta and assorted sandwiches. **Bar:** Full bar. **Reservations:** accepted. **Hours:** 11 am-midnight, Sun-10 pm. Closed major holidays. **Address:** 2079 50th Ave T4R 1Z4 **Location:** Hwy 2, exit 394 (Gaetz Ave), just n. **Parking:** on-site.

ROCKY MOUNTAIN HOUSE pop. 6,874

BEST WESTERN ROCKY MOUNTAIN HOUSE   *Book great rates at AAA.com*   Phone: (403)844-3100

Hotel
$135-$145 All Year

Address: 4407 41st Ave T4T 1A5 **Location:** Hwy 11 and 22, just w on 42nd Ave, then just s; east end of town. **Facility:** 81 units. 74 one-bedroom standard units, some with whirlpools. 7 one-bedroom suites, some with whirlpools. 4 stories, interior corridors. *Bath:* combo or shower only. **Parking:** on-site, winter plug-ins. **Amenities:** high-speed Internet, voice mail, irons, hair dryers. *Some:* DVD players. **Pool(s):** heated indoor. **Leisure Activities:** whirlpool, waterslide, exercise room. **Guest Services:** valet and coin laundry, wireless Internet. **Business Services:** PC. **Free Special Amenities: continental breakfast and local telephone calls.**

AAA Benefit:
Members save up to 20%, plus 10% bonus points with rewards program.

CHINOOK INN   Phone: 403/845-2833

Motel
Rates not provided

Address: 5321 59th Ave T4T 1J4 **Location:** 0.8 mi (1.3 km) w on Hwy 11, then s. **Facility:** 19 one-bedroom standard units, some with whirlpools. 1 story, interior corridors. **Parking:** on-site, winter plug-ins. **Amenities:** high-speed Internet (fee), voice mail, hair dryers. *Some:* irons. **Leisure Activities:** bicycles. **Guest Services:** valet laundry, wireless Internet.

HOLIDAY INN EXPRESS ROCKY MOUNTAIN HOUSE   *Book great rates at AAA.com*   Phone: (403)845-2871

Hotel
$99-$119 All Year

Address: 4715 45th St T4T 1B1 **Location:** Hwy 11 and 22, just e on 47th Ave, then just n. **Facility:** 40 units. 39 one-bedroom standard units. 1 one-bedroom suite with kitchen. 2 stories (no elevator), interior corridors. **Parking:** on-site, winter plug-ins. **Amenities:** dual phone lines, voice mail, irons, hair dryers. **Guest Services:** valet laundry, wireless Internet. **Business Services:** PC. **Free Special Amenities: full breakfast and high-speed Internet.**

SUPER 8   *Book at AAA.com*

Hotel
Rates not provided

Phone: 403/846-0088

Address: 4406 41st Ave T4T 1J6 **Location:** Hwy 11 and 22, just w on 42nd Ave, then just s; east end of town. **Facility:** 97 units. 91 one-bedroom standard units, some with efficiencies and/or whirlpools. 6 one-bedroom suites. 3 stories, interior/exterior corridors. *Bath:* combo or shower only. **Parking:** on-site, winter plug-ins. **Amenities:** high-speed Internet, voice mail, irons, hair dryers. *Some:* DVD players, video games. **Pool(s):** heated indoor. **Leisure Activities:** whirlpool, waterslide, exercise room. **Guest Services:** coin laundry, wireless Internet. **Business Services:** meeting rooms.

[ECO] [🛗] CALL [&M] [🛥] [✕] [🔌] [🖥] [💻] / SOME UNITS FEE [🐾] [✕]

------ **WHERE TO DINE** ------

MARTESA DI LUME

(CAA)

Italian
$12-$22

Phone: 403/845-7197

Considered one of the best in town, this restaurant is well loved for its great food and gracious owner. A classic Italian menu is prepared exclusively by the chef and features fresh seafood, chicken, veal and pastas; meals are well worth the time they take to prepare, but guests should allow plenty of time. House desserts are constantly changing. Casual dress. **Bar:** Full bar. **Reservations:** suggested. **Hours:** 5 pm-9 pm. Closed major holidays; also Sun & Mon. **Address:** 4925 50th St T4T 1A3 **Location:** Between 49th and 50th sts; centre. **Parking:** street.

ST. ALBERT—See Edmonton p. 465.

SASKATCHEWAN RIVER CROSSING

COLUMBIA ICEFIELD CHALET AT COLUMBIA ICEFIELD

Hotel
$115-$275 4/21-10/16

Phone: 780/852-6550

Address: Hwy 93 N T1L 1J3 **Location:** 31.3 mi (50 km) n on Hwy 93 (Icefield Pkwy). **Facility:** Smoke free premises. 32 units. 10 one- and 22 two-bedroom standard units. 3 stories, interior corridors. **Parking:** on-site. **Terms:** open 4/21-10/16, check-in 4 pm, cancellation fee imposed. **Amenities:** hair dryers. **Leisure Activities:** hiking trails. **Business Services:** PC (fee). [🍽] [✕] [🅰] [📺] [💻]

SHERWOOD PARK—See Edmonton p. 466.

SLAVE LAKE pop. 6,703

HOLIDAY INN EXPRESS HOTEL & SUITES   *Book great rates at AAA.com*

(CAA) [SAVE]

Hotel
$126-$146 All Year

Phone: (780)849-4819

Address: 1551 Main St SE T0G 2A0 **Location:** Hwy 2, just s. **Facility:** 96 units. 92 one-bedroom standard units, some with whirlpools. 4 one-bedroom suites. 4 stories, interior corridors. **Parking:** on-site, winter plug-ins. **Amenities:** high-speed Internet, voice mail, irons, hair dryers. **Leisure Activities:** whirlpool, exercise room. **Guest Services:** valet and coin laundry, wireless Internet. **Business Services:** business center. **Free Special Amenities: expanded continental breakfast and high-speed Internet.** *(See color ad on insert)* [🛗] CALL [&M] [🍴] [🔌] [💻] / SOME UNITS [✕] [🖥]

LAKEVIEW INNS & SUITES   *Book great rates at AAA.com*

(CAA) [SAVE]

Hotel
Rates not provided

Phone: 780/849-9500

Address: 1550 Holmes Tr SE T0G 2A3 **Location:** Hwy 2, just n, east end of town. **Facility:** 68 units. 59 one-bedroom standard units, some with whirlpools. 9 one-bedroom suites. 3 stories, interior corridors. *Bath:* combo or shower only. **Parking:** on-site, winter plug-ins. **Amenities:** video library, DVD players, high-speed Internet, voice mail, irons, hair dryers. *Some:* CD players. **Leisure Activities:** whirlpool, exercise room. **Guest Services:** valet and coin laundry, wireless Internet. **Business Services:** PC. **Free Special Amenities: expanded continental breakfast and local telephone calls.** [📽] [🔌] [🖥] [💻] / SOME UNITS FEE [🐾] [✕]

------ **WHERE TO DINE** ------

TAO RESTAURANT & LOUNGE

Asian
$10-$32

Phone: 780/849-6658

A fireplace greets arriving patrons in this trendily decorated restaurant. An Asian-inspired menu tempts with Indonesian samosas made with pineapple and shrimp followed by calypso chicken, Thai halibut or lemon grass pork loin. Wrap up the meal with a decadent hugs-and-kisses cake. Casual dress. **Bar:** Full bar. **Reservations:** suggested. **Hours:** 11 am-10 pm. Closed major holidays; also Sun. **Address:** 109 2nd Ave NW T0G 2A1 **Location:** Just e of Main St; downtown. **Parking:** street. CALL [&M]

STETTLER pop. 5,418

BEST WESTERN CRUSADER INN   *Book great rates at AAA.com*

(CAA) [SAVE]

Hotel
$119-$129 All Year

Phone: (403)742-3371

Address: 6020 50th Ave T0C 2L2 **Location:** Hwy 12 (50th Ave); at 61st St. **Facility:** 62 units. 46 one-bedroom standard units, some with whirlpools. 16 one-bedroom suites, some with efficiencies and/or whirlpools. 2-3 stories, interior/exterior corridors. *Bath:* combo or shower only. **Parking:** on-site, winter plug-ins. **Amenities:** voice mail, irons, hair dryers. *Some:* DVD players, high-speed Internet. **Pool(s):** heated indoor. **Leisure Activities:** whirlpool, waterslide, exercise room. **Guest Services:** coin laundry, wireless Internet. **Business Services:** PC. **Free Special Amenities: local telephone calls and high-speed Internet.**

[🍽] [🍸] CALL [&M] [🛥] [✕] [🔌] [🖥] [💻] / SOME UNITS FEE [🐾] [✕]

AAA Benefit:
Members save up to 20%, plus 10% bonus points with rewards program.

STONY PLAIN—See Edmonton p. 467.

STRATHMORE—See Calgary p. 430.

TABER pop. 7,591

HERITAGE INN TABER — *Book at AAA.com* — **Phone: (403)223-4424**

Hotel
$105-$165 1/1-2/28
$100-$160 3/1-12/31

Address: 4830 46th Ave T1G 2A4 **Location:** Just s of jct Hwy 3 and 36 S, on Hwy 3. **Facility:** 74 units. 72 one-bedroom standard units. 2 one-bedroom suites, some with whirlpools. 2 stories (no elevator), interior corridors. **Parking:** on-site, winter plug-ins. **Terms:** cancellation fee imposed. **Amenities:** high-speed Internet. *Some:* CD players, irons, hair dryers. **Leisure Activities:** sauna, whirlpool. *Fee:* game room. **Guest Services:** wireless Internet. **Business Services:** conference facilities.

SUPER 8, TABER — *Book at AAA.com* — **Phone: (403)223-8181**

Hotel
$89 All Year

Address: 5700 46th Ave T1G 2B1 **Location:** Hwy 3; west end of town. **Facility:** 48 one-bedroom standard units. 2 stories (no elevator), interior/exterior corridors. **Parking:** on-site, winter plug-ins. **Amenities:** hair dryers. *Some:* irons. **Guest Services:** coin laundry, wireless Internet. **Business Services:** PC.

THREE HILLS pop. 3,089

BEST WESTERN DIAMOND INN — *Book great rates at AAA.com* — **Phone: (403)443-7889**

Hotel
$110-$125 All Year

Address: 351 7th Ave N T0M 2A0 **Location:** Hwy 21 and 27, 1.1 mi (1.9 km) w. **Facility:** 52 one-bedroom standard units, some with whirlpools. 3 stories, interior corridors. *Bath:* combo or shower only. **Parking:** on-site, winter plug-ins. **Amenities:** high-speed Internet, voice mail, irons, hair dryers. *Some:* DVD players. **Leisure Activities:** whirlpools, exercise room. **Guest Services:** valet and coin laundry, wireless Internet. **Business Services:** PC. **Free Special Amenities:** expanded continental breakfast and room upgrade (subject to availability with advance reservations).

AAA Benefit:
Members save up to 20%, plus 10% bonus points with rewards program.

TWIN BUTTE pop. 10

——— WHERE TO DINE ———

TWIN BUTTE COUNTRY GENERAL STORE — **Phone: 403/627-4035**

Mexican
$5-$13

Halfway between Pincher Creek and Waterton on the Cowboy Trail, the small but cheerful Mexican-themed diner is located at the back of a country store. Its menu features simple but tasty Western and Mexican dishes. Casual dress. **Bar:** Full bar. **Reservations:** suggested. **Hours:** 10 am-10 pm; hours may vary. Closed major holidays; also Mon, Tues 9/1-5/31. **Address:** Box 461 T0K 2J0 **Location:** 16.9 mi (27 km) s of Dinchis Creek, on Hwy 6 (Cowboy Tr). **Parking:** on-site.

VALLEYVIEW pop. 1,725

WESTERN VALLEY INN — **Phone: 780/524-4000**

Motel
$89-$149 All Year

Address: 5402 Highway St T0H 3N0 **Location:** Just w of jct Hwy 43 and 49. **Facility:** 50 units. 47 one-bedroom standard units, some with efficiencies. 3 one-bedroom suites with efficiencies. 2 stories (no elevator), exterior corridors. **Parking:** on-site, winter plug-ins. **Amenities:** high-speed Internet, voice mail. *Some:* irons, hair dryers. **Guest Services:** coin laundry, airport transportation-Valleyview Airport, wireless Internet. **Business Services:** PC. **Free Special Amenities:** expanded continental breakfast and high-speed Internet.

WAINWRIGHT pop. 5,426

——— WHERE TO DINE ———

THE HONEY POT EATERY & PUB — **Phone: 780/842-4094**

American
$8-$27

Diners receive a good meal and excellent value at the tucked-away restaurant. Its friendly, casual ambience enhances the country charm of its Western-style barnwood exterior. The extensive menu lists homemade bread, pies, soup and sandwiches. Casual dress. **Bar:** Full bar. **Reservations:** suggested. **Hours:** 11 am-9:30 pm. Closed major holidays; also Sun. **Address:** 823 2nd Ave T9W 1C5 **Location:** 0.6 mi (1 km) s on Main St from jct Hwy 14, just w at clock tower. **Parking:** street.

WATERTON PARK pop. 160

ASPEN VILLAGE INN

Book great rates at AAA.com

Phone: (403)859-2255

Motel
$120-$295 5/1-9/30

Address: 111 Windflower Ave T0K 2M0 **Location:** Centre. **Facility:** Smoke free premises. 51 units. 38 one- and 1 two-bedroom standard units, some with efficiencies. 11 one- and 1 two-bedroom suites, some with kitchens. 1-2 stories (no elevator), exterior corridors. **Parking:** on-site. **Terms:** open 5/1-9/30, office hours 7 am-11 pm, 3 day cancellation notice. **Amenities:** hair dryers. **Leisure Activities:** barbecues, playground. **Guest Services:** wireless Internet.

BAYSHORE INN

Book great rates at AAA.com

Phone: (403)859-2211

Motel
$119-$249 4/30-10/12

Address: 111 Waterton Ave T0K 2M0 **Location:** Centre. **Facility:** Smoke free premises. 70 units. 65 one- and 3 two-bedroom standard units, some with whirlpools. 2 one-bedroom suites. 2 stories (no elevator), interior/exterior corridors. *Bath:* combo or shower only. **Parking:** on-site. **Terms:** open 4/30-10/12, 3 day cancellation notice. **Amenities:** DVD players, voice mail, safes, irons, hair dryers. **Dining:** Bayshore Lakeside Chophouse, see separate listing, nightclub. **Leisure Activities:** hiking trails, spa. **Guest Services:** coin laundry, wireless Internet. **Business Services:** meeting rooms, PC. **Free Special Amenities:** local telephone calls and early check-in/late check-out.
(See color ad below)

CRANDELL MOUNTAIN LODGE

Book great rates at AAA.com

Phone: (403)859-2288

Hotel
$99-$229 All Year

Address: 102 Mt. View Rd T0K 2M0 **Location:** Centre. **Facility:** Smoke free premises. 17 units. 13 one-bedroom standard units, some with efficiencies and/or whirlpools. 4 one-bedroom suites with kitchens. 2 stories (no elevator), interior corridors. *Bath:* combo or shower only. **Parking:** on-site. **Terms:** office hours 8 am-10 pm, 3 day cancellation notice. **Amenities:** video library, hair dryers. **Leisure Activities:** hiking trails. **Guest Services:** wireless Internet.

SHINTANGLE SPRING BED & BREAKFAST INN

Phone: 403/627-5751

Bed & Breakfast
Rates not provided

Address: Hwy 6 T0K 2M0 **Location:** 4.5 mi (7.5 km) n of park entrance, then just w at Nixon Rd, follow sign. **Facility:** Smoke free premises. 4 one-bedroom standard units. 1 story, interior corridors. **Parking:** on-site, winter plug-ins. **Terms:** check-in 4 pm. **Guest Services:** TV in common area.

WATERTON GLACIER SUITES   *Book great rates at AAA.com*   Phone: (403)859-2004

Hotel
$139-$279 All Year

Address: 107 Windflower Ave T0K 2M0 **Location:** Centre. **Facility:** Smoke free premises. 25 units. 13 one-bedroom standard units with whirlpools. 12 one-bedroom suites with whirlpools. 2 stories (no elevator), exterior corridors. **Parking:** on-site. **Terms:** office hours 7 am-midnight, 3 day cancellation notice. **Amenities:** video library (fee). **Guest Services:** wireless Internet. **Free Special Amenities: local telephone calls and early check-in/late check-out.** *(See color ad p 499)*

WATERTON LAKES RESORT   *Book great rates at AAA.com*   Phone: (403)859-2150

Hotel
$125-$255 All Year

Address: 101 Clematis Ave T0K 2M0 **Location:** Centre. **Facility:** Smoke free premises. 80 units. 75 one-bedroom standard units, some with efficiencies and/or whirlpools. 5 one-bedroom suites with efficiencies. 2 stories (no elevator), interior/exterior corridors. *Bath:* combo or shower only. **Parking:** on-site. **Terms:** 3 day cancellation notice. **Amenities:** voice mail, hair dryers. *Some:* CD players, irons. **Pool(s):** heated indoor. **Leisure Activities:** sauna, whirlpool, steamroom, recreation programs, hiking trails. *Fee:* aerobic facilities. **Guest Services:** wireless Internet. **Business Services:** meeting rooms.

▼ See AAA listing p 501 ▼

———— *The following lodging was either not evaluated or did not* ————
meet AAA rating requirements but is listed for your information only.

PRINCE OF WALES HOTEL
Phone: 403-859-2231

[fyi]

Not evaluated. Address: Waterton Lakes National Park T0K 2M0 **Location:** Through park gates, about 5 mi (8 km), then just se. Facilities, services, and decor characterize a mid-scale property. *(See color ad p 500)*

———— **WHERE TO DINE** ————

BAYSHORE LAKESIDE CHOPHOUSE
Phone: 403-859-2211

Canadian
$9-$38

Diners can often view deer grazing outside the windows of the dining room, which boasts a wonderful view of Waterton Lake. The menu lists a variety of Alberta beef, salmon, trout and chicken dishes. Casual dress. **Bar:** Full bar. **Reservations:** suggested. **Hours:** Open 4/15-10/15; 7 am-11 pm. **Address:** 111 Waterton Ave T0K 2M0 **Location:** Centre; in Bayshore Inn. **Parking:** on-site.

WESTEROSE

VILLAGE CREEK COUNTRY INN
Phone: 780-586-0006

Hotel
Rates not provided

Address: 15 Village Dr, RR2 T0C 2V0 **Location:** Hwy 2, exit 482, 17.5 mi (28 km) w on Hwy 13; in Village at Pigeon Lake. **Facility:** 35 units. 32 one- and 2 two-bedroom standard units, some with kitchens and/or whirlpools. 1 condominium. 2 stories, interior/exterior corridors. **Parking:** on-site, winter plug-ins. **Amenities:** voice mail, irons, hair dryers. *Some:* DVD players. **Leisure Activities:** whirlpool, spa. **Guest Services:** wireless Internet. **Business Services:** meeting rooms, PC.

———— **WHERE TO DINE** ————

ECO CAFE
Phone: 780-586-2627

Canadian
$9-$15

In the Village of Pigeon Lake development, near the beaches, the intimate cafe is easy to miss among other coffee shops and gift stores. However, it's worth finding for its cheerfully decorated dining area and standard mix of coffee and treats, in addition to flavorful regional cuisine made from organically grown and raised foods, ranging from elk to bison. Curried elk pasta stands out. Owners raise their own lamb, pork and chicken, while other ingredients are raised down the road. Casual dress. **Bar:** Wine only. **Hours:** 6:30 am-8 pm. Closed: 12/25. **Address:** 10 Village Dr T0C 2V0 **Location:** Hwy 2, exit 482, 17.5 mi (28 km) w on Hwy 13. **Parking:** on-site.

WETASKIWIN pop. 11,673

BEST WESTERN WAYSIDE INN *Book great rates at AAA.com*
Phone: (780)312-7300

Hotel
$125-$145 All Year

Address: 4103 56th St T9A 1V2 **Location:** On Hwy 2A, just n of jct Hwy 13 W. **Facility:** Smoke free premises. 28 one-bedroom standard units. 2 stories (no elevator), interior corridors. **Parking:** on-site, winter plug-ins. **Terms:** check-in 4 pm. **Amenities:** irons, hair dryers. *Some:* high-speed Internet. **Dining:** nightclub. **Leisure Activities:** exercise room. **Guest Services:** wireless Internet. **Business Services:** meeting rooms, PC (fee). **Free Special Amenities:** newspaper and early check-in/late check-out.

AAA Benefit:
Members save up to 20%, plus 10% bonus points with rewards program.

SUPER 8 *Book at AAA.com*
Phone: (780)361-3808

Hotel
$109-$129 All Year

Address: 3820 56th St T9A 2B2 **Location:** On Hwy 2A, just s of jct Hwy 13 W. **Facility:** 49 one-bedroom standard units. 2 stories (no elevator), interior/exterior corridors. **Parking:** on-site, winter plug-ins. **Amenities:** hair dryers. *Some:* irons. **Guest Services:** coin laundry, wireless Internet. **Business Services:** meeting rooms.

———— **WHERE TO DINE** ————

HUCKLEBERRY'S CAFE
Phone: 780-352-3111

Continental
$8-$30

This popular restaurant features a homelike country and Western decor and offers up quick, efficient service. On the menu is a wide variety of burgers, pasta dishes and sandwiches that emphasize local ingredients. Find Alberta turkey and beef as well as the famous huckleberry, a berry from the mountains. Not surprisingly, the berry, which is plumper and juicier than the blueberry, found its way into the cafe's name and desserts, including the homemade pie. Casual dress. **Bar:** Full bar. **Reservations:** suggested. **Hours:** 11:30 am-9 pm, Sun-8 pm. Closed: 12/25, 12/26. **Address:** 3840 56th St, 103 St T9A 2B2 **Location:** Just e of Hwy 2A; s of jct Hwy 13 W; behind Super 8. **Parking:** on-site.

PIPESTONE FOOD COMPANY STEAK HOUSE   Phone: 780/352-9596

Canadian
$11-$40

A sophisticated menu contrasts the rustic interior at this inviting steakhouse. The menu features local naturally-raised meats and fresh wild-caught fish as well as king crab and lobster. Steaks can be enhanced with such decadent toppings as blue cheese au poivre or bacon and brie. Rounding out the menu is lamb, chicken and pasta entrées as well as gourmet burgers. Casual dress. **Bar:** Full bar. **Reservations:** suggested. **Hours:** 5 pm-9 pm, Fri & Sat-10 pm. Closed major holidays; also Mon. **Address:** 4911 51st St T9A 2A4 **Location:** Between 49th and 50th aves; downtown. **Parking:** street. CALL ⬤M

WHITECOURT pop. 8,971

LAKEVIEW INNS & SUITES   *Book great rates at AAA.com*   Phone: (780)706-3349

CAA SAVE

Hotel
$99-$130 All Year

Address: 3325 Caxton St T7S 1P2 **Location:** Hwy 43, just n of Park Dr. **Facility:** 50 one-bedroom standard units, some with whirlpools. 2 stories (no elevator); interior corridors. **Parking:** on-site, winter plug-ins. **Terms:** check-in 4 pm, cancellation fee imposed. **Amenities:** video library, DVD players, high-speed Internet, irons, hair dryers. **Leisure Activities:** whirlpool, limited exercise equipment. **Guest Services:** coin laundry. **Business Services:** PC. **Free Special Amenities: continental breakfast and local telephone calls.** ECO ⬤ ⬤ ⬤ / SOME UNITS ⬤

SUPER 8   *Book great rates at AAA.com*   Phone: (780)778-8908

CAA SAVE

Hotel
$129-$139 All Year

Address: 4121 Kepler St T7S 0A3 **Location:** On Hwy 43, just e of Hwy 32. **Facility:** 59 units. 57 one-bedroom standard units. 2 one-bedroom suites with whirlpools. 3 stories, interior corridors. **Parking:** on-site, winter plug-ins. **Terms:** cancellation fee imposed. **Amenities:** video games (fee), voice mail, irons, hair dryers. *Some:* high-speed Internet. **Leisure Activities:** exercise room. **Guest Services:** valet and coin laundry, wireless Internet. **Business Services:** PC. **Free Special Amenities: expanded continental breakfast and high-speed Internet.** ECO ⬤ ⬤ ⬤ ⬤ / SOME UNITS FEE ⬤ ⬤ ⬤

―――― WHERE TO DINE ――――

MOUNTAIN PIZZA & STEAK HOUSE   Phone: 780/778-3600

Steak
$10-$28

This casually elegant restaurant features steaks, shish kebabs, Italian veal and chicken dishes as well as pizza, all served by a friendly and efficient staff. The highly-secret steak spice is apparently world famous; customers from around the world come back to sample it. Casual dress. **Bar:** Full bar. **Reservations:** suggested. **Hours:** 11 am-11 pm. Closed major holidays. **Address:** 3827 Caxton St T7S 1P3 **Location:** Hwy 43, just s on Pine Rd. **Parking:** on-site. CALL ⬤M

British Columbia

Gulf Islands National Park
Reserve of Canada
© Chris Cheadle
age fotostock

100 MILE HOUSE

100 MILE HOUSE SUPER 8

Motel
$120-$150 3/1-10/31
$100-$120 11/1-2/28

Phone: 250/395-8888

Address: 989 Alder Ave V0K 2E0 **Location:** 0.6 mi (1 km) s on Hwy 97. **Facility:** 28 one-bedroom standard units. 2 stories (no elevator), exterior corridors. **Parking:** on-site, winter plug-ins. **Terms:** office hours 7 am-11 pm, 2 night minimum stay - weekends, 7 day cancellation notice-fee imposed. **Amenities:** hair dryers. **Guest Services:** wireless Internet. **Business Services:** PC.

ASK CALL 🔊M ▣ ▢ ▢ / SOME UNITS FEE 🐾 ✕ ▨

RAMADA LIMITED   *Book at AAA.com*

Motel
$90-$179 All Year

Phone: (250)395-2777

Address: 917 Alder Ave V0K 2E0 **Location:** 0.6 mi (1 km) s on Hwy 97. **Facility:** Smoke free premises. 36 one-bedroom standard units, some with efficiencies and/or whirlpools. 3 stories, interior corridors. *Bath:* combo or shower only. **Parking:** on-site. **Terms:** office hours 6 am-11 pm. **Amenities:** voice mail, irons, hair dryers. **Guest Services:** coin laundry, wireless Internet. **Business Services:** PC. ASK ▥ CALL 🔊M ✕ ▣ ▢ ▢ / SOME UNITS FEE 🐾

——— WHERE TO DINE ———

HAPPY LANDING RESTAURANT

Swiss
$10-$20

Phone: 250/395-5359

Behind the village restaurant's charming blue shutters, diners are welcomed to savor the flavors of traditional Swiss cuisine. Among choices are steaks, wonderful schnitzels, roestis and other European favorites. Casual dress. **Bar:** Full bar. **Reservations:** suggested. **Hours:** 11:30 am-2 & 5-9 pm, Mon, Thurs & Sat from 5 pm. Closed major holidays; also Sun. **Address:** 725 Alder Ave V0K 2E0 **Location:** Hwy 97, 0.6 mi (1 km) s on Service Rd. **Parking:** on-site.

SMITTY'S

Canadian
$7-$20

Phone: 250/395-4655

The family-oriented restaurant satisfies patrons with its ever-popular all-day breakfast items, as well as tasty and wholesome soups and salads at lunchtime. A relaxed mood characterizes the dining space. Casual dress. **Bar:** Full bar. **Hours:** 5:30 am-9 pm. Closed: 12/25. **Address:** Box 1217, 451 Caribou Hwy V0K 2E0 **Location:** On Hwy 97; by tourist information booth. **Parking:** on-site.

108 MILE HOUSE

108 RESORT & CONFERENCE CENTRE

CAA SAVE

Resort
Hotel
$95-S135 All Year

Phone: 250/791-5211

Address: 4816 Telqua Dr V0K 2Z0 **Location:** Hwy 97, 1 mi (1.6 km) nw on access road, follow signs. Located on 108 Recreational Ranch. **Facility:** Many activities are offered at this 600-acre resort, which features spacious guest rooms overlooking a golf course and lake. Smoke free premises. 42 units. 41 one-bedroom standard units. 1 one-bedroom suite. 2 stories (no elevator), exterior corridors. **Parking:** on-site, winter plug-ins. **Terms:** 30 day cancellation notice-fee imposed. **Amenities:** hair dryers. **Pool(s):** heated outdoor. **Leisure Activities:** saunas, whirlpool, beach access, rental canoes, 2 lighted tennis courts, rental bicycles, hiking trails, jogging, playground. *Fee:* golf-18 holes, driving range, cross country skiing, snowmobiling, horseback riding. **Guest Services:** coin laundry, wireless Internet. **Business Services:** conference facilities, PC. **Free Special Amenities:** local telephone calls and high-speed Internet. ▥ ▨ CALL 🔊M ▨ ✕ ✕ ▢ / SOME UNITS FEE 🐾 ▣

ABBOTSFORD pop. 115,463

BEST WESTERN BAKERVIEW INN *Book great rates at AAA.com* **Phone: (604)859-1341**

Motel
$116-$146 All Year

Address: 1821 Sumas Way V2S 4L5 **Location:** Trans-Canada Hwy 1, exit 92 (Town Centre), just n on Hwy 11. **Facility:** 61 one-bedroom standard units, some with efficiencies. 2 stories (no elevator), exterior corridors. **Parking:** on-site. **Terms:** cancellation fee imposed. **Amenities:** irons, hair dryers. **Pool(s):** heated indoor. **Leisure Activities:** whirlpool. **Guest Services:** coin laundry, wireless Internet. **Business Services:** PC. **Free Special Amenities: room upgrade (subject to availability with advance reservations) and high-speed Internet.**

AAA Benefit:
Members save up to 20%, plus 10% bonus points with rewards program.

BEST WESTERN REGENCY INN & CONFERENCE CENTRE *Book great rates at AAA.com* **Phone: (604)853-3111**

Hotel
$120-$150 3/1-9/7
$110-$140 9/8-2/28

Address: 32110 Marshall Rd V2T 1A1 **Location:** Trans-Canada Hwy 1, exit 87 (Clearbrook Rd). Located behind an elementary school. **Facility:** Smoke free premises. 128 one-bedroom standard units, some with efficiencies and/or whirlpools. 2-3 stories, interior corridors. **Parking:** on-site. **Terms:** cancellation fee imposed. **Amenities:** video games (fee), voice mail, irons, hair dryers. *Some:* high-speed Internet. **Pool(s):** 2 heated indoor. **Leisure Activities:** whirlpools, exercise room. **Guest Services:** valet and coin laundry, wireless Internet. **Business Services:** conference facilities, business center. *(See color ad below)*

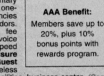

AAA Benefit:
Members save up to 20%, plus 10% bonus points with rewards program.

FREE expanded continental breakfast and high-speed Internet

COAST ABBOTSFORD HOTEL & SUITES *Book at AAA.com* **Phone: 604/853-1880**

Hotel
Rates not provided

Address: 2020 Sumas Way V2S 2C7 **Location:** Trans-Canada Hwy 1, exit 92 (Town Centre), just n on Hwy 11. **Facility:** Smoke free premises. 60 one-bedroom standard units, some with whirlpools. 4 stories, interior corridors. **Parking:** on-site. **Amenities:** high-speed Internet, voice mail, irons, hair dryers. **Pool(s):** heated indoor. **Leisure Activities:** whirlpool, exercise room. **Guest Services:** valet laundry, wireless Internet. **Business Services:** meeting rooms, PC (fee).

▼ See AAA listing above ▼

SUPER 8 ABBOTSFORD

Hotel
$99-$399 All Year

Book great rates at AAA.com

Phone: (604)853-1141

Address: 1881 Sumas Way V2S 4L5 **Location:** Trans-Canada Hwy 1, exit 92 (Town Centre), just n on Hwy 11. **Facility:** 99 units. 82 one-bedroom standard units. 17 one-bedroom suites with kitchens. 2-4 stories, interior/exterior corridors. **Parking:** on-site. **Terms:** check-in 4 pm, cancellation fee imposed. **Amenities:** voice mail, hair dryers. *Some:* high-speed Internet. **Pool(s):** heated indoor. **Leisure Activities:** whirlpool, waterslide, exercise room. **Guest Services:** valet and coin laundry, wireless Internet. **Business Services:** meeting rooms, business center. *(See color ad below)*

FREE expanded continental breakfast and high-speed Internet

▼ *See AAA listing above* ▼

▼ *See AAA listing p 641* ▼

—— **WHERE TO DINE** ——

MILESTONE'S GRILL AND BAR
Phone: 604/850-3826

▼▼▼
Canadian
$8-$27

Popular with locals, the bustling eatery is a great gathering place. Diners enjoy the relaxed setting and casual menu featuring pasta, pizza, roasted chicken and a tasty choice of egg and brunch options. A nice wine list complements the food choices. Casual dress. **Bar:** Full bar. **Hours:** 11 am-10 pm, Fri-11 pm, Sat 10 am-11 pm, Sun 10 am-9:30 pm. **Address:** 200-2070 Sumas Way V2S 2C7 **Location:** Corner of S Fraser Way and Sumas Way (Hwy 11); in Abbotsford Village Mall. **Parking:** on-site. CALL 🚿M

SWISS CHALET
Phone: 604/864-4002

▼▼▼
Canadian
$6-$18

The popular restaurant is known for its rotisserie chicken and ribs and the tangy Chalet sauce that gives food its special zip. Diners munch on a half or quarter chicken with sides such as steamed vegetables, fries, baked potatoes and salads. Lunch guests often go for the great soup and sandwich combination. Take-out and delivery service are popular options. Casual dress. **Bar:** Full bar. **Hours:** 11:30 am-10 pm, Sun 11 am-9:30 pm. Closed: 12/25. **Address:** 32470 S Fraser Way V2T 1X3 **Location:** S Fraser Way at Trethewey. **Parking:** on-site.

AINSWORTH HOT SPRINGS

AINSWORTH HOT SPRINGS RESORT
Phone: (250)229-4212

(CAA) (SAVE)
♦♦ ♦♦
Hotel
$129-$199 All Year

Address: 3609 Hwy 31 V0G 1A0 **Location:** On Hwy 31. **Facility:** Smoke free premises. 43 one-bedroom standard units, some with efficiencies. 4 stories, interior/exterior corridors. **Parking:** on-site. **Amenities:** hair dryers. *Some:* irons. **Leisure Activities:** hot springs pool. *Fee:* massage. **Guest Services:** complimentary laundry, wireless Internet. **Business Services:** meeting rooms, PC. **Free Special Amenities: local telephone calls and high-speed Internet.**
🍴 🍷 CALL 🚿M ✖ 📷 🖥 / SOME UNITS 🖥

ALDERGROVE—See Vancouver p. 641.

ARMSTRONG—See Okanagan Valley p. 551.

BARRIERE

MOUNTAIN SPRINGS MOTEL & RV PARK
Phone: (250)672-0090

♦♦ ♦♦
Motel
$75-$80 All Year

Address: 4253 Yellowhead Hwy V0E 1E0 **Location:** 0.6 mi (1 km) s on Hwy 5 (Yellowhead Hwy). **Facility:** Smoke free premises. 12 one-bedroom standard units, some with efficiencies. 1 story, exterior corridors. **Parking:** on-site, winter plug-ins. **Terms:** office hours 7 am-midnight, 7 day cancellation notice-fee imposed. **Guest Services:** coin laundry, wireless Internet. **Business Services:** PC. (ASK) CALL 🚿M ✖ 📷 🖥 🖥 / SOME UNITS 🖥

BIG WHITE

SUNDANCE RESORT   *Book at AAA.com*
Phone: 250/491-3272

▼▼▼
Condominium
Rates not provided

Address: 255 Feathertop Way V1Y 2E5 **Location:** Jct Hwy 33 and Big White Rd, 15 mi (24 km) n on Big White Rd. Located at Big White Ski Resort. **Facility:** Offering ski-in and ski-out privileges, these attractive units are steps from the bullet ski lift and a short walk from the village center. Smoke free premises. 96 units. 50 one-bedroom standard units. 18 one- and 28 two-bedroom suites, some with kitchens. 3-4 stories, interior corridors. *Bath:* combo or shower only. **Parking:** on-site. **Terms:** open 3/1-4/18 & 11/26-2/28, check-in 4 pm. **Amenities:** DVD players, voice mail, hair dryers. *Some:* irons. **Pool(s):** heated outdoor. **Leisure Activities:** whirlpools, steamroom, waterslide, exercise room. *Fee:* downhill & cross country skiing, snowmobiling, tobogganing. **Guest Services:** wireless Internet. **Business Services:** PC. 🚫 ✖ ✖ 🖥 🖥 🖥

BLUE RIVER

GLACIER MOUNTAIN LODGE
Phone: (250)673-2393

▼▼
Motel
$99-$209 All Year

Address: 869 Shell Rd V0E 1J0 **Location:** On Hwy 5 (Yellowhead Hwy); at Shell Rd, follow signs. **Facility:** 35 units. 34 one-bedroom standard units. 1 two-bedroom suite with kitchen. 2 stories (no elevator), interior corridors. **Parking:** on-site, winter plug-ins. **Amenities:** hair dryers. **Leisure Activities:** whirlpool. **Guest Services:** wireless Internet.
(ASK) 🍴 📷 🖥 / SOME UNITS FEE 🐾 ✖

BOSTON BAR pop. 188

—— **WHERE TO DINE** ——

SIMON'S CAFE
Phone: 604/867-9277

▼
Canadian
$9-$15

This restaurant is accessed via a thrilling Hell's Gate Airtram ride over the mighty Fraser River. Regular Airtram admission, which is discounted for CAA/AAA members, applies. On the menu are homemade salmon chowder, salmon lasagna, sandwiches and burgers. Casual dress. **Bar:** Beer & wine. **Hours:** Open 4/15-10/15; 10 am-4 pm; to 5 pm 5/16-9/1. **Address:** 43111 Trans-Canada Hwy V0K 1C0 **Location:** 6.9 mi (11 km) s on Trans-Canada Hwy 1; at Hell's Gate Airtram. **Parking:** on-site. CALL 🚿M

BOWEN ISLAND (See map and index starting on p. 594)

WILDWOOD LANE COTTAGES

Phone: 604/947-2253

Vacation Rental Cottage
Rates not provided

Address: 1321 Adams Rd V0N 1G0 **Location:** From ferry terminal, 3.5 mi (5.6 km) w on Grafton Rd, then 0.6 mi (1 km) n. **Facility:** A short, 20-minute ferry ride from the Horseshoe Bay Terminal, these separate cottages offer good privacy, efficiencies and private decks. Smoke free premises. 4 cottages. 1 story, exterior corridors. *Bath:* shower only. **Parking:** on-site. **Terms:** office hours 8 am-10 pm. **Amenities:** video library, DVD players, hair dryers. **Leisure Activities:** whirlpool.

BRENTWOOD BAY—See Victoria p. 694.

BURNABY—See Vancouver p. 642.

CACHE CREEK pop. 1,037

BONAPARTE MOTEL

Phone: (250)457-9693

Motel
$69-$129 3/1-10/31
$49-$99 11/1-2/28

Address: 1395 Hwy 97 N V0K 1H0 **Location:** Just n of jct Trans-Canada Hwy 1. **Facility:** 24 units. 20 one- and 4 two-bedroom standard units, some with efficiencies or kitchens. 1 story, exterior corridors. **Parking:** on-site, winter plug-ins. **Terms:** office hours 7 am-midnight. **Pool(s):** heated outdoor. **Leisure Activities:** sauna, whirlpool. **Guest Services:** wireless Internet. **Free Special Amenities:** local telephone calls and high-speed Internet.

—— WHERE TO DINE ——

WANDER INN RESTAURANT   *Menu on AAA.com*

Phone: 250/457-6511

Chinese
$8-$16

Fare includes Cantonese dishes-such as the emperor's plate with chicken, beef and stir-fry-as well as burgers, sandwiches, soups, steaks and chops. Seniors and visitors like this roadside spot, which has a coffee shop, dining room section and ample parking. While the decor may hint at its age, the restaurant is clean and well maintained. Casual dress. **Bar:** Full bar. **Hours:** 11:30 am-9 pm; 11 am-2 & 5-9 pm 11/1-3/31. Closed: 12/25, 12/26. **Address:** 1034 Trans-Canada Hwy 1 V0K 1H0 **Location:** Just s of jct Hwy 97. **Parking:** on-site.

CAMPBELL RIVER pop. 28,456

ANCHOR INN & SUITES   *Book at AAA.com*

Phone: 250/286-1131

Hotel
Rates not provided

Address: 261 Island Hwy V9W 2B3 **Location:** On Island Hwy 19A, 1.3 mi (2 km) s. **Facility:** 77 one-bedroom standard units, some with whirlpools. 7 stories, interior corridors. **Parking:** on-site. **Amenities:** voice mail, irons, hair dryers. **Pool(s):** heated indoor. **Leisure Activities:** whirlpool, exercise room. **Guest Services:** valet and coin laundry, wireless Internet. **Business Services:** meeting rooms, PC.

ARBOUR'S GUEST HOUSE

Phone: (250)287-9873

Bed & Breakfast
$90-$120 All Year

Address: 375 S Murphy St V9W 1Y8 **Location:** 1.3 mi (2 km) s on Island Hwy 19A, just e on 1st Ave, then 0.5 mi (0.8 km) s on Murphy St; on water side of street. Located in a residential area. **Facility:** Smoke free premises. 4 one-bedroom standard units. 2 stories (no elevator), interior corridors. *Bath:* some shared or private. **Parking:** on-site. **Terms:** office hours 8 am-10 pm, age restrictions may apply, 14 day cancellation notice-fee imposed. **Amenities:** hair dryers. **Guest Services:** TV in common area.

BEST WESTERN AUSTRIAN CHALET   *Book great rates at AAA.com*

Phone: (250)923-4231

Motel
$124-$175 All Year

Address: 462 S Island Hwy V9W 1A5 **Location:** 2 mi (3.2 km) s on Island Hwy 19A. **Facility:** 59 one-bedroom standard units, some with efficiencies and/or whirlpools. 2-3 stories (no elevator), interior/exterior corridors. **Parking:** on-site. **Amenities:** voice mail, irons, hair dryers. *Some:* high-speed Internet. **Pool(s):** heated indoor. **Leisure Activities:** sauna, whirlpool, putting green, table tennis, barbecue, exercise room. **Guest Services:** valet and coin laundry, wireless Internet. **Business Services:** meeting rooms, PC.

AAA Benefit:
Members save up to 20%, plus 10% bonus points with rewards program.

FREE continental breakfast and high-speed Internet

CAMPBELL RIVER LODGE FISHING & ADVENTURE RESORT

Phone: (250)287-7446

Motel
$74-$129 All Year

Address: 1760 N Island Hwy V9W 2E7 **Location:** On Island Hwy 19A, 1.3 mi (2 km) nw of downtown; just e from Hwy 19 and 28. **Facility:** Smoke free premises. 28 one-bedroom standard units, some with efficiencies. 2 stories (no elevator), interior/exterior corridors. **Parking:** on-site. **Terms:** office hours 7:30 am-11:30 pm, 3 day cancellation notice-fee imposed. **Amenities:** voice mail, hair dryers. **Leisure Activities:** whirlpool, saltwater & freshwater charter fishing with guides. *Fee:* custom fish canning, freezing & shipping. **Guest Services:** coin laundry, wireless Internet. **Business Services:** meeting rooms, PC. **Free Special Amenities: local telephone calls and high-speed Internet.**

OCEAN RESORT

Phone: 250/923-4281

Motel
Rates not provided

Address: 4834 S Island Hwy V9H 1E8 **Location:** 11 mi (18 km) s on Island Hwy 19A. **Facility:** Smoke free premises. 29 units. 28 one-bedroom standard units. 1 one-bedroom suite with kitchen. 2 stories (no elevator), interior corridors. **Parking:** on-site. **Terms:** office hours 7 am-9 pm. **Amenities:** DVD players, voice mail. **Leisure Activities:** saunas, limited exercise equipment.

TOWN CENTRE INN

Phone: 250/287-8866

Motel
$79-$99 3/1-10/31
$74-$94 11/1-2/28

Address: 1500 Dogwood St V9W 3A6 **Location:** Follow Island Hwy 19A through town, watch for signs, just e on Dogwood St; corner of 16th Ave. **Facility:** 34 one-bedroom standard units, some with efficiencies. 2 stories (no elevator), exterior corridors. **Parking:** on-site. **Terms:** office hours 7:30 am-midnight, cancellation fee imposed. **Amenities:** voice mail, hair dryers. **Leisure Activities:** sauna. **Guest Services:** coin laundry, wireless Internet.

TRAVELODGE CAMPBELL RIVER   *Book at AAA.com*

Phone: (250)286-6622

Motel
$85-$125 3/1-9/30
$85-$99 10/1-2/28

Address: 340 S Island Hwy V9W 1A5 **Location:** 1.9 mi (3 km) s on Island Hwy 19A. **Facility:** 40 one-bedroom standard units. 2 stories (no elevator), interior corridors. **Parking:** on-site. **Terms:** cancellation fee imposed. **Amenities:** hair dryers. **Pool(s):** heated indoor. **Leisure Activities:** whirlpool. **Guest Services:** coin laundry, wireless Internet.

──────── *The following lodging was either not evaluated or did not* ────────
meet AAA rating requirements but is listed for your information only.

HERON'S LANDING, A BOUTIQUE HOTEL

Phone: 250/923-2848

[fyi]

Not evaluated. **Address:** 492 S Island Hwy V9W 1A5 **Location:** 2 mi (3.2 km) s on Island Hwy 19A. Facilities, services, and decor characterize a mid-scale property.

—— **WHERE TO DINE** ——

BAAN THAI RESTAURANT   Phone: 250/286-485■
ⓦⓦ ⓦⓦ
Thai   The traditional flavors and aromas of Thailand's distinctive cuisine are honored at this contemporar■
$8-$15   downtown restaurant. The second-floor spot also features a small rooftop patio. Casual dress. **Bar:** Full ba■
Reservations: suggested, for dinner. **Hours:** 11:30 am-2 & 4:30-9 pm, Fri & Sat-9:30 pm. Closed majo■
holidays; also Sun. **Address:** 1090B Shoppers Row V9W 2C6 **Location:** At 11th Ave; downtown. **Parking**
street.

BEST WOK   Phone: 250/287-283■
ⓦⓦ ⓦⓦ
Chinese   Contemporary Chinese and Western food is on the menu at the downtown restaurant. Combination meal■
$5-$16   serve two, four, six or eight to 10 diners. Plenty of on-site parking is available, but for those who can't din■
in, take-out and delivery also are offered. Casual dress. **Bar:** Full bar. **Reservations:** accepted. **Hours:** 1■
am-9:30 pm. Closed: 10/11, 12/25. **Address:** 968 Alder St V9W 2P9 **Location:** From Shoppers Row, just ■
on 10th Ave, then just s. **Parking:** on-site. CALL ⒼⓂ

THE DRIFTWOOD RESTAURANT   Phone: 250/923-550■
ⓦⓦ ⓦⓦ
Chinese   A 15-minute drive south along scenic Island Highway and across from the Oyster Bay rest area, thi■
$8-$18   Chinese restaurant sets up a nightly dinner buffet, as well as a lunch buffet on weekends. Guests also hav■
the option of ordering from the extensive menu. Dishes are prepared with 100 percent vegetable oil and n■
monosodium glutamate. Casual dress. **Bar:** Full bar. **Hours:** 11:30 am-9 pm. Closed: 12/25. **Address:** 432■
S Island Hwy V9H 1B7 **Location:** 10 mi (16 km) s on Island Hwy 19A. **Parking:** on-site.

FUSILLI GRILL   Phone: 250/830-009■
ⓦⓦ ⓦⓦ
Pacific Northwest   Contemporary West Coast creations inspired by Italian cuisine highlight the menu of this youthful and casu■
$9-$26   bistro-restaurant. The place is in a small strip mall, away from the busy town center and highways. Dail■
specials and British Columbia wines are featured. Casual dress. **Bar:** Full bar. **Reservations:** suggeste■
for dinner Fri & Sat. **Hours:** 11 am-9:30 pm, Fri-10:30 pm, Sat 4:30 pm-10 pm, Sun & Mon 4:30 pm-9 pm■
Closed: 1/1, 12/25. **Address:** 4-220 Dogwood St V9W 2X9 **Location:** Island Hwy 19A, 1.5 mi (2.4 km) se■
in Dogwood Plaza. **Parking:** on-site. CALL ⒼⓂ

LOOKOUT WEST COAST GRILL & SEAFOOD
  HOUSE   Phone: 250/286-681■
ⓦⓦ ⓦⓦ
Seafood   Near the start of the downtown shopping district, the waterfront restaurant offers views of Quadra Island jus■
$8-$26   across the water. In addition to local seafood, such as oysters, mussels, salmon and halibut, the men■
includes tapas and tidbits, gourmet soup and salads and pastas. All are priced reasonably. Casual dress■
Bar: Full bar. **Hours:** 11:30 am-10 pm. Closed: 12/25. **Address:** 921 Island Hwy V9W 2C2 **Location:** Just ■
on Island Hwy 19A from downtown. **Parking:** on-site. CALL ⒼⓂ

MOXIE'S CLASSIC GRILL   Phone: 250/830-150■
ⓦⓦ ⓦⓦ
Canadian   This sleek, funky and popular restaurant presents an extensive menu of creatively prepared dishes■
$8-$18   including pizza, pasta, rice, noodles, signature salads and burgers. Other menus include one for childre■
and one for Sunday brunch. Lending to the upbeat, stylish decor are dark wood appointments and river roc■
fireplaces. Casual dress. **Bar:** Full bar. **Hours:** 9:30 am-midnight. **Address:** 1360 Island Hwy V9W 8C■
Location: From Island Hwy 19A, just n on Discovery Cres; in Discovery Harbour Mall. **Parking:** on-site.

RICKY'S ALL DAY GRILL   Phone: 250/286-344■
ⓦⓦ ⓦⓦ
Canadian   The comfortable eatery, which employs friendly servers, presents a varied menu that includes pasta dishes■
$6-$15   wraps, omelets, stir-fry preparations and burgers. Portions are generous. Children's and senior selection■
are offered. Guests can request seating in a booth or at a table. Casual dress. **Bar:** Full bar. **Hours:** 6 am-■
pm, Sun from 7 am. **Address:** 811 13th Ave V9W 4G9 **Location:** Island Hwy 19A, just s on Dogwood S■
then just e. **Parking:** on-site.

CASTLEGAR pop. 7,002

QUALITY INN CASTLEGAR   *Book at AAA.com*   Phone: (250)365-217■
ⓦⓦ ⓦ
Hotel   **Address:** 1935 Columbia Ave V1N 2W8 **Location:** Jct Hwy 3A and 3B, just s. **Facility:** Smoke fre■
$110-$160 6/1-2/28   premises. 48 units. 47 one-bedroom standard units. 1 two-bedroom suite with kitchen. 2 stories (n■
$90-$110 3/1-5/31   elevator), interior/exterior corridors. **Parking:** on-site. **Terms:** office hours 7 am-11 pm■
Amenities: voice mail, irons, hair dryers. **Leisure Activities:** limited exercise equipment. **Gues■
Services: wireless Internet. **Business Services:** meeting rooms, PC.
ⒶⓈⓀ 🍴 ✕ 🛢 🖼 🖥 / SOME UNITS FEE 🐾

SUPER 8-CASTLEGAR   *Book at AAA.com*   Phone: (250)365-270■
ⓦⓦ ⓦ
Hotel   **Address:** 651 18th St V1N 2N1 **Location:** Hwy 3, exit city centre. **Facility:** Smoke free premises. 5■
$135-$329 5/2-2/28   units. 52 one-bedroom standard units, some with efficiencies and/or whirlpools. 4 one-bedroom suite■
$125-$299 3/1-5/1   with efficiencies. 3 stories, interior corridors. *Bath:* combo or shower only. **Parking:** on-site. **Terms■
cancellation fee imposed. **Amenities:** voice mail, irons, hair dryers. *Some:* high-speed Interne■
Pool(s): heated indoor. **Leisure Activities:** whirlpool, waterslide. **Guest Services:** valet and coi■
laundry, wireless Internet. **Business Services:** meeting rooms, PC.
ⒺⒸⓄ ⒶⓈⓀ 🍴 🛏 ✕ 🎣 🛢 🖼 🖥 / SOME UNITS FEE 🐾

—— **WHERE TO DINE** ——

BLACK ROOSTER CLASSIC BAR & GRILL   Phone: 250/365-777■
ⓦⓦ ⓦⓦ
Canadian   A giant black rooster dominates the entrance to this casual establishment, where the varied menu range■
$10-$30   from sandwiches, burgers and pizza to more serious fare such as rack of lamb or seared wild salmon■
Casual dress. **Bar:** Full bar. **Reservations:** suggested. **Hours:** 11 am-10 pm, Fri & Sat-11 pm. Closed: 1/1■
12/25. **Address:** 651 18th St V1N 2N1 **Location:** Jct Hwy 3, just n on Hwy 22; next to Super 8. **Parking**
on-site. CALL ⒼⓂ

CHASE pop. 2,460

CHASE COUNTRY INN MOTEL

Phone: (250)679-3333

Motel
$79-$99 3/1-10/31
$69-$89 11/1-2/28

Address: 576 Coburn St V0E 1M0 **Location:** Trans-Canada Hwy 1 and Coburn St. **Facility:** 21 one-bedroom standard units, some with efficiencies or kitchens. 2 stories (no elevator), exterior corridors. **Parking:** on-site, winter plug-ins. **Terms:** office hours 8 am-11 pm, cancellation fee imposed. **Amenities:** voice mail, hair dryers. **Guest Services:** coin laundry, wireless Internet.

ASK ⊤⊤ 🔲 🔲 / SOME UNITS FEE 🐾 ✕ 📷

TALKING ROCK RESORT AND QUAAOUT LODGE

Phone: (250)679-3090

Resort
Hotel
$100-$250 All Year

Address: 1663 Little Shuswap Lake Rd W V0E 1M0 **Location:** Trans-Canada Hwy 1, exit Squilax Bridge, 1.5 mi (2.5 km) w. Located in a quiet secluded area. **Facility:** Native interpretative trails crisscross the grounds of this lakefront lodge offering brightly decorated guest rooms. 72 one-bedroom standard units, some with whirlpools. 3 stories, interior corridors. **Parking:** on-site. **Terms:** office hours 7 am-11 pm. **Amenities:** voice mail, hair dryers. **Pool(s):** heated indoor/outdoor. **Leisure Activities:** whirlpool, steamroom, boat dock, rental bicycles, exercise room. **Guest Services:** coin laundry, wireless Internet. **Business Services:** conference facilities, PC.

ASK ⊤⊤ 🍸 CALL ᏝM 🏊 ✕ 🎦 🔲 / SOME UNITS FEE 🐾 ✕ 🔲

CHEMAINUS pop. 2,937

BEST WESTERN CHEMAINUS FESTIVAL INN

Book great rates at AAA.com

Phone: (250)246-4181

CAA SAVE

Hotel
$133-$160 3/1-8/31
$132-$150 9/1-2/28

Address: 9573 Chemainus Rd V0R 1K5 **Location:** Trans-Canada Hwy 1, exit Henry Rd, 0.9 mi (1.4 km) e. **Facility:** Smoke free premises. 75 units. 24 one-bedroom standard units, some with efficiencies. 51 one-bedroom suites with efficiencies. 4 stories, interior corridors. **Parking:** on-site. **Amenities:** high-speed Internet, voice mail, safes, irons, hair dryers. **Pool(s):** heated indoor. **Leisure Activities:** whirlpool, exercise room. **Guest Services:** coin laundry, wireless Internet. **Business Services:** meeting rooms, PC.

AAA Benefit:
Members save up to 20%, plus 10% bonus points with rewards program.

ECO CALL ᏝM 🏊 ✕ 🎦 🔲 🔲 / SOME UNITS FEE 🐾 📷

FREE expanded continental breakfast and early check-in/late check-out

CHETWYND pop. 2,633

LAKEVIEW INNS & SUITES

Book great rates at AAA.com

Phone: (250)788-3000

CAA SAVE

Hotel
$129 All Year

Address: 4820 N Access Rd V0C 1J0 **Location:** Hwy 29 and 97, just n on 48th St, then just e. **Facility:** 57 units. 53 one-bedroom standard units, some with kitchens, kitchens and/or whirlpools. 4 one-bedroom suites with kitchens and whirlpools. 4 stories, interior corridors. **Parking:** on-site, winter plug-ins. **Amenities:** video library, DVD players, high-speed Internet, irons, hair dryers. **Leisure Activities:** exercise room. **Guest Services:** wireless Internet. **Business Services:** meeting rooms, business center. **Free Special Amenities:** expanded continental breakfast and local telephone calls.

ECO ⊤⊤ 🔲 📷 🔲 / SOME UNITS FEE 🐾 ✕

POMEROY INN & SUITES

Book at AAA.com

Phone: 250/788-4800

Extended Stay
Hotel
Rates not provided

Address: 5200 N Access Rd V0C 1J0 **Location:** Hwy 29 and 97, just n on 52nd St. **Facility:** 87 units. 43 one-bedroom standard units, some with kitchens. 44 one-bedroom suites with kitchens, some with whirlpools. 4 stories, interior corridors. *Bath:* combo or shower only. **Parking:** on-site, winter plug-ins. **Amenities:** high-speed Internet, voice mail, irons, hair dryers. **Pool(s):** heated indoor. **Leisure Activities:** whirlpool, waterslide, exercise room. **Guest Services:** valet and coin laundry, wireless Internet. **Business Services:** meeting rooms, PC.

⊤⊤ 🏊 ✕ 🎦 🔲 📷 🔲 / SOME UNITS FEE 🐾 ✕

CHILLIWACK pop. 62,927

BEST WESTERN RAINBOW COUNTRY INN

Book great rates at AAA.com

Phone: (604)795-3828

CAA SAVE

Hotel
$140-$270 3/1-10/31
$120-$250 11/1-2/28

Address: 43971 Industrial Way V2R 3A4 **Location:** Trans-Canada Hwy 1, exit 116 (Lickman Rd). **Facility:** Smoke free premises. 74 one-bedroom standard units, some with whirlpools. 2 stories (no elevator), interior corridors. **Parking:** on-site. **Amenities:** voice mail, irons, hair dryers. *Some:* high-speed Internet. **Dining:** 2 restaurants. **Pool(s):** heated indoor. **Leisure Activities:** sauna, whirlpool. **Guest Services:** valet and coin laundry, wireless Internet. **Business Services:** meeting rooms, PC. **Free Special Amenities:** local telephone calls and high-speed Internet.

AAA Benefit:
Members save up to 20%, plus 10% bonus points with rewards program.

⊤⊤ 🍸 CALL ᏝM 🏊 ✕ 🎦 🔲 / SOME UNITS FEE 🐾 🔲

CHILLIWACK TRAVELODGE *Book great rates at AAA.com*   Phone: (604)792-424█

Hotel
$91-$225 All Year

Address: 45466 Yale Rd W V2R 3Z8 **Location:** Trans-Canada Hwy 1, exit 119, just n. **Facility:** 8█ units. 81 one- and 1 two-bedroom standard units, some with efficiencies. 2 stories (no elevator) interior corridors. **Parking:** on-site. **Terms:** 7 day cancellation notice. **Amenities:** voice mail, irons, ha█ dryers. **Pool(s):** heated indoor. **Leisure Activities:** whirlpool. **Guest Services:** coin laundry, wireles█ Internet. **Business Services:** meeting rooms, PC. **Free Special Amenities: local telephone call█ and high-speed Internet.**

COMFORT INN *Book at AAA.com*   Phone: (604)858-063█

Motel
$105-$155 7/1-2/28
$95-$135 3/1-6/30

Address: 45405 Luckakuck Way V2R 3C7 **Location:** Trans-Canada Hwy 1, exit 119, s on Vedder Rd then 0.6 mi (1 km) w. **Facility:** 83 one-bedroom standard units. 2 stories (no elevator), interic█ corridors. **Parking:** on-site. **Amenities:** irons, hair dryers. **Guest Services:** valet laundry, wireles█ Internet. **Business Services:** PC (fee).

DAYS INN CHILLIWACK *Book at AAA.com*   Phone: (604)792-195█

Motel
$89-$170 All Year

Address: 8583 Young Rd S V2P 4P3 **Location:** Hwy 1, exit 119 eastbound, 0.6 mi (1 km) n on Yal█ Rd, then just e on Hocking Ave; exit 120 (Young Rd) westbound, 0.6 mi (1 km) n. **Facility:** 29 one█ bedroom standard units. 2 stories (no elevator), interior corridors. **Parking:** on-site. **Amenities:** voic█ mail, hair dryers. **Guest Services:** wireless Internet. **Business Services:** PC.

─── WHERE TO DINE ───

EARLS RESTAURANT   Phone: 604/858-336█

Canadian
$10-$28

Offering an experience that falls between fast food and fine dining, the fun, relaxed restaurant prepare█ great food at a great price. Choices range from juicy burgers, hearty sandwiches, fresh salads, wings an█ pizza to full entrees of steak, chops and seafood. Made-from-scratch soups and assorted breads, as well a█ a nice choice of wines and beers, round out the offerings. This is a fitting spot for impromptu get-together█ and festive occasions. Casual dress. **Bar:** Full bar. **Hours:** 11:30 am-11 pm. Closed: 12/25█ **Address:** 45585 Luckakuck Way V2R 1A1 **Location:** Trans-Canada Hwy 1, exit 119, just w on Vedder R█ in Cottonwood Shopping Center. **Parking:** on-site.

RICKY'S ALL DAY GRILL   Phone: 604/858-566█

Canadian
$6-$15

The comfortable eatery, which employs friendly servers, presents a varied menu that includes pasta dishes█ wraps, omelets, stir-fry preparations and burgers. Portions are generous. Children's and senior selection█ are offered. Guests can request seating in a booth or at a table. Casual dress. **Bar:** Full bar. **Hours:** 6:3█ am-9:30 pm. **Address:** 45389 Luckakuck Way V2R 3C7 **Location:** Trans-Canada Hwy 1, exit 119, just s o█ Vedder Rd, then 0.6 mi (1 km) n. **Parking:** on-site.

CHRISTINA LAKE pop. 986

NEW HORIZON MOTEL   Phone: (250)447-931█

Motel
$105-$190 All Year

Address: 2037 Hunter Frontage Rd (Hwy 3) V0H 1E2 **Location:** Just e. **Facility:** Smoke free█ premises. 25 units. 19 one-bedroom standard units, some with kitchens and/or whirlpools. 6 one█ bedroom suites with kitchens. 1-2 stories (no elevator), exterior corridors. *Bath:* combo or shower only█ **Parking:** on-site. **Terms:** office hours 7 am-9 pm, 2-4 night minimum stay - seasonal and/o█ weekends, 90 day cancellation notice-fee imposed. **Amenities:** irons, hair dryers. *Some:* high-spee█ Internet. **Leisure Activities:** basketball, volleyball. **Guest Services:** wireless Internet.

CLEARWATER

CLEARWATER VALLEY RESORT & KOA
KAMPGROUND *Book great rates at AAA.com*   Phone: (250)674-390█

Cottage
$92-$152 5/1-10/12

Address: 373 Clearwater Valley Rd V0E 1N0 **Location:** Jct Hwy 5 (Yellowhead Hwy) and Clearwate█ Valley Rd. **Facility:** Smoke free premises. 18 one-bedroom standard units. 1-2 stories (no elevator)█ exterior corridors. **Parking:** on-site. **Terms:** open 5/1-10/12, office hours 7:30 am-10 pm, cancellatio█ fee imposed. **Amenities:** hair dryers. **Pool(s):** heated outdoor. **Leisure Activities:** miniature gol█ playground, horseshoes, volleyball. *Fee:* game room. **Guest Services:** coin laundry, wireless Internet█ **Business Services:** PC. **Free Special Amenities: local telephone calls and high-speed Internet.**

DUTCH LAKE MOTEL AND CAMPGROUND   Phone: 250/674-332█

Motel
$65-$98 All Year

Address: 333 Roy Rd V0E 1N0 **Location:** Hwy 5 (Yellowhead Hwy) at Roy Rd. **Facility:** 27 units. 19█ one- and 2 two-bedroom standard units, some with efficiencies (utensils extra charge). 6 one-bedroom█ suites with efficiencies (utensils extra charge). 2 stories (no elevator), exterior corridors. **Parking:** on█ site, winter plug-ins. **Terms:** office hours 7 am-11 pm, cancellation fee imposed. **Amenities:** hai█ dryers. **Leisure Activities:** rental canoes. **Guest Services:** coin laundry, wireless Internet.

COMOX pop. 11,172

ORT AUGUSTA INN & SUITES   *Book great rates at AAA.com*   Phone: (250)339-2277

Motel
$85-$165 All Year

Address: 2082 Comox Ave V9M 1P8 **Location:** Hwy 19A (Cliffe Ave), follow signs to Comox Ave, then 2.5 mi (4 km) e. **Facility:** 69 one-bedroom standard units, some with efficiencies, kitchens and/or whirlpools. 2 stories (no elevator), interior/exterior corridors. *Bath:* combo or shower only. **Parking:** on-site. **Terms:** office hours 7:30 am-11 pm, 3 day cancellation notice-fee imposed. **Amenities:** irons, hair dryers. *Some:* high-speed Internet. **Pool(s):** heated outdoor. **Guest Services:** wireless Internet. **Free Special Amenities:** continental breakfast and high-speed Internet.

---- WHERE TO DINE ----

MITTY'S   Phone: 250/339-3911

Canadian
$7-$20

The family-oriented restaurant satisfies patrons with its ever-popular all-day breakfast items, as well as tasty and wholesome soups and salads at lunchtime. A relaxed mood characterizes the dining space. Casual dress. **Bar:** Full bar. **Hours:** 7:30 am-8 pm. Closed: 12/25, 12/26. **Address:** 1747 Comox Ave V9M 3M2 **Location:** Between Port Augusta and Nordin sts. **Parking:** on-site.

COQUITLAM—See Vancouver p. 645.

COURTENAY pop. 18,304

HE ANCO MOTEL   Phone: 250/334-2451

Motel
$70-$90 All Year

Address: 1885 Cliffe Ave V9N 2K9 **Location:** Just s of Hwy 19 Connector. **Facility:** 67 one-bedroom standard units, some with efficiencies. 2 stories (no elevator), exterior corridors. *Bath:* combo or shower only. **Parking:** on-site. **Terms:** cancellation fee imposed. **Amenities:** *Some:* high-speed Internet, hair dryers. **Pool(s):** heated outdoor. **Guest Services:** coin laundry, wireless Internet. **Business Services:** meeting rooms.

BEST WESTERN THE WESTERLY HOTEL   *Book great rates at AAA.com*   Phone: (250)338-7741

Hotel
$144-$209 All Year

Address: 1590 Cliffe Ave V9N 2K4 **Location:** Corner of Cliffe Ave and Island Hwy 19A N. **Facility:** Smoke free premises. 144 units. 141 one-bedroom standard units, some with whirlpools. 3 one-bedroom suites. 3-4 stories, interior corridors. *Bath:* combo or shower only. **Parking:** on-site. **Terms:** cancellation fee imposed. **Amenities:** voice mail, irons, hair dryers. **Pool(s):** heated indoor. **Leisure Activities:** saunas, whirlpool, exercise room. **Guest Services:** valet and coin laundry, wireless Internet. **Business Services:** meeting rooms, business center. *(See color ad below)*

AAA Benefit:
Members save up to 20%, plus 10% bonus points with rewards program.

FREE newspaper and high-speed Internet

CROWN ISLE RESORT & GOLF COMMUNITY

Phone: 250/703-505▮

Resort
Hotel
$144-$288 5/1-2/28
$117-$225 3/1-4/30

Address: 399 Clubhouse Dr V9N 9G3 **Location:** Island Hwy 19A N, 0.9 mi (1.5 km) n on Comox Ave then 1.6 mi (2.5 km) ne on Ryan Rd, follow signs. **Facility:** A spectacular golf course and wonderf condominium-like rooms await at this resort, which is just a short drive from the business distric Smoke free premises. 90 units. 83 one- and 7 two-bedroom standard units, some with efficiencie kitchens and/or whirlpools. 2-3 stories (no elevator), exterior corridors. **Parking:** on-site. **Terms:** offic hours 6 am-11 pm, cancellation fee imposed. **Amenities:** video library, DVD players, CD players, high speed Internet, voice mail, irons, hair dryers. **Leisure Activities:** whirlpool, steamrooms, exercis room. *Fee:* golf-18 holes. **Guest Services:** complimentary laundry, wireless Internet. **Busines Services:** conference facilities, PC.

GREYSTONE MANOR BED & BREAKFAST

Phone: 250/338-142▮

Historic Bed
& Breakfast
$105 All Year

Address: 4014 Haas Rd V9N 9T4 **Location:** 2.5 mi (4 km) s on Island Hwy 19A S to Hilton R Located in a quiet secluded area. **Facility:** The secluded B&B features a wonderful English-styl garden, a common area with original hardwood floors, and cozy rooms with simple decor. Smoke fre premises. 3 one-bedroom standard units. 2 stories (no elevator), interior corridors. *Bath:* combo o shower only. **Parking:** on-site. **Terms:** office hours 7:30 am-10 pm, check-in 4 pm, age restriction may apply. **Amenities:** hair dryers. **Guest Services:** TV in common area.

KINGFISHER OCEANSIDE RESORT & SPA

Phone: 250/338-132▮

Hotel
Rates not provided

Address: 4330 S Island Hwy V9N 9R9 **Location:** 3.8 mi (6 km) s on Island Hwy 19A S, watch fo signs. **Facility:** Smoke free premises. 64 units. 44 one-bedroom standard units, some with efficiencie and/or whirlpools. 20 one-bedroom suites with efficiencies, some with whirlpools. 2 stories, exterio corridors. *Bath:* combo or shower only. **Parking:** on-site. **Terms:** office hours 7 am-11 pm **Amenities:** video library (fee), DVD players, irons, hair dryers. **Dining:** restaurant, see separate listing **Pool(s):** heated outdoor. **Leisure Activities:** sauna, whirlpool, steamroom, tennis court, renta bicycles, exercise room, spa. **Guest Services:** valet laundry, wireless Internet. **Business Services** meeting rooms, PC.

OLD HOUSE VILLAGE HOTEL & SPA   *Book great rates at AAA.com*

Phone: (250)703-020▮

(CAA) (SAVE)

Hotel
$99-$289 All Year

Address: 1730 Riverside Ln V9N 8C7 **Location:** Island Hwy 19A, just n on 19th St. **Facility:** Smok free premises. 79 units. 30 one-bedroom standard units. 47 one- and 2 two-bedroom suites wit kitchens, some with whirlpools. 3 stories, interior corridors. *Bath:* combo or shower only. **Parking:** on site. **Terms:** check-in 4 pm, cancellation fee imposed. **Amenities:** video library (fee), DVD players high-speed Internet, voice mail, irons, hair dryers. **Dining:** restaurant, see separate listing **Pool(s):** heated outdoor. **Leisure Activities:** sauna, whirlpool, exercise room, spa. **Guest Services** wireless Internet. **Business Services:** meeting rooms, PC.

TRAVELODGE COURTENAY   *Book at AAA.com*

Phone: (250)334-449▮

Motel
$93-$118 All Year

Address: 2605 Cliffe Ave V9N 2L8 **Location:** 0.8 mi (1.2 km) s on Island Hwy 19A S. Adjacent t Driftwood Mall. **Facility:** 91 one-bedroom standard units, some with efficiencies. 2 stories (n elevator), exterior corridors. **Parking:** on-site. **Amenities:** voice mail, hair dryers. *Some:* high-spee Internet, irons. **Pool(s):** heated outdoor. **Guest Services:** coin laundry, wireless Internet. **Busines Services:** meeting rooms, PC (fee).

—— WHERE TO DINE ——

ATLAS CAFE

Phone: 250/338-983▮

Southwestern
$10-$17

This funky downtown cafe presents an eclectic menu with a mix of Italian dishes, Mexican entrees an global cuisine such as curry-glazed wild salmon, vegetable lasagna and Asian soba noodles. This plac opens early for breakfast. Casual dress. **Bar:** Full bar. **Reservations:** accepted. **Hours:** 8:30 am-9:30 pm Fri-10:30 pm, Sat-10 pm, Sun-9 pm, Mon-3:30 pm. Closed major holidays. **Address:** 250 6th St V9N 1M **Location:** Jct Island Hwy 19A N, 0.5 mi (0.8 km) n on Cliffe Ave. **Parking:** street.

KINGFISHER DINING ROOM

Phone: 250/338-132▮

Pacific Northwest
$12-$35

Amazing water views from every table in a warm and inviting atmosphere await both guests staying at th resort and those simply stopping in for a delightful meal. Dishes feature fresh local ingredients that includ seafood, meats and vegetables grown locally from area farmers in addition to vegetables grown in th property's own gardens. Particularly popular are the weekly gala seafood buffet and the Sunday brunch which starts at 9:30 am; reservations are recommended. Casual dress. **Bar:** Full ba **Reservations:** suggested. **Hours:** 7 am-9 pm, Fri & Sat-10 pm. **Address:** 4330 S Island Hwy V9N 9R **Location:** 3.8 mi (6 km) s on Island Hwy 19A; in Kingfisher Oceanside Resort & Spa. **Parking:** on-site.

MONTE CHRISTO ON THE RIVER

Phone: 250/338-1468

Canadian
$9-$21

Along the river, the well-established restaurant presents a casual lunch menu with daily specials an homemade soups. At the heart of the dinner menu are steak, seafood, pasta and barbecue dishes. Als offered are many seniors' and children's choices. Casual dress. **Bar:** Full bar. **Hours:** 11:30 am-10 pm, Fri 11 pm, Sat 4 pm-11 pm, Sun 4 pm-10 pm. Closed: 1/1, 12/25, 12/26. **Address:** 975 Comox Rd V9N 3P **Location:** Island Hwy 19A N. **Parking:** on-site.

HE OLD HOUSE RESTAURANT

Phone: 250/338-5406

Canadian
$9-$30

This locally popular dining spot is housed in a rustic 1938 home that has been renovated inside and now features very modern decor. Sitting alongside the river, the exterior still features an old farmhouse-like charm. Patrons will find friendly, attentive service and plenty of parking. Casual dress. **Bar:** Full bar. **Reservations:** suggested. **Hours:** 11:30 am-9:30 pm, Fri & Sat-10 pm. Closed: 12/25. **Address:** 1760 Riverside Ln V9N 8C7 **Location:** Island Hwy 19A, just n on 19th St. **Parking:** on-site. CALL

RICKY'S ALL DAY GRILL

Phone: 250/334-9638

Canadian
$6-$15

The comfortable eatery, which employs friendly servers, presents a varied menu that includes pasta dishes, wraps, omelets, stir-fry preparations and burgers. Portions are generous. Children's and senior selections are offered. Guests can request seating in a booth or at a table. Casual dress. **Bar:** Full bar. **Hours:** 7 am-8:30 pm. **Address:** 795 Ryan Rd V9N 3R6 **Location:** Island Hwy 19A N, just ne; in Washington Park Centre Mall. **Parking:** on-site.

CRANBROOK pop. 18,476

BEST WESTERN CRANBROOK HOTEL *Book great rates at AAA.com*

Phone: (250)417-4002

Hotel
$169-$199 3/1-9/30
$139-$199 10/1-2/28

Address: 1019 Cranbrook St N V1C 3S4 **Location:** Hwy 3 and 95; centre. **Facility:** 94 units. 86 one-bedroom standard units. 4 one- and 4 two-bedroom suites, some with whirlpools. 4 stories, interior corridors. **Parking:** on-site. **Amenities:** high-speed Internet, voice mail, irons, hair dryers. **Pool(s):** indoor. **Leisure Activities:** waterslide, exercise room. *Fee:* game room. **Guest Services:** coin laundry, wireless Internet. **Business Services:** PC. **Free Special Amenities:** newspaper and high-speed Internet.

AAA Benefit:
Members save up to 20%, plus 10% bonus points with rewards program.

DAYS INN CRANBROOK *Book at AAA.com*

Phone: (250)426-6683

Hotel
$119-$154 All Year

Address: 600 Cranbrook St N V1C 3R7 **Location:** Corner of 6th St and Cranbrook St N. **Facility:** 87 units. 86 one-bedroom standard units. 1 one-bedroom suite with kitchen and whirlpool. 4 stories, interior corridors. **Parking:** on-site, winter plug-ins. **Terms:** check-in 4 pm. **Amenities:** voice mail, irons, hair dryers. *Some:* DVD players. **Dining:** Bavarian Chalet, see separate listing. **Pool(s):** heated outdoor. **Leisure Activities:** sauna, whirlpool. **Guest Services:** valet laundry, area transportation, wireless Internet. **Business Services:** meeting rooms, PC (fee).

HERITAGE INN CRANBROOK *Book at AAA.com*

Phone: (250)489-4301

Hotel
$135-$210 All Year

Address: 803 Cranbrook St N V1C 3S2 **Location:** Hwy 3 and 95; centre. **Facility:** 100 units. 97 one-bedroom standard units. 2 one- and 1 two-bedroom suites. 3 stories (no elevator), interior corridors. **Parking:** on-site, winter plug-ins. **Terms:** cancellation fee imposed. **Amenities:** voice mail. *Some:* DVD players, high-speed Internet (fee), safes, irons, hair dryers. **Pool(s):** heated indoor. **Leisure Activities:** whirlpool, limited exercise equipment. **Guest Services:** wireless Internet. **Business Services:** conference facilities.

ST. EUGENE GOLF RESORT & CASINO *Book great rates at AAA.com*

Phone: (250)420-2000

Historic Resort Hotel
$132-$190 All Year

Address: 7731 Mission Rd V1C 7E5 **Location:** Hwy 3, exit Kimberley/Airport (Hwy 95A) to Mission Rd, 2.8 mi (4.5 km) n. **Facility:** This upscale hotel, in a picturesque setting, was built in an old mission school dating to the 1800s. Designated smoking area. 125 units. 122 one-bedroom standard units. 3 one-bedroom suites, some with whirlpools. 3 stories, interior corridors. **Parking:** on-site. **Terms:** check-in 4 pm, cancellation fee imposed. **Amenities:** video games (fee), high-speed Internet, dual phone lines, voice mail, irons, hair dryers. **Dining:** Purcell Grill, see separate listing. **Pool(s):** heated outdoor. **Leisure Activities:** sauna, whirlpools, steamroom, fishing, cross country skiing, ice skating, billiards, helitours, rafting, tepee fire pit area, interpretive centre, hiking trails, horseback riding, exercise room. *Fee:* golf-18 holes. **Guest Services:** valet laundry, airport transportation-Canadian Rockies International Airport, area transportation-spa. **Business Services:** conference facilities, business center. **Free Special Amenities:** high-speed Internet.

SUPER 8 *Book at AAA.com*

Phone: (250)489-8028

Hotel
$90-$115 3/1-10/1
$90-$95 10/2-2/28

Address: 2370 Cranbrook St N V1C 3T2 **Location:** Just w of jct Hwy 93 and 95. **Facility:** 48 one-bedroom standard units. 2 stories (no elevator), interior corridors. **Parking:** on-site, winter plug-ins. **Terms:** cancellation fee imposed. **Amenities:** hair dryers. *Some:* irons. **Guest Services:** coin laundry, wireless Internet. **Business Services:** PC (fee).

--- **WHERE TO DINE** ---

ALLEGRA MEDITERRANEAN CUISINE

Phone: 250/426-8812

Mediterranean
$13-$27

This bright, bistro-style restaurant has an interesting take on French, Italian and Spanish Mediterranean cuisines thanks to its Swiss chef/owner. The menu lists a variety of pastas, chicken, veal, pork tenderloin and lamb dishes, all offering good value. Service is simple, yet friendly. Casual dress. **Bar:** Full bar. **Reservations:** suggested. **Hours:** 5 pm-9 pm. Closed: 12/25; also Mon & Tues. **Address:** 1225B Cranbrook St N V1C 3S6 **Location:** Hwy 3 and 95, just s of Theatre Rd; in strip mall. **Parking:** on-site.

BAVARIAN CHALET

Continental
$8-$26

Phone: 250/489-330

The restaurant is a favorite for good, hearty food, a relaxing atmosphere and European touches. Among menu choices are ribs, chicken cordon bleu, schnitzels and German spaetzle, as well as excellent prime rib specials Thursday through Saturday nights. Save room for the delicious apple strudel. Casual dress. **Bar:** Full bar. **Reservations:** required. **Hours:** 7 am-3 & 5-9 pm, Thurs-Sat to 10 pm. Closed major holidays. **Address:** 600 Cranbrook St N V1C 3R7 **Location:** Corner of 6th St and Cranbrook St N; in Days Inn Cranbrook. **Parking:** on-site.

HEIDI'S EUROPEAN & INTERNATIONAL CUISINE   *Menu on AAA.com*

(AAA)

International
$8-$34

Phone: 250/426-792

Located in the heart of Cranbrook, the cozy, comfortable, European-style restaurant serves an extensive menu of international fare, including rotisserie chicken, schnitzel, bratwurst and steak. Prime rib is offered Fridays and Saturdays. Dim lights add to an intimate ambience, and charming, friendly servers will recommend their favorite dishes. Casual dress. **Bar:** Full bar. **Reservations:** suggested. **Hours:** 11 am-2:30 & 5-9 pm, Fri-10 pm, Sat 11:30 am-10 pm. Closed major holidays; also Sun. **Address:** 821 C Baker St V1C 1A3 **Location:** On 9th Ave S; centre. **Parking:** street. CALL (&M)

MR MIKE'S STEAKHOUSE & BAR

Steak
$10-$30

Phone: 250/417-254

The family-oriented restaurant satisfies patrons with its ever-popular all-day breakfast items, as well as tasty and wholesome soups and salads at lunchtime. A relaxed mood characterizes the dining space. Casual dress. **Bar:** Full bar. **Hours:** 11 am-10 pm, Thurs-Sat to midnight. Closed: 12/25. **Address:** 1028 Cranbrook St N V1C 3S3 **Location:** Between 6th St NW and Theatre Rd. **Parking:** on-site.

PURCELL GRILL

Regional
Canadian
$18-$42

Phone: 250/420-202

Creative, artistic dishes are created with many regional ingredients. The setting, in the old St. Eugene Mission school, lends to a sense of history with exposed brick walls, heavy overhead beams and views of the golf course. Service is friendly and attentive. Casual dress. **Bar:** Full bar. **Reservations:** suggested. **Hours:** 7 am-11 & 5-10 pm; hours vary off season. **Address:** 7731 Mission Rd V1C 7E5 **Location:** Hwy 3 exit Kimberley/Airport (Hwy 95A) to Mission Rd, 2.8 mi (4.5 km) n; in St. Eugene Golf Resort & Casino. **Parking:** on-site. CALL (&M)

CRESTON pop. 4,826

DOWNTOWNER MOTOR INN

(AAA) (SAVE)

Motel
$55-$80 All Year

Phone: 250/428-2238

Address: 1218 Canyon St V0B 1G0 **Location:** Corner of 12th Ave N; centre. **Facility:** 23 one-bedroom standard units. 2 stories (no elevator), interior corridors. **Parking:** on-site. **Terms:** office hours 7 am-11 pm, cancellation fee imposed. **Leisure Activities:** sauna, whirlpool. **Guest Services:** wireless Internet. **Business Services:** meeting rooms. **Free Special Amenities:** local telephone calls and high-speed Internet.

SKIMMERHORN INN

(AAA) (SAVE)

Motel
$87-$157 All Year

Phone: (250)428-4009

Address: 2711 Hwy 3 V0B 1G0 **Location:** On Hwy 3, 0.8 mi (1.3 km) e. **Facility:** Smoke free premises. 25 units. 16 one- and 5 two-bedroom standard units, some with kitchens. 4 two-bedroom suites with kitchens. 2 stories (no elevator), exterior corridors. **Parking:** on-site, winter plug-ins. **Amenities:** hair dryers. *Some:* irons. **Pool(s):** heated outdoor. **Leisure Activities:** picnic tables, gas barbecue, playground, horseshoes. **Guest Services:** wireless Internet. **Free Special Amenities:** local telephone calls and high-speed Internet.

SUNSET MOTEL

(AAA) (SAVE)

Motel
$79-$109 All Year

Phone: 250/428-2229

Address: 2705 Canyon St (Hwy 3 E) V0B 1G0 **Location:** On Hwy 3, 0.8 mi (1.3 km) e. **Facility:** Smoke free premises. 24 one-bedroom standard units, some with efficiencies, kitchens and/or whirlpools. 1-2 stories (no elevator), exterior corridors. **Parking:** on-site, winter plug-ins. **Amenities:** video library. *Some:* irons, hair dryers. **Pool(s):** heated outdoor. **Guest Services:** wireless Internet. **Free Special Amenities:** local telephone calls and high-speed Internet.

———— **WHERE TO DINE** ————

ALDO & CO ITALIAN RESTAURANT

Italian
$7-$33

Phone: 250/402-6895

This casually elegant restaurant is a nice little surprise in this small town. Although the dinner menu isn't large, it assembles Italian-style appetizers, salads, soups, pasta dishes and one or two meat entrees presented with a contemporary flourish. Interestingly, the lunch menu is a little more in depth. All desserts are prepared in house. Dressy casual. **Bar:** Full bar. **Reservations:** suggested. **Hours:** 11:30 am-1:30 & 5-9 pm. Closed major holidays; also Sun & Mon. **Address:** 1821 Canyon St V0B 1G5 **Location:** Just e on Hwy 3. **Parking:** on-site.

COFFEE CREEK CAFE

Sandwiches
$4-$9

Phone: 250/428-9511

This little cafe makes everything from scratch, right down to the croutons. Kootenay Rose salad and the signature Russian borscht are among the fresh and healthful soups, salads and build-your-own sandwiches, which taste great with organic coffee. Guests order from the friendly counter staff and can enjoy the lively art displays. Public parking is available at the back of the building. Casual dress. **Reservations:** accepted. **Hours:** 8 am-4 pm. Closed major holidays; also Sat & Sun. **Address:** 1127A Canyon St V0B 1G0 **Location:** Downtown. **Parking:** street. CALL (&M)

DAWSON CREEK pop. 10,994

BEST WESTERN DAWSON CREEK HOTEL & SUITES
Book great rates at AAA.com

Phone: (250)782-6226

CAA SAVE

Hotel
$179 All Year

Address: 500 Hwy 2 V1G 0A4 **Location:** 1.8 mi (3 km) e of center. **Facility:** 100 units. 55 one-bedroom standard units, some with efficiencies and/or whirlpools. 45 one-bedroom suites, some with whirlpools. 3 stories, interior corridors. *Bath:* combo or shower only. **Parking:** on-site, winter plug-ins. **Amenities:** high-speed Internet, voice mail, irons, hair dryers. **Pool(s):** heated indoor. **Leisure Activities:** whirlpool, waterslide, exercise room. **Guest Services:** valet laundry, wireless Internet. **Business Services:** meeting rooms, PC. **Free Special Amenities: expanded continental breakfast and newspaper.**

CALL / SOME UNITS FEE

AAA Benefit:
Members save up to 20%, plus 10% bonus points with rewards program.

DAWSON CREEK DAYS INN
Book great rates at AAA.com

Phone: (250)782-8887

CAA SAVE

Hotel
$117-$144 All Year

Address: 640 122nd Ave V1G 0A4 **Location:** Hwy 49, just n on 122nd Ave; centre. **Facility:** 85 units. 77 one-bedroom standard units. 8 one-bedroom suites, some with efficiencies and/or whirlpools. 4 stories, interior corridors. **Parking:** on-site, winter plug-ins. **Amenities:** high-speed Internet, voice mail, hair dryers. *Some:* irons. **Leisure Activities:** exercise room. **Guest Services:** valet and coin laundry, wireless Internet. **Business Services:** PC. *(See color ad below)*

ECO / SOME UNITS

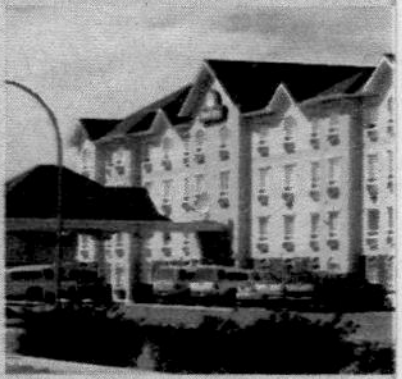

FREE expanded continental breakfast and high-speed Internet

DAWSON CREEK SUPER 8
Book great rates at AAA.com

Phone: (250)782-8899

CAA SAVE

Hotel
$135-$220 3/1-9/30
$140-$200 10/1-2/28

Address: 1440 Alaska Ave V1G 1Z5 **Location:** Just s of jct Hwy 97 S (Hart Hwy) and 97 N (Alaska Hwy). **Facility:** 66 units. 62 one-bedroom standard units, some with efficiencies and/or whirlpools. 4 one-bedroom suites. 2 stories (no elevator), interior corridors. **Parking:** on-site, winter plug-ins. **Amenities:** irons, hair dryers. *Some:* high-speed Internet. **Dining:** Sola's Bar & Grill, see separate listing. **Leisure Activities:** limited exercise equipment. **Guest Services:** coin laundry, wireless Internet. **Business Services:** meeting rooms, PC. **Free Special Amenities: continental breakfast and high-speed Internet.**

/ SOME UNITS FEE

▼ See AAA listing above ▼

Days Inn - Dawson Creek
640 - 122nd Ave.
Dawson Creek, BC V1G 0A4

CAA/AAA Members Save 10% Off Published Rates*

See what the new day brings.

- FREE Daybreak® Café breakfast
- FREE high-speed Internet
- Earn Wyndham Rewards® points on qualified stays**
- All rooms with mini-fridge & microwave
- Coin operated laundry

Days Inn
DAWSON CREEK

daysinn.ca 1-800-Days-Inn® 250-782-8887

*Advanced reservations required. Certain restrictions apply. See daysinn.ca for details. Rooms at this discount are limited and subject to availability at participating properties. Blackout dates and other restrictions may apply. Stay must be completed by 2/28/11. **A qualified stay is defined as a stay at a qualifying rate at one of the participating Wyndham Hotel Group properties. ©2009 Days Inns Worldwide, Inc. All Rights Reserved. All Days Inn hotels are independently owned and operated.

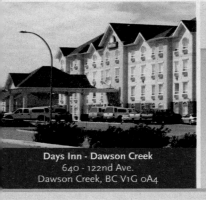

POMEROY INN & SUITES *Book at AAA.com*   **Phone:** (250)782-370●

Hotel
$189-$329 All Year

Address: 540 Hwy #2 V1G 0A4 **Location:** 1.8 mi (3 km) e of centre. **Facility:** 94 units. 41 one- and ● two-bedroom standard units, some with whirlpools. 45 one-bedroom suites with kitchens, some with whirlpools. 4 stories, interior corridors. **Bath:** combo or shower only. **Parking:** on-site, winter plug-ins ● **Amenities:** high-speed Internet, voice mail, irons, hair dryers. **Pool(s):** heated indoor. **Leisure** ● **Activities:** whirlpool, waterslide, exercise room. **Guest Services:** valet laundry, wireless Internet ● **Business Services:** PC. (ASK) [icons] / SOME UNITS FEE [icons]

—— **WHERE TO DINE** ——

SOLA'S BAR & GRILL   **Phone:** 250/782-889●

Canadian
$10-$28

A large stone fireplace dominates the popular and bustling restaurant's contemporary dining room. On the menu is a little something for everyone, including a variety of burgers and sandwiches such as the open-faced honey ham and Swiss on French bread, as well as classic entrees of prime rib, lemon pepper chicken or grilled salmon. The friendly staff provides swift service. Casual dress. **Bar:** Full bar. **Reservations:** no● accepted. **Hours:** 11:30 am-11 pm, Fri & Sat-midnight, Sun 10 am-11 pm. Closed: 12/25. **Address:** 1440 Alaska Ave V1G 1Z5 **Location:** Just s of jct Hwy 97 S (Hart Hwy) and 97 N (Alaska Hwy); in Dawson Creek Super 8. **Parking:** on-site. CALL [icon]

DELTA—See Vancouver p. 646.

DUNCAN pop. 4,986

BEST WESTERN COWICHAN VALLEY INN *Book great rates at AAA.com*   **Phone:** (250)748-2722

(CAA) (SAVE)

Hotel
$124-$161 All Year

Address: 6474 Trans-Canada Hwy 1 V9L 6C6 **Location:** 1.8 mi (3 km) n. **Facility:** 42 one-bedroom standard units. 2 stories (no elevator), interior corridors. **Parking:** on-site. **Amenities:** voice mail, irons, hair dryers. **Pool(s):** heated outdoor. **Leisure Activities:** exercise room. **Guest Services:** valet laundry, wireless Internet. **Business Services:** meeting rooms, PC. **Free Special Amenities:** full breakfast and high-speed Internet. [icons] / SOME UNITS FEE [icons]

AAA Benefit:
Members save up to 20%, plus 10% bonus points with rewards program.

TRAVELODGE SILVER BRIDGE INN DUNCAN *Book at AAA.com*   **Phone:** (250)748-4311

Hotel
$109-$249 All Year

Address: 140 Trans-Canada Hwy 1 V9L 3P7 **Location:** Just n of Silver Bridge. **Facility:** 33 one-bedroom standard units, some with efficiencies, kitchens and/or whirlpools. 2 stories (no elevator) exterior corridors. **Parking:** on-site. **Terms:** cancellation fee imposed. **Amenities:** high-speed Internet, irons, hair dryers. **Guest Services:** valet laundry, wireless Internet. **Business Services:** conference facilities, PC. (ECO) (ASK) [icons] / SOME UNITS FEE [icons]

—— **WHERE TO DINE** ——

DOGHOUSE A FAMILY RESTAURANT   **Phone:** 250/746-4614

Canadian
$5-$17

Patrons have been coming to the Doghouse since 1955, and it's easy to see why. Quality homestyle cooking, generous family servings and reasonable prices might make a regular out of you, too. Fish and chips is a specialty not to be missed, and the veal cutlets and homemade desserts are worth mentioning. Casual dress. **Bar:** Full bar. **Hours:** 6 am-10 pm. Closed: 12/25. **Address:** 271 Trans-Canada Hwy 1 V9L 3R1 **Location:** Corner of Trans-Canada Hwy 1 and Trunk Rd. **Parking:** on-site. CALL [icon]

ENDERBY—See Okanagan Valley p. 551.

FAIRMONT HOT SPRINGS pop. 489

FAIRMONT HOT SPRINGS RESORT   **Phone:** (250)345-6311

Resort
Hotel
$114-$324 All Year

Address: 5225 Fairmont Resort Rd V0B 1L1 **Location:** 1 mi (1.6 km) e off Hwy 93 and 95. **Facility:** The resort's outstanding feature is its landscaped grounds, which includes an area with natural hot springs pools. Smoke free premises. 140 units. 125 one- and 4 two-bedroom standard units, some with efficiencies. 6 one-bedroom suites, some with whirlpools. 5 cottages. 3 stories, interior/exterior corridors. **Parking:** on-site, winter plug-ins. **Terms:** check-in 4 pm, 3 day cancellation notice-fee imposed. **Amenities:** high-speed Internet, voice mail, irons, hair dryers. **Leisure Activities:** sauna, steamroom, fishing, 2 tennis courts, cross country skiing, recreation programs in summer, jogging, playground, spa. **Fee:** golf-45 holes, miniature golf, downhill skiing, horseback riding. **Guest Services:** coin laundry, wireless Internet. **Business Services:** conference facilities, PC (fee). [icons] FEE [icons] / SOME UNITS [icon]

No matter which destination you choose, we'll be there.

As familiar a sight as these great Canadian landmarks, we span the country from coast to coast. With over 280 locations and 7 great brands across Canada, we're never far from where you want to go. Plus, with amenities such as free high-speed Internet, free breakfast and free local newspapers at most hotels, we'll make you feel right at home.

Check-in to value today at Choice Hotels.®
choicehotels.ca • 800.228.1222

choicehotels.ca
800.228.1222

       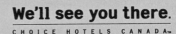

We'll see you there.
CHOICE HOTELS CANADA™

CHOICEprivileges
REWARDS PROGRAM

Go places.
Treat yourself often.

The places you have to go can get you to the places you want to go fast.

Join the **Choice Privileges**® rewards program and watch your points add up. With every qualifying stay at a Choice hotel, you'll earn points toward free stays at any of our 5,500 locations – including Hawaii, Europe*, Australasia**, the Caribbean or one of dozens of luxury resorts. Or use your points for airline rewards, gift cards and more. See our website for program details. **Choice Privileges**. Go places. Treat yourself often.

Visit choiceprivileges.ca or call 866.283.3510 to join today.

*Excluding Denmark, Estonia, Finland, Iceland, Latvia, Lithuania, Norway and Sweden.
**Including Australia, New Zealand, Singapore, Papua New Guinea and Fiji.

choicehotels.ca

We'll see you there.

CHOICE HOTELS CANADA℠

FANNY BAY pop. 766

SHIPS POINT INN B&B

Bed & Breakfast
$135-$185 All Year

Phone: 250/335-1004

Address: 7584 Ships Point Rd V0R 1W0 **Location:** Hwy 19, exit 87 to Hwy 19A, 4.3 mi (7 km) n, then 1.8 mi (3 km) e, follow signs. **Facility:** Along the edge of Fanny Bay, the secluded property enables guests to enjoy clam-farming activities and occasionally the seals and otters. Smoke free premises. 6 one-bedroom standard units. 2 stories (no elevator); interior corridors. *Bath:* combo or shower only. **Parking:** on-site. **Terms:** office hours 8 am-10 pm, age restrictions may apply, 7 day cancellation notice-fee imposed. **Amenities:** hair dryers. **Leisure Activities:** whirlpool. **Guest Services:** TV in common area, wireless Internet.

FERNIE pop. 4,217

BEST WESTERN FERNIE MOUNTAIN LODGE

Book great rates at AAA.com

Phone: (250)423-5500

(AAA) (SAVE)

Hotel
$136-$176 All Year

Address: 1622 7th Ave V0B 1M0 **Location:** Jct Hwy 3 and 7th Ave; east end of town. **Facility:** 95 units. 85 one-bedroom standard units, some with efficiencies and/or whirlpools. 10 one-bedroom suites, some with efficiencies and/or whirlpools. 3 stories, interior corridors. **Parking:** on-site, winter plug-ins. **Amenities:** high-speed Internet, voice mail, irons, hair dryers. **Dining:** 2 restaurants. **Pool(s):** heated indoor. **Leisure Activities:** whirlpools, exercise room. **Guest Services:** valet and coin laundry, wireless Internet. **Business Services:** meeting rooms, PC (fee). **Free Special Amenities:** local telephone calls and high-speed Internet.

AAA Benefit:
Members save up to
20%, plus 10%
bonus points with
rewards program.

CORNERSTONE LODGE

Phone: 250/423-6855

Condominium
$216-$382 12/24-2/28
$149-$294 3/1-12/23

Address: 5339 Ski Hill Rd V0B 1M6 **Location:** 4 mi (6.5 km) w on Hwy 3, then 0.8 mi (1.4 km) n. **Facility:** Smoke free premises. 26 units. 8 one- and 18 two-bedroom suites with kitchens. 3 stories, interior corridors. **Parking:** on-site, winter plug-ins. **Terms:** off-site registration, check-in 4 pm, 2 night minimum stay, 30 day cancellation notice-fee imposed. **Amenities:** high-speed Internet, hair dryers. *Some:* DVD players. **Leisure Activities:** whirlpool, downhill & cross country skiing, snowmobiling, limited exercise equipment. **Guest Services:** complimentary laundry.

LIZARD CREEK LODGE AND CONDOMINIUMS AT FERNIE ALPINE RESORT

Phone: 250/423-2057

(AAA) (SAVE)

Condominium
$145-$570 All Year

Address: 5346 Highline Dr V0B 1M6 **Location:** 4 mi (6.5 km) w on Hwy 3, 0.8 mi (1.4 km) on Ski Area Rd, follow signs. **Facility:** Featuring ski-in/ski-out access, this luxurious property offers a mix of lodge rooms in the main building as well as upscale, fully equipped condos. Smoke free premises. 99 units. 7 one-bedroom standard units with kitchens. 47 one-, 34 two- and 11 three-bedroom suites with kitchens. 3 stories, interior corridors. **Parking:** on-site. **Terms:** check-in 4 pm, 5 night minimum stay - seasonal, 30 day cancellation notice. **Amenities:** DVD players, dual phone lines, voice mail, irons, hair dryers. *Some:* high-speed Internet. **Dining:** Lizard Creek Lodge Dining Room, see separate listing. **Pool(s):** heated outdoor. **Leisure Activities:** whirlpools, steamroom, cross country skiing, ski lockers, recreation programs, hiking trails, exercise room. *Fee:* downhill skiing, snowmobiling, horseback riding, massage. **Guest Services:** valet and coin laundry, area transportation (fee)-within town, wireless Internet. **Business Services:** meeting rooms, PC (fee).

PARK PLACE LODGE

Book great rates at AAA.com

Phone: (250)423-6871

(AAA) (SAVE)

Hotel
$148-$298 12/12-2/28
$129-$269 3/1-12/11

Address: 742 Hwy 3 V0B 1M0 **Location:** At 7th St. **Facility:** 64 one-bedroom standard units, some with efficiencies or kitchens. 3 stories, interior corridors. **Parking:** on-site, winter plug-ins. **Terms:** check-in 4 pm, cancellation fee imposed. **Amenities:** DVD players, video games, CD players, high-speed Internet, voice mail, irons, hair dryers. **Pool(s):** heated indoor. **Leisure Activities:** sauna, whirlpool, hiking trails, exercise room. **Guest Services:** valet laundry, wireless Internet. **Business Services:** meeting rooms.

FREE local telephone calls and high-speed Internet

STANFORD HOTELS & RESORTS

Phone: 250/423-5000

Condominium
Rates not provided

Address: 100 Riverside Way V0B 1M1 **Location:** 1.2 mi (2 km) on Hwy 3. **Facility:** Smoke free premises. 144 units. 57 one-bedroom standard units. 11 one-, 47 two- and 29 three-bedroom suites with kitchens, some with whirlpools. 3 stories, interior/exterior corridors. **Parking:** on-site, winter plug-ins. **Terms:** check-in 5 pm. **Amenities:** voice mail, irons. *Some:* DVD players, CD players, high-speed Internet (fee), hair dryers. **Pool(s):** heated indoor. **Leisure Activities:** sauna, whirlpools, waterslide, fishing, downhill & cross country skiing, ice skating, hiking trails, playground, exercise room, spa. **Guest Services:** coin laundry, area transportation, wireless Internet. **Business Services:** meeting rooms, PC (fee).

SUPER 8-FERNIE   *Book at AAA.com*   Phone: (250)423-6788

▼▼ ▼▼
Hotel
$85-$119 All Year

Address: 2021 Hwy 3 V0B 1M1 **Location:** On Hwy 3; west end of town. **Facility:** Smoke free premises. 43 one-bedroom standard units. 3 stories, interior corridors. **Parking:** on-site, winter plug-ins. **Amenities:** hair dryers. **Leisure Activities:** whirlpool. **Guest Services:** coin laundry, wireless Internet.

—————— **WHERE TO DINE** ——————

THE BLUE TOQUE DINER   Phone: 250/423-4637

▼▼ ▼▼
Breakfast
$8-$10

In The Art Station, a historic Canadian Pacific Railway station, this tiny spot is a favorite with locals and visitors. It's known for all-day, one-of-a-kind breakfasts that are both delicious and beautifully presented. Fresh made-in-house soups, salads, sandwiches and desserts complete the lunch menu. Diners should expect a short wait at this popular spot. Casual dress. **Bar:** Full bar. **Hours:** 9 am-3 pm; seasonal hours vary. Closed: 12/25; also Tues & Wed. **Address:** 601 1st Ave V0B 1M0 **Location:** Corner of 6th St and 1st Ave. **Parking:** street.

KELSEY'S   Phone: 250/423-2444

▼▼ ▼▼
Canadian
$10-$24

A fun, relaxed atmosphere and tasty menu of casual fare make the restaurant a popular favorite with locals. Diners might start a meal with some tempting appetizers, such as wings, loaded potato skins or nachos, and follow them with an old-time favorite, such as a burger, wrap, pizza or pasta dish. For a heartier meal, it's hard to beat pork back ribs or a steak. The diverse menu has broad appeal. Casual dress. **Bar:** Full bar. **Reservations:** accepted. **Hours:** noon-8 pm, Fri & Sat-9 pm; winter hours vary. **Address:** 5339 Ski Hill Rd, Fernie Alpine Resort V0B 1M0 **Location:** At base of ski hill. **Parking:** on-site.

LIZARD CREEK LODGE DINING ROOM   Phone: 250/423-2057

▼▼ ▼▼ ▼▼
Canadian
$13-$42

Considered to be one of the best places in Fernie, this upscale dining room is a superb place for a fine meal. After a day on the ski hill, guests can explore a regional menu of creative dishes or more casual lunch offerings. During the winter, Sunday brunch is offered. Casual dress. **Bar:** Full bar. **Reservations:** suggested. **Hours:** 7 am-2:30 & 5:30-9 pm. **Address:** 5346 Highline Dr V0B 1M1 **Location:** 4 mi (6.5 km) w on Hwy 3, 0.8 mi (1.4 km) on Ski Area Rd, follow signs; in Lizard Creek Lodge and Condominiums at Fernie Alpine Resort. **Parking:** on-site. CALL Ⓛ Ⓜ

MUGSHOTS BISTRO   Phone: 250/423-8018

▼▼
Coffee/Tea
$4-$8

Quirky and eclectic best describe the funky coffeehouse, which prepares a wide selection of soups, sandwiches, ground coffees and sumptuous desserts. The downtown spot is popular with locals and visitors alike not only for its hearty, healthy food but also for the Internet cafe. Casual dress. **Reservations:** not accepted. **Hours:** 7 am-5 pm, Sun-4 pm. Closed: 10/11, 12/25. **Address:** 592 3rd Ave V0B 1M0 **Location:** Corner of 5th St and 3rd Ave; downtown. **Parking:** street. CALL Ⓛ Ⓜ

FORT NELSON pop. 4,514

LAKEVIEW INNS & SUITES   *Book great rates at AAA.com*   Phone: (250)233-5001

ⒸⒶⒶ SAVE
▼▼ ▼▼
Hotel
$137-$149 All Year

Address: 4507-50th Ave S V0C 1R0 **Location:** Just off Hwy 97 (Alaska Hwy); at 44th St. **Facility:** 82 units. 70 one-bedroom standard units, some with efficiencies and/or whirlpools. 8 one- and 4 two-bedroom suites with efficiencies and whirlpools. 4 stories, interior corridors. *Bath:* combo or shower only. **Parking:** on-site. **Terms:** cancellation fee imposed. **Amenities:** video library, DVD players, high-speed Internet, voice mail, irons, hair dryers. **Leisure Activities:** whirlpool, steamroom, limited exercise equipment. **Guest Services:** coin laundry, airport transportation-Fort Nelson Airport, wireless Internet. **Business Services:** meeting rooms, business center. **Free Special Amenities:** expanded continental breakfast and local telephone calls.

WOODLANDS INN   *Book great rates at AAA.com*   Phone: (250)774-6669

ⒸⒶⒶ SAVE
▼▼ ▼▼
Hotel
$149-$169 All Year

Address: 3995 50th Ave S V0C 1R0 **Location:** On Hwy 97 (Alaska Hwy). **Facility:** 131 units. 117 one-bedroom standard units. 14 one-bedroom suites, some with efficiencies or kitchens. 4 stories, interior corridors. **Parking:** on-site, winter plug-ins. **Terms:** 7 day cancellation notice-fee imposed. **Amenities:** video games (fee), high-speed Internet, hair dryers. **Dining:** The One, see separate listing. **Leisure Activities:** whirlpool, steamroom, exercise room. **Guest Services:** coin laundry. **Business Services:** meeting rooms, PC.

—————— **WHERE TO DINE** ——————

THE ONE   Phone: (250)774-6669

▼▼ ▼▼
Canadian
$12-$39

Newly designed, this contemporary dining room features comfortable banquettes with blue lights along the baseboards to lead the way, great lighting and dark wood accents. Menu highlights include a variety of Alberta beef, salmon, halibut, burgers, pasta, pizza and other Canadian fare. Service is friendly. Casual dress. **Bar:** Full bar. **Hours:** 6 am-1:30 & 5-9 pm, Sun from 6:30 am. Closed: 12/24, 12/25. **Address:** 3995 50th Ave S V0C 1R0 **Location:** On Hwy 97 (Alaska Hwy); in Woodlands Inn. **Parking:** on-site. CALL Ⓛ Ⓜ

FORT ST. JOHN pop. 16,034

COACHMAN INN   Phone: (250)787-0651

ⒸⒶⒶ SAVE
▼▼ ▼▼
Hotel
$150 All Year

Address: 8540 Alaska Rd V1J 5L6 **Location:** 1.2 mi (2 km) s on Hwy 97 (Alaska Hwy). **Facility:** 70 one-bedroom standard units. 2 stories (no elevator), interior corridors. **Parking:** on-site, winter plug-ins. **Amenities:** irons, hair dryers. *Some:* DVD players. **Leisure Activities:** sauna, whirlpool, limited exercise equipment. **Guest Services:** valet laundry, wireless Internet. **Business Services:** meeting rooms, PC. **Free Special Amenities:** local telephone calls and high-speed Internet.

LAKEVIEW INNS & SUITES   *Book great rates at AAA.com*   Phone: (250)787-0779

Hotel
$109-$129 All Year

Address: 10103 98th Ave V1J 1P8 **Location:** Corner of 100th Ave; centre of downtown. **Facility:** 72 one-bedroom standard units, some with efficiencies and/or whirlpools. 3 stories (no elevator), interior corridors. *Bath:* combo or shower only. **Parking:** on-site, winter plug-ins. **Terms:** cancellation fee imposed. **Amenities:** video library, DVD players, high-speed Internet, voice mail, irons, hair dryers. **Leisure Activities:** whirlpool, exercise room. **Guest Services:** valet and coin laundry, wireless Internet. **Business Services:** meeting rooms, PC. **Free Special Amenities: expanded continental breakfast and local telephone calls.**

POMEROY HOTEL   *Book great rates at AAA.com*   Phone: (250)262-3233

Hotel
$169-$249 6/1-2/28
$169-$229 3/1-5/31

Address: 11308 Alaska Rd V1J 5T5 **Location:** Just w on Hwy 97 (Alaska Hwy). **Facility:** This sparkling hotel offers a wide variety of guest rooms, all with wet bar areas, large desks and the hotel's signature Opulence Sleep System. 125 units. 86 one-bedroom standard units, some with kitchens and/or whirlpools. 39 one-bedroom suites, some with kitchens. 3 stories, interior corridors. *Bath:* combo or shower only. **Parking:** on-site, winter plug-ins. **Amenities:** high-speed Internet, voice mail, irons, hair dryers. **Pool(s):** heated indoor. **Leisure Activities:** whirlpool, waterslide, exercise room. **Guest Services:** coin laundry, airport transportation-Fort St. John Regional Airport, wireless Internet. **Business Services:** PC.

POMEROY INN & SUITES   Phone: (250)262-3030

Extended Stay Hotel
$149-$169 All Year

Address: 9304 Alaska Rd V1J 6Z5 **Location:** Just s on Hwy 97 (Alaska Hwy). **Facility:** 92 units. 60 one-bedroom standard units, some with kitchens and/or whirlpools. 32 one-bedroom suites with kitchens. 4 stories, interior corridors. *Bath:* combo or shower only. **Parking:** on-site. **Amenities:** video games (fee), high-speed Internet, voice mail, irons, hair dryers. **Leisure Activities:** exercise room. **Guest Services:** valet laundry, wireless Internet. **Business Services:** PC.

QUALITY INN NORTHERN GRAND   *Book at AAA.com*   Phone: (250)787-0521

Hotel
$129-$174 All Year

Address: 9830 100th Ave V1J 1Y5 **Location:** Centre. **Facility:** Smoke free premises. 125 units. 124 one-bedroom standard units, some with whirlpools. 1 one-bedroom suite. 6 stories, interior corridors. **Parking:** on-site, winter plug-ins. **Amenities:** voice mail, irons, hair dryers. *Some:* DVD players, CD players. **Pool(s):** heated indoor. **Leisure Activities:** sauna, whirlpool, exercise room. **Guest Services:** valet laundry, wireless Internet. **Business Services:** conference facilities, PC.

SUPER 8-FORT ST. JOHN   *Book great rates at AAA.com*   Phone: (250)785-7588

Hotel
$150-$160 All Year

Address: 9500 Alaska Hwy V1J 6S7 **Location:** Just s on Hwy 97 (Alaska Hwy). **Facility:** 93 units. 85 one-bedroom standard units. 8 one-bedroom suites, some with whirlpools. 4 stories, interior corridors. *Bath:* combo or shower only. **Parking:** on-site, winter plug-ins. **Terms:** cancellation fee imposed. **Amenities:** high-speed Internet, voice mail, irons, hair dryers. **Pool(s):** heated indoor. **Leisure Activities:** whirlpool, waterslide, exercise room. **Guest Services:** valet and coin laundry, airport transportation-Fort St. John Regional Airport. **Business Services:** meeting rooms, PC. **Free Special Amenities: expanded continental breakfast and high-speed Internet.**

WHERE TO DINE

MASTARO SUSHI   Phone: 250/261-6595

Japanese
$10-$20

Almost a thousand kilometers from the nearest coast, the restaurant nevertheless prepares an expansive selection of sushi and sashimi, in addition to classic appetizers such as edamame (salted soy beans) and gyoza (dumplings). The menu also lists many noodle dishes, pan-fried yakisoba and udon soups, rice items and teriyaki. Casual dress. **Bar:** Full bar. **Reservations:** accepted. **Hours:** 11:30 am-3 & 5-10 pm, Sat & Sun from 5 pm. Closed: 1/1, 12/24, 12/25. **Address:** 9823-100th St V1J 3Y2 **Location:** Downtown. **Parking:** on-site.

UPTOWN GRILL   Phone: 250/787-9085

International
$8-$34

The chef-owner prides himself on making everything from scratch, and it shows in the quality. The menu creatively blends items from around the world, including Creole or tandoori chicken, Moroccan chickpea stew and St. Louis barbecue ribs. King crab, lobster and steaks are also available. Entrees all start off with a salad or soup, and the made-in-house desserts here are a must. Diners can eat from the lunchtime buffet, order from the menu or opt for the weeknight international set menu. Casual dress. **Bar:** Full bar. **Reservations:** suggested. **Hours:** 11:30 am-2:30 & 4-9 pm, Sat & Sun from 4 pm. Closed major holidays. **Address:** 9924 101st Ave V1J 2B2 **Location:** Downtown. **Parking:** street.

FORT STEELE

BULL RIVER GUEST RANCH   Phone: 250/429-3760

Resort Hotel
Rates not provided

Address: 2975 Bull River Rd V1C 4H7 **Location:** Hwy 95, 12.9 mi (21.4 km) se of town on Ft Steele-Wardner Rd, 7.2 mi (12 km) ne on gravel road; Hwy 3 W, 24.6 mi (41 km) e of Cranbrook, 5 mi (8.2 km) n on Ft Steele-Wardner Rd, 7.2 mi (12 km) ne on gravel road. Located in a quiet rustic area. **Facility:** This working ranch offers one-bedroom log cabins in a scenic mountain setting; a two-night minimum stay is required. Smoke free premises. 12 units. 4 one-bedroom standard units. 8 cabins. 1 story, exterior corridors. *Bath:* shower only. **Parking:** on-site. **Amenities:** hair dryers. **Leisure Activities:** sauna, whirlpools, canoeing, fishing, bicycles, hiking trails, jogging, playground, horseshoes, volleyball. *Fee:* horseback riding. **Guest Services:** complimentary laundry, wireless Internet. **Business Services:** meeting rooms, PC.

GALIANO ISLAND—See Gulf Islands p. 524.

GIBSONS pop. 4,182

BONNIEBROOK LODGE OCEANFRONT INN

Phone: (604)886-2887

Country Inn
$129-$299 All Year

Address: 1532 Ocean Beach Esplanade V0N 1V5 **Location:** Hwy 101, 3.8 mi (6 km) s on Veterans Rd to Fichett St, just sw to King St, 0.6 mi (1 km) sw to Chaster, then 5 mi (8 km) sw to Gowers Pt Rd, follow signs. **Facility:** Guest suites in the 1922 lodge are reserved strictly for adults while the cottages behind the lodge are ideal for families. Smoke free premises. 7 one-bedroom standard units with whirlpools. 1-3 stories (no elevator), interior/exterior corridors. **Parking:** on-site. **Terms:** office hours 9 am-6 pm, check-in 4 pm, 1-5 night minimum stay, 7 day cancellation notice-fee imposed. **Amenities:** video library (fee), DVD players, high-speed Internet, hair dryers. **Leisure Activities:** beach access. **Guest Services:** wireless Internet.

CEDARS INN HOTEL & CONVENTION CENTRE

Phone: (604)886-3008

Motel
$94-$156 All Year

Address: 895 Gibsons Way V0N 1V0 **Location:** Hwy 101 and Shaw Rd; 3.8 mi (6 km) n from ferry terminal. Opposite Sunnycrest Mall. **Facility:** 45 one-bedroom standard units, some with efficiencies. 2 stories (no elevator), interior/exterior corridors. *Bath:* combo or shower only. **Parking:** on-site. **Terms:** office hours 7 am-11 pm, cancellation fee imposed. **Amenities:** voice mail, irons, hair dryers. **Pool(s):** heated outdoor. **Leisure Activities:** sauna, whirlpool, limited exercise equipment. **Guest Services:** valet laundry, wireless Internet. **Business Services:** meeting rooms, PC. **Free Special Amenities:** continental breakfast and high-speed Internet.

------ **WHERE TO DINE** ------

MOLLY'S REACH RESTAURANT

Phone: 604/886-9710

Canadian
$6-$17

The famous landmark originally was built as a set for "The Beachcombers," a popular CBC TV series of the late '70s and early '80s. Today, it's a family restaurant that serves a mix of seafood, steaks, sandwiches and soups. This place is well worth the stop for the memories alone. Casual dress. **Bar:** Full bar. **Reservations:** accepted. **Hours:** 9 am-9 pm. Closed: 12/25. **Address:** 647 School Rd V0N 1V0 **Location:** School Rd and Gibsons Way; on waterfront. **Parking:** on-site.

GOLD BRIDGE

MORROW CHALETS

Phone: 250/238-2462

Vacation Rental Cottage
$275-$375 All Year

Address: 2440 Gun Creek Rd V0K 1P0 **Location:** 5 mi (8 km) n from the Tyaughton Lake turnoff, follow signs. **Facility:** These huge, self-contained log cabins on the shores of Tyaughton Lake can accommodate six or more persons; summer and winter activities are available. Smoke free premises. 3 cottages. 2 stories (no elevator), exterior corridors. **Parking:** on-site. **Terms:** office hours 8 am-8 pm, check-in 4 pm, 30 day cancellation notice-fee imposed. **Amenities:** video library, DVD players, hair dryers. **Leisure Activities:** canoeing. **Guest Services:** complimentary laundry, wireless Internet.

TYAX MOUNTAIN LAKE RESORT

Phone: (250)238-2221

Resort
Hotel
$169-$203 5/15-10/15

Address: Tyaughton Lake Rd V0K 1P0 **Location:** 5 mi (8 km) n from the Tyaughton Lake turnoff, follow signs. **Facility:** A log lodge and log chalets are featured at this resort offering family-oriented wilderness activities. Smoke free premises. 32 units. 28 one-bedroom standard units. 4 cottages. 2 stories (no elevator), interior corridors. **Parking:** on-site. **Terms:** open 5/15-10/15, office hours 7 am-11 pm, check-in 4 pm, 60 day cancellation notice-fee imposed. **Amenities:** voice mail, hair dryers. **Leisure Activities:** sauna, whirlpool, canoeing, paddleboats, fishing, hiking trails, playground, limited exercise equipment. **Fee:** bicycles, horseback riding. **Guest Services:** coin laundry. **Business Services:** meeting rooms, PC.

GOLDEN pop. 3,811

BEST WESTERN MOUNTAIN VIEW INN

Book great rates at AAA.com

Phone: (250)344-2333

Hotel
$139-$189 3/1-9/30
$129-$179 10/1-2/28

Address: 1024 11th St N V0A 1H2 **Location:** Just w of jct Hwy 95 and Trans-Canada Hwy 1; on S Service Rd. **Facility:** 71 one-bedroom standard units. 3 stories, interior corridors. **Parking:** on-site, winter plug-ins. **Amenities:** video games (fee), irons, hair dryers. *Some:* high-speed Internet. **Pool(s):** heated indoor. **Leisure Activities:** ATV tours. *Fee:* whitewater rafting, snowmobile tours. **Guest Services:** valet and coin laundry, wireless Internet. **Business Services:** PC. **Free Special Amenities:** early check-in/late check-out and high-speed Internet.

COLUMBIA VALLEY B&B

Phone: 250/348-2508

Bed & Breakfast
$95-$145 All Year

Address: 2304 Hwy 95 S V0A 1H4 **Location:** 14.4 mi (24 km) s of jct Trans-Canada Hwy 1. **Facility:** Smoke free premises. 4 units. 3 one- and 1 two-bedroom standard units. 2 stories (no elevator), interior/exterior corridors. **Parking:** on-site, winter plug-ins. **Terms:** office hours 7 am-midnight, check-in 4 pm, 3 day cancellation notice-fee imposed. **Leisure Activities:** rental canoes. **Guest Services:** wireless Internet.

GOLDEN RIM MOTOR INN

Phone: (250)344-2216

Motel
$79-$185 All Year

Address: 1416 Golden View Rd V0A 1H1 **Location:** On Trans-Canada Hwy 1, 1 mi (1.6 km) e of jct Hwy 95. **Facility:** 81 units. 78 one-bedroom standard units, some with kitchens and/or whirlpools. 3 two-bedroom suites with whirlpools. 2-3 stories (no elevator), exterior corridors. **Parking:** on-site, winter plug-ins. **Amenities:** hair dryers. *Some:* DVD players, irons. **Pool(s):** heated indoor. **Leisure Activities:** sauna, whirlpool, waterslide. **Guest Services:** coin laundry, wireless Internet. **Business Services:** PC.

HILLSIDE LODGE & CHALETS

Phone: (250)344-7281

Cabin
$138-$260 All Year

Address: 1740 Seward Frontage Rd V0A 1H0 **Location:** 9.4 mi (15 km) w on Hwy 1, follow signs n off highway. Located in a quiet area. **Facility:** Spectacular mountain scenery and the sound of moving water give this lodge's grounds a serene sense of place; offerings include cabins and B&B rooms. Smoke free premises. 12 units. 4 one-bedroom standard units. 8 cabins. 1-2 stories, exterior corridors. *Bath:* combo or shower only. **Parking:** on-site, winter plug-ins. **Terms:** 5 day cancellation notice-fee imposed. **Amenities:** hair dryers. *Some:* DVD players. **Leisure Activities:** sauna, whirlpool, steamroom, cross country skiing, hiking trails, limited exercise equipment. **Free Special Amenities:** full breakfast.

—————— **WHERE TO DINE** ——————

CEDAR HOUSE CAFE & RESTAURANT

Phone: 250/344-4679

Canadian
$15-$38

Rocky Mountain organic dining is what's to be expected at the small, bistro-style restaurant. The cozy, comfortable dining room has many rustic features, yet a surprising elegance. Menu selections ranging from salmon to lamb to other Canadian specialties often incorporate produce grown in the chef's own garden. Service is laid-back and friendly, and even the owner has been known to come out and greet guests. Casual dress. **Bar:** Full bar. **Reservations:** suggested. **Hours:** Open 3/1-4/12 & 6/4-2/28; 5 pm-10:30 pm. Closed: 1/1; also Mon. **Address:** 735 Hefti Rd V0A 1H2 **Location:** 4.6 mi (7.4 km) s of town, just e at Almberg Rd, follow signs. **Parking:** on-site.

ELEVEN 22 GRILL & LIQUIDS

Phone: 250/344-2443

Western Canadian
$11-$25

The charming eatery's international menu lists health-conscious curries, pastas, salads, hummus, tzatziki, spanakopita and burgers. A weekly fondue is a treat in winter. The restored centennial home nurtures a warm, casual ambience. Casual dress. **Bar:** Full bar. **Reservations:** suggested. **Hours:** 5 pm-10 pm; call for days in spring & fall. **Address:** 1122 10th Ave S V0A 1H0 **Location:** Just e at 12th St; centre. **Parking:** on-site.

GOLDEN BAKERY & DELI

Phone: 250/344-2928

Deli
$3-$7

One of the town's best-kept secrets, the simple delicatessen and bakery serves homemade soups, salads and sandwiches, along with a huge selection of sweets. Just off the highway, the eatery invites guests to dine in or get their food to go. Don't bypass the display case of treats. Casual dress. **Hours:** 6 am-6 pm. Closed: Sun. **Address:** 415 N 9th Ave V0A 1H0 **Location:** Just w off Hwy 95; downtown. **Parking:** street.

THE KICKING HORSE GRILL

Phone: 250/344-2330

International
$19-$38

The restaurant's small lodge-like interior is perfect for a casual meal with friends. Dark wood beams criss-cross the ceiling and line the walls, creating a true Rocky Mountain feel. Interesting and eclectic menu choices draw on many influences, ranging from Asian to Swedish and even some Canadian elements. Casual dress. **Bar:** Full bar. **Reservations:** suggested. **Hours:** 4:30 pm-10 pm. Closed: 1/1. **Address:** 1105 9th St S V0A 1H0 **Location:** Hwy 95, just e; downtown. **Parking:** on-site.

LEGENDZ DINER

Phone: 250/344-5059

Canadian
$8-$18

Appointed in a 1950s theme, the diner is a popular stopover for residents and those just passing through. In addition to an extensive list of diner classics, this place prepares burgers, steaks and some hot entrees. The homemade pies are legendary. Casual dress. **Bar:** Beer & wine. **Reservations:** accepted. **Hours:** 7 am-11 pm. Closed: 12/24, 12/25. **Address:** 1405 N Trans-Canada Hwy V0A 1H0 **Location:** Jct Trans-Canada Hwy 1 and 95, 0.6 mi (1 km) n. **Parking:** on-site.

GRAND FORKS pop. 4,036

RAMADA LIMITED

Book at AAA.com

Phone: 250/442-2127

Motel
Rates not provided

Address: 2729 Central Ave V0H 1H2 **Location:** West end of town on Hwy 3. **Facility:** 45 units. 38 one- and 5 two-bedroom standard units, some with efficiencies, kitchens and/or whirlpools. 1 one- and 1 two-bedroom suites with kitchens. 2 stories (no elevator), exterior corridors. **Parking:** on-site. **Amenities:** voice mail, irons, hair dryers. **Pool(s):** heated outdoor. **Guest Services:** wireless Internet. **Business Services:** PC.

WESTERN TRAVELLER MOTEL

Phone: (250)442-5566

Motel
$64-$139 All Year

Address: 1591 Central Ave V0H 1H0 **Location:** West end of town on Hwy 3. **Facility:** 34 units. 32 one-bedroom standard units, some with efficiencies. 2 one-bedroom suites. 2 stories (no elevator), exterior corridors. **Parking:** on-site. **Terms:** office hours 7 am-midnight, cancellation fee imposed. **Amenities:** irons, hair dryers. **Guest Services:** wireless Internet. **Business Services:** meeting rooms, PC (fee). **Free Special Amenities:** local telephone calls and high-speed Internet.

Gulf Islands

GALIANO ISLAND pop. 1,258

GALIANO OCEANFRONT INN & SPA

Phone: (250)539-3388

Hotel
$199-$425 All Year

Address: 134 Madrona Dr V0N 1P0 **Location:** From Sturdies Bay ferry terminal, just ne on Sturdies Bay Rd. **Facility:** Smoke free premises. 20 units. 10 one-bedroom standard units, some with whirlpools. 10 one-bedroom suites with kitchens and whirlpools. 2 stories (no elevator), interior/exterior corridors. **Parking:** on-site. **Terms:** office hours 8 am-4:6 pm, 7 day cancellation notice-fee imposed. **Amenities:** CD players, hair dryers. *Some:* DVD players, irons. **Dining:** eat@ Galiano Inn Restaurant, see separate listing. **Leisure Activities:** whirlpool, spa, yoga classes. **Guest Services:** wireless Internet. **Business Services:** meeting rooms.

ASK 🍴 🍽 CALL 🚵M ✖ 🐦 📞 📋 / SOME UNITS FEE 🐾 📱

------ **WHERE TO DINE** ------

EAT@ GALIANO INN RESTAURANT

Phone: 250/539-3388

Pacific Rim
$9-$30

The waterfront restaurant serves delightful West Coast cuisine prepared with fresh local ingredients, including Salt Spring Island organic goat cheese and West Coast seafood. A fine selection of British Columbia wines complements the fare. Hours vary in the off-season, so call ahead. Casual dress. **Bar:** Full bar. **Reservations:** required, for dinner. **Hours:** 6 pm-10 pm; also 9 am-3 pm 7/1-9/4. Closed: 12/25. **Address:** 134 Madrona Dr V0N 1P0 **Location:** From Sturdies Bay ferry terminal, just ne on Sturdies Bay Rd; in Galiano Oceanfront Inn & Spa. **Parking:** on-site. 🐦

GALIANO GRAND CENTRAL EMPORIUM

Phone: 250/539-9885

Canadian
$7-$18

Not far from the Sturdies Bay ferry terminal, this simple restaurant is one of few open all year long. The building isn't much to look at, but the food is really good, and it's a great place to stop while waiting for the ferry. Guests are invited to order from the wall-mounted, blackboard-style menu, grab a seat and enjoy daily homemade soups, lunch sandwiches and morning breakfasts. Casual dress. **Bar:** Full bar. **Hours:** 7 am-8 pm; to midnight 6/15-9/4. Closed: 12/25. **Address:** 2740 Sturdies Bay, S24 C31 Rd V0N 1P0 **Location:** Just nw of Sturdies Bay Ferry Terminal. **Parking:** on-site. 🐦

HUMMINGBIRD INN PUB

Phone: 250/539-5472

Canadian
$7-$18

Dining choices on the island are limited, but those who visit the adult-oriented pub can expect pub-style food. Casual dress. **Bar:** Full bar. **Hours:** 11 am-11 pm. Closed: 12/25. **Address:** 47 Sturdies Bay Rd V0N 1P0 **Location:** From Sturdies Bay ferry terminal, 1.8 mi (3 km) nw. **Parking:** on-site. 🐦

PENDER ISLAND

POETS COVE RESORT & SPA

Phone: (250)629-2100

CAA SAVE

Hotel
$189-$299 All Year

Address: 9801 Spalding Rd, South Pender Island V0N 2M3 **Location:** From Otter Bay Ferry Terminal, follow signs to South Pender Island, then 10 mi (16 km) s; Otter Bay Rd to Bidwell Harbour Rd to Canal Rd. **Facility:** Smoke free premises. 46 units. 22 one-bedroom standard units. 24 cottages. 1-3 stories, interior/exterior corridors. **Parking:** on-site and valet. **Terms:** check-in 4 pm, 3 day cancellation notice-fee imposed. **Amenities:** DVD players, high-speed Internet, voice mail, irons, hair dryers. **Pool(s):** 2 heated outdoor. **Leisure Activities:** whirlpools, exercise room, spa. *Fee:* marina. **Guest Services:** coin laundry, wireless Internet. **Business Services:** meeting rooms, PC.

🍴 🍽 🏊 ✖ ✖ 🐦 📞 📋 / SOME UNITS FEE 🐾 📱

------ **WHERE TO DINE** ------

AURORA RESTAURANT

Phone: 250/629-2115

Canadian
$25-$45

You will find this restaurant inside Pender Island's newest upscale lodging; all tables overlook the marina. Enjoy a cuisine that uses only the highest quality ingredients specially brought in just for this restaurant. Dinner is very popular so reservations are a must. Casual dress. **Bar:** Full bar. **Reservations:** required, for dinner. **Hours:** 7:30 am-11:30 & 6-9 pm. **Address:** 9801 Spalding Rd V0N 2M3 **Location:** From Otter Bay Ferry Terminal, follow signs to South Pender Island, then 10 mi (16 km) s; Otter Bay Rd to Bidwell Harbour Rd to Canal Rd; in Poets Cove Resort & Spa. **Parking:** on-site and valet. CALL 🚵M 🐦

QUADRA ISLAND

TAKU RESORT & MARINA

Phone: (250)285-3031

Motel
$89-$305 All Year

Address: 616 Taku Rd V0P 1H0 **Location:** From Campbell River ferry terminal, 4.1 mi (6.6 km) n on West Rd, then just e on Heriot Bay Rd, follow signs to Heriot Bay. **Facility:** Smoke free premises. 14 units. 5 one- and 4 two-bedroom standard units, some with efficiencies, kitchens and/or whirlpools. 5 cabins. 1 story, exterior corridors. **Parking:** on-site. **Terms:** office hours 8 am-8 pm, check-in 4 pm, 2 night minimum stay - seasonal, 30 day cancellation notice-fee imposed. **Amenities:** hair dryers. *Some:* DVD players. **Leisure Activities:** whirlpool, fishing, tennis court, basketball, horseshoes, volleyball. *Fee:* boat dock. **Guest Services:** coin laundry, wireless Internet. **Business Services:** PC.

🍴 ✖ ✖ 🐦 📞 📋 / SOME UNITS FEE 🐾 🌮

TSA-KWA-LUTEN LODGE

Phone: (250)285-2042

Hotel
$105-$380 4/18-10/12

Address: 1 Lighthouse Rd V0P 1N0 **Location:** From Campbell River ferry terminal, just se on Green Rd, 0.6 mi (1 km) e on Noble Rd, 1.8 mi (2.9 km) se on Cape Mudge Rd to Joyce Rd, 0.6 mi (1 km) sw, then 1.4 mi (2.2 km) s. **Facility:** Smoke free premises. 36 units. 30 one-bedroom standard units, some with whirlpools. 6 cottages. 1-2 stories (no elevator), interior/exterior corridors. **Parking:** on-site. **Terms:** open 4/18-10/12, 3 day cancellation notice-fee imposed. **Amenities:** voice mail, irons, hair dryers. **Dining:** Hama Elas Dining Room, see separate listing. **Leisure Activities:** sauna, whirlpool, bicycles, exercise room, horseshoes. *Fee:* charter fishing. **Guest Services:** TV in common area, wireless Internet. **Business Services:** meeting rooms, PC.

ASK ❘¶ 🍸 CALL M ✕ ✕ ✕ W ▭ / SOME UNITS ❚ ▭

WHERE TO DINE

HAMA ELAS DINING ROOM

Phone: 250/285-2042

Seafood
$12-$28

The menu centers on a native theme and lists North American dishes familiar to many guests, such as steak, pasta and chicken. Casual dress. **Bar:** Full bar. **Reservations:** suggested. **Hours:** Open 4/15-10/15; 7:30 am-9 pm. **Address:** 1 Lighthouse Rd V0P 1N0 **Location:** From Campbell River ferry terminal, just se on Green Rd, 0.6 mi (1 km) e on Noble Rd, 1.8 mi (2.9 km) se on Cape Mudge Rd to Joyce Rd, 0.6 mi (1 km) sw, then 1.4 mi (2.2 km) s; in Tsa-Kwa-Luten Lodge. **Parking:** on-site. CALL M

SALT SPRING ISLAND pop. 9,780

ANNE'S OCEANFRONT HIDEAWAY B & B

Phone: 250/537-0851

Bed & Breakfast
$185-$225 All Year

Address: 168 Simson Rd V8K 1E2 **Location:** From Ganges Township, just n, 1.8 mi (3 km) w on Vesuvius Bay Rd, 3.7 mi (6 km) n on Sunset Dr. Located in a quiet secluded area. **Facility:** As the name suggests, this is truly a hideaway; on a hillside overlooking the ocean, the inn offers a wrap-around veranda, perfect for boat watching. Smoke free premises. 3 one-bedroom standard units with whirlpools. 2 stories, interior corridors. **Parking:** on-site. **Terms:** office hours 6 am-11 pm, 2 night minimum stay - seasonal and/or weekends, 10 day cancellation notice-fee imposed. **Amenities:** CD players, hair dryers. **Guest Services:** wireless Internet. CALL M ✕ 📷 ❚

HARBOUR HOUSE HOTEL

Phone: 250/537-5571

Hotel
$79-$199 All Year

Address: 121 Upper Ganges Rd V8K 2S2 **Location:** 0.6 mi (1 km) n on Lower Ganges Rd, then just e, towards Long Harbour ferry terminal. **Facility:** Designated smoking area. 36 one-bedroom standard units, some with whirlpools. 2 stories (no elevator), interior/exterior corridors. *Bath:* combo or shower only. **Parking:** on-site. **Terms:** cancellation fee imposed. **Amenities:** voice mail, hair dryers. *Some:* irons. **Dining:** restaurant, see separate listing. **Guest Services:** wireless Internet. **Business Services:** meeting rooms. ASK ❘¶ 🍸 CALL M ✕ 📷 ▭ / SOME UNITS FEE 🐾 ✕ ❚ ▭

SALT SPRINGS SPA RESORT

Phone: 250/537-4111

Vacation Rental Cottage
Rates not provided

Address: 1460 N Beach Rd V8K 1J4 **Location:** From Ganges Township, 4.9 mi (8 km) n on North End Rd, 0.6 mi (1 km) ne on Fernwood Rd, then 0.6 mi (1.8 km) nw. **Facility:** Each self-contained cottage features a hydro-jet tub filled with healing mineral water that is drawn from an underground spring. Smoke free premises. 13 units. 1 two-bedroom suite with kitchen. 12 cottages. 1 story, exterior corridors. **Parking:** on-site. **Terms:** office hours 8:30 am-8:30 pm, check-in 4 pm. **Amenities:** hair dryers. **Leisure Activities:** bicycles, spa, yoga. **Guest Services:** coin laundry, wireless Internet.

✕ ✕ W 🏊 ❚ ▭ ▭

SEABREEZE INNE

Phone: 250/537-4145

Motel
Rates not provided

Address: 101 Bittancourt Rd V8K 2K2 **Location:** From Ganges Township, 0.6 mi (1 km) s on Fulford-Ganges Rd. **Facility:** Smoke free premises. 25 one-bedroom standard units, some with efficiencies and/or whirlpools. 2 stories (no elevator), exterior corridors. **Parking:** on-site. **Terms:** office hours 8 am-8 pm. **Amenities:** voice mail, irons, hair dryers. **Leisure Activities:** whirlpool. **Guest Services:** coin laundry, wireless Internet. ✕ 📷 ❚ ▭ / SOME UNITS FEE 🐾 ✕ ▭

The following lodging was either not evaluated or did not meet AAA rating requirements but is listed for your information only.

HASTINGS HOUSE COUNTRY HOUSE HOTEL

Phone: 250/537-2362

fyi

Not evaluated. **Address:** 160 Upper Ganges Rd V8K 2S2 **Location:** 0.6 mi (1 km) n on Lower Ganges Rd, then just e; towards Long Harbour ferry terminal. Facilities, services, and decor characterize an upscale property.

WHERE TO DINE

BARB'S BUNS/BAKERY & BISTRO

Phone: 250/537-4491

Breads/Pastries
$9-$20

The mouthwatering aromas of fresh bread, pastries and coffee hang in the air at the vibrant and busy bohemian spot, where healthy vegetarian breakfasts and lunches are built around organic ingredients. Leaving without a bag of carry-out baked goods should be a crime. Casual dress. **Hours:** 7 am-5 pm. Closed: 1/1, 12/25, 12/26; also Sun. **Address:** 1-121 McPhillips Ave V8K 2T6 **Location:** In Ganges Township; from Lower Ganges Rd, just w; centre. **Parking:** street. ✕

CALVIN'S SALTSPRING ISLAND BISTRO
Phone: 250/538-555

◇◇ ◇◇
Canadian
$10-$30

In the heart of the Ganges township right near the water, this simple bistro-style restaurant offers heart' meals like burgers, sandwiches and soups as well as a number of desserts. There's a choice of boot' seating or tables set up near the large windows, which boast a great view of the water. Casual dress. Bar Full bar. Reservations: suggested. Hours: Open 3/1-12/31 & 2/1-2/28; 11:30 am-2 & 5-9 pm, Sun from pm 5/8-9/6; seasonal hours & days may vary. Closed: 12/25; also Mon. Address: 133 Lower Ganges R V8K 2T2 Location: In Ganges Township; corner of Hereford Ave. Parking: street. 🅰️

HARBOUR HOUSE RESTAURANT & LOUNGE
Phone: 250/537-470

◇◇ ◇◇
Canadian
$6-$22

Views of Ganges Harbour are excellent both from the nicely decorated dining room, which has tables se against the window, and the spacious garden patio. The menu focuses on down-home Canadian fare including daily specials. Servers merit acknowledgement for their attentiveness. Casual dress. Bar: Full ba Reservations: accepted. Hours: 7 am-11 pm. Address: 121 Upper Ganges Rd V8K 2S2 Location: 0.6 m (1 km) n on Lower Ganges Rd, then just e, towards Long Harbour ferry terminal; in Harbour House Parking: on-site. 🅰️

HASTINGS HOUSE DINING ROOM
Phone: 250/537-236 2

CAA

◇◇ ◇◇ ◇◇ ◇◇
Pacific Northwest
$36-$45

This restaurant holds a truly wonderful dining experience. Each dinner guest receives his or her ow personalized menu, which features a pre-set, four-course chef's tasting meal as well as an a la carte menu The last seating is at 8 pm. Dressy casual. Bar: Full bar. Reservations: suggested. Hours: Open 3/15 11/15; 5:30 pm-8 pm. Address: 160 Upper Ganges Rd V8K 2S2 Location: 0.6 mi (1 km) n on Lowe Ganges Rd, then just e, towards Long Harbour ferry terminal; in Hastings House Country House Hotel Parking: on-site. 🅰️

RESTAURANT HOUSE PICCOLO
Phone: 250/537-184

◇◇ ◇◇
Continental
$27-$36

Reservations are a good idea at the cozy restaurant. Its location in a small house nestled away from th busy shops of Ganges offers limited seats amid its tightly spaced tables. An impressive selection c reasonably priced wines pair with delightful Scandinavian and European standards and seafoo preparations. Casual dress. Bar: Full bar. Reservations: suggested, required 8/1-9/30. Hours: 5 pm-9:3 pm. Closed: 12/25, 12/26; also Sun & Mon. Address: 108 Hereford Ave V8K 2V9 Location: In Gange Township; cross street Lower Ganges Rd. Parking: street. 🅰️

The previous listings were for the Gulf Islands.
This page resumes the alphabetical listings of cities in British Columbia.

HALFMOON BAY pop. 417

——— *The following lodging was either not evaluated or did not* ———
meet AAA rating requirements but is listed for your information only.

ROCKWATER SECRET COVE RESORT
Phone: 604/885-703

Hotel

Did not meet all AAA rating requirements for locking devices in some guest rooms at time of las evaluation on 05/19/2009. Address: 5356 Ole Rd V0N 1Y2 Location: 4.4 mi (7 km) n on Hwy 101 follow signs. Facilities, services, and decor characterize a mid-scale property.

——— WHERE TO DINE ———

ROCKWATER SECRET COVE RESORT
RESTAURANT
Phone: 604/885-703

CAA

◇◇ ◇◇
Pacific Northwest
$12-$32

Diners are treated to stunning water views from every table. Among offerings of wonderful West Coas cuisine are a fish of the day, as well as rack of lamb and hearty steaks. The homemade chuck steak burge is a good lunch choice. Casual dress. Bar: Full bar. Reservations: suggested, for dinner. Hours: 11:30 am 3 & 5:30-9 pm, Wed & Thurs 5:30 pm-8 pm, Mon & Tues 8 am-2 & 5:30-9:30 pm. Address: 5356 Ole' Cove Rd V0N 1Y2 Location: 4.4 mi (7 km) n on Hwy 101, follow signs; in Rockwater Secret Cove Resor Parking: on-site. 🅰️

HARRISON HOT SPRINGS pop. 1,573

HARRISON BEACH HOTEL   *Book great rates at AAA.com*   Phone: (604)796-1111

Hotel
$99-$249 All Year

Address: 160 Esplanade Ave V0M 1K0 **Location:** Just w; on lakefront. **Facility:** Smoke free premises. 42 units. 39 one-bedroom standard units with efficiencies. 3 one-bedroom suites with efficiencies and whirlpools. 4 stories, interior corridors. *Bath:* combo or shower only. **Parking:** on-site (fee). **Terms:** cancellation fee imposed. **Amenities:** video library (fee), DVD players, high-speed Internet, voice mail, irons, hair dryers. **Pool(s):** heated indoor. **Leisure Activities:** limited exercise equipment. **Guest Services:** coin laundry, wireless Internet. **Business Services:** meeting rooms, PC (fee). **Free Special Amenities:** local telephone calls and high-speed Internet.

HARRISON HOT SPRINGS RESORT & SPA   *Book great rates at AAA.com*   Phone: (604)796-2244

Resort
Hotel
$139-$249 All Year

Address: 100 Esplanade Ave V0M 1K0 **Location:** Just w; on lakefront. **Facility:** Along the shores of Harrison Lake, this property is well known for its wonderful hot pools and therapeutic mineral spa. Smoke free premises. 337 one-bedroom standard units. 8 stories, interior corridors. *Bath:* combo or shower only. **Parking:** on-site (fee) and valet. **Terms:** check-in 4 pm, 1-2 night minimum stay - seasonal and/or weekends, 3 day cancellation notice-fee imposed. **Amenities:** voice mail, irons, hair dryers. *Some:* video games (fee), high-speed Internet. **Dining:** The Copper Room, see separate listing, entertainment. **Pool(s):** 3 heated outdoor, 2 heated indoor. **Leisure Activities:** steamrooms, rental boats, indoor/outdoor hot therapeutic mineral pools, 2 tennis courts, hiking trails, jogging, exercise room, spa. *Fee:* golf-9 holes. **Guest Services:** valet laundry, wireless Internet. **Business Services:** conference facilities, business center. *(See color ad below)*

FREE newspaper

--------- **WHERE TO DINE** ---------

BLACK FOREST RESTAURANT   Phone: 604/796-9343

German
$10-$26

Black Forest's warm, cozy atmosphere appeals to both tourists and locals, as does a menu that lists steak, West Coast salmon and German specialties of beef rouladen and schnitzel. A central European flair punctuates the Alpine-style dining room, which incorporates paintings and murals into the decor. Casual dress. **Bar:** Full bar. **Reservations:** suggested, in summer. **Hours:** 5 pm-10 pm; also 11:30 am-3 pm 6/1-9/30. Closed: 12/25. **Address:** 180 Esplanade Ave V0M 1K0 **Location:** Just w; on lakefront. **Parking:** street.

_____ ▼ *See AAA listing above* ▼ _____

THE COPPER ROOM

Phone: 604/796-224

Pacific Rim
$25-$36

Rich, pleasant decor fills the welcoming dining room, which overlooks outdoor pools. A dress code i imposed at this place, which is known for its delicious prime rib and Fraser Valley local produce, in additio to many comfort food dishes, steaks, chops and chicken. From Tuesday through Saturday, guests can enjo dancing with their meal, and tables are set up to accommodate a lingering visit. Dressy casua Entertainment. **Bar:** Full bar. **Reservations:** required. **Hours:** 6 pm-10 pm, Fri & Sat-11 pm. **Address:** 10 Esplanade Ave V0M 1K0 **Location:** Just w; on lakefront; in Harrison Hot Springs Resort & Spa. **Parking** valet. CALL ⟨M⟩

HOPE pop. 6,185

ALPINE MOTEL

Phone: (604)869-993

Motel
$95-$115 3/1-9/30
$78-$89 10/1-2/28

Address: 505 Old Hope-Princeton Way V0X 1L0 **Location:** Trans-Canada Hwy 1, exit 17 westbound; exit 170 eastbound, just n from lights. **Facility:** 14 one-bedroom standard units, some wit efficiencies. 1 story, exterior corridors. **Parking:** on-site. **Terms:** office hours 7 am-midnigh **Amenities:** high-speed Internet. **Free Special Amenities:** local telephone calls and high-spee Internet.

BEST CONTINENTAL MOTEL

Phone: 604/869-972

Motel
$69-$125 All Year

Address: 860 Fraser Ave V0X 1L0 **Location:** Trans-Canada Hwy 1, exit 170 to downtown; at Fort S **Facility:** 14 one-bedroom standard units. 2 stories (no elevator), exterior corridors. **Parking:** on-site **Terms:** office hours 8 am-midnight, cancellation fee imposed. **Guest Services:** wireless Internet. **Fre Special Amenities:** local telephone calls and high-speed Internet.

COLONIAL '900' MOTEL

Phone: (604)869-522

Motel
$75-$115 All Year

Address: 900 Old Hope-Princeton Way V0X 1L0 **Location:** Trans-Canada Hwy 1, exit 17 westbound; exit 170 eastbound, 0.6 mi (1 km) n from lights. **Facility:** Smoke free premises. 16 one bedroom standard units, some with efficiencies or kitchens. 1 story, exterior corridors. **Parking:** on site, winter plug-ins. **Terms:** office hours 8 am-11 pm. **Amenities:** hair dryers. **Guest Services** wireless Internet. **Free Special Amenities:** local telephone calls and room upgrade (subject t availability with advance reservations).

HERITAGE INN

Phone: (604)869-7166

Motel
$89-$116 All Year

Address: 570 Old Hope-Princeton Way V0X 1L0 **Location:** Trans-Canada Hwy 1, exit 173 westbound; exit 170 eastbound, just n from lights. **Facility:** Smoke free premises. 27 one-bedroom standard units, some with kitchens. 1-2 stories (no elevator), exterior corridors. **Parking:** on-site. **Amenities:** high-speed Internet, irons, hair dryers. **Leisure Activities:** whirlpool. **Guest Services:** coin laundry, wireless Internet. **Business Services:** PC.

FREE local telephone calls and high-speed Internet

QUALITY INN

Book great rates at AAA.com

Phone: (604)869-995

Motel
$115-$145 6/15-2/28
$80-$95 3/1-6/14

Address: 350 Old Hope-Princeton Way V0X 1L0 **Location:** Trans-Canada Hwy 1, exit 17 westbound; exit 170 eastbound, just n from lights. **Facility:** 25 one-bedroom standard units, some wit efficiencies. 2 stories (no elevator), interior corridors. **Parking:** on-site. **Terms:** office hours 8 am midnight. **Amenities:** voice mail, hair dryers. **Pool(s):** heated indoor. **Leisure Activities:** sauna whirlpool. **Guest Services:** wireless Internet. **Business Services:** PC.

SKAGIT MOTOR INN

Phone: (604)869-522

Motel
$108-$118 All Year

Address: 655 3rd Ave V0X 1L0 **Location:** Trans-Canada Hwy 1, exit 170 to downtown, just e of Wate Ave. Located in a residential area. **Facility:** 31 one-bedroom standard units, some with efficiencies. story, exterior corridors. **Parking:** on-site. **Terms:** office hours 7 am-11 pm, 3 day cancellation notic fee imposed. **Amenities:** voice mail, hair dryers. **Leisure Activities:** whirlpool. **Guest Services:** coi laundry, wireless Internet. **Business Services:** meeting rooms. **Free Special Amenities:** roo upgrade (subject to availability with advance reservations) and high-speed Internet.

—— WHERE TO DINE ——

THE GOLDRUSH PUB
Phone: 604/860-4333

Canadian
$9-$16

Examples of the good pub food include burgers, sandwiches and many appetizers. Various beers on tap or in the bottle are available. Provincial liquor laws do not allow entry to those under age 19. Casual dress. **Bar:** Full bar. **Hours:** 11 am-11 pm. Closed: 1/1, 12/25. **Address:** 629 Old Hope-Princeton Way V0X 1L2 **Location:** Trans-Canada Hwy 1, exit 170 eastbound; exit 173 westbound. **Parking:** on-site.

HOME RESTAURANT
Phone: 604/869-5558

Canadian
$8-$15

Burgers, meatloaf, club-house sandwiches, mountain-man breakfasts and homemade soup, sauce and pie make up much of the menu at the popular family-friendly restaurant. The hearty food brings back patrons for many returns. Casual dress. **Bar:** Beer & wine. **Hours:** 6 am-9 pm; to 11 pm 7/1-8/31. Closed: 12/25. **Address:** 665 Old Hope-Princeton Way V0X 1L4 **Location:** Trans-Canada Hwy 1, exit 173 westbound; exit 170 eastbound, just n from lights. **Parking:** on-site. CALL

HOPE DRIVE-IN & RESTAURANT
Phone: 604/869-5380

Canadian
$6-$15

The casual drive-in is a good stop for good food at reasonable prices. Guests can eat in or order from the take-out window. On the menu are freshly made sandwiches, burgers and homemade soups and desserts. Casual dress. **Bar:** Full bar. **Hours:** 6 am-10 pm. Closed: 1/1, 12/25, 12/26. **Address:** 590 Old Hope-Princeton Way V0X 1L0 **Location:** Trans-Canada Hwy 1, exit 173 westbound; exit 170 eastbound, just n from lights. **Parking:** on-site. CALL

PAPANDREAS GREEK TAVERNA
Phone: 604/869-7218

Greek
$8-$18

On the north end of town next door to Colonial 900 Motel, this restaurant features fine Greek dishes along with steaks and some really good pizza. Guests can dine in or take out. Casual dress. **Bar:** Full bar. **Reservations:** accepted. **Hours:** 4 pm-10 pm; 11:30 am-11 pm 6/1-9/30. Closed: 12/25, 12/26. **Address:** 904 Old Hope-Princeton Way V0X 1L0 **Location:** Trans-Canada Hwy 1, exit 173 westbound; exit 170 eastbound, 0.6 mi (1 km) n from lights. **Parking:** on-site.

HOLLY'S RESTAURANT
Phone: 604/869-7448

Canadian
$6-$15

The great family-dining restaurant serves breakfast all day. Its menu of homestyle cooking lists dishes such as chicken teriyaki, halibut, salmon, pasta, Angus beef and fish and chips. The casual, open setting has a comfortable feel. Casual dress. **Bar:** Full bar. **Hours:** 6 am-8:30 pm, Fri-Sun to 9 pm. Closed: 12/25. **Address:** 888 Fraser Ave V0X 1L0 **Location:** Trans-Canada Hwy 1, exit 170 to downtown; jct Hudson Bay St. **Parking:** on-site.

INVERMERE pop. 3,002

BEST WESTERN INVERMERE INN *Book great rates at AAA.com*
Phone: (250)342-9246

Hotel
$120-$210 All Year

Address: 1310 7th Ave V0A 1K0 **Location:** Hwy 93 and 95, exit Invermere, 1.8 mi (3 km) w; centre. **Facility:** Smoke free premises. 45 units. 44 one-bedroom standard units. 1 one-bedroom suite. 3 stories, interior corridors. **Terms:** check-in 4 pm. **Parking:** on-site, winter plug-ins. **Amenities:** high-speed Internet, voice mail, irons, hair dryers. **Dining:** nightclub. **Leisure Activities:** whirlpool, exercise room. **Guest Services:** coin laundry, wireless Internet. **Business Services:** meeting rooms, PC (fee). **Free Special Amenities:** continental breakfast and high-speed Internet.

AAA Benefit:
Members save up to 20%, plus 10% bonus points with rewards program.

INVERMERE SUPER 8 *Book at AAA.com*
Phone: (250)342-8888

Hotel
$125-$195 All Year

Address: 8888 Arrow Rd V0A 1K0 **Location:** On Hwy 95. **Facility:** 49 one-bedroom standard units. 3 stories, interior corridors. **Parking:** on-site. **Amenities:** voice mail, hair dryers. *Some:* irons. **Leisure Activities:** whirlpool. **Guest Services:** coin laundry, wireless Internet. **Business Services:** PC (fee).

—— WHERE TO DINE ——

BLACK FOREST STEAK & SCHNITZEL HOUSE
Phone: 250/342-9417

Continental
$15-$30

On the menu is a good selection of schnitzels, bratwurst, steak and seafood finely prepared with a respect for tradition. Table d'hotes are offered daily, and the decor and relaxed ambience are inspired by Europe. The restaurant is a favorite with birders, who can enjoy watching the owner's pets while dining. **Bar:** Full bar. **Reservations:** suggested. **Hours:** 5 pm-11 pm; to 10 pm off season. **Address:** 540 Hwy 93 & 95 V0A 1K0 **Location:** On Hwy 93 and 95. **Parking:** on-site.

BLUE DOG CAFE
Phone: 250/342-3814

Sandwiches
$8-$10

A favorite of the locals, this small cafe prepares fresh and wholesome soups, salads, wraps and sandwiches, staying as far away from monosodium glutamate and preservatives as it can. Baked goods, chutneys, dressings and vinaigrettes all are prepared from scratch. Breakfast is served with a variety of Kicking Horse coffees. Casual dress. **Bar:** Beer & wine. **Reservations:** not accepted. **Hours:** 10 am-5 pm. Closed: 1/1, 12/24, 12/25. **Address:** 1213 7th Ave V0A 1K0 **Location:** On Main St; downtown. **Parking:** street.

PORTABELLA RESTAURANT

International
$20-$40

Phone: 250/342-060(

On a side street just off downtown, the small converted house decorated in a casual Mediterranean style can seem a little tight for elbow room. Regardless, the dining room is surprisingly intimate and moments of silence indicate guests are enjoying the creatively prepared dishes. It isn't hard to see the commitment to quality, as many things seem to be made in-house and the restaurant has built its reputation on using local seasonal ingredients and merging them with Mediterranean accents. Dressy casual. **Bar:** Full bar. **Reservations:** suggested. **Hours:** 5 pm-8:30 pm. Closed: Mon. **Address:** 722 13th St V0A 1K(**Location:** Just e of Main St; downtown. **Parking:** street.

STRAND'S OLD HOUSE RESTAURANT

Continental
$16-$36

Phone: 250/342-634(

The restaurant offers intimate dining in a recently restored historic house. The varied menu includes such offerings as lamb, game, seafood, a selection of pastas and dinner-size salads. A good number of daily specials complements the menu. A covered porch provides a bright, airy alternative to the more secluded corners of the main dining room. Servers are friendly and courteous. Casual dress. **Bar:** Full bar. **Reservations:** suggested. **Hours:** 5 pm-9 pm; Mon-Fri to 10:30 pm in summer. Closed: 12/25. **Address:** 818 12th St V0A 1K0 **Location:** Centre. **Parking:** on-site. **Historic** CALL 🛗

KAMLOOPS pop. 80,376

ACCENT INNS

Book great rates at AAA.com

Motel
$99-$179 All Year

Phone: (250)374-8877

Address: 1325 Columbia St W V2C 6P4 **Location:** Trans-Canada Hwy 1, exit 369 (Columbia St eastbound, at Notre Dame Dr; exit 370 (Summit Dr) westbound. **Facility:** 83 one-bedroom standard units, some with efficiencies. 3 stories, exterior corridors. **Parking:** on-site, winter plug-ins. **Amenities:** voice mail, irons, hair dryers. **Pool(s):** heated outdoor. **Leisure Activities:** sauna, whirlpool, limited exercise equipment. **Guest Services:** valet and coin laundry, wireless Internet. **Business Services:** meeting rooms, PC. **Free Special Amenities:** newspaper and high-speed Internet. 🌿 CALL 🛗 🏊 ❌ 🎥 📶 💻 / SOME UNITS FEE 🐾 ❌ 📷

BEST WESTERN KAMLOOPS

Hotel
Rates not provided

Phone: 250/374-787(

Too new to rate, opening scheduled for December 2009. **Address:** 660 Columbia St W V2C 1L1 **Location:** Trans-Canada Hwy 1, exit 369 (Columbia St) eastbound, 1.3 mi (2 km) n; exit 370 (Summit Dr) westbound to Columbia St via City Centre, then just n. **Amenities:** 81 units, coffeemakers, refrigerators, pool. *(See color ad below)*

AAA Benefit:
Members save up to 20%, plus 10% bonus points with rewards program.

▼ *See AAA listing above* ▼

COMFORT INN & SUITES   *Book great rates at AAA.com*

Phone: (250)372-0987

Hotel
$110-$189 All Year

Address: 1810 Rogers Pl V1S 1T7 **Location:** Trans-Canada Hwy 1, exit 368 (Hillside Ave), just w. **Facility:** 128 units. 118 one-bedroom standard units, some with efficiencies and/or whirlpools. 10 one-bedroom suites, some with efficiencies and/or whirlpools. 3 stories, interior corridors. **Parking:** on-site, winter plug-ins. **Amenities:** voice mail, irons, hair dryers. **Dining:** Vittorio's Italian Restaurant, see separate listing. **Pool(s):** heated outdoor, heated indoor. **Leisure Activities:** whirlpools, waterslide, exercise room. **Guest Services:** valet and coin laundry, wireless Internet. **Business Services:** meeting rooms, PC (fee). *(See color ad below)*

FREE expanded continental breakfast and high-speed Internet

ECONO LODGE INN & SUITES   *Book great rates at AAA.com*

Phone: (250)372-8533

Motel
$59-$129 All Year

Address: 1773 Trans-Canada Hwy E V2C 3Z6 **Location:** 1.5 mi (2.4 km) e on Trans-Canada Hwy 1, south side of service access road. **Facility:** 45 one-bedroom standard units, some with kitchens. 2 stories (no elevator), exterior corridors. **Parking:** on-site, winter plug-ins. **Terms:** office hours 7 am-midnight. **Amenities:** hair dryers. **Pool(s):** heated indoor. **Leisure Activities:** whirlpool. **Guest Services:** coin laundry, wireless Internet.

FREE local telephone calls and high-speed Internet

▼ See AAA listing above ▼

Get a Fresh Perspective on AAATravelViews.com

- Blogs from our experts on popular and unique destinations
- The latest in helpful travel advice and news
- Photos, videos, maps and special member offers
- Comments and Q&A with AAA experts

Share travel at
AAATravelViews.com

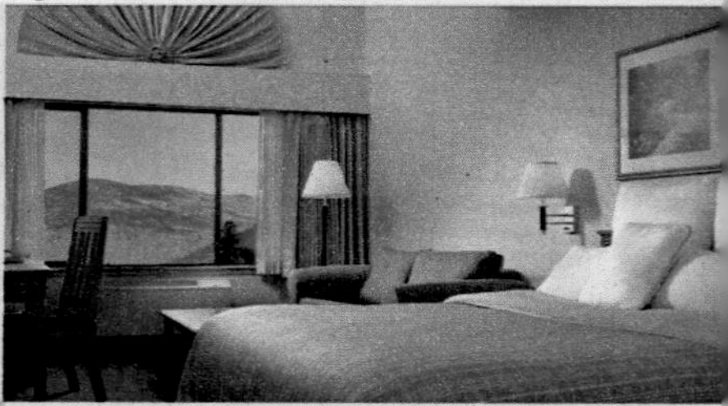

FOUR POINTS BY SHERATON *Book great rates at AAA.com* **Phone:** 250/374-4144

CAA SAVE

Hotel
Rates not provided

Address: 1175 Rogers Way V1S 1R5 **Location:** Trans-Canada Hwy 1, exit 368 (Hillside Ave), just s. **Facility:** Smoke free premises. 78 units. 77 one- and 1 two-bedroom standard units, some with efficiencies, kitchens and/or whirlpools. 4 stories, interior corridors. **Parking:** on-site, winter plug-ins. **Amenities:** dual phone lines, voice mail, irons, hair dryers. **Dining:** Ric's Grill, see separate listing. **Pool(s):** heated indoor. **Leisure Activities:** sauna, whirlpool, waterslide, exercise room. **Guest Services:** valet and coin laundry, wireless Internet. **Business Services:** meeting rooms, business center. *(See color ad below)*

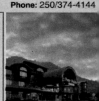

ECO CALL / SOME UNITS

FOUR POINTS BY SHERATON

AAA Benefit:
Members get up to 15% off, plus Starwood Preferred Guest® bonuses.

FREE local telephone calls and high-speed Internet

HAMPTON INN BY HILTON *Book great rates at AAA.com* **Phone:** 250/571-7897

CAA SAVE

Hotel
Rates not provided

Address: 1245 Rogers Way V1S 1R9 **Location:** Trans-Canada Hwy 1, exit 368 (Hillside Ave), just s via Hillside Way. **Facility:** Smoke free premises. 81 one-bedroom standard units, some with whirlpools. 3 stories, interior corridors. *Bath:* combo or shower only. **Parking:** on-site, winter plug-ins. **Amenities:** video games (fee), high-speed Internet, voice mail, irons, hair dryers. **Pool(s):** heated indoor. **Leisure Activities:** whirlpool, waterslide, exercise room. **Guest Services:** valet and coin laundry, wireless Internet. **Business Services:** meeting rooms, business center. *(See color ad p 533)*

ECO CALL / SOME UNITS FEE

Hampton Inn

AAA Benefit:
Members save up to 10% everyday!

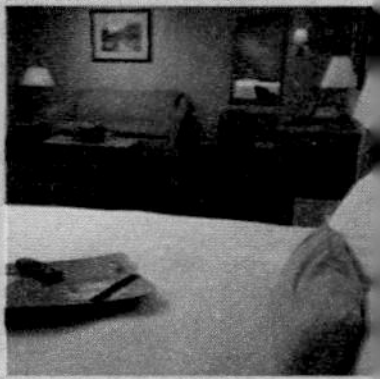

▼ *See AAA listing above* ▼

HOLIDAY INN & SUITES   *Book great rates at AAA.com*   **Phone:** 250/376-8288

[fyi]
Hotel
Rates not provided

Too new to rate, opening scheduled for October 2009. **Address:** 675 Tranquille Rd V2B 3H7 **Location:** Victoria St W, just n on Fortune Dr, then 1 mi (1.6 km) w. **Amenities:** 89 units, restaurant, coffeemakers, microwaves, refrigerators, pool. *(See color ad p 534)*

HOLIDAY INN EXPRESS KAMLOOPS   *Book at AAA.com*   **Phone:** 250/372-3474

Hotel
Rates not provided

Address: 1550 Versatile Dr V1S 1X4 **Location:** Trans-Canada Hwy 1, exit 367 (Pacific Way), just w. **Facility:** Smoke free premises. 80 units. 79 one-bedroom standard units. 1 one-bedroom suite with whirlpool. 4 stories, interior corridors. **Parking:** on-site, winter plug-ins. **Amenities:** high-speed Internet, voice mail, irons, hair dryers. **Pool(s):** heated indoor. **Leisure Activities:** whirlpool, exercise room. **Guest Services:** valet laundry. **Business Services:** meeting rooms, business center.

ECO [↑] CALL [M] ⚄ ✕ [⚑] [▣] / SOME UNITS FEE [⌂] [▤]

KAMLOOPS SUPER 8   *Book at AAA.com*   **Phone:** (250)374-8688

Motel
$119-$149 All Year

Address: 1521 Hugh Allan Dr V1S 1P4 **Location:** Trans-Canada Hwy 1, exit 367 (Pacific Way). **Facility:** 47 one-bedroom standard units. 2 stories (no elevator), interior corridors. **Parking:** on-site. **Amenities:** hair dryers. **Guest Services:** wireless Internet.

[↑] CALL [M] [▤] [▣] / SOME UNITS FEE [⌂] ✕

KAMLOOPS TOWNELODGE   *Book great rates at AAA.com*   **Phone:** (250)828-6660

(CAA) (SAVE)
▼▼▼
Hotel
$150-$185 3/1-9/30
$140-$165 10/1-2/28

Address: 1250 Rogers Way V1S 1N5 **Location:** Trans-Canada Hwy 1, exit 368 (Hillside Ave), just s. **Facility:** Smoke free premises. 203 units. 189 one-bedroom standard units. 8 one- and 6 two-bedroom suites, some with whirlpools. 3 stories, interior corridors. *Bath:* combo or shower only. **Parking:** on-site. **Amenities:** high-speed Internet, voice mail, irons, hair dryers. *Some:* safes. **Pool(s):** heated indoor. **Leisure Activities:** sauna, whirlpool, exercise room. **Guest Services:** valet laundry, wireless Internet. **Business Services:** conference facilities, business center. *(See color ad p 534)*

ECO [↑] [⚐] CALL [M] ⚄ ✕ ✕ [⚑] [▣] [▣]
/ SOME UNITS FEE [⌂] [▦]

FREE local telephone calls and high-speed Internet

▼ See AAA listing p 532 ▼

▼ See AAA listing p 533 ▼

▼ See AAA listing p 533 ▼

MAVERICK MOTOR INN

Motel
$69-$249 All Year

Phone: 250/374-9666

Address: 1250 W Trans-Canada Hwy 1 V2C 6R3 **Location:** Trans-Canada Hwy 1, exit 368 (Hillside Ave). **Facility:** Smoke free premises. 42 one-bedroom standard units, some with efficiencies. 2 stories (no elevator), interior corridors. **Parking:** on-site. **Terms:** cancellation fee imposed. **Amenities:** video library (fee), voice mail, irons, hair dryers. **Pool(s):** heated indoor. **Leisure Activities:** whirlpool, waterslide. **Guest Services:** coin laundry, wireless Internet. **Business Services:** meeting rooms, PC.

QUALITY INN

Book great rates at AAA.com

Motel
$70-$180 All Year

Phone: (250)851-0111

Address: 1860 Rogers Pl V1S 1T7 **Location:** Trans-Canada Hwy 1, exit 368 (Hillside Ave). **Facility:** 63 one-bedroom standard units, some with efficiencies and/or whirlpools. 2 stories (no elevator), interior corridors. **Parking:** on-site, winter plug-ins. **Amenities:** irons, hair dryers. **Pool(s):** heated outdoor. **Leisure Activities:** sauna, whirlpool, limited exercise equipment. **Guest Services:** coin laundry, wireless Internet. **Business Services:** PC.

FREE continental breakfast and high-speed Internet

RAMADA KAMLOOPS

Book great rates at AAA.com

Hotel
$109-$270 All Year

Phone: (250)374-0358

Address: 555 W Columbia St V2C 1K7 **Location:** Trans-Canada Hwy 1, exit 369 (Columbia St) eastbound, 1.3 mi (2 km) n; exit 370 (Summit Dr) westbound to Columbia St via City Centre. **Facility:** Smoke free premises. 90 one-bedroom standard units. 2-3 stories, interior corridors. **Parking:** on-site, winter plug-ins. **Amenities:** voice mail, irons, hair dryers. **Leisure Activities:** whirlpool, exercise room. **Guest Services:** valet and coin laundry, wireless Internet. **Business Services:** meeting rooms, business center. *(See color ad below)*

RANCHLAND MOTEL

Book at AAA.com

Motel
$69-$110 All Year

Phone: (250)828-8787

Address: 2357 Trans-Canada Hwy E V2C 4A8 **Location:** 2.8 mi (4.5 km) e on Trans-Canada Hwy 1, exit River Rd, then just w along service access road. **Facility:** 36 one-bedroom standard units, some with efficiencies. 2 stories (no elevator), exterior corridors. **Parking:** on-site, winter plug-ins. **Terms:** office hours 7 am-11 pm, cancellation fee imposed. **Amenities:** hair dryers. **Leisure Activities:** sauna, whirlpool. **Guest Services:** coin laundry, wireless Internet.

▼ *See AAA listing above* ▼

SCOTT'S INN & RESTAURANT   *Book great rates at AAA.com*

Phone: (250)372-8221

CAA SAVE

Motel
$90-$120 3/1-9/6
$80-$110 9/7-2/28

Address: 551 11th Ave V2C 3Y1 **Location:** Trans-Canada Hwy 1, exit 369 (Columbia St) eastbound, 3.1 mi (5 km) n; exit City Centre westbound, 1 mi (1.6 km) s on Columbia St. Located in a residential area across from a playground. **Facility:** 51 units. 48 one- and 3 two-bedroom standard units, some with efficiencies or kitchens. 2 stories (no elevator), exterior corridors. **Bath:** combo or shower only. **Parking:** on-site, winter plug-ins. **Terms:** office hours 7 am-11 pm, cancellation fee imposed. **Amenities:** voice mail, hair dryers. **Pool(s):** heated indoor. **Leisure Activities:** whirlpool. **Guest Services:** coin laundry, wireless Internet. **Business Services:** PC (fee). *(See color ad below)*

🍽 🏊 📶 💻 / SOME UNITS FEE 🐕 ✕ 📠

THE THOMPSON HOTEL & CONFERENCE CENTRE   *Book at AAA.com*

Phone: (250)374-199...

Hotel
$139-$179 All Year

Address: 650 Victoria St V2C 2B4 **Location:** Trans-Canada Hwy 1, exit 369 (Columbia St) eastbou... to City Centre; exit 370 (Summit Dr) westbound, just n on 6th Ave; downtown. **Facility:** Smoke fr... premises. 98 one-bedroom standard units. 3 stories, interior corridors. **Parking:** on-site, winter plu... ins. **Terms:** cancellation fee imposed. **Amenities:** voice mail, irons, hair dryers. **Pool(s):** heat... indoor. **Leisure Activities:** whirlpool, exercise room, game room. **Guest Services:** valet laund... wireless Internet. **Business Services:** meeting rooms, PC.

ECO ASK 📶 ✕ ✕ 🎥 💻 / SOME UNITS 📶

---- **WHERE TO DINE** ----

CHAPTERS VIEWPOINT RESTAURANT & CATERING

Phone: 250/374-322...

Canadian
$8-$40

This restaurant's great location offers a spectacular view of the city and surrounding hills. The well-prepar... menu features New Mexican cuisine, beef and prime rib, chicken and seafood. The decor is Pac... Northwest and makes use of the Douglas fir for beams. Casual dress. **Bar:** Full b... **Reservations:** suggested. **Hours:** 11:30 am-9 pm. Closed: 12/25, 12/26. **Address:** 610 W Columbia V2C 1L1 **Location:** Trans-Canada Hwy 1, exit 369 (Columbia St) eastbound, 1.2 mi (2 km) n; exit 3... (Summit Dr) westbound to Columbia St via City Centre; in Panorama/Howard Johnson Inn. **Parking** on-site.

ON THE ROCKS PUB & GRILL

Phone: 250/374-976...

Canadian
$9-$19

The sports bar and grill features tons of appetizers, burgers, sandwiches, pitas and wraps, plus da... specials and lots of beers on tap. No one younger than 19 is permitted. Casual dress. **Bar:** Full b... **Reservations:** accepted. **Hours:** 11 am-11:30 pm. Closed: 12/25. **Address:** 1265 Rogers Way V1S 1... **Location:** Trans-Canada Hwy 1, exit 368 (Hillside Ave), just s. **Parking:** on-site. CALL 🅼

ORIENTAL GARDENS RESTAURANT

Chinese
$10-$20

Phone: 250/372-2344

Delicious Japanese and Chinese entrees are featured at this restaurant, where a full sushi bar and Japanese-style, private dining booths are also offered. The restaurant will validate parking for those guests who park in the lot to the side. Casual dress. **Bar:** Full bar. **Reservations:** accepted. **Hours:** Open 3/1-12/23 & 1/23-2/28; 5 pm-10 pm, Fri & Sat-11 pm. Closed: 10/11. **Address:** 545 Victoria St V2C 2B1 **Location:** Victoria St at 5th Ave; downtown. **Parking:** on-site (fee).

RIC'S GRILL

Steak
$12-$32

Phone: 250/377-3113

"Funky and modern" describes the decor and the food at the upscale steakhouse, which bustles with activity. Steaks are well worth it, but then again, so are the salmon, chicken and pasta dishes. A wide variety of distinctive appetizers rounds out the menu. Servers are friendly and attentive. Casual dress. **Bar:** Full bar. **Hours:** 6:30 am-10:30 pm. Closed: 12/25. **Address:** 1175 Rogers Way V1S 1R5 **Location:** Trans-Canada Hwy 1, exit 368 (Hillside Ave), just s; in Four Points by Sheraton. **Parking:** on-site. CALL Ⓜ

RIC'S MEDITERRANEAN GRILL

Steak
$11-$30

Phone: 250/372-7771

A youthful, bustling ambience characterizes the popular downtown restaurant. The food blends Mediterranean ingredients with seafood, fish and steaks to create dishes that show sensitivity to international influences. The long list of appetizers and by-the-glass wine choices let diners turn dinner into a sampling event. Casual dress. **Bar:** Full bar. **Reservations:** suggested. **Hours:** 11 am-9:30 pm, Sat & Sun from 4 pm. Closed: 12/25. **Address:** 227 Victoria St V2C 2A1 **Location:** Between 2nd and 3rd aves. **Parking:** street. CALL Ⓜ

VITTORIO'S ITALIAN RESTAURANT

Italian
$13-$25

Phone: 250/851-2112

"Come hungry, leave full!" is the motto of the family-friendly restaurant. Portions are huge, and the staff often sends diners on their way with doggie bags. Pizza dough is made from scratch, and the entree selection lists all the Italian favorites. Casual dress. **Bar:** Full bar. **Reservations:** suggested. **Hours:** 5 pm-10 pm. **Address:** 1820 Rogers Pl V1S 1T7 **Location:** Trans-Canada Hwy 1, exit 368 (Hillside Ave), just w; in Comfort Inn & Suites. **Parking:** on-site. CALL Ⓜ

KELOWNA—See Okanagan Valley p. 551.

KIMBERLEY pop. 6,139

INNWEST KIRKWOOD INN

Condominium
Rates not provided

Phone: 250/427-7616

Address: 880 North Star Dr V1A 2Y6 **Location:** From Gerry Sorensen Way, follow signs. **Facility:** Smoke free premises. 45 units. 7 one-bedroom standard units. 18 one- and 20 two-bedroom suites with kitchens, some with whirlpools. 2 stories (no elevator), exterior corridors. **Parking:** on-site. **Terms:** office hours 8 am-8 pm, check-in 4 pm. **Amenities:** video library (fee), voice mail. Some: irons, hair dryers. **Pool(s):** heated outdoor. **Leisure Activities:** sauna, whirlpool, downhill & cross country skiing. **Guest Services:** coin laundry, wireless Internet. **Business Services:** PC.

TRICKLE CREEK LODGE

Book great rates at AAA.com

Extended Stay Hotel
$163-$272 All Year

Phone: (250)427-5175

Address: 500 Stemwinder Dr V1A 2Y6 **Location:** From Gerry Sorensen Way, follow signs. **Facility:** Smoke free premises. 80 units. 19 one-bedroom standard units with kitchens. 41 one- and 20 two-bedroom suites with kitchens. 3 stories, interior corridors. *Bath:* combo or shower only. **Parking:** on-site. **Terms:** check-in 4 pm, 14 day cancellation notice-fee imposed. **Amenities:** high-speed Internet, dual phone lines, voice mail, irons, hair dryers. **Pool(s):** heated outdoor. **Leisure Activities:** whirlpools, downhill skiing, outdoor barbecue, hiking trails, exercise room. *Fee:* golf-18 holes. **Guest Services:** coin laundry. **Business Services:** meeting rooms, PC (fee). **Free Special Amenities:** newspaper and high-speed Internet.

——— WHERE TO DINE ———

THE BEAN TREE CAFE

Sandwiches
$6-$7

Phone: 250/427-7889

This casual spot offers counter service for a quick lunch or just cup of coffee or tea. Homemade fresh soups, salads, interesting grilled sandwiches (like the grilled Marrakesh on rye), wraps and baked goodies are the mainstay here. Beverages range from 15 types of tea to Italian sodas, wine, beer and, of course, coffee. Entertainment is on tap some evenings. Casual dress. **Bar:** Beer & wine. **Reservations:** not accepted. **Hours:** 7 am-5 pm, Sat from 8 am, Sun from 9 am. Closed: 1/1, 12/25. **Address:** 295 Spokane St V1A 2E6 **Location:** Hwy 95A, just n on Wallinger Ave. **Parking:** street.

KELSEY'S

Canadian
$9-$21

Phone: 250/427-1600

A fun, relaxed atmosphere and tasty menu of casual fare make the restaurant a popular favorite with locals. Diners might start a meal with some tempting appetizers, such as wings, loaded potato skins or nachos, and follow them with an old-time favorite, such as a burger, wrap, pizza or pasta dish. For a heartier meal, it's hard to beat pork back ribs or a steak. The diverse menu has broad appeal. Casual dress. **Bar:** Full bar. **Reservations:** accepted. **Hours:** 11 am-midnight, Sun-11 pm; seasonal hours vary. **Address:** 101-500 Stemwinder Dr V1A 2Y6 **Location:** Downtown. **Parking:** on-site.

LANGLEY—See Vancouver p. 647.

LUND pop. 243

―――― WHERE TO DINE ――――

THE LUND HOTEL RESTAURANT

Canadian
$10-$22

Phone: 604/414-047

At the gateway to Desolation Sound, an up-and-coming kayak and boating area on the Sunshine Coast, t restaurant presents a menu of fresh, creatively presented local seafood. Views of the water and dista mountains are breathtaking. Casual dress. **Bar:** Full bar. **Hours:** 11:30 am-9 pm; to 8 pm 10/1-4/30. Close 1/1, 12/25, 12/26. **Address:** 1436 Hwy 101 V0N 2G0 **Location:** End of Hwy 101; on Sunshine Coast; The Historic Lund Hotel. **Parking:** on-site.

MADEIRA PARK

PAINTED BOAT RESORT SPA & MARINA

Vacation Rental
Condominium
$240-$440 All Year

Phone: 604/883-245

Address: 12849 Lagoon Dr V0N 2H0 **Location:** Hwy 101, just w on Gonzales Rd, then just s, follc signs. **Facility:** Located near a marina, the hotel offers two-bedroom units, some with a loft or den. units include a gourmet kitchen and private patio or balcony. Smoke free premises. 31 two-bedroc suites with kitchens. 2-3 stories (no elevator), exterior corridors. **Parking:** on-site. **Terms:** office hou 8 am-11 pm, check-in 4 pm, 14 day cancellation notice-fee imposed. **Amenities:** video library, DV players, high-speed Internet, irons, hair dryers. **Dining:** The Restaurant at Painted Boat, see separa listing. **Pool(s):** heated outdoor. **Leisure Activities:** whirlpool, exercise room, spa. **Guest Service** complimentary laundry, wireless Internet. **Business Services:** meeting rooms, PC (fee).

SUNSHINE COAST RESORT & MARINA

Vacation Rental
Condominium
$150-$495 3/1-9/21
$95-$295 9/22-2/28

Phone: (604)883-917

Address: 12695 Sunshine Coast Hwy V0N 2H0 **Location:** Just n of Madeira Park Rd, follow sigr **Facility:** Comprised of condo units plus the original four self-contained cottage-style rooms, overlooking the deep-water marina and surrounding mountains. Smoke free premises. 17 units. 3 on bedroom standard units. 9 one- and 1 two-bedroom suites with kitchens, some with whirlpools. cottages. 3 stories, interior/exterior corridors. *Bath:* combo or shower only. **Parking:** on-site. **Term** office hours 8 am-midnight, 2 night minimum stay - seasonal and/or weekends, 21 day cancellati notice-fee imposed. **Amenities:** video library, DVD players, high-speed Internet, voice mail, irons, h dryers. **Leisure Activities:** sauna, whirlpool, rental boats, rental canoes, fishing. *Fee:* marina, chart fishing. **Guest Services:** coin laundry, wireless Internet.

―――― WHERE TO DINE ――――

THE RESTAURANT AT PAINTED BOAT

Pacific Northwest
$12-$35

Phone: 604/883-300

This contemporary, casually elegant bistro is open for lunch and dinner. The menu focuses on abundance of fresh, local ingredients available on the Sunshine Coast. The views of the private marina a stunning from the waterfront deck. Casual dress. **Bar:** Full bar. **Reservations:** suggested. **Hours:** 11 am pm; from 5 pm 11/1-4/30. Closed: 1/1, 12/25, 12/26; also Mon & Tues 1/1-4/30. **Address:** 12849 Lagoon V0N 2H0 **Location:** Hwy 101, just w on Gonzales Rd, then just s, follow signs; in Painted Boat Sp & Marina. **Parking:** on-site.

MALAHAT—See Victoria p. 695.

MAPLE RIDGE—See Vancouver p. 650.

MCBRIDE pop. 660

NORTH COUNTRY LODGE

CAA SAVE

Motel
$85-$100 All Year

Phone: 250/569-00

Address: 868 Frontage Rd N V0J 2E0 **Location:** Just w of village main exit, on Hwy 16 north servi road. **Facility:** 48 units. 44 one-bedroom standard units, some with efficiencies. 4 one-bedroom suite with efficiencies. 2 stories (no elevator), exterior corridors. **Parking:** on-site, winter plug-ins. **Term** office hours 7:30 am-11 pm, 3 day cancellation notice-fee imposed. **Amenities:** hair dryers. **Leisu** **Activities:** whirlpool. **Guest Services:** wireless Internet. **Business Services:** PC.

MERRITT pop. 6,998

BEST WESTERN NICOLA INN *Book great rates at AAA.com*

CAA SAVE

Hotel
$99-$217 3/1-10/31
$89-$169 11/1-2/28

Phone: (250)378-425

AAA Benefit:
Members save up to
20%, plus 10%
bonus points with
rewards program.

Address: 4025 Walters St V1K 1K1 **Location:** Hwy 5, exit 290, 0.6 mi (1 km) w. **Facility:** 56 units. 52 one-bedroom standard units. 4 one-bedroom suites. 2 stories (no elevator), exterior corridors. **Parking:** on-site, winter plug-ins. **Terms:** cancellation fee imposed. **Amenities:** high-speed Internet, irons, hair dryers. **Pool(s):** heated indoor. **Leisure Activities:** whirlpool, exercise room. **Guest Services:** coin laundry, wireless Internet. **Business Services:** meeting rooms, PC. Free Special Amenities: local telephone calls and high-speed Internet.

SUPER 8 MERRITT *Book at AAA.com*

Motel
$110-$130 3/1-9/30
$95-$110 10/1-2/28

Phone: (250)378-942

Address: 3561 Voght St V1K 1C5 **Location:** Hwy 5, exit 290, just w. **Facility:** 35 one-bedroo standard units, some with efficiencies or kitchens. 2 stories (no elevator), exterior corridors. **Parkin** on-site. **Terms:** office hours 6 am-11 pm. **Amenities:** hair dryers. **Pool(s):** heated indoor. **Leisu** **Activities:** whirlpool. **Guest Services:** wireless Internet.

MISSION—See Vancouver p. 650.

NAKUSP pop. 1,524

THE SELKIRK INN

Motel
$59-$95 All Year

Phone: 250/265-3666

Address: 210 W 6th Ave V0G 1R0 **Location:** Centre. **Facility:** Smoke free premises. 39 one-bedroom standard units, some with efficiencies (utensils extra charge). 2 stories (no elevator), interior corridors. *Bath:* combo or shower only. **Parking:** on-site. **Terms:** office hours 7 am-11 pm. **Amenities:** voice mail. *Some:* irons. **Leisure Activities:** sauna. **Guest Services:** wireless Internet. **Business Services:** meeting rooms. **Free Special Amenities: local telephone calls and high-speed Internet.**

NANAIMO pop. 78,692

BEST WESTERN DORCHESTER HOTEL

   Book great rates at AAA.com

Hotel
$135-$200 All Year

Phone: (250)754-6835

Address: 70 Church St V9R 5H4 **Location:** Hwy 19A (Island Hwy) to Comox Rd; downtown. **Facility:** Smoke free premises. 70 units. 67 one-bedroom standard units. 3 one-bedroom suites. 4 stories, interior corridors. **Parking:** on-site. **Terms:** cancellation fee imposed. **Amenities:** voice mail, safes, irons, hair dryers. *Some:* high-speed Internet. **Leisure Activities:** bicycles, exercise room. **Guest Services:** valet laundry, wireless Internet. **Business Services:** meeting rooms, PC. *(See color ad below)*

AAA Benefit:
Members save up to 20%, plus 10% bonus points with rewards program.

FREE local telephone calls and high-speed Internet

————— ▼ *See AAA listing above* ▼ —————

Conveniently Located in the
Heart of Downtown Nanaimo

- 70 guest rooms and suites with Harbour and City view
- 5 minutes from Departure Bay Ferry Terminal
- Complimentary bicycle use
- Only steps away from the Seawall, Old City Quarter, Nanaimo District Museum and the Great Canadian Casino

**BEST WESTERN DORCHESTER
DOWNTOWN NANAIMO**

70 Church Street, Nanaimo
1.800.661.2449
www.dorchesternanaimo.com

BEST WESTERN NORTHGATE INN

Book great rates at AAA.com

Phone: (250)390-2222

ⒶⒶ SAVE

▽▽▽
Hotel
$104-$142 3/1-9/30
$94-$122 10/1-2/28

Address: 6450 Metral Dr V9T 2L8 **Location:** Hwy 19A (Island Hwy), just w on Aulds Rd, then just s. **Facility:** Smoke free premises. 72 one-bedroom standard units, some with efficiencies and/or whirlpools. 3 stories, interior corridors. **Parking:** on-site. **Terms:** cancellation fee imposed. **Amenities:** voice mail, safes, irons, hair dryers. **Leisure Activities:** sauna, whirlpool, limited exercise equipment. **Guest Services:** valet and coin laundry, wireless Internet. **Business Services:** meeting rooms, PC. *(See color ad below)*

AAA Benefit:
Members save up to 20%, plus 10% bonus points with rewards program.

🍴 🍸 ⊠ ✕ 🏋 🛗 🖥 💻 /SOME UNITS FEE 🐾

FREE local telephone calls and high-speed Internet

BUCCANEER INN

Phone: 250/753-1246

ⒶⒶ SAVE

▽▽▽
Motel
$70-$199 All Year

Address: 1577 Stewart Ave V9S 4E3 **Location:** 1 mi (1.5 km) e; just before the ferry terminal. **Facility:** Smoke free premises. 13 units. 2 one-bedroom standard units. 11 one-bedroom suites with kitchens. 2 stories (no elevator), exterior corridors. *Bath:* combo or shower only. **Parking:** on-site. **Terms:** office hours 9 am-9 pm, 7 day cancellation notice-fee imposed. **Amenities:** irons, hair dryers. **Leisure Activities:** barbecue. **Guest Services:** coin laundry, wireless Internet. **Business Services:** PC. **Free Special Amenities:** local telephone calls and high-speed Internet.

✕ 🏋 🛗 🖥 💻

DAYS INN NANAIMO HARBOURVIEW

Book at AAA.com

Phone: (250)754-8171

▽▽
Hotel
$99-$129 3/1-9/30
$89-$119 10/1-2/28

Address: 809 Island Hwy S V9R 5K1 **Location:** On Island Hwy 1, 1.3 mi (2 km) s. **Facility:** 79 one-bedroom standard units, some with efficiencies. 2 stories (no elevator), interior corridors. **Parking:** on-site. **Amenities:** hair dryers. *Some:* high-speed Internet, safes, irons. **Pool(s):** heated indoor. **Leisure Activities:** whirlpool. **Guest Services:** valet and coin laundry, wireless Internet. **Business Services:** meeting rooms, PC (fee). ECO ASK 🍴 🍸 🏊 🛗 🖥 💻 /SOME UNITS FEE 🐾 ✕

▼ See AAA listing above ▼

THE GRAND HOTEL NANAIMO   *Book at AAA.com*   Phone: (250)758-3000

Hotel
$129-$350 All Year

Address: 4898 Rutherford Rd V9T 4Z4 **Location:** 3.8 mi (6 km) n on Hwy 19A (Island Hwy) from Departure Bay ferry terminal, then just e. **Facility:** Smoke free premises. 72 one-bedroom standard units, some with whirlpools. 4 stories, interior corridors. **Parking:** on-site. **Terms:** cancellation fee imposed. **Amenities:** high-speed Internet, voice mail, irons, hair dryers. **Pool(s):** heated indoor. **Leisure Activities:** exercise room. **Guest Services:** valet laundry. **Business Services:** meeting rooms, PC (fee). (ASK) [ICONS]

INN ON LONG LAKE   Phone: (250)758-1144

(CAA) (SAVE)

Hotel
$109-$299 All Year

Address: 4700 Island Hwy N V9T 1W6 **Location:** 3.1 mi (5 km) n on Hwy 19A (Island Hwy) from Departure Bay ferry terminal. **Facility:** 62 one-bedroom standard units, some with efficiencies, kitchens and/or whirlpools. 3 stories, exterior corridors. **Parking:** on-site. **Terms:** cancellation fee imposed. **Amenities:** voice mail, irons, hair dryers. **Leisure Activities:** sauna, whirlpool, rental canoes, rental paddleboats, boat dock, limited exercise equipment, horseshoes, volleyball. **Guest Services:** valet and coin laundry, wireless Internet. **Business Services:** meeting rooms, PC. *(See color ad below)* [ICONS]

FREE expanded continental breakfast and newspaper

RAMADA INN NANAIMO   *Book at AAA.com*   Phone: (250)716-2009

Hotel
$103-$150 All Year

Address: 315 Rosehill St V9S 1E3 **Location:** 1 mi (1.6 km) n on Hwy 19A (Island Hwy). **Facility:** Smoke free premises. 65 one-bedroom standard units, some with whirlpools. 4 stories, interior corridors. **Parking:** on-site. **Terms:** cancellation fee imposed. **Amenities:** high-speed Internet, voice mail, safes, irons, hair dryers. **Leisure Activities:** exercise room. **Guest Services:** valet and coin laundry, wireless Internet. **Business Services:** meeting rooms, business center. (ASK) [ICONS]

▼ See AAA listing above ▼

TRAVELODGE NANAIMO   *Book great rates at AAA.com*   Phone: (250)754-6355

CAA SAVE

Hotel
$119-$139 3/1-9/30
$105-$129 10/1-2/28

Address: 96 Terminal Ave N V9S 4J2 **Location:** Jct Terminal Ave and Hwy 19A (Island Hwy). **Facility:** 76 one-bedroom standard units, some with efficiencies. 3 stories, interior corridors. **Parking:** on-site. **Amenities:** voice mail, hair dryers. *Some:* high-speed Internet, irons. **Leisure Activities:** sauna. **Guest Services:** valet and coin laundry, wireless Internet. **Business Services:** meeting rooms, PC (fee). **Free Special Amenities:** expanded continental breakfast and high-speed Internet.

ECO 📶 🍽 💻 / SOME UNITS FEE 🛒 ⊠ 🐾 🚪 📷

------ WHERE TO DINE ------

BLUE GINGER SUSHI BAR & SATAY GRILL   Phone: 250/751-8238

Japanese
$6-$20

The restaurant represents an interesting idea. It combines three Asian tastes—Japanese, Chinese and Thai—on a single menu. Dishes reflect a melange of flavors and are a fun twist on the typical Asian dining experience. Casual dress. **Bar:** Full bar. **Hours:** 11:30 am-10 pm, Fri-11 pm, Sun noon-10 pm. Closed: 12/25. **Address:** 5769 Turner Rd, Unit 1 V9T 6L8 **Location:** Hwy 19A (Island Hwy), at Turner Rd; in Longwood Station. **Parking:** on-site.

CACTUS CLUB CAFE   Phone: 250/729-0011

Canadian
$9-$29

This bustling, casual restaurant serves huge burgers, sandwiches, pasta, salads, soups, quesadillas, fajitas, vegetarian dishes, steak, ribs, chicken and fish. Featured are certified Angus beef and fresh wild British Columbia salmon. The thick and creamy milk shakes come highly recommended. Casual dress. **Bar:** Full bar. **Hours:** 11 am-midnight, Fri & Sat-1 am. Closed: 12/25. **Address:** 801, 5800 Turner Rd V9T 6J4 **Location:** Hwy 19A (N Island Hwy), just e before Uplands Dr. **Parking:** on-site.

EARLS RESTAURANT   Phone: 250/756-4100

Canadian
$9-$25

Offering an experience that falls between fast food and fine dining, the fun, relaxed restaurant prepares great food at a great price. Choices range from juicy burgers, hearty sandwiches, fresh salads, wings and pizza to full entrees of steak, chops and seafood. Made-from-scratch soups and assorted breads, as well as a nice choice of wines and beers, round out the offerings. This is a fitting spot for impromptu get-togethers and festive occasions. Casual dress. **Bar:** Full bar. **Hours:** 11 am-11 pm, Fri & Sat-midnight, Sun 10:30 am-10 pm. Closed: 12/25. **Address:** 100-2980 N Island Hwy V9T 5V4 **Location:** 2.5 mi (4 km) n on Hwy 19A (Island Hwy) from Departure Bay ferry terminal. **Parking:** on-site. CALL 📞M

GINA'S MEXICAN CAFE
Phone: 250/753-5411

Mexican
$8-$17

One of the busiest restaurants in downtown, Gina's has been serving Mexican food to hungry diners for more than 20 years in one of the gaudiest houses imaginable! Lines out the door are not uncommon, and the cramped interior and tacky Mexican decor add to its popularity. Nothing on the menu is more than $16, and portions are large. Parking is at street meters or in a nearby pay lot. Casual dress. **Bar:** Full bar. **Hours:** 11 am-9 pm, Fri-10 pm, Sat noon-10 pm, Sun noon-8 pm. Closed: 12/25, 12/26. **Address:** 47 Skinner St V9R 5K4 **Location:** Hwy 19A (Island Hwy), just e on Comox Rd, then just s on Chapel St. **Parking:** street.

KELSEY'S
Phone: 250/729-8882

Canadian
$7-$21

A fun, relaxed atmosphere and tasty menu of casual fare make the restaurant a popular favorite with locals. Diners might start a meal with some tempting appetizers, such as wings, loaded potato skins or nachos, and follow them with an old-time favorite, such as a burger, wrap, pizza or pasta dish. For a heartier meal, it's hard to beat pork back ribs or a steak. The diverse menu has broad appeal. Casual dress. **Bar:** Full bar. **Hours:** 11:30 am-11 pm, Sun-10 pm. **Address:** 4711 Rutherford Rd V9T 4K6 **Location:** In Rutherford Mall. **Parking:** on-site.

LONGWOOD BREWPUB
Phone: 250/729-8225

Canadian
$9-$27

Families are welcomed in the restaurant section, but the pub, which offers all the amenities of the restaurant, is strictly for adults. Patrons can sample hand-crafted lagers and ales, as well as hearty pub food, such as sandwiches, burgers, pastas and varied dinner entrees. Casual dress. **Bar:** Full bar. **Hours:** 11 am-11 pm, Sun 10 am-10 pm. Closed: 1/1, 12/25. **Address:** 5775 Turner Rd V9T 6L8 **Location:** Hwy 19A (Island Hwy) at Turner Rd; in Longwood Station. **Parking:** on-site. CALL

MOXIE'S CLASSIC GRILL
Phone: 250/390-1079

Canadian
$8-$18

This sleek, funky and popular restaurant presents an extensive menu of creatively prepared dishes, including pizza, pasta, rice, noodles, signature salads and burgers. Other menus include one for children and one for Sunday brunch. Lending to the upbeat, stylish decor are dark wood appointments and river rock fireplaces. Casual dress. **Bar:** Full bar. **Hours:** 11 am-11 pm, Fri & Sat-midnight. **Address:** 6750 Island Hwy N, #102 V9V 1S3 **Location:** Hwy 19A (Island Hwy); in Nored Plaza. **Parking:** on-site.

RICKY'S ALL DAY GRILL
Phone: 250/390-1227

Canadian
$6-$15

The comfortable eatery, which employs friendly servers, presents a varied menu that includes pasta dishes, wraps, omelets, stir-fry preparations and burgers. Portions are generous. Children's and senior selections are offered. Guests can request seating in a booth or at a table. Casual dress. **Bar:** Full bar. **Hours:** 6:30 am-9 pm. **Address:** 6550 Island Hwy N V9V 1K8 **Location:** Corner of Hwy 19A (Island Hwy) and Hammond Bay Rd. **Parking:** on-site.

SMITTY'S
Phone: 250/716-8887

Canadian
$7-$20

The family-oriented restaurant satisfies patrons with its ever-popular all-day breakfast items, as well as tasty and wholesome soups and salads at lunchtime. A relaxed mood characterizes the dining space. Casual dress. **Bar:** Full bar. **Hours:** 6:30 am-9 pm. Closed: 12/25. **Address:** 50 10th St V9R 6L1 **Location:** Hwy 19A (Island Hwy S), just w. **Parking:** on-site.

SWISS CHALET
Phone: 250/729-7120

Canadian
$6-$18

The popular restaurant is known for its rotisserie chicken and ribs and the tangy Swiss Chalet sauce that gives food its special zip. Diners munch on a half or quarter chicken with sides such as steamed vegetables, fries, baked potatoes and salads. Lunch guests often go for the great soup and sandwich combination. Take-out and delivery service are popular options. Casual dress. **Bar:** Full bar. **Hours:** 11:30 am-10 pm, Sun 11 am-9:30 pm. Closed: 12/25. **Address:** 3290 N Island Hwy V9T 1W1 **Location:** Hwy 19A (Island Hwy) at Bowen Rd. **Parking:** on-site.

ZOUGLA
Phone: 250/716-3233

Mediterranean
$12-$30

Diners will enjoy this restaurant's steak and seafood as well as such Mediterranean specialties as moussaka, spanakopita and souvlaki. Floor-to-ceiling windows offer a great view of the ocean and mountains. Couples and travelers like the relaxing ambience. Casual dress. **Bar:** Full bar. **Hours:** 11 am-10 pm, Fri-11 pm, Sat 11:30 am-11 pm, Sun 4 pm-10 pm. Closed: 12/25, 12/26. **Address:** 2021 Estevan Rd V9S 3Y9 **Location:** Hwy 19A (Island Hwy) and Brechin Rd, on road to Departure Bay ferry terminal. **Parking:** on-site.

NANOOSE BAY pop. 5,246

——— **WHERE TO DINE** ———

THE LANDING WEST COAST GRILL
Phone: 250/468-2400

Pacific Rim
$12-$35

Two large, 6,000-gallon saltwater aquariums dominate this restaurant, and each is stocked with local salmon, crab, sea urchins, herring, perch and abalone. The menu focuses on local ingredients with West Coast and Mediterranean influences. Casual dress. **Bar:** Full bar. **Reservations:** suggested. **Hours:** 11 am-9 pm, Sat & Sun from 10 am. **Address:** 1-1600 Stroulger Rd V9P 9B7 **Location:** Hwy 19, exit 46 (Parksville), 0.5 mi (0.8 km) n on Old Island Hwy (19A), just e on Franklin's Gull Rd, 1.5 mi (2.4 km) s on Northwest Bay Rd, then just e on Beaver Creek Wharf Rd; in Pacific Shores Resort & Spa. **Parking:** on-site. CALL

NARAMATA—See Okanagan Valley p. 559.

NELSON pop. 9,298

BEST WESTERN BAKER STREET INN & CONVENTION CENTRE   *Book great rates at AAA.com*

Phone: (250)352-3525

Hotel
$109-$149 All Year

Address: 153 Baker St V1L 4H1 **Location:** Jct Hwy 6 and 3A. **Facility:** Smoke free premises. 70 one-bedroom standard units, some with whirlpools. 4 stories, interior corridors. **Parking:** on-site. **Amenities:** high-speed Internet, voice mail, irons, hair dryers. **Leisure Activities:** whirlpool, exercise room. **Guest Services:** coin laundry, wireless Internet. **Business Services:** meeting rooms, PC. **Free Special Amenities:** local telephone calls and high-speed Internet.

AAA Benefit:
Members save up to 20%, plus 10% bonus points with rewards program.

NORTH SHORE INN

Phone: (250)352-6606

Motel
$62-$85 All Year

Address: 687 Hwy 3A V1L 5P7 **Location:** 1.9 mi (3 km) n on Hwy 3A via Nelson Bridge. **Facility:** 30 units. 29 one-bedroom standard units, some with kitchens. 1 one-bedroom suite. 3 stories (no elevator), interior corridors. **Parking:** on-site. **Terms:** office hours 7:30 am-11:30 pm. **Leisure Activities:** whirlpool. **Guest Services:** wireless Internet. **Business Services:** PC.

—— WHERE TO DINE ——

ALL SEASONS CAFE

Phone: 250/352-0101

Canadian
$19-$32

True to its name, this funky restaurant features a regional and seasonal menu, incorporating the best of the area and time of year in terms of ingredients. Everything is made from scratch, and dishes are beautiful. In a small house-like setting a block away from downtown, this is a true gem in the heart of Nelson. Guests can eat in the dimly lit, romantic dining room or in the glass-enclosed veranda, with a view of the rock garden. Casual dress. **Bar:** Full bar. **Reservations:** suggested. **Hours:** 5 pm-10 pm. Closed: 12/25. **Address:** 620 Herridge Ln V1L 6A7 **Location:** Just e of Baker St; between Josephine and Hall sts, down alleyway. **Parking:** street.

REDFISH GRILL

Phone: 250/352-3456

International
$6-$19

Behind windows that overlook the town's main street, this deceptively large and eclectic restaurant has developed a reputation for itself. This place often touted as one of the more creative restaurants in town has a kitchen unafraid of taking chances in creating new interpretations of almost any global dish. The varied menu features a little bit of everything from all four corners of the world and uses fresh, local and homemade ingredients. Casual dress. **Bar:** Full bar. **Reservations:** accepted. **Hours:** 8 am-10 pm, Fri & Sat-11 pm. Closed major holidays. **Address:** 479 Baker St V1L 4H7 **Location:** Between Stanley and Ward sts; downtown. **Parking:** street.

THOR'S PIZZA

Phone: 250/352-1212

Pizza
$5-$15

Named after the owner's dog, the eatery uses the freshest quality ingredients and Italian-style bread crust. Surely the pooch has impeccable taste in pizza, what with a certified chef de cuisine in front of the oven. Most ingredients in the fabulous pizzas are sourced locally or made in house, so there is no wonder why customers line up out the door on weekends. Ciabatta subs, grilled panini sandwiches, calzones and individual slices also are available. Guests can take advantage of the limited seating or grab their food to go. Casual dress. **Reservations:** not accepted. **Hours:** 11 am-10 pm, Fri & Sat-midnight, Sun 4 pm-9 pm. Closed major holidays. **Address:** 303 Victoria St V1L 4K3 **Location:** Between Kootenay and Stanley sts; downtown. **Parking:** street.

NEW DENVER pop. 512

SWEET DREAMS GUESTHOUSE

Phone: (250)358-2415

Bed & Breakfast
$65-$95 All Year

Address: 702 Eldorado St V0G 1S0 **Location:** Just w of Hwy 6 on Slocan Ave. Located across street from lake. **Facility:** Smoke free premises. 5 one-bedroom standard units. 2 stories (no elevator), interior corridors. *Bath:* some shared or private, shower only. **Parking:** on-site. **Terms:** office hours 10 am-7 pm, check-in 5 pm, 2 night minimum stay - seasonal, 14 day cancellation notice-fee imposed.

NEW WESTMINSTER—See Vancouver p. 650.

NORTH VANCOUVER—See Vancouver p. 651.

OAK BAY—See Victoria p. 695.

Destination Okanagan Valley

*T*he Okanagan Valley is a year-round recreation destination. Whether your pleasure is boating, biking, camping, fishing, golf, hiking or skiing, you'll find plenty of opportunities for outdoor pursuits.

*T*he valley's cities offer all sorts of diversions for visitors, from museums to theater to casinos. Stroll around a farmers market or head out to one of the local wineries.

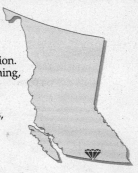

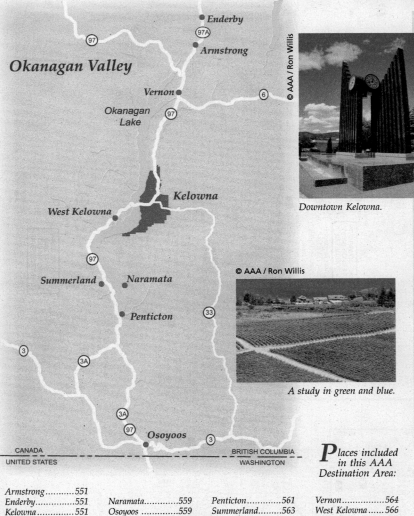

© AAA / Ron Willis

Downtown Kelowna.

© AAA / Ron Willis

A study in green and blue.

*P*laces included in this AAA Destination Area:

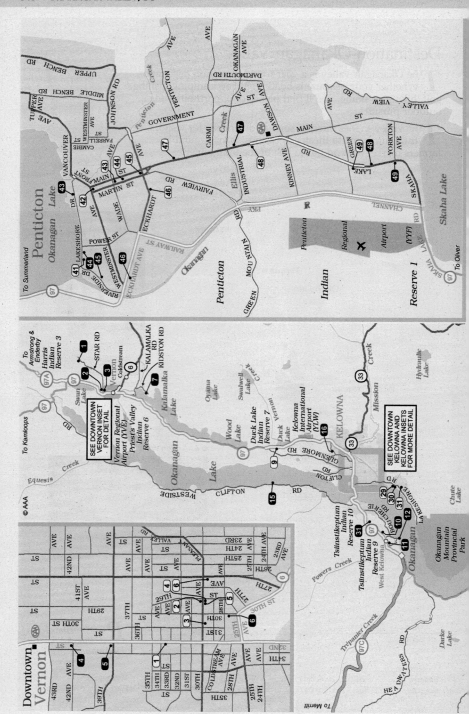

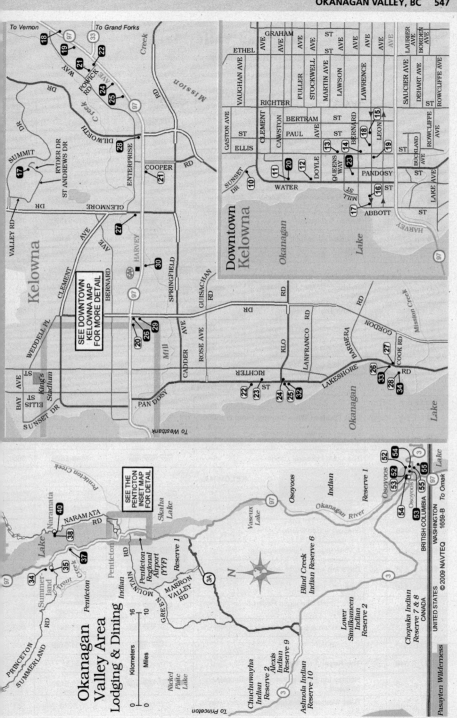

Okanagan Valley Area

This index helps you "spot" where approved lodgings and restaurants are located on the corresponding detailed maps. Lodging daily rate range is for comparison only and show the property's high season. Restaurant rate range is a combination of lunch and/or dinner. Turn to the listing page for more detailed rate information and consult display ads for special promotions.

VERNON

Map Page	OA	Lodgings	Diamond Rated	High Season	Page
1 / p. 546		Castle on the Mountain B & B	▽▽▽	$120-$250	565
2 / p. 546	CAA	**Best Western Villager Motor Inn**	▽▽	$96-$141 SAVE	565
3 / p. 546	CAA	**Holiday Inn Express Hotel & Suites Vernon** - see color ad on insert	▽▽▽	$109-$189 SAVE	565
4 / p. 546		Super 8 Vernon	▽▽	$95-$225	565
5 / p. 546	CAA	**Best Western Vernon Lodge & Conference Centre** - see color ad p 564	▽▽▽	$111-$159 SAVE	564
6 / p. 546		Vernon Travelodge	▽	$85-$159	565
7 / p. 546		LakeSide Illahee Inn	▽▽▽	$149-$389	565

Map Page	OA	Restaurants	Diamond Rated	Cuisine	Meal Range	Page
① / p. 546		Intermezzo Restaurant	▽▽▽	Italian	$11-$39	566
② / p. 546		The Eclectic Med Restaurant Inc	▽▽▽	Mediterranean	$16-$32	565
③ / p. 546		Amarin Thai Restaurant	▽▽	Thai	$10-$16	565
④ / p. 546		The Italian Kitchen Company	▽▽	Italian	$12-$25	566
⑤ / p. 546		Los Huesos	▽▽	Mexican	$9-$16	566
⑥ / p. 546		El Portillo Coffee House	▽	Deli	$4-$6	566

WEST KELOWNA

Map Page	OA	Lodgings	Diamond Rated	High Season	Page
10 / p. 546	CAA	**Best Western Wine Country Hotel & Suites**	▽▽▽	$119-$180 SAVE	566
11 / p. 546	CAA	**Holiday Inn West Kelowna** - see color ad on insert	▽▽▽	$99-$375 SAVE	566
12 / p. 546		The Cove Lakeside Resort	▽▽▽	$149-$889	566

KELOWNA

Map Page	OA	Lodgings	Diamond Rated	High Season	Page
15 / p. 546		Lake Okanagan Resort	▽▽▽	$159-$499	555
16 / p. 546		Grapevine Bed & Breakfast	▽▽▽	Rates not provided	553
17 / p. 546		A Vista Villa Bed and Barbecue	▽▽▽	$289-$409	551
18 / p. 546	CAA	**Days Inn** - see color ad p 553	▽▽	$99-$179 SAVE	552
19 / p. 546		Super 8	▽▽	$85-$150	555
20 / p. 546		Delta Grand Okanagan Resort & Conference Centre	▽▽▽	Rates not provided	552
21 / p. 546		Fairfield Inn & Suites by Marriott Kelowna	▽▽▽	$135-$215	553
22 / p. 546		Vineyard Inn	▽▽	$104-$189	556
23 / p. 546	CAA	**The Royal Anne Hotel**	▽▽	$89-$189 SAVE	555
24 / p. 546		Holiday Inn Express Kelowna - see color ad on insert	▽▽▽	$119-$199	554
25 / p. 546	CAA	**Best Western Inn-Kelowna** - see color ad p 552	▽▽▽	$150-$289 SAVE	551

KELOWNA (cont'd)

Map Page	OA	Lodgings (cont'd)	Diamond Rated	High Season	Page
26 / p. 546		Kelowna Inn	◆◆	$95-$195	554
27 / p. 546	◆◆◆	**Recreation Inn & Suites** - see color ad p 554	◆◆	$139-$242 [SAVE]	555
28 / p. 546	◆◆◆	**Dilworth Inn** - see color ad p 554	◆◆	$135-$195 [SAVE]	553
29 / p. 546	◆◆◆	**Traveller's Choice Motor Inn**	◆◆	$86-$234 [SAVE]	556
30 / p. 546	◆◆◆	**Accent Inns**	◆◆	$99-$189 [SAVE]	551
31 / p. 546	◆◆◆	**Comfort Inn Kelowna-Westside**	◆◆	$149-$229 [SAVE]	551
32 / p. 546		Siesta Inn	◆◆	$134-$279	555
33 / p. 546		Manteo Resort-Waterfront Hotel & Villas	◆◆◆	$170-$300	555
34 / p. 546		Hotel Eldorado	◆◆◆	Rates not provided	554

Map Page	OA	Restaurants	Diamond Rated	Cuisine	Meal Range	Page
9 / p. 546		The Jammery	◆◆	Canadian	$8-$14	557
10 / p. 546	◆◆◆	**Bouchons Bistro**	◆◆◆	French	$19-$35	556
11 / p. 546		Grand Bay Cafe	◆◆◆	Canadian	$12-$29	556
12 / p. 546		Hanna's Lounge & Grill	◆◆◆	Pacific Northwest	$11-$35	557
13 / p. 546		Dawett Fine Indian Cuisine	◆◆	Indian	$6-$17	556
14 / p. 546		The Grateful Fed Bar & Grill	◆	Deli	$5-$10	556
15 / p. 546		Mamma Rosa	◆◆	Italian	$13-$34	557
16 / p. 546		Christopher's	◆◆	Seafood	$15-$40	556
17 / p. 546		Ric's Grill	◆◆◆	Steak	$14-$37	558
18 / p. 546		The Yellowhouse Restaurant	◆◆◆	Canadian	$11-$36	559
19 / p. 546		Yamas Taverna Restaurant	◆◆	Greek	$11-$35	558
20 / p. 546		Mekong Restaurant	◆◆	Traditional Chinese	$6-$15	557
21 / p. 546		Pearson's European Deli	◆	Deli	$7-$12	558
22 / p. 546		Mizu Japanese Restaurant	◆◆	Sushi	$8-$14	557
23 / p. 546		The Marmalade Cat Cafe	◆	Vegetarian	$6-$8	557
24 / p. 546		Jakx Neighbourhood Grill	◆◆	Canadian	$8-$24	557
25 / p. 546		Pheasant & Quail Pub	◆◆	American	$10-$22	558
26 / p. 546	◆◆◆	**Wild Apple Restaurant**	◆◆◆	Pacific Northwest	$12-$28	558
27 / p. 546		Cabana Bar and Grille	◆◆◆	Canadian	$10-$33	556
28 / p. 546		Eldorado Dining Room & Bar	◆◆◆	Regional Canadian	$10-$50	556
29 / p. 546		Seven Six Four Restaurant	◆◆◆	Pacific Northwest	$11-$28	558
30 / p. 546		Minstrel Cafe & Bar	◆◆◆	International	$8-$30	557
31 / p. 546	◆◆◆	**Summerhill Sunset Bistro**	◆◆◆	Regional Canadian	$12-$33	558

SUMMERLAND

Map Page	OA	Lodging	Diamond Rated	High Season	Page
37 / p. 546	◆◆◆	**Summerland Motel**	◆◆	$80-$150 [SAVE]	563

Map Page	OA	Restaurants	Diamond Rated	Cuisine	Meal Range	Page
㉞ / p. 546	CAA	**Cellar Door Bistro At Sumac Ridge Estate Winery**	◈◈◈	Regional Canadian	$12-$28	563
㉟ / p. 546		Vanilla Pod Restaurant	◈◈◈	Canadian	$8-$28	564

NARAMATA

Map Page	OA	Lodging	Diamond Rated	High Season	Page
㊵ / p. 546		The Village Motel	◈◈	$90-$145	559

Map Page	OA	Restaurant	Diamond Rated	Cuisine	Meal Range	Page
㊳ / p. 546	CAA	**Cobblestone Wine Bar & Restaurant**	◈◈◈	Canadian	$9-$34	559

PENTICTON

Map Page	OA	Lodgings	Diamond Rated	High Season	Page
㊸ / p. 546	CAA	**Penticton Lakeside Resort, Convention Centre & Casino - see color ad p 561**	◈◈◈	$165-$235 [SAVE]	562
㊹ / p. 546	CAA	**Spanish Villa Resort**	◈	$68-$350 [SAVE]	562
㊺ / p. 546	CAA	**Days Inn & Conference Centre Penticton**	◈◈	$99-$299 [SAVE]	561
㊻ / p. 546	CAA	**Ramada Inn & Suites**	◈◈◈	$109-$269 [SAVE]	562
㊼ / p. 546		Super 8 Penticton	◈◈	Rates not provided	562
㊽ / p. 546	CAA	**Best Western Inn at Penticton**	◈◈◈	$99-$199 [SAVE]	561
㊾ / p. 546		Empire Motel	◈◈	$59-$164	561

Map Page	OA	Restaurants	Diamond Rated	Cuisine	Meal Range	Page
㊶ / p. 546		Salty's Beach House	◈◈	Caribbean	$12-$26	563
㊷ / p. 546		Fibonacci Roastery & Cafe	◈	Deli	$7-$10	562
㊸ / p. 546		Navratan	◈◈	Indian	$10-$17	563
㊹ / p. 546		Amante Bistro	◈◈◈	International	$9-$34	562
㊺ / p. 546		Theo's Restaurant	◈◈	Greek	$6-$30	563
㊻ / p. 546		Bogner's of Penticton	◈◈◈	Continental	$22-$40	562
㊼ / p. 546		La Casa Ouzeria	◈◈	Italian	$9-$26	563
㊽ / p. 546		Shades Family Restaurant	◈◈	American	$6-$12	563
㊾ / p. 546		Iyara Thai Restaurant	◈◈	Thai	$8-$16	563

OSOYOOS

Map Page	OA	Lodgings	Diamond Rated	High Season	Page
㊾ / p. 546		Spirit Ridge Vineyard Resort & Spa	◈◈◈	Rates not provided	560
㊾ / p. 546		The Coast Osoyoos Beach Hotel	◈◈	$79-$219	560
㊾ / p. 546	CAA	**Best Western Sunrise Inn**	◈◈◈	$99-$255 [SAVE]	559
㊾ / p. 546	CAA	**Walnut Beach Resort**	◈◈◈	$169-$799 [SAVE]	560

Map Page	OA	Restaurants	Diamond Rated	Cuisine	Meal Range	Page
㊾ / p. 546		Passa Tempo	◈◈◈	Canadian	$10-$26	560
㊾ / p. 546		Wildfire Grill	◈◈	Canadian	$9-$24	560
㊾ / p. 546		Diamond Steak and Seafood House	◈◈	Steak	$10-$55	560
㊾ / p. 546		Campo Marina	◈◈	Italian	$14-$23	560

ARMSTRONG pop. 4,241

—— **WHERE TO DINE** ——

VILLAGE CHEESE COMPANY **Phone:** 250/546-8651

Deli
$5-$7

Inside a working cheese factory, the bistro has a small seating area. As they nosh on pre-made sandwiches and desserts, guests can watch cheese being made and browse the vast choice of retail cheeses and cheese-related knick-knacks. Casual dress. **Reservations:** not accepted. **Hours:** 8 am-5 pm, Sun from 8:30 am, Sun 10 am-4 pm. Closed major holidays. **Address:** 3475 Smith Dr V0E 1B0 **Location:** Centre. **Parking:** on-site.

ENDERBY pop. 2,828

HOWARD JOHNSON INN FORTUNES LANDING   *Book great rates at AAA.com*   **Phone:** (250)838-6825

CAA SAVE
Hotel
$99-$109 3/1-9/16
$69-$79 9/17-2/28

Address: 1510 George St V0E 1V0 **Location:** 0.6 mi (1 km) n on Hwy 974. **Facility:** Smoke free premises. 32 units. 31 one-bedroom standard units. 1 one-bedroom suite with kitchen. 2 stories (no elevator), exterior corridors. **Parking:** on-site. **Pool(s):** heated outdoor. **Guest Services:** wireless Internet. **Business Services:** meeting rooms. **Free Special Amenities:** local telephone calls and newspaper.

KELOWNA pop. 106,707   (See map and index starting on p. 546)

ACCENT INNS   *Book great rates at AAA.com*   **Phone:** (250)862-8888   **30**

CAA SAVE
Hotel
$99-$189 All Year

Address: 1140 Harvey Ave V1Y 6E7 **Location:** Corner of Hwy 97 N (Harvey Ave) and Gordon Dr. Located across from a shopping mall. **Facility:** Smoke free premises. 102 units. 90 one-bedroom standard units, some with efficiencies. 12 one-bedroom suites with efficiencies. 3 stories, exterior corridors. **Parking:** on-site, winter plug-ins. **Amenities:** voice mail, irons, hair dryers. **Pool(s):** heated outdoor. **Leisure Activities:** sauna, whirlpool, limited exercise equipment. **Guest Services:** valet and coin laundry, wireless Internet. **Business Services:** meeting rooms, PC. **Free Special Amenities:** newspaper and high-speed Internet.

A VISTA VILLA BED AND BARBECUE **Phone:** (250)762-7837   **17**

Bed & Breakfast
$289-$409 All Year

Address: 962 Ryder Dr V1Y 7T5 **Location:** Hwy 97 (Harvey Ave), 1.6 mi (2 km) n on Spall St to Summit Rd, just e to Valley Rd, follow Valley Rd (which becomes Ryder Dr). Located in a residential area. **Facility:** A Continental breakfast is served in your room but the true highlight at this spa retreat is the nightly barbecue dinner served promptly at 6 pm. Smoke free premises. 4 one-bedroom standard units with whirlpools. 2 stories (no elevator), interior/exterior corridors. **Parking:** on-site. **Terms:** office hours 8 am-8 pm, check-in 4 pm, 3 night minimum stay - seasonal, age restrictions may apply, 30 day cancellation notice-fee imposed. **Amenities:** video library, CD players, hair dryers. *Some:* DVD players. **Pool(s):** heated outdoor. **Leisure Activities:** sauna, spa. **Guest Services:** complimentary laundry, wireless Internet. **Business Services:** PC.

BEST WESTERN INN-KELOWNA   *Book great rates at AAA.com*   **Phone:** (250)860-1212   **25**

CAA SAVE
Hotel
$150-$289 All Year

Address: 2402 Hwy 97 N V1X 4J1 **Location:** 0.6 mi (1 km) s of jct Hwy 33 and 97 N (Harvey Ave); corner of Leckie Rd. **Facility:** Smoke free premises. 154 units. 128 one-bedroom standard units, some with whirlpools. 26 one-bedroom suites, some with efficiencies or kitchens. 8 stories, interior/exterior corridors. *Bath:* combo or shower only. **Parking:** on-site. **Terms:** check-in 4 pm. **Amenities:** video games (fee), high-speed Internet, voice mail, irons, hair dryers. *Some:* honor bars. **Pool(s):** heated indoor. **Leisure Activities:**

AAA Benefit:
Members save up to 20%, plus 10% bonus points with rewards program.

whirlpools, steamroom, exercise room, spa. **Guest Services:** valet and coin laundry, wireless Internet. **Business Services:** conference facilities, business center. *(See color ad p 552)*

FREE expanded continental breakfast and high-speed Internet

COMFORT INN KELOWNA-WESTSIDE   *Book great rates at AAA.com*   **Phone:** (250)769-2355   **31**

CAA SAVE
Hotel
$149-$229 3/1-9/18
$89-$169 9/19-2/28

Address: 1655 Westgate Rd V1Z 3P1 **Location:** Jct Hwy 97 (Harvey Ave) and Bartley Rd, s to Ross Rd. **Facility:** Smoke free premises. 81 units. 80 one-bedroom standard units, some with efficiencies and/or whirlpools. 1 one-bedroom suite with kitchen. 2 stories (no elevator), interior corridors. **Parking:** on-site. **Terms:** cancellation fee imposed. **Amenities:** irons, hair dryers. **Pool(s):** heated indoor. **Leisure Activities:** whirlpool, exercise room. **Guest Services:** valet and coin laundry, wireless Internet. **Business Services:** meeting rooms, PC. **Free Special Amenities:** expanded continental breakfast and high-speed Internet.

(See map and index starting on p. 546)

DAYS INN   *Book great rates at AAA.com*   Phone: (250)868-3297   **18**

Motel
$99-S179 All Year

Address: 2649 Hwy 97 N V1X 4J6 **Location:** Jct Hwy 97 (Harvey Ave) and 33, just n. **Facility:** 91 units. 68 one-bedroom standard units, some with efficiencies. 23 one-bedroom suites. 2 stories, interior/exterior corridors. *Bath:* combo or shower only. **Parking:** on-site. **Terms:** cancellation fee imposed. **Amenities:** voice mail, irons, hair dryers. **Pool(s):** heated outdoor. **Leisure Activities:** whirlpool. **Guest Services:** coin laundry, wireless Internet. **Business Services:** meeting rooms, PC. *(See color ad p 553)*

FREE continental breakfast and high-speed Internet

DELTA GRAND OKANAGAN RESORT &
CONFERENCE CENTRE   *Book at AAA.com*   Phone: 250/763-4500   **20**

Resort
Hotel
Rates not provided

Address: 1310 Water St V1Y 9P3 **Location:** Hwy 97 (Harvey Ave), 0.6 mi (1 km) w along Water St. **Facility:** Featuring a spa, a casino and waterfront views, this luxurious, full-service, resort hotel has a retreat-like ambience. Smoke free premises. 391 units. 254 one-bedroom standard units, some with whirlpools. 30 one-, 101 two- & 6 three-bedroom suites with kitchens, some with whirlpools. 3-10 stories, interior corridors. *Bath:* combo or shower only. **Parking:** on-site (fee) and valet. **Terms:** check-in 4 pm. **Amenities:** video games (fee), voice mail, irons, hair dryers. *Some:* DVD players, CD players, high-speed Internet (fee). **Dining:** Grand Bay Cafe, see separate listing. **Pool(s):** heated outdoor, heated indoor/outdoor. **Leisure Activities:** sauna, whirlpools, steamroom, rental boats, rental canoes, rental paddleboats, rental bicycles, spa. *Fee:* waterskiing. **Guest Services:** valet and coin laundry, wireless Internet. **Business Services:** conference facilities, business center.

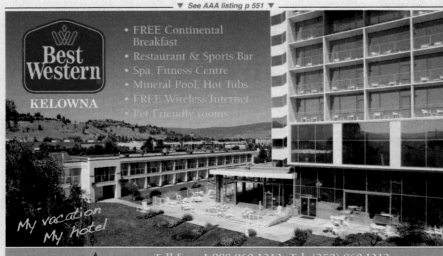

(See map and index starting on p. 546)

DILWORTH INN *Book great rates at AAA.com* Phone: (250)762-9666

Motel
$135-$195 All Year

Address: 1755 Dilworth Dr V1Y 8R1 **Location:** Hwy 97 N (Harvey Ave), just w. Located behind White Spot Restaurant. **Facility:** Smoke free premises. 50 units. 48 one-bedroom standard units, some with efficiencies or kitchens. 2 one-bedroom suites with kitchens. 3 stories (no elevator), interior corridors. **Parking:** on-site. **Terms:** cancellation fee imposed. **Amenities:** voice mail, hair dryers. **Pool(s):** heated indoor. **Leisure Activities:** sauna, whirlpool, sun decks, barbecue, limited exercise equipment. **Guest Services:** coin laundry, wireless Internet. **Business Services:** PC. **Free Special Amenities:** newspaper and high-speed Internet. (See color ad p 554)

FAIRFIELD INN & SUITES BY MARRIOTT KELOWNA *Book great rates at AAA.com* Phone: (250)763-2800

Hotel
$135-$215 All Year

Address: 1655 Powick Rd V1X 4L1 **Location:** Just s of Jct Hwy 97 N (Harvey Ave) and 33 W. **Facility:** Smoke free premises. 116 one-bedroom standard units. 4 stories, interior corridors. *Bath:* combo or shower only. **Parking:** on-site. **Terms:** check-in 4 pm, cancellation fee imposed. **Amenities:** video library, high-speed Internet, voice mail, irons, hair dryers. *Some:* DVD players. **Pool(s):** heated outdoor. **Leisure Activities:** whirlpool, waterslide, exercise room. **Guest Services:** valet and coin laundry, wireless Internet. **Business Services:** meeting rooms, PC.

AAA Benefit:
Members save a minimum 5% off the best available rate.

GRAPEVINE BED & BREAKFAST Phone: 250/860-5580

Bed & Breakfast
Rates not provided

Address: 2621 Longhill Rd V1V 2G5 **Location:** Hwy 97 N (Harvey Ave), 2.5 mi (4 km) w on Dilworth Dr, then just n. **Facility:** True to its name, the Grapevine is surrounded by vineyards and features a private garden, both of which add country charm to its near-city location. Smoke free premises. 4 one-bedroom standard units. 2 stories (no elevator), interior corridors. *Bath:* combo or shower only. **Parking:** on-site. **Terms:** check-in 4 pm, age restrictions may apply. **Amenities:** DVD players, hair dryers. **Pool(s):** heated outdoor. **Leisure Activities:** whirlpool. **Guest Services:** wireless Internet.

▼ See AAA listing p 552 ▼

(See map and index starting on p. 546)

HOLIDAY INN EXPRESS KELOWNA *Book at AAA.com* **Phone:** (250)763-0500 **24**

Hotel
$119-$199 3/1-9/30
$109-$129 10/1-2/28

Address: 2429 Hwy 97 N V1X 4J2 **Location:** 0.6 mi (1 km) s of jct Hwy 97 N (Harvey Ave) and 33. **Facility:** 120 one-bedroom standard units, some with whirlpools. 4 stories, interior corridors. *Bath:* combo or shower only. **Parking:** on-site. **Terms:** check-in 4 pm, cancellation fee imposed. **Amenities:** video games (fee), high-speed Internet, voice mail, irons, hair dryers. **Dining:** Ricky's All Day Grill, see separate listing. **Pool(s):** heated indoor. **Leisure Activities:** whirlpool, exercise room. **Guest Services:** valet laundry, wireless Internet. **Business Services:** meeting rooms, PC. *(See color ad on insert)*

HOTEL ELDORADO *Book at AAA.com* **Phone:** 250/763-7500 **34**

Hotel
Rates not provided

Address: 500 Cook Rd V1W 3G9 **Location:** Hwy 97 (Harvey Ave), 2.5 mi (4 km) s on Pandosy (which becomes Lakeshore Rd). **Facility:** Smoke free premises. 55 units. 49 one-bedroom standard units, some with whirlpools. 6 one-bedroom suites with whirlpools. 3-4 stories, interior corridors. *Bath:* combo or shower only. **Parking:** on-site. **Amenities:** video library (fee), voice mail, irons, hair dryers. *Some:* DVD players, high-speed Internet. **Dining:** Eldorado Dining Room & Bar, see separate listing. **Pool(s):** heated indoor. **Leisure Activities:** whirlpool, steamroom, rental boats, marina, waterskiing, exercise room, spa. **Guest Services:** valet laundry, wireless Internet. **Business Services:** meeting rooms, PC.

KELOWNA INN *Book at AAA.com* **Phone:** (250)762-2533 **26**

Motel
$95-$195 All Year

Address: 1070 Harvey Ave V1Y 8S4 **Location:** Corner of Hwy 97 N (Harvey Ave) and Gordon Dr. Located across from the mall. **Facility:** 112 units. 92 one- and 10 two-bedroom standard units, some with efficiencies, kitchens and/or whirlpools. 6 one- and 4 two-bedroom suites, some with efficiencies. 2 stories (no elevator), exterior corridors. **Parking:** on-site. **Amenities:** voice mail. *Some:* hair dryers. **Dining:** Mekong Restaurant, see separate listing. **Pool(s):** heated indoor. **Leisure Activities:** whirlpool, steamroom. **Guest Services:** coin laundry, wireless Internet. **Business Services:** PC.

(See map and index starting on p. 546)

LAKE OKANAGAN RESORT *Book at AAA.com* Phone: (250)769-3511 **15**

▼▼▼▼
Resort Hotel
$159-$499 All Year

Address: 2751 Westside Rd V1Z 3T1 **Location:** From floating bridge, 1.5 mi (2.5 km) sw on Hwy 97 (Harvey Ave), 10.6 mi (17 km) nw on Westside Rd (narrow winding road), follow signs. **Facility:** This older resort along the shores of Okanagan Lake features a mix of unit styles and sizes, including some newer upscale villas. Smoke free premises. 149 units. 12 one-bedroom standard units with efficiencies. 114 one-, 3 two- and 19 three-bedroom suites, some with efficiencies, kitchens and/or whirlpools. 1 house. 3-6 stories, interior/exterior corridors. **Parking:** on-site. **Terms:** office hours 7 am-11 pm, check-in 4 pm, 2 night minimum stay - seasonal and/or weekends, 14 day cancellation notice, 7/1-8/31-fee imposed. **Amenities:** video library (fee), DVD players, voice mail, irons, hair dryers. *Some:* high-speed Internet. **Pool(s):** 4 heated outdoor. **Leisure Activities:** saunas, whirlpool, rental boats, rental canoes, rental paddleboats, 7 tennis courts (3 lighted), recreation programs, hiking trails, jogging, playground, exercise room, spa, horseshoes, volleyball. *Fee:* marina, waterskiing, horseback riding. **Guest Services:** coin laundry, wireless Internet. **Business Services:** conference facilities, PC (fee). ECO ASK CALL / SOME UNITS

MANTEO RESORT-WATERFRONT HOTEL & VILLAS *Book at AAA.com* Phone: (250)860-1031 **33**

▼▼▼▼
Resort Hotel
$170-$300 All Year

Address: 3762 Lakeshore Rd V1W 3L4 **Location:** Hwy 97 N (Harvey Ave), 2.5 mi (4 km) s on Pandosy (which becomes Lakeshore Rd). **Facility:** Set along the lake, this resort offers extensive recreational facilities as well as large, upscale rooms ranging from studio to condo style. Smoke free premises. 102 units. 48 one-bedroom standard units. 30 one-, 17 two- and 7 three-bedroom suites with kitchens. 4 stories, interior/exterior corridors. **Parking:** on-site. **Terms:** check-in 4 pm, cancellation fee imposed. **Amenities:** video library (fee), voice mail, irons, hair dryers. *Some:* DVD players, CD players, high-speed Internet. **Dining:** Wild Apple Restaurant, see separate listing. **Pool(s):** 2 heated outdoor, heated indoor. **Leisure Activities:** saunas, whirlpools, steamrooms, waterslide, rental boats, rental canoes, rental paddleboats, boat dock, putting green, 2 lighted tennis court, recreation programs in season, playground, exercise room. *Fee:* massage, game room. **Guest Services:** valet and coin laundry, wireless Internet. **Business Services:** meeting rooms, PC. ASK CALL / SOME UNITS

RECREATION INN & SUITES *Book great rates at AAA.com* Phone: (250)860-3982 **27**

CAA SAVE
▼▼▼
Motel
$139-$242 3/1-9/30
$92-$189 10/1-2/28

Address: 1891 Parkinson Way V1Y 7V6 **Location:** Hwy 97 N (Harvey Ave), just w on Spall Rd. **Facility:** 50 units. 31 one- and 8 two-bedroom standard units, some with efficiencies or kitchens. 10 one- and 1 three-bedroom suites with kitchens. 2 stories (no elevator), exterior corridors. **Parking:** on-site. **Terms:** cancellation fee imposed. **Amenities:** hair dryers. *Some:* irons. **Pool(s):** heated outdoor. **Leisure Activities:** sauna, whirlpool. **Guest Services:** coin laundry, wireless Internet. **Business Services:** PC. **Free Special Amenities:** newspaper and high-speed Internet. *(See color ad p 554)* / SOME UNITS FEE

THE ROYAL ANNE HOTEL *Book great rates at AAA.com* Phone: (250)763-2277 **23**

CAA SAVE
▼▼▼
Hotel
$89-$189 All Year

Address: 348 Bernard Ave V1Y 6N5 **Location:** Corner of Pandosy and Bernard Ave; downtown. **Facility:** 64 one-bedroom standard units. 5 stories, interior corridors. **Parking:** on-site. **Terms:** cancellation fee imposed. **Amenities:** voice mail, irons, hair dryers. **Leisure Activities:** saunas, exercise room. **Guest Services:** valet laundry, airport transportation (fee)-Kelowna International Airport, wireless Internet. **Business Services:** meeting rooms, PC. FEE / SOME UNITS FEE

FREE expanded continental breakfast and high-speed Internet

SIESTA INN Phone: (250)763-5013 **32**

▼▼
Motel
$134-$279 3/1-9/20
$92-$182 9/21-2/28

Address: 3152 Lakeshore Rd V1W 3T1 **Location:** Hwy 97 (Harvey Ave), 1.8 mi (2.8 km) s on Pandosy (which becomes Lakeshore Rd). **Facility:** Smoke free premises. 96 units. 24 one-bedroom standard units, some with efficiencies. 68 one- and 4 two-bedroom suites with kitchens. 2 stories (no elevator), exterior corridors. **Parking:** on-site. **Terms:** 3 night minimum stay - seasonal and/or weekends, cancellation fee imposed. **Amenities:** voice mail, hair dryers. *Some:* irons. **Pool(s):** heated outdoor, heated indoor. **Leisure Activities:** sauna, whirlpools, exercise room. **Guest Services:** coin laundry, wireless Internet. **Business Services:** PC. / SOME UNITS

SUPER 8 *Book at AAA.com* Phone: (250)762-8222 **19**

Motel
$85-$150 3/1-9/30
$85-$120 10/1-2/28

Address: 2592 Hwy 97 N V1X 4J4 **Location:** Jct Hwy 33, just n on Hwy 97 N (Harvey Ave). **Facility:** 61 one-bedroom standard units. 2 stories (no elevator), exterior corridors. **Parking:** on-site. **Terms:** cancellation fee imposed. **Amenities:** hair dryers. **Pool(s):** heated outdoor. **Leisure Activities:** whirlpool. **Guest Services:** valet laundry, wireless Internet. **Business Services:** PC (fee). ECO ASK CALL / SOME UNITS

(See map and index starting on p. 546)

TRAVELLER'S CHOICE MOTOR INN

Motel
$86-$234 All Year

Phone: 250-762-3221 [29]

Address: 1780 Gordon Dr V1Y 3H2 **Location:** Hwy 97 N (Harvey Ave), just e. Located across from the mall. **Facility:** Smoke free premises. 43 units. 34 one-bedroom standard units, some with kitchens. 7 one- and 2 two-bedroom suites, some with kitchens. 2 stories (no elevator), exterior corridors. **Parking:** on-site. **Terms:** office hours 7 am-midnight, cancellation fee imposed. **Amenities:** voice mail, hair dryers. *Some:* irons. **Pool(s):** heated indoor. **Leisure Activities:** whirlpool, barbecue. **Guest Services:** coin laundry, wireless Internet. **Free Special Amenities:** continental breakfast and local telephone calls. [icons] / SOME UNITS FEE [icons]

VINEYARD INN

Motel
$104-$189 3/1-9/30
$94-$154 10/1-2/28

Phone: 250-860-5703 [22]

Address: 2486 Hwy 97 N V1X 4J3 **Location:** Southwest corner of jct Hwy 97 (Harvey Ave) and 33. **Facility:** Smoke free premises. 26 units. 10 one-bedroom standard units. 14 one- and 2 two-bedroom suites, some with efficiencies or kitchens. 1 story, exterior corridors. **Parking:** on-site. **Terms:** office hours 7:30 am-11:30 pm, 3 day cancellation notice-fee imposed. **Amenities:** voice mail, hair dryers. **Pool(s):** heated outdoor. **Leisure Activities:** whirlpool, putting green, playground. **Guest Services:** coin laundry, wireless Internet. ASK [icons] / SOME UNITS FEE [icons]

—— WHERE TO DINE ——

BOUCHONS BISTRO   *Menu on AAA.com*

French
$19-$35

Phone: 250/763-6595 [10]

Located a few blocks from the waterfront and downtown, the restaurant could have been lifted directly off the streets of Nice or Rennes. Offering classic bistro fare, meals are prepared using fresh, local ingredients. Cassoulet, the house specialty, is superb. The wine list consists of healthy doses of both French and local Okanagan wines. Decor features cork flooring, ochre walls, stained-glass panels and handwritten menus. Service is decidedly professional and many staff speak French. Dressy casual. **Bar:** Full bar. **Reservations:** suggested. **Hours:** Open 3/16-2/15; 5:30 pm-10 pm. Closed major holidays. **Address:** 105-1180 Sunset Dr V1Y 9W6 **Location:** Jct Water St; centre. **Parking:** street. CALL [icons]

CABANA BAR AND GRILLE

Canadian
$10-$33

Phone: 250/763-1955 [27]

This ultra-cool space has deluxe banquettes and bar seating along the open kitchen. Taste buds perk up at the unusual twists that pop up in the appealing appetizers, burgers, sandwiches, pizzas and pastas, as well as meat and seafood entrees with a choice of sauces such as peppercorn and truffle butter or local apple barbecue. The pastry chef prepares an array of equally delicious desserts. Also on site are a huge seasonal patio with flaming grills and a trendy lounge for more casual dining. Casual dress. **Bar:** Full bar. **Reservations:** accepted. **Hours:** 11:30 am-midnight. Closed: 12/24-12/26. **Address:** 3799 Lakeshore Rd V1W 3K5 **Location:** Hwy 97 (Harvey Ave), 2.5 mi (4 km) s on Pandosy (which becomes Lakeshore Rd). **Parking:** on-site. CALL [icons]

CHRISTOPHER'S

Seafood
$15-$40

Phone: 250/861-3464 [16]

Patrons appreciate the charming restaurant's quaint dining room, personalized attention and fresh seafood. Selections also include steak, salad bar offerings and desserts. Large groups are accommodated at this local favorite, and the atmosphere can be boisterous. Casual dress. **Bar:** Full bar. **Reservations:** suggested. **Hours:** 4:30 pm-10 pm, Fri & Sat-midnight. Closed: 12/25. **Address:** 242 Lawrence Ave V1Y 6L3 **Location:** Downtown. **Parking:** street.

DAWETT FINE INDIAN CUISINE

Indian
$6-$17

Phone: 250/717-1668 [13]

Considered one of the best Indian restaurants in the Okanagan Valley, this place doesn't disappoint with its traditional ethnic cuisine. Guests can tantalize their taste buds with tandoori chicken, chicken masala, pakoras and samosas, all made with top-quality ingredients. Vegetarians will find many choices of fine food to enjoy in a simple, comfortable dining room. Casual dress. **Bar:** Full bar. **Reservations:** suggested. **Hours:** 11 am-2:30 & 4:30-9:45 pm, Fri-10:45 pm, Sat 12:30 pm-3 & 4-10:45 pm, Sun 12:30 pm-3 & 4-9:45 pm. Closed: 12/25. **Address:** 1435 Ellis St V1Y 2A3 **Location:** Between Bernard and Doyle aves; downtown. **Parking:** street.

ELDORADO DINING ROOM & BAR

Regional
Canadian
$10-$50

Phone: 250/763-7500 [28]

The casual yet elegant restaurant is right along the water and offers views of Lake Okanagan and the valley. Preparations of regionally diverse cuisine exceed expectations. In addition to seafood and pasta options, diners can select from several meat dishes. Known for its brunch, this place is a must stop for those visiting Kelowna. Casual dress. **Bar:** Full bar. **Reservations:** suggested. **Hours:** 7 am-11 pm. Closed: 12/25. **Address:** 500 Cook Rd V1W 3G9 **Location:** Hwy 97 (Harvey Ave), 2.5 mi (4 km) s on Pandosy (which becomes Lakeshore Rd); in Hotel Eldorado. **Parking:** on-site. CALL [icons]

GRAND BAY CAFE

Canadian
$12-$29

Phone: 250/763-4500 [11]

This restaurant's menu lines up a wide variety of fare, ranging from seafood to pasta to prime rib. Most tables offer a view overlooking the lake and river paths, and the service is attentive. Casual dress. **Bar:** Full bar. **Reservations:** suggested. **Hours:** 6:30 am-10 pm. **Address:** 1310 Water St V1Y 9P3 **Location:** Hwy 97 (Harvey Ave), 0.6 mi (1 km) w along Water St; in The Grand Okanagan Lakefront Resort & Conference Centre. **Parking:** on-site (fee) and valet.

THE GRATEFUL FED BAR & GRILL

Deli
$5-$10

Phone: 250/862-8621 [14]

Popular with the late-night crowd, the small, unassuming delicatessen is a must stop for visiting rock stars and concertgoers. The menu comprises traditional deli fare. Live music of many genres is featured most nights. Casual dress. **Bar:** Full bar. **Reservations:** accepted. **Hours:** 7 am-11 pm, Mon-4 pm. Closed major holidays; also Sun. **Address:** 509 Bernard Ave V1Y 6N9 **Location:** Jct Ellis St; centre. **Parking:** street.

(See map and index starting on p. 546)

HANNA'S LOUNGE & GRILL   **Phone:** 250/860-1266   ⑫

Pacific Northwest
$11-$35

Patrons can access the restaurant from the waterfront entrance or walk through the Grand Okanagan Hotel. Inside they'll find a modern, upbeat atmosphere and a menu that features dishes prepared with a West Coast flair, along with many local Okanagan wines. The second-floor location offers wonderful views of the lake and distant hills. Parking is at street meters or in the nearby yacht club pay lot. Casual dress. **Bar:** Full bar. **Hours:** 11 am-10 pm, Fri & Sat-11 pm. Closed: 12/25. **Address:** 1352 Water St V1Y 9P3 **Location:** Hwy 97 (Harvey Ave), 0.6 mi (1 km) w; at The Grand Okanagan Lakefront, above Rose's. **Parking:** street.

JAKX NEIGHBOURHOOD GRILL   **Phone:** 250/763-0773   ㉔

Canadian
$8-$24

A favorite among locals, the family-owned restaurant is on the second floor of a shopping center, with wheelchair access via an elevator. A wine list focused on bottles from area wineries matches with pizzas and pasta and meat entrees. Families are welcomed. Casual dress. **Bar:** Full bar. **Reservations:** suggested. **Hours:** 11 am-9 pm. Closed major holidays; also Sun & Mon. **Address:** 203-595 KLO Rd V1Y 8E7 **Location:** 1.9 mi (3 km) e on Pandosy St (which becomes Lakeshore Rd); at Pandosy and KLO Rd; in shopping plaza. **Parking:** on-site. CALL ♿Ⓜ

THE JAMMERY   **Phone:** 250/766-1139   ⑨

Canadian
$8-$14

A play on the winery concept, the restaurant uses locally grown fruits in its creations. Guests can learn about the jam made on site or just come for afternoon tea. The menu lays out an excellent selection of breakfast choices, sandwiches, wraps and afternoon tea service. Casual dress. **Reservations:** not accepted. **Hours:** 7:30 am-4 pm; to 5 pm in summer. Closed: 1/1, 12/25, 12/26. **Address:** 8038 Hwy 97 N V1X 6A6 **Location:** Hwy 97 N (Harvey Ave), 7.4 mi (12 km) n. **Parking:** on-site. CALL ♿Ⓜ

JOEY RESTAURANTS   **Phone:** 250/860-8999

Mediterranean
$11-$29

The cuisine blends Mediterranean and Asian cooking styles and emphasizes finger foods for sharing. Those who aren't big fans of tapas can consider full meal offerings centered on steaks and chops. Casual dress. **Bar:** Full bar. **Reservations:** not accepted. **Hours:** 11:30 am-1 am, Sun-midnight. Closed: 12/24, 12/25. **Address:** 300-2475 Hwy 97 V1X 4J2 **Location:** Hwy 97 (Harvey Ave); between Banks and Powick rds. **Parking:** on-site. CALL ♿Ⓜ

KELSEY'S   **Phone:** 250/762-4774

Canadian
$9-$21

A fun, relaxed atmosphere and tasty menu of casual fare make the restaurant a popular favorite with locals. Diners might start a meal with some tempting appetizers, such as wings, loaded potato skins or nachos, and follow them with an old-time favorite, such as a burger, wrap, pizza or pasta dish. For a heartier meal, it's hard to beat pork back ribs or a steak. The diverse menu has broad appeal. Casual dress. **Bar:** Full bar. **Reservations:** accepted. **Hours:** 11 am-11 pm, Sun from 10 am. Closed: 12/25. **Address:** 1755 Capri St V1Y 6E8 **Location:** Capri St and Gordon Ave. **Parking:** on-site.

MAMMA ROSA   **Phone:** 250/763-4114   ⑮

Italian
$13-$34

As the name suggests, the restaurant is known for Italian food, just as Mama might have made it. The extensive menu lists homemade in various forms, ranging from cannelloni and lasagna to manicotti and penne. Also tempting is a fine selection of pizzas. Red-and-white-checked tablecloths and Italian decor lend to the cozy atmosphere. The service is super. Casual dress. **Bar:** Full bar. **Reservations:** suggested. **Hours:** 5 pm-close, Sun from 5:30 pm. Closed: Mon. **Address:** 561 Lawrence Ave V1Y 6L8 **Location:** Downtown. **Parking:** street. CALL ♿Ⓜ

THE MARMALADE CAT CAFE   **Phone:** 250/861-4158   ㉓

Vegetarian
$6-$8

Many people accidentally discover this cute and tiny restaurant as they wander through the aisles of the gift shop that seems to surround it. Guests line up to order choices from a good selection of hearty and creative sandwiches, hot daily specials that seem to sell out quickly, and assorted small tasty desserts. Casual dress. **Reservations:** not accepted. **Hours:** 7:30 am-5 pm, Sat from 8 am, Sun 9 am-4 pm. Closed major holidays. **Address:** 2903 Pandosy St V1Y 1W1 **Location:** Jct West Ave. **Parking:** street.

MEKONG RESTAURANT   **Phone:** 250/763-8000   ⑳

Traditional
Chinese
$6-$15

The restaurant prepares fresh, mouthwatering Szechuan cuisine. Patrons are encouraged to ask about the signature deluxe meals, which involve ginger chicken or steak strips with black pepper sauce for two to 10 people. The decor is bright, fresh and contemporary. Peak meal times can be busy. Casual dress. **Bar:** Full bar. **Reservations:** accepted. **Hours:** 11:30 am-10 pm. Closed: 12/25. **Address:** 1030 Harvey Ave V1Y 8S4 **Location:** Corner of Hwy 97 N (Harvey Ave) and Gordon Dr; in Kelowna Motor Inn. **Parking:** on-site.

MINSTREL CAFE & BAR   **Phone:** 250/764-2301   ㉚

International
$8-$30

A little off the beaten path, the distinctive cafe is considered to be one of Kelowna's best-kept secrets, especially for lunch. Upon entry, guests notice a large tree in the middle of the dining room, set against soft olive walls boasting original local art. The menu lists a wide range of soups, salads and frittatas, which can be enjoyed in the open, airy dining room or on the patio outside. Live entertainment is featured on weekends. Casual dress. **Bar:** Full bar. **Reservations:** suggested. **Hours:** 11:30 am-11 pm. Closed: 12/25. **Address:** 4638 Lakeshore Rd V1W 1X5 **Location:** Hwy 97 (Harvey Ave), 5.6 mi (9 km) s at Pandosy St (which becomes Lakeshore Rd). **Parking:** on-site. CALL ♿Ⓜ

MIZU JAPANESE RESTAURANT   **Phone:** 250/862-8022   ㉒

Sushi
$8-$14

The eat-in/take-out eatery has but seven small tables, and diners can watch sushi and sashimi being made at the counter. Many locals patronize the popular, busy spot for take-out sushi. Regardless of where the food is eaten, patrons are tempted by artistic, traditional displays of delicious Japanese fare. Casual dress. **Reservations:** not accepted. **Hours:** 11:30 am-8:30 pm. Closed: 1/1, 12/25, 12/26; also Mon. **Address:** 2684 Pandosy St V1Y 1V6 **Location:** Hwy 97 (Harvey Ave), 1.8 mi (3 km) s on Pandosy St (which becomes Lakeshore Rd); in South Gate Plaza. **Parking:** on-site.

(See map and index starting on p. 546)

MOXIE'S CLASSIC GRILL
Phone: 250/861-6110

Canadian
$10-$29

This sleek, funky and popular restaurant presents an extensive menu of creatively prepared dishes, including pizza, pasta, rice, noodles, signature salads and burgers. Other menus include one for children and one for Sunday brunch. Lending to the upbeat, stylish decor are dark wood appointments and river rock fireplaces. Casual dress. **Bar:** Full bar. **Reservations:** accepted. **Hours:** 11 am-midnight, Fri & Sat-1 am. Closed: 12/25. **Address:** 1730 Cooper Rd V1Y 8V5 **Location:** Hwy 97 (Harvey Ave), just e; corner of Enterprise Way. **Parking:** on-site.

PEARSON'S EUROPEAN DELI
Phone: 250/762-0800   21

Deli
$7-$12

Aromas of fresh bread fill the small delicatessen, which offers a case of salads, ranging from pasta to curried chicken. Behind the counter is a chalkboard with several sandwich options, as well as such listings as cabbage rolls and pierogies. Made on thick slabs of fresh bread, sandwiches are incredible. This spot fits the bill for a healthy, quick meal. Casual dress. **Reservations:** not accepted. **Hours:** 6:30 am-6 pm, Sat 9 am-4 pm. Closed major holidays; also Sun. **Address:** #30-2070 Harvey Ave V1Y 8P8 **Location:** Hwy 95 S; jct Cooper Ave; in strip mall. **Parking:** on-site.

PHEASANT & QUAIL PUB
Phone: 250/860-1066   25

American
$10-$22

Modeled after an English ale house, the cozy restaurant invites patrons to drop in for a pint and some good pub food. Comfortable armchairs for lounging, a bar area and an enclosed smoking area encourage relaxing. Fish and chips, sandwiches, pastas and salads make up the menu, and the friendly servers share information about the local brews. Casual dress. **Bar:** Full bar. **Reservations:** accepted, except Fri. **Hours:** 11 am-10 pm, Fri & Sat-11 pm. Closed: 1/1, 12/25. **Address:** 3110 Lakeshore Rd V1W 3T1 **Location:** 1.8 mi (3 km) s on Pandosy (which becomes Lakeshore Rd). **Parking:** on-site.

RICKY'S ALL DAY GRILL
Phone: 250/763-4141

Canadian
$9-$26

The comfortable eatery, which employs friendly servers, presents a varied menu that includes pasta dishes, wraps, omelets, stir-fry preparations and burgers. Portions are generous. Children's and senior selections are offered. Guests can request seating in a booth or at a table. Casual dress. **Bar:** Full bar. **Reservations:** accepted. **Hours:** 7 am-8:30 pm. Closed: 12/25. **Address:** 2435 Hwy 97 N V1X 4J2 **Location:** 0.6 mi (1 km) s of jct Hwy 97 N (Harvey Ave) and 33; in Holiday Inn Express. **Parking:** on-site.

RIC'S GRILL
Phone: 250/869-1586   17

Steak
$14-$37

"Funky and modern" describes the decor and the food at the upscale steakhouse, which bustles with activity. Steaks are well worth it, but then again, so are the salmon, chicken and pasta dishes. A wide variety of distinctive appetizers rounds out the menu. Servers are friendly and attentive. Casual dress. **Bar:** Full bar. **Reservations:** suggested. **Hours:** 11:30 am-11 pm, Sat & Sun from 4:30 pm. Closed: 12/25. **Address:** 210 Lawrence Ave V1Y 6L3 **Location:** Corner of Lawrence Ave and Abbott St; downtown. **Parking:** street.

SEVEN SIX FOUR RESTAURANT
Phone: 250/764-7645   29

Pacific Northwest
$11-$28

The distinctive restaurant's simple dining room pipes with live local music on weekends. Although the menu is not extensive, its meals, which incorporate a blend of fresh and local ingredients, are fantastic. The wine list features a wide selection of excellent British Columbian wines by the glass or bottle. Casual dress. **Bar:** Full bar. **Reservations:** suggested. **Hours:** 10 am-4 pm, Sat & Sun from 8:30 am. Closed: 1/1, 12/25; also Mon. **Address:** 12-4600 Lakeshore Rd V1W 1X4 **Location:** 4.4 mi (7 km) w at Pandosy (which becomes Lakeshore Rd). **Parking:** on-site.

SUMMERHILL SUNSET BISTRO
Phone: 250/764-8000   31

Regional
Canadian
$12-$33

Overlooking the Okanagan Valley, the winery restaurant affords nice views. Food presentations are artistic. Guests can make their way to the eatery after a tour and tasting or come directly for a special meal. Several menu items incorporate regional ingredients and a Bavarian smokehouse cooking technique. Starters are large enough to share, and meals are exquisite. Casual dress. **Bar:** Full bar. **Reservations:** suggested. **Hours:** 11 am-9 pm. Closed: 12/25. **Address:** 4870 Chute Lake Rd V1W 4M3 **Location:** 9 mi (15 km) e at Pandosy (which becomes Lakeshore Rd), just s at Chute Lake Rd, follow signs. **Parking:** on-site.

CALL

SWISS CHALET
Phone: 250/762-6362

Canadian
$7-$18

The popular restaurant is known for its rotisserie chicken and ribs and the tangy Chalet sauce that gives food its special zip. Diners munch on a half or quarter chicken with sides such as steamed vegetables, fries, baked potatoes and salads. Lunch guests often go for the great soup and sandwich combination. Take-out and delivery service are popular options. Casual dress. **Bar:** Full bar. **Reservations:** accepted. **Hours:** 11 am-10 pm, Fri & Sat-11 pm. Closed: 12/25. **Address:** 1475 Harvey Ave V1Y 6E9 **Location:** Jct Burtch Rd. **Parking:** on-site.

WILD APPLE RESTAURANT   *Menu on AAA.com*
Phone: 250/860-4488   26

Pacific Northwest
$12-$28

A fresh, bright, contemporary dining room awaits guests of the restaurant along the waterfront. Featuring an open-concept kitchen and light, bright colors, the dining room transforms in the evening to become a bit more intimate. Upbeat, creative meals include pasta and sandwiches at lunch and creative seafood and meat preparations at dinner. Casual dress. **Bar:** Full bar. **Reservations:** suggested. **Hours:** 6 am-10 pm; from 7 am 11/1-2/28. **Address:** 3762 Lakeshore Rd V1W 3L4 **Location:** Hwy 97 N (Harvey Ave), 2.5 mi (4 km) s on Pandosy (which becomes Lakeshore Rd); in Manteo Resort-Waterfront Hotel & Villas. **Parking:** on-site. CALL

YAMAS TAVERNA RESTAURANT
Phone: 250/763-5823   19

Greek
$11-$35

A typical and traditional Greek feel envelops the downtown restaurant, which is popular with the business crowd at lunch. Guests can choose from the all-you-can-eat lunch buffet or from delicious entrees on the menu. Casual dress. **Bar:** Full bar. **Reservations:** suggested. **Hours:** 11 am-11 pm, Sat & Sun from 4:30 pm. Closed major holidays. **Address:** 1630 Ellis St V1Y 8L1 **Location:** Hwy 97 (Harvey Ave), just w at Ellis St. **Parking:** street.

(See map and index starting on p. 546)

THE YELLOWHOUSE RESTAURANT
Phone: 250/763-5136   (18)

▼▼◆▼▼
Canadian
$11-$36

In a Victorian heritage house, the restaurant gives guests a warm welcome. The freshest ingredients are used in delicious dishes that are made from scratch in house. Taste buds will be tantalized with entrees such as duck with pecan, spinach and thyme stuffing or the signature seafood linguine with lemon pepper dill cream. Service is attentive and professional. Casual dress. **Bar:** Full bar. **Reservations:** suggested. **Hours:** 11:30 am-2:30 & 5-9 pm, Sat & Sun from 5 pm. Closed major holidays. **Address:** 526 Lawrence Ave V1Y 6L7 **Location:** Hwy 97 (Harvey Ave), just n on Bertram St, then just w; downtown. **Parking:** street.

CALL 🖭M

NARAMATA pop. 1,787   (See map and index starting on p. 546)

THE VILLAGE MOTEL
Phone: (250)496-5535   (40)

▼▼◆▼▼
Motel
$90-$145 3/1-12/31

Address: 244 Robinson Dr V0H 1N0 **Location:** 8.8 mi (14 km) n on Naramata Rd from Penticton. **Facility:** Smoke free premises. 9 units. 5 one-bedroom standard units, some with efficiencies. 4 one-bedroom suites with efficiencies. 1 story, exterior corridors. **Parking:** on-site. **Terms:** open 3/1-12/31, office hours 8 am-9 pm, 2-3 night minimum stay - seasonal and/or weekends, 14 day cancellation notice. **Amenities:** hair dryers. 📶 ✕ 🖃 🖾 🖾 🖥 🖳 / SOME UNITS FEE 🐕 🖃

━━━━━━━━━ **WHERE TO DINE** ━━━━━━━━━

COBBLESTONE WINE BAR & RESTAURANT
Phone: 250/496-5064   (38)

(CAA)
▼▼◆▼▼
Canadian
$9-$34

There is an intimate, cozy feel among the brick floors and walls of this restaurant, set in the basement of the Naramata Heritage Inn & Spa. This is casual dining at its best, with a menu that features many artistic dishes with regional ingredients. Servers will impress with an extensive wine knowledge, helping to create a lovely and enjoyable meal. Casual dress. **Hours:** Open 3/1-10/31 & 2/8-2/28; 11 am-9 pm; Fri-Sun to 8 pm 2/8-3/31. **Address:** 3625 First St V0H 1N0 **Location:** 11.4 mi (19 km) ne of Penticton; from Naramata Rd, w along Robinson to 1st St, just s; in Naramata Heritage Inn & Spa. **Parking:** on-site. CALL 🖭M

OSOYOOS pop. 4,752   (See map and index starting on p. 546)

BEST WESTERN SUNRISE INN   *Book great rates at AAA.com*
Phone: (250)495-4000   (54)

(CAA) (SAVE)
▼▼◆▼▼
Hotel
$99-$255 All Year

Address: 5506 Main St V0H 1V0 **Location:** Jct Hwy 97, 1.9 mi (3 km) on Hwy 3 (Main St). **Facility:** Smoke free premises. 66 units. 37 one-bedroom standard units, some with efficiencies and/or whirlpools. 29 one-bedroom suites with kitchens. 3 stories, interior corridors. *Bath:* combo or shower only. **Parking:** on-site. **Terms:** check-in 4 pm, 7 day cancellation notice-fee imposed. **Amenities:** voice mail, irons, hair dryers. **Pool(s):** heated indoor. **Leisure Activities:** whirlpool, exercise room. **Guest Services:** coin laundry, wireless Internet. **Business Services:** PC. **Free Special Amenities:** continental breakfast and high-speed Internet.

🍴 🍸 CALL 🖭M 🏊 ✕ 🖾 🖥 🖳 / SOME UNITS FEE 🐕 🖃

AAA Benefit:
Members save up to 20%, plus 10% bonus points with rewards program.

Theme park fun:
SMART.

Theme park discounts: **INGENIOUS.**

(See map and index starting on p. 546)

THE COAST OSOYOOS BEACH HOTEL   *Book at AAA.com*   Phone: (250)495-6525   53

▼▼▼ ▼▼▼
Motel
$79-$219 All Year

Address: 7702 Main St (Hwy 3 E) V0H 1V0 **Location:** Jct Hwy 97, 1.2 mi (2 km) e. **Facility:** Smoke free premises. 60 units. 47 one-bedroom standard units, some with kitchens. 9 one- and 4 two-bedroom suites with kitchens. 3 stories, interior/exterior corridors. **Parking:** on-site. **Terms:** office hours 7 am-11 pm, check-in 4 pm, 14 day cancellation notice-fee imposed. **Amenities:** voice mail, hair dryers. *Some:* high-speed Internet. **Pool(s):** heated indoor. **Leisure Activities:** whirlpool, waterslide, exercise room. **Guest Services:** coin laundry, wireless Internet. **Business Services:** PC.

ECO ASK ▮▮+ 🏊 ✕ ✕ ▯ 🖥 / SOME UNITS 🖨

SPIRIT RIDGE VINEYARD RESORT & SPA   Phone: 250/495-5445   52

▼▼▼ ▼▼
Condominium
Rates not provided

Address: 1200 Rancher Creek Rd V0H 1V6 **Location:** Hwy 97 S, e on Hwy 3 (Main St), cross bridge, left on 45th St, 0.9 mi (1.5 km) e. **Facility:** Tuscan-style villas and traditional condo units border an award-winning vineyard, offering beautiful views of the town and nearby lake. Smoke free premises. 127 units. 96 one- and 2 three-bedroom suites with kitchens. 2-4 stories, interior/exterior corridors. **Parking:** on-site. **Terms:** check-in 4 pm. **Amenities:** video library, DVD players, CD players, high-speed Internet, voice mail, safes, irons, hair dryers. **Dining:** Passa Tempo, see separate listing. **Pool(s):** heated outdoor. **Leisure Activities:** whirlpool, waterslide, beach access, rental boats, rental canoes, rental paddleboats, exercise room, spa. *Fee:* marina. **Guest Services:** coin laundry, area transportation, wireless Internet. **Business Services:** meeting rooms.

▮▮ CALL 🔊M 🏊 ✕ ✕ ▯ 🖨 🖥 / SOME UNITS FEE 🐾

WALNUT BEACH RESORT   *Book great rates at AAA.com*   Phone: (250)495-5400   55

CAA SAVE

▼▼▼ ▼▼
Hotel
$169-$799 All Year

Address: 4200 Lakeshore Dr V0H 1V6 **Location:** 0.9 mi (1.5 km) s off Hwy 3 (Main St). **Facility:** Smoke free premises. 112 units. 39 one-bedroom standard units with efficiencies. 42 one- and 31 two-bedroom suites with kitchens. 3 stories, interior corridors. **Parking:** on-site. **Terms:** check-in 4 pm, 7 day cancellation notice-fee imposed. **Amenities:** DVD players, CD players, high-speed Internet, voice mail, irons, hair dryers. **Pool(s):** heated outdoor. **Leisure Activities:** sauna, whirlpools, steamroom, limited beach access, boat dock, barbecues, exercise room. *Fee:* massage. **Guest Services:** wireless Internet. **Business Services:** meeting rooms, business center.

▮▮ ▼ CALL 🔊M 🏊 ✕ ✕ ▯ 🖨 🖥

—— WHERE TO DINE ——

CAMPO MARINA   Phone: 250/495-7650   55

▼▼▼ ▼▼▼
Italian
$14-$23

The established, family-run restaurant is sure to please with its hearty Italian dishes. The cozy, comfortable dining room welcomes guests to linger over linguine, tantalize their taste buds with tiramisu and savor pan-seared scallops. Casual dress. **Bar:** Full bar. **Reservations:** accepted. **Hours:** 5 pm-9 pm. Closed: 12/24-12/26. **Address:** 5907 Main St, RR 3 V0H 1V3 **Location:** East end of town on Hwy 3 (Main St). **Parking:** on-site. CALL 🔊M

DIAMOND STEAK AND SEAFOOD HOUSE   Phone: 250/495-6223   54

◆◆◆ ◆◆
Steak
$10-$55

Tasty food and attentive service are hallmarks at the excellent family restaurant. The menu lists a nice selection of pasta, pizza and Greek specialties. Broiled chicken breast with peppercorn and brandy demi-glace sauce is simply delectable. Casual dress. **Bar:** Full bar. **Reservations:** suggested, in summer. **Hours:** 4 pm-10 pm. Closed: 12/25; also Mon. **Address:** 8903 Main St V0H 1V0 **Location:** Hwy 3 (Main St) at 89th St; centre. **Parking:** street.

PASSA TEMPO   Phone: 250/495-8007   52

◆◆◆ ◆◆◆
Canadian
$10-$26

Unusual multidimensional decor characterizes this restaurant, which offers a lovely patio and fantastic views of the lake. High-quality local produce influences the menu, which gravitates around a tapas and appetizer core, such as a daily terrine or pear and goat cheese spread. Entrees might include braised beef short ribs with Stilton cheese cornbread. The made-in-house desserts are mouthwatering. Among the individual tables is a long, custom-built wood table that dominates the room. Casual dress. **Bar:** Full bar. **Reservations:** suggested. **Hours:** 8 am-9 pm. **Address:** 1200 Rancher Creek Rd V0H 1V6 **Location:** Hwy 97 S, e on Hwy 3 (Main St), cross bridge, left on 45th St, 0.9 mi (1.5 km) e; in Spirit Ridge Vineyard Resort & Spa. **Parking:** on-site. CALL 🔊M

WILDFIRE GRILL   Phone: 250/495-2215   53

▼▼ ▼▼
Canadian
$9-$24

As patrons enter the downtown restaurant's small dining room, they are greeted by warm orange walls and tables that sparkle. The dining patio opens seasonally. "Globally inspired" is the motto of the contemporary bistro, which serves salmon, chicken and pasta dishes, as well as hearty salads. Casual dress. **Bar:** Full bar. **Reservations:** accepted. **Hours:** 11 am-3 & 5-9 pm, Sat & Sun from 5 pm. Closed: 12/25. **Address:** 8526 Main St V0H 1V0 **Location:** Just e of jct Hwy 97 and 3 (Main St); downtown. **Parking:** street.

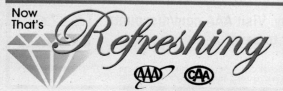

PENTICTON pop. 31,909   (See map and index starting on p. 546)

BEST WESTERN INN AT PENTICTON   *Book great rates at AAA.com*   **Phone:** (250)493-0311

Hotel
$99–$199 All Year

Address: 3180 Skaha Lake Rd V2A 6G4 **Location:** 2.5 mi (4 km) s. **Facility:** Smoke free premises. 67 units. 55 one-bedroom standard units, some with whirlpools. 9 one- and 3 two-bedroom suites, some with efficiencies or kitchens. 2 stories (no elevator), exterior corridors. **Parking:** on-site. **Amenities:** voice mail, irons, hair dryers. *Some:* high-speed Internet. **Pool(s):** heated outdoor, heated indoor. **Leisure Activities:** whirlpool, playground. **Guest Services:** valet and coin laundry, wireless Internet. **Business Services:** meeting rooms, PC. **Free Special Amenities:** continental breakfast and high-speed Internet.

AAA Benefit:
Members save up to 20%, plus 10% bonus points with rewards program.

DAYS INN & CONFERENCE CENTRE PENTICTON   *Book great rates at AAA.com*   **Phone:** (250)493-6616

Hotel
$99–$299 All Year

Address: 152 Riverside Dr V2A 5Y4 **Location:** Hwy 97, just n. **Facility:** Smoke free premises. 104 one-bedroom standard units, some with kitchens and/or whirlpools. 2 stories (no elevator), interior corridors. *Bath:* combo or shower only. **Parking:** on-site. **Terms:** cancellation fee imposed. **Amenities:** voice mail, irons, hair dryers. *Some:* high-speed Internet, safes. **Pool(s):** heated outdoor, heated indoor. **Leisure Activities:** whirlpool, children spray park, limited exercise equipment, spa. **Guest Services:** coin laundry, wireless Internet. **Business Services:** conference facilities, PC (fee).

FREE continental breakfast and local telephone calls

EMPIRE MOTEL   **Phone:** 250/493-2323

Motel
$59–$164 All Year

Address: 3495 Skaha Lake Rd V2A 6G6 **Location:** From centre, 2.8 mi (4.5 km) s. **Facility:** Smoke free premises. 32 units. 17 one- and 5 two-bedroom standard units, some with efficiencies. 10 one-bedroom suites with kitchens. 2 stories (no elevator), exterior corridors. **Parking:** on-site. **Terms:** office hours 8 am-10 pm, 30 day cancellation notice-fee imposed. **Amenities:** hair dryers. **Pool(s):** heated outdoor. **Leisure Activities:** playground. **Guest Services:** wireless Internet.

▼ See AAA listing p 562 ▼

PENTICTON LAKESIDE RESORT, CONVENTION CENTRE & CASINO

Book great rates at AAA.com

Phone: (250)493-8221 **43**

Hotel
$165-$235 All Year

Address: 21 Lakeshore Dr W V2A 7M5 **Location:** Main St at Lakeshore Dr W. **Facility:** With an on-site casino, lakeside location and balconies in some rooms, this full-service, resort-style hotel is a destination property. Smoke free premises. 204 units. 196 one-bedroom standard units, some with whirlpools. 8 one-bedroom suites. 6 stories, interior corridors. **Parking:** on-site (fee) and valet. **Terms:** check-in 4 pm, 7 day cancellation notice-fee imposed. **Amenities:** voice mail, irons, hair dryers. **Dining:** 2 restaurants. **Pool(s):** heated indoor. **Leisure Activities:** whirlpool, rental boats, rental canoes, rental paddleboats, boat dock, recreation programs in summer. **Guest Services:** valet laundry, wireless Internet. **Business Services:** conference facilities, PC (fee). *(See color ad p 561)*

RAMADA INN & SUITES

Book great rates at AAA.com

Phone: (250)492-8926 **46**

Hotel
$109-$269 3/1-10/13
$89-$269 10/14-2/28

Address: 1050 Eckhardt Ave W V2A 2C3 **Location:** 0.8 mi (1.2 km) w on Hwy 97. **Facility:** Smoke free premises. 125 units. 110 one-bedroom standard units, some with whirlpools. 15 one-bedroom suites with kitchens. 1-3 stories, interior/exterior corridors. **Parking:** on-site. **Terms:** cancellation fee imposed. **Amenities:** voice mail, irons, hair dryers. *Some:* high-speed Internet. **Pool(s):** heated outdoor. **Leisure Activities:** whirlpool, playground, exercise room. **Guest Services:** valet and coin laundry, wireless Internet. **Business Services:** meeting rooms, PC. **Free Special Amenities:** newspaper and high-speed Internet.

SPANISH VILLA RESORT

Phone: (250)492-2922 **44**

Motel
$68-$350 All Year

Address: 890 Lakeshore Dr W V2A 1C1 **Location:** Corner of Power St and Lakeshore Dr W. **Facility:** Smoke free premises. 60 units. 16 one-bedroom standard units. 38 one-, 5 two- and 1 three-bedroom suites with kitchens. 2 stories (no elevator), exterior corridors. **Parking:** on-site. **Terms:** office hours 8 am-10 pm, 2-7 night minimum stay - seasonal and/or weekends, 14 day cancellation notice-fee imposed. **Amenities:** hair dryers. **Pool(s):** heated indoor. **Guest Services:** coin laundry, wireless Internet. **Free Special Amenities:** newspaper and high-speed Internet.

SUPER 8 PENTICTON

Book at AAA.com

Phone: 250/492-3829 **47**

Motel
Rates not provided

Address: 1706 Main St V2A 5G8 **Location:** Jct Main St and Industrial Ave. **Facility:** 54 units. 43 one-bedroom standard units, some with efficiencies and/or whirlpools. 6 one- and 5 two-bedroom suites, some with efficiencies or kitchens. 2 stories (no elevator), interior/exterior corridors. *Bath:* combo or shower only. **Parking:** on-site. **Amenities:** hair dryers. **Pool(s):** heated indoor. **Leisure Activities:** whirlpool. **Guest Services:** coin laundry, wireless Internet. **Business Services:** PC.

—— **WHERE TO DINE** ——

AMANTE BISTRO

Phone: 250/493-1961 **44**

International
$9-$34

"Urban chic" describes the decor at this cozy little bistro, where the delightful menu features a variety of tapas-style appetizers and antipasti made from fresh specialty items such as hickory-smoked duck breast or pork cheeks. A great choice for the adventurous is the "challenge the chef" tapas. Entrees range from weekly fish to rack of lamb. The hospitable and warm setting is conducive to lingering, and the owner and sometimes her chef husband chat at guests' tables. Casual dress. **Bar:** Full bar. **Reservations:** suggested. **Hours:** Open 3/1-12/31 & 2/1-2/28; 5:30 pm-9 pm, Fri also 11:30 am-2:30 pm. Closed: 12/24, 12/25; also Sun 11/1-6/30 & Mon. **Address:** 101-483 Main St V2A 5C4 **Location:** Corner of Padmore Ave W and Main St; downtown. **Parking:** on-site and street.

BOGNER'S OF PENTICTON

Phone: 250/493-2711 **46**

Continental
$22-$40

For somewhere special to eat, the 100-year-old heritage mansion fits the bill. On a quiet residential street, the rustic restaurant has an elegant dining room and attentive servers. Guests can sit back and enjoy flavorful creations from the kitchen. Drawing largely on regional ingredients, the chef also chooses many local wines for the menu. Casual dress. **Bar:** Full bar. **Reservations:** accepted. **Hours:** 5:30 pm-11 pm. Closed: Mon. **Address:** 302 Eckhardt Ave W V2A 2A9 **Location:** 2 blks w of Main St; corner of Argyle St. **Parking:** on-site.

FIBONACCI ROASTERY & CAFE

Phone: 250/770-1913 **42**

Deli
$7-$10

A small Italian-style red coffee roaster is the centerpiece of this large, open-concept coffee shop. The aroma of freshly roasting coffee, brewed in small batches, wafts through the dining room. More than 40 types of loose-leaf teas come from organic and fair-trade roasted green beans. As for food, patrons find sandwiches and a limited selection of entrees, which are prepared to order. Staff call out customers names when the order is ready. Casual dress. **Bar:** Beer & wine. **Reservations:** not accepted. **Hours:** 7 am-8 pm, Sun-6 pm. Closed: 12/25. **Address:** 219 Main St V2A 5B1 **Location:** Centre. **Parking:** street.

IYARA THAI RESTAURANT

Thai
$8-$16

Phone: 250/770-9791   49

In the south end of town toward Skaha Lake, the friendly restaurant serves authentic Thai cuisine from an extensive menu that includes dishes from mild to hot and spicy. Bangkok-trained chefs prepare fresh, delicious food, while eschewing the use of monosodium glutamate. Casual dress. **Bar:** Full bar. **Reservations:** accepted. **Hours:** 11:30 am-2:30 & 5-9 pm, Fri-Sun 5 pm-9:30 pm. Closed: 12/25. **Address:** 2985 Skaha Lake Rd V2A 5J6 **Location:** From centre, 2.2 mi (3.5 km) s. **Parking:** on-site.

CALL

LA CASA OUZERIA

Italian
$9-$26

Phone: 250/492-9144   47

A family-run operation, the homey restaurant satisfies those who can't decide what to have. The menu lists both Greek and Italian cuisine. The service and ambience merge to create a cozy, comfortable experience. Casual dress. **Bar:** Full bar. **Reservations:** suggested, weekends. **Hours:** 11:30 am-2 & 5-10 pm, Sat & Sun from 5 pm. Closed: 1/1, 12/25, 12/26; also Mon. **Address:** 1090 Main St V2A 5E5 **Location:** Corner of Main St and Nelson Ave. **Parking:** on-site.

NAVRATAN

Indian
$10-$17

Phone: 250/490-4746   43

Diners step into another world at this small restaurant, where the Indian cuisine includes tandoori chicken and many other dishes cooked in the clay oven, in addition to well-prepared curries, vindaloos, korma, biryani and a choice of naan breads. Casual dress. **Bar:** Full bar. **Reservations:** accepted. **Hours:** 11 am-2 & 4:30-10 pm, Sun from 4:30 pm. Closed major holidays. **Address:** 413 Main St V2A 5C4 **Location:** Corner of Wade Ave W and Main St; downtown. **Parking:** street.

RICKY'S ALL DAY GRILL

Canadian
$9-$26

Phone: 250/490-0375

The comfortable eatery, which employs friendly servers, presents a varied menu that includes pasta dishes, wraps, omelets, stir-fry preparations and burgers. Portions are generous. Children's and senior selections are offered. Guests can request seating in a booth or at a table. Casual dress. **Bar:** Full bar. **Reservations:** not accepted. **Hours:** 8 am-9 pm. Closed: 12/25. **Address:** 2111 Main St V2A 6W6 **Location:** Between Warren and McDougall aves; in Cherry Lane Shopping Centre. **Parking:** on-site.

SALTY'S BEACH HOUSE

Caribbean
$12-$26

Phone: 250/493-5001   41

During his travels, the owner collected recipes for all kinds of fish and other seafood, including the daily fresh catch, in addition to ribs, Sterling Silver AAA beef and jerk chicken. The dishes reflect the flavors of the Caribbean, Hawaii, Thailand and other island destinations. An island theme punctuates the fun restaurant, which has an inviting summer patio overlooking the lake and the Black Pearl Lounge and Oyster Bar upstairs. Casual dress. **Bar:** Full bar. **Reservations:** suggested. **Hours:** 11 am-11 pm, Fri & Sat-midnight; to 9 pm, Fri & Sat-11 pm 10/1-5/31. Closed: 12/25. **Address:** 1000 Lakeshore Dr V2A 1C1 **Location:** Hwy 97, 0.5 mi (0.8 km) n. **Parking:** street.

SHADES FAMILY RESTAURANT

American
$6-$12

Phone: 250/493-0465   48

For a quick, affordable meal that will please everyone in the family, the family-run restaurant hits the mark. On the menu is everything from grilled cheese sandwiches to burgers and fries. Guests shouldn't be surprised if the server addresses them as "honey" and knows almost all the regulars by name. Casual dress. **Bar:** Full bar. **Hours:** 6:30 am-8:30 pm, Fri & Sat-9:30 pm. Closed: 1/1, 4/4, 12/25. **Address:** 1909 Main St V2A 5H5 **Location:** Corner of Main St and Okanagan Rd. **Parking:** on-site.

THEO'S RESTAURANT

Greek
$6-$30

Phone: 250/492-4019   45

The established downtown restaurant is a favorite with the locals. This place adds its own little twists to classics made from the freshest ingredients. On the menu are choices such as Greek salads, dolmades, souvlaki, moussaka and roast lamb, as well as steak and seafood. The Mediterranean decor is warm and family oriented. Parking is available on the street or behind the restaurant. Casual dress. **Bar:** Full bar. **Reservations:** suggested. **Hours:** 11 am-10 pm, Fri & Sat-11 pm, Sun 4 pm-10 pm. Closed: 12/25. **Address:** 687 Main St V2A 5C9 **Location:** Main St at Eckhardt Ave. **Parking:** on-site.

SUMMERLAND pop. 10,713   (See map and index starting on p. 546)

SUMMERLAND MOTEL

CAA SAVE

Motel
$80-$150 All Year

Phone: 250/494-4444   37

Address: 2107 Tait St V0H 1Z4 **Location:** 3.1 mi (5 km) s on Hwy 97. **Facility:** Smoke free premises. 58 units. 49 one-bedroom standard units, some with efficiencies. 9 one-bedroom suites with kitchens. 2 stories, exterior corridors. **Bath:** combo or shower only. **Parking:** on-site. **Terms:** office hours 8 am-10 pm, 2 night minimum stay - seasonal and/or weekends, 10 day cancellation notice. **Amenities:** voice mail. Some: high-speed Internet, hair dryers. **Pool(s):** heated outdoor. **Leisure Activities:** exercise room. **Guest Services:** coin laundry, wireless Internet. **Free Special Amenities:** local telephone calls and high-speed Internet.

———— WHERE TO DINE ————

CELLAR DOOR BISTRO AT SUMAC RIDGE ESTATE WINERY

CAA

Regional
Canadian
$12-$28

Phone: 250/494-0451   34

The restaurant at Sumac Ridge is perched atop the ridge, and some tables afford stunning views of the vineyard and valley below. After entering the wine and tasting shop, patrons notice the upscale, bistro-style eatery at the back. Local ingredients go into the marvelous, artistic dishes. The seasonal menu may feature a sandwich of the day, soup and a decadent dessert, and patrons also can opt to try a flight of wine. Casual dress. **Bar:** Full bar. **Reservations:** suggested. **Hours:** Open 3/1-12/19 & 1/14-2/28; 11:30 am-2:30 & 5:30-8 pm; seasonal hours vary. **Address:** Hwy 97 V0H 1Z0 **Location:** On Hwy 97, follow signs for Sumac Ridge Estate Winery. **Parking:** on-site. CALL

(See map and index starting on p. 546)

VANILLA POD RESTAURANT

Canadian
$8-$28

Phone: 250/494-8222   ㉟

While traffic whizzes by on Highway 97, the pace slows down inside this small, slightly eclectic main street restaurant. The menu revolves around tapas dishes meant to be shared among friends, and along with some decided Spanish influences, many dishes employ some of the finest ingredients to be found in the surrounding Okanagan Valley. The smart wine list features only British Columbia-produced wines, many of which are produced within a stone's throw of the restaurant. Casual dress. **Bar:** Full bar. **Reservations:** accepted. **Hours:** Open 3/1-1/1 & 2/14-2/28; noon-midnight; 5:30 pm-close 10/9-5/21. Closed major holidays; also Mon; Sun 10/9-5/21. **Address:** 9917A Main St V0H 1Z8 **Location:** Jct Henry St; downtown. **Parking:** street.

VERNON pop. 33,494   (See map and index starting on p. 546)

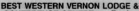

**BEST WESTERN VERNON LODGE &
CONFERENCE CENTRE**   *Book great rates at AAA.com*

Phone: (250)545-3385   **5**

AAA Benefit:
Members save up to 20%, plus 10% bonus points with rewards program.

CAA SAVE

Hotel
$111-$159 All Year

Address: 3914 32nd St V1T 5P1 **Location:** 1 mi (1.5 km) n on Hwy 97 (32nd St). **Facility:** Smoke free premises. 127 units. 119 one-bedroom standard units. 8 one-bedroom suites, some with whirlpools. 3 stories (no elevator), interior corridors. **Parking:** on-site. **Amenities:** video games (fee), voice mail, irons, hair dryers. **Pool(s):** heated indoor/outdoor. **Leisure Activities:** whirlpool, exercise room. **Guest Services:** valet laundry, wireless Internet. **Business Services:** conference facilities, PC. *(See color ad below)*

 / SOME UNITS FEE

FREE local telephone calls and high-speed Internet

(See map and index starting on p. 546)

BEST WESTERN VILLAGER MOTOR INN *Book great rates at AAA.com* Phone: (250)549-2224

Motel
$96-$141 All Year

Address: 5121 26th St V1T 8G4 Location: 1.5 mi (2.5 km) n on 27th St. Located across from Village Green Mall. Facility: 53 one-bedroom standard units, some with efficiencies. 2 stories (no elevator), exterior corridors. Parking: on-site. Amenities: irons, hair dryers. Pool(s): heated indoor. Leisure Activities: whirlpool. Guest Services: wireless Internet. Business Services: PC. Free Special Amenities: expanded continental breakfast and high-speed Internet.

AAA Benefit:
Members save up to 20%, plus 10% bonus points with rewards program.

CASTLE ON THE MOUNTAIN B & B Phone: 250/542-4593

Bed & Breakfast
$120-$250 All Year

Address: 8227 Silver Star Rd V1B 3M8 Location: Hwy 97A, exit 48th Ave (which becomes Silver Star Rd), 6.3 mi (10 km) e. Facility: Home to spectacular views and gracious hosts, this comfortable property overlooks the scenic Okanagan Valley. Smoke free premises. 6 units. 4 one-bedroom standard units, some with whirlpools. 1 one-bedroom suite with kitchen. 1 cottage. 3 stories (no elevator), interior/exterior corridors. Bath: combo or shower only. Parking: on-site, winter plug-ins. Terms: office hours 8 am-10 pm, check-in 4 pm, 14 day cancellation notice-fee imposed. Amenities: video library, DVD players, hair dryers. Some: CD players. Leisure Activities: whirlpool. Guest Services: coin laundry, wireless Internet. Business Services: meeting rooms.

HOLIDAY INN EXPRESS HOTEL & SUITES VERNON *Book great rates at AAA.com* Phone: (250)550-7777

Hotel
$109-$189 All Year

Address: 4716 34th St V1T 5Y9 Location: Hwy 97 (32nd St) northbound at 48th Ave. Facility: 85 one-bedroom standard units, some with whirlpools. 3 stories, interior corridors. Bath: combo or shower only. Parking: on-site. Amenities: high-speed Internet, dual phone lines, voice mail, irons, hair dryers. Pool(s): heated indoor. Leisure Activities: whirlpool, exercise room. Guest Services: valet and coin laundry. Business Services: meeting rooms, business center. (See color ad on insert)

LAKESIDE ILLAHEE INN *Book at AAA.com* Phone: (250)260-7896

Bed & Breakfast
$149-$389 3/1-10/31
$109-$309 11/1-2/28

Address: 15010 Tamarack Dr V1B 2E1 Location: Hwy 97 (32nd St), s of town, 1.5 mi (2.5 km) se on College Way, 1.2 mi (2 km) e on Kalamalka Rd, then 1.8 mi (3 km) s on Kidston Rd, follow signs. Located in a quiet residential area. Facility: Luxurious rooms, all with balconies, and a lake setting give this upscale inn a relaxed atmosphere; a scenic provincial park is nearby. Smoke free premises. 5 one-bedroom standard units, some with whirlpools. 3 stories (no elevator), interior/exterior corridors. Bath: combo or shower only. Parking: on-site. Terms: office hours 8 am-10 pm, 2 night minimum stay - seasonal, age restrictions may apply, 7 day cancellation notice-fee imposed. Amenities: DVD players, CD players, irons, hair dryers. Leisure Activities: whirlpool, paddleboats, boat dock. Fee: spa treatments. Guest Services: valet laundry, wireless Internet. Business Services: meeting rooms.

SUPER 8 VERNON *Book at AAA.com* Phone: (250)542-4434

Motel
$95-$225 All Year

Address: 4204 32nd St V1T 5P4 Location: Hwy 97 (32nd St); jct 43rd Ave. Facility: Smoke free premises. 62 units. 60 one- and 2 two-bedroom standard units. 3 stories, interior corridors. Parking: on-site. Amenities: voice mail, hair dryers. Some: irons. Pool(s): heated indoor. Leisure Activities: whirlpool. Guest Services: wireless Internet. Business Services: PC.

VERNON TRAVELODGE *Book at AAA.com* Phone: (250)545-2161

Motel
$85-$159 All Year

Address: 3000 28th Ave V1T 1W1 Location: Hwy 97 (32nd St), just e on 28th Ave. Near Polson Park. Facility: 39 one-bedroom standard units. 2 stories (no elevator), exterior corridors. Bath: combo or shower only. Parking: on-site. Terms: office hours 7 am-11 pm, cancellation fee imposed. Amenities: Some: irons, hair dryers. Pool(s): heated outdoor. Guest Services: wireless Internet. Business Services: PC.

——— WHERE TO DINE ———

AMARIN THAI RESTAURANT Phone: 250/542-9300

Thai
$10-$16

Lining the extensive menu are many salads, some with meat, as well as beef, seafood, chicken and pork dishes. The stylish decor, including Thai artifacts and art, is warm and appealing. Service is fine. Parking is limited to the street. Casual dress. Bar: Full bar. Reservations: suggested. Hours: 5 pm-9:30 pm. Closed: 12/25; also Sun & Mon. Address: 2903 31st St V1T 5H6 Location: Between 29th and 30th aves. Parking: street.

THE ECLECTIC MED RESTAURANT INC Phone: 250/558-4646

Mediterranean
$16-$32

In a word, the restaurant can be summed up as "funky," with a varied and eclectic menu of Mediterranean food. The many tempting food choices entice diners to return repeatedly. Appetizers are big enough to enjoy as a meal, and entrees incorporate everything from seafood to vegetarian staples. A superb wine list, a warm atmosphere and friendly service add up to a fantastic evening. Dressy casual. Bar: Full bar. Reservations: suggested. Hours: 5 pm-10 pm. Closed: major holidays, 12/26. Address: 2915 30th Ave V1T 5Z1 Location: Corner of Hwy 97 (32nd St) and 32nd Ave. Parking: street.

(See map and index starting on p. 546)

EL PORTILLO COFFEE HOUSE Phone: 250/545-9599 ⑥

Deli
$4-$6

It's an old adage that police officers know the best places in town to eat. This indeed may be the safest spot in town. While the contemporary space with cozy nooks and a patio is well known for its coffee and baked goods, it also serves freshly made soups and sandwiches. Casual dress. **Bar:** Beer only. **Reservations:** not accepted. **Hours:** 6 am-10 pm. **Address:** 2706 30th Ave V1T 2B6 **Location:** Jct 32nd St, just e; centre. **Parking:** on-site.

INTERMEZZO RESTAURANT Phone: 250/542-3853 ①

Italian
$11-$39

You'll enjoy the wide variety of pasta, chicken, seafood, barbecue ribs and the specialty veal, prepared in six classic ways, at Intermezzo, which is located downtown behind a small shopping complex. Meals are delicious and attractively presented. Casual dress. **Bar:** Full bar. **Reservations:** accepted. **Hours:** 5 pm-9 pm. Closed: 12/24, 12/25; also Mon. **Address:** 3206 34th Ave V1T 6M1 **Location:** Hwy 97 (32nd St), just w. **Parking:** street.

THE ITALIAN KITCHEN COMPANY Phone: 250/558-7899 ④

Italian
$12-$25

Hearty, delicious food awaits at the funky, upbeat restaurant along the main street downtown. Among offerings are traditional dishes, ranging from pastas to salads to savory soups. Hardwood floors and an exposed brick wall are accentuated by large local art in a bright and cheery decor. Service is friendly and attentive. Casual dress. **Bar:** Full bar. **Reservations:** suggested. **Hours:** 11 am-2 & 5-9 pm, Sat & Sun from 5 pm. Closed: 10/11, 12/24, 12/25. **Address:** 2916 30th Ave V1T 2B7 **Location:** Between 29th and 30th sts. **Parking:** street.

LOS HUESOS Phone: 250/275-4820 ⑤

Mexican
$9-$16

Mexican tunes greet patrons as they step off the street into the warm and inviting dining room. The straightforward menu lists classic burritos, chimichangas, tacos and fajitas, as well as daily specials. Margaritas are made with fresh fruit. Live music pumps up the atmosphere on weekends and every night during the summer. Casual dress. **Bar:** Full bar. **Reservations:** suggested. **Hours:** 11:30 am-2 & 5-9 pm, Fri & Sat-10 pm. Closed: 12/24, 12/25; also Sun. **Address:** 2918 30th Ave V1T 2B7 **Location:** Downtown. **Parking:** street. CALL 🖑M

WEST KELOWNA pop. 28,793 (See map and index starting on p. 546)

BEST WESTERN WINE COUNTRY HOTEL & SUITES *Book great rates at AAA.com* Phone: (250)707-1637 ⑩

ⓐⓐ SAVE

Hotel
$119-$180 All Year

Address: 3460 Carrington Rd V4T 3C1 **Location:** Hwy 97 (Dobbin Rd), just e on Elk Rd. **Facility:** Smoke free premises. 99 units. 89 one-bedroom standard units. 10 one-bedroom suites, some with whirlpools. 4 stories, interior corridors. **Parking:** on-site, winter plug-ins. **Terms:** cancellation fee imposed. **Amenities:** high-speed Internet, voice mail, safes, irons, hair dryers. **Pool(s):** heated indoor. **Leisure Activities:** whirlpool, waterslide, exercise room. **Guest Services:** valet and coin laundry, wireless Internet. **Business Services:** meeting rooms, PC.

AAA Benefit:
Members save up to 20%, plus 10% bonus points with rewards program.

FREE expanded continental breakfast and high-speed Internet

THE COVE LAKESIDE RESORT *Book at AAA.com* Phone: (250)707-1800 ⑫

Resort
Hotel
$149-$889 All Year

Address: 4205 Gellatly Rd V4T 2K2 **Location:** Hwy 97 (Dobbin Rd), 1 mi (1.6 km) s, follow signs. **Facility:** Tastefully-appointed suites feature a gourmet kitchen, separate bedrooms, a large living area and spectacular views of Okanagan Lake. Smoke free premises. 105 units. 12 one-, 78 two- and 15 three-bedroom suites with kitchens. 4 stories, interior corridors. **Parking:** on-site. **Terms:** 3 day cancellation notice-fee imposed. **Amenities:** video library, DVD players, voice mail, irons, hair dryers. **Pool(s):** 2 heated outdoor. **Leisure Activities:** whirlpools, waterslide, limited beach access, putting green, tennis court, exercise room, spa. *Fee:* marina. **Guest Services:** complimentary and valet laundry, wireless Internet. **Business Services:** meeting rooms, PC (fee).

ECO ASK 🍴 🍸 CALL 🖑M 🛏 ✕ ✕ 🎣 📱 📠 💻 / SOME UNITS FEE 🐕

HOLIDAY INN WEST KELOWNA *Book great rates at AAA.com* Phone: (250)768-8879 ⑪

ⓐⓐ SAVE

Hotel
$99-$375 All Year

Address: 2569 Dobbin Rd V4T 2J6 **Location:** Hwy 97 (Dobbin Rd) and Herbert Rd. **Facility:** Smoke free premises. 77 units. 75 one-bedroom standard units, some with whirlpools. 2 two-bedroom suites with kitchens and whirlpools. 3 stories, interior corridors. **Parking:** on-site. **Amenities:** voice mail, irons, hair dryers. **Pool(s):** heated indoor/outdoor. **Leisure Activities:** whirlpool, exercise room. **Guest Services:** valet laundry, wireless Internet. **Business Services:** meeting rooms. **Free Special Amenities:** newspaper and high-speed Internet. *(See color ad on insert)*

ECO 🍴 🍸 CALL 🖑M 🛏 ✕ 🎣 💻 / SOME UNITS 📱 📠

This ends listings for the Okanagan Valley.
The following page resumes the alphabetical listings of cities in British Columbia.

OSOYOOS—See Okanagan Valley p. 559.

PARKSVILLE pop. 10,993

ARBUTUS GROVE MOTEL

Phone: 250/248-6422

Motel
Rates not provided

Address: 1182 E Island Hwy V9P 1W3 **Location:** Island Hwy 19, exit 46 (Parksville), 1 mi (1.6 km) n on Hwy 19A. **Facility:** Smoke free premises. 10 one-bedroom standard units, some with efficiencies. 1 story, exterior corridors. **Parking:** on-site. **Terms:** office hours 9 am-11 pm. **Amenities:** high-speed Internet, hair dryers. / SOME UNITS

BEACH ACRES RESORT

Phone: 250/248-3424

Vacation Rental Cottage
Rates not provided

Address: 1051 Resort Dr, #25 V9P 2E4 **Location:** Island Hwy 19, exit 46 (Parksville), 1.6 mi (2.5 km) n on Hwy 19A. **Facility:** A mix of condos is dispersed over several acres; some are set back and secluded, some sit on a cliff overlooking the ocean and others are beachfront. Smoke free premises. 57 units. 2 one- and 21 two-bedroom standard units with kitchens. 34 cottages. 1-2 stories (no elevator), exterior corridors. *Bath:* combo or shower only. **Parking:** on-site. **Terms:** office hours 8 am-9 pm, check-in 4 pm. **Amenities:** video library, voice mail, irons. *Some:* DVD players. **Pool(s):** heated indoor. **Leisure Activities:** sauna, whirlpool, 3 tennis courts, recreation programs, playground, basketball, horseshoes, shuffleboard, volleyball. **Guest Services:** coin laundry, wireless Internet. **Business Services:** meeting rooms, PC.

THE BEACH CLUB RESORT

Phone: (250)248-8999

Contemporary Resort Hotel
$134-$450 All Year

Address: 181 Beachside Dr V9P 2H5 **Location:** Island Hwy 19, exit 51 (Parksville/Coombs), 1.2 mi (2 km), then just n on Hwy 19A. **Facility:** Smoke free premises. 149 units. 74 one-bedroom standard units. 75 one-bedroom suites with kitchens. 4-9 stories, interior/exterior corridors. **Parking:** on-site. **Terms:** check-in 4 pm, 5 day cancellation notice-fee imposed. **Amenities:** DVD players, voice mail, safes, irons, hair dryers. **Pool(s):** heated indoor. **Leisure Activities:** whirlpool, exercise room, spa. **Guest Services:** valet laundry, wireless Internet. **Business Services:** meeting rooms, business center.

 / SOME UNITS

FREE high-speed Internet

OCEANSIDE VILLAGE RESORT

Phone: 250/248-8961

Extended Stay Cottage
Rates not provided

Address: 1080 Resort Dr V9P 2E3 **Location:** Island Hwy 19, exit 46 (Parksville), 1.8 mi (2.5 km) n on Hwy 19A. **Facility:** A short walk away from beautiful Rathtrevor Park, a great spot for beachcombing, these wonderfully modern, newly constructed individual cottages are sprinkled over several acres and comfortably sleep six to eight people in a home-away-from-home setting. Smoke free premises. 50 two-bedroom suites with kitchens. 1 story, exterior corridors. **Parking:** on-site. **Terms:** office hours 9 am-5 pm, check-in 4 pm. **Amenities:** DVD players, CD players, irons, hair dryers. **Pool(s):** heated indoor. **Leisure Activities:** whirlpool, exercise room. **Guest Services:** complimentary laundry, wireless Internet. / SOME UNITS FEE

QUALITY RESORT BAYSIDE

Phone: (250)248-8333

Hotel
$129-$179 7/1-2/28
$119-$159 3/1-6/30

Address: 240 Dogwood St V9P 2H5 **Location:** Island Hwy 19, exit 51 (Parksville/Coombs), 1.3 mi (2 km) e, then 0.6 mi (1 km) n on Hwy 19A. **Facility:** Smoke free premises. 59 one-bedroom standard units. 3 stories, interior corridors. **Parking:** on-site. **Amenities:** voice mail, irons, hair dryers. **Pool(s):** heated indoor. **Leisure Activities:** whirlpool, beach access, squash, exercise room. **Guest Services:** valet laundry, wireless Internet. **Business Services:** meeting rooms, PC.

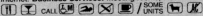 / SOME UNITS

FREE continental breakfast and high-speed Internet

SANDCASTLE INN

Phone: 250/248-2334

Hotel
$79-$139 All Year

Address: 374 W Island Hwy V9P 1K8 **Location:** Island Hwy 19, exit 51 (Parksville/Coombs), 1.3 mi (2 km) e, then just n on Hwy 19A. **Facility:** Smoke free premises. 36 one-bedroom standard units, some with efficiencies. 3 stories, interior corridors. *Bath:* combo or shower only. **Parking:** on-site. **Terms:** office hours 7 am-11 pm, 7 day cancellation notice-fee imposed. **Amenities:** voice mail. **Leisure Activities:** barbecue area. **Guest Services:** coin laundry, wireless Internet. **Business Services:** meeting rooms, PC. / SOME UNITS

SKYLITE MOTEL

Phone: (250)248-4271

Motel
$89-$139 All Year

Address: 459 E Island Hwy V9P 2G5 **Location:** Island Hwy 19, exit 46 (Parksville), 2.2 mi (3.5 km) n on Hwy 19A. **Facility:** 25 one-bedroom standard units, some with efficiencies or kitchens. 1-2 stories (no elevator), exterior corridors. **Parking:** on-site. **Terms:** office hours 7 am-11 pm. **Amenities:** irons, hair dryers. **Guest Services:** valet laundry, wireless Internet.

ASK / SOME UNITS FEE

SUNRISE RIDGE WATERFRONT RESORT

Book great rates at AAA.com

Phone: 250/248-4674

Hotel
Rates not provided

Address: 1175 Resort Dr V9P 2E3 **Location:** Island Hwy 19, exit 46 (Parksville), 1.6 mi (2.5 km) n on Hwy 19A. **Facility:** Smoke free premises. 64 units. 23 one-bedroom standard units, 28 one-, 11 two- and 2 three-bedroom suites with kitchens, some with whirlpools. 2-3 stories, interior/exterior corridors. *Bath:* combo or shower only. **Parking:** on-site. **Terms:** check-in 4 pm. **Amenities:** video library, DVD players, voice mail, irons, hair dryers. *Some:* high-speed Internet. **Guest Services:** wireless Internet. **Business Services:** meeting rooms.

FREE local telephone calls and high-speed Internet

TIGH-NA-MARA SEASIDE SPA RESORT & CONFERENCE CENTER

Phone: (250)248-2072

Resort
Hotel
$119-$359 All Year

Address: 1155 Resort Dr V9P 2E5 **Location:** Island Hwy 19, exit 46 (Parksville), 1.3 mi (2 km) n on Hwy 19A. **Facility:** This all-season resort features a cluster of lovely log cottages and deluxe condo-style units set in a forestlike setting or along a sandy beach. Smoke free premises. 192 units. 89 one-bedroom standard units, some with efficiencies and/or whirlpools. 66 one- and 4 two-bedroom suites, some with kitchens and/or whirlpools. 33 cottages. 1-3 stories (no elevator), exterior corridors. **Parking:** on-site. **Terms:** check-in 4 pm, 2 night minimum stay - seasonal and/or weekends, 5 day cancellation notice-fee imposed. **Amenities:** voice mail, irons, hair dryers. **Dining:** Cedar Dining Room at Tigh-Na-Mara Seaside Spa Resort, see separate listing. **Pool(s):** heated indoor. **Leisure Activities:** sauna, whirlpool, tennis court, recreation programs, rental bicycles, playground, exercise room, spa, horseshoes, volleyball. **Guest Services:** valet and coin laundry, area transportation, wireless Internet. **Business Services:** conference facilities, business center.

ASK / SOME UNITS FEE

TRAVELODGE PARKSVILLE

Book at AAA.com

Phone: (250)248-2232

Hotel
$129-$239 3/1-9/30
$99-$219 10/1-2/28

Address: 424 W Island Hwy V9P 1K8 **Location:** Island Hwy 19, exit 51 (Parksville/Coombs), 1.3 mi (2 km) e, then just n on Hwy 19A. **Facility:** Smoke free premises. 84 one-bedroom standard units, some with whirlpools. 3 stories, interior corridors. **Parking:** on-site. **Terms:** cancellation fee imposed. **Amenities:** voice mail, irons, hair dryers. **Pool(s):** heated indoor. **Leisure Activities:** whirlpool, exercise room. **Guest Services:** coin laundry, wireless Internet. **Business Services:** meeting rooms, PC. ASK CALL / SOME UNITS FEE

V.I.P. MOTEL

Phone: (250)248-3244

Motel
$69-$169 All Year

Address: 414 W Island Hwy V9P 1K8 **Location:** Island Hwy 19, exit 51 (Parksville/Coombs), 1.3 mi (2 km) e, then just n on Hwy 19A. **Facility:** 21 one-bedroom standard units, some with efficiencies. 1 story, exterior corridors. **Parking:** on-site. **Terms:** office hours 7 am-11 pm, cancellation fee imposed. **Amenities:** hair dryers. **Leisure Activities:** barbecue patio. **Guest Services:** coin laundry, wireless Internet. **Free Special Amenities: continental breakfast and high-speed Internet.**

/ SOME UNITS

—— WHERE TO DINE ——

AMRIKKO'S FINE INDIAN CUISINE

Phone: 250/951-0682

Indian
$8-$15

The goal of this Indian restaurant is simple: Offer a warm, casual atmosphere, polite service and superb food in generous portions. The menu offers tandoori barbecue, lamb, beef and vegetarian dishes and, of course, chicken specials such as butter chicken or chicken vindaloo. Belly dancers perform every Friday and Saturday nights. Casual dress. **Bar:** Full bar. **Hours:** 11 am-2:30 & 4-9 pm, Fri & Sat-10 pm. Closed: 1/1, 12/25. **Address:** 487 E Island Hwy V9P 2H6 **Location:** Island Hwy 19, exit 46 (Parksville), 2.2 mi (3.5 km) n on Hwy 19A. **Parking:** on-site.

BUGSYS BAR & GRILL

Phone: 250/248-4545

Canadian
$8-$23

In gangster circles, the name Bugsy is a term of endearment or honor; here, Bugsy translates to pizza, calzones, ribs, chicken, pasta and burgers. A large bar features big screen TVs for all the sporting events you can handle, and the restaurant is open late. Casual dress. **Bar:** Full bar. **Hours:** 11 am-11 pm, Sun from 10 am. Closed: 12/25. **Address:** 332 W Island Hwy V9P 1K8 **Location:** Island Hwy 19, exit 51 (Parksville/Coombs), 1.3 mi (2 km) e, then just n on Hwy 19A. **Parking:** on-site. CALL

CEDAR DINING ROOM AT TIGH-NA-MARA SEASIDE SPA RESORT

Phone: 250/248-2333

Pacific Rim
$12-$36

Although the menu focuses on West Coast seafood, it also lists pasta and steak dishes and more casual breakfast and lunch offerings, including daily soup and sandwich specials. Sunday brunch is popular. The authentic log restaurant is nestled in a forest by the sea. The country-elegant setting is informal, warm and friendly, and the decor matches the complex's rustic log cabin look, complete with a wood-burning fireplace in the dining room's center. Casual dress. **Bar:** Full bar. **Reservations:** suggested, for dinner & Sunday brunch. **Hours:** 7 am-9:30 pm. **Address:** 1155 Resort Dr V9P 2E5 **Location:** Island Hwy 19, exit 46 (Parksville), 1.3 mi (2 km) n on Hwy 19A; in Tigh-Na-Mara Seaside Spa Resort & Conference Center. **Parking:** on-site. CALL

KALVAS RESTAURANT

Phone: 250/248-6933

Steak
$20-$40

In a cozy Alpine-style setting appointed in log cabin decor, guests sit down to high-quality home cooking. Fresh ingredients factor into seafood and steak dishes. Casual dress. **Bar:** Full bar. **Reservations:** suggested. **Hours:** 5 pm-10 pm. **Address:** 180 Moilliet St, Island Hwy N V9P 2H4 **Location:** Island Hwy 19, exit 51 (Parksville/Coombs), 1.3 mi (2 km) e, then just n on Hwy 19A. **Parking:** on-site. CALL

LEFTY'S FRESH FOOD RESTAURANT

Phone: 250/954-3886

Canadian
$9-$20

Three friends realized they all were left-handed, and a new restaurant was born. The kitchen is committed to fresh ingredients in such dishes as the signature "southpawtatoes," which are oven roasted in special seasoning, and the made-from-scratch desserts. The motto here: "Everyone is born right-handed; only the greatest overcome it.". Casual dress. **Bar:** Full bar. **Reservations:** accepted. **Hours:** 8 am-8 pm, Fri & Sat-9 pm. Closed: 12/25. **Address:** 101-280 E Island Hwy V9P 2G3 **Location:** Island Hwy 19, exit 46 (Parksville), 2.5 mi (4 km) n on Hwy 19A. **Parking:** on-site.

PARSON

ALEXA CHALETS-TIMBER INN & RESTAURANT

Phone: 250/348-2228

Hotel
Rates not provided

Address: 3483 Hwy 95 V0A 1L0 **Location:** Just off Hwy 95; 21.3 mi (34 km) s of Golden. **Facility:** Smoke free premises. 11 units. 5 one-bedroom standard units. 1 house and 5 cabins. 2 stories (no elevator), interior/exterior corridors. **Bath:** combo or shower only. **Parking:** on-site. **Terms:** open 3/1-10/15 & 12/1-2/28, office hours 7 am-11 pm, check-in 4 pm. **Amenities:** hair dryers. **Leisure Activities:** sauna, whirlpool, hiking trails, limited exercise equipment, basketball. *Fee:* massage. **Guest Services:** TV in common area, complimentary laundry. **Business Services:** PC.

PEMBERTON pop. 1,637

PEMBERTON VALLEY LODGE *Book great rates at AAA.com*

Phone: (604)894-2000

Hotel
$139-$409 All Year

Address: 1490 Portage Rd V0N 2L1 **Location:** Just e on Hwy 99 from Pioneer Junction. **Facility:** Smoke free premises. 85 units. 43 one-bedroom standard units with efficiencies. 32 one- and 10 two-bedroom suites with kitchens. 3 stories, interior corridors. **Parking:** on-site. **Terms:** check-in 4 pm, cancellation fee imposed. **Amenities:** video library, DVD players, voice mail, irons, hair dryers. **Pool(s):** heated outdoor. **Leisure Activities:** whirlpool, limited exercise equipment. **Guest Services:** complimentary laundry, area transportation, wireless Internet. **Business Services:** meeting rooms, PC (fee). *(See color ad p 706)*

PENDER ISLAND—See Gulf Islands p. 524.

PENTICTON—See Okanagan Valley p. 561.

PITT MEADOWS—See Vancouver p. 653.

PORT ALBERNI pop. 17,743

BEST WESTERN BARCLAY HOTEL *Book great rates at AAA.com*

Phone: (250)724-7171

Hotel
$109-$159 All Year

Address: 4277 Stamp Ave V9Y 7X8 **Location:** Johnston Rd (Hwy 4), just s on Gertrude St. **Facility:** Smoke free premises. 86 one-bedroom standard units, some with whirlpools. 5 stories, interior corridors. **Parking:** on-site. **Amenities:** voice mail, irons, hair dryers. *Some:* high-speed Internet. **Pool(s):** heated outdoor. **Leisure Activities:** sauna, whirlpool, exercise room. **Guest Services:** valet laundry, wireless Internet. **Business Services:** meeting rooms, business center. **Free Special Amenities:** local telephone calls and high-speed Internet.

AAA Benefit:
Members save up to 20%, plus 10% bonus points with rewards program.

CEDAR WOOD LODGE BED AND BREAKFAST INN

Bed & Breakfast
$90-$149 All Year

Phone: (250)724-6800

Address: 5895 River Rd V9Y 6Z5 **Location:** 1.9 mi (3 km) w on River Rd (Hwy 4) from Johnston Rd. **Facility:** Smoke free premises. 8 one-bedroom standard units with whirlpools. 2 stories (no elevator), interior corridors. **Parking:** on-site. **Terms:** office hours 7 am-11 pm. **Amenities:** video library, DVD players, high-speed Internet, hair dryers. **Guest Services:** valet laundry, wireless Internet. **Business Services:** meeting rooms.

THE HOSPITALITY INN *Book at AAA.com*

Hotel
$129-$155 All Year

Phone: (250)723-8111

Address: 3835 Redford St V9Y 3S2 **Location:** 2 mi (3.2 km) sw of jct Hwy 4 via City Centre/Port Alberni South Route. **Facility:** 50 one-bedroom standard units. 2 stories (no elevator), interior corridors. **Parking:** on-site. **Terms:** cancellation fee imposed. **Amenities:** high-speed Internet, voice mail, irons, hair dryers. **Pool(s):** heated outdoor. **Leisure Activities:** whirlpool, exercise room. **Guest Services:** valet laundry, wireless Internet. **Business Services:** meeting rooms, PC.

RIVERSIDE MOTEL

(CAA) (SAVE)

Motel
$69-$139 All Year

Phone: (250)724-9916

Address: 5065 Roger St V9Y 3Y9 **Location:** Johnston Rd (Hwy 4), just s on Gertrude St, then just w. **Facility:** 10 one-bedroom units. 1 story, exterior corridors. **Bath:** combo or shower only. **Parking:** on-site. **Terms:** office hours 7:30 am-11 pm, cancellation fee imposed. **Amenities:** voice mail, hair dryers. **Guest Services:** coin laundry, wireless Internet. **Free Special Amenities:** local telephone calls and high-speed Internet.

SOMASS MOTEL

Motel
$60-$130 All Year

Phone: (250)724-3236

Address: 5279 River Rd V9Y 6Z3 **Location:** 2 mi (3.2 km) on River Rd (Hwy 4) from Johnston Rd. **Facility:** Smoke free premises. 14 units. 6 one-bedroom standard units. 6 one- and 2 two-bedroom suites with kitchens. 1 story, exterior corridors. **Parking:** on-site. **Terms:** office hours 7 am-11 pm. **Amenities:** hair dryers. *Some:* high-speed Internet. **Pool(s):** outdoor. **Guest Services:** coin laundry, wireless Internet. **Business Services:** PC.

——— **WHERE TO DINE** ———

LITTLE BAVARIA RESTAURANT *Menu on AAA.com*

(CAA)

German
$8-$20

Phone: 250/724-4242

This quaint restaurant features a pleasant Bavarian decor with an accent on good old-fashioned German food. Schnitzel, Hungarian goulash, cabbage rolls, steak, seafood, and fondue for two are on the menu. Couples and business people like this place. Casual dress. **Bar:** Full bar. **Reservations:** suggested. **Hours:** 11 am-2 & 5-9 pm, Sat & Sun from 5 pm. Closed: 7/1; also 12/24-12/29. **Address:** 3035 4th Ave V9Y 2B8 **Location:** Between Argyle and Angus. **Parking:** street.

SMITTY'S

Canadian
$7-$20

Phone: 250/724-5022

The family-oriented restaurant satisfies patrons with its ever-popular all-day breakfast items, as well as tasty and wholesome soups and salads at lunchtime. A relaxed mood characterizes the dining space. Casual dress. **Bar:** Full bar. **Hours:** 6:30 am-9 pm. Closed: 12/25. **Address:** 3426 3rd Ave V9Y 7M8 **Location:** Between Napier St and the Quadrant. **Parking:** on-site.

PORT COQUITLAM—See Vancouver p. 653.

PORT HARDY pop. 3,822

AIRPORT INN

Hotel
Rates not provided

Phone: 250/949-9434

Address: 4030 Byng Rd V0N 2P0 **Location:** Hwy 19, 3.1 mi (5 km) ne, follow signs. **Facility:** Smoke free premises. 45 one-bedroom standard units, some with efficiencies. 2 stories (no elevator), interior corridors. **Parking:** on-site. **Amenities:** voice mail, hair dryers. *Some:* irons. **Dining:** Seto's Wok & Grill, see separate listing. **Guest Services:** coin laundry, wireless Internet. **Business Services:** meeting rooms.

GLEN LYON INN

Hotel
$105-$180 All Year

Phone: (250)949-7115

Address: 6435 Hardy Bay Rd V0N 2P0 **Location:** Hwy 19, 0.9 mi (1.5 km) n, follow signs. **Facility:** Smoke free premises. 44 one-bedroom units, some with efficiencies and/or whirlpools. 3 stories, exterior corridors. **Parking:** on-site. **Terms:** office hours 4:30 am-1 am, 3 day cancellation notice-fee imposed. **Amenities:** voice mail, hair dryers. **Leisure Activities:** limited exercise equipment. **Guest Services:** coin laundry, wireless Internet. **Business Services:** meeting rooms, PC (fee).

——— *The following lodging was either not evaluated or did not* ———
meet AAA rating requirements but is listed for your information only.

QUARTERDECK INN

fyi

Phone: 250/902-0455

Not evaluated. **Address:** 6555 Hardy Bay Rd V0N 2P0 **Location:** Hwy 19, 0.9 mi (1.5 km) n. Facilities, services, and decor characterize a mid-scale property.

—— WHERE TO DINE ——

MALONE'S BISTRO

Canadian
$10-$25

Phone: 250/949-3050

In a former shopping mall now housing North Island College, the popular family restaurant presents a menu of local seafood, steak, pizza and traditional Greek specialties. Casual dress. **Bar:** Full bar. **Reservations:** suggested. **Hours:** 11 am-2 & 5-9 pm; 11 am-9 pm 7/1-8/31. Closed: major holidays, 12/24; also Sun. **Address:** 9300 Trustee Rd V0N 2P0 **Location:** 0.6 mi (1 km) se on Hwy 19, just sw; in The North Island Mall. **Parking:** on-site.

MARKET STREET CAFE

Canadian
$5-$12

Phone: 250/949-8110

Serving homemade soup and sandwiches along with mouthwatering pastries, pie and muffins, the downtown cafe is in the heart of the business district. Booths line the walls. Casual dress. **Hours:** 7 am-5:30 pm. Closed: 12/25. **Address:** 7030 Market St V0N 2P0 **Location:** Hwy 19, 0.6 mi (1 km) nw (towards water) on Granville St, then just ne. **Parking:** street.

SETO'S WOK & GRILL

Chinese
$9-$22

Phone: 250/949-8381

Locals and visitors alike enjoy this restaurant, near Port Hardy's airport. It prepares many Cantonese/Chinese selections, as well as some Western fare, including burgers, hot and cold sandwiches and appetizers. Families are welcomed. Casual dress. **Bar:** Full bar. **Hours:** 7 am-9 pm. Closed major holidays. **Address:** 4030 Byng Rd V0N 2P0 **Location:** Hwy 19, 3.1 mi (5 km) ne, follow signs; in Airport Inn. **Parking:** on-site. CALL

TOUDAI RESTAURANT

Japanese
$4-$13

Phone: 250/949-8755

The popular sushi restaurant featuring favorites such as maki, nigiri, sashimi, sushi combinations and bento box dinners. It's a good idea to come early, as this place fills up quickly. Casual dress. **Bar:** Beer & wine. **Hours:** 5 pm-9 pm; also 11 am-2 pm 7/1-9/15. Closed: 12/25; also Mon 10/1-5/31. **Address:** 7370 Market St V0N 2P0 **Location:** Corner of Market and Douglas sts; downtown; in Northshore Inn. **Parking:** on-site.

PORT MCNEILL pop. 2,623

BLACK BEAR RESORT

Motel
$135-$255 All Year

Phone: (250)956-4900

Address: 1812 Campbell Way V0N 2R0 **Location:** Hwy 19, 1.3 mi (2 km) e. **Facility:** Smoke free premises. 40 one-bedroom standard units, some with efficiencies. 2 stories (no elevator), exterior corridors. **Parking:** on-site. **Terms:** office hours 6 am-midnight, cancellation fee imposed. **Amenities:** high-speed Internet, voice mail, safes, hair dryers. **Leisure Activities:** sauna, whirlpool, exercise room, spa. **Guest Services:** coin laundry, wireless Internet. **Business Services:** meeting rooms, PC.

HAIDA-WAY MOTOR INN

Motel
$85-$129 All Year

Phone: (250)956-3373

Address: 1817 Campbell Way V0N 2R0 **Location:** Hwy 19, 1.3 mi (2 km) e. **Facility:** 52 one-bedroom standard units. 3 stories (no elevator), interior corridors. **Parking:** on-site. **Terms:** office hours 6 am-1 am, check-in 4 pm, cancellation fee imposed. **Dining:** Northern Lights Restaurant, see separate listing. **Guest Services:** coin laundry, wireless Internet. **Business Services:** meeting rooms, PC.

—— WHERE TO DINE ——

NORTHERN LIGHTS RESTAURANT

Canadian
$15-$25

Phone: 250/956-3263

Popular among the locals for tasty food, the restaurant offers summer choices that include fresh local seafood as well as some steak, chicken or pasta dishes. Save room for dessert, as there is always a nice selection. Casual dress. **Bar:** Full bar. **Reservations:** suggested, 6/15-9/15. **Hours:** 5 pm-10 pm. Closed: 12/23-1/3. **Address:** 1817 Campbell Way V0N 2R0 **Location:** Hwy 19, 1.3 mi (2 km) e; in Haida-Way Motor Inn. **Parking:** on-site.

POWELL RIVER pop. 12,957

POWELL RIVER TOWN CENTRE HOTEL   *Book at AAA.com*

Hotel
$99-$200 All Year

Phone: (604)485-3000

Address: 4660 Joyce Ave V8A 3B6 **Location:** 0.5 mi (0.8 km) e on Duncan St (BC ferry terminal), then 0.6 mi (1 km) n. **Facility:** Smoke free premises. 71 one-bedroom standard units, some with whirlpools. 2 stories, interior corridors. **Parking:** on-site. **Terms:** cancellation fee imposed. **Amenities:** video games (fee), voice mail, hair dryers. **Leisure Activities:** whirlpool, limited exercise equipment. **Guest Services:** valet laundry, area transportation, wireless Internet. **Business Services:** meeting rooms.

—— WHERE TO DINE ——

THE SHINGLEMILL PUB & BISTRO

Canadian
$9-$24

Phone: 604/483-2001

The popular, longstanding pub and bistro sits on the shores of Powell Lake, and large bay windows overlook the marina. The view is best from the second floor. Food is typical bistro fare: burgers, sandwiches and soups. Although it's a bit of a drive to get here, it's worth the trip. Casual dress. **Bar:** Full bar. **Reservations:** accepted. **Hours:** 11 am-2:30 & 5-9 pm; 11 am-9 pm 7/1-9/5. Closed: 12/25. **Address:** 6233 Powell Pl V8A 4S6 **Location:** From Duncan St (BC ferry terminal), 2.2 mi (3.5 km) n on Marine Ave, 0.9 mi (1.5 km) e on Arbutus Ave. **Parking:** on-site.

WESTVIEW RESTAURANT & PIZZA

Phone: 604/485-6162

Pizza
$8-$20

The menu blends Greek dishes, such as souvlaki and moussaka, with Italian fare, including baked lasagna and many pizza varieties. Large bay windows overlook the ocean. Casual dress. **Bar:** Full bar. **Reservations:** accepted. **Hours:** 11 am-9 pm, Sat & Sun from 4 pm. Closed: 1/1, 12/25, 12/26. **Address:** 4553 Marine Ave V8A 2K5 **Location:** From Duncan St (BC ferry terminal), just n; between Burton and Courtney sts. **Parking:** on-site. CALL 🛗M

PRINCE GEORGE pop. 70,981

BEST WESTERN CITY CENTRE   *Book great rates at AAA.com*

Phone: (250)563-1267

Motel
$110-$140 All Year

Address: 910 Victoria St V2L 2K8 **Location:** Just n of Victoria St (Hwy 16) and Patricia Blvd; downtown. **Facility:** 53 units. 49 one-bedroom standard units. 4 one-bedroom suites. 2 stories (no elevator), exterior corridors. **Parking:** on-site, winter plug-ins. **Terms:** office hours 6 am-11 pm. **Amenities:** irons, hair dryers. **Pool(s):** heated indoor. **Leisure Activities:** exercise room. **Guest Services:** valet and coin laundry, wireless Internet. **Business Services:** PC. Free Special Amenities: local telephone calls and high-speed Internet.

AAA Benefit:
Members save up to 20%, plus 10% bonus points with rewards program.

DAYS INN - PRINCE GEORGE   *Book at AAA.com*

Phone: (250)562-7072

Hotel
$95-$105 All Year

Address: 600 Quebec St V2L 1W7 **Location:** From Victoria St (Hwy 16), just n on 7th Ave. **Facility:** 76 one-bedroom standard units. 2 stories, interior corridors. **Parking:** on-site. **Terms:** 7 day cancellation notice-fee imposed. **Amenities:** voice mail. *Some:* irons, hair dryers. **Leisure Activities:** exercise room. **Guest Services:** valet and coin laundry, wireless Internet. **Business Services:** meeting rooms, PC (fee). ECO ASK 🍴 🍸 🖥 💻 / SOME UNITS ✕

FOUR POINTS BY SHERATON PRINCE GEORGE   *Book great rates at AAA.com*

Phone: 250/564-7100

Hotel
Rates not provided

Address: 1790 Hwy 97 S V2L 5L3 **Location:** Hwy 97, exit Spruce northbound; exit city centre via Queensway southbound. **Facility:** Smoke free premises. 74 units. 65 one-bedroom standard units. 9 one-bedroom suites, some with whirlpools. 3 stories, interior corridors. **Parking:** on-site, winter plug-ins. **Amenities:** high-speed Internet, voice mail, irons, hair dryers. **Pool(s):** heated indoor. **Leisure Activities:** whirlpool, exercise room. **Guest Services:** valet laundry, wireless Internet. **Business Services:** meeting rooms, PC. 🍴 🍸 CALL 🛗M 🛏 ✕ 📷 🖥 💻 💻 / SOME UNITS FEE 🐾

FOUR POINTS BY SHERATON

AAA Benefit:
Members get up to 15% off, plus Starwood Preferred Guest® bonuses.

TREASURE COVE CASINO HOTEL   *Book at AAA.com*

Phone: (250)614-9111

Hotel
$149-$199 All Year

Address: 2005 Hwy 97 S V2N 7A3 **Location:** Corner of Hwy 97 and 16. **Facility:** Smoke free premises. 82 one-bedroom standard units, some with whirlpools. 4 stories, interior corridors. **Parking:** on-site. **Terms:** check-in 4 pm, cancellation fee imposed. **Amenities:** high-speed Internet, voice mail, irons, hair dryers. **Pool(s):** heated indoor. **Leisure Activities:** whirlpool, waterslide, exercise room. **Guest Services:** valet laundry. **Business Services:** meeting rooms, PC. ECO ASK 🍴 🍸 CALL 🛗M 🛏 ✕ ✕ 📷 🖥 💻

--- **WHERE TO DINE** ---

CHINA SAIL RESTAURANT

Phone: 250/564-2828

Chinese
$9-$15

A local favorite for more than 20 years, this restaurant continues to serve delicious Chinese and Canadian dishes. Diners can select an individual meal, family dinner or combination plate; all are reasonably priced. Casual dress. **Bar:** Full bar. **Hours:** 11:30 am-11 pm, Fri & Sat-midnight, Sun 2 pm-9 pm. Closed: 12/25, 12/26. **Address:** 4288 5th Ave V2M 7A2 **Location:** Hwy 97, 1 mi (1.7 km) w; corner of 5th Ave and Tabor. **Parking:** on-site. CALL 🛗M

EARLS RESTAURANT

Phone: 250/562-1527

Canadian
$8-$19

Offering an experience that falls between fast food and fine dining, the fun, relaxed restaurant prepares great food at a great price. Choices range from juicy burgers, hearty sandwiches, fresh salads, wings and pizza to full entrees of steak, chops and seafood. Made-from-scratch soups and assorted breads, as well as a nice choice of wines and beers, round out the offerings. This is a fitting spot for impromptu get-togethers and festive occasions. Casual dress. **Bar:** Full bar. **Hours:** 11 am-midnight, Sun 10 am-11 pm. Closed: 12/25. **Address:** 1440 E Central St V2M 3C1 **Location:** Corner of Hwy 97 and 15th Ave. **Parking:** on-site. CALL 🛗M

MOXIE'S CLASSIC GRILL

Phone: 250/564-4700

Canadian
$8-$18

This sleek, funky and popular restaurant presents an extensive menu of creatively prepared dishes, including pizza, pasta, rice, noodles, signature salads and burgers. Other menus include one for children and one for Sunday brunch. Lending to the upbeat, stylish decor are dark wood appointments and river rock fireplaces. Casual dress. **Bar:** Full bar. **Hours:** 11 am-midnight, Sat & Sun from 10 am. **Address:** 1804 E Central St V2M 3C3 **Location:** Hwy 97 and 19th Ave. **Parking:** on-site.

RIC'S GRILL   *Menu on AAA.com*   Phone: 250/614-9096

Steak
$9-$45

"Funky and modern" describes the decor and the food at the upscale steakhouse, which bustles with activity. Steaks are well worth it, but then again, so are the salmon, chicken and pasta dishes. A wide variety of distinctive appetizers rounds out the menu. Servers are friendly and attentive. Casual dress. **Bar:** Full bar. **Reservations:** suggested. **Hours:** 4:30 pm-10 pm, Wed & Thurs from 11:30 am, Fri 11:30 am-11 pm, Sat 4:30 pm-11 pm. Closed: 12/25. **Address:** 547 George St V2L 1R8 **Location:** Between 5th and 6th aves; downtown. **Parking:** street. CALL ⌖M

PRINCE RUPERT pop. 12,815

ALEEDA MOTEL   Phone: (250)627-1367

CAA SAVE

Motel
$50-$105 All Year

Address: 900 3rd Ave W V8J 1M8 **Location:** Corner of 3rd Ave W and 8th St. **Facility:** 31 one-bedroom standard units, some with efficiencies. 2 stories (no elevator), interior corridors. **Parking:** on-site. **Amenities:** voice mail. **Guest Services:** wireless Internet. **Free Special Amenities:** continental breakfast and high-speed Internet.

THE COAST PRINCE RUPERT HOTEL   *Book at AAA.com*   Phone: (250)624-6711

Hotel
$125-$197 3/1-9/30
$116-$179 10/1-2/28

Address: 118 6th St V8J 3L7 **Location:** Between 1st and 2nd aves W. **Facility:** 92 one-bedroom standard units. 8 stories, interior corridors. **Parking:** on-site. **Terms:** cancellation fee imposed. **Amenities:** high-speed Internet, voice mail, irons, hair dryers. **Guest Services:** valet laundry. **Business Services:** meeting rooms, PC.

ECO ASK ⌖M

INN ON THE HARBOUR   Phone: (250)624-9107

Motel
$85-$145 All Year

Address: 720 1st Ave W V8J 3V6 **Location:** Corner of 6th St. **Facility:** Smoke free premises. 49 one-bedroom standard units. 3 stories (no elevator), interior corridors. *Bath:* combo or shower only. **Parking:** on-site. **Amenities:** voice mail, hair dryers. **Guest Services:** valet and coin laundry, wireless Internet. ASK ⌖M

TOTEM LODGE MOTEL   Phone: (250)624-6761

CAA SAVE

Motel
$89-$99 3/1-10/1
$69-$79 10/2-2/28

Address: 1335 Park Ave V8J 1K3 **Location:** 1 mi (1.6 km) w on Hwy 16 (2nd Ave W) from downtown. **Facility:** 31 one-bedroom standard units, some with kitchens. 3 stories (no elevator), interior corridors. **Parking:** on-site. **Terms:** 7 day cancellation notice. **Guest Services:** coin laundry, wireless Internet. **Free Special Amenities:** continental breakfast and high-speed Internet.

------ WHERE TO DINE ------

OPA SUSHI   Phone: 250/627-4560

Japanese
$5-$30

The sushi restaurant occupies an old loft originally used for taking the main conk lines off the nets and putting them into a pot filled with tar, which helped preserve the rope from rot and salt damage. The tar pot is still here, as is the tar on the floor. Seating is limited. Prices listed are for individual sushi rolls. Casual dress. **Bar:** Beer & wine. **Reservations:** suggested. **Hours:** 11:30 am-2 & 5-9 pm, Sat noon-3 & 5-9 pm. Closed major holidays; also Sun & Mon. **Address:** 34 Cow Bay Rd V8J 1A5 **Location:** From 3rd Ave E, 0.6 mi (1 km) n; in Cow Bay. **Parking:** street.

RAIN DINING LOUNGE   Phone: 250/627-8272

Pacific Rim
$12-$25

Different for Prince Rupert, this restaurant offers a fine dining experience with a funky Vancouver feel. The decor incorporates bright colors, waterfalls and an open cocktail lounge and kitchen. Intense flavors and textures characterize dishes intended to share. Casual dress. **Bar:** Full bar. **Reservations:** suggested. **Hours:** 5 pm-1:30 am, Sun 10 am-2 am. Closed: 12/25, 12/26. **Address:** 737 2nd Ave W V8J 1H4 **Location:** Between 8th and 7th sts. **Parking:** street. CALL ⌖M

SMILES SEAFOOD CAFE   Phone: 250/624-3072

Seafood
$6-$20

In business since 1934, the distinctive diner-style restaurant serves locals and tourists alike with a variety of seafood, steaks, chops, sandwiches and salads. Any local can point the way to the cafe, in the city's Cow Bay area. Casual dress. **Bar:** Full bar. **Hours:** Open 3/1-12/25 & 2/1-2/28; 11 am-9 pm; 9 am-10 pm 6/1-9/6. Closed: 10/11, 12/25, 12/26. **Address:** 113 Cow Bay Rd V8J 1A4 **Location:** From 3rd Ave E, 0.6 mi (1 km) n; in Cow Bay. **Parking:** street.

STARDUST RESTAURANT   Phone: 250/627-1221

Chinese
$8-$20

Specializing in Mandarin and Western-style food, the downtown restaurant prepares combination plates for one person, as well as easy-to-share preparations of seafood, beef, pork, fried rice, chow mein, chop suey, chicken and duck. Casual dress. **Hours:** 11:30 am-9:30 pm. Closed: 1/1, 12/25, 12/26. **Address:** 627 3rd Ave W V8J 1M3 **Location:** Between 6th and 5th sts. **Parking:** street.

THE WATERFRONT RESTAURANT   Phone: 250/624-6771

Canadian
$10-$34

This restaurant offers absolutely the best, most incredible view of the harbor and mountains as the hotel sits atop a cliff overlooking the strait. This all-day restaurant serves traditional dishes such as pasta, burgers, steak and specializes in seafood. Casual dress. **Bar:** Full bar. **Hours:** 6:30 am-10 pm, Sat & Sun from 7 am. Closed: 12/25. **Address:** 222 1st Ave W V8J 3P6 **Location:** Hwy 16, just nw on 2nd St; in Crest Hotel. **Parking:** on-site. CALL ⌖M

PRINCETON pop. 2,677

CANADAS BEST VALUE PRINCETON INN & SUITES

Phone: (250)295-3537

(CAA) (SAVE)

▼▼▼▼

Motel

$99-$139 All Year

Address: 169 Hwy 3 V0X 1W0 **Location:** On Hwy 3. **Facility:** 44 one-bedroom standard units, some with kitchens. 2 stories (no elevator), exterior corridors. **Parking:** on-site, winter plug-ins. **Amenities:** high-speed Internet, irons, hair dryers. **Pool(s):** heated outdoor. **Leisure Activities:** sauna, whirlpool. **Guest Services:** wireless Internet. **Business Services:** meeting rooms, PC. **Free Special Amenities: continental breakfast and high-speed Internet.**

📶 CALL 🅜 🍳 🚫 🖥 💻 / SOME UNITS FEE 🐾 ✕

VILLAGER INN

Book great rates at AAA.com

Phone: (250)295-6996

(CAA) (SAVE)

▼▼

Motel

$69-$95 All Year

Address: 244 4th St V0X 1W0 **Location:** Just off Hwy 3. **Facility:** Smoke free premises. 26 one-bedroom standard units, some with efficiencies. 2 stories (no elevator), exterior corridors. **Parking:** on-site. **Terms:** office hours 7 am-11 pm, cancellation fee imposed. **Amenities:** irons, hair dryers. **Pool(s):** heated outdoor. **Guest Services:** coin laundry, wireless Internet. **Business Services:** PC. **Free Special Amenities: local telephone calls and high-speed Internet.**

📶 🍳 ✕ 🖥 💻 / SOME UNITS FEE 🐾

QUADRA ISLAND—See Gulf Islands p. 524.

QUALICUM BAY pop. 397

—— **WHERE TO DINE** ——

SANDBAR CAFE

▼▼

Canadian

$7-$15

Phone: 778/424-4478

The Sandbar Cafe is a roadside-style diner with a very nice view of the water. The traditional fare of very good food includes a daily selection of tasty sandwiches and homemade soup. The coffee is always fresh, and service is friendly and prompt. Casual dress. **Bar:** Full bar. **Hours:** 7 am-8 pm. Closed: 12/25, 12/26. **Address:** 6087 W Island Hwy V0R 1G0 **Location:** Hwy 19, exit 75 (Qualicum Bay/Bowser), 1.8 mi (3 km) e, follow Hwy 19A signs, then 1.5 mi (2.5 km) n on Hwy 19A. **Parking:** on-site. 🏧

QUALICUM BEACH pop. 6,921

OCEAN CREST MOTEL

▼▼▼

Motel

$59-$104 All Year

Phone: 250/752-5518

Address: 3292 W Island Hwy V9K 2C6 **Location:** Hwy 19, exit 60 (Qualicum Beach/Port Alberni), 2.5 mi (4 km) e on Memorial Ave, then 1.9 mi (3 km) n on Hwy 19A. **Facility:** Smoke free premises. 19 one-bedroom standard units, some with efficiencies. 2 stories (no elevator), exterior corridors. **Parking:** on-site. **Terms:** office hours 8 am-10 pm. **Amenities:** hair dryers. **Guest Services:** wireless Internet. ✕ 🖥 💻 / SOME UNITS 🍳

OLD DUTCH INN (BY THE SEA)

▼▼▼

Hotel

$80-$140 6/1-2/28

$80-$100 3/1-5/31

Phone: (250)752-6914

Address: 2690 Island Hwy W V9K 1G8 **Location:** Hwy 19, exit 60 (Qualicum Beach/Port Alberni), 2.5 mi (4 km) on Memorial Ave at jct Hwy 19A. **Facility:** Smoke free premises. 35 one-bedroom standard units. 2 stories (no elevator), interior corridors. *Bath:* combo or shower only. **Parking:** on-site. **Amenities:** irons, hair dryers. **Dining:** restaurant, see separate listing. **Pool(s):** heated indoor. **Leisure Activities:** sauna, whirlpool. **Guest Services:** wireless Internet. **Business Services:** meeting rooms.

(ASK) 📶 🍽 🍳 ✕ 🏧 🖥 💻 / SOME UNITS FEE 🐾

—— **WHERE TO DINE** ——

GARY'S BISTRO

▼▼▼

Canadian

$9-$18

Phone: 250/752-5800

Open early for breakfast and staying busy through lunch and dinner, the downtown bistro serves a host of burgers and a great selection of appetizers with great beers on tap. The signature egg-bennys incorporate free-range eggs. Casual dress. **Bar:** Full bar. **Hours:** 8 am-9 pm. Closed: 1/1, 12/25. **Address:** Box 145, 115 W Second Ave V9K 1S7 **Location:** Between Primrose St and Memorial Ave. **Parking:** street.

OLD DUTCH INN DINING ROOM

▼▼▼

Dutch

$10-$25

Phone: 250/752-6914

Guests are treated to great ocean views from Old Dutch Inn's dining room, which stays true to the restaurant's name with Dutch decor and servers dressed in Dutch costumes. The menu lists creatively prepared pastries, in addition to early-bird specials and Dutch specialties. Casual dress. **Bar:** Full bar. **Reservations:** suggested, for dinner. **Hours:** 7 am-9:30 pm. Closed: 12/25. **Address:** 2690 Island Hwy W V9K 1G8 **Location:** Hwy 19, exit 60 (Qualicum Beach/Port Alberni), 2.5 mi (4 km) on Memorial Ave at Hwy 19A; in Old Dutch Inn (By The Sea). **Parking:** on-site. CALL 🅜 🏧

THE SHADY REST WATERFRONT PUB RESTAURANT

▼▼▼

Canadian

$12-$22

Phone: 250/752-9111

The waterfront restaurant and pub features all the usual favorites, such as burgers and sandwiches for lunch and more hearty fare for dinner. The dining section directly overlooks the ocean. Casual dress. **Bar:** Full bar. **Hours:** 11 am-9 pm, Sat & Sun from 8 am. Closed: 12/25. **Address:** 3109 Island Hwy W V9K 2C5 **Location:** Hwy 19, exit 60 (Qualicum Beach/Port Alberni), 2.4 mi (4 km) e on Memorial Ave, then 1.2 mi (2 km) n on Hwy 19A. **Parking:** on-site. CALL 🅜

QUEEN CHARLOTTE ISLANDS

——— *The following lodgings were either not evaluated or did not* ———
meet AAA rating requirements but are listed for your information only.

GRACIE'S PLACE
Phone: 250/559-4262

[fyi]
Motel

Did not meet all AAA rating requirements for locking devices in some guest rooms at time of last evaluation on 05/07/2008. **Address:** 3113 3rd Ave V0T 1S0 **Location:** On Graham Island; in Queen Charlotte; from BC Ferries and Skidegate Landing, 1.8 mi (3 km) s on Oceanview Dr. Facilities, services, and decor characterize an economy property.

HECATE INN
Phone: 250/559-4543

[fyi]
Motel

Did not meet all AAA rating requirements for locking devices in some guest rooms at time of last evaluation on 05/07/2008. **Address:** 321 3rd Ave V0T 1S0 **Location:** On Graham Island; in Queen Charlotte; from BC Ferries and Skidegate Landing, 2.5 mi (4 km) s on Oceanview Dr. Facilities, services, and decor characterize an economy property.

PREMIER CREEK LODGING
Phone: 250/559-8415

[fyi]
Motel

Did not meet all AAA rating requirements for locking devices in some guest rooms at time of last evaluation on 05/07/2008. **Address:** 3101 3rd Ave V0T 1S0 **Location:** On Graham Island; in Queen Charlotte; from BC Ferries and Skidegate Landing, 1.9 mi (3 km) s on Oceanview Dr. Facilities, services, and decor characterize an economy property.

——— **WHERE TO DINE** ———

JAGS BEANSTALK
Phone: 250/559-8826

Coffee/Tea
$5-$15

Fresh coffee, pastries and wrapped sandwiches can be purchased at this coffee shop housed inside a garden store. A few tables and chairs are set up inside as well as on the deck, which offers views of the ocean strait. Casual dress. **Hours:** 7:30 am-5 pm, Sat from 9 am, Sun 10 am-4 pm. Closed major holidays; also Sun 9/1-4/30. **Address:** 100 Hwy 110 V0T 1S1 **Location:** On Graham Island; in Skidegate; 1 mi (1.6 km) n of BC Ferry Terminal, on Hwy 16. **Parking:** on-site.

OCEANA
Phone: 250/559-8683

Chinese
$8-$18

Popular with locals looking for good Chinese food, this restaurant offers take-out yogurt, sherbet and ice cream. Casual dress. **Bar:** Beer & wine. **Hours:** 11:30 am-2 & 5-9 pm. Closed major holidays. **Address:** 3119 3rd Ave V0T 1S0 **Location:** On Graham Island; in Queen Charlotte; from BC Ferries and Skidegate Landing, 1.8 mi (3 km) s on Oceanview Dr. **Parking:** on-site.

QUESNEL pop. 9,326

BEST WESTERN TOWER INN
Book great rates at AAA.com
Phone: (250)992-2201

Hotel
$115-$120 All Year

Address: 500 Reid St V2J 2M9 **Location:** Hwy 97, just e on Shepherd Ave; downtown. **Facility:** Smoke free premises. 63 units. 62 one- and 1 two-bedroom standard units, some with whirlpools. 4 stories, interior corridors. **Parking:** on-site. **Amenities:** high-speed Internet, voice mail, irons, hair dryers. **Leisure Activities:** exercise room. **Guest Services:** valet laundry, wireless Internet. **Business Services:** meeting rooms, business center. **Free Special Amenities:** newspaper and high-speed Internet.

Best Western
AAA Benefit: Members save up to 20%, plus 10% bonus points with rewards program.

TALISMAN INN
Phone: 250/992-7247

Motel
$69-$149 All Year

Address: 753 Front St V2J 2L2 **Location:** Hwy 97, 0.6 mi (1 km) n of Carson Ave. **Facility:** 83 one-bedroom standard units, some with efficiencies, kitchens and/or whirlpools. 2 stories, interior corridors. *Bath:* combo or shower only. **Parking:** on-site, winter plug-ins. **Terms:** office hours 6:30 am-midnight, cancellation fee imposed. **Amenities:** voice mail, irons. *Some:* hair dryers. **Leisure Activities:** whirlpool, limited exercise equipment. **Guest Services:** coin laundry, wireless Internet. **Business Services:** meeting rooms, PC. **Free Special Amenities:** continental breakfast and local telephone calls.

——— **WHERE TO DINE** ———

GRANVILLE'S COFFEE
Phone: 250/992-3667

Canadian
$4-$9

Patrons easily can become too busy viewing the eatery's eclectically decorated walls to finish their coffee. Good choices include jumbo muffins, deli sandwiches and homemade soups. Located downtown where fluent espresso is spoken. Casual dress. **Hours:** 7 am-10 pm, Sun 8 am-5 pm. Closed: 12/25. **Address:** 383 Reid St V2J 2M5 **Location:** Reid St at St Laurent Ave; downtown. **Parking:** street.

RADIUM HOT SPRINGS pop. 735

BIGHORN MEADOWS RESORT *Book great rates at AAA.com*   Phone: (250)347-2323

Condominium
$119-$139 All Year

Address: 10 Bighorn Blvd V0A 1M0 **Location:** Hwy 93/95, 0.5 mi (0.9 km) sw on Stanley St; in Springs Golf Course. **Facility:** From smaller studio units to large units, the resort includes varied rooms, including some lofts that let guests walk right from onto the golf course. Smoke free premises. 189 units. 66 one-bedroom standard units. 64 one- and 59 two-bedroom suites with whirlpools. 3 stories, exterior corridors. **Parking:** on-site, winter plug-ins. **Terms:** office hours 8 am-8 pm, check-in 4 pm, 3 day cancellation notice. **Amenities:** video library, DVD players, high-speed Internet, voice mail, irons, hair dryers. **Pool(s):** heated outdoor. **Leisure Activities:** whirlpool. *Fee:* golf-18 holes. **Guest Services:** complimentary laundry, wireless Internet. **Business Services:** PC (fee).

FREE high-speed Internet

CEDAR MOTEL   Phone: 250/347-9463

Motel
$75-$140 All Year

Address: 7593 Main St W V0A 1M0 **Location:** Hwy 93 and 95, just s of jct Hwy 93, on service road (Main St). **Facility:** 17 units. 8 one- and 9 two-bedroom standard units, some with efficiencies. 2 stories (no elevator), exterior corridors. **Parking:** on-site, winter plug-ins. **Terms:** office hours 8 am-11 pm. **Amenities:** *Some:* hair dryers. **Guest Services:** wireless Internet.

CHALET EUROPE   Phone: 250/347-9305

Motel
$89-$189 All Year

Address: 5063 Madsen Rd V0A 1M0 **Location:** Hwy 95, just w on Hwy 93, then 0.4 mi (0.7 km) s, up the hill. **Facility:** Smoke free premises. 17 one-bedroom suites. 3 stories (no elevator), exterior corridors. **Parking:** on-site. **Terms:** office hours 7 am-10:30 pm, 7 day cancellation notice-fee imposed. **Amenities:** DVD players, hair dryers. *Some:* irons. **Leisure Activities:** whirlpool, cross country skiing, barbecue area, table tennis, foosball, hiking trails, jogging, game room. **Guest Services:** coin laundry, wireless Internet.

FREE continental breakfast and high-speed Internet

▼ See AAA listing p 577 ▼

Village Country Inn
Radium Hot Springs, B.C.

Charming and elegant Victorian style Country Inn offering warm, cozy rooms for romantic getaways. Located in the heart of the Columbia Valley with world class Golfing, Hiking & Skiing at your doorstep. Come for a revitalizing weekend retreat or stay longer to visit Banff and Lake Louise, which are only 1 1/2 hours away. Finish your day at the famous Radium Hot Springs pool.

1-877-466-4680
(250)347-9392
www.villagecountryinn.bc.ca

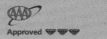
Approved

LIDO MOTEL

Phone: 250/347-9533

Motel
$65-$95 All Year

Address: 4876 McKay St V0A 1M0 **Location:** Jct Hwy 93 and 95, just e, just s along Main St, then just e. **Facility:** Smoke free premises. 10 units. 2 one- and 8 two-bedroom standard units, some with efficiencies. 1 story, exterior corridors. *Bath:* combo or shower only. **Parking:** on-site, winter plug-ins. **Terms:** office hours 7:30 am-11 pm, 7 day cancellation notice. **Amenities:** *Some:* DVD players. **Leisure Activities:** miniature golf, horseshoes. **Guest Services:** wireless Internet.

PRESTIGE RADIUM HOT SPRINGS   *Book great rates at AAA.com*

Phone: (250)347-2300

CAA SAVE

Hotel
$169-$209 3/1-9/30
$129-$189 10/1-2/28

Address: 7493 Main St W V0A 1M0 **Location:** Jct Hwy 93 and 95. **Facility:** Smoke free premises. 87 units. 82 one- and 2 two-bedroom standard units, some with efficiencies or kitchens. 3 one-bedroom suites with whirlpools, some with kitchens. 3 stories, interior corridors. **Parking:** on-site, winter plug-ins. **Terms:** cancellation fee imposed. **Amenities:** video games (fee), voice mail, irons, hair dryers. **Pool(s):** heated indoor. **Leisure Activities:** whirlpool, exercise room, spa. **Guest Services:** wireless Internet. **Business Services:** meeting rooms, PC (fee). **Free Special Amenities:** newspaper and high-speed Internet.

VILLAGE COUNTRY INN & TEA ROOM

Phone: 250/347-9392

CAA SAVE

Country Inn
$95-$175 All Year

Address: 7557 Canyon Ave V0A 1M0 **Location:** Jct Hwy 93 and 95, just w along Main St, then just s on St Joseph St. Located in a residential area across from playground. **Facility:** From the luxurious duvets to the serene setting, the Victorian property is suitable for short- or long-term stays and offers a retreat-like ambience. Smoke free premises. 14 one-bedroom standard units. 2 stories (no elevator), interior corridors. *Bath:* combo or shower only. **Parking:** on-site, winter plug-ins. **Terms:** office hours 7:30 am-9 pm, check-in 4 pm, 7 day cancellation notice-fee imposed. **Amenities:** video library (fee). *Some:* DVD players, hair dryers. **Leisure Activities:** board games, chess and cards available in tea room, local art display. **Guest Services:** wireless Internet. *(See color ad p 576)*

FREE high-speed Internet

—— WHERE TO DINE ——

BACK COUNTRY JACKS

Phone: 250/347-0009

Canadian
$10-$27

This Western-themed restaurant is a local hot spot for good eats. Canadian barbecue chicken, ribs, steaks, seafood, trout and salmon feature prominently on the menu, complemented by soups, salads, hot sandwiches, meatloaf, chili and homemade pies. Designed to resemble a corral, the dining room is decorated with Western-style murals and memorabilia. Booming music keeps the atmosphere lively. Casual dress. **Bar:** Full bar. **Hours:** Open 3/1-10/31 & 12/1-2/28; 11:30 am-11 pm; 4 pm-10 pm in winter. Closed: 12/24, 12/25. **Address:** 7355 W Main St V0A 1M0 **Location:** Hwy 93 and 95, just s of jct Hwy 93, on service road (Main St). **Parking:** on-site.

THE OLD SALZBURG RESTAURANT

Phone: 250/347-6553

CAA

Austrian
$10-$30

Guests are immediately greeted with a friendly hello at this mountainside restaurant, which boasts a warm, mountain village ambience and lovely views. The menu lists traditional Austrian and Continental dishes, like schnitzel, hearty spaetzle, pasta, chicken and steak. Patio seating is an option in the summer, but in the winter, a window seat is a good spot to take in views of the valley and mountain ranges. Expect attentive service. Casual dress. **Bar:** Full bar. **Reservations:** suggested, in summer. **Hours:** 11:30 am-4 & 5-10 pm; from 5 pm 9/15-4/15. Closed: 12/25; also Mon, Tues 9/15-4/15. **Address:** 4943 Hwy 93 V0A 1M0 **Location:** Hwy 93 and 95, just w; centre. **Parking:** on-site.

REVELSTOKE pop. 7,230

THE COAST HILLCREST RESORT HOTEL   *Book great rates at AAA.com*

Phone: (250)837-3322

CAA SAVE

Hotel
$159-$239 All Year

Address: 2100 Oak Dr V0E 2S0 **Location:** 2.7 mi (4.3 km) e on Trans-Canada Hwy 1, 0.6 mi (0.9 km) sw. **Facility:** Smoke free premises. 75 one-bedroom standard units, some with whirlpools. 3 stories, interior corridors. **Parking:** on-site, winter plug-ins. **Amenities:** video library, safes, irons, hair dryers. *Some:* DVD players, CD players. **Leisure Activities:** sauna, whirlpools, steamroom, helicopter skiing, ATV tours, pool table, exercise room, spa. *Fee:* white water rafting. **Guest Services:** valet laundry, wireless Internet. **Business Services:** meeting rooms, PC (fee).

FREE local telephone calls

DAYS INN & SUITES REVELSTOKE

Book great rates at AAA.com

Phone: (250)837-2191

CAA SAVE

Hotel
$89-$199 All Year

Address: 301 Wright St V0E 2S0 **Location:** South side of Trans-Canada Hwy 1, just e of Columbia River Bridge at Victoria Rd, then just se. **Facility:** Smoke free premises. 56 units. 33 one-bedroom standard units. 22 one- and 1 two-bedroom suites, some with efficiencies or kitchens. 2 stories (no elevator), interior/exterior corridors. **Parking:** on-site, winter plug-ins. **Terms:** cancellation fee imposed. **Amenities:** voice mail, irons, hair dryers. *Some:* DVD players, high-speed Internet. **Leisure Activities:** whirlpools, exercise room. **Guest Services:** coin laundry, wireless Internet. **Business Services:** PC.

FREE continental breakfast and local telephone calls

MONASHEE LODGE

Motel
Rates not provided

Phone: 250/837-6778

Address: 1601 3rd St W V0E 2S0 **Location:** South side of Trans-Canada Hwy 1, just e of Columbia River Bridge at Victoria Rd, then just se on Wright St. **Facility:** Smoke free premises. 18 one-bedroom standard units, some with kitchens (utensils extra charge). 2 stories (no elevator), exterior corridors. **Parking:** on-site, winter plug-ins. **Terms:** office hours 7 am-11 pm. **Amenities:** voice mail. *Some:* DVD players, irons, hair dryers. **Leisure Activities:** whirlpool. **Guest Services:** complimentary laundry, wireless Internet. **Business Services:** PC.

SANDMAN HOTEL

CAA SAVE

Hotel
Rates not provided

Phone: 250/837-5271

Address: 1901 LaForme Blvd V0E 2S0 **Location:** North side of Trans-Canada Hwy 1, at intersection nearest east end of Columbia River Bridge. Located in a quiet area. **Facility:** 172 units. 170 one-bedroom standard units, some with efficiencies. 1 one- and 1 two-bedroom suites with kitchens. 2 stories (no elevator), interior/exterior corridors. **Parking:** on-site, winter plug-ins. **Terms:** check-in 4 pm. **Amenities:** irons, hair dryers. *Some:* high-speed Internet. **Pool(s):** 2 heated indoor. **Leisure Activities:** whirlpools. **Guest Services:** valet laundry, wireless Internet. **Business Services:** meeting rooms, PC. **Free Special Amenities:** local telephone calls and high-speed Internet.

SUPER 8 REVELSTOKE

Book at AAA.com

Hotel
Rates not provided

Phone: 250/837-0888

Address: 1700 W Victoria Rd V0E 2S0 **Location:** South side of Trans-Canada Hwy 1, just e of Columbia River Bridge at Victoria Rd (town centre exit). **Facility:** 44 units. 35 one-bedroom standard units. 9 one-bedroom suites. 2 stories (no elevator), interior corridors. **Parking:** on-site, winter plug-ins. **Terms:** check-in 4 pm. **Amenities:** hair dryers. *Some:* irons. **Pool(s):** heated indoor. **Leisure Activities:** whirlpool. **Guest Services:** coin laundry, wireless Internet. **Business Services:** PC.

SWISS CHALET MOTEL

CAA SAVE

Motel
$89-$155 All Year

Phone: 250/837-4650

Address: 1101 Victoria Rd V0E 2S0 **Location:** 0.6 mi (1 km) s from Trans-Canada Hwy 1. **Facility:** Smoke free premises. 22 units. 20 one- and 2 two-bedroom standard units, some with whirlpools. 1-2 stories (no elevator), exterior corridors. **Bath:** combo or shower only. **Parking:** on-site, winter plug-ins. **Terms:** office hours 7:30 am-10 pm. **Amenities:** *Some:* hair dryers. **Guest Services:** wireless Internet. **Business Services:** PC (fee). **Free Special Amenities:** expanded continental breakfast and high-speed Internet.

─── WHERE TO DINE ───

THE NOMAD FOOD CO.

Canadian
$5-$13

Phone: 250/837-4211

There's something for everyone at this little spot easily accessed from the Trans-Canada Highway. The friendly staff serves great, freshly made paninis, wraps, burgers, fried chicken, fish and chips and homemade soup. Dishes boast fresh veggies, real meat, real cheese and no MSG. Best yet, there's an ice cream bar for dessert. Casual dress. **Hours:** 11 am-8 pm, Fri & Sat-9 pm; hours vary in winter. Closed: 12/25; also Tues. **Address:** 1601 Victoria Rd W V0E 3K0 **Location:** South side of Trans-Canada Hwy 1, just e of Columbia River Bridge at Victoria Rd. **Parking:** on-site.

THE ONE TWELVE RESTAURANT & LOUNGE

CAA

American
$10-$40

Phone: 250/837-2107

This restaurant maintains a cozy but elegant atmosphere with the help of subdued lighting, soft music, an antique fireplace and friendly service. Diners' taste buds are tempted with specialties such as Alberta steak, veal, lamb and seafood. Lunchtime offerings include a soup of the day, as well as quiche Lorraine and several chicken sandwiches. Casual dress. **Bar:** Full bar. **Reservations:** suggested. **Hours:** 5:30 pm-9 pm. Closed major holidays. **Address:** 112 1st St E V0E 2S0 **Location:** 1.2 mi (2 km) s from Trans-Canada Hwy 1, at Victoria Rd; downtown; in The Regent Inn. **Parking:** on-site.

THREE VALLEY LAKE CHATEAU

Canadian
$8-$22

Phone: 250/837-2109

This easily accessible restaurant is a good place to stop for a rest and let the children browse. Fast, simple food is served in ample portions. A ghost town and antique train are next door. Casual dress. **Bar:** Full bar. **Reservations:** not accepted. **Hours:** Open 4/9-10/15; 7 am-8 pm. **Address:** 8903 Trans-Canada Hwy 1 V0E 2S0 **Location:** 11.5 mi (19.2 km) w on Trans-Canada Hwy 1; on Three Valley Lake; in Three Valley Gap Lake Chateau. **Parking:** on-site.

ZALAS STEAK & PIZZA HOUSE

Steak
$14-$35

Phone: 250/837-5555

A popular place to dine in town, this restaurant features a varied menu with some Greek twists and all the classic Canadian favorites. Entrees come with offerings from the little salad bar. Casual dress. **Bar:** Full bar. **Reservations:** suggested. **Hours:** 4:30 pm-11 pm, Fri & Sat-midnight. Closed: 12/24, 12/25. **Address:** 1601 Victoria Rd W V0E 2S0 **Location:** South side of Trans-Canada Hwy 1, just e of Columbia River Bridge at Victoria Rd. **Parking:** on-site.

RICHMOND—See Vancouver p. 654.

ROSSLAND pop. 3,278

CASA ALPINA

Motel
$99-$109 12/1-2/28
$89-$99 3/1-11/30

Phone: (250)362-7364

Address: 1199 Nancy Greene Hwy V0G 1Y0 **Location:** 0.6 mi (1 km) w on Hwy 3B; jct Hwy 22. **Facility:** 42 units. 40 one-bedroom standard units, some with efficiencies or kitchens. 2 one-bedroom suites with kitchens. 2 stories (no elevator), exterior corridors. **Parking:** on-site. **Terms:** office hours 6 am-10 pm, 3 day cancellation notice-fee imposed. **Amenities:** voice mail. *Some:* irons, hair dryers. **Leisure Activities:** whirlpool. **Guest Services:** coin laundry, wireless Internet.

SAANICH—See Victoria p. 696.

SALMON ARM pop. 16,012

BEST WESTERN SALMON ARM INN   *Book great rates at AAA.com*

Motel
$99-$149 All Year

Phone: (250)832-9793

AAA Benefit:
Members save up to 20%, plus 10% bonus points with rewards program.

Address: 61 10th St SW V1E 1E4 **Location:** 0.7 mi (1.1 km) w on Trans-Canada Hwy 1. **Facility:** 77 one-bedroom standard units, some with efficiencies. 2 stories (no elevator), exterior corridors. **Parking:** on-site. **Amenities:** voice mail, irons, hair dryers. *Some:* DVD players. **Pool(s):** heated indoor. **Leisure Activities:** whirlpool. **Guest Services:** valet laundry, wireless Internet. **Business Services:** PC. **Free Special Amenities: expanded continental breakfast and high-speed Internet.**

HOLIDAY INN EXPRESS HOTEL & SUITES SALMON ARM   *Book at AAA.com*

Hotel
$123-$176 All Year

Phone: (250)832-7711

Address: 1090 22nd St NE V1E 2V5 **Location:** 0.5 mi (0.8 km) e on Trans-Canada Hwy 1. **Facility:** 114 units. 85 one-bedroom standard units, some with whirlpools. 29 one-bedroom suites. 5 stories, interior corridors. *Bath:* combo or shower only. **Parking:** on-site. **Terms:** check-in 4 pm, cancellation fee imposed. **Amenities:** video games (fee), high-speed Internet, dual phone lines, voice mail, irons, hair dryers. **Pool(s):** heated indoor/outdoor. **Leisure Activities:** whirlpool, waterslide, exercise room. **Guest Services:** valet and coin laundry. **Business Services:** meeting rooms, business center.

SUPER 8   *Book at AAA.com*

Hotel
$75-$200 All Year

Phone: (250)832-8812

Address: 2901 10th Ave NE V1E 2S3 **Location:** 0.6 mi (1 km) e on Trans-Canada Hwy 1. **Facility:** Smoke free premises. 40 units. 39 one-bedroom standard units, some with whirlpools. 1 one-bedroom suite with kitchen. 2 stories (no elevator), interior corridors. **Parking:** on-site. **Amenities:** hair dryers. *Some:* DVD players, irons. **Guest Services:** coin laundry, wireless Internet. **Business Services:** PC.

—— WHERE TO DINE ——

CHIANG MAI ORCHID THAI RESTAURANT

Northern Thai
$9-$17

Phone: 250/832-0699

Chefs trained in Thailand prepare both spicy and mild dishes in the classic northern style and from fresh ingredients. The entire family manages and staffs the simple dining room, and the chef often comes out to see how guests' meals are. Patrons need look no further for a taste of Thailand in the middle of British Columbia. Casual dress. **Bar:** Full bar. **Reservations:** accepted. **Hours:** 11:30 am-2:30 & 5-8:30 pm, Sat & Sun from 5 pm. Closed: 12/25, 12/26. **Address:** 131 Hudson Ave NE V1E 4N7 **Location:** Trans-Canada Hwy 1, just sw at Alexander St to Hudson Ave, then just e. **Parking:** street.

PRIMAVERA RISTORANTE ITALIANO

Italian
$10-$25

Phone: 250/833-0065

A small, authentic piece of Italy can be found just off the highway. Red-checkered tablecloths, vine-covered walls and Italian music create a cozy environment in which patrons can savor hearty dishes ranging from veal to seafood fettuccine. The restaurant is busy on weekends and when entertainers perform some nights of the week. Casual dress. **Bar:** Full bar. **Reservations:** suggested, weekends. **Hours:** 11 am-9 pm, Fri-10 pm, Sat 5 pm-10 pm. Closed major holidays; also Sun. **Address:** 260 Ross St NE V0E 1H1 **Location:** Trans-Canada Hwy 1, exit Ross St, just n. **Parking:** street.

SALT SPRING ISLAND—See Gulf Islands p. 525.

SAVONA

LAKESIDE COUNTRY INN   *Book at AAA.com*   **Phone:** (250)373-2528

Motel
$110-$190 6/1-10/15
$90-$160 4/15-5/31

Address: 7001 Savona Access Rd V0K 2J0 **Location:** Trans-Canada Hwy 1, exit Savona; along business frontage road. **Facility:** Smoke free premises. 9 one-bedroom efficiencies or kitchens. 2 stories (no elevator), exterior corridors. *Bath:* combo or shower only. **Parking:** on-site, winter plug-ins. **Terms:** open 4/15-10/15, office hours 8 am-10 pm, age restrictions may apply, 3 day cancellation notice. **Amenities:** hair dryers. **Leisure Activities:** rental canoes, rental paddleboats, boat dock, bicycles. **Guest Services:** wireless Internet.

ASK ⊠ ⊠ 🛢 ▣ / SOME UNITS ▣

SICAMOUS pop. 2,676

BEST WESTERN SICAMOUS INN   *Book great rates at AAA.com*   **Phone:** (250)836-4117

(CAA) (SAVE)

Motel
$156-$279 3/1-9/7
$129-$230 9/8-2/28

Address: 806 Trans-Canada Hwy 1 V0E 2V0 **Location:** Jct Trans-Canada Hwy 1 and 97; at east end of town. **Facility:** Smoke free premises. 65 units. 57 one-bedroom standard units. 8 one-bedroom suites, some with whirlpools. 2 stories (no elevator), interior/exterior corridors. **Parking:** on-site. **Amenities:** high-speed Internet, voice mail, irons, hair dryers. **Pool(s):** heated indoor. **Leisure Activities:** whirlpools. **Guest Services:** coin laundry, wireless Internet. **Business Services:** PC.

AAA Benefit:
Members save up to 20%, plus 10% bonus points with rewards program.

🍴↑ CALL 🕭M ⊠ ⊠ 🛢 ▣ ▣

FREE continental breakfast and high-speed Internet

SICAMOUS SUPER 8   *Book at AAA.com*   **Phone:** (250)836-4988

Motel
$70-$170 3/1-10/31 & 2/1-2/28

Address: 1120 Riverside Ave V0E 2V0 **Location:** Trans-Canada Hwy 1, s on Hwy 97A, just w on Main St to traffic circle, then just s. **Facility:** Smoke free premises. 22 units. 18 one-bedroom standard units. 4 one-bedroom suites. 2 stories (no elevator), exterior corridors. **Parking:** on-site, winter plug-ins. **Terms:** open 3/1-10/31 & 2/1-2/28, office hours 7 am-10 pm, cancellation fee imposed. **Amenities:** hair dryers. **Leisure Activities:** whirlpool. **Guest Services:** wireless Internet.

🍴↑ ⊠ 🎦 ▣ / SOME UNITS FEE 🐕 🛢 ▣

SIDNEY—See Victoria p. 696.

SILVERTON pop. 185

WILLIAM HUNTER CABINS   **Phone:** (250)358-2844

Cabin
$98-$128 6/1-2/28
$88-$108 3/1-5/31

Address: 303 Lake Ave V0G 2B0 **Location:** Centre. **Facility:** Smoke free premises. 6 one-bedroom suites with efficiencies. 1 story, exterior corridors. **Parking:** on-site, winter plug-ins. **Terms:** office hours 8 am-8 pm, 14 day cancellation notice-fee imposed. **Guest Services:** wireless Internet.

ASK 🍴↑ ⊠ 🎦 🎦 🕭 🛢 ▣ ▣ / SOME UNITS FEE 🐕

SMITHERS pop. 5,217

ASPEN INN & SUITES   **Phone:** 250/847-4551

Motel
Rates not provided

Address: 4628 Yellowhead Hwy V0J 2N0 **Location:** 0.9 mi (1.5 km) w on Hwy 16 (Yellowhead Hwy). **Facility:** Smoke free premises. 60 units. 55 one-bedroom standard units, some with efficiencies. 5 one-bedroom suites with efficiencies. 2 stories, exterior corridors. **Parking:** on-site, winter plug-ins. **Amenities:** voice mail, hair dryers. **Pool(s):** heated indoor. **Leisure Activities:** saunas, whirlpool. **Guest Services:** wireless Internet. **Business Services:** meeting rooms, PC.

🍴 🍸 ⊠ ⊠ 🎦 🛢 ▣ ▣ / SOME UNITS FEE 🐕

SOOKE—See Victoria p. 698.

SORRENTO pop. 1,360

———— WHERE TO DINE ————

HOME RESTAURANT   **Phone:** 250/675-3552

Canadian
$6-$15

Friendly servers deliver large portions at this basic diner, known for delicious, homestyle cooking and scrumptious homemade desserts. Reasonable prices make eating here a good value. Casual dress. **Bar:** Beer & wine. **Reservations:** not accepted. **Hours:** 7 am-8 pm. Closed: 12/25. **Address:** 1235C Trans-Canada Hwy V0E 2W0 **Location:** Trans-Canada Hwy 1; in Petro Canada Gas Station. **Parking:** on-site.

SQUAMISH pop. 14,949

EXECUTIVE SUITES GARIBALDI SPRINGS GOLF RESORT

Book great rates at AAA.com

Phone: (604)815-0048

Hotel
$119-$389 All Year

Address: 40900 Tantalus Rd V8B 0R3 **Location:** Hwy 99, just e on Garibaldi Way, then 0.6 mi (1 km) n. **Facility:** Smoke free premises. 111 units. 24 one-bedroom standard units with efficiencies. 73 one- and 14 two-bedroom suites with kitchens, some with whirlpools. 4 stories, interior corridors. **Parking:** on-site. **Terms:** cancellation fee imposed. **Amenities:** DVD players, voice mail, irons, hair dryers. **Dining:** Rockwell's Bar & Grill, see separate listing. **Pool(s):** heated indoor/outdoor. **Leisure Activities:** whirlpool, exercise room. *Fee:* golf-18 holes. **Guest Services:** complimentary laundry, wireless Internet. **Business Services:** meeting rooms, PC (fee). **Free Special Amenities:** local telephone calls and newspaper.

MOUNTAIN RETREAT HOTEL & SUITES

Book great rates at AAA.com

Phone: (604)815-0883

Hotel
$125-$140 All Year

Address: 38922 Progress Way V8B 0K5 **Location:** 0.9 mi (1.5 km) n on Hwy 99 at Industrial Way. **Facility:** 87 one-bedroom standard units, some with efficiencies. 4 stories, interior corridors. **Parking:** on-site. **Terms:** check-in 4 pm, cancellation fee imposed. **Amenities:** video games (fee), voice mail, irons, hair dryers. **Pool(s):** heated indoor. **Leisure Activities:** whirlpool, waterslide, exercise room. **Guest Services:** coin laundry, wireless Internet. **Business Services:** meeting rooms, PC (fee). **Free Special Amenities:** local telephone calls and high-speed Internet.

SEA TO SKY HOTEL

Book great rates at AAA.com

Phone: (604)898-4874

Hotel
$179-$375 3/1-3/31
$99-$189 4/1-2/28

Address: 40330 Tantalus Way V0N 1T0 **Location:** 2.9 mi (4.5 km) n on Hwy 99 at Garibaldi Way. **Facility:** Smoke free premises. 52 units. 44 one- and 8 two-bedroom standard units. 3 stories, interior corridors. **Parking:** on-site. **Terms:** cancellation fee imposed. **Amenities:** voice mail, irons, hair dryers. **Leisure Activities:** sauna, whirlpool, exercise room. **Guest Services:** coin laundry, wireless Internet. **Business Services:** meeting rooms, PC. *(See color ad below)*

FREE local telephone calls and high-speed Internet

—— WHERE TO DINE ——

PARKSIDE RESTAURANT

Canadian
$9-$38

Phone: 604/892-2273

The cozy restaurant serves breakfast, lunch and dinner, including salads, tapas, sandwiches, wraps, pasta and such hearty dinner entrees as chicken Marsala, prosciutto halibut and grilled salmon. The motto is, "Fresh ingredients made to order. Please be patient; the best things are worth waiting for!". Casual dress. **Reservations:** suggested, for dinner Fri & Sat. **Hours:** 10 am-3 & 5:30-11 pm. Closed: 12/25, 12/26. **Address:** 36996 Cleveland Rd V8B 0C2 **Location:** Hwy 99, 0.6 mi (1 km) w on Cleveland Ave; corner of Victoria St. **Parking:** on-site. [AC]

ROCKWELL'S BAR & GRILL

Canadian
$8-$19

Phone: 604/815-0999

In a newer lodging, the restaurant overlooks the golf course and distant mountains. The menu features casual fare such as burgers, soups and various sandwiches, with more complex menu items at dinner. Casual dress. **Bar:** Full bar. **Hours:** 7 am-10 pm. Closed: 12/25. **Address:** 40900 Tantalus Rd V8B 0R3 **Location:** Hwy 99, just e on Garibaldi Way, then 0.6 mi (1 km) n; in Executive Suites Garibaldi Springs Golf Resort. **Parking:** on-site. CALL [&M]

SUMMERLAND—See Okanagan Valley p. 563.

SUN PEAKS

COAST SUNDANCE LODGE   *Book great rates at AAA.com*

Hotel
$89-$269 11/20-2/28
$75-$199 3/1-11/19

Phone: (250)578-0200

Address: 3160 Creekside Way V0E 5N0 **Location:** Hwy 5, 19.4 mi (31 km) ne on Todd Mountain Rd, follow signs to village. **Facility:** Smoke free premises. 84 units. 64 one-bedroom standard units, some with efficiencies. 15 one- and 5 two-bedroom suites, some with efficiencies or kitchens. 4 stories, interior corridors. **Parking:** on-site (fee). **Terms:** 30 day cancellation notice, in winter-fee imposed. **Amenities:** high-speed Internet, irons, hair dryers. **Leisure Activities:** whirlpool, ski lockers, hiking trails, exercise room. *Fee:* downhill & cross country skiing, snowmobiling. **Guest Services:** coin laundry. **Business Services:** meeting rooms. **Free Special Amenities: local telephone calls and high-speed Internet.** [ECO] [YI] [Y] CALL [&M] [pool] [X] [X] [AC] [camera] [B] [microwave] [fridge]

DELTA SUN PEAKS RESORT   *Book at AAA.com*

Resort
Hotel
$99-$399 All Year

Phone: (250)578-6000

Address: 3240 Village Way V0E 5N0 **Location:** Hwy 5, 19.4 mi (31 km) ne on Todd Mountain Rd, follow signs to village. **Facility:** Within the Sun Peaks Village, the resort hotel strives for superb service and offers ritzy accommodations done up in a Rocky Mountain theme. Smoke free premises. 261 units. 205 one-bedroom standard units. 34 one- and 22 two-bedroom suites, some with kitchens. 4-5 stories, interior corridors. **Parking:** on-site (fee) and valet. **Terms:** check-in 4 pm, cancellation fee imposed. **Amenities:** high-speed Internet (fee), dual phone lines, voice mail, irons, hair dryers. *Note:* DVD players, video games (fee). **Dining:** Mantles Restaurant, see separate listing. **Pool(s):** heated outdoor. **Leisure Activities:** sauna, whirlpools, steamroom, recreation programs, hiking trails, jogging, exercise room, game room. *Fee:* downhill & cross country skiing, massage. **Guest Services:** valet and coin laundry. **Business Services:** conference facilities, business center.
[ECO] [ASK] [YI] [Y] [accessible] CALL [&M] [pool] [X] [X] [AC] [B] [microwave] / SOME UNITS FEE [pets] [fridge]

HEFFLEY BOUTIQUE INN   *Book at AAA.com*

Hotel
$99-$425 4/14-2/28
$99-$359 3/1-4/13

Phone: (250)578-8343

Address: 3185 Creekside Way V0E 5N0 **Location:** Hwy 5, 19.4 mi (31 km) ne on Todd Mountain Rd, follow signs to village. **Facility:** Smoke free premises. 26 one-bedroom standard units, some with efficiencies and/or whirlpools. 3 stories, interior corridors. **Parking:** on-site (fee). **Terms:** check-in 4 pm, 30 day cancellation notice-fee imposed. **Amenities:** irons, hair dryers. **Leisure Activities:** sauna, whirlpool, steamroom. **Guest Services:** wireless Internet. **Business Services:** PC (fee).
[ASK] [YI] [Y] CALL [&M] [X] [X] [AC] [B] [microwave] [fridge]

NANCY GREENE'S CAHILTY LODGE   *Book at AAA.com*

Hotel
$99-$399 All Year

Phone: (250)578-7454

Address: 3220 Village Way V0E 5N0 **Location:** Hwy 5, 19.4 mi (31 km) ne on Todd Mountain Rd, follow signs to village. **Facility:** Smoke free premises. 192 units. 147 one-bedroom standard units, some with efficiencies or kitchens. 38 one-, 6 two- and 1 three-bedroom suites, some with kitchens. 4 stories, interior corridors. **Parking:** on-site (fee), winter plug-ins. **Terms:** check-in 4 pm, cancellation fee imposed. **Amenities:** video library (fee), DVD players, voice mail, hair dryers. **Leisure Activities:** whirlpools, hiking trails, jogging, exercise room. *Fee:* downhill & cross country skiing. **Guest Services:** coin laundry, wireless Internet. **Business Services:** meeting rooms, PC.
[ASK] [YI] [Y] CALL [&M] [X] [X] [AC] [microwave] / SOME UNITS [B] [fridge]

SUN PEAKS LODGE

Hotel
$109-$299 12/3-2/28
$89-$209 3/1-9/30

Phone: (250)578-7878

Address: 3180 Creekside Way V0E 5N0 **Location:** Hwy 5, 19.4 mi (31 km) ne on Todd Mountain Rd, follow signs to village. **Facility:** Smoke free premises. 44 one-bedroom standard units, some with whirlpools. 3 stories, interior corridors. **Parking:** on-site (fee). **Terms:** open 3/1-9/30 & 12/3-2/28, 30 day cancellation notice-fee imposed. **Amenities:** voice mail, irons, hair dryers. **Leisure Activities:** sauna, whirlpool, steamroom. **Guest Services:** wireless Internet. **Business Services:** PC (fee). **Free Special Amenities: high-speed Internet.** [YI] [Y] [X] [X] [AC] [camera] [B] [microwave]

—— WHERE TO DINE ——

MANTLES RESTAURANT   **Phone:** 250/578-6060

Pacific Northwest
$11-$35

Pacific Northwest fare is made in the vibrant family restaurant. The funky, upscale dining room, complete with an open-concept demonstration kitchen, sets the scene after a day on the ski hills. Among tempting starters are varied distinctive appetizers, ranging from scallops and portobello mushrooms to Caesar salad. The entrees are a piece of art. Good choices include salmon woven on a stalk of lemongrass, rack of lamb and oven-fired pizzas. Casual dress. **Bar:** Full bar. **Reservations:** suggested. **Hours:** 7 am-9 pm. **Address:** 3240 Village Way V0E 5N0 **Location:** Hwy 5, 19.4 mi (31 km) ne on Todd Mountain Rd, follow signs to village; in Delta Sun Peaks Resort. **Parking:** on-site and valet.

SURREY—See Vancouver p. 660.

TELEGRAPH COVE

TELEGRAPH COVE MARINA & RV PARK   **Phone:** 250/928-3163

Motel
$75-$160 3/1-9/8
$75-$105 9/9-2/28

Address: 1642B Telegraph Cove Rd V0N 3J0 **Location:** 9 mi (15 km) e on Beaver Cove Rd. **Facility:** Smoke free premises. 20 one-bedroom standard units with efficiencies. 68 one-bedroom standard units with efficiencies. 2 stories (no elevator), exterior corridors. *Bath:* shower only. **Parking:** on-site. **Terms:** office hours 8 am-9 pm, 30 day cancellation notice-fee imposed. **Guest Services:** coin laundry, wireless Internet.

TERRACE pop. 11,320

BEST WESTERN TERRACE INN   *Book great rates at AAA.com*   **Phone:** (250)635-0083

Hotel
$139-$248 All Year

Address: 4553 Greig Ave V8G 1M7 **Location:** Hwy 16, just e on Greig Ave, follow city centre signs. **Facility:** Smoke free premises. 61 one-bedroom standard units, some with whirlpools. 5 stories, interior corridors. **Parking:** on-site. **Terms:** cancellation fee imposed. **Amenities:** high-speed Internet, voice mail, irons, hair dryers. **Leisure Activities:** exercise room. **Guest Services:** valet laundry, wireless Internet. **Business Services:** meeting rooms, PC. **Free Special Amenities: continental breakfast and high-speed Internet.**

AAA Benefit:
Members save up to 20%, plus 10% bonus points with rewards program.

COAST INN OF THE WEST   *Book at AAA.com*   **Phone:** (250)638-8141

Hotel
$109-$229 All Year

Address: 4620 Lakelse Ave V8G 1R1 **Location:** Hwy 16 to city centre; between Emerson and Kalum sts; downtown. **Facility:** 66 one-bedroom standard units. 2-4 stories, interior corridors. **Parking:** on-site. **Terms:** cancellation fee imposed. **Amenities:** irons, hair dryers. **Guest Services:** valet laundry, wireless Internet. **Business Services:** meeting rooms, PC.

—— WHERE TO DINE ——

THE BAVARIAN INN STEAK & SEAFOOD GRILL   **Phone:** 250/635-9161

German
$20-$35

Downstairs is The Black Eddy Pub, while the more formal dining room, which offers great views, is upstairs. In addition to the expected German specialties, the menu lists steaks, seafood and pasta. This place is just east of the downtown mall. Casual dress. **Bar:** Full bar. **Reservations:** suggested. **Hours:** 4:30 pm-10 pm. Closed major holidays. **Address:** 4332 Lakelse Ave V8G 1N8 **Location:** Hwy 16 to City Centre, 0.6 mi (1 km) e. **Parking:** on-site.

BISTRO L'AMBIANCE   **Phone:** 250/615-0486

French
$9-$20

This little French bistro is next to the Coast Inn of the West, and parking is anywhere on the street. A French flair punctuates the food offerings, which range from fondues and appetizers to seafood, lunch sandwiches, children's choices and desserts. Casual dress. **Bar:** Full bar. **Hours:** 11 am-9 pm. Closed major holidays; also Sun. **Address:** 4608 Lakelse Ave V8G 1R1 **Location:** Hwy 16 to city centre, between Emerson and Kalum sts; downtown. **Parking:** street.

HOT HOUSE FLAVOURFUL FOOD   **Phone:** 250/615-5800

Indian
$7-$16

In a small strip mall, this simple eat-in-or-take-out restaurant presents a menu with worldwide influences, ranging from East Indian and Mexican to Asian and Cajun. Something extra distinguishes the flavorful food. Ask about the signature dishes. Casual dress. **Bar:** Beer & wine. **Hours:** 11:30 am-9 pm. Closed major holidays; also Sun. **Address:** 107-4717 Lakelse Ave V8G 1R5 **Location:** Corner of Spark St and Lakelse Ave; in small shopping complex. **Parking:** on-site.

TOFINO pop. 1,655

BEST WESTERN TIN WIS RESORT   *Book great rates at AAA.com*

Phone: (250)725-4445

CAA SAVE

Hotel
$165-$395 All Year

Address: 1119 Pacific Rim Hwy V0R 2Z0 **Location:** 1.8 mi (3.5 km) s on Hwy 4. **Facility:** Smoke free premises. 85 units. 82 one-bedroom standard units, some with efficiencies. 3 one-bedroom suites with efficiencies and whirlpools. 2-3 stories, exterior corridors. **Parking:** on-site. **Amenities:** high-speed Internet, voice mail, irons, hair dryers. **Leisure Activities:** sauna, whirlpool, exercise room. **Guest Services:** coin laundry, wireless Internet. **Business Services:** meeting rooms, PC. **Free Special Amenities:** local telephone calls and high-speed Internet.

AAA Benefit:
Members save up to 20%, plus 10% bonus points with rewards program.

HIMWITSA LODGE

Phone: 250/725-2017

Hotel
$175-$280 All Year

Address: 300 Main St V0R 2Z0 **Location:** Just n of centre via First St. **Facility:** Smoke free premises. 4 one-bedroom standard units, some with whirlpools. 2 stories (no elevator), interior corridors. **Parking:** on-site. **Terms:** office hours 9:30 am-9:30 pm, 14 day cancellation notice-fee imposed. **Amenities:** video library, DVD players, irons, hair dryers. **Guest Services:** wireless Internet.

LONG BEACH LODGE RESORT

Phone: 250/725-2442

Contemporary Hotel
Rates not provided

Address: 1441 Pacific Rim Hwy V0R 2Z0 **Location:** 4.7 mi (7.5 km) s on Hwy 4. **Facility:** Smoke free premises. 61 units. 41 one-bedroom standard units, some with whirlpools. 20 cottages. 2-3 stories, interior/exterior corridors. **Parking:** on-site. **Terms:** check-in 4 pm. **Amenities:** video library, DVD players, high-speed Internet, voice mail, safes, irons, hair dryers. **Dining:** restaurant, see separate listing. **Leisure Activities:** exercise room. **Guest Services:** coin laundry, wireless Internet. **Business Services:** meeting rooms, business center.

PACIFIC SANDS BEACH RESORT   *Book great rates at AAA.com*

Phone: (250)725-3322

CAA SAVE

Hotel
$185-$600 All Year

Address: 1421 Pacific Rim Hwy V0R 2Z0 **Location:** 4.7 mi (7.5 km) s on Hwy 4. Located next to Pacific Rim National Park. **Facility:** Smoke free premises. 77 units. 50 one-bedroom standard units with kitchens, some with whirlpools. 26 two- and 1 three-bedroom suites with kitchens, some with whirlpools. 1-3 stories (no elevator), exterior corridors. **Parking:** on-site. **Terms:** office hours 8 am-9 pm, 2-3 night minimum stay - seasonal and/or weekends, cancellation fee imposed. **Amenities:** video library (fee), DVD players, irons, hair dryers. *Some:* high-speed Internet, voice mail. **Leisure Activities:** recreation programs in summer, barbecue, hiking trails. **Guest Services:** coin laundry, wireless Internet. **Business Services:** PC. **Free Special Amenities:** preferred room (subject to availability with advance reservations).

SCHOONER MOTEL

Phone: 250/725-3478

CAA SAVE

Motel
$85-$245 All Year

Address: 315-321 Campbell St V0R 2Z0 **Location:** Campbell and 2nd sts; downtown. **Facility:** Smoke free premises. 18 one-bedroom standard units, some with efficiencies. 2 stories, exterior corridors. *Bath:* combo or shower only. **Parking:** on-site. **Terms:** office hours 8 am-9 pm, 14 day cancellation notice-fee imposed. **Amenities:** hair dryers. **Guest Services:** coin laundry, wireless Internet.

TOFINO MOTEL

Phone: 250/725-2055

Motel
Rates not provided

Address: 542 Campbell St V0R 2Z0 **Location:** Campbell and 4th sts; downtown. **Facility:** Smoke free premises. 13 units. 12 one- and 1 two-bedroom standard units. 2 stories (no elevator), exterior corridors. **Parking:** on-site. **Terms:** office hours 8:30 am-10 pm. **Amenities:** hair dryers. **Guest Services:** wireless Internet.

WICKANINNISH INN   *Book great rates at AAA.com*

Phone: (250)725-3100

CAA SAVE

Contemporary Hotel
$300-$560 All Year

Address: 500 Osprey Ln at Chesterman Beach V0R 2Z0 **Location:** 2.7 mi (4.3 km) e on Hwy 4. Located in a quiet area. **Facility:** The inn is on an oceanfront rock outcropping in an area known for its wild winter storms; rooms feature a fireplace and a soaker tub. Closed 1/3-1/6. Smoke free premises. 75 units. 64 one-bedroom standard units, some with whirlpools. 11 one-bedroom suites, some with kitchens. 3 stories, interior corridors. **Parking:** on-site and valet. **Terms:** check-in 4 pm, 2 night minimum stay - seasonal and/or weekends, 14 day cancellation notice-fee imposed. **Amenities:** video library, DVD players, CD players, high-speed Internet, dual phone lines, voice mail, safes, honor bars, irons, hair dryers. **Dining:** Pointe Restaurant, see separate listing. **Leisure Activities:** steamroom, exercise room, spa. **Guest Services:** wireless Internet. **Business Services:** meeting rooms, PC. **Free Special Amenities:** local telephone calls and high-speed Internet.

The following lodging was either not evaluated or did not meet AAA rating requirements but is listed for your information only.

WEIGH WEST MARINE RESORT TOFINO

Phone: 250/725-3277

Not evaluated. **Address:** 634 Campbell St V0R 2Z0 **Location:** 0.6 mi (1 km) s from downtown. Facilities, services, and decor characterize an economy property.

WHERE TO DINE

BLUE HERON RESTAURANT

Phone: 250/725-3277

Canadian
$10-$28

On the shores of Porpoise Bay, the restaurant treats patrons to wonderful views. The specialty is wonderful fresh seafood, as well as chicken and steak—but mostly it's the seafood that keeps people coming back. Casual dress. **Bar:** Full bar. **Hours:** 7 am-9 pm. Closed: 12/25. **Address:** 634 Campbell St V0R 2Z0 **Location:** 0.6 mi (1 km) s of downtown; in Weigh West Marine Resort Tofino. **Parking:** on-site. CALL &M

POINTE RESTAURANT

Phone: 250/725-3106

Pacific Northwest
$16-$42

Built above the rocks and jutting out into the ocean, this restaurant offers breathtaking scenery of wild waves in the winter. The Canadian West Coast cuisine features fresh seafood and a good selection of wines. Walk-ins are welcome for breakfast and lunch. Casual dress. **Bar:** Full bar. **Reservations:** required, for dinner. **Hours:** 8-11 am, 11:30-2:30 & 5-9 pm. Closed: 1/2-1/10. **Address:** 500 Osprey Ln at Chesterman Beach V0R 2Z0 **Location:** 2.7 mi (4.3 km) e on Hwy 4; in Wickaninnish Inn. **Parking:** on-site and valet. CALL &M

RESTAURANT AT LONG BEACH LODGE RESORT

Phone: 250/725-2442

Pacific Northwest
$8-$42

This restaurant is in a lodge right along the beach, each table offering wonderful views of the waves and sand. The menu offers a wide range of items, and many ingredients are found locally or are strictly from the province, such as salmon, Salt Spring Island goat cheese, free-range chickens and locally grown beef. Casual dress. **Bar:** Full bar. **Reservations:** required, for dinner. **Hours:** noon-9 pm. **Address:** 1441 Pacific Rim Hwy V0R 2Z0 **Location:** 4.7 mi (7.5 km) s on Hwy 4; in Long Beach Lodge Resort. **Parking:** on-site. CALL &M AX

SCHOONER RESTAURANT

Phone: 250/725-3444

Seafood
$10-$30

Great food has been a part of this building since 1949. Ask about "Morris the Ghost," who lived here in the early '70s and always made the chowder. Open for breakfast, lunch and dinner, the downtown restaurant prepares "out to sea" and "land ho" entrees. Casual dress. **Bar:** Full bar. **Reservations:** suggested, for dinner. **Hours:** 9 am-3 & 5-9 pm. Closed: 12/25. **Address:** 331 Campbell St V0R 2Z0 **Location:** Corner of 2nd St; downtown. **Parking:** on-site. AX

SHELTER RESTAURANT

Phone: 250/725-3353

Pacific Northwest
$11-$45

On the edge of town, the tastefully renovated old village house welcomes diners with regional cuisine featuring market produce and local seafood. Seating is offered by the stone fireplace in the lounge or in the candlelit upstairs loft. Casual dress. **Bar:** Full bar. **Reservations:** suggested. **Hours:** 11:30 am-midnight. Closed: 1/1, 12/25, 12/26. **Address:** 601 Campbell St V0R 2Z0 **Location:** Campbell and Gibson sts; downtown. **Parking:** on-site. AX

SOBO RESTAURANT

Phone: 250/725-2341

Pacific Rim
$6-$26

Locals are quick to rave about the food, which was once prepared from an old catering truck parked in the Tofino Botanical Gardens. The eatery has a new home in town, and the truck has been retired. Diners can still order seasonal specials, which are displayed on a colorful chalkboard, or such daily features as killer fish tacos, organic bean tostadas, crispy shrimp cakes, soba noodle salad and Caesar salad. Casual dress. **Bar:** Full bar. **Hours:** 11 am-9 pm, Mon & Tues-5:30 pm. Closed: 12/25, 12/26. **Address:** 311 Neill St V0R 2Z0 **Location:** Corner of Neill and 1st sts. **Parking:** on-site. CALL &M

SPOTTED BEAR BISTRO

Phone: 250/725-2215

Pacific Northwest
$18-$32

In a shopping complex, the small, intimate bistro prepares wonderfully distinctive Pacific Northwest cuisine from fresh ingredients, including local seafood, pasta, vegetarian dishes and such red meats as veal and lamb. Due to limited seating, reservations are a must. Casual dress. **Bar:** Full bar. **Reservations:** required. **Hours:** Open 3/1-12/31 & 2/1-2/28; 5:30 pm-10 pm; to 9 pm in winter; Saturday & Sunday brunch 10 am-2 pm; 11:30 am-2 pm 7/1-9/15. Closed: 12/25. **Address:** 101-120 Fourth St V0R 2Z0 **Location:** Fourth and Campbell sts; downtown. **Parking:** on-site and street. CALL &M AX

TRAIL pop. 7,237

BEST WESTERN TERRA NOVA HOTEL
Book great rates at AAA.com

Phone: (250)368-3355

Hotel
$160-$180 All Year

Address: 1001 Rossland Ave V1R 3N7 **Location:** On Hwy 3B; just n of city centre. **Facility:** Smoke free premises. 58 units. 56 one-bedroom standard units. 2 one-bedroom suites with whirlpools. 4 stories, interior corridors. *Bath:* combo or shower only. **Parking:** on-site. **Terms:** cancellation fee imposed. **Amenities:** high-speed Internet, voice mail, irons, hair dryers. **Leisure Activities:** whirlpool, exercise room. **Guest Services:** valet laundry, wireless Internet. **Business Services:** meeting rooms, PC (fee). **Free Special Amenities:** local telephone calls and high-speed Internet.

AAA Benefit:
Members save up to 20%, plus 10% bonus points with rewards program.

——— WHERE TO DINE ———

COLANDER RESTAURANT (1999) LTD   *Menu on AAA.com*   Phone: 250/364-1816

Italian
$5-$19

At lunch, Colander offers a small pasta buffet and items such as burgers, subs and sandwiches, while the dinner menu is more extensive. The menu also lists regional beers. While the atmosphere is pleasant, the eatery serves the masses, so guests may have to flag down the waitress for any special requests, like refills or dessert. To-go containers are available for a fee. Casual dress. **Bar:** Full bar. **Reservations:** suggested, for dinner. **Hours:** 11:30 am-2 & 4:30-8:30 pm, Sat & Sun from 4:30 pm. Closed: 12/25. **Address:** 1475 Cedar Ave V1R 4C5 **Location:** Centre. **Parking:** street.

UCLUELET pop. 1,487

BLACK ROCK OCEANFRONT RESORT   *Book at AAA.com*   Phone: 250/726-4800

Contemporary
Hotel
Rates not provided

Address: 596 Marine Dr V0R 3A0 **Location:** 1 mi (1.6 km) e on Peninsula Rd, just s on Materson Rd, then just w. **Facility:** Smoke free premises. 133 units. 64 one-bedroom standard units. 64 one- and 5 two-bedroom suites with kitchens. 2-4 stories, interior/exterior corridors. **Parking:** on-site and valet. **Terms:** check-in 4 pm. **Amenities:** DVD players, voice mail, safes, irons, hair dryers. **Dining:** Fetch Restaurant, see separate listing. **Leisure Activities:** whirlpools, exercise room, spa. **Guest Services:** wireless Internet. **Business Services:** meeting rooms, business center.

THORNTON MOTEL   Phone: 250/726-7725

Motel
$81-$192 All Year

Address: 1861 Peninsula Rd V0R 3A0 **Location:** E on Peninsula Rd at Bay St. **Facility:** Smoke free premises. 16 units. 12 one- and 4 two-bedroom standard units, some with efficiencies. 2 stories (no elevator), exterior corridors. **Parking:** on-site. **Terms:** office hours 8 am-10 pm, 5 day cancellation notice-fee imposed. **Amenities:** hair dryers. *Some:* irons. **Guest Services:** coin laundry, wireless Internet.

——— *The following lodgings were either not evaluated or did not* ———
meet AAA rating requirements but are listed for your information only.

A SNUG HARBOUR INN   Phone: 250/726-2686

(fyi)

Not evaluated. **Address:** 460 Marine Dr V0R 3A0 **Location:** 1 mi (1.6 km) e on Peninsula Rd, just s. Facilities, services, and decor characterize a mid-scale property.

TAUCA LEA BY THE SEA   Phone: 250/726-4625

(fyi)

Vacation Rental
Condominium

Did not meet all AAA rating requirements for locking devices in some guest rooms at time of last evaluation on 05/26/2009. **Address:** 1971 Harbour Dr V0R 3A0 **Location:** From Peninsula Rd, just n on Sea Plane Base Rd, then just e. Facilities, services, and decor characterize a mid-scale property.

——— WHERE TO DINE ———

DELICADO'S SURFSIDE CAFE   Phone: 250/726-4246

Southwestern
$6-$11

Near the township's entryway, the newer restaurant serves fresh, daily made dishes, such as roll-ups, Southwestern burritos, enchiladas, homemade soups and salads. Those seeking healthful alternatives should seek out the menu's low-carbohydrate and dairy- and wheat-free dishes. Casual dress. **Bar:** Beer & wine. **Hours:** 11 am-7 pm; to 9 pm 5/1-9/30. Closed: 1/1, 12/24, 12/26; also Wed. **Address:** 2082 Peninsula Rd V0R 3A0 **Location:** At Forbes Rd; west end of town. **Parking:** on-site.

FETCH RESTAURANT

Phone: 250/726-4800

▼▼▼
Pacific Northwest
$10-$30

Floor-to-ceiling windows overlook the stunning ocean, where crashing waves wash over the rocky shoreline. The West Coast-inspired menu features a wide selection of West Coast fish, along with hearty meat dishes of beef and chicken. The extensive wine cellar offer many bottle choices. Casual dress. **Bar:** Full bar. **Reservations:** suggested. **Hours:** 7:30-10:30 am, 11:30-2:30 & 5:30-8:30 pm. **Address:** 596 Marine Dr V0R 3A0 **Location:** 1 mi (1.6 km) e on Peninsula Rd, just s on Materson Rd, then just w; in Black Rock Oceanfront Resort. **Parking:** on-site. CALL 🔊Ⓜ Ⓐ

MATTERSON HOUSE RESTAURANT

Phone: 250/726-2200

▼▼▼
Canadian
$6-$25

This casual restaurant is in a converted house along the main road through town. The menu features regular Canadian-type cuisine, such as soups and sandwiches for lunch and more complex entrees for dinner. Guests can come for breakfast on the weekend. Casual dress. **Bar:** Full bar. **Reservations:** suggested, for dinner. **Hours:** 11 am-8:30 pm, Fri-Sun from 9 am. Closed: 12/25, 12/26; also Mon. **Address:** 1682 Peninsula Rd V0R 3A0 **Location:** Just e. **Parking:** on-site. Ⓐ

VALEMOUNT pop. 1,195

BEST WESTERN VALEMOUNT INN & SUITES

Book great rates at AAA.com

Phone: (250)566-0086

Ⓐ SAVE

▼▼▼
Hotel
$155-$193 3/1-9/6
$107-$150 9/7-2/28

Address: 1950 Hwy 5 S V0E 2Z0 **Location:** 0.9 mi (1.5 km) s on Hwy 5 (Yellowhead Hwy). Located near wildlife sanctuary. **Facility:** Smoke free premises. 77 units. 54 one- and 2 two-bedroom standard units, some with whirlpools. 21 one-bedroom suites. 2 stories, interior corridors. *Bath:* combo or shower only. **Parking:** on-site, winter plug-ins. **Terms:** check-in 4 pm, cancellation fee imposed. **Amenities:** dual phone lines, voice mail, irons, hair dryers. **Pool(s):** heated indoor. **Leisure Activities:** whirlpool, waterslide, cross country skiing, bird-watching, hiking trails, exercise room. **Guest Services:** coin laundry, wireless Internet. **Business Services:** meeting rooms, PC. *(See color ad below)*

AAA Benefit:
Members save up to 20%, plus 10% bonus points with rewards program.

🍴 🏊 ✖ ✕ 📞 💻 / SOME UNITS FEE 🐾 📠

FREE local telephone calls and high-speed Internet

▼ *See AAA listing above* ▼

Best Western Valemount Inn & Suites

- Exclusive loyalty program for AAA members! (See back cover for details)

- Bird watching and Wildlife Sanctuary adjacent

- Golf -.1 km, ATV Trails -.5 km, Snowmobile Trails - 20 km

- Horseback Riding - 2 km

- Full Service Restaurant and Lounge on site

- Ample Parking for Trailers and Buses

To Jasper, Prince George & Edmonton

⑤   5TH AVE

BW Valemount Inn & Suites

YELLOWHEAD HWY

To Kamloops

Best Western Valemount Inn & Suites
1950 Hwy 5 South • Valemount, BC V0E 2Z0
250.566.0086
866.777.1120 | bestwesternvalemount.com

Show Your Card & Save

▼▼▼

CHALET CONTINENTAL MOTEL

Phone: (250)566-9787

Hotel
$79-$149 All Year

Address: 1450 5th Ave V0E 2Z0 **Location:** Off Hwy 5 (Yellowhead Hwy), just e. **Facility:** 37 units. 35 one-bedroom standard units, some with kitchens and/or whirlpools. 2 one-bedroom suites. 2 stories (no elevator), interior corridors. **Parking:** on-site, winter plug-ins. **Terms:** office hours 7 am-11 pm, cancellation fee imposed. **Amenities:** high-speed Internet, hair dryers. *Some:* DVD players (fee), irons. **Pool(s):** heated indoor. **Leisure Activities:** sauna, whirlpool, steamroom, sun deck, barbecue area. **Guest Services:** airport transportation-Valemont Airport, area transportation-rail station, wireless Internet. **Free Special Amenities:** continental breakfast and high-speed Internet.

-------- WHERE TO DINE --------

CARIBOU GRILL

Phone: 250/566-8244

Canadian
$12-$30

About five blocks off Highway 97 in a beautiful log cabin toward the end of the main street, the restaurant prepares casual fare. The menu centers on Canadian cuisine, including traditional pasta and meat dishes, including venison. Service is attentive and friendly service in a setting marked by original log house decor. Casual dress. **Bar:** Full bar. **Reservations:** not accepted. **Hours:** Open 3/1-10/15 & 12/1-2/28; 4:30 pm-10 pm. Closed: 12/25. **Address:** 1002 5th Ave V0C 2Z0 **Location:** Hwy 5 (Yellowhead Hwy), 0.6 mi (1 km) e at 5th Ave. **Parking:** on-site.

Destination Vancouver
pop. 545,671

*L*ose yourself in Vancouver. There's much to do, and getting there is half the fun.

*Y*ou can walk to downtown attractions, parks and shops; let SkyTrain whisk you to suburban destinations; or ride a ferry to the outer limits for recreation.

Waterfront dining, Vancouver.

Bicycling in Stanley Park, Vancouver. (See listing page 167)

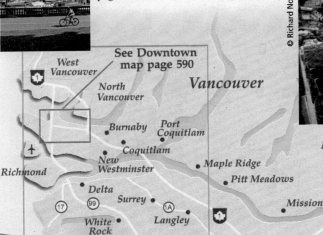

West Vancouver

North Vancouver

See Downtown map page 590

Vancouver

Burnaby

Port Coquitlam

Coquitlam

New Westminster

Maple Ridge

Pitt Meadows

Richmond

Delta

Surrey

Mission

White Rock

Langley

Aldergrove

See Vicinity map page 594

UNITED STATES
CANADA

BRITISH COLUMBIA
WASHINGTON

Granville Island Market, Vancouver. (See mention page 175)

*P*laces included in this AAA Destination City:

Chinatown, Vancouver. (See listing page 175)

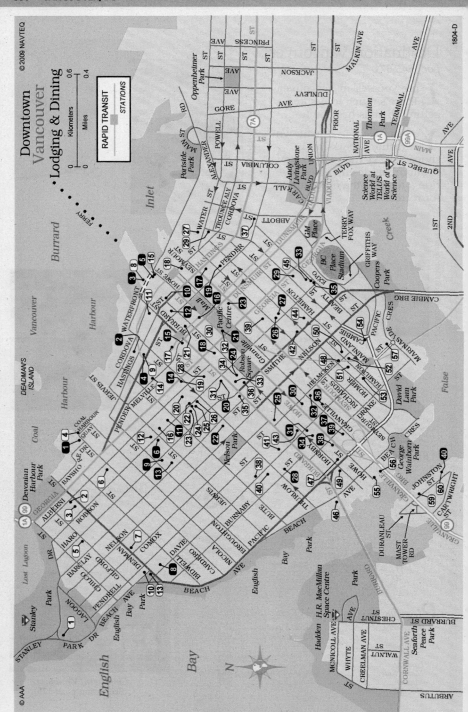

Downtown
Vancouver
• Lodging & Dining

©2009 NAVTEQ

1804-D

Downtown Vancouver

This index helps you "spot" where approved lodgings and restaurants are located on the corresponding detailed maps. Lodging daily rate range is for comparison only and show the property's high season. Restaurant rate range is a combination of lunch and/or dinner. Turn to the listing page for more detailed rate information and consult display ads for special promotions.

DOWNTOWN VANCOUVER

Map Page	OA	Lodgings	Diamond Rated	High Season	Page
1 / p. 590	CAA	**The Westin Bayshore Vancouver** - see color ad p 622	◇◇◇◇	$195-$580 SAVE	622
2 / p. 590	CAA	**Renaissance Vancouver Hotel Harbourside** - see color ad p 618	◇◇◇	$219-$299 SAVE	617
3 / p. 590	CAA	**Pan Pacific Vancouver** - see color ad p 616	◇◇◇◇	$269-$449 SAVE	614
4 / p. 590	CAA	**Vancouver Marriott Pinnacle Downtown**	◇◇◇◇	$219-$299 SAVE	621
5 / p. 590	CAA	**The Fairmont Waterfront**	◇◇◇◇	Rates not provided SAVE	607
6 / p. 590	CAA	**The Listel Hotel**	◇◇◇	$139-$299 SAVE	613
8 / p. 590	CAA	**Best Western Sands by the Sea** - see color ad p 604	◇◇◇	$149-$259 SAVE	605
9 / p. 590	CAA	**West End Guest House**	◇◇◇	$150-$325 SAVE	622
10 / p. 590		Terminal City Tower Hotel	◇◇◇	Rates not provided	621
11 / p. 590	CAA	**Blue Horizon Hotel** - see color ad p 605	◇◇◇	$109-$329 SAVE	605
12 / p. 590	CAA	**Days Inn Vancouver Downtown** - see color ad p 606	◇◇◇	$119-$375 SAVE	606
13 / p. 590		Barclay House in the West End	◇◇◇	Rates not provided	600
14 / p. 590	CAA	**Shangri-La Hotel Vancouver**	◇◇◇◇	$311-$428 SAVE	619
15 / p. 590	CAA	**Hyatt Regency Vancouver**	◇◇◇◇	$159-$439 SAVE	611
16 / p. 590	CAA	**Hotel Le Soleil** - see color ad p 613	◇◇◇◇	$375-$475 SAVE	610
17 / p. 590	CAA	**Delta Vancouver Suites**	◇◇◇	$159-$299 SAVE	607
18 / p. 590	CAA	**The Fairmont Hotel Vancouver**	◇◇◇◇	Rates not provided SAVE	607
19 / p. 590		Ramada Limited Downtown Vancouver	◇◇	$79-$400	617
20 / p. 590	CAA	**The Sutton Place Hotel** - see color ad p 621	◇◇◇◇	$169-$599 SAVE	621
21 / p. 590	CAA	**Four Seasons Hotel Vancouver**	◇◇◇◇	$245-$820 SAVE	607
22 / p. 590		'O Canada' House B&B	◇◇◇	Rates not provided	613
23 / p. 590	CAA	**St. Regis Hotel**	◇◇◇	$134-$318 SAVE	617
24 / p. 590	CAA	**The Wedgewood Hotel & Spa**	◇◇◇◇	$298-$418 SAVE	622
25 / p. 590	CAA	**Sheraton Vancouver Wall Centre Hotel** - see color ad p 620	◇◇◇◇	Rates not provided SAVE	619
26 / p. 590	CAA	**L'Hermitage Hotel**	◇◇◇	Rates not provided SAVE	613
27 / p. 590	CAA	**The Westin Grand, Vancouver**	◇◇◇◇	$169-$679 SAVE	623
28 / p. 590	CAA	**Sunset Inn & Suites** - see color ad p 601	◇◇◇	$99-$475 SAVE	619
29 / p. 590		Sandman Hotel Vancouver City Center	◇◇	$109-$209	619
30 / p. 590	CAA	**Holiday Inn Hotel & Suites Vancouver-Downtown** - see color ad on insert	◇◇◇	$89-$299 SAVE	609
31 / p. 590	CAA	**Landis Hotel & Suites** - see color ad p 615	◇◇◇	$179-$359 SAVE	611

DOWNTOWN VANCOUVER (cont'd)

Map Page	OA	Lodgings (cont'd)	Diamond Rated	High Season	Page
32 / p. 590	CAA	Best Western Chateau Granville - see color ad p 602	◆◆◆	$89-$249 SAVE	602
33 / p. 590	CAA	The Georgian Court Hotel - see color ad p 608	◆◆◆	$179-$419 SAVE	608
34 / p. 590	CAA	Cascadia Hotel & Suites	◆◆◆	$189-$289 SAVE	605
35 / p. 590	CAA	Hampton Inn & Suites by Hilton, Downtown Vancouver - see color ad p 603	◆◆◆	Rates not provided SAVE	609
36 / p. 590	CAA	Howard Johnson Hotel Downtown Vancouver - see color ad p 614	◆◆	$149-$279 SAVE	610
37 / p. 590	CAA	Ramada Inn & Suites Downtown Vancouver - see color ad p 617	◆◆	$109-$279 SAVE	616
38 / p. 590		Quality Hotel Downtown-The Inn at False Creek	◆◆	$129-$259	615
39 / p. 590	CAA	Best Western Downtown Vancouver - see color ad p 603	◆◆◆	$99-$199 SAVE	602
40 / p. 590	CAA	Granville Island Hotel - see color ad p 609	◆◆◆	$189-$550 SAVE	608

Map Page	OA	Restaurants	Diamond Rated	Cuisine	Meal Range	Page
1 / p. 590	CAA	The Fish House in Stanley Park	◆◆◆	Seafood	$15-$33	625
2 / p. 590	CAA	Ciao Bella Ristorante	◆◆	Italian	$8-$29	624
3 / p. 590		Cafe de Paris	◆◆◆	French	$13-$35	624
4 / p. 590		Cardero's Restaurant	◆◆	Pacific Northwest	$9-$29	624
5 / p. 590		L'Altro Buca	◆◆◆	Italian	$20-$36	627
6 / p. 590		Le Gavroche Restaurant Francais	◆◆◆	French	$13-$45	627
7 / p. 590		Delilah's	◆◆	Pacific Northwest	$33-$45	625
8 / p. 590	CAA	Five Sails Restaurant	◆◆◆◆	Pacific Northwest	$28-$39	625
9 / p. 590		Show Case Restaurant	◆◆◆	Pacific Northwest	$15-$30	629
10 / p. 590		Rain City Grill	◆◆◆	Pacific Northwest	$14-$32	628
11 / p. 590		Imperial Chinese Seafood Restaurant	◆◆◆	Chinese	$15-$58	626
12 / p. 590		Ezogiku Noodle Cafe	◆	Japanese	$6-$9	625
13 / p. 590		Won More Szechuan Cuisine	◆◆	Chinese	$7-$16	630
14 / p. 590		Voya Restaurant & Lounge	◆◆◆	Pacific Northwest	$15-$30	629
15 / p. 590		Herons Restaurant	◆◆◆	Pacific Northwest	$12-$35	626
16 / p. 590		Zin Restaurant & Lounge	◆◆◆	International	$10-$30	630
17 / p. 590		Rex Rotisserie & Grill	◆◆◆	Southwestern	$12-$36	628
18 / p. 590		Aqua Riva Restaurant & Bar	◆◆◆	Pacific Rim	$12-$35	623
19 / p. 590		Market by Jean-Georges	◆◆◆	Pacific Northwest	$14-$38	627
20 / p. 590		Oysi Oysi Japanese Restaurant	◆◆	Japanese	$7-$19	628
21 / p. 590		Copper Chimney	◆◆◆	Indian	$14-$30	624
22 / p. 590	CAA	The Hermitage	◆◆◆	Traditional French	$15-$36	626
23 / p. 590		CINCIN	◆◆◆	Mediterranean	$19-$40	624
24 / p. 590		Zefferelli's Restaurant	◆◆	Italian	$11-$25	630

Map Page	OA	Restaurants (cont'd)	Diamond Rated	Cuisine	Meal Range	Page
25 / p. 590	⊙	**Tropika Malaysian & Thai Cuisine**	◈◈	Asian	$8-$20	629
26 / p. 590	⊙	**Joe Fortes Seafood & Chop House**	◈◈	Seafood	$12-$40	626
27 / p. 590		Al Porto Ristorante	◈◈◈	Northern Italian	$12-$27	623
28 / p. 590		Kobe Japanese Steak House	◈◈	Japanese	$33-$58	627
29 / p. 590		Water St. Cafe	◈◈	Italian	$11-$24	629
30 / p. 590		Diva at the Met	◈◈◈◈	Pacific Northwest	$18-$47	625
31 / p. 590		Fleuri Restaurant - see color ad p 621	◈◈◈◈	Pacific Northwest	$16-$46	626
32 / p. 590	⊙	**Yew Restaurant & Bar**	◈◈◈	Pacific Northwest	$15-$42	630
33 / p. 590	⊙	**Don Francesco Restaurant**	◈◈◈	Italian	$14-$40	625
34 / p. 590	⊙	**Bacchus Restaurant**	◈◈◈◈	French	$15-$35	623
35 / p. 590		Le Crocodile	◈◈◈◈	French	$15-$40	627
36 / p. 590	⊙	**Cafe Presto Panini**	◈◈	Italian	$9-$15	624
37 / p. 590		Wild Rice	◈◈	Asian	$11-$21	630
38 / p. 590		India Bistro	◈◈	Indian	$9-$14	626
39 / p. 590		Kingston Taphouse & Grille	◈◈	Canadian	$10-$19	627
40 / p. 590		Stepho's Souvlaki Greek Taverna	◈◈	Greek	$8-$12	629
41 / p. 590		Kam's Place Singaporean Cuisine	◈◈	Asian	$9-$15	626
42 / p. 590		Subeez Cafe	◈◈	Canadian	$11-$27	629
43 / p. 590		Lickerish	◈◈	Pacific Northwest	$7-$25	627
44 / p. 590		Villa de Lupo Restaurant	◈◈◈	Italian	$20-$36	629
45 / p. 590	⊙	**The William Tell -** see color ad p 608	◈◈◈	Swiss	$27-$39	630
46 / p. 590		Chilli House Thai Bistro	◈◈	Thai	$11-$16	624
47 / p. 590		Il Giardino	◈◈◈	Italian	$19-$40	626
48 / p. 590		Blue Water Cafe & Raw Bar	◈◈◈◈	Seafood	$31-$46	623
49 / p. 590	⊙	**A Kettle Of Fish**	◈◈◈	Seafood	$20-$39	623
50 / p. 590	⊙	**Glowbal Grill & Satay Bar**	◈◈◈	International	$10-$35	626
51 / p. 590		Brix Restaurant & Wine Bar	◈◈◈	Pacific Northwest	$22-$37	623
52 / p. 590		Yaletown Brewing Company	◈◈	Canadian	$9-$29	630
53 / p. 590		Elixir Restaurant - Opus Bar	◈◈◈	French	$16-$38	625
54 / p. 590		La Terrazza	◈◈◈	Northern Italian	$18-$38	627
55 / p. 590		C Restaurant	◈◈◈	Seafood	$18-$40	624
56 / p. 590		Nu	◈◈◈	Continental	$13-$37	628
57 / p. 590		Provence Marinaside	◈◈◈	Pacific Rim	$12-$35	628
59 / p. 590		The Sandbar Seafood Restaurant	◈◈	Seafood	$11-$29	629
60 / p. 590		Dockside Restaurant & Brewing Company	◈◈	Canadian	$14-$38	625

© AAA

1803-D

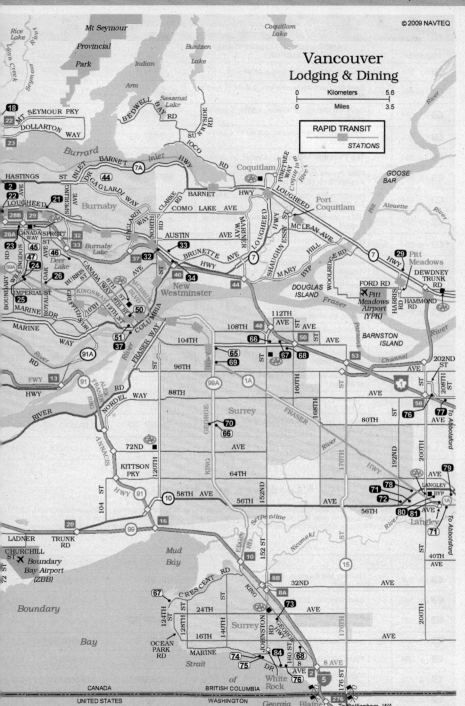

Vancouver
Lodging & Dining

RAPID TRANSIT
STATIONS

Kilometers 5.6

Miles 3.5

© 2009 NAVTEQ

✈ Airport Accommodations

Map Page	OA	VANCOUVER INTERNATIONAL AIRPORT	Diamond Rated	High Season	Page
49 / p. 594	CAA	Accent Inns, 3 mi (5 km) e of airport	◆◆	$89-$179 SAVE	654
45 / p. 594	CAA	Best Western Abercorn Inn, 2.4 mi (4 km) e of airport	◆◆	$125-$160 SAVE	654
42 / p. 594		Days Inn Vancouver Airport, 1.8 mi (3 km) e of airport	◆◆	$99-$250	654
47 / p. 594	CAA	Delta Vancouver Airport, 0.9 mi (1.4 km) e of airport	◆◆◆	$159-$329 SAVE	654
41 / p. 594	CAA	The Fairmont Vancouver Airport, at airport	◆◆◆◆	$319-$429 SAVE	654
52 / p. 594	CAA	Four Points by Sheraton Vancouver Airport, 3 mi (5 km) se of airport	◆◆◆	$135-$300 SAVE	655
44 / p. 594	CAA	Hampton Inn - by Hilton Vancouver Airport, 1.8 mi (3 km) e of airport	◆◆◆	$125-$480 SAVE	655
53 / p. 594	CAA	Hilton Vancouver Airport, 3 mi (5 km) se of airport	◆◆◆	$159-$799 SAVE	655
43 / p. 594	CAA	Holiday Inn Express Vancouver-Airport, 2.4 mi (4 km) e of airport	◆◆◆	$129-$179 SAVE	655
51 / p. 594	CAA	Holiday Inn International Vancouver Airport, 3 mi (5 km) e of airport	◆◆◆	$115-$189 SAVE	656
56 / p. 594	CAA	Quality Hotel Airport (South), 3 mi (5 km) se of airport	◆◆	$89-$139 SAVE	656
50 / p. 594	CAA	Radisson Hotel Vancouver Airport, 2.4 mi (4 km) se of airport	◆◆◆	$139-$219 SAVE	656
40 / p. 594	CAA	River Rock Casino Resort, 3 mi (5 km) e of airport	◆◆◆◆	Rates not provided SAVE	657
48 / p. 594		Sandman Hotel Vancouver Airport, 3 mi (5 km) e of airport	◆◆	$119-$159	657
54 / p. 594	CAA	Sheraton Vancouver Airport, 3 mi (5 km) se of airport	◆◆◆	$139-$349 SAVE	658
46 / p. 594	CAA	Travelodge Hotel Vancouver Airport, 3 mi (5 km) e of airport	◆◆	$119-$399 SAVE	658
55 / p. 594	CAA	Vancouver Airport Marriott, 3 mi (5 km) se of airport	◆◆◆	$259-$289 SAVE	658
N/A		The Westin Wall Centre Vancouver Airport, 3 mi (5 km) e of airport		$140-$229	658

Vancouver and Vicinity

This index helps you "spot" where approved lodgings and restaurants are located on the corresponding detailed maps. Lodging daily rate range is for comparison only and show the property's high season. Restaurant rate range is a combination of lunch and/or dinner. Turn to the listing page for more detailed rate information and consult display ads for special promotions.

VANCOUVER

Map Page	OA	Lodgings	Diamond Rated	High Season	Page
1 / p. 594	CAA	Holiday Inn Express Vancouver - see color ad p 611	◆◆◆	$119-$309 SAVE	633
2 / p. 594	CAA	Best Western Exhibition Park	◆◆	$89-$189 SAVE	632
3 / p. 594		Holiday Inn Vancouver-Centre (Broadway) - see color ad on insert	◆◆◆	$115-$249	636
4 / p. 594	CAA	Best Western Uptown - see color ad p 631	◆◆◆	$90-$190 SAVE	632
5 / p. 594	CAA	Plaza 500 Hotel	◆◆◆	$189-$329 SAVE	636
6 / p. 594	CAA	Days Inn-Vancouver Metro - see color ad p 607	◆◆	$79-$189 SAVE	633
7 / p. 594	CAA	2400 Motel	◆	$81-$199 SAVE	631

Map Page	OA	Restaurants	Diamond Rated	Cuisine	Meal Range	Page
① / p. 594		Tea House in Stanley Park	◇◇◇	Pacific Northwest	$17-$39	640
② / p. 594	CAA	**The Cannery**	◇◇◇	Seafood	$15-$40	638
③ / p. 594		Pink Pearl Chinese Restaurant	◇◇	Chinese	$4-$19	639
④ / p. 594		Abigail's Party	◇◇	Canadian	$8-$22	638
⑤ / p. 594		Lombardo's Ristorante Pizzeria	◇◇	Pizza	$12-$20	639
⑥ / p. 594		Quattro on Fourth	◇◇◇	Italian	$20-$39	640
⑦ / p. 594		Bishop's	◇◇◇◇	Pacific Northwest	$34-$38	638
⑧ / p. 594		Monk McQueen's	◇◇	Seafood	$15-$40	639
⑨ / p. 594	CAA	**Sophie's Cosmic Cafe**	◇◇	Canadian	$7-$17	640
⑩ / p. 594		Hell's Kitchen	◇◇	Canadian	$9-$25	638
⑪ / p. 594		Las Margaritas Restaurante & Cantina	◇◇	Mexican	$12-$19	638
⑫ / p. 594		FUEL Restaurant	◇◇◇	Pacific Northwest	$12-$30	638
⑬ / p. 594		Mistral French Bistro	◇◇◇	French	$14-$29	639
⑭ / p. 594	CAA	**Lumiere**	◇◇◇◇	French	$65-$175	639
⑮ / p. 594		Tomato Fresh Food Cafe	◇◇	Canadian	$8-$23	641
⑯ / p. 594		Provence Mediterranean Grill	◇◇◇	Mediterranean	$10-$29	640
⑰ / p. 594		Maurya Indian Cuisine	◇◇	Indian	$12-$25	639
⑱ / p. 594		Rasputin	◇◇	Russian	$13-$25	640
⑲ / p. 594		Tojo's Restaurant	◇◇◇	Japanese	$17-$34	641
⑳ / p. 594		Rugby Beach Club Grille	◇◇	Canadian	$8-$18	640
㉑ / p. 594		Gramercy Grill	◇◇	Pacific Rim	$9-$33	638
㉒ / p. 594		West Restaurant	◇◇◇◇	Pacific Northwest	$30-$45	641
㉓ / p. 594		Red Door Pan Asian Grill	◇◇	Asian	$7-$18	640
㉔ / p. 594		The Ouisi Bistro	◇◇	Cajun	$8-$23	639
㉕ / p. 594		Trafalgars Bistro	◇◇	Regional Continental	$12-$27	641
㉖ / p. 594		Sawasdee Thai Restaurant	◇◇	Thai	$8-$13	640
㉗ / p. 594		Seasons in the Park Restaurant	◇◇◇	Pacific Northwest	$11-$34	640
㉘ / p. 594		Shaughnessy Restaurant At VanDusen Garden	◇◇	Pacific Northwest	$14-$30	640
㉙ / p. 594		Avenue Grill	◇◇	Italian	$8-$20	638

BOWEN ISLAND

Map Page	OA	Lodging	Diamond Rated	High Season	Page
⑩ / p. 594		Wildwood Lane Cottages	◇◇	Rates not provided	508

NORTH VANCOUVER

Map Page	OA	Lodgings	Diamond Rated	High Season	Page
⑬ / p. 594	CAA	**North Vancouver Hotel** - see color ad p 636	◇◇	$99-$169 SAVE	652
⑭ / p. 594	CAA	**Comfort Inn and Suites**	◇◇	$130-$140 SAVE	651
⑮ / p. 594		Lionsgate Travelodge	◇	$59-$149	652

NORTH VANCOUVER (cont'd)

Map Page	OA	Lodgings (cont'd)	Diamond Rated	High Season	Page
16 / p. 594	CAA	**Grouse Inn** - see color ad p 610	♦♦	$79-$169 SAVE	651
17 / p. 594	CAA	**Best Western Capilano Inn & Suites**	♦♦	$99-$149 SAVE	651
18 / p. 594	CAA	**Holiday Inn Hotel & Suites North Vancouver** - see color ad on insert, p 635, p 652	♦♦♦	$199-$350 SAVE	652

Map Page	OA	Restaurants	Diamond Rated	Cuisine	Meal Range	Page
38 / p. 594		The Edge Bistro	♦♦	Mediterranean	$8-$26	653
39 / p. 594		Moustache Cafe	♦♦♦	Pacific Northwest	$10-$32	653
40 / p. 594		Jagerhof Schnitzel House	♦♦	German	$9-$17	653
41 / p. 594		Gusto di Quattro	♦♦♦	Italian	$14-$35	653

BURNABY

Map Page	OA	Lodgings	Diamond Rated	High Season	Page
21 / p. 594	CAA	**Lake City Inn & Suites**	♦♦	$89-$109 SAVE	644
22 / p. 594	CAA	**Accent Inns**	♦♦	$119-$179 SAVE	642
23 / p. 594	CAA	**Delta Burnaby Hotel and Conference Centre** - see color ad p 643	♦♦♦	$139-$279 SAVE	642
24 / p. 594	CAA	**Hilton Vancouver Metrotown** - see color ad p 644	♦♦♦	$119-$799 SAVE	643
25 / p. 594		Holiday Inn Express Metrotown - see color ad on insert	♦♦♦	$109-$199	644
26 / p. 594	CAA	**Best Western Kings Inn and Conference Centre** - see color ad p 642	♦♦♦	$159-$169 SAVE	642

Map Page	OA	Restaurants	Diamond Rated	Cuisine	Meal Range	Page
44 / p. 594		HORIZONS	♦♦♦	Pacific Rim	$12-$32	645
45 / p. 594		Ebo Restaurant and Lounge	♦♦♦	Pacific Northwest	$12-$40	645
46 / p. 594	CAA	**Hart House Restaurant**	♦♦♦	Pacific Northwest	$14-$36	645
47 / p. 594	CAA	**Crystal Bar and Grille**	♦♦	Continental	$9-$30	644

PITT MEADOWS

Map Page	OA	Lodging	Diamond Rated	High Season	Page
29 / p. 594		Ramada Inn	♦♦	$89-$112	653

COQUITLAM

Map Page	OA	Lodgings	Diamond Rated	High Season	Page
32 / p. 594	CAA	**Best Western Coquitlam Inn Convention Centre**	♦♦♦	$149-$289 SAVE	645
33 / p. 594		Ramada Coquitlam	♦♦	$110-$150	646
34 / p. 594	CAA	**Best Western Chelsea Inn**	♦♦♦	$125 SAVE	645

NEW WESTMINSTER

Map Page	OA	Lodging	Diamond Rated	High Season	Page
37 / p. 594	CAA	**Inn at the Quay**	♦♦♦	$200-$235 SAVE	650

Map Page	OA	Restaurants	Diamond Rated	Cuisine	Meal Range	Page
50 / p. 594		La Rustica Ristorante	♦♦	Italian	$12-$28	651
51 / p. 594		Burger Heaven	♦	American	$7-$18	651

RICHMOND

Map Page	OA	Lodgings	Diamond Rated	High Season	Page
40 / p. 594	CAA	**River Rock Casino Resort** - see color ad p 657	♦♦♦♦	Rates not provided SAVE	657
41 / p. 594	CAA	**The Fairmont Vancouver Airport** - see color ad p 632	♦♦♦♦	$319-$429 SAVE	654

RICHMOND (cont'd)

Map Page	OA	Lodgings (cont'd)	Diamond Rated	High Season	Page
42 / p. 594		Days Inn Vancouver Airport	◆◆	$99-$250	654
43 / p. 594	CAA	Holiday Inn Express Vancouver-Airport	◆◆◆	$129-$179 SAVE	655
44 / p. 594	CAA	Hampton Inn - by Hilton Vancouver Airport	◆◆◆	$125-$480 SAVE	655
45 / p. 594	CAA	Best Western Abercorn Inn - see color ad p 631	◆◆	$125-$160 SAVE	654
46 / p. 594	CAA	Travelodge Hotel Vancouver Airport	◆◆◆	$119-$399 SAVE	658
47 / p. 594	CAA	Delta Vancouver Airport	◆◆◆	$159-$329 SAVE	654
48 / p. 594		Sandman Hotel Vancouver Airport	◆◆	$119-$159	657
49 / p. 594	CAA	Accent Inns	◆◆	$89-$179 SAVE	654
50 / p. 594	CAA	Radisson Hotel Vancouver Airport - see color ad p 656	◆◆◆	$139-$219 SAVE	656
51 / p. 594	CAA	Holiday Inn International Vancouver Airport - see color ad on insert, p 633	◆◆◆	$115-$189 SAVE	656
52 / p. 594	CAA	Four Points by Sheraton Vancouver Airport	◆◆◆	$135-$300 SAVE	655
53 / p. 594	CAA	Hilton Vancouver Airport - see color ad p 634	◆◆◆	$159-$799 SAVE	655
54 / p. 594	CAA	Sheraton Vancouver Airport	◆◆◆	$139-$349 SAVE	658
55 / p. 594	CAA	Vancouver Airport Marriott	◆◆◆	$259-$289 SAVE	658
56 / p. 594	CAA	Quality Hotel Airport (South)	◆◆	$89-$139 SAVE	656
57 / p. 594	CAA	Holiday Inn Express & Suites Riverport - see color ad on insert	◆◆◆	$109-$299 SAVE	655

Map Page	OA	Restaurants	Diamond Rated	Cuisine	Meal Range	Page
54 / p. 594		Tramonto	◆◆◆	Italian	$27-$45	659
55 / p. 594		Globe @ YVR	◆◆◆	Pacific Northwest	$15-$42	659
56 / p. 594		Flying Beaver	◆◆	Canadian	$9-$20	659
57 / p. 594		Steveston Seafood House	◆◆◆	Seafood	$18-$43	659
58 / p. 594		Tapenade Bistro	◆◆	Mediterranean	$11-$26	659
59 / p. 594		Correlis Mediterranean Grill	◆◆	Mediterranean	$7-$21	658

DELTA

Map Page	OA	Lodgings	Diamond Rated	High Season	Page
60 / p. 594	CAA	Delta Town & Country Inn	◆◆◆	$102-$112 SAVE	646
61 / p. 594	CAA	Clair's Bed & Breakfast	◆◆	$135-$185 SAVE	646
62 / p. 594		River Run Cottages	◆◆◆	$170-$225	646
63 / p. 594	CAA	The Coast Tsawwassen Inn	◆◆◆	$113-$128 SAVE	646

Map Page	OA	Restaurant	Diamond Rated	Cuisine	Meal Range	Page
62 / p. 594	CAA	La Belle Auberge	◆◆◆	French	$23-$35	647

SURREY

Map Page	OA	Lodgings	Diamond Rated	High Season	Page
66 / p. 594	CAA	Sheraton Vancouver Guildford Hotel - see color ad p 662	◆◆◆	Rates not provided SAVE	663
67 / p. 594		Ramada Hotel & Suites Surrey/Guildford	◆◆	$99-$159	663
68 / p. 594		Holiday Inn Express Hotel & Suites	◆◆◆	$99-$149	661
69 / p. 594	CAA	Compass Point Inn - see color ad p 661	◆◆	$99-$129 SAVE	661
70 / p. 594	CAA	Best Western King George Inn & Suites - see color ad p 660	◆◆◆	$86-$170 SAVE	660

SURREY (cont'd)

Map Page	OA	Lodgings (cont'd)	Diamond Rated	High Season	Page
71 / p. 594	CAA	**Hampton Inn & Suites Langley/Surrey** - see color ad p 649	▽▽▽	$129-$189 SAVE	661
72 / p. 594	CAA	**Ramada Langley-Surrey**	▽▽▽	$119-$169 SAVE	663
73 / p. 594	CAA	**Best Western Peace Arch Inn**	▽▽	$100-$169 SAVE	660

Map Page	OA	Restaurants	Diamond Rated	Cuisine	Meal Range	Page
65 / p. 594		Yokohama Japanese Restaurant	▽▽	Japanese	$7-$21	664
66 / p. 594		Villa Verdi Ristorante Italiano	▽▽▽	Italian	$15-$32	664
67 / p. 594		Crescent Beach Bistro	▽▽	Seafood	$10-$26	663
68 / p. 594		The Turkey House & Deli	▽	Deli	$7-$12	664

LANGLEY

Map Page	OA	Lodgings	Diamond Rated	High Season	Page
76 / p. 594		Sandman Hotel Langley	▽▽	$129-$169	649
77 / p. 594	CAA	**Holiday Inn Express Hotel & Suites Langley** - see color ad on insert	▽▽▽	$115-$199 SAVE	649
78 / p. 594	CAA	**Best Value Westward Inn**	▽	$89-$99 SAVE	647
79 / p. 594	CAA	**Best Western Langley Inn** - see color ad p 647	▽▽▽	$110-$231 SAVE	648
80 / p. 594	CAA	**Days Inn & Suites Langley** - see color ad p 648	▽▽	$125-$189 SAVE	648
81 / p. 594	CAA	**Coast Hotel & Convention Centre**	▽▽▽	$125-$175 SAVE	648

Map Page	OA	Restaurant	Diamond Rated	Cuisine	Meal Range	Page
71 / p. 594		Sonoma Grill	▽▽▽	Continental	$10-$30	650

WHITE ROCK

Map Page	OA	Lodging	Diamond Rated	High Season	Page
84 / p. 594	CAA	**Ocean Promenade Hotel** - see color ad p 665	▽▽▽	$139-$469 SAVE	665

Map Page	OA	Restaurants	Diamond Rated	Cuisine	Meal Range	Page
74 / p. 594	CAA	**Pearl On The Rock**	▽▽▽▽	Pacific Northwest	$13-$45	665
75 / p. 594		Giraffe	▽▽▽	Pacific Rim	$10-$28	665
76 / p. 594		La Baia Italian Restaurant	▽▽	Italian	$14-$25	665

WEST VANCOUVER

Map Page	OA	Restaurants	Diamond Rated	Cuisine	Meal Range	Page
32 / p. 594		Fraiche	▽▽▽	Pacific Northwest	$14-$45	664
33 / p. 594		Salmon House on the Hill	▽▽	Seafood	$29-$35	664
35 / p. 594		La Regalade French Bistro	▽▽	French	$19-$25	664

DOWNTOWN VANCOUVER   (See map and index starting on p. 590)

BARCLAY HOUSE IN THE WEST END   **Phone:** 604/605-1351   **13**

Historic Bed
& Breakfast
Rates not provided

Address: 1351 Barclay St V6E 1H6 **Location:** Between Broughton and Jervis sts. Located in a residential area. **Facility:** The Victorian home is on a tree-lined street in the West End district; a lovely front porch overlooks the garden, and rooms have a masculine motif. Smoke free premises. 6 one-bedroom standard units. 3 stories (no elevator), interior/exterior corridors. *Bath:* combo or shower only. **Parking:** on-site. **Terms:** office hours 7 am-7 pm, age restrictions may apply. **Amenities:** video library, DVD players, CD players, voice mail, safes, irons, hair dryers. **Guest Services:** wireless Internet.
Business Services: PC. 📠 🖨 📶 💳

(See map and index starting on p. 590)

▼ *See AAA listing p 619* ▼

(See map and index starting on p. 590)

BEST WESTERN CHATEAU GRANVILLE   *Book great rates at AAA.com*   Phone: (604)669-7070

Hotel
$89-$249 All Year

Address: 1100 Granville St V6Z 2B6 **Location:** Between Davie and Helmcken sts. **Facility:** 150 units. 55 one-bedroom standard units. 95 one-bedroom suites. 3-15 stories, interior corridors. **Parking:** on-site (fee). **Terms:** cancellation fee imposed. **Amenities:** dual phone lines, voice mail, irons, hair dryers. **Guest Services:** valet laundry, wireless Internet. **Business Services:** meeting rooms, PC. *(See color ad below)*

AAA Benefit:
Members save up to 20%, plus 10% bonus points with rewards program.

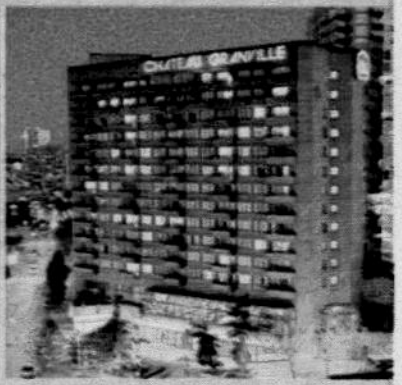

FREE early check-in/late check-out and high-speed Internet

BEST WESTERN DOWNTOWN VANCOUVER   *Book great rates at AAA.com*   Phone: (604)669-9888

Hotel
$99-$199 All Year

Address: 718 Drake St V6Z 2W6 **Location:** Corner of Drake and Granville sts. Located in the Granville Street Entertainment District. **Facility:** Smoke free premises. 143 one-bedroom standard units, some with efficiencies and/or whirlpools. 12 stories, interior corridors. **Parking:** on-site (fee). **Terms:** cancellation fee imposed. **Amenities:** high-speed Internet, voice mail, safes, irons, hair dryers. **Leisure Activities:** saunas, whirlpool, exercise room. **Guest Services:** valet and coin laundry, area transportation within downtown, wireless Internet. **Business Services:** meeting rooms, PC. **Free Special Amenities:** local telephone calls and high-speed Internet.** *(See color ad p 603)*

AAA Benefit:
Members save up to 20%, plus 10% bonus points with rewards program.

▼ *See AAA listing above* ▼

Overlooking the Beautiful
False Creek Area

- Situated in the heart of fine dining, shopping & entertainment
- Downtown drop off shuttle
- Complimentary cruise ship terminal drop off
- Kitchenettes available
- Legendary White Spot Restaurant and Lounge

**BEST WESTERN
DOWNTOWN VANCOUVER**

718 Drake Street, Vancouver
1.888.669.9888
www.bestwesterndowntown.com

Heart of Vancouver's
Shopping District

- Located right on Robson Street
- Complimentary hot breakfast buffet
- Rooftop fitness facilities, whirlpool and sauna
- One bedroom kitchen suites available
- Complimentary downtown drop-off shuttle service

**HAMPTON INN & SUITES
DOWNTOWN VANCOUVER**

111 Robson Street, Vancouver

www.hamptoninnvancouver.com   1.877.602.1008

▼ See AAA listing p 605 ▼

(See map and index starting on p. 590)

BEST WESTERN SANDS BY THE SEA   *Book great rates at AAA.com*   **Phone:** (604)682-1831   **8**

Hotel
$149-$259 3/1-9/30
$99-$159 10/1-2/28

Address: 1755 Davie St V6G 1W5 **Location:** Between Bidwell and Denman sts. **Facility:** Smoke free premises. 121 one-bedroom standard units, some with efficiencies. 6 stories, interior corridors. **Parking:** on-site (fee). **Terms:** check-in 4 pm, cancellation fee imposed. **Amenities:** video games (fee), voice mail, irons, hair dryers. **Leisure Activities:** sauna, exercise room. **Guest Services:** valet and coin laundry, wireless Internet. **Business Services:** meeting rooms, PC. *(See color ad p 604)*

AAA Benefit:
Members save up to 20%, plus 10% bonus points with rewards program.

FREE local telephone calls and high-speed Internet

BLUE HORIZON HOTEL   *Book great rates at AAA.com*   **Phone:** (604)688-1411   **11**

Hotel
$109-$329 All Year

Address: 1225 Robson St V6E 1C3 **Location:** Between Jervis and Bute sts. **Facility:** Smoke free premises. 214 one-bedroom standard units. 31 stories, interior corridors. **Parking:** on-site (fee). **Terms:** cancellation fee imposed. **Amenities:** high-speed Internet, voice mail, safes, irons, hair dryers. **Pool(s):** heated indoor. **Leisure Activities:** sauna, whirlpool, exercise room. **Guest Services:** valet laundry. **Business Services:** meeting rooms, PC (fee). *(See color ad below)*

FREE high-speed Internet

CASCADIA HOTEL & SUITES   *Book great rates at AAA.com*   **Phone:** (604)688-1234   **34**

Hotel
$189-$289 All Year

Address: 1234 Hornby St V6Z 1W2 **Location:** Between Drake and Davie sts. **Facility:** Smoke free premises. 200 one-bedroom standard units, some with efficiencies or kitchens. 22 stories, interior corridors. **Parking:** on-site (fee). **Terms:** check-in 4 pm, cancellation fee imposed. **Amenities:** high-speed Internet, voice mail, irons, hair dryers. **Pool(s):** heated indoor. **Leisure Activities:** whirlpool, exercise room. **Guest Services:** valet and coin laundry, wireless Internet. **Business Services:** meeting rooms, PC. **Free Special Amenities:** full breakfast and high-speed Internet.

▼ See AAA listing above ▼

(See map and index starting on p. 590)

DAYS INN VANCOUVER DOWNTOWN *Book great rates at AAA.com* **Phone:** (604)681-4335 **12**

Hotel
$119-$375 All Year

Address: 921 W Pender St V6C 1M2 **Location:** Between Burrard and Hornby sts. Located in the financial district. **Facility:** Smoke free premises. 85 one-bedroom standard units. 6 stories, interior corridors. *Bath:* combo or shower only. **Parking:** valet. **Terms:** cancellation fee imposed. **Amenities:** high-speed Internet, voice mail, safes, irons, hair dryers. **Guest Services:** valet and coin laundry, wireless Internet. **Business Services:** meeting rooms, PC (fee). *(See color ad below)*

FREE early check-in/late check-out and high-speed Internet

▼ *See AAA listing above* ▼

Days Inn - Vancouver Downtown

- 85 boutique-style guestrooms with contemporary colour, modern decor and amenities
- Free high-speed Internet access and bottled water
- Chelsea Restaurant & Lounge and Smiley O'Neal's Irish Whisky Pub
- Valet parking and other touches of West Coast hospitality to ensure your stay is as comfortable as possible
- Within walking distance of Canada Place/Convention Centre and Cruise Ship Terminal
- Free downtown drop-off shuttle service
- 100% non-smoking
- Hotel Association of Canada "Green Key" eco-rated hotel

Approved

DAYS INN - VANCOUVER
921 Pender Street
Vancouver Tel: 604.681.4335

Days Inn.
VANCOUVER DOWNTOWN

www.daysinnvancouver.com Toll Free: 1.877.681.4335 U.S. and Canada

(See map and index starting on p. 590)

DELTA VANCOUVER SUITES *Book great rates at AAA.com* **Phone:** (604)689-8188 **17**

CAA SAVE

Hotel

$159-$299 All Year

Address: 550 W Hastings St V6B 1L6 **Location:** Between Seymour and Richards sts; entrance in alley way. **Facility:** Smoke free premises. 225 units. 40 one-bedroom standard units. 185 one-bedroom suites. 23 stories, interior corridors. **Parking:** on-site (fee) and valet. **Terms:** cancellation fee imposed. **Amenities:** dual phone lines, voice mail, safes, irons, hair dryers. *Fee:* video games, high-speed Internet. **Leisure Activities:** exercise room. **Guest Services:** valet laundry, wireless Internet. **Business Services:** meeting rooms, business center.

ECO 24 CALL / SOME UNITS FEE

THE FAIRMONT HOTEL VANCOUVER *Book great rates at AAA.com* **Phone:** 604/684-3131 **18**

CAA SAVE

Classic Historic Hotel

Rates not provided

Address: 900 W Georgia St V6C 2W6 **Location:** Corner of Burrard at W Georgia St; enter from Hornby St. **Facility:** Opened by the Queen Mother in 1939, the historic downtown landmark hotel features wonderfully restored rooms and suites as well as lobby boutiques. 556 units. 520 one-bedroom standard units. 36 one-bedroom suites, some with whirlpools. 15 stories, interior corridors. **Parking:** on-site (fee) and valet. **Amenities:** voice mail, honor bars, irons, hair dryers. *Fee:* video games, high-speed Internet. **Dining:** entertainment. **Pool(s):** heated indoor. **Leisure Activities:** saunas, whirlpool, spa. **Guest Services:** valet laundry, wireless Internet. **Business Services:** conference facilities, business center.

CALL / SOME UNITS FEE

THE FAIRMONT WATERFRONT *Book great rates at AAA.com* **Phone:** 604/691-1991 **5**

CAA SAVE

Hotel

Rates not provided

Address: 900 Canada Place Way V6C 3L5 **Location:** Howe St at Cordova St. Opposite Canada Place. **Facility:** Near the cruise ship terminal and convention center, this guest-oriented property features attractive guest rooms with either a harbor or city view. 489 units. 477 one-bedroom standard units. 12 one-bedroom suites. 23 stories, interior corridors. **Parking:** on-site (fee) and valet. **Amenities:** voice mail, honor bars, irons, hair dryers. *Fee:* video games, high-speed Internet. *Some:* CD players, safes. **Dining:** Herons Restaurant, see separate listing. **Pool(s):** heated outdoor. **Leisure Activities:** whirlpool, steamrooms. *Fee:* massage. **Guest Services:** valet laundry, wireless Internet. **Business Services:** conference facilities, business center.

ECO 24 CALL / SOME UNITS FEE

FOUR SEASONS HOTEL VANCOUVER *Book great rates at AAA.com* **Phone:** (604)689-9333 **21**

CAA SAVE

Hotel

$245-$820 All Year

Address: 791 W Georgia St V6C 2T4 **Location:** Between Howe and Granville sts. Connected to a shopping complex. **Facility:** Known for providing lovely accommodations and impeccable service, the downtown hotel's lobby offers access to an adjacent large shopping complex. Smoke free premises. 372 units. 304 one-bedroom standard units. 68 one-bedroom suites. 28 stories, interior corridors. **Parking:** on-site (fee) and valet. **Terms:** cancellation fee imposed. **Amenities:** DVD players, high-speed Internet (fee), dual phone lines, voice mail, safes, honor bars, irons, hair dryers. **Dining:** Yew Restaurant & Bar, see separate listing. **Pool(s):** heated indoor/outdoor. **Leisure Activities:** saunas, whirlpool. **Guest Services:** valet laundry, wireless Internet. **Business Services:** conference facilities, business center. 24 CALL / SOME UNITS

▼ See AAA listing p 633 ▼

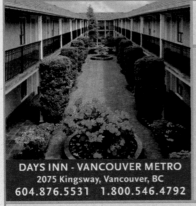

(See map and index starting on p. 590)

THE GEORGIAN COURT HOTEL   *Book great rates at AAA.com*   Phone: (604)682-5555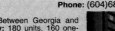

Hotel
$179-$419 All Year

Address: 773 Beatty St V6B 2M4 **Location:** Between Georgia and Robson sts. Opposite BC Place Stadium. **Facility:** 180 units. 160 one-bedroom standard units. 20 one-bedroom suites. 12 stories, interior corridors. **Parking:** on-site (fee). **Terms:** cancellation fee imposed. **Amenities:** high-speed Internet, voice mail, safes, irons, hair dryers. **Dining:** 2 restaurants, also, The William Tell, see separate listing. **Leisure Activities:** whirlpool, steamroom, exercise room. **Guest Services:** valet laundry, area transportation-downtown, wireless Internet. **Business Services:** meeting rooms, business center. *(See color ad below)*

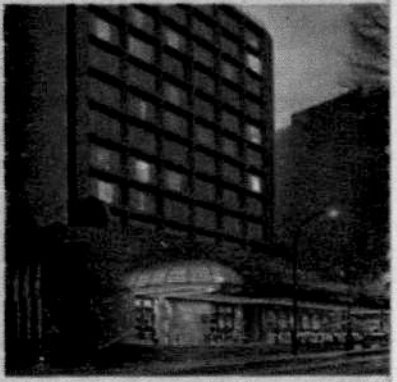

FREE local telephone calls and high-speed Internet

GRANVILLE ISLAND HOTEL   *Book great rates at AAA.com*   Phone: (604)683-7373

Hotel
$189-$550 All Year

Address: 1253 Johnston St V6H 3R9 **Location:** Granville Island; below the bridge, follow signs. **Facility:** 82 one-bedroom standard units, some with whirlpools. 3-4 stories, interior corridors. **Parking:** on-site (fee). **Terms:** cancellation fee imposed. **Amenities:** high-speed Internet, dual phone lines, voice mail, safes, honor bars, irons, hair dryers. **Dining:** Dockside Restaurant & Brewing Company, see separate listing. **Leisure Activities:** sauna, whirlpool, rental bicycles, exercise room. **Guest Services:** valet laundry, wireless Internet. **Business Services:** meeting rooms, PC. *(See color ad p 609)*

FREE newspaper and high-speed Internet

──────── ▼ See AAA listing above ▼ ────────

GEORGIAN COURT
HOTEL

A World Apart in
Downtown Vancouver

- Boutique style hotel in downtown Vancouver
- Spacious guest rooms and suites
- Fitness facility with jacuzzi and steam room
- Fine dining at the William Tell Restaurant and casual dining at The Bistro and Beatty St. Bar & Grill

GEORGIAN COURT HOTEL
DOWNTOWN VANCOUVER

773 Beatty Street, Vancouver

www.georgiancourt.com   1.800.663.1155

(See map and index starting on p. 590)

HAMPTON INN & SUITES BY HILTON, DOWNTOWN VANCOUVER

Book great rates at AAA.com

Phone: 604/602-1008 [35]

Hotel
Rates not provided

AAA Benefit:
Members save up to
10% everyday!

Address: 111 Robson St V6B 2A8 **Location:** Between Cambie and Beatty sts. Opposite BC Place Stadium. **Facility:** Smoke free premises. 132 units. 110 one-bedroom standard units, some with whirlpools. 22 one-bedroom suites with kitchens. 16 stories, interior corridors. **Parking:** on-site (fee). **Amenities:** video games (fee), high-speed Internet, dual phone lines, voice mail, safes, irons, hair dryers. **Leisure Activities:** sauna, whirlpool, exercise room. **Guest Services:** valet and coin laundry, area transportation-downtown, wireless Internet. **Business Services:** meeting rooms, PC. **Free Special Amenities:** expanded continental breakfast and high-speed Internet. *(See color ad p 603)*

HOLIDAY INN HOTEL & SUITES VANCOUVER-DOWNTOWN

Book great rates at AAA.com

Phone: (604)684-2151 [30]

Hotel
$89-$299 All Year

Address: 1110 Howe St V6Z 1R2 **Location:** Between Helmcken and Davie sts. **Facility:** 245 one-bedroom standard units, some with efficiencies, kitchens and/or whirlpools. 7 stories, interior corridors. *Bath:* combo or shower only. **Parking:** on-site (fee). **Terms:** check-in 4 pm, cancellation fee imposed. **Amenities:** voice mail, irons, hair dryers. *Some:* honor bars. **Pool(s):** heated indoor. **Leisure Activities:** saunas, exercise room. **Guest Services:** valet and coin laundry, wireless Internet. **Business Services:** meeting rooms, PC (fee). **Free Special Amenities:** newspaper and high-speed Internet. *(See color ad on insert)*

▼ See AAA listing p 608 ▼

(See map and index starting on p. 590)

HOTEL LE SOLEIL

Book great rates at AAA.com

Phone: (604)632-3000 **16**

(AAA) (SAVE)

▽▽▽ ▽▽▽

Boutique Hotel
$375-$475 All Year

Address: 567 Hornby St V6C 2E8 **Location:** Between Dunsmuir and Pender sts. **Facility:** One of Vancouver's most exclusive boutique hotels, the property prides itself on its amazing attention to detail. Guests can expect to be pampered. 109 units. 9 one-bedroom standard units. 100 one-bedroom suites, some with whirlpools. 16 stories, interior corridors. *Bath:* combo or shower only. **Parking:** valet. **Terms:** cancellation fee imposed. **Amenities:** high-speed Internet, dual phone lines, voice mail, safes, honor bars, irons, hair dryers. **Dining:** Copper Chimney, see separate listing. **Guest Services:** valet laundry, wireless Internet. **Business Services:** meeting rooms, business center. *(See color ad p 613)*

ECO 🍴 🍸 CALL 🛗M 🛗 🐾 🖨 / SOME UNITS FEE 🐕 ✖

FREE newspaper and high-speed Internet

HOWARD JOHNSON HOTEL DOWNTOWN VANCOUVER

Book great rates at AAA.com

Phone: (604)688-8701 **36**

(AAA) (SAVE)

▽▽ ▽▽

Hotel
$149-$279 3/1-9/30
$79-$169 10/1-2/28

Address: 1176 Granville St V6Z 1L8 **Location:** Between Davie and Helmcken sts. Located in Granville Street Entertainment District. **Facility:** Smoke free premises. 110 units. 105 one-bedroom standard units. 5 one-bedroom suites. 5 stories, interior corridors. **Parking:** on-site (fee). **Terms:** cancellation fee imposed. **Amenities:** voice mail, hair dryers. *Some:* fax, irons. **Guest Services:** valet and coin laundry, wireless Internet. **Business Services:** PC (fee). *(See color ad p 614)*

ECO 🍴 🍸 🛗 ✖ 🐾 🖨 / SOME UNITS FEE 🐕 📠 🖨

▼ See AAA listing p 651 ▼

(See map and index starting on p. 590)

HYATT REGENCY VANCOUVER   *Book great rates at AAA.com*   Phone: (604)683-1234   **15**

Hotel
$159-$439 All Year

Address: 655 Burrard St V6C 2R7 **Location:** Between W Georgia and Melville sts. Connected to shopping centre. **Facility:** Guest rooms on the 20th floor and higher feature unusual rain shower systems that come down from the ceiling rather than a wall-mounted shower head. 644 units. 634 one-bedroom standard units. 10 one-bedroom suites. 34 stories, interior corridors. *Bath:* combo or shower only. **Parking:** on-site (fee) and valet. **Terms:** check-in 4 pm, cancellation fee imposed. **Amenities:** high-speed Internet (fee), dual phone lines, voice mail, safes, honor bars, irons, hair dryers. **Pool(s):** heated outdoor. **Leisure Activities:** whirlpool, exercise room. **Guest Services:** valet laundry, wireless Internet. **Business Services:** conference facilities, business center.

AAA Benefit:
Ask for the AAA rate
and save 10%.

LANDIS HOTEL & SUITES   *Book great rates at AAA.com*   Phone: (604)681-3555   **31**

Extended Stay
Hotel
$179-$359 3/1-8/31
$209-$249 9/1-2/28

Address: 1200 Hornby St V6Z 1W2 **Location:** Between Drake and Davie sts. **Facility:** Smoke free premises. 50 two-bedroom suites with kitchens. 18 stories, interior corridors. **Parking:** on-site (fee). **Amenities:** DVD players, high-speed Internet, dual phone lines, voice mail, safes, irons, hair dryers. **Pool(s):** heated indoor. **Leisure Activities:** whirlpool, exercise room. **Guest Services:** valet and coin laundry, area transportation-within downtown, wireless Internet. **Business Services:** PC. *(See color ad p 615)*

FREE continental breakfast and high-speed Internet

▼ See AAA listing p 633 ▼

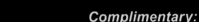

(See map and index starting on p. 590)

L'HERMITAGE HOTEL   *Book great rates at AAA.com*   Phone: 778/327-4100

Boutique Hotel
Rates not provided

Address: 788 Richards St V6B 3A4 **Location:** Between Robson and W Georgia sts. **Facility:** Just blocks from BC Place Stadium and the hot Robson Street shopping district, the sophisticated boutique hotel appoints its studio rooms and suites with stylish furnishings and leading-edge technology. Smoke free premises. 60 units. 34 one-bedroom standard units. 24 one- and 2 two-bedroom suites, some with kitchens. 7 stories, interior corridors. **Parking:** on-site (fee) and valet. **Terms:** check-in 4 pm. **Amenities:** high-speed Internet, voice mail, safes, irons, hair dryers. **Pool(s):** heated outdoor. **Leisure Activities:** whirlpool, steamrooms, exercise room. **Guest Services:** valet laundry, area transportation-downtown area, wireless Internet. **Business Services:** meeting rooms, PC. **Free Special Amenities:** newspaper and high-speed Internet.

THE LISTEL HOTEL   *Book great rates at AAA.com*   Phone: (604)684-8461

Hotel
$139-$299 All Year

Address: 1300 Robson St V6E 1C5 **Location:** Between Broughton and Jervis sts. **Facility:** Smoke free premises. 130 one-bedroom standard units. 6 stories, interior corridors. **Parking:** valet. **Terms:** cancellation fee imposed. **Amenities:** high-speed Internet, dual phone lines, voice mail, honor bars, irons, hair dryers. *Some:* DVD players. **Leisure Activities:** whirlpool, exercise room. **Guest Services:** valet laundry, wireless Internet. **Business Services:** meeting rooms, PC.

'O CANADA' HOUSE B&B   Phone: 604/688-0555

Historic Bed & Breakfast
Rates not provided

Address: 1114 Barclay St V6E 1H1 **Location:** Between Thurlow and Bute sts. Located in a residential area. **Facility:** This beautifully restored 1897 Victorian home is in the West End within easy walking distance of many restaurants and shops. Smoke free premises. 7 units. 6 one-bedroom standard units. 1 cottage. 3 stories (no elevator), interior corridors. *Bath:* combo or shower only. **Parking:** on-site. **Terms:** office hours 7 am-7 pm, age restrictions may apply. **Amenities:** video library, DVD players, hair dryers. **Guest Services:** wireless Internet.

▼ *See AAA listing p 610* ▼

(See map and index starting on p. 590)

PAN PACIFIC VANCOUVER   *Book great rates at AAA.com*   Phone: (604)662-8111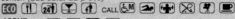

Hotel
$269-$449 3/1-10/31
$179-$359 11/1-2/28

Address: 300-999 Canada Pl V6C 3B5 **Location:** Motor entrance off Burrard St. Located at Canada Place. **Facility:** This service-oriented hotel is attached to the convention center as well as a pier where huge cruise ships dock during summer months. 504 units. 473 one-bedroom standard units. 29 one- and 2 two-bedroom suites, some with kitchens and/or whirlpools. 23 stories, interior corridors. **Parking:** on-site (fee) and valet. **Terms:** check-in 4 pm. **Amenities:** video library, CD players, high-speed Internet (fee), dual phone lines, voice mail, safes, honor bars, irons, hair dryers. *Some:* DVD players. **Dining:** Five Sails Restaurant, see separate listing, entertainment. **Pool(s):** heated outdoor. **Leisure Activities:** saunas, whirlpool, steamrooms, spa. **Guest Services:** valet laundry, wireless Internet. **Business Services:** meeting rooms, business center. *(See color ad p 616)*

FREE newspaper and early check-in/late check-out

QUALITY HOTEL DOWNTOWN-THE INN AT FALSE
CREEK   *Book at AAA.com*   Phone: (604)682-0229   **38**

Hotel
$129-$259 3/1-9/30
$80-$159 10/1-2/28

Address: 1335 Howe St V6Z 1R7 **Location:** Between Drake and Pacific sts. **Facility:** Smoke free premises. 157 units. 137 one-bedroom standard units. 20 one-bedroom suites, some with kitchens. 7 stories, interior corridors. **Parking:** on-site (fee). **Terms:** cancellation fee imposed. **Amenities:** voice mail, irons, hair dryers. **Pool(s):** heated outdoor. **Guest Services:** valet laundry, wireless Internet. **Business Services:** meeting rooms, PC (fee).

▼ *See AAA listing p 610* ▼

▼ See AAA listing p 611 ▼

Modern Convenience
Downtown Vancouver

THE LANDiS
HOTEL & SUITES

- Beautiful, fully furnished 800 & 1,000 sq ft 2-bedroom suites
- Complete kitchens with microwave and dishwasher
- Fitness centre, heated indoor swimming pool and whirlpool
- Complimentary continental breakfast
- Complimentary wireless high speed internet
- Just blocks from the city's best restaurants, shops & attractions

THE LANDiS HOTEL & SUITES DOWNTOWN VANCOUVER
1200 Hornby Street, Vancouver

www.landissuitesvancouver.com   1.877.291.6111

(See map and index starting on p. 590)

▼ See AAA listing p 614 ▼

(See map and index starting on p. 590)

RAMADA LIMITED DOWNTOWN VANCOUVER   *Book at AAA.com*   Phone: (604)488-1088   **19**

Hotel
$79-$400 All Year

Address: 435 W Pender St V6B 1V2 **Location:** Between Homer and Richards sts. **Facility:** Smoke free premises. 80 one-bedroom standard units. 6 stories, interior corridors. **Parking:** valet. **Terms:** cancellation fee imposed. **Amenities:** voice mail, irons, hair dryers. **Guest Services:** valet and coin laundry, wireless Internet. **Business Services:** meeting rooms, PC.

ECO ASK T+ CALL &M X 🎦 💻

RENAISSANCE VANCOUVER HOTEL HARBOURSIDE   *Book great rates at AAA.com*   Phone: (604)689-9211   **2**

CAA SAVE

Hotel
$219-$299 All Year

Address: 1133 W Hastings St V6E 3T3 **Location:** Between Bute and Thurlow sts. **Facility:** Smoke free premises. 442 units. 434 one-bedroom standard units. 8 one-bedroom suites. 19 stories, interior corridors. **Parking:** on-site (fee) and valet. **Terms:** cancellation fee imposed. **Amenities:** high-speed Internet (fee), voice mail, safes, irons, hair dryers. **Pool(s):** heated indoor. **Leisure Activities:** whirlpool. **Guest Services:** valet laundry, wireless Internet. **Business Services:** meeting rooms, business center. *(See color ad p 618)*

AAA Benefit:
Members save a minimum 5% off the best available rate.

ECO T Y CALL &M 🛗 X 🎦 🔋 💻 / SOME UNITS FEE 🐕

FREE newspaper and room upgrade (subject to availability with advance reservations)

ST. REGIS HOTEL   *Book great rates at AAA.com*   Phone: (604)681-1135   **23**

CAA SAVE

Hotel
$134-$318 All Year

Address: 602 Dunsmuir St V6B 1Y6 **Location:** Between Granville and Seymour sts. **Facility:** Smoke free premises. 65 units. 50 one-bedroom standard units. 15 one-bedroom suites. 5 stories, interior corridors. *Bath:* combo or shower only. **Parking:** on-site (fee) and valet. **Terms:** 3 day cancellation notice, in summer-fee imposed. **Amenities:** high-speed Internet, dual phone lines, voice mail, safes, irons, hair dryers. **Guest Services:** valet laundry, wireless Internet. **Business Services:** meeting rooms, business center. **Free Special Amenities: full breakfast and high-speed Internet.**

T Y CALL &M 🛗 X 🎦 💻 / SOME UNITS 🔋

▼ See AAA listing p 616 ▼

(See map and index starting on p. 590)

▼ *See AAA listing p 617* ▼

(See map and index starting on p. 590)

SANDMAN HOTEL VANCOUVER CITY CENTER   *Book at AAA.com*   Phone: (604)681-2211    29

Hotel
$109-$209 All Year

Address: 180 W Georgia St V6B 4P4 **Location:** Between Cambie and Beatty sts. **Facility:** 303 one-bedroom standard units. 11-14 stories, interior corridors. **Parking:** on-site (fee). **Terms:** check-in 4 pm, cancellation fee imposed. **Amenities:** video games (fee), voice mail, irons, hair dryers. **Dining:** Moxie's Classic Grill, see separate listing. **Pool(s):** heated indoor. **Leisure Activities:** whirlpool. **Guest Services:** valet laundry, wireless Internet. **Business Services:** meeting rooms, business center.

SHANGRI-LA HOTEL VANCOUVER   *Book great rates at AAA.com*   Phone: (604)689-1120   14

Contemporary
Hotel
$311-$428 All Year

Address: 1128 W Georgia St V6E 0A8 **Location:** Between Thurlow and Bute sts. **Facility:** Luxurious guest rooms feature the latest and greatest amenities, from automatically closing drapes and sheers to centrally controlled lighting. Smoke free premises. 119 units. 80 one-bedroom standard units. 39 one-bedroom suites, some with whirlpools. 15 stories, interior corridors. **Parking:** on-site (fee) and valet. **Terms:** cancellation fee imposed. **Amenities:** DVD players, high-speed Internet, dual phone lines, voice mail, safes, honor bars, irons, hair dryers. *Some:* fax. **Dining:** Market by Jean-Georges, see separate listing, entertainment. **Pool(s):** heated outdoor. **Leisure Activities:** sauna, whirlpool, steamroom, spa. **Guest Services:** valet laundry, wireless Internet. **Business Services:** meeting rooms, business center.

FREE local telephone calls and high-speed Internet

SHERATON VANCOUVER WALL CENTRE HOTEL   *Book great rates at AAA.com* Phone: 604/331-1000   25

Hotel
Rates not provided

Address: 1088 Burrard St V6Z 2R9 **Location:** Between Helmcken and Nelson sts. **Facility:** The hotel's two tall black towers rise above Vancouver's skyline; inside, rooms offer floor-to-ceiling windows and wonderful views of the city. Smoke free premises. 733 units. 661 one-bedroom standard units, some with whirlpools. 40 one- and 32 two-bedroom suites, some with kitchens. 28-35 stories, interior corridors. *Bath:* combo or shower only. **Parking:** on-site (fee) and valet. **Amenities:** high-speed Internet (fee), dual phone lines, voice mail, safes, irons, hair dryers. **Dining:** 2 restaurants. **Pool(s):** heated indoor. **Leisure Activities:** sauna, whirlpools, steamroom, spa. **Guest Services:** valet laundry, area transportation-downtown, wireless Internet. **Business Services:** conference facilities, business center. *(See color ad p 620)*

S Sheraton
HOTELS & RESORTS

AAA Benefit:
Members get up to 15% off, plus Starwood Preferred Guest® bonuses.

FREE newspaper

SUNSET INN & SUITES   *Book great rates at AAA.com*   Phone: (604)688-2474   28

Address: 1111 Burnaby St V6E 1P4 **Location:** Between Thurlow and Bute sts. **Facility:** Smoke free premises. 50 units. 10 one-bedroom standard units with kitchens. 40 one-bedroom suites with kitchens. 11 stories, interior corridors. *Bath:* combo or shower only. **Parking:** on-site. **Terms:** check-in 4 pm, cancellation fee imposed. **Amenities:** DVD players, voice mail, safes, irons, hair dryers. **Leisure Activities:** exercise room. **Guest Services:** coin laundry, wireless Internet. *(See color ad p 601)*

FREE continental breakfast and high-speed Internet

(See map and index starting on p. 590)

▼ See AAA listing p 619 ▼

(See map and index starting on p. 590)

THE SUTTON PLACE HOTEL *Book great rates at AAA.com* **Phone:** (604)682-5511 **20**

Hotel
$169-$599 All Year

Address: 845 Burrard St V6Z 2K6 **Location:** Between Smithe and Robson sts. **Facility:** Attractive yet understated rooms incorporate superior residential-style furnishings at this service-oriented hotel near Robson Street. Smoke free premises. 397 units. 350 one-bedroom standard units. 47 one-bedroom suites. 21 stories, interior corridors. **Parking:** on-site (fee) and valet. **Terms:** cancellation fee imposed. **Amenities:** video library, DVD players, CD players, dual phone lines, voice mail, safes, honor bars, irons, hair dryers. *Fee:* video games, high-speed Internet. **Dining:** Fleuri Restaurant, see separate listing, entertainment. **Pool(s):** heated indoor. **Leisure Activities:** sauna, whirlpool, steamrooms, exercise room, spa. **Guest Services:** valet laundry, area transportation-downtown, wireless Internet. **Business Services:** meeting rooms, business center. *(See color ad below)*

FREE newspaper

TERMINAL CITY TOWER HOTEL *Book at AAA.com* **Phone:** 604/681-4121 **10**

Hotel
Rates not provided

Address: 837 W Hastings St V6C 1B6 **Location:** Between Howe and Hornby sts. **Facility:** Smoke free premises. 60 units. 30 one-bedroom standard units. 30 one-bedroom suites. 30 stories, interior corridors. **Parking:** on-site (fee). **Amenities:** high-speed Internet (fee), dual phone lines, voice mail, safes, irons, hair dryers. **Pool(s):** heated indoor. **Leisure Activities:** saunas, whirlpool, steamrooms, racquetball courts. **Guest Services:** valet laundry, wireless Internet. **Business Services:** meeting rooms, PC.

VANCOUVER MARRIOTT PINNACLE DOWNTOWN *Book great rates at AAA.com* **Phone:** (604)684-1128 **4**

Hotel
$219-$299 All Year

Address: 1128 W Hastings St V6E 4R5 **Location:** Between Thurlow and Bute sts. **Facility:** Located in the heart of the downtown business district, guest rooms offer breathtaking views of the mountains, water and downtown Vancouver. Smoke free premises. 434 one-bedroom standard units. 31 stories, interior corridors. **Parking:** on-site (fee) and valet. **Terms:** check-in 4 pm, cancellation fee imposed. **Amenities:** dual phone lines, voice mail, safes, irons, hair dryers. *Fee:* video games, high-speed Internet. *Some:* CD players. **Dining:** Show Case Restaurant, see separate listing. **Pool(s):** heated indoor. **Leisure Activities:** sauna, whirlpool, steamroom, exercise room. **Guest Services:** valet laundry, wireless Internet. **Business Services:** conference facilities, business center.

Marriott
HOTELS & RESORTS

AAA Benefit:
Members save a minimum 5% off the best available rate.

▼ *See AAA listing above* ▼

(See map and index starting on p. 590)

THE WEDGEWOOD HOTEL & SPA   *Book great rates at AAA.com*   Phone: (604)689-7777 ㉔

(AAA) (SAVE)

▽▽▽ ▽▽▽

Boutique
Hotel

$298-$418 3/1-9/30
$238-$298 10/1-2/28

Address: 845 Hornby St V6Z 1V1 **Location:** Between Smithe and Robson sts. **Facility:** An intimate and stylish boutique hotel, The Wedgewood is a must-visit thanks to the wonderfully attentive staff. Smoke free premises. 83 units. 45 one-bedroom standard units. 38 one-bedroom suites, some with whirlpools. 13 stories, interior corridors. **Parking:** valet. **Terms:** cancellation fee imposed. **Amenities:** CD players, high-speed Internet, dual phone lines, voice mail, safes, honor bars, irons, hair dryers. **Dining:** Bacchus Restaurant, see separate listing, entertainment. **Leisure Activities:** steamroom, exercise room, spa. **Guest Services:** valet laundry, wireless Internet. **Business Services:** meeting rooms, business center.

🍴 24↑ 🍷 CALL &M 🐾 🗙 📽 💻

FREE newspaper and high-speed Internet

WEST END GUEST HOUSE   Phone: (604)681-2889 ⑨

(AAA) (SAVE)

▽▽ ▽▽

Historic Bed
& Breakfast

$150-$325 All Year

Address: 1362 Haro St V6E 1G2 **Location:** Between Broughton and Jervis sts. Located in a quiet residential area. **Facility:** A resident ghost allegedly lives in this well-preserved Victorian home in the residential neighborhood known as the West End. Smoke free premises. 7 one-bedroom standard units. 2 stories (no elevator), interior corridors. *Bath:* combo or shower only. **Terms:** office hours 8 am-7 pm, 2-3 night minimum stay - weekends, age restrictions may apply, 7 day cancellation notice-fee imposed. **Amenities:** video library, DVD players, voice mail, hair dryers. **Leisure Activities:** bicycles. **Guest Services:** wireless Internet. **Business Services:** PC. Free **Special Amenities:** full breakfast and high-speed Internet. 🗙 ℳ

THE WESTIN BAYSHORE VANCOUVER   *Book great rates at AAA.com*   Phone: (604)682-3377 ❶

(AAA) (SAVE)

▽▽▽ ▽▽▽

Hotel

$195-$580 All Year

Address: 1601 Bayshore Dr V6G 2V4 **Location:** W Georgia and Cardero sts. **Facility:** Manicured grounds surround the downtown, harborside hotel where every room offers excellent views; the outdoor pool is set amid lush landscaping. Smoke free premises. 510 units. 482 one-bedroom standard units. 28 one-bedroom suites. 9-16 stories, interior corridors. **Parking:** on-site (fee) and valet. **Terms:** check-in 4 pm, cancellation fee imposed. **Amenities:** video games (fee), dual phone lines, voice mail, safes, honor bars, irons, hair dryers. *Some:* high-speed Internet (fee). **Dining:** 2 restaurants. **Pool(s):** heated outdoor, heated indoor. **Leisure Activities:** saunas, whirlpool, steamroom, jogging, exercise room, spa. **Guest Services:** valet laundry, area transportation-downtown, wireless Internet. **Business Services:** conference facilities, business center. *(See color ad below)*

WESTIN
HOTELS & RESORTS

AAA Benefit:
Enjoy up to 15% off
your next stay, plus
Starwood Preferred
Guest® bonuses.

ECO 🍴 24↑ 🍷 CALL &M 🏊 🗙 🗙 💻 / SOME UNITS 🐾

▼ *See AAA listing above* ▼

(See map and index starting on p. 590)

THE WESTIN GRAND, VANCOUVER *Book great rates at AAA.com* Phone: (604)602-1999 **27**

Hotel
$169-$679 All Year

Address: 433 Robson St V6B 6L9 **Location:** Between Homer and Richards sts. **Facility:** Shaped like a baby grand piano, this chic, all-suite hotel has floor-to-ceiling windows that offer city views from every unit. Smoke free premises. 207 units. 23 one-bedroom standard units. 184 one-bedroom suites. 26 stories, interior corridors. **Parking:** on-site (fee) and valet. **Amenities:** high-speed Internet (fee), dual phone lines, voice mail, safes, honor bars, irons, hair dryers. **Pool(s):** heated outdoor. **Leisure Activities:** sauna, whirlpool, steamrooms, exercise room. *Fee:* massage. **Guest Services:** valet laundry, wireless Internet. **Business Services:** meeting rooms, business center.

WESTIN
HOTELS & RESORTS

AAA Benefit:
Enjoy up to 15% off your next stay, plus Starwood Preferred Guest® bonuses.

—— WHERE TO DINE ——

A KETTLE OF FISH *Menu on AAA.com* Phone: 604/682-6661 **49**

Seafood
$20-$39

The enchanting, casually elegant restaurant, which occupies a lush garden setting, has been serving Vancouver for more than 28 years. It is known for fresh seafood, including the specialty kettle fish soup, as well as wild British Columbia sockeye salmon, Atlantic Coast lobster and Pacific Coast Dungeness crab. A pay parking lot is about a half-block down on Hornby Street. Casual dress. **Bar:** Full bar. **Reservations:** suggested. **Hours:** 5:30 pm-9:30 pm; Sunday brunch 10:30 am-2:30 pm. Closed: 1/1, 12/25, 12/26. **Address:** 900 Pacific St V6Z 2E3 **Location:** Corner of Hornby and Pacific sts. **Parking:** street.

AL PORTO RISTORANTE Phone: 604/683-8376 **27**

Northern Italian
$12-$27

In the heart of Old Gastown, this restaurant is housed in a century-old Hudson Bay Trading Co. warehouse. Tables upstairs offer a great harbor view; the downstairs area is like dining in a Tuscan villa. Prosciutto di parma is excellent. Parking can be found in a nearby lot or at street meters. Casual dress. **Bar:** Full bar. **Reservations:** suggested. **Hours:** 11:30 am-10:30 pm, Sat & Sun from 5 pm. Closed: 1/1, 12/25, 12/26; also for lunch on holidays. **Address:** 321 Water St V6B 1B8 **Location:** Between Richards and Cambie sts; in Gastown. **Parking:** street.

AQUA RIVA RESTAURANT & BAR Phone: 604/683-5599 **18**

Pacific Rim
$12-$35

Wood-fired pizza and Pacific tuna and salmon stand out on a menu of seafood and rotisserie dishes at this downtown waterfront restaurant. Guests can watch cruise ships dock at the terminal through floor-to-ceiling windows as they enjoy tasty fare. Funky decor and an open kitchen distinguish the space. Casual dress. **Bar:** Full bar. **Reservations:** suggested. **Hours:** 11:30 am-2:30 & 5-10 pm, Sat & Sun from 5 pm. Closed: 12/24, 12/25. **Address:** 200 Granville St V6C 1S4 **Location:** Between Cordova and Howe sts. **Parking:** on-site (fee).

BACCHUS RESTAURANT Phone: 604/608-5319 **34**

French
$15-$35

The elegant establishment occupies a wonderful, boutique-style downtown hotel. On warm summer evenings, the windows are opened so diners can people-watch. The creative menu reflects a heavy French influence, and each night a special entree is prepared in the classical French style along with a la carte menu items. The staff is highly attentive. Dressy casual. Entertainment. **Bar:** Full bar. **Reservations:** suggested. **Hours:** 6:30 am-11 pm. **Address:** 845 Hornby St V6Z 1V1 **Location:** Between Smithe and Robson sts; in The Wedgewood Hotel & Spa. **Parking:** valet and street.

BLUE WATER CAFE & RAW BAR Phone: 604/688-8078 **48**

Seafood
$31-$46

In the hip Yaletown district, this highly recognized restaurant offers a fantastic dining experience centered on the ocean's wonderful harvests of fresh seafood. Diners can sample fresh oysters from the oyster bar or fresh sushi items, and those not into fish can try at least three meat dishes. During warmer weather, the patio becomes a hot spot for people-watching. Casual dress. **Bar:** Full bar. **Reservations:** suggested. **Hours:** 5 pm-midnight. Closed: 1/1, 12/24, 12/25. **Address:** 1095 Hamilton St V6B 5T4 **Location:** Between Nelson and Helmcken sts. **Parking:** valet and street.

THE BOATHOUSE RESTAURANT Phone: 604/669-2225

Seafood
$10-$25

The restaurant's fantastic heated and covered patio, which is open all year and in all kinds of weather, affords spectacular views of English Bay. Casual bar food makes up the menu in the downstairs pub, while the more formal upstairs dining room serves fresh seafood. Casual dress. **Bar:** Full bar. **Reservations:** suggested. **Hours:** 11 am-11 pm. Closed: 12/25. **Address:** 1795 Beach Ave V6G 1Y9 **Location:** Between Bidwell and Denman sts. **Parking:** valet and street.

BRIX RESTAURANT & WINE BAR Phone: 604/915-9463 **51**

Pacific Northwest
$22-$37

A nice place to drop in for a glass of wine and a bite, the restaurant is pure Yaletown—a funky old space with wood floors and high ceilings. A wine list with 50-odd by-the-glass choices complements the tapas selections, as well as items on the varied main menu. Casual dress. **Bar:** Full bar. **Reservations:** suggested. **Hours:** 5 pm-midnight. Closed major holidays; also Sun. **Address:** 1138 Homer St V6B 2X6 **Location:** Between Helmcken and Davie sts. **Parking:** street.

(See map and index starting on p. 590)

CACTUS CLUB CAFE

Phone: 604/685-8070

Canadian
$9-$29

This bustling, casual restaurant serves huge burgers, sandwiches, pasta, salads, soups, quesadillas, fajitas, vegetarian dishes, steak, ribs, chicken and fish. Featured are certified Angus beef and fresh wild British Columbia salmon. The thick and creamy milk shakes come highly recommended. Casual dress. **Bar:** Full bar. **Hours:** 11 am-midnight, Fri & Sat-1 am. Closed: 12/25. **Address:** 357 Davie St V6B 1R2 **Location:** Between Homer and Hamilton sts. **Parking:** street.

CACTUS CLUB CAFE

Phone: 604/687-3278

Canadian
$9-$29

This bustling, casual restaurant serves huge burgers, sandwiches, pasta, salads, soups, quesadillas, fajitas, vegetarian dishes, steak, ribs, chicken and fish. Featured are certified Angus beef and fresh wild British Columbia salmon. The thick and creamy milk shakes come highly recommended. Casual dress. **Bar:** Full bar. **Hours:** 11 am-midnight, Fri & Sat-1 am. Closed: 12/25. **Address:** 1136 Robson St V6E 1B2 **Location:** Between Bute and Thurlow sts. **Parking:** street.

CAFE DE PARIS

Phone: 604/687-1418 ③

French
$13-$35

A West End staple since 1977, the bistro-style French restaurant lets guests choose from among longtime menu favorites and daily chef's creations. The wonderful wine list includes a nice selection of both French and British Columbia wines. Guests who can't find a spot in the free lot behind the building can feed a meter on the street. Casual dress. **Bar:** Full bar. **Reservations:** suggested, weekends. **Hours:** 11:30 am-2 & 5:30-10 pm, Sat from 5:30 pm, Sun 5 pm-9 pm. Closed: 1/1, 12/25, 12/26. **Address:** 751 Denman St V6G 2L6 **Location:** Between Robson and Alberni sts. **Parking:** on-site and street.

CAFE PRESTO PANINI *Menu on AAA.com*

Phone: 604/684-4445 ㊱

CAA

Italian
$9-$15

In business for more than 20 years, this small cafe satisfies cravings for reasonably priced homemade Italian food, with nothing more than $15. Choices range from delicious grilled panini sandwiches on focaccia bread to penne or linguine pasta with any of six sauces. Vegetarian choices also are available. Parking is at street meters or in nearby lots across from the courthouse. Casual dress. **Bar:** Beer & wine. **Reservations:** suggested, for lunch. **Hours:** 11:30 am-2 & 5-8 pm. Closed major holidays; also Sun. **Address:** 895 Hornby St V6Z 1T9 **Location:** Between Robson and Smithe sts. **Parking:** street.

CALL

CARDERO'S RESTAURANT

Phone: 604/669-7666 ④

Pacific Northwest
$9-$29

At the north end of Cardero and Nicola streets where the seawall weaves around the various condos sits this distinctive warehouse-like restaurant overlooking a marina and Vancouver's north shore. This place is known for its wonderfully prepared fish dishes and mouthwatering pizzas, which are baked in a wood oven. For oyster lovers, there's an open oyster bar. Comfy leather chairs in the cozy lounge are right next to a wood-burning fireplace. Casual dress. **Bar:** Full bar. **Reservations:** suggested. **Hours:** 11:30 am-11 pm, Sun-10 pm. Closed: 12/25. **Address:** 1583 Coal Harbour Quay V6G 3E7 **Location:** Between Cardero and Nicola sts. **Parking:** valet and street. CALL

CHILLI HOUSE THAI BISTRO

Phone: 604/685-8989 ㊻

Thai
$11-$16

Just under the Burrard Street Bridge and along the picturesque marina, the restaurant prepares spicy Thai favorites, including satays, pad thai noodles and coconut rice. The friendly staff will help guests pick dishes, which can be requested in milder varieties. Free underground parking is available. Casual dress. **Bar:** Full bar. **Reservations:** suggested. **Hours:** 3 pm-10 pm. Closed: 12/25. **Address:** 1018 Beach Ave V6E 3N9 **Location:** Between Thurlow and Hornby sts. **Parking:** on-site. CALL

CIAO BELLA RISTORANTE

Phone: 604/688-5771 ②

CAA

Italian
$8-$29

Patrons can taste some excellent Italian food. Convenient parking is at the rear of the building, just off Alberni Street. The menu lists many classics—including pasta dishes with authentic sauces and hearty main courses. This place is well worth the stop. Casual dress. **Bar:** Full bar. **Reservations:** suggested. **Hours:** 11:30 am-2:30 & 4:30-10:30 pm. **Address:** 703 Denman St V6G 2L6 **Location:** Between Robson and Alberni sts. **Parking:** on-site.

CINCIN

Phone: 604/688-7338 ㉓

Mediterranean
$19-$40

The menu at this restaurant blends the Mediterranean and Italian dishes that have been delighting patrons for years. Choices include tasty pasta or thin-crust pizza cooked in a wood-fired oven. On the second floor overlooking Robson Street, the bustling spot has a trendy feel that sometimes lures film stars. Service is prompt and attentive. Casual dress. **Bar:** Full bar. **Reservations:** suggested. **Hours:** 5 pm-11 pm. Closed: 1/1, 12/25, 12/26. **Address:** 1154 Robson St V6E 1B5 **Location:** Between Bute and Thurlow sts. **Parking:** street.

COPPER CHIMNEY

Phone: 604/689-8862 ㉑

Indian
$14-$30

West Coast and Italian influences fuse to create a wonderful blend of interesting flavors. The bustling bi-level dining room features a large, open kitchen, a pleasant bar area and a loft dining area overlooking an artistic hanging light fixture. Casual dress. **Bar:** Full bar. **Reservations:** suggested. **Hours:** 6:30 am-10 pm, Sat & Sun 6:30 am-noon & 5-10 pm. **Address:** 567 Hornby St V6C 2E8 **Location:** Between Dunsmuir and Pender sts; in Hotel Le Soleil. **Parking:** valet and street. CALL

C RESTAURANT

Phone: 604/681-1164 (55)

Seafood
$18-$40

Along the seawall at the end of Howe Street, the restaurant avails guests of a nice treat in offering patio seating during the summer. An extensive wine list complements its wonderful array of fresh fish and other seafood. Because area parking is limited, it's a good idea to use the valet service. Casual dress. **Bar:** Full bar. **Reservations:** required, for dinner. **Hours:** 11:30 am-2:30 & 5:30-10 pm, Sat & Sun from 5:30 pm. Closed: 12/25. **Address:** 2-1600 Howe St V6Z 2L9 **Location:** 1 blk below Beach Ave. **Parking:** valet and street. CALL

(See map and index starting on p. 590)

DELILAH'S
Phone: 604/687-3424   [7]

Pacific Northwest
$33-$45

Just off trendy Denman Street, the tucked-away restaurant is known for its martinis and over-the-top atmosphere. All dinners—from the small, two-course selection to the full, four-course feast—are prix fixe. Casual dress. **Bar:** Full bar. **Reservations:** suggested. **Hours:** 5 pm-10 pm, Fri & Sat-11 pm. Closed: 1/1, 12/25, 12/26; also Mon. **Address:** 1789 Comox St V6G 1P5 **Location:** Between Denman and Bidwell sts. **Parking:** street. CALL 🅼

DIVA AT THE MET
Phone: 604/602-7788   [30]

Pacific Northwest
$18-$47

An affluent clientele patronizes the fashionable fine-dining establishment. Creative nouvelle cuisine, which is equal parts health-conscious and delicious, is elevated to an art form. Dressy casual. **Bar:** Full bar. **Reservations:** suggested. **Hours:** 6:30 am-10 pm. **Address:** 645 Howe St V6C 2Y9 **Location:** Between Georgia and Dunsmuir sts; in Metropolitan Hotel. **Parking:** on-site and valet. CALL 🅼

DOCKSIDE RESTAURANT & BREWING COMPANY
Phone: 604/685-7070   [60]

Canadian
$14-$38

Floor-to-ceiling windows offer views of the marina, and a 50-foot aquarium adds to the restaurant's charm. In the heart of the kitchen is a wood-fired grill where breakfast, lunch and dinner dishes are prepared. Casual dress. **Bar:** Full bar. **Reservations:** suggested. **Hours:** 7 am-10 pm; Sunday brunch. **Address:** 1253 Johnston St V6H 3R9 **Location:** Granville Island; below the bridge, follow signs; in Granville Island Hotel. **Parking:** on-site. CALL 🅼

DON FRANCESCO RESTAURANT   *Menu on AAA.com*
Phone: 604/685-7770   [33]

Italian
$14-$40

In the heart of the vibrant downtown area, this wonderful Italian restaurant offers excellent pasta dishes and market-fresh specialties of wild game, including boar, ostrich, quail and partridge, all prepared with a Mediterranean flair. An accomplished staff and warm, inviting atmosphere add to a memorable experience. Dressy casual. **Bar:** Full bar. **Reservations:** suggested. **Hours:** 11:30 am-11 pm, Sat & Sun from 5 pm. Closed: 1/1, 12/25, 12/26. **Address:** 860 Burrard St V6Z 1X9 **Location:** Between Smithe and Robson sts. **Parking:** on-site (fee). CALL 🅼

EARLS RESTAURANT
Phone: 604/682-6700

Canadian
$10-$19

Offering an experience that falls between fast food and fine dining, the fun, relaxed restaurant prepares great food at a great price. Choices range from juicy burgers, hearty sandwiches, fresh salads, wings and pizza to full entrees of steak, chops and seafood. Made-from-scratch soups and assorted breads, as well as a nice choice of wines and beers, round out the offerings. This is a fitting spot for impromptu get-togethers and festive occasions. Casual dress. **Bar:** Full bar. **Hours:** 11:30 am-midnight. Closed: 12/25. **Address:** 905 Hornby St V6Z 1V3 **Location:** Corner of Hornby and Smithe sts. **Parking:** street.

EARLS RESTAURANT
Phone: 604/669-0020

Canadian
$10-$19

Offering an experience that falls between fast food and fine dining, the fun, relaxed restaurant prepares great food at a great price. Choices range from juicy burgers, hearty sandwiches, fresh salads, wings and pizza to full entrees of steak, chops and seafood. Made-from-scratch soups and assorted breads, as well as a nice choice of wines and beers, round out the offerings. This is a fitting spot for impromptu get-togethers and festive occasions. Casual dress. **Bar:** Full bar. **Hours:** 11:30 am-midnight, Fri & Sat-1 am. Closed: 12/25. **Address:** 1185 Robson St V6E 1B5 **Location:** Between Bute and Thurlow sts. **Parking:** street. CALL 🅼

ELIXIR RESTAURANT - OPUS BAR
Phone: 604/642-0557   [53]

French
$16-$38

The restaurant takes guests on a figurative trip to Paris. The design is pure Parisian, and the funky lounge is known for its martinis. Delightful surprises abound on the classic French brasserie menu. Casual dress. **Bar:** Full bar. **Reservations:** suggested. **Hours:** 6:30 am-11 pm, Fri & Sat-midnight. **Address:** 350 Davie St V6B 5Z6 **Location:** Between Hamilton and Mainland sts. **Parking:** valet and street. CALL 🅼

EZOGIKU NOODLE CAFE
Phone: 604/685-8606   [12]

Japanese
$6-$9

The Japanese noodle shop offers something different from standard restaurants. For less than $10, diners can order a steaming bowl of egg noodles served with a choice of three mouthwatering broths and a choice of such complementary items as teriyaki chicken, wontons or seafood. The restaurant offers mostly counter service. Casual dress. **Hours:** 11 am-10 pm. Closed major holidays. **Address:** 1329 Robson St V6E 1C6 **Location:** Between Jervis and Broughton sts. **Parking:** street.

THE FISH HOUSE IN STANLEY PARK   *Menu on AAA.com*
Phone: 604/681-7275   [1]

Seafood
$15-$33

Located in the lush and quiet surroundings of Stanley Park, this restaurant features a wide variety of fresh seafood wonderfully prepared with a Canadian West Coast influence. Its casual atmosphere offers patio dining in season. Pay parking lot in effect at all times. Casual dress. **Bar:** Full bar. **Reservations:** suggested. **Hours:** 11:30 am-10 pm, Sat & Sun from 11 am; Saturday & Sunday brunch. Closed: 12/24-12/26. **Address:** 8901 Stanley Park Dr V6G 3E2 **Location:** Beach Ave entrance to Stanley Park; next to tennis courts. **Parking:** on-site (fee). CALL 🅼 Ⓧ

FIVE SAILS RESTAURANT
Phone: 604/844-2855   [8]

Pacific Northwest
$28-$39

Long hailed as one of the city's finest restaurants, this place is a must for its combination of stunning third-story waterfront views and spectacular food. Patrons can watch cruise ships docking in the summer or just take in the water and mountain vistas from window tables. The sea inspires exquisite menu choices, which celebrate the best seafood the Pacific Northwest has to offer. Complementing the food are diverse hand-selected wines from both distant vineyards and British Columbia wineries. Dressy casual. **Bar:** Full bar. **Reservations:** suggested. **Hours:** 5:30 pm-10 pm. Closed: 12/26; also 1/1-1/15. **Address:** 999 Canada Pl V6C 3B5 **Location:** Motor entrance off Burrard St; in The Pan Pacific Vancouver. **Parking:** on-site (fee) and valet. CALL 🅼

(See map and index starting on p. 590)

FLEURI RESTAURANT

Phone: 604/682-5511 **31**

Pacific Northwest
$16-$46

In the elegant hotel, the restaurant offers quiet seclusion from the bustling city streets. Diners enjoy consistently professional, personable service and a delightful menu that includes both a la carte choices and a chef's tasting selection. Dressy casual. **Bar:** Full bar. **Reservations:** suggested. **Hours:** 6:30 am-10:30 pm. **Address:** 845 Burrard St V6Z 2K6 **Location:** Between Smithe and Robson sts; in The Sutton Place Hotel. **Parking:** on-site (fee) and valet. *(See color ad p 621)* CALL &M

GLOWBAL GRILL & SATAY BAR

Phone: 604/602-0835 **50**

International
$10-$35

In the funky Yaletown district, the hip grill might make visitors feel like they're in a 1970s time warp. Lending to the mood are amazing hanging lamps that look like sea anemones and '70s-style carpet. The satay bar offers a nice selection of individually priced items, as well as a $23 sampler. Some of the wines are not badly priced, as are a number of entrees. Casual dress. **Bar:** Full bar. **Reservations:** suggested. **Hours:** 11 am-midnight, Sat & Sun from 10:30 am; Saturday & Sunday brunch. Closed: 1/1, 12/25. **Address:** 1079 Mainland St V6B 5P9 **Location:** Between Helmcken and Nelson sts. **Parking:** valet and street. CALL &M

THE HERMITAGE   *Menu on AAA.com*

Phone: 604/689-3237 **22**

Traditional
French
$15-$36

A former chef to King Leopold of Belgium, the chef/owner offers a menu that includes delicious rack of lamb, crepes Suzette and many French specialties. Servers are trained to be proper and exact. Patio dining is available in fair weather. The restaurant occupies a tiny courtyard setting along trendy Robson Street. Casual dress. **Bar:** Full bar. **Reservations:** suggested. **Hours:** 11:30 am-2:30 & 5:30-10 pm, Sat & Sun from 5:30 pm. Closed: 1/1, 12/25, 12/26; also for lunch holidays. **Address:** 115/1025 Robson St V6E 4A9 **Location:** Between Thurlow and Burrard sts; in courtyard area. **Parking:** street. CALL &M

HERONS RESTAURANT

Phone: 604/691-1991 **15**

Pacific Northwest
$12-$35

Across from the cruise ship terminal of Canada Place, the restaurant presents a menu that's a showcase for the best of seasonal British Columbian cuisine. The open kitchen enables guests to view the staff as they prepare breakfast, lunch and dinner for hungry diners. Sunday brunch is a popular choice. Dressy casual. **Bar:** Full bar. **Reservations:** suggested. **Hours:** 6:30 am-10 pm. **Address:** 900 Canada Place Way V6C 3L5 **Location:** Howe St at Cordova St; in The Fairmont Waterfront. **Parking:** on-site (fee) and valet. CALL &M

IL GIARDINO

Phone: 604/669-2422 **47**

Italian
$19-$40

This nice restaurant, which specializes in game, fowl and pasta, is designed to look like the Tuscan villa of its owner, Umberto Menghi. The charming decor features bright colors, open beams and exquisite furniture. Flowers surround the patio, which opens during the warmer months. Wonderful wine and good service further set this place apart. Casual dress. **Bar:** Full bar. **Reservations:** suggested. **Hours:** 11:30 am-11 pm, Sat from 5:30 pm. Closed major holidays; also Sun. **Address:** 1382 Hornby St V6Z 1W5 **Location:** Corner of Pacific and Hornby sts. **Parking:** valet and street. [AC]

IMPERIAL CHINESE SEAFOOD RESTAURANT

Phone: 604/688-8191 **11**

Chinese
$15-$58

Diners at the long-established restaurant should request a table next to one of the floor-to-ceiling windows. Also lending appeal to the dining room are fancy tablecloths with matching napkins and chandeliers hanging from the soaring ceilings. Choices include fresh lobster and crab, shark fin and bird's Chinese dishes, with prices that can range from $15 to $300 for shark fin soup. Casual dress. **Bar:** Full bar. **Reservations:** suggested. **Hours:** 11 am-10:30 pm, Sat & Sun from 10:30 am. **Address:** 355 Burrard St V6C 2G8 **Location:** Between W Hastings and Cordova sts. **Parking:** street.

INDIA BISTRO

Phone: 604/684-6342 **38**

Indian
$9-$14

In the Davie Village, this wonderful Indian restaurant serves well-known and reasonably priced favorites, including naan bread, savory tandoori chicken and a good choice of vegetarian options. Friendly servers circulate through the bright, colorful dining area. Parking is at street meters or in nearby pay lots. Casual dress. **Bar:** Full bar. **Reservations:** suggested, weekend evenings. **Hours:** 11:30 am-11 pm. Closed: 1/1, 12/25. **Address:** 1157 Davie St V6E 1N2 **Location:** Between Bute and Thurlow sts. **Parking:** street.

JOE FORTES SEAFOOD & CHOP HOUSE   *Menu on AAA.com*

Phone: 604/669-1940 **26**

Seafood
$12-$40

Along trendy Robson Street, the San Francisco-style seafood grill allows for delightful rooftop garden dining in season. Also on site are a popular oyster bar and fireplace lounge. Diners are encouraged to ask about turn-of-the-20th-century legend Joe Fortes. Valet service is available weekdays and after 6 pm on weekends. Casual dress. **Bar:** Full bar. **Reservations:** suggested. **Hours:** 11 am-11 pm. Closed: 12/25. **Address:** 777 Thurlow St V6E 3V5 **Location:** Between Robson and Alberni sts. **Parking:** valet and street. CALL &M

KAM'S PLACE SINGAPOREAN CUISINE

Phone: 604/669-3389 **41**

Asian
$9-$15

In the part of West End known as Davie Village, the restaurant dishes up food in huge portions. Lines are not uncommon, and reservations are taken only for large groups. Lunch and dinner specials are worth asking about. Parking can be a challenge, as only metered street spaces and public pay lots are available. Casual dress. **Bar:** Full bar. **Reservations:** accepted. **Hours:** 11 am-2:30 & 5-9:30 pm. Closed: 12/25. **Address:** 1043 Davie St V6E 1M5 **Location:** Between Thurlow and Burrard sts. **Parking:** street.

(See map and index starting on p. 590)

KINGSTON TAPHOUSE & GRILLE   **Phone:** 604/681-7011   39

♦♦♦ ♦♦♦
Canadian
$10-$19

Near BC Place Stadium, the restaurant entices sports enthusiasts to enjoy wood-plank pizzas, burgers and steaks before or after sporting events. When the weather permits, patrons can dine al fresco on one of two large outdoor patios, one being on the rooftop. Casual dress. **Bar:** Full bar. **Reservations:** accepted. **Hours:** 11:30 am–midnight. Closed: 1/1, 12/25. **Address:** 755 Richards St V6B 3A6 **Location:** Between Robson and W Georgia sts. **Parking:** street.

KOBE JAPANESE STEAK HOUSE   **Phone:** 604/684-2451   28

♦♦♦ ♦♦♦
Japanese
$33-$58

Visitors and locals alike enjoy this restaurant's style of dinner, which seats several guests at a teppan table where the chef prepares meals of steak, chicken, shrimp or lobster on the grill in front of them. Casual dress. **Bar:** Full bar. **Reservations:** required. **Hours:** 5:30 pm-9 pm, Thurs-Sat to 10 pm. Closed major holidays. **Address:** 1042 Alberni St V6E 1A3 **Location:** Between Burrard and Thurlow sts. **Parking:** street.

L'ALTRO BUCA   **Phone:** 604/683-6912   5

◆◆◆◆◆◆
Italian
$20-$36

In the lower level of the Buccan Hotel in Vancouver's West End, the restaurant invites guests to sample fine Italian food in a fun, lively setting. Although valet parking is recommended, public pay parking can be found under the West End Community Centre at Haro and Denman streets. Casual dress. **Bar:** Full bar. **Reservations:** required. **Hours:** 5 pm-10 pm, Fri & Sat-11 pm. Closed: major holidays, 12/26. **Address:** 1906 Haro St V6G 1H7 **Location:** Between Gilford and Chilco sts. **Parking:** valet and street.
CALL 🅖🅜 🅚

LA TERRAZZA   **Phone:** 604/899-4449   54

◆◆◆◆◆◆
Northern Italian
$18-$38

Near the Cambie Street bridge in Yaletown, the lovely restaurant features an impressive wine list with many bottles displayed in a huge rack against one wall. On the menu is an array of meat dishes—such as grilled venison, rack of lamb and Cornish game hen—along with some seafood and a choice of pasta. Dressy casual. **Bar:** Full bar. **Reservations:** suggested. **Hours:** 5 pm-11 pm. Closed: 4/4, 12/24-12/26. **Address:** 1088 Cambie St & Pacific Blvd V6B 6J5 **Location:** By Cambie St Bridge. **Parking:** valet and street. CALL 🅖🅜

LE CROCODILE   **Phone:** 604/669-4298   35

◆◆◆◆◆◆◆◆◆
French
$15-$40

The French restaurant's menu emphasizes beef and seafood. The signature dish is Alsatian onion pie; other offerings include grilled lamb chops and pan-fried Dover sole filleted tableside. The atmosphere is bustling, and attentive, longtime servers warmly recognize many returning guests. The trained steward helps match meals to wonderful bottles of wine. Although the decor is simple and table spacing is tight, this popular spot fills quickly. Dressy casual. **Bar:** Full bar. **Reservations:** suggested. **Hours:** 11:30 am-2 & 5:30-10 pm, Sat from 5:30 pm. Closed major holidays; also Sun. **Address:** 100-909 Burrard St on Smithe St V6Z 2N2 **Location:** Smithe and Burrard sts. **Parking:** on-site (fee) and valet. CALL 🅖🅜

LE GAVROCHE RESTAURANT FRANCAIS   **Phone:** 604/685-3924   6

◆◆◆◆◆◆
French
$13-$45

In a small, character house, this charming French restaurant's second-floor dining room affords views of the harbor and North Shore. Try the lamb, beef tenderloin, veal or veal sweetbread. For seafood lovers, there is salmon, prawns and the ever-popular lobster. Dressy casual. **Bar:** Full bar. **Reservations:** suggested. **Hours:** 11:30 am-2:30 & 5:30-10:30 pm, Sat & Sun from 5:30 pm. Closed: 1/1, 12/25, 12/26. **Address:** 1616 Alberni St V6G 1A6 **Location:** Between Cardero and Bidwell sts. **Parking:** street.

LICKERISH   **Phone:** 604/696-0725   43

♦♦♦ ♦♦♦
Pacific Northwest
$7-$25

One of several trendy restaurants on Davie Street, this place sets itself apart by emphasizing food rather than decor. The menu features a wide selection of tapas made for sharing, in addition to more filling main dishes such as cobb salad, AAA-grade beef tenderloin or wonderful mushroom risotto, all reasonably priced. Casual dress. **Bar:** Full bar. **Reservations:** suggested. **Hours:** 4 pm-midnight. Closed: 1/1, 12/25. **Address:** 903 Davie St V62 1B8 **Location:** Between Burrard and Hornby sts. **Parking:** street.

MARKET BY JEAN-GEORGES   **Phone:** 604/695-1115   19

♦♦♦ ♦♦♦
Pacific Northwest
$14-$38

Internationally acclaimed chef Jean-Georges Vongerichten has put his name on this exciting restaurant on the third floor of the Shangri-La Hotel. Offering a truly West Coast experience, this place has four distinct dining areas: the casual cafe, the heated terrace, the fine-dining room and the always busy bar. The reasonably priced six-course market prix fixe offers a sampling of everything this spot has to offer. Dressy casual. **Bar:** Full bar. **Reservations:** suggested. **Hours:** 11:30 am-2:30 & 5-10:30 pm, Sat from 5:30 pm. Closed: 1/1, 5/24, 12/25, 12/26; also Sun. **Address:** 1115 Alberni St V6E 4T9 **Location:** Between Thurlow and Bute sts; in Shangri-La Hotel Vancouver. **Parking:** on-site (fee) and valet. CALL 🅖🅜

MILESTONE'S GRILL AND BAR   **Phone:** 604/684-9111

♦♦ ♦♦
Canadian
$8-$27

Popular with locals, the bustling eatery is a great gathering place. Diners enjoy the relaxed setting and casual menu featuring pasta, pizza, roasted chicken and a tasty choice of egg and brunch options. A nice wine list complements the food choices. Casual dress. **Bar:** Full bar. **Reservations:** accepted. **Hours:** 11 am-11 pm. **Address:** 1109 Hamilton St V6B 2Y1 **Location:** Between Helmcken and Davie sts. **Parking:** street.

MILESTONE'S GRILL AND BAR   **Phone:** 604/682-4477

♦♦ ♦♦
Canadian
$8-$27

Popular with locals, the bustling eatery is a great gathering place. Diners enjoy the relaxed setting and casual menu featuring pasta, pizza, roasted chicken and a tasty choice of egg and brunch options. A nice wine list complements the food choices. Casual dress. **Bar:** Full bar. **Reservations:** suggested, evenings. **Hours:** 11 am-11 pm. **Address:** 1145 Robson St V6E 1B5 **Location:** Between Bute and Thurlow sts. **Parking:** street.

(See map and index starting on p. 590)

MOXIE'S CLASSIC GRILL

Canadian
$9-$25

Phone: 604/678-8043

This sleek, funky and popular restaurant presents an extensive menu of creatively prepared dishes, including pizza, pasta, rice, noodles, signature salads and burgers. Other menus include one for children and one for Sunday brunch. Lending to the upbeat, stylish decor are dark wood appointments and river rock fireplaces. Casual dress. **Entertainment. Hours:** 6:30 am-1 am, Sun-midnight. Closed: 12/25. **Address:** 1160 Davie St V6E 1N1 **Location:** Between Bute and Thurlow sts. **Parking:** on-site (fee) and street. CALL &M

MOXIE'S CLASSIC GRILL

Canadian
$8-$18

Phone: 604/684-8434

This sleek, funky and popular restaurant presents an extensive menu of creatively prepared dishes, including pizza, pasta, rice, noodles, signature salads and burgers. Other menus include one for children and one for Sunday brunch. Lending to the upbeat, stylish decor are dark wood appointments and river rock fireplaces. Casual dress. **Bar:** Full bar. **Hours:** 6 am-midnight, Fri & Sat-1 am. Closed: 12/25. **Address:** 180 W Georgia St V6B 4P4 **Location:** Between Cambie and Beatty sts; in Sandman Hotel Downtown Vancouver. **Parking:** street.

MOXIE'S CLASSIC GRILL

Canadian
$8-$18

Phone: 604/696-9986

This sleek, funky and popular restaurant presents an extensive menu of creatively prepared dishes, including pizza, pasta, rice, noodles, signature salads and burgers. Other menus include one for children and one for Sunday brunch. Lending to the upbeat, stylish decor are dark wood appointments and river rock fireplaces. Casual dress. **Bar:** Full bar. **Hours:** 11 am-midnight, Fri-1 am, Sat 9:30 am-1 am, Sun 9:30 am-11 pm. Closed: 12/25. **Address:** 808 Bute St V6E 1Y4 **Location:** Between Robson and Haro sts. **Parking:** street.

NU

Continental
$13-$37

Phone: 604/646-4668   56

Set along the shoreline, the restaurant has a large bay window overlooking the marina. Cool lights and low, funky chairs re-create the look and feel of the 1970s. Reinventing chicken wings, Nu's removes the meat from the bone, mixes the meat with a sharp cheese, places the meat back on the bone and then deep fries the wings to perfection. Casual dress. **Bar:** Full bar. **Reservations:** suggested. **Hours:** 11:30 am-11 pm, Sat & Sun from 10:30 am. Closed: 12/25. **Address:** 1661 Granville St V6Z 1N3 **Location:** Just off Beach Crescent; under the Granville St Bridge. **Parking:** on-site.

OYSI OYSI JAPANESE RESTAURANT

Japanese
$7-$19

Phone: 604/682-0011   20

The downtown restaurant's menu lists fresh seafood, barbecue and sushi, as well as take-out combination trays. Guests can park in metered street spots or in a limited number of free spaces in underground parking lot stalls 200 through 300 available weekdays after 5 pm and all day Saturday and Sunday. Casual dress. **Bar:** Beer & wine. **Reservations:** accepted, for dinner. **Hours:** 11 am-10:30 pm, Fri-11:30 pm, Sat noon-11:30 pm, Sun noon-10 pm. **Address:** 1136 Alberni St V6E 1A5 **Location:** Between Bute and Thurlow sts. **Parking:** on-site (fee) and street.

PROVENCE MARINASIDE

Pacific Rim
$12-$35

Phone: 604/681-4144   57

The delightful restaurant faces the seawall and a small marina in an area known as Falsecreek. The menu spans breakfast, lunch and dinner, so guests can fit this place into any part of their day. In addition to choices from the antipasti display case, selections include wonderful pasta and panini, as well as beef, chicken and fish entrees. Casual dress. **Bar:** Full bar. **Reservations:** suggested. **Hours:** 8 am-10 pm, Fri & Sat-10:30 pm; seasonal hours may vary. Closed: 12/25. **Address:** 1177 Marinaside Crescent V6Z 2Y3 **Location:** End of Davie St, towards water. **Parking:** street.

RAIN CITY GRILL

Pacific Northwest
$14-$32

Phone: 604/685-7337   10

Pacific Northwest cuisine makes up a menu that includes fresh ingredients and weekly changes. The atmosphere is simple yet stately, the service staff attentive and nicely attired, and the wine list extensive. Seating is limited, so it's a good idea to make a reservation, especially on the weekend. Dressy casual. **Bar:** Full bar. **Reservations:** suggested. **Hours:** 11:30 am-2:30 & 5-11 pm, Sat & Sun from 10:30 am. Closed: 12/25, 12/26. **Address:** 1193 Denman St V6G 2N1 **Location:** Just n of jct Denman and Davie sts. **Parking:** valet and street.

REX ROTISSERIE & GRILL

Southwestern
$12-$36

Phone: 604/683-7390   17

Catering to the area's business crowd, the restaurant is busy during lunch and less hectic around dinnertime. Choices include hot rotisserie chicken and prime rib, in addition to freshly made sandwiches and some pasta dishes. Patio seating is a seasonal option. Guests can have parking validated after 5 pm. Casual dress. **Bar:** Full bar. **Reservations:** suggested, for lunch. **Hours:** 11:30 am-3 & 5-9:30 pm. Closed major holidays; also Sat & Sun. **Address:** 1055 Dunsmuir St V7X 1G4 **Location:** Between Thurlow and Burrard sts; plaza level of Bentall Centre. **Parking:** street.

RICKY'S ALL DAY GRILL

Canadian
$6-$15

Phone: 604/602-9233

The comfortable eatery, which employs friendly servers, presents a varied menu that includes pasta dishes, wraps, omelets, stir-fry preparations and burgers. Portions are generous. Children's and senior selections are offered. Guests can request seating in a booth or at a table. Casual dress. **Bar:** Full bar. **Hours:** 7 am-8 pm, Sat & Sun from 8 am. **Address:** 104-111 Dunsmuir St V6B 6A3 **Location:** Corner of Dunsmuir and Beatty sts. **Parking:** on-site (fee).

RICKY'S ALL DAY GRILL

Canadian
$6-$15

Phone: 604/669-2781

The comfortable eatery, which employs friendly servers, presents a varied menu that includes pasta dishes, wraps, omelets, stir-fry preparations and burgers. Portions are generous. Children's and senior selections are offered. Guests can request seating in a booth or at a table. Casual dress. **Bar:** Full bar. **Hours:** 7 am-8 pm, Sat & Sun from 8 am. **Address:** 23-200 Burrard St V6C 3L6 **Location:** Between W Hastings and Cordova sts. **Parking:** on-site (fee).

(See map and index starting on p. 590)

THE SANDBAR SEAFOOD RESTAURANT   Phone: 604/669-9030   59

Seafood
$11-$29

More than a century ago, Granville Island was known as "the great sandbar," where native tribes came to fish. Today, the 300-seat fresh seafood restaurant perches on the waterfront and offers great views from every seat. Complimentary parking is available for three hours during the day and all night after 7 pm. Casual dress. **Bar:** Full bar. **Reservations:** suggested, for dinner. **Hours:** 11:30 am-10 pm, Fri & Sat-11 pm. Closed: 12/25. **Address:** 1535 Johnston St V6H 3R9 **Location:** Below the bridge, follow signs to Granville Island. **Parking:** on-site. CALL &M

SHOW CASE RESTAURANT   Phone: 604/639-4040   9

Pacific Northwest
$15-$30

Natural light shining through floor-to-ceiling windows illuminates the restaurant and adjoining bar. Distinctive presentations characterize offerings of West Coast cuisine. Breakfast, lunch and dinner are available daily. Casual dress. **Bar:** Full bar. **Reservations:** suggested. **Hours:** 6:30 am-2 & 5-10 pm. **Address:** 1128 W Hastings St V6E 4R5 **Location:** Between Bute and Thurlow sts; in Vancouver Marriott Pinnacle Downtown. **Parking:** on-site and valet. CALL &M

STEPHO'S SOUVLAKI GREEK TAVERNA   Phone: 604/683-2555   40

Greek
$8-$12

Amid the many shops, bars and coffee houses on bustling Davie Street, the longstanding restaurant is a favorite for its generous plates of reasonably priced rice, roasted potatoes, souvlaki, lamb and chicken. There's often a line, so diners are encouraged to arrive early. Casual dress. **Bar:** Full bar. **Hours:** 11:30 am-11:30 pm. Closed: 12/25. **Address:** 1124 Davie St V6E 1N1 **Location:** Between Bute and Thurlow sts. **Parking:** street.

SUBEEZ CAFE   Phone: 604/687-6107   42

Canadian
$11-$27

Around for more than 12 years, the restaurant serves casual fare to the masses. On the menu are sandwiches, all-day breakfast items, pasta, salads and larger entrees for those who are particularly hungry. The patio opens on warmer days. Casual dress. **Bar:** Full bar. **Hours:** 11 am-1 am, Sun-midnight. Closed: 12/25. **Address:** 891 Homer St V6B 2W2 **Location:** Between Smithe and Robson sts, **Parking:** street. CALL &M

TROPIKA MALAYSIAN & THAI CUISINE   Phone: 604/737-6002   25

Asian
$8-$20

A quick trip through the extensive menu, which combines Malaysian, Thai and Singapore cuisine, turns up Thai curries that are eight hours in preparation, pan-fried roti bread that disappears within seconds of reaching the table and Malaysian chili sauce dishes. The restaurant is on trendy Robson Street. Casual dress. **Bar:** Full bar. **Reservations:** suggested. **Hours:** 11:30 am-10:30 pm. **Address:** 1128 Robson St V6E 1B2 **Location:** Between Bute and Thurlow sts. **Parking:** street.

VERA'S BURGER SHACK   Phone: 604/893-8372

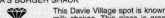
Canadian
$5-$11

This Davie Village spot is known for freshly ground beef burgers, juicy hot dogs, huge onion rings and thick milk shakes. This place is great for something different. Guests can eat in or order for take-out. Casual dress. **Hours:** 11 am-11 pm, Fri & Sat-midnight. Closed: 1/1, 12/25. **Address:** 1030 Davie St V6E 1M3 **Location:** Between Thurlow and Burrard sts. **Parking:** street. CALL &M

VERA'S BURGER SHACK   Phone: 604/228-8372

Canadian
$5-$9

Vera's, as it has come to be known, has received kudos for its burgers for the past few years. The secret to its success is simple, freshly ground beef that's cooked to perfection. In addition to burgers, guests might want to try the dogs, fries, onion rings or daily specials. A children's menu is available. Casual dress. **Hours:** 11 am-11 pm. Closed: 1/1, 12/25. **Address:** 1925 Cornwall Ave V6J 1C8 **Location:** Between Walnut and Cypress sts. **Parking:** street.

VILLA DE LUPO RESTAURANT   Phone: 604/688-7436   44

Italian
$20-$36

A romantic feel envelops the lovely restaurant, where the menu of fine cuisine lists homemade pasta, lamb osso buco and other dishes prepared from fresh, local ingredients. Also offered is a wide range of fine wines. Parking is only at street meters. Casual dress. **Bar:** Full bar. **Reservations:** suggested. **Hours:** 5:30 pm-10 pm. Closed: 1/1, 12/25, 12/26. **Address:** 869 Hamilton St V6B 2R7 **Location:** Between Robson and Smithe sts. **Parking:** street.

VOYA RESTAURANT & LOUNGE   Phone: 604/639-8692   14

Pacific Northwest
$15-$30

This intimate 80-seat restaurant and lounge is where funky meets upscale; it's the only way to describe this distinctive lobby-level restaurant in one of the city's newest boutique hotels. French and Asian inspirations weave through dishes made from ingredients only found locally or from organic growers around the lower mainland of the province. The restaurant is a member of Oceanwise, a sustainable fishing program. Dressy casual. **Bar:** Full bar. **Reservations:** suggested. **Hours:** 6:30 am-2:30 & 5:30-10 pm, Sun-noon. **Address:** 1177 Melville St V6E 0A3 **Location:** Between Bute and Thurlow sts. **Parking:** valet and street. CALL &M

WATER ST. CAFE   Phone: 604/689-2832   29

Italian
$11-$24

In a Victorian building across the street from Old Gastown's steam clock landmark, the elegant yet casual restaurant prepares Continental and Italian cuisine with British Columbia and Canadian West Coast touches. A corner location makes this trendy spot perfect for people-watching. The wonderful selection of warmed breads makes mouths water. With its remnants of red brick walls and large bay windows, the interior evokes an old warehouse. Casual dress. **Bar:** Full bar. **Reservations:** suggested. **Hours:** 11:30 am-10 pm. Closed: 1/1, 12/25. **Address:** 300 Water St V6B 1B6 **Location:** Corner of Cambie and Water sts; in Gastown. **Parking:** street.

(See map and index starting on p. 590)

WHITE SPOT

Phone: 604/681-8034

▼▼ ▼▼
Canadian
$8-$18

Open for three meals a day, the popular casual restaurant prepares offerings such as sandwiches and burgers, fresh salads, pastas and stir-fries, fish and chips, chargrilled sirloin steaks and chicken, in addition to a selection of yummy desserts. Casual dress. **Bar:** Full bar. **Hours:** 6:30 am-11 pm. Closed: 12/25. **Address:** 1616 W Georgia St V6G 2V5 **Location:** Corner of W Georgia and Cardero sts. **Parking:** on-site.

WHITE SPOT

Phone: 604/605-0045

▼▼ ▼▼
Canadian
$8-$18

Open for three meals a day, the popular casual restaurant prepares offerings such as sandwiches and burgers, fresh salads, pastas and stir-fries, fish and chips, chargrilled sirloin steaks and chicken, in addition to a selection of yummy desserts. Casual dress. **Bar:** Full bar. **Hours:** 7 am-10 pm. Closed: 12/25. **Address:** 718 Drake St V6Z 2W6 **Location:** Between Granville and Hornby sts. **Parking:** street.

WHITE SPOT

Phone: 604/662-3066

▼▼ ▼▼
Canadian
$8-$18

Open for three meals a day, the popular casual restaurant prepares offerings such as sandwiches and burgers, fresh salads, pastas and stir-fries, fish and chips, chargrilled sirloin steaks and chicken, in addition to a selection of yummy desserts. Casual dress. **Bar:** Full bar. **Hours:** 6:30 am-11 pm. Closed: 12/25. **Address:** 580 W Georgia St V6B 2A3 **Location:** Corner of W Georgia and Seymour sts. **Parking:** on-site (fee).

WILD RICE

Phone: 604/642-2882   37

▼▼ ▼▼
Asian
$11-$21

The funky eastside bar and Asian eatery caters to the nightclub crowd looking for appetizers to share with fancy and innovative drinks. Just up the street from Tinseltown Cinema, this place is a great pre- or post-movie stop. Street parking is limited, but spots are ample in the nearby parkade. Casual dress. **Bar:** Full bar. **Hours:** 5 pm-11 pm, Fri 11:30 am-midnight, Sat 5 pm-midnight. Closed major holidays. **Address:** 117 W Pender St V6B 1S4 **Location:** Between Beatty and Abbott sts. **Parking:** street. CALL

THE WILLIAM TELL   *Menu on AAA.com*

Phone: 604/688-3504   45

(CAA)
▼▼▼▼
Swiss
$27-$39

The menu, which focuses on Swiss dishes prepared with a French influence, stands out at this long-established restaurant, a favorite of Vancouverites for years. A privacy walls separates the cozy, intimate dining room, which exudes European-style elegance, from the more casual bistro. Among menu favorites are tiger prawns, rack of lamb, steak tartare and Chateaubriand. Attentive staffers serve all tables. Casual dress. **Bar:** Full bar. **Reservations:** suggested. **Hours:** 5:30 pm-9 pm, Sun-8 pm. Closed major holidays; also Mon. **Address:** 765 Beatty St V6B 2M4 **Location:** Between Georgia and Robson sts; in The Georgian Court Hotel. **Parking:** on-site (fee) and valet. *(See color ad p 608)* CALL

WON MORE SZECHUAN CUISINE

Phone: 604/688-8856   13

▼▼ ▼▼
Chinese
$7-$16

The second-floor restaurant overlooks English Bay. The wonderful eatery is known for its dry ginger beef and salt and pepper squid. Those who like it hot and spicy should look for the highlighted items on the menu. Casual dress. **Bar:** Beer & wine. **Hours:** 4 pm-10 pm. Closed: 12/24, 12/25. **Address:** 201-1184 Denman St V6G 2M9 **Location:** Between Davie and Pendrell sts. **Parking:** street.

YALETOWN BREWING COMPANY

Phone: 604/681-2739   52

▼▼ ▼▼
Canadian
$9-$29

In the trendy Yaletown District, the distinctive brewpub offers homemade beers to accompany its thin-crust pizzas and wonderful burgers. On warm days, patrons can unwind on the large outdoor patio. Casual dress. **Bar:** Full bar. **Reservations:** suggested. **Hours:** 11:30 am-10 pm, Fri & Sat-11 pm. Closed: 12/25. **Address:** 1111 Mainland St V6B 5P2 **Location:** Between Helmcken and Davie sts. **Parking:** street. CALL

YEW RESTAURANT & BAR

Phone: 604/692-4939   32

(CAA)
▼▼▼▼
Pacific Northwest
$15-$42

A unique dining room offers extra lofty ceilings, thick beams, wood-paneled walls and a floor-to-ceiling sandstone fireplace to enhance a West Coast feel. Capturing the essence of British Columbia, the chef relies on ingredients from the entire Pacific region. The menu features four meat choices, four fish choices and some pasta choices, and an extensive wine list highlights old world classics as well as favorites from British Columbia, the Pacific Northwest and California. Dressy casual. **Bar:** Full bar. **Reservations:** suggested. **Hours:** 6:30 am-2:30 & 5-10 pm. **Address:** 791 W Georgia St V6C 2T4 **Location:** Between Howe and Granville sts; in Four Seasons Hotel Vancouver. **Parking:** on-site (fee) and valet. CALL

ZEFFERELLI'S RESTAURANT

Phone: 604/687-0655   24

▼▼ ▼▼
Italian
$11-$25

On the second floor above the Cactus Club, many tables offer spectacular views of bustling Robson Street. In operation since 1989, the restaurant boasts it is the best place for delicious pasta dishes, offering reasonably priced menu options with a fine selection of local wines. Casual dress. **Bar:** Full bar. **Reservations:** suggested. **Hours:** 11:30 am-11 pm, Sat from 5 pm, Sun 5 pm-10 pm. Closed: 1/1, 12/25. **Address:** 1136 Robson St V6E 1B2 **Location:** Between Bute and Thurlow sts. **Parking:** street.

ZIN RESTAURANT & LOUNGE

Phone: 604/408-1700   16

▼▼▼▼
International
$10-$30

On trendy Robson Street, the funky restaurant gets its name from zinfandel wines, which servers say pair well with the global cuisine on the wonderful, meant-for-sharing tapas menu. Casual dress. **Bar:** Full bar. **Reservations:** suggested. **Hours:** 7 am-midnight. Closed: 12/25, 12/26. **Address:** 1277 Robson St V6E 1C4 **Location:** Between Jervis and Bute sts; in Pacific Palisades Hotel. **Parking:** on-site (fee) and valet. CALL

VANCOUVER pop. 578,041   (See map and index starting on p. 594)

2400 MOTEL

◇◇◇

Motel
$81-$199 All Year

Phone: (604)434-2464   **7**

Address: 2400 Kingsway V5R 5G9 **Location:** 4.5 mi (7.2 km) se on Hwy 1A and 99A (Kingsway and 33rd Ave). **Facility:** 65 units. 32 one- and 33 two-bedroom standard units, some with kitchens. 1 story, exterior corridors. *Bath:* combo or shower only. **Parking:** on-site. **Terms:** cancellation fee imposed. **Free Special Amenities:** room upgrade (subject to availability with advance reservations) and high-speed Internet. ⓘ X / SOME UNITS FEE ♨ X ▯ ▭

▼ See AAA listing p 654 ▼

Staying at the Best Western in Richmond is more rewarding than ever.

- Complimentary Airport Shuttle Service
- Free Wireless Internet Access
- Free Parking for your Stay
- 100% Non-Smoking Hotel
- Restaurant & Pub On Site

Best Western Abercorn Inn

9260 Bridgeport Road, Richmond, BC V6X 1S1

604.270.7576

1.800.663.0085 | abercorn-inn.com

▼ See AAA listing p 632 ▼

Staying at the Best Western in Vancouver is more rewarding than ever.

- Fitness Solarium
- Free Secured Underground Parking
- Complimentary High Speed Wired & Wireless Internet
- Continental Breakfast Daily
- Heart of Mount Pleasant Close to Downtown

Best Western Uptown

205 Kingsway, Vancouver, BC V5T 3J5

604.267.2000

1.888.234.9111 | bestwesternvancouver.ca

(See map and index starting on p. 594)

BEST WESTERN EXHIBITION PARK

 *Book great rates at AAA.com*

Phone: (604)294-4751

Hotel
$89-$189 3/1-9/30
$79-$169 10/1-2/28

Address: 3475 E Hastings St V5K 2A5 **Location:** Trans-Canada Hwy 1, exit 26; jct Trans-Canada Hwy 1 and 7A. **Facility:** 58 one-bedroom standard units. 3 stories, interior corridors. **Parking:** on-site. **Amenities:** voice mail, irons, hair dryers. **Leisure Activities:** saunas, whirlpool. **Guest Services:** valet and coin laundry, wireless Internet. **Business Services:** PC (fee). **Free Special Amenities:** expanded continental breakfast and early check-in/late check-out.

AAA Benefit:
Members save up to 20%, plus 10% bonus points with rewards program.

BEST WESTERN UPTOWN

Book great rates at AAA.com

Phone: (604)267-2000   4

Hotel
$90-$190 All Year

Address: 205 Kingsway V5T 3J5 **Location:** Corner of E 10th St. **Facility:** Smoke free premises. 69 one-bedroom standard units, some with whirlpools. 4 stories, interior corridors. **Parking:** on-site. **Amenities:** high-speed Internet, voice mail, irons, hair dryers. *Some:* dual phone lines. **Leisure Activities:** limited exercise equipment. **Guest Services:** valet laundry, wireless Internet. **Business Services:** PC. *(See color ad p 631)*

AAA Benefit:
Members save up to 20%, plus 10% bonus points with rewards program.

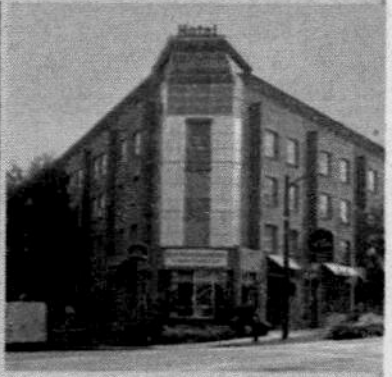

FREE continental breakfast and high-speed Internet

(See map and index starting on p. 594)

DAYS INN-VANCOUVER METRO   *Book great rates at AAA.com*   Phone: (604)876-5531

Motel
$79-$189 3/1-9/30
$59-$129 10/1-2/28

Address: 2075 Kingsway V5N 2T2 **Location:** 3.8 mi (6 km) se on Hwy 1A and 99A (Kingsway and Victoria Dr). **Facility:** 66 one-bedroom standard units. 3 stories (no elevator), exterior corridors. *Bath:* combo or shower only. **Parking:** on-site. **Terms:** cancellation fee imposed. **Amenities:** irons, hair dryers. *Some:* high-speed Internet. **Guest Services:** wireless Internet. **Business Services:** PC (fee).
(See color ad p 607)

FREE continental breakfast and high-speed Internet

HOLIDAY INN EXPRESS VANCOUVER   *Book great rates at AAA.com*   Phone: (604)254-1000

Hotel
$119-$309 3/1-9/30
$119-$189 10/1-2/28

Address: 2889 E Hastings St V5K 2A1 **Location:** Between Renfrew and Kaslo sts. **Facility:** Smoke free premises. 100 units. 99 one-bedroom standard units. 1 one-bedroom suite. 4 stories, interior corridors. **Parking:** on-site. **Terms:** check-in 4 pm, cancellation fee imposed. **Amenities:** video games (fee), dual phone lines, voice mail, irons, hair dryers. **Leisure Activities:** sauna, exercise room. **Guest Services:** valet and coin laundry, wireless Internet. **Business Services:** meeting rooms.
(See color ad p 611)

FREE expanded continental breakfast and high-speed Internet

▼ See AAA listing p 656 ▼

(See map and index starting on p. 594)

▼ See AAA listing p 652 ▼

(See map and index starting on p. 594)

HOLIDAY INN VANCOUVER-CENTRE (BROADWAY)   *Book at AAA.com*   Phone: (604)879-0511   **3**

Hotel
$115-$249 All Year

Address: 711 W Broadway V5Z 3Y2 **Location:** Between Heather and Willow sts. **Facility:** Smoke free premises. 200 one-bedroom standard units. 16 stories, interior corridors. **Parking:** on-site (fee). **Terms:** cancellation fee imposed. **Amenities:** high-speed Internet, voice mail, irons, hair dryers. **Pool(s):** heated indoor. **Leisure Activities:** sauna, exercise room. **Guest Services:** valet and coin laundry. **Business Services:** meeting rooms, PC (fee). *(See color ad on insert)*

ECO ASK 〒 ▽ CALL ⬅M 🏊 ✕ 🎥 💻 / SOME UNITS 🛗

PLAZA 500 HOTEL   *Book great rates at AAA.com*   Phone: (604)873-1811   **5**

CAA SAVE

Hotel
$189-$329 All Year

Address: 500 W 12th Ave V5Z 1M2 **Location:** Corner of W 12th Ave at Cambie St. **Facility:** Smoke free premises. 153 one-bedroom standard units. 17 stories, interior corridors. **Parking:** on-site (fee) and valet. **Terms:** check-in 4 pm, 14 day cancellation notice-fee imposed. **Amenities:** dual phone lines, voice mail, irons, hair dryers. *Some:* high-speed Internet (fee). **Guest Services:** valet laundry, wireless Internet. **Business Services:** conference facilities, business center. **Free Special Amenities:** room upgrade and preferred room (each subject to availability with advance reservations).

〒 ▽ CALL ⬅M ➕ ✕ 🎥 💻 / SOME UNITS 🛗

▼ See AAA listing p 652 ▼

▼ See AAA listing p 658 ▼

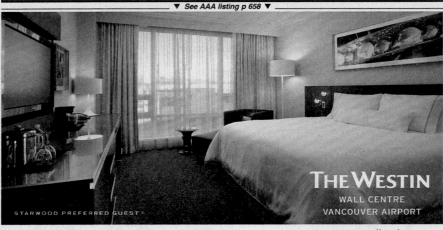

(See map and index starting on p. 594)

——— WHERE TO DINE ———

ABIGAIL'S PARTY

Phone: 604/739-4677 ④

▼▼▼

Canadian
$8-$22

The owners of the cheeky Kitsilano tapas eatery chose this name because it's fun and sexy, as is the warm interior with low lighting and cool music. Selections from the small, selective wine list complement a monthly changing menu. Tapas dishes are big enough to share, and servers are attentive and friendly. Parking is at street meters or in two-hour spots around the neighborhood. Casual dress. **Bar:** Full bar. **Reservations:** suggested. **Hours:** 5:30 pm-2 am, Sat also 9 am-2:30 pm, Sun 9 am-2:30 & 5:30-11 pm; Saturday & Sunday brunch. Closed: 1/1, 12/25. **Address:** 1685 Yew St V6K 3E6 **Location:** Between Cornwall and 1st Ave; in Kitsiland District. **Parking:** street.

AVENUE GRILL

Phone: 604/266-8183 ㉙

▼▼▼

Italian
$8-$20

In the trendy Kerrisdale neighborhood, the long-established restaurant has limited space, making reservations a good idea, especially on weekends. Tables are tightly spaced, but seating is comfortable. The main draw is the food: standard breakfast selections, fresh sandwiches, daily soups and blue-plate specials for lunch; and many pasta dishes made from more than 40 toppings on the dinner menu. Most parking is along the street. Casual dress. **Bar:** Full bar. **Reservations:** required, weekends. **Hours:** 8 am-10 pm, Sun-3:30 pm. Closed: 12/25. **Address:** 2114 W 41st Ave V6M 1Z1 **Location:** Between Yew St and W Boulevard. **Parking:** street.

BISHOP'S

Phone: 604/738-2025 ⑦

▼▼▼ ▼▼▼

Pacific Northwest
$34-$38

The long-established restaurant has been serving wonderful contemporary North American cuisine for more than 20 years. The weekly changing menu highlights the season's freshest ingredients, such as British Columbia salmon, which has a short season. Try the signature death by chocolate dessert. Dressy casual. **Bar:** Full bar. **Reservations:** required. **Hours:** 5:30 pm-11 pm, Sun-10 pm. Closed: 12/24-12/26; also 1/1-1/15. **Address:** 2183 W 4th Ave V6K 1N7 **Location:** Between Arbutus and Yew sts. **Parking:** street.

CACTUS CLUB CAFE

Phone: 604/733-0434

▼▼▼

Canadian
$9-$29

This bustling, casual restaurant serves huge burgers, sandwiches, pasta, salads, soups, quesadillas, fajitas, vegetarian dishes, steak, ribs, chicken and fish. Featured are certified Angus beef and fresh wild British Columbia salmon. The thick and creamy milk shakes come highly recommended. Casual dress. **Bar:** Full bar. **Hours:** 11 am-midnight, Fri & Sat-1 am. Closed: 12/25. **Address:** 1530 W Broadway V6J 5K9 **Location:** Between W Broadway and Fir St. **Parking:** street.

CACTUS CLUB CAFE

Phone: 604/714-6000

▼▼▼

Canadian
$9-$29

This bustling, casual restaurant serves huge burgers, sandwiches, pasta, salads, soups, quesadillas, fajitas, vegetarian dishes, steak, ribs, chicken and fish. Featured are certified Angus beef and fresh wild British Columbia salmon. The thick and creamy milk shakes come highly recommended. Casual dress. **Bar:** Full bar. **Hours:** 11 am-midnight, Fri & Sat-1 am. Closed: 12/25. **Address:** 575 W Broadway V5Z 1E6 **Location:** Corner of W Broadway and Ash St. **Parking:** street.

THE CANNERY

Menu on AAA.com

Phone: 604/254-9606 ②

Seafood
$15-$40

For 40 years, the restaurant has set the standard for fresh seafood. In an industrial section of town, it's well worth the visit. The setting offers a memorable view of the harbor, mountains and sea lions at play. The many fresh seafood dishes, such as salmon Wellington, and local wines are excellent. Casual dress. **Bar:** Full bar. **Reservations:** suggested. **Hours:** 11:30 am-2:30 & 5:30-9 pm, Fri-9:30 pm, Sat 10:30 am-2 & 5-9:30 pm, Sun 10:30 am-2 & 5-9 pm; Saturday & Sunday brunch. Closed: 12/24-12/26. **Address:** 2205 Commissioner St V5L 1A4 **Location:** E Hastings St to Renfrew St, just n to McGill St, just e to Commissioner St, then 0.9 mi (1.5 km) n. **Parking:** on-site.

FUEL RESTAURANT

Phone: 604/288-7905 ⑫

▼▼▼ ▼

Pacific Northwest
$12-$30

Along trendy Fourth Avenue, the restaurant prepares weekly changing offerings of superb regional cuisine from ingredients purchased from local farmers and purveyors. The kitchen looks right out onto the street, providing a hook for captivated passers-by. Dressy casual. **Bar:** Full bar. **Reservations:** suggested. **Hours:** noon-2:30 & 5:30-10 pm, Sat & Sun from 5:30 pm. Closed major holidays. **Address:** 1944 W 4th Ave V6J 1M5 **Location:** Between Cypress and Maple sts. **Parking:** street. 🗝

GRAMERCY GRILL

Phone: 604/730-5666 ㉑

▼▼▼ ▼

Pacific Rim
$9-$33

Named after a New York district, the restaurant offers a dark-wood interior, comfortable booths and tables and a showpiece bar. During warm days and evenings, patrons gather on the pleasant patio. Prices for such dishes as osso buco, roast lamb sirloin, game hen and, of course, West Coast salmon are reasonable. Several wines by the glass are available. Casual dress. **Bar:** Full bar. **Reservations:** suggested. **Hours:** 11:30 am-11 pm, Sun from 10 am. Closed: 12/25. **Address:** 2685 Arbutus St V6J 3Y4 **Location:** Between W 10th and W 11th aves. **Parking:** street. CALL ♿Ⓜ

HELL'S KITCHEN

Phone: 604/736-4355 ⑩

▼▼▼

Canadian
$9-$25

This busy publike restaurant features hearty food to go with the beers on tap. Among good choices are the burger with sweet yam fries and a delightful dipping sauce, or the "pizza from hell," made in the classic New York thin crust style. Diners can choose from a wide array of toppings (perhaps the "Daisy Duke" or "The Naked Chef"?) or create their own. Parking is in metered street spots only. Casual dress. **Bar:** Full bar. **Hours:** 11:30 am-1 am, Fri-2 am, Sat & Sun 10 am-2 am. Closed: 12/25. **Address:** 2041 W 4th Ave V6J 1N3 **Location:** Between Arbutus and Maple sts. **Parking:** street. CALL ♿Ⓜ

LAS MARGARITAS RESTAURANTE & CANTINA

Phone: 604/734-7117 ⑪

▼▼▼

Mexican
$12-$19

Mexican appointments accent the bright, festive dining room, where diners scan a menu of healthy choices, as well as fajitas, grilled salmon burritos and chipotle chicken. Servers are prompt and attentive. Those who don't secure one of the six parking stalls behind the building can opt for metered street parking. Casual dress. **Bar:** Full bar. **Reservations:** suggested, except Fri-Sun. **Hours:** 11:30 am-10 pm, Fri & Sat-11 pm. Closed: 12/25. **Address:** 1999 W 4th Ave V6J 1M7 **Location:** Between Cypress and Maple sts. **Parking:** on-site and street.

(See map and index starting on p. 594)

LOMBARDO'S RISTORANTE PIZZERIA

Phone: 604/251-2240

Pizza
$12-$20

Located in the Il Mercata Mall, Lombardo's is known as one of the oldest brick-oven pizza houses in town, and it offers 20 types of pizza. The lasagna is very good also. Locals and visitors alike enjoy the family-style atmosphere, though seating is a bit limited. Casual dress. **Bar:** Beer & wine. **Hours:** 11 am-11 pm, Sun-10 pm. Closed: 1/1, 12/25. **Address:** 120 1641 Commercial Dr V5L 3A4 **Location:** Corner of 1st St and Commercial Dr; in Il Mercato Mall. **Parking:** on-site (fee) and street.

LUMIERE

Phone: 604/739-8185

French
$65-$175

The restaurant merges European elegance, North American flair and Asian minimalism. Food critics worldwide have bestowed accolades on this place, a must for visitors to the city. Superstar New York chef Daniel Boulud lends his expertise as an owner/partner. Valet parking is available Thursday through Sunday. Dressy casual. **Bar:** Full bar. **Reservations:** required. **Hours:** 5:30 pm-10:30 pm. Closed: 1/1, 12/25, 12/26; also Mon & Tues. **Address:** 2551 W Broadway V6K 2E9 **Location:** Between Trafalgar and Larch sts. **Parking:** valet and street.   CALL

MAURYA INDIAN CUISINE

Phone: 604/742-0622

Indian
$12-$25

Representative of the cuisine are moist, flavorful tandoori chicken, vindaloo lamb and a number of vegetarian dishes. Yummy naan bread comes with three dipping sauces. Lending to the warm, inviting atmosphere are rich wood accents and professional decoration down to the last detail. Parking is at the back of the restaurant or at street meters. Casual dress. **Bar:** Full bar. **Reservations:** suggested. **Hours:** 11:30 am-2:30 & 5-11 pm, Sun 11:30 am-3 & 5-11 pm. **Address:** 1643 W Broadway V6J 1W9 **Location:** Between Fir and Pine sts. **Parking:** on-site and street.

MEMPHIS BLUES BARBEQUE HOUSE

Phone: 604/215-2599

Barbecue
$8-$25

A sure sign that diners are likely to get messy fingers and faces is the roll of paper towels at each table. Savory favorites include slabs of ribs, pulled pork, Cornish game hens and, of course, heaps of barbecue wings. Casual dress. **Bar:** Full bar. **Hours:** 11 am-10 pm, Sat noon-11 pm, Sun noon-10 pm. Closed: 12/25, 12/26. **Address:** 1342 Commercial Dr V5L 3X6 **Location:** Between Kitchener and Charles sts. **Parking:** street.

MEMPHIS BLUES BARBEQUE HOUSE

Phone: 604/738-6806

Barbecue
$8-$25

A sure sign that diners are likely to get messy fingers and faces is the roll of paper towels at each table. Savory favorites include slabs of ribs, pulled pork, Cornish game hens and, of course, heaps of barbecue wings. Casual dress. **Bar:** Full bar. **Hours:** 11 am-10 pm, Sat noon-11 pm, Sun noon-10 pm. Closed: 12/25, 12/26. **Address:** 1465 W Broadway V6H 1H6 **Location:** Between Granville and Hemlock sts. **Parking:** street.

MISTRAL FRENCH BISTRO

Phone: 604/733-0046

French
$14-$29

The quaint French bistro serves wonderful lunches and dinners with a heavy reliance on meats such as roast chicken, veal and New York grade A beef. Amazing desserts made on the premises are the highlight here. Parking is offered at metered spots along the street. Casual dress. **Bar:** Full bar. **Reservations:** suggested. **Hours:** 11:30 am-2 & 5:30-10 pm. Closed: 1/1, 12/25, 12/26; also Sun & Mon. **Address:** 2585 W Broadway V6K 2E9 **Location:** Between Trafalgar and Larch sts. **Parking:** street.
CALL

MONK MCQUEEN'S

Phone: 604/877-1351

Seafood
$15-$40

The restaurant affords great views of the mountains and the south shore of False Creek, with its numerous moored sailboats and condominiums. Two moods are sustained: casual in the downstairs area and more upscale upstairs, where the sounds of live jazz filter out on Wednesday through Sunday evenings in summer and on weekends in winter. Casual dress. **Bar:** Full bar. **Reservations:** suggested. **Hours:** 11:30 am-9:30 pm, Sat & Sun 11 am-10 pm. Closed: 12/25, 12/26. **Address:** 601 Stamps Landing V5Z 3Z1 **Location:** W 6th Ave and Moberly Rd; just w of Cambie St Bridge. **Parking:** valet and street.   CALL

MOXIE'S CLASSIC GRILL

Phone: 604/678-9973

Canadian
$8-$18

This sleek, funky and popular restaurant presents an extensive menu of creatively prepared dishes, including pizza, pasta, rice, noodles, signature salads and burgers. Other menus include one for children and one for Sunday brunch. Lending to the upbeat, stylish decor are dark wood appointments and river rock fireplaces. Casual dress. **Bar:** Full bar. **Hours:** 11 am-midnight, Fri & Sat-1 am. **Address:** 1759 W Broadway V6J 4S5 **Location:** Between Burrard and Pine sts. **Parking:** on-site (fee).

THE OUISI BISTRO

Phone: 604/732-7550

Cajun
$8-$23

In the mix of high-end shops and restaurants along trendy Granville Street, the low-key restaurant serves Louisiana Creole and Cajun dishes from its open kitchen. Certain times of the year usher in live jazz in the evenings. Parking is at street meters. Casual dress. **Bar:** Full bar. **Reservations:** suggested. **Hours:** 11 am-1 am, Sat & Sun from 9 am. Closed: 12/25. **Address:** 3014 Granville St V6H 3J8 **Location:** Between W 15th and W 14th sts. **Parking:** street.

PINK PEARL CHINESE RESTAURANT

Phone: 604/253-4316

Chinese
$4-$19

Pink Pearl's focus is on fresh ingredients, local produce and West Coast seafood. An excellent and varied array of dim sum items is offered 9 am-3 pm This restaurant has received numerous write-ups in newspapers, magazines and travel guides. Casual dress. **Bar:** Full bar. **Reservations:** accepted. **Hours:** 9 am-10 pm, Fri & Sat-11 pm. **Address:** 1132 E Hastings St V6A 1S2 **Location:** Just w of Clark St; between Glen and Vernon sts. **Parking:** on-site.   CALL

(See map and index starting on p. 594)

PROVENCE MEDITERRANEAN GRILL
Phone: 604/222-1980   16

Mediterranean
$10-$29

The pleasant restaurant serves casual southern French and Italian cuisine in a warm neighborhood atmosphere. At the end of the month, the owners have a culinary tasting or chef's sampling at a set price. Guests can walk off their meal afterward by checking out the nearby shops. Casual dress. **Bar:** Full bar. **Reservations:** suggested. **Hours:** 11:30 am-10 pm, Sat-11 pm, Sun 10 am-10 pm. Closed: 12/25. **Address:** 100-4473 W 10th Ave V6R 2H2 **Location:** Between Sasamat and Trimble sts. **Parking:** street.

QUATTRO ON FOURTH
Phone: 604/734-4444   6

Italian
$20-$39

In the heart of Kitsilano, this restaurant features an airy, fun and lively decor; it makes you feel like you're in Tuscany. This place has a great local reputation, with menu highlights such as Cornish game hen or pistachio-crusted sable fish. Diners here with a group should try the made-for-sharing antipasto platter. During warmer weather, this place opens its large patio. Service is good, too. Casual dress. **Bar:** Full bar. **Reservations:** suggested. **Hours:** 5 pm-10 pm, Fri & Sat-11 pm. Closed: 1/1, 12/25, 12/26. **Address:** 2611 W 4th Ave V6K 1P8 **Location:** Between MacDonald and Trafalgar sts. **Parking:** street. CALL &M

RASPUTIN
Phone: 604/879-6675   18

Russian
$13-$25

The restaurant's Russian cuisine is as rich and varied as the land it comes from. A typical meal usually features several appetizers accompanied by shots of vodka. Representative of the fare are Ukrainian borscht, black caviar and pirozhki, Russia's famous stuffed buns. Dinner entrees include kebabs, chicken Kiev and "the feast," a mixed grill of several items. Casual dress. **Bar:** Full bar. **Reservations:** suggested, weekends. **Hours:** 5 pm-11 pm, Fri & Sat-midnight. Closed: 1/1, 12/25; also Mon. **Address:** 457 W Broadway V5Y 1R4 **Location:** Between Cambie and Yukon sts. **Parking:** street.

RED DOOR PAN ASIAN GRILL
Phone: 604/733-5699   23

Asian
$7-$18

Across the bridge from downtown and along a trendy part of Granville Street, the distinctive Asian restaurant designs plates for sharing, which allows patrons to sample a variety of reasonably priced dishes. The decor incorporates plenty of black and red, and service is fast and friendly. Casual dress. **Bar:** Full bar. **Hours:** 11:30 am-11 pm, Fri & Sat-midnight, Sun 11:30 am-10 pm. Closed: 12/25. **Address:** 2996 Granville St V6H 3J7 **Location:** Corner of W 14th St. **Parking:** on-site. CALL &M

RUGBY BEACH CLUB GRILLE
Phone: 604/736-2438   20

Canadian
$8-$18

The 250-seat restaurant is spacious and comfortable, but when this place gets going, it gets noisy. The energy buzz is a big part of the appeal, as is the food, which is priced a la carte. Drink prices are among the cheapest in town. Pay parking can be found on the street or in lots. Casual dress. **Bar:** Full bar. **Reservations:** suggested. **Hours:** 4:24 pm-11 pm. Closed: 12/25. **Address:** 201-950 W Broadway V5Z 1K7 **Location:** Between Oak and Laurel sts. **Parking:** street. CALL &M

SAWASDEE THAI RESTAURANT
Phone: 604/876-4030   26

Thai
$8-$13

Flavorful food and pleasant service are hallmarks of the popular restaurant, which is outside the downtown core on a street with various other shops and restaurants. Decor includes pale walls with various framed posters of Thailand, and clean, comfortable surroundings. Casual dress. **Bar:** Full bar. **Reservations:** suggested, weekends. **Hours:** 11:30 am-2:30 & 5-10 pm, Sat & Sun from 5 pm. Closed: 10/11, 12/25. **Address:** 4250 Main St V5V 3P9 **Location:** Main St and 27th Ave. **Parking:** street.

SEASONS IN THE PARK RESTAURANT
Phone: 604/874-8008   27

Pacific Northwest
$11-$34

Atop a small hill in Queen Elizabeth Park, the restaurant affords lovely views of the park and its flowers. Fish and meat preparations stand out on the menu. Access to the park and restaurant is via either Cambie or Main streets. Dressy casual. **Bar:** Full bar. **Reservations:** suggested. **Hours:** 11:30 am-10 pm, Sun from 10:30 am. Closed: 12/25. **Address:** 33rd Ave & Cambie St V6G 3E7 **Location:** Between Main and Cambie sts; at 33rd Ave; in Queen Elizabeth Park. **Parking:** on-site (fee) and valet. CALL &M

SHAUGHNESSY RESTAURANT AT VANDUSEN GARDEN
Phone: 604/261-0011   28

Pacific Northwest
$14-$30

Overlooking the wonderful Vandusen Gardens, the quiet haven uses fresh ingredients in beautiful lunch and dinner entrees. Among daily specials are homemade soups. Ask about the chicken pot pie, a longtime favorite. After the meal, enjoy a stroll through the gardens. Casual dress. **Bar:** Full bar. **Reservations:** suggested. **Hours:** 11:30 am-9 pm, Sat & Sun from 11 am. Closed: 12/25. **Address:** 5251 Oak St V6M 4H1 **Location:** Between W 33rd and W 37th aves. **Parking:** on-site. CALL &M K

SOPHIE'S COSMIC CAFE
Phone: 604/732-6810   9

Canadian
$7-$17

Guests should be prepared to stand in line for this popular restaurant, the walls of which are covered with decorations that serve as reminders of a bygone time. Breakfast is the specialty meal—and portions are plentiful—but burgers, sandwiches and daily specials rarely disappoint. Parking is only at meters. Casual dress. **Bar:** Full bar. **Hours:** 8 am-9 pm. Closed: 12/25; also for dinner 12/24. **Address:** 2095 W 4th Ave V6J 1N3 **Location:** Between Arbutus and Maple sts. **Parking:** street.

SWISS CHALET
Phone: 604/732-8100

Swiss
$6-$19

The popular restaurant is known for its rotisserie chicken and ribs and the tangy Chalet sauce that gives food its special zip. Diners munch on a half or quarter chicken with sides such as steamed vegetables, fries, baked potatoes and salads. Lunch guests often go for the great soup and sandwich combination. Take-out and delivery service are popular options. Casual dress. **Bar:** Full bar. **Hours:** 11 am-10 pm, Fri & Sat-11 pm. Closed: 12/25. **Address:** 3204 W Broadway V6K 2H4 **Location:** Between Blenheim and Trutch sts. **Parking:** on-site. CALL &M

TEA HOUSE IN STANLEY PARK
Phone: 604/669-3281   1

Pacific Northwest
$17-$39

In the charming country-garden setting of Stanley Park, the restaurant affords spectacular views of English Bay and the mountains. The menu standout is the fabulous roasted rack of lamb. Couples and visitors especially enjoy the atmosphere of casual elegance. Pay parking is in effect. Casual dress. **Bar:** Full bar. **Reservations:** suggested. **Hours:** 11:30 am-2:30 & 5:30-9:45 pm, Sun from 11 am, Sun from 10:30 am; Saturday & Sunday brunch. Closed: 12/25. **Address:** 7501 Stanley Park Dr V6G 3E2 **Location:** Ferguson Point; in Stanley Park. **Parking:** on-site (fee). CALL &M

(See map and index starting on p. 594)

TOJO'S RESTAURANT   **Phone:** 604/872-8050

Japanese
$17-$34

Each item on the menu is prepared using traditional Japanese methods, the freshest ingredients and no monosodium glutamate. Locals rave about the food, and patrons might spot celebrities dining alongside them. Worth a try are the omakase dinners, similar to a chef's tasting menu, where the restaurant arranges a meal for $60, $80 or $110. If that's not appealing, guests can simply order a la carte. Street meters are the best parking option, as there's no on-site parking. Casual dress. **Bar:** Full bar. **Reservations:** required. **Hours:** 5 pm-10 pm. Closed: 12/25; also Sun & 1/1-1/15. **Address:** 1133 W Broadway V6H 1G1 **Location:** Between Spruce and Alder sts. **Parking:** street. CALL

TOMATO FRESH FOOD CAFE   **Phone:** 604/874-6020

Canadian
$8-$23

Near the shops and businesses along trendy Broadway Street, the distinctive neighborhood bistro prepares incredibly fresh comfort food with an innovative spin. Table spacing is a bit tight, but the atmosphere and service are pleasant. A small sidewalk patio opens on warm pleasant days. Casual dress. **Bar:** Beer & wine. **Reservations:** accepted. **Hours:** 9 am-10 pm. Closed: 12/25. **Address:** 2486 Bayswater St V6K 4B3 **Location:** Corner of Broadway and Bayswater St. **Parking:** on-site and street. CALL

TRAFALGARS BISTRO   **Phone:** 604/739-0555   ②⑤

Regional
Continental
$12-$27

The lamb and ground pork burger, fresh-made soups of the day and all-day egg dishes are popular choices at the inviting bistro, which occupies a small neighborhood shopping complex. This place serves brunch daily, and reservations are all but a must at dinnertime, when the tightly spaced tables fill quickly. The owners describe the food as being "French based with some Asian influences," but most patrons would describe it as being good and reasonably priced. Casual dress. **Bar:** Full bar. **Reservations:** suggested, evenings. **Hours:** 11 am-10 pm, Fri-11 pm, Sat 10 am-11 pm, Sun 10 am-4 pm. Closed: 12/25, 12/26. **Address:** 2603 W 16th Ave V6K 3C2 **Location:** Between Trafalgar and Stephens sts. **Parking:** street.

WEST RESTAURANT   **Phone:** 604/738-8938   ②②

Pacific Northwest
$30-$45

On trendy South Granville Street, this restaurant has been recognized with several awards, especially for its innovative wine list and magnificent "wall of wine," which holds some 3,000 wines from 750 labels. The menu highlights British Columbia's finest seafood, game, organic and local ingredients. The in-house pastry chef makes all the fresh breads, sorbets, ice creams, chocolates and desserts. Dressy casual. **Bar:** Full bar. **Reservations:** suggested. **Hours:** 11:30 am-2 & 5:30-11 pm, Sat & Sun from 5:30 pm. Closed: 1/1, 12/25. **Address:** 2881 Granville St V6H 3J4 **Location:** Between 12th and 13th aves. **Parking:** valet and street.

CALL

WHITE SPOT   **Phone:** 604/261-2820

Canadian
$8-$18

Open for three meals a day, the popular casual restaurant prepares offerings such as sandwiches and burgers, fresh salads, pastas and stir-fries, fish and chips, chargrilled sirloin steaks and chicken, in addition to a selection of yummy desserts. Casual dress. **Bar:** Full bar. **Hours:** 7:30 am-10 pm, Fri & Sat-11 pm. Closed: 4/4, 12/25. **Address:** 613A-650 41st Ave V5Z 2M9 **Location:** 41st Ave and Cambie St; in Oakridge Mall. **Parking:** on-site.

WHITE SPOT   **Phone:** 604/873-1252

Canadian
$8-$18

Open for three meals a day, the popular casual restaurant prepares offerings such as sandwiches and burgers, fresh salads, pastas and stir-fries, fish and chips, chargrilled sirloin steaks and chicken, in addition to a selection of yummy desserts. Casual dress. **Bar:** Full bar. **Hours:** 6:30 am-10 pm, Fri & Sat-11 pm. Closed: 12/25. **Address:** 2850 Cambie St V5Z 1V5 **Location:** Corner of Cambie and 13th sts. **Parking:** on-site and street.

The Vancouver Vicinity

ALDERGROVE pop. 12,363

BURNABY   pop. 202,799   (See map and index starting on p. 594)

ACCENT INNS
Book great rates at AAA.com   Phone: (604)473-5000   22

(CAA) (SAVE)

▼▼

Hotel

$119-$179 All Year

Address: 3777 Henning Dr V5C 6N5 **Location:** Trans-Canada Hwy 1, exit 28 (Grandview Hwy), just n on Boundary Rd. **Facility:** Smoke free premises. 128 one-bedroom standard units, some with efficiencies. 3 stories, exterior corridors. **Parking:** on-site. **Amenities:** voice mail, irons, hair dryers. **Leisure Activities:** sauna, whirlpool, exercise room. **Guest Services:** valet and coin laundry, wireless Internet. **Business Services:** meeting rooms, business center. **Free Special Amenities: newspaper and high-speed Internet.**

ECO 🍴 CALL &M ⊠ ✕ 🎥 🔒 📠 💻 / SOME UNITS FEE 🐾

BEST WESTERN KINGS INN AND CONFERENCE CENTRE
Book great rates at AAA.com   Phone: (604)438-1383   26

(CAA) (SAVE)

▼▼▼

Hotel

$159-$169 3/1-9/30
$119-$139 10/1-2/28

Address: 5411 Kingsway V5H 2G1 **Location:** Trans-Canada Hwy 1, exit 29 (Willingdon Ave), 1.9 mi (3 km) s to Kingsway, then 1.2 mi (2 km) e. **Facility:** 137 one-bedroom standard units, some with efficiencies, kitchens and/or whirlpools. 2 stories (no elevator), exterior corridors. **Parking:** on-site. **Amenities:** high-speed Internet, voice mail, irons, hair dryers. **Pool(s):** heated outdoor. **Guest Services:** valet and coin laundry, wireless Internet. **Business Services:** meeting rooms, PC. *(See color ad below)*

AAA Benefit:
Members save up to 20%, plus 10% bonus points with rewards program.

🍴 🏊 ♿ 🎥 🔒 💻 / SOME UNITS FEE 🐾 ✕ 📠

FREE continental breakfast and local telephone calls

DELTA BURNABY HOTEL AND CONFERENCE CENTRE
Book great rates at AAA.com   Phone: (604)453-0750   23

(CAA) (SAVE)

▼▼▼▼

Hotel

$139-$279 All Year

Address: 4331 Dominion St V5G 1B2 **Location:** Trans-Canada Hwy 1, exit 29 (Willingdon Ave S), just w on Canada Way, then n on Sumner St. **Facility:** Among the city's newest hotels, this luxurious spot offers two floors of fun in its on-site casino, which is open around the clock. Smoke free premises. 200 units. 189 one-bedroom standard units. 10 one- and 1 two-bedroom suites. 21 stories, interior corridors. *Bath:* combo or shower only. **Parking:** on-site (fee) and valet. **Terms:** cancellation fee imposed. **Amenities:** high-speed Internet (fee), dual phone lines, voice mail, irons, hair dryers. *Some:* safes. **Dining:** Ebo Restaurant and Lounge, see separate listing. **Leisure Activities:** whirlpool, steamroom, exercise room. **Guest Services:** valet laundry, wireless Internet. **Business Services:** conference facilities, business center. *(See color ad p 643)*

🌀 🍴 🍸 CALL &M ⊠ ✕ 🎥 💻 / SOME UNITS FEE 🐾 🔒

▼ See AAA listing above ▼

(See map and index starting on p. 594)

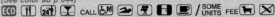
▼ See AAA listing p 642 ▼

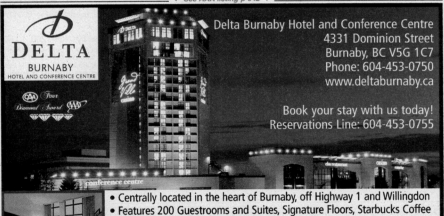

(See map and index starting on p. 594)

HOLIDAY INN EXPRESS METROTOWN *Book at AAA.com* Phone: (604)438-1881 **25**

Hotel
$109-$199 1/1-2/28
$99-$189 3/1-12/31

Address: 4405 Central Blvd V5H 4M3 **Location:** Trans-Canada Hwy 1, exit 29 (Willingdon Ave), 3.1 mi (5 km) s to Central Blvd, then just e. Adjacent to a large shopping centre. **Facility:** Smoke free premises. 100 one-bedroom standard units. 6 stories, interior corridors. **Parking:** on-site. **Terms:** check-in 4 pm, cancellation fee imposed. **Amenities:** voice mail, irons, hair dryers. **Pool(s):** heated outdoor. **Leisure Activities:** exercise room. **Guest Services:** valet and coin laundry, wireless Internet. **Business Services:** meeting rooms, PC (fee). *(See color ad on insert)*

LAKE CITY INN & SUITES Phone: (604)294-5331 **21**

Motel
$89-$109 All Year

Address: 5415 Lougheed Hwy V5B 2Z7 **Location:** Trans-Canada Hwy 1, exit 29 (Willingdon Ave), just n, 0.6 mi (1 km) e on Lougheed Hwy, just n on Springer Ave, then just e on Broadway. Located in a residential area. **Facility:** 48 units. 42 one- and 6 two-bedroom standard units, some with efficiencies. 2 stories (no elevator), exterior corridors. **Parking:** on-site. **Terms:** cancellation fee imposed. **Amenities:** voice mail, irons, hair dryers. **Pool(s):** heated outdoor. **Leisure Activities:** whirlpool. **Guest Services:** coin laundry, wireless Internet. **Business Services:** meeting rooms, PC. **Free Special Amenities:** early check-in/late check-out and high-speed Internet.

WHERE TO DINE

CACTUS CLUB CAFE Phone: 604/291-6606

Canadian
$9-$29

This bustling, casual restaurant serves huge burgers, sandwiches, pasta, salads, soups, quesadillas, fajitas, vegetarian dishes, steak, ribs, chicken and fish. Featured are certified Angus beef and fresh wild British Columbia salmon. The thick and creamy milk shakes come highly recommended. Casual dress. **Bar:** Full bar. **Hours:** 11 am-midnight, Fri & Sat-1 am. Closed: 12/25. **Address:** 4219B Lougheed Hwy V5C 3Y6 **Location:** Between Gilmore and Madison aves. **Parking:** on-site.

CRYSTAL BAR AND GRILLE Phone: 604/438-1200 **47**

Continental
$9-$30

On the third floor of the Hilton Vancouver Metrotown, the 80-seat restaurant is open for breakfast, lunch and dinner and also serves a fabulous Sunday brunch. Creative dishes center on fish, beef or pasta. Casual dress. **Bar:** Full bar. **Reservations:** suggested. **Hours:** 6 am-11 pm. **Address:** 6083 McKay Ave V5H 2W7 **Location:** Trans-Canada Hwy 1, exit 29 (Willingdon Ave), 1.8 mi (3 km) s to Kingsway, then just e; in Hilton Vancouver Metrotown. **Parking:** on-site and valet.

EARLS RESTAURANT Phone: 604/205-5025

Canadian
$10-$28

Offering an experience that falls between fast food and fine dining, the fun, relaxed restaurant prepares great food at a great price. Choices range from juicy burgers, hearty sandwiches, fresh salads, wings and pizza to full entrees of steak, chops and seafood. Made-from-scratch soups and assorted breads, as well as a nice choice of wines and beers, round out the offerings. This is a fitting spot for impromptu get-togethers and festive occasions. Casual dress. **Bar:** Full bar. **Hours:** 11:30 am-11 pm, Fri & Sat-midnight. Closed: 12/25. **Address:** 3850 Lougheed Hwy V5C 6N4 **Location:** Just e of Boundary Rd. **Parking:** on-site.

▼ See AAA listing p 643 ▼

(See map and index starting on p. 594)

EBO RESTAURANT AND LOUNGE

Phone: 604/453-0750 ④⑤

Pacific Northwest
$12-$40

Patrons enjoy panoramic views of Burnaby and the North Shore Mountains from this second-floor dining room. Vancouver Aquarium recommends this place, which participates in sustainable food practices, as a choice for ocean-friendly seafood, specifically the freshest bounty of the Pacific Northwest. Breakfast comes in the form of a full buffet, while lunch and dinner are a la carte. Casual dress. **Bar:** Full bar. **Reservations:** suggested. **Hours:** 6 am-10 pm, Fri & Sat-midnight. **Address:** 4331 Dominion St V5G 1B2 **Location:** Trans-Canada Hwy 1, exit 29 (Willingdon Ave S), just w on Canada Way, then n on Sumner St; in Delta Burnaby Hotel and Conference Centre. **Parking:** on-site and valet. CALL ⑤Ⓜ

HART HOUSE RESTAURANT

Phone: 604/298-4278 ④⑥

Pacific Northwest
$14-$36

The turn-of-the-20th-century, Tudor-style country home has been turned into a lovely restaurant overlooking Deer Lake and two acres of lush lawn. The menu features rack of lamb, fish and pasta, along with lighter fare for lunch. Casual dress. **Bar:** Full bar. **Reservations:** suggested. **Hours:** 11:30 am-2:30 & 5:30-9 pm, Fri-10 pm, Sat 5:30 pm-10 pm, Sun 11 am-2 & 5:30-9 pm; Sunday brunch. Closed: 1/1, 12/26; also Mon. **Address:** 6664 Deer Lake Ave V5E 4H3 **Location:** Trans-Canada Hwy 1, exit 33 (Kensington S), 0.6 mi (1 km) e on Canada Way to Sperling Ave, follow signs to Burnaby Village Museum. **Parking:** on-site. CALL ⑤Ⓜ

HORIZONS

Phone: 604/299-1155 ④④

Pacific Rim
$12-$32

Views of the city and mountains are wonderful from the restaurant's hilltop location in Burnaby Mountain Park. Specialties of alderwood-fired fresh seafood and steak, as well as rack of lamb and roasted duck, line the menu at this casual spot for fine dining. Dressy casual. **Bar:** Full bar. **Reservations:** suggested. **Hours:** 11:30 am-2 & 5-close, Sun from 11 am; Sunday brunch. Closed: 12/24, 12/25. **Address:** 100 Centennial Way V5A 2X9 **Location:** Lougheed Hwy, 3.1 mi (5 km) n on Gaglardi Way, 0.6 mi (1 km) w on Burnaby Mountain Pkwy, then just n, follow signs. **Parking:** on-site.

MILESTONE'S GRILL AND BAR

Phone: 604/291-7393

Canadian
$8-$27

Popular with locals, the bustling eatery is a great gathering place. Diners enjoy the relaxed setting and casual menu featuring pasta, pizza, roasted chicken and a tasty choice of egg and brunch options. A nice wine list complements the food choices. Casual dress. **Bar:** Full bar. **Hours:** 11 am-11 pm, Sat & Sun from 10 am. Closed: 12/25. **Address:** 4420 Lougheed Hwy V5C 3Z3 **Location:** Between Rosser and Willingdon aves. **Parking:** on-site. CALL ⑤Ⓜ

SWISS CHALET

Phone: 604/299-1761

Canadian
$6-$18

The popular restaurant is known for its rotisserie chicken and ribs and the tangy Chalet sauce that gives food its special zip. Diners munch on a half or quarter chicken with sides such as steamed vegetables, fries, baked potatoes and salads. Lunch guests often go for the great soup and sandwich combination. Take-out and delivery service are popular options. Casual dress. **Bar:** Full bar. **Hours:** 11:30 am-10 pm, Sun 11 am-9:30 pm. Closed: 12/25. **Address:** 3860 Lougheed Hwy V5C 6N4 **Location:** Lougheed Hwy at Boundary Rd. **Parking:** on-site.

COQUITLAM pop. 114,565   (See map and index starting on p. 594)

BEST WESTERN CHELSEA INN   *Book great rates at AAA.com*

Phone: (604)525-7777 ㉞

Motel
$125 All Year

Address: 725 Brunette Ave V3K 1C3 **Location:** Trans-Canada Hwy 1, exit 40B (Brunette Ave N). **Facility:** Smoke free premises. 61 units. 60 one-bedroom standard units, some with efficiencies and/or whirlpools. 1 two-bedroom suite with kitchen and whirlpool. 3 stories, interior corridors. **Parking:** on-site. **Amenities:** voice mail, irons, hair dryers. **Pool(s):** heated outdoor. **Leisure Activities:** sauna, limited exercise equipment. **Guest Services:** coin laundry, wireless Internet. **Business Services:** PC. **Free Special Amenities:** continental breakfast and high-speed Internet.

AAA Benefit:
Members save up to 20%, plus 10% bonus points with rewards program.

CALL ⑤Ⓜ

BEST WESTERN COQUITLAM INN CONVENTION CENTRE   *Book great rates at AAA.com*

Phone: (604)931-9011 ㉜

Hotel
$149-$289 All Year

Address: 319 North Rd V3K 3V8 **Location:** Trans-Canada Hwy 1, exit 37 (Cariboo Rd/Gaglardi Way), 1.2 mi (2 km) e on Lougheed Hwy (Hwy 7), then just s. **Facility:** Smoke free premises. 106 units. 90 one-bedroom standard units, some with whirlpools. 16 two-bedroom suites with kitchens. 2 stories, interior/exterior corridors. **Parking:** on-site. **Amenities:** voice mail, irons, hair dryers. **Dining:** 2 restaurants. **Pool(s):** heated indoor. **Leisure Activities:** sauna, whirlpool, limited exercise equipment. **Guest Services:** valet laundry, wireless Internet. **Business Services:** conference facilities, PC. **Free Special Amenities:** local telephone calls and high-speed Internet.

AAA Benefit:
Members save up to 20%, plus 10% bonus points with rewards program.

(See map and index starting on p. 594)

RAMADA COQUITLAM　　*Book at AAA.com*　　　　　　　　Phone: (604)931-4433　**33**

▼▼▼ ▼▼▼
Hotel
$110-$150 3/1-9/30
$90-$120 10/1-2/28

Address: 631 Lougheed Hwy V3K 3S5 **Location:** Trans-Canada Hwy 1, exit 44 (Coquitlam), 1.9 mi (3 km) w on Lougheed Hwy (Hwy 7). **Facility:** 84 one-bedroom standard units, some with whirlpools. 2 stories (no elevator), interior/exterior corridors. **Parking:** on-site. **Amenities:** voice mail, irons, hair dryers. **Pool(s):** heated indoor. **Leisure Activities:** whirlpool, exercise room. **Guest Services:** valet and coin laundry, wireless Internet. **Business Services:** meeting rooms, PC.

[ASK] [❙↑] [☎] [⇄] [♣] [▦] / SOME UNITS FEE [🐾] [✕] [▤] [▱]

──────── **WHERE TO DINE** ────────

CACTUS CLUB CAFE　　　　　　　　　　　　　　　　Phone: 604/777-0440

▼▼▼ ▼▼▼
Canadian
$9-$29

This bustling, casual restaurant serves huge burgers, sandwiches, pasta, salads, soups, quesadillas, fajitas, vegetarian dishes, steak, ribs, chicken and fish. Featured are certified Angus beef and fresh wild British Columbia salmon. The thick and creamy milk shakes come highly recommended. Casual dress. **Bar:** Full bar. **Hours:** 11 am-midnight, Fri & Sat-1 am. Closed: 12/25. **Address:** 110-101 Schoolhouse St V3K 4X8 **Location:** From Lougheed Hwy, just n. **Parking:** on-site.

JOEY RESTAURANTS　　　　　　　　　　　　　　　　Phone: 604/939-3077

▼▼▼ ▼▼▼
Canadian
$8-$24

The cuisine blends Mediterranean and Asian cooking styles and emphasizes finger foods for sharing. Those who aren't big fans of tapas can consider full meal offerings centered on steaks and chops. Casual dress. **Bar:** Full bar. **Hours:** 11 am-1 am, Sun & Mon-midnight. Closed: 12/25. **Address:** 550 Lougheed Hwy V3K 353 **Location:** Trans-Canada Hwy 1, exit 37 (Gaglardi Way) eastbound, 2.3 mi (3.8 km) e on Hwy 7 (Lougheed Hwy); exit 44 (Coquitlam) westbound, 1.9 mi (3.2 km) w. **Parking:** on-site. CALL [⓶M]

RICKY'S ALL DAY GRILL　　　　　　　　　　　　　　Phone: 604/468-8000

▼▼▼ ▼▼▼
Canadian
$6-$15

The comfortable eatery, which employs friendly servers, presents a varied menu that includes pasta dishes, wraps, omelets, stir-fry preparations and burgers. Portions are generous. Children's and senior selections are offered. Guests can request seating in a booth or at a table. Casual dress. **Bar:** Full bar. **Hours:** 7:30 am-8 pm, Wed & Thurs-9 pm, Fri & Sat-10 pm. **Address:** 2929 Barnet Hwy, Unit 2660 V3B 5R5 **Location:** Just off Barnet Hwy; in Coquitlam Centre Mall. **Parking:** on-site.

DELTA pop. 96,723　(See map and index starting on p. 594)

CLAIR'S BED & BREAKFAST　　　　　　　　　　　　　Phone: 604/940-8867　**61**

[CAA] [SAVE]
▼▼▼ ▼▼▼
Historic Bed
& Breakfast
$135-$185 3/1-9/30
$115-$165 10/1-2/28

Address: 4919 48th Ave V4K 1V4 **Location:** Hwy 17, 1.1 mi (1.8 km) w on Ladner Trunk Rd to Elliott St, just n. Located in Ladner Village. **Facility:** Built in 1913, this Edwardian-style house served as a family home for its first 60 years. In 1994 the home was purchased and converted into a B&B. Smoke free premises. 6 one-bedroom standard units, some with whirlpools. 2 stories (no elevator), interior corridors. *Bath:* combo, shower or tub only. **Parking:** on-site. **Terms:** office hours 8 am-8 pm, check-in 3:30 pm, 10 day cancellation notice-fee imposed. **Guest Services:** TV in common area. **Free Special Amenities: full breakfast and high-speed Internet.** [❙↑] [✕] [⚿] [⚿] [☎]

THE COAST TSAWWASSEN INN　　*Book great rates at AAA.com*　　Phone: (604)943-8221　**63**

[CAA] [SAVE]
▼▼▼ ▼▼▼
Hotel
$113-$128 10/1-2/28
$111-$123 3/1-9/30

Address: 1665 56th St V4L 2B2 **Location:** Hwy 99, exit 28 (Tsawwassen Ferries), 5 mi (8 km) w on Hwy 17; 3.1 mi (5 km) from the BC ferry terminal. **Facility:** 90 one-bedroom suites, some with kitchens and/or whirlpools. 3 stories, interior corridors. **Parking:** on-site. **Amenities:** video games (fee), voice mail, irons, hair dryers. **Pool(s):** heated indoor. **Leisure Activities:** sauna, whirlpool, exercise room. **Guest Services:** valet and coin laundry, area transportation-ferry terminal, wireless Internet. **Business Services:** meeting rooms, business center. **Free Special Amenities: newspaper and high-speed Internet.** [ECO] [❙↑] [☎] CALL [⓶M] [⇄] [✕] [♣] [▤] [▱] [▦] / SOME UNITS FEE [🐾] [✕]

DELTA TOWN & COUNTRY INN　　*Book great rates at AAA.com*　　Phone: (604)946-4404　**60**

[CAA] [SAVE]
▼▼▼ ▼▼▼
Hotel
$102-$112 All Year

Address: 6005 Hwy 17 V4K 5B8 **Location:** Hwy 17 at Hwy 99, exit 28 (River Rd). Located in a quiet rural area. **Facility:** Smoke free premises. 49 one-bedroom standard units. 2 stories (no elevator), interior corridors. **Parking:** on-site. **Terms:** cancellation fee imposed. **Amenities:** voice mail, irons, hair dryers. *Some:* high-speed Internet (fee). **Pool(s):** heated outdoor. **Leisure Activities:** exercise room. *Fee:* 5 tennis courts (4 indoor, 5 lighted). **Guest Services:** valet and coin laundry, wireless Internet. **Business Services:** conference facilities, business center. **Free Special Amenities: local telephone calls and early check-in/late check-out.** [❙↑] [☎] [⇄] [✕] [▦] / SOME UNITS [▤] [▱]

RIVER RUN COTTAGES　　　　　　　　　　　　　　Phone: (604)946-7778　**62**

▼▼▼ ▼▼▼
Bed & Breakfast
$170-$225 3/1-9/30
$149-$180 10/1-2/28

Address: 4551 River Rd W V4K 1R9 **Location:** Hwy 17, 1.6 mi (2.5 km) n on Ladner Trunk Rd (which becomes 47A St, then becomes River Rd W). Located in Ladner Village. **Facility:** These three self-contained cottages with decks are built on pillars over tidal mud flats on the Fraser River; one floating cottage is tied to a dock. Smoke free premises. 4 one-bedroom standard units. 1 story, exterior corridors. *Bath:* combo or shower only. **Parking:** on-site. **Terms:** office hours 7 am-10 pm, check-in 4 pm, 21 day cancellation notice-fee imposed. **Amenities:** CD players, hair dryers. **Leisure Activities:** bicycles. [ASK] [❙↑] [✕] [⚿] [⚿] [☎] [▤] [▱] [▦] / SOME UNITS FEE [🐾]

(See map and index starting on p. 594)

──── WHERE TO DINE ────

CACTUS CLUB CAFE   Phone: 604/591-1707

Canadian
$9-$29

This bustling, casual restaurant serves huge burgers, sandwiches, pasta, salads, soups, quesadillas, fajitas, vegetarian dishes, steak, ribs, chicken and fish. Featured are certified Angus beef and fresh wild British Columbia salmon. The thick and creamy milk shakes come highly recommended. Casual dress. **Bar:** Full bar. **Hours:** 11 am-midnight, Fri & Sat-1 am. Closed: 12/25. **Address:** 7907 120th St V4C 6P6 **Location:** Just s from 80th Ave. **Parking:** on-site.

LA BELLE AUBERGE   *Menu on AAA.com*   Phone: 604/946-7717   [62]

French
$23-$35

Situated in a charming, 100-year-old Victorian home, the restaurant is owned and operated by a chef who competed with the Canadian Culinary Olympic team in the 1980s and judged the competition in the 1990s. His specialty is French cuisine, and an eight-course meal costs $95. A la carte ordering is another option. Casual dress. **Bar:** Full bar. **Reservations:** suggested. **Hours:** 6 pm-11 pm. Closed: Sun, Mon & 1/1-1/15. **Address:** 4856 48th Ave V4K 1V2 **Location:** Hwy 17, 1.1 mi (1.8 km) w on Ladner Trunk Rd to Elliott St, then just n. **Parking:** on-site.

RICKY'S ALL DAY GRILL   Phone: 604/599-1784

Canadian
$6-$15

The comfortable eatery, which employs friendly servers, presents a varied menu that includes pasta dishes, wraps, omelets, stir-fry preparations and burgers. Portions are generous. Children's and senior selections are offered. Guests can request seating in a booth or at a table. Casual dress. **Bar:** Full bar. **Hours:** 6 am-9 pm, Sun from 7 am. **Address:** 7135 120th St V4E 2A9 **Location:** Just s of 72nd Ave. **Parking:** on-site.

LANGLEY pop. 23,606   (See map and index starting on p. 594)

BEST VALUE WESTWARD INN   *Book great rates at AAA.com*   Phone: (604)534-9238   [78]

Motel
$89-$99 All Year

Address: 19650 Fraser Hwy V3A 4C7 **Location:** Trans-Canada Hwy 1, exit 58 (200th St/Langley City), 3.1 mi (5 km) s on 200th St, 0.6 mi (1 km) w on Hwy 10, then just w. **Facility:** 55 one-bedroom standard units, some with kitchens. 1 story, exterior corridors. **Parking:** on-site. **Guest Services:** coin laundry. **Business Services:** PC. [11+] [] / [SOME UNITS] FEE [] [] []

▼ See AAA listing p 648 ▼

(See map and index starting on p. 594)

BEST WESTERN LANGLEY INN

Book great rates at AAA.com

Phone: (604)530-9311   **79**

Hotel
$110-$231 All Year

Address: 5978 Glover Rd V3A 4H9 **Location:** Trans-Canada Hwy 1, exit 66 (232nd St), 6 km s, follow signs. **Facility:** 78 units. 77 one-bedroom standard units, some with efficiencies. 1 two-bedroom suite with kitchen. 2 stories (no elevator), interior corridors. **Parking:** on-site. **Amenities:** video games (fee), voice mail, irons, hair dryers. **Pool(s):** heated indoor. **Leisure Activities:** whirlpool, exercise room. **Guest Services:** valet and coin laundry, wireless Internet. **Business Services:** meeting rooms, business center. *(See color ad p 647)*

AAA Benefit:
Members save up to 20%, plus 10% bonus points with rewards program.

FREE expanded continental breakfast and high-speed Internet

COAST HOTEL & CONVENTION CENTRE

Book great rates at AAA.com

Phone: (604)530-1500 **81**

Hotel
$125-$175 All Year

Address: 20393 Fraser Hwy V3A 7N2 **Location:** Trans-Canada Hwy 1, exit 58 (200th St/Langley City), 3.9 mi (6.3 km) s on 200th St, then just e. **Facility:** Comfortable guest rooms with contemporary West Coast-style decor give guests easy access to the large casino, 420-seat theater and dining outlets. Smoke free premises. 77 one-bedroom standard units. 6 stories, interior corridors. **Parking:** on-site. **Amenities:** CD players, high-speed Internet, dual phone lines, voice mail, irons, hair dryers. **Dining:** 2 restaurants. **Leisure Activities:** steamrooms, exercise room. **Guest Services:** valet laundry. **Business Services:** conference facilities, business center. **Free Special Amenities: local telephone calls and high-speed Internet.**

DAYS INN & SUITES LANGLEY

Book great rates at AAA.com

Phone: (604)539-0100 **80**

Hotel
$125-$189 1/1-2/28
$89-$169 3/1-12/31

Address: 20250 Logan Ave V3A 4L6 **Location:** Trans-Canada Hwy 1, exit 58 (200th St/Langley City), 3.9 mi (6.3 km) s on 200th St, then just e. **Facility:** 62 units. 48 one-bedroom standard units. 14 one-bedroom suites, some with whirlpools. 4 stories, interior corridors. **Parking:** on-site. **Terms:** cancellation fee imposed. **Amenities:** voice mail, irons, hair dryers. **Leisure Activities:** exercise room. **Guest Services:** coin laundry, wireless Internet. **Business Services:** PC (fee). *(See color ad below)*

FREE expanded continental breakfast and high-speed Internet

▼ *See AAA listing above* ▼

(See map and index starting on p. 594)

HOLIDAY INN EXPRESS HOTEL & SUITES
LANGLEY   *Book great rates at AAA.com*   Phone: (604)882-2000   **77**

Hotel
$115-$199 All Year

Address: 8750 204th St V1M 2Y5 **Location:** Trans-Canada Hwy 1, exit 58 (200th St/Langley City), just e on 88th Ave. **Facility:** Smoke free premises. 85 one-bedroom standard units, some with whirlpools. 4 stories, interior corridors. **Parking:** on-site. **Amenities:** video games, high-speed Internet, dual phone lines, voice mail, irons, hair dryers. **Pool(s):** heated indoor. **Leisure Activities:** sauna, whirlpool, steamroom, exercise room. **Guest Services:** valet and coin laundry, wireless Internet. **Business Services:** meeting rooms, PC (fee). **Free Special Amenities: expanded continental breakfast and high-speed Internet.** *(See color ad on insert)*

SANDMAN HOTEL LANGLEY   Phone: 604/888-7263   **76**

Hotel
$129-$169 2/1-2/28
$119-$159 3/1-1/31

Address: 8855 202nd St V1M 2N9 **Location:** Trans-Canada Hwy 1, exit 58 (200th St/Langley City), just e on 88th Ave. **Facility:** 145 units. 129 one-bedroom standard units, some with efficiencies. 16 one-bedroom suites. 4 stories, interior corridors. **Amenities:** high-speed Internet, voice mail, irons, hair dryers. **Leisure Activities:** limited exercise equipment. **Guest Services:** valet laundry, wireless Internet. **Business Services:** meeting rooms, business center.

SUPER 8 LANGLEY/ALDERGROVE   *Book at AAA.com*   Phone: (604)856-8288

Motel
$139-$169 5/1-2/28
$109-$129 3/1-4/30

Address: 26574 Gloucester Way V4W 4A8 **Location:** Trans-Canada Hwy 1, exit 73 (264th St/Aldergrove), just e on 56th Ave. **Facility:** Smoke free premises. 81 units. 69 one-bedroom standard units. 12 one-bedroom suites. 4 stories, interior corridors. **Parking:** on-site. **Amenities:** high-speed Internet, voice mail, irons, hair dryers. **Pool(s):** heated indoor. **Leisure Activities:** whirlpool, waterslide, limited exercise equipment. **Guest Services:** valet and coin laundry, wireless Internet. **Business Services:** meeting rooms, PC.

────────────── ▼ WHERE TO DINE ▼ ──────────────

MOXIE'S CLASSIC GRILL   Phone: 604/539-9491

Canadian
$8-$18

This sleek, funky and popular restaurant presents an extensive menu of creatively prepared dishes, including pizza, pasta, rice, noodles, signature salads and burgers. Other menus include one for children and one for Sunday brunch. Lending to the upbeat, stylish decor are dark wood appointments and river rock fireplaces. Casual dress. **Bar:** Full bar. **Hours:** 11 am-midnight, Fri & Sat-1 am. **Address:** 19777 Willowbrook Dr V3A 8H2 **Location:** Trans-Canada Hwy 1, exit 58 (200th St/Langley City), just e on 88th Ave. **Parking:** on-site.

▼ See AAA listing p 661 ▼

(See map and index starting on p. 594)

RICKY'S ALL DAY GRILL

Canadian
$9-$22

Phone: 604/530-4317

The comfortable eatery, which employs friendly servers, presents a varied menu that includes pasta dishes, wraps, omelets, stir-fry preparations and burgers. Portions are generous. Children's and senior selections are offered. Guests can request seating in a booth or at a table. Casual dress. **Bar:** Full bar. **Hours:** 6:30 am-9 pm, Fri & Sat-10 pm. **Address:** 22314 Fraser Hwy V3A 8M6 **Location:** Between 222nd and 223A sts. **Parking:** on-site.

RICKY'S ALL DAY GRILL

Canadian
$9-$22

Phone: 604/888-4211

The comfortable eatery, which employs friendly servers, presents a varied menu that includes pasta dishes, wraps, omelets, stir-fry preparations and burgers. Portions are generous. Children's and senior selections are offered. Guests can request seating in a booth or at a table. Casual dress. **Bar:** Full bar. **Hours:** 6 am-9 pm. Closed: 12/25. **Address:** 8720 204th St V3A 8G5 **Location:** Trans-Canada Hwy 1, exit 58 (200th St/Langley City), just e on 88th Ave. **Parking:** on-site.

SONOMA GRILL

Continental
$10-$30

Phone: 604/534-2104   (71)

Named after the famous wine valley in Northern California, the Sonoma Grill features seafood, pasta, chicken, steak, pork and popular schnitzels. Guests can take the advice of the restaurant's slogan: try, taste and indulge. Casual dress. **Bar:** Full bar. **Reservations:** suggested. **Hours:** 11:30 am-2 & 5-10 pm. Closed: 12/25. **Address:** 20598 Fraser Hwy V3A 4G2 **Location:** Corner of Fraser Hwy and 206th St; downtown. **Parking:** on-site.

MAPLE RIDGE pop. 68,949

MAPLE RIDGE INN & SUITES   *Book great rates at AAA.com*

(CAA) (SAVE)

Hotel
$109-$129 3/1-9/30
$89-$119 10/1-2/28

Phone: (604)463-5111

Address: 21735 Lougheed Hwy V2X 2S2 **Location:** 1.2 mi (2 km) w on Lougheed Hwy (Hwy 7). **Facility:** 61 one-bedroom standard units, some with kitchens and/or whirlpools. 2 stories (no elevator), exterior corridors. **Parking:** on-site. **Terms:** cancellation fee imposed. **Amenities:** high-speed Internet, voice mail, irons, hair dryers. **Leisure Activities:** whirlpool, limited exercise equipment. **Guest Services:** coin laundry, wireless Internet. **Business Services:** meeting rooms, PC. **Free Special Amenities:** local telephone calls and high-speed Internet.

（free image icons）CALL (&M) / SOME UNITS FEE (X) (icons)

TRAVELODGE MAPLE RIDGE   *Book great rates at AAA.com*

(CAA) (SAVE)

Motel
$99-$169 3/1-9/15
$89-$149 9/16-2/28

Phone: (604)467-1511

Address: 21650 Lougheed Hwy V2X 2S1 **Location:** 1.2 mi (2 km) w on Lougheed Hwy (Hwy 7). **Facility:** 56 one-bedroom standard units, some with efficiencies. 2 stories (no elevator), interior corridors. **Parking:** on-site. **Terms:** cancellation fee imposed. **Amenities:** voice mail, hair dryers. **Leisure Activities:** sauna, limited exercise equipment. **Guest Services:** valet and coin laundry, wireless Internet. **Business Services:** meeting rooms. **Free Special Amenities: continental breakfast and high-speed Internet.** (icons) CALL (&M) / SOME UNITS FEE (icons)

—— **WHERE TO DINE** ——

SWISS CHALET

Canadian
$6-$18

Phone: 604/460-8033

The popular restaurant is known for its rotisserie chicken and ribs and the tangy Chalet sauce that gives food its special zip. Diners munch on a half or quarter chicken with sides such as steamed vegetables, fries, baked potatoes and salads. Lunch guests often go for the great soup and sandwich combination. Take-out and delivery service are popular options. Casual dress. **Bar:** Full bar. **Hours:** 11:30 am-10 pm, Sun 11 am-9:30 pm. Closed: 12/25. **Address:** 20395 Lougheed Hwy V2X 2P9 **Location:** Lougheed Hwy (Hwy 7) at 203rd St. **Parking:** on-site.

MISSION pop. 34,505

BEST WESTERN MISSION CITY LODGE   *Book great rates at AAA.com*

(CAA) (SAVE)

Hotel
$95-$249 All Year

Phone: (604)820-5500

Address: 32281 Lougheed Hwy V2V 1A3 **Location:** Just w of Hwy 11; corner of Lougheed Hwy (Hwy 7) and Hurd St. **Facility:** Smoke free premises. 80 one-bedroom standard units, some with efficiencies and/or whirlpools. 4 stories, interior corridors. **Bath:** combo or shower only. **Parking:** on-site. **Amenities:** high-speed Internet, voice mail, irons, hair dryers. **Pool(s):** heated indoor. **Leisure Activities:** sauna, whirlpool, exercise room. **Guest Services:** valet and coin laundry, wireless Internet. **Business Services:** meeting rooms, PC. **Free Special Amenities: local telephone calls and high-speed Internet.**

(icons) CALL (&M) (icons) / SOME UNITS FEE (icon)

AAA Benefit:
Members save up to 20%, plus 10% bonus points with rewards program.

NEW WESTMINSTER pop. 58,549   (See map and index starting on p. 594)

INN AT THE QUAY   *Book great rates at AAA.com*

(CAA) (SAVE)

Hotel
$200-$235 3/1-9/30
$192-$225 10/1-2/28

Phone: (604)520-1776   (37)

Address: 900 Quayside Dr V3M 6G1 **Location:** Along waterfront, follow signs to Westminster Quay. Adjacent to public market. **Facility:** Smoke free premises. 126 one-bedroom standard units, some with whirlpools. 9 stories, interior corridors. **Bath:** combo or shower only. **Parking:** on-site. **Amenities:** voice mail, honor bars, irons, hair dryers. **Leisure Activities:** sauna, whirlpool, exercise room. **Guest Services:** valet laundry, wireless Internet. **Business Services:** conference facilities, PC. **Free Special Amenities: newspaper and high-speed Internet.**

(icons) CALL (&M) (X) (icons)

(See map and index starting on p. 594)

─── WHERE TO DINE ───

THE BOATHOUSE RESTAURANT   **Phone: 604/525-3474**

Seafood
$12-$40

Along the water at Westminster Quay and next to the Inn at Westminster Quay, the relaxed restaurant lets diners look out over the Fraser River. An extensive selection of wines and cocktails complements the great seafood dishes. Casual dress. **Bar:** Full bar. **Reservations:** suggested. **Hours:** 6:30 am-3 & 5-10 pm, Sat & Sun 8:30 am-3 & 5-9 pm. Closed: 12/25. **Address:** 900 Quayside Dr V3M 6G1 **Location:** Along the waterfront, follow signs to Westminster Quay. **Parking:** on-site (fee).

BURGER HEAVEN   **Phone: 604/522-8339**   51

American
$7-$18

This locally popular dining spot features all kinds of burgers—chicken, veggie or beef—cooked to order and served with many different, fresh toppings. The menu also lists a wide variety of sandwiches, beer, wine and coolers. Guests should watch their heads in the living room-style dining room, as the ceiling has several hanging plants. Both the walls and tabletops are adorned with hundreds of customer pictures. Expect casual service by a friendly staff. Casual dress. **Bar:** Beer & wine. **Hours:** 11 am-9 pm, Fri & Sat-10 pm. Closed: 12/25. **Address:** 77 10th St V3M 3X4 **Location:** From Royal Ave, just e. **Parking:** street.

LA RUSTICA RISTORANTE   **Phone: 604/525-6355**   50

Italian
$12-$28

The setting of this Italian restaurant was converted from two older side-by-side houses. The menu lists many popular pasta dishes, along with traditional fare such as pepper steak. Friendly servers can assist with recommendations. On the weekends, live entertainment enhances the atmosphere. Casual dress. **Bar:** Full bar. **Reservations:** suggested, weekends. **Hours:** 11:30 am-2 & 5-10 pm, Fri-10:30 pm, Sat 5 pm-10:30 pm, Sun 5 pm-10 pm. Closed: 1/1, 12/25, 12/26. **Address:** 228 6th St V3L 3A4 **Location:** Between 3rd and 2nd aves. **Parking:** on-site and street.

NORTH VANCOUVER pop. 44,303   (See map and index starting on p. 594)

BEST WESTERN CAPILANO INN & SUITES   *Book great rates at AAA.com*   **Phone: (604)987-8185**   17

Motel
$99-$149 All Year

Address: 1634 Capilano Rd V7P 3B4 **Location:** Trans-Canada Hwy 1, exit 14 (Capilano Rd), 0.9 mi (1.5 km) s; from north end of Lions Gate Bridge, 0.6 mi (1 km) e on Marine Dr, then just n. **Facility:** 74 units. 73 one- and 1 two-bedroom standard units, some with efficiencies, kitchens and/or whirlpools. 2 stories (no elevator), exterior corridors. **Parking:** on-site. **Amenities:** voice mail, irons, hair dryers. *Some:* high-speed Internet. **Pool(s):** heated outdoor. **Guest Services:** coin laundry, wireless Internet. **Business Services:** meeting rooms, PC. **Free Special Amenities: local telephone calls and high-speed Internet.**

AAA Benefit:
Members save up to 20%, plus 10% bonus points with rewards program.

COMFORT INN AND SUITES   *Book great rates at AAA.com*   **Phone: (604)988-3181**   14

Motel
$130-$140 6/1-2/28
$80-$90 3/1-5/31

Address: 1748 Capilano Rd V7P 3B4 **Location:** Trans-Canada Hwy 1, exit 14 (Capilano Rd), 0.9 mi (1.5 km) s; from north end of Lions Gate Bridge, 0.6 mi (1 km) e on Marine Dr, then just n. **Facility:** 94 units. 91 one- and 3 two-bedroom standard units, some with efficiencies or kitchens. 2 stories (no elevator), exterior corridors. **Parking:** on-site. **Terms:** check-in 4 pm, cancellation fee imposed. **Amenities:** voice mail, irons, hair dryers. *Some:* high-speed Internet. **Pool(s):** heated outdoor. **Leisure Activities:** whirlpool. **Guest Services:** valet and coin laundry, wireless Internet. **Business Services:** meeting rooms, PC.

GROUSE INN   *Book great rates at AAA.com*   **Phone: (604)988-7101**   16

Motel
$79-$169 All Year

Address: 1633 Capilano Rd V7P 3B3 **Location:** Trans-Canada Hwy 1, exit 14 (Capilano Rd), 0.9 mi (1.5 km) s; from north end of Lions Gate Bridge, 0.6 mi (1 km) e on Marine Dr. **Facility:** 80 units. 73 one- and 7 two-bedroom standard units, some with efficiencies, kitchens and/or whirlpools. 2 stories (no elevator), exterior corridors. **Parking:** on-site. **Terms:** cancellation fee imposed. **Amenities:** voice mail, irons, hair dryers. **Pool(s):** heated outdoor. **Guest Services:** coin laundry, wireless Internet. **Business Services:** meeting rooms, PC (fee). *(See color ad p 610)*

FREE continental breakfast and high-speed Internet

(See map and index starting on p. 594)

HOLIDAY INN HOTEL & SUITES NORTH VANCOUVER *Book great rates at AAA.com*

Phone: (604)985-3111 18

CAA SAVE

Hotel
$199-$350 All Year

Address: 700 Old Lillooet Rd V7J 2H5 **Location:** Trans-Canada Hwy 1, exit 22 (Mt Seymour Pkwy), follow signs. **Facility:** 162 one-bedroom standard units, some with efficiencies and/or whirlpools. 6 stories, interior corridors. **Parking:** on-site. **Terms:** cancellation fee imposed. **Amenities:** video games (fee), high-speed Internet, dual phone lines, voice mail, safes, irons, hair dryers. **Pool(s):** heated indoor. **Leisure Activities:** sauna, whirlpool, exercise room, spa. **Guest Services:** valet and coin laundry, wireless Internet. **Business Services:** meeting rooms, PC. *(See color ad on insert, p 635 & below)*

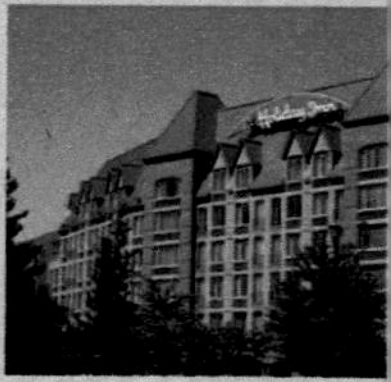

FREE local telephone calls and high-speed Internet

LIONSGATE TRAVELODGE *Book at AAA.com*

Phone: (604)985-5311 15

Motel
$59-$149 All Year

Address: 2060 Marine Dr V7P 1V7 **Location:** Trans-Canada Hwy 1, exit 14 (Capilano Rd), 0.9 mi (1.5 km) s, then just w; from north end of Lions Gate Bridge, just e. **Facility:** 61 one-bedroom standard units. 2 stories (no elevator), exterior corridors. *Bath:* combo or shower only. **Parking:** on-site. **Amenities:** voice mail, irons, hair dryers. **Pool(s):** heated outdoor. **Guest Services:** wireless Internet.

NORTH VANCOUVER HOTEL *Book great rates at AAA.com*

Phone: (604)987-4461 13

CAA SAVE

Motel
$99-$169 3/1-9/30
$79-$129 10/1-2/28

Address: 1800 Capilano Rd V7P 3B6 **Location:** Trans-Canada Hwy 1, exit 14 (Capilano Rd), 0.9 mi (1.5 km) s; from north end of Lions Gate Bridge, 0.6 mi (1 km) e on Marine Dr, then just n. **Facility:** Smoke free premises. 72 one-bedroom standard units, some with kitchens. 2 stories (no elevator), exterior corridors. **Parking:** on-site. **Amenities:** high-speed Internet, voice mail, irons, hair dryers. **Pool(s):** heated outdoor. **Guest Services:** valet and coin laundry, wireless Internet. **Business Services:** PC (fee). *(See color ad p 636)*

▼ See AAA listing above ▼

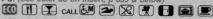

(See map and index starting on p. 594)

—— WHERE TO DINE ——

CACTUS CLUB CAFE

Phone: 604/986-5776

Canadian
$9-$29

This bustling, casual restaurant serves huge burgers, sandwiches, pasta, salads, soups, quesadillas, fajitas, vegetarian dishes, steak, ribs, chicken and fish. Featured are certified Angus beef and fresh wild British Columbia salmon. The thick and creamy milk shakes come highly recommended. Casual dress. **Bar:** Full bar. **Hours:** 11 am-midnight, Fri & Sat-1 am. Closed: 12/25. **Address:** 1598 Pemberton Ave V7P 2S2 **Location:** From Marine Dr, just w at W 16th St. **Parking:** on-site.

THE EDGE BISTRO

Phone: 604/985-9125 (38)

Mediterranean
$8-$26

In the Edgemont Shopping Village on the road to Grouse Mountain, the quaint restaurant prepares a large selection of pastas in the $14 range and poultry, meats and seafood in the $20 range. Selections from an interesting wine list are reasonably priced. The amazing tiramisu merits serious consideration. Casual dress. **Bar:** Full bar. **Reservations:** suggested. **Hours:** 11 am-2:30 & 5-9:30 pm, Sun from 5 pm. Closed major holidays. **Address:** 3135 Edgemont Blvd V7R 2N7 **Location:** 1.1 mi (1.8 km) n on Capilano Rd, 0.6 mi (1 km) e on Ridgewood Dr, then just s; in Edgemont Village. **Parking:** street.

GUSTO DI QUATTRO

Phone: 604/924-4444 (41)

Italian
$14-$35

Translated, Gusto di Quattro means "a taste of Quattro." The North Shore favorite, which has a small dining space, is by Lonsdale Quay Market. Wonderful pastas and freshly made breads await. Patrons likely will have to wait for a table if they didn't make a reservation. A pay parking lot is right across the street. Casual dress. **Bar:** Full bar. **Reservations:** suggested. **Hours:** 11 am-2 & 5-10 pm, Sat & Sun from 5 pm. Closed: 1/1, 12/25, 12/26. **Address:** 1 Lonsdale Ave V7M 2E4 **Location:** Trans-Canada Hwy 1, exit 18 (Lonsdale Ave), 1.6 mi (2.5 km) s to Lonsdale Quay Market. **Parking:** street. CALL

JAGERHOF SCHNITZEL HOUSE

Phone: 604/980-4316 (40)

German
$9-$17

Just north of the Sea Bus terminal on Lonsdale and near the shops of Lonsdale Quay Market, the cozy little restaurant lures a loyal clientele for wonderful schnitzels. The only available parking is on the street. Casual dress. **Bar:** Full bar. **Reservations:** suggested, for dinner. **Hours:** 11:30 am-1:30 & 5-9:30 pm, Sat & Sun from 5 pm. Closed: 12/25, 12/26; also Mon. **Address:** 71 Lonsdale Ave V7M 2E5 **Location:** Between 1st St and Esplanade. **Parking:** street. CALL

MOUSTACHE CAFE

Phone: 604/987-8461 (39)

Pacific Northwest
$10-$32

The decor is bright and colorful inside the cozy 1918 home that serves as the setting for this cafe. A West Coast flair is evident in preparations made from ingredients found only in British Columbia. Casual dress. **Bar:** Full bar. **Reservations:** suggested. **Hours:** 11 am-11 pm. Closed major holidays; also Mon. **Address:** 129 W 2nd St V7M 1C5 **Location:** Between Chesterfield and Lonsdale aves. **Parking:** on-site and street.

RICKY'S ALL DAY GRILL

Phone: 604/904-4430

Canadian
$6-$15

The comfortable eatery, which employs friendly servers, presents a varied menu that includes pasta dishes, wraps, omelets, stir-fry preparations and burgers. Portions are generous. Children's and senior selections are offered. Guests can request seating in a booth or at a table. Casual dress. **Bar:** Full bar. **Hours:** 7 am-9 pm, Fri & Sat-10 pm. **Address:** 1995 Lonsdale Ave V7M 2K3 **Location:** Between 20th and 19th sts. **Parking:** on-site.

SWISS CHALET

Phone: 604/986-1858

Canadian
$6-$18

The popular restaurant is known for its rotisserie chicken and ribs and the tangy Chalet sauce that gives food its special zip. Diners munch on a half or quarter chicken with sides such as steamed vegetables, fries, baked potatoes and salads. Lunch guests often go for the great soup and sandwich combination. Take-out and delivery service are popular options. Casual dress. **Bar:** Full bar. **Hours:** 11:30 am-10 pm, Sun 11 am-9:30 pm. Closed: 12/25. **Address:** 801 Marine Dr V7P 3K6 **Location:** Marine Dr at Fell Ave. **Parking:** on-site.

PITT MEADOWS pop. 15,623   (See map and index starting on p. 594)

RAMADA INN   *Book at AAA.com*

Phone: (604)460-9859 (29)

Hotel
$89-$112 All Year

Address: 19267 Lougheed Hwy V3Y 2J5 **Location:** Lougheed Hwy (Hwy 7) and Harris Rd. **Facility:** 80 one-bedroom standard units, some with efficiencies and/or whirlpools. 3 stories, interior corridors. **Parking:** on-site. **Terms:** check-in 4 pm. **Amenities:** high-speed Internet, voice mail, irons, hair dryers. **Pool(s):** heated outdoor. **Leisure Activities:** whirlpool, exercise room. **Guest Services:** valet and coin laundry, wireless Internet. **Business Services:** meeting rooms.

PORT COQUITLAM pop. 52,687

—— WHERE TO DINE ——

EARLS RESTAURANT

Phone: 604/941-1733

Canadian
$8-$15

Offering an experience that falls between fast food and fine dining, the fun, relaxed restaurant prepares great food at a great price. Choices range from juicy burgers, hearty sandwiches, fresh salads, wings and pizza to full entrees of steak, chops and seafood. Made-from-scratch soups and assorted breads, as well as a nice choice of wines and beers, round out the offerings. This is a fitting spot for impromptu get-togethers and festive occasions. Casual dress. **Bar:** Full bar. **Hours:** 11:30 am-11 pm, Fri & Sat-midnight. Closed: 12/25. **Address:** 2850 Shaughnessy St V3C 6K5 **Location:** Corner of Shaughnessy St and Lougheed Hwy (Hwy 7). **Parking:** on-site. CALL

RICHMOND pop. 174,461 (See map and index starting on p. 594)

ACCENT INNS

Book great rates at AAA.com

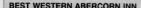

Phone: (604)273-3311 49

CAA SAVE

Hotel

$89-$179 All Year

Address: 10551 St Edwards Dr V6X 3L8 **Location:** Hwy 99, exit 39 (Bridgeport Rd/Airport) northbound to St Edwards Dr; exit 39A (Richmond/Airport) southbound to St Edwards Dr. **Facility:** Smoke free premises. 206 one-bedroom standard units, some with efficiencies. 3 stories, exterior corridors. **Parking:** on-site. **Amenities:** voice mail, irons, hair dryers. *Some:* high-speed Internet. **Leisure Activities:** whirlpool, limited exercise equipment. **Guest Services:** valet and coin laundry, airport transportation-Vancouver International Airport, wireless Internet. **Business Services:** meeting rooms, PC. **Free Special Amenities: newspaper and high-speed Internet.**

ECO CALL / SOME UNITS FEE

BEST WESTERN ABERCORN INN

Book great rates at AAA.com

Phone: (604)270-7576 45

CAA SAVE

Hotel

$125-$160 All Year

Address: 9260 Bridgeport Rd V6X 1S1 **Location:** Hwy 99, exit 39 (Bridgeport Rd/Airport) northbound; exit 39A (Richmond/Airport) southbound. **Facility:** Smoke free premises. 98 one-bedroom standard units, some with whirlpools. 3 stories, interior corridors. **Parking:** on-site. **Amenities:** voice mail, irons, hair dryers. **Leisure Activities:** limited exercise equipment. **Guest Services:** valet laundry, airport transportation-Vancouver International Airport, wireless Internet. **Business Services:** meeting rooms, PC (fee). *(See color ad p 631)*

ECO CALL / SOME UNITS FEE

AAA Benefit:

Members save up to 20%, plus 10% bonus points with rewards program.

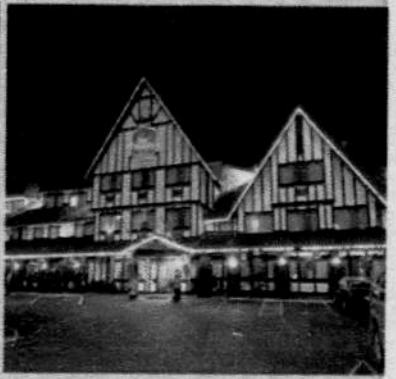

FREE local telephone calls and high-speed Internet

DAYS INN VANCOUVER AIRPORT

Book at AAA.com

Phone: (604)207-8000 42

Hotel

$99-$250 All Year

Address: 2840 Sexsmith Rd V6X 2H3 **Location:** Hwy 99, exit 39 (Bridgeport Rd/Airport) northbound; exit 39A (Richmond/Airport) southbound, just w on Bridgeport Rd. **Facility:** Smoke free premises. 66 one-bedroom standard units. 5 stories, interior corridors. **Parking:** on-site. **Terms:** check-in 4 pm. **Amenities:** high-speed Internet, voice mail, safes, irons, hair dryers. **Leisure Activities:** exercise room. **Guest Services:** valet laundry, wireless Internet. **Business Services:** PC (fee).

ECO ASK CALL

DELTA VANCOUVER AIRPORT

Book great rates at AAA.com

Phone: (604)278-1241 47

CAA SAVE

Hotel

$159-$329 All Year

Address: 3500 Cessna Dr V7B 1C7 **Location:** Corner of Russ Baker Way and Cessna Dr; near Moray Bridge. **Facility:** Smoke free premises. 415 one-bedroom standard units. 10 stories, interior corridors. **Parking:** on-site (fee) and valet. **Amenities:** high-speed Internet (fee), voice mail, irons, hair dryers. **Dining:** 2 restaurants. **Pool(s):** heated outdoor. **Leisure Activities:** exercise room. **Guest Services:** valet laundry, airport transportation-Vancouver International Airport. **Business Services:** conference facilities, business center.

ECO 24 CALL / SOME UNITS FEE

THE FAIRMONT VANCOUVER AIRPORT

Book great rates at AAA.com

Phone: (604)207-5200 41

CAA SAVE

Hotel

$319-$429 3/1-1/17

Address: 3111 Grant McConachie Way V7B 1X9 **Location:** In Vancouver International Airport. **Facility:** Luxurious rooms feature sound-insulated windows and high-tech temperature and lighting controls; a full spa and jetted lap pool are on the premises. 392 one-bedroom standard units, some with whirlpools. 14 stories, interior corridors. **Parking:** on-site (fee) and valet. **Terms:** open 3/1-1/17, cancellation fee imposed. **Amenities:** dual phone lines, voice mail, safes, honor bars, irons, hair dryers. *Fee:* video games, high-speed Internet. *Some:* CD players. **Dining:** Globe @ YVR, see separate listing. **Pool(s):** heated indoor. **Leisure Activities:** saunas, whirlpool, spa. **Guest Services:** valet laundry, wireless Internet. **Business Services:** meeting rooms, business center. *(See color ad p 632)*

ECO 24 CALL / SOME UNITS FEE

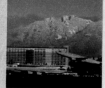

FREE newspaper

(See map and index starting on p. 594)

FOUR POINTS BY SHERATON VANCOUVER AIRPORT   *Book great rates at AAA.com*

Phone: (604)214-0888   **52**

Hotel
$135-$300 All Year

Address: 8368 Alexandra Rd V6X 4A6 **Location:** No 3 Rd, just e on Alderbridge Way, then just n on Hazelbridge Way. **Facility:** Smoke free premises. 139 one-bedroom standard units. 6 stories, interior corridors. **Parking:** on-site (fee). **Terms:** 3 day cancellation notice. **Amenities:** video games (fee), high-speed Internet, dual phone lines, voice mail, irons, hair dryers. **Leisure Activities:** exercise room. **Guest Services:** valet laundry, airport transportation-Vancouver International Airport, wireless Internet. **Business Services:** meeting rooms, PC.

FOUR POINTS BY SHERATON

AAA Benefit:
Members get up to 15% off, plus Starwood Preferred Guest® bonuses.

FREE newspaper and high-speed Internet

HAMPTON INN - BY HILTON VANCOUVER AIRPORT   *Book great rates at AAA.com*

Phone: (604)232-5505   **44**

Hotel
$125-$480 All Year

Address: 8811 Bridgeport Rd V6X 1R9 **Location:** Hwy 99, exit 39 (Bridgeport Rd/Airport) northbound; exit 39A (Richmond/Airport) southbound. **Facility:** Smoke free premises. 112 one-bedroom standard units. 5 stories, interior corridors. **Parking:** on-site. **Terms:** 1-7 night minimum stay, cancellation fee imposed. **Amenities:** video games (fee), voice mail, irons, hair dryers. *Some:* dual phone lines. **Leisure Activities:** exercise room. **Guest Services:** valet laundry, airport transportation-Vancouver International Airport, wireless Internet. **Business Services:** meeting rooms, business center.

Hampton Inn

AAA Benefit:
Members save up to 10% everyday!

FREE expanded continental breakfast and high-speed Internet

HILTON VANCOUVER AIRPORT   *Book great rates at AAA.com*

Phone: (604)273-6336   **53**

Hotel
$159-$799 All Year

Address: 5911 Minoru Blvd V6X 4C7 **Location:** Corner of Minoru Blvd and Westminster Hwy. **Facility:** 237 units. 235 one-bedroom standard units. 2 two-bedroom suites. 15 stories, interior corridors. **Parking:** on-site (fee). **Terms:** 1-7 night minimum stay, cancellation fee imposed. **Amenities:** high-speed Internet (fee), dual phone lines, voice mail, irons, hair dryers. **Pool(s):** heated outdoor. **Leisure Activities:** whirlpool, tennis court, exercise room. **Guest Services:** valet laundry, airport transportation-Vancouver International Airport, wireless Internet. **Business Services:** meeting rooms, business center. *(See color ad p 634)*

Hilton

AAA Benefit:
Members save 5% or more everyday!

FREE local telephone calls and newspaper

HOLIDAY INN EXPRESS & SUITES RIVERPORT   *Book great rates at AAA.com*   Phone: (604)241-1830   **57**

Hotel
$109-$299 All Year

Address: 10688 No 6 Rd V6W 1E7 **Location:** Hwy 99, exit 32 (Steveston Hwy), just e. **Facility:** Smoke free premises. 105 units. 98 one-bedroom standard units, some with efficiencies and/or whirlpools. 6 one- and 1 two-bedroom suites, some with efficiencies or kitchens. 4 stories, interior corridors. *Bath:* combo or shower only. **Parking:** on-site. **Amenities:** high-speed Internet, voice mail, irons, hair dryers. **Pool(s):** heated indoor. **Leisure Activities:** whirlpool, exercise room. **Guest Services:** valet and coin laundry, airport transportation-Vancouver International Airport, wireless Internet. **Business Services:** meeting rooms, business center. **Free Special Amenities:** expanded continental breakfast and high-speed Internet. *(See color ad on insert)*

HOLIDAY INN EXPRESS VANCOUVER-AIRPORT   *Book great rates at AAA.com*   Phone: (604)273-8080   **43**

Hotel
$129-$179 All Year

Address: 9351 Bridgeport Rd V6X 1S3 **Location:** Hwy 99, exit 39 (Bridgeport Rd/Airport) northbound; exit 39A (Richmond/Airport) southbound. **Facility:** 107 one-bedroom standard units, some with whirlpools. 8 stories, interior corridors. **Parking:** on-site. **Terms:** check-in 4 pm. **Amenities:** dual phone lines, voice mail, irons, hair dryers. **Guest Services:** valet laundry, airport transportation-Vancouver International Airport, wireless Internet. **Business Services:** PC (fee).

(See map and index starting on p. 594)

HOLIDAY INN INTERNATIONAL VANCOUVER AIRPORT
Book great rates at AAA.com

Phone: (604)821-1818 **51**

Hotel
$115-$189 All Year

Address: 10720 Cambie Rd V6X 1K8 **Location:** Hwy 99, exit 39A (Bridgeport Rd/Airport) northbound to St. Edwards Dr, then 0.6 mi (1 km) n; exit 39B (No 4 Rd) southbound, just e. **Facility:** Smoke free premises. 162 one-bedroom standard units. 6 stories, interior corridors. **Parking:** on-site (fee). **Terms:** check-in 4 pm, cancellation fee imposed. **Amenities:** high-speed Internet, dual phone lines, voice mail, irons, hair dryers. **Leisure Activities:** whirlpool, exercise room. **Guest Services:** valet laundry, airport transportation-Vancouver International Airport, wireless Internet. **Business Services:** meeting rooms, PC (fee). *(See color ad on insert & p 633)*

QUALITY HOTEL AIRPORT (SOUTH)
Book great rates at AAA.com

Phone: (604)244-3051 **56**

Hotel
$89-$139 All Year

Address: 7228 Westminster Hwy V6X 1A1 **Location:** Between Gilbert Rd and Alderbridge Way. **Facility:** 70 one-bedroom standard units, some with whirlpools. 4 stories, interior corridors. **Parking:** on-site. **Amenities:** high-speed Internet, voice mail, irons, hair dryers. **Guest Services:** valet laundry, wireless Internet. **Business Services:** meeting rooms, PC. **Free Special Amenities: expanded continental breakfast and high-speed Internet.**

RADISSON HOTEL VANCOUVER AIRPORT
Book great rates at AAA.com

Phone: (604)276-8181 **50**

Hotel
$139-$219 All Year

Address: 8181 Cambie Rd V6X 3X9 **Location:** Corner of No 3 and Cambie rds. **Facility:** Smoke free premises. 185 units. 149 one-bedroom standard units. 36 one-bedroom suites, some with kitchens. 12 stories, interior corridors. **Parking:** on-site (fee). **Terms:** cancellation fee imposed. **Amenities:** high-speed Internet, voice mail, safes, irons, hair dryers. **Pool(s):** heated indoor. **Leisure Activities:** whirlpool, exercise room. **Guest Services:** valet laundry, airport transportation-Vancouver International Airport, wireless Internet. **Business Services:** conference facilities, business center. *(See color ad below)*

FREE full breakfast and high-speed Internet

—————— ▼ See AAA listing above ▼ ——————

(See map and index starting on p. 594)

RIVER ROCK CASINO RESORT   *Book great rates at AAA.com*   Phone: 604/247-8900

Hotel
Rates not provided

Address: 8811 River Rd V6X 3P8 **Location:** Hwy 99, exit 39 (Bridgeport Rd/Airport) northbound; exit 39A (Richmond/Airport) southbound, just w on Bridgeport Rd, then just n on Great Canadian Way. **Facility:** Features include a large show lounge, conference facilities, a full-service spa and a 24-hour casino; kids will love the pool's water slide. 203 units. 174 one- and 29 two-bedroom suites. 9-11 stories, interior corridors. *Bath:* combo or shower only. **Parking:** on-site and valet. **Terms:** check-in 4 pm. **Amenities:** video games (fee), CD players, high-speed Internet, dual phone lines, voice mail, safes, irons, hair dryers. **Dining:** Tramonto, see separate listing, entertainment. **Pool(s):** heated indoor. **Leisure Activities:** whirlpool, waterslide, exercise room, spa. *Fee:* marina. **Guest Services:** valet laundry, wireless Internet. **Business Services:** conference facilities, business center. *(See color ad below)*

FREE early check-in/late check-out and high-speed Internet

SANDMAN HOTEL VANCOUVER AIRPORT   *Book at AAA.com*   Phone: (604)303-8888

Hotel
$119-$159 3/1-9/30
$99-$139 10/1-2/28

Address: 3233 St Edwards Dr V6X 3K4 **Location:** Hwy 99, exit 39 (Bridgeport Rd/Airport) northbound to St Edwards Dr; exit 39A (Richmond/Airport) southbound. **Facility:** 172 one-bedroom standard units, some with whirlpools. 5 stories, interior corridors. **Parking:** on-site. **Terms:** cancellation fee imposed. **Amenities:** video games (fee), high-speed Internet, voice mail, irons, hair dryers. **Dining:** Moxie's Classic Grill, see separate listing. **Pool(s):** heated indoor. **Leisure Activities:** whirlpool, exercise room. **Guest Services:** valet laundry, wireless Internet. **Business Services:** meeting rooms, business center.

▼ *See AAA listing above* ▼

(See map and index starting on p. 594)

SHERATON VANCOUVER AIRPORT *Book great rates at AAA.com*   **Phone:** (604)273-7878   **54**

Hotel
$139-$349 All Year

Address: 7551 Westminster Hwy V6X 1A3 **Location:** Corner of Minoru Blvd and Westminster Hwy. **Facility:** Smoke free premises. 390 one-bedroom standard units. 6-7 stories, interior corridors. *Bath:* combo or shower only. **Parking:** on-site (fee). **Amenities:** high-speed Internet, voice mail, irons, hair dryers. **Pool(s):** heated outdoor. **Leisure Activities:** whirlpool, exercise room. **Guest Services:** valet laundry, airport transportation-Vancouver International Airport, wireless Internet. **Business Services:** conference facilities, business center. **Free Special Amenities: newspaper and preferred room (subject to availability with advance reservations).**

(S) **Sheraton**
HOTELS & RESORTS

AAA Benefit:
Members get up to 15% off, plus Starwood Preferred Guest® bonuses.

TRAVELODGE HOTEL VANCOUVER AIRPORT *Book great rates at AAA.com*   **Phone:** (604)278-5155   **46**

Hotel
$119-$399 7/1-2/28
$99-$159 3/1-6/30

Address: 3071 St Edwards Dr V6X 3K4 **Location:** Hwy 99, exit 39 (Bridgeport Rd/Airport) northbound to St Edwards Dr; exit 39A (Richmond Rd/Airport) southbound. **Facility:** 160 one-bedroom standard units. 10 stories, interior corridors. **Parking:** on-site. **Terms:** cancellation fee imposed. **Amenities:** video games (fee), voice mail, irons, hair dryers. **Pool(s):** heated indoor. **Leisure Activities:** whirlpool. **Guest Services:** valet laundry, airport transportation-Vancouver International Airport, wireless Internet. **Business Services:** meeting rooms, PC (fee).

VANCOUVER AIRPORT MARRIOTT *Book great rates at AAA.com*   **Phone:** (604)276-2112   **55**

Hotel
$259-$289 All Year

Address: 7571 Westminster Hwy V6X 1A3 **Location:** Corner of Minoru Blvd and Westminster Hwy. **Facility:** Smoke free premises. 237 units. 235 one-bedroom standard units. 2 two-bedroom suites. 18 stories, interior corridors. **Parking:** on-site (fee). **Terms:** cancellation fee imposed. **Amenities:** dual phone lines, voice mail, irons, hair dryers. *Fee:* video games, high-speed Internet. **Pool(s):** heated outdoor. **Leisure Activities:** whirlpool, exercise room. **Guest Services:** valet and coin laundry, airport transportation-Vancouver International Airport, wireless Internet. **Business Services:** meeting rooms, business center. **Free Special Amenities: early check-in/late check-out and preferred room (subject to availability with advance reservations).**

Marriott
HOTELS & RESORTS

AAA Benefit:
Members save a minimum 5% off the best available rate.

THE WESTIN WALL CENTRE VANCOUVER AIRPORT *Book great rates at AAA.com*   **Phone:** 604/303-6565

fyi
Hotel
$140-$229 All Year

Too new to rate, opening scheduled for January 2010. **Address:** 3099 Corvette Way V6X 3L8 **Location:** Sea Island Way; at No 3 Rd. **Amenities:** 188 units. **Terms:** cancellation fee imposed. *(See color ad p 636)*

WESTIN
HOTELS & RESORTS

AAA Benefit:
Enjoy up to 15% off your next stay, plus Starwood Preferred Guest® bonuses.

———— WHERE TO DINE ————

CACTUS CLUB CAFE   **Phone:** 604/244-9969

Canadian
$9-$29

This bustling, casual restaurant serves huge burgers, sandwiches, pasta, salads, soups, quesadillas, fajitas, vegetarian dishes, steak, ribs, chicken and fish. Featured are certified Angus beef and fresh wild British Columbia salmon. The thick and creamy milk shakes come highly recommended. Casual dress. **Bar:** Full bar. **Hours:** 11 am-midnight, Fri & Sat-1 am. Closed: 12/25. **Address:** 5500 No 3 Rd V6X 2C8 **Location:** Corner of No 3 and Lansdowne rds. **Parking:** on-site.

CORRELIS MEDITERRANEAN GRILL   **Phone:** 604/272-7264   **59**

Mediterranean
$7-$21

Traditional Greek dishes with a hint of Italian influence are what guests will find at Correlis. This spot specializes in large portions of fresh local seafood, lamb and chicken. Modern decor, a casual atmosphere and friendly service all add up to a good dining experience. Guests may dine on the patio in warmer weather. Casual dress. **Bar:** Full bar. **Reservations:** suggested, for dinner. **Hours:** 11 am-10 pm; seasonal hours may vary. Closed: 12/25. **Address:** 160-3900 Bayview St V7E 4R7 **Location:** At No 1 Rd. **Parking:** on-site.

(See map and index starting on p. 594)

FLYING BEAVER

Canadian
$9-$20

Phone: 604/273-0278 56

The pub is in the terminal of Harbour Air, a small float plane operation. While chowing down on a good burger or some appetizers, patrons can gaze through large bay windows to watch planes land and take off. Signs to the South Terminal lead to this place, where there's plenty of free parking. Casual dress. **Bar:** Full bar. **Hours:** 11 am-midnight, Sat & Sun from 8 am. Closed: 1/1, 12/25. **Address:** 4760 Inglis Dr V7B 1W4 **Location:** Russ Baker Way, 0.6 mi (1 km) w on Inglis Dr towards south terminal. **Parking:** on-site.

GLOBE @ YVR

Pacific Northwest
$15-$42

Phone: 604/207-5200 55

This restaurant treats diners to a memorable view of air traffic creeping in and out of the gates as service vehicles buzz around like bees. In addition to complete lunch and dinner service, the restaurant offers a wonderful Sunday brunch. The skilled culinary team keeps up the pace in the open-activity kitchen. Casual dress. **Bar:** Full bar. **Reservations:** suggested. **Hours:** 6 am-11 pm. **Address:** 3111 Grant McConachie Way V7B 1X9 **Location:** In Vancouver International Airport; in The Fairmont Vancouver Airport. **Parking:** on-site (fee) and valet. CALL 🛗♿M

KELSEY'S

Canadian
$7-$21

Phone: 604/274-7404

A fun, relaxed atmosphere and tasty menu of casual fare make the restaurant a popular favorite with locals. Diners might start a meal with some tempting appetizers, such as wings, loaded potato skins or nachos, and follow them with an old-time favorite, such as a burger, wrap, pizza or pasta dish. For a heartier meal, it's hard to beat pork back ribs or a steak. The diverse menu has broad appeal. Casual dress. **Bar:** Full bar. **Hours:** 11:30 am-11 pm, Sun-10 pm. **Address:** 100-11300 Steveston Hwy V7A 5J5 **Location:** Steveston Hwy and No 5 Rd; in Ironwood Plaza. **Parking:** on-site.

MOXIE'S CLASSIC GRILL

Canadian
$8-$18

Phone: 604/303-1111

This sleek, funky and popular restaurant presents an extensive menu of creatively prepared dishes, including pizza, pasta, rice, noodles, signature salads and burgers. Other menus include one for children and one for Sunday brunch. Lending to the upbeat, stylish decor are dark wood appointments and river rock fireplaces. Casual dress. **Bar:** Full bar. **Hours:** 6 am-midnight. **Address:** 3233 St Edwards Dr V6X 3K4 **Location:** Hwy 99, exit 39 (Bridgeport Rd/Airport) northbound to St Edwards Dr; exit 39A (Richmond/Airport) southbound; in Sandman Hotel Vancouver Airport. **Parking:** on-site.

RICKY'S ALL DAY GRILL

Canadian
$6-$15

Phone: 604/233-7705

The comfortable eatery, which employs friendly servers, presents a varied menu that includes pasta dishes, wraps, omelets, stir-fry preparations and burgers. Portions are generous. Children's and senior selections are offered. Guests can request seating in a booth or at a table. Casual dress. **Bar:** Full bar. **Hours:** 7 am-8 pm, Fri & Sat-9 pm. **Address:** 9100 Blundell Rd, #490 V6V 1K3 **Location:** Between Garden City Rd and Heather St. **Parking:** on-site. 🔖

STEVESTON SEAFOOD HOUSE

Seafood
$18-$43

Phone: 604/271-5252 57

Voted the city's best seafood restaurant for 8 years in a row, the fine-dining establishment resides in the historic Steveston village. The menu lists ocean-fresh seafood, based on availability. Prawns and scallops are delicious, and the warm and friendly decor is pleasant. Casual dress. **Bar:** Full bar. **Reservations:** suggested. **Hours:** 5:30 pm-9 pm, Fri & Sat-10 pm. Closed major holidays. **Address:** 3951 Moncton St V7E 3A2 **Location:** Jct Moncton St and No 1 Rd; in Steveston Village. **Parking:** street.

TAPENADE BISTRO

Mediterranean
$11-$26

Phone: 604/275-5188 58

An urban bistro features a unique menu including seafood and chicken crepes, panini, daily pasta dishes, fresh fish, chicken, steak and pork. To complement your meal, a large selection of local wines are offered. Casual dress. **Bar:** Full bar. **Reservations:** for dinner. **Hours:** 11:30 am-2:30 & 5-9 pm, Sat & Sun 11 am-3 & 5-9 pm. Closed: 12/25; also Mon. **Address:** 3711 Bayview St V7E 3B6 **Location:** Between 2nd and 3rd aves; in Historic Steveston. **Parking:** street. CALL 🛗♿M

TRAMONTO

Italian
$27-$45

Phone: 604/247-8900 54

Spectacular views of the Fraser River await those who dine at this third-floor dining room, which is perfect for an intimate evening or entertaining an important client. The menu lines up a selection of delicious Southern Italian cuisine, and the extensive wine cellar boasts more than 500 red and white wines from many wine-producing countries. Casual dress. **Bar:** Full bar. **Reservations:** suggested. **Hours:** 6:30 am-2:30 & 5-11 pm. **Address:** 8811 River Rock Rd V6X 3P8 **Location:** Hwy 99, exit 39 (Bridgeport Rd/Airport) northbound; exit 39A (Richmond/Airport) southbound, just w on Bridgeport Rd, then just n on Great Canadian Way; in River Rock Casino Resort. **Parking:** on-site and valet. CALL 🛗♿M

SURREY pop. 347,825 (See map and index starting on p. 594)

BEST WESTERN KING GEORGE INN & SUITES

Book great rates at AAA.com

Phone: (604)502-9000 **70**

Hotel

$86-$170 All Year

Address: 8033 King George Hwy V3W 5B4 **Location:** Jct Fraser Hwy (Hwy 1A), 2.5 mi (4 km) s to 80th Ave. **Facility:** 72 one-bedroom standard units, some with efficiencies. 3 stories, interior corridors. **Parking:** on-site. **Amenities:** high-speed Internet, voice mail, irons, hair dryers. *Some:* dual phone lines. **Pool(s):** heated indoor. **Leisure Activities:** whirlpool, limited exercise equipment. **Guest Services:** valet and coin laundry, wireless Internet. **Business Services:** PC. *(See color ad below)*

CALL / SOME UNITS

AAA Benefit: Members save up to 20%, plus 10% bonus points with rewards program.

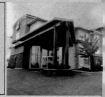

FREE continental breakfast and high-speed Internet

BEST WESTERN PEACE ARCH INN

Book great rates at AAA.com

Phone: (604)541-8100 **73**

Motel

$100-$169 All Year

Address: 2293 King George Hwy V4A 5A4 **Location:** Hwy 99, exit 10 southbound, 2.8 mi (4.5 km) s; exit 2 northbound, 2.1 mi (3.5 km) n. **Facility:** Smoke free premises. 42 one-bedroom standard units, some with whirlpools. 3 stories, interior corridors. **Parking:** on-site. **Terms:** 7 day cancellation notice. **Amenities:** high-speed Internet, voice mail, irons, hair dryers. **Pool(s):** indoor. **Leisure Activities:** sauna, whirlpool, exercise room. **Guest Services:** coin laundry, wireless Internet. **Business Services:** meeting rooms, PC.

CALL

AAA Benefit: Members save up to 20%, plus 10% bonus points with rewards program.

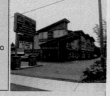

FREE expanded continental breakfast and high-speed Internet

▼ See AAA listing above ▼

Best Western King George Inn & Suites

- Complimentary continental breakfast
- Indoor swimming pool, hot tub and fitness room
- Free above ground parking
- Long Term Stay discounts
- Free Wireless Internet

Best Western King George Inn & Suites

8033 King George Hwy, Surrey, BC V3W 5B4, Canada

604.502.9000 | info@bestwesternsurrey.com

1.866.502.5025 | www.bestwesternsurrey.com

Show Your Card & Save

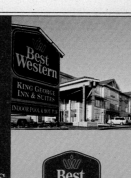

(See map and index starting on p. 594)

COMPASS POINT INN   *Book great rates at AAA.com*   Phone: (604)588-9511

Hotel
$99-$129 All Year

Address: 9850 King George Hwy V3T 4Y3 **Location:** Jct Fraser Hwy (Hwy 1A) and Hwy 99A (King George Hwy). **Facility:** Smoke free premises. 81 one-bedroom standard units. 6 stories, interior corridors. *Bath:* combo or shower only. **Parking:** on-site. **Terms:** cancellation fee imposed. **Amenities:** voice mail, irons, hair dryers. **Dining:** 2 restaurants. **Pool(s):** heated indoor. **Leisure Activities:** whirlpool, exercise room. **Guest Services:** valet and coin laundry, wireless Internet. **Business Services:** meeting rooms, PC (fee). *(See color ad below)*

HAMPTON INN & SUITES LANGLEY/SURREY   *Book great rates at AAA.com*   Phone: (604)530-6545

Hotel
$129-$189 All Year

AAA Benefit:
Members save up to 10% everyday!

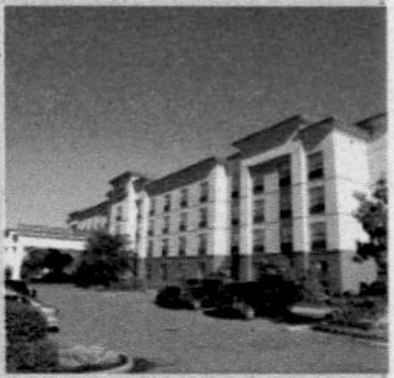

Address: 19500 Langley Bypass V3S 7R2 **Location:** Trans-Canada Hwy 1, exit 58 (200th St/Langley City), 3.1 mi (5 km) s, then 0.7 mi (1.2 km) w on Hwy 10. **Facility:** Smoke free premises. 96 units. 78 one-bedroom standard units. 18 one-bedroom suites with efficiencies. 4 stories, interior corridors. **Parking:** on-site. **Terms:** cancellation fee imposed. **Amenities:** video games, high-speed Internet, voice mail, irons, hair dryers. *Some:* dual phone lines. **Pool(s):** heated indoor. **Leisure Activities:** whirlpool, waterslide, exercise room. **Guest Services:** valet and coin laundry, wireless Internet. **Business Services:** meeting rooms, business center. *(See color ad p 649)*

FREE expanded continental breakfast and high-speed Internet

HOLIDAY INN EXPRESS HOTEL & SUITES   *Book at AAA.com*   Phone: (604)930-8510

Hotel
$99-$149 All Year

Address: 15808 104th Ave V4N 5L2 **Location:** Trans-Canada Hwy 1, exit 50 (160th St), just w. **Facility:** Smoke free premises. 85 one-bedroom standard units, some with whirlpools. 4 stories, interior corridors. **Parking:** on-site. **Amenities:** video games (fee), high-speed Internet, voice mail, irons, hair dryers. **Pool(s):** heated indoor. **Leisure Activities:** sauna, whirlpool, exercise room. **Guest Services:** coin laundry, wireless Internet. **Business Services:** meeting rooms, business center.

▼ See AAA listing p 663 ▼

(See map and index starting on p. 594)

RAMADA HOTEL & SUITES SURREY/GUILDFORD   *Book at AAA.com*   Phone: (604)930-4700   67

Hotel
$99-$159 3/1-9/30
$89-$129 10/1-2/28

Address: 10410 158th St V4N 5C2 **Location:** Trans-Canada Hwy 1, exit 50 (160th St), just w on 104th Ave. **Facility:** 77 one-bedroom standard units. 3 stories, interior corridors. *Bath:* combo or shower only. **Parking:** on-site. **Terms:** cancellation fee imposed. **Amenities:** voice mail, irons, hair dryers. **Pool(s):** heated outdoor. **Leisure Activities:** whirlpool, exercise room. **Guest Services:** valet laundry, wireless Internet. **Business Services:** meeting rooms, PC (fee).

RAMADA LANGLEY-SURREY   *Book great rates at AAA.com*   Phone: (604)576-8388   72

Hotel
$119-$169 All Year

Address: 19225 Hwy 10 V3S 8V9 **Location:** Trans-Canada Hwy 1, exit 58 (200th St/Langley City), 3.1 mi (5 km) s on 200th St, then 1.2 mi (2 km) w on Rt 10; corner of 192nd St and Rt 10. **Facility:** Smoke free premises. 85 one-bedroom standard units, some with efficiencies. 3 stories, interior corridors. **Parking:** on-site. **Terms:** cancellation fee imposed. **Amenities:** voice mail, safes, irons, hair dryers. *Some:* high-speed Internet. **Pool(s):** heated indoor. **Leisure Activities:** whirlpool, exercise room. **Guest Services:** valet and coin laundry, wireless Internet. **Business Services:** meeting rooms, business center.

FREE expanded continental breakfast and high-speed Internet

SHERATON VANCOUVER GUILDFORD HOTEL   *Book great rates at AAA.com*   Phone: 604/582-9288   66

Hotel
Rates not provided

Address: 15269 104th Ave V3R 1N5 **Location:** Trans-Canada Hwy 1, exit 48 eastbound, 0.6 mi (1 km) s on 152nd St, just e; exit 50 westbound, then just w. **Facility:** Smoke free premises. 279 one-bedroom standard units, some with whirlpools. 20 stories, interior corridors. **Parking:** on-site (fee) and valet. **Amenities:** voice mail. *Some:* video games (fee), irons, hair dryers. **Pool(s):** heated outdoor. **Leisure Activities:** whirlpool, exercise room. **Guest Services:** valet laundry, wireless Internet. **Business Services:** meeting rooms, business center. *(See color ad p 662)*

Sheraton
HOTELS & RESORTS

AAA Benefit:
Members get up to 15% off, plus Starwood Preferred Guest® bonuses.

FREE early check-in/late check-out and room upgrade (subject to availability with advance reservations)

—— WHERE TO DINE ——

CRESCENT BEACH BISTRO   Phone: 604/531-1882   67

Seafood
$10-$26

Diners here enjoy a delightful setting either on the lovely outdoor terrace or the quaint indoor dining room. Plants adorn both sections and the lively Mediterranean background music adds to the atmosphere. Menu highlights include Spanish paella, shrimp and scallops with tangy mango chutney, or a more traditional rack of lamb. Its best to phone ahead for reservations as it's very popular with the locals. Casual dress. **Bar:** Full bar. **Reservations:** suggested. **Hours:** 11:30 am-2 & 5-10 pm, Sat from 5 pm. Closed major holidays; also Sun. **Address:** 12251 Beecher St V4A 3A4 **Location:** 2 blks from Crescent Beach at McKenzie Ave. **Parking:** street.

MOXIE'S CLASSIC GRILL   Phone: 604/495-7020

Canadian
$8-$18

This sleek, funky and popular restaurant presents an extensive menu of creatively prepared dishes, including pizza, pasta, rice, noodles, signature salads and burgers. Other menus include one for children and one for Sunday brunch. Lending to the upbeat, stylish decor are dark wood appointments and river rock fireplaces. Casual dress. **Bar:** Full bar. **Hours:** 11 am-midnight, Fri & Sat-1 am. **Address:** 10608 151A St V3R 1J8 **Location:** Trans-Canada Hwy 1, exit 48 eastbound, 0.6 mi (1 km) s on 152nd St; exit 50 westbound, 0.6 mi (1 km) s on 104th Ave. **Parking:** on-site.

RICKY'S ALL DAY GRILL   Phone: 604/582-2545

Canadian
$10-$29

The comfortable eatery, which employs friendly servers, presents a varied menu that includes pasta dishes, wraps, omelets, stir-fry preparations and burgers. Portions are generous. Children's and senior selections are offered. Guests can request seating in a booth or at a table. Casual dress. **Bar:** Full bar. **Hours:** 7 am-9 pm, Mon & Tues-8 pm. **Address:** 1076 Central City V3T 2W1 **Location:** Between King George Hwy and 100th Ave. **Parking:** on-site.

RICKY'S ALL DAY GRILL   Phone: 604/581-3212

Canadian
$10-$29

The comfortable eatery, which employs friendly servers, presents a varied menu that includes pasta dishes, wraps, omelets, stir-fry preparations and burgers. Portions are generous. Children's and senior selections are offered. Guests can request seating in a booth or at a table. Casual dress. **Bar:** Full bar. **Hours:** 6 am-9 pm. **Address:** 8958 152nd St V3R 4L7 **Location:** Between Fraser Hwy and 88th Ave. **Parking:** on-site.

(See map and index starting on p. 594)

RICKY'S ALL DAY GRILL

Canadian
$10-$29

Phone: 604/535-1789

The comfortable eatery, which employs friendly servers, presents a varied menu that includes pasta dishes, wraps, omelets, stir-fry preparations and burgers. Portions are generous. Children's and senior selections are offered. Guests can request seating in a booth or at a table. Casual dress. **Bar:** Full bar. **Hours:** 6 am-9 pm. **Address:** 3189 King George Hwy V4P 1B8 **Location:** Hwy 99, exit 10, 1.9 mi (3 km) s. **Parking:** on-site.

SWISS CHALET

Canadian
$6-$18

Phone: 604/583-0883

The popular restaurant is known for its rotisserie chicken and ribs and the tangy Chalet sauce that gives food its special zip. Diners munch on a half or quarter chicken with sides such as steamed vegetables, fries, baked potatoes and salads. Lunch guests often go for the great soup and sandwich combination. Take-out and delivery service are popular options. Casual dress. **Bar:** Full bar. **Hours:** 11:30 am-10 pm, Sun 11 am-9:30 pm. Closed: 12/25. **Address:** 9666 King George Hwy V3T 2V4 **Location:** King George Hwy at 96th Ave. **Parking:** on-site.

THE TURKEY HOUSE & DELI

Deli
$7-$12

Phone: 604/531-6222 68

Since 1973, the distinctive combination restaurant and delicatessen has been serving 100 percent turkey products and unforgettable home-cooked meals. On the menu are varied sandwiches and soups, as well as hot items that can be eaten here or taken out. Visitors can purchase turkey deli meats and pre-made dishes that can be warmed at home, including turkey pies, sausage rolls and lasagna. Casual dress. **Hours:** 9 am-6 pm. Closed major holidays; also Sun & Mon. **Address:** 1433 King George Hwy V4A 4Z5 **Location:** Hwy 99, exit 2B southbound; from Canada/US border, exit 2 northbound, then 0.6 mi (1 km) n. **Parking:** on-site.

VILLA VERDI RISTORANTE ITALIANO

Italian
$15-$32

Phone: 604/591-2123 66

Open for lunch and dinner, the Italian restaurant offers a choice among a wide selection of pasta dishes, including a pasta bar option that lets patrons customize a specialty dish from a list of pastas and sauces. Free parking is plentiful. Casual dress. **Bar:** Full bar. **Reservations:** suggested. **Hours:** 11:30 am-2 & 5:30-10 pm, Sat from 5:30 pm. Closed major holidays; also Sun. **Address:** 13620 80th Ave V3W 6M1 **Location:** Jct Fraser Hwy (Hwy 1A), 2.5 mi (4 km) s on King George Hwy. **Parking:** on-site. CALL &M

YOKOHAMA JAPANESE RESTAURANT

Japanese
$7-$21

Phone: 604/584-4555 65

Tatami rooms and a full sushi bar contribute to the cozy environment, which occupies a slightly hard-to-find location in a small strip mall. The combination dinner includes beef teriyaki, tempura, noodles, rice and dessert. Another option is the all-you-can-eat lunch and dinner menu. Service is pleasant. Casual dress. **Bar:** Beer & wine. **Reservations:** suggested, weekends. **Hours:** 11:30 am-2:30 & 5-10 pm, Fri & Sat-10:30 pm, Sun noon-3 & 5-10 pm. Closed: 1/1, 12/24, 12/25. **Address:** 10356 137th St V3T 4H4 **Location:** Just off Hwy 99A (King George Hwy) at 104th Ave on Whalley Ring Rd. **Parking:** on-site.

WEST VANCOUVER pop. 42,131 (See map and index starting on p. 594)

─── **WHERE TO DINE** ───

CACTUS CLUB CAFE

Canadian
$9-$29

Phone: 604/922-1707

This bustling, casual restaurant serves huge burgers, sandwiches, pasta, salads, soups, quesadillas, fajitas, vegetarian dishes, steak, ribs, chicken and fish. Featured are certified Angus beef and fresh wild British Columbia salmon. The thick and creamy milk shakes come highly recommended. Casual dress. **Bar:** Full bar. **Hours:** 11 am-midnight, Fri & Sat-1 am. Closed: 12/25. **Address:** 855 Main St V7T 2Z3 **Location:** Just off Marine Dr; in Village at Park Royal. **Parking:** on-site.

FRAICHE

Pacific Northwest
$14-$45

Phone: 604/925-7595 32

On a hillside in a newly constructed residential neighborhood sits this wonderful restaurant owned by a chef who worked the Four Seasons resorts for 16 years until opening his own place. Stunning views, inviting decor and delicious food await those who head up the mountain. The menu is a showcase for fresh seasonal and regional cuisine, such as an organic beef burger, grilled bison rib-eye, arctic char and local sablefish. Dressy casual. **Bar:** Full bar. **Reservations:** suggested. **Hours:** 11:30 am-2:30 & 5-10 pm, Sat & Sun 11 am-3 pm. Closed major holidays; also Mon. **Address:** 2-2240 Chippendale Rd V7S 3J5 **Location:** Trans-Canada Hwy 1, exit 10 (21st St), just w to Folkstone Way, 0.9 mi (1.5 km) n, then just e. **Parking:** valet and street. CALL &M

LA REGALADE FRENCH BISTRO

French
$19-$25

Phone: 604/921-2228 35

The tiny, family-run bistro blends fantastically fresh ingredients in heaping plates of great food. The chef/owner hails from France and has cooked at fine restaurants both in France and here in the city. Daily specials are listed on the wall chalkboard. The many homemade desserts on display deserve serious consideration. Casual dress. **Bar:** Full bar. **Reservations:** suggested. **Hours:** 11:30 am-2 & 5:30-10 pm, Sat from 5:30 pm. Closed: Sun & Mon. **Address:** #103 2232 Marine Dr V7V 1K4 **Location:** Trans-Canada Hwy 1, exit 10 (22nd St), 0.9 mi (1.5 km) s, then just w. **Parking:** street.

SALMON HOUSE ON THE HILL

Seafood
$29-$35

Phone: 604/926-3212 33

You'll certainly appreciate the incredible panoramic view of the city and harbor from the Salmon House's hilltop location. The restaurant's cuisine specializes in Pacific Rim influences, with fresh British Columbia salmon as the house specialty. Casual dress. **Bar:** Full bar. **Reservations:** suggested. **Hours:** 5 pm-10 pm, Sat & Sun also 10:30 am-2:30 pm. Closed: 12/24, 12/25. **Address:** 2229 Folkestone Way V7S 2Y6 **Location:** Trans-Canada Hwy 1, exit 10 (21st St), follow signs. **Parking:** on-site. CALL &M

WHITE ROCK pop. 18,755   (See map and index starting on p. 594)

OCEAN PROMENADE HOTEL   *Book great rates at AAA.com*   **Phone:** (604)542-0102   84

Hotel

$139-$469 3/1-10/1
$129-$469 10/2-2/28

Address: 15611 Marine Dr V4B 1E1 **Location:** Hwy 99, exit 2B southbound; exit 2 (White Rock/8th Ave) northbound, 1.3 mi (2 km) w. **Facility:** 51 one-bedroom standard units, some with kitchens and/or whirlpools. 3 stories, interior/exterior corridors. **Parking:** on-site. **Terms:** check-in 4 pm, cancellation fee imposed. **Amenities:** DVD players, high-speed Internet, voice mail, safes, irons, hair dryers. **Leisure Activities:** exercise room. **Guest Services:** valet and coin laundry. **Business Services:** meeting rooms. *(See color ad below)*

FREE local telephone calls and high-speed Internet

------ **WHERE TO DINE** ------

GIRAFFE   **Phone:** 604/538-6878   75

Pacific Rim
$10-$28

All tables at the lovely, intimate restaurant face the water. Giraffe-centric decor, including the noteworthy napkin holders, suits this place's name. Daily specials, which are printed on a blackboard at the entrance, are can't-miss choices. The dining room's small size accounts for tight table spacing. Pay parking is in effect at all times. Casual dress. **Bar:** Full bar. **Reservations:** suggested. **Hours:** 5:30 pm-9 pm, Thurs-Sat also 11:30 am-2 pm, Sun 11 am-2 & 5:30-9 pm; Sunday brunch. Closed major holidays. **Address:** 15053 Marine Dr V4B 1C5 **Location:** Hwy 99, exit 2B southbound; exit 2 northbound, 1.8 mi (3 km) w. **Parking:** street.

LA BAIA ITALIAN RESTAURANT   **Phone:** 604/531-6261   76

Italian
$14-$25

Delicious rack of lamb and veal Marsala are among choices at the bright and airy restaurant, which displays antiques and offers a nice view of the park. The atmosphere is cozy, and service is friendly and attentive. Those who can't nab a free parking spot at the back can pay to park on the street. Casual dress. **Bar:** Full bar. **Reservations:** suggested. **Hours:** 5 pm-10 pm. Closed major holidays. **Address:** 15791 Marine Dr V4B 1E5 **Location:** Hwy 99, exit 2B southbound; exit 2 northbound, 0.9 mi (1.5 km) w. **Parking:** on-site.

PEARL ON THE ROCK   *Menu on AAA.com*   **Phone:** 604/542-1064   74

Pacific Northwest
$13-$45

Across from the beach, where there is plenty of pay parking in lots or at street meters, the restaurant has an open patio that makes it a hot spot for people-watching. However, one sampling from the spectacular menu makes clear the real draw: the food. With or without wine pairings, the tasting menu highlights wonderfully creative seafood dishes. Casual dress. **Bar:** Full bar. **Reservations:** suggested. **Hours:** 11:30 am-2:30 & 5-9 pm. Closed: 1/1, 10/11, 12/24, 12/25. **Address:** 14955 Marine Dr V4B 1C3 **Location:** Hwy 99, exit 2B southbound; exit 2 northbound, 2.1 mi (3.5 km) w. **Parking:** street.

The previous listings were for the Vancouver Vicinity.
This page resumes the alphabetical listings of cities in British Columbia.

VANDERHOOF pop. 4,064

——— WHERE TO DINE ———

RICKY'S ALL DAY GRILL

Canadian
$6-$15

Phone: 250/567-6080

The comfortable eatery, which employs friendly servers, presents a varied menu that includes pasta dishes, wraps, omelets, stir-fry preparations and burgers. Portions are generous. Children's and senior selections are offered. Guests can request seating in a booth or at a table. Casual dress. **Bar:** Full bar. **Hours:** 7 am-8 pm, Fri & Sat-9 pm. **Address:** 2351 Church St V0J 3A0 **Location:** Corner of Church St and Stewart Ave. **Parking:** on-site.

VERNON—See Okanagan Valley p. 564.

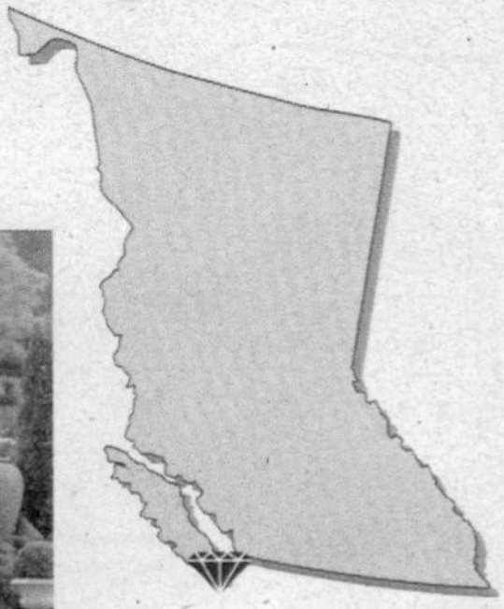

Destination Victoria
pop. 74,125

*T*he Trans-Canada Highway ends in Victoria, but your journey isn't complete until you've seen the city and its surroundings.

*W*ander down cobblestone streets lined with Victorian lampposts. Tour one glorious English garden after another. Do the town in a double-decker bus. Or cruise to neighboring islands.

Butchart Gardens, Brentwood Bay.
(See listing page 200)

Bastion Square, Victoria.
(See listing page 194)

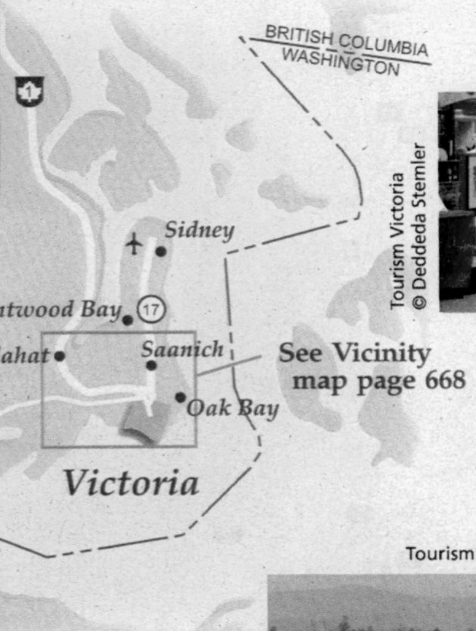

Shopping in Victoria.

See Vicinity map page 668

Tourism Victoria © Frank Leung

*P*laces included in this AAA Destination City:

Whale-watching in Victoria.

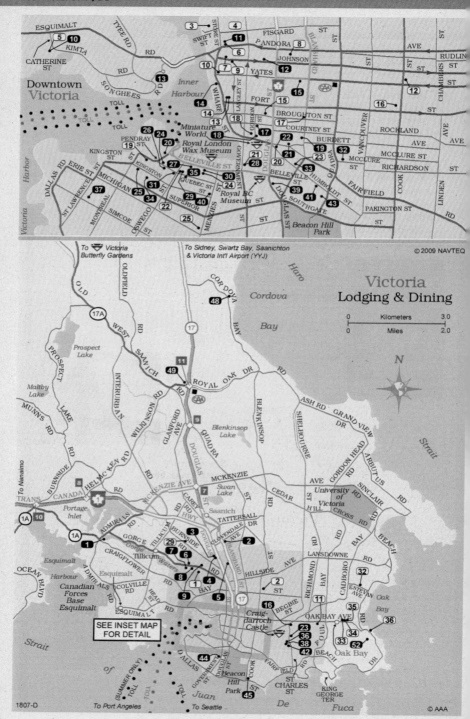

Downtown Victoria

Victoria
Lodging & Dining

© 2009 NAVTEQ

SEE INSET MAP
FOR DETAIL

1807-D

© AAA

✈ Airport Accommodations

Map Page	OA	VICTORIA AIRPORT	Diamond Rated	High Season	Page
N/A	(AAA)	Quality Inn Waddling Dog, 0.6 mi (1 km) se of airport	◇◇	$125-$145 SAVE	696
N/A	(AAA)	Victoria Airport Super 8, 0.6 mi (1 km) e of airport	◇◇	Rates not provided SAVE	696
N/A	(AAA)	Best Western Emerald Isle Motor Inn, 1.2 mi (2 km) n of airport	◇◇◇	$135-$349 SAVE	697
N/A	(AAA)	The Cedarwood Inn & Suites, 1.2 mi (2 km) se of airport	◇◇◇	$95-$255 SAVE	697
N/A	(AAA)	Victoria Airport Travelodge Sidney, 1.2 mi (2 km) e of airport	◇◇	$129-$199 SAVE	697

Victoria

is index helps you "spot" where approved lodgings and restaurants are located on the corresponding detailed maps. Lodging
lly rate range is for comparison only and show the property's high season. Restaurant rate range is a combination of lunch
d/or dinner. Turn to the listing page for more detailed rate information and consult display ads for special promotions.

VICTORIA

Map Page	OA	Lodgings	Diamond Rated	High Season	Page
1 / p. 668	(AAA)	Comfort Inn & Suites	◇◇	$139-$299 SAVE	677
2 / p. 668	(AAA)	Accent Inns	◇◇	$99-$189 SAVE	672
3 / p. 668	(AAA)	Mayfair Motel	◇◇	$49-$119 SAVE	683
4 / p. 668	(AAA)	Blue Ridge Inns	◇◇	$69-$129 SAVE	676
5 / p. 668	(AAA)	Comfort Hotel & Conference Centre	◇◇◇	$143-$259 SAVE	676
6 / p. 668	(AAA)	Robin Hood Motel - see color ad p 685	◇◇	$66-$109 SAVE	685
7 / p. 668		Ramada Victoria	◇◇	$125-$185	684
8 / p. 668	(AAA)	Travelodge Victoria - see color ad p 688	◇◇	$79-$189 SAVE	687
9 / p. 668	(AAA)	Howard Johnson Hotel-City of Victoria	◇◇	$69-$159 SAVE	682
10 / p. 668		Spinnakers Gastro Brewpub and Guesthouses	◇◇◇	$129-$249	685
11 / p. 668		Swans Suite Hotel - see color ad p 687	◇◇◇	$149-$359	686
12 / p. 668	(AAA)	Best Western Carlton Plaza Hotel - see color ad p 674	◇◇◇	$114-$199 SAVE	675
13 / p. 668	(AAA)	Delta Victoria Ocean Pointe Resort and Spa	◇◇◇◇	$129-$328 SAVE	678
14 / p. 668	(AAA)	Victoria Regent Waterfront Hotel & Suites - see color ad p 689	◇◇◇	$139-$309 SAVE	687
15 / p. 668	(AAA)	Dalton Hotel & Suites	◇	$85-$229 SAVE	677
16 / p. 668	(AAA)	Amethyst Inn at Regents Park	◇◇◇	$119-$269 SAVE	674
17 / p. 668	(AAA)	The Magnolia Hotel & Spa	◇◇◇◇	$149-$349 SAVE	683
18 / p. 668		Union Club of British Columbia	◇◇◇	$179-$409	687
19 / p. 668		Quality Inn Downtown	◇◇◇	$69-$169	684
20 / p. 668	(AAA)	Admiral Inn - see color ad p 673	◇◇	$99-$269 SAVE	673
21 / p. 668		Chateau Victoria Hotel and Suites - see color ad p 677	◇◇◇	$105-$229	676

VICTORIA (cont'd)

Map Page	OA	Lodgings (cont'd)	Diamond Rated	High Season	Page
22 / p. 668	CAA	**Executive House Hotel** - see color ad p 679	◆◆	$99-$215 [SAVE]	679
23 / p. 668		Villa Marco Polo Inn	◆◆◆	$145-$335	690
24 / p. 668	CAA	**Huntingdon Hotel & Suites**	◆◆	$99-$389 [SAVE]	682
25 / p. 668		Haterleigh Heritage Inn	◆◆◆	$150-$250	680
26 / p. 668	CAA	**Harbour Towers Hotel & Suites**	◆◆◆	$94-$450 [SAVE]	680
27 / p. 668	CAA	**Days Inn Victoria on the Harbour** - see color ad p 678	◆◆	$79-$213 [SAVE]	678
28 / p. 668		The Fairmont Empress	◆◆◆◆	Rates not provided	679
29 / p. 668	CAA	**Best Western Inner Harbour Hotel** - see color ad p 675	◆◆◆	$95-$275 [SAVE]	675
30 / p. 668	CAA	**Hotel Grand Pacific** - see color ad p 681	◆◆◆◆	$149-$329 [SAVE]	682
31 / p. 668	CAA	**The Oswego Hotel**	◆◆◆	$159-$599 [SAVE]	684
32 / p. 668	CAA	**Abigail's Hotel** - see color ad p 672	◆◆◆	$189-$480 [SAVE]	672
33 / p. 668	CAA	**Marriott Victoria Inner Harbour** - see color ad p 683	◆◆◆◆	$209-$339 [SAVE]	683
34 / p. 668		Andersen House Bed & Breakfast	◆◆◆	$125-$275	674
35 / p. 668	CAA	**Royal Scot Hotel & Suites** - see color ad p 686	◆◆◆	$145-$265 [SAVE]	685
36 / p. 668		Abbeymoore Manor Bed & Breakfast Inn	◆◆◆	$139-$249	672
37 / p. 668		Heathergate House Bed & Breakfast	◆◆	$85-$145	681
38 / p. 668		Fairholme Manor	◆◆◆	$175-$325	679
39 / p. 668	CAA	**Queen Victoria Hotel and Suites** - see color ad p 684	◆◆◆	$130-$450 [SAVE]	684
40 / p. 668	CAA	**Embassy Inn**	◆◆	$99-$370 [SAVE]	678
41 / p. 668		Humboldt House Bed & Breakfast	◆◆	$147-$295	682
42 / p. 668	CAA	**Prior House B&B Inn**	◆◆◆◆	$159-$259 [SAVE]	684
43 / p. 668		Ambrosia Historic Bed & Breakfast Retreat	◆◆◆	$115-$275	673
44 / p. 668	CAA	**James Bay Inn Hotel & Suites** - see color ad p 682	◆	$76-$165 [SAVE]	683
45 / p. 668		Dashwood Seaside Heritage Manor	◆◆	$135-$285	677

Map Page	OA	Restaurants	Diamond Rated	Cuisine	Meal Range	Page
1 / p. 668		Glo Euro Pub	◆◆	Canadian	$9-$20	692
2 / p. 668		Haultain's Fish & Chips	◆	Fish & Chips	$10-$18	692
3 / p. 668		Canoe Brewpub Marina Restaurant	◆◆	Canadian	$9-$28	691
4 / p. 668		Hunan Village	◆◆	Chinese	$8-$15	692
5 / p. 668	CAA	**Spinnakers Gastro Brewpub & Restaurant**	◆◆	Canadian	$10-$23	694
6 / p. 668		Wild Saffron Bistro & Wine Bar	◆◆◆	Pacific Rim	$15-$34	694
7 / p. 668		Cafe Mexico	◆◆	Mexican	$11-$19	691

Map Page	OA	Restaurants (cont'd)	Diamond Rated	Cuisine	Meal Range	Page
8 / p. 668	AA	**The Black Olive**	◈◈◈	Mediterranean	$10-$34	691
9 / p. 668		Il Terrazzo	◈◈◈	Italian	$10-$35	692
10 / p. 668		Restaurant Matisse	◈◈◈	French	$20-$33	693
11 / p. 668		White Heather Tea Room	◈◈	Breads/Pastries	$8-$14	694
12 / p. 668		Passero's Mediterranean Cuisine	◈◈	Mediterranean	$7-$19	693
13 / p. 668		Siam Thai Restaurant	◈◈	Thai	$8-$18	693
14 / p. 668		Koto Japanese Restaurant	◈◈	Japanese	$6-$20	692
15 / p. 668		Pagliacci's	◈◈	Italian	$6-$24	693
16 / p. 668		Pluto's	◈◈	Canadian	$7-$15	693
17 / p. 668		The Pink Bicycle	◈◈	Burgers	$12-$15	693
18 / p. 668		Pescatore's Seafood & Grill	◈◈◈	Seafood	$10-$32	693
19 / p. 668		Niche	◈◈◈	Pacific Northwest	$18-$24	693
20 / p. 668		Barkley's Steak & Seafood	◈◈◈	Steak	$22-$45	691
21 / p. 668		The Empress Room	◈◈◈◈	Pacific Northwest	$14-$45	691
22 / p. 668		Victoria Harbour House Restaurant	◈◈	Steak	$16-$35	694
23 / p. 668		Fire & Water Fish & Chop House	◈◈◈	Pacific Northwest	$12-$36	691
24 / p. 668	AA	**The Mark**	◈◈◈	Regional Canadian	$32-$42	692
25 / p. 668	AA	**James Bay Tea Room & Restaurant**	◈◈	Canadian	$8-$14	692

SAANICH

Map Page	OA	Lodgings	Diamond Rated	High Season	Page
48 / p. 668		Sunnymeade House B&B	◈◈	Rates not provided	696
49 / p. 668		Howard Johnson Hotel & Suites	◈◈◈	$117-$153	696

Map Page	OA	Restaurants	Diamond Rated	Cuisine	Meal Range	Page
29 / p. 668		Brady's Fish & Chips	◈	Fish & Chips	$7-$13	696

OAK BAY

Map Page	OA	Lodging	Diamond Rated	High Season	Page
52 / p. 668		Oak Bay Guest House Bed & Breakfast	◈◈	$139-$199	695

Map Page	OA	Restaurants	Diamond Rated	Cuisine	Meal Range	Page
32 / p. 668		Paprika Bistro	◈◈◈	Continental	$20-$32	695
33 / p. 668		Penny Farthing Public House	◈◈	Canadian	$8-$17	695
34 / p. 668		The Blethering Place Tea Room & Restaurant	◈◈	Canadian	$6-$17	695
35 / p. 668		Ottavio Italian Bakery & Delicatessen	◈◈	Italian	$7-$14	695
36 / p. 668		The Marina Restaurant	◈◈◈	Seafood	$12-$32	695

VICTORIA pop. 78,057 (See map and index starting on p. 668)

ABBEYMOORE MANOR BED & BREAKFAST INN

Historic Bed
& Breakfast
$139-$249 3/1-10/28
$109-$219 10/29-2/28

Phone: (250)370-1470

Address: 1470 Rockland Ave V8S 1W2 **Location:** Blanshard St (Hwy 17), 1.2 mi (2 km) e on Fort just s on St Charles St, then just w. **Facility:** Once the residence of a lieutenant governor, renovated B&B is in a neighborhood dotted with stately Victorian homes. Smoke free premises units. 5 one-bedroom standard units. 2 one-bedroom suites with efficiencies and whirlpools. 3 stor (no elevator), interior/exterior corridors. **Bath:** combo or shower only. **Parking:** on-site. **Terms:** off hours 7 am-10 pm, check-in 4 pm, 14 day cancellation notice-fee imposed. **Amenities:** CD playe hair dryers. *Some:* DVD players. **Guest Services:** wireless Internet. **Business Services:** PC.

ABIGAIL'S HOTEL　　*Book great rates at AAA.com*

Boutique
Hotel
$189-$480 All Year

Phone: (250)388-5363

Address: 906 McClure St V8V 3E7 **Location:** Blanshard St (Hwy 17), just e on Fairfield Rd, then just n on Vancouver St. Located in a quiet residential area. **Facility:** The European-style boutique hotel has newer rooms with TVs, refrigerators and coffee makers; older rooms boast fireplaces and large, claw-foot tubs. Smoke free premises. 23 one-bedroom standard units, some with whirlpools. 2-3 stories (no elevator), interior corridors. **Bath:** combo or shower only. **Parking:** on-site. **Terms:** 14 day cancellation notice-fee imposed. **Amenities:** video library, DVD players, voice mail, hair dryers. *Some:* irons. **Leisure Activities:** spa. **Guest Services:** valet laundry, wireless Internet. **Business Services:** PC. *(See color ad below)*

FREE full breakfast and high-speed Internet

ACCENT INNS　　*Book great rates at AAA.com*

Hotel
$99-$189 All Year

Phone: (250)475-7500

Address: 3233 Maple St V8X 4Y9 **Location:** 1.9 mi (3 km) n on Blanshard St (Hwy 17); corner Blanshard St and Cloverdale Ave. **Facility:** 118 one-bedroom standard units, some with efficiencies stories, exterior corridors. **Parking:** on-site. **Amenities:** high-speed Internet, voice mail, irons, h dryers. **Guest Services:** valet and coin laundry, wireless Internet. **Business Services:** meet rooms, PC. **Free Special Amenities:** newspaper and high-speed Internet.

▼ *See AAA listing above* ▼

HOTEL

**AAA/CAA
Approved**

Escape to Abigail's Hotel and see what breathtaking Victoria, BC has to offer!

This boutique style B&B is located just steps from downtown Victoria's famous attractions, museums, theatres, fine restaurants, and parks. Includes gourmet breakfast personally presented by the Executive Chef, plus evening hors d'oeuvres, 24 hr parkin & internet service. Spa services on-site. Some packages include attractions passes!

906 McClure Street, Victoria BC · 1-800-561-6565 · www.abigailshotel.com

ee map and index starting on p. 668)

ADMIRAL INN

Motel
S99-$269 All Year

Phone: (250)388-6267 **20**

Address: 257 Belleville St V8V 1X1 **Location:** Corner of Belleville and Quebec sts. **Facility:** Smoke free premises. 32 units. 21 one-bedroom standard units, some with kitchens. 11 one-bedroom suites with kitchens. 3 stories, exterior corridors. **Parking:** on-site. **Terms:** office hours 7:30 am-11 pm, 15 day cancellation notice-fee imposed. **Amenities:** irons, hair dryers. **Guest Services:** coin laundry, wireless Internet. **Business Services:** PC. *(See color ad below)*

FREE expanded continental breakfast and high-speed Internet

AMBROSIA HISTORIC BED & BREAKFAST RETREAT

Historic Bed & Breakfast
$115-$275 All Year

Phone: 250/380-7705 **43**

Address: 522 Quadra St V8V 3S3 **Location:** Between Southgate and Humboldt sts. **Facility:** Located within walking distance of downtown and Beacon Hill Park, the inn offers spacious rooms in a fully restored Victorian-style home. Smoke free premises. 4 one-bedroom standard units, some with whirlpools. 2 stories (no elevator), interior corridors. *Bath:* combo or shower only. **Parking:** on-site. **Terms:** office hours 8 am-10 pm, check-in 4 pm, 2 night minimum stay - seasonal and/or weekends, age restrictions may apply, 14 day cancellation notice-fee imposed. **Amenities:** CD players, hair dryers. **Guest Services:** wireless Internet.

▼ See AAA listing above ▼

(See map and index starting on p. 668)

AMETHYST INN AT REGENTS PARK　　　　　　　　　　　　Phone: (250)595-2053

Historic Bed
& Breakfast

$119-$269 All Year

Address: 1501 Fort St V8S 1Z6 **Location:** Blanshard St (Hwy 17), 1.2 mi (2 km) e on Fort St to Charles St. Located in a residential area. **Facility:** Located in a charming residential neighborhood, Victorian mansion features antiques, stained glass windows and a magnificent staircase. Smoke fr premises. 13 one-bedroom standard units, some with whirlpools. 3 stories (no elevat interior/exterior corridors. **Parking:** on-site. **Terms:** office hours 7 am-11 pm, age restrictions m apply, 14 day cancellation notice-fee imposed. **Amenities:** DVD players, CD players, hair drye **Guest Services:** wireless Internet. **Business Services:** PC. **Free Special Amenities: full breakfa and high-speed Internet.**

ANDERSEN HOUSE BED & BREAKFAST　　　　　　　　　Phone: 250/388-4565

Historic Bed
& Breakfast

$125-$275 All Year

Address: 301 Kingston St V8V 1V5 **Location:** Between Pendray and Montreal sts. **Facility:** T 1891 home in Victoria's Inner Harbour blends rich historic details with comfortable, contempora furnishings and original artwork. Smoke free premises. 4 one-bedroom standard units, some w whirlpools. 3 stories (no elevator), interior/exterior corridors. *Bath:* combo or shower only. **Parking:** site. **Terms:** office hours 8 am-10 pm, 2 night minimum stay - seasonal and/or weekends, a restrictions may apply, 14 day cancellation notice-fee imposed. **Amenities:** DVD players, CD playe irons, hair dryers. **Guest Services:** wireless Internet.

▼ *See AAA listing p 675* ▼

Close to Just About Everything!
Downtown Victoria

- Bright, spacious and well-appointed guestrooms and suites
- Suites offer full kitchen facilities
- De Dutch Pannekoek House Restaurant
- Complimentary high-speed internet access, bottled water & local calls
- Fitness facility
- Valet parking

BEST WESTERN CARLTON PLAZA
642 Johnson Street, Victoria V8W 1M6

www.bestwesterncarlton.com　　　1.800.663.7241

ee map and index starting on p. 668)

BEST WESTERN CARLTON PLAZA HOTEL *Book great rates at AAA.com* Phone: (250)388-5513 12

Hotel
$114-$199 All Year

Address: 642 Johnson St V8W 1M6 **Location:** Between Douglas and Broad sts. **Facility:** Smoke free premises. 103 units. 97 one-bedroom standard units, some with efficiencies or kitchens. 6 one-bedroom suites with kitchens. 7 stories, interior corridors. **Parking:** on-site (fee) and valet. **Terms:** cancellation fee imposed. **Amenities:** voice mail, safes, irons, hair dryers. *Some:* high-speed Internet. **Leisure Activities:** exercise room. **Guest Services:** valet and coin laundry, wireless Internet. **Business Services:** PC. *(See color ad p 674)*

FREE local telephone calls and high-speed Internet

BEST WESTERN INNER HARBOUR HOTEL *Book great rates at AAA.com* Phone: (250)384-5122 29

Hotel
$95-$275 All Year

Address: 412 Quebec St V8V 1W5 **Location:** Between Oswego and Menzies sts. **Facility:** Smoke free premises. 74 units. 66 one-bedroom standard units, some with kitchens (utensils extra charge). 7 one- and 1 two-bedroom suites with whirlpools, some with efficiencies or kitchens (utensils extra charge). 8 stories, interior corridors. **Parking:** on-site. **Terms:** check-in 4 pm, cancellation fee imposed. **Amenities:** video library (fee), high-speed Internet, voice mail, irons, hair dryers. *Some:* DVD players (fee). **Pool(s):** heated outdoor. **Leisure Activities:** sauna, whirlpool, steamroom, exercise room. **Guest Services:** valet and coin laundry, wireless Internet. **Business Services:** PC. **Free Special Amenities:** expanded continental breakfast and high-speed Internet. *(See color ad below)*

(See map and index starting on p. 668)

BLUE RIDGE INNS — *Book great rates at AAA.com* — Phone: (250)388-4345

Motel
$69-$129 All Year

Address: 3110 Douglas St V8Z 3K4 **Location:** Between Finlayson St and Speed Ave. **Facility:** units. 61 one-bedroom standard units, some with efficiencies or kitchens. 1 two-bedroom suite w kitchen. 1 cottage. 2 stories (no elevator), exterior corridors. *Bath:* combo or shower only. **Parking:** o site. **Amenities:** voice mail. **Pool(s):** heated indoor. **Leisure Activities:** sauna. **Guest Services:** cc laundry, wireless Internet. **Business Services:** meeting rooms, PC. **Free Special Amenitie** newspaper and high-speed Internet.

CHATEAU VICTORIA HOTEL AND SUITES — *Book great rates at AAA.com* — Phone: (250)382-4221

Hotel
$105-$229 3/1-9/30
$95-$120 10/1-2/28

Address: 740 Burdett Ave V8W 1B2 **Location:** Between Douglas and Blanshard (Hwy 17) sts. **Facility:** Smoke free premises. 177 units. 59 one-bedroom standard units. 111 one- and 7 two-bedroom suites, some with efficiencies, kitchens and/or whirlpools. 19 stories, interior corridors. **Parking:** on-site. **Terms:** cancellation fee imposed. **Amenities:** video games (fee), voice mail, safes, irons, hair dryers. **Pool(s):** heated indoor. **Leisure Activities:** whirlpool, exercise room. **Guest Services:** valet laundry, area transportation, wireless Internet. **Business Services:** meeting rooms, PC. *(See color ad p 677)*

COMFORT HOTEL & CONFERENCE CENTRE — *Book great rates at AAA.com* — Phone: (250)382-4400

Hotel
$143-$259 6/1-2/28
$98-$139 3/1-5/31

Address: 3020 Blanshard St V8T 5C7 **Location:** 1.6 mi (2.6 km) n on Blanshard St (Hwy 17), just s Finlayson St. **Facility:** Smoke free premises. 152 units. 143 one-bedroom standard units, some wi efficiencies. 9 one-bedroom suites, some with efficiencies. 3-4 stories, interior/exterior corridor **Parking:** on-site. **Terms:** cancellation fee imposed. **Amenities:** video games (fee), voice mail, iron hair dryers. *Some:* high-speed Internet. **Leisure Activities:** sauna, whirlpool, exercise room. **Gue Services:** valet and coin laundry, wireless Internet. **Business Services:** meeting rooms, PC (fee **Free Special Amenities:** newspaper.

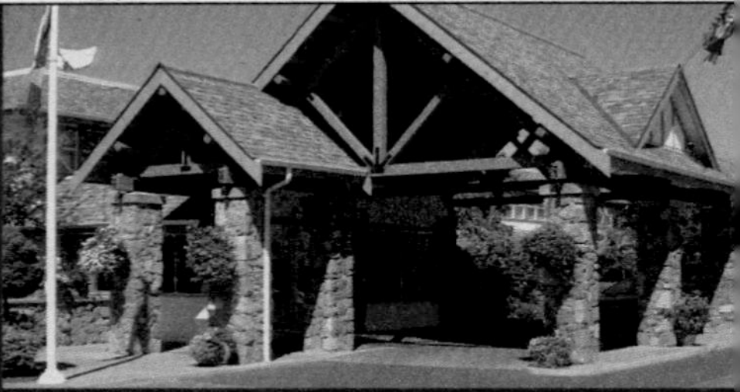

▼ *See AAA listing p 697* ▼

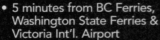

● map and index starting on p. 668)

MFORT INN & SUITES   *Book great rates at AAA.com*   **Phone:** (250)388-7861

CAA SAVE
WWW WWW
Motel
●39-$299 7/1-2/28
●19-$249 3/1-6/30

Address: 101 Island Hwy V9B 1E8 **Location:** Douglas St, 3.1 mi (5 km) w on Gorge Rd, then just s on Admirals Rd. **Facility:** 106 units. 84 one-bedroom standard units, some with efficiencies. 16 one- and 6 two-bedroom suites, some with kitchens. 2 stories (no elevator), interior/exterior corridors. **Parking:** check-in 4 pm. **Amenities:** voice mail, irons, hair dryers. **Pool(s):** heated outdoor. **Leisure Activities:** rental bicycles. *Fee:* kayaks. **Guest Services:** valet and coin laundry, wireless Internet. **Business Services:** meeting rooms, PC (fee). [icons] / SOME UNITS FEE [icons]

TON HOTEL & SUITES   *Book great rates at AAA.com*   **Phone:** (250)384-4136   15

CAA SAVE
WWW
Hotel
●85-$229 All Year

Address: 759 Yates St V8W 1L6 **Location:** Between Blanshard (Hwy 17) and Douglas sts. **Facility:** Smoke free premises. 93 units. 89 one-bedroom standard units. 4 one-bedroom suites with efficiencies. 4 stories, interior corridors. *Bath:* combo or shower only. **Parking:** on-site (fee). **Terms:** cancellation fee imposed. **Amenities:** voice mail. **Guest Services:** valet laundry, wireless Internet. **Free Special Amenities: expanded continental breakfast and high-speed Internet.**
ECO [icons] / SOME UNITS [icons]

HWOOD SEASIDE HERITAGE MANOR   **Phone:** (250)385-5517   45

WWW WWW
Historic Bed
& Breakfast
●35-$285 All Year

Address: 1 Cook St V8V 3W6 **Location:** 0.6 mi (1 km) e of Douglas St on Dallas Rd. Located in a residential area across from Beacon Hill Park. **Facility:** Built in 1912, this charming Tudor-style mansion sits at the end of Cook Street and is the only B&B with an ocean view and a peek at Mt. Baker. Smoke free premises. 11 one-bedroom standard units, some with whirlpools. 3 stories (no elevator), interior corridors. **Parking:** on-site. **Terms:** office hours 8 am-9 pm, check-in 4 pm, 2 night minimum stay - seasonal and/or weekends, age restrictions may apply, 14 day cancellation notice-fee imposed. **Amenities:** hair dryers. **Guest Services:** wireless Internet. ASK [icons]

▼ See AAA listing p 676 ▼

ateau Victoria
HOTEL & SUITES

Inquire about our AAA/CAA rates

www.chateauvictoria.com

lassic comfort in a convenient
wntown Victoria location.

1-800-663-5891
reservations@chateauvictoria.com

(See map and index starting on p. 668)

DAYS INN VICTORIA ON THE HARBOUR *Book great rates at AAA.com* **Phone:** (250)386-3451

Hotel
$79-$213 All Year

Address: 427 Belleville St V8V 1X3 **Location:** Between Oswego and Menzies sts. **Facility:** Smoke free premises. 71 one-bedroom standard units, some with kitchens. 4 stories, interior corridors. *Bath:* combo or shower only. **Parking:** on-site. **Amenities:** voice mail, safes, irons, hair dryers. **Pool(s):** heated indoor. **Leisure Activities:** whirlpool. **Guest Services:** valet laundry, wireless Internet. **Business Services:** PC (fee). *(See color ad below)*

 / SOME UNITS FEE

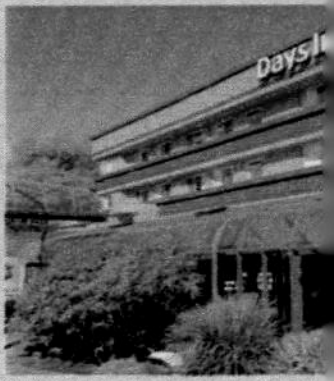

FREE local telephone calls and high-speed Internet

DELTA VICTORIA OCEAN POINTE RESORT AND SPA *Book great rates at AAA.com* **Phone:** (250)360-2999

Hotel
$129-$328 3/1-9/30
$129-$309 10/1-2/28

Address: 45 Songhees Rd V9A 6T3 **Location:** Just w of Johnson St Bridge, Esquimalt at Tyee **Facility:** Rooms at the waterfront hotel are comfortable and nicely decorated; watching sea pl land and take off from the harbor is an added treat. Smoke free premises. 244 units. 239 one-bed standard units, some with efficiencies. 5 one-bedroom suites, some with efficiencies and/or whirlp 8 stories, interior corridors. **Parking:** on-site (fee) and valet. **Terms:** check-in 4 pm, cancellatio imposed. **Amenities:** dual phone lines, voice mail, honor bars, irons, hair dryers. *Fee:* video ga high-speed Internet. **Pool(s):** heated indoor. **Leisure Activities:** sauna, whirlpool, 2 lighted te courts, racquetball court, spa. **Guest Services:** valet laundry, area transportation-downtown/ harbour, wireless Internet. **Business Services:** conference facilities, business center.

   / SOME UNITS FEE

EMBASSY INN *Book great rates at AAA.com* **Phone:** (250)382-8161

Hotel
$99-$370 7/1-2/28
$89-$349 3/1-6/30

Address: 520 Menzies St V8V 2H4 **Location:** Corner of Quebec St. Adjacent to Parliament buildings. **Facility:** Smoke free premises. 103 one-bedroom standard units, some with efficiencies or kitchens. 3-4 stories, interior/exterior corridors. **Parking:** on-site. **Terms:** check-in 3:30 pm, cancellation fee imposed. *Some:* irons. **Pool(s):** heated outdoor. **Leisure Activities:** sauna. **Guest Services:** valet and coin laundry, wireless Internet. **Business Services:** meeting rooms.

/ SOME UNITS

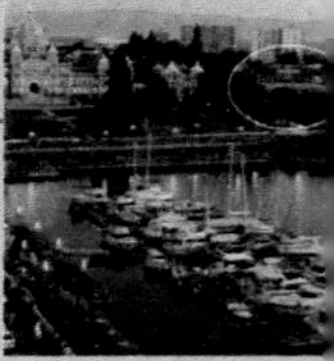

FREE local telephone calls and high-speed Internet

▼ *See AAA listing above* ▼

(See map and index starting on p. 668)

EXECUTIVE HOUSE HOTEL   *Book great rates at AAA.com*   Phone: (250)388-5111   **22**

(CAA) (SAVE)

Hotel
$99-$215 All Year

Address: 777 Douglas St V8W 2B5 **Location:** Between Blanshard (Hwy 17) and Douglas sts; downtown. **Facility:** Smoke free premises. 181 units. 98 one-bedroom standard units, some with efficiencies and/or whirlpools. 78 one- and 5 two-bedroom suites, some with kitchens and/or whirlpools. 17 stories, interior corridors. **Parking:** on-site (fee) and valet. **Terms:** cancellation fee imposed. **Amenities:** voice mail, irons, hair dryers. *Some:* CD players. **Dining:** Barkley's Steak & Seafood, see separate listing. **Leisure Activities:** whirlpool, steamroom, exercise room. **Guest Services:** valet and coin laundry, area transportation-Inner Harbour & downtown, wireless Internet. **Business Services:** meeting rooms, PC. *(See color ad below)*

FREE local telephone calls and high-speed Internet

FAIRHOLME MANOR   Phone: (250)598-3240   **38**

Historic Bed
& Breakfast

$175-$325 3/1-10/15
$135-$250 10/16-2/28

Address: 638 Rockland Pl V8S 3R2 **Location:** Blanshard St (Hwy 17), 1.2 mi (2 km) e on Fort St, just s on St. Charles St to Rockland Ave, look for Rockland Pl sign, then down alley. Located in historic Rockland District. **Facility:** Built in 1885, the restored mansion—surrounded by an acre of park-like gardens and lawn—has been converted into luxury suites with upscale baths. Smoke free premises. 6 units. 5 one- and 1 two-bedroom standard units. 2 stories (no elevator), interior/exterior corridors. **Parking:** on-site. **Terms:** office hours 8 am-10 pm, check-in 4 pm, age restrictions may apply, 14 day cancellation notice-fee imposed. **Amenities:** video library, DVD players, CD players, irons, hair dryers. **Guest Services:** wireless Internet.

THE FAIRMONT EMPRESS   *Book at AAA.com*   Phone: 250/384-8111   **28**

Classic Historic
Hotel

Rates not provided

Address: 721 Government St V8W 1W5 **Location:** Between Belleville and Humboldt sts. Located on Inner Harbour. **Facility:** Known for its tradition of afternoon tea, this landmark Victorian property offers views of the harbor; rooms vary in style and size, as do the views. 476 one-bedroom standard units, some with whirlpools. 8 stories, interior corridors. **Parking:** on-site (fee) and valet. **Terms:** check-in 4 pm. **Amenities:** voice mail, irons, hair dryers. *Fee:* video games, high-speed Internet. *Some:* CD players, safes. **Dining:** The Empress Room, see separate listing. **Pool(s):** heated indoor. **Leisure Activities:** saunas, whirlpool, exercise room, spa. **Guest Services:** valet laundry. **Business Services:** conference facilities, business center.

(See map and index starting on p. 668)

FOUR POINTS BY SHERATON　　*Book great rates at AAA.com*

Phone: 250/474-6063

Hotel
Rates not provided

Address: 829 McCallum Rd V9B 6W6 **Location:** Trans-Canada Hwy 1, exit 14 (Highlands), just n on Millstream Rd, then just w. **Facility:** Smoke free premises. 117 units. 114 one-bedroom standard units, some with efficiencies and/or whirlpools. 3 one-bedroom suites with efficiencies and whirlpools. 4 stories, interior corridors. *Bath:* combo or shower only. **Parking:** on-site. **Amenities:** high-speed Internet, voice mail, safes, irons, hair dryers. **Pool(s):** heated indoor. **Leisure Activities:** sauna, whirlpool, exercise room. **Guest Services:** valet laundry, wireless Internet. **Business Services:** meeting rooms, PC. **Free Special Amenities:** local telephone calls and high-speed Internet.

FOUR ⸙ POINTS
BY SHERATON

AAA Benefit:
Members get up to
15% off, plus
Starwood Preferred
Guest® bonuses.

HARBOUR TOWERS HOTEL & SUITES　　*Book great rates at AAA.com*

Phone: (250)385-2405　26

Hotel
$94-$450 All Year

Address: 345 Quebec St V8V 1W4 **Location:** Between Oswego and Pendray sts. **Facility:** Smoke free premises. 196 units. 123 one-bedroom standard units, some with efficiencies. 45 one- and 28 two-bedroom suites, some with efficiencies, kitchens and/or whirlpools. 12 stories, interior corridors. **Parking:** on-site (fee). **Terms:** cancellation fee imposed. **Amenities:** high-speed Internet, voice mail, irons, hair dryers. *Some:* CD players. **Pool(s):** heated indoor. **Leisure Activities:** sauna, whirlpool. **Guest Services:** valet and coin laundry, area transportation-downtown. **Business Services:** conference facilities, business center. **Free Special Amenities:** newspaper and high-speed Internet.

HATERLEIGH HERITAGE INN　　*Book at AAA.com*

Phone: (250)384-9995　25

Historic Bed
& Breakfast
$150-$250 All Year

Address: 243 Kingston St V8V 1V5 **Location:** Corner of Pendray and Kingston sts. Located in the Inner Harbour. **Facility:** A sweeping staircase, semicircular porch and stained-glass and leaded windows distinguish this restored, early 20th-century Victorian home. Smoke free premises. 7 one-bedroom standard units, some with whirlpools. 2 stories (no elevator), interior corridors. **Parking:** on-site. **Terms:** office hours 8 am-9 pm, check-in 4 pm, age restrictions may apply, 14 day cancellation notice. **Amenities:** hair dryers. **Guest Services:** wireless Internet. **Business Services:** PC.

(See map and index starting on p. 668)

HEATHERGATE HOUSE BED & BREAKFAST

Bed & Breakfast
$85-$145 3/1-9/1
$90-$125 9/2-2/28

Phone: (250)383-0068 **37**

Address: 122 Simcoe St V8V 1K4 **Location:** Between St. Lawrence and Montreal sts. **Facility:** Smoke free premises. 5 units. 4 one- and 1 two-bedroom standard units, some with kitchens. 2 stories (no elevator), interior/exterior corridors. *Bath:* combo or shower only. **Parking:** on-site. **Terms:** office hours 8 am-11 pm, 2 night minimum stay - seasonal, 14 day cancellation notice-fee imposed. **Amenities:** hair dryers. **Guest Services:** wireless Internet. **Business Services:** PC. ⊠ 🔏 / SOME UNITS 🛗

▼ *See AAA listing p 682* ▼

(See map and index starting on p. 668)

HOTEL GRAND PACIFIC

Hotel
$149-$329 All Year

Book great rates at AAA.com

Phone: (250)386-0450 ⓪

Address: 463 Belleville St V8V 1X3 **Location:** Between Oswego and Menzies sts. **Facility:** The upscale high-rise building offers a variety of views, and modern rooms with private balconies overlook the Olympic Mountains or the Inner Harbour. Smoke free premises. 304 units. 266 one-bedroom standard units. 38 one-bedroom suites, some with whirlpools. 8-10 stories, interior corridors. **Parking:** on-site (fee) and valet. **Terms:** cancellation fee imposed. **Amenities:** video games (fee), high-speed Internet, voice mail, safes, honor bars, irons, hair dryers. **Dining:** 2 restaurants, also, The Mark, see separate listing. **Pool(s):** heated indoor. **Leisure Activities:** sauna, whirlpool, steamroom, spa. *Fee:* squash court. **Guest Services:** valet laundry, wireless Internet. **Business Services:** conference facilities, business center. *(See color ad p 681)*

FREE newspaper and high-speed Internet

HOWARD JOHNSON HOTEL-CITY OF VICTORIA

Book great rates at AAA.com

Phone: (250)382-2151 ⑨

Hotel
$69-$159 3/1-9/30
$59-$159 10/1-2/28

Address: 310 Gorge Rd E V8T 2W2 **Location:** From Douglas St, 0.6 mi (1.4 km) w; between Jutland St and Washington Ave. **Facility:** Smoke free premises. 80 one-bedroom standard units, some with kitchens. 3 stories, interior corridors. **Parking:** on-site. **Terms:** cancellation fee imposed. **Amenities:** voice mail, irons, hair dryers. *Some:* high-speed Internet. **Pool(s):** heated indoor. **Leisure Activities:** saunas, exercise room. **Guest Services:** valet and coin laundry, wireless Internet. **Business Services:** meeting rooms, PC.

HUMBOLDT HOUSE BED & BREAKFAST

Historic Bed
& Breakfast
$147-$295 All Year

Phone: (250)383-0152 ㊶

Address: 867 Humboldt St V8V 2Z6 **Location:** Jct Humboldt and Quadra sts. Located in a quiet area. **Facility:** A retreat-like ambience makes this B&B well-suited for romantic getaways. Smoke free premises. 6 one-bedroom standard units, some with whirlpools. 2 stories (no elevator), interior corridors. *Bath:* combo or shower only. **Parking:** on-site. **Terms:** office hours 7 am-11 pm, 7 day cancellation notice-fee imposed. **Amenities:** CD players, hair dryers. *Some:* DVD players. **Guest Services:** wireless Internet.

HUNTINGDON HOTEL & SUITES

Book great rates at AAA.com

Hotel
$99-$389 All Year

Phone: (250)381-3456 ㉔

Address: 330 Quebec St V8V 1W3 **Location:** Between Oswego and Pendray sts. **Facility:** Smoke free premises. 115 units. 114 one- and 1 two-bedroom standard units, some with kitchens (utensils extra charge). 3 stories, interior corridors. **Parking:** on-site (fee). **Amenities:** voice mail, irons, hair dryers. **Leisure Activities:** sauna, whirlpool. **Guest Services:** valet and coin laundry, wireless Internet. **Business Services:** meeting rooms, PC.

▼ See AAA listing p 683 ▼

(See map and index starting on p. 668)

JAMES BAY INN HOTEL & SUITES

Book great rates at AAA.com — **Phone:** (250)384-7151 — 44

CAA SAVE

Hotel
$76-$165 All Year

Address: 270 Government St V8V 2L2 **Location:** Between Toronto and Marifield sts. **Facility:** Smoke free premises. 45 one-bedroom standard units, some with kitchens. 4 stories (no elevator), interior corridors. *Bath:* combo or shower only. **Parking:** on-site. **Guest Services:** wireless Internet. **Business Services:** PC. *(See color ad p 682)*

ECO / SOME UNITS

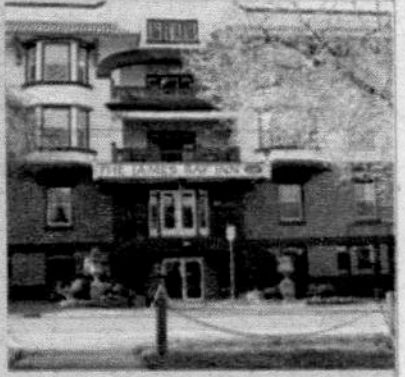

FREE high-speed Internet

THE MAGNOLIA HOTEL & SPA

Book great rates at AAA.com — **Phone:** (250)381-0999 — 17

CAA SAVE

Hotel
$149-$349 All Year

Address: 623 Courtney St V8W 1B8 **Location:** Corner of Courtney and Gordon sts. Located on the Inner Harbour. **Facility:** The luxury hotel offers elegant guest rooms with large bay windows; located within walking distance of shops and restaurants. Smoke free premises. 63 one-bedroom standard units. 7 stories, interior corridors. **Parking:** valet. **Terms:** check-in 4 pm, cancellation fee imposed. **Amenities:** CD players, high-speed Internet, dual phone lines, voice mail, honor bars, irons, hair dryers. **Leisure Activities:** exercise room, spa. **Guest Services:** valet laundry, wireless Internet. **Business Services:** meeting rooms, PC (fee). **Free Special Amenities: continental breakfast and high-speed Internet.** CALL / SOME UNITS FEE

MARRIOTT VICTORIA INNER HARBOUR

Book great rates at AAA.com — **Phone:** (250)480-3800 — 33

CAA SAVE

Hotel
$209-$339 All Year

Marriott
HOTELS & RESORTS

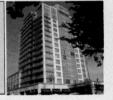

AAA Benefit:
Members save a minimum 5% off the best available rate.

Address: 728 Humboldt St V8W 3Z5 **Location:** Between Blanshard (Hwy 17) and Douglas sts. **Facility:** Near downtown and the Inner Harbour, the full-service hotel features spacious guest units that offer wonderful views of the downtown area. Smoke free premises. 236 units. 228 one-bedroom standard units. 8 one-bedroom suites. 16 stories, interior corridors. **Parking:** on-site (fee) and valet. **Terms:** check-in 4 pm, cancellation fee imposed. **Amenities:** CD players, high-speed Internet, dual phone lines, voice mail, safes, irons, hair dryers. **Dining:** Fire & Water Fish & Chop House, see separate listing. **Pool(s):** heated indoor. **Leisure Activities:** whirlpool, steamroom, exercise room. **Guest Services:** valet and coin laundry, wireless Internet. **Business Services:** meeting rooms, business center. **Free Special Amenities: newspaper and high-speed Internet.** *(See color ad below)*

ECO 24 CALL / SOME UNITS FEE

MAYFAIR MOTEL

Phone: (250)388-7337 — 3

CAA SAVE

Extended Stay Motel
$49-$119 All Year

Address: 650 Speed Ave V8Z 1A4 **Location:** From downtown, 1.6 mi (2.5 km) n on Douglas St. **Facility:** Smoke free premises. 22 one-bedroom standard units with kitchens (utensils extra charge). 4 stories, interior corridors. **Parking:** on-site. **Terms:** office hours 8 am-11:30 pm. **Guest Services:** coin laundry, wireless Internet. **Free Special Amenities: local telephone calls and high-speed Internet.**

▼ See AAA listing above ▼

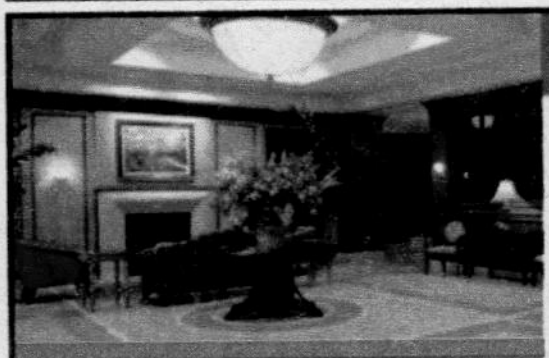

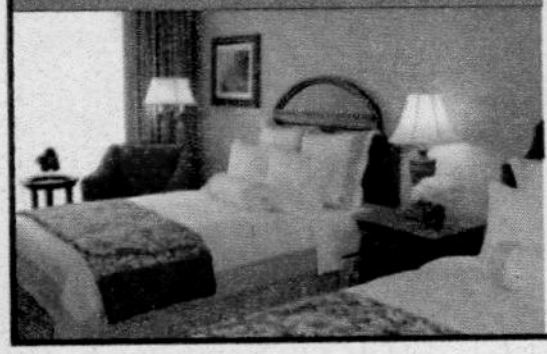

(See map and index starting on p. 668)

THE OSWEGO HOTEL   *Book great rates at AAA.com*   Phone: (250)294-7500   **31**

(CAA) [SAVE]

◆◆◆ ◆◆◆

Hotel
$159-$599 3/1-9/21
$139-$569 9/22-2/28

Address: 500 Oswego St V8V 5C1 **Location:** Between Kingston and Quebec sts. **Facility:** Smoke free premises. 80 units. 21 one-bedroom standard units with efficiencies. 44 one- and 15 two-bedroom suites with kitchens. 10 stories, interior corridors. **Parking:** on-site (fee) and valet. **Terms:** cancellation fee imposed. **Amenities:** CD players, high-speed Internet, voice mail, irons, hair dryers. **Leisure Activities:** whirlpool, exercise room. **Guest Services:** valet and coin laundry, wireless Internet. **Business Services:** meeting rooms, PC. **Free Special Amenities:** newspaper and high-speed Internet. [ECO] [TI] [Y] CALL [&M] [X] [X/] [🐾] [🖥] [🖦] [🖵] / SOME UNITS FEE [🐕]

PRIOR HOUSE B&B INN   Phone: 250/592-8847   **42**

(CAA) [SAVE]

◆◆◆ ◆◆◆

· Historic Bed
& Breakfast
$159-$259 All Year

Address: 620 St. Charles St V8S 3N7 **Location:** Blanshard St (Hwy 17), 1.2 mi (2 km) e on Fort St, then just s. Located in a quiet area. **Facility:** Set on lush, landscaped grounds in a tree-lined neighborhood, the Prior House is a wonderfully restored 1912 manor home featuring antique furnishings. Smoke free premises. 6 units. 3 one-bedroom standard units with whirlpools. 2 one- and 2 two-bedroom suites with whirlpools. 3 stories (no elevator), interior corridors. **Parking:** on-site. **Terms:** office hours 7 am-9 pm, 2 night minimum stay - seasonal and/or weekends, age restrictions may apply, 14 day cancellation notice-fee imposed. **Amenities:** video library, DVD players, CD players, high-speed Internet, voice mail, irons, hair dryers. **Guest Services:** valet laundry, wireless Internet. **Business Services:** PC. **Free Special Amenities:** full breakfast and high-speed Internet.
[X] [X/] [🖥] [🖦] [🖵] / SOME UNITS FEE [🐕]

QUALITY INN DOWNTOWN   *Book at AAA.com*   Phone: (250)385-6787   **19**

◆◆◆

Hotel
$69-$169 All Year

Address: 850 Blanshard St V8W 2H2 **Location:** Between Courtney St and Burnett Ave; downtown. **Facility:** Smoke free premises. 63 units. 61 one-bedroom standard units, some with efficiencies and/or whirlpools. 2 one-bedroom suites with whirlpools. 3 stories, interior corridors. **Parking:** on-site. **Terms:** cancellation fee imposed. **Amenities:** voice mail, irons, hair dryers. *Some:* high-speed Internet. **Pool(s):** heated indoor. **Leisure Activities:** steamroom, limited exercise equipment. **Guest Services:** valet and coin laundry, wireless Internet. **Business Services:** meeting rooms, PC.
[ECO] [ASK] [TI] [Y] [🛏] [X] [X/] [🐾] [🖥] [🖵] / SOME UNITS FEE [🐕] [🖦]

QUEEN VICTORIA HOTEL AND SUITES   *Book great rates at AAA.com*   Phone: (250)386-1312   **39**

(CAA) [SAVE]

◆◆◆

Hotel
$130-$450 All Year

Address: 655 Douglas St V8V 2P9 **Location:** Between Belleville and Superior sts. **Facility:** Smoke free premises. 146 units. 125 one-bedroom standard units, some with efficiencies and/or whirlpools. 14 one- and 7 two-bedroom suites, some with whirlpools. 7 stories, interior corridors. **Parking:** on-site (fee). **Terms:** check-in 4 pm, cancellation fee imposed. **Amenities:** voice mail, safes, irons, hair dryers. **Pool(s):** heated indoor. **Leisure Activities:** sauna, whirlpool, exercise room. **Guest Services:** valet and coin laundry, area transportation-downtown area, wireless Internet. **Business Services:** PC. **Free Special Amenities:** local telephone calls and high-speed Internet. *(See color ad below)*
[ECO] [TI] [Y] CALL [&M] [🛏] [X] [X/] [🖵] / SOME UNITS [🖥] [🖦]

RAMADA VICTORIA   *Book at AAA.com*   Phone: (250)386-1422   **7**

◆◆

Hotel
$125-$185 3/1-9/30
$59-$149 10/1-2/28

Address: 123 Gorge Rd E V9A 1L1 **Location:** From Douglas St, 1.2 mi (2.4 km) w. **Facility:** Smoke free premises. 91 one-bedroom standard units, some with efficiencies or kitchens. 4 stories, interior corridors. **Parking:** on-site. **Terms:** cancellation fee imposed. **Amenities:** voice mail, irons, hair dryers. **Pool(s):** heated outdoor. **Leisure Activities:** exercise room. **Guest Services:** valet and coin laundry, wireless Internet. **Business Services:** meeting rooms, business center.
[ECO] [ASK] [TI] [Y] [🛏] [X] [🐾] [🖵] / SOME UNITS FEE [🐕] [🖥] [🖦]

▼ *See AAA listing above* ▼

(See map and index starting on p. 668)

ROBIN HOOD MOTEL

Phone: (250)388-4302 · 6

Motel
$66-$109 3/1-9/30
$66-$82 10/1-2/28

Address: 136 Gorge Rd E V9A 1L4 **Location:** Douglas St, 1.2 mi (2.4 km) w. **Facility:** 54 one-bedroom standard units, some with kitchens. 3 stories (no elevator), exterior corridors. **Parking:** on-site. **Terms:** office hours 8 am-11 pm. **Amenities:** voice mail. **Guest Services:** coin laundry, wireless Internet. *(See color ad below)*

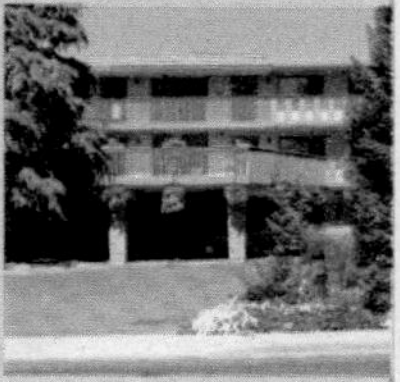

FREE local telephone calls and preferred room (subject to availability with advance reservations)

ROYAL SCOT HOTEL & SUITES   *Book great rates at AAA.com*

Phone: (250)388-5463 · 35

Hotel
$145-$265 All Year

Address: 425 Quebec St V8V 1W7 **Location:** Between Menzies and Oswego sts. **Facility:** Smoke free premises. 176 units. 94 one-bedroom standard units, some with kitchens. 78 one- and 4 two-bedroom suites with kitchens. 4 stories, interior corridors. **Terms:** cancellation fee imposed. **Amenities:** high-speed Internet, voice mail, safes, irons, hair dryers. **Pool(s):** heated indoor. **Leisure Activities:** saunas, whirlpool, billiards, exercise room, shuffleboard, game room. **Guest Services:** valet and coin laundry, area transportation-downtown. **Business Services:** meeting rooms, PC (fee). *(See color ad p 686)*

FREE local telephone calls and high-speed Internet

SPINNAKERS GASTRO BREWPUB AND GUESTHOUSES

Phone: (250)386-2739 · 10

Country Inn
$129-$249 All Year

Address: 308 Catherine St V9A 3S8 **Location:** 1.3 mi (2 km) nw over Johnson St Bridge, then just s. **Facility:** Traditional guest rooms make up the restored 1884 guesthouse, which has five adult-oriented garden suites and four one-bedroom villa suites. Smoke free premises. 10 units. 9 one-bedroom standard units, some with efficiencies, kitchens and/or whirlpools. 1 cottage. 2 stories (no elevator), interior/exterior corridors. *Bath:* combo or shower only. **Parking:** on-site. **Terms:** office hours 8 am-11 pm, age restrictions may apply, 7 day cancellation notice-fee imposed. **Amenities:** voice mail, irons, hair dryers. **Dining:** restaurant, see separate listing. **Guest Services:** wireless Internet.

───── ▼ *See AAA listing above* ▼ ─────

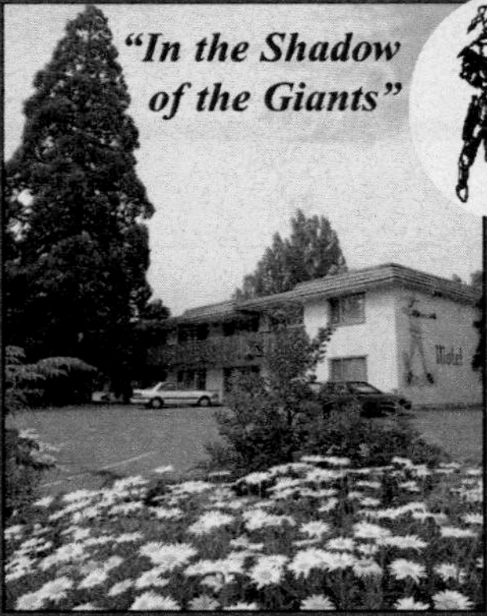

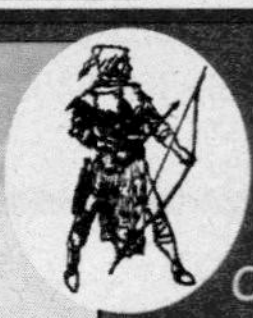

(See map and index starting on p. 668)

SWANS SUITE HOTEL

Hotel
$149-$359 All Year

Phone: (250)361-3310 ⓫

Address: 506 Pandora Ave V8W 1N6 **Location:** Corner of Pandora Ave and Store St. **Facility:** Smoke free premises. 30 units. 18 one- and 12 two-bedroom suites with kitchens. 2 stories, interior corridors. **Parking:** street. **Terms:** check-in 4 pm, 7 day cancellation notice, in summer-fee imposed. **Amenities:** video library, DVD players, voice mail, irons, hair dryers. **Some:** high-speed Internet. **Guest Services:** valet and coin laundry, wireless Internet. **Business Services:** meeting rooms. **(See color ad p 687)** ASK 🍽 🍸 ✕ 🅰 🖥 📠 🖨

▼ See AAA listing p 685 ▼

(See map and index starting on p. 668)

TRAVELODGE VICTORIA   *Book great rates at AAA.com*   Phone: (250)388-6611   **8**

Hotel
$79-$189 All Year

Address: 229 Gorge Rd E V9A 1L1 **Location:** From Douglas St, 1.2 mi (2 km) w on Gorge Rd E; at Washington Ave. **Facility:** 73 one-bedroom standard units, some with efficiencies or kitchens. 3 stories (no elevator), exterior corridors. **Parking:** on-site. **Terms:** cancellation fee imposed. **Amenities:** voice mail, safes, irons, hair dryers. **Pool(s):** heated indoor. **Leisure Activities:** saunas, exercise room. **Guest Services:** valet and coin laundry, wireless Internet. **Business Services:** meeting rooms, PC (fee). *(See color ad p 688)*

UNION CLUB OF BRITISH COLUMBIA   *Book at AAA.com*   Phone: (250)384-1151   **18**

Classic Historic
Hotel
$179-$409 All Year

Address: 805 Gordon St V8W 1Z6 **Location:** Between Courtney and Humboldt sts. **Facility:** Part of an international club system, the former gentlemen's club has historic elements that serve as reminders of the days when women had their own separate entrance and waiting lounge. Guest rooms range from spacious two-room suites to smaller rooms perfect for short stays. A dress code is in effect. Smoke free premises. 22 one-bedroom standard units. 4 stories, interior corridors. **Parking:** on-site (fee). **Terms:** office hours 7 am-11 pm, age restrictions may apply. **Amenities:** high-speed Internet, voice mail, irons, hair dryers. **Leisure Activities:** steamroom, exercise room. **Guest Services:** valet laundry, wireless Internet. **Business Services:** meeting rooms, business center.

VICTORIA REGENT WATERFRONT HOTEL & SUITES   *Book great rates at AAA.com*   Phone: (250)386-2211   **14**

Vacation Rental
Condominium
$139-$309 All Year

Address: 1234 Wharf St V8W 3H9 **Location:** Wharf and Yates sts. Located on the Inner Harbour. **Facility:** These wonderful downtown condominium units all have spectacular harbor views, modern kitchens and super-large bedrooms. Smoke free premises. 47 units. 9 one-bedroom standard units, some with whirlpools. 12 one- and 26 two-bedroom suites with kitchens, some with whirlpools. 8 stories, interior corridors. **Parking:** on-site. **Terms:** cancellation fee imposed. **Amenities:** high-speed Internet, voice mail, safes, honor bars, irons, hair dryers. **Guest Services:** valet and coin laundry, wireless Internet. **Business Services:** meeting rooms, PC. *(See color ad p 689)*

FREE expanded continental breakfast and high-speed Internet

▼ See AAA listing p 686 ▼

(See map and index starting on p. 668)

▼ See AAA listing p 687 ▼

(See map and index starting on p. 668)

▼ See AAA listing p 687 ▼

(See map and index starting on p. 668)

VILLA MARCO POLO INN

Bed & Breakfast
$145-$335 All Year

Phone: 250/370-1524 23

Address: 1524 Shasta Pl V8S 1X9 **Location:** Blanshard St (Hwy 17), 1.3 mi (2 km) e on Fort St, then just s on St. Charles St. Located in a residential area. **Facility:** The renovated home is in one of Victoria's oldest neighborhoods; many of the spacious, nicely decorated bedrooms overlook the manicured grounds. Smoke free premises. 4 one-bedroom standard units, some with whirlpools. 2 stories (no elevator), interior corridors. **Parking:** on-site. **Terms:** office hours 7 am-11 pm, check-in 4 pm, 2 night minimum stay - weekends, age restrictions may apply, 14 day cancellation notice. **Amenities:** voice mail, irons, hair dryers. **Guest Services:** wireless Internet. **Business Services:** PC. (ASK) ✕ [AC]

▼ See AAA listing p 691 ▼

Plan. Map. Go. TripTik® Travel
Planner on AAA.com or CAA.ca

See map and index starting on p. 668)

THE WESTIN BEAR MOUNTAIN GOLF RESORT & SPA *Book great rates at AAA.com*

Phone: 250/391-7160

Hotel
Rates not provided

Address: 1999 Country Club Way V9B 6R3 **Location:** Trans-Canada Hwy 1, exit 14 (Highlands), 1.1 mi (1.7 km) n on Millstream Rd, then 1.9 mi (3 km) ne on Bear Mountain Pkwy, follow signs. **Facility:** In the up-and-coming area of Bear Mountain, the newer resort offers standard-style rooms and large one-bedroom suites with full kitchens. Smoke free premises. 156 units. 83 one-bedroom standard units. 73 one-bedroom suites with kitchens. 3-5 stories, interior corridors. **Parking:** on-site and valet. **Amenities:** DVD players, video games (fee), high-speed Internet, voice mail, safes, irons, hair dryers. *Some:* dual phone lines. **Dining:** 4 restaurants. **Pool(s):** heated outdoor. **Leisure Activities:** sauna, whirlpool, walking trails, hiking trails, spa. **Fee:** golf-39 holes, 2 tennis courts, racquetball court, bicycles. **Guest Services:** complimentary and valet laundry, wireless Internet. **Business Services:** conference facilities, business center. *(See color ad p 690)*

AAA Benefit:
Enjoy up to 15% off your next stay, plus Starwood Preferred Guest® bonuses.

ECO ▯ 24 ▯ CALL ▯ ▯ FEE ▯ ▯ ▯ ▯ ▯ ▯ ▯ / SOME UNITS FEE ▯

FREE local telephone calls and high-speed Internet

—— WHERE TO DINE ——

BARKLEY'S STEAK & SEAFOOD

Phone: 250/382-7111 (20)

Steak
$22-$45

Barkley's has an elegant, Victorian atmosphere and an attentive, professional service staff. The restaurant's dishes include steak and seafood, of course, but the menu also offers pasta selections and a choice of Continental items. Dressy casual. **Bar:** Full bar. **Reservations:** suggested. **Hours:** 4:30 pm-10:30 pm, Fri & Sat-11 pm, Sun-10 pm. Closed: 12/26. **Address:** 777 Douglas St V8W 2B5 **Location:** Between Blanshard (Hwy 17) and Douglas sts; downtown; in Executive House Hotel. **Parking:** on-site and valet.

THE BLACK OLIVE

Phone: 250/384-6060 (8)

Mediterranean
$10-$34

This charming downtown restaurant serves an interesting mix of Mediterranean dishes, some reflecting Italian influences. During the week, the restaurant features a daily specials sheet at lunch for those pressed for time. Parking is available on the street or in nearby pay lots. Casual dress. **Bar:** Full bar. **Reservations:** suggested. **Hours:** 11:30 am-2:30 & 5-10 pm, Sat & Sun from 5 pm. Closed: 12/25, 12/26. **Address:** 739 Pandora Ave V8W 1N9 **Location:** Between Douglas and Blanshard (Hwy 17) sts. **Parking:** street. CALL ▯

CACTUS CLUB CAFE

Phone: 250/361-3233

Canadian
$9-$29

This bustling, casual restaurant serves huge burgers, sandwiches, pasta, salads, soups, quesadillas, fajitas, vegetarian dishes, steak, ribs, chicken and fish. Featured are certified Angus beef and fresh wild British Columbia salmon. The thick and creamy milk shakes come highly recommended. Casual dress. **Bar:** Full bar. **Hours:** 11 am-midnight, Fri & Sat-1 am. Closed: 12/25. **Address:** 1125 Douglas St V8W 3L7 **Location:** Between Fort and View sts. **Parking:** street.

CAFE MEXICO

Phone: 250/386-1425 (7)

Mexican
$11-$19

This Mexican restaurant presents an extensive menu of really good food. Bright colors spring forth from all over the vibrant dining room. Casual dress. **Bar:** Full bar. **Reservations:** accepted. **Hours:** 11 am-10 pm, Fri & Sat-11 pm. Closed: 1/1, 12/25. **Address:** 1425 Store St V8W 3C6 **Location:** Between Pandora and Johnson sts; in Market Square. **Parking:** street. ▯

CANOE BREWPUB MARINA RESTAURANT

Phone: 250/361-1940 (3)

Canadian
$9-$28

The waterfront brew pub offers freshly brewed beers along with fresh fish, tasty pasta, burgers, sandwiches and pizza. Casual dress. **Bar:** Full bar. **Reservations:** suggested. **Hours:** 11:30 am-11 pm, Thurs-midnight, Fri & Sat-1 am. Closed: 1/1, 12/25. **Address:** 450 Swift St V8W 1S3 **Location:** Corner of Stone and Fisgard sts. **Parking:** on-site. ▯

THE EMPRESS ROOM

Phone: 250/384-8111 (21)

Pacific Northwest
$14-$45

Topping the list for fine dining in Victoria, the restaurant enables guests to relax and enjoy a meal surrounded by tapestry walls and richly carved ceilings that are truly amazing. The menu, which changes seasonally to showcase the best cuisine the province has to offer, might offer such selections as British Columbia salmon, Alberta beef and local area seafood. The Empress Room is perfect for a special occasion. Semi-formal attire. **Bar:** Full bar. **Reservations:** suggested. **Hours:** 7 am-11 & 6-10 pm. **Address:** 721 Government St V8W 1W5 **Location:** Between Belleville and Humboldt sts; in The Fairmont Empress. **Parking:** on-site and valet. **Historic** CALL ▯

FIRE & WATER FISH & CHOP HOUSE

Phone: 250/480-3828 (23)

Pacific Northwest
$12-$36

The restaurant offers a comfortable yet casual atmosphere. On the menu are premium-quality steaks and seasonal local seafood, such as Pacific rockfish, halibut and wild British Columbia salmon. Dishes are served with a choice of signature sauces and accompaniments, which makes every entree distinctive. Dressy casual. **Bar:** Full bar. **Reservations:** suggested. **Hours:** 6:30 am-3 & 5-10 pm; Sunday brunch. **Address:** 728 Humboldt St V8W 3Z5 **Location:** Between Blanshard (Hwy 17) and Douglas sts; in Marriott Victoria Inner Harbour. **Parking:** on-site and valet. CALL ▯

(See map and index starting on p. 668)

GLO EURO PUB

Canadian
$9-$20

Phone: 250/385-5643   ① 1

Open late every night, this distinctive pub/restaurant is a little tricky to find, but it's well worth the trouble. A tables in the dining room and on the large patio overlook the Gorge Waterway. Fun and tasty food choices range from flatbread pizza, entree salads and burgers to sandwiches and pasta. Parking is along the street but the pub will validate tickets for those who use pay lots. Casual dress. **Bar:** Full bar. **Reservations:** suggested. **Hours:** 11 am-close. Closed: 12/25. **Address:** 104-2940 Jutland Rd V8T 5K. **Location:** Just sw of Gorge Rd. **Parking:** street.

HAULTAIN'S FISH & CHIPS

Fish & Chips
$10-$18

Phone: 250/383-8332   ② 2

Patrons can dine in or take out from this small, neighborhood-favorite restaurant that's been in the same quiet residential area for 32 years. Fish 'n' chips is the specialty, but burgers and specialty dinners also are served. Seating can be limited, but it's well worth the wait. Casual dress. **Bar:** Beer & wine. **Hours:** 11 am-7:30 pm. Closed: 1/1, 12/25, 12/26; also Sun & Mon. **Address:** 1127 Haultain St V8T 1V4 **Location:** Blanshard St (Hwy 17), 0.6 mi (1 km) e on Bay St, then just n on Cook St. **Parking:** on-site. 🅰️🅲

HUNAN VILLAGE

Chinese
$8-$15

Phone: 250/382-0661   ④ 4

Located in Victoria's Chinatown district, this restaurant specializes in Hunan and Cantonese meals. Hot and spicy beef, smoked duck or ham dishes are the local favorites. There's metered street parking or spaces nearby in pay parking lots. Casual dress. **Bar:** Full bar. **Hours:** 11 am-11 pm, Sun 5 pm-10 pm. Closed 10/11, 12/25. **Address:** 546 Fisgard St V8W 1R4 **Location:** Between Government and Store sts. **Parking:** street. CALL 🅲🅼

IL TERRAZZO

Italian
$10-$35

Phone: 250/361-0028   ⑨ 9

Situated in an old courtyard, Il Terrazzo offers excellent meals such as Australian lamb, ostrich, pasta and seafood, with emphasis on wood-burning oven specialties. Wine choices are extensive, with a nice by-the-glass selection. Fast, friendly service. Casual dress. **Bar:** Full bar. **Reservations:** suggested. **Hours:** 11:30 am-3 & 5-10 pm, Fri & Sat-10:30 pm, Sun 5 pm-10 pm. Closed: 12/25; also for lunch Sat & Sun 10/1-5/1. **Address:** 555 Johnson St V8W 1M2 **Location:** Jct Wharf St; near Market Square; main entrance off Waddington Alley. **Parking:** street. CALL 🅲🅼 🅰️🅲

JAMES BAY TEA ROOM & RESTAURANT   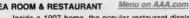 *Menu on AAA.com*

Canadian
$8-$14

Phone: 250/382-8282   ㉕ 25

Inside a 1907 home, the popular restaurant displays memorabilia and photographs of Britain's royal family. The menu lists omelets, pot pies, bangers and kidney pie. Afternoon tea is $14 and high tea is served on Saturdays and Sundays for $17.25. Casual dress. **Bar:** Beer & wine. **Reservations:** suggested. **Hours:** 7 am-5 pm, Sun from 8 am. Closed: 12/24, 12/25. **Address:** 332 Menzies St V8V 2G9 **Location:** Corner of Superior; just s of the Parliament buildings. **Parking:** street.

KELSEY'S

Canadian
$7-$21

Phone: 250/978-5550

A fun, relaxed atmosphere and tasty menu of casual fare make the restaurant a popular favorite with locals. Diners might start a meal with some tempting appetizers, such as wings, loaded potato skins or nachos, and follow them with an old-time favorite, such as a burger, wrap, pizza or pasta dish. For a heartier meal, it's hard to beat pork back ribs or a steak. The diverse menu has broad appeal. Casual dress. **Bar:** Full bar. **Hours:** 11:30 am-11 pm, Sun-10 pm. **Address:** 325 Burnside Rd W V8Z 7L6 **Location:** Burnside and Tillicum rds. **Parking:** on-site.

KOTO JAPANESE RESTAURANT

Japanese
$6-$20

Phone: 250/382-1514   ⑭ 14

Offerings include an extensive array of sushi and sashimi dishes, as well as teriyaki steak, ginger pork and a wide selection of tempura. Casual dress. **Bar:** Full bar. **Reservations:** suggested. **Hours:** 11:30 am-2 & 5-9 pm, Sat & Sun from 5 pm. Closed: 1/1, 12/25. **Address:** 510 Fort St V8W 1E6 **Location:** Between Government and Wharf sts. **Parking:** street. CALL 🅲🅼

THE MARK   *Menu on AAA.com*

Regional Canadian
$32-$42

Phone: 250/386-0450   ㉔ 24

With only 28 seats, the restaurant offers the discriminating guest a very intimate dining experience. The menu is constantly changing, but it always offers the finest in local ingredients. An excellent selection of wines will complement any meal. Dressy casual. **Bar:** Full bar. **Reservations:** required. **Hours:** 6 pm-10 pm. **Address:** 463 Belleville St V8V 1X3 **Location:** Between Oswego and Menzies sts; in Hotel Grand Pacific. **Parking:** on-site and valet.

MILESTONE'S GRILL AND BAR

Canadian
$8-$27

Phone: 250/381-2244

Popular with locals, the bustling eatery is a great gathering place. Diners enjoy the relaxed setting and casual menu featuring pasta, pizza, roasted chicken and a tasty choice of egg and brunch options. A nice wine list complements the food choices. Casual dress. **Bar:** Full bar. **Reservations:** suggested, evenings. **Hours:** 11 am-11 pm. Closed: 12/25. **Address:** 812 Wharf St V8W 1T3 **Location:** Corner of Government and Humboldt sts. **Parking:** street. CALL 🅲🅼

MOXIE'S CLASSIC GRILL

Canadian
$8-$18

Phone: 250/360-1660

This sleek, funky and popular restaurant presents an extensive menu of creatively prepared dishes, including pizza, pasta, rice, noodles, signature salads and burgers. Other menus include one for children and one for Sunday brunch. Lending to the upbeat, stylish decor are dark wood appointments and river rock fireplaces. Casual dress. **Bar:** Full bar. **Hours:** 11 am-11 pm, Fri & Sat-midnight. **Address:** 1010 Yates St, #1 V8V 3M6 **Location:** Between Vancouver and Cook sts. **Parking:** on-site.

(See map and index starting on p. 668)

NICHE

Phone: 250/388-4255   ⑲

▼▼▼

Pacific Northwest
$18-$24

In a renovated heritage home close to Inner Harbour hotels, the restaurant employs an exciting, young chef who prepares unique daily changing menus based on his mood and the fresh, local ingredients he acquires. The result is a new example of Pacific Northwest cuisine. Plate presentations are exquisite, and pairings from a wine list feature many wonderful British Columbian wines. Semi-formal attire. **Bar:** Full bar. **Hours:** 5 pm-10 pm, Wed-Fri also 11 am-2 pm. Closed: 1/1, 12/25. **Address:** 225 Quebec St V8V 1W2 **Location:** Corner of Pendray and Quebec sts. **Parking:** on-site.

PAGLIACCI'S

Phone: 250/386-1662   ⑮

▼▼▼

Italian
$6-$24

A New York-style Italian eatery with a bustling Big Apple ambience, this place has the food to match. Flavorful pasta dishes include the exceptional ravioli or spaghetti Western, made with fresh tomatoes and topped with a couple of large meatballs. It's as Italian as it gets. Casual dress. **Bar:** Full bar. **Hours:** 11:30 am-3 & 5:30-10 pm, Fri & Sat-11 pm, Sun 10 am-3 pm; Sunday brunch. Closed: 12/25; also Yom Kippur. **Address:** 1011 Broad St V8W 2A1 **Location:** Between Fort and Broughton sts. **Parking:** street.

PASSERO'S MEDITERRANEAN CUISINE

Phone: 250/384-6474   ⑫

▼▼▼

Mediterranean
$7-$19

The family-run restaurant serves a fine combination of Greek and Italian cuisine in large portions. Lending to the bistro theme are lots of color and live plants. The patio opens seasonally. Casual dress. **Bar:** Full bar. **Reservations:** accepted. **Hours:** 11 am-9 pm, Fri-10 pm, Sat 4 pm-10 pm. Closed major holidays; also Sun. **Address:** 1102 Yates St V8V 3M8 **Location:** Corner of Cook St. **Parking:** on-site.

PESCATORE'S SEAFOOD & GRILL

Phone: 250/385-4512   ⑱

▼▼▼

Seafood
$10-$32

The chic bistro prepares excellent fresh seafood and great beverage choices, such as espresso, cappuccino and martinis. Patrons can look forward to hip and funky fine dining with parking at street meters or in pay lots. Casual dress. **Bar:** Full bar. **Reservations:** suggested. **Hours:** 11:30 am-11 pm, Sat & Sun from 11 am; Saturday & Sunday brunch. Closed: 1/1, 12/25. **Address:** 614 Humboldt St V8W 1A4 **Location:** Between Gordon and Government sts. **Parking:** street.

THE PINK BICYCLE

Phone: 250/384-1008   ⑰

▼▼

Burgers
$12-$15

This tiny but often packed spot is distinguished not only by its trademark pink bicycle parked outside the door but also by its menu packed with hand-made, mouthwatering gourmet burgers. The house specialty is the Pink Bike cheeseburger made from naturally raised Vancouver Island beef, but the adventurous are urged to try burger options such as the blue cheese lamb, mutton, bison, halibut or chicken with sauteed leeks. Among accompaniments are truffle fries, poutine and pink lemonade cheesecake. Casual dress. **Bar:** Full bar. **Reservations:** not accepted. **Hours:** 11:30 am-7:30 pm, Mon-2:30 pm. Closed major holidays; also Sun. **Address:** 1008 Blanshard St V8W 2H5 **Location:** Jct Broughton Rd. **Parking:** street.

PLUTO'S

Phone: 250/385-4747   ⑯

▼▼

Canadian
$7-$15

The funky-looking, turquoise and pink art deco structure used to be a gas station. In addition to the extensive breakfast menu, which is served until 2 pm, there are also varied wraps and burgers and a few Mexican items. Casual dress. **Bar:** Full bar. **Hours:** 8 am-9 pm, Fri & Sat-10 pm. Closed: 12/25. **Address:** 1150 Cook St V8V 3Z9 **Location:** Corner of Cook and View sts. **Parking:** on-site.

RESTAURANT MATISSE

Phone: 250/480-0883   ⑩

▼▼▼

French
$20-$33

This eatery is a wonderful French restaurant located downtown. The first thing you'll notice is the bright sunlight-yellow decor that is warm and inviting. Daily specials along with what they do best include duck, beef and fish. Casual dress. **Bar:** Full bar. **Reservations:** suggested. **Hours:** 5:30 pm-10 pm. Closed: 12/25; also Mon & Tues. **Address:** 512 Yates St V8W 1K8 **Location:** Between Government and Wharf sts. **Parking:** street.

RICKY'S ALL DAY GRILL

Phone: 250/383-9925

▼▼

Canadian
$6-$15

The comfortable eatery, which employs friendly servers, presents a varied menu that includes pasta dishes, wraps, omelets, stir-fry preparations and burgers. Portions are generous. Children's and senior selections are offered. Guests can request seating in a booth or at a table. Casual dress. **Bar:** Full bar. **Hours:** 7 am-9 pm. **Address:** 1501 Admirals Rd V9A 2P8 **Location:** Corner of Admirals and Glentana rds; on Admirals Walk Mall. **Parking:** on-site.

SIAM THAI RESTAURANT

Phone: 250/383-9911   ⑬

▼▼

Thai
$8-$18

The secret of Thai cooking is to maintain a delicate balance between the spices and main ingredients. The restaurant accomplishes this in its soups, as well as dishes of fried rice, noodles, chicken, beef, pork, seafood and vegetarian items. Lunch specials are available. Casual dress. **Bar:** Full bar. **Reservations:** suggested. **Hours:** 11:30 am-2 & 4:30-10 pm, Sun 4:30 pm-9 pm. Closed: 12/25. **Address:** 512 Fort St V8W 1E6 **Location:** Between Government and Wharf sts. **Parking:** street.

SMITTY'S

Phone: 250/383-5612

▼▼▼

Canadian
$7-$20

The family-oriented restaurant satisfies patrons with its ever-popular all-day breakfast items, as well as tasty and wholesome soups and salads at lunchtime. A relaxed mood characterizes the dining space. Casual dress. **Bar:** Full bar. **Hours:** 6:30 am-9 pm. Closed: 12/25. **Address:** 850 Douglas St V8W 2B6 **Location:** Between Burdett Ave and Courtney St. **Parking:** on-site.

(See map and index starting on p. 668)

SPINNAKERS GASTRO BREWPUB & RESTAURANT   **Phone:** 250/386-2739   [5]

Canadian
$10-$23

The fun and lively pub and restaurant features terrific breads, a wonderful mile-high apple pie and delicious homemade soups. Guests can tour the brew house, said to be Canada's first in-house brewery, or brin home treats from the on-site bakery. Casual dress. **Bar:** Full bar. **Reservations:** suggested. **Hours:** 11 am 11 pm. Closed: 12/25. **Address:** 308 Catherine St V9A 3S8 **Location:** 1.3 mi (2 km) nw over Johnson $ Bridge, then just s; in Spinnakers Gastro Brewpub and Guesthouses. **Parking:** on-site. CALL [M]

SWISS CHALET   **Phone:** 250/475-033

Canadian
$7-$19

The popular restaurant is known for its rotisserie chicken and ribs and the tangy Chalet sauce that give food its special zip. Diners munch on a half or quarter chicken with sides such as steamed vegetables, frie baked potatoes and salads. Lunch guests often go for the great soup and sandwich combination. Take-ou and delivery service are popular options. Casual dress. **Bar:** Full bar. **Hours:** 11 am-10 pm. Closed: 12/25 **Address:** 3233 Douglas St V8Z 3K8 **Location:** Between Tolmie and Roderick sts. **Parking:** on-site.

CALL [M]

VICTORIA HARBOUR HOUSE RESTAURANT   **Phone:** 250/386-1244   [2]

Steak
$16-$35

Just up from the U.S. Ferry terminal in Victoria's Inner Harbour and surrounded by many hotels sits thi long-established restaurant that serves fresh seafood and fine steaks. If on-site parking is full, diners ca park along the street. Casual dress. **Bar:** Full bar. **Reservations:** suggested. **Hours:** 4:30 pm-10 pm **Address:** 607 Oswego St V8V 4W9 **Location:** Corner of Oswego and Quebec sts. **Parking:** on-site.

WHITE HEATHER TEA ROOM   **Phone:** 250/595-8020   [11]

Breads/Pastries
$8-$14

In the Oak Bay area, the wonderful tea room serves lunch and afternoon tea starting at 1:30 pm. Amon choices are wee tea for $12.45, not-so-wee tea for $15.95 and the big muckle $37.95 for hearty appetites Among favorites are the sconewiches, freshly-baked scones with varied fillings. Everything is baked on site Casual dress. **Bar:** Beer & wine. **Reservations:** required, for lunch. **Hours:** 10 am-5 pm. Closed: 12/25 12/26; also Sun & Mon. **Address:** 1885 Oak Bay Ave V8R 1C6 **Location:** Corner of Davie St. **Parking** on-site.

WILD SAFFRON BISTRO & WINE BAR   **Phone:** 250/361-3310   [6]

Pacific Rim
$15-$34

The warm, contemporary bistro pairs its large selection of local and international wines—not to mentio beers from the on-site brewery—with wonderful West Coast cuisine, including the seafood dishes for whic this place is known, in addition to hearty lamb, game, poultry and vegetarian options. Artistic fla characterizes the plate presentations. Casual dress. **Bar:** Full bar. **Reservations:** suggested. **Hours:** 5 pm 10 pm. Closed: Sun & Mon. **Address:** 1605 Store St V8W 1N6 **Location:** At Pandora St. **Parking:** street.

The Victoria Vicinity

BRENTWOOD BAY

BRENTWOOD BAY LODGE & SPA   *Book great rates at AAA.com*   **Phone:** (250)544-207

Hotel
$179-$549 All Year

Address: 849 Verdier Ave V8M 1C5 **Location:** Hwy 17, exit Brentwood Bay, 1.8 mi (3 km) w o Keating Rd, 0.9 mi (1.5 km) n on W Saanich Rd, then 0.6 mi (1 km) w to the Mill Bay Ferry **Facility:** Luxurious oceanview suites feature fine linens, awesome beds, soaker tubs with slidin panels overlooking the ocean, gas fireplaces and private decks. Smoke free premises. 33 units. 3 one-bedroom standard units with whirlpools. 3 one-bedroom suites with whirlpools. 3 stories, exterio corridors. **Parking:** on-site. **Terms:** 7 day cancellation notice-fee imposed. **Amenities:** video library DVD players, CD players, high-speed Internet, voice mail, safes, honor bars, irons, hair dryers **Dining:** Seagrille, see separate listing. **Pool(s):** heated outdoor. **Leisure Activities:** whirlpool exercise room, spa. *Fee:* marina. **Guest Services:** valet and coin laundry, wireless Internet. **Business Services:** meeting rooms, PC. **Free Special Amenities:** preferred room (subject to availability with advance reservations) and high-speed Internet. Affiliated with A Preferred Hotel.

---- **WHERE TO DINE** ----

SEAGRILLE   **Phone:** 250/544-207

Seafood
$15-$35

In one of the city's finest luxury oceanfront resorts, the restaurant is just minutes from famous Butcha Gardens. Fresh fish, Alberta beef and local produce factor in exquisite, creatively prepared dishes. A extensive wine list features many award-winning British Columbia wines. Dressy casual. **Bar:** Full ba **Reservations:** suggested. **Hours:** 5:30 pm-11 pm. **Address:** 849 Verdier Ave V8M 1C5 **Location:** Hwy 17 exit Brentwood Bay, 1.8 mi (3 km) w on Keating Rd, 0.9 mi (1.5 km) n on W Saanich Rd, then 0.6 mi (1 km w to the Mill Bay Ferry; in Brentwood Bay Lodge & Spa. **Parking:** on-site. CALL [M]

SMITTY'S   **Phone:** 250/652-176

Canadian
$8-$20

The family-oriented restaurant satisfies patrons with its ever-popular all-day breakfast items, as well as tasty and wholesome soups and salads at lunchtime. A relaxed mood characterizes the dining space. Casua dress. **Bar:** Full bar. **Hours:** 7 am-8 pm. Closed: 12/25. **Address:** Box 249, 6719 W Saanich Rd V0S 1A0 **Location:** Corner of Saanich and Keating Cross rds. **Parking:** on-site.

MALAHAT

MALAHAT BUNGALOWS MOTEL

Vintage Motel
$62-$165 All Year

Phone: (250)478-3011

Address: 300 Trans-Canada Hwy V0R 2L0 **Location:** Trans-Canada Hwy 1, 16.3 mi (26 km) n of Victoria, follow signs. **Facility:** A half-hour drive from Victoria is this mix of bungalows; while the decor is older, the setting is delightful, and some have fireplaces. 18 units. 13 one-bedroom standard units, some with kitchens. 5 two-bedroom suites with kitchens. 1 story, exterior corridors. **Bath:** combo or shower only. **Parking:** on-site. **Terms:** office hours 8 am-midnight, 3 day cancellation notice-fee imposed. **Leisure Activities:** whirlpool. **Guest Services:** coin laundry.

—— WHERE TO DINE ——

MALAHAT MOUNTAIN INN

Regional
Canadian
$15-$36

Phone: 250/478-1944

Gourmet dining is the mode in the relaxed setting. Set 600 feet above Saanich Inlet, the dining room affords a stunning view of the mountains and ocean. Food choices exhibit a delightful Pacific Northwest influence. Casual dress. **Bar:** Full bar. **Reservations:** suggested. **Hours:** 11:30 am-8:30 pm, Sat-9 pm, Sun 11 am-8 pm. Closed: 12/25. **Address:** 265 Trans-Canada Hwy 1 V0R 2L0 **Location:** Trans-Canada Hwy 1, 16 mi (26 km) n of Victoria, watch for signs. **Parking:** on-site.

OAK BAY pop. 17,908   (See map and index starting on p. 668)

OAK BAY GUEST HOUSE BED & BREAKFAST

Historic Bed
& Breakfast
$139-$199 3/1-9/15
$99-$179 9/16-2/28

Phone: (250)598-3812   **52**

Address: 1052 Newport Ave V8S 5E2 **Location:** 3 mi (4.8 km) e on Oak Bay Ave (which becomes Newport Ave). **Facility:** In keeping with the age of this historic building, the guest rooms are average-size and some bathrooms are compact. Smoke free premises. 11 one-bedroom standard units. 2 stories (no elevator), interior corridors. **Bath:** combo or shower only. **Parking:** on-site. **Terms:** office hours 8 am-10 pm, age restrictions may apply, 3 day cancellation notice-fee imposed. **Amenities:** hair dryers. **Guest Services:** wireless Internet.

—— WHERE TO DINE ——

THE BLETHERING PLACE TEA ROOM & RESTAURANT

Canadian
$6-$17

Phone: 250/598-1413   **34**

Built in 1912, this building is the oldest in the "village." Its English-style decor matches its English-style fare featuring roast beef and Yorkshire pudding and Welsh rarebit. Afternoon tea is served 11 am-7:30 pm Families are welcomed here. Casual dress. **Bar:** Beer & wine. **Reservations:** accepted. **Hours:** 8 am-9 pm. **Address:** 2250 Oak Bay Ave V8R 1G5 **Location:** Corner of Monterey and Oak Bay aves; in Oak Bay Village. **Parking:** on-site.

THE MARINA RESTAURANT

Seafood
$12-$32

Phone: 250/598-8555   **36**

Located in the Oak Bay Marina, this restaurant provides beautiful, sweeping views of the ocean, harbor and mountains. Its menu features a Pacific Northwest cuisine, showcasing fresh, local and exotic seafood as well as items from a sushi bar and cafe deli. Casual dress. **Bar:** Full bar. **Reservations:** suggested. **Hours:** 11:30 am-2:30 & 5-10 pm, Sun 9:30 am-9 pm. Closed: 12/25. **Address:** 1327 Beach Dr V8S 2N4 **Location:** 3.8 mi (6 km) e via Oak Bay Ave, just s. **Parking:** on-site.

OTTAVIO ITALIAN BAKERY & DELICATESSEN

Italian
$7-$14

Phone: 250/592-4080   **35**

This pleasant cafe in the heart of Oak Bay offers a wide variety of fresh salads, grilled panini sandwiches and wonderful soups. The homemade gelato with fresh fruit is a hit. Choose dining inside or out on a lovely terrazzo overlooking a busy street scene. Casual dress. **Bar:** Beer & wine. **Hours:** 8 am-6 pm. Closed: 12/25, 12/26; also Sun & Mon. **Address:** 2272 Oak Bay Ave V8R 1G7 **Location:** At Monterey Ave. **Parking:** on-site. CALL

PAPRIKA BISTRO

Continental
$20-$32

Phone: 250/592-7424   **32**

In the small Estevan Shopping Centre, the bistro prepares some superb dishes from fresh ingredients. Because this place can be tricky to find, it's wise to ask a concierge or other hotel staffer for directions. The drive is worthwhile. Casual dress. **Bar:** Full bar. **Reservations:** suggested. **Hours:** 5 pm-10 pm. Closed major holidays; also Sun. **Address:** 2524 Estevan Ave V8R 2S7 **Location:** Between Dunlevy and Musgrave sts; in Estevan Shopping Centre; in Oak Bay area. **Parking:** street.

PENNY FARTHING PUBLIC HOUSE

Canadian
$8-$17

Phone: 250/370-9008   **33**

The classic, relaxed British-style pub is decorated in rich dark wood with brass accents. Fine pub fare pairs with a wide selection of stouts, ales and lagers. Patrons younger than age 19 are not permitted. Casual dress. **Bar:** Full bar. **Hours:** 11 am-midnight, Sun & Mon-11 pm. Closed: 12/25. **Address:** 2228 Oak Bay Ave V8R 1G5 **Location:** Between Monterey Ave and Hampshire Rd. **Parking:** street.

SAANICH   (See map and index starting on p. 668)

HOWARD JOHNSON HOTEL & SUITES   *Book at AAA.com*   Phone: (250)704-4656   **49**

Hotel
$117-$153 All Year

Address: 4670 Elk Lake Dr V8Z 5M2 **Location:** Blanshard St (Hwy 17), just w on Royal Oak Dr, the just n. **Facility:** Smoke free premises. 88 one-bedroom standard units, some with kitchens. 3 stories interior/exterior corridors. *Bath:* combo or shower only. **Parking:** on-site. **Terms:** cancellation fee imposed. **Amenities:** high-speed Internet, voice mail, irons, hair dryers. **Pool(s):** heated outdoor **Leisure Activities:** whirlpool, exercise room. **Guest Services:** valet and coin laundry, wireless Internet. **Business Services:** meeting rooms, PC (fee).

ECO ASK 🍴 🍽 CALL 🅵M 🏊 ❌ 🔌 💻 / SOME UNITS FEE 🐾 📷

QUALITY INN WADDLING DOG   *Book great rates at AAA.com*   Phone: (250)652-1146

Ⓐ SAVE

Hotel
$125-$145 7/1-2/28
$109-$139 3/1-6/30

Address: 2476 Mt Newton Crossroad V8M 2B8 **Location:** Corner of Blanshard St (Hwy 17) and Mt Newton Crossroad. **Facility:** Smoke free premises. 30 one-bedroom standard units. 3 stories, interior corridors. **Parking:** on-site. **Amenities:** voice mail, irons, hair dryers. **Guest Services:** wireless Internet. **Business Services:** meeting rooms, PC (fee). 🍴 🍽 ❌ 💻 / SOME UNITS FEE 🐾

FREE continental breakfast and high-speed Internet

SUNNYMEADE HOUSE B&B   Phone: 250-658-1414   **48**

Bed & Breakfast
Rates not provided

Address: 1002 Fenn Ave V8Y 1P3 **Location:** 7.2 mi (12 km) n on Blanshard St (Hwy 17), exit Cordova Bay Rd, then 1.8 mi (3 km) e on Sayward/Cordova Bay Rd; across from service station. **Facility:** Smoke free premises. 4 one-bedroom standard units, some with whirlpools. 2 stories (no elevator), interior corridors. *Bath:* combo or shower only. **Parking:** on-site. **Terms:** open 3/1-11/1, office hours 9 am-10 pm, age restrictions may apply. **Amenities:** hair dryers. ❌ 🅺 🆆 🆉

VICTORIA AIRPORT SUPER 8   *Book great rates at AAA.com*   Phone: 250-652-6888

Ⓐ SAVE

Hotel
Rates not provided

Address: 2477 Mt Newton Crossroad V8M 2B7 **Location:** Just e of Blanshard St (Hwy 17). **Facility:** 51 one-bedroom standard units, some with whirlpools. 2 stories (no elevator), interior corridors. **Parking:** on-site. **Amenities:** safes, hair dryers. **Guest Services:** wireless Internet. **Free Special Amenities:** continental breakfast and high-speed Internet.

🍴⁺ CALL 🅵M 💻 / SOME UNITS FEE 🐾 ❌

——— WHERE TO DINE ———

BRADY'S FISH & CHIPS   Phone: 250-382-3695   **29**

Fish & Chips
$7-$13

The casual family restaurant serves English-style fish and chips, as well as mouthwatering halibut and cod and fine chowder. Guests can order for dine-in or take-out. Casual dress. **Bar:** Beer & wine. **Hours:** 11 am-7 pm, Fri & Sat-8 pm, Sun noon-7 pm. Closed major holidays. **Address:** 1-50 Burnside Rd W V9A 1B9 **Location:** Just w of Harriet Rd; in Albion Mall. **Parking:** on-site. CALL 🅵M

SIDNEY pop. 11,315

BEACON INN AT SIDNEY   Phone: (250)655-3288

Bed & Breakfast
$119-$259 All Year

Address: 9724 3rd St V8L 3A2 **Location:** Hwy 17, exit Sidney, 0.6 mi (1 km) e on Beacon Ave, then just s. **Facility:** The stately B&B features spacious guest rooms intricately appointed with have rich wood furnishings, plush velvet trim and regal feather beds. Smoke free premises. 9 one-bedroom standard units, some with whirlpools. 3 stories (no elevator), interior corridors. **Parking:** on-site. **Terms:** office hours 8 am-8 pm, age restrictions may apply, cancellation fee imposed. **Amenities:** CD players, hair dryers. **Guest Services:** wireless Internet. ASK ❌

BEST WESTERN EMERALD ISLE MOTOR INN   *Book great rates at AAA.com*   Phone: (250)656-4441

Hotel
$135-$349 3/1-9/30
$109-$299 10/1-2/28

Address: 2306 Beacon Ave V8L 1X2 **Location:** Hwy 17, exit Sidney, just e. **Facility:** 65 one-bedroom standard units, some with efficiencies, kitchens and/or whirlpools. 2 stories, interior corridors. **Parking:** on-site. **Amenities:** voice mail, irons, hair dryers. **Dining:** Smitty's, see separate listing. **Leisure Activities:** sauna, whirlpool, exercise room. **Guest Services:** valet and coin laundry, wireless Internet. **Business Services:** PC. *(See color ad p 676)*

AAA Benefit: Members save up to 20%, plus 10% bonus points with rewards program.

FREE newspaper and early check-in/late check-out

THE CEDARWOOD INN & SUITES   Phone: (250)656-5551

Hotel
$95-$255 All Year

Address: 9522 Lochside Dr V8L 1N8 **Location:** Hwy 17, just e on McTavish Rd, then 0.8 mi (1.4 km) n. **Facility:** Smoke free premises. 46 units. 45 one- and 1 two-bedroom standard units, some with efficiencies, kitchens and/or whirlpools. 2 stories (no elevator), exterior corridors. **Parking:** on-site. **Terms:** office hours 7 am-11 pm, 3 day cancellation notice-fee imposed. **Amenities:** video library (fee), voice mail, hair dryers. *Some:* high-speed Internet, irons. **Guest Services:** coin laundry, wireless Internet. **Free Special Amenities: newspaper and high-speed Internet.**

MIRALOMA ON THE COVE   Phone: (250)656-6622

Hotel
$159-$449 All Year

Address: 2326 Harbour Rd V8L 2P8 **Location:** Beacon Ave, 1.3 mi (2 km) n on Resthaven Dr, then 0.6 mi (1 km) e. **Facility:** Smoke free premises. 22 units. 9 one-bedroom standard units. 9 one- and 4 two-bedroom suites, some with efficiencies, kitchens and/or whirlpools. 3 stories, interior corridors. *Bath:* combo or shower only. **Parking:** on-site. **Amenities:** video library, DVD players, CD players, high-speed Internet, voice mail, irons, hair dryers. **Leisure Activities:** sauna, whirlpool, bicycles, exercise room. **Guest Services:** valet laundry, wireless Internet. **Business Services:** meeting rooms, PC.

THE SIDNEY PIER HOTEL & SPA   *Book great rates at AAA.com*   Phone: (250)655-9445

Hotel
$119-$649 All Year

Address: 9805 Seaport Pl V8L 4X3 **Location:** Hwy 17, 0.6 mi (1 km) e on Beacon Ave. **Facility:** Smoke free premises. 55 units. 46 one-bedroom standard units. 9 one-bedroom suites with kitchens. 3 stories, interior corridors. *Bath:* combo or shower only. **Parking:** on-site (fee). **Terms:** check-in 4 pm, cancellation fee imposed. **Amenities:** video library (fee), DVD players, high-speed Internet, voice mail, safes, irons, hair dryers. **Dining:** Haro's Restaurant & Bar, see separate listing. **Leisure Activities:** steamrooms, exercise room, spa. **Guest Services:** valet and coin laundry, wireless Internet. **Business Services:** meeting rooms, PC. **Free Special Amenities: local telephone calls and high-speed Internet.**

VICTORIA AIRPORT TRAVELODGE SIDNEY   *Book great rates at AAA.com*   Phone: (250)656-1176

Hotel
$129-$199 3/1-9/30
$99-$169 10/1-2/28

Address: 2280 Beacon Ave V8L 1X1 **Location:** Hwy 17, exit Sidney, just e. **Facility:** 90 one-bedroom standard units, some with efficiencies (utensils extra charge). 2-4 stories, interior corridors. *Bath:* combo or shower only. **Parking:** on-site. **Amenities:** voice mail, hair dryers. *Some:* high-speed Internet. **Pool(s):** heated outdoor. **Guest Services:** valet laundry, wireless Internet. **Business Services:** meeting rooms, PC (fee). **Free Special Amenities: early check-in/late check-out and room upgrade (subject to availability with advance reservations).**

——— WHERE TO DINE ———

BLUE PETER PUB & RESTAURANT   Phone: 250/656-4551

Canadian
$7-$17

Along the wharf, this pub affords a great view of the harbor. Fresh seafood, steak and pasta are featured, and the laid-back environment offers three seating options: one area for families with kids; one on the pub side, which has a fireplace; and a third on the warm-weather patio. Casual dress. **Bar:** Full bar. **Hours:** 11 am-10 pm, Fri & Sat-midnight. **Address:** 2270 Harbour Rd V8L 2P6 **Location:** Beacon Ave, 1.3 mi (2 km) n on Resthaven Dr to Harbour Rd, then just e. **Parking:** on-site.

DEEP COVE CHALET   Phone: 250/656-3541

French
$18-$45

Visitors and locals alike enjoy this delightful restaurant tucked away in a setting offering a lovely, manicured lawn and garden and spectacular views of the inlet. It may be a bit difficult to reach, but it's well worth the drive to sample the French cuisine. Fresh seafood, lamb, ostrich, caribou, wild boar and a nice variety of wines round out the menu. Casual dress. **Bar:** Full bar. **Reservations:** suggested. **Hours:** Open 3/1-12/31 & 2/1-2/28; 5:30 pm-10 pm, Wed-Sun also noon-2:30 pm. Closed: 12/24; also Mon & Tues. **Address:** 11190 Chalet Rd V8L 4R4 **Location:** Hwy 31, exit Wain Rd/Deep Cove, 0.6 mi (1 km) w on Wain Rd, then 1.8 mi (3 km) nw on Tatlow Rd. **Parking:** on-site.

HARO'S RESTAURANT & BAR

Pacific Rim
$10-$36

Phone: 250/655-9700

Affording sweeping views of Haro Strait, this relaxed waterfront restaurant has a heated outdoor terrace, comfortable lounge and bustling cafe-like atmosphere that appeals to almost anyone. The menu highlights ultra-fresh seafood, which is obtained from sustainable fishery practices and combined with local and organic produce, homemade pasta and local meats to create wonderful seasonal specialties. Casual dress. **Bar:** Full bar. **Reservations:** suggested. **Hours:** 11 am-10 pm. **Address:** 9805 Seaport Pl V8L 4X7. **Location:** Hwy 17, 0.6 mi (1 km) e on Beacon Ave; in The Sidney Pier Hotel & Spa. **Parking:** on-site.
CALL 🆑ᴹ

SMITTY'S

ⒸⒶⒶ

Canadian
$7-$20

Phone: 250/656-2423

The family-oriented restaurant satisfies patrons with its ever-popular all-day breakfast items, as well as tasty and wholesome soups and salads at lunchtime. A relaxed mood characterizes the dining space. Casual dress. **Bar:** Full bar. **Hours:** 7 am-8 pm. Closed: 12/25. **Address:** 2306 Beacon Ave V8L 1X2. **Location:** Hwy 17, exit Sidney, just e; in Best Western Emerald Isle Motor Inn. **Parking:** on-site.

SOOKE pop. 9,704

MARKHAM HOUSE BED & BREAKFAST

Bed & Breakfast
$120-$250 All Year

Phone: (250)642-7542

Address: 1775 Connie Rd V9Z 1C8 **Location:** 6.2 mi (10 km) e on Hwy 14. Located in a quiet rural area. **Facility:** Just a short drive from Victoria, the 10-acre, Tudor estate is home to three large, elegant rooms; a private cottage features its own outdoor hot tub. Smoke free premises. 4 one-bedroom standard units, some with whirlpools. 2 stories (no elevator), interior corridors. *Bath:* combo or shower only. **Parking:** on-site. **Terms:** 7 day cancellation notice-fee imposed. **Amenities:** video library, DVD players, CD players, hair dryers. **Leisure Activities:** whirlpool. **Guest Services:** complimentary laundry, wireless Internet. ⒶⓈⓀ ✕ 🅺 / SOME UNITS 🔲 🖥

OCEAN WILDERNESS INN   *Book at AAA.com*

Bed & Breakfast
$130-$220 All Year

Phone: (250)646-2116

Address: 9171 W Coast Rd V9Z 1G3 **Location:** 8.6 mi (14 km) w on Hwy 14. Located in a secluded area. **Facility:** Smoke free premises. 7 one-bedroom standard units. 2 stories (no elevator), interior/exterior corridors. **Parking:** on-site. **Terms:** office hours 8 am-8 pm, 2 night minimum stay - seasonal and/or weekends, 7 day cancellation notice-fee imposed. **Amenities:** hair dryers. **Leisure Activities:** whirlpool. **Guest Services:** wireless Internet.
ⒶⓈⓀ ✕ 🅺 🆆 🅩 🔲 / SOME UNITS FEE 🐾

SOOKE HARBOUR HOUSE   *Book great rates at AAA.com*

ⒸⒶⒶ ⓈⒶⓋⒺ

Country Inn
$315-$675 3/1-1/4
$315-$585 2/4-2/28

Phone: (250)642-3421

Address: 1528 Whiffen Spit Rd V9Z 0T4 **Location:** 1.2 mi (2 km) w on Hwy 14. **Facility:** A colorful garden enhances this small inn, where guest rooms are cozy—many have wood fireplaces, and all feature gorgeous views of the ocean. Smoke free premises. 28 one-bedroom standard units, some with whirlpools. 4 stories, interior/exterior corridors. *Bath:* combo or shower only. **Parking:** on-site. **Terms:** open 3/1-1/4 & 2/4-2/28, 7 day cancellation notice-fee imposed. **Amenities:** CD players, voice mail, irons, hair dryers. **Leisure Activities:** saunas. **Guest Services:** wireless Internet. **Business Services:** meeting rooms, PC. **Free Special Amenities:** continental breakfast and newspaper.
🍴 🍸 CALL 🆑ᴹ ✕ 🅺 🆆 🔲 🖥 / SOME UNITS FEE 🐾

——— **WHERE TO DINE** ———

STONE PIPE GRILL

▽▽ ▽▽

Canadian
$7-$19

Phone: 250/642-0566

The casual restaurant offers homestyle cooking with flair. The menu includes options from burgers and sandwiches to fine steaks and seafood, plus daily specials and homemade desserts. Portions are ample and incorporate the use of local ingredients in season. Casual dress. **Bar:** Full bar. **Reservations:** accepted. **Hours:** 11 am-9 pm. Closed: 12/25. **Address:** 2038 Otter Point Rd V9Z 0S9. **Location:** Hwy 14; center. **Parking:** on-site. CALL 🆑ᴹ 🅺

This ends listings for the Victoria Vicinity.
The following resumes the alphabetical listings of cities in British Columbia.

WEST KELOWNA—See Okanagan Valley p. 566.

WEST VANCOUVER—See Vancouver p. 664.

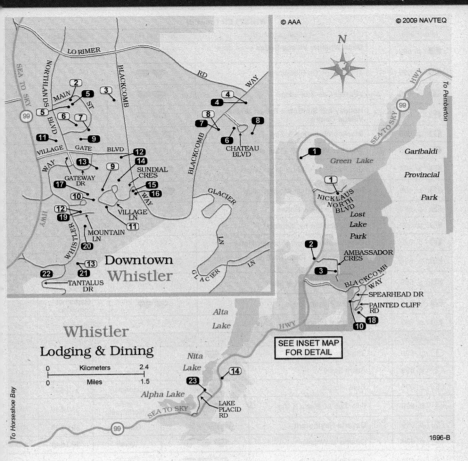

© AAA © 2009 NAVTEQ

SEE INSET MAP
FOR DETAIL

Whistler
Lodging & Dining

1696-B

Whistler

This index helps you "spot" where approved lodgings and restaurants are located on the corresponding detailed maps. Lodging daily rate range is for comparison only and show the property's high season. Restaurant rate range is a combination of lunch and/or dinner. Turn to the listing page for more detailed rate information and consult display ads for special promotions.

WHISTLER

Map Page	OA	Lodgings	Diamond Rated	High Season	Page
1 / above	AAA	**Edgewater Lodge -** see color ad p 703	▽▽	$124-$225 SAVE	702
2 / above		The Durlacher Hof Alpine Inn	▽▽▽	$109-$399	702
3 / above		Chalet Luise	▽▽	$119-$179	701
4 / above	AAA	**Four Seasons Resort Whistler**	▽▽▽▽▽	$265-$920 SAVE	703
5 / above		Summit Lodge & Spa	▽▽▽	$150-$599	708
6 / above		Glacier Lodge	▽▽▽	Rates not provided	703
7 / above	AAA	**Le Chamois**	▽▽▽	$179-$595 SAVE	706
8 / above	AAA	**The Fairmont Chateau Whistler**	▽▽▽▽	$179-$900 SAVE	703

WHISTLER (cont'd)

Map Page	OA	Lodgings (cont'd)	Diamond Rated	High Season	Page
9 / p. 699	CAA	**Delta Whistler Village Suites** - see color ad p 702	◇◇◇	$99-$409 SAVE	702
10 / p. 699		The Aspens On Blackcomb	◇◇	Rates not provided	700
11 / p. 699		Whistler Cascade Lodge	◇◇	Rates not provided	708
12 / p. 699	CAA	**Holiday Inn SunSpree Resort Whistler Village Centre**	◇◇◇	$109-$899 SAVE	705
13 / p. 699	CAA	**Blackcomb Lodge & Spa**	◇◇◇	$152-$503 SAVE	701
14 / p. 699	CAA	**Whistler Village Inn + Suites**	◇◇	$119-$489 SAVE	708
15 / p. 699		Pan Pacific Whistler Village Centre	◇◇◇	Rates not provided	707
16 / p. 699		Pan Pacific Whistler Mountainside	◇◇◇	Rates not provided	706
17 / p. 699	CAA	**Crystal Lodge & Suites**	◇◇◇	$99-$339 SAVE	701
18 / p. 699	CAA	**Residence Inn by Marriott**	◇◇◇	$449-$549 SAVE	707
19 / p. 699	CAA	**Best Western Listel Whistler Hotel**	◇◇	$89-$349 SAVE	701
20 / p. 699	CAA	**Hilton Whistler Resort & Spa** - see color ad p 704	◇◇◇◇	$185-$799 SAVE	705
21 / p. 699	CAA	**The Westin Resort & Spa**	◇◇◇◇	Rates not provided SAVE	708
22 / p. 699		Tantalus Resort Lodge	◇◇	Rates not provided	708
23 / p. 699	CAA	**Nita Lake Lodge** - see color ad p 705	◇◇◇	$269-$799 SAVE	706

Map Page	OA	Restaurants	Diamond Rated	Cuisine	Meal Range	Page
1 / p. 699		The Den Restaurant	◇◇	Canadian	$11-$35	709
2 / p. 699		Sachi Sushi	◇◇	Japanese	$6-$24	710
3 / p. 699		Brew House	◇◇	Canadian	$12-$37	709
4 / p. 699		Fifty Two 80 Bistro & Bar	◇◇◇	Pacific Northwest	$12-$40	709
5 / p. 699	CAA	**Bavaria Restaurant**	◇◇	German	$21-$39	709
6 / p. 699		Quattro at Whistler	◇◇◇	Italian	$20-$40	710
7 / p. 699		The Mountain Club	◇◇◇	Pacific Northwest	$21-$32	709
8 / p. 699		La Rua Restaurante	◇◇◇	Pacific Northwest	$19-$45	709
9 / p. 699		Araxi Restaurant & Bar	◇◇◇	Continental	$12-$46	708
10 / p. 699		LaBocca Restaurant & Bar	◇◇	Canadian	$7-$38	709
11 / p. 699		Sushi Village Japanese Cuisine	◇◇	Japanese	$6-$38	710
12 / p. 699		Bear Foot Bistro	◇◇◇	Pacific Northwest	$98-$148	709
13 / p. 699		The Aubergine Grille	◇◇◇	Pacific Northwest	$10-$36	708
14 / p. 699		Rimrock Cafe	◇◇◇	Seafood	$36-$52	710

WHISTLER pop. 9,248 (See map and index starting on p. 699)

THE ASPENS ON BLACKCOMB　*Book at AAA.com*　　Phone: 604/932-7222　**10**

◇◇
Vacation Rental
Condominium
Rates not provided

Address: 4800 Spearhead Dr V0N 1B4 **Location:** Hwy 99, 0.6 (1 km) e on Lorimer Rd (Upper Village), just se on Blackcomb Way, then just w. **Facility:** These fully self-contained condo's feature lots of space to move around, there geared for families or for a group of friends not afraid to share. Smoke free premises. 77 units. 56 one- and 21 two-bedroom suites with kitchens. 4-5 stories, interior corridors. **Parking:** on-site (fee). **Terms:** check-in 4 pm. **Amenities:** video library, DVD players, voice mail, irons, hair dryers. *Some:* high-speed Internet. **Pool(s):** heated outdoor. **Leisure Activities:** sauna, whirlpools, exercise room. **Guest Services:** coin laundry, wireless Internet. **Business Services:** meeting rooms.

(See map and index starting on p. 699)

BEST WESTERN LISTEL WHISTLER HOTEL   *Book great rates at AAA.com*   Phone: (604)932-1133   **19**

CAA SAVE

♦♦♦ ♦♦♦

Hotel
$89-$349 All Year

Address: 4121 Village Green V0N 1B4 **Location:** Hwy 99, just e on Village Gate Blvd, then follow Whistler Way. **Facility:** Smoke free premises. 98 units. 96 one-bedroom standard units. 2 one-bedroom suites with whirlpools. 3 stories, interior corridors. **Parking:** on-site (fee). **Terms:** check-in 4 pm, 3-5 night minimum stay - seasonal, cancellation fee imposed. **Amenities:** voice mail, safes, irons, hair dryers. **Dining:** Bear Foot Bistro, see separate listing. **Pool(s):** heated outdoor. **Leisure Activities:** saunas, whirlpool. **Guest Services:** valet and coin laundry, wireless Internet. **Business Services:** meeting rooms, PC. **Free Special Amenities: room upgrade (subject to availability with advance reservations) and high-speed Internet.**

AAA Benefit:
Members save up to 20%, plus 10% bonus points with rewards program.

🍴 🍷 🖥 ✕ 🎦 🖥 💻 / SOME UNITS FEE 🐕 🅺

BLACKCOMB LODGE & SPA   *Book great rates at AAA.com*   Phone: (604)932-4155   **13**

CAA SAVE

♦♦♦ ♦♦♦

Hotel
$152-$503 All Year

Address: 4220 Gateway Dr V0N 1B4 **Location:** Hwy 99, just e on Village Gate Blvd, then just s. **Facility:** Smoke free premises. 71 one-bedroom standard units, some with efficiencies. 3 stories, interior corridors. **Parking:** on-site (fee). **Terms:** check-in 4 pm, 2-3 night minimum stay - seasonal, 30 day cancellation notice-fee imposed. **Amenities:** DVD players, voice mail, safes, irons, hair dryers. **Pool(s):** heated indoor. **Leisure Activities:** sauna, whirlpool, spa. **Guest Services:** coin laundry, wireless Internet. **Business Services:** meeting rooms, PC (fee). **Free Special Amenities: room upgrade and preferred room (each subject to availability with advance reservations).**

🍴📶 🖥 ✕ 💻 / SOME UNITS 🖥

CHALET LUISE   Phone: 604/932-4187   **3**

♦♦♦ ♦♦♦

Bed & Breakfast
$119-$179 All Year

Address: 7461 Ambassador Crescent V0N 1B7 **Location:** Hwy 99, exit Nancy Green Dr, follow road to Ambassador Crescent. Located in a residential area. **Facility:** Smoke free premises. 8 one-bedroom standard units. 3 stories (no elevator), interior corridors. **Bath:** combo or shower only. **Parking:** on-site. **Terms:** office hours 8 am-10 pm, 14 day cancellation notice-fee imposed. **Amenities:** hair dryers. **Leisure Activities:** sauna, whirlpool. **Guest Services:** TV in common area, coin laundry, wireless Internet. **Business Services:** PC. ✕ 🅺 📺 📶 / SOME UNITS 🖥

CRYSTAL LODGE & SUITES   *Book great rates at AAA.com*   Phone: (604)932-2221   **17**

CAA SAVE

♦♦♦ ♦♦♦

Hotel
$99-$339 4/26-2/28
$130-$268 3/1-4/25

Address: 4154 Village Green V0N 1B4 **Location:** Hwy 99, just e on Village Gate Blvd, then follow road to Whistler Way. **Facility:** Smoke free premises. 158 units. 135 one-bedroom standard units, some with efficiencies and/or whirlpools. 15 one-, 5 two- and 3 three-bedroom suites, some with kitchens and/or whirlpools. 5 stories, interior corridors. **Parking:** on-site (fee). **Terms:** check-in 4 pm, 2-5 night minimum stay - seasonal and/or weekends, 3 day cancellation notice, 30 day in winter-fee imposed. **Amenities:** voice mail, hair dryers. *Some:* high-speed Internet (fee), safes, irons. **Dining:** 2 restaurants, also, Ric's Grill, see separate listing. **Pool(s):** heated outdoor. **Leisure Activities:** sauna, whirlpool, exercise room. **Guest Services:** valet and coin laundry, wireless Internet. **Business Services:** meeting rooms, business center.

ECO 🍴 🍷 CALL 📶 🖥 ✕ ✕ 🎦 🖥 💻 / SOME UNITS FEE 🐕 📷

FREE local telephone calls and newspaper

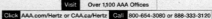

(See map and index starting on p. 699)

DELTA WHISTLER VILLAGE SUITES   *Book great rates at AAA.com*   **Phone:** (604)905-3987

Extended Stay
Hotel
$99-$409 All Year

Address: 4308 Main St V0N 1B4 **Location:** Hwy 99, just e on Village Gate Blvd, just n on Northlands Blvd, then just e. **Facility:** Smoke free premises. 205 units. 22 one-bedroom standard units. 131 one- and 52 two-bedroom suites with kitchens. 6 stories, interior corridors. **Parking:** on-site (fee) and valet. **Terms:** check-in 4 pm, 30 day cancellation notice-fee imposed. **Amenities:** voice mail, irons, hair dryers. *Fee:* video games, high-speed Internet. **Pool(s):** heated outdoor. **Leisure Activities:** sauna, whirlpools, exercise room, spa. *Fee:* ski equipment. **Guest Services:** valet and coin laundry, area transportation-ski hills, wireless Internet. **Business Services:** meeting rooms, PC (fee). *(See color ad below)*

THE DURLACHER HOF ALPINE INN   **Phone:** (604)932-1924

Bed & Breakfast
$109-$399 All Year

Address: 7055 Nesters Rd V0N 1B7 **Location:** 0.9 mi (1.5 km) n on Hwy 99. **Facility:** Goose-down duvets and hand-carved pine furniture are featured in the guest rooms, which are kept meticulous thanks to the caring housekeeping staff. Smoke free premises. 8 one-bedroom standard units, some with whirlpools. 3 stories (no elevator), interior corridors. *Bath:* combo or shower only. **Parking:** on-site. **Terms:** office hours 8 am-8 pm, 3 night minimum stay - seasonal, 14 day cancellation notice, 30 day in winter-fee imposed. **Amenities:** hair dryers. **Leisure Activities:** sauna, whirlpool. **Guest Services:** TV in common area, wireless Internet.

EDGEWATER LODGE   **Phone:** 604/932-0688

Hotel
$124-$225 All Year

Address: 8020 Alpine Way V0N 1B0 **Location:** 2.5 mi (4 km) n of Whistler Village via Hwy 99, then just e. **Facility:** Smoke free premises. 12 one-bedroom standard units. 1 story, exterior corridors. *Bath:* combo or shower only. **Parking:** on-site. **Terms:** office hours 8:30 am-10 pm, 14 day cancellation notice-fee imposed. **Amenities:** video library, hair dryers. **Leisure Activities:** whirlpool. **Guest Services:** wireless Internet. *(See color ad p 703)*

(See map and index starting on p. 699)

THE FAIRMONT CHATEAU WHISTLER — *Book great rates at AAA.com* — **Phone:** (604)938-8000 **8**

(AA) SAVE

Hotel
$179-$900 All Year

Address: 4599 Chateau Blvd V0N 1B4 **Location:** Hwy 99, 0.6 mi (1 km) e on Lorimer Rd (Upper Village), just w on Blackcomb Way. **Facility:** A luxurious chateau at one of North America's premier ski resorts, the property includes amenities such as a golf course and spa. 550 units. 490 one-bedroom standard units, some with whirlpools. 55 one- and 5 two-bedroom suites, some with whirlpools. 12 stories, interior corridors. **Parking:** on-site (fee) and valet. **Terms:** check-in 4 pm, 3 day cancellation notice-fee imposed. **Amenities:** video library, voice mail, safes, irons, hair dryers. *Fee:* video games, high-speed Internet. *Some:* DVD players, CD players. **Dining:** 4 restaurants. **Pool(s):** 2 heated outdoor. **Leisure Activities:** sauna, whirlpools, steamrooms, 3 tennis courts, spa. *Fee:* golf-18 holes, tennis instruction, ski & sports equipment. **Guest Services:** valet and coin laundry, area transportation-Whistler Township and golf course, wireless Internet. **Business Services:** conference facilities, business center.

ECO ⊠ 24 ⊠ CALL ⊠M ⊠ ⊠ ⊠ ⊠ ⊠ / SOME UNITS FEE ⊠ ⊠

FOUR SEASONS RESORT WHISTLER — *Book great rates at AAA.com* — **Phone:** (604)935-3400 **4**

(AA) SAVE

Hotel
$265-$920 All Year

Address: 4591 Blackcomb Way V0N 1B4 **Location:** Hwy 99, 0.6 mi (1 km) e on Lorimer Rd (Upper Village). **Facility:** Situated near Blackcomb Mountain, this stunning hotel offers warmly decorated guest rooms with rich wood accents, a cozy fireplace and a balcony. Smoke free premises. 298 units. 178 one-bedroom standard units. 90 one-, 20 two- and 10 three-bedroom suites, some with kitchens and/or whirlpools. 6-9 stories, interior corridors. **Parking:** valet. **Terms:** 30 day cancellation notice, in winter-fee imposed. **Amenities:** video library, DVD players, video games (fee), CD players, high-speed Internet, dual phone lines, voice mail, safes, irons, hair dryers. **Dining:** Fifty Two 80 Bistro & Bar, see separate listing. **Pool(s):** heated outdoor. **Leisure Activities:** whirlpools, steamrooms, rental bicycles, jogging, spa. **Guest Services:** valet laundry, area transportation-Whistler Village & golf course, wireless Internet. **Business Services:** meeting rooms, business center.

⊠ 24 ⊠ CALL ⊠M ⊠ ⊠ ⊠ ⊠ ⊠ ⊠ ⊠ / SOME UNITS ⊠ ⊠

GLACIER LODGE — *Book at AAA.com* — **Phone:** 604/905-0518 **6**

Boutique
Hotel
Rates not provided

Address: 4573 Chateau Blvd V0N 1B4 **Location:** Hwy 99, 0.6 mi (1 km) e on Lorimer Rd (Upper Village), then just w on Blackcomb Way. **Facility:** About half of the units are one bedrooms with kitchens, while the other half are standard hotel rooms with double beds and small kitchenettes. Smoke free premises. 73 units. 34 one-bedroom standard units, some with efficiencies. 34 one-, 4 two- and 1 three-bedroom suites with kitchens. 3 stories, interior corridors. **Parking:** on-site (fee). **Terms:** check-in 4 pm. **Amenities:** video library, DVD players, voice mail, irons, hair dryers. **Pool(s):** heated outdoor. **Leisure Activities:** whirlpools, exercise room. **Guest Services:** coin laundry, wireless Internet. **Business Services:** meeting rooms.

⊠ CALL ⊠M ⊠ ⊠ ⊠ ⊠ ⊠ / SOME UNITS ⊠

▼ See AAA listing p 702 ▼

(See map and index starting on p. 699)

▼ See AAA listing p 705 ▼

Hilton
Whistler Resort & Spa

Experience luxury & serenity at Whistler's Newest Four Diamond Resort property

- A ski in ski out property nestled at the base of Whistler & Blackcomb mountains.
- Many suites include full kitchens, deep soaker tubs & balconies
- Pet Friendly
- Full service Spa & Health Club facilities

www.hiltonwhistler.com

4050 Whistler Way Whistler BC V0N 1B4   1-800-515-4050   reservations@hiltonwhistler.com

(See map and index starting on p. 699)

HILTON WHISTLER RESORT & SPA

Book great rates at AAA.com

Hotel
$185-$799 All Year

Phone: (604)932-1982   **20**

Address: 4050 Whistler Way V0N 1B4 **Location:** Hwy 99, just e on Village Gate Blvd, then follow Whistler Way. **Facility:** The newly renovated hotel boasts some of the town's largest hotel rooms; the chair lifts at Whistler Mountain are within easy walking distance. Smoke free premises. 289 units. 265 one-bedroom standard units, some with efficiencies. 15 one- and 9 two-bedroom suites with kitchens, some with whirlpools. 5-8 stories, interior corridors. *Bath:* combo or shower only. **Parking:** on-site (fee) and valet. **Terms:** check-in 4 pm, 1-7 night minimum stay, cancellation fee imposed. **Amenities:** dual phone lines, voice mail, safes, irons, hair dryers. *Fee:* video games, high-speed Internet. **Pool(s):** heated outdoor. **Leisure Activities:** sauna, whirlpools, exercise room, spa. **Guest Services:** valet and coin laundry, area transportation-Whistler Village and golf courses, wireless Internet. **Business Services:** conference facilities, business center. *(See color ad p 704)*

AAA Benefit:
Members save 5%
or more everyday!

HOLIDAY INN SUNSPREE RESORT WHISTLER VILLAGE CENTRE

Book great rates at AAA.com

Hotel
$109-$899 All Year

Phone: (604)938-0878   **12**

Address: 4295 Blackcomb Way V0N 1B4 **Location:** Hwy 99, just e on Village Gate Blvd. **Facility:** Smoke free premises. 115 units. 105 one- and 10 two-bedroom standard units with whirlpools, some with efficiencies or kitchens. 6 stories, interior corridors. **Parking:** on-site (fee). **Terms:** check-in 4 pm, 30 day cancellation notice-fee imposed. **Amenities:** high-speed Internet, voice mail, irons, hair dryers. **Leisure Activities:** whirlpool, exercise room. **Free Special Amenities:** local telephone calls and high-speed Internet.

▼ See AAA listing p 706 ▼

WHISTLER'S PREMIER BOUTIQUE HOTEL

Whistler's premier full service boutique hotel; nestled on the shore of picturesque Nita Lake. Enjoy lake and mountain views from any of the 77 suites fully equipped with; king beds, soaker tubs, and fireplaces. Indulge yourself at the full service spa and health club, or dine lakeside at Jordan's Crossing.

Toll Free: 1-888-755-6482 • www.nitalakelodge.com

2131 Lake Placid Road, Whistler, B.C., V0N 1B2

(See map and index starting on p. 699)

LE CHAMOIS

Hotel
$179-$595 11/23-2/28
$115-$299 3/1-4/20

Phone: (604)932-4113 **7**

Address: 4557 Blackcomb Way V0N 1B4 **Location:** Hwy 99, 0.6 mi (1 km) e on Lorimer Rd (Upper Village), then just w. **Facility:** Smoke free premises. 45 units. 43 one-bedroom standard units, some with whirlpools. 2 three-bedroom suites with kitchens, some with whirlpools. 6 stories, interior corridors. **Parking:** on-site (fee). **Terms:** open 3/1-4/20 & 11/23-2/28, check-in 4 pm, 2-7 night minimum stay - seasonal, 30 day cancellation notice-fee imposed. **Amenities:** DVD players, voice mail, irons, hair dryers. **Dining:** La Rua Restaurante, see separate listing. **Pool(s):** heated outdoor. **Leisure Activities:** whirlpool, limited exercise equipment. **Guest Services:** coin laundry, wireless Internet. **Business Services:** meeting rooms. **Free Special Amenities:** local telephone calls and high-speed Internet.

NITA LAKE LODGE

Hotel
$269-$799 12/1-2/28
$159-$499 3/1-11/30

Phone: 604/966-5700 **23**

Address: 2131 Lake Placid Rd V0N 1B2 **Location:** 1.8 mi (3 km) s on Hwy 99, just w. **Facility:** Smoke free premises. 77 units. 64 one- and 13 two-bedroom standard units. 4 stories, interior corridors. **Parking:** on-site (fee) and valet. **Terms:** 2-5 night minimum stay - seasonal and/or weekends, 30 day cancellation notice, in winter-fee imposed. **Amenities:** DVD players, CD players, high-speed Internet (fee), voice mail, irons, hair dryers. **Dining:** 2 restaurants. **Leisure Activities:** whirlpools, exercise room, spa. **Guest Services:** valet and coin laundry, area transportation-ski hills & Whistler Township. **Business Services:** meeting rooms. *(See color ad p 705)*

FREE local telephone calls and high-speed Internet

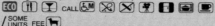

PAN PACIFIC WHISTLER MOUNTAINSIDE *Book at AAA.com* **Phone:** 604/905-2999 **16**

Extended Stay
Contemporary Hotel
Rates not provided

Address: 4320 Sundial Crescent V0N 1B4 **Location:** Hwy 99, just e on Village Gate Blvd, then just s on Blackcomb Way. **Facility:** Smoke free premises. 121 units. 45 one-bedroom standard units with kitchens. 51 one- and 25 two-bedroom suites with kitchens. 8 stories, interior corridors. **Parking:** on-site (fee) and valet. **Amenities:** video games (fee), CD players, high-speed Internet, dual phone lines, voice mail, safes, irons, hair dryers. **Pool(s):** heated outdoor. **Leisure Activities:** whirlpools, steamroom, exercise room, spa. **Guest Services:** valet and coin laundry, area transportation, wireless Internet. **Business Services:** meeting rooms.

────────── ▼ See AAA listing p 569 ▼ ──────────

(See map and index starting on p. 699)

PAN PACIFIC WHISTLER VILLAGE CENTRE   *Book at AAA.com*   Phone: 604/966-5500   **15**

Extended Stay
Contemporary Hotel
Rates not provided

Address: 4299 Blackcomb Way V0N 1B4 **Location:** Hwy 99, just e on Village Gate Blvd. **Facility:** Smoke free premises. 83 units. 45 one-, 35 two- and 3 three-bedroom suites with kitchens. 8 stories, interior corridors. **Parking:** on-site (fee) and valet. **Amenities:** video games (fee), CD players, high-speed Internet, dual phone lines, voice mail, safes, irons, hair dryers. **Pool(s):** heated outdoor. **Leisure Activities:** sauna, whirlpools, exercise room, spa. **Guest Services:** valet and coin laundry, area transportation, wireless Internet. **Business Services:** meeting rooms, PC (fee).

ECO 📶 CALL &M 🏊 ✕ ✕ 🍴 🔒 🖥 💻 / SOME UNITS FEE 🐾

RESIDENCE INN BY MARRIOTT   *Book great rates at AAA.com*   Phone: (604)905-3400   **18**

(CAA) (SAVE)
♦♦♦♦
Vacation Rental
Condominium
$449-$549 All Year

Address: 4899 Painted Cliff Rd V0N 1B4 **Location:** Hwy 99, 0.6 mi (1 km) e on Lorimer Rd (Upper Village), just se on Blackcomb Way, then just w, follow road all the way to the end. **Facility:** Studio units and one- or two-bedroom condominiums, each with a gas fireplace, occupy this facility on Blackcomb Mountain. Smoke free premises. 186 units. 84 one-bedroom standard units with kitchens. 57 one- and 45 two-bedroom suites with kitchens. 6 stories, interior corridors. **Parking:** on-site (fee). **Terms:** check-in 4 pm, 60 day cancellation notice-fee imposed. **Amenities:** voice mail, irons, hair dryers. **Pool(s):** heated outdoor. **Leisure Activities:** whirlpools, exercise room. **Guest Services:** valet and coin laundry, wireless Internet. **Business Services:** meeting rooms, PC.

AAA Benefit:
Members save a
minimum 5% off the
best available rate.

ECO CALL &M 🏊 ✕ 🎿 🍴 🔒 🖥 💻 / SOME UNITS FEE 🐾

FREE expanded continental breakfast and high-speed Internet

(See map and index starting on p. 699)

SUMMIT LODGE & SPA

▼◆▼◆▼

Hotel
$150-$599 All Year

Phone: (604)932-2778 **5**

Address: 4359 Main St V0N 1B4 **Location:** Hwy 99, just n on Village Gate Blvd, then just w on Northlands Blvd. **Facility:** Smoke free premises. 81 units. 75 one-bedroom standard units with efficiencies. 6 one-bedroom suites with efficiencies. 5 stories, interior corridors. **Parking:** on-site (fee). **Terms:** check-in 4 pm, 2-5 night minimum stay - seasonal and/or weekends, 30 day cancellation notice, in season-fee imposed. **Amenities:** high-speed Internet, voice mail, irons, hair dryers. **Dining:** Sachi Sushi, see separate listing. **Pool(s):** heated outdoor. **Leisure Activities:** sauna, whirlpool, spa. **Guest Services:** valet and coin laundry, wireless Internet. **Business Services:** meeting rooms, PC (fee).

ECO ASK ⑪ ☎ CALL ⓂSM ⚲ ✖ ✖ 🎦 🖥 🖨 🖵 / SOME UNITS 🐾

TANTALUS RESORT LODGE   *Book at AAA.com*

▼◆▼ ▼◆▼

Condominium
Rates not provided

Phone: 604/932-4146 **22**

Address: 4200 Whistler Way V0N 1B4 **Location:** Hwy 99, just e on Village Gate Blvd, then follow Whistler Way to the end. **Facility:** Smoke free premises. 64 two-bedroom suites with kitchens. 5 stories, interior corridors. **Parking:** on-site (fee). **Terms:** check-in 4 pm. **Amenities:** voice mail, safes, hair dryers. **Pool(s):** heated outdoor. **Leisure Activities:** sauna, whirlpools, 2 tennis courts, playground, volleyball. **Guest Services:** coin laundry, area transportation, wireless Internet. **Business Services:** meeting rooms, PC (fee).

⚲ ✖ ✖ ⚖ 🎦 🖥 🖨 🖵 / SOME UNITS FEE 🐾

THE WESTIN RESORT & SPA   *Book great rates at AAA.com*

ⓒAA SAVE

▼◆▼ ▼◆▼

Hotel
Rates not provided

Phone: 604/905-5000 **21**

Address: 4090 Whistler Way V0N 1B4 **Location:** Hwy 99, just e on Village Gate Blvd, then s. **Facility:** The upscale lodging comprises shops, conference facilities, a spa and health club as well as ski-in, ski-out convenience to Whistler Mountain. Smoke free premises. 400 units. 199 one-bedroom standard units with efficiencies. 183 one- and 18 two-bedroom suites with kitchens, some with whirlpools. 11 stories, interior corridors. **Parking:** on-site (fee) and valet. **Terms:** check-in 4 pm. **Amenities:** dual phone lines, voice mail, safes, honor bars, irons, hair dryers. *Fee:* video games, high-speed Internet. **Dining:** The Aubergine Grille, see separate listing. **Pool(s):** heated outdoor. **Leisure Activities:** sauna, whirlpools, steamrooms, spa. **Guest Services:** valet and coin laundry, area transportation-within Whistler Township, wireless Internet. **Business Services:** conference facilities, business center. **Free Special Amenities:** newspaper.

ECO ⑪ 24⑪ ☎ CALL ⓂSM ⚲ ⛵ ✖ ✖ 🎦 🖥 🖨 🖵 / SOME UNITS 🐾

WESTIN
HOTELS & RESORTS

AAA Benefit:
Enjoy up to 15% off your next stay, plus Starwood Preferred Guest® bonuses.

WHISTLER CASCADE LODGE

▼◆▼ ▼◆▼

Vacation Rental
Condominium
Rates not provided

Phone: 604/905-4875 **11**

Address: 4315 Northlands Blvd V0N 1B0 **Location:** Hwy 99, just e on Village Gate Blvd, then just n. **Facility:** Select from standard-style hotel rooms with a small kitchenette or a one-bedroom condo unit with a full kitchen and large living room area. Smoke free premises. 112 units. 30 one-bedroom standard units with efficiencies. 80 one- and 2 two-bedroom suites with kitchens. 6 stories, interior corridors. **Parking:** on-site (fee). **Terms:** check-in 4 pm. **Amenities:** video library, DVD players, voice mail, irons, hair dryers. **Pool(s):** heated outdoor. **Leisure Activities:** saunas, whirlpools, limited exercise equipment. **Guest Services:** coin laundry, wireless Internet. **Business Services:** meeting rooms, PC (fee). ⚲ ✖ ✖ 🖥 🖨 🖵

WHISTLER VILLAGE INN + SUITES   *Book great rates at AAA.com*

ⓒAA SAVE

▼◆▼ ▼◆▼

Hotel
$119-$489 All Year

Phone: (604)932-4004 **14**

Address: 4429 Sundial Pl V0N 1B4 **Location:** Hwy 99, just e on Village Gate Blvd, then just s on Blackcomb Way to Sundial Pl. **Facility:** Smoke free premises. 87 units. 83 one-bedroom standard units, some with efficiencies. 4 one-bedroom suites with efficiencies. 3 stories, interior corridors. **Parking:** on-site (fee). **Terms:** check-in 4 pm, 2 night minimum stay - seasonal and/or weekends, 14 day cancellation notice-fee imposed. **Amenities:** DVD players, voice mail, irons, hair dryers. **Pool(s):** heated outdoor. **Leisure Activities:** saunas, whirlpools, exercise room. **Guest Services:** valet and coin laundry, wireless Internet. **Business Services:** meeting rooms, PC (fee).

⛏ CALL ⓂSM ⚲ ✖ ✖ 🖵 / SOME UNITS 🖥 🖨

─────── **WHERE TO DINE** ───────

ARAXI RESTAURANT & BAR

▼◆▼◆▼

Continental
$12-$46

Phone: 604/932-4540 **9**

The restaurant exudes a vibrant, theatrical atmosphere. Fresh items punctuate upscale, diverse and creative menu selections. Diners are sure to enjoy tuna tartare, Tofino salmon filet and smoked pork loin. An impressive wine list and enticing desserts round out the offerings. Patio dining is a nice option during the summer months. Casual dress. **Bar:** Full bar. **Reservations:** suggested. **Hours:** 5 pm-11 pm. **Address:** 4222 Village Square V0N 1B4 **Location:** In Whistler Village Square, by the Blackcomb Lodge. **Parking:** on-site (fee). CALL ⓂSM 🍷

THE AUBERGINE GRILLE

▼◆▼◆▼

Pacific Northwest
$10-$36

Phone: 604/905-5000 **13**

French for "eggplant," Aubergine houses a show kitchen where guests can watch chefs assemble breakfast, lunch and dinner selections. The eclectic menu centers on West Coast seafood, including British Columbia salmon, but it also lists such comfort foods as steak, pizza and pasta. Casual dress. **Bar:** Full bar. **Reservations:** suggested, for dinner & in winter. **Hours:** 7 am-10 pm. **Address:** 4090 Whistler Way V0N 1B4 **Location:** Hwy 99, just e on Village Gate Blvd, then s; in The Westin Resort & Spa. **Parking:** on-site (fee) and valet. CALL ⓂSM

(See map and index starting on p. 699)

BAVARIA RESTAURANT

Phone: 604/932-7518

German beers and schnapps complement pork and veal schnitzels and fondues. The three-course dinner includes an appetizer, choice of schnitzel and dessert. Metered street parking is in effect at all times. Casual dress. **Bar:** Full bar. **Reservations:** suggested. **Hours:** 5 pm-9:30 pm; 4 pm-11 pm 12/1-4/30. **Address:** 101-4369 Main St V0N 1B4 **Location:** Hwy 99, just n on Village Gate Blvd, then just w on Northland Blvd; in Alpenglow Lodge. **Parking:** street. CALL

German
$21-$39

BEAR FOOT BISTRO

Phone: 604/932-3433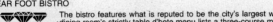

The bistro features what is reputed to be the city's largest wine cellar, with more than 20,000 bottles. The dining room's strictly table d'hote menu lists a three-course meal at $39 (in summer) and $98 (in winter) and a five-course meal at $95 (in summer) and $148 (in winter). Those not inclined to eat in the dining room can visit the wine bar, where meals often are served with by-the-glass wines. Casual dress. **Bar:** Full bar. **Reservations:** suggested. **Hours:** 6 pm-10 pm. **Address:** 4121 Village Green V0N 1B4 **Location:** Hwy 99, just e on Village Gate Blvd, then follow Whistler Way; in Best Western Listel Whistler Hotel. **Parking:** valet.

Pacific Northwest
$98-$148

CALL

BREW HOUSE

This brewpub brews beer solely for consumption on the premises. Four flagship brews are always available, and the menu features a variety of tapas, pizza, pasta and rotisserie foods—all chosen to complement the beers. Casual dress. **Bar:** Full bar. **Reservations:** suggested. **Hours:** 11:30 am-midnight, Fri & Sat-1 am. **Address:** 4355 Blackcomb Way V0N 1B4 **Location:** Hwy 99, 0.6 mi (1 km) e on Lorimer Rd (Upper Village), then just w. **Parking:** on-site (fee). CALL

Canadian
$12-$37

THE DEN RESTAURANT

Phone: 604/938-9898

Open for breakfast, lunch and dinner, the publike restaurant overlooks the golf course and nearby lake. Offerings range from tapas, burgers and sandwiches at lunch to more sophisticated dinner fare, including preparations of Alberta beef and great seafood. Many microbrews are on tap. Casual dress. **Bar:** Full bar. **Reservations:** suggested. **Hours:** Open 3/1-10/14 & 12/1-2/28; 6:30 am-10 pm; from 4 pm 12/1-3/31. **Address:** 8080 Nicklaus North Blvd V0N 1B8 **Location:** 2 mi (3.5 km) n of Whistler Village via Hwy 99, then just e; in The Nicklaus North Golf Course Clubhouse. **Parking:** on-site. CALL

Canadian
$11-$35

EARLS RESTAURANT

Phone: 604/935-3222

Offering an experience that falls between fast food and fine dining, the fun, relaxed restaurant prepares great food at a great price. Choices range from juicy burgers, hearty sandwiches, fresh salads, wings and pizza to full entrees of steak, chops and seafood. Made-from-scratch soups and assorted breads, as well as a nice choice of wines and beers, round out the offerings. This is a fitting spot for impromptu get-togethers and festive occasions. Casual dress. **Bar:** Full bar. **Hours:** 11:30 am-11 pm. **Address:** 4295 Blackcomb Way, Unit 220 V0N 1B4 **Location:** Hwy 99, just e on Village Gate Blvd, then just s. **Parking:** street.

Canadian
$10-$28

CALL

FIFTY TWO 80 BISTRO & BAR

Phone: 604/966-5280

The restaurant is named for the number of feet in the vertical mile that can be skied on Blackcomb Mountain. The casual bistro welcomes guests for breakfast, lunch and dinner. British Columbia wines match with items from the seafood bar, including freshly shucked oysters, crab, lobster and prawns. Stylish, casual resort wear is recommended for evenings. Casual dress. **Bar:** Full bar. **Reservations:** suggested. **Hours:** 6:30 am-10 pm. **Address:** 4591 Blackcomb Way V0N 1B4 **Location:** Hwy 99, 0.6 mi (1 km) e on Lorimer Rd (Upper Village); in Four Seasons Resort Whistler. **Parking:** valet. CALL

Pacific Northwest
$12-$40

LABOCCA RESTAURANT & BAR

Phone: 604/932-2112

This restaurant is busy and popular with both the young and mature. The menu features fondue, rack of lamb, pizza, pasta and wok cooking—a real mix of different items to suit almost every taste. The huge outdoor patio is open during the summer. Casual dress. **Bar:** Full bar. **Reservations:** suggested, during ski season. **Hours:** 10 am-11 pm. **Address:** 4232 Village Stroll V0N 1B0 **Location:** In Whistler Village Square. **Parking:** no self-parking. CALL

Canadian
$7-$38

LA RUA RESTAURANTE

Phone: 604/932-5011

In the Upper Village, the wonderful restaurant affords wonderful views of Blackcomb Mountain. This place is known for its wild game and fish, warm and inviting atmosphere and great service. Complimentary parking is available in Le Chamois Hotel. Casual dress. **Bar:** Full bar. **Reservations:** suggested. **Hours:** Open 3/1-10/9 & 11/23-2/28; 6 pm-10 pm. **Address:** 4557 Blackcomb Way V0N 1B0 **Location:** Hwy 99, 0.6 mi (1 km) e on Lorimer Rd (Upper Village), then just w; in Le Chamois. **Parking:** on-site.

Pacific Northwest
$19-$45

THE MOUNTAIN CLUB

Phone: 604/932-6009

This cozy, fun restaurant sits on the corner of a pedestrian walkway, and large floor-to-ceiling windows facilitate the great people-watching. The menu features wonderful comfort foods, such as the signature mac 'n' cheese and the M.C. burger with sweet yam fries. Those who can't find metered street parking can use the large free day lot and walk into the village. Casual dress. **Bar:** Full bar. **Reservations:** suggested. **Hours:** 6 pm-11 pm; from 5 pm 11/1-3/31. **Address:** 40 4314 Main St V0N 1B4 **Location:** Just n of Village Gate Blvd; in Whistler Village North. **Parking:** street. CALL

Pacific Northwest
$21-$32

(See map and index starting on p. 699)

QUATTRO AT WHISTLER   Phone: 604/905-4844

Italian
$20-$40

Next to Pinnacle International Resort, the restaurant offers a cozy atmosphere and a wonderful wine list that represents several regions and includes some reasonably priced selections. Adventurous diners might try Fraser Valley duck, rack of lamb, pan-seared beef tenderloin, baked salmon wrapped in phyllo pastry or pazza a pezzi—a combination of five pastas. Casual dress. **Bar:** Full bar. **Reservations:** suggested. **Hours:** 5:30 pm-11 pm. **Address:** 4319 Main St V0N 1B4 **Location:** Hwy 99, just e on Village Gate Blvd, then just n on Northlands Blvd. **Parking:** street. CALL

RIC'S GRILL   Phone: 604/932-7427

Steak
$20-$35

"Funky and modern" describes the decor and the food at the upscale steakhouse, which bustles with activity. Steaks are well worth it, but then again, so are the salmon, chicken and pasta dishes. A wide variety of distinctive appetizers rounds out the menu. Servers are friendly and attentive. Casual dress. **Bar:** Full bar. **Reservations:** suggested, for dinner. **Hours:** 4:30 pm-10 pm. **Address:** 4154 Village Green V0N 1B4 **Location:** Hwy 99, just e on Village Gate Blvd, then follow road to Whistler Way; in Crystal Lodge & Suites. **Parking:** street.

RIMROCK CAFE   Phone: 604/932-5565

Seafood
$36-$52

The hidden gem may be hard to find, but the locals know and love this place. Open for dinner with the last seating at 9:30 pm, the restaurant serves many seafood items, including swordfish, salmon and halibut, in addition to an interesting selection of wild game such as buffalo and grilled caribou. This place is so popular that reservations are a must. Casual dress. **Bar:** Full bar. **Reservations:** required. **Hours:** 6 pm-9:30 pm. Closed: 10/15-11/20. **Address:** 2117 Whistler Rd V0N 1B0 **Location:** From Whistler Village; Village Gate Blvd, 2.1 mi (3.5 km) s on Hwy 99, just e; in The Highland Lodge. **Parking:** on-site.

SACHI SUSHI   Phone: 604/935-5649

Japanese
$6-$24

At Summit Lodge, the cozy Japanese restaurant prepares interesting fresh sushi selections. Diners can pay for street parking for 2 hours. Casual dress. **Bar:** Full bar. **Hours:** noon-2:30 & 5:30-10 pm; 5:30 pm-10 pm 12/1-4/15. Closed: 12/25. **Address:** 106-4359 Main St V0N 1B4 **Location:** Hwy 99, just n on Village Gate Blvd, then just w on Northlands Blvd; in Summit Lodge & Spa. **Parking:** street.

SUSHI VILLAGE JAPANESE CUISINE   Phone: 604/932-3330

Japanese
$6-$38

Opposite the Blackcomb Gondola, this restaurant specializes in fresh, tasty sushi and sashimi but also lists green salad, steamed rice, steamed vegetables and ice cream. Small or large groups might feel comfy in the tatami rooms. The relaxed, friendly setting was one of the original six restaurants in Whistler. Casual dress. **Bar:** Full bar. **Reservations:** suggested. **Hours:** 5:30 pm-10 pm, Fri-Sun also noon-2:30 pm; 5 pm-10 pm, Fri-Sun also noon-2:30 pm in winter. **Address:** 4272 Mountain Square V0N 1B4 **Location:** Hwy 99, just e on Village Gate Blvd, then just s on Blackcomb Way; in Sundial Boutique Hotel. **Parking:** street.

WHITE ROCK—See Vancouver p. 665.

WILLIAMS LAKE pop. 10,744

DRUMMOND LODGE MOTEL   Phone: 250/392-5334

Motel
$72-$140 All Year

Address: 1405 Cariboo Hwy V2G 2W3 **Location:** 0.6 mi (1 km) s on Hwy 97. **Facility:** 24 units. 23 one-bedroom standard units, some with efficiencies or kitchens (utensils extra charge). 1 one-bedroom suite with kitchen (utensils extra charge). 1-2 stories (no elevator), exterior corridors. **Parking:** on-site, winter plug-ins. **Terms:** office hours 7:30 am-11 pm, cancellation fee imposed. **Amenities:** high-speed Internet. **Guest Services:** coin laundry, wireless Internet.

WILLIAMS LAKE SUPER 8   *Book great rates at AAA.com*   Phone: (250)398-8884

(AAA) (SAVE)

Motel
$82-$120 All Year

Address: 1712 Broadway Ave S V2G 2W4 **Location:** 1.2 mi (2 km) s on Hwy 97. **Facility:** Smoke free premises. 53 one-bedroom standard units, some with whirlpools. 3 stories (no elevator), interior corridors. **Parking:** on-site, winter plug-ins. **Amenities:** high-speed Internet, hair dryers. **Guest Services:** coin laundry, wireless Internet. **Business Services:** PC. **Free Special Amenities:** continental breakfast and high-speed Internet.

WINDERMERE pop. 1,259

WINDERMERE CREEK BED AND BREAKFAST
CABINS   Phone: (250)342-0356

Cabin
$109-$159 All Year

Address: 1658 Windermere Loop Rd V0B 2L2 **Location:** Hwy 93/95 (south end of town), 0.6 mi (1 km) e on Kootenay 3 Rd, keep left at fork for 1.3 mi (2.2 km). Located in a quiet area. **Facility:** Set in a mountain valley, the property offers four modern cabins with kitchenettes as well as one rustic yet well-appointed 1887 cabin. Smoke free premises. 5 cabins. 1 story, interior/exterior corridors. **Parking:** on-site, winter plug-ins. **Terms:** age restrictions may apply, 30 day cancellation notice-fee imposed. **Amenities:** CD players, hair dryers. *Some:* DVD players. **Leisure Activities:** cross country skiing, hiking trails. **Guest Services:** wireless Internet.

Manitoba

BEAUSEJOUR pop. 2,823

SUPERIOR INN
Book at AAA.com
Phone: (204)268-9050

Hotel
$94-$99 All Year

Address: 1055 Park Ave R0E 0C0 **Location:** On Hwy 215; jct Hwy 12/44/302. Located in a rural area. **Facility:** 36 units. 32 one-bedroom standard units, some with whirlpools. 4 one-bedroom suites with whirlpools. 2 stories (no elevator), interior corridors. **Parking:** on-site, winter plug-ins. **Terms:** cancellation fee imposed. **Amenities:** voice mail, hair dryers. *Some:* irons. **Pool(s):** heated indoor. **Leisure Activities:** sauna, whirlpool. **Guest Services:** coin laundry, wireless Internet. **Business Services:** meeting rooms, PC.

BRANDON pop. 41,511

CANAD INNS-DESTINATION CENTRE BRANDON
Book great rates at AAA.com
Phone: (204)727-1422

CAA SAVE

Hotel
$105-$230 All Year

Address: 1125 18th St R7A 7C5 **Location:** On Hwy 10 (18th St); jct Brandon Ave. **Facility:** Smoke free premises. 159 units. 152 one-bedroom standard units, some with whirlpools. 7 one-bedroom suites. 11 stories, interior corridors. *Bath:* combo or shower only. **Parking:** on-site, winter plug-ins. **Amenities:** video games (fee), high-speed Internet, voice mail, hair dryers. *Some:* CD players. **Dining:** 2 restaurants, nightclub. **Pool(s):** heated indoor. **Leisure Activities:** waterslide, hot tubs, exercise room. **Guest Services:** valet laundry, wireless Internet. **Business Services:** meeting rooms, business center. **Free Special Amenities:** newspaper and high-speed Internet.

COMFORT INN
Book at AAA.com
Phone: (204)727-6232

Hotel
$107-$147 5/1-2/28
$97-$137 3/1-4/30

Address: 925 Middleton Ave R7C 1A8 **Location:** Trans-Canada Hwy 1; between Hwy 10 (18th St) N and Hwy 10 S; on northside of service road. Located in a commercial area. **Facility:** 81 one-bedroom standard units. 2 stories (no elevator), interior corridors. **Parking:** on-site, winter plug-ins. **Amenities:** irons, hair dryers. **Guest Services:** valet laundry, wireless Internet. **Business Services:** PC (fee).

DAYS INN BRANDON
Book at AAA.com
Phone: (204)727-3600

Hotel
$104-$139 All Year

Address: 2130 Currie Blvd R7B 4E7 **Location:** Jct Trans-Canada Hwy 1, 4.9 mi (7.9 km) w on Hwy 10 (18th St). Located in a commercial area. **Facility:** 61 units. 58 one-bedroom standard units. 3 one-bedroom suites. 3 stories, interior corridors. **Parking:** on-site, winter plug-ins. **Terms:** check-in 4 pm. **Amenities:** video library (fee), high-speed Internet, voice mail, hair dryers. *Some:* DVD players (fee), irons. **Pool(s):** heated indoor. **Leisure Activities:** whirlpool, limited exercise equipment. **Guest Services:** valet and coin laundry, wireless Internet. **Business Services:** meeting rooms, PC.

LAKEVIEW INNS & SUITES BRANDON
Book great rates at AAA.com
Phone: (204)728-1880

CAA SAVE

Hotel
$95-$140 All Year

Address: 1880 18th St N R7C 1A5 **Location:** On Hwy 10 (18th St), just s of jct Trans-Canada Hwy 1. Located in a commercial area. **Facility:** 66 units. 50 one-bedroom standard units, some with whirlpools. 16 one-bedroom suites. 3 stories, interior corridors. **Parking:** on-site, winter plug-ins. **Terms:** cancellation fee imposed. **Amenities:** video library, DVD players, voice mail, irons, hair dryers. *Some:* dual phone lines. **Pool(s):** heated indoor. **Leisure Activities:** exercise room. **Guest Services:** valet and coin laundry, wireless Internet. **Business Services:** meeting rooms, PC. **Free Special Amenities:** continental breakfast and local telephone calls.

ROYAL OAK INN & SUITES
Book at AAA.com
Phone: (204)728-5775

Hotel
$120-$125 All Year

Address: 3130 Victoria Ave R7B 0N2 **Location:** 3.1 mi (5 km) s on Hwy 10 (18th St) from jct Trans-Canada Hwy 1, then 1.1 mi (1.8 km) w. Located in a commercial area. **Facility:** 156 units. 96 one-bedroom standard units, some with whirlpools. 60 one-bedroom suites, some with whirlpools. 2-5 stories, interior corridors. **Parking:** on-site, winter plug-ins. **Terms:** cancellation fee imposed. **Amenities:** video library, DVD players, high-speed Internet, voice mail, irons, hair dryers. *Some:* CD players. **Pool(s):** heated indoor. **Leisure Activities:** whirlpool, waterslide, exercise room. **Guest Services:** valet and coin laundry, wireless Internet. **Business Services:** conference facilities, PC.

SUPER 8 BRANDON
Book at AAA.com
Phone: (204)729-8024

Hotel
$115-$160 All Year

Address: 1570 Highland Ave R7C 1A7 **Location:** Jct Trans-Canada Hwy 1, just s on Hwy 10 (18th St), then just e. Located in a commercial area. **Facility:** 79 units. 77 one-bedroom standard units. 2 one-bedroom suites. 2 stories (no elevator), interior corridors. **Parking:** on-site, winter plug-ins. **Terms:** cancellation fee imposed. **Amenities:** video library (fee), DVD players, high-speed Internet, voice mail, irons, hair dryers. **Pool(s):** heated indoor. **Leisure Activities:** whirlpool, exercise room. **Guest Services:** valet and coin laundry, wireless Internet. **Business Services:** meeting rooms.

VICTORIA INN
Book at AAA.com
Phone: (204)725-1532

Hotel
$103-$199 All Year

Address: 3550 Victoria Ave R7B 2R4 **Location:** Jct Trans-Canada Hwy 1, 3.1 mi (5 km) s on Hwy 10 (18th St), then 0.9 mi (1.4 km) w. Located in a residential/commercial area. **Facility:** Smoke free premises. 131 one-bedroom standard units, some with whirlpools. 2 stories (no elevator), interior corridors. *Bath:* combo or shower only. **Parking:** on-site, winter plug-ins. **Terms:** cancellation fee imposed. **Amenities:** video library, DVD players, high-speed Internet, voice mail, irons, hair dryers. **Pool(s):** heated indoor. **Leisure Activities:** whirlpool, exercise room. **Guest Services:** valet and coin laundry, wireless Internet. **Business Services:** conference facilities, PC.

—— WHERE TO DINE ——

DOUBLE HAPPINESS RESTAURANT   Phone: 204/728-6388

♦♦ ♦♦
Chinese
$6-$12

Bright and clean, the little spot is where locals head when they get a craving for Chinese food. Casual dress. **Bar:** Full bar. **Reservations:** accepted. **Hours:** 11 am-10 pm, Fri & Sat-11 pm, Sun 4 pm-10 pm. Closed: 12/25. **Address:** 608 Rosser Ave R7A 0K7 **Location:** Between 7th and 6th sts. **Parking:** street.

THE GREEN OLIVE   Phone: 204/726-0207

♦♦ ♦♦
Canadian
$8-$28

From the name alone, one would expect to find Italian fare but the menu also is made up of good 'ol Canadian foods, like ribs, steaks and pastas. Casual dress. **Bar:** Full bar. **Reservations:** suggested. **Hours:** 10 am-9 pm. Closed major holidays; also Sun. **Address:** 612 Rosser Ave R7A 0K7 **Location:** Between 6th and 7th sts; downtown. **Parking:** street.

LADY OF THE LAKE CAFE & PUB   Phone: 204/726-8785

♦♦ ♦♦
Canadian
$8-$20

This unique combination of a 50s-style diner, a modern pub and a 7,000-square-foot gift shop is a little quirky but interesting. The menu is multi-faceted with an emphases on local and organic products and a host to "gourmet comfort" foods that are as tasty as they are healthy. The pub features live jazz most nights and more high-energy entertainment on Friday and Saturday. Casual dress. **Bar:** Full bar. **Reservations:** accepted. **Hours:** 9 am-midnight, Mon-5 pm, Tues & Wed-10 pm. Closed major holidays; also Sun. **Address:** 135-B 17th St N R7A 1G6 **Location:** Just e on Maple Ave from jct Hwy 10 (18th St). **Parking:** on-site.

CHURCHILL pop. 923

POLAR INN & SUITES   Phone: (204)675-8878

♦♦ ♦♦
Motel
$119-$245 All Year

Address: 153 Kelsey Blvd R0B 0E0 **Location:** Centre. **Facility:** 26 units. 23 one-bedroom standard units, some with kitchens. 3 one-bedroom suites with kitchens. 1 story, interior corridors. **Parking:** on-site, winter plug-ins. **Terms:** office hours 8 am-8 pm. **Amenities:** video library, voice mail, hair dryers. *Some:* DVD players, irons. **Guest Services:** wireless Internet. **Business Services:** meeting rooms.

THE TUNDRA INN   Phone: 204/675-8831

♦♦ ♦♦
Hotel
$111-$220 All Year

Address: 34 Franklin St R0B 0E0 **Location:** Centre. Located in a commercial area. **Facility:** 31 one-bedroom standard units. 2 stories (no elevator), interior corridors. **Parking:** on-site, winter plug-ins. **Terms:** office hours 8 am-5 pm, 30 day cancellation notice-fee imposed. **Amenities:** high-speed Internet, hair dryers. **Guest Services:** coin laundry. **Business Services:** PC.

—— *The following lodgings were either not evaluated or did not* ——
meet AAA rating requirements but are listed for your information only.

BEAR COUNTRY INN   Phone: 204/675-8299

[fyi]

Not evaluated. **Address:** 126 Kelsey Blvd R0B 0E0 **Location:** Just w of train station. Facilities, services, and decor characterize an economy property.

CHURCHILL MOTEL   Phone: 204/675-8853

[fyi]

Not evaluated. **Address:** 152 Kelsey Blvd R0B 0E0 **Location:** Centre. Facilities, services, and decor characterize an economy property.

SEAPORT HOTEL   Phone: 204/675-8807

[fyi]

Not evaluated. **Address:** 299 Kelsey Blvd R0B 0E0 **Location:** Centre. Facilities, services, and decor characterize a mid-scale property.

—— WHERE TO DINE ——

GYPSY BAKERY, RESTAURANT & COFFEE SHOP   Phone: 204/675-2322

♦
American
$4-$19

This incredibly popular eatery features an extensive selection of fresh baked goods, steak, shrimp, fish, chicken, sandwiches, soup, salad, pizza and pirogies. It is THE place for to-go lunches. Fine wines and cigars are also available. Polite service. Casual dress. **Bar:** Full bar. **Hours:** Open 3/1-12/15 & 2/1-2/28; 7 am-9 pm. Closed major holidays; also Sun. **Address:** 253 Kelsey Blvd R0B 0E0 **Location:** Centre. **Parking:** on-site.

FLIN FLON pop. 5,836

VICTORIA INN NORTH   Phone: 204/687-7555

♦♦ ♦♦
Hotel
Rates not provided

Address: 160 Hwy 10A N R8A 0C6 **Location:** Jct Hwy 10 and 10A, 0.6 mi (1 km) nw (eastern approach to city). Located in a commercial area. **Facility:** 93 one-bedroom standard units, some with whirlpools. 3 stories (no elevator), interior corridors. **Parking:** on-site, winter plug-ins. **Amenities:** video games (fee), voice mail, irons, hair dryers. **Dining:** The Kelsey Dining Room, see separate listing. **Pool(s):** heated indoor. **Leisure Activities:** whirlpool, exercise room. **Guest Services:** coin laundry, wireless Internet. **Business Services:** meeting rooms, PC.

—— **WHERE TO DINE** ——

THE KELSEY DINING ROOM Phone: 204/687-7555

Canadian
$8-$29

Friendly, efficient service and generous portions keep locals and visitors returning to this restaurant. The menu is varied and offers selections such as steak, chicken, fish and pasta. Booth and table seating are available. Casual dress. **Bar:** Full bar. **Reservations:** accepted. **Hours:** 6:30 am-10 pm, Sat & Sun from 7 am. Closed: 12/24-12/26. **Address:** 160 Hwy 10A N R8A 0C6 **Location:** Jct Hwy 10 and 10A, 0.6 mi (1 km) nw (eastern approach to city); in Victoria Inn North. **Parking:** on-site.

GIMLI pop. 1,891

LAKEVIEW RESORT & CONFERENCE CENTRE   *Book great rates at AAA.com*   Phone: (204)642-8565

Hotel
$92-$285 All Year

Address: 10 Centre St R0C 1B0 **Location:** Centre. **Facility:** Smoke free premises. 99 units. 42 one-bedroom standard units. 52 one- and 5 two-bedroom suites, some with efficiencies, kitchens and/or whirlpools. 3 stories, interior corridors. **Parking:** on-site, winter plug-ins. **Terms:** cancellation fee imposed. **Amenities:** video library, DVD players, voice mail, irons, hair dryers. **Pool(s):** heated outdoor, heated indoor. **Leisure Activities:** sauna, whirlpool, exercise room. *Fee:* game room. **Guest Services:** coin laundry, area transportation-within 6 mi (10 km), wireless Internet. **Business Services:** conference facilities, PC. **Free Special Amenities: local telephone calls and high-speed Internet.**

HECLA

RADISSON HECLA OASIS RESORT   *Book at AAA.com*   Phone: (204)279-2041

Resort
Hotel
$149-$242 6/1-2/28
$165-$209 3/1-5/31

Address: Hwy 8 R0C 2R0 **Location:** Hwy 8, n of Hecla Village. **Facility:** Located in a park on Hecla Island, the property is fashioned in a Nordic design and offers well-appointed guest rooms with Sleep Number beds. Smoke free premises. 90 units. 68 one-bedroom standard units. 22 one-bedroom suites. 2 stories, interior corridors. *Bath:* combo or shower only. **Parking:** on-site. **Terms:** 7 day cancellation notice-fee imposed. **Amenities:** high-speed Internet, dual phone lines, voice mail, safes, irons, hair dryers. *Some:* CD players. **Dining:** RoK Restaurant and Lounge, see separate listing. **Pool(s):** heated indoor, heated indoor/outdoor. **Leisure Activities:** sauna, whirlpools, steamrooms, waterslide, limited beach access, cross country skiing, snowmobiling, ice skating, recreation programs in summer, rental bicycles, hiking trails, spa, volleyball. *Fee:* golf-18 holes. **Guest Services:** wireless Internet. **Business Services:** conference facilities, business center.

—— **WHERE TO DINE** ——

ROK RESTAURANT AND LOUNGE Phone: 204/279-2041

Canadian
$10-$20

Steaks, ribs, chicken, burgers and gourmet-style pizzas are offered at this pleasant, casual restaurant. Outdoor terrace dining is available in season. Casual dress. **Bar:** Full bar. **Reservations:** accepted. **Hours:** 7 am-11 pm. **Address:** Hwy 8 R0C 2R0 **Location:** On Hwy 8, n of Hecla Village; in Radisson Hecla Oasis Resort. **Parking:** on-site.

NEEPAWA pop. 3,298

BAY HILL INNS & SUITES Phone: 204/476-8888

Hotel
Rates not provided

Address: 160 Main St W R0J 1H0 **Location:** On Hwy 16, just w of jct Rt 5. Located in a quiet area. **Facility:** 34 units. 32 one-bedroom standard units. 2 one-bedroom suites, some with whirlpools. 2 stories (no elevator), interior corridors. **Parking:** on-site, winter plug-ins. **Pool(s):** heated indoor. **Leisure Activities:** whirlpool. **Guest Services:** wireless Internet. **Business Services:** PC.

PORTAGE LA PRAIRIE pop. 12,728

CANAD INNS DESTINATION CENTRE PORTAGE LA PRAIRIE Phone: (204)857-9745

Hotel
$95-$255 All Year

Address: 2401 Saskatchewan Ave W R1N 3L5 **Location:** Jct Hwy 1A and 24th St W. Located in a commercial area. **Facility:** Smoke free premises. 92 units. 71 one-bedroom standard units. 21 one-bedroom suites, some with whirlpools. 2 stories, interior corridors. *Bath:* combo or shower only. **Parking:** on-site, winter plug-ins. **Amenities:** irons, hair dryers. *Some:* high-speed Internet. **Pool(s):** heated indoor. **Leisure Activities:** whirlpool, waterslide, hot tub, exercise room. **Guest Services:** valet laundry, wireless Internet. **Business Services:** conference facilities, PC. **Free Special Amenities: newspaper and high-speed Internet.**

SUPER 8 Phone: (204)857-8883

Hotel
$90-$101 All Year

Address: 2668 Hwy 1A W R1N 3B2 **Location:** On Hwy 1A, 0.9 mi (1.5 km) w. Located in a commercial area. **Facility:** 58 units. 56 one-bedroom standard units. 2 one-bedroom suites. 2 stories (no elevator), interior corridors. **Parking:** on-site, winter plug-ins. **Amenities:** voice mail, hair dryers. *Some:* high-speed Internet, irons. **Pool(s):** heated indoor. **Leisure Activities:** whirlpool, waterslide. **Guest Services:** valet and coin laundry, wireless Internet. **Business Services:** meeting rooms, PC.

WESTGATE INN MOTEL

Phone: (204)239-5200

Motel
$60-$89 All Year

Address: 1010 Saskatchewan Ave E R1N 0K1 **Location:** 0.6 mi (1 km) e on Hwy 1A. Located in a commercial area. **Facility:** 25 one-bedroom standard units, some with efficiencies. 2 stories (no elevator), exterior corridors. **Parking:** on-site, winter plug-ins. **Terms:** office hours 7 am-midnight. **Guest Services:** wireless Internet. [ASK] [♦] [🍴] [🖨] / SOME UNITS [🐾] [✕] [🖥]

------ WHERE TO DINE ------

BILL'S STICKY FINGERS

Phone: 204/857-9999

Canadian
$6-$25

The comfortable, casual, older restaurant offers a wide-ranging menu that includes ribs, chicken, steak, lasagna, gyros and pizza, as well as daily specials. The service is friendly and prompt. Casual dress. **Bar:** Full bar. **Reservations:** accepted. **Hours:** 11 am-midnight, Sat & Sun from 4 pm. Closed: 1/1, 12/25, 12/26. **Address:** 210 Saskatchewan Ave E R1N 0K9 **Location:** Just w of Main St. **Parking:** on-site.

GARDEN GATE GRILL AND BAKERY

Phone: 204/856-0540

Canadian
$6-$16

This rather nondescript restaurant stands out amidst the town's many chain restaurants by serving up a little bit of everything and a whole lot of friendly, small-town service. Everything from soups and sandwiches to burgers and steaks can be found on the menu. Casual dress. **Bar:** Full bar. **Reservations:** not accepted. **Hours:** 11 am-9 pm, Sat & Sun from 10 am. Closed major holidays. **Address:** 2380 Sissons Dr R1N 0G5 **Location:** Jct Hwy 1A and 24th St W. **Parking:** on-site.

RUSSELL pop. 1,428

THE RUSSELL INN HOTEL & CONFERENCE CENTRE

Phone: (204)773-2186

Hotel
$105-$196 12/1-2/28
$98-$129 3/1-11/30

Address: Hwy 16 R0J 1W0 **Location:** 0.8 mi (1.2 km) se on Hwy 16 and 83. Located in a commercial area. **Facility:** 97 units. 73 one-bedroom standard units, some with whirlpools. 24 one-bedroom suites. 1 story, interior corridors. **Parking:** on-site, winter plug-ins. **Terms:** 2 night minimum stay - seasonal and/or weekends, 14 day cancellation notice, 30 day in winter-fee imposed. **Amenities:** video library, DVD players, voice mail, irons, hair dryers. *Some:* high-speed Internet. **Dining:** restaurant, see separate listing. **Pool(s):** heated indoor. **Leisure Activities:** whirlpool, waterslide, playground, exercise room. *Fee:* game room. **Guest Services:** coin laundry, wireless Internet. **Business Services:** conference facilities, PC. [ASK] [⊞] [🍴] [▼] [🏊] [✕] [🛎] [🖨] / SOME UNITS [🐾] [✕] [🖥]

------ WHERE TO DINE ------

RUSSELL INN DINING ROOM

Phone: 204/773-7507

Canadian
$7-$30

This popular local dining room offers generous portions and efficient service in a family atmosphere. The varied menu includes such items as pasta, seafood, chicken and ribs, as well as veal, steaks and quesadillas. Some light meals are also available. Casual dress. **Bar:** Full bar. **Reservations:** accepted. **Hours:** 7 am-10 pm, Sun-9 pm. Closed: 12/25. **Address:** Hwy 16 R0J 1W0 **Location:** 0.8 mi (1.2 km) se on Hwy 16 and 83; in The Russell Inn Hotel & Conference Centre. **Parking:** on-site.

SCANTERBURY

SOUTH BEACH CASINO & RESORT

Book great rates at AAA.com

Phone: (204)766-2100

Hotel
$85 All Year

Address: One Ocean Dr R0E 1W0 **Location:** On Rt 59, just s of town. **Facility:** Reminiscent of South Beach, the restaurant boast an Art Deco decor. 95 units. 85 one-bedroom standard units, some with whirlpools. 10 one-bedroom suites. 6 stories, interior corridors. *Bath:* combo or shower only. **Parking:** on-site and valet. **Terms:** cancellation fee imposed. **Amenities:** high-speed Internet, voice mail, irons, hair dryers. *Some:* dual phone lines. **Pool(s):** heated indoor. **Guest Services:** valet laundry, wireless Internet. **Business Services:** conference facilities, PC. **Free Special Amenities:** early check-in/late check-out and high-speed Internet. [ECO] [♦] [🍴] [▼] [🏊] [📷] [🖨] / SOME UNITS [✕] [⊞]

STEINBACH pop. 11,066

DAYS INN

Book at AAA.com

Phone: 204/320-9200

Hotel
Rates not provided

Address: 75 Hwy 12 N R5G 1T3 **Location:** 0.5 mi (0.8 km) n of jct Hwy 52. Located in a commercial area. **Facility:** 49 one-bedroom standard units. 3 stories, interior corridors. *Bath:* combo or shower only. **Parking:** on-site, winter plug-ins. **Amenities:** voice mail, hair dryers. *Some:* DVD players (fee). **Pool(s):** heated indoor. **Leisure Activities:** whirlpool, waterslide, exercise room. **Guest Services:** valet and coin laundry, wireless Internet. **Business Services:** meeting rooms, PC (fee). [🏊] [✕] [✕] [⊞] [🖥] [🖨] / SOME UNITS FEE [🐾]

THE PAS pop. 5,589

KIKIWAK INN

Phone: 204/623-1800

Hotel
Rates not provided

Address: Hwy 10 N R0B 2J0 **Location:** On Hwy 10, 0.4 mi (0.6 km) n. Located in a commercial area. **Facility:** 60 one-bedroom standard units, some with whirlpools. 3 stories, interior corridors. **Parking:** on-site, winter plug-ins. **Amenities:** voice mail, irons, hair dryers. *Some:* high-speed Internet. **Dining:** Niska Dining Room, see separate listing. **Pool(s):** heated indoor. **Leisure Activities:** whirlpool, exercise room. **Guest Services:** valet laundry, wireless Internet. **Business Services:** conference facilities. [♦] [🍴] [▼] CALL [📞M] [🏊] [⊞] [🖨] / SOME UNITS [🐾] [✕] [🖥]

SUPER 8   *Book at AAA.com*   Phone: (204)623-1888

Hotel
$115 All Year

Address: 1717 Gordon Ave R9A 1K3 **Location:** At southern approach to town. Located in a commercial area. **Facility:** 70 units. 53 one-bedroom standard units. 17 one-bedroom suites. 2 stories (no elevator), interior corridors. **Parking:** on-site, winter plug-ins. **Amenities:** voice mail, hair dryers. *Some:* DVD players (fee). **Pool(s):** heated indoor. **Leisure Activities:** whirlpool, waterslide. **Guest Services:** coin laundry, wireless Internet. **Business Services:** meeting rooms.

—— **WHERE TO DINE** ——

NISKA DINING ROOM   Phone: 204/623-1800

Canadian
$9-$23

The menu lists such choices as pickerel, stir-fried beef, steak, chicken, ribs, pasta and salads. Also offered are heart-healthy choices and dishes recommended for diabetics. Native art is displayed in the dining room. Casual dress. **Bar:** Full bar. **Reservations:** accepted. **Hours:** 6:30 am-10 pm, Sun 8 am-8 pm. Closed: 12/25. **Address:** Hwy 10 N R0B 2J0 **Location:** On Hwy 10, 0.4 mi (0.6 km) n; in Kikiwak Inn. **Parking:** on-site.

THOMPSON pop. 13,446

COUNTRY INN & SUITES BY CARLSON   *Book at AAA.com*   Phone: 204/778-8879

Hotel
Rates not provided

Address: 70 Thompson Dr N R8N 1Y8 **Location:** Just w of Hwy 6. Located in a commercial area. **Facility:** 60 units. 23 one-bedroom standard units. 37 one-bedroom suites. 2 stories (no elevator), interior corridors. **Parking:** on-site, winter plug-ins. **Amenities:** video library, DVD players, voice mail, irons, hair dryers. **Leisure Activities:** sauna, exercise room. **Guest Services:** valet and coin laundry, wireless Internet. **Business Services:** meeting rooms, PC.

DAYS INN & SUITES   *Book at AAA.com*   Phone: (204)778-6000

Hotel
$134-$149 All Year

Address: 21 Thompson Dr N R8N 2B5 **Location:** Just e of Hwy 6. Located in a commercial area. **Facility:** Smoke free premises. 60 units. 56 one-bedroom standard units. 4 one-bedroom suites, some with whirlpools. 2 stories (no elevator), interior corridors. **Parking:** on-site, winter plug-ins. **Terms:** cancellation fee imposed. **Amenities:** high-speed Internet, voice mail, irons, hair dryers. **Leisure Activities:** limited exercise equipment. **Guest Services:** valet and coin laundry, wireless Internet. **Business Services:** PC.

——— *The following lodgings were either not evaluated or did not* ———
meet AAA rating requirements but are listed for your information only.

INTERIOR INN & EXECUTIVE SUITES   Phone: 204/778-5535

[fyi]

Not evaluated. **Address:** 180 Thompson Dr R8N 1Y8 **Location:** Thompson Dr at Riverside St. Facilities, services, and decor characterize a mid-scale property.

BURNTWOOD HOTEL   Phone: 204/677-4551

[fyi]

Not evaluated. **Address:** 146 Selkirk Ave R8N 0N1 **Location:** Jct Cree Rd. Facilities, services, and decor characterize a mid-scale property.

—— **WHERE TO DINE** ——

THE HUB   Phone: 204/778-5630

Canadian
$7-$27

The restaurant is a meeting spot for local folks. Fish and chips, burgers, sandwiches, salads and pizza are served in generous portions, and heartier options, like steak and seafood, are available on the dinner menu. Casual dress. **Bar:** Full bar. **Reservations:** accepted. **Hours:** 11 am-10 pm. Closed major holidays. **Address:** 111 Churchill Dr R8N 1M9 **Location:** Centre. **Parking:** on-site.

WINKLER pop. 9,106

DAYS INN & SUITES   *Book at AAA.com*   Phone: 204/325-8888

Hotel
Rates not provided

Address: 395 Boundary Tr R6W 4B1 **Location:** Main St and Hwy 14; centre. Located in a commercial area. **Facility:** 52 units. 40 one-bedroom standard units. 12 one-bedroom suites, some with whirlpools. 3 stories, interior corridors. **Parking:** on-site, winter plug-ins. **Amenities:** high-speed Internet, voice mail, irons, hair dryers. **Pool(s):** heated indoor. **Leisure Activities:** whirlpool, waterslide, exercise room. **Guest Services:** coin laundry, wireless Internet. **Business Services:** meeting rooms, PC.

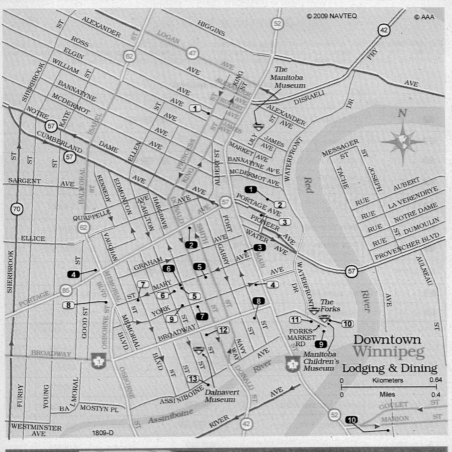

© 2009 NAVTEQ   © AAA

Downtown
Winnipeg
Lodging & Dining

Downtown Winnipeg

This index helps you "spot" where approved lodgings and restaurants are located on the corresponding detailed maps. Lodging daily rate range is for comparison only and show the property's high season. Restaurant rate range is a combination of lunch and/or dinner. Turn to the listing page for more detailed rate information and consult display ads for special promotions.

DOWNTOWN WINNIPEG

Map Page	OA	Lodgings	Diamond Rated	High Season	Page
1 / p. 717		The Fairmont Winnipeg	▽▽▽	Rates not provided	722
2 / p. 717	CAA	**Radisson Hotel Winnipeg Downtown**	▽▽▽	$120-$182 SAVE	723
3 / p. 717		Hampton Inn & Suites	▽▽▽	$119-$169	723
4 / p. 717	CAA	**Holiday Inn Hotel & Suites Winnipeg Downtown** - see color ad on insert	▽▽▽	$109-$119 SAVE	723
5 / p. 717		Place Louis Riel Suite Hotel - see color ad p 219	▽▽	$125-$400	723
6 / p. 717	CAA	**Delta Winnipeg** - see color ad p 722	▽▽▽	$89-$399 SAVE	722
7 / p. 717	CAA	**Best Western Charterhouse Hotel Downtown Winnipeg**	▽▽	$119-$165 SAVE	721
8 / p. 717		The Fort Garry	▽▽▽	Rates not provided	723
9 / p. 717	CAA	**Inn at the Forks**	▽▽▽	$149-$279 SAVE	723
10 / p. 717	CAA	**Norwood Hotel**	▽▽	$114-$155 SAVE	723

Map Page	OA	Restaurants	Diamond Rated	Cuisine	Meal Range	Page
1 / p. 717		Mirlycourtois	▽▽▽	French	$24-$54	724
2 / p. 717	CAA	**The Velvet Glove**	▽▽▽▽	Continental	$26-$36	725
3 / p. 717		Hu's on First	▽▽	Asian	$10-$16	724
4 / p. 717		Ivory Restaurant & Bar	▽▽	Indian	$12-$25	724
5 / p. 717		Blaze Bistro & Lounge	▽▽▽	Canadian	$9-$35	724
6 / p. 717		Ichiban Japanese Steak House & Sushi Bar	▽▽	Japanese	$15-$38	724
7 / p. 717		Hy's Steakhouse	▽▽▽	Steak	$10-$50	724
8 / p. 717		Storm Restaurant & Catering	▽▽	Canadian	$9-$15	724
9 / p. 717		East India Company Pub & Eatery	▽▽	Indian	$10-$20	724
10 / p. 717		The Current	▽▽▽	Canadian	$10-$39	724
11 / p. 717		Beachcombers	▽▽	Canadian	$10-$37	724
12 / p. 717		Amici	▽▽▽	Italian	$10-$42	723
13 / p. 717		Restaurant Dubrovnik	▽▽▽	Continental	$28-$50	724

Get a Fresh Perspective on AAATravelViews.com

- Blogs from our experts on popular and unique destinations
- The latest in helpful travel advice and news
- Photos, videos, maps and special member offers
- Comments and Q&A with AAA experts

Share travel at
AAATravelViews.com

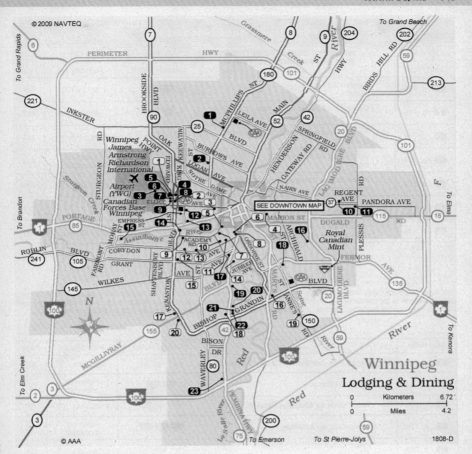

Winnipeg
Lodging & Dining

✈ Airport Accommodations

Map Page	OA	WINNIPEG JAMES ARMSTRONG RICHARDSON INTERNATIONAL AIRPORT	Diamond Rated	High Season	Page
9 / p. 719		Comfort Inn Airport, 1.4 mi (2.3 km) e of airport	◆◆	$112-$122	726
7 / p. 719		Country Inn & Suites By Carlson, 1.2 mi (1.9 km) e of airport	◆◆	$105-$135	727
3 / p. 719	CAA	**Four Points by Sheraton Hotel Winnipeg, at airport**	◆◆◆	$125-$145 SAVE	727
4 / p. 719		Greenwood Inn & Suites, 0.9 mi (1.5 km) e of airport	◆◆◆	Rates not provided	728
5 / p. 719	CAA	**Hilton Suites Winnipeg Airport, 1 mi (1.6 km) e of airport**	◆◆◆	$139-$229 SAVE	728
8 / p. 719		Sandman Hotel & Suites Winnipeg Airport, 0.9 mi (1.5 km) e of airport	◆◆◆	$144-$214	728
6 / p. 719	CAA	**Victoria Inn Hotel & Convention Centre, 0.8 mi (1.2 km) e of airport**	◆◆◆	$129-$174 SAVE	730

Winnipeg

This index helps you "spot" where approved lodgings and restaurants are located on the corresponding detailed maps. Lodging daily rate range is for comparison only and show the property's high season. Restaurant rate range is a combination of lunch and/or dinner. Turn to the listing page for more detailed rate information and consult display ads for special promotions.

WINNIPEG

Map Page	OA	Lodgings	Diamond Rated	High Season	Page
1 / p. 719	CAA	**Canad Inns Destination Centre Garden City**	◆◆◆	$85-$259 SAVE	725
2 / p. 719		Days Inn Winnipeg	◆◆	Rates not provided	727
3 / p. 719	CAA	**Four Points by Sheraton Hotel Winnipeg**	◆◆◆	$125-$145 SAVE	727
4 / p. 719		Greenwood Inn & Suites	◆◆◆	Rates not provided	728
5 / p. 719	CAA	**Hilton Suites Winnipeg Airport** - see color ad p 729	◆◆◆	$139-$229 SAVE	728
6 / p. 719	CAA	**Victoria Inn Hotel & Convention Centre**	◆◆◆	$129-$174 SAVE	730
7 / p. 719		Country Inn & Suites By Carlson	◆◆	$105-$135	727
8 / p. 719		Sandman Hotel & Suites Winnipeg Airport	◆◆◆	$144-$214	728
9 / p. 719		Comfort Inn Airport	◆◆	$112-$122	726
10 / p. 719	CAA	**Canad Inns Destination Centre Club Regent Casino Hotel** - see color ad p 219	◆◆◆	$119-$299 SAVE	725
11 / p. 719	CAA	**Canad Inns Destination Centre Transcona**	◆◆	$89-$259 SAVE	726
12 / p. 719	CAA	**Canad Inns Destination Centre Polo Park**	◆◆◆	$104-$279 SAVE	726
13 / p. 719		Clarion Hotel & Suites	◆◆◆	$149-$209	726
14 / p. 719	CAA	**Best Western Viscount Gort Hotel**	◆◆	$110-$200 SAVE	725
15 / p. 719	CAA	**Holiday Inn Winnipeg Airport West**	◆◆◆	$129-$169 SAVE	728
16 / p. 719	CAA	**Canad Inns Destination Centre Windsor Park**	◆◆	$99-$259 SAVE	726
17 / p. 719	CAA	**Quality Inn & Suites**	◆◆	$90-$270 SAVE	728
18 / p. 719	CAA	**Travelodge Winnipeg**	◆◆	$82-$159 SAVE	730

WINNIPEG (cont'd)

Map Page	OA	Lodgings (cont'd)	Diamond Rated	High Season	Page
19 / p. 719		Holiday Inn Winnipeg South	▼▼▼	Rates not provided	728
20 / p. 719	CAA	**Best Western Pembina Inn & Suites**	▼▼	$122-$126 SAVE	725
21 / p. 719	CAA	**Express by Canad Inns**	▼▼	$74-$124 SAVE	727
22 / p. 719	CAA	**Canad Inns Destination Centre Fort Garry**	▼▼	$99-$299 SAVE	725
23 / p. 719	CAA	**Comfort Inn South**	▼▼	$113-$175 SAVE	726

Map Page	OA	Restaurants	Diamond Rated	Cuisine	Meal Range	Page
1 / p. 719		Bistro 1800 - see color ad p 729	▼▼	Canadian	$12-$30	730
2 / p. 719		Chop Steak Fish Bar	▼▼▼	Steak	$11-$39	730
3 / p. 719		India Palace	▼▼	Indian	$10-$21	731
4 / p. 719		Beaujena's	▼▼▼	French	$17-$36	730
5 / p. 719		Restaurant Bistro Dansk	▼▼	European	$5-$16	732
6 / p. 719		Miyabi	▼▼	Japanese	$7-$19	732
7 / p. 719		529 Wellington	▼▼▼	Steak	$12-$49	730
8 / p. 719		Dandelion Eatery	▼▼	Natural/Organic	$10-$22	731
9 / p. 719		Fusion Grill	▼▼▼	Canadian	$10-$39	731
10 / p. 719		Spuntino Cafe	▼▼	Italian	$12-$22	732
11 / p. 719		Fresh Café	▼▼	Natural/Organic	$5-$12	731
12 / p. 719		Mona Lisa Ristorante	▼▼	Northern Italian	$7-$29	732
13 / p. 719	CAA	**Bonfire Bistro**	▼▼	Italian	$9-$23	730
14 / p. 719		The Round Table Steak House & Pub	▼▼	Steak	$9-$37	732
15 / p. 719		Stella's Cafe	▼	Breakfast	$5-$10	732
16 / p. 719		Maxime's	▼▼	Continental	$10-$28	731
17 / p. 719		Joeys	▼▼	Mediterranean	$11-$32	731
18 / p. 719		Meiji Sushi Japanese Restaurant & G. Martini Bar	▼▼	Japanese	$10-$25	731
19 / p. 719		La Fiesta Cafecito	▼▼	Salvadoran	$7-$18	731
20 / p. 719		Dacquisto	▼▼	Italian	$10-$50	730

DOWNTOWN WINNIPEG   (See map and index starting on p. 717)

BEST WESTERN CHARTERHOUSE HOTEL
DOWNTOWN WINNIPEG   *Book great rates at AAA.com*   **Phone:** (204)942-0101   7

CAA SAVE

▼▼▼ ▼▼
Hotel
$119-$165 All Year

Address: 330 York Ave R3C 0N9 **Location:** Between Hargrave and Donald sts. Located in business district. **Facility:** 87 one-bedroom standard units. 5 stories, interior corridors. **Parking:** on-site (fee), winter plug-ins. **Amenities:** high-speed Internet, voice mail, irons, hair dryers. *Some:* DVD players (fee). **Leisure Activities:** exercise room. **Guest Services:** valet and coin laundry, airport transportation-Winnipeg James Armstrong Richardson International Airport, area transportation-bus depot & train station, wireless Internet. **Business Services:** meeting rooms, PC. **Free Special Amenities:** local telephone calls and high-speed Internet.

AAA Benefit:
Members save up to 20%, plus 10% bonus points with rewards program.

(See map and index starting on p. 717)

DELTA WINNIPEG

Phone: (204)942-0551

Hotel
$89-$399 All Year

Address: 350 St. Mary Ave R3C 3J2 **Location:** At Hargrave St. Adjacent to convention centre. **Facility:** Smoke free premises. 393 units. 377 one- and 6 two-bedroom standard units. 10 one-bedroom suites, some with whirlpools. 18 stories, interior corridors. *Bath:* combo or shower only. **Parking:** on-site (fee) and valet. **Amenities:** video games (fee), high-speed Internet, voice mail, irons, hair dryers. *Some:* CD players. *Fee:* DVD players. **Dining:** Blaze Bistro & Lounge, see separate listing. **Pool(s):** heated outdoor, heated indoor. **Leisure Activities:** sauna, whirlpool. **Guest Services:** valet and coin laundry, wireless Internet. **Business Services:** conference facilities, business center. *(See color ad below)*

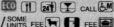

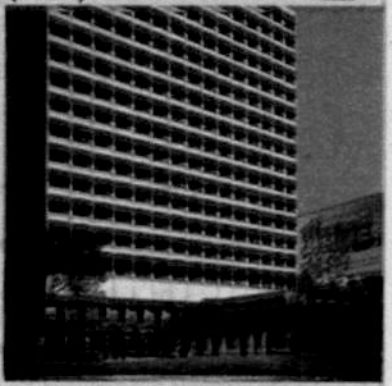

THE FAIRMONT WINNIPEG

Phone: 204/957-1350

Hotel
Rates not provided

Address: 2 Lombard Pl R3B 0Y3 **Location:** Just e of Portage Ave and Main St. Located in a commercial area. **Facility:** 340 units. 328 one-bedroom standard units, some with whirlpools. 12 one-bedroom suites. 21 stories, interior corridors. *Bath:* combo or shower only. **Parking:** on-site (fee) and valet, winter plug-ins. **Amenities:** voice mail, honor bars, irons, hair dryers. *Some:* DVD players, CD players. **Dining:** The Velvet Glove, see separate listing. **Pool(s):** heated indoor. **Leisure Activities:** whirlpool, steamroom, exercise room. *Fee:* massage. **Guest Services:** valet laundry, wireless Internet. **Business Services:** conference facilities, business center.

▼ See AAA listing above ▼

(See map and index starting on p. 717)

THE FORT GARRY
Book at AAA.com

Phone: 204/942-8251 **8**

Classic Historic Hotel
Rates not provided

Address: 222 Broadway Ave R3C 0R3 **Location:** Just w of Main St. **Facility:** Impressive hotel built in the Chicago block-style tradition. Gracious appointments in the public areas. Rooms range from small to spacious. Smoke free premises. 240 units. 224 one-bedroom standard units. 16 one-bedroom suites, some with whirlpools. 10 stories, interior corridors. *Bath:* combo or shower only. **Parking:** on-site (fee) and valet, winter plug-ins. **Amenities:** video games, dual phone lines, voice mail, irons, hair dryers. *Some:* DVD players (fee), CD players, high-speed Internet, safes. **Pool(s):** heated indoor. **Leisure Activities:** sauna, whirlpool, steamroom, jogging, exercise room, spa. **Guest Services:** valet laundry, wireless Internet. **Business Services:** conference facilities, business center.

HAMPTON INN & SUITES
Book great rates at AAA.com

Phone: (204)942-4222 **3**

Hotel
$119-$169 All Year

Address: 260 Main St R3C 1A9 **Location:** Corner of St. Mary Ave. Located in business district. **Facility:** Smoke free premises. 128 one-bedroom standard units, some with whirlpools. 6 stories, interior corridors. *Bath:* combo or shower only. **Parking:** on-site, winter plug-ins. **Terms:** 1-7 night minimum stay, cancellation fee imposed. **Amenities:** high-speed Internet, dual phone lines, voice mail, hair dryers. **Pool(s):** heated indoor. **Leisure Activities:** whirlpool, steamroom, exercise room. **Guest Services:** valet and coin laundry, wireless Internet. **Business Services:** meeting rooms, business center.

AAA Benefit:
Members save up to 10% everyday!

HOLIDAY INN HOTEL & SUITES WINNIPEG DOWNTOWN
Book great rates at AAA.com

Phone: (204)786-7011 **4**

Hotel
$109-$119 6/2-2/28
$99-$109 3/1-6/1

Address: 360 Colony St R3B 2P3 **Location:** Corner of Portage Ave. **Facility:** 140 units. 120 one-bedroom standard units. 20 one-bedroom suites. 11 stories, interior corridors. *Bath:* combo or shower only. **Parking:** on-site (fee) and valet, winter plug-ins. **Amenities:** video games (fee), high-speed Internet, dual phone lines, voice mail, irons, hair dryers. **Pool(s):** heated indoor. **Leisure Activities:** whirlpool, exercise room. **Guest Services:** valet and coin laundry, wireless Internet. **Business Services:** meeting rooms, PC (fee). *(See color ad on insert)*

INN AT THE FORKS
Book great rates at AAA.com

Phone: (204)942-6555 **9**

Hotel
$149-$279 All Year

Address: 75 Forks Market Rd R3C 0A2 **Location:** At the Forks. Located in a park and entertainment area. **Facility:** Smoke free premises. 117 units. 114 one-bedroom standard units, some with whirlpools. 3 one-bedroom suites. 5 stories, interior corridors. **Parking:** on-site (fee) and valet, winter plug-ins. **Terms:** cancellation fee imposed. **Amenities:** video games (fee), high-speed Internet, dual phone lines, voice mail, safes, irons, hair dryers. **Dining:** The Current, see separate listing. **Leisure Activities:** exercise room, spa. **Guest Services:** valet laundry, area transportation-downtown area, wireless Internet. **Business Services:** conference facilities, PC. **Free Special Amenities:** local telephone calls and high-speed Internet.

NORWOOD HOTEL
Book great rates at AAA.com

Phone: (204)233-4475 **10**

Hotel
$114-$155 All Year

Address: 112 Marion St R2H 0T1 **Location:** On Rt 115, just e of St. Mary's Rd. Located in a commercial area. **Facility:** Smoke free premises. 52 one-bedroom standard units. 5 stories, interior corridors. **Parking:** on-site, winter plug-ins. **Terms:** cancellation fee imposed. **Amenities:** voice mail, irons, hair dryers. *Some:* DVD players (fee), high-speed Internet. **Guest Services:** valet laundry, wireless Internet. **Business Services:** meeting rooms, PC. **Free Special Amenities:** local telephone calls and high-speed Internet.

PLACE LOUIS RIEL SUITE HOTEL
Book at AAA.com

Phone: (204)947-6961 **5**

Extended Stay Hotel
$125-$400 All Year

Address: 190 Smith St R3C 1J8 **Location:** At St. Mary Ave. **Facility:** Smoke free premises. 300 units. 111 one-bedroom standard units with kitchens. 172 one- and 17 two-bedroom suites with kitchens. 23 stories, interior corridors. *Bath:* combo or shower only. **Parking:** on-site (fee), winter plug-ins. **Terms:** cancellation fee imposed. **Amenities:** video games (fee), high-speed Internet, voice mail, irons, hair dryers. *Some:* CD players. **Leisure Activities:** exercise room. *Fee:* game room. **Guest Services:** valet and coin laundry, wireless Internet. **Business Services:** meeting rooms, business center. *(See color ad p 219)*

RADISSON HOTEL WINNIPEG DOWNTOWN
Book great rates at AAA.com

Phone: (204)956-0410 **2**

Hotel
$120-$182 All Year

Address: 288 Portage Ave R3C 0B8 **Location:** At Smith St. Located in a commercial area. **Facility:** Smoke free premises. 263 units. 254 one-bedroom standard units. 9 one-bedroom suites. 29 stories, interior corridors. *Bath:* combo or shower only. **Parking:** on-site (fee) and valet, winter plug-ins. **Amenities:** high-speed Internet, voice mail, irons, hair dryers. *Some:* CD players. **Pool(s):** heated indoor. **Leisure Activities:** saunas, whirlpool, terrace, exercise room. **Guest Services:** valet and coin laundry, area transportation-within 1.2 mi (2 km), wireless Internet. **Business Services:** conference facilities, business center. **Free Special Amenities:** local telephone calls and newspaper.

—— WHERE TO DINE ——

AMICI

Phone: 204/943-4997 **12**

Italian
$10-$42

You'll find this restaurant offers fine dining in contemporary surroundings upstairs, and casual dining and more moderate pricing at the Bombolini Wine Bar downstairs. The innovative menu features dishes with complex preparation and creative presentation. Dressy casual. **Bar:** Full bar. **Reservations:** suggested. **Hours:** 11:30 am-2 & 5-10 pm, Sat from 5 pm. Closed major holidays; also Sun. **Address:** 326 Broadway R3C 0S5 **Location:** At Hargrave St. **Parking:** street.

(See map and index starting on p. 717)

BEACHCOMBERS
Canadian
$10-$37

Phone: 204/948-0020   (11)

You'll enjoy the very good menu at this restaurant; it offers daily made soups and breads, fresh salad, classic and unique sandwiches, creative pasta, tender chicken and veal dishes, mouthwatering ribs, sizzling steaks and succulent seafood. Located in a bustling market, it also has outdoor seating. Casual dress. **Bar:** Full bar. **Reservations:** accepted. **Hours:** 11 am-midnight; hours may vary. Closed: 12/25. **Address:** 162-1 Forks Market Rd R3C 4L8 **Location:** Behind Union Station. **Parking:** on-site.

BLAZE BISTRO & LOUNGE
Canadian
$9-$35

Phone: 204/944-7259   (5)

This bistro offers an inviting atmosphere with oil paintings that truly depict the prairies. The menu is also regionally inspired and draws on local products for dishes such as Manitoba pickerel bruschetta and corn crusted turkey medallions. Casual dress. **Bar:** Full bar. **Reservations:** suggested. **Hours:** 6:30 am-10 pm, Sat 7 am-noon & 5-10 pm, Sun 7 am-noon. Closed major holidays. **Address:** 350 St. Mary Ave R3C 3J2 **Location:** At Hargrave St; in Delta Winnipeg. **Parking:** on-site.

THE CURRENT
Canadian
$10-$39

Phone: 204/944-2445   (10)

Large windows in the rear section of the dining room allow guests to overlook part of the interesting Forks Market area. Service is attentive and professional and the menu offers a good variety of items that are carefully and creatively prepared. Dressy casual. **Bar:** Full bar. **Reservations:** accepted. **Hours:** 6:30 am-11 pm, Fri & Sat-midnight, Sun 7 am-11 pm. **Address:** 75 Forks Market Rd R3C 0A2 **Location:** At the Forks; in Inn at the Forks. **Parking:** on-site.

EAST INDIA COMPANY PUB & EATERY
Indian
$10-$20

Phone: 204/947-3097   (9)

Decorated in brightly colored Indian murals and carved wood, the dining room is home to a large selection of traditional Indian fare, which guests will find on an extensive lunch and dinner buffet. Biryanis, masalas, curries and vegetarian options and can be ordered off the menu as well. Classic naan bread is always a hit, but more adventurous diners should can try the garlic- or cheese-flavored naan. Casual dress. **Bar:** Full bar. **Reservations:** accepted. **Hours:** 11 am-3 & 5-10 pm, Sat from 5 pm, Sun noon-8 pm. Closed major holidays. **Address:** 349 York Ave R3C 3S9 **Location:** Jct Carlton St. **Parking:** on-site and street.

HU'S ON FIRST
Asian
$10-$16

Phone: 204/982-7426   (3)

Opt for any one of the many Asian dishes—Chinese, Thai and Vietnamese—on the menu at this trendy urban bistro. Extremely popular, the place can get noisy when it's packed full, which tends to happen often, especially game nights during baseball season. Reservations are suggested. Outdoor patio seating is available. Casual dress. **Bar:** Full bar. **Reservations:** suggested. **Hours:** 11 am-10 pm, Fri-11 pm, Sat 4:30 pm-11 pm, Sun 4:30 pm-9 pm. Closed major holidays. **Address:** 1 Portage Ave E R3B 3N3 **Location:** Corner of Waterfront Dr and Pioneer Ave; at CanWest Global Park. **Parking:** on-site.

HY'S STEAKHOUSE
Steak
$10-$50

Phone: 204/942-1000   (7)

A popular and long-established dining tradition, the steakhouse lines up a good selection of grilled steaks, most of which are cut large. However, a lighter filet is likely to appeal to diners with lesser appetites. The pleasingly varied wine list includes some by-the-glass choices. The upscale decor resembles that of a private club, but the atmosphere remains warm and friendly. Dressy casual. **Bar:** Full bar. **Reservations:** suggested. **Hours:** 11:30 am-2 & 5-9 pm, Sat-10 pm, Sun 5 pm-9 pm. Closed major holidays. **Address:** 1 Lombard Pl R3B 0X3 **Location:** Jct Main St and Portage Ave; main floor of Richardson Building. **Parking:** on-site.

ICHIBAN JAPANESE STEAK HOUSE & SUSHI BAR
Japanese
$15-$38

Phone: 204/925-7400   (6)

Ichiban features a sushi bar and teppan-style cooking, where your meal is prepared in an entertaining manner at your table. Offerings also include North American dishes of steak, chicken and seafood. The server staff is pleasant, cordial and attentive. Before leaving, the staff will happily validate parking after 5:30 pm for the Delta Parkade, accessible from St. Mary Ave. Casual dress. **Bar:** Full bar. **Reservations:** accepted. **Hours:** 4:30 pm-10 pm. Closed major holidays. **Address:** 189 Carlton St R3C 3H7 **Location:** Corner of St. Mary Ave. **Parking:** street.

IVORY RESTAURANT & BAR
Indian
$12-$25

Phone: 204/944-1600   (4)

An East Indian treat, the restaurant offers diners the option of choices from a nicely developed menu or from the buffet line, which is a showcase for high-quality, well-presented, hot and cold dishes. Food is delightfully seasoned and reflects the diner's preference for spiciness. The decor blends "art gallery" and "bistro". Dressy casual. **Bar:** Full bar. **Reservations:** suggested. **Hours:** 11 am-11 pm, Sat from 5 pm, Sun 5 pm-10 pm. Closed major holidays; also Sun, for lunch 11/11 & Good Friday. **Address:** 200 Main St R3C 4V9 **Location:** Between St. Mary and York aves. **Parking:** on-site.

MIRLYCOURTOIS
French
$24-$54

Phone: 204/942-7332   (1)

The restaurant offers creative but traditional cuisine. Dressy casual. **Bar:** Full bar. **Reservations:** suggested. **Hours:** 5 pm-8:30 pm. Closed major holidays; also Sun & Mon. **Address:** 188 Princess St R3B 1L2 **Location:** Corner of James Ave; in exchange district; centre. **Parking:** on-site (fee) and street.

RESTAURANT DUBROVNIK
Continental
$28-$50

Phone: 204/944-0594   (13)

Located in a beautifully restored mansion near the Assiniboine River, this restaurant provides a warm and inviting dining room and an excellent menu with 20 artfully presented entrees such as pork tenderloin, chicken goyko with shrimp, beef and seafood. Dressy casual. **Bar:** Full bar. **Reservations:** suggested. **Hours:** 11:30 am-2 pm, Wed-Fri also 5 pm-10:30 pm. Closed: 12/25; also Sun. **Address:** 390 Assiniboine Ave R3C 0Y1 **Location:** Between Carlton and Hargrave sts. **Parking:** on-site. Historic

STORM RESTAURANT & CATERING
Canadian
$9-$15

Phone: 204/948-0085   (8)

This restaurant features a progressive menu with some Pacific Rim influences. The Caesar salad and barbecue chicken wrap with salsa are delightful choices, with attractive presentations. The decor is funky, with an open kitchen and outdoor patio. Casual dress. **Bar:** Full bar. **Reservations:** suggested. **Hours:** 11 am-2 pm. Closed major holidays; also Mon. **Address:** 300 Memorial Blvd R3C 1V1 **Location:** Just s of Portage Ave; top floor in the Winnipeg Art Gallery. **Parking:** street.

(See map and index starting on p. 717)

THE VELVET GLOVE *Menu on AAA.com* Phone: 204/957-1350 ②

Continental
$26-$36

The dining room has a warm finish of wood, large chandeliers and a fireplace. Unpretentious servers are attentive, professional and keen to share their knowledge of the well-developed wine list. Guests can order from the main menu, which lists favorite steak and fish dishes, or the seasonal menu, which centers on creative and artistically presented alternatives. Dressy casual. **Bar:** Full bar. **Reservations:** suggested. **Hours:** 6:30 am-2 & 5:30-9:30 pm, Sat & Sun 7 am-11:30 & 5:30-9:30 pm. **Address:** 2 Lombard Pl R3B 0Y3 **Location:** Just e of Portage Ave and Main St; in The Fairmont Winnipeg. **Parking:** on-site and valet.

WINNIPEG pop. 633,451 (See map and index starting on p. 719)

BEST WESTERN PEMBINA INN & SUITES *Book great rates at AAA.com* Phone: (204)269-8888 ⑳

Hotel
$122-$126 All Year

Address: 1714 Pembina Hwy R3T 2G2 **Location:** 0.6 mi (1 km) n of jct Bishop Grandin Blvd. Located in a commercial area. **Facility:** Smoke free premises. 104 units. 91 one-bedroom standard units. 13 one-bedroom suites, some with whirlpools. 4 stories, interior corridors. **Parking:** on-site, winter plug-ins. **Amenities:** high-speed Internet, voice mail, safes, irons, hair dryers. *Some:* dual phone lines. **Pool(s):** heated indoor. **Leisure Activities:** whirlpool, waterslide, exercise room. **Guest Services:** valet and coin laundry, airport transportation-Winnipeg James Armstrong Richardson International Airport, area transportation-University of Manitoba, wireless Internet. **Business Services:** meeting rooms, PC.

AAA Benefit:
Members save up to 20%, plus 10% bonus points with rewards program.

FREE expanded continental breakfast and high-speed Internet

BEST WESTERN VISCOUNT GORT HOTEL *Book great rates at AAA.com* Phone: (204)775-0451 ⑭

Hotel
$110-$200 All Year

Address: 1670 Portage Ave R3J 0C9 **Location:** Jct Rt 90. Located in a commercial area. **Facility:** Smoke free premises. 135 units. 129 one-bedroom standard units. 6 one-bedroom suites, some with whirlpools. 4-6 stories, interior corridors. **Parking:** on-site, winter plug-ins. **Amenities:** video games (fee), voice mail, irons, hair dryers. **Dining:** 2 restaurants. **Pool(s):** heated indoor. **Leisure Activities:** sauna, whirlpool, waterslide, limited exercise equipment. **Guest Services:** valet laundry, airport transportation-Winnipeg James Armstrong Richardson International Airport, area transportation-bus & train station, wireless Internet. **Business Services:** conference facilities, PC. **Free Special Amenities:** local telephone calls and high-speed Internet.

AAA Benefit:
Members save up to 20%, plus 10% bonus points with rewards program.

CANAD INNS DESTINATION CENTRE CLUB
REGENT CASINO HOTEL *Book great rates at AAA.com* Phone: (204)667-5560 ⑩

Hotel
$119-$299 All Year

Address: 1415 Regent Ave W R2C 3B2 **Location:** 1.1 mi (1.8 km) e of Lagimodiere Blvd (Hwy 20). **Facility:** With direct access to an adjacent casino, this property offers well-appointed guest units. Smoke free premises. 146 units. 142 one-bedroom standard units. 4 one-bedroom suites with whirlpools. 6 stories, interior corridors. *Bath:* combo or shower only. **Parking:** on-site, winter plug-ins. **Amenities:** video games (fee), high-speed Internet, dual phone lines, voice mail, irons, hair dryers. *Some:* CD players. **Pool(s):** heated indoor. **Leisure Activities:** whirlpool, exercise room. **Guest Services:** valet laundry, wireless Internet. **Business Services:** conference facilities, PC. **Free Special Amenities:** newspaper and high-speed Internet. *(See color ad p 219)*

CANAD INNS DESTINATION CENTRE FORT GARRY *Book great rates at AAA.com* Phone: (204)261-7450 ㉒

Hotel
$99-$299 All Year

Address: 1824 Pembina Hwy R3T 2G2 **Location:** Just n of Bishop Grandin Blvd. **Facility:** Smoke free premises. 107 units. 64 one-bedroom standard units, some with whirlpools. 39 one- and 4 two-bedroom suites. 2 stories, interior corridors. *Bath:* combo or shower only. **Parking:** on-site, winter plug-ins. **Amenities:** high-speed Internet, voice mail, irons, hair dryers. *Some:* DVD players, video games, CD players. **Dining:** nightclub. **Pool(s):** heated indoor. **Leisure Activities:** whirlpool, waterslide. **Guest Services:** valet laundry, airport transportation-Winnipeg James Armstrong Richardson International Airport, wireless Internet. **Business Services:** meeting rooms, business center. **Free Special Amenities:** newspaper and high-speed Internet.

CANAD INNS DESTINATION CENTRE GARDEN
CITY *Book great rates at AAA.com* Phone: (204)633-0024 ①

Hotel
$85-$259 All Year

Address: 2100 McPhillips St R2V 3T9 **Location:** At Jefferson Ave. Located in a commercial area. **Facility:** Smoke free premises. 72 units. 61 one-bedroom standard units. 9 one- and 2 two-bedroom suites. 3 stories, interior corridors. **Parking:** on-site, winter plug-ins. **Amenities:** voice mail, irons, hair dryers. *Some:* DVD players, video games, CD players. **Dining:** 2 restaurants, entertainment. **Pool(s):** heated indoor. **Leisure Activities:** whirlpool, waterslide. **Guest Services:** valet laundry, wireless Internet. **Business Services:** conference facilities. **Free Special Amenities:** newspaper and high-speed Internet.

(See map and index starting on p. 719)

CANAD INNS DESTINATION CENTRE POLO PARK

Phone: (204)775-8791 **12**

Hotel
$104-$279 All Year

Address: 1405 St. Matthews Ave R3G 0K5 **Location:** Just e of St. James St. Located opposite Canad Inns Stadium. **Facility:** Smoke free premises. 105 units. 95 one-bedroom standard units, some with whirlpools. 10 one-bedroom suites, some with whirlpools. 6 stories, interior corridors. *Bath:* combo or shower only. **Parking:** on-site, winter plug-ins. **Amenities:** video games (fee), high-speed Internet, voice mail, irons, hair dryers. **Dining:** 2 restaurants. **Pool(s):** heated indoor. **Leisure Activities:** whirlpool, waterslide, exercise room. **Guest Services:** valet laundry, airport transportation-Winnipeg James Armstrong Richardson International Airport, area transportation, wireless Internet. **Business Services:** conference facilities, PC. **Free Special Amenities: newspaper and high-speed Internet.**

CANAD INNS DESTINATION CENTRE TRANSCONA

Phone: (204)224-1681 **11**

Hotel
$89-$259 All Year

Address: 826 Regent Ave W R2C 3A8 **Location:** At Plessis Rd. **Facility:** Smoke free premises. 50 units. 43 one- and 4 two-bedroom standard units. 3 two-bedroom suites. 2 stories, interior corridors. **Parking:** on-site, winter plug-ins. **Amenities:** voice mail, irons, hair dryers. *Some:* DVD players, video games. **Dining:** 2 restaurants, nightclub. **Pool(s):** heated indoor. **Leisure Activities:** whirlpool, waterslide. **Guest Services:** valet laundry, wireless Internet. **Business Services:** conference facilities, PC. **Free Special Amenities: newspaper and high-speed Internet.**

CANAD INNS DESTINATION CENTRE WINDSOR PARK

Phone: (204)253-2641 **16**

Hotel
$99-$259 All Year

Address: 1034 Elizabeth Rd R2J 1B3 **Location:** Jct s of Maginot St and w of Lagimodiere Blvd. Located in a residential/commercial area. **Facility:** 54 units. 47 one- and 5 two-bedroom standard units. 2 two-bedroom suites. 2 stories (no elevator), interior corridors. **Parking:** on-site, winter plug-ins. **Amenities:** voice mail, irons, hair dryers. *Some:* DVD players. **Dining:** **Pool(s):** heated indoor. **Leisure Activities:** whirlpool, waterslide. **Guest Services:** valet laundry, wireless Internet. **Business Services:** meeting rooms. **Free Special Amenities: newspaper and high-speed Internet.**

CLARION HOTEL & SUITES

Phone: (204)774-5110 **13**

Hotel
$149-$209 All Year

Address: 1445 Portage Ave R3G 3P4 **Location:** Jct Empress St. Located in a commercial area. **Facility:** 139 units. 89 one-bedroom standard units, some with whirlpools. 50 one-bedroom suites. 6 stories, interior corridors. **Parking:** on-site, winter plug-ins. **Amenities:** video games (fee), high-speed Internet, dual phone lines, voice mail, irons, hair dryers. *Some:* safes. **Pool(s):** heated indoor. **Leisure Activities:** whirlpool, steamroom, waterslide, exercise room, spa. **Guest Services:** valet laundry, wireless Internet. **Business Services:** conference facilities, business center.

COMFORT INN AIRPORT

Phone: (204)783-5627 **9**

Hotel
$112-$122 7/1-2/28
$108-$121 3/1-6/30

Address: 1770 Sargent Ave R3H 0C8 **Location:** At King Edward St. Located in a commercial area. **Facility:** 81 one-bedroom standard units. 2 stories (no elevator), interior corridors. **Parking:** on-site (fee), winter plug-ins. **Amenities:** high-speed Internet, voice mail, irons, hair dryers. **Guest Services:** valet laundry. **Business Services:** PC.

COMFORT INN SOUTH

Phone: (204)269-7390 **23**

Hotel
$113-$175 All Year

Address: 3109 Pembina Hwy R3T 4R6 **Location:** Just n of jct Perimeter Hwy 100 and 75. Located in a residential commercial area. **Facility:** 85 one-bedroom standard units, some with whirlpools. 2 stories (no elevator), interior corridors. **Parking:** on-site, winter plug-ins. **Amenities:** voice mail, irons, hair dryers. **Guest Services:** valet laundry, wireless Internet. **Business Services:** PC.

(See map and index starting on p. 719)

COUNTRY INN & SUITES BY CARLSON *Book at AAA.com* **Phone:** (204)783-6900 **7**

◈◈ ◈◈
Hotel
$105-$135 All Year

Address: 730 King Edward St R3H 1B4 **Location:** Just s of Wellington Ave. Located in a commercial area. **Facility:** Smoke free premises. 76 units. 40 one-bedroom standard units. 36 one-bedroom suites. 3 stories, interior corridors. **Parking:** on-site, winter plug-ins. **Terms:** 4 day cancellation notice-fee imposed. **Amenities:** video library, DVD players, CD players, voice mail, irons, hair dryers. **Leisure Activities:** exercise room. **Guest Services:** valet and coin laundry, wireless Internet. **Business Services:** PC. (ASK) (┃┫) CALL (🄼) ✕ 🔒 🖳 / SOME UNITS FEE 🐾 🛏 🖂

DAYS INN WINNIPEG *Book at AAA.com* **Phone:** 204/586-8525 **2**

◈◈ ◈◈
Hotel
Rates not provided

Address: 550 McPhillips St R2X 2H2 **Location:** Just n of Logan Ave. Located in a commercial area. **Facility:** 66 one-bedroom standard units. 2 stories (no elevator), interior corridors. **Parking:** on-site, winter plug-ins. **Amenities:** voice mail, irons, hair dryers. **Pool(s):** heated indoor. **Leisure Activities:** whirlpool, waterslide. **Guest Services:** coin laundry, wireless Internet.
🛏 🍽 🏊 🐾 🖳 / SOME UNITS FEE 🐾 ✕ 🔒 🖂

EXPRESS BY CANAD INNS **Phone:** (204)269-6955 **21**

(CAA) (SAVE)
◈◈ ◈◈
Hotel
$74-$124 All Year

Address: 1792 Pembina Hwy R3T 2G2 **Location:** Just n of Bishop Grandin Blvd. **Facility:** Smoke free premises. 36 one-bedroom standard units. 2 stories (no elevator), interior/exterior corridors. **Parking:** on-site, winter plug-ins. **Amenities:** voice mail, irons, hair dryers. **Dining:** nightclub. **Guest Services:** valet laundry, wireless Internet. **Business Services:** meeting rooms. **Free Special Amenities:** newspaper and high-speed Internet. (ECO) (┃┫) 🍽 ✕ 🔒 🖂 🖳

FOUR POINTS BY SHERATON HOTEL WINNIPEG *Book great rates at AAA.com* **Phone:** (204)775-5222 **3**

(CAA) (SAVE)
◈◈ ◈◈
Hotel
$125-$145 All Year

Address: 1999 Wellington Ave R3H 1H5 **Location:** At Winnipeg James Armstrong Richardson International Airport. **Facility:** Smoke free premises. 132 units. 114 one-bedroom standard units. 18 one-bedroom suites. 7 stories, interior corridors. *Bath:* combo or shower only. **Parking:** on-site (fee), winter plug-ins. **Amenities:** video library, high-speed Internet, voice mail, irons, hair dryers. **Leisure Activities:** exercise room. *Fee:* pool tables. **Guest Services:** valet laundry, wireless Internet. **Business Services:** meeting rooms, business center.
(ECO) (┃┫) (24┃) 🍽 ✕ 🔒 🖂 🖳

FOUR ⅄ POINTS
· BY SHERATON ·

AAA Benefit:
Members get up to
15% off, plus
Starwood Preferred
Guest® bonuses.

(See map and index starting on p. 719)

GREENWOOD INN & SUITES   *Book at AAA.com*   Phone: 204/775-9889   **4**

Hotel
Rates not provided

Address: 1715 Wellington Ave R3H 0G1 **Location:** At Century St. Located in a commercial area. **Facility:** 213 units. 203 one-bedroom standard units. 10 one-bedroom suites, some with whirlpools. 6 stories, interior corridors. *Bath:* combo or shower only. **Parking:** on-site, winter plug-ins. **Amenities:** high-speed Internet, voice mail, irons, hair dryers. *Some:* CD players. **Pool(s):** heated indoor. **Leisure Activities:** whirlpool, steamroom, exercise room. **Guest Services:** valet laundry, wireless Internet. **Business Services:** conference facilities, PC.

HILTON SUITES WINNIPEG AIRPORT   *Book great rates at AAA.com*   Phone: (204)783-1700   **5**

Hotel
$139-$229 All Year

Address: 1800 Wellington Ave R3H 1B2 **Location:** At Berry St. Located in a commercial area. **Facility:** Smoke free premises. 160 units. 11 one-bedroom standard units. 149 one-bedroom suites, some with whirlpools. 6 stories, interior corridors. **Parking:** on-site (fee), winter plug-ins. **Terms:** 1-7 night minimum stay, cancellation fee imposed. **Amenities:** dual phone lines, voice mail, irons, hair dryers. **Dining:** Bistro 1800, see separate listing. **Pool(s):** heated outdoor, heated indoor. **Leisure Activities:** sauna, whirlpool, exercise room. **Guest Services:** valet laundry, airport transportation-Winnipeg James Armstrong Richardson International Airport, wireless Internet. **Business Services:** conference facilities, business center. *(See color ad p 729)*

 Hilton

AAA Benefit:
Members save 5%
or more everyday!

HOLIDAY INN WINNIPEG AIRPORT WEST   *Book great rates at AAA.com*   Phone: (204)885-4478   **15**

Hotel
$129-$169 All Year

Address: 2520 Portage Ave R3J 3T6 **Location:** Just e of Moray St. Located in a residential/commercial area. **Facility:** 226 units. 208 one-bedroom standard units. 18 one-bedroom suites, some with kitchens and/or whirlpools. 15 stories, interior corridors. *Bath:* combo or shower only. **Parking:** on-site, winter plug-ins. **Amenities:** video games (fee), dual phone lines, voice mail, irons, hair dryers. *Some:* DVD players, CD players. **Pool(s):** heated indoor. **Leisure Activities:** saunas, whirlpool, children's activity centre, exercise room. *Fee:* game room. **Guest Services:** valet and coin laundry, airport transportation-Winnipeg James Armstrong Richardson International Airport, area transportation-Polo Park, wireless Internet. **Business Services:** conference facilities, business center. **Free Special Amenities:** local telephone calls and high-speed Internet.

HOLIDAY INN WINNIPEG SOUTH   *Book at AAA.com*   Phone: 204/452-4747   **19**

Hotel
Rates not provided

Address: 1330 Pembina Hwy R3T 2B4 **Location:** At McGillivray Blvd. Located in a commercial area. **Facility:** 170 units. 169 one-bedroom standard units. 1 one-bedroom suite with whirlpool. 11 stories, interior corridors. **Parking:** on-site, winter plug-ins. **Amenities:** dual phone lines, voice mail, irons, hair dryers. *Some:* CD players. **Pool(s):** heated indoor. **Leisure Activities:** whirlpool, exercise room. **Guest Services:** valet and coin laundry, wireless Internet. **Business Services:** conference facilities, PC.

QUALITY INN & SUITES   *Book great rates at AAA.com*   Phone: (204)453-8247   **17**

Hotel
$90-$270 All Year

Address: 635 Pembina Hwy R3M 2L4 **Location:** Jct s of Grant Ave. **Facility:** 69 units. 55 one-bedroom standard units, some with whirlpools. 14 one-bedroom suites with efficiencies. 4 stories, interior corridors. **Parking:** on-site, winter plug-ins. **Amenities:** voice mail, irons, hair dryers. *Some:* DVD players, CD players, high-speed Internet, dual phone lines. **Leisure Activities:** exercise room. **Guest Services:** valet laundry, wireless Internet. **Business Services:** meeting rooms, business center.

FREE full breakfast and high-speed Internet

SANDMAN HOTEL & SUITES WINNIPEG AIRPORT   *Book at AAA.com*   Phone: (204)775-7263   **8**

Hotel
$144-$214 All Year

Address: 1750 Sargent Ave R3H 0C7 **Location:** Between King Edward and Century sts. Located in a commercial area. **Facility:** 210 units. 123 one-bedroom standard units. 87 one-bedroom suites, some with whirlpools. 4 stories, interior corridors. *Bath:* combo or shower only. **Parking:** on-site, winter plug-ins. **Amenities:** video games (fee), high-speed Internet, voice mail, irons, hair dryers. **Dining:** Chop Steak Fish Bar, see separate listing. **Guest Services:** valet laundry, wireless Internet. **Business Services:** business center.

(See map and index starting on p. 719)

TRAVELODGE WINNIPEG   *Book great rates at AAA.com*   Phone: (204)255-6000   [18]

Hotel
$82-$159 All Year

Address: 20 Alpine Ave R2M 0Y5 **Location:** Just e of jct Fermor Ave and St. Anne's Rd. Located in a residential/commercial area. **Facility:** 75 units. 71 one-bedroom standard units. 4 one-bedroom suites, some with whirlpools. 2 stories (no elevator), interior corridors. **Parking:** on-site, winter plug-ins. **Amenities:** voice mail, hair dryers. *Some:* irons. **Dining:** nightclub. **Pool(s):** heated indoor. **Leisure Activities:** sauna, whirlpool, limited exercise equipment. *Fee:* bowling lanes, game room. **Guest Services:** valet and coin laundry, wireless Internet. **Business Services:** meeting rooms, PC. **Free Special Amenities: local telephone calls and high-speed Internet.**

VICTORIA INN HOTEL & CONVENTION CENTRE   *Book great rates at AAA.com*   Phone: (204)786-4801   [6]

Hotel
$129-$174 All Year

Address: 1808 Wellington Ave R3H 0G3 **Location:** At Berry St. Located in a commercial area. **Facility:** Smoke free premises. 260 units. 247 one-bedroom standard units. 5 one-bedroom suites. 5 stories, interior corridors. *Bath:* combo or shower only. **Parking:** on-site, winter plug-ins. **Terms:** cancellation fee imposed. **Amenities:** video games (fee), high-speed Internet, voice mail, irons, hair dryers. *Some:* CD players. **Pool(s):** heated indoor. **Leisure Activities:** whirlpool, waterslide, exercise room. **Guest Services:** valet and coin laundry, airport transportation-Winnipeg James Armstrong Richardson International Airport, wireless Internet. **Business Services:** conference facilities, business center. **Free Special Amenities: local telephone calls and newspaper.**

------- WHERE TO DINE -------

529 WELLINGTON   Phone: 204/487-8325   [7]

Steak
$12-$49

The restaurant encourages patrons to think big: big steaks, that is. Also huge on quality are lobster and jumbo prawns. Only Canadian Prime certified Alberta beef is served. Service matches the detailed old dining rooms, which are paneled in rich wood and fitting of a grand old mansion. Dressy casual. **Bar:** Full bar. **Reservations:** suggested. **Hours:** 11:30 am-2 & 5-11 pm, Sat from 5 pm, Sun 5 pm-9 pm. Closed: 12/24, 12/25. **Address:** 529 Wellington Crescent R3M 0A5 **Location:** Just s of Academy Rd. **Parking:** on-site.

BEAUJENA'S   Phone: 204/233-4841   [4]

French
$17-$36

This intimate restaurant is a hidden gem within a quiet residential area. Vibrant colors and rich, gauzy fabrics create an inviting spot where guests can enjoy French-flavored cuisine with local Manitoban ingredients. Each month the restaurant offers a unique, seven-course chef's menu, which is expertly paired with wines. Dressy casual. **Bar:** Full bar. **Reservations:** suggested. **Hours:** 5 pm-10 pm. Closed major holidays; also Sun-Wed. **Address:** 302 Hamel Ave R2H 0K9 **Location:** Jct Provencher Blvd and St. Jean Baptiste St. **Parking:** no self-parking.

BISTRO 1800   Phone: 204/783-1700   [1]

Canadian
$12-$30

Convenient to the airport, this is an excellent spot for a good meal in a quiet, relaxing setting. Casual dress. **Bar:** Full bar. **Reservations:** accepted. **Hours:** 6 am-2 & 5-12:30 am. **Address:** 1800 Wellington Ave R3H 1B2 **Location:** At Berry St; in Hilton Suites Winnipeg Airport. **Parking:** on-site. *(See color ad p 729)*

BONFIRE BISTRO   *Menu on AAA.com*   Phone: 204/487-4440   [13]

Italian
$9-$23

Diners can expect comfortable, simple decor and a friendly atmosphere. Management and staff are focused on creating well-prepared dishes. Among choices are wonderful thin-crust gourmet pizzas baked in a wood-fired oven, assorted pasta creations and varied daily specials posted on a blackboard. Casual dress. **Bar:** Beer & wine. **Reservations:** not accepted. **Hours:** 11:30 am-2:30 & 5-10 pm, Fri & Sat-11 pm. Closed major holidays; also Sun. **Address:** 1433 Corydon Ave R3N 0J2 **Location:** At Waterloo St. **Parking:** on-site.

CHEZ CORA   Phone: 204/928-1200

Canadian
$6-$13

Eggs, omelets, waffles, crepes (sorry, no American-style pancakes here), French toast, fruit platters and all the breakfast meats—that's the specialty here, all day. However, at lunchtime the menu lists a selection of soups, salads, quiches, sandwiches and a dish called the grilled panini crepe. Casual dress. **Reservations:** accepted, except Sat & Sun. **Hours:** 6 am-3 pm, Sun from 7 am. Closed: 12/25. **Address:** 840 Waverley St R3T 5Z7 **Location:** Jct Wilkes Ave. **Parking:** on-site.

CHOP STEAK FISH BAR   Phone: 204/788-2015   [2]

Steak
$11-$39

High ceilings, dark subdued colors, plush velours and earthy woods contrasting with modern glass light fixtures all contribute to the casually chic decor at this modern steakhouse. A recent addition to the city's restaurant scene, Chop offers the choicest cuts of certified Angus beef and the freshest fish and seafood. Dressy casual. **Bar:** Full bar. **Reservations:** accepted. **Hours:** 11 am-midnight, Mon-Fri 11 am, Sat 4 pm-1 am, Sun 4 pm-11 pm. Closed: 12/25. **Address:** 1750 Sargent Ave R3H 0C7 **Location:** Between King Edward and Century sts; in Sandman Hotel & Suites Winnipeg Airport. **Parking:** on-site.

DACQUISTO   Phone: 204/938-2229   [20]

Italian
$10-$50

Risotto, gnocchi, spaghetti and osso buco are all selections found on this truly Italian menu. There is also a nice selection of gourmet wood-fired pizzas and an extensive list of Italian wines. Bon appetito! Casual dress. **Bar:** Full bar. **Reservations:** required. **Hours:** 5 pm-11 pm. Closed: 12/25. **Address:** 1715 Kenaston Blvd R3Y 1V5 **Location:** Just s of McGillivray Blvd. **Parking:** on-site.

(See map and index starting on p. 719)

DANDELION EATERY
Phone: 204/453-5755

Natural/Organic
$10-$22

"Organic, seasonal, natural" is indeed the case at this mostly vegetarian restaurant. The frequently-changing menu is fabulously creative and still offers several meat dishes that may include elk, duck or lamb. Emphasis is on regional products and the owner/chef is a strong supporter of producers who support sustainable agriculture. The sangria is simply delicious. Casual dress. **Bar:** Full bar. **Reservations:** suggested. **Hours:** 11 am-10 pm, Fri-11 pm, Sat 10 am-11 pm, Sun & Mon 11 am-4 pm. Closed major holidays. **Address:** 230 Osborne St R3L 1Z5 **Location:** At Corydon Ave/Donald St; in Organza Market. **Parking:** on-site.

EARLS RESTAURANT
Phone: 204-275-1250

Canadian
$10-$32

Offering an experience that falls between fast food and fine dining, the fun, relaxed restaurant prepares great food at a great price. Choices range from juicy burgers, hearty sandwiches, fresh salads, wings and pizza to full entrees of steak, chops and seafood. Made-from-scratch soups and assorted breads, as well as a nice choice of wines and beers, round out the offerings. This is a fitting spot for impromptu get-togethers and festive occasions. Casual dress. **Bar:** Full bar. **Hours:** 11 am-midnight, Wed-Sat to 1 am. Closed: 12/25. **Address:** 2005 Pembina Hwy R3T 5W7 **Location:** Jct Bishop Grandin Blvd, just s. **Parking:** on-site.

CALL

FRESH CAFÉ
Phone: 204/221-5775

Natural/Organic
$5-$12

From the cheery sunlit decor right down to the delectable desserts, everything here is "fresh." With an emphasis on natural, organic and local foods, this little jewel-of-a-daytime eatery offers day-long breakfasts, lunch and a juice bar. Take advantage of a nice sunny day and dine on the large, streetside outdoor terrace. Casual dress. **Bar:** Beer & wine. **Reservations:** not accepted. **Hours:** 7 am-4 pm. Closed major holidays. **Address:** 775 Corydon Ave R3M 0W5 **Location:** Between Cockburn and Arbuthnot sts; in Corydon Village. **Parking:** street.

FUSION GRILL
Phone: 204/489-6963

Canadian
$10-$39

This comfortable little restaurant affords a wonderful opportunity to experience fine Canadian food. Manitoba produce is often used and the list of Canadian wines is notable. Casual dress. **Bar:** Full bar. **Reservations:** suggested. **Hours:** 11:30 am-2 & 5:30-10 pm. Closed major holidays; also Sun & Mon. **Address:** 550 Academy Rd R3N 0E3 **Location:** Just e of jct Kenaston Blvd. **Parking:** street.

INDIA PALACE
Phone: 204/774-6061

Indian
$10-$21

You'll enjoy the fresh, flavorful cuisine at this restaurant, where the tandoori chicken is exceptional. The menu is so extensive that it will satisfy the most discerning tastes. It has a softly lit decor, and warm, caring and friendly service. Casual dress. **Bar:** Full bar. **Reservations:** suggested. **Hours:** 11 am-10 pm, Sun from 2 pm; hours may vary. Closed: 12/25. **Address:** 770 Ellice Ave R3G 0B8 **Location:** Corner of Simcoe St. **Parking:** street.

JOEYS
Phone: 204/477-5639

Mediterranean
$11-$32

Immensely popular and frantically busy at times, this chic, recently-opened Mediterranean grill offers a varied choice of well-prepared dishes that include everything from sandwiches to chicken, ribs, fish and steak. A seasonal patio is available. Casual dress. **Bar:** Full bar. **Reservations:** not accepted. **Hours:** 11 am-1:30 am. Closed: 12/25. **Address:** 1550 Kenaston Blvd R3P 0Y4 **Location:** On Rt 90; just n of McGillivray Blvd. **Parking:** on-site.

KELSEY'S
Phone: 204/668-6689

Canadian
$7-$20

A fun, relaxed atmosphere and tasty menu of casual fare make the restaurant a popular favorite with locals. Diners might start a meal with some tempting appetizers, such as wings, loaded potato skins or nachos, and follow them with an old-time favorite, such as a burger, wrap, pizza or pasta dish. For a heartier meal, it's hard to beat pork back ribs or a steak. The diverse menu has broad appeal. Casual dress. **Bar:** Full bar. **Hours:** 11 am-midnight, Thurs-Sat to 1 am, Sun-11 pm. Closed: 12/25. **Address:** 1582 Regent Ave W R2C 3B4 **Location:** Just e of jct Lagimodiere Blvd. **Parking:** on-site. CALL

LA FIESTA CAFECITO
Phone: 204/257-7108

Salvadoran
$7-$18

This little (and we mean "little") family-run restaurant offers true Salvadoran cuisine and the friendliest service. A delicious blend of new and traditional Latin American dishes is served up in a pretty, festively colored dining room. Two must-try items include pupusas and corn tamale. Casual dress. **Bar:** Full bar. **Reservations:** suggested. **Hours:** 4 pm-10 pm. Closed major holidays; also Sun & Mon. **Address:** 730 St. Anne's Rd, Unit M R2N 0A2 **Location:** Just n of Perimeter Hwy; in South Glen Mall. **Parking:** on-site.

MAXIME'S
Phone: 204/257-1521

Continental
$10-$28

This restaurant is a favorite with locals. Its menu features pasta, pizza, Greek specialties, steak, chicken and seafood entrees, which are served in large portions. The service is polite, professional and efficient, and the decor is upscale. Casual dress. **Bar:** Full bar. **Reservations:** accepted. **Hours:** 11 am-midnight, Sun 10:30 am-10 pm. Closed: 1/1, 12/25, 12/26. **Address:** 1131 St Mary's Rd R2M 3T9 **Location:** Corner of Bishop Grandin Blvd. **Parking:** on-site.

MEIJI SUSHI JAPANESE RESTAURANT & G.
MARTINI BAR
Phone: 204-453-1120

Japanese
$10-$25

This restaurant does an excellent job of combining a martini bar with a Japanese restaurant. As a complement to the extensive Japanese menu of sushi, teriyaki, tempura and udon is an exhaustive list of over 50 martinis. Guests can opt for tatami or conventional seating. Casual dress. **Bar:** Full bar. **Reservations:** accepted. **Hours:** 11:30 am-2:30 & 5-10:30 pm, Fri-11:30 pm, Sat 5 pm-11:30 pm, Sun 5 pm-10:30 pm. Closed major holidays. **Address:** 10-1875 Pembina Hwy R3T 2G7 **Location:** Just n of Bishop Grandin Blvd. **Parking:** on-site.

(See map and index starting on p. 719)

MIYABI

Japanese
$7-$19

Phone: 204/888-0028   ⑥

Servers at this casual-style Japanese restaurant are quite knowledgeable and eager to guide patrons through the menu. The food is served in smaller, tapas-style portions, which provides diners an excellent opportunity of sampling a variety of dishes with friends. Free parking is available across the street, behind the Urban Barn. Casual dress. **Bar:** Full bar. **Reservations:** accepted. **Hours:** 5 pm-10 pm, Thurs & Fri also noon-3 pm, Sat 1 pm-11 pm, Sun 1 pm-10 pm. Closed major holidays. **Address:** 159 Osborne St R3L 1Y7 **Location:** Between Stradbrook and Wardlaw aves; in Osborne Village. **Parking:** on-site and street.

MONA LISA RISTORANTE
Northern Italian
$7-$29

Phone: 204/488-3687   ⑫

This popular neighborhood restaurant features an extensive cuisine of Northern Italian fare, including mezza lune, melengane alla parmigiana, veal and jumbo prawns. Local hockey hero memorabilia adorn the walls in the lounge, and there's a sidewalk patio. Casual dress. **Bar:** Full bar. **Reservations:** suggested. **Hours:** 11 am-11 pm, Fri & Sat-midnight, Sun 4 pm-10 pm. Closed: 1/1, 12/25. **Address:** 1697 Corydon Ave R3N 0J9 **Location:** Corner of Renfrew St. **Parking:** street.

RESTAURANT BISTRO DANSK
European
$5-$16

Phone: 204/775-5662   ⑤

What started as a popular Danish restaurant in the '70s has, over the years, morphed into a well frequented restaurant serving much-loved Eastern European fare. Although many Danish favorites—such as frikadeller and marinated herring—continue to appear on the menu, many regulars now come for the tender schnitzels and mouth-watering chicken paprika. A decent variety of European wines and beers is available to complement any dish. Casual dress. **Bar:** Full bar. **Reservations:** accepted. **Hours:** 11 am-2:30 & 5-9 pm. Closed: 12/25; also Sun & Mon. **Address:** 63 Sherbrook St R3C 2B2 **Location:** Corner of Wolseley Ave. **Parking:** street.

THE ROUND TABLE STEAK HOUSE & PUB
Steak
$9-$37

Phone: 204/453-3631   ⑭

You'll enjoy the casual atmosphere at this restaurant, which has an English-manor decor that includes glowing fireplaces. The house specialty is prime rib, and the menu also offers a very good variety of steak, seafood, chicken and pasta dishes. Casual dress. **Bar:** Full bar. **Reservations:** accepted. **Hours:** 11:30 am-10 pm, Sat & Sun from 4:30 pm. Closed: 1/1, 9/6, 12/25. **Address:** 800 Pembina Hwy R3M 2M7 **Location:** Just s of Taylor St. **Parking:** on-site.

ROYAL FORK BUFFET RESTAURANT
Comfort Food
$10-$13

Phone: 204/668-1960

The Royal Fork features buffet-style dining with a wide variety of freshly made choices, including sugar-free desserts. Families can be fed for an excellent value. Dinner prices are in effect starting at 4 pm Monday through Saturday and all day on Sunday and major holidays. Casual dress. **Hours:** 11 am-8:30 pm, Fri & Sat-9 pm, Sun 10 am-8 pm. Closed: 12/25. **Address:** 900-1615 Regent Ave W R2C 5C6 **Location:** Jct Lagimodiere Blvd (Metro Rt 20) and Regent Ave W; in Kildonan Crossing Shopping Centre. **Parking:** on-site.

SPUNTINO CAFE
Italian
$12-$22

Phone: 204/475-4447   ⑩

The delightful little cafe features wonderful pasta dishes, veal and some seafood, which are accompanied by fresh bread that's prepared in-house. Casual dress. **Reservations:** suggested. **Hours:** 11:30 am-2 & 5-9 pm, Thurs & Fri 11:30 am-9:30 pm, Sat noon-10 pm, Sun 5 pm-9 pm. Closed major holidays; also Mon. **Address:** 926 Grosvenor Ave R3M 0N4 **Location:** Jct Stafford St. **Parking:** street.

STELLA'S CAFE
Breakfast
$5-$10

Phone: 204/453-8562   ⑮

Start the day with homemade breads and pastries or one of Stella's many signature omelettes—this is an all-day breakfast place—and then take advantage of some fabulous area shopping. But get here early on weekend mornings if you want to avoid waiting in line. Free parking is available behind the Urban Barn. Casual dress. **Bar:** Beer & wine. **Reservations:** not accepted. **Hours:** 7 am-8:30 pm, Sun 8 am-5 pm. Closed: 12/25. **Address:** 166 Osborne St R3L 1Y8 **Location:** Corner of Wardlaw Ave; in Osborne Village. **Parking:** on-site.

Northwest Territories and Nunavut

South Nahanni River,
Nahanni National Park
Reserve of Canada
© Daryl Benson
Masterfile

YELLOWKNIFE pop. 18,700

CHATEAU NOVA HOTEL & SUITES *Book great rates at AAA.com* **Phone:** (867)873-9700

Hotel
$149-$199 All Year

Address: 4401 50th Ave X1A 2N2 **Location:** Downtown. **Facility:** 80 units. 72 one-bedroom standard units, some with efficiencies and/or whirlpools. 8 one-bedroom suites with kitchens. 4 stories, interior corridors. **Parking:** on-site, winter plug-ins. **Terms:** cancellation fee imposed. **Amenities:** voice mail, irons, hair dryers. *Some:* high-speed Internet. **Leisure Activities:** whirlpool, steamroom, exercise room. **Guest Services:** valet laundry, airport transportation-Yellowknife International Airport, wireless Internet. **Business Services:** meeting rooms, business center. **Free Special Amenities:** local telephone calls and high-speed Internet.

COAST FRASER TOWER *Book at AAA.com* **Phone:** 867/873-8700

Hotel
Rates not provided

Address: 5303 52nd St X1A 1V1 **Location:** Corner of 52nd St and 53rd Ave. **Facility:** 58 units. 40 one- and 18 two-bedroom suites with kitchens. 10 stories, interior corridors. **Parking:** on-site, winter plug-ins. **Amenities:** dual phone lines, voice mail, irons, hair dryers. *Some:* high-speed Internet. **Leisure Activities:** steamroom, exercise room. **Guest Services:** coin laundry, wireless Internet. **Business Services:** meeting rooms, PC.

THE EXPLORER HOTEL *Book at AAA.com* **Phone:** (867)873-3531

Hotel
$185-$205 All Year

Address: 4825 49th Ave X1A 2R3 **Location:** Downtown. **Facility:** 187 units. 185 one-bedroom standard units. 2 one-bedroom suites. 8 stories, interior corridors. **Parking:** on-site, winter plug-ins. **Terms:** check-in 4 pm, cancellation fee imposed. **Amenities:** voice mail, irons, hair dryers. **Leisure Activities:** exercise room. **Guest Services:** valet laundry, wireless Internet. **Business Services:** conference facilities, PC.

YELLOWKNIFE SUPER 8 *Book at AAA.com* **Phone:** (867)669-8888

Motel
$169-$199 All Year

Address: 308 Old Airport Rd X1A 3G3 **Location:** 1.2 mi (2 km) s on Franklin Ave, 0.6 mi (1 km) w; in Wal-Mart Plaza. **Facility:** Smoke free premises. 66 units. 41 one-bedroom standard units. 25 one-bedroom suites. 4 stories, interior corridors. **Parking:** on-site, winter plug-ins. **Terms:** cancellation fee imposed. **Amenities:** high-speed Internet, voice mail, irons, hair dryers. **Leisure Activities:** exercise room. **Guest Services:** coin laundry, wireless Internet. **Business Services:** PC.

—— WHERE TO DINE ——

THE BLACK KNIGHT PUB **Phone:** 867/920-4041

Canadian
$8-$24

The bustling Scottish pub, geared for those 19 and older, is packed at mealtimes. Diners will find classic Old World fare, like Guinness steak and kidney pie, fish and chips, shepherd's pie and bangers and mash. Lots of burgers (including caribou), steaks and sandwiches finish off the menu, and there's a huge Scottish "whisky" selection. Classic, pub-style decor includes dark wood accents, bar towels, beer mats, a suit of armor and an old sword encased on the wall. Casual dress. **Bar:** Full bar. **Reservations:** not accepted. **Hours:** 11 am-9 pm, Wed-Fri to 11 pm. Closed: 12/25; also Sun & Good Friday. **Address:** 4910 49th St X1A 2N8 **Location:** Downtown. **Parking:** street.

BULLOCK'S BISTRO **Phone:** 867/873-3474

Regional
Canadian
$15-$43

Ask locals for a place to eat, and this seafood joint is usually mentioned. Casual service includes guests being asked to grab a drink from the cooler. The menu features freshly caught northern fish like Arctic char, lake trout, northern pike, pickerel and Great Slave cod as well as dishes with caribou, musk ox and buffalo. Fish chowder and musk ox or caribou stew are specialties. Service can be slow, so rustic decor provides things to view: Walls are covered with snapshots and a caribou head. Casual dress. **Bar:** Beer & wine. **Reservations:** suggested, for dinner. **Hours:** noon-9 pm, Sun from 2 pm; hours may vary. Closed: 1/1, 4/4, 12/24, 12/25; also 12/31. **Address:** 3534 Weaver Dr X1A 2H2 **Location:** 1 mi (1.6 km) ne on Franklin Ave, then just n; in Old Town. **Parking:** on-site.

LE FROLIC BISTRO/BAR **Phone:** 867/669-9852

French
$13-$35

Creative, colorful and regionally inspired cuisine with a French twist is on the menu at this bustling bistro. Locals frequent the restaurant after work and on weekends for its casual, relaxed environment. Guests can mingle with the locals and sample such appetizers as escargot and entrees ranging from venison to Arctic char. All the desserts are made in house. Casual dress. **Bar:** Full bar. **Reservations:** accepted, except for lunch Fri & Sat. **Hours:** 11 am-11 pm. Closed major holidays; also Sun. **Address:** 5019 49th St X1A 2N6 **Location:** Downtown; underneath L'Heritage Restaurant Francais. **Parking:** street.

L'HERITAGE MEDITERRANEAN **Phone:** 867/873-9561

French
$34-$50

One of the city's best-kept downtown secrets, this quaint French restaurant is a pleasant surprise. Small touches of France are incorporated into the decor. Each dish is a delight, with creativity and color, and the menu is heavily influenced with regional ingredients. This spot shouldn't be missed for a fine, elegant meal in lovely surroundings. Casual dress. **Bar:** Full bar. **Reservations:** suggested. **Hours:** 5 pm-10 pm. Closed major holidays; also Sun. **Address:** 349 Old Airport Rd X1A 2N6 **Location:** Downtown. **Parking:** street.

OUR PLACE FAMILY DINING ROOM **Phone:** 867/920-2265

International
$11-$40

The intimate, dimly lit restaurant nurtures a lounge-like atmosphere. Varied offerings of regional cuisine include preparations of char, seafood and game meats, such as venison. Casual dress. **Bar:** Full bar. **Reservations:** suggested. **Hours:** Open 3/1-6/30 & 8/1-2/28; 11 am-2 & 5-9:30 pm, Sat from 5 pm. Closed major holidays; also Sun. **Address:** 5006 50th Ave X1A 2P5 **Location:** Corner of 50th Ave and 50th St; second level. **Parking:** street.

WILDCAT CAFE **Phone:** 867/873-4004

Regional
Canadian
$12-$28

This historic café is a popular spot at meal times, both with locals and tourists. One of the city's original buildings, the small log cabin has large picnic tables inside, and guests who can't find their own are invited to partake in a city tradition and join another party's table. Among offerings of regional cuisine are musk-ox stew and awesome milkshakes. Casual dress. **Bar:** Full bar. **Reservations:** accepted, except Friday. **Hours:** Open 5/20-8/31; 7 am-10 pm, Sat & Sun from 10 am. **Address:** 3904 Wiley Rd X1A 2N2 **Location:** In Old Town. **Parking:** on-site. **Historic**

Saskatchewan

Rural Saskatchewan
© John E. Marriott
age fotostock

CARONPORT pop. 919

THE PILGRIM INN

Hotel
Rates not provided

Phone: 306/756-5002

Address: Hwy 1 W S0H 0S0 **Location:** On Trans-Canada Hwy 1. Located near Briercrest College & Seminary. **Facility:** Smoke free premises. 41 units. 40 one-bedroom standard units, some with kitchens. 1 one-bedroom suite with efficiency. 2 stories, interior corridors. **Parking:** on-site, winter plug-ins. **Terms:** office hours 7 am-11 pm. **Leisure Activities:** 4 tennis courts. **Guest Services:** complimentary laundry, wireless Internet. **Business Services:** meeting rooms.

ESTEVAN pop. 10,084

DAYS INN   *Book at AAA.com*

Hotel
Rates not provided

Phone: 306/634-6456

Address: 1305 9th St S4A 1J1 **Location:** Jct Hwy 39, just n on 13th Ave; centre. **Facility:** 75 units. 68 one-bedroom standard units, some with whirlpools. 7 one-bedroom suites, some with whirlpools. 3 stories, interior corridors. **Parking:** on-site, winter plug-ins. **Amenities:** high-speed Internet, voice mail, irons, hair dryers. **Leisure Activities:** whirlpool, exercise room. **Guest Services:** wireless Internet. **Business Services:** meeting rooms, PC.

MOTEL 6 ESTEVAN   *Book great rates at AAA.com*

fyi
Hotel
$100-$113 All Year

Phone: 306/634-8666

Too new to rate. **Address:** 88 King St E S4A 2A4 **Location:** Hwy 39, 1 mi (1.7 km) n at Kensington Ave, then just e. **Amenities:** 68 units, pets, microwaves, refrigerators. *(See color ad below)*

PERFECT INNS & SUITES

CAA SAVE

Hotel
$100-$130 All Year

Phone: (306)634-8585

Address: 134 2nd Ave S4A 2W6 **Location:** Just n of jct Hwy 39. Located next to Tim Horton's. **Facility:** 70 units. 65 one-bedroom standard units. 5 one-bedroom suites, some with whirlpools. 3 stories, interior corridors. **Parking:** on-site, winter plug-ins. **Amenities:** high-speed Internet, voice mail, irons, hair dryers. *Some:* dual phone lines. **Leisure Activities:** whirlpool, exercise room. **Guest Services:** valet and coin laundry, wireless Internet. **Business Services:** meeting rooms, PC. **Free Special Amenities:** expanded continental breakfast and high-speed Internet.

——— WHERE TO DINE ———

EDDIE'S NEIGHBOURHOOD GRILL & BAR Phone: 306/634-5656

▼▼ ▼▼
Canadian
$9-$25

This popular, casual restaurant provides efficient, friendly service in a pleasant atmosphere. The menu offers a good variety. Patio seating can be requested in season. Casual dress. **Bar:** Full bar. **Reservations:** accepted. **Hours:** 11 am-10 pm. Closed: 12/25. **Address:** 122 4th St S4A 0T4 **Location:** Just e of jct Hwy 39 E and 2nd Ave. **Parking:** on-site.

KINDERSLEY pop. 4,412

NOVA INN Phone: 306/463-4687

▼▼ ▼▼
Hotel
Rates not provided

Address: 100 12th Ave NW S0L 1S0 **Location:** Jct of Hwy 7 and 21. **Facility:** 43 one-bedroom standard units. 2 stories (no elevator), interior/exterior corridors. **Parking:** on-site, winter plug-ins. **Amenities:** high-speed Internet, voice mail, irons, hair dryers. **Leisure Activities:** sauna. **Guest Services:** wireless Internet. **Business Services:** meeting rooms.

🍽 ⊤ 🐾 🖥 💻 / SOME UNITS 🐾 ✕ 📠

LANGENBURG pop. 1,048

LANGENBURG COUNTRY INN Phone: 306/743-2638

▼
Motel
$65-$75 All Year

Address: 1041 Kaiser William Ave E S0A 2A0 **Location:** On Hwy 16, 0.6 mi (1 km) e. Located in a rural area. **Facility:** 14 one-bedroom standard units. 1 story, exterior corridors. **Parking:** on-site, winter plug-ins. **Terms:** office hours 7:30 am-10 pm. **Amenities:** Some: irons, hair dryers. **Guest Services:** coin laundry, wireless Internet. 🖥 📠 💻 / SOME UNITS ✕

LLOYDMINSTER —See nearby AB city of LLOYDMINSTER.

MOOSE JAW pop. 32,132

COMFORT INN   *Book at AAA.com* Phone: (306)692-2100

▼▼ ▼▼
Hotel
$120-$170 All Year

Address: 155 Thatcher Dr W S6J 1M1 **Location:** 0.8 mi (1.2 km) s on Hwy 2 from jct Trans-Canada Hwy 1, then just w. Located in a commercial area. **Facility:** 60 units. 58 one-bedroom standard units, some with whirlpools. 2 one-bedroom suites with whirlpools. 3 stories, interior corridors. **Parking:** on-site, winter plug-ins. **Terms:** cancellation fee imposed. **Amenities:** high-speed Internet, voice mail, hair dryers. Some: irons. **Leisure Activities:** limited exercise equipment. **Guest Services:** valet and coin laundry. **Business Services:** meeting rooms, PC.

ASK 🍽 🐾 💻 / SOME UNITS FEE 🐾 ✕ 🖥 📠

HERITAGE INN MOOSE JAW   *Book at AAA.com* Phone: (306)693-7550

▼▼ ▼▼
Hotel
$115-$210 1/1-2/28
$112-$209 3/1-12/31

Address: 1590 Main St N S6J 1L3 **Location:** On Hwy 2, 0.9 mi (1.4 km) s of jct Trans-Canada Hwy 1. **Facility:** 104 units. 102 one-bedroom standard units. 2 one-bedroom suites with whirlpools. 2 stories (no elevator), interior corridors. *Bath:* combo or shower only. **Parking:** on-site, winter plug-ins. **Terms:** cancellation fee imposed. **Amenities:** voice mail, irons, hair dryers. Some: DVD players (fee), high-speed Internet. **Pool(s):** heated indoor. **Leisure Activities:** whirlpool. **Guest Services:** valet laundry, wireless Internet. **Business Services:** conference facilities, PC.

ASK 🍽 ⊤ 🛁 💻 / SOME UNITS FEE 🐾 ✕ 🖥 📠

PRAIRIE OASIS MOTEL Phone: (306)692-4894

▼
Motel
$86-$96 All Year

Address: 955 Thatcher Dr E S6H 4N9 **Location:** Just s of jct Trans-Canada Hwy 1. Located next to Prairie Oasis Tourist Complex. **Facility:** 40 units. 36 one-bedroom standard units, some with efficiencies. 4 one-bedroom suites with efficiencies. 1 story, exterior corridors. **Parking:** on-site, winter plug-ins. **Terms:** check-in 4 pm. **Amenities:** high-speed Internet. **Pool(s):** heated indoor. **Leisure Activities:** whirlpool, waterslide. Fee: miniature golf. **Guest Services:** coin laundry, wireless Internet. **Business Services:** meeting rooms, PC. 🍽 🛁 ✕ 🖥 💻 / SOME UNITS 🐾 ✕ 📠

SUPER 8-MOOSE JAW   *Book at AAA.com* Phone: 306/692-8888

▼▼ ▼▼
Hotel
Rates not provided

Address: 1706 Main St N S6J 1L4 **Location:** On Hwy 2, 0.7 mi (1.1 km) s of jct Trans-Canada Hwy 1. **Facility:** 60 units. 58 one-bedroom standard units, some with whirlpools. 2 one-bedroom suites. 3 stories, interior corridors. **Parking:** on-site, winter plug-ins. **Amenities:** voice mail, hair dryers. Some: high-speed Internet. **Guest Services:** coin laundry, wireless Internet. **Business Services:** PC.

ECO 🍽 CALL 📺 🐾 🖥 💻 / SOME UNITS FEE 🐾 ✕ 📠

TEMPLE GARDENS MINERAL SPA RESORT   *Book at AAA.com* Phone: (306)694-5055

▼▼ ▼▼▼
Hotel
$135-$396 All Year

Address: 24 Fairford St E S6H 0C7 **Location:** Just e of Main St (Hwy 2); centre. Next to Crescent Park. **Facility:** Smoke free premises. 179 units. 168 one-bedroom standard units, some with whirlpools. 11 one-bedroom suites, some with whirlpools. 5 stories, interior corridors. **Parking:** on-site (fee), winter plug-ins. **Terms:** check-in 4 pm, cancellation fee imposed. **Amenities:** video games (fee), high-speed Internet, voice mail, hair dryers. Some: irons. **Dining:** Harwood's, see separate listing. **Leisure Activities:** steamroom, rental bicycles, exercise room, spa. **Guest Services:** valet laundry, wireless Internet. **Business Services:** conference facilities, business center.

ASK 🍽 ⊤ ✕ ✕ 🐾 🖥 💻

── WHERE TO DINE ──

HARWOOD'S

Steak
$9-$45

Phone: 306/693-7778

Known for its high-quality cuts of beef, the restaurant is a popular spot with locals. Casual dress. **Bar:** Full bar. **Reservations:** suggested. **Hours:** 7 am-11 pm. **Address:** 24 Fairford St E S6H 0C7 **Location:** Just e of Main St (Hwy 2); centre; in Temple Gardens Mineral Spa Resort. **Parking:** on-site (fee).

HOUSTON PIZZA

American
$9-$30

Phone: 306/693-3934

A nice spot for couples or families, this restaurant presents a menu of steaks, spaghetti, lasagna, ribs, barbecue chicken, seafood, stir-fry and salads, as well as yummy pizza. Servers are prompt. Casual dress. **Bar:** Full bar. **Reservations:** accepted. **Hours:** 11 am-11 pm, Fri & Sat-midnight. Closed: 12/24, 12/25. **Address:** 117 Main St N S6H 0V9 **Location:** Just s of High St; 2 mi (3.5 km) s of Trans-Canada Hwy 1. **Parking:** street.

NORTH BATTLEFORD pop. 13,190

GOLD EAGLE LODGE   *Book great rates at AAA.com*

Hotel
$139-$289 10/1-2/28
$132-$282 3/1-9/30

Phone: (306)446-8877

Address: 12004 Railway Ave E S9A 3W3 **Location:** Jct Hwy 46 and 16 (Yellowhead Hwy), just w. **Facility:** Smoke free premises. 112 units. 93 one- and 10 two-bedroom standard units. 9 one-bedroom suites, some with kitchens and/or whirlpools. 4 stories, interior corridors. *Bath:* combo or shower only. **Parking:** on-site, winter plug-ins. **Terms:** cancellation fee imposed. **Amenities:** high-speed Internet, voice mail, irons, hair dryers. **Pool(s):** heated indoor. **Leisure Activities:** sauna, whirlpools, steamroom, exercise room. **Guest Services:** coin laundry. **Business Services:** meeting rooms, business center. **Free Special Amenities: continental breakfast and high-speed Internet.**

SUPER 8   *Book at AAA.com*

Hotel
$100-$125 3/1-8/31
$95-$115 9/1-2/28

Phone: (306)446-8888

Address: 1006 Hwy 16 Bypass S9A 3W2 **Location:** 0.3 mi (0.5 km) nw of jct Hwy 16. **Facility:** 72 one-bedroom standard units. 2-3 stories, interior corridors. **Parking:** on-site, winter plug-ins. **Terms:** cancellation fee imposed. **Amenities:** high-speed Internet, hair dryers. **Guest Services:** wireless Internet.

TROPICAL INN

Hotel
$90-$94 All Year

Phone: 306/446-4700

Address: 1001 Hwy 16 Bypass S9A 3W2 **Location:** Corner of Battleford Rd. **Facility:** 119 units. 113 one- and 2 two-bedroom standard units, some with whirlpools. 4 one-bedroom suites with whirlpools. 2 stories, interior corridors. **Parking:** on-site, winter plug-ins. **Terms:** check-in 4 pm, cancellation fee imposed. **Amenities:** video games (fee), voice mail, irons, hair dryers. *Some:* high-speed Internet. **Pool(s):** heated indoor. **Leisure Activities:** sauna, whirlpool, waterslide. **Guest Services:** valet laundry, wireless Internet. **Business Services:** meeting rooms, PC.

PRINCE ALBERT pop. 34,138

BEST WESTERN MARQUIS INN & SUITES   *Book great rates at AAA.com*

Hotel
$110-$150 All Year

Phone: (306)922-9595

Address: 602 36th St E S6V 7P2 **Location:** Jct Hwy 3 (6th Ave E) and Marquis Rd. **Facility:** 77 units. 75 one-bedroom standard units. 2 one-bedroom suites. 2 stories, interior corridors. **Parking:** on-site, winter plug-ins. **Terms:** check-in 4 pm. **Amenities:** high-speed Internet, voice mail, irons, hair dryers. **Leisure Activities:** exercise room. **Business Services:** meeting rooms, PC. **Free Special Amenities: full breakfast and high-speed Internet.**

AAA Benefit:
Members save up to 20%, plus 10% bonus points with rewards program.

COMFORT INN   *Book at AAA.com*

Hotel
$98-$125 All Year

Phone: (306)763-4466

Address: 3863 2nd Ave W S6W 1A1 **Location:** 1.6 mi (2.6 km) s on Hwy 2. **Facility:** 62 one-bedroom standard units. 2 stories (no elevator), interior corridors. **Parking:** on-site, winter plug-ins. **Amenities:** irons, hair dryers. **Guest Services:** valet laundry, wireless Internet.

DAYS INN   *Book at AAA.com*

Hotel
Rates not provided

Phone: 306/763-8988

Address: 150 34th St W S6V 8E9 **Location:** On Hwy 2, jct Marquis Rd. Located in a commercial area. **Facility:** 80 units. 72 one-bedroom standard units, some with whirlpools. 8 one-bedroom suites. 4 stories, interior corridors. **Parking:** on-site, winter plug-ins. **Amenities:** high-speed Internet, voice mail, irons, hair dryers. **Pool(s):** heated indoor. **Leisure Activities:** whirlpool, waterslide, limited exercise equipment. **Guest Services:** valet and coin laundry. **Business Services:** business center.

RAMADA PRINCE ALBERT

Book great rates at AAA.com

Phone: (306)922-1333

(CAA) (SAVE)

Hotel
$105 All Year

Address: 3245 2nd Ave W S6V 5G1 **Location:** 1.2 mi (2 km) s on Hwy 2. **Facility:** 66 units. 64 one-bedroom standard units, some with whirlpools. 2 one-bedroom suites with whirlpools. 3 stories, interior corridors. **Parking:** on-site, winter plug-ins. **Terms:** check-in 4 pm, cancellation fee imposed. **Amenities:** voice mail, irons, hair dryers. *Some:* high-speed Internet, safes. **Leisure Activities:** exercise room. **Guest Services:** valet laundry, airport transportation-Prince Albert Airport, wireless Internet. **Business Services:** meeting rooms, business center. **Free Special Amenities: expanded continental breakfast and high-speed Internet.**

SUPER 8

Book at AAA.com

Phone: (306)953-0088

Hotel
$114-$129 All Year

Address: 4444 2nd Ave W S6V 5R7 **Location:** 1.7 mi (2.7 km) s on Hwy 2. **Facility:** 60 one-bedroom standard units. 3 stories, interior corridors. **Parking:** on-site, winter plug-ins. **Amenities:** voice mail, irons, hair dryers. **Guest Services:** valet and coin laundry, wireless Internet.

TRAVELODGE PRINCE ALBERT

Book at AAA.com

Phone: (306)764-6441

Hotel
$110-$175 All Year

Address: 3551 2nd Ave W S6V 5G1 **Location:** 1.4 mi (2.2 km) s on Hwy 2. **Facility:** 80 units. 57 one-bedroom standard units. 23 one-bedroom suites, some with whirlpools. 2 stories (no elevator), interior corridors. **Parking:** on-site, winter plug-ins. **Amenities:** high-speed Internet, voice mail, irons, hair dryers. *Some:* DVD players. **Leisure Activities:** exercise room. **Guest Services:** valet laundry, wireless Internet. **Business Services:** meeting rooms, PC.

------ WHERE TO DINE ------

AMY'S ON SECOND

Phone: 306-763-1515

Continental
$13-$27

Nestled into a warm, intimate setting to enjoy homemade cuisine and regional specialties prepared using fresh ingredients. Try the wild rice soup, rack of lamb, Saskatchewan pickerel and cheesecake. Casual dress. **Bar:** Full bar. **Reservations:** suggested. **Hours:** 11 am-9 pm. Closed major holidays; also Sun. **Address:** 2990 2nd Ave W S6V 7E9 **Location:** 0.9 mi (1.4 km) s on Hwy 2. **Parking:** on-site.

VENICE HOUSE

Phone: 306-764-6555

Greek
$8-$39

A casual, family-dining experience awaits you at the restaurant. The menu offers steak, pizza, spaghetti and seafood dishes, but the house specialty is Greek-style ribs. The very relaxed atmosphere is quite comfortable and appealing. A lighter senior menu is offered. Casual dress. **Bar:** Full bar. **Reservations:** accepted. **Hours:** 11 am-10 pm, Fri & Sat-11 pm. Closed: 12/25; also for lunch holidays. **Address:** 1498 Central Ave S6V 4W5 **Location:** 15th St and Central Ave. **Parking:** on-site and street.

REGINA pop. 179,246

BEST WESTERN SEVEN OAKS INN

Book great rates at AAA.com

Phone: (306)757-0121

(CAA) (SAVE)

Hotel
$135 All Year

Address: 777 Albert St S4R 2P6 **Location:** On Hwy 6; jct 2nd Ave. Located in a commercial area. **Facility:** 157 units. 154 one-bedroom standard units. 3 one-bedroom suites. 3 stories, interior corridors. **Parking:** on-site, winter plug-ins. **Amenities:** high-speed Internet, voice mail, irons, hair dryers. **Dining:** Ricky's All Day Grill, see separate listing. **Pool(s):** heated indoor. **Leisure Activities:** sauna, whirlpool, waterslide, exercise room. **Guest Services:** valet and coin laundry, airport transportation (fee)-Regina International Airport, wireless Internet. **Business Services:** conference facilities, business center. *(See color ad p 740)*

AAA Benefit:
Members save up to 20%, plus 10% bonus points with rewards program.

FREE newspaper and high-speed Internet

COMFORT INN

Book great rates at AAA.com

Phone: (306)789-5522

(CAA) (SAVE)

Hotel
$119-$125 All Year

Address: 3221 E Eastgate Dr S4Z 1A4 **Location:** Trans-Canada Hwy 1, 1.3 mi (2 km) e of Ring Rd; at eastern approach to city. Opposite a shopping centre and Eastgate Park. **Facility:** 99 one-bedroom standard units. 2 stories (no elevator), interior corridors. **Parking:** on-site, winter plug-ins. **Amenities:** irons, hair dryers. **Guest Services:** valet laundry, wireless Internet. **Business Services:** PC.

COUNTRY INN & SUITES BY CARLSON

Book at AAA.com

Phone: (306)789-9117

Hotel
$125-$155 1/1-2/28
$120-$150 3/1-12/31

Address: 3321 Eastgate Bay S4Z 1A4 **Location:** Trans-Canada Hwy 1, 1.3 mi (2 km) e of Ring Rd; at eastern approach to city. Opposite a shopping centre. **Facility:** 76 units. 39 one-bedroom standard units. 37 one-bedroom suites. 3 stories, interior corridors. **Parking:** on-site, winter plug-ins. **Terms:** 3 day cancellation notice. **Amenities:** video library, DVD players, voice mail, irons, hair dryers. *Some:* high-speed Internet, dual phone lines. **Leisure Activities:** exercise room. **Guest Services:** valet and coin laundry, wireless Internet. **Business Services:** PC.

DAYS INN   *Book great rates at AAA.com*   **Phone:** (306)522-3297

Hotel
$130-$180 All Year

Address: 3875 Eastgate Dr S4Z 1A4 **Location:** Jct Ring Rd, 1.5 mi (2.4 km) e on Trans-Canada Hwy 1, just n; at eastern approach to city. Located in a commercial area. **Facility:** 129 one-bedroom standard units, some with efficiencies and/or whirlpools. 3-4 stories, interior corridors. *Bath:* combo or shower only. **Parking:** on-site, winter plug-ins. **Terms:** check-in 4 pm, cancellation fee imposed. **Amenities:** voice mail, irons, hair dryers. *Some:* high-speed Internet. **Pool(s):** heated indoor. **Leisure Activities:** whirlpools, waterslide, exercise room. **Guest Services:** valet and coin laundry, wireless Internet. **Free Special Amenities: continental breakfast and high-speed Internet.**

DELTA REGINA   *Book at AAA.com*   **Phone:** (306)525-5255

Hotel
$165-$230 All Year

Address: 1919 Saskatchewan Dr S4P 4H2 **Location:** At Rose St; centre. Across from Casino Regina. **Facility:** 274 units. 251 one-bedroom standard units. 23 one-bedroom suites, some with whirlpools. 25 stories, interior corridors. **Parking:** on-site (fee), winter plug-ins. **Amenities:** high-speed Internet, voice mail, irons, hair dryers. *Some:* CD players. **Pool(s):** heated indoor. **Leisure Activities:** whirlpool, waterslide, exercise room, spa. **Guest Services:** valet laundry, wireless Internet. **Business Services:** conference facilities, business center.

HOLIDAY INN EXPRESS & SUITES   *Book at AAA.com*   **Phone:** 306/789-5888

Hotel
$162-$200 All Year

Too new to rate. **Address:** 4255 Albert St S4S 3R6 **Location:** On Hwy 6, 1 mi (1.6 km) n of jct Trans-Canada Hwy 1. **Amenities:** 102 units, coffeemakers, microwaves, refrigerators, pool.

HOLIDAY INN EXPRESS HOTEL & SUITES REGINA   *Book at AAA.com*   **Phone:** (306)569-4600

Hotel
$145-$195 All Year

Address: 1907 11th Ave S4P 0J2 **Location:** Corner of Rose St; centre. Located near Casino Regina. **Facility:** 78 units. 70 one-bedroom standard units. 8 one-bedroom suites, some with whirlpools. 5 stories, interior corridors. **Parking:** on-site (fee), winter plug-ins. **Amenities:** dual phone lines, voice mail, irons, hair dryers. **Leisure Activities:** exercise room. **Guest Services:** valet laundry, wireless Internet. **Business Services:** meeting rooms, business center.

▼ *See AAA listing p 739* ▼

Best Western Seven Oaks Inn - One of The Best Family Hotels in Town.

- Exclusive loyalty program for AAA members!
- 240 Foot Waterslide
- Fitness Room & Sauna
- Wireless High Speed Internet in all rooms

- Free Shuttle to and from Airport
- Ricky's All Day Grill & Corner Pub

Best Western Seven Oaks Inn
777 Albert St, Regina, SK S4R 2P6
306.757.0121
1.800.667.8063 | www.bestwesternsevenoaks.com

HOLIDAY INN HOTEL & SUITES   *Book at AAA.com*   Phone: (306)789-3883

Hotel
$169-$224 1/1-2/28
$159-$214 3/1-12/31

Address: 1800 Prince of Wales Dr S4Z 1A4 **Location:** 1.2 mi (1.9 km) e on Trans-Canada Hwy 1, jct Ring Rd, then just n; at eastern approach to city. Opposite a shopping centre. **Facility:** 120 units. 107 one-bedroom standard units. 13 one-bedroom suites. 4 stories, interior corridors. **Parking:** on-site, winter plug-ins. **Amenities:** video games (fee), high-speed Internet, voice mail, irons, hair dryers. **Pool(s):** heated indoor. **Leisure Activities:** whirlpool, waterslide, exercise room. **Guest Services:** valet and coin laundry, wireless Internet. **Business Services:** meeting rooms, business center.

HOWARD JOHNSON INN   *Book great rates at AAA.com*   Phone: (306)565-0455

Hotel
$100-$110 All Year

Address: 1110 Victoria Ave E S4N 7A9 **Location:** On Trans-Canada Hwy 1, just w of Ring Rd; at eastern approach to city. **Facility:** Smoke free premises. 120 units. 96 one-bedroom standard units. 24 one-bedroom suites, some with whirlpools. 3 stories, interior corridors. **Parking:** on-site, winter plug-ins. **Terms:** cancellation fee imposed. **Amenities:** video games (fee), voice mail, irons, hair dryers. **Pool(s):** heated indoor. **Leisure Activities:** whirlpool. **Guest Services:** valet and coin laundry, wireless Internet. **Business Services:** meeting rooms. **Free Special Amenities:** local telephone calls and high-speed Internet.

QUALITY HOTEL   *Book great rates at AAA.com*   Phone: (306)569-4656

Hotel
$99-$169 All Year

Address: 1717 Victoria Ave S4P 0P9 **Location:** Just e of Broad St; downtown. **Facility:** 126 one-bedroom standard units. 7 stories, interior corridors. **Parking:** on-site, winter plug-ins. **Amenities:** video games (fee), voice mail, irons, hair dryers. **Leisure Activities:** sauna, exercise room. **Guest Services:** valet and coin laundry, wireless Internet. **Business Services:** meeting rooms, PC.

RADISSON PLAZA HOTEL SASKATCHEWAN   *Book great rates at AAA.com*   Phone: (306)522-7691

Hotel
$173-$280 All Year

Address: 2125 Victoria Ave S4P 0S3 **Location:** At Scarth St; centre. Opposite Victoria Park. **Facility:** Smoke free premises. 224 units. 198 one-bedroom standard units. 26 one-bedroom suites, some with whirlpools. 10 stories, interior corridors. **Bath:** combo or shower only. **Parking:** on-site and valet, winter plug-ins. **Terms:** cancellation fee imposed. **Amenities:** video games (fee), dual phone lines, voice mail, honor bars, irons, hair dryers. **Some:** CD players, high-speed Internet. **Dining:** Cortlandt Hall Dining Room, see separate listing. **Leisure Activities:** whirlpool, steamroom, spa. **Guest Services:** valet laundry, wireless Internet, beauty salon. **Fee:** airport transportation-Regina International Airport, area transportation-within city limits. **Business Services:** conference facilities, business center. *(See color ad below)*

FREE newspaper and high-speed Internet

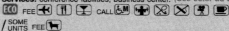

RAMADA HOTEL & CONVENTION CENTRE *Book at AAA.com* Phone: (306)569-1666

Hotel
$134-$194 All Year

Address: 1818 Victoria Ave S4P 0R1 **Location:** At Broad St; centre. **Facility:** 232 units. 219 one-bedroom standard units. 13 one-bedroom suites, some with whirlpools. 15 stories, interior corridors. **Parking:** on-site (fee). **Terms:** cancellation fee imposed. **Amenities:** voice mail, irons, hair dryers. *Some:* high-speed Internet. **Pool(s):** heated indoor. **Leisure Activities:** sauna, whirlpool, exercise room. **Guest Services:** valet laundry, wireless Internet. **Business Services:** conference facilities, PC.

REGINA INN HOTEL & CONFERENCE CENTRE *Book great rates at AAA.com* Phone: (306)525-6767

Hotel
$129-$210 All Year

Address: 1975 Broad St S4P 1Y2 **Location:** Jct Victoria Ave; centre. **Facility:** 235 units. 230 one-bedroom standard units. 5 one-bedroom suites, some with whirlpools. 15 stories, interior corridors. **Parking:** on-site, winter plug-ins. **Terms:** check-in 4 pm, cancellation fee imposed. **Amenities:** video games (fee), voice mail, irons, hair dryers. *Some:* CD players. **Leisure Activities:** exercise room. **Guest Services:** valet laundry, wireless Internet. **Business Services:** conference facilities, business center. **Free Special Amenities:** local telephone calls and high-speed Internet.

SANDMAN HOTEL SUITES & SPA *Book at AAA.com* Phone: 306/757-2444

Hotel
Rates not provided

Address: 1800 Victoria Ave E S4N 7K3 **Location:** On Trans-Canada Hwy 1, just e of Ring Rd; at eastern approach to city. Located in a commercial area. **Facility:** 132 units. 49 one-bedroom standard units. 83 one-bedroom suites, some with whirlpools. 4 stories, interior corridors. *Bath:* combo or shower only. **Parking:** on-site, winter plug-ins. **Terms:** check-in 4 pm. **Amenities:** high-speed Internet, voice mail, irons, hair dryers. **Pool(s):** heated indoor. **Leisure Activities:** whirlpool, exercise room. **Guest Services:** valet laundry, wireless Internet. **Business Services:** meeting rooms, business center.

SUPER 8 REGINA *Book at AAA.com* Phone: (306)789-8833

Hotel
$104-$135 All Year

Address: 2730 Victoria Ave E S4N 6M5 **Location:** On Trans-Canada Hwy 1, 1 mi (1.6 km) e of Ring Rd; at eastern approach to city. Opposite a shopping centre. **Facility:** 60 units. 59 one-bedroom standard units. 1 one-bedroom suite. 3 stories (no elevator), interior corridors. **Parking:** on-site, winter plug-ins. **Terms:** check-in 4 pm. **Amenities:** video games (fee), hair dryers. **Guest Services:** valet laundry, wireless Internet.

THE TRAVELODGE HOTEL & CONFERENCE CENTRE
Book great rates at AAA.com

Phone: (306)586-3443

Hotel
$110-$160 All Year

Address: 4177 Albert St S S4S 3R6 **Location:** On Hwy 6, 1 mi (1.6 km) n of jct Trans-Canada Hwy 1. **Facility:** Smoke free premises. 200 one-bedroom standard units, some with whirlpools. 4 stories, interior corridors. **Parking:** on-site, winter plug-ins. **Terms:** check-in 4 pm, cancellation fee imposed. **Amenities:** high-speed Internet, voice mail, irons, hair dryers. **Pool(s):** heated indoor. **Leisure Activities:** whirlpool, waterslide, children's play cave, exercise room. **Guest Services:** valet laundry, wireless Internet. **Business Services:** conference facilities, business center. *(See color ad below)*

FREE local telephone calls and high-speed Internet

WEST HARVEST INN *Book at AAA.com*

Phone: 306/586-6755

Hotel
Rates not provided

Address: 4025 Albert St S S4S 3R6 **Location:** On Hwy 6, 1.3 mi (2 km) n of jct Trans-Canada Hwy 1. **Facility:** Smoke free premises. 105 one-bedroom standard units, some with whirlpools. 5 stories, interior corridors. **Parking:** on-site, winter plug-ins. **Amenities:** video games (fee), voice mail, irons, hair dryers. **Leisure Activities:** exercise room. **Guest Services:** valet and coin laundry, wireless Internet. **Business Services:** meeting rooms, business center.

WINGATE BY WYNDHAM *Book great rates at AAA.com*

Phone: (306)584-7400

Hotel
$162-$200 All Year

Address: 1700 Broad St S4P 1X4 **Location:** Corner of Saskatchewan Dr; centre. Located across from Casino Regina. **Facility:** 118 one-bedroom standard units. 7 stories, interior corridors. *Bath:* combo or shower only. **Parking:** on-site (fee), winter plug-ins. **Terms:** cancellation fee imposed. **Amenities:** high-speed Internet, voice mail, safes, irons, hair dryers. **Leisure Activities:** exercise room. **Guest Services:** valet laundry, wireless Internet. **Business Services:** meeting rooms, business center. **Free Special Amenities:** expanded continental breakfast and high-speed Internet.

——— WHERE TO DINE ———

CATHEDRAL VILLAGE FREEHOUSE

Phone: 306/359-1661

Canadian
$8-$24

The young and young at heart appreciate the sometimes boisterous atmosphere at the upscale tavern. Servers are friendly. The menu lists an interesting mix of dishes, such as ribs, steak, burritos, tandoori chicken stir fry, soups, salads, sandwiches and pizzas cooked in a wood-fired oven. The patio is open seasonally. Casual dress. **Bar:** Full bar. **Reservations:** accepted. **Hours:** 11 am-midnight; hours may vary. Closed: 10/11, 12/25; also Sun 1/1-3/31. **Address:** 2062 Albert St S4P 2T7 **Location:** On Hwy 6; jct 13th Ave. **Parking:** on-site and street.

▼ *See AAA listing above* ▼

CORTLANDT HALL DINING ROOM
Phone: 306/337-4311

Canadian
$10-$38

The restaurant's award-winning chefs prepare a wide-ranging menu of delicious meals and a good selection of in-house desserts and pastries. The buffet is a popular choice for breakfast and lunch as well as on Sunday nights. Attractive Victorian decor provides for intimate dining. Dressy casual. **Bar:** Full bar. **Reservations:** suggested, required for Sunday brunch. **Hours:** 7 am-2 & 5-9 pm; Sunday brunch seatings 10 am & 12:30 pm. **Address:** 2125 Victoria Ave S4P 0S3 **Location:** At Scarth St; centre; in Radisson Plaza Hotel Saskatchewan. **Parking:** on-site.

CRAVE KITCHEN & WINE BAR
Phone: 306/525-8777

International
$12-$36

Located in one of Regina's oldest clubs, the modern restaurant and lounge offers tempting tapas and a number of delicious entrées. Popular with the downtown crowd, at times the eatery can be loud and jovial. Casual dress. **Bar:** Full bar. **Reservations:** accepted, except Friday. **Hours:** 11 am-10 pm, Sat from 4 pm. Closed major holidays; also Sun. **Address:** 1925 Victoria Ave S4P 0R3 **Location:** Victoria Ave and Broad St; centre of downtown. **Parking:** street.

CREEK IN CATHEDRAL BISTRO
Phone: 306/352-4448

Continental
$10-$29

Located in a residential area close to downtown, the charming bistro has a tasteful decor with local artwork adorning the walls and friendly, capable servers. Creatively prepared and artfully presented food, prepared using market-fresh ingredients, keeps the locals returning. Casual dress. **Bar:** Full bar. **Reservations:** suggested. **Hours:** 11 am-4 & 5-9 pm, Fri-close, Sat 10 am-4 pm. Closed major holidays; also Sun. **Address:** 3414 13th Ave S4T 1P7 **Location:** Just e of Elphinstone St. **Parking:** street.

THE DIPLOMAT STEAKHOUSE
Phone: 306/359-3366

Steak
$10-$50

On the menu at this establishment is wonderful steak, filet mignon, coq au vin and seafood, as well as an impressive choice of wine and cognac. Elegant surroundings and knowledgeable servers are characteristic. Dressy casual. **Bar:** Full bar. **Reservations:** suggested, weekends. **Hours:** 11 am-2 & 4-midnight, Sat from 4 pm, Sun 4 pm-9 pm. Closed: 7/1, 12/25. **Address:** 2032 Broad St S4P 1Y3 **Location:** Just s of jct Broad St and Victoria Ave. **Parking:** on-site.

EARLS RESTAURANT
Phone: 306/584-7733

Canadian
$10-$28

Offering an experience that falls between fast food and fine dining, the fun, relaxed restaurant prepares great food at a great price. Choices range from juicy burgers, hearty sandwiches, fresh salads, wings and pizza to full entrees of steak, chops and seafood. Made-from-scratch soups and assorted breads, as well as a nice choice of wines and beers, round out the offerings. This is a fitting spot for impromptu get-togethers and festive occasions. Casual dress. **Bar:** Full bar. **Reservations:** accepted, except Fri & Sat for dinner. **Hours:** 11:30 am-midnight, Fri & Sat-1 am. Closed: 12/25. **Address:** 2606 28th Ave S4S 6P3 **Location:** Jct Albert St S. **Parking:** on-site.

FIRESIDE BISTRO
Phone: 306/761-2305

Canadian
$7-$32

The menu lists creative choices alongside such favorites as pasta, chicken, fish and steak. The bistro's dining areas are in the rooms of a large old house. The patio opens seasonally. Casual dress. **Bar:** Full bar. **Reservations:** suggested. **Hours:** 11 am-10 pm, Fri & Sat-11 pm. Closed major holidays. **Address:** 2305 Smith St S4P 2P7 **Location:** 3 blks s of Victoria Ave, just e of Hwy 6 (Albert St). **Parking:** street.

GOLF'S STEAK HOUSE
Phone: 306/525-5808

Steak
$10-$50

The restaurant features hearty portions of tasty AAA Angus Pride steak and prime rib, as well as seafood, chicken and rack of lamb. The menu includes a good variety. Professional service and traditional formal decor characterize the restaurant, which signifies when it's open for business by lighting the torch out front. Casual dress. **Bar:** Full bar. **Reservations:** accepted. **Hours:** 11 am-11 pm, Sat from 4 pm, Sun 4 pm-10 pm. Closed: 12/25. **Address:** 1945 Victoria Ave S4P 0R3 **Location:** Corner of Victoria Ave and Hamilton St. **Parking:** on-site.

LA BODEGA
Phone: 306/546-3660

Mediterranean
$11-$50

Those who enjoy a variety of taste sensations surely will be pleased with the varied tapas menu. The atmosphere is cozy in the dining room and on the seasonal patio. Casual dress. **Bar:** Full bar. **Reservations:** accepted. **Hours:** 11 am-2 am, Sun from 10:30 am. Closed: 12/25, 12/26. **Address:** 2228 Albert St S4P 2V2 **Location:** Just n of jct 15th Ave. **Parking:** street.

THE LAST SPIKE
Phone: 306/781-7000

American
$8-$20

In the old Regina train station, the restaurant has one dining room section in a rail passenger car. Reservations are required to dine in the car. The menu centers on simple, filling fare along the lines of ribs, chicken and fish 'n' chips. Casual dress. **Bar:** Full bar. **Reservations:** accepted. **Hours:** 9 am-10:30 pm, Fri & Sat-midnight. Closed: 12/24, 12/25. **Address:** 1880 Saskatchewan Dr S4P 0A8 **Location:** Centre; in Casino Regina. **Parking:** on-site (fee).

LUIGGI'S PASTA HOUSE
Phone: 306/949-7427

Italian
$7-$25

The family-oriented eatery serves traditional Italian food in a fun and lively atmosphere. Casual dress. **Bar:** Full bar. **Reservations:** accepted. **Hours:** 11 am-9 pm, Fri & Sat-10 pm, Sun 4 pm-9 pm. Closed: 4/4, 12/25. **Address:** 470 Albert St N S4R 3C1 **Location:** Corner of 9th Ave, just s of Ring Rd. **Parking:** on-site.

MEDITERRANEAN BISTRO
Phone: 306/757-1666

Continental
$9-$32

This casual yet upscale bistro/market uses fresh products and offers a good variety of carefully prepared and creatively presented fish, chicken, red meat and pasta dishes. Dressy casual. **Bar:** Full bar. **Reservations:** suggested. **Hours:** 11 am-close, Sun from 10:30 am. Closed major holidays. **Address:** 2589 Quance St E S4V 2Y7 **Location:** Trans-Canada Hwy 1, just se of jct Fleet St; at eastern approach to city. **Parking:** on-site.

MICHI

Japanese
$7-$16

Phone: 306/565-0141

Most of the fish and seafood served at this pleasant eatery is imported directly from Japan. One bite of this authentic sushi, teriyaki and tempura and there's no denying that Michi's five chefs hail from Japan. Casual dress. **Bar:** Full bar. **Reservations:** accepted. **Hours:** 11:30 am-2 & 5-9 pm, Sun from 5 pm. Closed major holidays. **Address:** 1943 Scarth St S4P 2H1 **Location:** Just n of Victoria Ave; centre. **Parking:** street.

MOXIE'S CLASSIC GRILL

Canadian
$9-$32

Phone: 306/781-5655

This sleek, funky and popular restaurant presents an extensive menu of creatively prepared dishes, including pizza, pasta, rice, noodles, signature salads and burgers. Other menus include one for children and one for Sunday brunch. Lending to the upbeat, stylish decor are dark wood appointments and river rock fireplaces. Casual dress. **Bar:** Full bar. **Reservations:** accepted. **Hours:** 11 am-11 pm, Thurs-Sat to 1 am. Closed: 12/25. **Address:** 1800A Victoria Ave S4N 7K3 **Location:** Jct Glen Carin Rd, just nw. **Parking:** on-site.

RICKY'S ALL DAY GRILL

Canadian
$9-$26

Phone: 306/775-3000

The comfortable eatery, which employs friendly servers, presents a varied menu that includes pasta dishes, wraps, omelets, stir-fry preparations and burgers. Portions are generous. Children's and senior selections are offered. Guests can request seating in a booth or at a table. Casual dress. **Bar:** Full bar. **Reservations:** accepted. **Hours:** 7 am-10 pm. Closed: 12/25. **Address:** 777 Albert St S4R 2P6 **Location:** On Hwy 6; jct 2nd Ave; in Best Western Seven Oaks Inn. **Parking:** on-site.

THE WILLOW ON WASCANA

Canadian
$11-$39

Phone: 306/585-3663

Here is an opportunity to enjoy a cozy restaurant in a park setting with super river views. Service is skilled and friendly and the menu offers a good variety of beautifully prepared dishes; a patio is available in season. Casual dress. **Bar:** Full bar. **Reservations:** suggested. **Hours:** 4:30 pm-9:30 pm, also Thurs-Sat 11:30 am-1:15 pm. Closed: 10/11, 12/25, 12/26; also first 2 weeks in Jan. **Address:** 3000 Wascana Dr S4P 3B2 **Location:** Jct S Broad St and Wascana Pkwy; next to marina. **Parking:** on-site.

SASKATOON pop. 202,425

✈ Airport Accommodations

OA	JOHN G DIEFENBAKER INTERNATIONAL	Diamond Rated	High Season	Page
CAA	**Best Western Harvest Inn, 2.5 mi (4 km) se of airport**	◈◈	$127-$230 SAVE	745
CAA	**Comfort Inn, 1.9 mi (3 km) se of airport**	◈◈	$124-$128 SAVE	745
	Country Inn & Suites By Carlson, 1.6 mi (2.5 km) se of airport	◈◈	$120-$140	746
CAA	Days Inn-Saskatoon, 1.9 mi (3 km) se of airport	◈◈	$136-$175 SAVE	746
	Sandman Hotel, 1.6 mi (2.5 km) se of airport	◈◈	Rates not provided	747
	Super 8, 2.5 mi (4 km) se of airport	◈◈	$110-$122	747
	Travelodge Hotel Saskatoon, 1.9 mi (3 km) se of airport	◈◈	$129-$189	747

BEST WESTERN HARVEST INN

Book great rates at AAA.com

Hotel
$127-$230 All Year

Phone: (306)244-5552

Address: 1715 Idylwyld Dr N S7L 1B4 **Location:** On Hwy 11 (Idylwyld Dr), 0.4 mi (0.7 km) s of jct Circle Dr. Located in a commercial area. **Facility:** Smoke free premises. 92 units. 83 one-bedroom standard units. 9 one-bedroom suites. 2 stories, interior corridors. **Parking:** on-site, winter plug-ins. **Amenities:** high-speed Internet, voice mail, irons, hair dryers. **Dining:** Ricky's All Day Grill, see separate listing. **Leisure Activities:** exercise room. **Guest Services:** valet laundry, airport transportation-John G Diefenbaker International Airport, wireless Internet. **Business Services:** meeting rooms, PC. **Free Special Amenities: local telephone calls and high-speed Internet.**

AAA Benefit:
Members save up to 20%, plus 10% bonus points with rewards program.

🛬 🍴 🍸 ✕ 🎦 💻 / SOME UNITS FEE 🐾 🔌 🖥

COLONIAL SQUARE INN & SUITES

Hotel
$99-$139 All Year

Phone: (306)343-1676

Address: 1301 8th St E S7H 0S7 **Location:** 1.5 mi (2.4 km) e of jct Hwy 11 (Idylwyld Dr); 1.4 mi (2.3 km) w of jct Circle Dr. Opposite Cumberland Park. **Facility:** Smoke free premises. 80 one-bedroom standard units. 2 stories (no elevator), interior corridors. **Parking:** on-site, winter plug-ins. **Terms:** 1-7 night minimum stay, 7 day cancellation notice-fee imposed. **Amenities:** voice mail, irons, hair dryers. **Guest Services:** valet laundry, wireless Internet. **Business Services:** meeting rooms. **Free Special Amenities: local telephone calls and high-speed Internet.**

🔌 ✕ 🔌 💻 / SOME UNITS FEE 🐾

COMFORT INN

Book great rates at AAA.com

Hotel
$124-$128 All Year

Phone: (306)934-1122

Address: 2155 Northridge Dr S7L 6X6 **Location:** Just ne of jct Hwy 11 (Idylwyld Dr) and Circle Dr. Located in a commercial area. **Facility:** 80 one-bedroom standard units. 2 stories (no elevator), interior corridors. **Parking:** on-site, winter plug-ins. **Terms:** check-in 4 pm, cancellation fee imposed. **Amenities:** irons, hair dryers. **Guest Services:** valet laundry, wireless Internet. **Business Services:** PC. ECO 🔌 CALL 🅂🄼 🎦 💻 / SOME UNITS FEE 🐾 ✕ 🔌 🖥

COUNTRY INN & SUITES BY CARLSON *Book at AAA.com*

Phone: (306)934-3900

Hotel
$120-$140 1/1-2/28
$112-$125 3/1-12/31

Address: 617 Cynthia St S7L 6B7 **Location:** Just w on Circle Dr from jct Hwy 11 (Idylwyld Dr), then just n on Ave CN. Located in a commercial area. **Facility:** Smoke free premises. 76 units. 37 one-bedroom standard units. 39 one-bedroom suites. 3 stories, interior corridors. *Bath:* combo or shower only. **Parking:** on-site, winter plug-ins. **Terms:** cancellation fee imposed. **Amenities:** video library, DVD players, voice mail, irons, hair dryers. **Leisure Activities:** exercise room. **Guest Services:** valet and coin laundry, wireless Internet. **Business Services:** meeting rooms, PC.

DAYS INN-SASKATOON *Book great rates at AAA.com*

Phone: (306)242-3297

(CAA) (SAVE)

Hotel
$136-$175 All Year

Address: 2000 Idylwyld Dr N S7L 7M7 **Location:** Just nw of jct Hwy 11 (Idylwyld Dr) and Circle Dr. Located in a commercial area. **Facility:** 102 units. 96 one-bedroom standard units, some with whirlpools. 9 one-bedroom suites, some with whirlpools. 4 stories, interior corridors. *Bath:* combo or shower only. **Parking:** on-site, winter plug-ins. **Amenities:** high-speed Internet, voice mail, irons, hair dryers. *Some:* safes. **Pool(s):** heated indoor. **Leisure Activities:** whirlpool, waterslide, exercise room. **Guest Services:** valet and coin laundry, airport transportation-John G Diefenbaker International Airport. **Business Services:** PC.

FREE expanded continental breakfast and high-speed Internet

DELTA BESSBOROUGH *Book at AAA.com*

Phone: (306)244-5521

Hotel
$122-$340 7/1-2/28
$142-$290 3/1-6/30

Address: 601 Spadina Crescent E S7K 3G8 **Location:** At 21st St E; centre. Located beside park & river. **Facility:** 225 units. 216 one-bedroom standard units, some with whirlpools. 9 one-bedroom suites, some with whirlpools. 6 stories, interior corridors. **Parking:** on-site (fee) and valet, winter plug-ins. **Terms:** cancellation fee imposed. **Amenities:** video games (fee), high-speed Internet, voice mail, irons, hair dryers. *Some:* dual phone lines. **Dining:** Samurai Japanese Restaurant, see separate listing. **Pool(s):** heated indoor. **Leisure Activities:** sauna, whirlpool, steamroom, jogging, exercise room. *Fee:* massage. **Guest Services:** valet laundry, wireless Internet. **Business Services:** conference facilities, business center.

HILTON GARDEN INN *Book great rates at AAA.com*

Phone: (306)244-2311

Hotel
$179-$364 All Year

Address: 90 22nd St E S7K 3X6 **Location:** Just e of jct Hwy 11 (Idylwyld Dr), at 1st Ave. Located in the downtown business district. **Facility:** Smoke free premises. 180 units. 166 one-bedroom standard units. 14 one-bedroom suites, some with whirlpools. 16 stories, interior corridors. *Bath:* combo or shower only. **Parking:** on-site (fee). **Terms:** 1-7 night minimum stay, cancellation fee imposed. **Amenities:** high-speed Internet, voice mail, irons, hair dryers. **Pool(s):** heated indoor. **Leisure Activities:** whirlpool, exercise room. **Guest Services:** valet and coin laundry, wireless Internet. **Business Services:** conference facilities, business center.

Hilton
Garden Inn

AAA Benefit:
Members save 5% or
more everyday!

HOLIDAY INN EXPRESS HOTEL & SUITES *Book at AAA.com*

Phone: (306)384-8844

Hotel
$144-$189 All Year

Address: 315 Idylwyld Dr N S7L 0Z1 **Location:** On Hwy 11 (Idylwyld Dr), just n of 23rd St. Located in a commercial area. **Facility:** Smoke free premises. 120 units. 114 one-bedroom standard units. 5 one- and 1 two-bedroom suites. 4 stories, interior corridors. **Parking:** on-site, winter plug-ins. **Amenities:** high-speed Internet, dual phone lines, voice mail, irons, hair dryers. **Pool(s):** heated indoor. **Leisure Activities:** whirlpool, exercise room. **Guest Services:** valet laundry, wireless Internet. **Business Services:** meeting rooms, business center.

MOTEL 6 SASKATOON *Book great rates at AAA.com*

Phone: (306)665-6688

Hotel
$106-$142 1/1-2/28
$102-$136 3/1-12/31

Address: 231 Marquis Dr S7R 1B7 **Location:** E of jct Trans-Canada Hwy 16; 0.4 mi (0.7 km) w of Hwy 11 (Idylwyld Dr). Opposite truck stop, close to Credit Union Centre. **Facility:** 67 one-bedroom standard units, some with efficiencies. 3 stories, interior corridors. *Bath:* combo or shower only. **Parking:** on-site, winter plug-ins. **Amenities:** high-speed Internet, voice mail. *Some:* irons. **Pool(s):** heated indoor. **Leisure Activities:** whirlpool. **Guest Services:** coin laundry, wireless Internet. **Business Services:** PC (fee). **(See color ad p 268)**

RADISSON HOTEL SASKATOON *Book at AAA.com* Phone: (306)665-3322

[fyi]
Hotel
$149-$229 All Year

Under major renovation, scheduled to be completed June 2009. **Last rated:** ▼▼▼ **Address:** 405 20th St E S7K 6X6 **Location:** At 4th Ave S; centre. Located close to a river side park. **Facility:** 291 units. 283 one-bedroom standard units. 8 one-bedroom suites with whirlpools. 19 stories, interior corridors. **Parking:** on-site (fee). **Amenities:** video games (fee), high-speed Internet, dual phone lines, voice mail, irons, hair dryers. **Pool(s):** heated indoor. **Leisure Activities:** sauna, whirlpool, waterslide, jogging, exercise room. *Fee:* game room. **Guest Services:** valet laundry, wireless Internet. **Business Services:** conference facilities, PC.

SANDMAN HOTEL *Book at AAA.com* Phone: 306/477-4844

▼▼▼
Hotel
Rates not provided

Address: 310 Circle Dr W S7L 2Y5 **Location:** Just w of Hwy 11 (Idylwyld Dr). Located in a commercial area. **Facility:** Smoke free premises. 190 units. 178 one-bedroom standard units, some with whirlpools. 12 one-bedroom suites. 4 stories, interior corridors. **Parking:** on-site, winter plug-ins. **Terms:** check-in 4 pm. **Amenities:** video games (fee), high-speed Internet, voice mail, irons, hair dryers. **Pool(s):** heated indoor. **Leisure Activities:** whirlpool, exercise room. **Guest Services:** valet laundry, wireless Internet. **Business Services:** meeting rooms, PC.

SHERATON CAVALIER SASKATOON HOTEL *Book great rates at AAA.com* Phone: 306/652-6770

(CAA) (SAVE)
▼▼▼▼
Hotel
Rates not provided

Address: 612 Spadina Crescent E S7K 3G9 **Location:** At 21st St E; centre. Opposite park and river. **Facility:** Smoke free premises. 249 units. 243 one-bedroom standard units, some with whirlpools. 6 one-bedroom suites with whirlpools. 8 stories, interior corridors. **Parking:** on-site (fee), winter plug-ins. **Amenities:** high-speed Internet, dual phone lines, voice mail, honor bars, irons, hair dryers. **Dining:** Carver's Steakhouse, see separate listing. **Pool(s):** heated indoor. **Leisure Activities:** whirlpools, waterslide, exercise room. **Guest Services:** valet laundry, wireless Internet. **Business Services:** conference facilities, business center. **Free Special Amenities:** local telephone calls and high-speed Internet.

(S) **Sheraton**
HOTELS & RESORTS

AAA Benefit:
Members get up to 15% off, plus Starwood Preferred Guest® bonuses.

SUPER 8 *Book at AAA.com* Phone: (306)384-8989

▼▼▼
Hotel
$110-$122 All Year

Address: 706 Circle Dr E S7K 3T7 **Location:** 1.3 mi (2 km) e of jct Hwy 11 (Idylwyld Dr). Located in a commercial area. **Facility:** Smoke free premises. 69 one-bedroom standard units, some with whirlpools. 3 stories, interior corridors. *Bath:* combo or shower only. **Parking:** on-site, winter plug-ins. **Amenities:** voice mail, irons, hair dryers. **Guest Services:** valet laundry, wireless Internet. **Business Services:** PC.

TRAVELODGE HOTEL SASKATOON *Book at AAA.com* Phone: (306)242-8881

▼▼
Hotel
$129-$189 All Year

Address: 106 Circle Dr W S7L 4L6 **Location:** Just w of jct Hwy 11 (Idylwyld Dr). Located in a commercial area. **Facility:** 261 units. 258 one-bedroom standard units, some with whirlpools. 3 one-bedroom suites with whirlpools. 2-6 stories, interior corridors. **Parking:** on-site, winter plug-ins. **Terms:** cancellation fee imposed. **Amenities:** voice mail, irons, hair dryers. *Some:* high-speed Internet. **Pool(s):** 2 heated indoor. **Leisure Activities:** whirlpools, waterslide, exercise room. *Fee:* game room. **Guest Services:** valet and coin laundry, wireless Internet. **Business Services:** conference facilities, business center.

─── **WHERE TO DINE** ───

2ND AVE GRILL Phone: 306-244-9899

▼▼
American
$10-$33

In the heart of the downtown business district, this upscale grill offers an inviting atmosphere and attentive service. The varied menu features items that range from soups and salads to jambalaya. Casual dress. **Bar:** Full bar. **Reservations:** accepted. **Hours:** 11:30 am-10 pm, Fri & Sat-midnight, Sun 4:30 pm-8:30 pm. Closed: 12/25, 12/26; also Sun. **Address:** 10-123 2nd Ave S S7K 7E6 **Location:** Just w of jct 22nd St; centre. **Parking:** street.

CARVER'S STEAKHOUSE Phone: 306/652-8292

▼▼▼
Steak
$26-$48

This popular restaurant serves Caesar salads that are prepared at the table to your taste, and top quality steaks are delivered sizzling on a skillet. Dressy casual. **Bar:** Full bar. **Reservations:** suggested. **Hours:** 5:30 pm-10 pm. Closed major holidays. **Address:** 612 Spadina Crescent E S7K 3G9 **Location:** At 21st St E; centre; in Sheraton Cavalier. **Parking:** on-site (fee) and street.

CHIANTI Phone: 306/665-8466

▼▼
Italian
$8-$17

Lining the menu is a good selection of fresh pasta creations, as well as veal, seafood and chicken dishes. Personable servers circulate in an atmosphere that suits families and couples. Located near downtown, the dining room boasts warm red walls and travel posters of Italy. Casual dress. **Bar:** Full bar. **Reservations:** suggested. **Hours:** 11 am-10 pm, Fri & Sat-11 pm. Closed: 12/25. **Address:** 102 Idylwyld Dr N S7L 0Y7 **Location:** Corner of 22nd St E; centre. **Parking:** on-site.

EARLS RESTAURANT Phone: 306/664-4060

▼▼
Canadian
$11-$29

Offering an experience that falls between fast food and fine dining, the fun, relaxed restaurant prepares great food at a great price. Choices range from juicy burgers, hearty sandwiches, fresh salads, wings and pizza to full entrees of steak, chops and seafood. Made-from-scratch soups and assorted breads, as well as a nice choice of wines and beers, round out the offerings. This is a fitting spot for impromptu get-togethers and festive occasions. Casual dress. **Bar:** Full bar. **Reservations:** not accepted. **Hours:** 11 am-midnight, Fri & Sat-1 am. Closed: 12/25. **Address:** 610 2nd Ave N S7K 2C8 **Location:** Jct Queen St. **Parking:** street.

GENESIS FAMILY RESTAURANT

Phone: 306/244-5516

Chinese
$8-$16

The restaurant features a progressive Chinese menu offering many healthy choices, all made with fresh ingredients. Portions are large, and the diverse and creative menu includes Western dishes. Dim sum is served daily 11 am-2:30 pm. Servers are friendly. Casual dress. **Bar:** Full bar. **Reservations:** accepted. **Hours:** 11 am-9 pm; hours may vary. Closed major holidays. **Address:** 901 D 22nd St W S7M 0R9 **Location:** 0.6 mi (1 km) w of Hwy 11 (Idylwyld Dr). **Parking:** on-site.

JOHN'S PRIME RIB HOUSE

Phone: 306/244-6384

Steak
$9-$54

A longstanding city favorite, the restaurant is known for top-quality prime rib and steak. Service is professional, and the rich wood paneling in the dining room creates a pleasant atmosphere. Casual dress. **Bar:** Full bar. **Reservations:** accepted. **Hours:** 11:30 am-11:30 pm, Sat from 4:30 pm; hours may vary. Closed major holidays; also Sun. **Address:** 401 21st St E S7K 0C5 **Location:** At 4th Ave S; centre. **Parking:** street.

MOXIE'S CLASSIC GRILL

Phone: 306/374-9800

Canadian
$12-$33

This sleek, funky and popular restaurant presents an extensive menu of creatively prepared dishes, including pizza, pasta, rice, noodles, signature salads and burgers. Other menus include one for children and one for Sunday brunch. Lending to the upbeat, stylish decor are dark wood appointments and river rock fireplaces. Casual dress. **Bar:** Full bar. **Hours:** 11 am-midnight, Fri & Sat-1 am, Sun 10 am-midnight. Closed: 12/25. **Address:** 3134 8th St E S7H 0W2 **Location:** Jct Circle Dr, just se. **Parking:** on-site.

RICKY'S ALL DAY GRILL

Phone: 306/652-3222

Canadian
$9-$25

The comfortable eatery, which employs friendly servers, presents a varied menu that includes pasta dishes, wraps, omelets, stir-fry preparations and burgers. Portions are generous. Children's and senior selections are offered. Guests can request seating in a booth or at a table. Casual dress. **Bar:** Full bar. **Reservations:** accepted. **Hours:** 7 am-9 pm, Fri & Sat-10 pm. Closed: 12/25. **Address:** 1715 Idylwyld Dr N S7L 1B4 **Location:** On Hwy 11 (Idylwyld Dr), 0.4 mi (0.7 km) s of jct Circle Dr; in Best Western Harvest Inn. **Parking:** on-site.

SAMURAI JAPANESE RESTAURANT

Phone: 306/683-6926

Japanese
$17-$36

Finely crafted sushi and authentic tableside Teppanyaki cuisine are featured at this dining room. Casual dress. **Bar:** Full bar. **Reservations:** suggested. **Hours:** 5 pm-10 pm. Closed major holidays. **Address:** 601 Spadina Crescent E S7K 3G8 **Location:** At 21st St E; centre of downtown; in Delta Bessborough. **Parking:** on-site (fee).

THE WILLOWS DINING ROOM

Phone: 306/956-1100

Canadian
$9-$32

Grand golf course views, friendly servers and a varied menu make this restaurant a good place to simply relax and enjoy good food. Casual dress. **Bar:** Full bar. **Reservations:** accepted. **Hours:** 11 am-9 pm; hours vary in winter. Closed: 12/25; also Family Day. **Address:** 382 Cartwright St S7T 1B1 **Location:** Jct Clarence and Cartwright St, just w. **Parking:** on-site.

SHAUNAVON pop. 1,691

HIDDEN HILTEN MOTEL

Phone: 306/297-4166

Motel
$68-$86 All Year

Address: 352 5th St W S0N 2M0 **Location:** 0.3 mi (0.5 km) e of jct Hwy 37, then just n. Located in a quiet area. **Facility:** 13 one-bedroom standard units. 1 story, exterior corridors. **Parking:** on-site, winter plug-ins. **Terms:** cancellation fee imposed. **Amenities:** irons, hair dryers. **Guest Services:** wireless Internet.

SWIFT CURRENT pop. 14,946

BEST WESTERN INN & SUITES

Book great rates at AAA.com

Phone: (306)773-4660

Hotel
$139-$169 All Year

Address: 105 George St W S9H 0K4 **Location:** Jct Trans-Canada Hwy 1 and Central Ave. **Facility:** 59 units. 47 one-bedroom standard units, some with whirlpools. 12 one-bedroom suites, some with whirlpools. 2 stories (no elevator), interior corridors. *Bath:* combo or shower only. **Parking:** on-site, winter plug-ins. **Amenities:** high-speed Internet, voice mail, irons, hair dryers. **Pool(s):** heated indoor. **Leisure Activities:** sauna, whirlpools, exercise room. **Guest Services:** valet and coin laundry. **Business Services:** meeting rooms, PC. **Free Special Amenities:** expanded continental breakfast and high-speed Internet.

AAA Benefit:
Members save up to 20%, plus 10% bonus points with rewards program.

COMFORT INN

Book at AAA.com

Phone: (306)778-3994

Hotel
$95-$105 All Year

Address: 1510 S Service Rd E S9H 3X6 **Location:** On south side service road of Trans-Canada Hwy 1, just w of 22nd Ave NE. **Facility:** 74 one-bedroom standard units. 2 stories (no elevator), interior corridors. **Parking:** on-site, winter plug-ins. **Terms:** 7 day cancellation notice-fee imposed. **Amenities:** irons, hair dryers. **Guest Services:** valet laundry, wireless Internet. **Business Services:** PC.

GREEN HECTARES BED & BREAKFAST

Phone: 306/773-7632

Bed & Breakfast
$90-$120 All Year

Address: Waker Rd S9H 4M7 **Location:** Trans-Canada Hwy 1, exit 22nd Ave NE, just n to Saskatchewan Dr, e to Adaris St, then to Waker Rd. Located on a small cattle ranch, close to Cypress Regional Hospital. **Facility:** Smoke free premises. 6 one-bedroom standard units. 1 story, interior/exterior corridors. *Bath:* some shared or private, combo or shower only. **Parking:** on-site, winter plug-ins. **Terms:** office hours 7 am-10 pm. **Guest Services:** TV in common area, coin laundry. **Business Services:** meeting rooms.

HOLIDAY INN EXPRESS & SUITES   *Book at AAA.com*   Phone: 306/773-8288

Hotel
$135 All Year

Too new to rate, opening scheduled for September 2009. **Address:** 1301 N Service Rd E S9H 3X6 **Location:** Trans-Canada Hwy 1, exit Hwy 4, just w. **Amenities:** 103 units, coffeemakers, microwaves, refrigerators, pool.

SAFARI INN MOTEL   Phone: (306)773-4608

Motel
$68-$77 All Year

Address: 810 S Service Rd E S9H 3T9 **Location:** On south side service road of Trans-Canada Hwy 1, just e of Central Ave. **Facility:** 18 units. 14 one- and 4 two-bedroom standard units, some with efficiencies. 1 story, exterior corridors. **Parking:** on-site, winter plug-ins. **Terms:** office hours 7 am-11 pm. **Leisure Activities:** gas grill, picnic table. **Guest Services:** valet laundry, wireless Internet. **Business Services:** PC. **Free Special Amenities:** local telephone calls and high-speed Internet.

SUPER 8   *Book at AAA.com*   Phone: (306)778-6088

Hotel
$121-$191 All Year

Address: 405 N Service Rd E S9H 3X6 **Location:** Trans-Canada Hwy 1, just e of Central Ave N; on north side of Service Rd. **Facility:** 63 one-bedroom standard units, some with whirlpools. 2 stories (no elevator), interior corridors. **Parking:** on-site, winter plug-ins. **Amenities:** voice mail, hair dryers. **Pool(s):** heated indoor. **Leisure Activities:** whirlpool, exercise room. **Guest Services:** valet and coin laundry, wireless Internet. **Business Services:** meeting rooms.

WESTWIND MOTEL   Phone: 306/773-1441

Motel
Rates not provided

Address: 155 N Service Rd W S9H 3X6 **Location:** On north side service road of Trans-Canada Hwy 1, just w of Central Ave N. **Facility:** 36 one-bedroom standard units, some with kitchens. 1 story, exterior corridors. **Parking:** on-site, winter plug-ins. **Terms:** office hours 8 am-midnight. **Amenities:** voice mail. **Dining:** TNT Family Restaurant, see separate listing. **Pool(s):** heated outdoor. **Guest Services:** valet and coin laundry, wireless Internet.

—— **WHERE TO DINE** ——

MISO HOUSE   Phone: 306/778-4411

Japanese
$8-$17

At this modern restaurant, guests find a good selection of reasonably priced entrées, many of which include miso soup, rice and kimchee. Couples prefer the sushi boat. Casual dress. **Bar:** Beer & wine. **Reservations:** accepted. **Hours:** 11 am-10 pm, Sun 11:30 am-9:30 pm; hours may vary. Closed: 12/25. **Address:** 285 N Service Rd W S9H 3S8 **Location:** Trans-Canada Hwy 1, 0.4 mi (0.6 km) w of Hwy 4 (Central Ave). **Parking:** on-site.

SPRINGS GARDEN   Phone: 306/773-2021

American
$7-$28

The Springs Garden's decor is casual, contemporary, bright and cheerful. The menu includes a variety of popular dishes: soup, steak, chicken, seafood, pizza, ribs and Greek specialties. The server staff is friendly, efficient and prompt. Casual dress. **Bar:** Full bar. **Reservations:** suggested, Thurs-Sun. **Hours:** 8:30 am-9 pm, Sun from 9 am. Closed major holidays. **Address:** 323 1 Springs Dr S9H 3X6 **Location:** Trans-Canada Hwy 1, on north service road; in Swift Current Shopping Mall. **Parking:** on-site.

TNT FAMILY RESTAURANT   *Menu on AAA.com*   Phone: 306/773-6002

Canadian
$7-$25

Locals have long frequented the family-owned-and-operated spot for generous portions of Canadian fare, including beef, chicken and pasta dishes, and Greek favorites, such as spanakopita (spinach pie). Most seating is in booths. Casual dress. **Bar:** Full bar. **Reservations:** accepted. **Hours:** 11 am-9:30 pm, Sat from 9 am, Sun 9 am-8 pm. Closed major holidays. **Address:** 155 N Service Rd W S9H 3X6 **Location:** On north side service road of Trans-Canada Hwy 1, just w of Central Ave N; in Westwind Motel. **Parking:** on-site.

WONG'S KITCHEN   Phone: 306/773-4636

Chinese
$11-$30

Wong's Kitchen is one of the best spots in town to visit. The locally popular restaurant features Cantonese-style preparation of its dishes. The menu also offers steak and seafood selections. A smorgasbord is served noon-2 pm each day. Helpful staff. Casual dress. **Bar:** Full bar. **Reservations:** accepted. **Hours:** 11:30 am-11 pm, Sun-9 pm. Closed: 12/25, 12/26. **Address:** 320 S Service Rd E S9H 3T6 **Location:** Just e of jct Trans-Canada Hwy 1 and Hwy 4 (Central Ave). **Parking:** on-site.

WEYBURN pop. 9,433

PERFECT INNS & SUITES   Phone: 306/842-2691

Motel
$74-$170 All Year

Address: 238 Sims Ave S4H 2J8 **Location:** 0.3 mi (0.5 km) w of jct Hwy 35 and 39. Located next to McDonalds. **Facility:** 59 units. 55 one-bedroom standard units. 4 one-bedroom suites with kitchens. 1 story, interior/exterior corridors. **Parking:** on-site, winter plug-ins. **Terms:** check-in 4 pm. **Amenities:** high-speed Internet. *Some:* irons, hair dryers. **Guest Services:** valet laundry. **Business Services:** PC. **Free Special Amenities:** expanded continental breakfast and high-speed Internet.

WHERE TO DINE

T & C FAMILY RESTAURANT/DALLAS PIZZA **Phone:** 306/842-2933

Canadian
$7-$25

This restaurant offers family dining in contemporary and friendly surroundings. The menu features a wide variety of sandwiches, stir-fry, steak, seafood, pizza, souvlakia and Greek ribs. Families, couples and business people alike enjoy this eatery. Casual dress. **Bar:** Full bar. **Reservations:** accepted. **Hours:** 10 am-10 pm. Closed: 12/24, 12/25. **Address:** 72 3rd St NE S4H 0V9 **Location:** Just n of Hwy 39; centre. **Parking:** street.

YORKTON pop. 15,038

COMFORT INN & SUITES *Book at AAA.com* **Phone:** (306)783-0333

Hotel
$125-$200 7/1-2/28
$120-$190 3/1-6/30

Address: 22 Dracup Ave S3N 3W1 **Location:** Just w of jct Hwy 9, 10 and 16 (Yellowhead Hwy). **Facility:** 80 units. 64 one-bedroom standard units. 16 one-bedroom suites, some with whirlpools. 4 stories, interior corridors. **Parking:** on-site, winter plug-ins. **Amenities:** voice mail, irons, hair dryers. *Some:* DVD players, high-speed Internet. **Pool(s):** heated indoor. **Leisure Activities:** exercise room. **Guest Services:** coin laundry, wireless Internet. **Business Services:** meeting rooms.

ASK / SOME UNITS FEE

DAYS INN *Book at AAA.com* **Phone:** (306)783-3297

Hotel
$120-$190 All Year

Address: 2 Kelsey Bay S3N 3Z4 **Location:** Just e of jct Hwy 9, 10 and 16 (Yellowhead Hwy). **Facility:** 74 one-bedroom standard units, some with whirlpools. 3 stories, interior corridors. **Parking:** on-site, winter plug-ins. **Terms:** check-in 4 pm. **Amenities:** voice mail, irons, hair dryers. *Some:* DVD players, high-speed Internet. **Pool(s):** heated indoor. **Leisure Activities:** whirlpool, waterslide. **Guest Services:** coin laundry, wireless Internet. **Business Services:** meeting rooms, PC.

ECO ASK CALL / SOME UNITS FEE

RAMADA *Book great rates at AAA.com* **Phone:** (306)783-9781

CAA SAVE

Hotel
$119-$149 All Year

Address: 100 Broadway St E S3N 0K9 **Location:** On Hwy 9, 10, and 16 (Yellowhead Hwy); downtown. **Facility:** 80 units. 79 one-bedroom standard units, some with whirlpools. 1 one-bedroom suite. 2 stories (no elevator), interior corridors. *Bath:* combo or shower only. **Parking:** on-site, winter plug-ins. **Terms:** cancellation fee imposed. **Amenities:** voice mail, irons, hair dryers. *Some:* DVD players (fee). **Pool(s):** heated indoor. **Leisure Activities:** sauna, whirlpool, waterslide, exercise room. **Guest Services:** valet and coin laundry, wireless Internet. **Business Services:** conference facilities.

/ SOME UNITS FEE

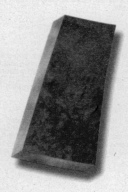

Yukon Territory

Off Dempster Hwy,
near the Arctic Circle
John E. Marriott
Getty Images

DAWSON CITY pop. 1,327

BONANZA GOLD MOTEL
Phone: 867/993-6789

Motel
$89-$189 All Year

Address: Bonanza Creek Rd Y0B 1G0 **Location:** 1.5 mi (2.4 km) s on Hwy 2. **Facility:** 45 one-bedroom standard units, some with efficiencies, kitchens and/or whirlpools. 2 stories (no elevator), exterior corridors. *Bath:* combo or shower only. **Parking:** on-site, winter plug-ins. **Terms:** office hours 7 am-8 pm, cancellation fee imposed. **Amenities:** *Some:* hair dryers. **Leisure Activities:** hiking trails. **Guest Services:** coin laundry, wireless Internet. **Business Services:** PC.

DAWSON CITY BED & BREAKFAST
Phone: 867/993-5649

(CAA) (SAVE)

Bed & Breakfast
$140-$165 All Year

Address: 451 Craig St Y0B 1G0 **Location:** Just off 7th Ave. **Facility:** Smoke free premises. 4 one-bedroom suites. 2 stories (no elevator), interior corridors. *Bath:* combo or shower only. **Parking:** on-site, winter plug-ins. **Terms:** cancellation fee imposed. **Amenities:** video library, DVD players, high-speed Internet, honor bars, hair dryers. **Leisure Activities:** library. **Guest Services:** airport transportation-Dawson City Airport, area transportation-bus station & town dock, wireless Internet. **Business Services:** PC. **Free Special Amenities:** full breakfast and high-speed Internet.

THE ELDORADO HOTEL
Phone: (867)993-5451

(CAA) (SAVE)

Motel
$130-$279 3/1-12/19 &
2/11-2/28

Address: 3rd Ave & Princess St Y0B 1G0 **Location:** Downtown. **Facility:** 40 units. 39 one-bedroom standard units, some with whirlpools. 1 one-bedroom suite with kitchen. 2 stories (no elevator), interior/exterior corridors. **Parking:** on-site, winter plug-ins. **Terms:** open 3/1-12/19 & 2/11-2/28, cancellation fee imposed. **Amenities:** voice mail. *Some:* DVD players, honor bars, irons, hair dryers. **Guest Services:** coin laundry, airport transportation-Dawson City Airport, wireless Internet. **Business Services:** PC. **Free Special Amenities:** local telephone calls and high-speed Internet.

KLONDIKE KATE'S CABINS
Phone: (867)993-6527

Cabin
$100-$160 4/15-9/30

Address: 1103 3rd Ave & King St Y0B 1G0 **Location:** Corner of 3rd Ave and King St. **Facility:** Smoke free premises. 15 cabins. 1 story, exterior corridors. *Bath:* combo or shower only. **Parking:** on-site. **Terms:** open 4/15-9/30, cancellation fee imposed. **Amenities:** voice mail. **Dining:** restaurant, see separate listing. **Guest Services:** valet laundry.

WESTMARK INN DAWSON CITY   *Book great rates at AAA.com*
Phone: (867)993-5542

(CAA) (SAVE)

Motel
$129-$169 5/18-9/7

Address: 5th Ave & Harper Y0B 1G0 **Location:** At 5th Ave and Harper St; downtown. **Facility:** Smoke free premises. 177 one-bedroom standard units. 2 stories (no elevator), interior/exterior corridors. *Bath:* combo or shower only. **Parking:** on-site. **Terms:** open 5/18-9/7, cancellation fee imposed. **Amenities:** voice mail, hair dryers. **Guest Services:** coin laundry, airport transportation-Dawson City Airport, wireless Internet. **Business Services:** PC. **Free Special Amenities:** local telephone calls.

YUKON HOTEL
Phone: (867)993-5451

Motel
$105-$160 3/1-12/19 &
2/11-2/28

Address: 5th Ave & Princess St Y0B 1G0 **Location:** Corner of 5th Ave; downtown. **Facility:** Smoke free premises. 6 one-bedroom standard units with efficiencies. 2 stories (no elevator), interior corridors. **Parking:** on-site, winter plug-ins. **Terms:** open 3/1-12/19 & 2/11-2/28, off-site registration, cancellation fee imposed. **Amenities:** voice mail. **Guest Services:** coin laundry, wireless Internet.

—— **WHERE TO DINE** ——

THE DRUNKEN GOAT TAVERNA
Phone: 867/993-5868

Traditional Greek
$12-$33

Guests can enjoy delicious, authentic Greek food created by the owner/chef amid a dining room plastered with a large, scenic mural of Greece covering the walls and ceiling. The eatery accepts only cash and traveler's checks. Casual dress. **Bar:** Beer & wine. **Reservations:** suggested. **Hours:** 5 pm-close. **Address:** 952 2nd Ave Y0B 1G0 **Location:** Center. **Parking:** street. CALL

KLONDIKE KATE'S RESTAURANT   *Menu on AAA.com*
Phone: 867/993-6527

(CAA)

American
$8-$32

Along the city's main drag a few blocks from the theater, this restaurant captures a sense of history and the gold rush era. During summer, guests can choose to eat inside or on the heated patio. The menu features an array of sandwiches, wraps and seafood and meat dishes. Casual dress. **Bar:** Full bar. **Reservations:** suggested. **Hours:** Open 4/4-9/30; 7 am-11 pm. **Address:** 3rd Ave & King St Y0B 1G0 **Location:** Corner of 3rd Ave and King St; in Klondike Kate's Cabins. **Parking:** on-site. **Historic**

HAINES JUNCTION pop. 589

ALCAN MOTOR INN
Phone: 867/634-2371

Motel
$121-$176 3/1-9/30
$110-$160 10/1-2/28

Address: Alaska & Haines Hwys Y0B 1L0 **Location:** Jct Hwy 1 (Alaska Hwy) and 3 (Haines Hwy). **Facility:** 23 units. 19 one-bedroom standard units. 4 one-bedroom suites, some with efficiencies and/or whirlpools. 2 stories (no elevator), exterior corridors. *Bath:* combo or shower only. **Parking:** on-site, winter plug-ins. **Terms:** 3 day cancellation notice-fee imposed. **Amenities:** irons, hair dryers. **Dining:** Northern Lights Steak & Seafood, see separate listing. **Guest Services:** coin laundry, wireless Internet.

——— WHERE TO DINE ———

NORTHERN LIGHTS STEAK & SEAFOOD

Phone: 867/634-2033

Steak
$8-$30

This dining room boasts a wooden interior, cathedral ceilings and views of the Alaska mountain range through each window. A talented chef creates artful presentations of in-house cuts of meat as well as fresh seafood from Haines, Ak., when available. Casual dress. **Bar:** Full bar. **Reservations:** accepted. **Hours:** 7 am-9 pm; hours may vary in winter. Closed: 12/25. **Address:** Alaska & Haines Hwys Y0B 1L0 **Location:** Jct Hwy 1 (Alaska Hwy) and 3 (Haines Hwy); in Alcan Motor Inn. **Parking:** on-site.

TESLIN pop. 141

——— WHERE TO DINE ———

DAWSON PEAKS RESORT

Phone: 867/390-2244

CAA

Canadian
$6-$27

A internationally acclaimed mystery novel made this rustic yet comfortable property renown worldwide, especially for its fresh-baked rhubarb pies. Casual dress. **Bar:** Beer & wine. **Reservations:** accepted. **Hours:** Open 6/1-8/30; 8 am-8 pm. **Address:** Box 80 Y0A 1B0 **Location:** 6 mi (10 km) s of town at KM 1232. **Parking:** on-site.

WHITEHORSE pop. 20,461

BEST WESTERN GOLD RUSH INN   *Book great rates at AAA.com*

Phone: (867)668-4500

CAA SAVE

Hotel
$145-$205 3/1-9/30
$115-$185 10/1-2/28

Address: 411 Main St Y1A 2B6 **Location:** Centre. **Facility:** Smoke free premises. 101 units. 97 one-bedroom standard units, some with whirlpools. 2 one- and 2 two-bedroom suites with kitchens. 4 stories, interior corridors. **Parking:** on-site, winter plug-ins. **Amenities:** voice mail, irons, hair dryers. **Leisure Activities:** exercise room, spa. **Guest Services:** coin laundry, airport transportation-Whitehorse International Airport, wireless Internet. **Business Services:** PC (fee). **Free Special Amenities:** local telephone calls and high-speed Internet.

AAA Benefit:
Members save up to 20%, plus 10% bonus points with rewards program.

EDGEWATER HOTEL

Phone: (867)667-2572

CAA SAVE

Hotel
$169-$189 All Year

Address: 101 Main St Y1A 2A7 **Location:** Opposite White Pass Rail Depot. **Facility:** Smoke free premises. 32 units. 27 one-bedroom standard units. 5 one-bedroom suites, some with kitchens. 3 stories (no elevator), interior corridors. **Parking:** on-site, winter plug-ins. **Terms:** 7 day cancellation notice-fee imposed. **Amenities:** high-speed Internet, dual phone lines, voice mail, irons, hair dryers. **Dining:** The Cellar Steakhouse and Wine Bar, see separate listing. **Leisure Activities:** roof top patio. **Guest Services:** valet laundry, airport transportation (fee)-Whitehorse International Airport, wireless Internet. **Business Services:** meeting rooms. **Free Special Amenities:** local telephone calls and high-speed Internet.

HIGH COUNTRY INN   *Book great rates at AAA.com*

Phone: (867)667-4471

CAA SAVE

Hotel
$169-$259 6/1-2/28
$129-$179 3/1-5/31

Address: 4051 4th Ave Y1A 1H1 **Location:** 0.4 mi (0.6 km) e of Main St. **Facility:** 83 one-bedroom standard units, some with efficiencies, kitchens and/or whirlpools. 4 stories, interior corridors. *Bath:* combo or shower only. **Parking:** on-site, winter plug-ins. **Terms:** 3 day cancellation notice-fee imposed. **Amenities:** voice mail, irons, hair dryers. *Some:* high-speed Internet. **Leisure Activities:** exercise room. **Guest Services:** valet and coin laundry, airport transportation-Whitehorse International Airport, wireless Internet. **Business Services:** conference facilities, PC (fee). **Free Special Amenities:** local telephone calls and high-speed Internet.

MIDNIGHT SUN INN/BED & BREAKFAST

Phone: (867)667-2255

Bed & Breakfast
$115-$140 All Year

Address: 6188 6th Ave Y1A 1N8 **Location:** Corner of Cook St. Located in a residential area. **Facility:** Smoke free premises. 4 one-bedroom standard units. 3 stories (no elevator), interior corridors. **Parking:** on-site, winter plug-ins. **Terms:** check-in 4 pm, 2 night minimum stay - seasonal, 7 day cancellation notice-fee imposed. **Amenities:** hair dryers. *Some:* high-speed Internet, voice mail. **Guest Services:** coin laundry, wireless Internet. **Business Services:** meeting rooms.

TOWN & MOUNTAIN HOTEL

Phone: (867)668-7644

CAA SAVE

Motel
$119-$159 3/1-10/31
$99-$119 11/1-2/28

Address: 401 Main St Y1A 2B6 **Location:** Centre. Located in downtown area. **Facility:** Smoke free premises. 30 one-bedroom standard units. 3 stories (no elevator), interior corridors. *Bath:* combo or shower only. **Parking:** on-site and street, winter plug-ins. **Terms:** 3 day cancellation notice. **Amenities:** voice mail, irons. *Some:* high-speed Internet, hair dryers. **Dining:** nightclub. **Guest Services:** airport transportation-Whitehorse International Airport, wireless Internet. **Free Special Amenities:** room upgrade (subject to availability with advance reservations) and high-speed Internet.

WESTMARK WHITEHORSE HOTEL & CONFERENCE CENTRE
Book great rates at AAA.com

Phone: (867)393-9700

Hotel
$169-$179 1/1-2/28
$159-$179 3/1-12/31

Address: 201 Wood St Y1A 2E4 **Location:** At 2nd Ave; centre. **Facility:** 180 units. 178 one-bedroom standard units. 2 one-bedroom suites. 3 stories, interior corridors. *Bath:* combo or shower only. **Parking:** on-site, winter plug-ins. **Terms:** cancellation fee imposed. **Amenities:** voice mail, irons, hair dryers. *Some:* high-speed Internet. **Leisure Activities:** exercise room. **Fee:** Frantic Follies Vaudeville Revue. **Guest Services:** valet and coin laundry, airport transportation-Whitehorse International Airport, wireless Internet, barber shop. **Business Services:** conference facilities, PC. **Free Special Amenities:** local telephone calls and high-speed Internet.

—— **WHERE TO DINE** ——

ALPINE BAKERY
Phone: 867-668-6871

Breads/Pastries
$8-$15

A short walk from the downtown core, this organic bakery features a handcrafted masonry oven that produces a whole range of fresh breads, baked goods and pizzas. Casual dress. **Hours:** 8 am-6 pm, Sat-4 pm. Closed major holidays; also Sun & Mon. **Address:** 411 Alexander St Y1A 2L8 **Location:** Jct 4th Ave. **Parking:** on-site.

THE CELLAR STEAKHOUSE AND WINE BAR
Phone: 867-667-2572

Steak
$26-$47

You'll enjoy offerings of prime rib, halibut, Alaskan king crab, steak, salmon, baby back ribs, chicken at this well-appointed, popular restaurant. Dressy casual. **Bar:** Full bar. **Reservations:** accepted. **Hours:** 3/1-12/31 & 2/15-2/28; 6 pm-10 pm. Closed major holidays; also Sun & Mon. **Address:** 101 Main St Y1A 2A7 **Location:** Opposite White Pass Rail Depot; in Edgewater Hotel. **Parking:** on-site and street.

THE CHOCOLATE CLAIM
Phone: 867-667-2202

Breads/Pastries
$5-$10

Tucked away on a side street a short distance from the downtown core, this small art gallery-style restaurant offers a range of delicious cakes and other desserts. Casual dress. **Reservations:** not accepted. **Hours:** 7:30 am-6 pm, Fri-7 pm, Sat 8:30 am-6 pm. Closed major holidays; also Sun. **Address:** 305 Strickland St Y1A 2J9 **Location:** Jct 4th Ave, just e. **Parking:** on-site.

THE DELI
Phone: 867-667-7583

Deli
$8-$9

A short walk from the downtown core, this unassuming little butcher shop offers a wide variety of prepackaged items, such as locally made sausages, pates and baked goods. Also tempting are traditional delicatessen salads and meats, which the sandwich corner uses in custom-made sandwiches that can be enjoyed on the limited tables inside or at picnic tables at the SS Klondike a few blocks away. Casual dress. **Reservations:** not accepted. **Hours:** 8:30 am-5:30 pm, Sat from 9 am. Closed major holidays; also Sun & Mon. **Address:** 203 Hanson St Y1A 1Y3 **Location:** Corner of 2nd Ave. **Parking:** street.

GIORGIO'S CUCCINA
Phone: 867-668-4050

Italian
$23-$45

The attractive dining room serves up Italian food, including thin crust pizza, fish, seafood, pasta and steaks. Many dishes are prepared on a mesquite-flavoring charbroiler. Fresh fruit smoothies and a wide selection of wines round out the menu. Casual dress. **Bar:** Full bar. **Reservations:** accepted. **Hours:** 4:30 pm-11 pm, Sun-10 pm. Closed: 12/25. **Address:** 206 Jarvis St Y1A 2H1 **Location:** Between 2nd and 3rd aves; downtown. **Parking:** on-site.

KLONDIKE RIB & SALMON BBQ
Phone: 867-667-7554

Seafood
$12-$28

This popular restaurant opens seasonally to serve regional cuisine prepared in memorable and creative manners. On the menu are Arctic char, halibut and salmon, as well as entrée-size salads and pasta dishes. Guests can eat inside, where they might share a table with other diners, or enjoy the midnight sun on the patio. **Bar:** Beer & wine. **Reservations:** suggested. **Hours:** Open 5/13-9/13; 11 am-10 pm. Closed: Sun. **Address:** 2116 2nd Ave Y1A 2B9 **Location:** Jct Main St; downtown. **Parking:** street.

MAINSTREET BACKEREI KAFFEE HAUS
Phone: 867/633-6291

Deli
$7-$10

Primarily an organic bakery, this main street mainstay is a popular gathering spot for those looking to enjoy a freshly baked pastry while sipping on a locally roasted cup of coffee. Casual dress. **Reservations:** not accepted. **Hours:** 7:30 am-6 pm. Closed major holidays. **Address:** 108-100 Main St Y1A 2A8 **Location:** Centre. **Parking:** street.

PHO LIEN
Phone: 867/633-6088

Vietnamese
$8-$12

The casual, family-run restaurant serves authentic Vietnamese cuisine. The specialty is pho, roasted meats and poultry in broth with vermicelli rice noodles. Casual dress. **Bar:** Beer & wine. **Reservations:** not accepted. **Hours:** 11 am-9 pm, Sun noon-8 pm; hours vary in winter. Closed: 1/1, 12/25. **Address:** 2190 2nd Ave, Unit 8 Y1A 5N6 **Location:** In Yukon Center Shopping Strip. **Parking:** on-site.

SANCHEZ CANTINA
Phone: 867-668-5858

Mexican
$12-$24

This casual restaurant with a seasonal terrace offers a variety of house-prepared authentic Mexican dishes, including tacos and enchiladas. Casual dress. **Bar:** Full bar. **Reservations:** suggested. **Hours:** Open 3/1-12/14 & 2/14-2/28; 11:30 am-2:30 & 5-9 pm, Sat from 5 pm. Closed major holidays; also Sun. **Address:** 211 Hanson St Y1A 1Y3 **Location:** Corner of 3rd Ave; downtown. **Parking:** street.

TASTE OF INDIA RESTAURANT
Phone: 867-668-5558

Indian
$8-$17

A short distance from the downtown area, a trip to this locally popular, family-run restaurant is well worth the effort. Guests will find vegetarian Indian cuisine using authentic spices brought from India. A buffet is offered for lunch, while dinner brings traditional dishes. Casual dress. **Bar:** Beer & wine. **Reservations:** accepted. **Hours:** 10 am-2 & 5-9 pm, Sat from 5 pm. Closed major holidays; also Sun. **Address:** 314 Ray St Y1A 5R3 **Location:** Between 3rd and 4th aves; behind Canadian Superstore. **Parking:** on-site.

Alaska

Tongass National Forest,
south of Juneau
© Mark Conlin
Larry Ulrich Stock

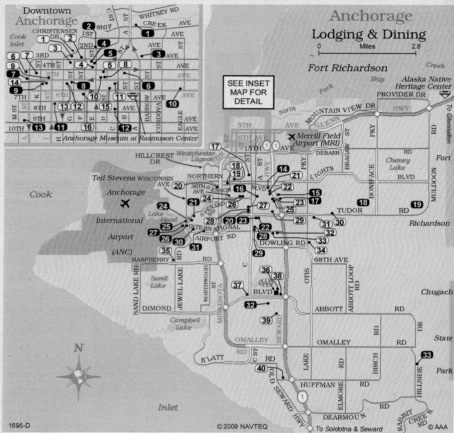

✈ Airport Accommodations

Map Page	OA	ANCHORAGE INTERNATIONAL	Diamond Rated	High Season	Page
26 / p. 756		Anchorage Airport Courtyard by Marriott, 1.7 mi e of airport	▼▼▼	$139-$249	759
27 / p. 756	AAA	**Coast International Inn, 1.8 mi e of airport**	▼▼	$74-$144 SAVE	761
30 / p. 756		Comfort Suites Anchorage International Airport, 1.6 mi e of airport	▼▼▼	Rates not provided	762
21 / p. 756		Holiday Inn Express Anchorage Airport, 1.9 mi e of airport	▼▼▼	$80-$242	765
31 / p. 756		Microtel Inn & Suites, 1.7 mi e of airport	▼▼	$160-$170	766
25 / p. 756	AAA	**Millennium Alaskan Hotel Anchorage, 1.8 mi e of airport**	▼▼▼	$149-$300 SAVE	766
24 / p. 756		Quality Inn & Suites, 1.8 mi e of airport	▼▼	$160-$180	767

Anchorage

This index helps you "spot" where approved lodgings and restaurants are located on the corresponding detailed maps. Lodging daily rate range is for comparison only and show the property's high season. Restaurant rate range is a combination of lunch and/or dinner. Turn to the listing page for more detailed rate information and consult display ads for special promotions.

ANCHORAGE

Map Page	OA	Lodgings	Diamond Rated	High Season	Page
1 / p. 756		Comfort Inn Ship Creek	▼▼▼	Rates not provided	762
2 / p. 756	AAA	**Anchorage Grand Hotel - see color ad p 760**	▼▼	$85-$205 SAVE	759
3 / p. 756	AAA	**Ramada Anchorage Downtown**	▼▼	$89-$339 SAVE	767
4 / p. 756		Hilton Anchorage .	▼▼▼	$99-$309	765
5 / p. 756	AAA	**Historic Anchorage Hotel**	▼▼	$149-$269 SAVE	765
6 / p. 756		Howard Johnson Plaza Hotel	▼▼	Rates not provided	766
7 / p. 756		Copper Whale Inn	▼▼	$85-$210	762
8 / p. 756	AAA	**Westmark Anchorage Hotel**	▼▼▼	$139-$249 SAVE	768
9 / p. 756	AAA	**Rodeway Inn Voyager Hotel**	▼▼	Rates not provided SAVE	767
10 / p. 756	AAA	**Sheraton Anchorage Hotel & SPA - see color ad p 768**	▼▼▼	$149-$369 SAVE	768
11 / p. 756		Anchorage Marriott Downtown	▼▼▼	$180-$290	759
12 / p. 756	AAA	**Quality Suites near Convention Center**	▼▼▼	$126-$209 SAVE	767
13 / p. 756	AAA	**Clarion Suites Downtown**	▼▼▼	$89-$232 SAVE	761
14 / p. 756		Embassy Suites - Anchorage	▼▼▼	$99-$399	762
15 / p. 756		Residence Inn by Marriott	▼▼▼	$169-$295	767
16 / p. 756		SpringHill Suites by Marriott	▼▼▼	$159-$269	768
17 / p. 756	AAA	**Best Western Golden Lion Hotel - see color ad p 760**	▼▼	$148-$192 SAVE	760
18 / p. 756		Camai Bed & Breakfast	▼▼▼	$55-$149	761
19 / p. 756	AAA	**Chugach Bed & Breakfast**	▼▼	$105-$140 SAVE	761
20 / p. 756		Hampton Inn-Anchorage	▼▼▼	Rates not provided	765
21 / p. 756		Holiday Inn Express Anchorage Airport	▼▼▼	$80-$242	765
22 / p. 756		Hilton Garden Inn	▼▼▼	$99-$329	765
23 / p. 756		Homewood Suites-Anchorage	▼▼▼	$229-$309	766
24 / p. 756		Quality Inn & Suites	▼▼	$160-$180	767

ANCHORAGE (cont'd)

Map Page	OA	Lodgings (cont'd)	Diamond Rated	High Season	Page
25 / p. 756	AAA	**Millennium Alaskan Hotel Anchorage** - see color ad p 766	◇◇◇	$149-$300 SAVE	766
26 / p. 756		Anchorage Airport Courtyard by Marriott	◇◇◇	$139-$249	759
27 / p. 756	AAA	**Coast International Inn**	◇◇	$74-$144 SAVE	761
28 / p. 756		Motel 6 - 4216	◇	$65-$150	766
29 / p. 756		Fairfield Inn & Suites by Marriott	◇◇◇	$119-$209	762
30 / p. 756		Comfort Suites Anchorage International Airport	◇◇◇	Rates not provided	762
31 / p. 756		Microtel Inn & Suites	◇◇	$160-$170	766
32 / p. 756	AAA	**Dimond Center Hotel** - see color ad p 763	◇◇◇	$135-$345 SAVE	762
33 / p. 756	AAA	**Highland Glen Lodge B&B**	◇◇◇	$89-$189 SAVE	765

Map Page	OA	Restaurants	Diamond Rated	Cuisine	Meal Range	Page
1 / p. 756		Snow Goose Restaurant	◇◇	American	$10-$27	772
2 / p. 756	AAA	**Marx Bros. Café**	◇◇◇◇	New American	$35-$40	771
3 / p. 756		Sack's Cafe & Restaurant	◇◇◇	International	$10-$34	771
4 / p. 756		Downtown Deli & Cafe	◇◇	Deli	$8-$15	769
5 / p. 756		Phyllis's Cafe and Salmon Bake	◇◇	American	$8-$39	771
6 / p. 756		Simon & Seaforts	◇◇◇	Regional American	$9-$46	772
7 / p. 756		Snow City Cafe	◇◇	American	$8-$13	772
8 / p. 756		Club Paris	◇◇	Steak	$9-$42	769
9 / p. 756	AAA	**Crow's Nest Restaurant**	◇◇◇	Continental	$28-$50	769
10 / p. 756		ginger	◇◇◇	Pacific Rim	$9-$33	770
11 / p. 756		Sullivan's Steakhouse	◇◇◇	Steak	$20-$40	772
12 / p. 756		Orso	◇◇◇	Regional Italian	$9-$37	771
13 / p. 756		Glacier Brewhouse	◇◇◇	American	$9-$29	770
14 / p. 756		Corsair Restaurant	◇◇◇	Continental	$23-$46	769
15 / p. 756		Crush Wine Bistro and Cellar	◇◇	Small Plates	$7-$18	769
16 / p. 756		Humpy's Great Alaskan Ale House	◇◇	American	$6-$18	770
17 / p. 756		The Greek Corner	◇◇	Greek	$9-$15	770
18 / p. 756		Sweet Basil Cafe	◇	Coffee/Tea	$5-$14	773
19 / p. 756		Middle Way Cafe	◇	Vegetarian	$5-$10	771
20 / p. 756		City Diner	◇◇	American	$8-$20	769
21 / p. 756		Kinley's Restaurant & Bar	◇◇◇	Fusion	$12-$32	770
22 / p. 756		Moose's Tooth Pub & Pizzeria	◇◇	American	$6-$10	771
23 / p. 756		Yen King Chinese Restaurant	◇	Chinese	$8-$20	773
24 / p. 756	AAA	**Jens' Restaurant**	◇◇◇	Continental	$10-$41	770
25 / p. 756		Nino's Italian Eatery	◇◇	Italian	$10-$28	771
26 / p. 756		Campobello Bistro	◇◇◇	Italian	$11-$25	769
27 / p. 756		Sea Galley	◇◇	Seafood	$10-$40	772

Map Page	OA	Restaurants (cont'd)	Diamond Rated	Cuisine	Meal Range	Page
(28) / p. 756		Pepper Mill	▼▼	American	$10-$40	771
(29) / p. 756		Aladdin's	▼▼	Mediterranean	$14-$24	769
(30) / p. 756		Thai Kitchen	▼	Thai	$8-$18	773
(31) / p. 756		Fu Do Chinese Restaurant	▼▼	Chinese	$8-$20	769
(32) / p. 756		Sourdough Mining Co	▼▼	American	$10-$30	772
(33) / p. 756		The Peanut Farm Sports Bar & Grill	▼▼	American	$10-$28	771
(34) / p. 756		Skyfire Cafe	▼▼	American	$8-$14	772
(35) / p. 756		Kincaid Grill	▼▼▼	Continental	$22-$32	770
(36) / p. 756		Henry's Great Alaskan Restaurant	▼▼	American	$8-$37	770
(37) / p. 756		Las Margaritas	▼▼	Mexican	$9-$20	770
(38) / p. 756		Sushi Ya Japanese Restaurant	▼▼	Japanese	$8-$23	772
(39) / p. 756		China Lights Oriental Cuisine	▼▼	Asian	$9-$18	769
(40) / p. 756	⟨AAA⟩	**Southside Bistro**	▼▼▼	American	$8-$33	772

ANCHORAGE pop. 260,283 (See map and index starting on p. 756)

ANCHORAGE AIRPORT COURTYARD BY MARRIOTT
Book great rates at AAA.com

Phone: (907)245-0322 **26**

▼▼▼
Hotel
$139-$249 All Year

Address: 4901 Spenard Rd 99517 **Location:** Just ne·of Jewell Lake and International Airport rds. **Facility:** Smoke free premises. 154 units. 150 one-bedroom standard units, some with whirlpools. 4 one-bedroom suites. 3 stories, interior corridors. *Bath:* combo or shower only. **Parking:** on-site. **Terms:** cancellation fee imposed. **Amenities:** high-speed Internet, dual phone lines, voice mail, irons, hair dryers. **Pool(s):** heated indoor. **Leisure Activities:** sauna, whirlpool, exercise room. **Guest Services:** valet and coin laundry, wireless Internet. **Business Services:** meeting rooms, PC.

AAA Benefit:
Members save a minimum 5% off the best available rate.

ANCHORAGE GRAND HOTEL
Book great rates at AAA.com

Phone: (907)929-8888 **2**

⟨AAA⟩ ⟨SAVE⟩
▼▼▼
Extended Stay Hotel
$85-$205 All Year

Address: 505 W 2nd Ave 99501 **Location:** Corner of 2nd Ave and E St; downtown. Across from Anchorage Market. **Facility:** Smoke free premises. 31 units. 6 one-bedroom standard units with kitchens. 25 one-bedroom suites with kitchens. 5 stories, interior corridors. **Parking:** street. **Amenities:** high-speed Internet, dual phone lines, voice mail, irons, hair dryers. **Guest Services:** coin laundry, wireless Internet. **Business Services:** business center. *(See color ad p 760)*

FREE continental breakfast and high-speed Internet

ANCHORAGE MARRIOTT DOWNTOWN
Book great rates at AAA.com

Phone: (907)279-8000 **11**

▼▼▼
Hotel
$180-$290 All Year

Address: 820 W 7th Ave 99501 **Location:** Between I and H sts. **Facility:** Smoke free premises. 392 one-bedroom standard units. 20 stories, interior corridors. *Bath:* combo or shower only. **Parking:** on-site (fee) and valet. **Terms:** cancellation fee imposed. **Amenities:** high-speed Internet (fee), dual phone lines, voice mail, irons, hair dryers. **Pool(s):** indoor. **Leisure Activities:** whirlpool, exercise room. **Guest Services:** valet laundry, wireless Internet. **Business Services:** meeting rooms, business center.

Marriott
HOTELS & RESORTS

AAA Benefit:
Members save a minimum 5% off the best available rate.

(See map and index starting on p. 756)

(See map and index starting on p. 756)

CAMAI BED & BREAKFAST

Bed & Breakfast
$55-$149 All Year

Phone: (907)333-2219   **18**

Address: 3838 Westminster Way 99508-4834 **Location:** SR 1 (Seward Hwy), 2.8 mi e on Benson/Northern Lights Blvd, 0.6 mi s on Wesleyn Dr to Queen Ct, then just e. Located in a residential area. **Facility:** The home-like B&B is located in a quiet residential area and provides guests with spacious, well-equipped rooms with a comfortable decor. Smoke free premises. 3 one-bedroom suites. 2 stories (no elevator), interior/exterior corridors. **Parking:** on-site. **Terms:** office hours 6 am-9 pm, 21 day cancellation notice-fee imposed. **Amenities:** video library, DVD players, high-speed Internet, voice mail, irons, hair dryers. **Guest Services:** wireless Internet. **Business Services:** PC.

CHUGACH BED & BREAKFAST

(AAA) (SAVE)

Bed & Breakfast
$105-$140 5/1-9/30

Phone: (907)333-4615   **19**

Address: 3901 Laron Ln 99504 **Location:** SR 1 (Seward Hwy), exit Tudor Rd, 5 mi e to Patterson St, just n to Madelynne Dr, then just e. **Facility:** Smoke free premises. 4 one-bedroom standard units, some with whirlpools. 2 stories (no elevator), interior corridors. *Bath:* some shared or private. **Parking:** on-site. **Terms:** open 5/1-9/30, office hours 8 am-8 pm, check-in 4 pm, 2 night minimum stay - seasonal, 7 day cancellation notice. **Amenities:** video library, DVD players, CD players, irons, hair dryers. **Leisure Activities:** sauna, picnic area. **Guest Services:** wireless Internet. **Business Services:** PC. **Free Special Amenities: full breakfast and high-speed Internet.**

CLARION SUITES DOWNTOWN   *Book great rates at AAA.com*

(AAA) (SAVE)

Hotel
$89-$232 All Year

Phone: (907)222-5005   **13**

Address: 1110 W 8th Ave 99501 **Location:** Corner of L St and W 8th Ave. **Facility:** Smoke free premises. 110 one-bedroom suites. 3 stories, interior corridors. *Bath:* combo or shower only. **Parking:** on-site. **Terms:** 3 day cancellation notice-fee imposed. **Amenities:** dual phone lines, voice mail, irons, hair dryers. *Fee:* video games, safes. **Pool(s):** heated indoor. **Leisure Activities:** whirlpool, limited exercise equipment. **Guest Services:** valet and coin laundry, airport transportation-Ted Stevens Anchorage International Airport, area transportation-within 3 mi, wireless Internet. **Business Services:** meeting rooms, business center. **Free Special Amenities: full breakfast and high-speed Internet.**

COAST INTERNATIONAL INN   *Book great rates at AAA.com*

(AAA) (SAVE)

Hotel
$74-$144 All Year

Phone: (907)243-2233   **27**

Address: 3450 Aviation Ave 99502 **Location:** Jct International Airport Rd, just n on Spenard Rd, then just w. **Facility:** 141 one-bedroom standard units. 2 stories (no elevator), interior corridors. *Bath:* combo or shower only. **Parking:** on-site. **Terms:** cancellation fee imposed. **Amenities:** video games (fee), high-speed Internet, dual phone lines, voice mail, irons, hair dryers. **Leisure Activities:** sauna, exercise room. **Guest Services:** valet and coin laundry, airport transportation-Ted Stevens Anchorage International Airport, wireless Internet. **Business Services:** meeting rooms, PC.

▼ See AAA listing p 798 ▼

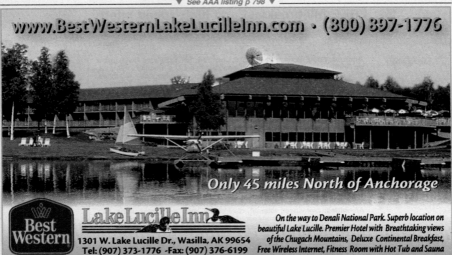

(See map and index starting on p. 756)

COMFORT INN SHIP CREEK   *Book at AAA.com*
Phone: 907/277-6887 ❶

▼▼◆▼▼
Hotel
Rates not provided

Address: 111 W Ship Creek Ave 99501 **Location:** At 3rd and E sts, 0.3 mi n on E St, across the railway, then just e; downtown. **Facility:** 100 units. 98 one-bedroom standard units, some with kitchens and/or whirlpools. 2 two-bedroom suites with kitchens and whirlpools. 3 stories, interior corridors. *Bath:* combo or shower only. **Parking:** on-site. **Terms:** check-in 4 pm. **Amenities:** video games (fee), dual phone lines, voice mail, irons, hair dryers. **Pool(s):** heated indoor. **Leisure Activities:** exercise room. **Guest Services:** valet and coin laundry, area transportation, wireless Internet. **Business Services:** PC.

COMFORT SUITES ANCHORAGE INTERNATIONAL AIRPORT   *Book at AAA.com*
Phone: 907/243-8080 ❸⓪

▼▼◆▼▼
Hotel
Rates not provided

Address: 2919 W International Airport Rd 99502 **Location:** Just e of Spenard Rd on Frontage Rd. **Facility:** Smoke free premises. 78 units. 72 one- and 4 two-bedroom standard units. 2 one-bedroom suites. 3 stories, interior corridors. *Bath:* combo or shower only. **Parking:** on-site. **Amenities:** high-speed Internet, voice mail, irons, hair dryers. **Pool(s):** heated indoor. **Leisure Activities:** whirlpool, exercise room. **Guest Services:** wireless Internet. **Business Services:** business center.

COPPER WHALE INN
Phone: (907)258-7999 ❼

▼▼ ▼▼
Bed & Breakfast
$85-$210 All Year

Address: 440 L St 99501 **Location:** Jct W 4th Ave; downtown. Located in a commercial area. **Facility:** Smoke free premises. 14 one-bedroom standard units. 2 stories (no elevator), interior corridors. *Bath:* some shared or private, shower or tub only. **Parking:** no self-parking. **Terms:** office hours 7 am-9 pm, 7 day cancellation notice. **Amenities:** hair dryers. *Some:* irons. **Leisure Activities:** rental bicycles. **Guest Services:** coin laundry, wireless Internet. **Business Services:** PC.

CROWNE PLAZA ANCHORAGE-MIDTOWN   *Book at AAA.com*
Phone: 907/433-4100

[fyi]
Hotel
$139-$249 All Year

Too new to rate. **Address:** 109 W International Airport Rd 99518 **Location:** Jct C St, just n on A St. **Amenities:** 165 units, restaurant, coffeemakers, microwaves, refrigerators, pool. **Terms:** cancellation fee imposed.

DIMOND CENTER HOTEL   *Book great rates at AAA.com*
Phone: (907)770-5000 ❸❷

(AAA) [SAVE]
▼▼◆▼▼
Hotel
$135-$345 All Year

Address: 700 E Dimond Blvd 99515 **Location:** SR 1 (Seward Hwy), exit Dimond Blvd, just w, then s on Dimond Center Dr. **Facility:** Smoke free premises. 109 one-bedroom standard units, some with whirlpools. 3 stories, interior corridors. **Parking:** on-site. **Terms:** 3 day cancellation notice-fee imposed. **Amenities:** CD players, high-speed Internet, dual phone lines, voice mail, irons, hair dryers. **Guest Services:** valet and coin laundry, airport transportation-Ted Stevens Anchorage International Airport, area transportation-train station, wireless Internet. **Business Services:** meeting rooms, business center. *(See color ad p 763)*

FREE full breakfast and high-speed Internet

EMBASSY SUITES - ANCHORAGE   *Book great rates at AAA.com*
Phone: (907)332-7000 ❶❹

▼▼◆▼▼
Hotel
$99-$399 All Year

Address: 600 E Benson Blvd 99503 **Location:** SR 1 (Seward Hwy), just w on Northern Lights Blvd, just s on Denali St, then just e. **Facility:** 169 units. 165 one- and 4 two-bedroom suites, some with whirlpools. 4 stories, interior corridors. *Bath:* combo or shower only. **Parking:** on-site. **Terms:** 1-7 night minimum stay, cancellation fee imposed. **Amenities:** dual phone lines, voice mail, irons, hair dryers. **Pool(s):** heated indoor. **Leisure Activities:** whirlpool, exercise room. **Guest Services:** valet and coin laundry, area transportation, wireless Internet. **Business Services:** meeting rooms, business center.

E
EMBASSY SUITES
HOTELS
AAA Benefit:
Members save 5% or more everyday!

FAIRFIELD INN & SUITES BY MARRIOTT   *Book great rates at AAA.com*
Phone: (907)222-9000 ❷❾

▼▼◆▼▼
Hotel
$119-$209 All Year

Address: 5060 A St 99503 **Location:** Jct C St, just e on International Airport Rd, then just n. **Facility:** Smoke free premises. 106 one-bedroom standard units, some with whirlpools. 4 stories, interior corridors. *Bath:* combo or shower only. **Parking:** on-site. **Terms:** cancellation fee imposed. **Amenities:** high-speed Internet, dual phone lines, voice mail, irons, hair dryers. **Pool(s):** heated indoor. **Leisure Activities:** whirlpool, limited exercise equipment. **Guest Services:** valet and coin laundry, wireless Internet. **Business Services:** PC.

FAIRFIELD
INN & SUITES
Marriott
AAA Benefit:
Members save a minimum 5% off the best available rate.

(See map and index starting on p. 756)

▼ See AAA listing p 762 ▼

(See map and index starting on p. 756)

▼ See AAA listing p 782 ▼

(See map and index starting on p. 756)

HAMPTON INN-ANCHORAGE *Book great rates at AAA.com* Phone: 907/550-7000 **20**

Hotel
Rates not provided

Address: 4301 Credit Union Dr 99503 **Location:** Corner of Tudor Rd and C St. **Facility:** Smoke free premises. 101 one-bedroom standard units, some with whirlpools. 3 stories, interior corridors. *Bath:* combo or shower only. **Parking:** on-site. **Amenities:** video games (fee), dual phone lines, voice mail, irons, hair dryers. **Pool(s):** heated indoor. **Leisure Activities:** whirlpool, exercise room. **Guest Services:** valet and coin laundry, area transportation, wireless Internet. **Business Services:** meeting rooms, PC.

AAA Benefit:
Members save up to 10% everyday!

HIGHLAND GLEN LODGE B&B Phone: (907)336-2312 **33**

Bed & Breakfast
$89-$189 All Year

Address: 11651 Hillside Dr 99507 **Location:** SR 1 (Seward Hwy), exit O'Mally Rd, 3.7 mi e, then 0.5 mi s. **Facility:** This lovely Tudor-style home offers guests comfortable accommodations in an attractive country setting; the rooms are spacious and well equipped. Smoke free premises. 5 one-bedroom standard units, some with whirlpools. 2 stories (no elevator), interior corridors. *Bath:* combo or shower only. **Parking:** on-site. **Terms:** office hours 6 am-8 pm, check-in 5 pm, 30 day cancellation notice-fee imposed. **Amenities:** video library, DVD players, hair dryers. *Some:* CD players, irons. **Leisure Activities:** whirlpool. **Guest Services:** wireless Internet. **Business Services:** PC. **Free Special Amenities:** full breakfast and high-speed Internet.

HILTON ANCHORAGE *Book great rates at AAA.com* Phone: (907)272-7411 **4**

Hotel
$99-$309 All Year

Address: 500 W 3rd Ave 99501 **Location:** At E St; downtown. **Facility:** 606 units. 596 one-bedroom standard units. 10 one-bedroom suites. 15-22 stories, interior corridors. *Bath:* combo or shower only. **Parking:** on-site (fee) and valet. **Terms:** 1-7 night minimum stay, cancellation fee imposed. **Amenities:** dual phone lines, voice mail, irons, hair dryers. *Fee:* video games, high-speed Internet. **Pool(s):** heated indoor. **Leisure Activities:** whirlpool, steamrooms, exercise room. **Guest Services:** valet laundry, wireless Internet. **Business Services:** conference facilities, business center.

Hilton
AAA Benefit:
Members save 5% or more everyday!

HILTON GARDEN INN *Book great rates at AAA.com* Phone: (907)729-7000 **22**

Hotel
$99-$329 All Year

Address: 4555 Union Square Dr 99503 **Location:** SR 1 (Seward Hwy), exit Tudor Rd, 0.8 mi w; U-turn at C St, then just s. **Facility:** 125 one-bedroom standard units, some with whirlpools. 4 stories, interior corridors. *Bath:* combo or shower only. **Parking:** on-site. **Terms:** 1-7 night minimum stay, cancellation fee imposed. **Amenities:** video games (fee), high-speed Internet, dual phone lines, voice mail, irons, hair dryers. **Pool(s):** heated indoor. **Leisure Activities:** whirlpool, exercise room. **Guest Services:** valet and coin laundry, area transportation, wireless Internet. **Business Services:** meeting rooms, business center.

Hilton Garden Inn
AAA Benefit:
Members save 5% or more everyday!

HISTORIC ANCHORAGE HOTEL *Book great rates at AAA.com* Phone: (907)272-4553 **5**

Historic
Hotel
$149-$269 All Year

Address: 330 E St 99501 **Location:** Between 4th and 3rd sts. **Facility:** The hotel was established in 1916, the inn features charming standard rooms that are compact, or more spacious suites that feature a sitting area. Smoke free premises. 26 one-bedroom standard units. 3 stories, interior corridors. **Parking:** no self-parking. **Terms:** 7 day cancellation notice-fee imposed. **Amenities:** voice mail, irons, hair dryers. **Leisure Activities:** limited exercise equipment. **Guest Services:** valet laundry, wireless Internet. **Business Services:** meeting rooms, PC. **Free Special Amenities:** expanded continental breakfast and high-speed Internet.

HOLIDAY INN EXPRESS ANCHORAGE AIRPORT *Book at AAA.com* Phone: (907)248-8848 **21**

Hotel
$80-$242 All Year

Address: 4411 Spenard Rd 99517 **Location:** 0.5 mi ne of Jewell Lake and International Airport rds. **Facility:** Smoke free premises. 129 one-bedroom standard units, some with whirlpools. 3 stories, interior corridors. *Bath:* combo or shower only. **Parking:** on-site. **Amenities:** video games (fee), high-speed Internet, dual phone lines, voice mail, irons, hair dryers. **Pool(s):** heated indoor. **Leisure Activities:** whirlpool, exercise room. **Guest Services:** valet and coin laundry, wireless Internet. **Business Services:** business center.

(See map and index starting on p. 756)

HOMEWOOD SUITES-ANCHORAGE   *Book great rates at AAA.com*   Phone: (907)762-7000   **23**

Extended Stay
Hotel
$229-$309 All Year

Address: 101 W 48th Ave 99503 **Location:** SR 1 (Seward Hwy), exit Tudor Rd, 0.8 mi w, U-turn at C St, then just s on Union Square Dr. **Facility:** 122 units. 47 one-bedroom standard units with efficiencies. 71 one- and 4 two-bedroom suites with efficiencies. 4 stories, interior corridors. *Bath:* combo or shower only. **Parking:** on-site. **Terms:** 1-7 night minimum stay, cancellation fee imposed. **Amenities:** video games (fee), high-speed Internet, dual phone lines, voice mail, irons, hair dryers. *Some:* DVD players (fee). **Pool(s):** heated indoor. **Leisure Activities:** whirlpool, exercise room, basketball. **Guest Services:** valet and coin laundry, area transportation, wireless Internet. **Business Services:** meeting rooms, business center.

AAA Benefit:
Members save 5% or
more everyday!

[icons] / SOME UNITS

HOWARD JOHNSON PLAZA HOTEL   *Book at AAA.com*   Phone: 907-793-5500   **6**

Hotel
Rates not provided

Address: 239 W 4th Ave 99501 **Location:** At 3rd Ave and C St; downtown. **Facility:** 247 one-bedroom standard units. 3 stories, interior corridors. *Bath:* combo or shower only. **Parking:** on-site. **Amenities:** voice mail, safes (fee), irons, hair dryers. **Pool(s):** heated indoor. **Leisure Activities:** exercise room. **Guest Services:** valet and coin laundry, wireless Internet. **Business Services:** meeting rooms, PC.

[icons] / SOME UNITS

MICROTEL INN & SUITES   *Book at AAA.com*   Phone: (907)245-5002   **31**

Motel
$160-$170 3/1-9/30
$75-$85 10/1-2/28

Address: 5205 Northwood Dr 99517 **Location:** Jct International Airport Rd, just n. **Facility:** 79 one-bedroom standard units, some with whirlpools. 3 stories, interior corridors. *Bath:* combo or shower only. **Parking:** on-site. **Terms:** check-in 4 pm. **Amenities:** video games (fee). *Some:* irons, hair dryers. **Leisure Activities:** whirlpools. **Guest Services:** valet and coin laundry, wireless Internet. **Business Services:** PC.

[icons] / SOME UNITS FEE

MILLENNIUM ALASKAN HOTEL ANCHORAGE   *Book great rates at AAA.com*   Phone: (907)243-2300   **25**

Hotel
$149-$300 All Year

Address: 4800 Spenard Rd 99517 **Location:** Jct International Airport Rd, just n. **Facility:** Smoke free premises. 245 one-bedroom standard units. 2 one-bedroom suites with whirlpools. 4 stories, interior corridors. *Bath:* combo or shower only. **Parking:** on-site. **Terms:** cancellation fee imposed. **Amenities:** dual phone lines, voice mail, irons, hair dryers. *Fee:* video games, high-speed Internet. **Leisure Activities:** sauna, whirlpool, rental bicycles, exercise room. **Guest Services:** valet and coin laundry, airport transportation-Ted Stevens Anchorage International Airport, area transportation-Dimond Center Mall and downtown, wireless Internet. **Business Services:** conference facilities, business center. *(See color ad below)*

[icons] / SOME UNITS FEE

MOTEL 6 - 4216   *Book at AAA.com*   Phone: (907)677-8000   **28**

Motel
$65-$150 All Year

Address: 5000 A St 99503 **Location:** Jct C St, just e on International Airport Rd, then just n. **Facility:** 85 one-bedroom standard units. 3 stories, interior corridors. *Bath:* combo or shower only. **Parking:** on-site. **Amenities:** high-speed Internet, voice mail. **Guest Services:** coin laundry, wireless Internet.

[icons] / SOME UNITS

▼ *See AAA listing above* ▼

(See map and index starting on p. 756)

QUALITY INN & SUITES   *Book at AAA.com*   Phone: (907)243-3131   **24**

Hotel
$160-$180 5/15-2/28
$70-$100 3/1-5/14

Address: 4615 Spenard Rd 99517-3299 **Location:** International Airport Rd; just ne of jct Jewel Lake and Spenard rds. **Facility:** Smoke free premises. 122 one-bedroom standard units, some with efficiencies. 2-5 stories, interior corridors. **Parking:** on-site. **Terms:** cancellation fee imposed. **Amenities:** voice mail, irons, hair dryers. **Leisure Activities:** exercise room. **Guest Services:** valet and coin laundry, area transportation, wireless Internet. **Business Services:** meeting rooms, PC.

QUALITY SUITES NEAR CONVENTION CENTER   *Book great rates at AAA.com*   Phone: (907)274-1000   **12**

Hotel
$126-$209 6/1-2/28
$108-$126 3/1-5/31

Address: 325 W 8th Ave 99501 **Location:** Corner of C St and W 8th Ave. **Facility:** Smoke free premises. 110 one-bedroom suites. 3 stories, interior corridors. *Bath:* combo or shower only. **Parking:** on-site. **Terms:** 3 day cancellation notice-fee imposed. **Amenities:** high-speed Internet, dual phone lines, voice mail, irons, hair dryers, safes. *Fee:* video games, safes. **Pool(s):** heated indoor. **Leisure Activities:** whirlpool, exercise room. **Guest Services:** valet and coin laundry, airport transportation-Ted Stevens Anchorage International Airport, area transportation-train depot, wireless Internet. **Business Services:** meeting rooms, business center. **Free Special Amenities: full breakfast and high-speed Internet.**

RAMADA ANCHORAGE DOWNTOWN   *Book great rates at AAA.com*   Phone: (907)272-7561   **3**

Motel
$89-$339 All Year

Address: 115 E 3rd Ave 99501 **Location:** Jct Barrow St; downtown. **Facility:** 90 one-bedroom standard units, some with whirlpools. 3 stories, interior/exterior corridors. *Bath:* combo or shower only. **Parking:** on-site. **Terms:** cancellation fee imposed. **Amenities:** high-speed Internet, voice mail, safes (fee), irons, hair dryers. **Leisure Activities:** exercise room. **Guest Services:** valet and coin laundry, wireless Internet. **Business Services:** meeting rooms, PC. **Free Special Amenities: expanded continental breakfast.**

RESIDENCE INN BY MARRIOTT   *Book great rates at AAA.com*   Phone: (907)563-9844   **15**

Extended Stay
Hotel
$169-$295 All Year

Address: 1025 E 35th Ave 99508 **Location:** Corner of SR 1 (Seward Hwy) and 36th Ave. **Facility:** Smoke free premises. 148 units. 56 one-bedroom standard units, some with efficiencies or kitchens. 56 one- and 36 two-bedroom suites, some with efficiencies or kitchens. 3 stories, interior corridors. *Bath:* combo or shower only. **Parking:** on-site. **Terms:** cancellation fee imposed. **Amenities:** video games (fee), high-speed Internet, voice mail, irons, hair dryers. *Some:* dual phone lines. **Pool(s):** heated indoor. **Leisure Activities:** whirlpool, exercise room, sports court. **Guest Services:** valet and coin laundry, area transportation, wireless Internet. **Business Services:** meeting rooms, business center.

AAA Benefit:
Members save a minimum 5% off the best available rate.

RODEWAY INN VOYAGER HOTEL   *Book great rates at AAA.com*   Phone: 907/277-9501   **9**

Hotel
Rates not provided

Address: 501 K St 99501 **Location:** At K St and 5th Ave; downtown. **Facility:** Smoke free premises. 40 one-bedroom standard units. 4 stories, interior corridors. *Bath:* combo or shower only. **Parking:** on-site (fee). **Amenities:** high-speed Internet, dual phone lines, voice mail, hair dryers. **Dining:** Corsair Restaurant, see separate listing. **Guest Services:** valet and coin laundry, wireless Internet. **Business Services:** PC. **Free Special Amenities: continental breakfast and high-speed Internet.**

(See map and index starting on p. 756)

SHERATON ANCHORAGE HOTEL & SPA   *Book great rates at AAA.com*   Phone: (907)276-8700   **10**

Hotel
$149-$369 All Year

Address: 401 E 6th Ave 99501 **Location:** 6th Ave and Denali St. **Facility:** Smoke free premises. 370 one-bedroom standard units. 16 stories, interior corridors. *Bath:* combo or shower only. **Parking:** on-site (fee) and valet. **Amenities:** high-speed Internet (fee), voice mail, irons, hair dryers. **Leisure Activities:** exercise room, spa. **Guest Services:** valet laundry, area transportation-downtown, wireless Internet. **Business Services:** conference facilities, business center. *(See color ad below)*

AAA Benefit:
Members get up to 15% off, plus Starwood Preferred Guest® bonuses.

FREE local telephone calls

SPRINGHILL SUITES BY MARRIOTT   *Book great rates at AAA.com*   Phone: (907)562-3247   **16**

Hotel
$159-$269 All Year

Address: 3401 A St 99503 **Location:** Corner of 36th Ave and A St. **Facility:** Smoke free premises. 101 one-bedroom standard units. 3 stories, interior corridors. *Bath:* combo or shower only. **Parking:** on-site. **Terms:** cancellation fee imposed. **Amenities:** high-speed Internet, voice mail, irons, hair dryers. **Pool(s):** heated indoor. **Leisure Activities:** whirlpool, limited exercise equipment. **Guest Services:** valet and coin laundry, wireless Internet. **Business Services:** business center.

AAA Benefit:
Members save a minimum 5% off the best available rate.

WESTMARK ANCHORAGE HOTEL   *Book great rates at AAA.com*   Phone: (907)276-7676   **8**

Hotel
$139-$249 All Year

Address: 720 W 5th Ave 99501 **Location:** At G St and W 5th Ave; downtown. **Facility:** Smoke free premises. 200 one-bedroom standard units. 14 stories, interior corridors. *Bath:* combo or shower only. **Parking:** on-site (fee). **Terms:** cancellation fee imposed. **Amenities:** dual phone lines, voice mail, irons, hair dryers. **Leisure Activities:** exercise room. **Guest Services:** valet laundry, wireless Internet. **Business Services:** meeting rooms, PC. **Free Special Amenities:** local telephone calls and high-speed Internet.

▼ See AAA listing above ▼

See map and index starting on p. 756)

—— WHERE TO DINE ——

ALADDIN'S
▼▼▼
Mediterranean
$14-$24

Phone: 907/561-2373 ㉙

Menu offerings range from Greek and Middle Eastern dishes to Indian and French-influenced fare. Vegetarians and vegans will find selections sharing menu space with lamb, chicken, beef and seafood selections. Casual dress. **Bar:** Beer & wine. **Reservations:** required. **Hours:** 5 pm-10 pm. Closed: 11/25, 12/25; also Sun-Tues. **Address:** 4240 Old Seward Hwy 99503 **Location:** Jct Tudor Rd, just n; in City Center Mall. **Parking:** on-site.

CAMPOBELLO BISTRO
▼▼▼
Italian
$11-$25

Phone: 907/563-2040 ㉖

A true gem is hidden in the Midtown roadside mall. The elegantly simple dining room is a perfect place for a casual yet romantic meal. Italian cooking, including various preparations of pasta and seafood, reflects an Alaskan flair. Casual dress. **Bar:** Beer & wine. **Reservations:** suggested. **Hours:** 11 am-2:30 & 5-9 pm, Sat from 5 pm, Mon 11 am-2:30 pm. Closed major holidays; also Sun. **Address:** 601 W 36th Ave 99503 **Location:** Jct Arctic Blvd, just e; in Bering Village Shopping Center. **Parking:** on-site. CALL &M ᴷ

CHINA LIGHTS ORIENTAL CUISINE
▼▼ ▼▼
Asian
$9-$18

Phone: 907/522-5888 ㊴

Diners can fill up at this Asian buffet boasting more than 100 dishes from China, Japan, Thailand and Vietnam. An a la carte menu also is available. Casual dress. **Bar:** Beer & wine. **Reservations:** accepted. **Hours:** 11 am-8:30 pm, Fri & Sat-9 pm, Sun 10 am-8 pm. Closed major holidays. **Address:** 9220 Old Seward Hwy 99515 **Location:** Just s of E Dimond Blvd. **Parking:** on-site.

CITY DINER
▼▼ ▼▼
American
$8-$20

Phone: 907/277-2489 ⑳

This slick, shiny, mirrored and glassed '50s-style diner offers all the classic items, like meatloaf, chicken fried steak, burgers, all kinds of sandwiches and a good variety of salads. The diner corn chowder is thick and scrumptious. The place is bustling, and folks gather in the mornings for great diner breakfasts. Soda fountain desserts, pies and cakes finish off the menu. Casual dress. **Bar:** Beer & wine. **Reservations:** not accepted. **Hours:** 6 am-11 pm. Closed: 1/1, 11/25, 12/25. **Address:** 3000 Minnesota Dr 99503 **Location:** Corner of Minnesota Dr and W Benson Blvd. **Parking:** on-site. CALL &M

CLUB PARIS
▼▼ ▼▼
Steak
$9-$42

Phone: 907/277-6332 ⑧

Home to the locally renowned four-inch filet mignon, the longstanding downtown restaurant—established in 1957 and said to be the oldest steakhouse in the city—is a favorite of visitors and locals alike. The dimly lit dining room, with its dark upholstery and padded booths, has a loungelike feel. In addition to a good selection of steaks, the menu also lists Alaskan seafood options. Casual dress. **Bar:** Full bar. **Reservations:** suggested. **Hours:** 11:30 am-2:30 & 5-10 pm, Fri & Sat-11 pm, Sun 5 pm-10 pm. Closed: 11/25, 12/25. **Address:** 417 W 5th Ave 99501 **Location:** Between D and E sts; downtown. **Parking:** street. ᴷ

CORSAIR RESTAURANT
▼▼ ▼▼
Continental
$23-$46

Phone: 907/278-4502 ⑭

The restaurant has provided its guests a fine dining experience since 1979. Fresh Alaskan seafood, veal, steak and rack of lamb are menu highlights. The dining room decor is nautical but romantic with impressive, fabric-upholstered booths acting as a focal point. The elegant table appointments and tuxedoed wait staff give hint to the special dining experience offered here. Casual dress. **Bar:** Full bar. **Reservations:** suggested. **Hours:** 5 pm-10 pm, Fri & Sat-11 pm. Closed major holidays; also Sun. **Address:** 944 W 5th Ave 99501 **Location:** At K St and 5th Ave; downtown; in The Voyager Hotel. **Parking:** street. CALL &M

CROW'S NEST RESTAURANT   *Menu on AAA.com*
◈◈◈
▼▼ ▼▼
Continental
$28-$50

Phone: 907/276-6000 ⑨

Perched high on the 20th floor of The Hotel Captain Cook, the restaurant affords panoramic mountain and Cook Inlet views, especially on long summer days. Service is attentive and formal but unstuffy. The menu's accent is on seafood, although it also offers an excellent variety of meats and exotic foods, such as Caspian Sea caviar, truffles, foie gras and seaweed. The excellent wine cellar houses more than 10,000 bottles. Casual dress. **Bar:** Full bar. **Reservations:** suggested. **Hours:** 5:30 pm-9:30 pm. Closed major holidays; also Sun. **Address:** 939 W 5th Ave 99501 **Location:** Between I and K sts; downtown; in The Hotel Captain Cook. **Parking:** on-site and valet. CALL &M

CRUSH WINE BISTRO AND CELLAR
▼▼ ▼▼
Small Plates
$7-$18

Phone: 907/865-9198 ⑮

This tiny but wonderfully delightful wine bar and tapas restaurant features first-class wines by the glass along with a menu of very reasonably priced items—lunch for $10, dinner items for $14—meant for sharing. Casual dress. **Bar:** Beer & wine. **Hours:** 11:30 am-2:30 & 5-10 pm, Fri-midnight, Sat 5 pm-midnight. Closed major holidays; also Sun. **Address:** 343 W 6th St 99501 **Location:** Corner of W 6th Ave and D St; across from Nordstrom. **Parking:** street. CALL &M

DOWNTOWN DELI & CAFE
▼▼ ▼▼
Deli
$8-$15

Phone: 907/276-7116 ④

Across from the downtown visitor's center, this popular eatery is known for its huge portions and all-day breakfast items. An excellent choice is the sourdough pancakes, prepared using a sourdough recipe received from an Alaskan gold miner in 1939. Casual dress. **Bar:** Wine only. **Reservations:** not accepted. **Hours:** 6 am-10 pm; 7 am-3 pm 10/1-4/30. Closed major holidays. **Address:** 525 W 4th Ave 99501-2211 **Location:** Between F and E sts; across from Log Cabin Visitors Center; downtown. **Parking:** street. ᴷ

FU DO CHINESE RESTAURANT
▼▼ ▼▼
Chinese
$8-$20

Phone: 907/561-6611 ㉛

A good mix of Cantonese, Mandarin and Szechuan selections is offered at this restaurant. The crispy duck, orange beef and sesame chicken are good choices. The attractive dining room is situated in a brightly decorated building in a commercial area. Casual dress. **Bar:** Full bar. **Reservations:** accepted. **Hours:** 11 am-10 pm, Fri & Sat-11 pm. Closed: 11/25; also Mon. **Address:** 2600 E Tudor Rd 99507 **Location:** Jct Old Seward Hwy, 1 mi e. **Parking:** on-site.

(See map and index starting on p. 756)

GINGER

Phone: 907/929-3680   10

WWWW
Pacific Rim
$9-$33

This contemporary, bustling restaurant features Pacific Rim cuisine utilizing regional and local produce and Alaskan seafood. Signature items include the panang beef curry, and the menu also lists duck breast, Alaskan sea scallops, ahi tuna and filet mignon. All the desserts are prepared in house. Casual dress. **Bar:** Beer & wine. **Reservations:** suggested. **Hours:** 11:30 am-2 & 5:30-9 pm. Closed: 4/4, 11/25, 12/25; also for lunch Sat & Sun. **Address:** 425 W 5th Ave 99501 **Location:** Between D and E sts; across from JC Penney. **Parking:** street.

GLACIER BREWHOUSE

Phone: 907/274-2739   13

WWWW
American
$9-$29

With a large stone fireplace as its focal point, the decor blends contemporary, industrial and rustic themes, creating an inviting, yet bustling, room. Large beer-brewing vats producing a number of tasty brews loom behind glass walls. Varied seafood and alder wood-fired rotisserie meat dishes, pizzas, sandwiches, salads and pastas are served in generous portions. Seasonal salmon is the standout, but dinner prime rib, barbecue pork ribs, bread pudding and peanut butter pie are plenty tempting. Casual dress. **Bar:** Full bar. **Reservations:** suggested. **Hours:** 11 am-10 pm, Sun from noon. Closed: 7/4, 11/25, 12/25. **Address:** 737 W 5th Ave, Suite 110 99501 **Location:** At H St; downtown. **Parking:** street.

THE GREEK CORNER

Phone: 907/276-2820   17

WWW
Greek
$9-$15

Folks might miss the small, family-run restaurant, one of the city's best-kept secrets. The menu lists both Greek and Italian cuisine, and there is something for everyone. Guests are greeted warmly, whether they are there all the time or for their first visit, and the service is friendly. Portions are hearty. The casual, traditional atmosphere is family-friendly. Casual dress. **Bar:** Beer & wine. **Hours:** 11 am-10 pm, Sat from noon, Sun from 4 pm. Closed major holidays. **Address:** 302 W Fireweed Ln 99503 **Location:** Corner of W Fireweed Ln and C St. **Parking:** on-site.

HENRY'S GREAT ALASKAN RESTAURANT

Phone: 907/770-0500   36

WWW
American
$8-$37

The lengthy menu draws a crowd at this casual eatery. Diners have a choice of burgers, sandwiches, steaks, pasta and such fresh seafood as Alaska scallops, salmon and halibut. Specialties include breaded and fried seafood, prime rib, barbecue baby back ribs and bouillabaisse. Casual dress. **Bar:** Full bar. **Hours:** 11:30 am-9:30 pm, Fri-10:30 pm, Sat noon-10:30 pm, Sun 3 pm-9:30 pm. Closed: 11/25, 12/25. **Address:** 8001 Old Seward Hwy 99518 **Location:** SR 1 (Seward Hwy), just w on Dimond Rd, then just n. **Parking:** on-site.

HUMPY'S GREAT ALASKAN ALE HOUSE

Phone: 907/276-2337   16

WWW
American
$6-$18

With an impressive selection of Alaskan microbrewed beers, this casual ale house is a favorite among locals. A menu with extraordinary pub fare lists a variety of sandwiches, burgers and pastas, plus dinner entrees of steak and Alaskan halibut and salmon. House-made desserts are worth the calories. Patio seating can be requested in season, and local bands often perform for an enthusiastic crowd. Those under 21 years of age are only allowed from 11 am-9 pm and must be accompanied by a parent. Casual dress. Entertainment. **Bar:** Full bar. **Reservations:** not accepted. **Hours:** 11 am-midnight, Fri & Sat-1 am. Closed: 1/1, 4/4, 12/25. **Address:** 610 W 6th Ave 99501 **Location:** Between F and G sts; downtown. **Parking:** street.

JENS' RESTAURANT

Phone: 907/561-5367   24

AAA
WWW
Continental
$10-$41

Danish by day and international by night, the cozy, bistro-style restaurant, which includes a casual tapas bar, is one of the city's finest. Local artists are featured, and the casual side has a stool bar where guests can enjoy a glass of wine from the extensive wine list. The eclectic, monthly changing menu relies heavily on local ingredients and flavors, which the talented chef prepares with his own twist. Casual dress. **Bar:** Full bar. **Reservations:** suggested. **Hours:** Open 3/1-12/31 & 2/1-2/28; 11:30 am-2 & 6-10 pm, Mon from 6 pm. Closed major holidays; also Sun. **Address:** 701 W 36th Ave 99503 **Location:** Just e of Arctic Blvd and W 36th Ave; in Olympic Center. **Parking:** on-site.

KINCAID GRILL

Phone: 907/243-0507   35

WWWW
Continental
$22-$32

It's no surprise that locals flock to this popular restaurant featuring a contemporary decor and innovative menu. Diners enjoy the carefully planned a la carte options or the chef's changing tasting menu paired with wines from the extensive wine list. Highlights include Alaska oyster or Kodiak scallops to start, followed by a seafood fusion soup or Caprese salad. A wide selection of local fish and seafood is paired with some creative sauces, and there are meat, game and poultry offerings. Casual dress. **Bar:** Full bar. **Reservations:** suggested. **Hours:** 5 pm-10 pm. Closed major holidays; also Sun & Mon. **Address:** 6700 Jewel Lake Rd 99502 **Location:** Jct Raspberry. **Parking:** on-site.

KINLEY'S RESTAURANT & BAR

Phone: 907/644-8953   21

WWWW
Fusion
$12-$32

Guests of this popular gathering spot will find an award-winning wine bar and innovative fare sure to tempt the taste buds. Examples of entrees that may be found include almond-crusted halibut with cherry and apple cider beurre blanc, or pan-seared pork tenderloin with brandied rhubarb pan jus. Hearty sandwiches and salads hit the spot at lunch. Casual dress. **Bar:** Beer & wine. **Hours:** 11:30 am-11 pm. Closed: 12/25; also Sun & Mon. **Address:** 3230 Seward Hwy 99503 **Location:** Jct 36th Ave, just n on SR 1. **Parking:** on-site.

LAS MARGARITAS

Phone: 907/349-4922   37

WWW
Mexican
$9-$20

A little out of the way but well worth the drive, this restaurant has a charming, casual country-style ambiance. The cuisine features popular Mexican and Italian specialties including burritos, spaghetti, pizza, steak and shrimp. Casual dress. **Bar:** Full bar. **Reservations:** suggested. **Hours:** 4 pm-10:30 pm, Sun-10 pm. Closed major holidays. **Address:** 541 W Dimond 99515 **Location:** Between Arctic Blvd and C St. **Parking:** on-site.

(See map and index starting on p. 756)

MARX BROS. CAFÉ

Phone: 907/278-2133 [2]

New American
$35-$40

For a truly exquisite meal, look no further than the dining rooms of this renovated 1916 home. Innovative and artistic selections of Alaskan seafood highlight the menu, and the locally renowned Caesar salad is prepared tableside. Choices include not only a wide selection of seafood, such as oysters, salmon and halibut, but also lamb and other meats. Save room for one of the divine desserts. The atmosphere is delightful, and the service friendly and genuine. Casual dress. **Bar:** Beer & wine. **Reservations:** required. **Hours:** 6 pm-9:30 pm, Fri & Sat 5:30 pm-10 pm; 5:30 pm-10 pm 5/31-9/6. Closed major holidays; also Sun & Mon. **Address:** 627 W 3rd Ave 99501 **Location:** Between F and G sts; downtown. **Parking:** street. **Historic**

MIDDLE WAY CAFE

Phone: 907/272-6433 [19]

Vegetarian
$5-$10

Considered one of the city's best vegetarian restaurants, this casual coffeehouse is tucked away from crowds in a small shopping plaza. Patrons can look to the blackboard for a choice of sandwiches, smoothies and homemade soups, most of which are organic. The funky, upbeat atmosphere draws on a variety of characters. It's not unusual to stumble upon musicians playing an impromptu concert out front. Casual dress. **Reservations:** not accepted. **Hours:** 7 am-7 pm, Sat & Sun from 8 am. Closed major holidays. **Address:** 1300 W Northern Lights Blvd 99503 **Location:** Jct Spenard Rd and Northern Lights Blvd; in shopping plaza. **Parking:** on-site. CALL

MOOSE'S TOOTH PUB & PIZZERIA

Phone: 907/258-2537 [22]

American
$6-$10

With a bustling, casual atmosphere, this rustic hangout is popular with locals and tourists alike and reservations are not accepted, so guests should expect a long wait. The specialty is gourmet pizzas, and they come with regular or thick crust; red sauce, green sauce or no sauce; assorted meats, steak, chicken, seafood or vegetable toppings; and cheeses ranging from mozzarella and provolone to Gorgonzola, Parmesan, cheddar and feta. Sodas and beers brewed in-house are a good accompaniment. Casual dress. **Bar:** Beer & wine. **Hours:** 10:30 am-11 pm, Fri-midnight, Sat 11 am-midnight, Sun 11 am-11 pm. Closed: 11/25, 12/25. **Address:** 3300 Old Seward Hwy 99503 **Location:** Old Seward Hwy at 34th St. **Parking:** on-site. CALL

NINO'S ITALIAN EATERY

Phone: 907/336-6466 [25]

Italian
$10-$28

Pizza is the specialty of the house at this casual, family-friendly eatery. Pasta dishes, veal, chicken and seafood entrees complete the menu. Popular dishes include veal parmigiana, chicken Marsala and spaghetti and meatballs. Casual dress. **Bar:** Beer & wine. **Reservations:** not accepted. **Hours:** 11 am-10 pm, Sat from 1 pm, Sun 4 pm-9 pm. Closed major holidays; also Mon. **Address:** 831 E 36th Ave 99503 **Location:** Jct SR 1 (Seward Hwy), just w. **Parking:** on-site.

ORSO

Phone: 907/222-3232 [12]

Regional Italian
$9-$37

The chef's creativity with regional Italian cuisine shines in such dishes as prosciutto-wrapped halibut with carmelized onion relish. Pasta lovers will enjoy the wild mushroom ravioli, and those with a sweet tooth should save room for the in-house prepared desserts, especially the marscapone chocolate cheesecake. Casual dress. **Bar:** Full bar. **Reservations:** suggested. **Hours:** 11:30 am-4 & 5-10 pm, Fri & Sat-11 pm. Closed: 11/25, 12/25. **Address:** 737 W 5th Ave 99501 **Location:** Jct G St, just w; downtown. **Parking:** on-site (fee) and street. CALL

THE PEANUT FARM SPORTS BAR & GRILL

Phone: 907/563-3283 [33]

American
$10-$28

Sports fanatics will be in heaven as flat-screen TVs dominate the walls, and those lucky enough to get a booth will have their own mini flat-screen TV, This sports bar is "the" place to be to watch any big game. Menu options include salads, hearty sandwiches, burgers and pizza, while dinner expands into steaks and seafood. A heated outdoor deck overlooks a picturesque wooded creek. Casual dress. **Bar:** Full bar. **Hours:** 6 am-2 am. Closed: 11/25, 12/25. **Address:** 5227 Old Seward Hwy 99518 **Location:** Jct International Airport Rd. **Parking:** on-site. CALL

PEPPER MILL

Phone: 907/561-0800 [28]

American
$10-$40

This restaurant offers gourmet pizzas and sandwiches, but the steaks are classic. Each can be topped off with a wide variety of exotic peppers. The owner has also collected some interesting pepper shakers that are displayed throughout the dining room. A deck is available in nice weather. Casual dress. **Bar:** Full bar. **Reservations:** accepted. **Hours:** 11 am-10 pm. Closed: 11/25, 12/25. **Address:** 4101 Credit Union Dr 99503 **Location:** Jct C and 40th sts. **Parking:** on-site. CALL

PHYLLIS'S CAFE AND SALMON BAKE

Phone: 907/274-6576 [5]

American
$8-$39

A large, covered outdoor patio lets guests enjoy the long days in the summer months. A simple menu lists hot and cold appetizers, the ever-popular chowder in a bread bowl, steaks, ribs and, of course, fresh Alaska halibut and salmon. A tasting of local beers is a great way to dine like an Alaskan. Casual dress. **Bar:** Full bar. **Hours:** 11 am-11 pm; hours may vary off season. Closed: 1/1, 11/25, 12/25. **Address:** 436 D St 99501 **Location:** Jct 5th Ave. **Parking:** street. CALL

SACK'S CAFE & RESTAURANT

Phone: 907/274-4022 [3]

International
$10-$34

In a word, the restaurant is delightful. The chic choice's menu draws largely on area ingredients, including fresh salmon, scallops and halibut. Thai and Asian influences are abundant. At lunch, sandwiches and casual fare are at the heart of the offerings; dinner is a bit more complex, with several entrees that change nightly as the season changes. Casual dress. **Bar:** Beer & wine. **Reservations:** suggested. **Hours:** 11 am-2:30 & 5-9 pm, Fri & Sat-10 pm, Sun 10 am-2:30 & 5-9 pm. Closed: major holidays, 12/24. **Address:** 328 G St 99501 **Location:** Between 3rd and 4th aves; downtown. **Parking:** street. CALL

(See map and index starting on p. 756)

SEA GALLEY

Phone: 907/563-3520 [27]

Seafood
$10-$40

A great place to dine for those in the mood for seafood, the restaurant features a distinct nautical decor complete with fish nets and a wide selection of fresh fish and seafood cooked up in a variety of ways Dinners include tasty chowder or an all-you-can-eat salad bar. Desserts are a highlight here; a huge display case filled with sweet treats sits near the dining room entrance. Casual dress. **Bar:** Full bar. **Hours:** 11 am 11 pm, Fri & Sat-1 am, Sun noon-10 pm. Closed: 11/25, 12/25. **Address:** 4101 Credit Union Dr 99503 **Location:** Jct C and 40th sts. **Parking:** on-site. CALL ⛄M

SIMON & SEAFORTS

Phone: 907/274-3502 [6]

Regional American
$9-$46

This local favorite specializes in fresh, creatively prepared seafood flown in daily from Homer. Angus beef from Nebraska, pasta and chicken and are also good. The dining room has a scenic inlet view. Try their world-famous sipping dessert, brandy ice! Casual dress. **Bar:** Full bar. **Reservations:** suggested. **Hours:** 11 am-2:30 & 5-9:30 pm, Fri-10 pm, Sat 4:30 pm-10 pm, Sun 4:30 pm-9 pm. Closed: 1/1, 12/25. **Address:** 420 L St 99501 **Location:** Between 4th and 5th aves; downtown; overlooking Cook Inlet. **Parking:** street. CALL ⛄M

SKYFIRE CAFE

Phone: 907/561-2969 [34]

American
$8-$14

In a small roadside mall, the simple cafe and bakery serves fantastic breakfasts and great sandwiches for lunch. Patrons find great value for the dollar. The menu offers a choice of various omelets and hearty sandwiches. Those in a hurry can grab one of the massive cinnamon buns or muffins. Casual dress. **Reservations:** not accepted. **Hours:** 11 am-3 pm; Sunday brunch 10 am-2 pm. Closed major holidays; also Sat & Mon. **Address:** 5701 Lake Otis Pkwy, Suite 600 99507 **Location:** Jct SR 1 (Seward Hwy), exit Dowling Rd, 0.5 mi e, then just n; in Manoog's Plaza. **Parking:** on-site.

SNOW CITY CAFE

Phone: 907/272-2489 [7]

American
$8-$13

It's all but guaranteed that a line will form on Saturday morning at the popular spot, and it is definitely worth the wait. Home to an all-day breakfast, this one has been ranked highly by city residents. The cafe bustles with energy during the breakfast and lunch hours and provides an upbeat atmosphere in which to enjoy hearty, delicious food. Casual dress. **Bar:** Beer & wine. **Reservations:** not accepted. **Hours:** 7 am-3 pm, Sat & Sun-4 pm. Closed major holidays. **Address:** 1034 W 4th Ave 99501 **Location:** Jct L St; downtown. **Parking:** street. CALL ⛄M 🅰️

SNOW GOOSE RESTAURANT

Phone: 907/277-7727 [1]

American
$10-$27

Those looking for a pint of locally brewed beer might visit this great stop, which also offers views of the Cook Inlet and shipyard. Upstairs is a casual pub-type atmosphere, and downstairs, though still casual, is more of a restaurant. Service can be unpredictable, but the food and view make a visit worthwhile. Casual dress. **Bar:** Full bar. **Reservations:** suggested. **Hours:** 11 am-10:30 pm, Sat & Sun 5 pm-11 pm. Closed: 1/1, 11/25, 12/25; also Sun, Mon 9/16-5/14. **Address:** 717 W 3rd Ave 99501 **Location:** Corner of 3rd Ave and G St; downtown. **Parking:** street. CALL ⛄M 🅰️

SOURDOUGH MINING CO

Phone: 907/563-2272 [32]

American
$10-$30

A close replica of the mill house at Independence Mine, the restaurant has a tunnel entrance made from mine-blasted rock. Mesquite-smoked ribs and succulent rotisserie chicken, Alaskan seafood, steaks, pot pies, stews and chowders line the menu. Corn fritters are tasty, and entrees include a trip to the all-you-can-eat ice cream bar. During the summer, the eatery offers two shows in the tent city, where guests can listen to the adventures of Dusty Sourdough and see a gold panning demonstration. Casual dress. **Bar:** Full bar. **Reservations:** suggested. **Hours:** 11 am-10 pm; to 9 pm in winter. Closed: 11/25, 12/25. **Address:** 5200 Juneau St 99518 **Location:** Just e of jct Old Seward Hwy and International Airport Rd. **Parking:** on-site. CALL ⛄M 🅰️

SOUTHSIDE BISTRO   *Menu on AAA.com*

Phone: 907/348-0088 [40]

AAA

American
$8-$33

Located in the heart of a southside Anchorage business park, this little strip mall eatery features an upbeat and contemporary decor. The menu features a wide variety of items to suit all tastes with cooking styles that defy classification. Fresh seafood, assorted meat dishes, pastas and thin-crust pizzas ooze with flavor and a creative bent. The lunch menu lists additional selections of sandwiches. The wine list focuses mainly on western U.S.A. product. Casual dress. **Bar:** Beer & wine. **Reservations:** suggested. **Hours:** 11:30 am-10 pm, Fri & Sat-11 pm. Closed major holidays; also Sun & Mon. **Address:** 1320 Huffman Park Dr 99515 **Location:** SR 1 (Seward Hwy), exit Huffman Rd, just w, then just n. **Parking:** on-site. CALL ⛄M 🅰️

SULLIVAN'S STEAKHOUSE

Phone: 907/258-2882 [11]

Steak
$20-$40

Named for John L. Sullivan, heavyweight champion of the world in the 1880s, the upscale steak house prepares a wide selection of steaks, chops and seafood. Decorated with black-and-white photographs of Sullivan, Jack Dempsey and other boxing legends. Casual dress. **Bar:** Full bar. **Reservations:** suggested. **Hours:** 11 am-11 pm, Sun from 4:30 pm. Closed: 11/25, 12/25. **Address:** 320 W 5th Ave, Suite 100 99501 **Location:** Corner 5th Ave and C St. **Parking:** street. CALL ⛄M

SUSHI YA JAPANESE RESTAURANT

Phone: 907/522-2244 [38]

Japanese
$8-$23

This delightful restaurant features a distinct Japanese decor complete with sushi bar and fine Asian ornamental artifacts throughout. In addition to an outstanding sushi selection, diners can also choose from traditional favorites such as tempura and teriyaki entrees and combination plates. Most entrees include miso soup and salad. Casual dress. **Bar:** Beer & wine. **Reservations:** accepted. **Hours:** noon-midnight, Sun noon-10 pm. Closed major holidays. **Address:** 1111 E Dimond Blvd 99515 **Location:** Jct Old Seward Hwy. **Parking:** on-site. CALL ⛄M

(See map and index starting on p. 756)

SWEET BASIL CAFE

Coffee/Tea
$5-$14

Phone: 907/274-0070 ⑱

Diners who enjoy homemade soups, freshly squeezed juices, large sandwiches and salads and sumptuous desserts might find the casual, bright and cheerful café an appealing spot. Locals and visitors alike frequent this place. The kitchen closes at 4 pm weekdays and 3 pm on Saturday for dine-in only service. Casual dress. **Bar:** Beer & wine. **Reservations:** not accepted. **Hours:** 10:30 am-4 pm, Sat 11 am-3 pm. Closed major holidays; also Sun. **Address:** 1021 W Northern Lights Blvd 99503 **Location:** Jct 10th St and W Northern Lights Blvd. **Parking:** street. CALL ⒼⓂ

THAI KITCHEN

Thai
$8-$18

Phone: 907/561-0082 ㉚

Set in a small strip mall, the eatery is the winner of many best-of-awards and has a strong local following. Tasty Thai fare comprises a lengthy menu of traditional dishes, including noodles, curries and many vegetarian options. Casual dress. **Hours:** 11 am-3 & 5-9 pm, Sat from 5 pm, Sun 5 pm-8:30 pm. Closed major holidays. **Address:** 3405 E Tudor Rd 99507 **Location:** SR 1 (Seward Hwy), 2.5 mi e; in Tudor Square Shopping Center. **Parking:** on-site. Ⓚ

YEN KING CHINESE RESTAURANT

Chinese
$8-$20

Phone: 907/563-2627 ㉓

A distinct Oriental decor and an expansive buffet of tasty Chinese cuisine make this place a favorite of both locals and tourists. The all-day buffet lines up a selection of soups, salads and Chinese favorites, including stir-fries, mixed Chinese greens and preparations of noodles, beef, chicken and pork. Those not in the mood for a buffet can browse the full a la carte menu or request food for takeout or hotel delivery. Casual dress. **Bar:** Full bar. **Reservations:** accepted. **Hours:** 11 am-10 pm, Fri & Sat-10:30 pm. Closed major holidays; also Mon. **Address:** 3501 Old Seward Hwy 99503 **Location:** Jct 36th St. **Parking:** on-site.
CALL ⒼⓂ

CANTWELL pop. 222—See also DENALI NATIONAL PARK AND PRESERVE.

COOPER LANDING pop. 369

KENAI PRINCESS WILDERNESS LODGE   *Book at AAA.com*   Phone: (907)595-1425

▼▼▼▼
Hotel
$179-$249 5/22-9/12

Address: 17245 Frontier Cir 99572 **Location:** SR 1 (Sterling Hwy) at Milepost 47.8, just n of bridge, then 2.1 mi w. **Facility:** Smoke free premises. 86 one-bedroom standard units. 1 story, exterior corridors. *Bath:* combo or shower only. **Parking:** on-site. **Terms:** open 5/22-9/12, check-in 3:30 pm, cancellation fee imposed. **Amenities:** hair dryers. **Dining:** Eagle's Crest Dining Room, see separate listing. **Leisure Activities:** whirlpool, fishing, hiking trails, exercise room, horseshoes, shuffleboard. *Fee:* charter fishing. **Guest Services:** coin laundry, wireless Internet. **Business Services:** PC.

〔ⓘ〕 〔Ⓨ〕 CALL 〔Ⓜ〕 〔✕〕 〔✕〕 〔Ⓐ〕 〔Ⓟ〕

---------- **WHERE TO DINE** ----------

EAGLE'S CREST DINING ROOM   Phone: 907/595-1425

▼▼ ▼▼
Pacific Northwest
$12-$30

Diners will enjoy the rustic lodge ambiance complete with country pine walls and ceilings and a huge stone fireplace. The main focus of the dining room is, however, the large panoramic windows that offer spectacular views of the mountains on a clear day. Light luncheon fare is featured including lots of salads, sandwiches and local fish and chips, and a more upscale dinner menu is also offered. Casual dress. **Bar:** Full bar. **Reservations:** suggested. **Hours:** Open 5/17-9/15; 7 am-11, noon-2:30 & 5:30-10 pm. **Address:** 17245 Frontier Cir 99572 **Location:** SR 1 (Sterling Hwy) at Milepost 47.8, just n of bridge, then 2.1 mi w; in Kenai Princess Wilderness Lodge. **Parking:** on-site. CALL 〔Ⓜ〕 〔Ⓐ〕

DENALI NATIONAL PARK AND PRESERVE —See also CANTWELL & HEALY.

DENALI BACKCOUNTRY LODGE   Phone: 907/376-1900

▼▼ ▼▼
Cabin
$810-$860 6/4-9/12

Address: MM 95 Denali Park Rd 99755 **Location:** End of the 90 mi Denali National Park Rd. **Facility:** Smoke free premises. 42 one-bedroom standard units. 1-2 stories (no elevator), exterior corridors. *Bath:* shower only. **Parking:** on-site. **Terms:** open 6/4-9/12, office hours 8 am-7 pm, check-out 6:15 am, 60 day cancellation notice-fee imposed. **Leisure Activities:** fishing, recreation programs, bicycles, hiking trails. **Guest Services:** area transportation. *(See color ad below, p 328 & p 330)*

〔Ⓐ〕 〔Ⓨ〕 〔✕〕 〔✕〕 〔Ⓐ〕 〔Ⓟ〕 〔☎〕

DENALI BLUFFS HOTEL   *Book great rates at AAA.com*   Phone: 907/683-7000

▼▼ ▼▼
Hotel
Rates not provided

Address: Milepost 238.4 Parks Hwy 99755 **Location:** 1 mi n of park entrance. **Facility:** Smoke free premises. 112 one-bedroom standard units. 2 stories (no elevator), exterior corridors. **Parking:** on-site. **Terms:** open 5/26-9/11. **Amenities:** voice mail, hair dryers. **Dining:** Mountaineer Bar & Grill, see separate listing. **Guest Services:** coin laundry, area transportation. **Business Services:** PC.

〔ⓘ〕 CALL 〔Ⓜ〕 〔✕〕 〔▣〕 / SOME UNITS 〔Ⓐ〕

DENALI CABINS   Phone: 907/376-1900

▼▼ ▼▼
Cabin
$159-$259 6/1-9/6
$136-$221 9/7-9/12

Address: Milepost 229 Parks Hwy 99755 **Location:** 9 mi s of park entrance, Milepost 229. **Facility:** Smoke free premises. 46 cabins. 1 story, exterior corridors. *Bath:* shower or tub only. **Parking:** on-site. **Terms:** open 6/1-9/12, office hours 6 am-10 pm, 60 day cancellation notice-fee imposed. **Amenities:** voice mail. **Leisure Activities:** whirlpools, hiking trails. **Guest Services:** area transportation. 〔Ⓐ〕 CALL 〔Ⓜ〕 〔✕〕 〔Ⓐ〕 〔Ⓟ〕

DENALI PRINCESS WILDERNESS LODGE   *Book at AAA.com*   **Phone:** (907)683-2282

Hotel

$199-$299 5/19-9/15

Address: Milepost 238.5 99755 **Location:** SR 3 (Parks Hwy), 1.5 mi n of park entrance. **Facility:** Smoke free premises. 656 units. 653 one-bedroom standard units, some with whirlpools. 3 one-bedroom suites with whirlpools. 2-3 stories, interior/exterior corridors. *Bath:* combo or shower only. **Parking:** on-site. **Terms:** open 5/19-9/15, cancellation fee imposed. **Amenities:** voice mail, hair dryers. **Dining:** King Salmon, see separate listing. **Leisure Activities:** whirlpools. *Fee:* massage. **Guest Services:** coin laundry, area transportation, beauty salon, tanning facilities. **Business Services:** meeting rooms, PC.

GRANDE DENALI PARK LODGE *Book at AAA.com*

Phone: 907/683-8500

△▽△▽ △▽
Hotel
Rates not provided

Address: Milepost 238.2 George Parks Hwy 99755 **Location:** SR 3 (Parks Hwy), at Milepost 238.2 on east side of road, 0.7 mi ne on Grande Dr. Located in a rustic area. **Facility:** Smoke free premises. 170 units. 164 one-bedroom standard units. 6 cabins. 4 stories, interior/exterior corridors. *Bath:* combo or shower only. **Parking:** on-site. **Terms:** open 5/17-9/14. **Amenities:** voice mail, hair dryers. **Dining:** Alpenglow, see separate listing. **Guest Services:** coin laundry, area transportation, wireless Internet. **Business Services:** meeting rooms, PC. *(See color ad p 775)*

🍴 🍸 CALL 🅢Ⓜ ⊠ ▣

MCKINLEY CREEKSIDE CABINS *Book great rates at AAA.com*

Phone: (907)683-2277

ⓐⓐⓐ [SAVE]
△▽△▽
Cabin
$139-$199 6/1-9/15
$79-$149 5/15-5/31

Address: Milepost 224 Parks Hwy 99755 **Location:** 13 mi s; Milepost 224 on SR 3 (Parks Hwy) **Facility:** Smoke free premises. 32 cabins. 1 story, exterior corridors. *Bath:* shower only. **Parking:** on-site. **Terms:** open 5/15-9/15, office hours 6 am-10 pm, check-in 4 pm, 14 day cancellation notice. **Dining:** Creekside Cafe, see separate listing. **Leisure Activities:** picnic & barbecue facilities, hiking trails, horseshoes. **Guest Services:** wireless Internet.

🍴 ⊠ ⊠ 🄺 🆆 ⊘ ▣ / SOME UNITS 🚽 🍽

The following lodgings were either not evaluated or did not meet AAA rating requirements but are listed for your information only.

CAMP DENALI

Phone: 907/683-2290

[fyi]

Not evaluated. Address: Milepost 89 Denali National Park Rd 99755. Facilities, services, and decor characterize an economy property.

NORTH FACE LODGE & CAMP DENALI

Phone: 907/683-2290

[fyi]

Not evaluated. Address: Milepost 89 Denali National Park Rd 99755 **Location:** Milepost 89 Denali National Park Rd. Facilities, services, and decor characterize an economy property.

WHERE TO DINE

ALPENGLOW

Phone: 907/683-8720

△▽ △▽
Regional American
$10-$32

Take the drive one mile up to enjoy this restaurant perched on the side of a mountain, featuring a full window dining room with spectacular panoramic views of Denali. Grilled, fresh Alaskan salmon is a favorite of many diners. Casual dress. **Bar:** Full bar. **Reservations:** accepted. **Hours:** Open 5/15-9/15; 5 am-10:30 pm. **Address:** Milepost 238.2 Parks Hwy 99755 **Location:** SR 3 (Parks Hwy), at Milepost 238.2, on east side of road, 0.7 mi ne on Grande Dr; in Grande Denali Lodge. **Parking:** on-site. CALL 🅢Ⓜ

CREEKSIDE CAFE

Phone: 907/683-2277

△▽
Regional American
$9-$23

Though the decor and service is simple, the cafe's food is hearty and delicious. You'll find a wide selection of sandwiches and salads, as well as one of the best breakfasts in the park. At the front of the restaurant is a large dessert case featuring selections such as cookies, squares, cinnamon buns and cakes. Casual dress. **Bar:** Beer & wine. **Reservations:** not accepted. **Hours:** Open 5/15-9/15; 6 am-10 pm. **Address:** Milepost 224 Parks Hwy 99755 **Location:** 13 mi s; Milepost 224 on SR 3 (Parks Hwy); in McKinley Creekside Cabins. **Parking:** on-site. 🄺

KING SALMON

Phone: 907/683-2282

△▽△▽△▽
Seafood
$12-$40

This spacious restaurant adjacent to the Princess Lodge satisfies those looking to feast on tasty Alaskan seafood dishes while enjoying a spectacular view. A custom-made, hand-blown glass salmon chandelier commands attention in the dining room. Sure to be a favorite at your table, the seafood sampler consists of tempura prawns, pan-seared halibut and Alaskan crab cake. Casual dress. **Bar:** Full bar. **Reservations:** suggested, for dinner. **Hours:** Open 5/19-9/15; 6 am-3 & 4:30-10 pm. **Address:** Milepost 238.5 99755 **Location:** SR 3 (Parks Hwy), 1.5 mi n of park entrance; in Denali Princess Wilderness Lodge. **Parking:** on-site. CALL 🅢Ⓜ 🄺

MORINO GRILL

Phone: 907/683-9246

△▽
American
$9-$12

This grill located adjacent to the Denali Visitor Center is comprised of a full-service coffeeshop barista station, a grill area in which your selection is made to order featuring grilled panini and a premade pack-and-go station for your picnic lunch in the park. Casual dress. **Bar:** Beer & wine. **Reservations:** not accepted. **Hours:** Open 5/31-9/15; 7:30 am-6 pm. **Address:** Denali Visitor Center 99755 **Location:** At Denali Visitor Center. **Parking:** on-site. CALL 🅢Ⓜ 🄺

MOUNTAINEER BAR & GRILL

Phone: 907/683-8889

△▽△▽
American
$13-$30

A simple menu lists burgers and pizza by day and such comfort foods as pot roast by night. The dining room has an early 1900s cabin theme, with log walls, antique outdoor decorative items and windows for viewing the mountains. Hours vary so call ahead to confirm they are open. Casual dress. **Bar:** Full bar. **Reservations:** accepted. **Hours:** Open 5/15-9/15; 5 am-10:30 pm. **Address:** Milepost 238.4 George Parks Hwy 99755 **Location:** 1 mi n of park entrance; in Denali Bluffs Hotel. **Parking:** on-site. CALL 🅢Ⓜ

NENANA VIEW GRILLE

Phone: 907/683-8258

△▽△▽△▽
American
$15-$32

Stunning mountain views await those who dine in this open-style restaurant. Choose from a wide variety of carefully selected Alaskan fare, such as wild Alaskan salmon, locally caught halibut and rockfish or try the free-range chicken or aged beef. After dinner, unwind and enjoy the views from the lounge. Casual dress. **Bar:** Full bar. **Reservations:** suggested. **Hours:** Open 5/15-9/15; 5 pm-10:30 pm. **Address:** Milepost 238.5 Parks Hwy 99755 **Location:** Milepost 238.5, on SR 3 (Parks Hwy); in McKinley Chalet Resort. **Parking:** on-site. CALL 🅢Ⓜ

THE PERCH

Phone: 907/683-2523

▼▼ ▼▼

Regional American
$11-$35

As the name suggests, the restaurant sits nestled up a gravel road on a side of a mountain, offering incredible views of the Denali mountain range. The aroma of fresh-baked bread and other enticing smells from the open kitchen fill the dining room. The planked Alaskan salmon and locally caught halibut is the specialty of the house. Other offerings include caribou medallions and beef rib-eye steak. There's always something wonderful for dessert so be sure to ask. Casual dress. **Bar:** Full bar. **Reservations:** accepted. **Hours:** Open 5/15-9/20; 6 am-9 & 5-9 pm. **Address:** Milepost 224 (George Parks Hwy) 99755 **Location:** 13 mi s, Milepost 224, on SR 3 (George Parks Hwy), follow signs up hill. **Parking:** on-site. [Ⓐ]

DENALI STATE PARK

MT. MCKINLEY PRINCESS WILDERNESS LODGE   *Book at AAA.com*

Phone: (907)733-2900

▼▼ ▼▼ ▼▼

Resort
Hotel
$149-$199 5/19-9/15

Address: Milepost 133.1 99683 **Location:** SR 3 (George Parks Hwy), Milepost 133.1, 1 mi e on Mt. McKinley View Rd. **Facility:** The hotel and some of the guest rooms offer exceptional views of Mt. McKinley when the mountain is not shrouded in clouds; the guest rooms feature a contemporary, mountain-wilderness motif. Smoke free premises. 460 units. 454 one-bedroom standard units. 6 one-bedroom suites, some with whirlpools. 2 stories (no elevator), interior/exterior corridors. *Bath:* combo or shower only. **Parking:** on-site. **Terms:** open 5/19-9/15, check-in 3:30 pm, cancellation fee imposed. **Amenities:** voice mail, hair dryers. **Leisure Activities:** whirlpools, recreation programs, hiking trails, limited exercise equipment. **Guest Services:** coin laundry, area transportation (fee), wireless Internet. **Business Services:** PC. [Ⓘ] [Ⓨ] CALL [Ⓜ] [Ⓧ] [Ⓧ] [Ⓐ] [Ⓥ]

EAGLE RIVER

EAGLE RIVER MICROTEL INN & SUITES   *Book great rates at AAA.com*

Phone: (907)622-6000

(AAA) [SAVE]
▼▼ ▼▼

Hotel
$120-$180 All Year

Address: 13049 Old Glenn Hwy 99577 **Location:** Jct Glenn Hwy (SR 1), exit Eagle River, 1.7 mi e. **Facility:** 60 one-bedroom standard units. 3 stories, interior corridors. *Bath:* combo or shower only. **Parking:** on-site, winter plug-ins. **Terms:** 7 day cancellation notice-fee imposed. **Amenities:** high-speed Internet, voice mail. **Guest Services:** coin laundry, wireless Internet. **Business Services:** meeting rooms. **Free Special Amenities:** continental breakfast. [Ⓘ] CALL [Ⓜ] [Ⓐ] [Ⓧ] / SOME UNITS FEE [Ⓗ] [Ⓧ] [Ⓘ] [Ⓘ] [Ⓘ]

EAGLE RIVER MOTEL

Phone: 907/694-5000

▼

Motel
Rates not provided

Address: 11111 Old Eagle River Rd 99577 **Location:** Glenn Hwy (SR 1), exit Eagle River, just e, just s on Monte Rd, then just w. Located in a residential area. **Facility:** Smoke free premises. 14 one-bedroom standard units, some with efficiencies or kitchens. 3 stories (no elevator), exterior corridors. **Parking:** on-site, winter plug-ins. **Terms:** office hours 7 am-midnight. **Amenities:** high-speed Internet, voice mail. **Guest Services:** coin laundry, wireless Internet. **Business Services:** PC. [Ⓧ] [Ⓐ] [Ⓘ] [Ⓘ] [Ⓘ] [Ⓘ] / SOME UNITS FEE [Ⓗ]

---------- **WHERE TO DINE** ----------

HAUTE QUARTER GRILL

Phone: 907/622-4745

▼▼▼

American
$8-$30

This locally-popular restaurant offers upscale cuisine in a relaxed, casual atmosphere. Food is well prepared using fresh ingredients and the kitchen shows its creative and innovative talent in many of the preparations. The flavorful creations and attentive staff combine to make this an enjoyable experience. Casual dress. **Bar:** Full bar. **Reservations:** accepted. **Hours:** 5 pm-10 pm. Closed major holidays; also Sun & Mon. **Address:** 11221 Old Glenn Hwy 99577 **Location:** Jct Glenn Hwy (SR 1), exit Eagle River, just e. **Parking:** on-site. CALL [Ⓜ]

FAIRBANKS pop. 30,224

A BED AND BREAKFAST INN ON MINNIE STREET

Phone: (907)456-1802

▼▼ ▼▼

Bed & Breakfast
$139-$269 3/1-9/30
$99-$179 10/1-2/28

Address: 345 Minnie St 99701 **Location:** Just n of downtown, follow Cushman St over bridge to Illinois St, 0.5 mi n, then just e. Located in a residential area. **Facility:** Comprised of two detached homes connected by a private garden and deck, the inn offers cozy guest rooms in a variety of sizes and styles. Smoke free premises. 12 units. 9 one-bedroom standard units, some with kitchens and/or whirlpools. 3 one-bedroom suites with kitchens. 2 stories (no elevator), interior/exterior corridors. *Bath:* some combo or shower only. **Parking:** on-site, winter plug-ins. **Terms:** 14 day cancellation notice-fee imposed. **Amenities:** video library, hair dryers. *Some:* DVD players, CD players, irons. **Guest Services:** coin laundry, wireless Internet. **Business Services:** PC. [Ⓧ] [Ⓐ] / SOME UNITS [Ⓘ] [Ⓘ] [Ⓘ]

ALL SEASONS INN   *Book great rates at AAA.com*

Phone: (907)451-6649

(AAA) [SAVE]
▼▼ ▼▼

Bed & Breakfast
$85-$199 All Year

Address: 763 7th Ave 99701 **Location:** Just w of Barnette St; downtown. Located in a residential area. **Facility:** This well-tended, European-style property features an attractive lobby and varied size rooms that are pleasantly and comfortably decorated. Smoke free premises. 8 one-bedroom standard units. 2 stories (no elevator), interior corridors. **Parking:** on-site, winter plug-ins. **Terms:** office hours 8 am-6 pm, 14 day cancellation notice-fee imposed. **Amenities:** video library, irons, hair dryers. *Some:* DVD players. **Leisure Activities:** board games in sun room, library. **Guest Services:** coin laundry, wireless Internet. **Business Services:** meeting rooms, PC. **Free Special Amenities:** full breakfast and high-speed Internet. [Ⓧ] [Ⓘ]

A TASTE OF ALASKA LODGE *Book great rates at AAA.com*   Phone: (907)488-785

Bed & Breakfast
$185-$235 All Year

Address: 551 Eberhardt Rd 99712 **Location:** Jct US 2 (Steese Hwy) and Johansen Expwy, 2.9 mi ne 5 mi e on Chena Hot Springs Rd, then 0.5 mi s, follow signs. Located in a quiet secluded area **Facility:** Located on the outskirts of town, the inn offers seclusion and a rustic elegance; an array o collectibles can be found throughout the property. Smoke free premises. 10 units. 8 one-bedroor standard units. 2 cottages. 2 stories (no elevator), interior/exterior corridors. *Bath:* combo or showe only. **Parking:** on-site, winter plug-ins. **Terms:** cancellation fee imposed. **Amenities:** video librar; high-speed Internet, voice mail, hair dryers. *Some:* CD players, irons. **Leisure Activities:** cros country skiing, hiking trails, horseshoes. *Fee:* dog mushing. **Guest Services:** wireless Interne **Business Services:** meeting rooms, PC. **Free Special Amenities: full breakfast and high-spee Internet.**

BEST WESTERN CHENA RIVER LODGE *Book great rates at AAA.com*   Phone: (907)328-350

Hotel
$81-$162 All Year

Address: 1255 Tvsa Way 99709 **Location:** Jct Airport and Sportsman ways, just w on Boat St. **Facility:** Smoke free premises. 67 one-bedroom standard units. 3 stories, interior corridors. *Bath:* combo or shower only. **Parking:** on-site, winter plug-ins. **Terms:** check-in 4 pm. **Amenities:** high-speed Internet, voice mail, irons, hair dryers. **Leisure Activities:** exercise room. **Guest Services:** coin laundry, airport transportation-Fairbanks International Airport, wireless Internet. **Business Services:** meeting rooms, business center. **Free Special Amenities: expanded continental breakfast and high-speed Internet.**

AAA Benefit:
Members save up to 20%, plus 10% bonus points with rewards program.

BRIDGEWATER HOTEL *Book at AAA.com*   Phone: (907)452-666

Hotel
$119-$169 5/15-9/15

Address: 723 1st Ave 99701 **Location:** Just w of Cushman St; downtown. **Facility:** Smoke free premises. 94 one-bedroom standard units. 5 stories, interior corridors. *Bath:* combo or shower onl; **Parking:** on-site, winter plug-ins. **Terms:** open 5/15-9/15, check-in 4 pm, cancellation fee imposed **Amenities:** hair dryers. *Some:* irons. **Guest Services:** valet laundry, area transportation, wireles Internet.

COMFORT INN-CHENA RIVER *Book at AAA.com*   Phone: 907/479-808

Hotel
Rates not provided

Address: 1908 Chena Landings Loop 99701 **Location:** Airport Way, just n on Peger Rd, then just on Phillips Field Rd, follow signs in wooded area south of road. Located in a quiet area. **Facility:** 7 one-bedroom standard units, some with whirlpools. 3 stories, interior corridors. *Bath:* combo or showe only. **Parking:** on-site, winter plug-ins. **Amenities:** video games (fee), irons, hair dryers **Pool(s):** heated indoor. **Leisure Activities:** whirlpool. **Guest Services:** valet and coin laundry, are transportation, wireless Internet. **Business Services:** meeting rooms, PC.

EXTENDED STAY DELUXE FAIRBANKS-OLD AIRPORT WAY *Book at AAA.com*   Phone: (907)457-228

Extended Stay Hotel
$134-$144 5/1-2/28
$89-$99 3/1-4/30

Address: 4580 Old Airport Rd 99709 **Location:** Near jct Parks Hwy and Airport Rd. **Facility:** 97 units 96 one-bedroom standard units, some with efficiencies. 1 one-bedroom suite with efficiency (n utensils). 2 stories, interior corridors. *Bath:* combo or shower only. **Parking:** on-site, winter plug-ins **Terms:** cancellation fee imposed. **Amenities:** DVD players, voice mail, irons, hair dryers **Pool(s):** heated indoor. **Leisure Activities:** whirlpool, limited exercise equipment. **Guest Services** coin laundry, area transportation, wireless Internet. **Business Services:** meeting rooms, PC.

FAIRBANKS DOWNTOWN BED & BREAKFAST *Book great rates at AAA.com*   Phone: (907)452-770

Bed & Breakfast
$95-$105 5/15-9/1

Address: 1461 Gillam Way 99701 **Location:** Jct Airport and Gillam ways, just s. Located in residential area. **Facility:** Smoke free premises. 5 one-bedroom standard units. 2 stories (no elevator interior corridors. *Bath:* combo or shower only. **Parking:** on-site, winter plug-ins. **Terms:** open 5/15-9/ 14 day cancellation notice-fee imposed. **Guest Services:** wireless Internet. **Business Services:** PC **Free Special Amenities: continental breakfast and high-speed Internet.**

FAIRBANKS HAMPTON INN & SUITES *Book great rates at AAA.com*   Phone: (907)451-150

Hotel
$89-$299 All Year

Address: 433 Harold Bentley Ave 99701 **Location:** Jct US 2 (Steese Hwy) and Johansen Expwy, 0.6 mi w, then just s at Hunter St. **Facility:** Smoke free premises. 101 one-bedroom standard units. 4 stories, interior corridors. *Bath:* combo or shower only. **Parking:** on-site, winter plug-ins. **Terms:** 1-7 night minimum stay, cancellation fee imposed. **Amenities:** high-speed Internet, voice mail, irons, hair dryers. **Pool(s):** heated indoor. **Leisure Activities:** whirlpool, exercise room. **Guest Services:** valet and coin laundry, wireless Internet. **Business Services:** meeting rooms, business center.

AAA Benefit:
Members save up to 10% everyday!

FAIRBANKS PRINCESS RIVERSIDE LODGE *Book at AAA.com*   Phone: (907)455-447

Hotel
$99-$199 All Year

Address: 4477 Pikes Landing Rd 99709 **Location:** Jct Airport Way and Pikes Landing rds, just nv **Facility:** Smoke free premises. 325 units. 322 one-bedroom standard units. 3 one-bedroom suites wit whirlpools, some with efficiencies. 3 stories, interior corridors. *Bath:* combo or shower only. **Parking** on-site, winter plug-ins. **Terms:** cancellation fee imposed. **Amenities:** voice mail, irons, hair dryers *Some:* DVD players, fax. **Leisure Activities:** steamrooms, exercise room, horseshoes. **Gues Services:** valet and coin laundry, area transportation, wireless Internet. **Business Services** conference facilities, PC.

HOLIDAY INN EXPRESS *Book at AAA.com* Phone: (907)328-1100

Hotel
$80-$207 All Year

Address: 400 Merhar Ave 99701 **Location:** Jct US 2 (Steese Hwy) and Johansen Expwy, 0.6 mi w, then just s at Hunter St. **Facility:** Smoke free premises. 114 one-bedroom standard units, some with whirlpools. 4 stories, interior corridors. *Bath:* combo or shower only. **Parking:** on-site, winter plug-ins. **Amenities:** high-speed Internet, voice mail, irons, hair dryers. **Pool(s):** heated indoor. **Leisure Activities:** whirlpool, exercise room. **Guest Services:** coin laundry, wireless Internet. **Business Services:** PC.

PIKE'S WATERFRONT LODGE *Book great rates at AAA.com* Phone: (907)456-4500

Hotel
$89-$450 All Year

Address: 1850 Hoselton Rd 99709 **Location:** Jct Airport Way and Hoselton rds. **Facility:** Smoke free premises. 208 units. 179 one-bedroom standard units, some with whirlpools. 1 one-bedroom suite. 28 cabins. 1-3 stories, interior/exterior corridors. *Bath:* combo or shower only. **Parking:** on-site, winter plug-ins. **Terms:** cancellation fee imposed. **Amenities:** voice mail, irons, hair dryers. *Some:* high-speed Internet. **Leisure Activities:** sauna, steamroom, exercise room. **Guest Services:** valet and coin laundry, airport transportation-Fairbanks International Airport, area transportation-train station & riverboat, wireless Internet. **Business Services:** meeting rooms, PC. *(See color ad below)*

FREE local telephone calls

REGENCY FAIRBANKS HOTEL *Book at AAA.com* Phone: (907)459-2700

Hotel
$89-$205 All Year

Address: 95 10th Ave 99701 **Location:** Just w of SR 2 (Steese Expwy). **Facility:** Smoke free premises. 128 units. 114 one- and 2 two-bedroom standard units with kitchens, some with whirlpools. 9 one- and 3 two-bedroom suites with kitchens, some with whirlpools. 3 stories, interior corridors. **Parking:** on-site, winter plug-ins. **Terms:** cancellation fee imposed. **Amenities:** voice mail, hair dryers. **Leisure Activities:** exercise room. **Guest Services:** valet and coin laundry, area transportation, wireless Internet. **Business Services:** meeting rooms, PC.

▼ *See AAA listing above* ▼

On the banks of the Chena River in Fairbanks, Alaska

Check our website for specials!
www.pikeslodge.com

- FREE high-speed wireless Internet
- FREE airport and railroad shuttle
- Pike's Landing Restaurant right next door

1-877-774-2400
pikeslodge.com

Approved Lodging

Comfortable rooms and friendly hospitality!

RIVER'S EDGE RESORT
Book great rates at AAA.com

Phone: (907)474-0286

Cabin
$149-$225 6/1-9/15
$109-$182 5/15-5/31

Address: 4200 Boat St 99709 **Location:** Airport Way, just n on Sportsman Way, then 0.5 mi w. **Facility:** Smoke free premises. 94 units. 8 one-bedroom standard units. 86 cabins. 2 stories (no elevator), interior/exterior corridors. **Parking:** on-site, winter plug-ins. **Terms:** open 5/15-9/15, cancellation fee imposed. **Amenities:** voice mail, hair dryers. *Some:* irons. **Dining:** Chena's Alaskan Grill, see separate listing. **Guest Services:** coin laundry, airport transportation-Fairbanks International Airport, area transportation-train station, wireless Internet. **Business Services:** meeting rooms, PC. *(See color ad below)*

FREE local telephone calls

SOPHIE STATION HOTEL
Book at AAA.com

Phone: (907)479-3650

Condominium
$120-$235 All Year

Address: 1717 University Ave S 99709 **Location:** Airport Way, just s. **Facility:** Comfortable and homey, this hotel has recently updated the guest rooms. Smoke free premises. 148 units. 8 one-bedroom standard units with efficiencies, some with whirlpools. 140 one-bedroom suites with kitchens 3 stories, interior corridors. *Bath:* combo or shower only. **Parking:** on-site, winter plug-ins. **Terms:** check-in 4 pm, cancellation fee imposed. **Amenities:** voice mail, irons, hair dryers. *Some:* high-speed Internet. **Leisure Activities:** exercise room. **Guest Services:** valet and coin laundry, area transportation, wireless Internet. **Business Services:** meeting rooms, PC.

SPRINGHILL SUITES BY MARRIOTT
Book great rates at AAA.com

Phone: (907)451-6552

Hotel
$104-$209 All Year

Address: 575 1st Ave 99701 **Location:** Downtown. Located across from visitors center. **Facility:** Smoke free premises. 140 one-bedroom standard units. 6 stories, interior corridors. *Bath:* combo or shower only. **Parking:** on-site, winter plug-ins. **Terms:** cancellation fee imposed. **Amenities:** high-speed Internet, voice mail, irons, hair dryers. **Dining:** Lavelle's Bistro, see separate listing. **Pool(s):** heated indoor. **Leisure Activities:** whirlpool, exercise room. **Guest Services:** valet and coin laundry, wireless Internet. **Business Services:** meeting rooms, PC, fax (fee).

AAA Benefit:
Members save a minimum 5% off the best available rate.

SUPER 8   *Book at AAA.com*   **Phone:** 907/451-8888

Motel
Rates not provided

Address: 1909 Airport Way 99701 **Location:** Airport Way at Wilbur St. Located near Pioneer Park. **Facility:** 77 one-bedroom standard units. 3 stories (no elevator), interior corridors. **Parking:** on-site, winter plug-ins. **Amenities:** safes, hair dryers. *Some:* irons. **Guest Services:** coin laundry, area transportation, wireless Internet.

WEDGEWOOD RESORT   *Book at AAA.com*   **Phone:** (907)452-1442

Condominium
$95-$195 All Year

Address: 212 Wedgewood Dr 99701 **Location:** Johansen Expwy, 1 mi w on College Rd to Margaret Dr, then just n. **Facility:** On the fringes of the bird sanctuary, this sprawling complex has a variety of rooms, ranging from suite style to standard, and impressive gardens. Smoke free premises. 460 units. 155 one-bedroom standard units. 233 one- and 72 two-bedroom suites with kitchens. 3 stories (no elevator), interior/exterior corridors. *Bath:* combo or shower only. **Parking:** on-site, winter plug-ins. **Terms:** check-in 4 pm, cancellation fee imposed. **Amenities:** voice mail, irons, hair dryers. *Some:* DVD players, high-speed Internet. **Leisure Activities:** cross country skiing, hiking trails. **Guest Services:** valet and coin laundry, area transportation, wireless Internet. **Business Services:** conference facilities, PC.

WESTMARK FAIRBANKS HOTEL & CONFERENCE CENTER   *Book great rates at AAA.com*   **Phone:** (907)456-7722

Hotel
$225-$550 3/1-9/15
$99-$550 9/16-2/28

Address: 813 Noble St 99701 **Location:** Just n of Airport Way at 10th Ave; just w of SR 2; downtown. **Facility:** Smoke free premises. 400 units. 391 one-bedroom standard units. 9 one-bedroom suites. 4-8 stories, interior corridors. *Bath:* combo or shower only. **Parking:** on-site, winter plug-ins. **Terms:** cancellation fee imposed. **Amenities:** voice mail, irons, hair dryers. *Some:* high-speed Internet, dual phone lines. **Leisure Activities:** exercise room. **Guest Services:** valet and coin laundry, airport transportation-Fairbanks International Airport, area transportation-train station, wireless Internet. **Business Services:** conference facilities, PC. **Free Special Amenities: local telephone calls and high-speed Internet.**

——— WHERE TO DINE ———

ALASKA COFFEE ROASTING CO   **Phone:** 907/457-5282

Coffee/Tea
$4-$7

Known for its huge selection of coffee roasted on the premises, this funky, upbeat and contemporary coffee house also serves a variety of light lunches. Diners can enjoy vegetable empanadas, wraps and pizzas at this locally popular spot, and there is a large dessert case to tempt a sweet tooth. Guests order at the counter and can either get food to go or linger in the cafe. Casual dress. **Hours:** 7 am-10 pm, Sat from 8 am, Sun from 9 am. **Address:** 4001 Geist Rd, Suite 2 99709 **Location:** Just w of University Ave; in West Valley Plaza. **Parking:** on-site.

ALASKA SALMON BAKE   **Phone:** 907/452-7274

Seafood
$31

Located in Pioneer Park, this traditional salmon bake offers all-you-can-eat, carved prime rib, deep-fried halibut, grilled salmon and Bering Sea cod with a simple salad bar. Guests pay for a ticket at the counter, then serve themselves at the salad bar, fish barbecue and dessert cabin. Seats can be had at the outdoor picnic tables or inside under a covered area. Casual dress. **Bar:** Beer & wine. **Reservations:** not accepted. **Hours:** Open 5/15-9/15; 5 pm-9 pm. **Address:** 3175 College Rd, #1 99709 **Location:** Airport Way; in Pioneer Park. **Parking:** on-site.

CHENA'S ALASKAN GRILL   **Phone:** 907/474-3644

American
$8-$31

Antiques and other decorative touches create a decor that suggests early 1900s Alaska. The menu emphasizes steaks and seafood, and items are very well prepared and nicely presented. Dining is casual and leisurely, with outside deck dining available in season. Casual dress. **Bar:** Full bar. **Reservations:** suggested, for dinner. **Hours:** Open 5/15-9/15; 6 am-9, noon-2 & 5-10 pm. **Address:** 4200 Boat St 99709 **Location:** Airport Way, just n on Sportsman Way, then 0.5 mi w; in River's Edge Resort. **Parking:** on-site.

THE COOKIE JAR RESTAURANT   **Phone:** 907/479-8319

American
$6-$17

Enjoy leisurely dining in a relaxed and casual atmosphere. The kitchen turns out a variety of selections prepared using fresh ingredients. Much is made on-site and when ordered. Save room for the restaurant's homemade cookies and pastries. Casual dress. **Reservations:** accepted. **Hours:** 6:30 am-8 pm, Fri & Sat-9 pm, Sun am-4 pm. Closed: 11/25, 12/25. **Address:** 1006 Cadillac Ct 99701 **Location:** Jct Johansen Expwy, just n on Danby St. **Parking:** on-site.

GAMBARDELLA'S PASTA BELLA   **Phone:** 907/457-4992

Italian
$7-$28

Business travelers and couples enjoy the excellent lasagna and tiramisu at the warm, comfortable restaurant. Among other good choices are homemade pizza, bread, pie, cheesecake, espresso and cappuccino. Seating is available on the covered patio in season. Casual dress. **Bar:** Beer & wine. **Reservations:** accepted. **Hours:** 11 am-9 pm, Fri & Sat-10 pm, Sun 4 pm-9 pm. Closed: 1/1, 11/25, 12/25. **Address:** 706 2nd Ave 99701 **Location:** Downtown. **Parking:** on-site and street.

LAVELLE'S BISTRO   **Phone:** 907/450-0555

Regional American
$10-$36

This upscale trendy restaurant is one of the best in the city. Featuring an impressive and extensive wine list, a funky modern interior and a varied menu, this is a great place for a reunion with a friend over a good meal. The menu can range from halibut to salmon to lamb to pasta, but everything is tasty, artistic and creative. Casual dress. **Bar:** Full bar. **Reservations:** suggested. **Hours:** 11 am-2 & 4:30-10 pm. Closed: 1/1, 11/25, 12/25; also Sun & Mon for lunch 9/16-5/14. **Address:** 575 1st Ave 99701 **Location:** Downtown; in SpringHill Suites by Marriott. **Parking:** on-site.

PIKE'S LANDING RESTAURANT & LOUNGE   Phone: 907/479-6500

▼▼ ▼▼

Regional American

$10-$39

One nice thing about Alaska in the summer is endless nights under the midnight sun, and one of the city's best places to enjoy the evenings is on the patio of this restaurant, which is set along the river bank. Patrons find an extensive selection of Alaskan seafood, but because it's such a popular place, the meal is best not rushed. Service is exceptionally friendly. Casual dress. **Bar:** Full bar. **Reservations:** suggested. **Hours:** 11 am-10 pm; hours vary in winter. Closed: 12/25. **Address:** 4438 Airport Way 99709 **Location:** Jct Airport Way and Hoselton; next to Pike's Waterfront Lodge. **Parking:** on-site. CALL 🅼

THE PUMP HOUSE RESTAURANT & SALOON   *Menu on AAA.com*   Phone: 907/479-8452

American

$11-$36

An authentic former tin pumphouse used in gold-mining operations, the restaurant is listed on the National Register of Historic Places. The decor exudes a warm Victorian mining era charm, and a deck affords a great view of the Chena River. Fresh oysters feature on the menu as well as a variety of Alaskan seafood, steaks and reindeer. Casual dress. **Bar:** Full bar. **Reservations:** suggested. **Hours:** 11:30 am-10 pm, Sunday brunch 10 am-2 pm; 5 pm-10 pm 9/16-5-31. Closed: 1/1. **Address:** 796 Chena Pump Rd 99708 **Location:** Jct Parks Hwy and Geist Rd (Chena Pump Rd), just e to Chena Pump Rd, then 1.3 mi s. **Parking:** on-site. **Historic** CALL 🅼

THAI HOUSE RESTAURANT   Phone: 907/452-6123

▼▼ ▼▼

Thai

$9-$16

This cozy, unassuming downtown spot is very popular with locals. Yellow curry powder, onion, egg, fresh ginger, chili and garlic are a few of the ingredients that bring the cuisine to life. The kitchen staff can accommodate your preferred level of spiciness. The servers dress in authentic and ornate Thai gowns and provide instructions and hints for first-time Thai diners. Casual dress. **Bar:** Beer & wine. **Reservations:** accepted. **Hours:** Open 3/1-12/24 & 1/15-2/28; 11 am-4 & 5-9:30 pm. Closed major holidays; also Sun. **Address:** 526 5th Ave 99701 **Location:** Downtown. **Parking:** street. 🅰

THE TURTLE CLUB   Phone: 907/457-3883

▼▼ ▼▼

American

$22-$34

Located about 15 minutes outside Fairbanks, this popular restaurant delivers bang for the buck with healthy portions. Menu selections are limited, but diners will find quality products with such specialties as prime rib and seafood. All dinners include a salad bar. Throughout the restaurant, curio cabinets are filled with turtle knick-knacks. The last reservation is taken for 9 pm. Casual dress. **Bar:** Full bar. **Reservations:** suggested. **Hours:** 6 pm-10 pm, Sun 5 pm-9 pm. Closed: 1/1, 11/25, 12/25; also 11/24 & 11/25. **Address:** 10 Mile Old Steese Hwy 99712 **Location:** 10 mi n on SR 2 (Steese Expwy), 0.6 mi w on SR 6 (Old Steese Hwy). **Parking:** on-site. CALL 🅼

WOLF RUN RESTAURANT   Phone: 907/458-0636

▼▼ ▼▼

American

$8-$25

Known for its decadent desserts, Wolf Run also features a good selection of homemade soups, sandwiches and salads. Dinner entrees include such classics as beef Wellington or chicken Kiev. Originally designed as a private home, the restaurant maintains a coziness with its simple decor. A very popular spot with the locals, this is a great place to sit and linger over a cup of coffee and dessert. Casual dress. **Bar:** Beer & wine. **Reservations:** suggested, for dinner. **Hours:** 11 am-9 pm, Fri & Sat-11 pm, Sun noon-9 pm, Mon 11 am-3 pm. Closed major holidays. **Address:** 3360 Wolf Run 99709 **Location:** Jct Johansen Expwy and University Ave. **Parking:** on-site. CALL 🅼 🅰

GIRDWOOD

THE HOTEL ALYESKA   *Book great rates at AAA.com*   Phone: (907)754-1111

🆂🆅 🆂🅰🆅🅴

▼▼ ▼▼ ▼

Resort
Hotel

$149-$500 All Year

Address: 1000 Arlberg Ave 99587 **Location:** SR 1 (Seward Hwy), 3 mi n on Alyeska Blvd, then 1 mi e. Located in a quiet area. **Facility:** The hotel sits at the base of a large mountain surrounded by seven glaciers. Recently renovated, guest rooms reflect the property's Alpine setting. Smoke free premises. 304 units. 300 one-bedroom standard units. 4 one-bedroom suites. 8 stories, interior corridors. *Bath:* combo or shower only. **Parking:** on-site and valet. **Terms:** check-in 4 pm. **Amenities:** video games (fee), high-speed Internet, voice mail, safes, irons, hair dryers. **Dining:** 5 restaurants, also, Seven Glaciers Restaurant, see separate listing. **Pool(s):** heated indoor. **Leisure Activities:** sauna, whirlpool, cross country skiing, ice skating, rental bicycles, hiking trails, exercise room, spa, game room. *Fee:* downhill skiing, snowmobiling. **Guest Services:** valet laundry, area transportation-within town, wireless Internet. **Business Services:** conference facilities, PC (fee). *(See color ad p 764)* 🍽 🍸 CALL 🅼 🛥 ✂ ✕ 🅰 🎦 📶 🖥

FREE preferred room (subject to availability with advance reservations) and high-speed Internet

—— WHERE TO DINE ——

DOUBLE MUSKY INN   Phone: 907/783-2822

▼▼ ▼▼

Regional Cajun

$22-$40

Guests are sure to enjoy the twist on New Orleans dishes prepared with fresh Alaskan seafood. Many savory delights-such as crab meat-stuffed halibut served with Creole burre blanc or shrimp etouffee-are among locals' favorites. A unique decor comprises Mardi Gras beads and masks surrounding locally made framed stained-glass create a festive atmosphere. This is a very popular spot and reservations are no accepted, so patrons should be prepared for a wait. Casual dress. **Bar:** Full bar. **Reservations:** no accepted. **Hours:** Open 3/1-10/27 & 12/8-2/28; 5 pm-10 pm, Fri-Sun from 4:30 pm. Closed: 12/25; also Mon. **Address:** Milepost 0.3 (Crow Creek Rd) 99587 **Location:** 1.9 mi n on Alyeska Blvd from SR 1 (Seward Hwy), 0.3 mi w. **Parking:** on-site. CALL 🅼

SEVEN GLACIERS RESTAURANT

Phone: 907/754-2237

Regional
American
$28-$58

The unusual mountaintop location is a spectacular setting, accessible only by an aerial tram from the hotel. The menu centers on creative Alaskan and West Coast preparations of seafood, beef and more exotic game. Decor is rather sparse, letting the views of the Seven Glaciers provide the "wow" factor. Casual dress. **Bar:** Full bar. **Reservations:** suggested. **Hours:** Open 3/1-4/27 & 5/15-2/28; 5:30 pm-9:30 pm; also Fri-Sun from noon in winter. Closed: 10/15-11/24, Sun-Wed 11/30-4/30. **Address:** 1000 Arlberg Ave 99587 **Location:** SR 1 (Seward Hwy), 3 mi n on Alyeska Blvd, then 1 mi e; in Hotel Alyeska. **Parking:** on-site and valet. *(See color ad p 764)* CALL ⬛M ⬛

GLENNALLEN pop. 554

LAKE LOUISE LODGE

Phone: (907)822-3311

Hotel
$95-$155 All Year

Address: Mile 16.1 Lake Louise Rd 99588 **Location:** Jct US 4 and 1, 29 mi w, 15.5 mi n, then 0.8 mi on gravel road. **Facility:** Designated smoking area. 7 one-bedroom standard units. 2 stories (no elevator), interior/exterior corridors. *Bath:* shower or tub only. **Terms:** winter plug-ins. **Terms:** check-in 4 pm, 14 day cancellation notice-fee imposed. **Amenities:** hair dryers. **Leisure Activities:** rental boats, boat dock, fishing, hiking trails. **Guest Services:** TV in common area.

⬛ ⬛ ⬛ ⬛ ⬛ ⬛ ⬛ ⬛

GUSTAVUS pop. 429

ANNIE MAE LODGE

Phone: (907)697-2346

Country Inn
$125-$200 All Year

Address: 2 Grandpa Rd 99826 **Location:** From airport, 3 mi w to Good River Rd, 0.5 mi to Grandpa's Farm Rd. Located in a quiet area. **Facility:** Smoke free premises. 11 one-bedroom standard units. 2 stories (no elevator), interior/exterior corridors. *Bath:* some shared or private, combo or shower only. **Parking:** on-site. **Terms:** office hours 5:30 am-10:30 pm, 30 day cancellation notice-fee imposed. **Leisure Activities:** fishing, bicycles, hiking trails. **Guest Services:** valet laundry, area transportation, wireless Internet.

GLACIER BAY LODGE

Phone: 907/697-4000

Motel
$199-$224 5/31-9/6

Address: 199 Bartlett Cove 99826 **Location:** 9 mi w of airport. **Facility:** Smoke free premises. 48 one-bedroom standard units. 2 stories (no elevator), exterior corridors. **Parking:** on-site. **Terms:** open 5/31-9/6, office hours 5 am-midnight, check-in 4 pm, 14 day cancellation notice-fee imposed. **Dining:** Fairweather Dining Room, see separate listing. **Leisure Activities:** hiking trails. **Guest Services:** coin laundry, wireless Internet. **Business Services:** PC.

GLACIER BAY'S BEAR TRACK INN   *Book at AAA.com*

Phone: (907)697-3017

Hotel
$790 5/20-9/10

Address: 255 Rink Creek Rd 99826 **Location:** 7 mi e of airport; at end of Rink Creek Rd. Located in a quiet area. **Facility:** Smoke free premises. 14 one-bedroom standard units. 2 stories (no elevator), interior corridors. **Parking:** on-site. **Terms:** open 5/20-9/10, office hours 7 am-10 pm, 90 day cancellation notice-fee imposed. **Amenities:** hair dryers. **Leisure Activities:** hiking trails. **Guest Services:** TV in common area, valet laundry, area transportation, wireless Internet. **Business Services:** meeting rooms, PC (fee).

ASK ⬛ ⬛ ⬛ ⬛ ⬛ ⬛ ⬛

―――― WHERE TO DINE ――――

FAIRWEATHER DINING ROOM

Phone: 907/697-4000

American
$10-$30

The hotel dining room offers both a wonderful view of the inlet and creatively prepared, locally caught seafood, as well as a variety of standards ranging from sandwiches to steaks. Casual dress. **Bar:** Full bar. **Reservations:** accepted. **Hours:** Open 5/31-9/6; 6-9:30 am, 11:30-2:30 & 5:30-10 pm. **Address:** 199 Bartlett Cove 99826 **Location:** 9 mi w of airport; in Glacier Bay Lodge. **Parking:** on-site. CALL ⬛M ⬛

HAINES pop. 1,811

CAPTAIN'S CHOICE INC MOTEL

Phone: (907)766-3111

Motel
$129-$192 All Year

Address: 108 2nd Ave N 99827 **Location:** Jct 2nd Ave and Dalton St. **Facility:** 37 units. 36 one-bedroom standard units, some with whirlpools. 1 one-bedroom suite. 2 stories (no elevator), exterior corridors. **Parking:** on-site. **Amenities:** voice mail, hair dryers. *Some:* irons. **Leisure Activities:** sun deck, sun deck. **Guest Services:** coin laundry, airport transportation-Haines Airport, area transportation-ferry. **Free Special Amenities:** continental breakfast and local telephone calls.

 / SOME UNITS FEE ⬛ ⬛

―――― WHERE TO DINE ――――

CHILKAT RESTAURANT & BAKERY

Phone: 907/766-3653

American
$6-$21

A few steps away from downtown, this local favorite offers a variety of well prepared and hearty dishes and features in-house bakery items. Casual dress. **Reservations:** accepted. **Hours:** Open 3/1-11/15; 7 am-3 pm, also Fri & Sat 4:30 pm-8 pm. Closed: 7/4, 11/25, 12/25; also Sun. **Address:** 25 5th Ave 99827 **Location:** Jct 5th Ave and Dalton St. **Parking:** on-site and street. ⬛

FORT SEWARD LODGE RESTAURANT & SALOON

Phone: 907/766-2009

American
$15-$26

The casual dining room has been restored to reflect its former gold rush saloon days and offers a variety of bar favorites including hamburgers and locally caught seafood. Casual dress. **Bar:** Full bar. **Reservations:** suggested. **Hours:** Open 5/1-10/31; 5 pm-9 pm. Closed: 1/1, 11/25, 12/25; also Mon & Tues. **Address:** 39 Mud Bay Rd 99827 **Location:** In Fort William H Seward. **Parking:** on-site.

LIGHTHOUSE RESTAURANT

Phone: 907/766-2442

Seafood
$8-$30

This casual spot overlooks the Lynn Canal, where the ferry and cruise ships dock in this small port town. Fresh seafood is a highlight in season. Casual dress. **Bar:** Full bar. **Reservations:** suggested. **Hours:** 6 am-9 pm. Closed: 11/25, 12/25. **Address:** 101 Front St 99827 **Location:** Waterfront; town center. **Parking:** on-site.

HEALY pop. 1,000—See also DENALI NATIONAL PARK AND PRESERVE.

DENALI DOME HOME BED & BREAKFAST

Phone: (907)683-1239

Bed & Breakfast
$110-$190 All Year

Address: 137 Healy Spur Rd 99743 **Location:** Jct SR 3 and Healy Spur Rd, 0.5 mi e. Located in a quiet area. **Facility:** In a scenic area, the dome-shaped inn offers cozy, comfortable rooms and spacious common areas; the owner's two Scottish terriers are on the premises. Smoke free premises. 7 one-bedroom standard units, some with whirlpools. 3 stories (no elevator), interior/exterior corridors. *Bath:* combo or shower only. **Parking:** on-site, winter plug-ins. **Terms:** check-in 4 pm, 30 day cancellation notice-fee imposed. **Amenities:** video library, DVD players, hair dryers. **Leisure Activities:** hiking trails, jogging. **Guest Services:** wireless Internet. **Business Services:** business center. **Free Special Amenities: full breakfast and high-speed Internet.**

DENALI LAKEVIEW INN

Phone: (907)683-4035

Bed & Breakfast
$89-$195 All Year

Address: Mile 1.2 Otto Lake Rd 99743 **Location:** SR 3, Milepost 247, 1.2 mi w. **Facility:** Ten minutes outside the township, this limited-service inn fronts tranquil Otto Lake. An in-room Continental breakfast is available each morning. Smoke free premises. 20 one-bedroom standard units, some with whirlpools. 2-3 stories, interior/exterior corridors. **Parking:** on-site, winter plug-ins. **Terms:** office hours 9 am-8 pm, check-in 4 pm, 14 day cancellation notice-fee imposed. **Amenities:** hair dryers. **Leisure Activities:** fishing. *Fee:* canoes. **Guest Services:** coin laundry. **Free Special Amenities: continental breakfast and high-speed Internet.**

HEALY HEIGHTS FAMILY CABINS

Phone: 907/683-2639

Cabin
$130-$220 6/1-9/20
$100-$180 5/15-5/31

Address: Hill Top Rd 99743 **Location:** SR 3, Milepost 247, 0.9 mi w on Otto Lake Rd, then 1.5 mi n, follow signs. **Facility:** Smoke free premises. 6 cabins. 1 story, exterior corridors. *Bath:* combo or shower only. **Parking:** on-site, winter plug-ins. **Terms:** open 5/15-9/20, office hours 8 am-10 pm, check-in 4 pm, 15 day cancellation notice-fee imposed.

---- WHERE TO DINE ----

BLACK DIAMOND GRILL

Phone: (907)683-4653

American
$6-$30

This casual restaurant sports simple decor and surprisingly good food, the likes of which includes salads, sandwiches, burgers and pastas, plus dinner entrees of Alaskan halibut and salmon, pork, steak and chicken. Diners can enjoy a great meal while drinking in scenic views from all the windows. Casual dress. **Bar:** Beer & wine. **Reservations:** accepted. **Hours:** Open 5/4-9/30; 11 am-11 pm. **Address:** 1 Mile Otto Lake Rd 99743 **Location:** SR 3, Milepost 247, 0.8 mi w. **Parking:** on-site.

HOMER pop. 3,946

BEST WESTERN BIDARKA INN   *Book great rates at AAA.com*

Phone: (907)235-8148

Hotel
$89-$199 All Year

Address: 575 Sterling Hwy 99603 **Location:** Just n of Pioneer Ave on Sterling Hwy (SR 1). **Facility:** 74 one-bedroom standard units, some with whirlpools. 2 stories (no elevator), interior/exterior corridors. **Parking:** on-site, winter plug-ins. **Terms:** check-in 4 pm. **Amenities:** irons, hair dryers. *Some:* high-speed Internet. **Leisure Activities:** exercise room. **Guest Services:** coin laundry, airport transportation-Homer Airport, area transportation-ferry, wireless Internet. **Business Services:** meeting rooms, PC.

AAA Benefit:
Members save up to 20%, plus 10% bonus points with rewards program.

FREE full breakfast and high-speed Internet

LANDS END RESORT

Phone: (907)235-0400

Hotel
$80-$245 All Year

Address: 4786 Homer Spit Rd 99603 **Location:** Oceanfront. 5 mi se; at end of Homer Spit Rd. Adjacent to ferry terminal. **Facility:** Smoke free premises. 113 units. 62 one- and 19 two-bedroom standard units. 3 one-bedroom suites. 29 condominiums. 3 stories, interior/exterior corridors. *Bath:* combo or shower only. **Parking:** on-site. **Terms:** check-in 4 pm, 3 day cancellation notice-fee imposed. **Amenities:** video library (fee), hair dryers. *Some:* DVD players, CD players. **Leisure Activities:** sauna, whirlpool, rental bicycles, limited exercise equipment, spa. *Fee:* fishing, charter fishing. **Guest Services:** wireless Internet. **Business Services:** meeting rooms, business center.

[ASK] [🍴] [📶] CALL [✒M] [🚫] [✕] [🐱] [🖥] / SOME UNITS [🅿] [🖨]

PIONEER INN

Phone: (907)235-5670

Motel
$119-$129 3/1-9/15
$79-$99 9/16-2/28

Address: 244 W Pioneer Ave 99603 **Location:** Jct Sterling Hwy (SR 1), just e. **Facility:** Smoke free premises. 7 units. 2 one-bedroom standard units. 5 one-bedroom suites with kitchens. 2 stories (no elevator), exterior corridors. **Parking:** on-site. **Terms:** office hours 8 am-10 pm, 7 day cancellation notice-fee imposed. **Guest Services:** wireless Internet.

[➕] [🍴] [✕] [🐱] [✒] [🅿] [🖥] / SOME UNITS [🖨]

VICTORIAN HEIGHTS BED AND BREAKFAST

Phone: (907)235-6357

Bed & Breakfast
$145-$175 6/1-8/31

Address: 1585 Race Rd 99603 **Location:** Sterling Hwy (SR 1), 1.8 mi ne on Pioneer Ave (which becomes East End Rd), 2.1 mi nw on East Hill Rd, then 0.3 mi e on Cottonwood, follow signs. **Facility:** Located in a quiet residential neighborhood, the home overlooks the distant bay and mountains offering stunning views from its hilltop location. Smoke free premises. 4 one-bedroom standard units, some with whirlpools. 2 stories (no elevator), interior corridors. *Bath:* combo or shower only. **Parking:** on-site. **Terms:** open 6/1-8/31, office hours 7 am-10 pm, check-in 4 pm, 2 night minimum stay, 14 day cancellation notice. **Amenities:** hair dryers. **Guest Services:** TV in common area, coin laundry, wireless Internet. [ASK] [✕] [🐱] [🐾] [🎥] [✒]

———— WHERE TO DINE ————

CAFE CUPS

Phone: 907/235-8330

American
$9-$35

Considered to be one of the best places in town, this eclectic, funky restaurant serves up a variety of homemade goods, and is well-known for its seafood options. There are only about fifteen tables at this funky place, which features a unique mosaic wall around the door. You can choose from salmon, shrimp and other seafood dishes, or try the feature of the day. The servers are efficient and personable. Casual dress. **Bar:** Beer & wine. **Reservations:** suggested. **Hours:** 4:30 pm-9:30 pm. Closed: 11/25, 12/25; also Sun & Mon. **Address:** 162 W Pioneer Ave 99603 **Location:** Jct Sterling Hwy (SR 1), just w. **Parking:** on-site. [🐱]

CAPTAIN PATTIE'S FISH HOUSE

Phone: 907/235-5135

Seafood
$7-$27

Those who spent the day fishing and can't wait to eat their catch can bring it in to the restaurant for preparation and cooking. Alaskan art contributes to the simple decor. The ever-changing menu boasts freshly caught fish dishes, along the lines of halibut, scallops and salmon. Early birds can take advantage of specials from 5 pm to 6 pm. On the famous Homer Spit, this spot is distinctive and casual. Casual dress. **Bar:** Beer & wine. **Reservations:** suggested. **Hours:** Open 3/20-9/30; 11 am-10 pm. Closed: 4/4. **Address:** 4241 Homer Spit Rd 99603 **Location:** 5 mi along Homer Spit Rd. **Parking:** on-site. [🐱]

CARIBOU FAMILY RESTAURANT

Phone: 907/235-5148

American
$7-$20

Hearty breakfasts are served all day at this casual eatery, along with other comfort food fare like chili cheeseburgers and patty melts. Seafood, steaks and chicken round out the menu. Homemade cakes and pies cause many guests to linger. Casual dress. **Hours:** 6 am-10 pm; Wed-Sat 24 hours in summer. **Address:** 672 East End Rd 99603 **Location:** Jct Sterling Hwy (SR 1), 0.4 mi e on Lake Rd. **Parking:** on-site. [🐱]

DON JOSE'S MEXICAN RESTAURANT & CANTINA

Phone: 907/235-7963

Mexican
$9-$17

This colorful cantina has been part of the Homer community since 1982. The menu includes all the traditional Mexican favorites like enchiladas, burritos, fajitas and chimichangas, along with house specialties like carne asada and coconut shrimp. Casual dress. **Bar:** Full bar. **Hours:** 11 am-10 pm, Sat & Sun from noon. Closed: 11/25, 12/25. **Address:** 127 W Pioneer Ave 99603 **Location:** Jct Sterling Hwy (SR 1), just e. **Parking:** on-site. [🐱]

DUNCAN HOUSE DINER

Phone: 907/235-5344

American
$4-$12

Well worth a visit for the hearty homestyle fare and cozy atmosphere, this country diner is known for its all-day breakfast that features hearty portions of freshly cooked fare. It's a great way to start the day. In addition to the breakfast options, a light lunch menu is offered from 11 am. Options there include hearty burgers, sandwiches, fresh soups and entrée salads. The decor is delightful, with a true, rustic Alaskan feel and a homelike touch. Casual dress. **Hours:** 6 am-3 pm; 7 am-2 pm in winter. Closed: 1/1, 11/25, 12/25. **Address:** 125 E Pioneer Ave 99603 **Location:** Jct Sterling Hwy (SR 1), just e. **Parking:** on-site. [🐱]

FAT OLIVES

Phone: 907/235-8488

Pizza
$8-$24

Wood-fired pizzas are the specialty of the house at this casual eatery. Huge sandwiches on house-made Tuscan bread and sizeable salads are featured at lunch, and the dinner menu expands to include seafood, lamb and beef as well as other tasty options. A lengthy wine list offers more than 30 wines by the glass. Casual dress. **Bar:** Beer & wine. **Hours:** 11 am-9 pm. **Address:** 376 Ohlson Ln 99603 **Location:** Jct W Pioneer Ave, just s on Sterling Hwy (SR 1). **Parking:** on-site. [🐱]

FRESH SOURDOUGH EXPRESS BAKERY & CAFE

Phone: 907/235-7571

Breads/Pastries
$6-$25

A popular spot with the locals, the Sourdough Express is a warm, inviting place serving up locally produced and some organic fare. Whether you're stopping in for a big breakfast, a sandwich for lunch or an evening bite to eat, you might also be tempted by the display case in the bakery, which features a wide array of delicious desserts. In the summer, outdoor patio dining is available, complete with a small play area for the kids. Casual dress. **Bar:** Beer & wine. **Reservations:** accepted. **Hours:** Open 3/1-10/31; 7 am-9 pm; 8 am-3 pm in fall & spring. **Address:** 1316 Ocean Dr 99603 **Location:** 3 mi sw on Sterling Hwy (SR 1), on way to Homer Spit Rd. **Parking:** on-site. CALL [✒M] [🐱]

THE HOMESTEAD RESTAURANT

Phone: 907/235-8723

WWW
Pacific Northwest
$19-$30

A bit hard to find, the restaurant is located 8 miles down East End Road across from Tesoro gas station. Diners enjoy wonderful views of the Homer Spit in this charming restaurant, which centers its menu on innovative preparations of fresh Alaskan seafood, steaks, duck, chicken and more. Casual dress. **Bar:** Full bar. **Reservations:** suggested. **Hours:** Open 3/15-12/31; 5 pm-10 pm. Closed: 11/25, 12/25. **Address:** Mile 8.2 East End Rd 99603 **Location:** Jct Pioneer Ave and Lake St, 8.2 mi e. **Parking:** on-site.

CALL 🔊M 🏍

TWO SISTERS BAKERY

Phone: 907/235-2280

WWW
Breads/Pastries
$4-$10

For healthy, organic baked goods and light lunches, the three sisters at the Two Sisters Bakery have what it takes. Located in a big house on the outskirts of downtown and near several galleries, the eatery offers giant cinnamon buns, scones, quiches, breakfast granola and, of course, a fine selection of fresh breads. Guests have the option to lounge for a few hours, or take their baked goods to go. Either way, service comes with a smile. Casual dress. **Reservations:** not accepted. **Hours:** 7 am-6 pm, Sat-4 pm, Sun 9 am-2 pm; hours vary in winter. Closed: 12/25. **Address:** 233 E Bunnell Ave 99603 **Location:** Sterling Hwy (SR 1), just s at Main St, then just e. **Parking:** on-site. 🏍

JUNEAU pop. 30,711

	✈ Airport Accommodations			
OA	**JUNEAU INTERNATIONAL AIRPORT**	Diamond Rated	High Season	Page
AAA	**Best Western Country Lane Inn, n of terminal**	WW	$130-$180 SAVE	786
AAA	**Best Western Grandma's Feather Bed, 1 mi n of terminal**	WW	$140-$180 SAVE	786
	Extended Stay Deluxe Juneau, n of terminal	WW	$144-$154	786

ALASKA WOLF LODGE

Phone: 907/586-2422

WW
Bed & Breakfast
Rates not provided

Address: 1900 Wickersham Dr 99801 **Location:** From Highland Dr, 0.9 mi n on Glacier Ave, just e; 2 mi n of downtown. Located in a quiet residential area. **Facility:** Smoke free premises. 6 one-bedroom standard units, some with kitchens and/or whirlpools. 2 stories (no elevator), interior corridors. *Bath:* some shared or private, combo or shower only. **Parking:** on-site. **Terms:** check-in 4 pm. **Amenities:** video library, hair dryers. *Some:* DVD players. **Leisure Activities:** massage. **Guest Services:** wireless Internet. / SOME UNITS 📺 📞 💻

BEST WESTERN COUNTRY LANE INN   *Book great rates at AAA.com*

Phone: (907)789-5005

AAA SAVE
WW
Motel
$130-$180 3/1-9/30
$110-$150 10/1-2/28

Address: 9300 Glacier Hwy 99801 **Location:** Just e off Egan Dr. **Facility:** Smoke free premises. 55 units. 50 one-bedroom standard units, some with efficiencies and/or whirlpools. 5 one-bedroom suites with efficiencies. 2 stories (no elevator), exterior corridors. **Parking:** on-site. **Amenities:** irons, hair dryers. *Some:* high-speed Internet. **Guest Services:** valet and coin laundry, airport transportation-Juneau International Airport, area transportation-within 10 mi, wireless Internet. **Business Services:** PC. **Free Special Amenities:** local telephone calls and high-speed Internet. 🚐 🛎 ❌ 🎦 💻 / SOME UNITS 📞 📠

AAA Benefit:
Members save up to 20%, plus 10% bonus points with rewards program.

BEST WESTERN GRANDMA'S FEATHER BED   *Book great rates at AAA.com*

Phone: (907)789-5566

AAA SAVE
WW
Country Inn
$140-$180 3/1-9/30
$130-$140 10/1-2/28

Address: 2358 Mendenhall Loop Rd 99801 **Location:** Just e off Egan Dr. **Facility:** Smoke free premises. 14 one-bedroom standard units with whirlpools. 2 stories, interior corridors. **Parking:** on-site. **Amenities:** high-speed Internet, voice mail, irons, hair dryers. **Guest Services:** valet laundry, airport transportation-Juneau International Airport, area transportation-within 10 mi, wireless Internet. **Business Services:** PC. **Free Special Amenities:** local telephone calls and high-speed Internet. 🚐 🍴 ❌ 🎦 📞 📠 💻

AAA Benefit:
Members save up to 20%, plus 10% bonus points with rewards program.

EXTENDED STAY DELUXE JUNEAU   *Book at AAA.com*

Phone: (907)790-6435

WW
Extended Stay
Hotel
$144-$154 5/1-2/28
$114-$124 3/1-4/30

Address: 1800 Shell Simmons Dr 99801 **Location:** At Juneau International Airport. **Facility:** 95 units. 92 one-bedroom standard units, some with efficiencies. 3 one-bedroom suites with efficiencies. 2 stories, interior corridors. *Bath:* combo or shower only. **Parking:** on-site. **Terms:** cancellation fee imposed. **Amenities:** DVD players, voice mail, irons, hair dryers. **Pool(s):** heated indoor. **Leisure Activities:** whirlpool, exercise room. **Guest Services:** valet and coin laundry, area transportation, wireless Internet. **Business Services:** meeting rooms, PC. ASK 🚐 🍴 CALL 🔊M 🏊 🎦 📞 📠 💻 / SOME UNITS FEE 🐾 ❌

GOLDBELT HOTEL JUNEAU *Book great rates at AAA.com* Phone: (907)586-6900

Hotel
$139-$199 All Year

Address: 51 Egan Dr 99801 **Location:** Just n of Main St; downtown. **Facility:** 105 one-bedroom standard units. 7 stories, interior corridors. **Parking:** on-site. **Terms:** cancellation fee imposed. **Amenities:** voice mail, irons, hair dryers. **Guest Services:** valet laundry, airport transportation-Juneau International Airport, wireless Internet. **Business Services:** meeting rooms, PC. *(See color ad below)* ⊞ 🍴 🍸 🅰 💻 / SOME UNITS ⊠ 🈁

PEARSON'S POND LUXURY INN & ADVENTURE SPA *Book great rates at AAA.com* Phone: (907)789-3772

Bed & Breakfast
$199-$599 All Year

Address: 4541 Sawa Cir 99801-8723 **Location:** From Egan Dr, 2.2 mi n on Mendenhall Loop Rd, 1.2 mi w on Mendenhall Loop Rd, 0.3 mi s on River Rd, just w on Kelly Ct, then just s. Located in a quiet residential area. **Facility:** A placid pond beautifies the property's grounds, while guest rooms offer luxurious amenities. The hosts can assist with activity planning. Smoke free premises. 5 one-bedroom standard units with efficiencies, some with whirlpools. 2 stories (no elevator), interior/exterior corridors. **Bath:** combo or shower only. **Parking:** on-site. **Terms:** 2 night minimum stay - seasonal, age restrictions may apply, 30 day cancellation notice-fee imposed. **Amenities:** video library, DVD players, CD players, high-speed Internet, voice mail, irons, hair dryers. *Some:* fax. **Leisure Activities:** whirlpools, boating, paddleboats, boat dock, fishing, fishing equipment, kayaks, cross country skiing, barbecue facility, bicycles, hiking trails, limited exercise equipment, yoga instruction. *Fee:* massage. **Guest Services:** complimentary laundry, wireless Internet. **Business Services:** meeting rooms, PC. **Free Special Amenities: expanded continental breakfast and high-speed Internet.**

⊠ ⊠ 🅰 🐾 🈁 🖨 💻

THE SILVERBOW INN BAKERY & RESTAURANT *Book at AAA.com* Phone: (907)586-4146

Historic Bed
& Breakfast
$88-$208 All Year

Address: 120 2nd St 99801 **Location:** Jct Main and 2nd sts; downtown. **Facility:** This restored 1914 building has quaint guest rooms with cheery, bright decor. Smoke free premises. 11 one-bedroom standard units, some with whirlpools. 3 stories (no elevator), interior corridors. **Bath:** combo or shower only. **Parking:** on-site. **Terms:** 7 day cancellation notice-fee imposed. **Amenities:** video library, high-speed Internet, voice mail, hair dryers. *Some:* DVD players. **Dining:** Silverbow Inn & Bakery, see separate listing. **Leisure Activities:** sauna, whirlpool. **Guest Services:** valet laundry, wireless Internet. **Business Services:** PC. ⒜ 🍴 ⊠ 🅰

WESTMARK BARANOF *Book great rates at AAA.com* Phone: (907)586-2660

Hotel
$149-$279 All Year

Address: 127 N Franklin St 99801 **Location:** At 2nd and Franklin sts; downtown. **Facility:** Smoke free premises. 195 units. 181 one-bedroom standard units, some with kitchens. 14 one-bedroom suites, some with efficiencies. 9 stories, interior corridors. **Bath:** combo or shower only. **Parking:** on-site. **Terms:** cancellation fee imposed. **Amenities:** high-speed Internet, voice mail, irons, hair dryers. **Dining:** 2 restaurants, also, The Gold Room, see separate listing. **Leisure Activities:** exercise room. **Guest Services:** valet laundry, wireless Internet. **Business Services:** conference facilities, PC. **Free Special Amenities: local telephone calls.** 🍴 ⊠ 🅰 / SOME UNITS 🐾 🈁 🖨

—— WHERE TO DINE ——

CHAN'S THAI KITCHEN
Phone: 907/789-9777

◆◆◆
Thai
$11-$15

This non-descript eatery tucked away in a small strip mall across from Auke Bay Marina will be worth finding. Authentic Thai cooking is served up hot and spicy. The spring rolls are some of the best to be had. This extremely popular restaurant does not take reservations and the seating is limited, so expect a wait for a table in the evening. Casual dress. **Reservations:** not accepted. **Hours:** 4:30 pm-8:30 pm, Sun-8 pm. Closed: 7/4, 11/25, 12/25; also Mon. **Address:** 11820 Glacier Hwy 99801 **Location:** 12 mi nw on Glacier Hwy; at Auke Bay, across from harbor. **Parking:** on-site.

GOLD CREEK SALMON BAKE
Phone: 907/586-1424

◆◆◆
American
$41

Catering to cruise ship customers, this outdoor buffet offers all-you-can-eat wood-grilled salmon filets in a forest mining camp setting. Casual dress. **Bar:** Full bar. **Reservations:** accepted. **Hours:** Open 5/1-9/30; 11 am-2 & 5-7:30 pm. **Address:** 1061 Salmon Creek Ln 99801 **Location:** Jct Glacier Hwy and Hospital Dr, just n. **Parking:** on-site.

THE GOLD ROOM
Phone: 907/586-2660

◆◆◆◆◆◆
Regional American
$25-$39

Find an upscale setting at this restaurant set in the Westmark Hotel, where a large wall painting depicts the gold rush days. An attentive staff serves artful presentations of such regional delicacies as salmon, halibut, prawns and crab. Casual dress. **Bar:** Full bar. **Reservations:** suggested. **Hours:** 5 pm-9 pm. Closed: 11/25, 12/25. **Address:** 127 N Franklin St 99801 **Location:** At 2nd and Franklin sts; downtown; at Westmark Baranof. **Parking:** on-site.

THE HANGAR ON THE WHARF
Phone: 907/586-5018

◆◆◆◆
American
$9-$27

Located on the wharf and popular with locals, the vibrant eatery offers no-frills dining. Guests can watch seaplanes take off and land while munching on fried halibut fingers and sipping an Alaskan Brewing Company amber ale. Casual dress. **Bar:** Full bar. **Hours:** 11 am-10 pm; hours may vary in winter. Closed: 11/25, 12/25. **Address:** 2 Marine Way, Suite 106 99801 **Location:** Downtown; on wharf at Sea Plane runway. **Parking:** on-site.

OLIVIA'S DE MEXICO
Phone: 907/586-6870

◆◆◆◆
Mexican
$11-$19

Tucked in the basement level, this little Mexican cantina has served authentic home-style cooking for over 30 years. After ordering, patrons are served homemade corn tortillas and salsa while waiting for the main course, which might include traditional soups, tacos, burritos, enchiladas, tostadas, chile verde and specials with fresh Alaskan halibut or shrimp. Tempting desserts include homemade creamy caramel-custard flan. Service is casual and food arrives incredibly fast. Casual dress. **Bar:** Beer & wine. **Reservations:** accepted. **Hours:** 11 am-9 pm. Closed major holidays; also Sun. **Address:** 222 Seward St 99801 **Location:** Between 2nd St and 3rd St; centre. **Parking:** on-site (fee).

SILVERBOW INN & BAKERY
Phone: 907/586-4146

◆◆
Deli
$5-$10

Silverbow, a restored historical structure with funky decor, is a fun spot where kids are allowed to color on the table covers. Classic and golden oldies films are shown two nights a week, and an adjacent New York-style bakery offers sinful desserts. Casual dress. **Bar:** Beer & wine. **Reservations:** not accepted. **Hours:** 6:30 am-8 pm, Sat & Sun from 8 am. Closed: 1/1, 12/25. **Address:** 120 2nd St 99801 **Location:** Jct Main and 2nd sts; downtown; in The Silverbow Inn Bakery & Restaurant. **Parking:** on-site.

TIMBERLINE BAR & GRILL
Phone: 907/463-3412

◆◆◆◆
American
$12-$29

Take a six-minute cable car ride to the top of Mount Roberts—separate fee—from which you'll be treated to stunning views of Juneau and the Gastineau Channel. It also takes you to this restaurant, which would be equally worthy at sea level. The Alaskan Alpine experience is sure to be memorable. Casual dress. **Bar:** Full bar. **Reservations:** accepted. **Hours:** Open 5/10-9/30; 11 am-8 pm. **Address:** 490 S Franklin 99801 **Location:** Downtown; at the top of Mount Roberts Tramway. **Parking:** on-site.

TWISTED FISH COMPANY
Phone: 907/463-5033

◆◆◆◆
Seafood
$9-$30

Alaskan seafood is the specialty at this restaurant, located on the pier near the cruise ship landing areas. Service is quick and friendly, and on those sunny days enjoy dining al fresco. Casual dress. **Bar:** Beer & wine. **Hours:** Open 5/1-9/30; 11 am-10 pm. **Address:** 550 S Franklin St 99801 **Location:** Downtown. **Parking:** on-site.

KENAI pop. 6,942

ASPEN EXTENDED STAY SUITES   *Book at AAA.com*
Phone: (907)283-2272

◆◆◆◆
Hotel
$99-$179 All Year

Address: 10431 Kenai Spur Hwy 99611 **Location:** 0.5 mi e; center; behind McDonald's. **Facility:** 78 one-bedroom standard units with efficiencies. 3 stories, interior corridors. **Bath:** combo or shower only. **Parking:** on-site, winter plug-ins. **Terms:** office hours 6 am-11 pm, cancellation fee imposed. **Amenities:** video library (fee), DVD players, voice mail, irons, hair dryers. **Leisure Activities:** exercise room. **Guest Services:** valet and coin laundry, wireless Internet. **Business Services:** meeting rooms, business center.

HARBORSIDE COTTAGES
Phone: (907)283-6162

[AAA] [SAVE]
◆◆◆◆
Cottage
$150-$195 5/1-10/1

Address: 813 Riverview Dr 99611 **Location:** Just s on Main St, then just e; center. **Facility:** Smoke free premises. 5 cottages. 1 story, exterior corridors. **Bath:** shower only. **Parking:** on-site. **Terms:** open 5/1-10/1, office hours 8 am-6 pm, check-in 4 pm, 3 night minimum stay - seasonal, 30 day cancellation notice. **Amenities:** irons. **Leisure Activities:** barbecue deck with picnic table. **Guest Services:** wireless Internet. **Free Special Amenities:** early check-in/late check-out and high-speed Internet.

——— WHERE TO DINE ———

CHARLOTTE'S

Sandwiches
$8-$12

Phone: 907/283-2777

A popular lunch spot, this cozy cafe features a menu of hearty salads and gourmet sandwiches, along with homemade desserts to tempt the sweet tooth. Casual dress. **Hours:** 7 am-4 pm, Sat 8 am-3 pm; 7 am-3 pm, Sat from 8 am in winter. Closed major holidays; also Sun. **Address:** 115 S Willow St, Suite 102 99611 **Location:** Jct Kenai Spur Hwy, just n. **Parking:** on-site.

PARADISOS RESTAURANT

Continental
$9-$30

Phone: 907/283-2222

A local favorite since 1971, Paradisos offers an extensive menu featuring Greek, Mexican and Italian selections along with steak and fresh local seafood like halibut and Alaskan king crab legs. Expect to be served good-size portions in a bustling, welcoming ambience. A separate enclosed lounge area offers area for smoking. Casual dress. **Bar:** Full bar. **Hours:** 11 am-11 pm, Fri & Sat-midnight. Closed: 11/25, 12/25. **Address:** 811 Frontage Rd 99611 **Location:** Jct Kenai Spur Hwy and Main St. **Parking:** on-site.

CALL

VERONICA'S

American
$6-$23

Phone: 907/283-2725

This charming bistro, located in the historic district, is the perfect spot to savor a homemade pastry with an aromatic cup of coffee or tea. Originally built as a private home in 1918, the restaurant serves delicious, specialty homemade items, including sandwiches and creative soups. Live music livens the place Friday and Saturday evenings. Casual dress. **Hours:** 9 am-8 pm, Fri & Sat-9:30 pm; 10 am-3 pm, Fri & Sat-9:30 pm 9/15-5/31. Closed major holidays; also Sun in winter. **Address:** 604 Peterson Way 99611 **Location:** Kenai Spur Hwy, just s on Main St, just w on Overland Ave, then just n on Mission; in the historic district. **Parking:** on-site. **Historic**

KETCHIKAN pop. 7,922

BEST WESTERN LANDING   *Book great rates at AAA.com*

Hotel
$195-$235 3/1-9/30
$142-$190 10/1-2/28

Phone: (907)225-5166

Address: 3434 Tongass Ave 99901 **Location:** Across from the Alaska Marine Hwy ferry terminal. **Facility:** 107 units. 90 one-bedroom standard units. 17 one-bedroom suites. 2-4 stories, interior/exterior corridors. *Bath:* combo or shower only. **Parking:** on-site. Amenities: voice mail, irons, hair dryers. *Some:* high-speed Internet. **Dining:** 2 restaurants, also, The Landing, see separate listing. **Leisure Activities:** exercise room. **Guest Services:** valet and coin laundry, airport transportation-Ketchikan International Airport, area transportation-ferry, wireless Internet. **Business Services:** conference facilities, business center. **Free Special Amenities: early check-in/late check-out and room upgrade (subject to availability with advance reservations).**

AAA Benefit:
Members save up to 20%, plus 10% bonus points with rewards program.

CAPE FOX LODGE   *Book great rates at AAA.com*

Hotel
$110-$210 All Year

Phone: (907)225-8001

Address: 800 Venetia Way 99901 **Location:** Above Creek St (tramway from Creek St). **Facility:** 72 units. 70 one-bedroom standard units. 2 one-bedroom suites with whirlpools. 3 stories, interior/exterior corridors. *Bath:* combo or shower only. **Parking:** on-site. **Amenities:** video games (fee), voice mail, irons, hair dryers. **Dining:** restaurant, see separate listing. **Guest Services:** valet and coin laundry, wireless Internet. **Business Services:** meeting rooms, PC (fee). **Free Special Amenities: local telephone calls and high-speed Internet.**

——— WHERE TO DINE ———

ANNABELLE'S FAMOUS KEG & CHOWDER HOUSE

Seafood
$10-$39

Phone: 907/225-9423

Located directly across from the cruise ship docks, diners can enjoy freshly caught seasonal seafood such as fresh salmon, clam chowder or halibut cheeks in either an attractive bar or classy dining room. Casual dress. **Bar:** Full bar. **Reservations:** suggested. **Hours:** 11 am-9 pm, Fri-Sun to 9:30 pm. Closed major holidays; also Sun 10/1-4/30. **Address:** 326 Front St 99901 **Location:** Center; across from cruise ship docks; in Gilmour Hotel. **Parking:** street. CALL

CAPE FOX LODGE DINING ROOM & LODGE

American
$10-$53

Phone: 907/225-8001

Perched 130 feet above Creek Street and high above the busy cruise ship harbor is the Westcoast Cape Fox Lodge and its reputable dining room, Heen Kahidi—meaning "house by the creek." This place is legendary for celebrating special events. Local seafood anchors the menu, which also includes aged beef, chicken and pasta. Spectacular views of the harbor are framed by pine boughs just outside the windows. Dressy casual. **Bar:** Full bar. **Reservations:** suggested. **Hours:** 7 am-9 pm, Fri & Sat-9:30 pm. Closed: 11/25, 12/24, 12/25. **Address:** 800 Venetia Way 99901 **Location:** Above Creek St (tramway from Creek St); in Cape Fox Lodge. **Parking:** on-site. CALL

THE LANDING

American
$8-$25

Phone: 907/225-5166

This 1950s-style diner offers an extensive menu of comfort foods as well as some of the best pies in the area. Casual dress. **Bar:** Full bar. **Hours:** 6 am-9 pm, Fri & Sat-9:30 pm. **Address:** 3434 Tongass Ave 99901 **Location:** Across from Alaska Marine Hwy ferry terminal; in Best Western Landing. **Parking:** on-site.

THE NARROWS INN RESTAURANT

Phone: 907/247-2600

American
$7-$25

Named for the Tongass Narrows on whose shores it is located, the restaurant offers casual dining about 1.5 miles north of town. The quiet rain-forest setting is adjacent to The Narrows Inn. The menu features fresh local seafood as well as pasta, steaks and chops. Casual dress. **Bar:** Full bar. **Reservations:** accepted **Hours:** 6:30 am-2 & 5-9 pm, Sun-2 pm; seasonal hours may vary. Closed: 12/25; also Sun 10/1-5/1. **Address:** 4871 N Tongass Hwy 99901 **Location:** 1.6 mi n from Alaska Marine Hwy ferry terminal; 1.2 mi n from Airport ferry terminal. **Parking:** on-site.

SALMON FALLS RESORT

Phone: 907/225-2752

Regional American
$19-$34

Fourteen miles outside town, the facility overlooks the Clarence Straits and Behm Canal of the Inland Passageway. Wide windows provide panoramic views, and a wooden ceiling adds ambiance. The menu lists fresh northern water seafood and grilled steaks. The friendly, young staff are culled from local communities and can offer exuberant information concerning the surrounding areas. Casual dress. **Bar:** Full bar. **Reservations:** suggested. **Hours:** Open 5/27-9/20; 5 pm-9 pm. **Address:** 16707 Tongass Hwy 99901 **Location:** 14.5 mi n from Alaska Marine Hwy ferry terminal; 14.1 mi n from Airport ferry terminal. **Parking:** on-site.

STEAMERS ON THE DOCK

Phone: 907/225-1600

Seafood
$13-$30

The casual third floor restaurant commands a magnificent view of Ketchikan harbor and features a variety of locally caught seafood including salmon and clams. **Reservations:** suggested. **Hours:** Open 5/1-9/30; 10 am-10 pm. **Address:** 76 Front St 99901 **Location:** Across from cruise ship dock; on 3rd floor of Commercial Building; center. **Parking:** street.

KLAWOCK pop. 854

*———— The following lodging was either not evaluated or did not ————
meet AAA rating requirements but is listed for your information only.*

FIREWEED LODGE

Phone: 907/755-2930

[fyi]

Not evaluated. **Address:** 6863 Klawock/Hollis Hwy 99925 **Location:** 4.5 mi w of Hollis ferry terminal. Facilities, services, and decor characterize a mid-scale property.

KODIAK pop. 6,334

✈ Airport Accommodations

KODIAK AIRPORT	Diamond Rated	High Season	Page
Comfort Inn Kodiak, adjacent to airport	◆◆	$161-$225	790

BEST WESTERN KODIAK INN   *Book great rates at AAA.com*

Phone: (907)486-5712

Hotel
$170-$260 3/1-10/31
$100-$169 11/1-2/28

Address: 236 W Rezanof Dr 99615 **Location:** 0.3 mi w of ferry terminal; center. **Facility:** 80 units. 78 one-bedroom standard units, some with whirlpools. 2 one-bedroom suites. 3 stories, interior/exterior corridors. **Parking:** on-site. **Terms:** cancellation fee imposed. **Amenities:** DVD players, voice mail, irons, hair dryers. *Some:* high-speed Internet. **Dining:** Chart Room Restaurant and Lounge, see separate listing. **Leisure Activities:** whirlpool, fish & game freezer, barbecue grills. **Guest Services:** coin laundry, airport transportation-Kodiak Airport, area transportation-ferry, wireless Internet. **Business Services:** meeting rooms, business center. **Free Special Amenities: expanded continental breakfast and local telephone calls.**

AAA Benefit:
Members save up to 20%, plus 10% bonus points with rewards program.

COMFORT INN KODIAK   *Book at AAA.com*

Phone: (907)487-2700

Hotel
$161-$225 5/1-2/28
$99-$135 3/1-4/30

Address: 1395 Airport Way 99615 **Location:** Adjacent to Kodiak Airport. **Facility:** 50 one-bedroom standard units, some with whirlpools. 2 stories, interior corridors. **Parking:** on-site. **Terms:** check-in 4 pm, 3 day cancellation notice-fee imposed. **Amenities:** voice mail, irons, hair dryers. **Leisure Activities:** exercise room. **Guest Services:** coin laundry, area transportation, wireless Internet. **Business Services:** meeting rooms, PC.

———— WHERE TO DINE ————

CHART ROOM RESTAURANT AND LOUNGE

Phone: 907/486-5712

Continental
$10-$30

Diners enjoy a lovely view from the large panoramic windows of this second-floor restaurant. The luncheon menu has a nice variety of casual fare including fresh chowder, tasty salads, sandwiches, pastas and burgers, as well as the ever-popular halibut and chips. Dinner features an extensive fish and seafood selection that is sure to please. Casual dress. **Bar:** Full bar. **Reservations:** suggested. **Hours:** 6 am-2 & 5-10 pm; 6 am-10 & 5-9 pm off season. Closed: 11/25, 12/25. **Address:** 236 W Rezanof Dr 99615 **Location:** 0.3 mi w of ferry terminal; center; in Best Western Kodiak Inn. **Parking:** on-site.

HENRY'S GREAT ALASKAN RESTAURANT Phone: 907/486-8844

American
$10-$35

The lengthy menu of burgers, sandwiches, steaks, fresh seafood and pasta draws a crowd at this casual downtown eatery. Specialties include breaded and fried seafood, prime rib and bouillabaisse. Casual dress. **Bar:** Full bar. **Hours:** 11:25 am-10 pm, Fri & Sat-10:30 pm, Sun noon-9:30 pm. Closed: 1/1, 4/4, 12/25. **Address:** 512 Marine Way 99615 **Location:** Just w of ferry terminal; on The Mall. **Parking:** on-site.

MOOSE PASS pop. 206

TRAIL LAKE LODGE *Book great rates at AAA.com* Phone: (907)288-3101

Motel
$109-$126 3/1-9/30
$69 10/1-2/28

Address: MM 29.5 Seward Hwy 99631 **Location:** US 9 (Seward Hwy) at MM 29.5. **Facility:** Smoke free premises. 21 one-bedroom standard units. 1-2 stories (no elevator), exterior corridors. **Bath:** shower only. **Parking:** on-site. **Terms:** office hours 8 am-midnight, 2 night minimum stay - seasonal and/or weekends, 7 day cancellation notice-fee imposed. **Guest Services:** wireless Internet.

PALMER pop. 4,533

—— WHERE TO DINE ——

THE INN CAFE Phone: 907/746-6118

American
$7-$9

Just a short distance from the tourist information center, this small restaurant overflows the lobby of the Inn B&B. Immensely popular with locals, the casual place is well known for its tastily prepared meals. Using a mix of local and seasonal ingredients, the chef/owner creates approachable food, such as daily quiches, light sandwiches and salads that are strong on flavor. Casual dress. **Reservations:** not accepted. **Hours:** 11 am-3 pm, Sun 9 am-2 pm. Closed major holidays; also Sat. **Address:** 325 E Elmwood Ave 99645 **Location:** 1 mi e of Glenn Hwy (SR 1) along Evergreen Ave (which becomes E Elmwood Ave); center. **Parking:** on-site.

SELDOVIA pop. 286

—— WHERE TO DINE ——

THE MAD FISH RESTAURANT Phone: 907/234-7676

American
$8-$28

A fun and vibrant eatery serving creative fare ranging from seafood to vegetarian dishes and homemade gourmet desserts. Casual dress. **Bar:** Beer & wine. **Reservations:** suggested. **Hours:** Open 5/1-9/5; 11:30 am-4 & 5:30-9 pm. **Address:** 221 Main St 99663 **Location:** Center. **Parking:** on-site.

SEWARD pop. 2,830

BEST WESTERN EDGEWATER HOTEL *Book great rates at AAA.com* Phone: (907)224-2700

Hotel
$90-$210 All Year

Address: 202 Fifth Ave 99664 **Location:** Just n of Alaska SeaLife Center. **Facility:** Smoke free premises. 76 one-bedroom standard units. 3 stories, interior corridors. **Bath:** combo or shower only. **Parking:** on-site. **Terms:** check-in 4 pm, 2 night minimum stay - seasonal, 3 day cancellation notice. **Amenities:** video library, DVD players, irons, hair dryers. **Leisure Activities:** sauna, whirlpool. **Guest Services:** coin laundry, area transportation-train depot & cruise terminal, wireless Internet. **Business Services:** meeting rooms, PC. **Free Special Amenities: continental breakfast and high-speed Internet.**

AAA Benefit:
Members save up to 20%, plus 10% bonus points with rewards program.

BOX CANYON CABINS Phone: (907)224-5046

Cabin
$155-$265 5/1-10/31

Address: 31515 Lois Way 99664 **Location:** 3.5 mi n on SR 9, just w on Herman Leirer Rd; 1 mi n on Old Exit Glacier Rd, then just e. **Facility:** Smoke free premises. 6 cabins. 1 story, exterior corridors. **Bath:** shower only. **Parking:** on-site. **Terms:** open 5/1-10/31, check-in 4 pm, 45 day cancellation notice-fee imposed. **Amenities:** hair dryers. **Leisure Activities:** *Fee:* charter fishing. **Guest Services:** coin laundry, wireless Internet.

HARBORVIEW INN *Book at AAA.com* Phone: (907)224-3217

Motel
$149-$299 6/1-9/30
$79-$119 5/1-5/31

Address: 804 Third Ave 99664 **Location:** Just n of Alaska SeaLife Center; downtown. **Facility:** Smoke free premises. 39 units. 36 one-bedroom standard units. 2 two-bedroom suites with kitchens. 1 condominium. 2 stories (no elevator), exterior corridors. **Bath:** combo or shower only. **Parking:** on-site. **Terms:** open 5/1-9/30, office hours 8 am-10 pm, check-in 4 pm, 3 day cancellation notice-fee imposed. **Amenities:** hair dryers. **Guest Services:** wireless Internet.

HOLIDAY INN EXPRESS SEWARD HARBOR HOTEL *Book at AAA.com* Phone: (907)224-2550

Hotel
$71-$265 All Year

Address: 1412 Fourth Ave 99664 **Location:** At Small Boat Harbor. **Facility:** Smoke free premises. 90 one-bedroom standard units. 3 stories, interior corridors. **Bath:** combo or shower only. **Parking:** on-site. **Terms:** check-in 4 pm. **Amenities:** high-speed Internet, voice mail, irons, hair dryers. **Pool(s):** heated indoor. **Leisure Activities:** whirlpool. **Guest Services:** coin laundry. **Business Services:** meeting rooms, PC.

HOTEL SEWARD

Hotel
$79-$359 All Year

Phone: (907)224-8001

Address: 221 Fifth Ave 99664 **Location:** Just n of Alaska SeaLife Center; downtown. **Facility:** Smoke free premises. 38 one-bedroom standard units. 2 stories, interior corridors. **Parking:** on-site and street. **Terms:** check-in 4 pm, 3 day cancellation notice. **Amenities:** irons, hair dryers. **Leisure Activities:** fishing, kayaking. **Guest Services:** coin laundry, area transportation-train depot & cruise terminal, wireless Internet. **Business Services:** conference facilities, PC. **Free Special Amenities:** local telephone calls and high-speed Internet.

SEWARD WINDSONG LODGE

Hotel
$149-$329 5/15-9/15

Phone: 907/224-7116

Address: 31772 Herman Leirer Rd 99664 **Location:** 3.5 mi n on SR 9, then 0.5 mi w. **Facility:** Smoke free premises. 180 one-bedroom standard units, some with whirlpools. 2 stories (no elevator), exterior corridors. *Bath:* combo or shower only. **Parking:** on-site. **Terms:** open 5/15-9/15, 14 day cancellation notice. **Amenities:** video library (fee), DVD players, voice mail, hair dryers. **Dining:** Resurrection Roadhouse, see separate listing. **Guest Services:** airport transportation-Seward Airport, area transportation-downtown & harbor, wireless Internet. **Business Services:** meeting rooms, PC. **Free Special Amenities:** local telephone calls and high-speed Internet.

—— WHERE TO DINE ——

CHINOOKS WATERFRONT RESTAURANT

Seafood
$8-$35

Phone: 907/224-2207

Diners will enjoy, on a clear day, the spectacular views of the mountains and harbor from the large panoramic windows. A great choice for both family and special occasion dining, the restaurant features two floors of dining with great views from all tables. The view is complemented by the chef's selection of fresh local seafood, pasta and steak selections. Casual dress. **Bar:** Full bar. **Hours:** Open 4/1-10/15; 11:30 am-10 pm. **Address:** 1404 Fourth Ave 99664 **Location:** At Small Boat Harbor. **Parking:** street.

CHRISTO'S PALACE

American
$12-$28

Phone: 907/224-5255

This popular downtown spot has a little something for everyone on its menu. Pizza is the house specialty but burgers, Mexican fare, pasta, steaks and such fresh Alaskan seafood as king crab legs, salmon and halibut round out the offerings. Casual dress. **Bar:** Full bar. **Hours:** 11 am-10:30 pm. Closed: 11/25, 12/25. **Address:** 133 Fourth Ave 99664 **Location:** Just n of Alaska SeaLife Center; downtown. **Parking:** street.

ORIENTAL GARDEN

Chinese
$8-$18

Phone: 907/224-7677

This casual restaurant boasts very authentic Oriental decor, complete with Chinese lanterns and a comfortable ambience. A tasty luncheon buffet is featured Monday through Saturday in addition to full a la carte selections. Both Japanese and Chinese cuisines are featured here, and the very reasonably priced combination meals are popular choices. Casual dress. **Bar:** Full bar. **Reservations:** accepted. **Hours:** 11 am-10 pm. **Address:** 313 4th Ave 99664 **Location:** Just n of Alaska SeaLife Center; downtown. **Parking:** street.

PEKING RESTAURANT

Phone: 907/224-5444

Chinese
$7-$15

The traditional restaurant serves a variety of dishes, including chicken balls and lemon chicken and rice, as well as dishes inspired by the area. For a new twist, try the kung pao halibut, a tasty dish that is sure to please. At lunch you satisfy any hunger at the all-you-can-eat buffet, or order a la carte off the menu. Casual dress. **Bar:** Full bar. **Reservations:** accepted. **Hours:** 10 am-11 pm. Closed major holidays. **Address:** 338 Fourth Ave 99664 **Location:** Downtown. **Parking:** street.

RESURRECTION ROADHOUSE

Phone: 907/224-7116

Regional American
$5-$32

Continuing the theme of the adjacent lodge, you'll be seated in a dining room with a natural wood decor while enjoying the views of the wooded setting overlooking a glacial stream. Heaping portions of tasty Alaskan seafood is the standout here. Dressy casual. **Bar:** Full bar. **Reservations:** suggested. **Hours:** Open 5/14-9/15; 6 am-2 & 5-10 pm. **Address:** 31772 Herman Leirer Rd 99664 **Location:** 3.5 mi n on SR 9, then 0.5 mi w; in Seward Windsong Lodge. **Parking:** on-site.

SITKA pop. 8,835

ALASKA OCEAN VIEW BED AND BREAKFAST INN

Book great rates at AAA.com   **Phone: (907)747-8310**

Bed & Breakfast
$99-$249 All Year

Address: 1101 Edgecumbe Dr 99835 **Location:** 1 mi n on Halibut Point Rd; 5.7 mi s of Alaska Marine Hwy ferry terminal, just e on Kashevaroff St, then just s. Located in a residential area. **Facility:** Attractively decorated rooms with excellent amenities are offered at this oceanview B&B; a garden pond enhances the setting. Smoke free premises. 3 one-bedroom standard units, some with whirlpools. 2 stories (no elevator), interior corridors. **Parking:** on-site. **Terms:** 2 night minimum stay - seasonal, cancellation fee imposed. **Amenities:** video library, DVD players, CD players, irons, hair dryers. **Leisure Activities:** whirlpool, badminton, croquet, library, horseshoes. **Guest Services:** wireless Internet. **Business Services:** PC. **Free Special Amenities: full breakfast and high-speed Internet.**

SHEE ATIKA TOTEM SQUARE INN

Book great rates at AAA.com   **Phone: (907)747-3693**

Hotel
$89-$179 All Year

Address: 201 Katlian St 99835 **Location:** Center; in Totem Square Complex, near Municipal Office. **Facility:** Smoke free premises. 68 units. 67 one-bedroom standard units. 1 one-bedroom suite with kitchen. 4 stories, interior corridors. *Bath:* combo or shower only. **Parking:** on-site. **Amenities:** high-speed Internet, voice mail, hair dryers. *Some:* irons. **Leisure Activities:** exercise room. **Guest Services:** coin laundry, airport transportation-Sitka Airport, area transportation-within 3 mi, wireless Internet. **Business Services:** meeting rooms, business center. **Free Special Amenities: expanded continental breakfast and high-speed Internet.**

SUPER 8-SITKA

Book at AAA.com   **Phone: (907)747-8804**

Hotel
$89-$185 All Year

Address: 404 Sawmill Creek Rd 99835 **Location:** Just e from corner of Lake St and Halibut Point/Sawmill Creek rds; center. **Facility:** 35 one-bedroom standard units. 2 stories (no elevator), interior corridors. **Parking:** on-site. **Amenities:** safes, hair dryers. *Some:* irons. **Leisure Activities:** whirlpool. **Guest Services:** coin laundry, wireless Internet.

WESTMARK SITKA

Book at AAA.com   **Phone: 907/747-6241**

Hotel
Rates not provided

Address: 330 Seward St 99835 **Location:** Center. **Facility:** Smoke free premises. 100 one-bedroom standard units, some with kitchens. 4 stories, interior corridors. *Bath:* combo or shower only. **Parking:** on-site. **Amenities:** *Some:* high-speed Internet. **Dining:** Raven Dining Room, see separate listing. **Guest Services:** valet laundry, wireless Internet. **Business Services:** meeting rooms, PC.

WILD STRAWBERRY LODGE FISHING RESORT

Phone: 907/747-3232

Resort Motel
$65-$145 All Year

Address: 724 Siginaka Way 99835 **Location:** 1 mi n on Halibut Point Rd, just w on Katlian (only traffic light on island). Located at Thomsen Harbor. **Facility:** This is not your typical "fishing lodge," as the owners encourage males and females of all ages to try their hand at catching "the big one." Smoke free premises. 10 units. 8 one-bedroom standard units. 1 two-bedroom suite with kitchen. 1 house. 1 story, interior/exterior corridors. *Bath:* combo or shower only. **Parking:** on-site. **Amenities:** video library. **Leisure Activities:** *Fee:* charter fishing. **Guest Services:** complimentary laundry, area transportation, wireless Internet. **Business Services:** business center.

---- **WHERE TO DINE** ----

CHANNEL CLUB

Phone: 907/747-7440

Regional American
$18-$54

A Sitka tradition since 1956, the restaurant's new owners completely rebuilt the establishment in 2008. It retained many of its original, best-loved menu offerings, so guests will still find signature cuts of organic meats and some salads, but the Culinary Institute-trained, local chef has added many new items: Delicious fresh seafood, salads using organic ingredients and decadent desserts. Every seat in the restaurant has a view of the bay, and a complimentary shuttle is available. Dressy casual. **Bar:** Full bar. **Reservations:** suggested. **Hours:** Open 3/1-12/25 & 2/1-2/28; 4:30 pm-9 pm, Fri & Sat-10 pm; hours vary in winter. **Address:** 2906 Halibut Point Rd 99835 **Location:** 2.9 mi n on Halibut Point Rd from 4-way stop; 3.4 mi s of Alaska Marine Hwy ferry terminal. **Parking:** on-site.

LEVEL II

Phone: 907/747-3900

◆◆◆◆ ◆◆◆◆
American
$11-$27

This second-level restaurant offers great harbor views. Seafood baskets, burgers with homemade potato chips and nicely prepared entrées are offered as well as a lunch-time salad bar. Service is casual and friendly. Casual dress. **Bar:** Full bar. **Reservations:** suggested, for lunch. **Hours:** 4:30 am-9 pm, Sun-7 pm; 9 am-6 pm 5/5-9/30. Closed: 1/1, 12/24-12/26. **Address:** 407 Lincoln St, #201 99835 **Location:** Downtown, second level. **Parking:** on-site (fee). 𝕂

LITTLE TOKYO

Phone: 907/747-5699

◆◆◆
Sushi
$8-$15

This small restaurant with a sushi bar sits just a short walk from the marina. Diners can watch chefs prepare their sushi and sashimi, or they can order from the standard menu. Casual dress. **Bar:** Beer only. **Hours:** noon-9 pm. Closed: 11/25, 12/25. **Address:** 315 Lincoln St 99835 **Location:** Center. **Parking:** street. 𝕂

LUDVIG'S BISTRO

Phone: 907/966-3663

◆◆◆◆ ◆◆◆◆ ◆◆◆◆
Mediterranean
$19-$32

A popular choice with locals and visitors alike, the restaurant serves a variety of Mediterranean fare prepared with regional influences. Dressy casual. **Bar:** Beer & wine. **Reservations:** suggested. **Hours:** 4 pm-10 pm. Closed major holidays; also Sun; Mon in winter. **Address:** 256 Katlian St 99835 **Location:** Center; 0.3 mi n of Totem Square. **Parking:** street.

RAVEN DINING ROOM

Phone: 907/747-6241

◆◆◆◆ ◆◆◆◆
American
$10-$39

This casual restaurant has long served as the training kitchen for chefs who later go on to work on the cruise ships that the restaurant overlooks. Diners can expect standard items ranging from sandwiches to steak as well as creative touches to locally caught and seasonal seafood. Casual dress. **Bar:** Full bar. **Reservations:** suggested. **Hours:** 6:30 am-2 & 5-9 pm, Fri & Sat-10 pm; to 10 pm 5/15-9/15. Closed: 12/25; also for dinner 12/24. **Address:** 330 Seward St 99835 **Location:** Center; in Westmark Sitka. **Parking:** on-site and street. CALL ♿ 𝕂

ROMA ITALIAN RESTAURANT

Phone: 907/966-4600

◆◆◆◆ ◆◆◆◆
Italian
$9-$17

Expect large portions of authentic Italian fare at this locally popular, convenient spot just across from the Westmark. A big draw is the homemade marinara sauce. Casual dress. **Bar:** Beer & wine. **Hours:** 11 am-9 pm, Fri-9:30 pm, Sat noon-9:30 pm, Sun noon-9 pm. Closed major holidays. **Address:** 327 Seward St 99835 **Location:** Center; across from Westmark Sitka. **Parking:** on-site. CALL ♿ 𝕂

VAN WINKLE & SONS

Phone: 907/747-7652

◆◆◆◆ ◆◆◆◆
American
$9-$26

Tasty regional cuisine awaits you at this popular eatery. Alaskan art adorns the walls, and you can gaze at the water while dining. Located upstairs of a small shopping mall near the bridge, the restaurant's view of the bay is spectacular and the food well prepared. Casual dress. **Bar:** Full bar. **Reservations:** suggested, in summer. **Hours:** 11:30 am-1:45 & 5-9:30 pm, Sat from 5 pm 9/15-5/1. Closed: 12/25; also Sun 9/15-5/1. **Address:** 205 Harbor Dr 99835 **Location:** Downtown; across from Crescent Harbor, just before O'Connell Bridge. **Parking:** on-site. CALL ♿ 𝕂 ◣

SKAGWAY pop. 862

WESTMARK INN SKAGWAY   *Book great rates at AAA.com*

Phone: (907)983-6000

(AAA) [SAVE]
◆◆◆
Motel
$135-$145 5/11-9/15

Address: 3rd & Spring St 99840 **Location:** Downtown. **Facility:** 151 one-bedroom standard units. 2 stories (no elevator), interior/exterior corridors. **Bath:** combo or shower only. **Parking:** on-site. **Terms:** open 5/11-9/15, cancellation fee imposed. **Amenities:** irons, hair dryers. **Guest Services:** coin laundry, airport transportation-Skagway Airport, area transportation-local area, wireless Internet. **Business Services:** meeting rooms, PC. **Free Special Amenities:** local telephone calls.

▦ 🍴 🍷 𝕂 ☂ 💻 / SOME UNITS 🛏 ✕ 📱

—— **WHERE TO DINE** ——

BONANZA BAR & GRILL

Phone: 907/983-6214

◆◆◆
American
$9-$20

Open seasonally, this sports bar can be loud and boisterous but is a popular spot for those looking for a wide selection of bar favorites. Certain areas are designated smoking sections. Casual dress. **Bar:** Full bar. **Reservations:** not accepted. **Hours:** Open 5/10-9/15; 10 am-midnight. **Address:** 3rd & Spring St 99840 **Location:** Jct 3rd and Broadway sts; downtown. **Parking:** street. CALL ♿ 𝕂 ◣

STARFIRE

Phone: 907/983-3663

◆◆◆◆ ◆◆◆◆
Thai
$13-$19

Just off Main Street, Starfire offers a casual setting and a chef trained in Thailand, so the twist is American. The spices are perfectly authentic, so diners should specify the heat level. Casual dress. **Bar:** Beer & wine. **Hours:** Open 4/15-10/15; 11 am-10 pm, Sat & Sun from 4 pm. **Address:** 4th & Spring St 99840 **Location:** 4th and Spring sts. **Parking:** street. 𝕂

SWEET TOOTH CAFE

Phone: 907/983-2405

◆◆◆
American
$7-$15

A local favorite, this casual Victorian-style restaurant offers few surprises but is well regarded for its well-prepared breakfasts and lunches. Casual dress. **Reservations:** accepted. **Hours:** 6 am-2 pm. Closed: 1/1, 11/25, 12/25. **Address:** 315 Broadway St 99840 **Location:** Jct 3rd St; downtown. **Parking:** street. 𝕂

SOLDOTNA pop. 3,759

ASPEN HOTEL-SOLDOTNA   *Book at AAA.com*

Hotel
$99-$179 All Year

Phone: (907)260-7736

Address: 326 Binkley Cir 99669 **Location:** Sterling Hwy (SR 1); center. **Facility:** 63 units. 58 one-and 2 two-bedroom standard units, some with whirlpools. 3 one-bedroom suites with efficiencies. 2 stories, interior corridors. *Bath:* combo or shower only. **Parking:** on-site, winter plug-ins. **Terms:** cancellation fee imposed. **Amenities:** video library (fee), DVD players, dual phone lines, voice mail, irons, hair dryers. **Pool(s):** heated indoor. **Leisure Activities:** whirlpool, limited exercise equipment. **Guest Services:** valet and coin laundry, wireless Internet. **Business Services:** meeting rooms, business center.

BEST WESTERN KING SALMON MOTEL   *Book great rates at AAA.com*

Motel
$79-$169 All Year

Phone: (907)262-5857

Address: 35546 A Kenai Spur Hwy 99669 **Location:** Jct Sterling Hwy (SR 1), 1 mi w on Kenai Spur Hwy. **Facility:** 48 one-bedroom standard units, some with efficiencies (no utensils). 2 stories (no elevator), exterior corridors. **Parking:** on-site, winter plug-ins. **Terms:** office hours 7 am-11 pm, check-in 4 pm, 3 day cancellation notice. **Amenities:** high-speed Internet, voice mail, irons, hair dryers. **Guest Services:** coin laundry. **Business Services:** PC. **Free Special Amenities:** local telephone calls and high-speed Internet.

AAA Benefit:
Members save up to 20%, plus 10% bonus points with rewards program.

KENAI RIVER RAVEN LODGE

Bed & Breakfast
$120-$250 All Year

Phone: 907/262-5818

Address: Mile 0.2 Funny River Rd 99669 **Location:** Sterling Hwy (SR 1) at Milepost 96.5, just e. **Facility:** A modern log home in a wooded area steps from Kenai River, this B&B offers bright, cheerful guest rooms; the breakfast room has a stone fireplace. Smoke free premises. 8 one-bedroom standard units, some with efficiencies and/or whirlpools. 3 stories (no elevator), interior corridors. **Parking:** on-site. **Terms:** check-in 4 pm, age restrictions may apply, cancellation fee imposed. **Leisure Activities:** *Fee:* fishing guides. **Guest Services:** wireless Internet. **Free Special Amenities:** full breakfast and high-speed Internet.

ORCA LODGE

Cottage
$190 5/1-9/30

Phone: (907)262-5649

Address: 44250 Oehler Dr 99669 **Location:** Sterling Hwy (SR 1) at Milepost 96.5, 0.8 mi e on Funny River Rd, just n. **Facility:** Smoke free premises. 6 cabins. 1 story, exterior corridors. **Parking:** on-site. **Terms:** open 5/1-9/30, office hours 9 am-10 pm, 30 day cancellation notice. **Leisure Activities:** fishing. *Fee:* charter fishing. **Guest Services:** wireless Internet. **Business Services:** PC.

------ **WHERE TO DINE** ------

BUCKETS SPORTS GRILL

American
$10-$20

Phone: 907/262-7220

This isn't the fanciest restaurant in town but it is the place to watch sports on the big screen while enjoying a cold one with friends. The menu is chock-full of tasty bar munchies like ribs and wings, not to mention awesome burgers and fries. Halibut, chicken, pasta dishes and salads ensure there will be something to satisfy everyone. Casual dress. **Bar:** Full bar. **Hours:** 7 am-10 pm, Fri & Sat-11 pm; hours vary off season. Closed: 12/25. **Address:** 43690 Sterling Hwy (SR 1) 99669 **Location:** Jct Kenai Spur Hwy, just n. **Parking:** on-site.

CHINA SEA RESTAURANT

Chinese
$8-$15

Phone: 907/262-5033

A local favorite for the all-day, all-you-can-eat Chinese buffet, this restaurant offers a nice mix of casual fare in a relaxed setting. The buffet includes a tasty salad bar, a choice of soups and mixed Chinese fare, including noodles, stir-fry, sweet and sour pork, chicken wings and rice. Soft drinks, tea and coffee help wash down the meal. Casual dress. **Hours:** 11 am-8:30 pm. Closed: 12/25. **Address:** 44539 Sterling Hwy, Suite 210 99669 **Location:** Sterling Hwy (SR 1); in the Blazy Soldotna Mall, 2nd Floor. **Parking:** on-site.

FINE THYME CAFE AT RIVER CITY BOOKS

American
$8-$11

Phone: 907/262-6620

Tucked in the back of a bookstore, the restaurant is one of the city's best-kept secrets. A limited menu lists a choice of sandwiches, wraps, soups and often a quiche of the day. Guests are welcomed to linger over a cup of coffee, then browse the bookstore. Casual dress. **Hours:** 9 am-5 pm, Sun 11 am-4 pm. Closed major holidays. **Address:** 43977 Sterling Hwy 99669 **Location:** Jct Sterling Hwy (SR 1) and Kenai Spur Hwy; in Cornerstone Marketplace. **Parking:** on-site.

FROSO'S FAMILY DINING

American
$8-$36

Phone: 907/262-7797

The family-oriented restaurant has a distinct Greek influence in its decor and menu selections. Guests enjoy the comfortable booths and ornate chandeliers that adorn the ceilings. The extensive menu includes fine steak and seafood options, freshly made pizzas and pasta dishes, and a full Mexican section. All entrees include soup or salad, or for an additional charge, diners can indulge in the salad bar. Casual dress. **Bar:** Full bar. **Hours:** 11 am-midnight. Closed major holidays. **Address:** 35433 Kenai Spur Hwy 99669 **Location:** Jct Sterling Hwy (SR 1), 0.7 mi w. **Parking:** on-site.

STERLING pop. 4,705

SUZIE'S CAFE

American
$7-$14

Phone: 907/260-5751

Ask anyone in Sterling for a great, inexpensive place to eat, and this place will be mentioned again and again. The diner-style eatery is conveniently located on the highway so guests can stop to enjoy huge burgers, fish and chips, sandwiches and salads. Breakfast is available on weekends, and the service is prompt and attentive. Casual dress. **Reservations:** not accepted. **Hours:** Open 5/15-9/15; 11:30 am-8 pm. **Address:** Milepost 82.7, Sterling Hwy 99672 **Location:** Milepost 83, Sterling Hwy (SR 1). **Parking:** on-site.

TALKEETNA pop. 772

TALKEETNA ALASKAN LODGE

Hotel
$189-$599 5/15-9/17

Phone: (907)733-9500

Address: 23601 S Talkeetna Spur Rd 99676 **Location:** 3.5 mi s of Talkeetna. **Facility:** Smoke free premises. 212 units. 209 one-bedroom standard units. 3 one-bedroom suites, some with whirlpools. 3 stories, interior/exterior corridors. *Bath:* combo or shower only. **Parking:** on-site. **Terms:** open 5/15-9/17, 15 day cancellation notice-fee imposed. **Amenities:** voice mail, irons, hair dryers. **Dining:** Foraker Dining Room, see separate listing. **Leisure Activities:** outdoor viewing deck, geocache course, hiking trails, limited exercise equipment. **Guest Services:** airport transportation-Talkeetna Airport, area transportation-train depot, wireless Internet. **Business Services:** meeting rooms, PC (fee). **Free Special Amenities:** local telephone calls.

CAFÉ MICHELE

Continental
$9-$27

Phone: 907/733-5300

A meal at this restaurant is a must when traveling to Talkeetna. The atmosphere is casual and fitting for this "Northern Exposure" town. The signature soy-ginger salmon features fresh Alaskan salmon marinated in Michele's own blend of soy sauce. Or, how about a "serious" Caesar salad topped with grilled herb chicken or fresh mesquite halibut. Choose from a selection of homemade desserts, including bourbon vanilla cheesecake. Casual dress. **Bar:** Beer & wine. **Reservations:** accepted. **Hours:** Open 5/1-10/1; 11 am-3 & 5:30-10 pm. **Address:** 2238 Talkeetna Spur Rd 99676 **Location:** Milepost 13.5 (Talkeetna Spur Rd) and Second St. **Parking:** on-site.

FORAKER DINING ROOM

American
$25-$40

Phone: 907/733-9500

The chef at Foraker creates dishes utilizing some of the state's great seafood. Lamb and tender venison also make appearances on the menu, and the in-house desserts—especially the chocolate mousse mole hill cake—are fabulous. The dining room offers great views of Mt. McKinley through large picture windows. Casual dress. **Bar:** Full bar. **Reservations:** suggested. **Hours:** Open 5/14-9/18; 5 pm-10 pm. **Address:** 23601 S Talkeetna Spur Rd 99676 **Location:** 1.5 mi s; in Talkeetna Alaskan Lodge. **Parking:** on-site.

TALKEETNA ROADHOUSE

Coffee/Tea
$4-$10

Phone: 907/733-1351

The food is simple and the decor basic, but the atmosphere and desserts are unforgettable. A city stop is not complete without a stop to the historic roadhouse. The dessert case is stocked with fresh, homemade goodies, ranging from huge hiker cookies to pies to the ultimate cinnamon bun. Guests seat themselves as they walk in the door and are entertained by the banter of the staff. Casual dress. **Bar:** Beer & wine. **Reservations:** not accepted. **Hours:** 7 am-2 & 4-9 pm; Sat & Sun 7 am-9 pm 10/1-4/30. Closed major holidays. **Address:** Main St 99676 **Location:** Downtown; in historic district. **Parking:** on-site. Historic

WILD FLOWER CAFE

American
$9-$35

Phone: 907/733-2695

This simply decorated little cafe in the heart of historic Talkeetna boasts an all-house-made menu, from the salad dressings to the hamburger buns. For lunch, the delicious Alaskan halibut sandwich with house mayo is a standout among fresh salads, pizza and burgers. Dinner entrees include fresh stuffed halibut and grilled salmon. Diners can enjoy a meal inside at one of the eight tables or on the deck to watch all the bustle of Main Street. Casual dress. **Bar:** Beer & wine. **Reservations:** not accepted. **Hours:** Open 5/23-9/30; 11:30 am-9 pm, Fri & Sat-9:30 pm, Sun noon-9 pm. **Address:** 1000 Main St 99676 **Location:** Center. **Parking:** street.

TOK pop. 1,393

CLEFT OF THE ROCK BED & BREAKFAST

Cabin
$95-$160 All Year

Phone: (907)883-4219

Address: 0.5 Sundog Tr 99780 **Location:** Jct SR 1 and 2 (Alaskan Hwy), 2.5 mi w on SR 2 (Alaskan Hwy) to Sundog Tr, then 0.5 mi n. **Facility:** Smoke free premises. 8 units. 3 one-bedroom standard units, some with whirlpools. 5 cabins. 2 stories (no elevator), interior/exterior corridors. *Bath:* some shared or private, combo or shower only. **Parking:** on-site, winter plug-ins. **Terms:** check-in 5 pm, 3 day cancellation notice-fee imposed. **Amenities:** video library. *Some:* DVD players. **Leisure Activities:** cross country skiing, play area, hiking trails, horseback riding, basketball. **Guest Services:** wireless Internet. **Business Services:** PC. **Free Special Amenities:** full breakfast and high-speed Internet.

WESTMARK INN TOK

Motel
Rates not provided

Book great rates at AAA.com

Phone: 907/883-5174

Address: Jct Alaska & Glenn Hwys 99780 **Location:** On SR 1; jct SR 2 (Alaskan Hwy). **Facility:** 93 one-bedroom standard units. 2 stories (no elevator), exterior corridors. **Parking:** on-site. **Terms:** open 5/15-9/9. **Amenities:** voice mail, irons, hair dryers. **Guest Services:** coin laundry. **Business Services:** PC. **Free Special Amenities:** local telephone calls.

------ WHERE TO DINE ------

FAST EDDY'S RESTAURANT

American
$7-$32

Phone: 907/883-4411

Decorated in contemporary appointments, the comfortable, family-oriented restaurant specializes in hoagies, steaks, halibut and handmade pizzas. Also on the diverse menu are gourmet burgers, sandwiches and pasta. The key word is fast—meals are served with remarkable speed by incredibly friendly servers who epitomize the idea of Northern hospitality. Casual dress. **Bar:** Beer & wine. **Reservations:** accepted. **Hours:** 6 am-11 pm; to 10 pm in winter. Closed: 1/1, 11/25, 12/25. **Address:** 1313 Alaska Hwy 99780 **Location:** Jct SR 1 and 2 (Alaskan Hwy), 1 mi e on SR 2 (Alaska Hwy). **Parking:** on-site. 🅰️🅲

TRAPPER CREEK pop. 423

GATE CREEK CABINS

Cottage
$120-$520 All Year

Phone: (907)733-1393

Address: Mile 10.5 Petersville Rd 99683 **Location:** From MM 114 (Parks Hwy), 10.5 mi w at Petersville Rd. **Facility:** Situated outside of town on a regularly stocked lake, the cottages feature an updated decor and offer easy access to swimming, canoeing and fishing. Smoke free premises. 8 cottages. 1-2 stories (no elevator), exterior corridors. *Bath:* combo or shower only. **Parking:** on-site, winter plug-ins. **Terms:** office hours 8 am-10 pm, check-in 4 pm, 2 night minimum stay - seasonal and/or weekends, 10 day cancellation notice. **Amenities:** video library (fee), DVD players. **Leisure Activities:** canoeing, paddleboats, bicycles, playground. *Fee:* snowmobiling.

(ASK) ⊠ ✕ 🅰️ 📺 🅩 🖥 💻 / SOME UNITS FEE 🐾

TRAPPER CREEK INN & RV PARK

Motel
$99-$139 All Year

Phone: 907/733-2302

Address: Mile 114.6 Parks Hwy 99683 **Location:** George Parks Hwy (SR 3), Milepost 114. **Facility:** 4 units. 1 one- and 2 two-bedroom standard units, some with kitchens. 1 three-bedroom suite with kitchen. 3 stories (no elevator), exterior corridors. *Bath:* combo or shower only. **Parking:** on-site. **Terms:** office hours 7 am-10 pm, 7 day cancellation notice. **Guest Services:** coin laundry, wireless Internet. (ASK) 🍴 ✕ 🅰️ 🅩 💻 / SOME UNITS FEE 🐾 🖥

VALDEZ pop. 4,036

BEST WESTERN VALDEZ HARBOR INN   *Book great rates at AAA.com*

(AAA) (SAVE)

Hotel
$170-$200 3/1-9/15
$150-$180 9/16-2/28

Phone: (907)835-3434

Address: 100 N Harbor Dr 99686 **Location:** Just s at Meals Ave. At small boat Harbor. **Facility:** 88 one-bedroom standard units, some with whirlpools. 2 stories (no elevator), interior corridors. *Bath:* combo or shower only. **Parking:** on-site. **Amenities:** video library (fee), DVD players, voice mail, irons, hair dryers. *Some:* high-speed Internet. **Dining:** Alaska's Bistro, see separate listing. **Leisure Activities:** exercise room. **Guest Services:** coin laundry, airport transportation-Valdez Airport, area transportation-ferry, wireless Internet, barbershop. **Business Services:** meeting rooms. **Free Special Amenities: expanded continental breakfast and high-speed Internet.**

✈️ 🍴 CALL &M 🅰️ 🐾 🖥 📠 💻 / SOME UNITS FEE 🐾 ✕

AAA Benefit:
Members save up to 20%, plus 10% bonus points with rewards program.

Get a Fresh Perspective
on AAATravelViews.com

· Blogs from our experts on popular and unique destinations · The latest in helpful travel advice and news · Photos, videos, maps and special member offers

Share travel at AAATravelViews.com.

MOUNTAIN SKY HOTEL & SUITES

Book at AAA.com

Phone: (907)835-4445

Hotel
$89-$199 All Year

Address: 100 Meals Ave 99686 **Location:** Richardson Hwy to Egan Dr; center. **Facility:** Smoke free premises. 103 units. 97 one- and 2 two-bedroom standard units, some with whirlpools. 4 one-bedroom suites with efficiencies. 3 stories (no elevator), interior corridors. *Bath:* combo or shower only. **Parking:** on-site, winter plug-ins. **Terms:** cancellation fee imposed. **Amenities:** video library (fee), voice mail, irons, hair dryers. **Pool(s):** heated indoor. **Leisure Activities:** whirlpool, exercise room. **Guest Services:** coin laundry, wireless Internet. **Business Services:** meeting rooms, PC.

—— WHERE TO DINE ——

ALASKA HALIBUT HOUSE

Phone: 907/835-2788

American
$7-$12

This restaurant located just steps from the harbor features fresh seafood, primarily halibut and salmon, prepared breaded and deep fried. Casual dress. **Reservations:** not accepted. **Hours:** 11 am-10 pm; hours vary off season. Closed major holidays. **Address:** 208 Meals Ave 99686 **Location:** Just n. **Parking:** on-site.

ALASKA'S BISTRO

Phone: 907/835-5688

Mediterranean
$20-$36

The nice restaurant offers fine service, a casually upscale atmosphere and a menu that centers on local seafood prepared with Italian influences. Casual dress. **Bar:** Full bar. **Reservations:** suggested. **Hours:** 5 pm-9 pm. Closed: 12/25; also Sun-Wed off season. **Address:** 100 N Harbor Dr 99686 **Location:** Just s at Meals Ave; in Best Western Valdez Harbor Inn. **Parking:** on-site.

WASILLA pop. 5,469

AGATE INN

Book at AAA.com

Phone: (907)373-2290

Hotel
$135-$375 All Year

Address: 4725 Begich Cir 99654 **Location:** 0.9 mi n of jct SR 3 (George Parks Hwy) and Seward Meridian Rd, 0.8 mi e, just s, then just e. **Facility:** Smoke free premises. 13 units. 8 one-bedroom standard units, some with whirlpools. 3 two- and 1 three-bedroom suites with kitchens. 1 house. 2 stories (no elevator), interior/exterior corridors. **Parking:** on-site, winter plug-ins. **Terms:** office hours 4:30 am-6 pm, check-in 4 pm, 14 day cancellation notice-fee imposed. **Amenities:** video library, high-speed Internet, voice mail, hair dryers. *Some:* irons. **Leisure Activities:** horseshoes. **Guest Services:** coin laundry. **Business Services:** meeting rooms.

BEST WESTERN LAKE LUCILLE INN

Book great rates at AAA.com

Phone: (907)373-1776

Hotel
$99-$200 All Year

Address: 1300 W Lake Lucille Dr 99654 **Location:** SR 3 (George Parks Hwy), just w on Hallea Ln; center. **Facility:** Smoke free premises. 54 units. 50 one-bedroom standard units. 4 one-bedroom suites with whirlpools. 2 stories (no elevator), interior corridors. **Parking:** on-site. **Amenities:** voice mail, irons, hair dryers. *Some:* high-speed Internet. **Leisure Activities:** sauna, whirlpool, boat dock, viewing decks, exercise room. **Guest Services:** coin laundry, wireless Internet. **Business Services:** business center. *(See color ad p 761 & p 331)*

AAA Benefit:
Members save up to 20%, plus 10% bonus points with rewards program.

FREE continental breakfast and early check-in/late check-out

—— WHERE TO DINE ——

EVANGELO'S RESTAURANT

Phone: 907/376-1212

Mediterranean
$8-$35

This open, airy, elegant restaurant has some lovely windows overlooking the scenery while still maintaining some privacy nooks. One of the most popular restaurants in town, it features a mainly Italian menu with a touch of Greek. Pastas, pizzas, steaks, seafood and a variety of sandwiches and calzones are standard fare. Casual dress. **Bar:** Full bar. **Reservations:** accepted. **Hours:** 10 am-10 pm. Closed: 11/25, 12/25. **Address:** 2530 E Parks Hwy 99654 **Location:** 1.2 mi n of jct Parks Hwy and Fairview Loop exit. **Parking:** on-site.

Offices

Cities with main offices are listed in **BOLD TYPE** and toll-free member service numbers in *ITALIC TYPE*.
All are closed Saturdays, Sundays and holidays unless otherwise indicated.
The addresses, phone numbers and hours for any AAA/CAA office are subject to change.
The type of service provided is designated below the name of the city where the office is located:

✦ Auto travel services, including books and maps, and on-demand TripTik® routings.
● Auto travel services, including selected books and maps, and on-demand TripTik® routings.
■ Books/maps only, no marked maps or on-demand TripTik® routings.
▲ Travel Agency Services, cruise, tour, air, car and rail reservations; domestic and international hotel reservations; passport photo services; international and domestic travel guides and maps; travel money products; and International Driving Permits. In addition, assistance with travel related insurance products including trip cancellation, travel accident, lost luggage, trip delay and assistance products.
✪ Insurance services provided.
✖ Car Care Plus Facility provides car care services.

AAA NATIONAL OFFICE: 1000 AAA DRIVE, HEATHROW, FLORIDA 32746-5063, (407) 444-7000

ALASKA

ANCHORAGE—AAA MOUNTAINWEST, 1005 E DIMOND BLVD ST 2A, 99515. WEEKDAYS (M-F) 8:30-5:30. (907) 344-4310, *(800) 391-4222.* ✦ ▲ ✪

PROVINCE OF ALBERTA

CALGARY—ALBERTA MOTOR ASSOCIATION, #100 530 8TH AVE SW, T2P 3S8. WEEKDAYS (M-F) 9:00-5:00. (403) 262-2345, *(800) 642-3810.* ● ▲ ✪

CALGARY—ALBERTA MOTOR ASSOCIATION, 3650 20 AVE NE, T1Y 6E8. WEEKDAYS (M-F) 9:00-5:00, SAT 9:00-5:00. (403) 590-0001, *(800) 642-3810.* ● ▲ ✪

CALGARY—ALBERTA MOTOR ASSOCIATION, 4700 17TH AVE SW, T3E 0E3. WEEKDAYS (M-F) 9:00-5:00, SAT 9:00-5:00. (403) 240-5300, *(800) 642-3810.* ● ▲ ✪

CALGARY—ALBERTA MOTOR ASSOCIATION, #600 85 SHAWVILLE BLVD SE, T2Y 3W5. WEEKDAYS (M-F) 9:00-5:00, SAT 9:00-5:00. (403) 254-2447, *(800) 642-3810.* ● ▲ ✪

CALGARY—ALBERTA MOTOR ASSOCIATION, 220 CROWFOOT CRES NW, T3G 3N5. WEEKDAYS (M-F) 9:00-5:00, SAT 9:00-5:00. (403) 239-6644, *(800) 642-3810.* ● ▲ ✪

CALGARY—ALBERTA MOTOR ASSOCIATION, 10816 MACLEOD TRL SE, T2J 5N8. WEEKDAYS (M-F) 9:00-5:00, SAT 9:00-5:00. (403) 278-3530, *(800) 642-3810.* ● ▲ ✪

CAMROSE—ALBERTA MOTOR ASSOCIATION, 6702 48 AVE, T4V 4S3. WEEKDAYS (M-F) 9:00-5:00, SAT 9:00-1:00. (780) 672-3391, *(800) 642-3810.* ● ▲ ✪

EDMONTON—ALBERTA MOTOR ASSOCIATION, 11220 109 ST NW, T5G 2T6. WEEKDAYS (M-F) 9:00-5:00, SAT 9:00-5:00. (780) 474-8601, *(800) 642-3810.* ✦ ▲ ✪

EDMONTON—ALBERTA MOTOR ASSOCIATION, 5040 MANNING DR NW, T5A 5B4. WEEKDAYS (M-F) 9:00-5:00, SAT 9:00-5:00. (780) 473-3112, *(800) 642-3810.* ● ▲ ✪

EDMONTON—**ALBERTA MOTOR ASSOCIATION**, 10310 G A MACDONALD AVE NW, T6J 6R7. WEEKDAYS (M-F) 9:00-5:30, SAT 9:00-5:00. (780) 430-5555. ● ▲ ✪

EDMONTON—ALBERTA MOTOR ASSOCIATION, 9938 170 ST, T5T 6G7. WEEKDAYS (M-F) 9:00-5:30, SAT 9:00-5:00. (780) 484-1221, *(800) 642-3810.* ● ▲ ✪

FORT MCMURRAY—ALBERTA MOTOR ASSOCIATION, 4 HOSPITAL ST, T9H 5E4. WEEKDAYS (M-F) 9:00-5:00. (780) 743-2433, *(800) 642-3810.* ● ▲ ✪

GRANDE PRAIRIE—ALBERTA MOTOR ASSOCIATION, 11401 99 ST, T8V 2H6. WEEKDAYS (M-F) 9:00-5:00, SAT 9:00-2:00. (780) 532-4421, *(800) 642-3810.* ● ▲ ✪

LETHBRIDGE—ALBERTA MOTOR ASSOCIATION, 120 SCENIC DR S, T1J 4R4. WEEKDAYS (M-F) 8:30-5:00, SAT 9:00-12:30. (403) 328-1181, *(800) 642-3810.* ● ▲ ✪

MEDICINE HAT—ALBERTA MOTOR ASSOCIATION, 2710 13 AVE SE, T1A 3P8. WEEKDAYS (M-F) 9:00-5:00, SAT 9:00-12:30. (403) 527-1166, *(800) 642-3810.* ● ▲ ✪

RED DEER—ALBERTA MOTOR ASSOCIATION, 141 2004 50TH AVE, T4R 3A2. WEEKDAYS (M-F) 9:00-5:00, SAT 9:00-12:30. (403) 342-6633, *(800) 642-3810.* ✦ ▲ ✪

SHERWOOD PARK—ALBERTA MOTOR ASSOCIATION, 236-222 BASELINE VILLAGE, T8H 1S8. WEEKDAYS (M-F) 9:00-5:00. (780) 467-8520. ✪

ST. ALBERT—ALBERTA MOTOR ASSOCIATION, 200 665 ST ALBERT TRAIL, T8N 3L3. WEEKDAYS (M-F) 8:30-05:30, SAT 9:00-5:00. (780) 418-8900, *(800) 642-3810.* ✦ ▲ ✪

PROVINCE OF BRITISH COLUMBIA

HEADQUARTERS CUSTOMER CONTACT CENTRE, 4567 CANADA WAY, V5G 4T1. WEEKDAYS (M-F) 9:00-5:00, SAT 9:00-5:00. (604) 268-5555, *(800) 663-1956.* ▲

ABBOTSFORD—CAA BRITISH COLUMBIA, 33338 S FRASER WAY, V2S 2B4. WEEKDAYS (M-F) 9:00-5:30, SAT 9:00-5:00. (604) 870-3850, *(800) 663-1956.* ■ ✪

BURNABY—CAA BRITISH COLUMBIA, 4567 CANADA WAY, V5G 4T1. WEEKDAYS (M-F) 9:00-5:30, SAT 9:00-5:00. (604) 268-5500, *(800) 663-1956.* ✦ ✪

CHILLIWACK—CAA BRITISH COLUMBIA, #190-45428 LUCKAKUCK WAY, V2R 3S9. WEEKDAYS (M-F) 9:00-5:30, SAT 9:00-5:00. (604) 824-2720, *(800) 663-1956.* ■ ✪

COQUITLAM—CAA BRITISH COLUMBIA, 50-2773 BARNET HWY, V3B 1C2. WEEKDAYS (M-F) 9:00-6:00, SAT 9:00-5:00. (604) 268-5750, *(800) 663-1956.* ■ ✪

COURTENAY—CAA BRITISH COLUMBIA, 17-1599 CLIFFE AVE, V9N 2K6. WEEKDAYS (M-F) 9:00-5:30, SAT 9:00-5:00. (250) 703-2328, *(800) 663-1956.* ■ ✪

DELTA—CAA BRITISH COLUMBIA, SCOTT 72 CTR 7343-120 ST, V4C 6P5. WEEKDAYS (M-F) 9:00-6:00, SAT 9:00-5:00. (604) 268-5900, *(800) 663-1956.* ■ ✪

KAMLOOPS—CAA BRITISH COLUMBIA, 400-500 NOTRE DAME DR, V2C 6T6. WEEKDAYS (M-F) 9:00-6:00, SAT 9:00-5:00. (250) 852-4600, *(800) 663-1956.* ■ ✪

KELOWNA—CAA BRITISH COLUMBIA, #18-1470 HARVEY AVE, V1Y 9K8. WEEKDAYS (M-F) 9:00-6:00, SAT 9:00-5:00. (250) 870-4900, *(800) 663-1956.* ■ ✪

LANGLEY—CAA BRITISH COLUMBIA, 10- 20190 LANGLEY BYPASS, V3A 9J9. WEEKDAYS (M-F) 9:00-6:00, SAT 9:00-5:00. (604) 268-5950, *(800) 663-1956.* ■ ○

MAPLE RIDGE—CAA BRITISH COLUMBIA, # 500 20395 LOUGHEED HWY, V2X 2P9. WEEKDAYS (M-F) 9:00-5:30, SAT 9:00-5:00. (604) 205-1200, *(800) 633-1956.* ■

NANAIMO—CAA BRITISH COLUMBIA, METRAL PL-6581 AULDS RD, V9T 6J6. WEEKDAYS (M-F) 9:00-6:00, SAT 9:00-5:00. (250) 390-7700, *(800) 663-1956.* ■ ○

NELSON—CAA BRITISH COLUMBIA, 596 BAKER ST, V1L 4H9. WEEKDAYS (M-F) 9:00-5:00, SAT 9:00-5:00. (250) 505-1720, *(800) 663-1956.* ■ ○

NEW WESTMINSTER—CAA BRITISH COLUMBIA, 501 SIXTH ST, V3L 3B9. WEEKDAYS (M-F) 9:00-5:30, SAT 9:00-5:00. (604) 268-5700, *(800) 663-1956.* ■ ○

NORTH VANCOUVER—CAA BRITISH COLUMBIA, 333 BROOKSBANK AVE, V7J 3S8. WEEKDAYS (M-F) 9:00-6:00, SAT 9:00-5:00. (604) 205-1050, *(800) 663-1956.* ■ ○

PENTICTON—CAA BRITISH COLUMBIA, 100-2100 MAIN ST, V2A 5H7. WEEKDAYS (M-F) 9:00-5:30, SAT 9:00-5:00. (250) 487-2450, *(800) 663-1956.* ■ ○

PRINCE GEORGE—CAA BRITISH COLUMBIA, 100- 2324 FERRY AVE, V2N 0B1. WEEKDAYS (M-F) 9:00-6:00, SAT 9:00-5:00. (250) 649-2399, *(800) 663-1956.* ■ ○

RICHMOND—CAA BRITISH COLUMBIA, 180 5951 NO 3 RD, V6X 2E3. WEEKDAYS (M-F) 9:00-5:30, SAT 9:00-5:00. (604) 268-5850, *(800) 663-1956.* ■ ○

SURREY—CAA BRITISH COLUMBIA, #C4-15285 101 AVE, V3R 9V8. WEEKDAYS (M-F) 9:00-6:00, SAT 9:00-5:00. (604) 205-1000, *(800) 663-1956.* ■ ○

SURREY—CAA BRITISH COLUMBIA, 130 2655 KING GEORGE HWY, V4P 1H7. WEEKDAYS (M-F) 9:00-6:00, SAT 9:00-5:00. (604) 205-1150, *(800) 663-1956.* ■ ○

VANCOUVER—CAA BRITISH COLUMBIA, 999 W BROADWAY, V5Z 1K5. WEEKDAYS (M-F) 9:00-5:30, SAT 9:00-5:00. (604) 268-5600, *(800) 663-1956.* ■ ○

VANCOUVER—CAA BRITISH COLUMBIA, 2347 W 41ST AVE, V6M 2A3. WEEKDAYS (M-F) 9:00-5:30, SAT 9:00-5:00. (604) 268-5800, *(800) 663-1956.* ■ ○

VERNON—CAA BRITISH COLUMBIA, #520 4400 32ND ST, V1T 9H2. WEEKDAYS (M-F) 9:00-6:00, SAT 9:00-5:00. (250) 550-2400, *(800) 663-1956.* ■ ○

VICTORIA—CAA BRITISH COLUMBIA, 169 2401C MILLSTREAM RD, V9B 3R5. WEEKDAYS (M-F) 9:00-5:30, SAT 9:00-5:00. (250) 391-3250, *(800) 663-1956.* + ○

VICTORIA—CAA BRITISH COLUMBIA, 1262 QUADRA ST, V8W 2K7. WEEKDAYS (M-F) 9:00-5:00, SAT 9:00-5:00. (250) 414-8320, *(800) 663-1956.* ■ ○

VICTORIA—CAA BRITISH COLUMBIA, #120-777 ROYAL OAK DR, V8X 4V1. WEEKDAYS (M-F) 8:30-5:30, SAT 9:00-5:00. (250) 704-1750, *(800) 663-1956.* ■ ○

WEST VANCOUVER—CAA BRITISH COLUMBIA, 608 PARK ROYAL N, V7T 1H9. WEEKDAYS (M-F) 9:00-6:00, SAT 9:00-5:00. (604) 268-5650, *(800) 663-1956.* ■ ○

WESTBANK—CAA BRITISH COLUMBIA, 301 3550 CARRINGTON RD, V4T 2Z1. WEEKDAYS (M-F) 9:00-6:00, SAT 9:00-5:00. (250) 707-4800, *(800) 663-1956.* ■ ○

PROVINCE OF MANITOBA

ALTONA—CAA MANITOBA, 61 2ND AVE NE, R0G 0B0. WEEKDAYS (M-F) 9:00-5:00, SAT 9:00-1:00. (204) 324-8474. ● ▲ ○

BRANDON—CAA MANITOBA, 305- 18TH ST N, R7A 6Z2. WEEKDAYS (M-F) 9:00-5:00, THU 9:00-8:00, SAT 9:00-4:00. (204) 571-4111. + ▲ ○

WINNIPEG—CAA MANITOBA, 501 ST ANNES RD, R2M 3E5. WEEKDAYS (M-F) 9:00-6:00, SAT 9:00-4:00. (204) 262-6201. ● ▲ ○

WINNIPEG—CAA MANITOBA, 2211 MCPHILLIPS ST UNIT C, R2V 3M5. WEEKDAYS (M-F) 9:00-6:00, SAT 9:00-4:00. (204) 262-6223. ● ▲

WINNIPEG—CAA MANITOBA, 870 EMPRESS ST, R3G 3H3. WEEKDAYS (M-F) 9:00-6:00, SAT 9:00-4:00. (204) 262-6100. + ▲

PROVINCE OF SASKATCHEWAN

ESTEVAN—CAA SASKATCHEWAN, 1340-400 KING ST, S4A 2B4. WEEKDAYS (M-F) 9:00-5:30, SAT 9:00-5:30. (306) 637-2185, *(800) 564-6222.* + ▲ ○

MOOSE JAW—CAA SASKATCHEWAN, 80 CARIBOU ST W, S6H 2J6. WEEKDAYS (M-F) 9:00-5:30, SAT 9:00-5:30. (306) 693-5195, *(800) 564-6222.* + ▲ ○

NORTH BATTLEFORD—CAA SASKATCHEWAN, 2002-100TH ST, S9A 0X5. WEEKDAYS (M-F) 9:00-5:30, SAT 9:00-5:30. (306) 445-9451, *(800) 564-6222.* + ▲ ○

PRINCE ALBERT—CAA SASKATCHEWAN, #29 2995 2ND AVE W, S6V 5V5. WEEKDAYS (M-F) 9:00-5:30, SAT 9:00-5:30. (306) 764-6818, *(800) 564-6222.* + ▲ ○

REGINA—CAA SASKATCHEWAN, 2510 E QUANCE ST, S4V 2X5. WEEKDAYS (M-F) 9:00-5:30, SAT 9:00-5:30. (306) 791-4323, *(800) 564-6222.* ● ▲ ○

REGINA—CAA SASKATCHEWAN, 200 ALBERT ST, S4R 2N4. WEEKDAYS (M-F) 9:00-5:30, SAT 9:00-5:30. (306) 791-4337, *(800) 564-6222.* + ▲ ○

REGINA—CAA SASKATCHEWAN, 4528 ALBERT ST, S4S 6B4. WEEKDAYS (M-F) 9:00-5:30, SAT 9:00-5:30. (306) 791-4322, *(800) 564-6222.* + ▲ ○

SASKATOON—CAA SASKATCHEWAN, 150- 1ST AVE S, S7K 1K2. WEEKDAYS (M-F) 9:00-5:30, SAT 9:00-5:30. (306) 668-3737, *(800) 564-6222.* ● ▲ ○

SASKATOON—CAA SASKATCHEWAN, 3110 8TH ST E #1, S7H 0W2. WEEKDAYS (M-F) 9:00-5:30, SAT 9:00-5:30. (306) 668-3770, *(800) 564-6222.* ● ▲ ○

SWIFT CURRENT—CAA SASKATCHEWAN, 15 DUFFERIN ST W, S9H 5A1. WEEKDAYS (M-F) 9:00-5:30, SAT 9:00-5:30. (306) 773-3193, *(800) 564-6222.* + ▲ ○

WEYBURN—CAA SASKATCHEWAN, 110 SOURIS AVE, S4H 2Z8. WEEKDAYS (M-F) 9:00-5:30, SAT 9:00-5:30. (306) 842-6651, *(800) 564-6222.* ● ▲ ○

YORKTON—CAA SASKATCHEWAN, 159 BROADWAY ST E, S3N 3K6. WEEKDAYS (M-F) 9:00-5:30, SAT 9:00-5:30. (306) 783-6536, *(800) 564-6222.* + ▲ ○

Population

Canadian population figures—Statistics Canada's 2001 GeoSuite, by permission of Canadian Minister of Industry.

Metric Equivalents Chart

TEMPERATURE

To convert Fahrenheit to Celsius, subtract 32 from the Fahrenheit temperature, multiply by 5 and divide by 9.
To convert Celsius to Fahrenheit, multiply by 9, divide by 5 and add 32.

ACRES

1 acre = 0.4 hectare (ha)	1 hectare = 2.47 acres

MILES AND KILOMETRES

Note: A kilometre is approximately 5/8 or 0.6 of a mile.
To convert kilometres to miles multiply by 0.6.

Miles/Kilometres		Kilometres/Miles	
15	24.1	30	18.6
20	32.2	35	21.7
25	40.2	40	24.8
30	48.3	45	27.9
35	56.3	50	31.0
40	64.4	55	34.1
45	72.4	60	37.2
50	80.5	65	40.3
55	88.5	70	43.4
60	96.6	75	46.6
65	104.6	80	49.7
70	112.7	85	52.8
75	120.7	90	55.9
80	128.7	95	59.0
85	136.8	100	62.1
90	144.8	105	65.2
95	152.9	110	68.3
100	160.9	115	71.4

LINEAR MEASURE

Customary	Metric
1 inch = 2.54 centimetres	1 centimetre = 0.4 inches
1 foot = 30 centimetres	1 metre = 3.3 feet
1 yard = 0.91 metres	1 metre = 1.09 yards
1 mile = 1.6 kilometres	1 kilometre = .62 miles

LIQUID MEASURE

Customary	Metric
1 fluid ounce = 30 millilitres	1 millilitre = .03 fluid ounces
1 cup = .24 litres	1 litre = 2.1 pints
1 pint = .47 litres	1 litre = 1.06 quarts
1 quart = .95 litres	1 litre = .26 gallons
1 gallon = 3.8 litres	

Celsius ° / Fahrenheit °

Celsius		Fahrenheit
100	BOILING	212
37		100
35		95
32		90
29		85
27		80
24		75
21		70
18		65
16		60
13		55
10		50
7		45
4		40
2		35
0	FREEZING	32
-4		25
-7		20
-9		15
-12		10
-15		5
-18		0
-21		-5
-24		-10
-27		-15

WEIGHT

If You Know:	Multiply By:	To Find:
Ounces	28	Grams
Pounds	0.45	Kilograms
Grams	0.035	Ounces
Kilograms	2.2	Pounds

PRESSURE

Air pressure in automobile tires is expressed in kilopascals. Multiply pound-force per square inch (psi) by 6.89 to find kilopascals (kPa).

24 psi = 165 kPa	28 psi = 193 kPa
26 psi = 179 kPa	30 psi = 207 kPa

GALLON AND LITRES

Gallons/Litres				Litres/Gallons			
5	19.0	12	45.6	10	2.6	40	10.4
6	22.8	14	53.2	15	3.9	50	13.0
7	26.6	16	60.8	20	5.2	60	15.6
8	30.4	18	68.4	25	6.5	70	18.2
9	34.2	20	76.0	30	7.8	80	20.8
10	38.0	25	95.0	35	9.1	90	23.4

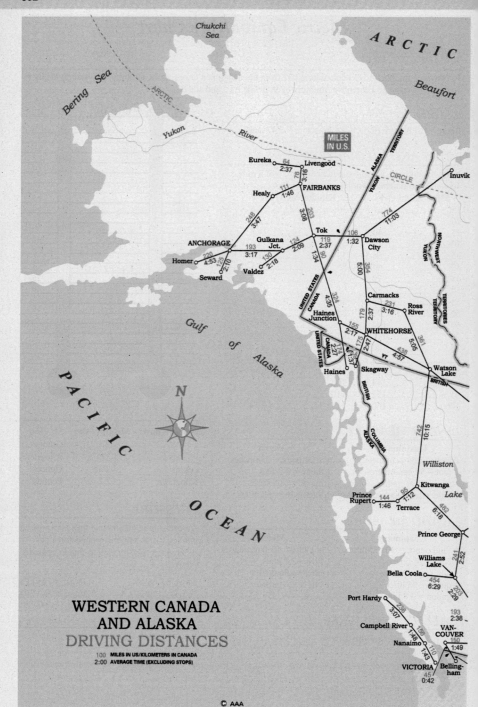

Chukchi Sea

Bering Sea

ARCTIC

Beaufort

Yukon River

MILES IN U.S.

ARCTIC CIRCLE

Eureka 64 Livengood
2:37
78
3:41
Healy 111 FAIRBANKS
1:46
Inuvik
246 3:08 203
3:47
774
11:03
ANCHORAGE 193 Gulkana 124 Tok 119 106 Dawson City
3:17 Jct. 2:09 2:37 1:32
Homer 220 125 130 90 5:00 354
4:53 2:10 2:18 1:34
Seward Valdez
4:35 304 Carmacks 231 Ross River
Haines 179 3:16
Junction 2:37
155 WHITEHORSE 361
2:17 438 5:05
174 175 4:57
1:37 2:47 YT Watson Lake
Haines Skagway BRITISH

Gulf of Alaska

742 10:15

Williston Lake

Kitwanga
Prince 144 1:12
Rupert 96 Terrace 482
1:46 6:18

Prince George

Williams 241
Lake 2:52
Bella Coola
454 203
6:29 2:29

Port Hardy
238 193
3:07 2:38
Campbell River VAN-
199 COUVER
1:48 150
Nanaimo 110 1:49
1:43
VICTORIA Belling-
45 ham
0:42

PACIFIC OCEAN

N

WESTERN CANADA
AND ALASKA
DRIVING DISTANCES

100 MILES IN US/KILOMETERS IN CANADA
2:00 AVERAGE TIME (EXCLUDING STOPS)

© AAA

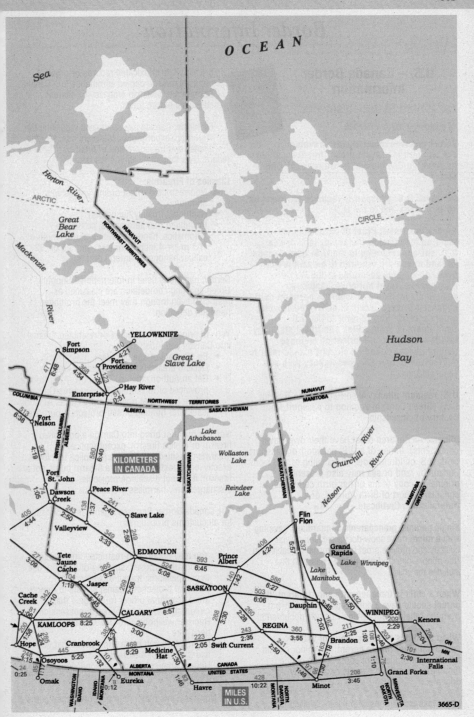

O C E A N

Sea

Horton River

ARCTIC

Great
Bear
Lake

CIRCLE

Mackenzie

NUNAVUT

NORTHWEST TERRITORIES

River

Hudson
Bay

YELLOWKNIFE

Fort
Simpson

310
4:21

Fort
Providence

Great
Slave Lake

471
6:48

388
4:54

1:28

Hay River

Enterprise

51
0:51

COLUMBIA

NORTHWEST   TERRITORIES

NUNAVUT

MANITOBA

SASKATCHEWAN

ALBERTA

513
6:38

Fort
Nelson

Lake
Athabasca

KILOMETERS
IN CANADA

381
4:19

BRITISH COLUMBIA
ALBERTA

880
6:40

ALBERTA
SASKATCHEWAN

Wollaston
Lake

Churchill   River

Nelson   River

Fort
St. John

1:05

Dawson
Creek

Peace River

241
2:45

Reindeer
Lake

SASKATCHEWAN
MANITOBA

243
2:50

138
1:37

Slave Lake

Flin
Flon

405
4:44

349
3:33

249
2:59

408
4:24

537
5:57

Grand
Rapids

271
3:09

Valleyview

Tete
Jaune
Cache

365
3:57

298
2:56

EDMONTON

593
6:45

Prince
Albert

140
1:42

586
6:27

Lake
Manitoba

Lake Winnipeg

336
3:45

432
4:32

104
1:19

Jasper

524
5:08

SASKATOON

503
6:06

Dauphin

WINNIPEG

Cache
Creek

342
4:10

413
3:45

CALGARY

613
6:57

288
3:30

228
2:28

260
2:50

211
2:25

209
1:03

Kenora

1:08
Brandon

2:29

1:06

81

622
8:25

3:00

REGINA

360

202
2:02

2:04

KAMLOOPS

285

223
2:05

Swift Current

243
2:35

241
3:55

ON

MN

Hope

445

Cranbrook

469
5:29

Medicine
Hat

144
1:30

2:50

1:10

Grand Forks

101
2:30

International
Falls

Osoyoos

3:15

5:25

1:32

101

ALBERTA
MONTANA

CANADA
UNITED   STATES

206
3:45

24
0:25

Omak

WASHINGTON

IDAHO

0:12

Eureka

MONTANA

Havre

428
10:22

MONTANA
NORTH DAKOTA

Minot

NORTH
DAKOTA
MINNESOTA

MILES
IN U.S.

3665-D

Border Information

U.S. – Canada Border Information

For United States Residents Traveling to Canada

Border crossing requirements: Travelers are required to present proper travel documents for travel to Canada and to return to the United States.

Air travel: U.S. passport is required for travel by air to Canada and to the U.S.

Land or sea travel: Proof of citizenship is required for travel to Canada by land or sea. U.S. citizens returning to the U.S. from Canada by land or sea are required to present proper travel documents according to the Western Hemisphere Travel Initiative. Approved documents include a passport or passport card, Enhanced Driver's License, or Trusted Traveler program card. Please refer to the U.S. Department of State's Web site travel.state.gov for the most current information on these requirements. Canadian citizens should refer to the Canada Border Services Agency Web site cbsa-asfc.gc.ca.

U.S. resident aliens: Alien Registration Receipt Card (Green Card) in addition to passport from country of citizenship.

Minors: All children must have their own travel documents. In lieu of a U.S. passport or passport card, U.S. children under 16 traveling to and from Canada by land or sea may also present an original or copy of his or her birth certificate, a consular Report of Birth Abroad, or a Naturalization Certificate.

Single parents, grandparents or guardians traveling with a minor must show documentation of legal custody and provide proof of citizenship for each child (the minor's passport or a parent's passport that includes the child).

When a child is traveling with only 1 parent, that parent should have a notarized letter of consent from the other parent or legal custody documents.

When a child is traveling alone or with an individual other than a parent, the minor should have a notarized letter of consent with phone number(s) from both parents or a custody document.

Legal Issues: Persons with felony convictions,

driving while intoxicated records or other offenses may be denied admittance into Canada. Contact the Canadian embassy or nearest consulate before travel.

Firearms: Canada has strict laws regarding the importing, exporting, possession, use, storage, display and transportation of firearms. These are federal laws that apply across the country.

Classes of Firearms:
- Non-restricted (most ordinary rifles and shotguns)
- Restricted (mainly handguns)
- Prohibited (full automatics, converted automatics, handguns with a barrel length of 105 m ($\approx$ 4 inches) or less, and .25 or .32 caliber handguns, among others)

Certain handguns used in International Shooting Union sporting competition are classified as restricted even though they meet the prohibited handgun definition.

Yes: To bring a non-restricted or restricted firearm into Canada you must:
- Be 18 years of age or older
- Declare firearm(s) at first point of entry
- Get an Authorization to Transport (ATT) from a provincial or territorial Chief Firearms Officer before arriving at point of entry (Note: ATT not issued for hunting or self-protection purposes)

No: You may not bring into Canada a prohibited firearm or replica firearm, except replicas of firearms classified as antiques (a replica that looks exactly, or almost exactly, like a firearm but is not a firearm; it cannot discharge projectiles or discharges only harmless projectiles).

The Canada Border Services Agency is responsible for all customs procedures.

Yes:
- You may import non-restricted firearms for legitimate purposes: sporting or hunting; use in competitions; transit movement; or personal protection against wildlife in remote areas (customs officer must agree that circumstances warrant firearm possession)
- Register weapons with U.S. Customs before departure
- Upon return you must show proof that you had the weapon before departure
- Under certain circumstances individuals and businesses may import firearms

No: Non-residents may not import prohibited items.

Fees (in Canadian funds):

- Non-Resident Firearm Declaration – $25 covers all firearms listed on declaration
- Possession and acquisition license – $60 for non-restricted firearms; valid for 5 years
- Temporary Firearms Borrowing License (for non-residents) – $30; may renew once in a 12-month period at no extra cost; $30 thereafter (800-731-4000)
- Imported firearm registration fee – No fee to register or transfer a firearm

Prohibited: Any large capacity cartridge magazine (limited to 5 rounds for semiautomatic rifles or shotguns, 10 rounds for handguns), any device designed to stop the sound of a firearm, any knife with a blade opened by spring pressure (e.g., switchblade), martial arts weapons (e.g., shuriken (shooting stars), nunchaku sticks), mace, blowguns, hand-held compact crossbows and any other weapons declared prohibited by regulation.

Yes: Hunters may bring in, duty-free, 200 rounds of ammunition; competition participants 1,500 rounds. Must show valid license or declaration to purchase ammunition. If planning to hunt in multiple provinces or territories, you must obtain a hunting license from each one.

No: Firearms forbidden in many of Canada's national and provincial parks, game reserves and adjacent areas.

Parks and Hunting Regulation Information:

Newfoundland and Labrador 800-563-6353 or 709-729-2830; Prince Edward Island 888-734-7529 or 902-629-2400; Nova Scotia 800-565-0000 ext 998 or 902-425-5781; New Brunswick 800-561-0123 or 506-789-4982; Quebec 800-363-7777 or 514-873-2015; Ontario 800-668-2746 or 416-314-0944; Manitoba 800-665-0040 or 204-945-3777; Saskatchewan 877-237-2273 or 306-787-2300; Alberta 800-661-8888 or 780-427-4321; British Columbia 800-663-6000 or 250-387-1642; Northwest Territories (Western NWT) 800-661-0788 or 867-873-4059; Nunavut (Eastern NWT) 800-491-7910 or 867-979-1261; Yukon 867-667-5340.

Note: Provinces and territories also have their own laws regulating the transportation of firearms through their areas, usually in connection with their hunting regulations. For further information on the entry of firearms, applying for a license or to obtain authorization to transport a firearm, contact: Canadian Firearms Centre at 800-731-4000.

Personal Baggage:

- Admissible into Canada on a temporary basis without payment of duty and taxes
- Customs may require a refundable security deposit at time of entry
- Deposits not normally required for health- or pleasure-related visits as long as all items are exported at trip's end

Personal baggage that may be taken into Canada on a duty- and tax-free basis includes clothing and personal items, sporting goods, automobiles, vessels, aircraft, snowmobiles, cameras, personal computers, food products and other items appropriate for the purpose and duration of the visit.

Tobacco products – Those meeting age requirements (18 years in Alberta, Manitoba, Northwest Territories and Nunavut, Saskatchewan, Quebec and Yukon Territory; 19 years in other provinces) may bring in 50 cigars, 200 cigarettes, 200 grams of tobacco and 200 tobacco sticks. **Alcohol** – Those meeting age requirements (18 years in Alberta, Manitoba and Quebec; 19 years in other provinces and territories) may bring in limited alcoholic beverages: 40 ounces (1.14 L) of liquor, 1.6 quarts (1.5 L) of wine or 9 quarts (8.5 L) of beer or ale (equivalent to 24 12-ounce bottles or cans).

- Amounts exceeding the allowable quantities noted above are subject to federal duty and taxes, and provincial/territorial liquor fees
- Pay provincial fees at customs at the time of entry in all provinces and the Yukon Territory
- Illegal to bring more than the allowable alcohol quantity into the Northwest Territories and Nunavut

Articles purchased at Canadian duty-free shops are subject to U.S. Customs exemptions and restrictions; those purchased at U.S. duty-free shops before entering Canada are subject to duty if brought back into the United States.

Prescription Drugs: Persons requiring medication while visiting Canada are permitted to bring it for their own use. Clearly identify and carry in original packaging with a label listing the drug and its intended use. Have a copy of the prescription and prescribing doctor's phone number.

Gifts: Items not exceeding $60 (CAN) in value, excluding tobacco, alcoholic beverages and advertising matter, taken into or mailed to Canada are allowed free entry. Gifts valued at more than $60 are subject to regular duty and taxes on the excess amount.

Pets and Plants: You must have a certificate for a dog or cat age 3 months and older. It must clearly describe the animal, declare that the animal is currently vaccinated against rabies and have a licensed veterinarian signature.

- Collar tags are not sufficient proof of immunization
- Be sure the vaccination does not expire while traveling in Canada
- The certificate is also required to bring the animal back into the United States

Exempt From These Rules: Assist dogs; healthy puppies and kittens under 3 months old with a health certificate, signed by a licensed veterinarian, indicating that the animal is too young to vaccinate.

Plants or plant material must be declared. For information, contact: Canadian Food Inspection Agency (CFIA), 59 Camelot Dr., Ottawa, ON K1A 0Y9; 613-225-2342.

Radio Communication Equipment
- Cell phone, PCS phone, citizens band (CB) or Family Radio Service radio allowed without prior registration
- Use of aircraft, marine or amateur radio allowed without prior authorization
- All other types of radio transmitting stations allowed with authorization letter from Industry Canada's Radio - communication and Broadcasting Regulatory Branch

Special Permits: A CITIES (Convention on International Trade in Endangered Species) permit is required for any endangered species brought into Canada, including those kept as pets, and for any items made from them (e.g., coats, handbags, shoes). For information contact: Environment Canada, Canadian Wildlife Service at 819-997-1840.

An Export Permit may be required to take out of Canada objects more than 50 years old (e.g., fossils, archaeological artifacts, fine and decorative art, technological objects or books and archival material). Contact: Movable Cultural Property Program of Canadian Heritage, 15 Eddy St., 3rd Floor, Gatineau,

Quebec, Canada K1A 0M5; 819-997-7761.

An Import Permit may be required for the importation of clothing, textiles, steel and certain agricultural products in excess of minimum quantities. For information contact: Department of Foreign Affairs and Int'l Trade, Export and Import Controls Bureau, Tower C, 4th Floor, LB Pearson Bldg., 125 Sussex Dr., Ottawa, ON K1A 0G2.

Vehicles
- Vehicles entering Canada for touring, including trailers not exceeding 8 feet 6 inches (2.6 m) in width are generally subject to quick and routine entry procedures.
- To leave or store a car, trailer or other goods in Canada while you leave the country you must pay import duty and taxes or present a valid permit. Canadian Customs officials. issue permits at point of entry
- You may not store a vacation trailer in Canada during the off-season.
- Vehicle registration cards required for Canadian travel.
- If driving a car other than your own, you must have written permission from the owner to use it.
- If driving a rented car, you must possess a copy of the contract.
- A valid U.S. driver's license is valid in Canada for time period specified by the individual provinces and territories.
  - In all Canadian provinces and territories it is illegal to use radar detectors, even if unplugged.
  - Seat belts required for the driver and all passengers throughout Canada.

Headlights: Driving with daytime running lights is required for all car models after 1990.
- In Alberta, British Columbia, New Brunswick, Nova Scotia and Prince Edward Island, lights must be turned on when light conditions restrict visibility to 500 feet (150 m).
- In Manitoba, lights must be turned on when light conditions restrict visibility to 200 feet (60 m).
- In Yukon Territory and Northwest Territories and Nunavut, headlights must remain on at all times.

- Elsewhere in Canada, driving with headlights on during all hours of the day is advised.

FINANCIAL RESPONSIBILITY LAWS IN CANADA

When an accident involves death, injury or property damage, Canadian provinces and territories require evidence of financial responsibility. You may be asked to show this evidence at any time.

U.S. motorists should check with their own U.S. insurance companies as to whether they are required to obtain and carry a yellow Non-Resident Inter-Province Motor Vehicle Liability Insurance Card (accepted as evidence of financial responsibility throughout Canada). Those not carrying proper proof may be subject to a substantial fine in some jurisdictions in Canada. If renting a vehicle, check with the rental car company.

The minimum liability insurance requirement is $200,000 (Canadian dollars) in all provinces and territories except Quebec, which requires $50,000. Should the courts' judgments exceed these figures, motorists held accountable are responsible for paying the full amount.

If traveling in Quebec, discuss your collision, disability and bodily injury coverages with your insurance agent. Since Quebec's minimum requirement does not include bodily injury, coverage of $200,000 or more is recommended. Consider additional coverage (i.e., trip accident policy).

For United States Residents Returning to the United States

U.S. citizens returning to the U.S. from Canada by land or sea are required to present proper travel documents according to the Western Hemisphere Travel Initiative.

Everyone who seeks entry into the United States – whether foreign visitors, U.S. citizens, or U.S. lawful permanent residents – must be inspected at the point of entry. Random searches may be conducted by U.S. Customs and Border Protection agents.

U.S. Exemptions for a Stay in Canada No Less Than 48 hours

- You may bring back tax- and duty-free articles not exceeding $800 in retail value
- Any amount over the $800 exemption is subject to duty
- The exemption is allowed once every 30 days
- A family (related persons living in the same household) may combine its exemptions (a family of 6 is entitled to $4,800 worth of goods duty-free on 1 declaration, even if articles claimed by 1 member exceed that individual's $800 amount)
- Exemptions based on fair retail value (keep receipts of all purchases as proof of fair retail value)
- Exemptions apply to articles acquired only for personal or household use or as gifts, but not intended for sale
- The exemption may include 100 cigars, 200 cigarettes and 1 liter of liquor per person over age 21 (customs enforces state liquor laws)
- All articles claimed under this exemption must accompany you on your return

U.S. Exemptions for a Stay in Canada Less Than 48 hours

- You may bring back tax- and duty-free articles not exceeding $200 in retail value
- The exemption may include no more than 50 cigarettes, 10 cigars, 5 fluid ounces (150 milliliters) of alcoholic beverage or 150 milliliters of perfume containing alcohol
  - A family may not combine purchases
  - If purchases exceed the $200 exemption, you lose the exemption and all purchases become subject to duty
  - All goods must be declared
- All articles claimed under this exemption must accompany you on your return

Gifts

- Gifts up to $100 fair retail value may be sent to friends or relatives in the United States provided no recipient receives more than 1 gift per day (need not be included in the $800 exemption)
- Gifts containing tobacco products, alcoholic beverages or perfume containing alcohol valued at more than $5 retail are excluded from this provision
- Write on outside of package the contents, retail value and "Unsolicited Gift"

Prohibited: Articles considered detrimental to the general welfare of the United States are prohibited entry: narcotics and dangerous drugs, drug paraphernalia, obscene articles and publications, seditious or treasonable matter, lottery tickets, hazardous items (fireworks, dangerous toys, toxic or poisonous substances) and switchblade knives. Any goods originating in the following countries are prohibited: Balkans, Burma, Cuba, Iran, Iraq, Liberia, Libya, North Korea, Sudan, Syria and Zimbabwe. Please note embargoes are not limited to these countries.

Restricted items include automobiles, biological materials (disease organisms and vectors for research), ceramic tableware, cultural treasures, firearms and ammunition, articles bearing marks or names copying or simulating trademarked articles or trade names (watches, cameras, perfumes), pirated copies of copyrighted articles (books, CDs, DVDs, audio- and video-tapes, computer programs), agricultural goods (plants and animal products) and pets, wildlife and fish.

You may bring into or take out of the United States an unlimited amount of money, however, if you transport more than $10,000 you must file a FinCen 105 with U.S. Customs. Failure to comply can result in civil, criminal and/or forfeiture penalties. Monies include currency, traveler's checks, U.S. or foreign coins in circulation, money orders and negotiable instruments or investment securities in bearer form. For a currency reporting flier contact: U.S. Customs, P.O. Box 7407, Washington, D.C. 20044.

While some agricultural products of Canadian origin (fruits, some plants with phyto-sanitary certificates, meats, etc.) may be brought into the United States, many are restricted to prevent the introduction of plant and animal pests and diseases. All must be declared at the U.S. border. Write to APHIS, Dept. of Agriculture, Room 1147-S, Wash., DC 20205, www.aphis.usda.gov, for a free copy of *Traveler's Tips*. Write to U.S. Customs, P.O. Box 7407, Washington, D.C. 20044 for other helpful leaflets: *Visiting the U.S.: Requirements for Non-Residents*, *Know Before You Go*, *Importing a Car*, and *Pets, Wildlife and U.S. Customs*.

For Canada Residents Traveling to the United States

Canadian citizens entering the U.S. by land or sea are required to present proper travel documents according to the Western Hemisphere Travel Initiative. Approved documents include a passport or passport card, Enhanced Driver's License, or Trusted Traveler program card. Please refer to the U.S. Department of State's Web site travel.state.gov or the Canada Border Services Agency Web site cbsa-asfc.gc.ca for the most current information on these requirements.

If traveling to the United States with a child, carry documentation proving your custodial rights. A person under age 18 traveling to the United States alone or with only 1 parent or another adult, must have certified documentation proving that the trip is permitted by both parents.

United States Customs permits Canadian residents to bring, free of duty, for personal use and not intended for sale: clothing, personal items and

equipment appropriate to the trip, including 200 cigarettes, 50 cigars or 2 kilograms of tobacco, or proportionate amounts of each, and 1 liter of alcoholic beverage.

Visitors in the United States for at least 72 hours who have not claimed this exemption in the preceding 6 months may bring gifts totaling $100 (US) retail value. Perfume containing alcohol and valued at more than $5 retail, tobacco products and alcoholic beverages are excluded from the gift provision.

Use of cell phones and General Radio Service Station (CB) is unrestricted.

For Canada Residents Returning to Canada

The Canada Border Services Agency allows Canadian residents to bring, free of duty and taxes, goods valued up to $400 (CAN) any number of times a year, provided the visit to the United States is 48 hours or more and all goods accompany the purchaser (written declaration may be required).

You may claim a $50 (CAN) exemption on goods, excluding alcoholic beverages and tobacco products, if returning after an absence of 24 hours or more and are not using any other exemption. If bringing back more than $50 worth of goods, the regular duty and tax rate is levied on the entire value. This exemption may apply any number of times in a year. No tobacco or alcohol may be carried if returning after an absence of less than 48 hours.

If returning after 7 days or more in the United States (not counting departure day from Canada) you may claim up to a $750 (CAN) exemption on goods. Goods, other than alcohol and tobacco products, need not accompany you (written declaration may be required).

Permitted within the $400 and $750 exemptions: up to 50 cigars, 200 cigarettes, 200 tobacco sticks and 200 grams (6.4 oz) of tobacco, and up to 1.14 liters (40 oz) of liquor or 1.5 liters (1.6 qts) of wine or 8.5 liters (9 qts) of beer or ale (or its equivalent of 24 12-ounce bottles or cans). You must meet the minimum age requirement of the province or territory entered to claim alcohol or tobacco products.

Special Tariff: When exceeding the $400 or $750 exemption, a special rate of 7 percent combined duty and taxes is levied on the next $300 value in goods (except tobacco and alcohol) exceeding the maximum exemptible amounts, provided goods are of U.S. origin. Regular duties apply on any additional amount. A 15 percent Harmonized Sales Tax (HST) (7 percent Goods and Services Tax (GST) and 8 percent provincial component) is charged on most goods and services supplied in Nova Scotia, New Brunswick and Newfoundland and Labrador. For information contact the Canada Border Services Agency before departing Canada. All extra goods must accompany you.

All exemptions are individual and may not be combined with those of other people. You may be asked to verify the length of your visit. Dated receipts normally constitute proof. Gifts (excluding alcoholic beverages, tobacco products and advertising matter) up to $60 (CAN) retail may be

sent from abroad free of duty or taxes. For gifts valued at more than $60 (CAN), duty and taxes apply to amount exceeding $60. Gifts sent from abroad do not count against personal exemptions; gifts brought back must be included in exemptions.

While AAA makes every effort to provide accurate and complete information, AAA makes no warranty, express or implied, and assumes no legal liability or responsibility for the accuracy or completeness of any information contained herein.

NATIONAL PARKS ENTRANCE FEES

At Canada's national parks, the basic per person or per family entry fee gives visitors access to the park, scenic outlooks, picnic areas and a variety of facilities. Additional fees are charged for visitors who choose to use other recreational services such as campgrounds, special interpretation programs and golf courses.

To receive a free Parks Canada vacation planner, phone (888) 773-8888. Detailed information about the services, benefits, entry fees and discounts at all national parks and historic sites is available by calling the following numbers:

(800) 748-7275 for Alberta;

(902) 426-3436 for Atlantic provinces (Newfoundland and Labrador, New Brunswick, Nova Scotia and Prince Edward Island);

(604) 513-4777 for British Columbia;

(888) 748-2928 for Manitoba;

(800) 748-7275 for Saskatchewan;

(800) 463-6769 for Québec;

(800) 661-0486 for Yukon Territory.

Points of Interest Index

Index Legend

NB.	national battlefield	NR.	national river
NBP.	national battlefield park	NS.	national seashore
NC.	national cemetery	NWR.	national wildlife refuge
NF.	national forest	PHP.	provincial historic(al) park
NHM.	national historic(al) monument	PHS.	provincial historic(al) site
NHP.	national historic(al) park	PP.	provincial park
NHS.	national historic(al) site	SF.	state forest
NL.	national lakeshore	SHM.	state historic(al) monument
NME.	national memorial	SHP.	state historic(al) park
NMO.	national monument	SHS.	state historic(al) site
NMP.	national military park	SME.	state memorial
NP.	national park	SP.	state park
NRA.	national recreation area	SRA.	state recreation area

▽ GEM: Points of Interest Offering a *Great Experience for Members*®

MUSIC HALLS & OPERA HOUSES

WALKING TOURS

🅢 *Attraction Admission Discount Index*

Bed & Breakfast Lodgings Index

Some bed and breakfasts listed below might have historical significance.
Those properties are also referenced in the Historical index.

Country Inns Index

Some of the following country inns can also be considered as bed-and-breakfast operations.

Historical Lodgings & Restaurants Index

Some of the following historical lodgings can also be considered as bed-and-breakfast operations.

Resorts Index

Many establishments are located in resort areas; however, the following places have extensive on-premises recreational facilities:

Comprehensive City Index

Here is an alphabetical list of all cities appearing in this TourBook® guide. Cities are presented by state province. Page numbers under the POI column indicate where points of interest text begins. Page numbers under the L&R column indicate where lodging and restaurant listings begin.

Comprehensive City Index (cont'd)

836

Comprehensive City Index (cont'd)

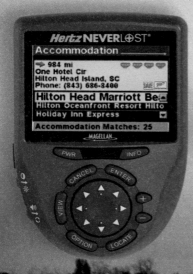

1000 BONUS or  **200 BONUS** or **25 BONUS**

Priority Club® Points   **Aeroplan® Miles***   **AIR MILES®† reward miles**

 INTERCONTINENTAL. HOTELS & RESORTS

 CROWNE PLAZA HOTELS & RESORTS

 hotel INDIGO

 Holiday Inn

 Holiday Inn Express

 STAYBRIDGE SUITES

 CANDLEWOOD SUITES

Earn extra rewards at participating hotels when you book the "Bonus CAA Package" and use the **IKCA1** promotional code.

Visit offers.ihg.com or call 1.877.512.8778 to book now!

*Or your preferred participating airline miles. Visit offers.ihg.com for participating hotels.

 aeroplan

 PRIORITY CLUB REWARDS — It's easier. Enjoy.®

 AIR MILES